Lecture Notes in Computer Science   8312

Commenced Publication in 1973
Founding and Former Series Editors:
Gerhard Goos, Juris Hartmanis, and Jan van Leeuwen

Editorial Board

David Hutchison, UK
Josef Kittler, UK
Alfred Kobsa, USA
John C. Mitchell, USA
Oscar Nierstrasz, Switzerland
Bernhard Steffen, Germany
Demetri Terzopoulos, USA
Gerhard Weikum, Germany

Takeo Kanade, USA
Jon M. Kleinberg, USA
Friedemann Mattern, Switzerland
Moni Naor, Israel
C. Pandu Rangan, India
Madhu Sudan, USA
Doug Tygar, USA

Advanced Research in Computing and Software Science
Subline of Lectures Notes in Computer Science

Subline Series Editors

Giorgio Ausiello, *University of Rome 'La Sapienza', Italy*
Vladimiro Sassone, *University of Southampton, UK*

Subline Advisory Board

Susanne Albers, *University of Freiburg, Germany*
Benjamin C. Pierce, *University of Pennsylvania, USA*
Bernhard Steffen, *University of Dortmund, Germany*
Madhu Sudan, *Microsoft Research, Cambridge, MA, USA*
Deng Xiaotie, *City University of Hong Kong*
Jeannette M. Wing, *Microsoft Research, Redmond, WA, USA*

Ken McMillan Aart Middeldorp
Andrei Voronkov (Eds.)

Logic for Programming, Artificial Intelligence, and Reasoning

19th International Conference, LPAR-19
Stellenbosch, South Africa, December 14-19, 2013
Proceedings

Springer

Volume Editors

Ken McMillan
Microsoft Research, Redmond, WA, USA
E-mail: kenmcml@microsoft.com

Aart Middeldorp
University of Innsbruck, Austria
E-mail: aart.middeldorp@uibk.ac.at

Andrei Voronkov
University of Manchester, UK
E-mail: andrei.voronkov@manchester.ac.uk

ISSN 0302-9743 e-ISSN 1611-3349
ISBN 978-3-642-45220-8 e-ISBN 978-3-642-45221-5
DOI 10.1007/978-3-642-45221-5
Springer Heidelberg New York Dordrecht London

Library of Congress Control Number: 2013954674

CR Subject Classification (1998): F.3, I.2, D.2, F.4.1, D.3, H.4, I.5

LNCS Sublibrary: SL 1 – Theoretical Computer Science and General Issues

© Springer-Verlag Berlin Heidelberg 2013
This work is subject to copyright. All rights are reserved by the Publisher, whether the whole or part of the material is concerned, specifically the rights of translation, reprinting, reuse of illustrations, recitation, broadcasting, reproduction on microfilms or in any other physical way, and transmission or information storage and retrieval, electronic adaptation, computer software, or by similar or dissimilar methodology now known or hereafter developed. Exempted from this legal reservation are brief excerpts in connection with reviews or scholarly analysis or material supplied specifically for the purpose of being entered and executed on a computer system, for exclusive use by the purchaser of the work. Duplication of this publication or parts thereof is permitted only under the provisions of the Copyright Law of the Publisher's location, in ist current version, and permission for use must always be obtained from Springer. Permissions for use may be obtained through RightsLink at the Copyright Clearance Center. Violations are liable to prosecution under the respective Copyright Law.
The use of general descriptive names, registered names, trademarks, service marks, etc. in this publication does not imply, even in the absence of a specific statement, that such names are exempt from the relevant protective laws and regulations and therefore free for general use.
While the advice and information in this book are believed to be true and accurate at the date of publication, neither the authors nor the editors nor the publisher can accept any legal responsibility for any errors or omissions that may be made. The publisher makes no warranty, express or implied, with respect to the material contained herein.

Typesetting: Camera-ready by author, data conversion by Scientific Publishing Services, Chennai, India

Printed on acid-free paper

Springer is part of Springer Science+Business Media (www.springer.com)

Preface

This volume contains the papers presented at the 19th International Conference on Logic for Programming, Artificial Intelligence and Reasoning (LPAR-19), held during December 14–19, 2013, in Stellenbosch, South Africa.

Following the call for papers, LPAR-19 received a record number of 152 submissions, materializing in 136 submissions with authors representing 31 different countries. Each submission was reviewed by at least three of the 37 Program Committee (PC) members. The PC was assisted by 174 additional reviewers and decided to accept 44 regular papers and eight tool descriptions and experimental papers. Once again the EasyChair system provided an indispensable platform for all matters related to the reviewing process, production of these proceedings, program and Web page generation, and registration of participants.

A record number of workshops were collocated with LPAR-19. The International Workshop on Algebraic Logic in Computer Science was organized by Clint van Alten of the University of the Witwatersrand and Petr Cintula and Carles Noguera of the Academy of Sciences of the Czech Republic. The 2nd Workshop on Automata, Logic, Formal languages, and Algebra (ALFA 2013) was organized by Volker Diekert, Manfred Kufleitner, and Michael Matthiesen of the University of Stuttgart. The 7th International Workshop on Analytic Proof Systems (APS-7) was organized by Matthias Baaz and Christian Fermüller of the Vienna University of Technology. The 10th International Workshop on the Implementation of Logics (IWIL-10) was organized by Stephan Schulz of the TU München, Geoff Sutcliffe of the University of Miami, and Boris Konev of the University of Liverpool. The First Workshop on Logics and Reasoning for Conceptual Models was organized by Maria Keet of the University of KwaZulu-Natal, Diego Calvanese of the Free University of Bolzano, and Szymon Klarman and Arina Britz of the CSIR-Meraka Institute in Pretoria. We were fortunate in having Laura Kovacs (Chalmers University of Technology) again as the LPAR-19 workshop chair.

Another key person in the LPAR community is Geoff Sutcliffe. This year, in his 5th LPAR organization, he teamed up with Bernd Fischer of the University of Stellenbosch. We thank them for the excellent organization.

LPAR-19 is greatful for the generous support by Microsoft Research, IBM South Africa, and VAS Tech.

October 2013

Ken Mcmillan
Aart Middeldorp
Andrei Voronkov

Organization

Program Committee

Franz Baader	Technical University of Dresden, Germany
Christel Baier	Technical University of Dresden, Germany
Josh Berdine	Microsoft Research
Armin Biere	Johannes Kepler University Linz, Austria
Nikolaj Bjorner	Microsoft Research
Sandrine Blazy	IRISA - Université Rennes 1, France
Krishnendu Chatterjee	IST Austria
Thierry Coquand	University of Gothenburg, Sweden
Joerg Endrullis	Vrije Universiteit Amsterdam, The Netherlands
Alberto Griggio	FBK-ICT IRST, Italy
Kim Guldstrand Larsen	Aalborg University, Denmark
John Harrison	Intel Corporation
Manuel Hermenegildo	IMDEA Software Institute, Spain
Stefan Hetzl	Vienna University of Technology, Austria
Nao Hirokawa	Japan Advanced Institute of Science and Technology
Martin Hofmann	LMU Munich, Germany
Gerwin Klein	NICTA and UNSW, Australia
Michael Kohlhase	Jacobs University, Germany
Laura Kovacs	Chalmers University of Technology, Sweden
Orna Kupferman	Hebrew University, Israel
Temur Kutsia	Johannes Kepler University Linz, Austria
Marta Kwiatkowska	University of Oxford, UK
P. Madhusudan	University of Illinois at Urbana-Champaign, USA
Rupak Majumdar	Max Planck Institute for Software Systems, Germany
Ken Mcmillan	Microsoft Research
Aart Middeldorp	University of Innsbruck, Austria
Albert Oliveras	Technical University of Catalonia, Spain
Axel Polleres	Vienna University of Economics and Business, Austria
Norbert Preining	Japan Advanced Institute of Science and Technology
Grigore Rosu	University of Illinois at Urbana-Champaign, USA
Philipp Ruemmer	Uppsala University, Sweden
Natarajan Shankar	SRI International

Geoff Sutcliffe University of Miami, USA
Naoyuki Tamura Kobe University, Japan
Helmut Veith Vienna University of Technology, Austria
Andrei Voronkov University of Manchester, UK
Christoph Weidenbach Max Planck Institute for Informatics, Germany

Additional Reviewers

A. Zonouz, Saman
Abío, Ignasi
Adams, Michael
Almagor, Shaull
Aminof, Benjamin
Andronick, June
Aoto, Takahito
Aravantinos, Vincent
Armas Romero, Ana
Asín Achá, Roberto Javier
Avanzini, Martin
Bacci, Giorgio
Bacci, Giovanni
Baelde, David
Banbara, Mutsunori
Baumgartner, Alexander
Beek, Wouter
Benzmueller, Christoph
Berardi, Stefano
Boker, Udi
Bonakdarpour, Borzoo
Bonatti, Piero
Borgwardt, Stefan
Boyton, Andrew
Brewka, Gerhard
Bruscoli, Paola
Chmelik, Martin
Ciobaca, Stefan
Cirstea, Horatiu
Classen, Jens
Cruanes, Simon
Cuenca Grau, Bernardo
Dalsgaard, Andreas Engelbredt
De Nivelle, Hans
Delahaye, Benoit
Dimitrova, Rayna
Dragan, Ioan

Dräger, Klaus
Eberhard, Sebastian
Emmi, Michael
Falke, Stephan
Fernandez Gil, Oliver
Fontaine, Pascal
Forejt, Vojtech
Fuhs, Carsten
Gammie, Peter
Gario, Marco
Gascón, Adrià
Gebler, Daniel
Gelfond, Michael
Gimenez, Stéphane
Gmeiner, Karl
Godo, Lluis
Gore, Rajeev
Greenaway, David
Guerrini, Stefano
Gundersen, Tom
Gupta, Ashustosh
Gurfinkel, Arie
Harrison, Amelia
Heule, Marijn
Hoder, Kryštof
Hojjat, Hossein
Holzmann, Gerard
Horbach, Matthias
Hose, Katja
Hutter, Dieter
Hölldobler, Steffen
Iancu, Mihnea
Jacquemard, Florent
Jovanovic, Dejan
Kakas, Antonis
Kaliszyk, Cezary
Kaminski, Mark

Kiefer, Stefan
Kifer, Michael
Kim, Jin Hyun
Klein, Joachim
Kloos, Johannes
Koenighofer, Robert
Konev, Boris
Kosta, Marek
Krause, Christian
Krennwallner, Thomas
Kuehlwein, Daniel
Lal, Akash
Leitsch, Alexander
Li, Wenchao
Lombardi, Carlos
Lopes, Nuno
Ludwig, Michel
Mainland, Geoffrey
Martins, Ruben
Matichuk, Daniel
Mereacre, Alexandru
Michaliszyn, Jakub
Micheli, Andrea
Montano Rivas, Omar
Moore, Brandon
Morales, Jose F.
Mosca, Alessandro
Murano, Aniello
Murray, Toby
Nabeshima, Hidetomo
Narizzano, Massimo
Nishida, Naoki
Noguera, Carles
Oikarinen, Emilia
Olesen, Mads Chr.
Oliva, Paulo
Ono, Hiroakira
Otop, Jan
Owre, Sam
Pagani, Michele
Palikareva, Hristina
Pan, Jeff Z.
Peltier, Nicolas
Polonsky, Andrew
Popescu, Andrei
Pozzato, Gian Luca
Pührer, Jörg
Qu, Hongyang
Rabe, Florian
Ranise, Silvio
Redl, Christoph
Reinecke, Philipp
Rubin, Sasha
Ryabokon, Anna
Rybalchenko, Andrey
Schaafsma, Bas
Schaub, Torsten
Schneider, Michael
Sebastiani, Roberto
Seidl, Martina
Serafini, Luciano
Serbanuta, Traian Florin
Serrano, Alejandro
Sewell, Thomas
Sheinvald, Sarai
Silva, Alexandra
Simaitis, Aistis
Simari, Guillermo
Simon, Laurent
Soh, Takehide
Stefanescu, Andrei
Stepanova, Dascha
Sternagel, Christian
Strassburger, Lutz
Stuckenschmidt, Heiner
Subotic, Pavle
Suda, Martin
Swift, Terrance
Thost, Veronica
Tompits, Hans
Tonetta, Stefano
Velner, Yaron
Vrgoc, Domagoj
Walsh, Toby
Wandelt, Sebastian
Weller, Daniel
Wenzel, Makarius
Williams, David
Wiltsche, Clemens
Wintersteiger, Christoph M.

Wojtczak, Dominik
Worrell, James
Xue, Bingtian
Yap, Roland
Zalinescu, Eugen

Zantema, Hans
Zeljić, Aleksandar
Zimmermann, Antoine
Zuleger, Florian
Zwirchmayr, Jakob

Table of Contents

An Algorithm for Enumerating Maximal Models of Horn Theories
with an Application to Modal Logics 1
  *Luca Aceto, Dario Della Monica, Anna Ingólfsdóttir,
  Angelo Montanari, and Guido Sciavicco*

May-Happen-in-Parallel Analysis for Priority-Based Scheduling 18
  Elvira Albert, Samir Genaim, and Enrique Martin-Martin

The Complexity of Clausal Fragments of LTL 35
  *Alessandro Artale, Roman Kontchakov, Vladislav Ryzhikov, and
  Michael Zakharyaschev*

A Semantic Basis for Proof Queries and Transformations.............. 53
  David Aspinall, Ewen Denney, and Christoph Lüth

Expressive Path Queries on Graphs with Data 71
  Pablo Barceló, Gaelle Fontaine, and Anthony Widjaja Lin

Proving Infinite Satisfiability 86
  Peter Baumgartner and Joshua Bax

SAT-Based Preprocessing for MaxSAT............................... 96
  Anton Belov, António Morgado, and Joao Marques-Silva

Dynamic and Static Symmetry Breaking in Answer Set
Programming.. 112
  Belaïd Benhamou

HOL Based First-Order Modal Logic Provers 127
  Christoph Benzmüller and Thomas Raths

Resourceful Reachability as HORN-LA 137
  *Josh Berdine, Nikolaj Bjørner, Samin Ishtiaq, Jael E. Kriener, and
  Christoph M. Wintersteiger*

A Seligman-Style Tableau System 147
  *Patrick Blackburn, Thomas Bolander, Torben Braüner, and
  Klaus Frovin Jørgensen*

Comparison of LTL to Deterministic Rabin Automata Translators 164
  František Blahoudek, Mojmír Křetínský, and Jan Strejček

Tree Interpolation in Vampire 173
  Régis Blanc, Ashutosh Gupta, Laura Kovács, and Bernhard Kragl

Polarizing Double-Negation Translations 182
  Mélanie Boudard and Olivier Hermant

Revisiting the Equivalence of Shininess and Politeness 198
  Filipe Casal and João Rasga

Towards Rational Closure for Fuzzy Logic: The Case of Propositional
Gödel Logic 213
  Giovanni Casini and Umberto Straccia

Multi-objective Discounted Reward Verification in Graphs
and MDPs 228
  Krishnendu Chatterjee, Vojtěch Forejt, and Dominik Wojtczak

Description Logics, Rules and Multi-context Systems 243
  Luís Cruz-Filipe, Rita Henriques, and Isabel Nunes

Complexity Analysis in Presence of Control Operators and Higher-Order
Functions 258
  Ugo Dal Lago and Giulio Pellitta

Zenon Modulo: When Achilles Outruns the Tortoise Using Deduction
Modulo 274
  David Delahaye, Damien Doligez, Frédéric Gilbert, Pierre
  Halmagrand, and Olivier Hermant

Long-Distance Resolution: Proof Generation and Strategy Extraction
in Search-Based QBF Solving 291
  Uwe Egly, Florian Lonsing, and Magdalena Widl

Verifying Temporal Properties in Real Models 309
  Tim French, John McCabe-Dansted, and Mark Reynolds

A Graphical Language for Proof Strategies 324
  Gudmund Grov, Aleks Kissinger, and Yuhui Lin

A Proof of Strong Normalisation of the Typed Atomic
Lambda-Calculus 340
  Tom Gundersen, Willem Heijltjes, and Michel Parigot

Relaxing Synchronization Constraints in Behavioral Programs 355
  David Harel, Amir Kantor, and Guy Katz

Characterizing Subset Spaces as Bi-topological Structures 373
  Bernhard Heinemann

Proof-Pattern Recognition and Lemma Discovery in ACL2 389
  *Jónathan Heras, Ekaterina Komendantskaya, Moa Johansson, and
  Ewen Maclean*

Semantic A-translations and Super-Consistency Entail Classical Cut
Elimination 407
  Lisa Allali and Olivier Hermant

Blocked Clause Decomposition..................................... 423
  Marijn J.H. Heule and Armin Biere

Maximal Falsifiability: Definitions, Algorithms, and Applications 439
  *Alexey Ignatiev, Antonio Morgado, Jordi Planes, and
  Joao Marques-Silva*

Solving Geometry Problems Using a Combination of Symbolic
and Numerical Reasoning 457
  Shachar Itzhaky, Sumit Gulwani, Neil Immerman, and Mooly Sagiv

On QBF Proofs and Preprocessing 473
  Mikoláš Janota, Radu Grigore, and Joao Marques-Silva

Partial Backtracking in CDCL Solvers 490
  Chuan Jiang and Ting Zhang

Lemma Mining over HOL Light 503
  Cezary Kaliszyk and Josef Urban

On Module-Based Abstraction and Repair of Behavioral Programs 518
  Guy Katz

Prediction and Explanation over DL-*Lite* Data Streams............... 536
  Szymon Klarman and Thomas Meyer

Forgetting Concept and Role Symbols in $\mathcal{ALCH}$-Ontologies 552
  Patrick Koopmann and Renate A. Schmidt

Simulating Parity Reasoning 568
  Tero Laitinen, Tommi Junttila, and Ilkka Niemelä

Herbrand Theorems for Substructural Logics 584
  Petr Cintula and George Metcalfe

On Promptness in Parity Games 601
  Fabio Mogavero, Aniello Murano, and Loredana Sorrentino

Defining Privacy Is Supposed to Be Easy.......................... 619
  Sebastian A. Mödersheim, Thomas Groß, and Luca Viganò

Reachability Modules for the Description Logic $\mathcal{SRIQ}$................. 636
  Riku Nortje, Katarina Britz, and Thomas Meyer

An Event Structure Model for Probabilistic Concurrent Kleene
Algebra 653
    Annabelle McIver, Tahiry Rabehaja, and Georg Struth

Three SCC-Based Emptiness Checks for Generalized Bchi
Automata 668
    *Etienne Renault, Alexandre Duret-Lutz, Fabrice Kordon, and
    Denis Poitrenaud*

PeRIPLO: A Framework for Producing Effective Interpolants
in SAT-Based Software Verification 683
    *Simone Fulvio Rollini, Leonardo Alt, Grigory Fedyukovich,
    Antti E.J. Hyvärinen, and Natasha Sharygina*

Incremental Tabling for Query-Driven Propagation of Logic Program
Updates 694
    Ari Saptawijaya and Luís Moniz Pereira

Tracking Data-Flow with Open Closure Types 710
    Gabriel Scherer and Jan Hoffmann

Putting Newton into Practice: A Solver for Polynomial Equations over
Semirings 727
    Maximilian Schlund, Michał Terepeta, and Michael Luttenberger

System Description: E 1.8 735
    Stephan Schulz

Formalization of Laplace Transform Using the Multivariable Calculus
Theory of HOL-Light 744
    Syeda Hira Taqdees and Osman Hasan

On Minimality and Integrity Constraints in Probabilistic Abduction 759
    *Calin-Rares Turliuc, Nataly Maimari, Alessandra Russo, and
    Krysia Broda*

POLAR: A Framework for Proof Refactoring 776
    Dominik Dietrich, Iain Whiteside, and David Aspinall

Author Index 793

An Algorithm for Enumerating Maximal Models of Horn Theories with an Application to Modal Logics[*]

Luca Aceto[1], Dario Della Monica[1], Anna Ingólfsdóttir[1], Angelo Montanari[2], and Guido Sciavicco[3]

[1] ICE-TCS, School of Computer Science
Reykjavik University, Reykjavik, Iceland
{luca,dariodm,annai}@ru.is
[2] Department of Mathematics and Computer Science
University of Udine, Udine, Italy
angelo.montanari@uniud.it
[3] Department of Information, Engineering and Communications
University of Murcia, Murcia, Spain
guido@um.es

Abstract. The fragment of propositional logic known as Horn theories plays a central role in automated reasoning. The problem of enumerating the maximal models of a Horn theory (MAXMOD) has been proved to be computationally hard, unless P = NP. To the best of our knowledge, the only algorithm available for it is the one based on a brute-force approach. In this paper, we provide an algorithm for the problem of enumerating the maximal subsets of facts that do not entail a distinguished atomic proposition in a definite Horn theory (MAXNOENTAIL). We show that MAXMOD is polynomially reducible to MAXNOENTAIL (and vice versa), making it possible to solve also the former problem using the proposed algorithm. Addressing MAXMOD via MAXNOENTAIL opens, inter alia, the possibility of benefiting from the monotonicity of the notion of entailment. (The notion of model does not enjoy such a property.) We also discuss an application of MAXNOENTAIL to expressiveness issues for modal logics, which reveals the effectiveness of the proposed algorithm.

Keywords: Horn theory, entailment, satisfiability, enumeration problems, modal logics.

---

[*] The authors acknowledge the support from the Spanish fellowship program *'Ramon y Cajal' RYC-2011-07821* and the Spanish MEC project *TIN2009-14372-C03-01* (G. Sciavicco), the project *Processes and Modal Logics* (project nr. 100048021) of the Icelandic Research Fund (L. Aceto, D. Della Monica, and A. Ingólfsdóttir), the project *Decidability and Expressiveness for Interval Temporal Logics* (project nr. 130802-051) of the Icelandic Research Fund (D. Della Monica), and the Italian GNCS project *Extended Game Logics* (A. Montanari).

1 Introduction

Propositional logic is the most basic tool in computer science and artificial intelligence. Despite its limited expressive power, it allows one to formalize several interesting scenarios. In particular, the fragment of propositional logic known as Horn theories [1] plays a central role in the search for efficient reasoning methods thanks to its good computational properties: the entailment problem can be solved in linear time [2,3], while it is NP-complete for full propositional logic. A Horn theory is a conjunction of clauses (that is, disjunctions of literals) such that every clause has, at most, one positive literal.

Horn theories can be applied to a number of different fields, such as planning [4], case based reasoning [5], or diagnosis [6]. A common problem is that of enumerating the models of a given theory with a particular property, e.g., maximality or minimality. As an example, the concepts of propositional circumscription and minimal/maximal diagnosis are related to this problem [7,8]. A model of a Horn theory is a truth assignment for all its atomic propositions that satisfies the theory. A model is maximal if extending its set of true propositions has the effect of losing the property of being a model. The problem of enumerating the maximal models of a given Horn theory, called here MAXMOD, has been studied in [9]. Since the problem has, in general, an output whose dimension (number of solutions returned) is exponential in the size of the input, one can hope, at best, to have an output-polynomial algorithm, that is, an algorithm whose complexity is polynomial in the size of both input and output. (A survey on the relationship between the output complexity hierarchy and the classical complexity hierarchy can be found in [10,11].) In [9], it has been proved that, unless P=NP, no output-polynomial algorithm can be devised for MAXMOD. This discouraged further investigation in the search for efficient algorithms for MAXMOD. As a consequence, to the best of our knowledge, the only algorithm available for it is the one based on a brute-force approach. It explores the space of truth assignments over the set of atomic propositions searching for maximal models. The trivial way to do so is in two steps: first, by identifying those assignments that are models, and then by checking them for maximality. Since the number of assignments is the size of the powerset of the set of propositions, the algorithm runs in exponential time.

In this paper, we establish a connection between MAXMOD and the problem of enumerating all maximal subsets of atomic propositions (facts) that do not entail a distinguished proposition in a given *definite* Horn theory (a theory where all clauses contain exactly one positive literal). The outcome of the latter problem, called here MAXNOENTAIL, can be intuitively interpreted as follows: *all maximal sets of facts that do not have atomic proposition X as a consequence.* We show that MAXMOD and MAXNOENTAIL are polynomially equivalent; thus, every algorithm for MAXNOENTAIL is also an algorithm for MAXMOD. It is worth noticing that the notion of entailment is monotone: if a set of facts entails a proposition, also each of its extensions does. Consequently, in order to check the maximality of a set F of facts that do not entail a given proposition X in a definite Horn theory, it is enough to check that every extension obtained by adding a *single* new proposition to F *does* entail X. On the other hand, the notion of model (and thus the notion of *non-model*) does not enjoy a similar property and thus, in order to verify the maximality of a model M of a Horn theory, it is necessary to verify that all the valuations *extending* M (i.e., the valuations for which the set of true propositions is an extension of the set of true propositions of M) are not models of the theory. Thanks to the monotonicity of entailment, the brute-force algorithm for MaxNoEntail performs better than the brute-force approach for MaxMod. Thus, reducing MaxMod to MaxNoEntail immediately gives us a faster, yet trivial, solution to Max-Mod. Furthermore, we present an alternative algorithm for MaxNoEntail that performs better than the brute-force approach, as it minimizes the number of candidate solutions that are tested before producing the next solution.

Another benefit resulting from approaching MaxMod via MaxNoEntail is that the latter problem is closely related to expressiveness issues for modal logics [12]. Indeed, such a relation between Horn theories and modal logics motivated this study in the first place [13,14]. A major issue in modal logic is that of finding out which modalities can be expressed in terms of others, in order to classify all expressively different sub-logics with respect to, e.g., expressive power or complexity of the satisfiability problem. A common approach to this problem consists of two steps: first, identifying as many inter-definabilities as possible, and then trying to prove completeness of such a set of inter-definabilities. The second step has two possible outcomes: either one is able to prove completeness, or the failure in proving it might suggest new inter-definabilities, giving rise to a new, extended set of inter-definabilities to be checked for completeness. In any case, the second step requires the identification of all maximal subsets of modalities that, within the current set of known inter-definabilities, do *not* express a specific modality. Since a set of inter-definabilities between modalities can be thought of as a definite Horn theory (where atomic propositions play the role of the modalities), identifying such maximal subsets of modalities amounts to solving MaxNoEntail. We provide empirical evidence that the proposed algorithm for MaxNoEntail is particularly efficient when applied to the study of the expressive power of modal logics, as described above, allowing us to solve instances that were intractable with the brute-force approach.

The paper is organized as follows. In Section 2, we give the preliminaries. In Section 3, we prove that MaxMod and MaxNoEntail are polynomially equivalent. We also present there the brute-force algorithm for MaxNoEntail, that gives us a more efficient solution for MaxMod. In Section 4, we present an alternative algorithm for MaxNoEntail and we prove its correctness. In Section 5, we give evidence of the effectiveness of the proposed method when applied to expressiveness issues for modal logics. Finally, in Section 6, we give an assessment of the work and outline future research directions.

2 Preliminaries

Throughout the paper, $\mathcal{P}$ denotes a finite, non-empty set of atomic propositions. A *Boolean expression* over $\mathcal{P}$ is a formula built using propositions from $\mathcal{P}$ and the classic Boolean operators of negation, conjunction, and disjunction. Every Boolean expression can be transformed into an equivalent formula in *conjunctive normal form* (CNF), where the outermost operator is the conjunction and each conjunct is a disjunction of *literals*, that is, atomic propositions (*positive literals*) or their negation (*negative literals*). A *Horn theory* (or *Horn expression*) over $\mathcal{P}$ is a Boolean expression over $\mathcal{P}$ in CNF whose conjuncts have at most one positive literal. Conjuncts of a Horn theory are referred to as *clauses*. It is common practice to think of a Horn theory $\mathcal{K}$ as the set $\{\delta_1, \ldots, \delta_k\}$ of its clauses. The atomic propositions occurring negated in a clause are called *antecedents* of the clause; the positive literal, if any, is called *consequent* of the clause. A clause $\delta_i = \neg A_1^i \vee \ldots \vee \neg A_{m_i}^i \vee A^i$ of a Horn theory can be seen as the implication of the consequent by the antecedents, written as $A_1^i, \ldots, A_{m_i}^i \Rightarrow A^i$. A clause with exactly one literal is a *fact*. A clause $\neg A_1^i \vee \ldots \vee \neg A_{m_1}^i$ with no positive literal can be seen as $A_1^i, \ldots, A_{m_i}^i \Rightarrow \bot$. Thus, it is useful to think of $\bot$ as a distinguished atomic proposition in $\mathcal{P}$, whose truth value is 0 in each truth assignment (see below for a formal definition of the notion of assignment). A theory in which every clause contains exactly one positive literal is said to be *definite*. Given a clause δ, we denote by ant_δ its set of antecedents, and by $cons_\delta$ the singleton containing the consequent. Finally, by $HT_\mathcal{P}$ (resp., $DHT_\mathcal{P}$), we denote the set of all (resp., definite) Horn theories over the set of atomic propositions $\mathcal{P}$.

An *assignment* M over $\mathcal{P}$ is defined as a function $M : \mathcal{P} \to \{0, 1\}$, assigning a truth value to every proposition in $\mathcal{P}$. An assignment M over $\mathcal{P}$ is a *model* of a Horn theory $\mathcal{K} \in HT_\mathcal{P}$, denoted by $M \models \mathcal{K}$, if and only if it satisfies all the clauses of $\mathcal{K}$. A Horn theory is *satisfiable* if and only if there exists a model for it. Moreover, we say that $\mathcal{K}$ *entails* a literal l, denoted $\models_\mathcal{K} l$, if and only if $\mathcal{K} \cup \{\neg l\}$ is not satisfiable. Here, we are mainly interested in entailment of *positive* literals. Given a Horn theory $\mathcal{K} \in HT_\mathcal{P}$, a subset of $\mathcal{P}$ is also referred to as a *fragment* (of $\mathcal{P}$). Thus, a fragment is a set of positive literals. Given a fragment F of $\mathcal{P}$, a positive literal $X \in \mathcal{P}$, and a Horn theory $\mathcal{K} \in HT_\mathcal{P}$, we say that F *entails* X in $\mathcal{K}$, denoted $F \models_\mathcal{K} X$, if and only if $\mathcal{K} \cup F \cup \{\neg X\}$ is unsatisfiable, that is, every model M of $\mathcal{K} \cup F$ is such that $M(X) = 1$. Given an assignment M over $\mathcal{P}$, we define the fragment *induced* by M, denoted $\eta(M)$, as the one containing exactly the propositions that are true in M. On the other hand, given a fragment F of $\mathcal{P}$, the assignment *induced* by F, denoted $\mu(F)$, is obtained by setting to 1 the propositions in F, and to 0 the ones in $\mathcal{P} \setminus F$. It obviously holds that $F = \eta(\mu(F))$ and $M = \mu(\eta(M))$, for each fragment F of $\mathcal{P}$ and for each assignment M over $\mathcal{P}$. The notion of entailment can now be extended from fragments to assignments: M *entails* X in $\mathcal{K}$, denoted $M \models_\mathcal{K} X$, if and only if $\eta(M) \models_\mathcal{K} X$. Similarly, the order over fragments induced by the set inclusion operation $\subset$ can be extended to assignments as follows: $M \prec M'$ if and only if $\eta(M) \subset \eta(M')$. Notice also that entailment is monotonic: if $F \models_\mathcal{K} X$ (resp., $M \models_\mathcal{K} X$) holds for some fragment F (resp., model M), then $F' \models_\mathcal{K} X$ (resp., $M' \models_\mathcal{K} X$) holds for every F' such that $F \subset F'$ (resp., M' such that $M \prec M'$).

Given a Horn theory $\mathcal{K}$, a model M of $\mathcal{K}$ is *maximal* if and only if $M' \not\models \mathcal{K}$ for every assignment M' such that $M \prec M'$. A fragment F is X-*incomplete* in $\mathcal{K}$ if

```
proc BruteForceMaxMod (P, K)
  S ← ∅
  for each assignment M over P
  do
    { if M ⊨ K
      then S ← S ∪ {M}
  for M ∈ S
  do
    { if ∃M' ∈ S s.t. M ≺ M'
      then S ← S \ {M}
  return S
```

```
proc BruteForceMaxNoEntail (P, K, X)
  S ← ∅
  for F ⊆ P
  do
    { if F ⊭_K X
      then
        { if ∀A ∈ P \ F it holds F ∪ {A} ⊨_K X
          then S ← S ∪ {F}
  return S
```

Fig. 1. The brute-force algorithm for MaxMod (left-hand side), and the one, more efficient, for MaxNoEntail (right-hand side)

and only if $F \not\models_K X$, and it is *maximally X-incomplete in K* if and only if it is X-incomplete in K and $F' \models_K X$ for every fragment F' such that $F \subset F'$. We will sometimes omit the specification of the Horn theory if it is clear from the context. Clearly, the monotonicity of entailment implies the monotonicity of X-incompleteness (if F is X-incomplete, then each of its subsets is X-incomplete, as well). Therefore, the notion of maximal incompleteness can be rephrased in the following equivalent way: F is maximally X-incomplete if and only if it is X-incomplete and $F \cup \{A\} \models_K X$ for each $A \in P \setminus F$. On the contrary, the notion of model of a generic theory does not enjoy such a property. As an example, consider the theory K, featuring the only clause $A, B \Rightarrow C$: the assignment M, which sets all the propositions to 0, is a model of K; the assignment M', which extends the set of true propositions of M by setting A and B to 1, is not a model of K; the assignment M'', which in turn extends the set of true propositions of M' by setting also C to 1, is another model of K.

We are now ready to formally define the enumeration problems MaxMod and MaxNoEntail, that are the aim of this study.

Definition 1. *Given a set of atomic propositions P and a Horn theory $K \in HT_P$, the problem MaxMod is defined as the problem of enumerating all and only the assignments over P that are maximal models of K. Similarly, given a set of atomic propositions P, a definite Horn theory $K \in DHT_P$, and a distinguished atomic proposition $X \in P$, the problem MaxNoEntail is defined as the problem of enumerating all and only the fragments F of P that are maximally X-incomplete in K.*

For the sake of completeness, before concluding the section we provide, in Fig. 1, left-hand side, the pseudo-code of a trivial, brute-force algorithm for MaxMod. It is clear that the algorithm described there is highly inefficient, and obviously not output-polynomial (in [9] it is proven that, unless P=NP, no output-polynomial algorithm exists for this problem): even if the set of solutions is small, or even empty, the algorithm requires an exponential number of steps. Moreover, the algorithm performs two iterations: the one on the space of the valuations over P, whose size is exponential in the one of the input, and the other on the space of the models of the Horn theory $\mathcal{K}$, whose size is possibly exponential in the one of the input, as well. In what follows, we first present a brute-force algorithm for MAXNOENTAIL (see Fig. 1, right-hand side) that, thanks to the monotonicity of entailment, avoids the second iteration step, thus having better performance than the one for MAXMOD. Then, we propose a more efficient solution for MAXNOENTAIL. Since, as we will show, MAXMOD is polynomially reducible to MAXNOENTAIL, the proposed algorithms for MAXNOENTAIL apply to MAXMOD, too.

3 Solving MAXMOD through MAXNOENTAIL

In this section, we provide a polynomial reduction from MAXMOD to MAX-NOENTAIL, and the other way around. This allows us to employ the brute-force algorithm for MAXNOENTAIL, depicted in Fig. 1 (right-hand side), to solve MAX-MOD, thus obtaining a more efficient, yet trivial, solution for it that benefits from the monotonicity of entailment. A MAXMOD *instance* is a pair $\langle \mathcal{P}, \mathcal{K} \rangle$, where $\mathcal{P}$ is a set of propositions and $\mathcal{K} \in HT_{\mathcal{P}}$. A MAXNOENTAIL *instance* is a triple $\langle \mathcal{P}, \mathcal{K}, X \rangle$, where $\mathcal{P}$ is a set of propositions, $\mathcal{K} \in DHT_{\mathcal{P}}$, and $X \in \mathcal{P}$. In what follows, we define the functions τ and γ that are used to transform MAXMOD instances into MAXNOENTAIL ones, and vice versa.

Definition 2. $\tau : HT_{\mathcal{P}} \to DHT_{\mathcal{P} \cup \{X\}}$, *where X is a distinguished atomic proposition not belonging to $\mathcal{P}$, is defined as follows: for each Horn theory $\mathcal{K} \in HT_{\mathcal{P}}$, $\tau(\mathcal{K})$ is the smallest theory such that: (i) for each clause $\delta \in \mathcal{K}$ that contains one positive literal, δ belongs to $\tau(\mathcal{K})$, and (ii) for each clause $\delta \in \mathcal{K}$ of the type $ant_\delta \Rightarrow \bot$ (i.e., δ does not contain positive literals), the clause $ant_\delta \Rightarrow X$ belongs to $\tau(\mathcal{K})$. $\gamma : DHT_{\mathcal{P}} \times \mathcal{P} \to HT_{\mathcal{P}}$ is defined as follows: for each definite Horn theory $\mathcal{K} \in DHT_{\mathcal{P}}$ and proposition $X \in \mathcal{P}$, $\gamma(\mathcal{K}, X) = \mathcal{K} \cup \{\neg X\}$.*

Our goal is to show that, for every MAXMOD instance $\langle \mathcal{P}, \mathcal{K} \rangle$, with $X \notin \mathcal{P}$, the set of solutions of MAXMOD on $\langle \mathcal{P}, \mathcal{K} \rangle$ coincides with the set of solutions of MAXNOENTAIL on $\langle \mathcal{P} \cup \{X\}, \tau(\mathcal{K}), X \rangle$, and that, for every MAXNOENTAIL instance $\langle \mathcal{P}, \mathcal{K}, X \rangle$, the set of solutions of MAXNOENTAIL on $\langle \mathcal{P}, \mathcal{K}, X \rangle$ coincides with the set of solutions of MAXMOD on $\langle \mathcal{P}, \gamma(\mathcal{K}, X) \rangle$. Let us give, first, a technical lemma.

Lemma 1. *Let $\mathcal{K} \in HT_{\mathcal{P}}$ and $A \in \mathcal{P}$. The following results hold.*

(a) Let F be a fragment of $\mathcal{P}$ that is maximally X-incomplete in $\mathcal{K}$. Then, $A \in F$ if and only if $F \models_\mathcal{K} A$.
(b) Let M be a model of $\mathcal{K}$. Then, $M(A) = 1$ if and only if $M \models_\mathcal{K} A$.

Proof. (a) Let F be a fragment of $\mathcal{P}$ that is maximally X-incomplete in $\mathcal{K}$. If $A \in F$, then $F \cup \{\neg A\}$ is unsatisfiable, and therefore $F \models_\mathcal{K} A$ follows by the definition of entailment. To prove the converse implication, let us suppose, for the sake of contradiction, that $F \models_\mathcal{K} A$ and $A \notin F$. By the definition of entailment, it follows that $\mathcal{K} \cup F \cup \{\neg A\}$ is unsatisfiable, that is, every model

M of $\mathcal{K} \cup F$ is such that $M(A) = 1$. Since F is X-incomplete, $F \not\models_\mathcal{K} X$ holds, which means that $\mathcal{K} \cup F \cup \{\neg X\}$ is satisfiable. Now, consider a model M that satisfies $\mathcal{K} \cup F \cup \{\neg X\}$. Clearly, it satisfies $\mathcal{K} \cup F$, as well. Thus, we have that $M(A) = 1$. Then, $\mathcal{K} \cup F \cup \{A\} \cup \{\neg X\}$ is satisfiable, which implies $F \cup \{A\} \not\models_\mathcal{K} X$, contradicting the assumption that F is maximally X-incomplete.

(b) Let M be a model of $\mathcal{K}$. If $M(A) = 1$, then $A \in \eta(M)$, which, in turn, implies $\eta(M) \models_\mathcal{K} A$, and thus $M \models_\mathcal{K} A$. To prove the converse implication, let us assume that $M \models_\mathcal{K} A$. By the definition of entailment, $\eta(M) \cup \mathcal{K} \cup \{\neg A\}$ is unsatisfiable. This means that each model of $\mathcal{K} \cup \eta(M)$ is such that $M(A) = 1$. Since M is a model of $\mathcal{K}$ (by our assumption) and M is a model of $\eta(M)$ (by the definition of $\eta(M)$), it follows that $M(A) = 1$, which was to be shown. □

Let us denote by $\mathcal{M}_{\langle\mathcal{P},\mathcal{K}\rangle}$ the set of solutions for MaxMod on the generic instance $\langle\mathcal{P},\mathcal{K}\rangle$ and by $\mathcal{I}_{\langle\mathcal{P},\mathcal{K},X\rangle}$ the set of solutions for MaxNoEntail on the generic instance $\langle\mathcal{P},\mathcal{K},X\rangle$. In the following two lemmas, we prove that MaxMod is reducible to MaxNoEntail (Lemma 2) and vice versa (Lemma 3).

Lemma 2. *Let $\langle\mathcal{P},\mathcal{K}\rangle$ be a generic instance of MaxMod, with $X \notin \mathcal{P}$. Then, $\mathcal{M}_{\langle\mathcal{P},\mathcal{K}\rangle} = \{\mu(F) \mid F \in \mathcal{I}_{\langle\mathcal{P}\cup\{X\},\tau(\mathcal{K}),X\rangle}\}$.*

Proof. We proceed in two steps: first, we show that $\mu(F) \in \mathcal{M}_{\langle\mathcal{P},\mathcal{K}\rangle}$, for each $F \in \mathcal{I}_{\langle\mathcal{P}\cup\{X\},\tau(\mathcal{K}),X\rangle}$; then, we prove that, for each model $M \in \mathcal{M}_{\langle\mathcal{P},\mathcal{K}\rangle}$, there exists a fragment $F \in \mathcal{I}_{\langle\mathcal{P}\cup\{X\},\tau(\mathcal{K}),X\rangle}$ such that $\mu(F) = M$.

To prove the former claim, let us assume $F \in \mathcal{I}_{\langle\mathcal{P}\cup\{X\},\tau(\mathcal{K}),X\rangle}$, which means that F is maximally X-incomplete in $\tau(\mathcal{K})$. We want to show that $\mu(F)$ belongs to $\mathcal{M}_{\langle\mathcal{P},\mathcal{K}\rangle}$, that is, $\mu(F)$ is a maximal model for $\mathcal{K}$.

- To prove that $\mu(F)$ is a model of $\mathcal{K}$, i.e., $\mu(F) \models \mathcal{K}$, let δ be a clause of $\mathcal{K}$. We shall argue show that $\mu(F)$ satisfies δ. We distinguish two cases.
  - δ is of the form $ant_\delta \Rightarrow A$, for some $A \in \mathcal{P}$. If $\mu(F)$ does not satisfy ant_δ, then we are done. Assume that $\mu(F)$ does satisfy ant_δ. We shall show that $\mu(F)(A) = 1$. Since $\mu(F)$ satisfies ant_δ, we have that $ant_\delta \subseteq F$. This means that $\{\delta\} \cup F \cup \{\neg A\}$ is unsatisfiable and thus $F \models_{\tau(\mathcal{K})} A$ holds, because δ is also a clause of $\tau(\mathcal{K})$, by construction. By Lemma 1(a), $A \in F$ and therefore $\mu(F)(A) = 1$, as claimed.
  - δ is of the form $ant_\delta \Rightarrow \bot$. We claim that $\mu(F)$ does not satisfy ant_δ. To see this, let us assume, towards a contradiction, that $\mu(F)$ satisfies ant_δ. Then, $ant_\delta \subseteq F$. By construction of $\tau(\mathcal{K})$, the clause $ant_\delta \Rightarrow X$ belongs to $\tau(\mathcal{K})$. Now, we have that $\{\delta\} \cup F \cup \{\neg X\}$ is unsatisfiable and thus $F \models_{\tau(\mathcal{K})} X$ holds, contradicting the X-incompleteness of F.

  Since $\mu(F)$ satisfies each clause of $\mathcal{K}$, we have that $\mu(F) \models \mathcal{K}$ holds.
- To prove the maximality of $\mu(F)$, let us assume, towards a contradiction, that there exists a model M of $\mathcal{K}$ such that $\mu(F) \prec M$. By the definition of $\eta(\cdot)$, this implies $F \subset \eta(M)$. We claim that $\eta(M)$ is X-incomplete in $\tau(\mathcal{K})$, thus obtaining a contradiction with the fact that F is maximally X-incomplete. Indeed, since M is a model of $\mathcal{K}$, it does not satisfy any of the sets ant_δ, where $\delta \in \mathcal{K}$ is of the form $ant_\delta \Rightarrow \bot$. Thus, $\eta(M) \not\subseteq ant_\delta$, for

every $\delta \in \tau(\mathcal{K})$ of the form $ant_\delta \Rightarrow X$, which yields $\eta(M) \not\models_\mathcal{K} X$. This, in turn, means that $\eta(M)$ is X-incomplete in $\tau(\mathcal{K})$, which contradicts the maximality of F.

To complete the proof, let us consider a model $M \in \mathcal{M}_{\langle \mathcal{P},\mathcal{K} \rangle}$, that is, M is a maximal model of $\mathcal{K}$. Our aim is to show that there exists a fragment $F \in \mathcal{I}_{\langle \mathcal{P} \cup \{X\}, \tau(\mathcal{K}), X \rangle}$ such that $\mu(F) = M$. We claim that $\eta(M) \in \mathcal{I}_{\langle \mathcal{P} \cup \{X\}, \tau(\mathcal{K}), X \rangle}$. Since $\mu(\eta(M)) = M$, the thesis follows from this claim. First, we prove that $\eta(M)$ is X-incomplete in $\tau(\mathcal{K})$, i.e., $\eta(M) \not\models_{\tau(\mathcal{K})} X$. To this end, let M' be the valuation over $\mathcal{P} \cup \{X\}$ obtained from M as follows: $M'(Y) = M(Y)$ for each $Y \in \mathcal{P}$ and $M'(X) = 0$. It is easy to see that M' is a model for $\tau(\mathcal{K}) \cup \eta(M) \cup \{\neg X\}$. Thus, $\tau(\mathcal{K}) \cup \eta(M) \cup \{\neg X\}$ is satisfiable, which implies $\eta(M) \not\models_{\tau(\mathcal{K})} X$. Now, in order to prove that $\eta(M)$ is maximally X-incomplete, we have to show that $\eta(M) \cup \{A\} \models_{\tau(\mathcal{K})} X$, for each $A \in (\mathcal{P} \cup \{X\}) \setminus \eta(M)$. If $A = X$, the thesis trivially follows from the definition of entailment. Otherwise, let us suppose, towards a contradiction, that $\eta(M) \cup \{A\} \not\models_{\tau(\mathcal{K})} X$, for some $A \in (\mathcal{P} \cup \{X\}) \setminus \eta(M)$, with $A \neq X$. This means that $\tau(\mathcal{K}) \cup \eta(M) \cup \{A\} \cup \{\neg X\}$ is satisfiable. Let M' be a model for it. Since M' is a model of $\tau(\mathcal{K})$ and $M'(X) = 0$, it is also a model of $\mathcal{K}$ (by construction of $\tau(\mathcal{K})$, X syntactically replaces the symbol $\bot$). Moreover, it is easy to convince oneself that $\eta(M') \supseteq \eta(M) \cup \{A\}$. Thus M' is a model of $\mathcal{K}$ such that $M \prec M'$, contradicting the maximality of M. Hence $\eta(M)$ is maximally X-incomplete in $\tau(\mathcal{K})$, and the thesis follows. □

Lemma 3. *Let $\langle \mathcal{P}, \mathcal{K}, X \rangle$ be a generic instance of* MAXNOENTAIL. *Then, $\mathcal{I}_{\langle \mathcal{P}, \mathcal{K}, X \rangle} = \{\eta(M) \mid M \in \mathcal{M}_{\langle \mathcal{P}, \gamma(\mathcal{K}, X) \rangle}\}$.*

Proof. We prove the statement in two steps: first, we show that $\eta(M) \in \mathcal{I}_{\langle \mathcal{P}, \mathcal{K}, X \rangle}$, for each $M \in \mathcal{M}_{\langle \mathcal{P}, \gamma(\mathcal{K}, X) \rangle}$; then, we show that, for each fragment $F \in \mathcal{I}_{\langle \mathcal{P}, \mathcal{K}, X \rangle}$, there exists a model $M \in \mathcal{M}_{\langle \mathcal{P}, \gamma(\mathcal{K}, X) \rangle}$ such that $\eta(M) = F$.

To prove the former claim, let us assume $M \in \mathcal{M}_{\langle \mathcal{P}, \gamma(\mathcal{K}, X) \rangle}$, which means that M is a maximal model of $\gamma(\mathcal{K}, X)$. As a preliminary step, we observe that, by construction of $\gamma(\mathcal{K}, X)$, every model of $\gamma(\mathcal{K}, X)$ is also a model of $\mathcal{K}$. We want to show that $\eta(M)$ belongs to $\mathcal{I}_{\langle \mathcal{P}, \mathcal{K}, X \rangle}$, that is, $\eta(M)$ is maximally X-incomplete in $\mathcal{K}$. First, we show that $\eta(M)$ is X-incomplete in $\mathcal{K}$, and then that it is maximally X-incomplete in $\mathcal{K}$. To show the X-incompleteness of $\eta(M)$, suppose, towards a contradiction, that $\eta(M) \models_\mathcal{K} X$. This means that $M \models_\mathcal{K} X$ and, by Lemma 1(b) and by the fact that M is also a model of $\mathcal{K}$, it follows that $M(X) = 1$, which implies that M is not a model of $\gamma(\mathcal{K}, X)$. This contradicts the assumption that $M \in \mathcal{M}_{\langle \mathcal{P}, \gamma(\mathcal{K}, X) \rangle}$. So, we have that $\eta(M)$ is X-incomplete in $\mathcal{K}$. Now, suppose, towards a contradiction, that $\eta(M)$ is not maximally X-incomplete. Thus, $\eta(M) \cup \{A\} \not\models_\mathcal{K} X$ holds, for some $A \in \mathcal{P} \setminus \eta(M)$. This means that $\mathcal{K} \cup \eta(M) \cup \{A\} \cup \{\neg X\}$ is satisfiable. Let M' be a model for it. Since M' satisfies $\mathcal{K}$ and $\{\neg X\}$, it is also a model of $\gamma(\mathcal{K}, X)$. Moreover, it is easy to see that $\eta(M) \subset \eta(M')$. Thus, M' is a model of $\gamma(\mathcal{K}, X)$ such that $M \prec M'$, which contradicts the maximality of M.

To complete the proof, let us consider a fragment $F \in \mathcal{I}_{\langle \mathcal{P}, \mathcal{K}, X \rangle}$, that is, F is maximally X-incomplete in $\mathcal{K}$. Our goal is to show that there exists a model

$M \in \mathcal{M}_{\langle \mathcal{P}, \gamma(\mathcal{K}, X) \rangle}$ such that $\eta(M) = F$. We claim that $\mu(F) \in \mathcal{M}_{\langle \mathcal{P}, \gamma(\mathcal{K}, X) \rangle}$. Since $\eta(\mu(F)) = F$, the thesis follows from this claim. First, we show that $\mu(F)$ is a model of $\gamma(\mathcal{K}, X)$. By construction, $\gamma(\mathcal{K}, X) = \mathcal{K} \cup \{\neg X\}$. By Lemma 1(a) and by the assumption that F is maximally X-incomplete, it follows $X \notin F$, which means that $\mu(F)(X) = 0$. Thus, $\mu(F)$ satisfies $\{\neg X\}$. Now, let us show that $\mu(F)$ also satisfies $\mathcal{K}$. Let δ be a generic clause in $\mathcal{K}$. It is of the form $A_1, \ldots, A_m \Rightarrow A$. We distinguish two cases. If $A_i \notin F$ for some $i \in \{1, \ldots, m\}$, then $\mu(F)(A_i) = 0$, which means that δ is satisfied by $\mu(F)$. Otherwise, $\{A_1, \ldots, A_m\} \subseteq F$, which means that $F \models_\mathcal{K} A$. Therefore, by Lemma 1(a), $A \in F$, which implies that $\mu(F)(A) = 1$. So, $\mu(F) \models \delta$ and, since δ was chosen arbitrarily, $\mu(F)$ is a model of $\mathcal{K}$. Since we showed that it is also a model of $\{\neg X\}$, we have that $\mu(F)$ is a model of $\gamma(\mathcal{K}, X)$. To prove the maximality of $\mu(F)$, let us suppose, towards a contradiction, that there exists a model M' of $\gamma(\mathcal{K}, X)$, such that $\mu(F) \prec M'$, which means $F \subset \eta(M')$. Since M' is a model of $\gamma(\mathcal{X}, X)$, it is both a model of $\mathcal{K}$ and $\{\neg X\}$. In particular, the latter implies $M'(X) = 0$. By Lemma 1(b), $M' \not\models_\mathcal{K} X$ holds, which means $\eta(M') \not\models_\mathcal{K} X$. Thus, $\eta(M')$ is a fragment that is X-incomplete in $\mathcal{K}$ such that $F \subset \eta(M')$. This contradicts the assumption that F is maximally X-incomplete. Hence, $\mu(F)$ is a maximal model of $\gamma(\mathcal{K}, X)$. □

The following theorem follows from Lemma 2, Lemma 3, and Definition 2.

Theorem 1. MAXMOD *and* MAXNOENTAIL *are polynomially equivalent.*

Thanks to the above reduction, it is possible to use the brute-force algorithm for MAXNOENTAIL, depicted in Fig. 1, right-hand side, to solve MAXMOD. While it is still based on a brute-force approach, such an algorithm turns out to be much more effective than the one described in Fig. 1, left-hand side. Indeed, in searching for fragments that are maximally X-incomplete in the given theory, one can easily verify the maximality of a candidate (i.e., an X-incomplete fragment) by checking if adding exactly one element to it preserves its incompleteness. This allows us to avoid a second pass on the set of potential results.

4 An Algorithm for MAXNOENTAIL

In this section we present an alternative algorithm for MAXNOENTAIL, called *AlgMaxNoEn* (see Fig. 2). We prove that our algorithm is correct and, in the next section, we give experimental evidence of its effectiveness when applied to expressiveness issues for modal logics (see the discussion in Sections 1 and 5).

We begin by giving some definitions that will be useful in what follows. Since only definite Horn theories occur in MAXNOENTAIL instances, throughout the section we assume that all Horn theories are definite, unless otherwise specified.

Definition 3. *Let $\mathcal{K} \in DHT_\mathcal{P}$ be a Horn theory, δ be a clause, and F be a fragment of $\mathcal{P}$, with $A \in F$. We say that: (i) A deactivates δ if A belongs to ant_δ; (ii) A is (F, δ)-useful if A deactivates δ and no other proposition in F does; (iii) A is $(F, \mathcal{K})$-useful if A is (F, δ')-useful for some $\delta' \in \mathcal{K}$; (iv) F is $\mathcal{K}$-useful if B is $(F, \mathcal{K})$-useful for every $B \in F$.*

```
proc ALGMAXNOENR (𝒩 = ⟨F, V⟩, ℒ, 𝒫, 𝒦, X)
  if compUtilityVec(𝒦, F) = false
    then return 'non-maximally incomplete'
  if (𝒫 \ (F ∪ V)) ⊨_𝒦 X
    then return 'no solution'
  if (𝒫 \ F) ⊭_𝒦 X
    then
      if ∄A ∈ F s.t. ((𝒫 \ F) ∪ {A}) ⊭_𝒦 X
        then
          { ℒ ← ℒ ∪ {𝒫 \ F}
            return 'solution found'
      else return 'non-maximally incomplete'
  // Here, F ∪ V is X-incomplete but F is not, thus V ≠ ∅
  flagSol ← false
  flagNoMax ← false
  keep ← true
  while V ≠ ∅ and keep
    let Y be an element of V
    V ← V \ {Y}
    F' ← F ∪ {Y}
    𝒩' ← ⟨F', V⟩
    AddChild(𝒩, 𝒩')
    ret ← AlgMaxNoEnR(𝒩', ℒ, 𝒫, 𝒦, X)
    if ret = 'solution found'
      then flagSol ← true
    if ret = 'non-maximally incomplete'
      then flagNoMax ← true
    if ret = 'no solution'
      then keep ← false
  if flagSol
    then return 'solution found'
  if flagNoMax
    then return 'non-maximally incomplete'
  return 'no solution'
```

```
proc ALGMAXNOEN (𝒫, 𝒦, X)
  ℒ ← ∅
  𝒫 ← 𝒫 \ {X}
  𝒩 ← ⟨∅, 𝒫⟩
  AlgMaxNoEnR(𝒩, ℒ, 𝒫, 𝒦, X)
  return ℒ
```

```
proc COMPUTILITYVEC (𝒦, F)
  F̂ ← F
  for i = 1 to k
    u[i] ← null
  for i = 1 to k
    let δ_i be the ith clause of 𝒦
    if |F ∩ ant_{δ_i}| = 1
      then u[i] ← F ∩ ant_{δ_i}
  for i = 1 to k
    F̂ ← F̂ \ u[i]
  if F̂ = ∅
    then return true
    else return false
```

Fig. 2. Pseudo-code for the algorithms *AlgMaxNoEn* (left-hand side, top), *compUtilityVec* (left-hand side, bottom), and *AlgMaxNoEnR* (right-hand side)

Notice that, for a given clause δ and fragment F, there can be at most one proposition in F that is (F, δ)-useful. More precisely, such a proposition exists if and only if $|F \cap ant_\delta| = 1$. In what follows, we will simply say that F is useful (in place of $\mathcal{K}$-useful) when the theory is clear from the context. The important property relating the notions of maximal X-incompleteness and usefulness is stated by the following lemma.

Lemma 4. *If a fragment F of $\mathcal{P}$ is maximally X-incomplete in $\mathcal{K}$, then its complement $\mathcal{P} \setminus F$ is useful.*

Notice that the the converse does not necessarily hold. Indeed, if F is X-incomplete and its complement is useful, then F is not necessarily maximally X-incomplete. As an example, consider the theory $\mathcal{K} = \{A, B \Rightarrow X, C \Rightarrow A\}$. The fragment A is X-incomplete and its complement BC is useful, but A is not maximally X-incomplete, as AC is X-incomplete, as well. Moreover, observe that, if a fragment F is not useful, then any fragment F' such that $F \subset F'$ is not useful, either. This follows from the fact that if a proposition $A \in F$ is not $(F, \mathcal{K})$-useful, then it is not $(F', \mathcal{K})$-useful for any F' such that $F \subset F'$.

Definition 4. *Given a Horn theory* $\mathcal{K} = \{\delta_1, \ldots, \delta_k\}$ *and a fragment* F, *the utility vector of* F *in* $\mathcal{K}$, *usually denoted by* $\boldsymbol{u}$, *is a vector of size* k *such that, for each index* i, $\boldsymbol{u}[i]$ *is equal to* $\{A\}$ *if* A *is* (F, δ_i)-*useful, and it is equal to* null *if* $|F \cap ant_{\delta_i}| \neq 1$.

Intuitively, the utility vector is the tool used to detect that a fragment is not useful: F is useful if and only if all the propositions in F occur in $\boldsymbol{u}$.

We are now ready to describe the proposed algorithm *AlgMaxNoEn* (Fig. 2). The intuitive idea of the algorithm is to produce candidate solutions (i.e., fragments) and verify whether they are actual solutions, that is, if they are maximally X-incomplete fragments. Candidate solutions are produced by incrementally removing propositions from the set $\mathcal{P}$, which from now on we assume does not contain X (as X cannot occur in any solution). Once a proposition is removed, the status of the resulting fragment is checked: if it is maximally X-incomplete, then it is added to the solution set; otherwise, either the computation continues by refining the candidate solution through the removal of another proposition or, if refining this candidate is considered not promising (according to criteria that will be defined later on), the analysis of this candidate ends and we focus on a new candidate.

The process is carried out in a recursive fashion, *AlgMaxNoEnR* being the recursive function and *AlgMaxNoEn* being the wrapper function, which executes the first call to *AlgMaxNoEnR* (see Fig. 2). The parameters of the recursion are the fragment F, representing the propositions that have been already removed (thus the candidate under analysis is its complement $\mathcal{P} \setminus F$), and the fragment V, which is a (not necessarily strict) subset of $\mathcal{P} \setminus F$ and represents the propositions that can still be removed to refine the current candidate. (The additional parameters of *AlgMaxNoEnR* can be thought of as global variables, as they are not involved in the recursion process: $\mathcal{L}$ collects the solutions, while $\mathcal{P}$, $\mathcal{K}$, and X represent the instance given as input to *AlgMaxNoEn*.) Thus, a generic recursive call on F and V analyses, as a candidate, the complement of F, which can be possibly refined, in successive recursive calls, through the removal of (some of) the propositions in V. In this way, the recursive function searches for solutions contained in the whole set of sub-fragment of $\mathcal{P} \setminus F$.

Given an instance $\langle \mathcal{P}, \mathcal{K}, X \rangle$ of MAXNOENTAIL as input, the wrapper function *AlgMaxNoEn* (Fig. 2, left-hand side, top) executes the first recursive call to *AlgMaxNoEnR* on the recursive parameters $F = \emptyset$ and $V = \mathcal{P}$. The function *AlgMaxNoEnR* recursively builds a tree isomorphic to its own recursion tree. Such a structure is actually useless for the purposes of the algorithm, but it will be handy for the correctness analysis. In what follows, nodes of the above-mentioned tree are identified by the pair $\langle F, V \rangle$ of recursive parameters on which the call is performed. Thus, there is a one-to-one correspondence between nodes and calls to *AlgMaxNoEnR*. For the sake of simplicity, we will sometimes refer to a call to *AlgMaxNoEnR* through its corresponding node, and vice versa. For example, we will say that "a node $\mathcal{N}$ returns the exit-value r", meaning that the corresponding call returns r. A call to *AlgMaxNoEnR* may produce one of three outcomes: 'solution found', 'no solution', or 'non-maximally incomplete'.

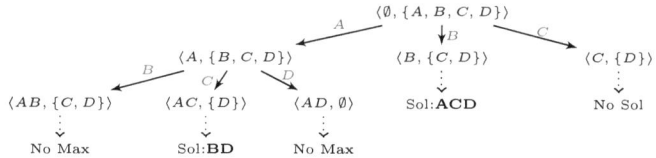

Fig. 3. Recursion tree of *AlgMaxNoEn* on $\mathcal{K}$

Intuitively, the value 'solution found' is returned by a node when a solution has been found in its own sub-tree (i.e., in the sub-tree rooted at it); if this is the case, we also say that the node *sees* a solution. Otherwise, if a fragment that is maximally X-incomplete in $\mathcal{K}$ has been analysed in its own sub-tree, the value 'non-maximally incomplete' is returned. The value 'no solution' is returned when none of the two cases above applies.

As a first step, the algorithm checks if one of the base-case conditions is met. Clearly, if a base-case condition is met inside a call, then that call corresponds to a leaf of the recursion tree. Base-case conditions allow the algorithm to end the analysis of a candidate, with no further refinements (and thus avoiding the exploration of the set of its sub-fragments), because either the candidate itself is a solution or its refinement is not promising. The refinement of a solution $\mathcal{P} \setminus F$ by removing propositions in V is not promising when the corresponding node $\langle F, V \rangle$ does not see any solution. Clearly, this is the case when $\mathcal{P} \setminus (F \cup V) \models_\mathcal{K} X$: if the weakest fragment $\mathcal{P} \setminus (F \cup V)$ of the set of sub-fragments of $\mathcal{P} \setminus F$ entails X, then, due to the monotonicity of entailment, all the fragments of the set do, meaning that none of them is X-incomplete. Another case in which refining a candidate is not promising is when the candidate F is X-incomplete but not maximally X-incomplete: if F is not maximally X-incomplete, then all its sub-fragments are not, either. We are interested in detecting such non-promising situations as soon as possible, to reduce the number of candidates analysed by the algorithm. To this end, we use the above-mentioned property that the complement of a maximally X-incomplete fragment is useful (Lemma 4). This implies that, if a fragment F is not useful, that is, some of its propositions do not occur in its utility vector, then neither $\mathcal{P} \setminus F$ nor any of its sub-fragments is a solution, and thus the analysis of $\mathcal{P} \setminus F$ ends with no further refinement. Thus, there are three base-case conditions. *(i)* If *compUtilityVec* (see Fig. 2, left-hand side, bottom) returns `false`, then F is not useful, and the function returns 'non-maximally incomplete'. *(ii)* If $\mathcal{P} \setminus (F \cup V)$ entails X, then refining $\mathcal{P} \setminus F$ cannot lead to a solution, and the function returns 'no solution'. *(iii)* If the complement of F is X-incomplete, then it may be a solution. Its maximality is checked, exploiting the monotonicity of entailment, and, depending on the result of this test, either it is added to the solution set $\mathcal{L}$ and 'solution found' is returned, or 'non-maximally incomplete' is returned.

If none of the above base-case conditions is met, the refinement of the candidate is performed (`while` loop in *AlgMaxNoEnR*, in Fig. 2). At each iteration, an element Y of V is selected. Each iteration corresponds to an attempt to extend F

with the new proposition Y and the new node $\langle F \cup \{Y\}, V \setminus \{Y\}\rangle$ (corresponding to the recursive call on $F \cup \{Y\}$ and $V \setminus \{Y\}$) is created as a child of the current one. Depending on the value returned from a recursive call, the local variables *flagSol*, *flagNoMax*, and *keep* are suitably updated. Intuitively, *FlagSol* is true if and only if the current node sees a solution. If the current node sees no solutions, but at least one of the nodes in its own sub-tree returned 'non-maximally incomplete', then *flagNoMax* is true. Finally, *keep* is set to false as soon as a call returns 'no solution'. In this last case, thanks to the monotonicity of the entailment, we can exit the current loop, as no other solution can be produced by refining the current candidate $\mathcal{P} \setminus F$. The return value after the loop is then returned depending on the values of *flagSol* and *flagNoMax*.

In Fig 3, we provide the recursion tree for the algorithm applied to the Horn theory

$$\mathcal{K} = \begin{cases} A, B \Rightarrow C \\ B \Rightarrow D \\ A, C \Rightarrow D \\ B, C \Rightarrow X \end{cases}$$

The figure shows that the algorithm is able to produce the only two solutions without exploring the whole space of fragments (only 7 fragments are processed out of $2^4 = 16$ possible ones).

In what follows, let $\mathcal{T}$ be the tree rooted at the node $\langle \emptyset, \mathcal{P}\rangle$, as generated by the first call to the recursive function *AlgMaxNoEn*. The following theorem states that the proposed algorithm is sound and complete.

Theorem 2. *Let $\langle \mathcal{P}, \mathcal{K}, X\rangle$ be an instance of* MaxNoEntail. *Then, a fragment is included in the set of solutions returned by the algorithm AlgMaxNoEn on input $\langle \mathcal{P}, \mathcal{K}, X\rangle$ if and only if it is maximally X-incomplete in $\mathcal{K}$.*

Proof. The soundness of *AlgMaxNoEn* follows from the description of the algorithm: a fragment is included in the set of solutions returned by *AlgMaxNoEn* only if the test for its maximal X-incompleteness succeeds.

To prove the completeness of *AlgMaxNoEn*, let us consider a generic maximally X-incomplete fragment F. We show that a node $\mathcal{N} = \langle \overline{F}, V\rangle$, where $\overline{F} = \mathcal{P} \setminus F$, is eventually created and processed, for some $V \subseteq F$. As F is indeed a maximally X-incomplete fragment, the corresponding base-case condition applies, and F is added to the solution set. Let us consider the ordering over $\mathcal{P}$ according to which the elements are selected inside the while loop of the algorithm *AlgMaxNoEnR* (see Fig. 2). Let A be the first occurrence in $\mathcal{P}$ of an element of $\overline{F}$ and let $B_1, \ldots, B_s$ be the elements preceding A in $\mathcal{P}$ (according to the above-mentioned ordering). We have to show that the child $\mathcal{N}_A = \langle \{A\}, V_A\rangle$, where $V_A = (\mathcal{P} \setminus \{A\}) \setminus \{B_i \mid 1 \leq i \leq s\}$, is eventually processed. Notice that $\mathcal{P} \setminus (V_A \cup \{A\}) \subseteq F$ holds, as $\overline{F} \subseteq V_A \cup \{A\}$. Thus, $\mathcal{P} \setminus (V_A \cup \{A\})$ is X-incomplete, as well (as F is and by monotonicity of the entailment). Suppose, towards a contradiction, that $\mathcal{N}_A$ is never processed. Then, one of its left siblings $\mathcal{N}_{B_i} = \langle \{B_i\}, V_{B_i}\rangle$, for some $i \in \{1, \ldots, s\}$, where $V_{B_i} = \mathcal{P} \setminus \{B_j \mid 1 \leq j \leq i\}$, has returned 'no solution'. Since $\mathcal{P} \setminus (V_A \cup \{A\})$ is X-incomplete and $V_A \cup \{A\} \subseteq V_{B_i}$

holds, there exists a path from $\mathcal{N}_{B_i}$ to a leaf corresponding to a candidate that is X-incomplete. Such a leaf returns either 'solution found' or 'non-maximally incomplete', and thus $\mathcal{N}_{B_i}$ does not return 'no solution', leading to contradiction. As the same argument can be iterated for every other element of $\overline{F}$, we can conclude that $\mathcal{N}_A$ is processed, and we are done. □

5 Applications and Experimental Results

The algorithm for MAXNOENTAIL given in Section 4 outperforms the brute-force ones given in Fig. 1. Moreover, thanks to the reduction provided in Section 3, it can also be exploited to solve MAXMOD. In this section, we show a further application of *AlgMaxNoEn* as a tool to compare the expressive power of modal logics (see Section 1).

Given a set of modalities, an *inter-definability* (among them) describes how to define a modality in terms of others. An inter-definability can be thought of as a clause of a definite Horn theory, where atomic propositions play the role of the modalities (e.g., the fact that combining the modality $\Diamond_1$ with the modality $\Diamond_2$ makes it possible to define the modality $\Diamond_3$ can be expressed by the Horn clause $\Diamond_1, \Diamond_2 \Rightarrow \Diamond_3$). Consequently, a set of inter-definabilities is nothing but a definite Horn theory. Now, a major issue in modal logic is to determine the complete set of inter-definabilities among a set of modalities (it is necessary, for example, in order to classify a family of modal logics with respect to their relative expressive power). As already pointed out in Section 1, the task of identifying the maximal subsets of modalities that, within a given set of inter-definabilities, do not express a specific modality is crucial in that respect. Since a set of inter-definabilities can be seen as a definite Horn theory, it easy to convince oneself that the latter task amounts to solving MAXNOENTAIL. Actually, it was this very problem that motivated us to carry out this study, in the search for a better solution than the one based on the brute-force approach. While in modal logics with few operators and inter-definabilities, the above-mentioned task can be easily carried out by hand (as it has been done, e.g., in [14]), in modal logics with many operators and several inter-definabilities, it may require a big and error-prone effort. Even though most modal logics have a small set of modalities, there are meaningful ones that feature tens of modalities (see, e.g., [15,16]). In [13], the authors proposed, and used, a naïve, brute-force algorithm similar to the ones presented in Fig. 1 to perform the aforementioned task. Even if this approach was efficient enough for the particular modal logic studied in [13], it turned out to be unsuitable to deal with logics with larger sets of modalities, such as the one studied in [15], featuring more than 20 modalities. As shown by our experimental results, the algorithm proposed here is efficient enough to deal also with those logics.

We have carried out an experimental comparison of the efficiency of the algorithm *AlgMaxNoEn* vis-a-vis those given in Fig. 1. We summarize the outcomes

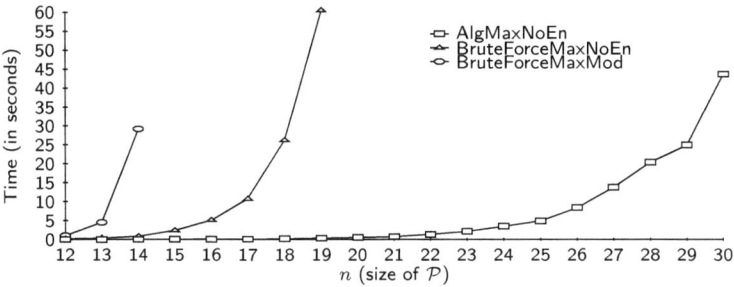

Fig. 4. Running times of the three algorithms on randomly-generated instances

of our experiments[1] in Fig. 4. For each pair of values n and k, ranging, respectively, between 12 and 30 and between $\lfloor n/3 \rfloor$ and n, the running times of the three algorithms presented in this papers (i.e., *BruteForceMaxMod*, *BruteForceMaxNoEntail*, and *AlgMaxNoEn*) are compared with respect to a set of seven randomly-generated Horn theories $\mathcal{K}$ over $\mathcal{P}$, where $|\mathcal{P}| = n$ and $|\mathcal{K}| = k$ (to be precise, *BruteForceMaxMod* is run on randomly-generated instances of the form $\langle \mathcal{P}, \mathcal{K} \rangle$, while *BruteForceMaxNoEntail* and *AlgMaxNoEn* on instances of the form $\langle \mathcal{P} \cup \{X\}, \tau(\mathcal{K}), X \rangle$, obtained from the instances used for testing *BruteForceMaxMod* through the reduction described in Section 3). The chart in Fig. 4 reports the average running times of the three algorithms for the different values of n (size of $\mathcal{P}$). In spite of a similar, exponential trend exhibited by the three algorithms (notice that such a behaviour is unavoidable as the problems can produce outputs whose size is, in general, exponential in the size of the input), our tests show that the two algorithms based on a brute-force approach become inefficient already for instances over set of propositions of size 15 and 20, respectively, and are thus unable to deal, for instance, with the logic studied in [15]. On the other hand, *AlgMaxNoEn* can deal with all tested instances in reasonable time.

6 Conclusions

In this paper we have studied the problem of enumerating the maximal models of a Horn theory (MAXMOD) and we established a connection between this problem and the problem of enumerating the maximal subsets of facts that do not entail a distinguished atomic proposition in a definite Horn theory (MAXNOENTAIL). We first showed that the two problems are polynomially equivalent and then we presented an algorithm for MAXNOENTAIL that performs better than the ones

---

[1] All the experiments were executed on a PC system with an Intel® Core™i3-2120 CPU @ 3.30GHz × 4 and 7.7 GB of RAM, under Ubuntu Linux 12.04 (precise) 64-bit. On the web-page http://www.di.unisa.it/dottorandi/dario.dellamonica/download/lpar13_code.zip it is possible to download the source code in C++.

based on a brute-force approach. As the problems can produce an output of size, in general, exponential in the size of the input, it not possible to avoid the exponential trend shown by the algorithms in Fig. 4. Moreover, in [9], it has been proved that, unless P=NP, no output-polynomial algorithm can be devised for MAXMOD (and thus for MAXNOENTAIL), meaning that it is not even possible to devise an algorithm that runs in polynomial time in terms of both the sizes of input and output. Nevertheless, our approach is efficient enough to allow us to deal with some expressiveness issues for modal logics that were intractable with the brute-force approach, as shown by empirical evidence.

The proposed algorithm can be improved by conceiving suitable heuristics to drive the construction of the candidate solution (e.g, heuristics for the choice of the next atomic proposition to be removed from the fragment) and by suitably reducing, on the fly, the Horn theory depending on the current candidate under analysis. We plan to explore both such possibilities in future work. We also intend to investigate the behaviour of the proposed algorithm on special instances of MAXNOENTAIL, i.e., on Horn theories whose clauses have the same consequent. Such a restriction makes the MAXNOENTAIL problem equivalent to the well-known problem of finding the minimal hitting sets of a hyper-graph, for which it is still an open question whether an output-polynomial algorithm exists.

References

1. Cook, S.: The complexity of theorem proving procedures. In: Proc. of the 3rd Annual ACM Symposium on Theory of Computing, pp. 151–158 (1971)
2. Chang, C., Lee, R.C.: Symbolic Logic and Mechanical Theorem Proving, 1st edn. Academic Press, Inc. (1997)
3. Lloyd, J.W.: Foundations of Logic Programming, 2nd edn. Springer (1987)
4. Kautz, H., Mcallester, D., Selman, B.: Encoding plans in propositional logic. In: Proc. of the 5th KR, pp. 374–384 (1996)
5. Riesbeck, C., Schank, R.: Inside Case-based Reasoning. Artificial intelligence series. Lawrence Erlbaum (1989)
6. Brachman, R., Levesque, H.: Knowledge Representation and Reasoning. Morgan Kaufmann Publishers Inc. (2004)
7. Brusoni, V., Console, L., Terenziani, P., Dupré, D.T.: Characterizing temporal abductive diagnosis. In: Proc. of the 6th DX, pp. 34–40 (1995)
8. Cadoli, M.: The complexity of model checking for circumscriptive formulae. Information Processing Letters 44, 113–118 (1992)
9. Kavvadias, D.J., Sideri, M., Stavropoulos, E.: Generating all maximal models of a Boolean expression. Inf. Process. Lett. 74(3-4), 157–162 (2000)
10. Knuth, D.: The Art of Computer Programming: Combinatorial Algorithms, Part 1, 1st edn., vol. 4A. Addison-Wesley Professional (2011)
11. Schmidt, J.: Enumeration: Algorithms and complexity. Unpublished (2009)
12. Blackburn, P., de Rijke, M., Venema, Y.: Modal Logic. Cambridge University Press (2002)
13. Aceto, L., Della Monica, D., Ingólfsdóttir, A., Montanari, A., Sciavicco, G.: A complete classification of the expressiveness of interval logics of Allen's relations over dense linear orders. In: Proc. of the 20th TIME (2013)

14. Della Monica, D., Goranko, V., Montanari, A., Sciavicco, G.: Expressiveness of the interval logics of Allen's relations on the class of all linear orders: Complete classification. In: Proc. of the 22nd IJCAI, pp. 845–850 (2011)
15. Balbiani, P., Goranko, V., Sciavicco, G.: Two-sorted point-interval temporal logics. Electr. Notes Theor. Comput. Sci. 278, 31–45 (2011)
16. Halpern, J., Shoham, Y.: A propositional modal logic of time intervals. Journal of the ACM 38(4), 935–962 (1991)

May-Happen-in-Parallel Analysis for Priority-Based Scheduling

Elvira Albert, Samir Genaim, and Enrique Martin-Martin

Complutense University of Madrid, Spain

Abstract. A *may-happen-in-parallel* (MHP) analysis infers the sets of pairs of program points that may execute in parallel along a program's execution. This is an essential piece of information to detect data races, and also to infer more complex properties of concurrent programs, e.g., deadlock freeness, termination and resource consumption analyses can greatly benefit from the MHP relations to increase their accuracy. Previous MHP analyses have assumed a worst case scenario by adopting a simplistic (non-deterministic) task scheduler which can select any available task. While the results of the analysis for a non-deterministic scheduler are obviously sound, they can lead to an overly pessimistic result. We present an MHP analysis for an asynchronous language with *prioritized* tasks buffers. *Priority-based scheduling* is arguably the most common scheduling strategy adopted in the implementation of concurrent languages. The challenge is to be able to take task priorities into account at static analysis time in order to filter out unfeasible MHP pairs.

1 Introduction

In asynchronous programming, programmers divide computations into shorter tasks which may create additional tasks to be executed asynchronously. Each task is placed into a task-buffer which can execute in *parallel* with other task-buffers. The use of a *synchronization* mechanism enables that the execution of a task is synchronized with the completion of another task. Synchronization can be performed via shared-memory [9] or via future variables [13,8]. Concurrent *interleavings* in a buffer can occur if, while a task is awaiting for the completion of another task, the processor is released such that another pending task can start to execute. This programming model captures the essence of the concurrency models in X10 [13], ABS [12], Erlang [1] and Scala [11], and it is the basis of actor-like concurrency [2,11]. The most common strategy to schedule tasks is undoubtedly *priority-based scheduling*. Each task has a priority level such that when the active task executing in the buffer releases the processor, a highest priority pending task is taken from its buffer and begins executing. Asynchronous programming with *prioritized tasks buffers* has been used to model real-world asynchronous software, e.g., Windows drivers, engines of modern web browsers, Linux's work queues, among others (see [9] and its references).

The higher level of abstraction that asynchronous programming provides, when compared to lower-level mechanisms like the use of multi-threading and locks, allows writing software which is more reliable and more amenable to be analyzed. In spite of this, proving error-freeness of these programs is still quite challenging. The difficulties are mostly related to: (1) *Tasks interleavings*, typically a programmer decomposes a task t into subtasks $t_1,\ldots,t_n$. Even if each of the sub-tasks would execute serially, it can happen that a task k unrelated to this computation interleaves its execution between t_i and t_{i+1}. If this task k changes the shared-memory, it can interfere with the computation in several ways, e.g., leading to non-termination, to an unbounded resource consumption, and to deadlocks. (2) *Buffers parallelism*, tasks executing across several task-buffers can run in parallel, this could lead to deadlocks and data races.

In this paper, we present a *may-happen-in-parallel* (MHP) analysis which identifies pairs of statements that can execute in parallel and in an interleaved way (see [13,3]). MHP is a crucial analysis to later prove the properties mentioned above. It directly allows ensuring absence of data races. Besides, MHP pairs allow us to greatly improve the accuracy of deadlock analysis [16,10] as it discards unfeasible deadlocks when the instructions involved in a possible deadlock cycle cannot happen in parallel. Also, it improves the accuracy of termination and cost analysis [5] since it allows discarding unfeasible interleavings. For instance, consider a loop like while (l!=null) {x=b.m(l.data); await x?; l=l.next;}, where x=b.m(e) posts an asynchronous task m(e) on buffer b, and the instruction await x? synchronizes with the completion of the asynchronous task by means of the future variable x. If the asynchronous task is not completed (x is not ready), the current task releases the processor and another task can take it. This loop terminates provided no instruction that increases the length of the list l *interleaves* or *executes in parallel* with the body of this loop.

Existing MHP analyses [13,3] assume a worst case scenario by adopting a simplistic (non-deterministic) task scheduler which can select any available task. While the results of the analysis for a non-deterministic scheduler are obviously sound, they can lead to an overly pessimistic result and report false errors due to unfeasible schedulings in the task order selection. For instance, consider two buffers b1 and b2 and assume we are executing a task in b1 with the following code "x=b1.m1(e1); y=b1.m2(e2); await x?; b2.m3(e3);". If the priority of the task executing m1 is smaller than that of m2, then it is ensured that task m2 and m3 will not execute in parallel even if the synchronization via **await** is on the completion of m1. This is because at the **await** instruction, when the processor is released, m2 will be selected by the priority-based scheduler before m1. A non-deterministic scheduler would give this spurious parallelism.

Our starting point is the MHP analysis for non-deterministic scheduling of [3], which distinguishes a local phase in which one inspects the code of each task locally, and ignores transitive calls, and a global phase in which the results of the local analysis are composed to build a global *MHP-graph* which captures the parallelism with transitive calls and among multiple task-buffers. The contribution of this paper is an MHP analysis for a priority-based scheduling which takes priorities into account both at the local and global levels of the analysis. As each buffer has its own scheduler which is independent of other buffer's schedulers, priorities can be only applied to establish the order of execution among the tasks executing on the same task-buffer (*intra-buffer* MHP pairs). Interestingly, even by only using priorities at the intra-buffer level, we are also able to implicitly eliminate unfeasible *inter-buffer* MHP pairs. We have implemented our analysis in the MayPar system [4] and evaluated it on some challenging examples, including some of the benchmarks used in [9]. The system can be used online through a web interface where the benchmarks used are also available.

2 Language

We consider asynchronous programs with priority-levels and multiple tasks buffers. Tasks can be synchronized with the completion of other tasks (of the same or of a different buffer) using futures. In this model, only highest-priority tasks may be dispatched, and tasks from different task buffers execute in parallel. The number of task buffers does not have to be known a priori and task buffers can be dynamically created. We keep the concept of task-buffer disconnected from physical entities, such as processes, threads, objects, processors, cores, etc. In [9], particular mappings of task-buffers to such entities in real-world asynchronous systems are described. Our model captures the essence of the concurrency and distribution models used in X10 [13] and in actor-languages (including ABS [12], Erlang [1] and Scala [11]). It also has many similarities with [9], the main difference being that the synchronization mechanism is by means of future variables (instead of using the shared-memory for this purpose).

2.1 Syntax

Each program declares a sequence of global variables $g_0, \ldots, g_n$ and a sequence of methods named $m_0, \ldots, m_i$ (that may declare local variables) such that one of the methods, named main, corresponds to the initial method which is never posted or called and it is executing in a buffer with identifier 0. The grammar below describes the syntax of our programs. Here, T are types, m procedure names, e expressions, x can be global or local variables, buffer identifiers b are local variables, f are future variables, and priority levels p are natural numbers.

$$M ::= T\ m(\bar{T}\ \bar{x})\{s;\textbf{return}\ e;\ \}$$
$$s\ ::= s;s \mid x = e \mid \textbf{if}\ e\ \textbf{then}\ s\ \textbf{else}\ s \mid \textbf{while}\ e\ \textbf{do}\ s \mid$$
$$\textbf{await}\ f? \mid b = \textsf{newBuffer} \mid f = b.m(\langle \bar{e} \rangle, p) \mid \textbf{release}$$

The notation $\bar{T}$ is used as a shorthand for $T_1, \ldots T_n$, and similarly for other names. We use the special buffer identifier *this* to denote the current buffer. For the sake of generality, the syntax of expressions is left free and also the set of types is not specified. We assume that every method ends with a **return** instruction.

The concurrency model is as follows. Each buffer has a lock that is shared by all tasks that belong to the buffer. Data synchronization is by means of future variables as follows. An **await** y? instruction is used to synchronize with the result of executing task $y=b.m(\langle \bar{z} \rangle, p)$ such that **await** y? is executed only when the future variable y is available (and hence the task executing m is finished). In the meantime, the buffer's lock can be released and some highest priority *pending* task on that buffer can take it. The instruction **release** can be used to unconditionally release the processor so that other pending task can take it. Therefore, our concurrency model is *cooperative* as processor release points are explicit in the code, in contrast to a *preemptive* model in which a higher priority task can interrupt the execution of a lower priority task at any point (see Sec. 7). W.l.o.g, we assume that all methods in a program have different names.

2.2 Semantics

A *program state* $St = \langle g, \texttt{Buf} \rangle$ is a mapping g from the global variables to their values along with all created buffers $\texttt{Buf}$. $\texttt{Buf}$ is of the form $buffer_1 \parallel \ldots \parallel buffer_n$ denoting the parallel execution of the created task-buffers. Each *buffer* is a term $buffer(bid, lk, \mathcal{Q})$ where bid is the buffer identifier, lk is the identifier of the *active task* that holds the buffer's lock or $\bot$ if the buffer's lock is free, and $\mathcal{Q}$ is the set of tasks in the buffer. Only one task can be *active* (running) in each buffer and has its *lock*. All other tasks are *pending* to be executed, or *finished* if they terminated and released the lock. A *task* is a term $tsk(tid, m, p, l, s)$ where tid is a unique task identifier, m is the method name executing in the task, p is the task priority level (the larger the number, the higher the priority), l is a mapping from local (possibly future) variables to their values, and s is the sequence of instructions to be executed or $s = \epsilon(v)$ if the task has terminated and the return value v is available. Created buffers and tasks never disappear from the state.

The execution of a program starts from an initial state where we have an initial buffer with identifier 0 executing task 0 of the form $S_0 = \langle g, buffer(0, 0, \{tsk(0, \textsf{main}, p, l, body(\textsf{main}))\}) \rangle$. Here, g contains initial values for the global variables, l maps parameters to their initial values and local reference and future variables to **null** (standard initialization), p is the priority given to main, and $body(m)$ refers to the sequence of instructions in the method m. The execution proceeds from S_0 by selecting *non-deterministically* one of the buffers and applying the semantic rules depicted in Fig. 1. We omit the treatment of the sequential instructions as it is standard, and we also omit the global memory g from the state as it is only modified by the sequential instructions.

NEWBUFFER: an active task tid in buffer bid creates a buffer bid' which is introduced to the state with a free lock. PRIORITY: Function $highestP$ returns a highest-priority task that is not finished, and it obtains its buffer's lock. ASYNC: A method call creates a new task (the initial state is created by $buildLocals$) with a fresh task identifier tid_1 which is associated to the corresponding future variable y in l'. We have assumed that $bid \neq bid_1$, but the case $bid = bid_1$ is analogous, the new task tid_1 is simply added to $\mathcal{Q}$ of bid. AWAIT1: If the future variable we are awaiting for points to a finished task, the **await** can be completed. The finished task t_1 is looked up in all buffers in the current state (denoted $\texttt{Buf}$). AWAIT2: Otherwise, the task yields the lock so that any other task of the same

(NEWBUFFER) $\dfrac{\text{fresh}(bid')\,,\ l' = l[x \to bid'],\ t = tsk(tid, m, p, l, \langle x = \mathsf{newBuffer}; s\rangle)}{buffer(bid, tid, \{t\} \cup \mathcal{Q}) \parallel B \rightsquigarrow}$
$buffer(bid, tid, \{tsk(tid, m, p, l', s)\} \cup \mathcal{Q}) \parallel buffer(bid', \bot, \{\}) \parallel B$

(PRIORITY) $\dfrac{highestP(\mathcal{Q}) = tid,\ t = tsk(tid, \_, \_, \_, s) \in \mathcal{Q},\ s \neq \epsilon(v)}{buffer(bid, \bot, \mathcal{Q}) \parallel B \rightsquigarrow buffer(bid, tid, \mathcal{Q}) \parallel B}$

(ASYNC) $\dfrac{l(x) = bid_1,\ \text{fresh}(tid_1),\ l' = l[y \to tid_1],\ l_1 = buildLocals(\bar{z}, m_1)}{buffer(bid, tid, \{tsk(tid, m, p, l, \langle y = x.m_1(\bar{z}, p_1); s\rangle)\} \cup \mathcal{Q}) \parallel buffer(bid_1, \_, \mathcal{Q}') \parallel B \rightsquigarrow}$
$buffer(bid, tid, \{tsk(tid, m, p, l', s)\} \cup \mathcal{Q}) \parallel$
$buffer(bid_1, \_, \{tsk(tid_1, m_1, p_1, l_1, body(m_1))\} \cup \mathcal{Q}') \parallel B$

(AWAIT1) $\dfrac{l(y) = tid_1,\ tsk(tid_1, \_, \_, \_, s_1) \in \mathsf{Buf},\ s_1 = \epsilon(v)}{buffer(bid, tid, \{tsk(tid, m, p, l, \langle \mathbf{await}\ y?; s\rangle)\} \cup \mathcal{Q}) \parallel B \rightsquigarrow}$
$buffer(bid, tid, \{tsk(tid, m, p, l, s)\} \cup \mathcal{Q}) \parallel B$

(AWAIT2) $\dfrac{l(y) = tid_1,\ tsk(tid_1, \_, \_, \_, s_1) \in \mathsf{Buf},\ s_1 \neq \epsilon(v)}{buffer(bid, tid, \{tsk(tid, m, p, l, \langle \mathbf{await}\ y?; s\rangle)\} \cup \mathcal{Q}) \parallel B \rightsquigarrow}$
$buffer(bid, \bot, \{tsk(tid, m, p, l, \langle \mathbf{await}\ y?; s\rangle)\} \cup \mathcal{Q}) \parallel B$

(RELEASE) $\overline{buffer(bid, tid, \{tsk(tid, m, p, l, \langle \mathbf{release}; s\rangle)\} \cup \mathcal{Q}) \parallel B \rightsquigarrow}$
$buffer(bid, \bot, \{tsk(tid, m, p, l, s)\} \cup \mathcal{Q}) \parallel B$

(RETURN) $\dfrac{v = l(x)}{buffer(bid, tid, \{tsk(tid, m, p, l, \langle \mathbf{return}\ x; \rangle)\} \cup \mathcal{Q}) \parallel B \rightsquigarrow}$
$buffer(bid, \bot, \{tsk(tid, m, p, l, \epsilon(v))\} \cup \mathcal{Q}) \parallel B$

Fig. 1. Summarized Semantics for a Priority-based Scheduling Async Language

buffer can take it. RELEASE: the current task frees the lock. RETURN: When **return** is executed, the return value is stored in v so that it can be obtained by the future variable that points to that task. Besides, the lock is released and will never be taken again by that task. Consequently, that task is *finished* (marked by adding the instruction $\epsilon(v)$) but it does not disappear from the state as its return value may be needed later on in an **await**.

Example 1. Figure 2 shows some simple methods which will illustrate different aspects of our analysis. In particular, non-termination of certain tasks and data races can occur if priorities are not properly assigned by the programmer, and later considered by the analysis. Our analysis will take the assigned priorities into account in order to gather the necessary MHP information to be able to guarantee termination and absence of data races. Let us by now only show some

```
 1 // g1 global variable        13 void m(){                    25 // main has priority 0
 2 // g2 global variable        14    while( g1 < 0 ){           26 main(){
 3 void task(){                 15       g1 = g1 + 1;            27    this.f(<>,10);
 4    g2 = g2 + 1;              16       release;                28    Fut x = this.m(<>,5);
 5 }                            17    }                          29    await x?;
 6 void f(){                    18 }                             30    this.h(<>,10);
 7    while( g1 > 0 ){          19 void h(){                     31    Buffer o=newbuffer;
 8       g1 = g1 - 1;           20    while(g1 > 0){             32    o.task(<>,0);
 9       g2 = g2 + 1;           21       g1 = g1 - 2;            33    ...
10       release;               22       release;                34 }
11    }                         23    }
12 }                            24 }
```

Fig. 2. Example for inter-buffer and intra-buffer may-happen-in-parallel relations

execution steps. The execution starts from a buffer 0 with a single task in which we are executing the main method. Let us assume that such task has been given the lowest priority 0. The global memory g is assumed to be properly initialized.

$St_0 \equiv \langle g, buffer(0, 0, \{tsk(0, \text{main}, 0, l, body(\text{main}))\})\rangle \xrightarrow{async}$
$St_1 \equiv \langle g, buffer(0, 0, \{tsk(0, ..), tsk(1, f, 10, ..)\})\rangle \xrightarrow{async}$
$St_2 \equiv \langle g, buffer(0, 0, \{tsk(0, ..), tsk(1, ..), tsk(2, m, 5..)\})\rangle \xrightarrow{await}$
$St_3 \equiv \langle g, buffer(0, \bot, \{tsk(0, .., await), tsk(1, ..), tsk(2, m, 5..)\})\rangle \xrightarrow{priority}$
$St_4 \equiv \langle g, buffer(0, 1, \{tsk(0, .., await), tsk(1, ..), tsk(2, m, 5..)\})\rangle \rightarrow^*$
$St_5 \equiv \langle g', buffer(0, 1, \{tsk(0, .., await), tsk(1, .., return), tsk(2, m, 5..)\})\rangle \xrightarrow{return}$
$St_6 \equiv \langle g', buffer(0, \bot, \{tsk(0, .., await), tsk(1, .., \epsilon(v)), tsk(2, m, 5..)\})\rangle \xrightarrow{priority}$
$St_7 \equiv \langle g', buffer(0, 2, \{tsk(0, .., await), tsk(1, .., \epsilon(v)), tsk(2, m, 5..)\})\rangle \rightarrow^*$
$St_8 \equiv \langle g'', buffer(0, 0, \{tsk(0, ..), tsk(1, .., \epsilon(v)), tsk(2, .., \epsilon(v)), tsk(3..)\})\rangle \xrightarrow{newbuf}$
$St_9 \equiv \langle g'', buffer(0, 0, \{tsk(0..), tsk(1..), tsk(2..), tsk(3..)\}), \rangle buffer(1, \bot, \{\})\rangle \xrightarrow{async}$
$St_{10} \equiv \langle g'', buffer(0, 0, \{tsk(0..), ..\}), \rangle buffer(1, \bot, \{task(4..)\})\rangle \xrightarrow{priority}$
$St_{11} \equiv \langle g'', buffer(0, 0, \{tsk(0..), ..\}), \rangle buffer(1, 4, \{task(4..)\})\rangle \dashrightarrow$

At St_1, we execute the instruction at Line 27 (L27 for short) that posts, in the current buffer **this**, a new task (with identifier 1) that will execute method f with priority 10. The next step St_2 posts another task (with identifier 2) in the current buffer with a lower priority (namely 5). At St_3, an **await** instruction (L29) is used to synchronize the execution with the completion of the task 2 spawned at L28. As the task executing f has higher priority than the one executing m, it will be selected for execution at St_4. After returning from the execution of task 1 in St_5, the PRIORITY rule selects task 2 for execution in St_6. An interesting aspect is that after creating buffer 1 at St_{10}, execution can non-deterministically choose buffer 0 or 1 (in St_{11} buffer 1 has been selected).

3 Definition of MHP

We first formally define the concrete property "MHP" that we want to approximate using static analysis. In what follows, we assume that instructions are labelled such that it is possible to obtain the corresponding program point identifiers. We also assume that program points are globally different. We use $p_{\dot{m}}$ to refer to the entry program point of method m, and $p_{\ddot{m}}$ to all program points after its **return** instruction. The set of all program points of P is denoted by P_p. We write $p \in m$ to indicate that program point p belongs to method m. Given a sequence of instructions s, we use $pp(s)$ to refer to the program point identifier associated with its first instruction and $pp(\epsilon(v)) = p_{\ddot{m}}$.

Definition 1 (concrete MHP). *Given a program P, its MHP is defined as $\mathcal{E}_P = \cup \{\mathcal{E}_S | S_0 \leadsto^* S\}$ where for $S = \langle g, \text{Buf} \rangle$, the set $\mathcal{E}_S$ is $\mathcal{E}_S = \{(pp(s_1), pp(s_2)) \mid buffer(bid_1, \_, \mathcal{Q}_1) \in \text{Buf}, buffer(bid_2, \_, \mathcal{Q}_2) \in \text{Buf}, t_1 = tsk(tid_1, \_, \_, \_, s_1) \in \mathcal{Q}_1, t_2 = tsk(tid_2, \_, \_, \_, s_2) \in \mathcal{Q}_2, tid_1 \neq tid_2\}$.*

The above definition considers the union of the pairs obtained from all derivations from S_0. This is because execution is non-deterministic in two dimensions: (1) in the selection of the buffer that is chosen for execution, since the buffers have access to the global memory different behaviours (and thus MHP pairs) can be obtained depending on the execution order, and (2) when there is more than one task with the highest priority, the selection is non-deterministic.

The MHP pairs can originate from *direct* or *indirect* task creation relationships. For instance, the parallelism between the points of the tasks executing h and task is *indirect* because they do not invoke one to the other directly, but a third task main invokes both of them. However, the parallelism between the points of the task main and those of task is *direct* because the first one invokes directly the latter one. Def. 1 captures all these forms of parallelism.

Importantly, $\mathcal{E}_P$ includes both *intra-buffer* and *inter-buffer* MHP pairs, each of which are relevant for different kinds of applications, as we explain below.

Intra-buffer MHP Pairs. Intra-buffer relations in Def. 1 are pairs in which $bid_1 \equiv bid_2$. We always have that the first instructions of all tasks which are pending in the buffer's queue may-happen-in-parallel among them, and also with the instruction of the task which is currently active (has the buffer's lock). This piece of information allows approximating the tasks interleavings that we may have in a considered buffer. In particular, when the execution is at a processor release point, we use the MHP pairs to see the instructions that may execute if the processor is released. Information about task interleavings is essential to infer termination and resource consumption in any concurrent setting (see [5]).

Example 2. Consider the execution trace in Ex. 1, we have the MHP pairs $(29, p_{\dot{f}})$ and $(29, p_{\dot{m}})$ since when the active task 0 is executing the **await** (point 29) in St_4, we have that tasks 1 and 2 are pending at their entry points. The following execution steps give rise to many other MHP pairs. The most relevant point to note is that in St_8 when the execution is at L30 and onwards, the tasks

(1) $\tau_\mathrm{p}(y=\mathsf{this}.m(\bar{x},p), M) = M[\langle y, O, Z, R\rangle/\langle\star, O, Z, R\rangle] \cup \{\langle y, \mathsf{t}, \tilde{m}, p\rangle\}$
(2) $\tau_\mathrm{p}(y=x.m(\bar{x},p), M) = M[\langle y, O, Z, R\rangle/\langle\star, O, Z, R\rangle] \cup \{\langle y, \mathsf{o}, \tilde{m}, p\rangle\}$
(3) $\tau_\mathrm{p}(\mathsf{release}, M) = \tau_\mathrm{p}(\mathsf{release}_1; \mathsf{release}_2, M)$
(4) $\tau_\mathrm{p}(\mathsf{release}_1, M) = M[\langle Y, \mathsf{t}, \tilde{m}, p\rangle/\langle Y, \mathsf{t}, \tilde{m}, \mathsf{p}\rangle]$ where $p \geq \mathsf{p}$
(5) $\tau_\mathrm{p}(\mathsf{release}_2, M) = M[\langle Y, \mathsf{t}, \tilde{m}, p\rangle/\langle Y, \mathsf{t}, \hat{m}, \mathsf{p}\rangle]$ where $p > \mathsf{p}$
(6) $\tau_\mathrm{p}(\mathsf{await}\ y?, M) = M'[\langle y, O, \tilde{m}, R\rangle/\langle y, O, \hat{m}, R\rangle]$
     where $M' = \tau_\mathrm{p}(\mathsf{release}_1; \mathsf{release}_2, M)$
(7) $\tau_\mathrm{p}(\mathsf{return}, M) = M[\langle Y, \mathsf{t}, \tilde{m}, R\rangle/\langle Y, \mathsf{t}, \tilde{m}, R\rangle]$
(8) $\tau_\mathrm{p}(b, M) = M$ otherwise

Fig. 3. Method-level MHP transfer function: $\tau_\mathrm{p} : s \times \mathcal{B} \mapsto \mathcal{B}$

1 and 2 are guaranteed to be at their exit program points $p_{\tilde{f}}$ and $p_{\tilde{m}}$. Thus, we will not have any MHP pair between the instructions that update the global variable g1 (L8 and L15 in tasks 1 and 2, resp.) and the release point at L22 of the task 3 executing h. This information is essential to prove the termination of h, as the analysis needs to be sure that the loop counter cannot be modified by instructions of other tasks that may execute in parallel with the body of this loop. The information is also needed to obtain an upper bound on the number of iterations of the loop and then infer the resource consumption of h.

Inter-buffer MHP Pairs. In addition to intra-buffer MHP relations, *inter-buffer* MHP pairs happen when $bid_1 \neq bid_2$. In this case, we obtain the instructions that may execute in parallel in different buffers. This information is relevant at least for two purposes: (1) to detect data-races in the access to the global memory and (2) to detect deadlocks and livelocks when one buffer is awaiting for the completion of one task running in another buffer, while such other task is awaiting for the completion of the current task, and the execution of these (synchronization) instructions happens in parallel (or simultaneously). If the language allows blocking the execution of the buffer such that no other pending task can take it, we have a deadlock, otherwise we have a livelock.

Example 3. Consider again the execution trace in Ex. 1, in St_{10} we have created a new buffer 1 in which task 4 starts to execute at St_{11}. We will have the inter-buffer pair (21,4) as we can have L21 executing in buffer 0 and L4 executing in buffer 1. Note that, if task had updated g1 instead of updating g2, we would have had a data race. Data races can lead to different types of errors, and static analyses that detect them are of utmost importance.

4 Method-Level Analysis with Priorities

In this section, we present the local phase of our MHP analysis which assigns to each program point, of a given method, an abstract state that describes the status of the tasks that have been locally invoked so far. The status of a task can be (1) *pending*, i.e., it is at the entry program point; (2) *finished*, i.e., it has executed a **return** instruction already; or (3) *active*, i.e., it can be executing at any program point (including the entry and the exit). The analysis uses *MHP atoms* which are syntactic objects of the form $\langle F, O, T, R \rangle$ where

- F is either a valid future variable name or $\star$. The value $\star$ indicates that the task might not be associated with any future variable, either because there is no need to synchronize with its result, or because the future has been reused and thus the association lost (this does not happen in our example);
- O is the *buffer name* that can be t or o, which resp. indicate that the task is executing on the same buffer or *maybe* on a different one;
- T can be $\check{m}$, $\tilde{m}$, or $\hat{m}$ where m is a method name. It indicates that the corresponding task is an instance of method m, and its status can be *pending*, *active*, or *finished* resp.;
- P is a natural number indicating the priority of the corresponding task.

Intuitively, an MHP atom $\langle F, O, T, R \rangle$ is read as follows: task T might be executing (in some status) on buffer O with priority P, and one can wait for it to finish using future variable F. The set of all MHP atoms is denoted by $\mathcal{A}$.

Example 4. The MHP atom $\langle x, \text{t}, \tilde{m}, 5 \rangle$ indicates that there is an instance of method m running in parallel, in the same buffer. This task is active (i.e., can be at any program point), has priority 5, and is associated with the future x. The MHP atom $\langle \star, \text{o}, \hat{task}, 0 \rangle$ indicates that there is an instance of method $task$ running in parallel, maybe in a different buffer. This task is finished (i.e., has executed **return**), has priority 0, and it is associated to any future variable.

An abstract state is a multiset of MHP atoms from $\mathcal{A}$. The set of all multisets over $\mathcal{A}$ is denoted by $\mathcal{B}$. Given $M \in \mathcal{B}$, we write $(a, i) \in M$ to indicate that a appears exactly $i > 0$ times in M. We omit i when it is 1. The local analysis is applied on each method and, as a result, it assigns an abstract state from $\mathcal{B}$ to each program point in the program. The analysis takes into account the priority of the method being analyzed. Thus, since a method might be called with different priorities $\text{p}_1, \ldots, \text{p}_n$, the analysis should be repeated for each p_i. For the sake of simplifying the presentation, we assume that each method is always called with the same priority. Handling several priorities is a context-sensitive analysis problem that can be done by, e.g., cloning the corresponding code.

The analysis of a given method, with respect to priority p, abstractly executes its code over abstract elements from $\mathcal{B}$. This execution uses a transfer function τ_p, depicted in Fig. 3, to rewrite abstract states. Given an instruction b and an abstract state $M \in \mathcal{B}$, $\tau_\text{p}(b, M)$ computes a new abstract state that results from abstractly executing b in state M. Note that the subscript p in τ_p is the priority of the method being analyzed. Let us explain the different cases of τ_p:

- (1) Posting a task on the same buffer adds a new MHP atom $\langle y, \text{t}, \check{m}, p \rangle$ to the abstract state. It indicates that an instance of m is pending, with priority p, on the *same* buffer as the analyzed method, and is associated

with future variable y. In addition, since y is assigned a new value, those atoms in M that were associated with y should now be associated with $\star$ in the new state. This is done by $M[\langle y, O, Z, R\rangle/\langle\star, O, Z, R\rangle]$ which replaces each atom that matches $\langle y, O, Z, R\rangle$ in M by $\langle\star, O, Z, R\rangle$;
- (2) It is similar to (1), the difference is that the new task might be posted on a buffer different from that of the method being analyzed. Thus, its status should be *active* since, unlike (1), it might start to execute immediately;
- (3)-(5) These cases highlight the use of priorities, and thus mark the main differences wrt [3]. They state that when releasing the processor, only tasks of equal or higher priorities are allowed to become active (simulated through **release**$_1$). Moreover, when taking the control back, any task with strictly higher priority is guaranteed to have been finished (simulated through **release**$_2$). Importantly, the abstract element after **release**$_1$ is associated to the program point of the **release** instruction, and that after **release**$_2$ is associated to the program point after the **release** instruction. These two auxiliary instructions are introduced to simulate the implicit "loop" (in the semantics) when the task is waiting at that point;
- (6) This instruction is similar to **release**, the only difference is that the status of the tasks that are associated with future variable y become finished in the following program point. Importantly, the abstract element after **release**$_1$ is associated to the program point of the **await** y?;
- (7) It changes the status of every pending task executing on the same buffer to active, this is because the processor is released. Note that we do not consider priorities in this case, since the task is finished.

In addition to using the transfer function for abstractly executing basic instructions, the analysis merges the results of paths (in conditions, loops, etc) using a join operator. We refer to [3] for formal definitions of the basic abstract interpretations operators. In what follows, we assume that the result of the local phase is given by means of a mapping $\mathcal{L}_P : P_p \mapsto \mathcal{B}$ which maps each program point p (including entry and exit points) to an abstract state $\mathcal{L}_P(p) \in \mathcal{B}$.

Example 5. Applying the local analysis on main, results in the following abstract states (initially the abstract state is $\emptyset$):

$$
\begin{array}{|l|}
\hline
28 : \{\langle \star, \mathsf{t}, \tilde{\mathsf{f}}, 10\rangle\} \\
29 : \{\langle \star, \mathsf{t}, \tilde{\mathsf{f}}, 10\rangle, \langle \mathsf{x}, \mathsf{t}, \tilde{\mathsf{m}}, 5\rangle\} \\
30 : \{\langle \star, \mathsf{t}, \hat{\mathsf{f}}, 10\rangle, \langle \mathsf{x}, \mathsf{t}, \hat{\mathsf{m}}, 5\rangle\} \\
31 : \{\langle \star, \mathsf{t}, \hat{\mathsf{f}}, 10\rangle, \langle \mathsf{x}, \mathsf{t}, \hat{\mathsf{m}}, 5\rangle, \langle \star, \mathsf{t}, \check{\mathsf{h}}, 10\rangle\} \\
32 : \{\langle \star, \mathsf{t}, \hat{\mathsf{f}}, 10\rangle, \langle \mathsf{x}, \mathsf{t}, \hat{\mathsf{m}}, 5\rangle, \langle \star, \mathsf{t}, \check{\mathsf{h}}, 10\rangle\} \\
33 : \{\langle \star, \mathsf{t}, \hat{\mathsf{f}}, 10\rangle, \langle \mathsf{x}, \mathsf{t}, \hat{\mathsf{m}}, 5\rangle, \langle \star, \mathsf{t}, \check{\mathsf{h}}, 10\rangle, \langle \star, \mathsf{o}, \tilde{\mathsf{task}}, 0\rangle\} \\
\hline
\end{array}
$$

Note that in the abstract state at program point 30 we have both f and m finished, this is because they have higher priority than main, and thus, while main is waiting at program point 29 both f and m must have completed their execution before main can proceed to the next instruction. If we ignore priorities, then we would infer that f might be active at program point 30 (which is less precise).

5 MHP Graph for Priority-Based Scheduling

In this section we will construct a MHP graph relating program points and methods in the program, that will be used to extract precise information on which program points might globally run in parallel. In order to build this graph, we use the local information computed in Sec. 4 which already takes priorities into account. In Sec. 5.2, we explain how to use the MHP graph to infer the MHP pairs in the program. Finally, in Sec. 5.3 we compare the inference method of MHP pairs using a priority-based scheduling with the technique introduced in [3] for programs with a non-deterministic scheduling.

5.1 Construction of the MHP Graph with Priorities

The MHP graph has different types of nodes and different types of edges. There are nodes that represent the status of methods (active, pending or finished) and nodes that represent the program points. Outgoing edges from method nodes are unweighted and unlabeled, they represent points of which at most one might be executing. Outgoing edges from program point nodes are *labeled*, written $\rightarrow_l$ where the label l is a tuple (O, R) that contains a priority R and a buffer name O. These edges represent tasks such that any of them might be running. Besides, when two nodes are directly connected by $i > 1$ edges, we connect them with a single edge superscripted with *weight i*, written as $\rightarrow_l^i$ where l is the label as before.

Definition 2 (MHP graph with priorities). *Given a program P, and its method-level MHP analysis result $\mathcal{L}_P$, the MHP graph of P is a directed graph $\mathcal{G}_P = \langle V, E \rangle$ with a set of nodes V and a set of edges $E = E_1 \cup E_2$ defined:*

$$V = \{\tilde{m}, \hat{m}, \breve{m} \mid m \in P_\mathcal{M}\} \cup P_\mathcal{P}$$
$$E_1 = \{\tilde{m} \rightarrow p \mid m \in P_\mathcal{M}, p \in P_\mathcal{P}, p \in m\} \cup \{\hat{m} \rightarrow p_{\tilde{m}}, \breve{m} \rightarrow p_{\tilde{m}} \mid m \in P_\mathcal{M}\}$$
$$E_2 = \{p \rightarrow_{(O,R)}^i x \mid p \in P_\mathcal{P}, (\langle \_, O, x, R \rangle, i) \in \mathcal{L}_P(p)\}$$

Example 6. Fig. 4 depicts the relevant fragment of the MHP graph for our running example. The graph only shows selected program points, namely all points of the main task and those points of the other tasks in which there is a **release** instruction, or in which the global memory is updated. For each task, we have three nodes which correspond to their possible status (except for h and task that we have omitted status that do not have incoming edges). In order to avoid cluttering the graph, in edges from program points, the labels only show the priority. The weight is omitted as it is always 1. The label corresponding to the buffer name is depicted using different types of arrows: normal arrows correspond to the buffer name o, while dashed arrows to t. From the pending (resp. finished) nodes, we always have an edge to the task entry (resp. exit) point. From the active nodes, we have edges to all program points in the corresponding method body, meaning that only one of them can be executing. The key aspect of the

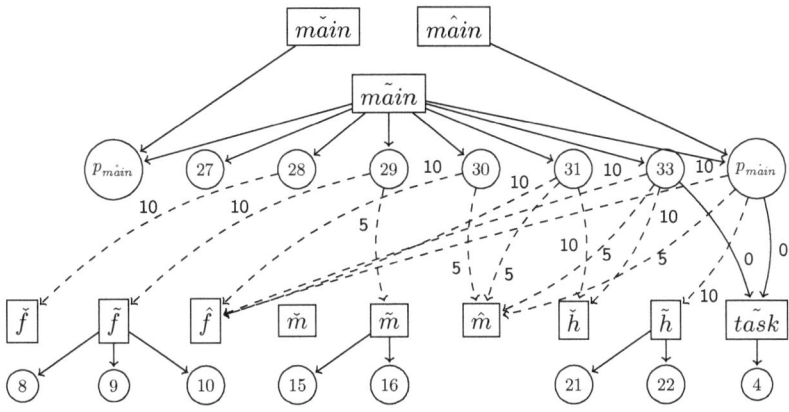

Fig. 4. MHP graph with priorities of the example

MHP graph is how we integrate the information gathered by the local analysis (with priorities) to build the edges from the program points: we can observe that node 28 has an edge to pending f, and at the **await** (node 29) the edges go to active f and m. After **await**, in nodes 30 and the next ones, the edges go to finished tasks. The remaining tasks only have edges to their program points since they do not make calls to other tasks.

5.2 Inference of Priority-Based MHP Pairs

The inference of MHP pairs is based on the notion of *intra-buffer path* in the MHP graph. A path from p_1 to p_2 is called *intra-buffer* if the program points p_1 and p_2 are reachable only through tasks in the same buffer. A simple way to ensure the intra-buffer condition is by checking that the buffer labels are always of type t (more accurate alternatives are discussed later). Intuitively, two program points $p_1, p_2 \in P_p$ may run in parallel if one of the following conditions hold:

1. there is a non-empty path in $\mathcal{G}_p$ from p_1 to p_2 or vice-versa; or
2. there is a program point $p_3 \in P_p$, and non-empty *intra-buffer* paths from p_3 to p_1 and from p_3 to p_2 that are either different in the first edge, or they share the first edge but it has weight $i > 1$, and the *minimum priority* in both paths is the same; or
3. there is a program point $p_3 \in P_p$, and non-empty paths from p_3 to p_1 and from p_3 to p_2 that are either different in the first edge, or they share the first edge but it has weight $i > 1$, and at least one of the paths is not intra-buffer.

The first case corresponds to *direct MHP* scenarios in which, when a task is running at p_1, there is another task running from which it is possible to *transitively* reach p_2, or vice-versa. For instance (33,4) is a direct MHP resulting from the direct call from main to task.

The second and third cases correspond to *indirect MHP* scenarios in which a task is running at p_3 and there are two other tasks p_1 and p_2 executing in parallel and both are reachable from p_3. However, the second condition takes advantage of the priority information in intra-buffer paths to discard potential MHP pairs: if the minimum priority of path $pt_1 \equiv p_3 \rightsquigarrow p_1$ is lower than the minimum priority of $pt_2 \equiv p_3 \rightsquigarrow p_2$, then we are sure that the task containing the program point p_2 will be finished before the task containing p_1 starts. For instance, consider the two paths from 29 to 8 and from 29 to 16, which form the potential MHP pair (8,16). They are both intra-buffer (executing on buffer 0) and the minimum priority is not the same (the one to 16 has lower priority). Thus, (16,8) is not an MHP pair. The intuition is that the task with minimum priority (m in this case) will be *pending* and will not start its execution until all the tasks in the other path are finished. Similarly, we obtain that the potential MHP pair (10,15) is not a real MHP pair. Knowing that (10,15) and (16,8) are not MHP pairs is important because this allows us to prove termination of both tasks executing m and f. This is an improvement over the standard MHP analysis in [3], where they are considered as MHP pairs—see Sect. 5.3. On the other hand, when a path involves tasks running in several buffers (condition 3), priorities cannot be taken into account, as the buffers (and their task schedulers) work independently. Observe that, in the second and third conditions, the first edge can only be shared if it has weight $i > 1$ because it denotes that there might be more than one instance of the same type of task running. For instance, if we add the instruction o.task(<>,0) at L33 we will infer the pair (4,4), reporting a potential data race in the access to g2.

Let us formalize the inference of the priority-based MHP pairs. We write $p_1 \rightsquigarrow p_2 \in \mathcal{G}_P$ to indicate that there is a path from p_1 to p_2 in $\mathcal{G}_P$ such that the sum of the edges weights is greater than or equal to 1, and $p_1 \to^i x \rightsquigarrow p_2 \in \mathcal{G}_P$ to mark that the path starts with an edge to x with weight i. We will say that a path $p_1 \rightsquigarrow p_2 \in \mathcal{G}_P$ is *intra-buffer* if all the edges from program points to methods have t labels. Similarly, we will say that p is the *lowest priority of the path* $p_1 \rightsquigarrow p_2 \in \mathcal{G}_P$, written $lowestP(p_1 \rightsquigarrow p_2) = p$, if p is the smallest priority of all those that appear in edges from program points to methods in the path. We now define the *priority-based MHP pairs* as follows.

Definition 3. *Given a program P, we let $\tilde{\mathcal{E}}_P = D \cup I_{intra} \cup I_{inter}$ where*

$$D = \{(p_1, p_2) \mid p_1, p_2 \in P_\mathcal{P}, p_1 \rightsquigarrow p_2 \in \mathcal{G}_P)\}$$

$$I_{intra} = \{(p_1, p_2) \mid p_1, p_2, p_3 \in P_\mathcal{P}, p_3 \xrightarrow{i} x_1 \rightsquigarrow p_1 \in \mathcal{G}_P, p_3 \xrightarrow{j} x_2 \rightsquigarrow p_2 \in \mathcal{G}_P,$$
$$p_3 \xrightarrow{i} x_1 \rightsquigarrow p_1 \text{ is intra}-\text{buffer}, lowestP(p_3 \xrightarrow{i} x_1 \rightsquigarrow p_1) = pr_1,$$
$$p_3 \xrightarrow{j} x_2 \rightsquigarrow p_2 \text{ is intra}-\text{buffer}, lowestP(p_3 \xrightarrow{j} x_2 \rightsquigarrow p_2) = pr_2,$$
$$(x_1 \neq x_2 \vee (x_1 = x_2 \wedge i = j > 1)) \wedge pr_1 = pr_2\}$$

$$I_{inter} = \{(p_1, p_2) \mid p_1, p_2, p_3 \in P_\mathcal{P}, p_3 \xrightarrow{i} x_1 \rightsquigarrow p_1 \in \mathcal{G}_P, p_3 \xrightarrow{j} x_2 \rightsquigarrow p_2 \in \mathcal{G}_P,$$
$$p_3 \xrightarrow{i} x_1 \rightsquigarrow p_1 \text{ or } p_3 \xrightarrow{j} x_2 \rightsquigarrow p_2 \text{ are not intra}-\text{buffer},$$
$$x_1 \neq x_2 \vee (x_1 = x_2 \wedge i = j > 1)\}$$

An interesting point is that even if priorities can only be taken into account at an intra-buffer level, due to the inter-buffer synchronization operations, they allow discarding unfeasible MHP pairs at an inter-buffer level. For instance, we can see that (4,9), which would report an spurious data race, is not an MHP pair. Note that 4 and 9 execute in different buffers. Still, the priority-based local analysis has allowed us to infer that after 29, task f will be finished and thus, it cannot happen in parallel with the execution of task in buffer o. Thus, it is ensured that there will not be a data-race in the access to g2 from the two different buffers.

The following theorem states the soundness of the analysis, namely, that $\tilde{\mathcal{E}}_P$ is an over-approximation of $\mathcal{E}_P$—the proof appears in the extended version of this paper [6]. Let $\mathcal{E}_P^{non-det}$ be the MHP pairs obtained by [3].

Theorem 1 (soundness). $\mathcal{E}_P \subseteq \tilde{\mathcal{E}}_P \subseteq \mathcal{E}_P^{non-det}$.

As we have discussed above, a sufficient condition for ensuring the intra-buffer condition of paths is to take priorities into account when all edges are labelled with the t buffer. However, if buffers can be uniquely identified at analysis time (as in the language of [9]), we can be more accurate. In particular, instead of using o to refer to any buffer, we would use the proper buffer name in the labels of the edges. Then, the intra-buffer condition will be ensured by checking that the buffer name along the considered paths is always the same.

In our language, buffers can be dynamically created, i.e., the number of buffers is not fixed a priori and one could have even an unbounded number of buffers (e.g., using newBuffer inside a loop). The standard way to handle this situation in static analysis is by incorporating points-to information [17,15] which allows us to over-approximate the buffers created. A well-known approximation is by buffer creation site such that all buffers created at the same program point are abstracted by a single abstract name. In this setting, we can take advantage of the priorities (and apply case 2 in Def. 3) only if we are sure that an abstract name is referring to a single concrete buffer. As the task scheduler of each buffer works independently, we cannot use knowledge on the priorities to discard pairs if the abstract buffer might correspond to several concrete buffers. The extension of our framework to handle these cases is subject if future work.

5.3 Comparison with Non-priority MHP Graphs

The new MHP graphs with priority information (Sec. 5.1), and the conditions to infer MHP pairs (Sec. 5.2), are extensions of the corresponding notions in [3]. The original MHP graphs were defined as in Def. 2 with the following differences:

- The edges in E_2 do not contain the label (O,R) with the buffer name and the priority, but only the weight.
- The method-level analysis $\mathcal{L}_p(p)$ in [3] does not take priorities into account, so after a **release** instruction, pending tasks are set to active. With the method-level analysis in this paper (Sect. 4), tasks with a higher priority in the same buffer are set to finished after a **release** instruction—case (4) in Fig. 3. This generates less paths in the resulting MHP graph with priorities and therefore less MHP pairs.

- In [3], there is another type of nodes (future variable nodes) used to increase the accuracy when the same future variable is re-used in several calls in branching instructions. For the sake of simplicity we have not included future nodes here as their treatment would be identical as in [3].

Regarding the conditions to infer MHP pairs, only two are considered in [3]:

1. there is a non-empty path in $\mathcal{G}_p$ from p_1 to p_2 or vice-versa; or
2. there is a program point $p_3 \in P_p$, and non-empty paths from p_3 to p_1 and from p_3 to p_2 that are either different in the first edge, or they share the first edge but it has weight $i > 1$.

The first case is the same as the first condition in Sect 5.2. The second case corresponds to indirect MHP scenarios and is a generalization of conditions 2 and 3 in Sect 5.2 without considering priorities and intra-buffer paths. With these conditions, we have that the **release** point 22 cannot happen in parallel with the instructions that modify the value of the loop counter g1 (namely 8 and 15), because there is no direct or indirect path connecting them starting from a program point. However, we have the indirect MHP pairs (10,15) and (16,8), meaning respectively that at the release point of f the counter g1 can be modified by an interleaved execution of m and that at the release point of m the counter g1 can be modified by an interleaved execution of f. Such spurious interleavings prevent us from proving termination of the tasks executing f and m and, as we have seen in Sec. 5.2, they are eliminated with the new MHP graphs with priorities and the new conditions for inferring MHP pairs.

6 Implementation in the MayPar System

We have implemented our analysis in a tool called MayPar [4], which takes as input a program written in the ABS language [12] extended with priority annotations. ABS is based on the concurrency model in Sec. 2 and uses the concept of *concurrent object* to realize the concept of task-buffer, such that object creation corresponds to buffer creation, and a method call o.m() posts a task executing m on the queue of object o. Currently the annotations are provided at the level of methods, instead of at the level of tasks. This is because we lacked the syntax in the ABS language to include annotations in the calls, but the adaptation to calls will be straightforward once we have the parser extended.

We have made our implementation and a series of examples available online at http://costa.ls.fi.upm.es/costabs/mhp. After selecting an example, the analysis options allow: the selection of the entry method, enabling the option to consider priorities in the analysis, and several other options related to the format for displaying the analysis results and the verbosity level. After the analysis, MayPar yields in the output the MHP pairs in textual format and also optionally a graphical representation of the MHP graph. Besides, MayPar can be used in an interactive way which allows the user to select a line and the tool highlights all program points that may happen in parallel with it.

The examples on the MayPar site that include priority annotations are within the folder priorities. It is also possible to upload new examples by writing them in the text area. In order to evaluate our proposal, we have included a series of small examples that contain challenging patterns for priority-based MHP analysis (including our running example) and we have also encoded the examples in the second experiment of [9] and adapted them to our language (namely we use **await** on futures instead of **assume** on heap values). MayPar with priority-scheduling can successfully analyze all of them. Although these examples are rather small programs, this is not due to scalability limits of MayPar. It is rather because of the modeling overhead required to set up actual programs for static analysis.

7   Conclusions and Related Work

May-happen-in-parallel relations are of utmost importance to guarantee the sound behaviour of concurrent and parallel programs. They are a basic component of other analyses that prove termination, resource consumption boundness, data-race and deadlock freeness. As our main contribution, we have leveraged an existing MHP analysis developed for a simplistic scenario in which any task could be selected for execution in order to take task-priorities into account. Interestingly, have succeeded to take priorities into account both at the intra-buffer level and, indirectly, also at an inter-buffer level.

To the best of our knowledge, there is no previous MHP analysis for a priority-based scheduling. Our starting point is the MHP analysis for concurrent objects in [3]. Concurrent objects are almost identical to our multi-buffer asynchronous programs. The main difference is that, instead of buffers, the concurrency units are the objects. The language in [3] is data-race free because it is not allowed to access an object field from a different object. Our main novelty w.r.t. [3] is the integration of the priority-based scheduler in the framework. Although we have considered a cooperative concurrency model in which processor release points are explicit in the program, it is straightforward to handle a preemptive scheduling at the intra-buffer level like in [9], by simply adding a release point after posting a new task. If the posted task has higher priority, the active task will be suspended and the posted task will become active. Thus, our analysis works directly for this model as well. As regards analyses for Java-like languages [14,7], we have that a fundamental difference with our approach is that they do not take thread-priorities into account nor consider any synchronization between the threads as we do. To handle preemptive scheduling at the inter-buffer level, one needs to assume processor release points at any instruction in the program, and then the main ideas of our analysis would be applicable. However, we believe that the loss of precision could be significant in this setting.

Acknowledgements. This work was funded partially by EU project FP7-ICT-610582 ENVISAGE: *Engineering Virtualized Services* (http://www.envisage-project.eu), by the Spanish projects TIN2008-05624, TIN2012-38137, PRI-AIBDE-2011-0900 and by the Madrid Regional

Government project S2009TIC-1465. We also want to acknowledge Antonio Flores-Montoya for his help and advice when implementing the analysis in the MayPar system.

References

1. Ericsson, A.: Erlang Efficiency Guide, 5.8.5 edn. (October 2011), http://www.erlang.org/doc/efficiency_guide/users_guide.html
2. Agha, G.A.: Actors: A Model of Concurrent Computation in Distributed Systems. MIT Press, Cambridge (1986)
3. Albert, E., Flores-Montoya, A.E., Genaim, S.: Analysis of May-Happen-in-Parallel in Concurrent Objects. In: Giese, H., Rosu, G. (eds.) FMOODS/FORTE 2012. LNCS, vol. 7273, pp. 35–51. Springer, Heidelberg (2012)
4. Albert, E., Flores-Montoya, A., Genaim, S.: Maypar: a May-Happen-in-Parallel Analyzer for Concurrent Objects. In: SIGSOFT/FSE 2012, pp. 1–4. ACM (2012)
5. Albert, E., Flores-Montoya, A., Genaim, S., Martin-Martin, E.: Termination and Cost Analysis of Loops with Concurrent Interleavings. In: Van Hung, D., Ogawa, M. (eds.) ATVA 2013. LNCS, vol. 8172, pp. 349–364. Springer, Heidelberg (2013)
6. Albert, E., Genaim, S., Martin-Martin, E.: May-Happen-in-Parallel Analysis for Priority-based Scheduling (Extended Version). Technical Report SIC 12/13. Univ. Complutense de Madrid (2013)
7. Barik, R.: Efficient computation of may-happen-in-parallel information for concurrent java programs. In: Ayguadé, E., Baumgartner, G., Ramanujam, J., Sadayappan, P. (eds.) LCPC 2005. LNCS, vol. 4339, pp. 152–169. Springer, Heidelberg (2006)
8. de Boer, F.S., Clarke, D., Johnsen, E.B.: A Complete Guide to the Future. In: De Nicola, R. (ed.) ESOP 2007. LNCS, vol. 4421, pp. 316–330. Springer, Heidelberg (2007)
9. Emmi, M., Lal, A., Qadeer, S.: Asynchronous programs with prioritized task-buffers. In: SIGSOFT FSE, p. 48. ACM (2012)
10. Flores-Montoya, A.E., Albert, E., Genaim, S.: May-Happen-in-Parallel based Deadlock Analysis for Concurrent Objects. In: Beyer, D., Boreale, M. (eds.) FMOODS/FORTE 2013. LNCS, vol. 7892, pp. 273–288. Springer, Heidelberg (2013)
11. Haller, P., Odersky, M.: Scala actors: Unifying thread-based and event-based programming. Theor. Comput. Sci. 410(2-3), 202–220 (2009)
12. Johnsen, E.B., Hähnle, R., Schäfer, J., Schlatte, R., Steffen, M.: ABS: A Core Language for Abstract Behavioral Specification. In: Aichernig, B.K., de Boer, F.S., Bonsangue, M.M. (eds.) FMCO 2010. LNCS, vol. 6957, pp. 142–164. Springer, Heidelberg (2011)
13. Lee, J.K., Palsberg, J.: Featherweight X10: A Core Calculus for Async-Finish Parallelism. In: Proc. of PPoPP 2010, pp. 25–36. ACM (2010)
14. Li, L., Verbrugge, C.: A practical mhp information analysis for concurrent java programs. In: Eigenmann, R., Li, Z., Midkiff, S.P. (eds.) LCPC 2004. LNCS, vol. 3602, pp. 194–208. Springer, Heidelberg (2005)
15. Milanova, A., Rountev, A., Ryder, B.G.: Parameterized Object Sensitivity for Points-to and Side-effect Analyses for Java. In: ISSTA, pp. 1–11 (2002)
16. Naik, M., Park, C., Sen, K., Gay, D.: Effective static deadlock detection. In: Proc. of ICSE, pp. 386–396. IEEE (2009)
17. Whaley, J., Lam, M.S.: Cloning-based context-sensitive pointer alias analysis using binary decision diagrams. In: PLDI, pp. 131–144. ACM (2004)

The Complexity of Clausal Fragments of LTL

Alessandro Artale[1], Roman Kontchakov[2], Vladislav Ryzhikov[1],
and Michael Zakharyaschev[2]

[1] KRDB Research Centre
Free University of Bozen-Bolzano
I-39100 Bolzano, Italy
{artale,ryzhikov}@inf.unibz.it

[2] Department of Computer Science and Information Systems
Birkbeck, University of London
London WC1E 7HX, UK
{roman,michael}@dcs.bbk.ac.uk

Abstract. We introduce and investigate a number of fragments of propositional temporal logic LTL over the flow of time $(\mathbb{Z}, <)$. The fragments are defined in terms of the available temporal operators and the structure of the clausal normal form of the temporal formulas. We determine the computational complexity of the satisfiability problem for each of the fragments, which ranges from NLOGSPACE to PTIME, NP and PSPACE.

1 Introduction

We consider the (PSPACE-complete) propositional temporal logic LTL over the flow of time $(\mathbb{Z}, <)$. Our aim is to investigate how the computational complexity of the satisfiability problem for LTL-formulas depends on the form of their clausal representation and the available temporal operators.

Sistla and Clarke [26] showed that satisfiability of LTL-formulas with all standard operators ('next-time', 'always in the future', 'eventually' and 'until') is PSPACE-complete; see also [18,19]. Ono and Nakamura [22] proved that for formulas with only 'always in the future' and 'eventually' the satisfiability problem becomes NP-complete. Since then a number of fragments of LTL of different complexity have been identified. For example, Chen and Lin [10] observed that the complexity does not change if we restrict attention to temporal Horn formulas. Demri and Schnoebelen [12] determined the complexity of fragments that depend on three parameters: the available temporal operators, the number of nested temporal operators, and the number of propositional variables in formulas. Markey [21] analysed fragments defined by the allowed set of temporal operators, their nesting and the use of negation. Dixon et al. [13] introduced a XOR fragment of LTL and showed its tractability. Bauland et al. [7] systematically investigated the complexity of fragments given by both temporal operators and Boolean connectives (using Post's lattice of sets of Boolean functions).

In this paper, we classify temporal formulas according to their clausal normal form. Recall [14] that any LTL-formula over $(\mathbb{N}, <)$ can be transformed into an equisatisfiable formula in the so-called *separated normal form* that consists of

Table 1. The complexity of clausal fragments of LTL

temporal operators α	$\boxdot, \Box_F, \Box_P, \bigcirc_F, \bigcirc_P$ $\mathsf{LTL}_\alpha^{\Box,\bigcirc}$	$\boxdot, \Box_F, \Box_P$ $\mathsf{LTL}_\alpha^{\Box}$	$\boxdot$ $\mathsf{LTL}_\alpha^{\boxdot}$
bool	PSPACE ($\leq$ [26])	NP ($\leq$ [22])	NP
horn	PSPACE ($\geq$ [10])	PTIME [$\leq$ Th. 3]	PTIME
krom	NP [$\leq$ Th. 1]	NP [$\geq$ Th. 5]	NLOGSPACE
core	NP [$\geq$ Th. 2]	NLOGSPACE [$\leq$ Th. 4]	NLOGSPACE

initial clauses (setting conditions at moment 0), step clauses (defining transitions between consecutive states), and eventuality clauses (defining the states that must be reached infinitely often). Our clausal normal form is a slight generalisation of the separated normal form. The main building blocks are *positive temporal literals* λ given by the following grammar:

$$\lambda ::= \bot \mid p \mid \bigcirc_F \lambda \mid \bigcirc_P \lambda \mid \Box_F \lambda \mid \Box_P \lambda \mid \boxdot \lambda, \qquad (1)$$

where p is a propositional variable, $\bigcirc_F$ and $\bigcirc_P$ are the next- and previous-time operators, and $\Box_F$, $\Box_P$, $\boxdot$ are the operators 'always in the future,' 'always in the past' and 'always.' We say that a temporal formula φ is in *clausal normal form* if

$$\varphi ::= \lambda \mid \neg\lambda \mid \boxdot(\neg\lambda_1 \vee \cdots \vee \neg\lambda_n \vee \lambda_{n+1} \vee \cdots \vee \lambda_{n+m}) \mid \varphi_1 \wedge \varphi_2. \qquad (2)$$

Conjunctions of positive and *negative* ($\neg\lambda$) literals can be thought of as initial clauses, while conjunctions of $\boxdot$-formulas generalise both step and eventuality clauses of the separated normal form. Similarly to [15] one can show that any LTL-formula over $(\mathbb{Z}, <)$ is equisatisfiable to a formula in clausal normal form.

We consider twelve fragments of LTL that will be denoted by $\mathsf{LTL}_\alpha^{\Box,\bigcirc}$, $\mathsf{LTL}_\alpha^{\Box}$ and $\mathsf{LTL}_\alpha^{\boxdot}$, for $\alpha \in \{\textit{bool, horn, krom, core}\}$. The superscript in the language name indicates the temporal operators that can be used in its positive literals. Thus, $\mathsf{LTL}_\alpha^{\Box,\bigcirc}$ uses all types of positive literals, $\mathsf{LTL}_\alpha^{\Box}$ can only use the $\Box$-operators:

$$\lambda ::= \bot \mid p \mid \Box_F \lambda \mid \Box_P \lambda \mid \boxdot \lambda,$$

and $\mathsf{LTL}_\alpha^{\boxdot}$ only the $\boxdot$-operator:

$$\lambda ::= \bot \mid p \mid \boxdot \lambda.$$

The subscript α in the language name refers to the form of the clauses

$$\neg\lambda_1 \vee \cdots \vee \neg\lambda_n \vee \lambda_{n+1} \vee \cdots \vee \lambda_{n+m} \qquad (3)$$

($m, n \geq 0$) that can be used in the formulas φ:

- *bool*-clauses are arbitrary clauses of the form (3),
- *horn*-clauses have at most one positive literal (that is, $m \leq 1$),

- *krom*-clauses are binary (that is, $n + m \leq 2$),
- *core*-clauses are binary with at most one positive literal ($n + m \leq 2$, $m \leq 1$).

The tight complexity bounds in Table 1 show how the complexity of the satisfiability problem for LTL-formulas depends on the form of clauses and the available temporal operators. The PSPACE upper bound for $\mathsf{LTL}_{bool}^{\Box,\bigcirc}$ is well-known [18,26,24,25]; the matching lower bound can be obtained already for $\mathsf{LTL}_{horn}^{\Box,\bigcirc}$ without $\Box_F$ and $\Box_P$ by a standard encoding of deterministic Turing machines with polynomial tape [10]. The NP upper bound for $\mathsf{LTL}_{bool}^{\Box}$ is also well-known [22], and the PTIME and NLOGSPACE lower bounds for $\mathsf{LTL}_{horn}^{\circledast}$ and $\mathsf{LTL}_{core}^{\circledast}$ coincide with the complexity of the respective non-temporal languages. The upper bounds for the $\mathsf{LTL}_\alpha^{\circledast}$ fragments can be obtained by embedding into the the underlying propositional fragments; see the full paper [6] for details.

The main contributions of this paper are the remaining complexity results in Table 1. The complexity of the $\mathsf{LTL}_\alpha^{\Box}$ fragments matches the complexity of the underlying non-temporal fragments except for the Krom case, where we can use the clauses $\neg p \vee \neg \Box_F q$ and $q \vee r$ to say that $p \to \Diamond_F r$ (if p then eventually r), which allows one to encode 3-colourability and results in NP-hardness. It is known that the addition of the operators $\bigcirc_F$ and $\bigcirc_P$ to the language with $\Box_F$ and $\Box_P$ usually increases the complexity (note that the proofs of the lower bounds for the $\mathsf{LTL}_\alpha^{\Box,\bigcirc}$ fragments require only $\circledast$ and $\bigcirc_F$). It is rather surprising that this does not happen in the case of the Krom fragment, while the complexity of the corresponding core fragment jumps from NLOGSPACE to NP.

We prove the upper bounds using two different techniques. The existence of models for $\mathsf{LTL}_{krom}^{\Box,\bigcirc}$-formulas is checked in Section 3 by guessing a small number of types and exponentially large distances between them (given in binary) and then using unary automata (and the induced arithmetic progressions) to verify correctness of the guess in polynomial time. In Section 4.1, we design a calculus for $\mathsf{LTL}_{core}^{\Box}$ in which derivations can be thought of as paths in a graph over the propositions labelled by moments of time. Thus, the existence of such derivations is essentially the graph reachability problem and can be solved in NLOGSPACE.

2 The Clausal Normal Form for LTL

The *propositional linear-time temporal logic* LTL (see, e.g., [16,17] and references therein) we consider in this paper is interpreted over the flow of time $(\mathbb{Z}, <)$. LTL-*formulas* are built from propositional variables $p_0, p_1, \ldots$, propositional constants $\top$ and $\bot$, the Boolean connectives $\wedge, \vee, \to$ and $\neg$, and two binary temporal operators $\mathcal{S}$ ('since') and $\mathcal{U}$ ('until'), which are assumed to be 'strict.' So, the other temporal operators mentioned in the introduction can be defined via $\mathcal{S}$ and $\mathcal{U}$ as follows:

$$\bigcirc_F \varphi = \bot \mathcal{U} \varphi, \quad \Diamond_F \varphi = \top \mathcal{U} \varphi, \quad \Box_F \varphi = \neg \Diamond_F \neg \varphi, \quad \circledast \varphi = \Diamond_P \Diamond_F \varphi,$$
$$\bigcirc_P \varphi = \bot \mathcal{S} \varphi, \quad \Diamond_P \varphi = \top \mathcal{S} \varphi, \quad \Box_P \varphi = \neg \Diamond_P \neg \varphi, \quad \circledast \varphi = \Box_P \Box_F \varphi.$$

A *temporal interpretation*, $\mathfrak{M}$, defines a truth-relation between moments of time $n \in \mathbb{Z}$ and propositional variables p_i. We write $\mathfrak{M}, n \models p_i$ to indicate that p_i is true at the moment n in the interpretation $\mathfrak{M}$. This truth-relation is extended to all LTL-formulas as follows (the Booleans are interpreted as expected):

$\mathfrak{M}, n \models \varphi \,\mathcal{U}\, \psi$ iff there is $k > n$ with $\mathfrak{M}, k \models \psi$ and $\mathfrak{M}, m \models \varphi$, for $n < m < k$,
$\mathfrak{M}, n \models \varphi \,\mathcal{S}\, \psi$ iff there is $k < n$ with $\mathfrak{M}, k \models \psi$ and $\mathfrak{M}, m \models \varphi$, for $k < m < n$.

An LTL-formula φ is *satisfiable* if there is an interpretation $\mathfrak{M}$ such that $\mathfrak{M}, 0 \models \varphi$; in this case we call $\mathfrak{M}$ a *model* of φ. We denote the length of φ by $|\varphi|$.

Recall that LTL-formulas of the form (2) were said to be in *clausal normal form*, and the class of such formulas was denoted by $\mathsf{LTL}_{bool}^{\Box,\bigcirc}$. The clauses (3) will often be represented as $\lambda_1 \wedge \cdots \wedge \lambda_n \to \lambda_{n+1} \vee \cdots \vee \lambda_{n+m}$ (where the empty disjunction is $\bot$ and the empty conjunction is $\top$).

Lemma 1 (clausal normal form). *For every LTL-formula, one can construct an equisatisfiable $\mathsf{LTL}_{bool}^{\Box,\bigcirc}$-formula. The construction requires logarithmic space.*

The proof of this lemma is similar to the proof of [15, Theorem 3.3.1] and uses fixed-point unfolding and renaming [15,23]. For example, we can replace every positive occurrence (that is, an occurrence in the scope of an even number of negations) of $p\,\mathcal{U}\,q$ in a given formula φ with a fresh propositional variable r and add the conjuncts $\boxasterisk(r \to \bigcirc_F q \vee \bigcirc_F p)$, $\boxasterisk(r \to \bigcirc_F q \vee \bigcirc_F r)$ and $\boxasterisk(r \to \Diamond_F q)$ to φ. The result contains no positive occurrences of $p\,\mathcal{U}\,q$ and is equisatisfiable with φ: the first two conjuncts are the fixed-point unfolding $(p\,\mathcal{U}\,q) \to \bigcirc_F q \vee (\bigcirc_F p \wedge \bigcirc_F (p\,\mathcal{U}\,q))$, while the last conjunct ensures that the fixed-point is eventually reached.

The next lemma allows us to consider an even more restricted classes of formulas. In what follows, we do not distinguish between a set of formulas and the conjunction of its members, and we write $\boxasterisk \Phi$ for the conjunction $\bigwedge_{\chi \in \Phi} \boxasterisk \chi$.

Lemma 2. *Let $\mathcal{L}$ be one of $\mathsf{LTL}_\alpha^{\Box,\bigcirc}$, $\mathsf{LTL}_\alpha^\Box$, $\mathsf{LTL}_\alpha^{\boxasterisk}$, for $\alpha \in \{bool, horn, krom, core\}$. For any $\mathcal{L}$-formula φ, one can construct, in log-space, an equisatisfiable $\mathcal{L}$-formula*

$$\Psi \wedge \boxasterisk \Phi, \qquad (4)$$

where Ψ is a conjunction of propositional variables from Φ, and Φ is a conjunction of clauses of the form (3) containing only $\bigcirc_F$, $\Box_P$, $\Box_F$ for $\mathsf{LTL}_\alpha^{\Box,\bigcirc}$, only $\Box_P$, $\Box_F$ for $\mathsf{LTL}_\alpha^\Box$, and only $\boxasterisk$ for $\mathsf{LTL}_\alpha^{\boxasterisk}$, in which the temporal operators are not nested.

Proof. First, we take a fresh variable p and replace all the conjuncts of the form λ and $\neg\lambda$ in φ by $\boxasterisk(\neg p \vee \lambda)$ and $\boxasterisk(\neg p \vee \neg\lambda)$, respectively; we set $\Psi = p$. For an $\mathsf{LTL}_\alpha^{\Box,\bigcirc}$ or $\mathsf{LTL}_\alpha^\Box$-formula, we replace the temporal literals $\boxasterisk \lambda$ with $\Box_F \Box_P \lambda$. Then, for each $\bigcirc_P \lambda$, we take a fresh variable, denoted $\overline{\bigcirc_P \lambda}$, replace each occurrence of $\bigcirc_P \lambda$ with $\overline{\bigcirc_P \lambda}$ and add the conjuncts $\boxasterisk(\bigcirc_F \overline{\bigcirc_P \lambda} \to \lambda)$ and $\boxasterisk(\lambda \to \bigcirc_F \overline{\bigcirc_P \lambda})$ to the resulting formula. In a similar manner, we use fresh

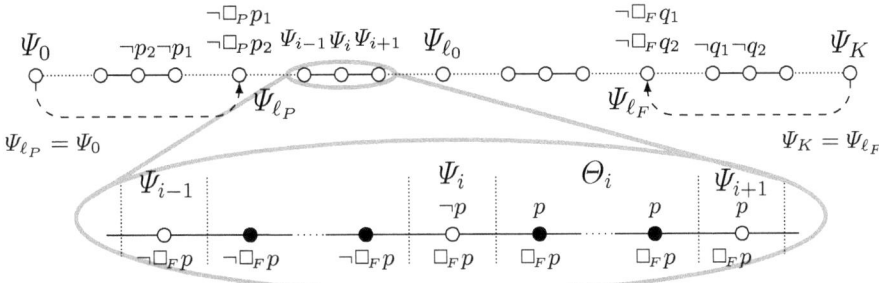

Fig. 1. The structure of a model in Lemma 3

propositional variables as abbreviations for nested temporal operators and obtain the required equisatisfiable formula. Clearly, this can be done in logarithmic space. □

We now characterise the structure of interpretations satisfying formulas φ^* of the form (4) in a way similar to other known descriptions of temporal models; see, e.g., [16,17]. This characterisation will be used in the upper bound proofs of Theorems 1 and 3. For each $\Box_F p$ in Φ, we take a fresh propositional variable, $\overline{\Box_F p}$, and call it the *surrogate* of $\Box_F p$; likewise, for each $\Box_P p$ in Φ we take its surrogate $\overline{\Box_P p}$. Let $\overline{\Phi}$ be the result of replacing all the $\Box$-literals in Φ with their surrogates. By a *type* for $\overline{\Phi}$ we mean any set of literals that contains either p or $\neg p$ (but not both), for each variable p in $\overline{\Phi}$ (including the surrogates).

The proof of the following lemma is standard and can be found in [6]. The reader may find useful Fig. 1 illustrating the conditions of the lemma.

Lemma 3 (structure of models). *Let φ be an $\mathsf{LTL}_{bool}^{\Box,\bigcirc}$-formula of the form (4) and $K = |\varphi| + 4$. Then φ is satisfiable iff there exist integers $m_0 < m_1 < \cdots < m_K$ and types $\Psi_0, \Psi_1, \ldots, \Psi_K$ for $\overline{\Phi}$ such that:*

(B$_0$) $m_{i+1} - m_i < 2^{|\overline{\Phi}|}$, for $0 \leq i < K$;

(B$_1$) *there exists ℓ_0, $0 < \ell_0 < K$, such that $\Psi \subseteq \Psi_{\ell_0}$;*

(B$_2$) $\overline{\Box_F p} \in \Psi_i \Rightarrow p, \overline{\Box_F p} \in \Psi_{i+1}$ *and* $\overline{\Box_F p} \in \Psi_{i+1} \setminus \Psi_i \Rightarrow p \notin \Psi_{i+1}$ $(0 \leq i < K)$,
$\overline{\Box_P p} \in \Psi_i \Rightarrow p, \overline{\Box_P p} \in \Psi_{i-1}$ *and* $\overline{\Box_P p} \in \Psi_{i-1} \setminus \Psi_i \Rightarrow p \notin \Psi_{i-1}$ $(0 < i \leq K)$;

(B$_3$) *there exist $\ell_F < K$ and $\ell_P > 0$ such that*
- $\Psi_{\ell_F} = \Psi_K$ *and, for each $\neg\overline{\Box_F p} \in \Psi_{\ell_F}$, there is $j \geq \ell_F$ with $\neg p \in \Psi_j$,*
- $\Psi_{\ell_P} = \Psi_0$ *and, for each $\neg\overline{\Box_P p} \in \Psi_{\ell_P}$, there is $j \leq \ell_P$ with $\neg p \in \Psi_j$;*

(B$_4$) *the following formulas are consistent, for $0 \leq i < K$:*

$$\psi_i = \Psi_i \wedge \bigwedge_{k=1}^{m_{i+1}-m_i-1} \bigcirc_F^k \Theta_i \wedge \bigcirc_F^{m_{i+1}-m_i} \Psi_{i+1} \wedge \boxasterisk \overline{\Phi},$$

where $\bigcirc_F^k \Psi$ is the result of attaching k operators $\bigcirc_F$ to each literal in Ψ and

$$\Theta_i = \{p, \overline{\Box_F p} \mid \overline{\Box_F p} \in \Psi_i\} \cup \{\neg\overline{\Box_F p} \mid \neg\overline{\Box_F p} \in \Psi_i\} \cup$$
$$\{p, \overline{\Box_P p} \mid \overline{\Box_P p} \in \Psi_{i+1}\} \cup \{\neg\overline{\Box_P p} \mid \neg\overline{\Box_P p} \in \Psi_{i+1}\}.$$

The intuition behind this lemma is as follows (see Fig. 1). If φ is satisfiable, then it has a model $\mathfrak{M}$ that consists of the initial fragments of models $\mathfrak{M}_i$ of the formulas ψ_i: namely, the types of the moments $m_i, \ldots, m_{i+1}$ in $\mathfrak{M}$ coincide with the types of the moments $0, \ldots, (m_{i+1} - m_i)$ in $\mathfrak{M}_i$. By $(\mathbf{B}_4)$, we have $\mathfrak{M}, 0 \models \boxdot \overline{\Phi}$. Then $(\mathbf{B}_1)$ makes sure that $\mathfrak{M}, 0 \models \Psi$. Conditions $(\mathbf{B}_2)$ and $(\mathbf{B}_3)$ guarantee that if $\overline{\Box_F p} \in \Psi_i$ then $p \in \Psi_j$ for all types Ψ_j located to the right of Ψ_i in Fig. 1 and, conversely, if $\overline{\Box_F p} \notin \Psi_i$ then $\neg p \in \Psi_j$, for some Ψ_j to the right of Ψ_i; and symmetrically for the $\Box_P$-literals. It follows that $\mathfrak{M}, 0 \models \boxdot \Phi$.

3 Binary-Clause LTL and Arithmetic Progressions

In this section, we prove NP-completeness of the satisfiability problem for $\mathsf{LTL}_{krom}^{\Box,\bigcirc}$ and $\mathsf{LTL}_{core}^{\Box,\bigcirc}$. The key ingredient of the proof of the upper bound is an encoding of condition $(\mathbf{B}_4)$ for *binary clauses* by means of arithmetic progressions (via unary automata). The proof of the lower bound is by reduction of the problem whether a given set of arithmetic progressions covers all the natural numbers.

Let φ be an $\mathsf{LTL}_{krom}^{\Box,\bigcirc}$-formula of the form (4). By Lemma 3, to check satisfiability of φ it suffices to guess $K+1$ types for $\overline{\Phi}$ and K natural numbers $n_i = m_{i+1} - m_i$, for $0 \le i < K$, whose binary representation, by $(\mathbf{B}_0)$, is polynomial in $|\overline{\Phi}|$. Evidently, $(\mathbf{B}_1)$–$(\mathbf{B}_3)$ can be checked in polynomial time. Our aim now is to show that $(\mathbf{B}_4)$ can also be verified in polynomial time, which will give a nondeterministic polynomial-time algorithm for checking satisfiability of $\mathsf{LTL}_{krom}^{\Box,\bigcirc}$-formulas.

Theorem 1. *The satisfiability problem for $\mathsf{LTL}_{krom}^{\Box,\bigcirc}$-formulas is in* NP.

Proof. In view of Lemma 2, we write $\bigcirc$ in place of $\bigcirc_F$. We denote propositional literals (p or $\neg p$) by L and temporal literals ($p, \neg p, \bigcirc p$ or $\neg \bigcirc p$) by D. We assume that $\bigcirc \neg p$ is the same as $\neg \bigcirc p$. We use '$\psi_1 \models \psi_2$' as a shorthand for '$\mathfrak{M}, 0 \models \psi_2$ whenever $\mathfrak{M}, 0 \models \psi_1$, for any interpretation $\mathfrak{M}$.' Thus, the problem is as follows: given a set Φ of binary clauses of the form $D_1 \vee D_2$, types Ψ and Ψ' for Φ, a set Θ of propositional literals and a number $n > 0$ (in binary), decide whether

$$\Psi \wedge \bigwedge_{k=1}^{n-1} \bigcirc^k \Theta \wedge \bigcirc^n \Psi' \wedge \boxdot \Phi \tag{5}$$

has a satisfying interpretation. For $0 \le k \le n$, we set:

$$F_\Phi^k(\Psi) = \{L' \mid L \wedge \boxdot \Phi \models \bigcirc^k L', \text{ for } L \in \Psi\},$$
$$P_\Phi^k(\Psi') = \{L \mid \bigcirc^k L \wedge \boxdot \Phi \models L, \text{ for } L' \in \Psi'\}.$$

Lemma 4. *Formula* (5) *is satisfiable iff the following conditions hold*:

(**L**$_1$) $F^0_\Phi(\Psi) \subseteq \Psi$, $F^n_\Phi(\Psi) \subseteq \Psi'$ and $P^0_\Phi(\Psi') \subseteq \Psi'$, $P^n_\Phi(\Psi') \subseteq \Psi$;
(**L**$_2$) $\neg L \notin F^k_\Phi(\Psi)$ and $\neg L \notin P^{n-k}_\Phi(\Psi')$, for all $L \in \Theta$ and $0 < k < n$.

Proof. Clearly, if (5) is satisfiable then the above conditions hold. For the converse direction, observe that if $L' \in F^k_\Phi(\Psi)$ then, since Φ is a set of binary clauses, there is a sequence of $\bigcirc$-prefixed literals $\bigcirc^{k_0} L_0 \rightsquigarrow \bigcirc^{k_1} L_1 \rightsquigarrow \cdots \rightsquigarrow \bigcirc^{k_m} L_m$ such that $k_0 = 0$, $L_0 \in \Psi$, $k_m = k$, $L_m = L'$, each k_i is between 0 and n and the $\rightsquigarrow$ relation is defined by taking $\bigcirc^{k_i} L_i \rightsquigarrow \bigcirc^{k_{i+1}} L_{i+1}$ just in one of the three cases: $k_{i+1} = k_i$ and $L_i \to L_{i+1} \in \Phi$ or $k_{i+1} = k_i + 1$ and $L_i \to \bigcirc L_{i+1} \in \Phi$ or $k_{i+1} = k_i - 1$ and $\bigcirc L_i \to L_{i+1} \in \Phi$ (we assume that, for example, $\neg q \to \neg p \in \Phi$ whenever Φ contains $p \to q$). So, suppose conditions (**L**$_1$)–(**L**$_2$) hold. We construct an interpretation satisfying (5). By (**L**$_1$), both $\Psi \wedge \boxdot \Phi$ and $\bigcirc^n \Psi' \wedge \boxdot \Phi$ are consistent. So, let $\mathfrak{M}_\Psi$ and $\mathfrak{M}_{\Psi'}$ be such that $\mathfrak{M}_\Psi, 0 \models \Psi \wedge \boxdot \Psi$ and $\mathfrak{M}_\Psi, n \models \Psi' \wedge \boxdot \Psi$, respectively. Let $\mathfrak{M}$ be an interpretation that coincides with $\mathfrak{M}_\Psi$ for all moments $k \leq 0$ and with $\mathfrak{M}_{\Psi'}$ for all $k \geq n$; for the remaining k, $0 < k < n$, it is defined as follows. First, for each $p \in \Theta$, we make p true at k and, for each $\neg p \in \Theta$, we make p false at k; such an assignment exists due to (**L**$_2$). Second, we extend the assignment by making L true at k if $L \in F^k_\Phi(\Psi) \cup P^{n-k}_\Phi(\Psi')$. Observe that we have $\{p, \neg p\} \not\subseteq F^k_\Phi(\Psi) \cup P^{n-k}_\Phi(\Psi')$: for otherwise $L \wedge \boxdot \Phi \models \bigcirc^k p$ and $\bigcirc^{n-k} L' \wedge \boxdot \Phi \models \neg p$, for some $L \in \Psi$ and $L' \in \Psi'$, whence $L \wedge \boxdot \Phi \models \bigcirc^n \neg L'$, contrary to (**L**$_1$). Also, by (**L**$_2$), any assignment extension at this stage does not contradict the choices made due to Θ. Finally, all propositional variables not covered in the previous two cases get their values from $\mathfrak{M}_\Psi$ (or $\mathfrak{M}_{\Psi'}$). We note that the last choice does not depend on the assignment that is fixed by taking account of the consequences of $\boxdot \Phi$ with Ψ, Ψ' and Θ (because if the value of a variable depended on those sets of literals, the respective literal would be among the logical consequences and would have been fixed before). □

Thus, it suffices to show that conditions (**L**$_1$) and (**L**$_2$) can be checked in polynomial time. First, we claim that there is a polynomial-time algorithm which, given a set Φ of binary clauses of the form $D_1 \vee D_2$, constructs a set Φ^* of binary clauses that is 'sound and complete' in the following sense:

(**S**$_1$) $\boxdot \Phi^* \models \boxdot \Phi$;
(**S**$_2$) if $\boxdot \Phi \models \boxdot(L \to \bigcirc^k L_k)$ then either $k = 0$ and $L \to L_0 \in \Phi^*$, or $k \geq 1$ and there are $L_0, L_1, \ldots, L_{k-1}$ with $L = L_0$ and $L_i \to \bigcirc L_{i+1} \in \Phi^*$, for $0 \leq i < k$.

Intuitively, the set Φ^* makes explicit the consequences of $\boxdot \Phi$ and can be constructed in time $(2|\Phi|)^2$ (the number of temporal literals in Φ^* is bounded by the doubled length $|\Phi|$ of Φ as each of its literal can only be prefixed by $\bigcirc$). Indeed, we start from Φ and, at each step, add $D_1 \vee D_2$ to Φ if it contains both $D_1 \vee D$ and $\neg D \vee D_2$; we also add $L_1 \vee L_2$ if Φ contains $\bigcirc L_1 \vee \bigcirc L_2$ (and *vice versa*). This procedure is sound since we only add consequences of $\boxdot \Phi$; completeness follows from the completeness proof for temporal resolution [15, Section 6.3].

Our next step is to encode Φ^* by means of unary automata. Let L, L' be literals. Consider a nondeterministic finite automaton $\mathfrak{A}_{L,L'}$ over $\{0\}$ such that the literals of Φ^* are its states, with L being the initial state and L' the only accepting state, and $\{(L_1, L_2) \mid L_1 \to \bigcirc L_2 \in \Phi^*\}$ is its transition relation. By **(S$_1$)** and **(S$_2$)**, for all $k > 0$, we have

$$\mathfrak{A}_{L,L'} \text{ accepts } 0^k \quad \text{iff} \quad \circledast \Phi \models \circledast(L \to \bigcirc^k L').$$

Then both $F_\Phi^k(\Psi)$ and $P_\Phi^k(\Psi')$ can be defined in terms of the language of $\mathfrak{A}_{L,L'}$:

$$F_\Phi^k(\Psi) = \{L' \mid \mathfrak{A}_{L,L'} \text{ accepts } 0^k, \text{ for } L \in \Psi\},$$
$$P_\Phi^k(\Psi') = \{L \mid \mathfrak{A}_{\neg L, \neg L'} \text{ accepts } 0^k, \text{ for } L' \in \Psi'\}$$

(recall that $\bigcirc^k L' \to L$ is equivalent to $\neg L \to \bigcirc^k \neg L'$). Note that the numbers n and k in conditions **(L$_1$)** and **(L$_2$)** are in general exponential in the length of Φ and, therefore, the automata $\mathfrak{A}_{L,L'}$ do not immediately provide a polynomial-time procedure for checking these conditions: although it can be shown that if **(L$_2$)** does not hold then it fails for a polynomial number k, this is not the case for **(L$_1$)**, which requires the accepting state to be reached in a fixed (exponential) number of transitions. Instead, we use the *Chrobak normal form* [11] to decompose the automata into a polynomial number of polynomial-sized arithmetic progressions (which can have an exponential common period; cf. the proof of Theorem 2). In what follows, given a and b, we denote by $a + b\mathbb{N}$ the set $\{a + bm \mid m \in \mathbb{N}\}$ (the arithmetic progression with initial term a and common difference b).

It is known that every N-state unary automaton $\mathfrak{A}$ can be converted (in polynomial time) into an equivalent automaton in Chrobak normal form (e.g., by using Martinez's algorithm [28]), which has $O(N^2)$ states and gives rise to M arithmetic progressions $a_1 + b_1 \mathbb{N}, \ldots, a_M + b_M \mathbb{N}$ such that

(A$_1$) $M \leq O(N^2)$ and $0 \leq a_i, b_i \leq N$, for $1 \leq i \leq M$;
(A$_2$) $\mathfrak{A}$ accepts 0^k iff $k \in a_i + b_i \mathbb{N}$, for some $1 \leq i \leq M$.

By construction, the number of arithmetic progressions is bounded by a quadratic function in the length of Φ.

We are now in a position to give a polynomial-time algorithm for checking **(L$_1$)** and **(L$_2$)**, which requires solving Diophantine equations. In **(L$_2$)**, for example, to verify that, for each $p \in \Theta$, we have $\neg p \notin F_\Phi^k(\Psi)$, for all $0 < k < n$, we take the automata $\mathfrak{A}_{L, \neg p}$, for $L \in \Psi$, and transform them into the Chrobak normal form to obtain arithmetic progressions $a_i + b_i \mathbb{N}$, for $1 \leq i \leq M$. Then there is k, $0 < k < n$, with $\neg p \in F_\Phi^k(\Psi)$ iff one of the equations $a_i + b_i m = k$ has an integer solution, for some k, $0 < k < n$. The latter can be verified by taking the integer $m = \lfloor -a_i/b_i \rfloor$ and checking whether either $a_i + b_i m$ or $a_i + b_i(m+1)$ belongs to the open interval $(0, n)$, which can clearly be done in polynomial time.

This completes the proof of Theorem 1. ❑

The matching lower bound for $\mathsf{LTL}_{core}^{\Box, \bigcirc}$-formulas, even without $\Box_F/\Box_P$, can be obtained using NP-hardness of deciding inequality of regular languages over a

	1	2	3	4	5	6	7	8	9	10	11	12	13	14	15	16	17	18	19	20	21	22	23	24	25	26	27	28	29	30
2	1	0	1	0	1	0	1	0	1	0	1	0	1	0	1	0	1	0	1	0	1	0	1	0	1	0	1	0	1	0
3	1			0	1			0	1			0	1			0	1			0	1			0	1			0	1	0
5	1				0	1				0	1				0	1				0	1				0	1				0

Fig. 2. Positive numbers encoding assignments for 3 variables p_1, p_2, p_3 (shaded)

unary alphabet [27]. In the proof of Theorem 2, we give a more direct reduction of the NP-complete problem 3SAT and repeat the argument of [27, Theorem 6.1] to construct a small number of arithmetic progressions (each with a small initial term and common difference) that give rise to models of exponential size.

Theorem 2. *The satisfiability problem for* $\mathsf{LTL}_{core}^{\Box,\bigcirc}$-*formulas is NP-hard.*

Proof. The proof is by reduction of 3SAT. Let $f = \bigwedge_{i=1}^{n} C_i$ be a 3CNF with variables $p_1, \ldots, p_m$ and clauses $C_1, \ldots, C_n$. By a propositional assignment for f we understand a function $\sigma \colon \{p_1, \ldots, p_m\} \to \{0, 1\}$. We represent such assignments by sets of positive natural numbers. More precisely, let $P_1, \ldots, P_m$ be the first m prime numbers; it is known that P_m does not exceed $O(m^2)$ [1]. A natural number $k > 0$ is said to *represent* an assignment σ if k is equivalent to $\sigma(p_i)$ modulo P_i, for all i, $1 \leq i \leq m$. Clearly, not every natural number represents an assignment since each element of

$$j + P_i \cdot \mathbb{N}, \qquad \text{for } 1 \leq i \leq m \text{ and } 2 \leq j < P_i, \tag{6}$$

is equivalent to j modulo P_i with $j \geq 2$. On the other hand, every natural number that does not represent an assignment belongs to one of those arithmetic progressions (see Fig. 2).

Let C_i be a clause in f, say, $C_i = p_{i_1} \vee \neg p_{i_2} \vee p_{i_3}$. Consider

$$P_{i_1}^1 P_{i_2}^0 P_{i_3}^1 + P_{i_1} P_{i_2} P_{i_3} \cdot \mathbb{N}. \tag{7}$$

A natural number represents an assignment that makes C_i true iff it does not belong to the progressions (6) and (7). In the same way we construct a progression of the form (7) for every clause in f. Thus, a natural number $k > 0$ *does not* belong to the constructed progressions of the form (6) and (7) iff k represents a satisfying assignment for f.

To complete the proof, we show that the defined progressions can be encoded in $\mathsf{LTL}_{core}^{\Box,\bigcirc}$. Take a propositional variable d (it will be shared by all formulas below). Given an arithmetic progression $a + b\mathbb{N}$ (with $a \geq 0$ and $b > 0$), let

$$\theta_{a,b} \;=\; u_0 \wedge \bigwedge_{j=1}^{a} \boxdot(u_{j-1} \to \bigcirc_F u_j) \wedge$$
$$\boxdot(u_a \to v_0) \wedge \bigwedge_{j=1}^{b} \boxdot(v_{j-1} \to \bigcirc_F v_j) \wedge \boxdot(v_b \to v_0) \wedge \boxdot(v_0 \to d),$$

where $u_0, \ldots, u_a$ and $v_0, \ldots, v_b$ are fresh propositional variables. It is not hard to see that, in every model of $\theta_{a,b}$, if k belongs to $a+b\mathbb{N}$, then d is true at moment k. Thus, we take a conjunction φ_f of the $\theta_{a,b}$ for arithmetic progressions (6) and (7)

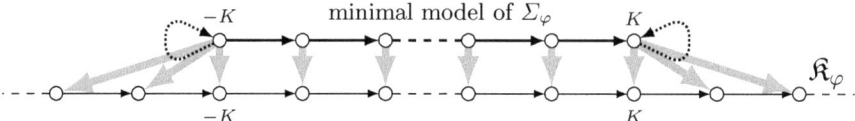

Fig. 3. The minimal model of Σ_φ and $\mathfrak{K}_\varphi$

together with $p \wedge \boxdot(\bigcirc_F p \to p) \wedge \boxdot(p \to d) \wedge \boxdot(\neg \boxdot d)$, where p is a fresh variable (the last formula makes both p and d true at all moments $k \leq 0$). The size of the $\mathsf{LTL}_{core}^{\Box,\bigcirc}$-formula φ_f is $O(n \cdot m^6)$. It is readily checked that φ_f is satisfiable iff f is satisfiable. □

4 Core and Horn Fragments without Next-Time

Let φ be an $\mathsf{LTL}_{horn}^{\Box}$-formula. By applying Lemma 2, we can transform φ to the form $\Psi \wedge \boxdot \Phi^+ \wedge \boxdot \Phi^-$, where Ψ is a set of propositional variables while Φ^+ and Φ^- are sets of *positive* and *negative* clauses of the form

$$\lambda_1 \wedge \lambda_2 \wedge \cdots \wedge \lambda_{k-1} \to \lambda_k \quad \text{and} \quad \neg\lambda_1 \vee \neg\lambda_2 \vee \cdots \vee \neg\lambda_k, \tag{8}$$

respectively. Trivially, $\Psi \wedge \boxdot \Phi^+$ is satisfiable. Since all clauses in Φ^+ have at most one positive literal and are constructed from variables possibly prefixed by $\Box_F$ or $\Box_P$, the formula $\Psi \wedge \boxdot \Phi^+$ has a *canonical model* $\mathfrak{K}_\varphi$ defined by taking

$$\mathfrak{K}_\varphi, n \models p \quad \text{iff} \quad \mathfrak{M}, n \models p, \quad \text{for every model } \mathfrak{M} \text{ of } \Psi \wedge \boxdot \Phi^+, \ n \in \mathbb{Z}$$

(indeed, $\mathfrak{K}_\varphi, 0 \models \Psi \wedge \boxdot \Phi^+$ follows from the observation that $\mathfrak{K}_\varphi, n \models \Box_F p$ iff $\mathfrak{M}, n \models \Box_F p$, for every model $\mathfrak{M}$ of $\Psi \wedge \boxdot \Phi^+$; and similarly for $\Box_P p$). If we consider the canonical model $\mathfrak{K}_\varphi$ in the context of Lemma 3 then, since the language does not contain $\bigcirc_F$ or $\bigcirc_P$, we have $m_{i+1} - m_i = 1$ for all i. Thus, $\mathfrak{K}_\varphi$ can be thought of as a sequence of $(\ell_F - \ell_P + 1)$-many states, the first and last of which repeat indefinitely. Let $K = |\varphi| + 4$.

Obviously, φ is satisfiable iff there is no negative clause $\neg\lambda_1 \vee \cdots \vee \neg\lambda_k$ in Φ^- such that all the λ_i are true in $\mathfrak{K}_\varphi$ at some moment n with $|n| \leq K$. This condition can be encoded by means of propositional Horn clauses in the following way. For each variable p, we take $2K + 1$ variables p^n, $|n| \leq K$, and, for each $\Box_F p$ and $\Box_P p$, we take $2K+1$ variables, denoted $(\Box_F p)^n$ and $(\Box_P p)^n$, $|n| \leq K$, respectively. Consider the following set Σ_φ of propositional Horn clauses, $|n| \leq K$:

(H$_0$) p^0, if $p \in \Psi$,

(H$_1$) $\lambda_1^n \wedge \cdots \wedge \lambda_{k-1}^n \to \lambda_k^n$, if $(\lambda_1 \wedge \cdots \wedge \lambda_{k-1} \to \lambda_k) \in \Phi^+$,

(H$_2$) $(\Box_F p)^n \to (\Box_F p)^{n+1}$ if $n < K$, $\quad (\Box_P p)^n \to (\Box_P p)^{n-1}$ if $n > -K$,

(H$_3$) $(\Box_F p)^n \to p^{n+1}$, $\quad (\Box_P p)^n \to p^{n-1}$,

(H$_4$) $(\Box_F p)^n \wedge p^n \to (\Box_F p)^{n-1}$ if $n > -K$, $\quad (\Box_P p)^n \wedge p^n \to (\Box_P p)^{n+1}$ if $n < K$,

(H$_5$) $(\Box_F p)^K \leftrightarrow p^K$, $\quad (\Box_P p)^{-K} \leftrightarrow p^{-K}$,

(H$_6$) $(\Box_F p)^{-K} \leftrightarrow p^{-K}$, $\quad (\Box_P p)^K \leftrightarrow p^K$.

Clearly, $|\Sigma_\varphi| \leq O(|\varphi|^2)$. It is readily seen that the minimal model of Σ_φ corresponds to the canonical model $\mathfrak{K}_\varphi$ as shown in Fig. 3. As propositional Horn satisfiability is PTIME-complete, we obtain the following:

Theorem 3. *The satisfiability problem for* $\mathsf{LTL}^{\Box}_{horn}$-*formulas is in* PTIME.

4.1 Temporal Derivations for $\mathsf{LTL}^{\Box}_{core}$ in NLogSpace

In $\mathsf{LTL}^{\Box}_{core}$-formulas, all clauses are binary: $k = 2$ in (8). Satisfiability of propositional binary clauses is known to be NLOGSPACE-complete. However, in the reduction $\varphi \mapsto \Sigma_\varphi$ above, the clauses (**H**$_4$) are ternary. In this section we show how to modify the reduction to ensure membership in NLOGSPACE. More precisely, we define two types of derivation from $\Psi \wedge \boxdot \Phi^+$: a 0-derivation of (λ, n) will mean that $\mathfrak{K}_\varphi, n \models \lambda$, while a $\forall$-derivation of λ from λ' that $\mathfrak{K}_\varphi, 0 \models \boxdot \lambda' \to \boxdot \lambda$. We then show that these derivations define $\mathfrak{K}_\varphi$ and that satisfiability of φ can be checked by a nondeterministic algorithm in logarithmic space.

Denote by $\to^*$ the transitive and reflexive closure of the relation $\to$ over literals given by the clauses of Φ^+. We require the following derivation rules over the pairs (λ, n), where λ is a positive temporal literal in φ and $n \in \mathbb{Z}$:

(**R**$_1$) $(\lambda_1, n) \Rightarrow (\lambda_2, n)$,   if $\lambda_1 \to^* \lambda_2$,

(**R**$_2$) $(\Box_F p, n) \Rightarrow (\Box_F p, n+1)$, $(\Box_P p, n) \Rightarrow (\Box_P p, n-1)$,

(**R**$_3$) $(\Box_F p, n) \Rightarrow (p, n+1)$, $(\Box_P p, n) \Rightarrow (p, n-1)$,

(**R**$_4$) $(\Box_F p, 0) \Rightarrow (\Box_F p, -1)$, $(\Box_P p, 0) \Rightarrow (\Box_P p, 1)$,   if $p' \to^* p$ for $p' \in \Psi$,

(**R**$_5$) $(p, n) \Rightarrow (\Box_F p, n-1)$, $(p, n) \Rightarrow (\Box_P p, n+1)$.

The rules in (**R**$_1$)–(**R**$_4$) mimic (**H**$_1$)–(**H**$_4$) above ((**H**$_4$) at moment 0 only) and reflect the semantics of LTL in the sense that whenever $(\lambda, n) \Rightarrow (\lambda', n')$ and $\mathfrak{K}_\varphi, n \models \lambda$ then $\mathfrak{K}_\varphi, n' \models \lambda'$. For example, consider (**R**$_4$). It only applies if p follows (by $\to^*$) from the initial conditions in Ψ, in which case $\mathfrak{K}_\varphi, 0 \models p$, and so $\mathfrak{K}_\varphi, 0 \models \Box_F p$ implies $\mathfrak{K}_\varphi, -1 \models \Box_F p$. The rules in (**R**$_5$) are different: for instance, we can only apply $(p, n) \Rightarrow (\Box_F p, n-1)$ if we know that p holds at all $m \geq n$.

A sequence $\mathfrak{d}: (\lambda_0, n_0) \Rightarrow \cdots \Rightarrow (\lambda_\ell, n_\ell)$, for $\ell \geq 0$, is called a 0-*derivation of* (λ_ℓ, n_ℓ) if $\lambda_0 \in \Psi$, $n_0 = 0$ and all applications of (**R**$_5$) are *safe* in the following sense: for any $(p, n_i) \Rightarrow_{(\mathbf{R}_5)} (\Box_F p, n_i - 1)$, there is $\lambda_j = \Box_F q$, for some q and $0 \leq j < i$; similarly, for any $(p, n_i) \Rightarrow_{(\mathbf{R}_5)} (\Box_P p, n_i + 1)$, there is $\lambda_j = \Box_P q$ with $0 \leq j < i$. In this case we write $\Psi \Rightarrow^0 (\lambda_\ell, n_\ell)$. For example, consider

$$\varphi = p \wedge \boxdot(p \to \Box_F q) \wedge \boxdot(q \to r) \wedge \boxdot(p \to r).$$

Evidently, $\mathfrak{K}_\varphi, -1 \models \Box_F r$. The following sequence is a 0-derivation of $(\Box_F r, -1)$ because the application of (**R**$_5$) is safe due to $\Box_F q$:

$$(p, 0) \Rightarrow_{(\mathbf{R}_1)} (\Box_F q, 0) \Rightarrow_{(\mathbf{R}_3)} (q, 1) \Rightarrow_{(\mathbf{R}_1)} (r, 1) \Rightarrow_{(\mathbf{R}_5)} (\Box_F r, 0) \Rightarrow_{(\mathbf{R}_4)} (\Box_F r, -1).$$

Intuitively, if we can derive $(r, 1)$ using $(\Box_F q, 0)$, then we can also derive (r, n) for any $n \geq 1$, and so we must also have $(\Box_F r, 0)$, which justifies the application of (**R**$_5$). This argument is formalised in the following lemma:

46 A. Artale et al.

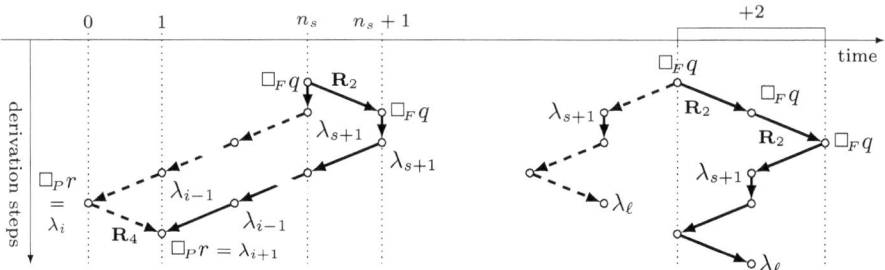

Fig. 4. Removing applications of **(R₄)** (left) and shifting a 0-derivation by 2 (right): dashed arrows show the original derivation and solid ones the resulting derivation

Lemma 5 (monotonicity). *Let $\mathfrak{d}$ be a 0-derivation of (λ_ℓ, n_ℓ) with a suffix*

$$\mathfrak{s}\colon (\Box_F q, n_s) \Rightarrow (\lambda_{s+1}, n_{s+1}) \Rightarrow \cdots \Rightarrow (\lambda_\ell, n_\ell), \qquad (9)$$

where none of the λ_i contains $\Box_F$. Then $\Psi \Rightarrow^0 (\lambda_\ell, m)$, for all $m \geq n_\ell$. Similarly, if there is a suffix beginning with some $\Box_P q$ then $\Psi \Rightarrow^0 (\lambda_\ell, m)$, for all $m \leq n_\ell$. Moreover, these 0-derivations only contain the rules used in $\mathfrak{d}$ and **(R₂)**.

Proof. We first remove all applications of **(R₄)** in $\mathfrak{s}$. Let $(\lambda_i, n_i) \Rightarrow_{(\mathbf{R_4})} (\lambda_{i+1}, n_{i+1})$ be the first one. By definition, $n_i = 0$ and, since $\Box_F q$ is the last $\Box_F$ in $\mathfrak{d}$, we have $n_{i+1} = 1$ and $\lambda_i = \lambda_{i+1} = \Box_P r$, for some r. So we can begin $\mathfrak{s}$ with $(\Box_F q, n_s) \Rightarrow_{(\mathbf{R_2})} (\Box_F q, n_s+1) \Rightarrow (\lambda_{s+1}, n_{s+1}+1) \Rightarrow \cdots \Rightarrow (\lambda_i, n_i+1) \Rightarrow (\lambda_{i+2}, n_{i+2})$; see Fig. 4 on the left-hand side. We repeatedly apply this operation to obtain a suffix $\mathfrak{s}$ of the form (9) that does not use **(R₄)**. We then replace $\mathfrak{s}$ in $\mathfrak{d}$ with $(\Box_F q, n_s) \Rightarrow_{(\mathbf{R_2})} \cdots \Rightarrow_{(\mathbf{R_2})} (\Box_F q, n_s+k) \Rightarrow (\lambda_{s+1}, n_{s+1}+k) \Rightarrow \cdots \Rightarrow (\lambda_\ell, n_\ell+k)$, where $k = m - n_\ell$; see Fig. 4 on the right-hand side. ❑

However, 0-derivations are not enough to obtain all literals that are true in $\mathfrak{K}_\varphi$. Indeed, consider the formula

$$\varphi \;=\; r \;\wedge\; \boxdot(r \to \Box_F q) \;\wedge\; \boxdot(\Box_F q \to q) \;\wedge\; \boxdot(\Box_P q \to p).$$

Clearly, $\mathfrak{K}_\varphi, n \models p$ for all $n \in \mathbb{Z}$, but neither (p, n) nor $(\Box_P q, n)$ is 0-derivable. On the other hand, for each $n \in \mathbb{Z}$, there is a 0-derivation of (q, n): for example,

$$(r, 0) \Rightarrow_{(\mathbf{R_1})} (\Box_F q, 0) \Rightarrow_{(\mathbf{R_1})} (q, 0) \Rightarrow_{(\mathbf{R_5})} (\Box_F q, -1) \Rightarrow_{(\mathbf{R_1})} (q, -1).$$

These 0-derivations correspond to $\mathfrak{K}_\varphi, 0 \models \boxdot q$, from which we can derive $\boxdot p$ by means of the second type of derivations. A sequence $\mathfrak{d}\colon (\lambda_0, n_0) \Rightarrow \cdots \Rightarrow (\lambda_\ell, n_\ell)$ is called a $\forall$-*derivation of λ_ℓ from λ_0* if it uses only **(R₁)**–**(R₃)** and **(R₅)**, whose applications are not necessarily safe. So we write $\Psi \Rightarrow^\forall \lambda$ if there is a $\forall$-derivation of λ from some q such that $\Psi \Rightarrow^0 (q, n)$, for all $n \in \mathbb{Z}$. In the example above, $(q, 0) \Rightarrow_{(\mathbf{R_5})} (\Box_P q, 1) \Rightarrow_{(\mathbf{R_1})} (p, 1)$ is a $\forall$-derivation of p from q, whence $\Psi \Rightarrow^\forall p$.

Lemma 6 (soundness). *If $\Psi \Rightarrow^0 (\lambda, n)$ then $\mathfrak{K}_\varphi, n \models \lambda$. If $\Psi \Rightarrow^\forall \lambda$ then $\mathfrak{K}_\varphi, 0 \models \boxdot \lambda$.*

Proof. By induction on the derivation length, using Lemma 5 for $(\mathbf{R_5})$. ☐

Lemma 7 (completeness). *If $\mathfrak{K}_\varphi, n \models \lambda$ then either $\Psi \Rightarrow^0 (\lambda, n)$ or $\Psi \Rightarrow^\forall \lambda$.*

Proof. Let $\mathfrak{M}$ be an interpretation such that, for all p and $n \in \mathbb{Z}$, we have $\mathfrak{M}, n \models p$ iff $\Psi \Rightarrow^0 (p, n)$ or $\Psi \Rightarrow^\forall p$. It suffices to show that $\mathfrak{M}, 0 \models \Psi \wedge \boxdot \Phi^+$. Indeed, if we assume that there are p' and n' such that $\mathfrak{K}_\varphi, n' \models p'$ but neither $\Psi \Rightarrow^0 (p', n')$ nor $\Psi \Rightarrow^\forall p'$, we will obtain $\mathfrak{M}, n' \models \neg p'$ contrary to our assumption (other types of literals are considered analogously).

Thus, we have to show that $\mathfrak{M}$ is a model of $\Psi \wedge \boxdot \Phi^+$. Suppose $p \in \Psi$. Then trivially $\Psi \Rightarrow^0 (p, 0)$, and so $\mathfrak{M}, 0 \models p$. Suppose $\lambda_1 \to \lambda_2 \in \Phi^+$ and $\mathfrak{M}, n \models \lambda_1$. We consider three cases depending on the shape of λ_1 and show that $\mathfrak{M}, n \models \lambda_2$.

$\lambda_1 = p$. If $\Psi \Rightarrow^\forall p$ then, by $(\mathbf{R_1})$, $\Psi \Rightarrow^\forall \lambda_2$. Otherwise, there is a 0-derivation of (p, n), and so $\Psi \Rightarrow^0 (\lambda_1, n) \Rightarrow_{(\mathbf{R_1})} (\lambda_2, n)$.

$\lambda_1 = \Box_F p$. Then $\mathfrak{M}, m \models p$ for all $m > n$. Consider $\mathfrak{M}, n+1 \models p$. If $\Psi \Rightarrow^\forall p$ then, by $(\mathbf{R_5})$, $(\mathbf{R_1})$, $\Psi \Rightarrow^\forall \lambda_2$. Otherwise, there is a 0-derivation $\mathfrak{d}$ of $(p, n+1)$.
  (F) If $\Box_F$ occurs in $\mathfrak{d}$ then $\Psi \Rightarrow^0 (p, n+1) \Rightarrow_{(\mathbf{R_5})} (\Box_F p, n) \Rightarrow_{(\mathbf{R_1})} (\lambda_2, n)$.
  (P) If $\Box_P$ occurs in $\mathfrak{d}$ then, by Lemma 5, $\Psi \Rightarrow^0 (p, m)$ for each $m \leq n+1$. Thus, $\Psi \Rightarrow^0 (p, m)$ for *all* $m \in \mathbb{Z}$, and so, by $(\mathbf{R_5})$ and $(\mathbf{R_1})$, $\Psi \Rightarrow^\forall \lambda_2$.
  (0) If $\mathfrak{d}$ contains neither $\Box_F$ nor $\Box_P$ then $n = -1$ and $\lambda \to^* p$, for some $\lambda \in \Psi$ (by $(\mathbf{R_1})$). As $\mathfrak{M}, 1 \models p$ and we assumed $\Psi \not\Rightarrow^\forall p$, there is a 0-derivation $\mathfrak{d}'$ of $(p, 1)$, which must contain $\Box_F$ or $\Box_P$. If $\mathfrak{d}'$ contains $\Box_F$ then $\Psi \Rightarrow^0 (p, 1) \Rightarrow_{(\mathbf{R_5})} (\Box_F p, 0) \Rightarrow_{(\mathbf{R_4})} (\Box_F p, -1) \Rightarrow_{(\mathbf{R_1})} (\lambda_2, n)$. If $\Box_P$ occurs in $\mathfrak{d}'$ then, by the argument in (P), $\Psi \Rightarrow^\forall \lambda_2$.

$\lambda_1 = \Box_P p$. The proof is symmetric.

In each of these cases, we have either $\Psi \Rightarrow^0 (\lambda_2, n)$ or $\Psi \Rightarrow^\forall \lambda_2$. Observe that $\Psi \Rightarrow^0 (\lambda_2, n)$ implies $\mathfrak{M}, n \models \lambda_2$. Indeed, this clearly holds for $\lambda_2 = p$. If $\lambda_2 = \Box_F p$ then, by repetitive applications of $(\mathbf{R_2})$ and an application of $(\mathbf{R_3})$, we obtain $\Psi \Rightarrow^0 (p, m)$, for all $m > n$, which means $\mathfrak{M}, n \models \Box_F p$. The case $\lambda_2 = \Box_P p$ is symmetric. If $\Psi \Rightarrow^\forall \lambda_2$ then, independently of whether λ_2 is p', $\Box_F p'$ or $\Box_P p'$, we have $\Psi \Rightarrow^\forall p'$, so $\mathfrak{M}, m \models p'$ for all $m \in \mathbb{Z}$, whence, $\mathfrak{M}, n \models \lambda_2$. ☐

Next, in Lemmas 8 and 9, we provide efficient criteria for checking the conditions $\Psi \Rightarrow^0 (\lambda, n)$ and $\Psi \Rightarrow^\forall \lambda$ by restricting the range of numbers that can be used in 0-derivations (numbers in $\forall$-derivations can simply be ignored). Given a 0-derivation $\mathfrak{d} \colon (\lambda_0, n_0) \Rightarrow \cdots \Rightarrow (\lambda_\ell, n_\ell)$, we define its *reach* as

$$r(\mathfrak{d}) = \max\{|n_i| \mid 0 \leq i \leq \ell\}.$$

We say that $\mathfrak{d}$ *right-stutters*, if there are $v < w$ such that $\lambda_v = \lambda_w$, $n_v < n_w$ and $n_i > 0$, for all i, $v \leq i \leq w$ (in particular, $(\mathbf{R_4})$ is not applied between v and w). Symmetrically, $\mathfrak{d}$ *left-stutters* if there are $v < w$ such that $\lambda_v = \lambda_w$, $n_v > n_w$ and $n_i < 0$, for all i, $v \leq i \leq w$.

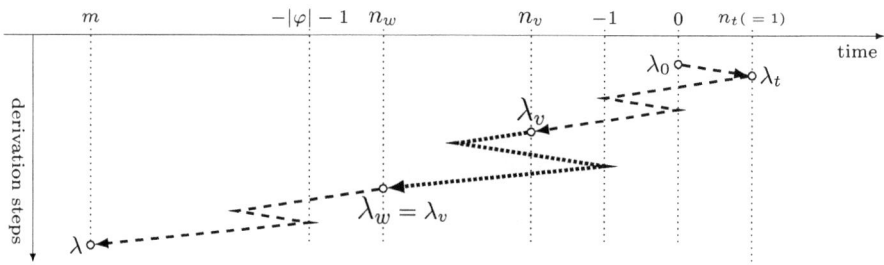

Fig. 5. Left-stuttering: n_v and n_w occur between -1 and $-|\varphi|-1$ (shaded) and the fragment of the derivation from n_v to n_w can be repeated any number of times (including 0)

Lemma 8 (checking $\Rightarrow^0$). $\Psi \Rightarrow^0 (\lambda, n)$ iff there exists a 0-derivation $\mathfrak{d}$ of (λ, m) such that $r(\mathfrak{d}) \leq 2|\varphi|$ and one of the following conditions holds:

(C$_1$) $m = n$;
(C$_2$) $\mathfrak{d}$ contains $\Box_F$ and either $m \leq n$ or $\mathfrak{d}$ left-stutters;
(C$_3$) $\mathfrak{d}$ contains $\Box_P$ and either $m \geq n$ or $\mathfrak{d}$ right-stutters.

Proof. ($\Rightarrow$) Let $\mathfrak{d}: (\lambda_0, n_0) \Rightarrow \cdots \Rightarrow (\lambda_\ell, n_\ell)$ be a 0-derivation of (λ, n). If $r(\mathfrak{d}) \leq |\varphi|$ then $\mathfrak{d}$ satisfies **(C$_1$)**. Otherwise, we take the first $\Box$-literal in $\mathfrak{d}$, say $\lambda_t = \Box_F q$ (the case of $\Box_P q$ is symmetric). Clearly, $|n_t| \leq 1$. Let $u > t$ be the smallest index with $|n_u| > |\varphi|$. Since adjacent n_i and n_{i+1} differ by at most 1, the segment between (λ_t, n_t) and (λ_u, n_u) contains a repeating literal: more precisely, there exist $v < w$ between t and u such that $\lambda_v = \lambda_w$ and

- either $n_v > n_w$ and $n_i < 0$, for $v \leq i \leq w$,
- or $n_v < n_w$ and $n_i > 0$, for $v \leq i \leq w$.

In the former case $\mathfrak{d}$ left-stutters, and we perform the following operations on the suffix $\mathfrak{s}: (\lambda_w, n_w) \Rightarrow \cdots \Rightarrow (\lambda_\ell, n_\ell)$ of $\mathfrak{d}$. First, we eliminate all applications of **(R$_4$)** in $\mathfrak{s}$: each suffix $(\Box_F q, 0) \Rightarrow_{(\mathbf{R_4})} (\Box_F q, -1) \Rightarrow (\lambda_s, n_s) \Rightarrow \cdots \Rightarrow (\lambda_\ell, n_\ell)$ is replaced by $(\Box_F q, 0) \Rightarrow (\lambda_s, n_s + 1) \Rightarrow \cdots \Rightarrow (\lambda_\ell, n_\ell + 1)$; and similarly for $\Box_P$. If each time we eliminate the last application of **(R$_4$)** then the result is clearly a 0-derivation. Second, we remove all duplicating literals: each suffix $(\lambda_s, n_s) \Rightarrow \cdots \Rightarrow (\lambda_{s'}, n_{s'}) \Rightarrow (\lambda_{s'+1}, n_{s'+1}) \Rightarrow \cdots \Rightarrow (\lambda_\ell, n_\ell)$ with $\lambda_s = \lambda_{s'}$ is replaced by $(\lambda_s, n_s) \Rightarrow (\lambda_{s'+1}, n_{s'+1}+k) \Rightarrow \cdots \Rightarrow (\lambda_\ell, n_\ell+k)$, where $k = n_s - n_{s'}$. This will give us a left-stuttering 0-derivation $\mathfrak{d}'$ of (λ, m), for some m. Since there are at most $|\varphi|$ distinct literals in $\mathfrak{s}$, we have $r(\mathfrak{d}') \leq 2|\varphi|$, thus satisfying the second option of **(C$_2$)**; see Fig. 5.

In the latter case $\mathfrak{d}$ right-stutters, and we construct a 0-derivation $\mathfrak{d}'$ of (p, n') by cutting out the segment $(\lambda_{v+1}, n_{v+1}) \Rightarrow \cdots \Rightarrow (\lambda_w, n_w)$ from $\mathfrak{d}$ and 'shifting' the tail using the construction above: eliminate applications of **(R$_4$)** and then decrease all numbers by $n_w - n_v > 0$. We then consider the obtained $\mathfrak{d}'$ as the original $\mathfrak{d}$. As the length of the derivations decreases and $n' \leq n$, by applying this procedure sufficiently many times, we shall finally construct a 0-derivation of reach $\leq 2|\varphi|$ and satisfying either $(\mathbf{C_1})$ or the first option of $(\mathbf{C_2})$.

($\Leftarrow$) is left to the reader. ☐

In a similar way we can show how to efficiently check the condition $\Psi \Rightarrow^\forall p$:

Lemma 9 (checking $\Rightarrow^\forall$). $\Psi \Rightarrow^0 (\lambda, n)$ holds for all $n \in \mathbb{Z}$ iff there are 0-derivations $\mathfrak{d}$ of (λ, m) and $\mathfrak{d}'$ of (λ, m') of reach at most $2|\varphi|$ such that one of the following conditions holds:

$(\mathbf{C'_1})$ $\mathfrak{d}$ contains $\square_F$, $\mathfrak{d}'$ contains $\square_P$ and $m \leq m' + 1$;
$(\mathbf{C'_2})$ $\mathfrak{d}$ contains $\square_F$ and left-stutters;
$(\mathbf{C'_3})$ $\mathfrak{d}$ contains $\square_P$ and right-stutters.

Proof. ($\Rightarrow$) Take a 0-derivation of $(q, 2|\varphi|+1)$. By Lemma 8, there is a derivation $\mathfrak{d}_0$ of (q, n_0) with $r(\mathfrak{d}_0) \leq 2|\varphi|$ satisfying either $(\mathbf{C_2})$ or $(\mathbf{C_3})$. If $\mathfrak{d}_0$ left- or right-stutters then we have $(\mathbf{C'_2})$ or $(\mathbf{C'_3})$, respectively. Otherwise, $\mathfrak{d}_0$ contains $\square_F$ and we can construct a finite sequence of 0-derivations $\mathfrak{d}_0, \mathfrak{d}_1, \mathfrak{d}_2, \ldots, \mathfrak{d}_k$ of reach at most $2|\varphi|$, where each $\mathfrak{d}_i$ is a 0-derivation of (q, n_i) containing $\square_F$, and such that $n_0 > n_1 > n_2 > \cdots > n_k$.

Suppose we have already constructed $\mathfrak{d}_i$. Since $\Psi \Rightarrow^0 (q, n)$, for all n, we have $\Psi \Rightarrow^0 (q, n_i - 1)$. By Lemma 8, there is a 0-derivation $\mathfrak{d}$ of (q, n_{i+1}), for some n_{i+1}, with one of $(\mathbf{C_1})$–$(\mathbf{C_3})$. If $(\mathbf{C_2})$ and $\mathfrak{d}$ left-stutters or $(\mathbf{C_3})$ and $\mathfrak{d}$ right-stutters then we obtain $(\mathbf{C'_2})$ or $(\mathbf{C'_3})$, respectively. If $(\mathbf{C_2})$ and $\mathfrak{d}$ contains $\square_F$ with $n_{i+1} \leq n_i - 1$ then $\mathfrak{d}$ becomes the next member $\mathfrak{d}_{i+1}$ in the sequence. If $(\mathbf{C_3})$ and $\mathfrak{d}$ contains $\square_P$ with $n_{i+1} \geq n_i - 1$ then $\mathfrak{d}_i$ and $\mathfrak{d}$ satisfy $(\mathbf{C'_1})$. Otherwise, we have $(\mathbf{C_1})$ with $n_{i+1} = n_i - 1$ (recall that $n_i > -2|\varphi|$). Consider three cases. If $\mathfrak{d}$ contains $\square_F$ then $\mathfrak{d}$ becomes the next member $\mathfrak{d}_{i+1}$ in the sequence. If $\mathfrak{d}$ contains $\square_P$ then $\mathfrak{d}_i$ and $\mathfrak{d}$ satisfy $(\mathbf{C'_1})$. Otherwise, that is, if $\mathfrak{d}$ contains neither $\square_P$ nor $\square_F$, we must have $n_{i+1} = 0$ and $p \to^* q$, for some $p \in \Psi$. Then we have $n_i = 1$ and, as $\mathfrak{d}_i$ contains $\square_F$, we can append $(q, 1) \Rightarrow_{(\mathbf{R_5})} (\square_F q, 0) \Rightarrow_{(\mathbf{R_4})} (\square_F q, -1) \Rightarrow_{(\mathbf{R_3})} (q, 0)$ to $\mathfrak{d}$ to obtain the next member $\mathfrak{d}_{i+1}$ in the sequence.

($\Leftarrow$) is left to the reader. ☐

We are now in a position to prove the main result of this section.

Theorem 4. *The satisfiability problem for* $\mathsf{LTL}^\square_{core}$*-formulas is in* NLOGSPACE.

Proof. An $\mathsf{LTL}^\square_{core}$-formula $\varphi = \Psi \wedge \boxasterisk \Phi^+ \wedge \boxasterisk \Phi^-$ is unsatisfiable iff Φ^- contains a clause $\neg \lambda_1 \vee \neg \lambda_2$ such that $\mathfrak{K}_\varphi, n \models \lambda_1 \wedge \lambda_2$, for some n with $|n| \leq K$. For each $\neg \lambda_1 \vee \neg \lambda_2$ in Φ^-, our algorithm guesses such an n (in binary) and, for both λ_1 and λ_2, checks whether $\Psi \Rightarrow^0 (\lambda_i, n)$ or $\Psi \Rightarrow^\forall \lambda_i$, which, by Lemmas 8 and 9, requires only logarithmic space. ☐

The initial clauses of $\mathsf{LTL}^\square_{core}$-formulas φ are propositional variables. If we slightly extend the language to allow for initial core-clauses (without $\boxasterisk$), then the satisfiability problem becomes PTIME-hard. This can be shown by reduction of satisfiability of propositional Horn formulas with clauses of the form p, $\neg p$ and

$p \wedge q \to r$, which is known to be PTIME-complete. Indeed, suppose $f = \bigwedge_{i=1}^{n} C_i$ is such a formula. We define a temporal formula φ_f to be the conjunction of all unary clauses of f with the following formulas, for each ternary clause C_i of the form $p \wedge q \to r$ in f:

$$c_i \;\wedge\; \boxdot(p \to \Box_F c_i) \;\wedge\; \boxdot(q \to \Box_P c_i) \;\wedge\; (\boxdot c_i \to r),$$

where c_i is a fresh variable. One can show that f is satisfiable iff φ_f is satisfiable.

We finish this section by an observation that if the language allows for non-Horn clauses (e.g., $p \vee q$) then the satisfiability problem becomes NP-hard:

Theorem 5. *The satisfiability problem for* $\mathsf{LTL}_{krom}^{\Box}$-*formulas is* NP-*hard.*

Proof. By reduction of graph 3-colourability. Given a graph $G = (V, E)$, consider the following $\mathsf{LTL}_{krom}^{\Box}$-formula φ_G with variables $p_0, \ldots, p_4$ and $\overline{v}_i$, for $v_i \in V$:

$$p_0 \;\wedge\; \bigwedge_{0 \leq i \leq 3} \boxdot(p_i \to \Box_F p_{i+1}) \;\wedge\; \bigwedge_{v_i \in V} \boxdot(p_0 \to \neg \Box_F \overline{v}_i) \;\wedge\; \bigwedge_{v_i \in V} \boxdot(p_4 \to \overline{v}_i) \;\wedge\; \bigwedge_{(v_i, v_j) \in E} \boxdot(\overline{v}_i \vee \overline{v}_j).$$

Intuitively, the first four conjuncts of this formula choose, for each vertex v_i of the graph, a moment of time $1 \leq n_i \leq 3$; the last conjunct makes sure that $n_i \neq n_j$ in case v_i and v_j are connected by an edge in G. It can be easily shown that φ_G is satisfiable iff G is 3-colourable. □

5 Conclusion

We have investigated the computational complexity of the satisfiability problem for the fragments of LTL over $(\mathbb{Z}, <)$ given by the form of the clauses—*bool*, *horn*, *krom* and *core*—in the clausal normal form and the temporal operators available for constructing temporal literals. Apart from $\mathsf{LTL}_{bool}^{\Box,\bigcirc}$, whose formulas are equisatisfiable to formulas in the full LTL, only $\mathsf{LTL}_{horn}^{\Box,\bigcirc}$ has PSPACE-complete satisfiability. For all other fragments, the complexity varies from NLOGSPACE to PTIME and NP.

The idea to consider sub-Boolean fragments of LTL comes from description logic, where the *DL-Lite* family [9,3] of logics has been designed and investigated with the aim of finding formalisms suitable for ontology-based data access (OBDA). It transpired that, despite their low complexity, *DL-Lite* logics were capable of representing basic conceptual data modelling constructs [8,2], and gave rise to the W3C standard ontology language *OWL 2 QL* for OBDA. One possible application of the results obtained in this paper lies in temporal conceptual modelling and temporal OBDA [5]. Temporal description logics (and other many-dimensional logics) are notorious for their bad computational properties [17,20]. We believe, however, that efficient practical reasoning can be achieved by considering sub-Boolean temporal extensions of *DL-Lite* logics; see [4] for first promising results.

References

1. Apostol, T.: Introduction to Analytic Number Theory. Springer (1976)
2. Artale, A., Calvanese, D., Kontchakov, R., Ryzhikov, V., Zakharyaschev, M.: Reasoning over extended ER models. In: Parent, C., Schewe, K.-D., Storey, V.C., Thalheim, B. (eds.) ER 2007. LNCS, vol. 4801, pp. 277–292. Springer, Heidelberg (2007)
3. Artale, A., Calvanese, D., Kontchakov, R., Zakharyaschev, M.: The DL-Lite family and relations. Journal of Artificial Intelligence Research 36, 1–69 (2009)
4. Artale, A., Kontchakov, R., Ryzhikov, V., Zakharyaschev, M.: Past and future of DL-Lite. In: Proc. of AAAI, pp. 243–248 (2010)
5. Artale, A., Kontchakov, R., Ryzhikov, V., Zakharyaschev, M.: Complexity of reasoning over temporal data models. In: Parsons, J., Saeki, M., Shoval, P., Woo, C., Wand, Y. (eds.) ER 2010. LNCS, vol. 6412, pp. 174–187. Springer, Heidelberg (2010)
6. Artale, A., Kontchakov, R., Ryzhikov, V., Zakharyaschev, M.: The Complexity of Clausal Fragments of LTL. CoRR abs/1306.5088 (2013)
7. Bauland, M., Schneider, T., Schnoor, H., Schnoor, I., Vollmer, H.: The complexity of generalized satisfiability for linear temporal logic. Logical Methods in Computer Science 5(1) (2009)
8. Berardi, D., Calvanese, D., De Giacomo, G.: Reasoning on UML class diagrams. Artificial Intelligence 168(1-2), 70–118 (2005)
9. Calvanese, D., De Giacomo, G., Lembo, D., Lenzerini, M., Rosati, R.: Tractable reasoning and efficient query answering in description logics: The DL-Lite family. Journal of Automated Reasoning 39(3), 385–429 (2007)
10. Chen, C.-C., Lin, I.-P.: The computational complexity of satisfiability of temporal Horn formulas in propositional linear-time temporal logic. Information Processing Letters 45(3), 131–136 (1993)
11. Chrobak, M.: Finite automata and unary languages. Theoretical Computer Science 47(2), 149–158 (1986)
12. Demri, S., Schnoebelen, P.: The complexity of propositional linear temporal logics in simple cases. Information and Computation 174(1), 84–103 (2002)
13. Dixon, C., Fisher, M., Konev, B.: Tractable temporal reasoning. In: Proc. of IJCAI, pp. 318–323 (2007)
14. Fisher, M.: A resolution method for temporal logic. In: Proc. of IJCAI, pp. 99–104. Morgan Kaufmann (1991)
15. Fisher, M., Dixon, C., Peim, M.: Clausal temporal resolution. ACM Transactions on Computational Logic 2(1), 12–56 (2001)
16. Gabbay, D., Hodkinson, I., Reynolds, M.: Temporal Logic: Mathematical Foundations and Computational Aspects, vol. 1. Oxford University Press (1994)
17. Gabbay, D., Kurucz, A., Wolter, F., Zakharyaschev, M.: Many-Dimensional Modal Logics: Theory and Applications. Elsevier (2003)
18. Halpern, J., Reif, J.: The propositional dynamic logic of deterministic, well-structured programs. In: Proc. of FOCS, pp. 322–334. IEEE (1981)
19. Lichtenstein, O., Pnueli, A., Zuck, L.D.: The glory of the past. In: Parikh, R. (ed.) Logic of Programs 1985. LNCS, vol. 193, pp. 196–218. Springer, Heidelberg (1985)
20. Lutz, C., Wolter, F., Zakharyaschev, M.: Temporal description logics: A survey. In: Proc. of TIME, pp. 3–14. IEEE Comp. Society (2008)
21. Markey, N.: Past is for free: On the complexity of verifying linear temporal properties with past. Acta Informatica 40(6-7), 431–458 (2004)

22. Ono, H., Nakamura, A.: On the size of refutation Kripke models for some linear modal and tense logics. Studia Logica 39, 325–333 (1980)
23. Plaisted, D.: A decision procedure for combinations of propositional temporal logic and other specialized theories. Journal of Automated Reasoning 2, 171–190 (1986)
24. Rabinovich, A.: Temporal logics over linear time domains are in PSPACE. In: Kučera, A., Potapov, I. (eds.) RP 2010. LNCS, vol. 6227, pp. 29–50. Springer, Heidelberg (2010)
25. Reynolds, M.: The complexity of decision problems for linear temporal logics. Journal of Studies in Logic 3(1), 19–50 (2010)
26. Sistla, A., Clarke, E.: The complexity of propositional linear temporal logics. In: Proc. of STOC, pp. 159–168. ACM (1982)
27. Stockmeyer, L., Meyer, A.: Word problems requiring exponential time: Preliminary report. In: Proc. of STOC, pp. 1–9. ACM (1973)
28. To, A.W.: Unary finite automata vs. arithmetic progressions. Information Processing Letters 109(17), 1010–1014 (2009)

A Semantic Basis for Proof Queries and Transformations

David Aspinall[1,*], Ewen Denney[2,**], and Christoph Lüth[3,***]

[1] LFCS, School of Informatics, University of Edinburgh
Edinburgh EH8 9AB, Scotland
[2] SGT, NASA Ames Research Center
Moffett Field, CA 94035, USA
[3] Deutsches Forschungszentrum für Künstliche Intelligenz & Universität Bremen
Bremen, Germany

Abstract. We add *updates* to the query language *PrQL*, designed for inspecting machine representations of proofs. PrQL natively supports *hiproofs* that express proof structure using hierarchically nested labelled trees, which we claim is a natural way of taming the complexity of huge proofs. Query-driven updates allow us to change this structure, in particular, to transform proofs produced by interactive theorem provers into forms that are easier for humans to understand, or that could be consumed by other tools. In this paper we motivate and define basic update operations, using an abstract denotational semantics of hiproofs and queries. This extends our previous semantics for queries based on syntactic tree representations. We define update operations that add and remove sub-proofs or manipulate the hierarchy to group and ungroup nodes. We show that these basic operations are well-behaved and hence can form a sound core for a hierarchical transformation language. Our study here is firmly in language design and semantics; implementation strategies and study of sub-languages of our query language with good complexity will come later.

1 Introduction

We are interested in ways to exploit machine representations of proofs constructed by interactive or automated theorem provers. These proof representations are produced so that they can be independently checked or imported into other systems. We believe that they can be exploited beyond this. For example, system inputs such as proof scripts are rarely given at the lowest level of detail, even with interactive theorem provers. Therefore it can be useful for proof developers to understand how the system has found a proof: which inference rules have been used, which axioms, which instantiations for existential variables, and

---

* Research supported by EPSRC grant EP/J001058/1.
** Research supported by NASA contract NNA10DE83C.
*** Research supported by BMBF grant 01IW10002 (SHIP).

so on. More complex questions are also interesting. For example, whether a proof contains unnecessary detours or replicated sub-proofs.

To this end, we recently introduced PrQL [3], a *proof query language* which treats a large formal proof as an object that can be examined in a systematic way. We are currently developing practical prototypes to experiment with proof queries, so far based on exporting from Isabelle [3] and HOL Light [21]. But it is clear already that as well asking questions, we also want to be able to *transform proofs* to alter their structure in various ways. This may be used to aid understanding (human or machine), by hiding certain kinds of details. Or it could be used for optimisation or adaptation, to change proofs to more efficient forms, or for consumption by different systems such as proof commentary tools or machine learning tools. This paper is a study of a rigorous foundation for such transformations, introducing *update* extensions for PrQL.

To study the foundations of updates, we need to have the right data model for hiproofs and define operations that preserve the hiproof structure. Some transformations may also preserve theoremhood of proved statements. This is why we design our own query and transformation language, rather than immediately encoding our concepts into a more general graph or tree model (such as XML) with an existing query and transformation language (such as XQuery Update [10] or XDuce [20]) that could make arbitrary dissections and rearrangement.

When it comes to implementing our query and update language, it is obviously desirable to reuse existing systems which have looser semantics but optimised implementations for query language fragments in good complexity classes. We may consider for example, graph databases, other tools in the "NoSQL" family or perhaps even SPARQL. We are conducting some early experiments in parallel with the work described here.

Contributions and Paper Outline. This paper contributes towards generic foundational aspects of theorem proving systems, in particular, the novel aspects of querying and transforming the proof objects which can be recorded by proof tools. Moreover, we contribute to the study of a *structured* representation for these objects. Sect. 2 introduces the idea of proof transformations that we are studying, with some informal examples and motivations. Sect. 3 recaps the technical background of hiproofs and PrQL. Sect. 4 introduces a revised denotational semantics for hiproofs; this extends previous work, connecting the syntactic strand of [2] with the previous denotational semantics of [14]. The new extensions add explicit orderings among subtrees and the ability to model *open*, i.e., incomplete, proofs. Sect. 5 gives a new denotational semantics to our query language. This interpretation provides two advances: (1) the ability to return locations in the hiproof where a query is satisfied, and (2) a close connection to a graph model that we can use to encode hiproofs. Sect. 6 builds on top of this to define our four kinds of update operations. We show that these operations are well-behaved and preserve proofs in certain senses. Finally, we give a more detailed comparison to related work in the concluding Sect. 7.

2 Querying and Transforming Hierarchical Trees

We start from *hiproofs* [14,2], which provide an abstract, generic notion of proof tree with hierarchical structure. Hiproofs are composed from atomic rules of inference from an unspecified underlying logic, but additionally provide a notion of *hierarchy*, by allowing labelling and nesting of subtrees inside boxes. This succinct notion of *structuring* in a proof can be used, for example, for noting where a lemma was applied, or where a particular tactic or external proof tool produced a subtree. The hierarchical structure of hiproofs and its interaction with the proof-tree is more complex than the straightforward tree structure, in particular because hiproofs allow nesting of partially completed proofs.

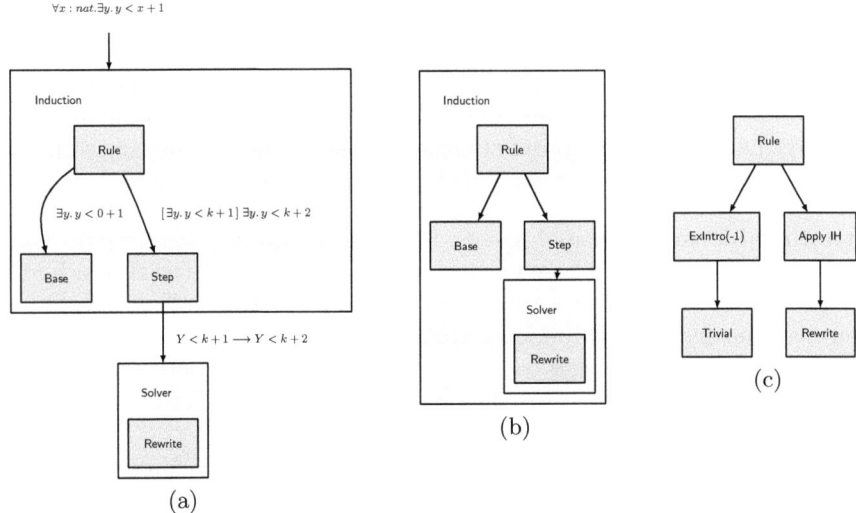

Fig. 1. Different hiproof structures on the same underlying proof

The picture shown in Fig. 1(a) is an example hiproof, shown at a certain level of abstraction. It corresponds with an ordinary (but upside-down) natural deduction style proof tree: the theorem being proved, $\forall x.\exists y.y < x + 1$ is shown at the top, and then the proof outline shows how the proof is achieved by decomposing the *goal* theorem into pieces. The labelled boxes correspond to *tactics* which have been applied to do this. Notice how the Induction box encapsulates an incomplete proof; it has the dangling edge which is passed into the Solver box. We suppose that boxes such as Base may contain further details, perhaps right down to atomic inferences in the underlying system; the diagram only hints at the full hiproof. Fig. 1(a) shows the statements being proved along edges. In a visualisation tool (such as the web-based HipCam [21]) the goals may be shown in pop-ups so as not to clutter the display, and boxes such as Base can be opened and closed dynamically.

Variations of hierarchy. Further right in Fig. 1 we see some alternative structuring of this simple inductive proof. Fig. 1(b) shows the complete step case being enclosed by the induction box; whereas Fig. 1(c) shows just the induction rule itself being boxed. These pictures motivate our main kind of desirable transformations: to alter and introduce hierarchical structure. For example, when an inductive proof appears in the proof tree, we might like to give it the uniform structure on the left so it can be easily picked apart. However, the proofs which arise by a naive labelling of tactics in HOL Light without hiproof adaptation [21], for example, have the form in Fig. 1(c).

Basic Transformations. Generally, the life cycle of data management is captured by functions to *create*, *read*, *update*, and *delete*. We already have mechanisms to create proof objects: abstractly, via the syntax for hiproofs reviewed in Sect. 3, and in practice by functions for exporting proof objects from systems like Isabelle [3] and HOL Light [21]. To inspect proof objects, PrQL provides a language of structured queries, reviewed further below. To manipulate existing hiproofs, we need to add update and delete operations. But we want to do this in a way that respects the proof structure, rather than as arbitrary edits to a tree or graph. This motivates the following four types of operation.

Introduce hierarchy is used moving from Fig. 1(c) to Fig. 1(a): we introduce a nested hiproof called Base for the two steps ExIntro and Trivial, which hides the detail. We also push in the children of Rule into the Induction box.

Remove hierarchy is the opposite transformation. Visualisation tools perform this reversibly under user control, but here we want to permanently transform the underlying structure by pulling out individual pieces, such as when moving from Fig 1(b) to Fig 1(a).

Remove subproof deletes part of a hiproof. This is a radical operation, and will change what is being proved, popping out an unproved subgoal to the top level. For example, if we remove the Solver tactic in Fig. 1(a), the proof is left unfinished with the subgoal $Y < k+1 \implies Y < k+2$ remaining.

Complete subproof is the inverse operation, and grafts on a new subtree. This can resolve a previously unproved subgoal, or generate new subgoals.

2.1 Finding Somewhere to Transform

First, to apply a transformation, we need to know *where* in a target hiproof it should be applied. A natural way to find a transformation point is to search for a node satisfying some properties: this is where *queries* enter the picture. (Similarly, update languages that have been defined elsewhere for semistructured data and graphs also use queries to position updates; see Sect. 7.)

We have already designed PrQL, a query language for hiproofs, so it is natural to reuse it. PrQL is a structured query language which combines property queries (that look at local properties on nodes) with structuring operations (that combine queries across connected nodes, decomposing the tree). These can be defined with recursion and logical connectives, giving a powerful language that can encode search in queries. For example, the PrQL query

somewhere (atomic ExIntro **then atomic** Trivial**)**

is satisfied by the hiproof in Fig. 1(c). The **atomic** operator examines a label on a bottom-most nested node. The **then** operator decomposes the target graph across the proof tree sequence. Similarly, we can decompose sibling hiproofs with **beside** and nested hiproofs with **inside**, building up patterns. Patterns may contain *match variables* that get instantiated with names of rules or box labels. Using recursion we can define operators like **somewhere** (finds a match in any subtree) and **nearby** (finds a match in any subtree at the same nesting depth). See Sect. 3.1 for more details of PrQL.

However, so far there is not yet a notion of *where* a query is satisfied; we do not have a way to describe where ExIntro or Trivial rules were actually found. To pick out specific nodes in a hiproof, we extend the query language to return positions: a new type of match variable standing for a (sub)hiproof where a query is satisfied. We add the new query term "**at** X" which matches X against the "currently examined" node in the tree. So

somewhere inside Induction **nearby (at** X ∧ **atomic** Trivial**)**

returns locations X where Trivial appears immediately inside an Induction box.

Unlike labels for boxes and atomic rule names, nodes in our proof trees are abstract: we do not need user-level syntax for writing their identities. So **at** can only locate a position by properties; it cannot pick out a specific node concretely. But the query language is precise enough that, for any specific node in the tree, there is a query which picks out that node uniquely (see Prop. 1 in Sect. 5).

2.2 Updating Proofs

Now we have a way to specify transformation points, we can show how our update operations are written. Several language design choices are possible. We have followed an SQL-like paradigm, matching positions then using one-shot operations which can update a large proof in-place, based on the selected positions. A more ambitious choice would be to design a hybrid query and update language, with looping and branching to build up complex transformations. But we first want to understand the update combinators that are common to both.

As a first example, to turn Fig. 1(c) into Fig. 1(b) we use a transformation which adds a box around a given subtree, called **box**:

$$\textbf{box } X \textbf{ to } Y \ Z \textbf{ as Induction where} \qquad (1)$$
$$(\textbf{at } X \wedge \textbf{atomic Rule}) \textbf{ then } (\textbf{seq } Y \textbf{ beside seq } Z)$$

where the recursive query **seq** X picks out a sequence ending at X:

$$\textbf{seq } X \stackrel{def}{=} \mu Q. \ * \textbf{ then } Q \vee (\textbf{at } X \wedge \neg(* \textbf{ then } *))$$

Besides adding boxes, we can remove them with **unbox**:

$$\textbf{unbox } X \textbf{ where at } X \wedge \textbf{inside Solver}$$

which removes the Solver box around the result of an automatic tactic. Instead we could rename it, simply writing: **rename** Solver **as** Auto.

So far, these operations have not changed what is proved in the hiproof. Other updates change the underlying proof tree, but maintain its validity. For example, maybe we are not interested in a particular subtree of a proof

$$\textbf{deletetree } X \textbf{ where inside Meson at } X$$

then this removes the subtree generated by an automatic procedure, just leaving the name of the procedure. In the hiproof structure, we do not forget that something is unproved; the subtree leaves a *dangling* edge.

Dually, we can fill in a proof for such a dangling edge; this is a *refinement* operation in the sense that it extends the proof:

$$\textbf{refine } X \textbf{ with } s \textbf{ where at } X \wedge \textbf{unproved } \gamma$$

Here, s is a literal term in the syntax for hiproofs, which proves the goal γ.

Finally, it can be useful to use a more general replacement transformation which is defined using **deletetree** then **refine**. For example, to find useless detours in a proof tree, we use the query:

$$\textbf{useless } X \ Y \ \stackrel{def}{=} (\textbf{at } X \wedge \textbf{goal } G) \textbf{ then nearby } (\textbf{at } Y \wedge \textbf{goal } G)$$

this identifies a path from X to Y where we hit the same goal $G = \gamma$. It might even be a tactic which is worse than useless, in that it has transformed a goal γ into several more goals to prove including γ again. Now the **replace** update

$$\textbf{replace } X \textbf{ by } Y \textbf{ where } (\textbf{useless } X \ Y)$$

removes this detour.

3 Syntactic Hiproofs and PrQL Queries

This section introduces previous material as background. We are as concise as possible and refer the reader to previous papers for more details [14,2,3].

Hiproofs add structure to an underlying *derivation system*, a simple kind of logical framework. A derivation system is given by a set $\mathcal{G}$ of *goals* (intuitively: possibly provable sequents or judgements), ranged over by γ, and a set of atomic inference rules ranged over by a. Atomic rules are composed to give hiproofs, which have a functional reading: a hiproof maps a finite list of input goals $g_1 = [\gamma_1, \ldots, \gamma_n]$ to a list of output subgoals $g_2 = [\gamma'_1, \ldots, \gamma'_m]$.

Informally, we draw hiproofs as inverted trees with a nested structure. Formally, a hiproof is given by two forests on the same set of nodes, as explained in Sect. 4. Syntactically, a hiproof can be written as a term:

$$
\begin{aligned}
s ::=\ & a \quad\mid \mathsf{id} & \text{atomic and identity} \\
\mid\ & [l]\, s \mid s_1\,;\, s_2 & \text{labelling and sequencing} \\
\mid\ & \langle\rangle \mid s_1 \otimes s_2 & \text{empty and tensor (juxtaposition)}
\end{aligned}
$$

where $l \in \mathcal{L}$, an arbitrary set of names and $a \in \mathcal{A}$ for some special subset $\mathcal{A} \subset \mathcal{L}$. We think of labels as standing for names of tactics or proof rules, or atomic steps; they have no semantic content. For example, the proofs in Fig. 1 are written syntactically as

$$([\mathsf{Induction}]\,\mathsf{Rule}\,;\,\mathsf{Base}\otimes\mathsf{Step})\,;\,[\mathsf{Solver}]\,\mathsf{Rewrite} \qquad (2)$$

$$[\mathsf{Induction}]\,\mathsf{Rule}\,;\,\mathsf{Base}\otimes(\mathsf{Step}\,;\,[\mathsf{Solver}]\,\mathsf{Rewrite}) \qquad (3)$$

$$\mathsf{Rule}\,;\,(\mathsf{ExIntro}\,;\,\mathsf{Trivial})\otimes(\mathsf{ApplyIH}\,;\,\mathsf{Rewrite}) \qquad (4)$$

3.1 Structured Queries in PrQL

The definition of PrQL starts with *matches* built from wildcards and match variables, constants (atoms, sets and predicates) and negation (to construct the complement of a match). Let Var_N be a set of schematic variables standing for names, ranged over by N in general and A when we suggest an atomic rule name or L a label name. Let Var_G be a set of variables standing for lists of goals. The name matches and goal matches are given by:

$$nm ::= a \mid l \mid \bullet \mid \xi \mid N \mid \neg nm \qquad gm ::= \gamma \mid \psi \mid G \mid \neg gm$$

where ξ stands for a logic-dependent predicate on names, and ψ stands for a logic-dependent predicate on goals used to check some structural property of the goal term. For example we might have a predicate that checks whether a goal γ is in the form of a horn clause, when $\phi_{horn}(\gamma)$ holds. The special name $\bullet$ is used to label unproved goals; the name $* = \neg\bullet$ serves as a wildcard.

We use matches to build up queries, q, as below. The extension to PrQL to locate vertices uses a set of match variables Var_H, ranged over by X.

$$
\begin{aligned}
q ::=\ & * & \text{anything non-empty} \\
\mid\ & \mathbf{at}\ X & \text{matches at node } X \\
\mid\ & \mathbf{atomic}\ nm & \text{atomic rule match} \\
\mid\ & \mathbf{inside}\ nm\ q & q \text{ satisfied inside box with label matching } nm \\
\mid\ & q_1\ \mathbf{then}\ q_2 & q_1 \text{ and } q_2 \text{ satisfied by successive nodes} \\
\mid\ & q_1\ \mathbf{beside}\ q_2 & q_1 \text{ and } q_2 \text{ satisfied by adjacent nodes} \\
\mid\ & \mathbf{goal}\ gm & \text{proved goal matches } gm \\
\mid\ & q_1 \wedge q_2 \mid q_1 \vee q_2 \mid \neg q & \text{compound queries} \\
\mid\ & \mu Q.q & \text{recursive query}
\end{aligned}
$$

Queries are built from schematic hiproof terms. They are posed against an implicit hiproof subject, instantiating the match variables and testing goals. Compound queries are built using logical connectives and recursion. This core language allows many useful derived forms, like the search operator **somewhere**. We can examine gaps in proofs too; to assert that the hiproof has γ as an unsolved goal we write:

$$\textbf{unproved } \gamma \stackrel{def}{=} \textbf{goal } \gamma \wedge \textbf{atomic } \bullet$$

This works because we model 'dangling' edges as empty boxes labelled with $\bullet$.

4 Denotational Hiproofs

A hiproof consists of two forests on the same set of nodes, with a distinguished root, satisfying some conditions [14]. To relate to a derivation system (where premises of inference rules have an ordering), we add a left-to-right ordering among siblings. To relate to the syntax, we use a more general forest notion first, then restrict to hiproofs. To model incomplete (partial) proofs, we add nodes corresponding to unproved goals. Lastly, we extend labelling to attach to each node the goal it validates, as shown on edges entering nodes in Fig. 1(a).

Given a forest F defined by a relation R on a set of vertices, we write $siblings_R(v, v')$ if v and v' are children of the same R-parent. Given a vertex v, we write $isroot_R(v)$ for the assertion that v is a root wrt R, i.e., $\forall v'.v'\ R\ v \implies v = v'$, and $isleaf_R(v)$ for the dual, i.e., $\forall v'.v\ R\ v' \implies v = v'$.

Definition 1 (Ordered Hiforest). *An ordered hiforest $H = \langle V, L, \leq_i, \to_s, \lesssim \rangle$ consists of a finite set of vertices V with a labelling function $L : V \to (\mathcal{L} \cup \{\bullet\}) \times \mathcal{G}$ and three relations on $V \times V$. The relations are an inclusion order $\leq_i$ (which captures the nesting of vertices; $>_i$ is proper containment), a sequencing relation $\to_s$ (which captures the functional composition of nodes) and a child order $\lesssim$. These are subject to the following conditions:*

0. *$\langle V, \leq_i \rangle$ and $\langle V, \to_s \rangle$ each form forests; $\leq_i$ and $\lesssim$ are partial orders.*
1. *arrows target outer nodes: $v \to_s w$ and $v' >_i w \implies v' >_i v$.*
2. *arrows emanate from inner nodes: $v \to_s w$ and $v' \leq_i v \implies v = v'$.*
3. *inclusion & sequence are mutually exclusive: $v \leq_i w$ and $v \to_s^* w \implies v = w$.*
4. *boxes have unique roots:*
   $siblings_{\leq_i}(v, v') \wedge isroot_{\to_s}(v) \wedge isroot_{\to_s}(v') \implies v = v'$.
5. *children or top-level roots are totally ordered:*
   $siblings_{\to_s}(v, v') \vee (isroot_{>_i}(v) \wedge isroot_{>_i}(v')) \implies v \lesssim v' \vee v' \lesssim v$.
6. *only leaves (wrt. sequencing and inclusion) may have $\bullet$ label:*
   $L(v) = (\bullet, \gamma) \implies leaf_{\to_s \cup >_i}(v)$.

Each node in a hiforest is given a name and a goal. The goal is the theorem proved at that node. The unproved parts are the 'dangling' holes labelled by $\bullet$. An ordered hiforest proves a sequence of top-level goals, whereas a hiproof proves just one.

Definition 2 (Ordered Hiproof). *An* ordered hiproof *is an ordered hiforest which satisfies the additional constraint:*

7. *Top-level roots are unique:* $\mathit{isroot}_{\to_s \cup >_i}(v) \wedge \mathit{isroot}_{\to_s \cup >_i}(v') \implies v = v'$.

We are mainly interested in *valid* hiproofs, which are those corresponding to a proof in the underlying derivation system.

Definition 3 (Validity). *A hiforest H is* valid *if it corresponds to a sequence of (possibly incomplete) proof trees in the underlying derivation system; we write $H \models g_1 \longrightarrow g_2$ if this holds and where g_1 is the list of goals on the outermost roots of H, and g_2 is the list of unproved goals on the holes, as ordered by extending $\lesssim$ to the leaves of the tree.*

A *map* between two hiforests is a map between the vertices and the labels which preserves the orderings and the labelling. We say a hiforest H_1 *refines to* a hiforest H_2, $H_1 \sqsubseteq H_2$, if there is an inclusion from H_1 to H_2 which also preserves the roots wrt $>_i$.

We now define some operations on the two dimensions of hiforests which will form the semantic foundations of our transformations. For brevity, definitions are given informally here, and made precise in the appendix. Given two hiforests H_1 and H_2 such that $H_1 \models g_1 \longrightarrow g$ and $H_2 \models g \longrightarrow g_2$, we define a composition operation $\mathit{graft}(H_1, H_2)$ that 'grafts' the roots of H_2 into the dangling goals of H_1, such that $\mathit{graft}(H_1, H_2) \models g_1 \longrightarrow g_2$; it can be characterised at the smallest hiforest H_3 which refines H_1, $H_1 \sqsubseteq H_3$, for which there is a (necessarily injective) map $\alpha : H_2 \longrightarrow H_3$. This is an instance of a more general operation $\mathit{graft}(H_1, H_2, v_1, \ldots, v_m)$ which grafts the m roots of H_2 into the specified danglers $v_1, \ldots, v_m$ of H_1, where H_1 may contain more than m danglers.

Given a vertex $v \in V$ in hiforest H, we define $\mathit{cover}(v, H)$ as the hiproof containing the set of vertices in H reachable from v by $>_i$ or $\to_s$, including v itself. If $H \models g_1 \longrightarrow g_2$ then $\mathit{cover}(v, H) \models \gamma_v \longrightarrow g_v$ where $L(v) = (l, \gamma_v)$ and $g_2 = g_2' \,{}^\wedge g_v \,{}^\wedge g_2''$ (with ${}^\wedge$ denoting list concatenation). The operation $\mathit{chop}(v, H)$ removes exactly these vertices, replacing them with a hole. So $\mathit{chop}(v, H) \models g_1 \longrightarrow g_3$ where g_3 is the list $g_2' \,{}^\wedge [\gamma_v] \,{}^\wedge g_2''$. Together, these operations are inverse to grafting, i.e. $\mathit{graft}(\mathit{chop}(v, H), \mathit{cover}(v, H), v) = H$ (modulo some technical restrictions). The final operations are $\mathit{box}(l, H)$ and $\mathit{unbox}(H)$ which add and remove 'boxes' around the roots of H, where a box is a node (labelled l) including all the other nodes (below that root). These are inverse as well: $\mathit{unbox}(\mathit{box}(l, H)) = H$. These two operations preserve validity and input and output goal lists.

5 Semantics for Queries

The query semantics we gave in [3] was based on querying syntax models directly. Since hiproofs are constructed syntactically, this is in a sense the most direct approach. However, syntactic representations are not canonical, because a particular underlying tree structure can be denoted by many terms in the syntax. E.g., the proof in Fig.1(c) can be expressed as in (4) or as

$$\text{Rule} \; ; \; (\text{ExIntro} \otimes \text{ApplyIH}) \; ; \; (\text{Trivial} \otimes \text{Rewrite})$$

For the definition of boolean satisfaction of a query given in [3], this is not problematic as we can close under the syntactic equivalence given by the algebraic structure of hiproofs. But to define updates it is more delicate, since we need a firm notion of *focus* in the hiproof to anchor changes; e.g., example (1) does not work with the syntactic form above. We could use normal forms for syntactic terms, but the denotational model is more direct and also fits well with parallel work on implementation using graph databases, building on [21].

The definition of query satisfaction in the denotational semantics uses a substitution to instantiate variables: $\sigma : (Var_N \rightharpoonup \mathcal{L}) \uplus (Var_G \rightharpoonup G) \uplus (Var_H \rightharpoonup V)$, where V is the set of vertices of the hiproof being queried. The base case for query satisfaction is for names and goals, treated very similarly:

$$
\begin{array}{llll}
n \models_\sigma n' & \text{iff} & n = n' & \quad \gamma \models_\sigma \gamma' \quad \text{iff} \quad \gamma = \gamma' \\
\xi \models_\sigma n & \text{iff} & \xi(n) & \quad \psi \models_\sigma \gamma \quad \text{iff} \quad \psi(\gamma) \\
N \models_\sigma n & \text{iff} & \sigma(N) = n & \quad G \models_\sigma \gamma \quad \text{iff} \quad \sigma(G) = \gamma \\
(\neg N) \models_\sigma n & \text{iff} & \neg(N \models_\sigma n) & \quad (\neg G) \models_\sigma \gamma \quad \text{iff} \quad \neg(G \models_\sigma \gamma)
\end{array}
$$

For a relation R and distinct a, b, we write $a \; R^1 \; b$ if $a \; R \; b$ and there is no intermediate c such that $a \; R \; c$ and $c \; R \; b$.

Definition 4 (Query satisfaction). *Let H be an ordered hiforest with vertices V and q a query. Satisfaction of q for H at a vertex $v \in V$ wrt a substitution σ is defined as the least relation $v \models_\sigma q$ satisfying the following clauses:*

$$
\begin{array}{lll}
v \models_\sigma * & always \\
v \models_\sigma \textbf{at } X & iff & \sigma(X) = v \\
v \models_\sigma \textbf{goal } gm & iff & gm \models_\sigma \gamma \text{ where } L(v) = (l, \gamma) \text{ for some } l \\
v \models_\sigma \textbf{inside } nm \; q & when & nm \models_\sigma l \text{ where } (v) = (l, \gamma) \text{ for some } \gamma \\
& & \text{and } \forall w. \; w \leq_i^1 v \Longrightarrow w \models_\sigma q \\
v \models_\sigma q_1 \textbf{ beside } q_2 & when & v \models_\sigma q_1 \text{ and } \exists w. v \leq_s^1 w \text{ with } w \models_\sigma q_2 \\
v \models_\sigma q_1 \textbf{ then } q_2 & when & v \models_\sigma q_1 \text{ and } \exists w. v \to_s^1 w \text{ with } w \models_\sigma q_2 \\
v \models_\sigma q_1 \land q_2 & when & v \models_\sigma q_1 \text{ and } v \models_\sigma q_2 \\
v \models_\sigma q_1 \lor q_2 & when & v \models_\sigma q_1 \text{ or } v \models_\sigma q_2 \\
v \models_\sigma \neg q & when & \neg(v \models_\sigma q) \\
v \models_\sigma \mu Q.q & when & v \models_\sigma q[\mu Q.q/Q]
\end{array}
$$

A query q is satisfied by a substitution σ on a hiforest H, written $H \models_\sigma q$, if it is satisfied on each outermost root vertex of H, i.e., $\forall v. \text{isroot}_{\to_s \cup >_i}(v) \Longrightarrow v \models_\sigma q$.

Def. 4 works by navigating in a fixed hiproof h to find satisfying vertices v. Because a vertex determines a sub-hiproof, this is equivalent to a structural definition as given in [3], which works by decomposing the subject hiproof during navigation, defining a relation $s \models_\sigma q$. Note that in this model **atomic** is defineable as an empty box: **atomic** $nm = $ **inside** $nm \; (\neg *)$.

Definition 5 (Query interpretation). *Let H be an ordered hiforest and q a query. Then we define the interpretation of q in H as the set of satisfying substitutions:* $[\![q]\!]_H = \{\,\sigma \mid H \models_\sigma q\,\}$.

Our language is expressive but queries can be expensive. In [3] we gave a naive algorithm for $[\![q]\!]$ using unification to instantiate variables, which is exponential in the number of match variables. Recursion and match variable unification unavoidably affect the data complexity of our queries (see basic results e.g., [12,18,1]). For large proofs, we would want a fragment that is more feasible but captures most desirable examples. The following proposition is the denotational counterpart of a similar proposition in [3].

Proposition 1. *Given a hiproof H, one of its vertices v and a variable X, there is a query $Q(v, X)$ which locates v at X, i.e., $[\![Q(v,X)]\!]_H = \{\sigma\}$ with $\sigma(X) = v$.*

6 Transformations and Their Semantics

We now introduce the core update operations formally. Note that we do *not* want to allow arbitrary "tree surgery" of the hiproof structure; we want update operations to preserve semantic validity. Updates have the syntax:

$u ::=$ **box** X_r **to** $X_1 \ldots X_n$ **as** l add nested box around $X_r \ldots X_1 \ldots X_n$
     unbox X unfold nested box at X
     rename X **as** l change label on box at X
     refine X **with** s add a new sub-hiproof at X
     deletetree X delete subtree at X
     replace X **by** Y replace subtree at X by that at Y

The **box** operation is the most interesting. It introduces a nested box, whose contents are nodes in the partial subtree with X_r as root and $X_1 \ldots X_n$ as leaves. This allows us to gather to an arbitrary depth, using a query to select either end of the path; this is useful to package up repeated applications of rules. The other update operations are straightforward to understand. An update is *applied* by combining with a query to instantiate node variables in a hiproof, written as **update** u q. This matches q to the root of the hiproof; a more common pattern is to search the hiproof for matches, as seen in the examples in Sect. 2.2. This is written and defined as u **where** q = **update** u (**somewhere** q).

6.1 Interpretation of Transformations

We can specify positions in a hiproof, but we still need to solve a well-known problem with tree and graph updates. Suppose a query picks out several nodes and a transformation changes the structure; then simultaneous updates may *overlap*. The result may be ill-defined, or may depend on the execution order. The semantics as given here is based on single-valued answers to queries; where a query has several answers, there may be several update results, representing applying the operation to different positions in the tree. To have a global effect, the update results may be *merged* if they do not conflict, or we may simply repeatedly apply a query and update. We are not yet investigating implementation in detail, so making any such choices for PrQL could be premature; we prefer to first pin down an accurate semantics. Later on, we plan to extend the language to allow more efficient constructs, avoiding multiple passes and using type systems to ensure safety; we will relate back to the present, intended semantics.

To interpret updates, we use the operations in Sect. 4 and extra definitions:

(i) A combinator to transform a subforest of H with a function f:
$$at(H, v, f) = graft(chop(H, v), f(cover(H, v)), v)$$

(ii) The *box* operator specialised to box only down to vertices $v_1, \ldots, v_n$:
$$addbox(H, l, v_1, \ldots, v_n) = graft(\ box(l, chop_n(H, v_1, \ldots, v_n)),$$
$$cover_n(H, v_1, \ldots, v_n), v_1, \ldots, v_n)$$

where $chop_n(H, v_1, \ldots, v_n)$ and $cover_n(H, v_1, \ldots, v_n)$ are the obvious generalisations of *chop* and *cover* to n arguments.

(iii) To add or remove boxes at the subforest given by v_r:
$$addboxat(H, v_r, v_1, \ldots, v_n) = at(H, v_r, \lambda H.addbox(H, l, v_1, \ldots, v_n))$$
$$unboxat(H, v_r) = at(H, v_r, unbox)$$

(iv) To change the label of a vertex: let $H = \langle V, L, \leq_i, \to_s, \lesssim \rangle$, $v \in V$ and $l \in L$, then L' is defined as $L'(v') = (l, \gamma)$ for $v' = v$, where $L(v) = (l', \gamma)$ and $L'(v') = L(v)$ otherwise. Then $relabel(l, H, v) = \langle V, L', <_i, \to_s, \lesssim \rangle$.

Definition 6 (Interpretation of transformations). *Let H be a hiproof and $q[X_1 \ldots X_n]$ a query with match variables instantiated by σ. The meaning of an update wrt σ is a partial function, defined when the RHS is defined:*

$$[\![\mathbf{box}\ X_r\ \mathbf{to}\ X_1 \ldots X_n\ \mathbf{as}\ l]\!]_H^\sigma = addboxat(H, l, \sigma(X_r), \sigma(X_1), \ldots, \sigma(X_n))$$
$$[\![\mathbf{unbox}\ X]\!]_H^\sigma = unboxat(H, \sigma(X))$$
$$[\![\mathbf{rename}\ X\ \mathbf{as}\ l]\!]_H^\sigma = relabel(H, \sigma(X), l)$$
$$[\![\mathbf{refine}\ X\ \mathbf{with}\ s]\!]_H^\sigma = graft(H, [\![s]\!], \sigma(X))$$
$$[\![\mathbf{deletetree}\ X]\!]_H^\sigma = chop(H, \sigma(X))$$
$$[\![\mathbf{replace}\ X_1\ \mathbf{by}\ X_2]\!]_H^\sigma = graft(chop(H, \sigma(X_1)), cover(H, \sigma(X_2)), \sigma(X_1))$$

$$[\![\mathbf{update}\ u\ q]\!]_H = \{\ [\![u]\!]_H^\sigma \mid \sigma \in [\![q]\!]_H\ and\ [\![u]\!]_H^\sigma\ is\ defined\ \}$$

Def. 6 gives a non-deterministic semantics; the result may be empty (if operations are undefined) or there may be several results (for different instantiations). We do not say anything here about how to combine several results into one, as this may depend on the implementation; as hinted above, an implementation may encode our core operations using a more general update language. In this setting, a better alternative would be to give criteria which guarantee a deterministic result. For the same reason, we do not yet investigate complexity results.

7 Related Work and Conclusions

This paper introduced an update extension of PrQL, a query language for hiproofs. We interpret queries and transformations using denotational semantics of hiproofs, which are graph-like structures subject to well-formedness constraints. We showed that the basic operations are enough to capture desirable transformations, and that they preserve well-formedness and the connection to underlying proof trees.

Connections in Theorem Proving. As larger proof developments are being constructed, people are starting to explore ways to investigate them. Besides PrQL, a query language has been proposed for OmDoc proofs [22]. The *Proviola* tool [23] provides another means for proof understanding, by recording the output issued by an interactive proof during its execution development; impressively, it has been used to annotate source code of large proofs in both Coq (the Feit-Thompson proof [17]) and HOL Light (Hales's Flyspeck proof [24]). However, Proviola sheds no light on a proof that proceeds in a single tactic execution step. A hiproof-based tool would allow more dynamic exploration, by zooming into proof objects to look at the fine detail — although the practical details of managing such large proof objects will be challenging. Other researchers have used proof as the subject for search and machine learning (e.g., [25,19]). Again this work might be usefully adapted to proof trees.

Conversely, we hope that our work can be adapted to transforming proof scripts. Rather than altering the extracted proof trees for HOL Light, we might want to impose the structural changes on the input proofs themselves, where possible. Work has been started on tools and foundations for *proof refactoring* towards this [5,27,15], but it is challenging: it requires understanding the meaning of input proof scripts, and how to transform them. By contrast, it is much easier to manipulate recorded output proof structures.

Update Languages for Structured Data. There is a large body of work from the last decade on query and update languages for general forms of structured data. PrQL was inspired by, among others, UnQL [7] and Graph Logic [9]; the latter was extended to Context Logic to consider updates [8] and the former extended to a language of functional transformations [11], in the setting of XML Update. The approach taken by the W3C to extend XQuery [10] has a more SQL-like flavour, similar to our approach.

Transformations and Hierarchy. To study PrQL updates and extensions further, fundamental results on tree queries [18], transformation operations [16] and complexity [4] should be possible to adapt. However, without restricting our language we are unlikely to improve on earlier complexity results [3], so instead we want to focus on translation into an efficient underlying XML or graph-based system. Having worked out the language design and semantics, we need to use the right level of abstraction before translation, taking *hierarchy* as a native construct. Hierarchical graphs have recently been studied in another setting, for structuring *safety cases* in a hierarchical way, providing a tool that performs transformations like those studied here [13]. Related ideas for managing hierarchy in understanding provenance have recently been proposed [6].

Future and Ongoing Work. Several extensions to our update language are desirable; at the least, to add constructs for composing and iterating transformations. Before pursuing that, we want to extend our practical experiments to transformations. Taking the implementation of hiproofs in HOL Light [21], we can output them in a form suitable for a graph database system such as Neo4j [26], which can store and process very large structures on disk. Some of our queries and transformations can be captured in Neo4j's query and update language *Cipher*, although it remains to investigate how efficient the encoding is; alongside practical experiments, we need to give a further theoretical analysis.

Acknowledgements. The authors thank James Cheney and Domagoj Vrgoc for helpful discussions.

References

1. Aho, A.V.: Algorithms for finding patterns in strings. In: van Leeuwen, J. (ed.) Handbook of Theoretical Computer Science, vol. A. MIT Press, Cambridge (1990)
2. Aspinall, D., Denney, E., Lüth, C.: Tactics for hierarchical proof. Mathematics in Computer Science 3(3), 309–330 (2010)
3. Aspinall, D., Denney, E., Lüth, C.: Querying proofs. In: Bjørner, N., Voronkov, A. (eds.) LPAR-18 2012. LNCS, vol. 7180, pp. 92–106. Springer, Heidelberg (2012)
4. Flesca, S., Greco, S.: Querying graph databases. In: Zaniolo, C., Grust, T., Scholl, M.H., Lockemann, P.C. (eds.) EDBT 2000. LNCS, vol. 1777, pp. 510–524. Springer, Heidelberg (2000)
5. Bourke, T., Daum, M., Klein, G., Kolanski, R.: Challenges and experiences in managing large-scale proofs. In: Jeuring, J., Campbell, J.A., Carette, J., Dos Reis, G., Sojka, P., Wenzel, M., Sorge, V. (eds.) CICM 2012. LNCS (LNAI), vol. 7362, pp. 32–48. Springer, Heidelberg (2012)
6. Buneman, P., Cheney, J., Kostylev, E.V.: Hierarchical models of provenance. In: Proceedings of the 4th USENIX Conference on Theory and Practice of Provenance, p. 10 (2012)
7. Buneman, P., Fernandez, M., Suciu, D.: UnQL: a query language and algebra for semistructured data based on structural recursion. The VLDB Journal 9(1), 76–110 (2000)
8. Calcagno, C., Gardner, P., Zarfaty, U.: Context logic and tree update. In: Proceedings of the 32nd ACM SIGPLAN-SIGACT Symposium on Principles of Programming Languages, pp. 271–282. ACM, New York (2005)
9. Cardelli, L., Gardner, P., Ghelli, G.: A spatial logic for querying graphs. In: Widmayer, P., Triguero, F., Morales, R., Hennessy, M., Eidenbenz, S., Conejo, R. (eds.) ICALP 2002. LNCS, vol. 2380, pp. 597–610. Springer, Heidelberg (2002)
10. Chamberlin, D.D., et al.: XQuery update facility 1.0 (W3C recommendation) (2011)
11. Cheney, J.: FLUX: functional updates for XML. SIGPLAN Not. 43(9), 3–14 (2008)

12. Cleaveland, R., Steffen, B.: A linear-time model-checking algorithm for the alternation-free modal mu-calculus. In: Larsen, K.G., Skou, A. (eds.) CAV 1991. LNCS, vol. 575, pp. 48–58. Springer, Heidelberg (1992)
13. Denney, E., Pai, G., Whiteside, I.: Hierarchical safety cases. In: Brat, G., Rungta, N., Venet, A. (eds.) NFM 2013. LNCS, vol. 7871, pp. 478–483. Springer, Heidelberg (2013)
14. Denney, E., Power, J., Tourlas, K.: Hiproofs: A hierarchical notion of proof tree. Electronic Notes in Theoretical Computer Science 155, 341–359 (2006)
15. Dietrich, D., Whiteside, I., Aspinall, D.: POLAR: A framework for proof refactoring. In: Logic for Programming, Artificial Intelligence, and Reasoning (2013)
16. Ehrig, H.: Fundamentals of algebraic graph transformation. Springer, Berlin (2006)
17. Gonthier, G., Asperti, A., Avigad, J., Bertot, Y., Cohen, C., Garillot, F., Le Roux, S., Mahboubi, A., O'Connor, R., Ould Biha, S., Pasca, I., Rideau, L., Solovyev, A., Tassi, E., Théry, L.: A machine-checked proof of the odd order theorem. In: Blazy, S., Paulin-Mohring, C., Pichardie, D. (eds.) ITP 2013. LNCS, vol. 7998, pp. 163–179. Springer, Heidelberg (2013)
18. Grohe, M., Schweikardt, N.: Comparing the succinctness of monadic query languages over finite trees. RAIRO - Theoretical Informatics and Applications 38(4), 343–373 (2004)
19. Heras, J., Komendantskaya, E.: ML4PG in computer algebra verification. In: Carette, J., Aspinall, D., Lange, C., Sojka, P., Windsteiger, W. (eds.) CICM 2013. LNCS (LNAI), vol. 7961, pp. 354–358. Springer, Heidelberg (2013)
20. Hosoya, H., Pierce, B.C.: XDuce: a statically typed XML processing language. ACM Trans. Internet Technol. 3(2), 117–148 (2003)
21. Obua, S., Adams, M., Aspinall, D.: Capturing hiproofs in HOL light. In: Carette, J., Aspinall, D., Lange, C., Sojka, P., Windsteiger, W. (eds.) CICM 2013. LNCS (LNAI), vol. 7961, pp. 184–199. Springer, Heidelberg (2013)
22. Rabe, F.: A query language for formal mathematical libraries. In: Jeuring, J., Campbell, J.A., Carette, J., Dos Reis, G., Sojka, P., Wenzel, M., Sorge, V. (eds.) CICM 2012. LNCS (LNAI), vol. 7362, pp. 143–158. Springer, Heidelberg (2012)
23. Tankink, C., Geuvers, H., McKinna, J., Wiedijk, F.: Proviola: A tool for proof re-animation. In: Autexier, S., Calmet, J., Delahaye, D., Ion, P.D.F., Rideau, L., Rioboo, R., Sexton, A.P. (eds.) AISC 2010. LNCS, vol. 6167, pp. 440–454. Springer, Heidelberg (2010)
24. Tankink, C., Kaliszyk, C., Urban, J., Geuvers, H.: Formal mathematics on display: A wiki for flyspeck. In: Carette, J., Aspinall, D., Lange, C., Sojka, P., Windsteiger, W. (eds.) CICM 2013. LNCS, vol. 7961, pp. 152–167. Springer, Heidelberg (2013)
25. Urban, J., Sutcliffe, G., Pudlák, P., Vyskočil, J.: MaLARea SG1 - machine learner for automated reasoning with semantic guidance. In: Armando, A., Baumgartner, P., Dowek, G. (eds.) IJCAR 2008. LNCS (LNAI), vol. 5195, pp. 441–456. Springer, Heidelberg (2008)
26. Vicknair, C., et al.: A comparison of a graph database and a relational database: a data provenance perspective. In: Proceedings of the 48th Annual Southeast Regional Conference, pp. 42:1–42:6. ACM, New York (2010)
27. Whiteside, I., Aspinall, D., Dixon, L., Grov, G.: Towards formal proof script refactoring. In: Davenport, J.H., Farmer, W.M., Urban, J., Rabe, F. (eds.) Calculemus/MKM 2011. LNCS (LNAI), vol. 6824, pp. 260–275. Springer, Heidelberg (2011)

A Additional Technical Details

Definition 7 (Grafting). *Let $H = \langle V, L, \leq_i, \to_s, \lesssim \rangle$ be a valid hiforest with $H \models g_1 \longrightarrow g$. Let $v_1, \ldots, v_n$ be distinct vertices in V, with $L(v_i) = (\bullet, \gamma_i)$ (and hence $n \leq length(g)$). Let $H' = \langle V', L', \leq_i', \to_s', \lesssim' \rangle$ be another hiforest with $H \models g' \longrightarrow g_2$, so it has n overall roots $\{v_{r1} \ldots v_{rn}\} \in V'$ ordered by $\lesssim'$ with $L(v_{ri}) = (l_i, \gamma_i)$. Suppose (wlog) $V \cap V' = \emptyset$.*

Then we can define a new hiforest by

$$graft(H, H', v_1, \ldots, v_n) = \langle V - \{v_1 \ldots v_n\} \cup V', L|_{V-\{v_1 \ldots v_n\}} \cup L', \leq_i'', \to_s'', \lesssim'' \rangle$$

The relations $\leq_i''$, $\to_s''$ and $\lesssim'$ are defined by:

$$v \leq_i'' w \text{ iff either} \begin{cases} v \leq_i w \land w \notin \{v_1 \ldots v_n\} \\ v \leq_i' v_{ri} \land v_i \leq_i w \\ v \leq_i' w \end{cases}$$

$$v \to_s'' w \text{ iff either} \begin{cases} v \to_s w \land w \notin \{v_1 \ldots v_n\} \\ v \to_s v_i \land v_{ri} \to_s' w \\ v \to_s' w \end{cases}$$

$$v \lesssim'' w \text{ iff either} \begin{cases} v \lesssim w \land w \notin \{v_1 \ldots v_n\} \\ (v \lesssim v_i \land v_{ri} = w) \lor (v = v_{ri} \land v_i \lesssim' w) \\ v \lesssim' w \end{cases}$$

If H has exactly n holes $v_1, \ldots, v_n$ (i.e., $g = [\gamma_1, \ldots, \gamma_n]$ and $L(v_i) = (\bullet, \gamma_i)$), then we write $graft(H, H')$ as an abbreviation.

Definition 8 (Cover). *Given a hiforest $H = \langle V, L, \leq_i, \to_s, \lesssim \rangle$ and vertex $v \in V$, we define the cover of v as all nodes below or inside v by $V' = cover_{\to_s \cup >_i}(v)$, where the cover of a relation R is defined as $cover_R(x) = \{y \mid x R^* y\}$. and the labellings and orderings restricted accordingly:*

$$cover(H, v) = \langle V', L|_{V'}, \leq_i|_{V' \times V'}, \to_s|_{V' \times V'}, \lesssim|_{V' \times V'} \rangle.$$

When defining the chopping operation, we do not take out the node v, but replace its label with $\bullet$ to make it a dangler:

Definition 9 (Chopping). *Given a hiforest (or hiproof) $H = \langle V, L, \leq_i, \to_s, \lesssim \rangle$ and vertex v, then we define a new hiforest without nodes below or inside v by setting $V' = (V - cover_{\to_s \cup >_i}(v)) \cup \{v\}$ and*

$$chop(H, v) = \langle V', L|_{V-cover_{\to_s \cup >_i}} \cup \{v \mapsto (\bullet, \gamma) \mid L(v) = (l, \gamma)\},$$
$$\leq_i|_{V' \times V'}, \to_s|_{V' \times V'}, \lesssim|_{V' \times V'} \rangle$$

We can generalise *chop* and *cover* to n arguments. Chopping n vertices removes them sequentially from H, whereas the cover of n vertices is a hiforest

$$\frac{\gamma_1 \cdots \gamma_n}{\gamma} a \text{ is an atomic inference} \qquad \qquad \frac{}{id \vdash \gamma \longrightarrow \gamma} \qquad \frac{s \vdash \gamma \longrightarrow g}{[l]\, s \vdash \gamma \longrightarrow g}$$

$$\frac{s_1 \vdash g_1 \longrightarrow g \quad s_2 \vdash g \longrightarrow g_2}{s_1\,;\,s_2 \vdash g_1 \longrightarrow g_2} \qquad \frac{s_1 \vdash g_1 \longrightarrow g_1' \quad s_2 \vdash g_2 \longrightarrow g_2'}{s_1 \otimes s_2 \vdash g_1 \wedge g_2 \longrightarrow g_1' \wedge g_2'}$$

Fig. 2. Validation of hiproof terms (the symbol $\wedge$ stands for list append)

with n roots:

$$chop_1(H, v_1) = chop(H, v_1)$$
$$chop_n(H, v_1, \ldots, v_n) = chop_{n-1}(chop(H, v_1), v_2, \ldots, v_n)$$
$$cover_1(H, v_1) = cover(H, v_1)$$
$$cover_n(H, v_1, \ldots, v_n) = cover(H, v_1) \cup cover_{n-1}(H, v_2, \ldots, v_n)$$

To avoid notational difficulties when dealing with more than one root simultaneously, we define boxing and unboxing only for hiproofs. The definitions extend easily to hiforests by boxing reach root of the forest separately (although that is not needed in this paper). Note how the danglers in H are not included in the box introduced with $box(l, H)$.

Definition 10 (Boxing and Unboxing). *Given a non-empty hiproof $H = \langle V, L, \leq_i, \rightarrow_s, \lesssim \rangle$ with overall root v_r, i.e., $isroot_{\rightarrow_s \cup >_i}(v_r)$, then the boxing of H with a label l is defined as*

$$box(l, H) = \langle V \cup \{*\}, L \cup \{* \mapsto (l, \gamma) \mid L(v_r) = (l', \gamma)\},$$
$$\leq_i \cup \{(v, *) \mid v \in V, L(v) = (l, \gamma) \wedge l \neq \bullet\}, \rightarrow_s, \lesssim \cup \{(*, *)\}\rangle$$

The unboxing removes such a box (if it exists): let $H = \langle V, L, \leq_i, \rightarrow_s, \lesssim \rangle$, then we define

$$V' = \begin{cases} V - \{r\} & isroot_{\rightarrow_s \cup >_i}(r), L(v) = (l, \gamma) \wedge l \neq \bullet \\ V & otherwise \end{cases}$$

Then:

$$unbox(H) = \langle V', L|_{V'}, \leq_i|_{V'}, \rightarrow_s, \lesssim|_{V'}\rangle$$

By careful inspection of the operation definitions we can show that the resulting hiforests indeed satisfy the conditions of Def. 1 and preserve semantic validity as stated earlier.

Proposition 2 (Operations and validity). *The semantic operations preserve the hiforest conditions and moreover, preserve semantic validity of hiproofs with the expected input-output goals.*

The final part of justifying our definitions is to show that the interpretation of updates is well-defined, when query results are given and refinement has the right shape. Specifically, **refine** X **with** s requires that when $\sigma(X) = v$ and the subtree at v has validity $chop(H,v) \models g_1 \longrightarrow g_2$, then the term given denotes a hiforest with the same input-output shape.

For this we need to show that syntactic hiproof terms denote valid tree structures. This is shown together with the definition of $[\![s]\!]$. Validity for syntactic hiproof terms is written as $s \vdash g_1 \longrightarrow g_2$, meaning that the hiproof s takes a list of input (proven) goals g_1 to produce a list of output (unproven) goals g_2, and is defined by the rules in Fig. 2.

Definition 11 (Interpretation of hiproof terms). *The definition of $[\![s]\!]$ is by induction on the syntactic validity* $s \vdash g_1 \longrightarrow g_2$, *defining $[\![s]\!]$ and establishing at the same time that $[\![s]\!] \models g_1 \longrightarrow g_2$. The cases are:*

- $\boxed{a \vdash \gamma \longrightarrow [\gamma_1, \ldots, \gamma_n\,].}$ *Then $[\![a]\!]$ is the $n+1$ point hiforest with nodes $a, x_1, \ldots, x_n$. We set $a \to_s x_i$, $L(a) = (a, \gamma)$ and each x_i is a "dangler", so $L(x_i) = (\bullet, [\gamma_i])$.*
- $\boxed{\mathrm{id} \vdash \gamma \longrightarrow \gamma.}$ *Then $[\![\mathrm{id}]\!]$ is the hiforest with one "dangler" node $*$, where $L(*) = (\bullet, [\gamma])$.*
- $\boxed{[l]\,s \vdash \gamma \longrightarrow g_2.}$ *Then $[\![[l]\,s]\!] = box(l, [\![s]\!])$ since $[\![s]\!]$ has a unique top-level root.*
- $\boxed{s_1\,;\,s_2 \vdash g_1 \longrightarrow g_2.}$ *Then $[\![s_1\,;\,s_2]\!] = graft([\![s_1]\!], [\![s_2]\!])$. The premises of the validity rule and the induction hypothesis ensure that the grafting operation is well-defined.*
- $\boxed{s_1 \otimes s_2 \vdash g_1 \wedge g_2 \longrightarrow g'_1 \wedge g'_2.}$ *Then $[\![s_1 \otimes s_2]\!]$ is the hiforest formed by disjoint union of $[\![s_1]\!]$ and $[\![s_2]\!]$, with the ordering relation $\lesssim$ extended on the roots and dangling nodes.*
- $\boxed{\langle\rangle \vdash [\,] \longrightarrow [\,].}$ *$[\![\langle\rangle]\!]$ is the empty hiforest.*

Note that denotational hiproofs are unique only up to the choice of node set V; two hiproofs which have the same structure and labelling but differ only on V are isomorphic [14]. The definitions above work with particular hiproofs, but it can be verified that the choice of node names (but not labels!) is unimportant.

Expressive Path Queries on Graphs with Data

Pablo Barceló[1], Gaelle Fontaine[1], and Anthony Widjaja Lin[2,3]

[1] Dept. of Computer Science, University of Chile
[2] Dept. of Computer Science, Oxford University
[3] Academia Sinica, Taipei, Taiwan

Abstract. Graph data models have recently become popular owing to their applications, e.g., in social networks, semantic web. Typical navigational query languages over graph databases — such as Conjunctive Regular Path Queries (CRPQs) — cannot express relevant properties of the interaction between the underlying data and the topology. Two languages have been recently proposed to overcome this problem: *walk logic* (WL) and *regular expressions with memory* (REM). In this paper, we begin by investigating fundamental properties of WL and REM, i.e., complexity of evaluation problems and expressive power. We first show that the data complexity of WL is nonelementary, which rules out its practicality. On the other hand, while REM has low data complexity, we point out that many natural data/topology properties of graphs expressible in WL cannot be expressed in REM. To this end, we propose *register logic*, an extension of REM, which we show to be able to express many natural graph properties expressible in WL, while at the same time preserving the elementariness of data complexity of REMs. It is also incomparable in expressive power against WL.

1 Introduction

Graph databases have recently gained renewed interest due to applications, such as the semantic web, social network analysis, crime detection networks, software bug detection, biological networks, and others (e.g., see [1] for a survey). Despite the importance of querying graph databases, no general agreement has been reached to date about the kind of features a practical query language for graph databases should support and about what can be considered a reasonable computational cost of query evaluation for the aforementioned applications.

Typical navigational query languages for graph databases — including the conjunctive regular path queries [6] and its many extensions [4] — suffer from a common drawback: they are well-suited for expressing relevant properties about the underlying topology of a graph database, but not about how it interacts with the data. This drawback is shared by common specification languages for verification [5] (e.g. CTL*), which are evaluated over a similar graph data model (a.k.a. transition systems). Examples of important queries that combine graph data and topology, but cannot be expressed in usual navigational languages for graph databases, include the following [7,11]: (Q1) *Find pairs of people in a social network connected by professional links restricted to people of the same* age. (Q2) *Find pairs of cities x and y in a transportation system, such that y can be reached from x using only services operated by the same company*. In each one of these queries, the connectivity between two nodes (i.e., the topology) is constrained by the data (from an infinite domain, e.g., $\mathbb{N}$), in the sense that we only consider paths in which all intermediate nodes satisfy a certain condition (e.g. they are people of the same age).

Two languages, *walk logic* and *regular expressions with memory*, have recently been proposed to overcome this problem. These languages aim at different goals:

(a) Walk logic (WL) was proposed by Hellings et al. [7] as a unifying framework for understanding the expressive power of path queries over graph databases. Its strength is on the expressiveness side. The underlying data model of WL is that of (node or edge)-labeled directed graphs. In this context, WL can be seen as a natural extension of FO with path quantification, plus the ability to check whether positions p and p' in paths π and π', respectively, have the same data values. In their paper, they assume the restriction that each node carries a distinct data value. However, as we shall see, this makes no difference in terms of the results that we can obtain.

(b) Regular expressions with memory (REMs) were proposed by Libkin and Vrgoč [9] as a formalism for comparing data values along a single path, while retaining a reasonable complexity for query evaluation. The strength of this language is on the side of efficiency. The data model of the class of REMs is that of edge-labeled directed graphs, in which each node is assigned a data value from an infinite domain. REMs define pairs of nodes in the graph database that are linked by a path satisfying a given condition c. Each such condition c is defined in a formalism inspired by the class of *register automata* [8], allowing some data values to be stored in the registers and then compared against other data values. The evaluation problem for REMs is PSPACE-complete (same than for FO over relational databases), and can be solved in polynomial time in *data complexity* [9], i.e., assuming queries to be fixed.[1] This shows that the language is, in fact, well-behaved in terms of the complexity of query evaluation.

The aim of this paper is to investigate the expressiveness and complexity of query evaluation for WL and the class of REMs with the hope of finding a navigational query language for data graphs that strikes a good balance between these two important aspects of query languages.

Contributions. We start by considering WL, which is known to be a powerful formalism in terms of expressiveness. Little is known about the cost of query evaluation for this language, save for the decidability of the evaluation problem and NP-hardness of its data complexity. Our first main contribution is to pinpoint the exact complexity of the evaluation problem for WL (and thus answering an open problem from [7]): we prove that it is non-elementary, and that this holds even in data complexity, which rules out the practicality of the language.

---

[1] Recall that data complexity is a reasonable measure of complexity in the database scenario [15], since queries are often much smaller than the underlying data.

We thus move to the class of REMs, which suffers from the opposite drawback: Although the complexity of evaluation for queries in this class is reasonable, the expressiveness of the language is too rudimentary for expressing some important path properties due to its inability to (i) compare data values in *different* paths and (ii) express branching properties of the graph database. An example of an interesting query that is not expressible as an REM is the following: (Q) *Find pairs of nodes x and y, such that there is a node z and a path π from x to y in which each node is connected to z*. Notice that this is the query that lies at the basis of the queries (Q1) and (Q2) we presented before.

Our second contribution then is to identify a natural extension of this language, called *register logic* (RL), that closes REMs under Boolean combinations and existential quantification over nodes, paths and register assignments. The latter allows the logic to express comparisons of data values appearing in different paths, as well as branching properties of the data. This logic is incomparable in expressive power to WL. Besides, many natural queries relating data and topology in data graphs can be expressed in RL including: the query (Q), hamiltonicity, the existence of an Eulerian trail, bipartiteness, and complete graphs with an even number of nodes. We then study the complexity of the problem of query evaluation for RL, and show that it can be solved in elementary time (in particular, that it is EXPSPACE-complete). This is in contrast to WL, for which even the data complexity is non-elementary. With respect to data complexity, we prove that RL is PSPACE-complete. We then identify a slight extension of its existential-positive fragment, which is tractable (NLOGSPACE) in data complexity and can express many queries of interest (including the query (Q)). The idea behind this extension is that atomic REMs can be enriched with an existential branching operator – in the style of the class of *nested regular expressions* [3] – that increases expressiveness without affecting the cost of evaluation.

Organization of the Paper. Section 2 defines our data model. In Section 3, we briefly recall the definition of walk logic and some basic results from [7]. In Section 4, we prove that the data complexity of WL is nonelementary. Section 5 contains our results concerning register logic. We conclude in Section 6 with future work.

2 The Data Model

We start with a definition of our data model: data graphs.

Definition 1 (Data graph). *Let Σ be a finite alphabet. A data graph G over Σ is a tuple (V, E, κ), where V is the finite set of nodes, $E \subseteq V \times \Sigma \times V$ is the set of directed edges labeled in Σ (that is, each triple $(v, a, v') \in E$ is to be understood as an edge from v to v' in G labeled a), and $\kappa : V \to \mathcal{D}$ is a function that assigns a data value in $\mathcal{D}$ to each node in V.*

This is the data model adopted by Libkin and Vrgoč [9] in their definition of REMs. In the case of WL [7], the authors adopted *graph databases* as their data model, i.e., data graphs $G = (V, E, \kappa)$ such that κ is injective (i.e. each node carries a different data value). We shall adopt the general model of [9] since none of our complexity results are affected by the data model: upper bounds hold for data graphs, while all lower bounds are proved in the more restrictive setting of graph databases.

There is also the issue of node-labeled vs edge-labeled data graphs. Our data model is edge-labeled, but the original one for WL is node-labeled [7]. We have chosen to use the former because it is the standard in the literature [2]. Again, this choice is inessential, since all the complexity results we present in the paper continue being true if the logics are interpreted over node-labeled graph databases or data graphs (applying the expected modifications to the syntax).

Finally, in several of our examples we use logical formulas to express properties of undirected graphs. In each such case we assume that an undirected graph H is represented as a graph database $G = (V, E, \kappa)$ over unary alphabet $\Sigma = \{a\}$, where V is the set of nodes of H and E is a symmetric relation (i.e. $(v, a, v') \in E$ iff $(v', a, v) \in E$).

3 Walk Logic

WL is an elegant and powerful formalism for defining properties of paths in graph databases, that was originally proposed in [7] as a yardstick for measuring the expressiveness of different path logics.

The syntax of WL is defined with respect to countably infinite sets Π of *path variables* (that we denote $\pi, \pi_1, \pi_2, \dots$) and $\mathcal{T}(\pi)$, for each $\pi \in \Pi$, of *position variables* of sort π. We assume that position variables of different sort are different. We denote position variables by $t, t_1, t_2, \dots$, and we write t^π when we need to reinforce that position variable t is of sort π.

Definition 2 (Walk logic (WL)). *The set of formulas of WL over finite alphabet Σ is defined by the following grammar, where (i) $a \in \Sigma$, (ii) t, t_1, t_2 are position variables of any sort, (iii) π is a path variable, and (iv) t_1^π, t_2^π are position variables of the same sort π:*

$$\phi, \phi' := E_a(t_1^\pi, t_2^\pi) \mid t_1^\pi < t_2^\pi \mid t_1 \sim t_2 \mid \neg \phi \mid \phi \vee \phi' \mid \exists t \phi \mid \exists \pi \phi$$

As usual, WL formulas without free variables are called Boolean.

To define the semantics of WL we need to introduce some terminology. A *path* (a.k.a. *walk* in [7]) in the data graph $G = (V, E, \kappa)$ is a finite, nonempty sequence $\rho = v_1 a_1 v_2 \cdots v_{n-1} a_{n-1} v_n$, such that $(v_i, a_i, v_{i+1}) \in E$ for each $1 \leq i < n$. The set of *positions* of ρ is $\{1, \dots, n\}$, and v_i is the node in position i of ρ, for $1 \leq i \leq n$. The intuition behind the semantics of WL formulas is as follows. Each path variable π is interpreted as a path $\rho = v_1 a_1 v_2 \cdots v_{n-1} a_{n-1} v_n$ in the data graph G, while each position variable t of sort π is interpreted as a position $1 \leq i \leq n$ in ρ (that is, position variables of sort π are interpreted as positions in the path that interprets π). The atomic formula $E_a(t_1^\pi, t_2^\pi)$ is true iff π is interpreted as path $\rho = v_1 a_1 v_2 \cdots v_{n-1} a_{n-1} v_n$, the position p_2 that interprets t_2

in ρ is the successor of the position p_1 that interprets t_1 (i.e. $p_2 = p_1 + 1$), and node in position p_1 is linked in ρ by an a-labeled edge to node in position p_2 (that is, $a_{p_1} = a$). In the same way, $t_1^\pi < t_2^\pi$ holds iff in the path ρ that interprets π the position that interprets t_1 is smaller than the one that interprets t_2. Furthermore, $t_1 \sim t_2$ is the case iff the data value carried by the node in the position assigned to t_1 is the same than the data value carried by the node in the position assigned to t_2 (possibly in different paths). We formalize the semantics of WL below.

Let $G = (V, E, \kappa)$ be a data graph and ϕ a WL formula. Assume that $\mathcal{S}_\phi$ is the set that consists of (i) all position variables t^π and path variables π such that t^π is a free variable of ϕ, and (ii) all path variables π such that π is a free variable of ϕ. Intuitively, $\mathcal{S}_\phi$ defines the set of (both path and position) variables that are relevant to define the semantics of ϕ over G. An *assignment* α for ϕ over G is a mapping that associates a path $\rho = v_1 a_1 v_2 \cdots v_{n-1} a_{n-1} v_n$ in G with each path variable $\pi \in \mathcal{S}_\phi$, and a position $1 \leq i \leq n$ with each position variable of the form t^π in $\mathcal{S}_\phi$ (notice that this is well-defined since $\pi \in \mathcal{S}_\phi$ every time a position variable of the form t^π is in $\mathcal{S}_\phi$). As usual, we denote by $\alpha[t \to i]$ and $\alpha[\pi \to \rho]$ the assignments that are equal to α except that t is now assigned position i and π the path ρ, respectively.

We say that G *satisfies* ϕ *under* α, denoted $(G, \alpha) \models \phi$, if one of the following holds (we omit Boolean combinations which are standard):

- $\phi = E_a(t_1^\pi, t_2^\pi)$, the path $\alpha(\pi)$ is $v_1 a_1 v_2 \cdots v_{n-1} a_{n-1} v_n$, and it is the case that $\alpha(t_2^\pi) = \alpha(t_1^\pi) + 1$ and $a = a_{\alpha(t_1^\pi)}$.
- $\phi = t_1^\pi < t_2^\pi$ and $\alpha(t_1^\pi) < \alpha(t_2^\pi)$.
- $\phi = (t_1 \sim t_2)$, t_1 is of sort π_1, t_2 is of sort π_2, and $\kappa(v_1) = \kappa(v_2)$, where v_i is the node in position $\alpha(t_i)$ of $\alpha(\pi_i)$, for $i = 1, 2$.
- $\phi = \exists t^\pi \psi$ and there is a position i in $\alpha(\pi)$ such that $(G, \alpha[t^\pi \to i]) \models \psi$.
- $\phi = \exists \pi \psi$ and there is a path ρ in G such that $(G, \alpha[\pi \to \rho]) \models \psi$.

Example 1. A simple example from [7] that shows that WL expresses NP-complete properties is the following query that checks if a graph has a Hamiltonian path:

$$\exists \pi \left(\forall t_1^\pi \forall t_2^\pi (t_1^\pi \neq t_2^\pi \to t_1^\pi \not\sim t_2^\pi) \land \forall \pi' \forall t_1^{\pi'} \exists t_2^\pi (t_1^{\pi'} \sim t_2^\pi) \right).$$

In fact, this query expresses that there is a path π that does not repeat nodes (because π satisfies $\forall t_1^\pi \forall t_2^\pi (t_1^\pi \neq t_2^\pi \to t_1^\pi \not\sim t_2^\pi)$), and every node belongs to such path (because π satisfies $\forall \pi' \forall t_1^{\pi'} \exists t_2^\pi (t_1^{\pi'} \sim t_2^\pi)$, and, thus, every node that occurs in some path π' in the graph database also occurs in π). □

4 WL Evaluation Is Non-elementary in Data Complexity

In this section we pinpoint the precise complexity of query evaluation for WL. It was proven in [7] that this problem is decidable. Although the precise complexity of this problem was left open in [7], one can prove that this is, in fact, a non-elementary problem by an easy translation from the satisfiability problem for FO formulas – which is known to be non-elementary [13,14]. In databases, however, one is often interested in a different measure of complexity – called *data complexity* [15] – that assumes the formula ϕ to be fixed. This is a reasonable assumption since databases are usually much bigger than formulas. Often in the setting of data complexity the cost of evaluating queries is much smaller than in the general setting in which formulas are part of the input. The main result of this section is that the data complexity of evaluating WL formulas is nonelementary even *over graph databases*, which rules out its practicality.

Theorem 1. *The evaluation problem for WL is non-elementary in data complexity. In particular, for each $k \in \mathbb{Z}_{>0}$, there is a finite alphabet Σ and a Boolean formula ϕ over Σ, such that the problem $\mathrm{EVAL}(WL,\phi)$ of evaluating the WL formula ϕ is k-EXPSPACE-hard. In addition, the latter holds even if the input is restricted to the class of graph databases.*

Proof (Sketch): We start by sketching the case $k = 1$ here, which provides insightful technical details about the nature of the proof. There is a Turing machine M such that the following problem is EXPSPACE-hard: given a word w of size n, is there an accepting run of M over w using at most 2^{cn} cells? We prove that there is a formula $\phi \in$ WL of size polynomial in the size of M such that for all words w of size n, we can compute a graph G_w such that

$$G_w \vDash \phi \quad \text{iff} \quad \text{there is an accepting run of } M \text{ over } w \text{ using } \leq 2^{cn} \text{ cells}. \quad (1)$$

The formula ϕ is of the form $\exists \pi \psi(\pi)$, where ψ is a formula that does not contain any quantification over path variables. Given a word w of size n, the label of the path π in the graph G_w will encode an accepting run of M over the word w in the following way. Suppose that in a configuration C, the content of the tape is the word $a_1 \ldots a_{2^{cn}}$, the head is scanning cell number j_0 and the state is q_0. The configuration C is encoded by the word e_C defined by

$$c(0)(\$, a_0) \ldots c(j_0 - 1)(\$, a_{j_0-1})c(j_0)(q_0, a_{j_0})c(j_0+1)(\$, a_{j_0+1}) \ldots c(2^n)(\$, a_{2^{cn}}),$$

where $c(j)$ is the binary representation of the number j. The pair $c(j)(q_j, a_j)$ (where $q_j = q_0$ if $j = j_0$ and $q_j = \$$ otherwise) is the *description* of cell number j in C. A run $C_0 C_1 \ldots$ is encoded as the word $e_{C_0} e_{C_1} \ldots$.

We think of a path π encoding a run as consisting of two parts: the first part contains the encoding e_{C_0} of the initial configuration and is a path through a subgraph I_w of G_w, while the second part contains the encoding $e_{C_1} e_{C_2} \ldots$ and is a path through the subgraph H_w of G_w. If Q is the set of states of M and Γ is the alphabet, we define H_w as the following graph

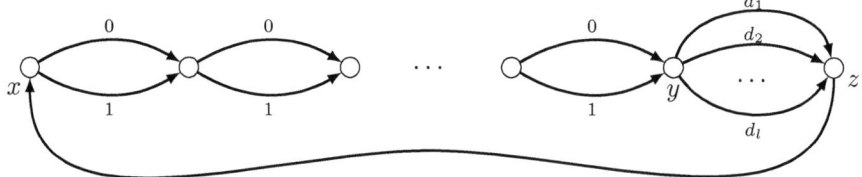

where $\{d_j : 1 \leq j \leq l\} = (Q \cup \{\$\}) \times \Gamma$ and the number of nodes with outgoing edges with labels 0 and 1 is equal to cn. The label of a path π' from the "left-most" node x to the "right-most" node z with only once occurrence of x is exactly the description of a cell in a configuration: it is the binary encoding of a number $\leq 2^{cn}$ followed by a pair of the form (q', a). We can define a formula $\phi_C \in \mathrm{WL}$ such that for all paths π starting in x and ending in z,

$$H_w \vDash \phi_C(\pi) \quad \text{iff} \quad \text{the label of } \pi \text{ is the encoding of a configuration.}$$

We do not give details; ϕ_C has to express that the first number encoded in binary is 0, that the last number is 2^{cn} and that the encoding of the description of cell number j is followed by the description of cell number $j+1$. Using the formula ϕ_C, we can define a formula ϕ_1 such that for all paths π,

$$H_w \vDash \phi_1(\pi) \quad \text{iff} \quad \text{the label of } \pi \text{ is the encoding of an accepting run.}$$

The formula ϕ_1 has to ensure that if $e_C e_{C'}$ occurs in the label of π, then C and C' are consecutive configurations according to M. Moreover, ϕ_1 has to express that eventually we reach the final state. In order to express ϕ_C and ϕ_1, we use the ability of WL to check whether two positions correspond to the same node. For example, in order to define ϕ_1, since we need to compare consecutive configurations e_C and $e_{C'}$, we need to be able to compare the content of a cell in configuration C and the content of that same cell in C'. In particular, we want to be able to express whether two subpaths π'_0 and π'_1 of π starting in x and ending in y correspond to the binary encoding of the same number. Since the length of such subpaths depends on n, we cannot check node by node whether the two subpaths are equal. However, it is sufficient to check that if $t_0^{\pi'_0}$ and $t_1^{\pi'_1}$ corresponds to the same node ($t_0^{\pi'_0} \sim t_1^{\pi'_1}$), then their successors also correpond to the same node ($t_0^{\pi'_0} + 1 \sim t_1^{\pi'_1} + 1$). Similarly, in the formula ϕ_C, we use the operator $\sim$ in order to express that two subpaths correspond to the binary encodings of numbers that are successors of each other.

Similarly to the way we define the graph H_w, we can introduce a graph I_w and a formula $\phi_0(\pi)$ such that

$$I_w \vDash \phi_0(\pi) \quad \text{iff} \quad \text{the label of } \pi \text{ is the encoding } e_{C_0},$$

where C_0 is the initial configuration of the run of M over w. By adding an "adequate edge" from I_w to H_w, we construct a graph G_w such that for all paths π, $G_w \vDash \phi_0(\pi) \wedge \phi_1(\pi)$ iff the label of π is the encoding of an accepting run over w. Hence, the formula $\phi := \exists \pi (\phi_0(\pi) \wedge \phi_1(\pi))$ satisfies (1).

For the case where $k > 1$, the problem to adapt the above proof is that we have to consider runs using a number of cells that is bound by a tower of exponentials of height k. If $k > 1$, the binary representation of such a bound is not polynomial. The trick is to represent such exponential towers by k-counters. A 1-counter is the binary representation of a number. If $k > 1$, a k-counter c is a word $\sigma_0 l_0 \ldots \sigma_{j_0} l_{j_0}$, where l_j is a $(k-1)$-counter and $\sigma_j \in \{0, 1\}$. The counter c represents the number $r(c) = \sum_{j=0}^{j_0} \sigma_j r(\sigma_j)$. In particular, a tower of exponentials of height k is represented by a k-counter of polynomial size.

We can show that there are a graph F_k and a formula $\chi_k(\pi)$ such that the label of π is a k-counter iff $F_k \models \chi_k(\pi)$. Using F_k and χ_k, we can then adapt the above proof to the cases where $k > 1$. □

As a corollary to the proof of Theorem 1, we obtain that data complexity is non-elementary even for simple WL formulas that talk about a single path in a graph database.

Corollary 1. *The evaluation problem for WL over graph databases is non-elementary in data complexity, even if restricted to Boolean WL formulas of the form $\exists \pi \psi$, where ψ uses no path quantification and contains no position variable of sort different that π.*

5 Register Logic

We saw in the previous section that WL is impractical due to its very high data complexity. In this section, we start by recalling the notion of regular expressions with memory (REM) and their basic results from [9]. The problem with this logic though is its limitation in expressive power. For instance, the query (Q) from the introduction cannot be expressed in REM. We then introduce an extension of REM, called regular logic (RL), that remedies this limitation in expressive power (in fact, it can express many natural examples of queries expressible in WL, e.g., those given in [7]) while retaining elementary complexity of query evaluation. Finally, we study which fragments of RL are well-behaved for database applications.

5.1 Regular Expressions with Memory

REMs define pairs of nodes in data graphs that are linked by a path that satisfies a constraint in the way in which the topology interacts with the underlying data. REMs allow to specify when data values are remembered and used. Data values are stored in k registers $r_1, \ldots, r_k$. At any point we can compare a data value with one previously stored in the registers. As an example, consider the REM $\downarrow r.a^+[r^=]$. It can be read as follows: Store the current data value in register r, and then check that after reading a word in a^+ we see the same data value again (condition $[r^=]$). We formally define REM next.

Let $r_1, \ldots, r_k$ be registers. The set of *conditions* c over $\{r_1, \ldots, r_k\}$ is recursively defined as: $c := r_i^= \mid c \wedge c \mid \neg c$, for $1 \leq i \leq k$. Assume that $\mathcal{D}_\bot$ is the extension of the set $\mathcal{D}$ of data values with a new symbol $\bot$. Satisfaction of conditions is defined with respect to a value $d \in \mathcal{D}$ (the data value that is currently being scanned) and a tuple $\tau = (d_1, \ldots, d_k) \in \mathcal{D}_\bot^k$ (the data values stored in the registers, assuming that $d_i = \bot$ represents the fact that register r_i has no value assigned) as follows (Boolean combinations omitted): $(d, \tau) \models r_i^=$ iff $d = d_i$.

Definition 3 (REMs). *The class of REMs over Σ and $\{r_1, \ldots, r_k\}$ is defined by the grammar:*

$$e := \varepsilon \mid a \mid e \cup e \mid e \cdot e \mid e^+ \mid e[c] \mid \downarrow \bar{r}.e$$

where a ranges over symbols in Σ, c over conditions over $\{r_1, \ldots, r_k\}$, and $\bar{r}$ over tuples of elements in $\{r_1, \ldots, r_k\}$.

That is, REM extends the class of regular expressions e – which is a popular mechanism for specifying topological properties of paths in graph databases (see, e.g., [16,2]) – with expressions of the form $e[c]$, for c a condition, and $\downarrow \bar{r}.e$, for $\bar{r}$ a tuple of registers – that define how such topology interacts with the data.

Semantics: To define the evaluation $e(G)$ of an REM e over a data graph $G = (V, E, \kappa)$, we use a relation $[\![e]\!]_G$ that consists of tuples of the form $(u, \lambda, \rho, v, \lambda')$, for u, v nodes in V, ρ a path in G from u to v, and λ, λ' two k-tuples over $\mathcal{D}_\bot$. The intuition is the following: the tuple $(u, \lambda, \rho, v, \lambda')$ belongs to $[\![e]\!]_G$ if and only if the data and topology of ρ can be parsed according to e, with λ being the initial assignment of the registers, in such a way that the final assignment is λ'. We then define $e(G)$ as the pairs (u, v) of nodes in G such that $(u, \bot^k, \rho, v, \lambda) \in [\![e]\!]_G$, for some path ρ in G from u to v and k-tuple λ over $\mathcal{D}_\bot$.

We inductively define relation $[\![e]\!]_G$ below. We assume that $\lambda_{\bar{r}=d}$, for $d \in \mathcal{D}$, is the tuple obtained from λ by setting all registers in $\bar{r}$ to be d. Also, if $\rho_1 = v_1 a_1 v_2 \cdots v_{k-1} a_{k-1} v_k$ and $\rho_2 = v_k a_k v_{k+1} \cdots v_{n-1} a_{n-1} v_n$ are paths, then $\rho_1 \rho_2$ is the path $v_1 a_1 v_2 \cdots v_{k-1} a_{k-1} v_k a_k v_{k+1} \cdots v_{n-1} a_{n-1} v_n$. Then:

- $[\![\varepsilon]\!]_G = \{(u, \lambda, \rho, u, \lambda) \mid u \in V, \rho = u, \lambda \in \mathcal{D}_\bot^k\}$.
- $[\![a]\!]_G = \{(u, \lambda, \rho, v, \lambda) \mid \rho = uav, \lambda \in \mathcal{D}_\bot^k\}$.
- $[\![e_1 \cup e_2]\!]_G = [\![e_1]\!]_G \cup [\![e_2]\!]_G$.
- $[\![e_1 \cdot e_2]\!]_G = [\![e_1]\!]_G \circ [\![e_2]\!]_G$, where $[\![e_1]\!]_G \circ [\![e_2]\!]_G$ is the set of tuples $(u, \lambda, \rho, v, \lambda')$ such that $(u, \lambda, \rho_1, w, \lambda'') \in [\![e_1]\!]_G$ and $(w, \lambda'', \rho_2, v, \lambda') \in [\![e_2]\!]_G$, for some $w \in V$, k-tuple λ'' over $\mathcal{D}_\bot$, and paths ρ_1, ρ_2 such that $\rho = \rho_1 \rho_2$.
- $[\![e^+]\!]_G = [\![e]\!]_G \cup ([\![e]\!]_G \circ [\![e]\!]_G) \cup ([\![e]\!]_G \circ [\![e]\!]_G \circ [\![e]\!]_G) \cdots$
- $[\![e[c]]\!]_G = \{(u, \lambda, \rho, v, \lambda') \in [\![e]\!]_G \mid (\kappa(v), \lambda') \models c\}$.
- $[\![\downarrow \bar{r}.e]\!]_G = \{(u, \lambda, \rho, v, \lambda') \mid (u, \lambda_{\bar{r}=\kappa(u)}, \rho, v, \lambda') \in [\![e]\!]_G\}$.

For each REM e, we will use the shorthand notation e^* to denote $\varepsilon \cup e^+$.

Example 2. The REM $\Sigma^* \cdot (\downarrow r.\Sigma^+[r^=]) \cdot \Sigma^*$ defines the pairs of nodes that are linked by a path in which two nodes have the same data value. The REM $\downarrow r.(a[\neg r^=])^+$ defines the pairs of nodes that are linked by a path ρ with label in a^+, such that the data value of the first node in the path is different from the data value of all other nodes in ρ. □

The problem EVAL(REM) is, given a data graph $G = (V, E, \kappa)$, a pair (v_1, v_2) of nodes in V, and an REM e, is $(v_1, v_2) \in e(G)$? The data complexity of the problem refers again to the case when ϕ is considered to be fixed. REMs are tractable in data complexity and have no worst combined complexity than FO over relational databases:

Proposition 1 ([9]). EVAL(REM) *is* PSPACE-*complete, and in* NLOGSPACE *in data complexity.*

5.2 Register Logic

REM is well-behaved in terms of the complexity of evaluation, but its expressive power is rather rudimentary for expressing several data/topology properties of interest in data graphs. As an example, the query (Q) from the introduction – which can be easily expressed in WL – cannot be expressed as an REM (we actually prove a stronger result later). The main shortcomings of REM in terms of its expressive power are its inability to (i) compare data values in different paths and (ii) express branching properties of the data.

In this section, we propose register logic (RL) as a natural extension of REM that makes up for this lack of expressiveness. We borrow ideas from the logic CRPQ¬, presented in [4], that closes the class of *regular path queries* [6] under Boolean combinations and existential *node* and *path* quantification. In the case of RL we start with REMs and close them not only under Boolean combinations and node and path quantification – which allow to express arbitrary patterns over the data – but also under *register assignment* quantification – which permits to compare data values in different paths. We also prove that the complexity of the evaluation problem for RL is elementary (EXPSPACE), and, thus, that in this regard RL is in stark contrast with WL.

To define RL we assume the existence of countably infinite sets of *node*, *path* and *register assignment variables*. Node variables are denoted $x, y, z, \ldots$, path variables are denoted $\pi, \pi', \pi_1, \pi_2, \ldots$, and register assignment variables are denoted $\nu, \nu_1, \nu_2, \ldots$

Definition 4 (Register logic (RL)). *We define the class of RL formulas ϕ over alphabet Σ and $\{r_1, \ldots, r_k\}$ using the following grammar:*

$$\texttt{atom} := x = y \mid \pi = \pi' \mid \nu = \nu' \mid \nu = \bar{\bot} \mid (x, \pi, y) \mid e(\pi, \nu_1, \nu_2)$$
$$\phi := \texttt{atom} \mid \neg \phi \mid \phi \vee \phi \mid \exists x \phi \mid \exists \pi \phi \mid \exists \nu \phi$$

Here x, y are node variables, π, π' are path variables, ν, ν' are register assignment variables, and e is an REM over Σ and $\{r_1, \ldots, r_k\}$.

Intuitively, $\nu = \bar{\bot}$ holds iff ν is the empty register assignment, (x, π, y) checks that π is a path from x to y, and $e(\pi, \nu, \nu')$ checks that π can be parsed according to e starting from register assignment ν and finishing in register assignment ν'. The quantifier $\exists \nu$ is to be read "there exists an assignment of data values in the data graph to the registers".

Let $G = (V, E, \kappa)$ be a data graph over Σ and ϕ a RL formula over Σ and $\{r_1 \ldots, r_k\}$. Assume that D is the set of data values that are mentioned in G, i.e., $D = \{\kappa(v) \mid v \in V\}$. An *assignment* α for ϕ over G is a mapping that assigns (i) a node in V to each free node variable x in ϕ, (ii) a path ρ in G to each free path variable π in ϕ, and (iii) a tuple λ in $(D \cup \{\bot\})^k$ to each register variable ν

that appears free in ϕ. That is, for safety reasons we assume that $\alpha(\nu)$ can only contain data values that appear in the underlying data graph. This represents no restriction for the expressiveness of the logic.

We inductively define $(G, \alpha) \models \phi$, for G a data graph, ϕ a RL formula, and α an assignment for ϕ over G, as follows (we omit equality atoms and Boolean combinations since they are standard):

- $(G, \alpha) \models \nu = \bar{\bot}$ iff $\alpha(\nu) = \bot^k$.
- $(G, \alpha) \models (x, \pi, y)$ iff $\alpha(\pi)$ is a path from $\alpha(x)$ to $\alpha(y)$ in G.
- $(G, \alpha) \models e(\pi, \nu, \nu')$ iff $(u, \alpha(\nu), \alpha(\pi), v, \alpha(\nu')) \in [\![e]\!]_G$, assuming $\alpha(\pi)$ goes from node u to v.
- $(G, \alpha) \models \exists x \phi$ iff there is node $v \in V$ such that $(G, \alpha[x \to v]) \models \phi$.
- $(G, \alpha) \models \exists \pi \phi$ iff there is path ρ in G such that $(G, \alpha[\pi \to \rho]) \models \phi$.
- $(G, \alpha) \models \exists \nu \phi$ iff there is tuple λ in $(D \cup \{\bot\})^k$ such that $(G, \alpha[\nu \to \lambda]) \models \phi$.

Thus, each REM e is expressible in RL using the formula:

$$\exists \pi \exists \nu \exists \nu' \, (\, \nu = \bar{\bot} \wedge e(\pi, \nu, \nu') \,).$$

Example 3. Recall query (Q) from the introduction: *Find pairs of nodes x and y in a graph database, such that there is a node z and a path π from x to y in which each node is connected to z.* This query can be expressed in RL over $\Sigma = \{a\}$ and a single register r as follows:

$$\exists \pi \, \big(\, (x, \pi, y) \wedge \exists z \forall \nu (e_1(\pi, \nu, \nu) \to \exists z' \exists \pi'((z', \pi', z) \wedge e_2(\pi', \nu, \nu))) \, \big),$$

where $e_1 := a^*[r^=] \cdot a^*$ is the REM that checks whether the node (i.e. data) stored in register r appears in a path, and $e_2 := \varepsilon[r^=] \cdot a^*$ is the REM that checks if the first node of a path is the one that is stored in register r.

In fact, this formula defines the pairs of nodes x and y such that there exists a path π that goes from x to y and a node z for which the following holds: for every register value ν (i.e., for every node ν) such that $e_1(\pi, \nu, \nu)$ (i.e. node ν is in π), it is the case that there is a path π' from some node z' to z such that $e_2(\pi', \nu, \nu)$ (i.e., $z' = \nu$ and π' connects ν to z). Notice that this uses the fact that the underlying data model is that of graph databases, in which each node is uniquely identified by its data value. □

Complexity of Evaluation for RL: The evaluation problem for RL, denoted EVAL(RL), is as follows: Given a data graph G, a RL formula ϕ, and an assignment α for ϕ over G, is it the case that $(G, \alpha) \models \phi$? As before, we denote by EVAL(RL,ϕ) the evaluation problem for the fixed RL formula ϕ.

We show next that, unlike WL, register logic RL can be evaluated in elementary time, and, actually, with only one exponential jump over the complexity of evaluation of REMs:

Theorem 2. EVAL(RL) *is* EXPSPACE-*complete. The lower bound holds even if the input is restricted to graph databases.*

Proof (Idea): For the upper bound, we adapt for RL the proof that CRPQ¬ formulas can be evaluated in PSPACE [4]. This requires some care in the way in which register values and atomic REM formulas are handled. The extra exponential blow up is produced by the fact that checking whether a path ρ in a data graph G does not satisfy an REM e (i.e. whether it is not the case that $(u, \bar{\bot}, \rho, v, \lambda) \in [\![e]\!]_G$, for some register assignment λ, assuming that ρ goes from u to v) requires exponential space. The lower bound is obtained by a reduction from the acceptance problem for a Turing machine that works in EXPSPACE. □

The increase in expressiveness of RL over REM has an important cost in data complexity, which becomes intractable:

Theorem 3. EVAL(RL) *is in* PSPACE *in data complexity. Furthermore, there is a finite alphabet Σ and a RL formula ϕ over Σ and a single register r, such that* EVAL(RL,ϕ) *is* PSPACE-*hard. In addition, the latter holds even if the input is restricted to graph databases.*

In the next section we introduce an interesting language, based on a restriction of RL, that is tractable in data complexity, and thus better suited for database applications. This language is a proper extension of REM. But before, we make some important remarks about the expresive power of RL.

Expressive Power of RL: We now look at the expressive power of the logic RL. It was proven in [7] that CRPQ is not subsumed in WL. Since RL subsumes CRPQ¬, it follows that RL is not subsumed in WL. On the other hand, WL is also not subsumed in RL due to Theorem 1, Theorem 2, and the standard time/space hierarchy theorem from complexity theory. Therefore, we have the following proposition:

Proposition 2. *The expressive powers of WL and RL are incomparable.*

On the other hand, we shall argue now that many natural queries about the interaction between data and topology are also expressible in RL. The aforementioned query (Q) is one such example. We shall now mention other examples: hamiltonicity (H), the existence of Eulerian trail (E), bipartiteness (B), and complete graphs with even number of nodes (C2). The first two are expressible in WL, while (B) and (C2) are not known to be expressible in WL. We conjecture that they are not.

We now show how to express in RL the existence of a hamiltonian path in a graph; the query (E) can be expressed in the same way but with two registers (to remember edges, i.e., consisting of two nodes). This is done with the following formula over $\Sigma = \{a\}$ and a single register r:

$$\exists \pi \left(\forall \lambda \forall \lambda' \neg e_1(\pi, \lambda, \lambda') \land \forall \lambda (\lambda \neq \bot \rightarrow e_2(\pi, \lambda, \lambda)) \right),$$

where $e_1 := a^* \cdot (\downarrow r.a^+[r^=]) \cdot a^*$ is the REM that checks whether in a path some node is repeated (i.e., that it is not a simple path), and $e_2 := a^*[r^=]a^*$ is the REM that checks that the node stored in register r appears in a path. In fact, this query expresses that there is a path π that it is simple (as expressed by the formula $\forall \lambda \forall \lambda' \neg e_1(\pi, \lambda, \lambda')$), and every node of the graph database is mentioned in π (as expressed by the formula $\forall \lambda (\lambda \neq \bot \rightarrow e_2(\pi, \lambda, \lambda)))$.

We now show how to express in RL the property bipartiteness from graph theory. An undirected $G = (V, E)$ is *bipartite* if its set of nodes can be partitioned into two sets S_1 and S_2 such that, for each edge $(v, w) \in E$, either (i) $v \in S_1$ and $w \in S_2$, or (ii) $v \in S_2$ and $w \in S_2$. It is well-known that a graph database is bipartite iff it does not have cycles of odd length. The latter is expressible in RL since the existence of an odd-length cycle can be expressed as $\exists \pi \exists \lambda \exists \lambda' e(\pi, \lambda, \lambda')$, where $e = \downarrow r.a(aa)^*[r^=]$.

We now show how to express in RL that a graph database is a complete graph with an even number of nodes. To this end, it is sufficient and necessary to express the existence of a hamiltonian path π with an odd number of edges in the graph. But this is a simple modification of our formula for expressing hamiltonicity: we add the check that π has an odd number of edges by adding the conjunct $e(\pi, \nu, \nu')$, where $e = a \cup a(aa)^+$, and close the entire formula under existential quantification of ν and ν'.

5.3 Tractability in Data Complexity

Let RL$^+$ be the positive fragment of RL (i.e. the logic obtained from RL by forbidding negation and adding conjunctions). It is easy to prove that the data complexity of the evaluation problem for RL$^+$ is tractable (NLOGSPACE). This fragment contains the class of *conjunctive* REMs, that has been previously identified as tractable in data complexity [9]. However, the expressive power of RL$^+$ is limited as the following proposition shows.

Proposition 3. *The query* (Q) *from the introduction is not expressible in RL$^+$.*

On the other hand, increasing the expressive power of RL$^+$ with some simple forms of negation leads to intractability of query evaluation in data complexity:

Proposition 4. *There is a finite alphabet Σ and REMs e_1, e_2, e_3, e_4 over Σ and a single register r, such that* EVAL(RL,ϕ) *is* PSPACE-*complete, where ϕ is either* $\exists \pi \exists \lambda \neg (e_1(\pi, \bot, \lambda) \vee e_2(\pi, \bot, \bot))$ *or* $\exists \pi \forall \lambda \neg (e_3(\pi, \bot, \lambda) \vee e_4(\pi, \bot, \bot))$.

In the case of basic navigational languages for graph databases, it is possible to increase the expressive power – without affecting the cost of evaluation – by extending formulas with a branching operator (in the style of the class of *nested regular expressions* [3]). The same idea can be applied in our scenario, by extending atomic REM formulas in RL$^+$ with such branching operator. The resulting language is more expressive than RL$^+$ (in particular, this extension can express query (Q)), yet remains tractable in data complexity. We formalize this idea below.

The class of *nested* REMs (NREM) extends REM with a nesting operator $\langle \cdot \rangle$ defined as follows: If e is an NREM then $\langle e \rangle$ is also an NREM. Intuitively, the formula $\langle e \rangle$ filters those nodes in a data graph that are the origin of a path that can be parsed according to e. Formally, if e is an NREM over k registers and G is a data graph, then $[\![\langle e \rangle]\!]_G$ consists of all tuples of the form $(u, \lambda, \rho = u, u, \lambda)$ such that $(u, \lambda, \rho', v, \lambda') \in [\![e]\!]_G$, for some node v in G, path ρ' in G, and k-tuple λ' over $\mathcal{D}_\bot$.

Let NRL$^+$ be the logic that is obtained from RL$^+$ by allowing atomic formulas of the form $e(\pi, \nu, \nu')$, for e an NREM. Given a data graph G and an assignment α for π, ν and ν' over G, we write as before $(G, \alpha) \models e(\pi, \nu, \nu')$ if and only if $\alpha(\pi)$ goes from u to v and $(u, \alpha(\nu), \alpha(\pi), v, \alpha(\nu')) \in [\![e]\!]_G$. The semantics of NRL$^+$ is thus obtained from the semantics of these atomic formulas in the expected way. The following example shows that query (Q) is expressible in NRL$^+$, and, therefore, that NRL$^+$ increases the expressiveness of RL$^+$.

Example 4. Over graph databases, the query (Q) from the introduction is expressible in NRL$^+$ using the following formula over $\Sigma = \{a\}$ and register r:

$$\phi = \exists \pi \exists \nu \big((x, \pi, y) \wedge e(\pi, \nu, \nu) \big),$$

where $e := (\langle e_1 \rangle \cdot a)^* \langle e_1 \rangle$, for $e_1 = a^*[r^=]$. Intuitively, e_1 checks in a path whether its last node is precisely the node stored in register r, and thus e checks whether every node in a path can reach the node stored in register r. Therefore, the formula ϕ defines the set of pairs (x, y) of nodes, such that there is a path π that goes from x to y and a register value ν (i.e., a node ν) that satisfy that every node in π is connected to ν. □

The extra expressive power of NRL$^+$ over RL$^+$ does not affect the data complexity of query evaluation:

Theorem 4. *Evaluation of NRL$^+$ formulas can be solved in* NLOGSPACE *in data complexity.*

From the proof of Theorem 4 it also follows that NRL$^+$ formulas can be evaluated in PSPACE in combined complexity.

6 Conclusions and Future Work

We have proven that the data complexity of walk logic is nonelementary, which rules out the practicality of the logic. We have proposed register logic, which is an extension of regular expressions with memory. Our results in this paper suggest that register logic is capable of expressing natural queries about interactions between data and topology in data graphs, while still preserving the elementary data complexity of query evaluation (PSPACE). Finally, we showed how to make register logic more tractable in data complexity (NLOGSPACE) through the logic NRL$^+$, while at the same time preserving some level of expressiveness of RL.

We leave open several problems for future work. One interesting question is to study the expressive power of extensions of walk logic, in comparison to RL and ECRPQ$^-$ from [4]. For example, we can consider extensions with regularity tests (i.e. an atomic formula testing whether a path belongs to a regular language).

Even in this simple case, the expressive power of the resulting logic, compared to RL and ECRPQ¬, is already not obvious. Secondly, we do not know whether NRL⁺ is strictly more expressive than RL. Finally, we will also mention that expressibility of bipartiteness in WL is still open (an open question from [7]). We also leave open whether the query that a graph database is a complete graph with an even number of nodes is expressible in WL.

Acknowledgements. We thank the reviewers for the useful comments. Barceló is funded by Fondecyt grant 1130104, Fontaine by Fondecyt postdoctoral grant 3130491, and Lin by EPSRC (EP/H026878/1). Part of this work was done when Lin visited Barceló funded by Fondecyt grant 1130104.

References

1. Angles, R., Gutiérrez, C.: Survey of graph database models. ACM Comput. Surv. 40(1) (2008)
2. Barceló, P.: Querying graph databases. In: PODS, pp. 175–188 (2013)
3. Barceló, P., Pérez, J., Reutter, J.L.: Relative expressiveness of nested regular expressions. In: AMW, pp. 180–195 (2012)
4. Barceló, P., Libkin, L., Lin, A.W., Wood, P.T.: Expressive languages for path queries over graph-structured data. ACM Trans. Database Syst. 37(4), 31 (2012)
5. Clarke, E.M., Grumberg, O., Peled, D.A.: Model checking. MIT Press (2000)
6. Cruz, I., Mendelzon, A.O., Wood, P.T.: A graphical query language supporting recursion. In: SIGMOD, pp. 323–330 (1987)
7. Hellings, J., Kuijpers, B., van den Bussche, J., Zhang, X.: Walk logic as a framework for path query languages on graph databases. In: ICDT, pp. 117–128 (2013)
8. Kaminski, M., Francez, N.: Finite memory automata. TCS 134(2), 329–363 (1994)
9. Libkin, L., Vrgoč, D.: Regular path queries on graphs with data. In: ICDT 2012, pp. 74–85 (2012)
10. Libkin, L., Vrgoč, D.: Regular expressions for data words. In: Bjørner, N., Voronkov, A. (eds.) LPAR-18 2012. LNCS, vol. 7180, pp. 274–288. Springer, Heidelberg (2012)
11. Libkin, L., Reutter, J.L., Vrgoc, D.: Trial for RDF: adapting graph query languages for RDF data. In: PODS, pp. 201–212 (2013)
12. Mendelzon, A.O., Wood, P.T.: Finding regular simple paths in graph databases. SIAM J. Comput. 24(6), 1235–1258 (1995)
13. Robertson, L.E.: Structure of complexity in the weak monadic second-order theories of the natural numbers. In: STOC, pp. 161–171 (1974)
14. Stockmeyer, L.: The complexity of decision problems in automata theory and logic. Ph.D. thesis. MIT (1974)
15. Vardi, M.Y.: The complexity of relational query languages. In: STOC, pp. 137–146 (1982)
16. Wood, P.T.: Query languages for graph databases. SIGMOD Record 41(1), 50–60 (2012)

Proving Infinite Satisfiability

Peter Baumgartner and Joshua Bax

NICTA* and Australian National University, Canberra, Australia
Firstname.Lastname@nicta.com.au

Abstract. We consider the problem of automatically disproving invalid conjectures over data structures such as lists and arrays over integers, in the presence of additional hypotheses over these data structures. We investigate a simple approach based on refutational theorem proving. We assume that the data structure axioms are satisfiable and provide a template language for additional hypotheses such that satisfiability is preserved. Then disproving is done by proving that the negated conjecture follows. By means of examples we demonstrate that our template language is reasonably expressive and that our approach works well with current theorem provers (Z3, SPASS+T and Beagle).

1 Introduction

We consider the problem of automatically disproving invalid conjectures over data structures such as lists and arrays over integers, in the presence of additional hypotheses over these data structures. Such invalid conjectures come up frequently in applications of automated reasoning to software verification and the analysis of data-rich state-based systems, for example. More formally, the disproving problem is to show that AX ∪ HYP does not entail a sentence CON, where AX are list and/or array axioms and CON is the conjecture in question. The obvious approach to disproving is to show satisfiability of AX ∪ HYP ∪ {¬CON} by means of a (complete) theorem prover. Unfortunately, current theorem proving technology is of limited usefulness for that: finite model finders cannot be used because the list axioms do not admit finite models, SMT-solvers are typically incomplete on quantified formulas and face the same problem, and theorem provers based on saturation often do not terminate on satisfiable input (let alone completeness issues in presence of arithmetic background theories).

We propose a different, conceptually simple approach based on refutational theorem proving. It consists in assuming that AX is satisfiable and providing templates for HYP that are guaranteed to preserve satisfiability of AX ∪ HYP. Then disproving is attempted simply by proving that AX ∪ HYP entails ¬CON, i.e., that AX ∪ HYP ∪ {CON} is unsatisfiable.

The main point of this paper is to demonstrate the practical feasibility of our approach. By means of examples, we demonstrate that our template language covers useful cases. We also report on our experiences disproving sample conjectures using current theorem provers (Z3 [11], SPASS+T [18] and Beagle [3]), and we compare their performance.

---

* NICTA is funded by the Australian Government as represented by the Department of Broadband, Communications and the Digital Economy and the Australian Research Council through the ICT Centre of Excellence program.

Related Work. Kapur and Zarba [8] show by way of reductions to sub-theories how to decide the satisfiability of conjunctions of ground literals wrt. various theories, including arrays and lists. Armando, Bonacina, Ranise and Schulz [2] use the superposition calculus as a decision procedure, again for conjunctions of ground literals wrt. these (and other) theories. In a similar way, Lynch and Morawska [9] aim at superposition as decision procedure based on finite saturation. Ihlemann, Jacobs and Sofronie-Stokkermans [7] develop decidability results for the theory of arrays and others using the framework of local theory extensions. DeMoura and Bjoerner [12] give decidability results for a theory extending the basic theory of arrays. McPeak and Necula [10] provide decision procedures for pointer data structures. Bradley, Manna and Sipma [4] give a decidability result for an expressive fragment of the theory of arrays, the *array property* fragment. Certain desirable formulas are not included in this fragment, for example totality axioms for functions or an injectivity predicate for arrays (see distinct in Section 4). Ghilardi, Nicolini, Ranise and Zucchelli [6] provide a decision procedure for an extension of the array theory and demonstrate how decision procedures may be derived for extensions to this theory, many of which lie outside the array property fragment. This relies on the existence of a "standard model" for the theory and extension, whose existence must be demonstrated a priori.

In contrast to these works, we do not provide decision procedures for specific fragments. This is intentionally so, in order to support disproving tasks in the presence of liberally formulated additional axioms (the set HYP above). Although we employ superposition-based provers in our experiments (like some of the approaches above), our approach does not hinge on finite saturation. Claessen and Lillieström [5] present a method for showing that a set of formulas does not admit finite models. It does not answer the question whether infinite models exists, and this way our work is complementary to theirs. Suter, Köksal and Kuncak [17] have developed a semi-decision procedure for checking satisfiability of correctness properties of recursive functional programs on algebraic data types. It overlaps with out method on lists (Section 3) by imposing similar syntactic restrictions. Their method works differently, by partial unrolling of function definitions into quantifier-free logic instead of theorem proving on (quantified) formulas. In [15], Rümmer and Shah use a program logic for Java to prove the incorrectness of programs. It utilizes a sequent calculus for unfolding lists and reasoning with arithmetic constraints, and this way is somewhat more spcialised than our approach.

Preliminaries. We work in the context of many-sorted logic with first-order signatures comprised of sorts and operator symbols (i.e., function symbols and predicate symbols) of given arities over these sorts. In this paper we focus on theorem proving modulo the fixed background theory of (linear) integer arithmetic. Our signatures Σ are comprised of sort symbols $s_1, \ldots, s_n$ where $s_n = \mathbb{Z}$, the integer sort. Let $sorts(\Sigma) = \{s_1, \ldots, s_n\}$. We assume Σ contains an equality symbol $\approx_{s_i}$ for each sort s_i. We usually drop the sort annotion from $\approx_{s_i}$. We also assume infinite supplies of variables of each sort. When x is a variable and s is a sort we write x_s to make clear that the sort of x is s.

We use the notions commonly used in automated theorem proving in a standard way. The (well-sorted Σ-) terms, atoms, and formulas are defined as usual. Let $x_1, \ldots, x_n$ be pairwise different variables of corresponding sorts $s_1, \ldots, s_n$. We write $F[x_1, \ldots, x_n]$ to indicate that the formula F has free variables at most $x_1, \ldots, x_n$, and we say that F has the *arity* $s_1 \times \cdots \times s_n$. We write $F[t_1, \ldots, t_n]$ for the formula obtained from $F[x_1, \ldots, x_n]$ by replacing every free occurrence of x_i in F by t_i, for all $1 \le i \le n$.

Our logical language is essentially the same as the TPTP-language TFA ("Typed Formulas with Arithmetic") and we adopt the semantics given for it in [16]. In brief, a *(Σ-)interpretation* I consists of a *(Σ-)domain* $D = D_{s_1} \uplus \ldots \uplus D_{s_n}$ with disjoint, non-empty sub-domains for each sort, and an arity-respecting mapping of function symbols to functions and predicate symbols to relations (representing the tuples of which the predicate holds true). We work with E-interpretations only. That is, $I(\approx_{s_i}) = \{(d,d) \mid d \in D_{s_i}\}$, where $I(op)$ is the interpretation of the operator op. Furthermore, we consider only interpretations that *extend arithmetic*, that is, (i) the domain $D_\mathbb{Z}$ of the integer sort $\mathbb{Z}$ is the set of all integer numbers and, (ii) the numeric operators such as $>$, $\ge$, $+$, $-$ and $\cdot$ are interpreted as expected. The usual notions of satisfaction, validity, model etc. apply in the standard way. In particular, when N is a set of sentences we write $I \models N$ to indicate that I is a model of (all elements of) N, and we say that N *entails* a formula F, written as $N \models F$ iff every model of N is a model of F.

2 Approach

Our approach consists in starting with a signature Σ and a set of Σ-sentences Ax that is known to be satisfiable. Our main interest is in lists and arrays, and so Ax will be corresponding axioms, see below. Then we stepwise expand Σ and Ax with new user-defined operators and additional definitions for these.

More formally, for two signatures Σ and Σ' over the same sorts we use set operators to relate the sets of their operators in the obvious way. For instance, we write $\Sigma' = \Sigma \cup \{op\}$ to indicate that Σ' is obtained from Σ by adding the operator op. We consider sequences $(Ax, \text{Def}_{op_1}, \ldots, \text{Def}_{op_n})$ such that Def_{op_i} is a set of Σ_i-sentences ("Definition for op_i") of a certain form explained below, where $\Sigma_0 = \Sigma$, $op_i \notin \Sigma_{i-1}$ and $\Sigma_i = \Sigma_{i-1} \cup \{op_i\}$ for all $1 \le i \le n$. We call any such sequence an *extension of Ax*.

Definition 2.1 (Admissible Definition). *Let Σ be a signature, D a Σ-domain, and $op \notin \Sigma$ an operator with an arity over sorts(Σ). We say that a set of $(\Sigma \cup \{op\})$-sentences N is an* admissible definition *of op (wrt. Σ and D) iff every Σ-interpretation I with domain D can be expanded to a $(\Sigma \cup \{op\})$-interpretation I' with domain D such that $I' \models N$.*

That is, I' differs from I only by adding an interpretation for op which satisfies N. We indicate this by writing $I' = I \cup I(op)$.

Proposition 2.2. *Let $(Ax, \text{Def}_{op_1}, \ldots, \text{Def}_{op_n})$ be an extension of Ax. Suppose there is a Σ_0-model $I \models Ax$ with domain D. If Def_{op_i} is an admissible definition of op_i wrt. Σ_{i-1} and D, for all $1 \le i \le n$, then there is a Σ_n-interpretation I' such that $I' \models Ax \cup \bigcup_{1 \le i \le n} \text{Def}_{op_i}$.*

Proof. By induction over the length n of extensions, using the given model I in the induction start and using admissibility in the induction step. □

As said, in this paper we are mainly interested in disproving conjectures. With the current terminology, the problem is to show that $N = Ax \cup \bigcup_{1 \le i \le n} \text{Def}_{op_i}$ does not entail a given Σ_n-sentence *Con*, the conjecture in question. Assuming admissible definitions, Proposition 2.2 gives us $I' \models N$, for some Σ_n-interpretation I'. Now, suppose we are able to *prove* (by a theorem prover) the entailment $N \models \neg Con$. It follows $I' \models \neg Con$, and so $I' \not\models Con$. By definition, then $N \not\models Con$, and so the conjecture is disproven.

Our intended application context is that of dynamically evolving systems. By this we mean computations that start in a (typically partially) specified initial state, modify some data until a final state is reached, and then the resulting (partially specified) final state is queried as to whether a property P holds in it. This leads to universally quantified implications *Con* in which the premise encodes both the initial state and computation, while the conclusion encodes property P.

A trivial example of this situation is the formula $Con = \forall l_{\mathsf{LIST}}\, l'_{\mathsf{LIST}}\,.\, l \not\approx \mathsf{nil} \wedge l' \approx \mathsf{tail}(l) \Rightarrow l' \not\approx \mathsf{nil}$. Here, $l \not\approx \mathsf{nil}$ is meant to represent the initial state; $l' \approx \mathsf{tail}(l)$ the computation; and $P = l' \not\approx \mathsf{nil}$. Where $\mathsf{Ax}_{\mathsf{LIST}}$ are the list axioms of Section 3 below, we wish to show $\mathsf{Ax}_{\mathsf{LIST}} \not\models Con$. With the approach indicated above, we have to prove $\mathsf{Ax}_{\mathsf{LIST}} \models \exists l_{\mathsf{LIST}}\, l'_{\mathsf{LIST}}\,.\, l \not\approx \mathsf{nil} \wedge l' \approx \mathsf{tail}(l)$ instead, which is a theorem proving task.

3 Lists

We consider lists over integers. To this end let the signature Σ_{LIST} consist of sorts LIST and $\mathbb{Z}$ and the operators $\mathsf{nil} : \mathsf{LIST}$, $\mathsf{cons} : \mathbb{Z} \times \mathsf{LIST} \mapsto \mathsf{LIST}$, $\mathsf{head} : \mathsf{LIST} \mapsto \mathbb{Z}$, $\mathsf{tail} : \mathsf{LIST} \mapsto \mathsf{LIST}$. The *list axioms* $\mathsf{AX}_{\mathsf{LIST}}$ are the following formulas, each implicitly universally quantified, where k is $\mathbb{Z}$-sorted and l is LIST-sorted:

$$\mathsf{head}(\mathsf{cons}(k,l)) \approx k \qquad\qquad \mathsf{cons}(k,l) \not\approx \mathsf{nil}$$
$$\mathsf{tail}(\mathsf{cons}(k,l)) \approx l \qquad\qquad \mathsf{cons}(\mathsf{head}(l), \mathsf{tail}(l)) \approx l \vee l \approx \mathsf{nil}$$

Structurally identical axioms have been mentioned in [13]. The satisfiability of the list axioms is well known. It can also be determined automatically. For example, the theorem prover Beagle [3] in a complete setting and after adding the axioms $\exists d_{\mathbb{Z}}\,.\, \mathsf{head}(\mathsf{nil}) \approx d$ and $\mathsf{tail}(\mathsf{nil}) \approx \mathsf{nil}$, terminates on $\mathsf{AX}_{\mathsf{LIST}}$ in a saturated state. Because the axioms satisfy a certain sufficient completeness requirement, this provides a proof of satisfiability. In particular, the list axioms are satisfied in the interpretation I_{LIST} with the domain $D_{\mathsf{LIST}} = \mathbf{LIST}$, the *finite length lists (over integers)*, which we assume to be freely generated by the constructors **nil** and $\mathbf{cons}(\cdot, \cdot)$, and the obvious interpretation for the Σ_{LIST}-operators.

We now turn to the templates for definitions.

Relations. Let Σ^+ be an expansion of Σ_{LIST} and $P \notin \Sigma^+$ a predicate symbol with arity $\mathbb{Z} \times \mathsf{LIST}$. Let Def_P a formula of the form

$$\forall k_{\mathbb{Z}}\, l_{\mathsf{LIST}}\,.\, P(k,l) \Leftrightarrow$$
$$l \approx \mathsf{nil} \wedge B[k] \tag{P1}$$
$$\vee\, \exists h_{\mathbb{Z}}\, t_{\mathsf{LIST}}\,.\, l \approx \mathsf{cons}(h,t) \wedge C[k,h,t] \tag{P2}$$
$$\vee\, \exists h_{\mathbb{Z}}\, t_{\mathsf{LIST}}\,.\, l \approx \mathsf{cons}(h,t) \wedge D[k,h,t] \wedge P(k,t) \tag{P3}$$

where B is a Σ^+-formula of arity $\mathbb{Z}$, and C and D are Σ^+-formulas of arity $\mathbb{Z} \times \mathbb{Z} \times \mathsf{LIST}$.

Lemma 3.1. *Let D be a Σ^+-domain with $D_{\mathsf{LIST}} = \mathbf{LIST}$. Then Def_P is an admissible definition of P wrt. Σ^+ and D.*

Proof. Briefly, the proof proceeds by constructing a canonical (minimal) model of the $\Leftarrow$-direction of Def_P, which is also always a model of the $\Rightarrow$-direction. From a logic-programming angle, the user could as well give only the $\Leftarrow$-direction of Def_P, then the system can add the completion ($\Rightarrow$-direction) for disproving purposes.

We assume Interpretations include a valuation component for variables. We write $I_{[x \mapsto d]}$ to indicate an update for the variable x to the domain element d.

Let I be a Σ^+-interpretation with domain D. We have to show that I can be expanded to a $(\Sigma^+ \cup \{P\})$-interpretation $I' = I \cup I(P)$, such that $I' \models \mathrm{Def}_P$.

The definition of $I(P)$ utilizes transfinite induction, and we need several orderings for that. Let $\geq_{\mathbb{Z}}$ be a (any) well-ordering on the integers and $\geq$ its extension to the quasi-lexicographic ordering on $\mathbf{LIST}$.[1] Because $\geq_{\mathbb{Z}}$ is well-founded and total, $\geq$ is well-founded and total, too (this is well-known). Let $>$ denote the strict subset of $\geq$.

Next, we define an ordering $\geq_P$ on pairs over integers and finite lists over integers as $(k_1, l_1) \geq_P (k_2, l_2)$ iff $l_1 > l_2$ or else $l_1 = l_2$ and $k_1 \geq_{\mathbb{Z}} k_2$. Notice that $\geq_P$ is also total and well-founded. Let $>_P$ denote the strict subset of $\geq_P$.

Let $(k, l) \in \mathbb{Z} \times \mathbf{LIST}$ be chosen arbitrarily. We need to decide whether to include (k, l) in $I'(P)$ or not, that is, whether to make $I'(P)(k, l)$ true or false, respectively. We do this by evaluating the body of Def_P, which resorts to evaluating smaller elements only.

More formally, for a given pair (k, l) we define subsets $\epsilon_P(k, l)$ and $I(P)_{(k,l)}$ of $\mathbb{Z} \times D_{\mathsf{LIST}}$. Assume that $\epsilon_P(k', l')$ has already been defined for all $(k', l') \in \mathbb{Z} \times D_{\mathsf{LIST}}$ with $(k, l) >_P (k', l')$. Where $I(P)_{(k,l)} = \bigcup_{(k,l) >_P (k',l')} \epsilon_P(k', l')$ define

$$\epsilon_P(k, l) = \{(k, l)\} \text{ if } \begin{cases} l = \mathbf{nil} \text{ and } I_{[k \mapsto k]} \models B[k] & \text{or} \\ l = \mathbf{cons}(h, t) \text{ and } I_{[k \mapsto k, h \mapsto h, t \mapsto t]} \models C[k, h, t], \\ \quad \text{for some } h \in \mathbb{Z} \text{ and } t \in D_{\mathsf{LIST}} & \text{or} \\ l = \mathbf{cons}(h, t), I_{[k \mapsto k, h \mapsto h, t \mapsto t]} \models D[k, h, t] \text{ and} \\ (I \cup I(P)_{(k,l)})_{[k \mapsto k, t \mapsto t]} \models P(k, t), \\ \quad \text{for some } h \in \mathbb{Z} \text{ and } t \in D_{\mathsf{LIST}} \end{cases}$$

In all other cases define $\epsilon_P(k, l) = \emptyset$. Finally define $I(P) = \bigcup_{(k,l)} \epsilon_P(k, l)$.

Notice that the conditions in the definition of $\epsilon_P(k, l)$ are all well-defined. In particular, we have $(k, l) >_P (k, t)$ in the last case. With the definition of $I(P)$ it is straightforward to show $(I \cup I(P)) \models \mathrm{Def}_P$ (assume a $>_P$-minimal pair (k, l) under which Def_P evaluates to false in $I \cup I(P)$ and lead this to a contradiction). □

Example. Let inRange : $\mathbb{Z} \times \mathbf{LIST}$ be a predicate symbol. Consider the extension of $\mathsf{Ax}_{\mathsf{LIST}}$ with the following (admissible) definition for P (the free variables are universally quantified with the obvious sorts).

$\mathsf{inRange}(n, l) \Leftrightarrow l \approx \mathsf{nil} \vee \exists h_{\mathbb{Z}} \, t_{\mathsf{LIST}}. (l \approx \mathsf{cons}(h, t) \wedge 0 \leq h \wedge h < n \wedge \mathsf{inRange}(n, t))$

---

[1] A quasi-lexicographic ordering, or shortlex ordering, compares firstly lists by their length, so that *nil* comes first, and then compares lists of the same length lexicographically.

This example comes from a case study with the first-order logic model checker from [1]. The inRange predicate is used there to specify lists of "ordered items" handled in a purchase order process, which must all be in a range $0..N - 1$, for some $N \geq 0$. The other examples in this paper are contrived.

The following table lists some sample problems together with the runtimes (in seconds) needed to *disprove* them with the provers mentioned.[2]

Problem	Beagle	Spass+T	Z3
inRange(4, cons(1, cons(5, cons(2, nil))))	6.2	0.3	0.2
$n > 4 \Rightarrow$ inRange$(n,$ cons$(1,$ cons$(5,$ cons$(2,$ nil$))))$	7.2	0.3	0.2
inRange$(n,$ tail$(l)) \Rightarrow$ inRange(n, l)	3.9	0.3	0.2
$\exists n_\mathbb{Z} \, l_\mathsf{LIST} \, . \, l \not\approx$ nil $\wedge$ inRange$(n, l) \wedge n -$ head$(l) < 1$	2.7	0.3	0.2
inRange$(n, l) \Rightarrow$ inRange$(n - 1, l)$	8.2	0.3	>60
$l \not\approx$ nil $\wedge$ inRange$(n, l) \Rightarrow n -$ head$(l) > 2$	2.8	0.3	0.2
$n > 0 \wedge$ inRange$(n, l) \wedge l' =$ cons$(n - 2, l) \Rightarrow$ inRange(n, l')	4.5	5.2	0.2

We remark that none of these problems are solvable by using any of the provers to directly establish consistency of the axioms, definitions and the conjecture. Even if only the $\Leftarrow$-direction is used, Z3 and Spass+T do not terminate. Because the universally quantified variables in the conjectures lead to Skolem constants, the resulting clause set is no longer sufficiently complete (see [3]), and a finite saturation obtained by Beagle does not allow one to conclude satisfiability.

Functions. Let $\Sigma^+ \supseteq \Sigma_\mathsf{LIST}$ be a signature, $s \in sorts(\Sigma)$ and $f \notin \Sigma^+$ a function symbol with arity $\mathbb{Z} \times \mathsf{LIST} \mapsto s$. Let Def_f be a set of (implicitly) universally quantified formulas of the form below, where k and h are $\mathbb{Z}$-sorted and t is LIST-sorted:

$$f(k, \mathsf{nil}) \approx b[k] \Leftarrow B[k] \qquad (f_0)$$

$$f(k, \mathsf{cons}(h, t)) \approx c_1[k, h, t, f(k, t)] \Leftarrow C_1[k, h, t, f(k, t)] \qquad (f_1)$$

$$\vdots$$

$$f(k, \mathsf{cons}(h, t)) \approx c_n[k, h, t, f(k, t)] \Leftarrow C_n[k, h, t, f(k, t)] \qquad (f_n)$$

where B is a Σ^+-formula of arity $\mathbb{Z}$, each C_i is a Σ^+-formula of arity $\mathbb{Z} \times \mathbb{Z} \times \mathsf{LIST} \times s$, b is a Σ^+-term of arity $\mathbb{Z} \mapsto s$, and each c_i is a Σ^+-term with arity $\mathbb{Z} \times \mathbb{Z} \times \mathsf{LIST} \times s \mapsto s$.

Lemma 3.2. *Let D be a Σ^+-domain with $D_\mathsf{LIST} = \mathbf{LIST}$. If for all $1 \leq i < j \leq n$ the formula*

$$\forall k_\mathbb{Z} \, h_\mathbb{Z} \, t_\mathsf{LIST} \, x_s \, . \, C_i[k, h, t, x] \wedge C_j[k, h, t, x] \Rightarrow c_i[k, h, t, x] \approx c_j[k, h, t, x]$$

is valid in all Σ^+-interpretations with domain D then Def_f is an admissible definition of f wrt. Σ^+ and D.

---

[2] Here and below, Beagle has been run with "cautious simplification on" and "ordinary variables on"; Z3, version 4.3.1 with the options "pull-nested-quantifiers", "mbqi" and "macro-finder" on; SPASS+T used Yices as a theory solver. All timings obtained on reasonable recent computer hardware. The input problems are available on the Beagle website http://users.cecs.anu.edu.au/~baumgart/systems/beagle/

Proof. The proof of Lemma 3.2 uses the same model construction technique as the proof of Lemma 3.1. Totality is obtained by interpreting f on an argument tuple such that none of the conditions f_0 to f_n holds true by an arbitrary domain element. The condition in the lemma statement enforces right-uniqueness (functionality). □

The condition in the statement of Lemma 3.2 is needed to make sure that all cases (f_i) and (f_j) for $i \neq j$ are consistent. For example, for $f(\text{cons}(h, t)) \approx 1 \Leftarrow h \approx 1$ and $f(\text{cons}(h, t)) \approx a \Leftarrow h \approx 1 + a$ this is not the case. Indeed, $\forall h_\mathbb{Z} \,.\, h \approx 1 \wedge h \approx 1 + a \Rightarrow 1 \approx a$ is not valid. Notice that establishing the condition is a theorem proving task, which fits well with our method. In the examples below it is trivial.

Example. Let length : LIST $\mapsto \mathbb{Z}$, count : $\mathbb{Z} \times$ LIST $\mapsto \mathbb{Z}$, append : LIST $\times$ LIST $\mapsto$ LIST and in : $\mathbb{Z}\times$LIST be operators. Consider the extension of Ax$_{\text{LIST}}$ with the following (admissible) definitions, in the given order.

$$\text{length}(\text{nil}) \approx 0 \qquad \text{append}(\text{nil}, l) \approx l$$
$$\text{length}(\text{cons}(h, t)) \approx 1 + \text{length}(t) \qquad \text{append}(\text{cons}(h, t), l) \approx \text{cons}(h, \text{append}(t, l))$$
$$\text{count}(k, \text{nil}) \approx 0$$
$$\text{count}(k, \text{cons}(h, t)) \approx \text{count}(k, t) \Leftarrow k \not\approx h \qquad \text{in}(k, l) \Leftrightarrow \text{count}(k, l) > 0$$
$$\text{count}(k, \text{cons}(h, t)) \approx \text{count}(k, t) + 1 \Leftarrow k \approx h$$

Here are some sample conjectures together with the times for disproving them.[3]

Problem	Beagle	Spass+T	Z3
$\text{length}(l_1) \approx \text{length}(l_2) \Rightarrow l_1 \approx l_2$	4.3	9.0	0.2
$n \geq 3 \wedge \text{length}(l) \geq 4 \Rightarrow \text{inRange}(n, l)$	5.4	1.1	0.2
$\text{count}(n, l) \approx \text{count}(n, \text{cons}(1, l))$	2.5	0.3	>60
$\text{count}(n, l) \geq \text{length}(l)$	2.7	0.3	>60
$l_1 \not\approx l_2 \Rightarrow \text{count}(n, l_1) \not\approx \text{count}(n, l_2)$	2.4	0.8	>60
$\text{length}(\text{append}(l_1, l_2)) \approx \text{length}(l_1)$	2.1	0.3	0.2
$\text{length}(l_1) > 1 \wedge \text{length}(l_2) > 1 \Rightarrow \text{length}(\text{append}(k, l)) > 4$	37	>60	>60
$\text{in}(n_1, l_1) \wedge \neg\text{in}(n_2, l_2) \wedge l_3 \approx \text{append}(l_1, \text{cons}(n_2, l_2)) \Rightarrow$ $\text{count}(n, l_3) \approx \text{count}(n, l_1)$	>60 (6.2)	9.1	>60

4 Arrays

The signature Σ_{ARRAY} consist of sorts ARRAY and $\mathbb{Z}$ and the operators read : ARRAY $\times$ $\mathbb{Z} \mapsto \mathbb{Z}$, write : ARRAY $\times \mathbb{Z} \times \mathbb{Z} \mapsto$ ARRAY, and init : $\mathbb{Z} \mapsto$ ARRAY. The *array axioms* AX$_{\text{ARRAY}}$ follow:

$$\text{read}(\text{write}(a, i, x), i) \approx x \qquad \text{read}(a, i) \approx \text{read}(b, i) \Rightarrow a \approx b$$
$$\text{read}(\text{write}(a, i, x), j) \approx \text{read}(a, j) \vee i \approx j \qquad \text{read}(\text{init}(x), i) \approx x$$

With the axiom $\text{read}(\text{init}(x), i) \approx x$, a term $\text{init}(t)$ represents an array that is initialized everywhere with t. As with the list axioms, the satisfiability of the array axioms can be established automatically with the Beagle prover by means of a finite saturation.

---

[3] The time of 6.2 seconds for the last problem is with "ordinary variables off".

Relations. Let $\Sigma^+ \supseteq \Sigma_{\mathsf{ARRAY}}$ be a signature and $P \notin \Sigma^+$ a new predicate symbol with arity $\mathbb{Z} \times \mathsf{ARRAY}$. Let Def_P be a formula of the form $\forall k_{\mathbb{Z}} \, x_{\mathsf{ARRAY}} \,.\, P(k, x) \Leftrightarrow C[k, x]$, where C is a Σ^+-formula with arity $\mathbb{Z} \times \mathsf{ARRAY}$.

This is a simpler definition than that for LIST, as it does not admit recursion with the new operator P. Of course, this is balanced by the strength of the read operator for arrays. Using it we can easily define useful predicates without recursion. For example the sorted predicate defines arrays in which the first N elements are sorted in increasing order: $\mathsf{sorted}(a, n) \Leftrightarrow (0 \leq i \wedge i < j \wedge j < n) \Rightarrow \mathsf{read}(a, i) \leq \mathsf{read}(a, j)$.

Lemma 4.1. Def_P *is an admissible definition of* P *wrt.* Σ^+ *and* D.

Proof. This must be so, since for any Σ^+-interpretation I over D and any x, k, I provides an evaluation of $\phi[k, x]$ and so the obvious interpretation $I(P)$ for $\Sigma^+ \cup \{P\}$ can be defined. □

Functions. Let $\Sigma^+ \supseteq \Sigma_{\mathsf{ARRAY}}$ be a signature, $s \in sorts(\Sigma)$ and $f \notin \Sigma^+$ a function symbol with arity $\mathbb{Z} \times \mathsf{ARRAY} \mapsto s$. Let Def_f be a set of (implicitly) universally quantified formulas of the form below, where k is $\mathbb{Z}$-sorted, a is ARRAY-sorted and y is s-sorted:

$$f(a, k) \approx y \Leftarrow C_1[a, k, y] \qquad (\mathrm{f}_1)$$

$$\vdots$$

$$f(a, k) \approx y \Leftarrow C_n[a, k, y] \qquad (\mathrm{f}_n)$$

where each C_i is a Σ^+-formula of arity $\mathsf{ARRAY} \times \mathbb{Z} \times s$. Note the differences between the LIST version and this definition. Here we do not allow recursion- each C_i is strictly over the signature Σ^+ and, instead of a term c_i we have a universally quantified variable y as the evaluation of f. While some functions on arrays are difficult or impossible to express in this way (for example, the sum of the first N elements of an array), many other interesting functions fit this framework. Consider the function $\mathsf{rev} : \mathsf{ARRAY} \times \mathbb{Z} \mapsto \mathsf{ARRAY}$ that returns a copy of an array with the order of the first N elements reversed:

$$\mathsf{rev}(a, n) \approx b \Leftarrow \forall i_{\mathbb{Z}} \,.\, 0 \leq i \wedge i < n \wedge \mathsf{read}(b, i) \approx \mathsf{read}(a, n - (i+1))$$
$$\vee \,((0 > i \vee i \geq n) \wedge \mathsf{read}(b, i) \approx \mathsf{read}(a, i))$$

Lemma 4.2. *Let* D *be a* Σ^+-*domain. If, for all* $1 \leq i \leq j \leq n$ *the formula*

$$C_i[a, k, y_1] \wedge C_j[a, k, y_2] \Rightarrow y_1 \approx y_2$$

is valid in all Σ^+-*interpretations with domain* D, *then* Def_f *is an admissible definition of* f *wrt.* Σ^+ *and* D.

Proof. Assume that the above condition is met and that I is a Σ^+ interpretation over D. For this particular $I(f)$, let f be a function which maps a tuple of domain elements $\mathbf{x}$ to a domain element y of the correct sort such that $I \models C_i[\mathbf{x}, y]$ for some i or to some arbitrary $d \in D$ of the correct sort if no such i and y exist. Since each C_i is a Σ^+ formula, it has an evaluation in I and by assumption any satisfying y is unique up to sort equivalence. Where an arbitrary element is selected no contradiction arises since $I(f) \not\models f(\mathbf{x}) = d \Rightarrow C[\mathbf{x}, d]$. Thus, Def_f is an admissible definition for f. □

Examples. Let the operators inRange : ARRAY × $\mathbb{Z}$ × $\mathbb{Z}$, max, distinct be defined as follows (sorted and rev are as defined previously):

inRange(a, r, n) ⇔
$\quad \forall i . (n > i \wedge i \geq 0)$
$\quad \Rightarrow (r \geq \text{read}(a, i) \wedge \text{read}(a, i) \geq 0)$
max$(a, n) \approx w \Leftarrow \forall i . (n > i \wedge i \geq 0) \Rightarrow w \geq \text{read}(a, i)) \wedge (\exists i . n > i \wedge i \geq 0 \wedge \text{read}(a, i) \approx w)$

distinct(a, n) ⇔
$\quad \forall i, j . (n > i \wedge n > j \wedge j \geq 0 \wedge i \geq 0)$
$\quad \Rightarrow \text{read}(a, i) \approx \text{read}(a, j) \Rightarrow i \approx j)$

Here are some sample conjectures together with the times for disproving them. [4] Note that u indicates termination with a status "unknown".

Problem	Beagle	Spass+T	Z3
$n \geq 0 \Rightarrow \text{inRange}(a, \max(a, n), n)$	1.40	0.16	u
distinct(init$(n), i$)	0.98	0.15	u
read(rev$(a, n + 1), 0) = \text{read}(a, n)$)	>60	>60(0.27)	>60
distinct$(a, n) \Rightarrow \text{distinct}(\text{rev}(a, n))$	>60	0.11	0.36
$\exists n_\mathbb{Z} . \neg\text{sorted}(\text{rev}(\text{init}(n), m), m)$	>60	0.16	u
sorted$(a, n) \wedge n > 0 \Rightarrow \text{distinct}(a, n)$	2.40	0.17	0.01

In addition, SPASS+T, Beagle and Z3 were used to prove the functionality condition in Lemma 4.2 for the max and rev operators. All provers verified the condition for max but only SPASS+T and Z3 verified that for rev.

5 Conclusions

The aim of this work is to provide a reasonably expressive language (in practical terms) that allows one to specify properties of data structures under consideration, like lists and arrays, and that supports disproving by existing theorem provers. The main idea is to capitalize on the strengths of these systems in theorem *proving* and use these for solving (appropriately phrased)disproving problems, instead of relying on their model-building capabilities. The latter, direct approach does not work well in the context of (integer) background theories: both saturation based and SMT methods are inherently incomplete, and so non-provability does not entail non-validity. See [3] for further details under which complete theorem proving is possible.

We gave some example problems and tested them with the theorem provers SPASS+T, Beagle and Z3. These examples are all non-solvable with the direct approach and solvable with our approach. All of them could be solved, and in short time. In general, the first-order solvers Beagle and SPASS+T worked most reliably, possibly thanks to handling quantified formulas natively instead of relying solely on instantiation heuristics. On the other hand, it is easy to find examples where our method does not work. A simple example is the conjecture $\exists n_\mathbb{Z} \; l_\text{LIST} . \text{length}(\text{cons}(n, l)) \approx 0$. (The direct approach does not work either, e.g., Beagle does not find a *finite* saturation.)

---

[4] SPASS+T used Yices as a theory solver. The time of 0.27s in the third problem is obtained by excluding the inRange definition.

Acknowledgements. We thank the reviewers for their helpful comments.

References

1. Bauer, A., Baumgartner, P., Diller, M., Norrish, M.: Tableaux for verification of datacentric processes. In: Galmiche, D., Larchey-Wendling, D. (eds.) TABLEAUX 2013. LNCS, vol. 8123, pp. 28–43. Springer, Heidelberg (2013)
2. Armando, A., Bonacina, M.P., Ranise, S., Schulz, S.: New results on rewrite-based satisfiability procedures. ACM Trans. Comput. Log. 10(1) (2009)
3. Baumgartner, P., Waldmann, U.: Hierarchic superposition with weak abstraction. In: Bonacina, M.P. (ed.) CADE 2013. LNCS (LNAI), vol. 7898, pp. 39–57. Springer, Heidelberg (2013)
4. Bradley, A.R., Manna, Z., Sipma, H.B.: Whats decidable about arrays? In: Emerson, E.A., Namjoshi, K.S. (eds.) VMCAI 2006. LNCS, vol. 3855, pp. 427–442. Springer, Heidelberg (2006)
5. Claessen, K., Lillieström, A.: Automated inference of finite unsatisfiability. J. Autom. Reasoning 47(2), 111–132 (2011)
6. Ghilardi, S., Nicolini, E., Ranise, S., Zucchelli, D.: Decision procedures for extensions of the theory of arrays. Ann. Math. Artif. Intell. 50(3-4), 231–254 (2007)
7. Ihlemann, C., Jacobs, S., Sofronie-Stokkermans, V.: On local reasoning in verification. In: Ramakrishnan, Rehof (eds.) [14], pp. 265–281
8. Kapur, D., Zarba, C.G.: A reduction approach to decision procedures (2005)
9. Lynch, C., Morawska, B.: Automatic decidability. In: LICS, pp. 7–16. IEEE Computer Society (2002)
10. McPeak, S., Necula, G.C.: Data structure specifications via local equality axioms. In: Etessami, K., Rajamani, S.K. (eds.) CAV 2005. LNCS, vol. 3576, pp. 476–490. Springer, Heidelberg (2005)
11. de Moura, L.M., Bjørner, N.: Z3: An efficient SMT solver. In: Ramakrishnan, Rehof (eds.) [14], pp. 337–340
12. de Moura, L.M., Bjørner, N.: Generalized, efficient array decision procedures. In: FMCAD, pp. 45–52. IEEE (2009)
13. Nelson, G., Oppen, D.C.: Fast decision procedures based on congruence closure. Journal of Association for Computer Machinery 27(2) (1980)
14. Ramakrishnan, C.R., Rehof, J. (eds.): TACAS 2008. LNCS, vol. 4963. Springer, Heidelberg (2008)
15. Rümmer, P., Shah, M.A.: Proving programs incorrect using a sequent calculus for java dynamic logic. In: Gurevich, Y., Meyer, B. (eds.) TAP 2007. LNCS, vol. 4454, pp. 41–60. Springer, Heidelberg (2007)
16. Sutcliffe, G., Schulz, S., Claessen, K., Baumgartner, P.: The TPTP typed first-order form with arithmetic. In: Bjørner, N., Voronkov, A. (eds.) LPAR-18 2012. LNCS, vol. 7180, pp. 406–419. Springer, Heidelberg (2012)
17. Suter, P., Köksal, A.S., Kuncak, V.: Satisfiability modulo recursive programs. In: Yahav, E. (ed.) SAS 2011. LNCS, vol. 6887, pp. 298–315. Springer, Heidelberg (2011)
18. Waldmann, U., Prevosto, V.: Spass+t. In: Geoff Sutcliffe, S.S., Schmidt, R. (eds.) ESCoR, Seattle, WA, USA. CEUR Workshop Proceedings, pp. 18–33 (2006)

SAT-Based Preprocessing for MaxSAT*

Anton Belov[1], António Morgado[2], and Joao Marques-Silva[1,2]

[1] Complex and Adaptive Systems Laboratory University College Dublin
[2] IST/INESC-ID, Technical University of Lisbon, Portugal

Abstract. State-of-the-art algorithms for industrial instances of MaxSAT problem rely on iterative calls to a SAT solver. Preprocessing is crucial for the acceleration of SAT solving, and the key preprocessing techniques rely on the application of resolution and subsumption elimination. Additionally, satisfiability-preserving clause elimination procedures are often used. Since MaxSAT computation typically involves a large number of SAT calls, we are interested in whether an input instance to a MaxSAT problem can be preprocessed *up-front*, i.e. prior to running the MaxSAT solver, rather than (or, in addition to) during each iterative SAT solver call. The key requirement in this setting is that the preprocessing has to be *sound*, i.e. so that the solution can be reconstructed correctly and efficiently after the execution of a MaxSAT algorithm on the preprocessed instance. While, as we demonstrate in this paper, certain clause elimination procedures are sound for MaxSAT, it is well-known that this is not the case for resolution and subsumption elimination. In this paper we show how to adapt these preprocessing techniques to MaxSAT. To achieve this we recast the MaxSAT problem in a recently introduced labelled-CNF framework, and show that within the framework the preprocessing techniques can be applied soundly. Furthermore, we show that MaxSAT algorithms restated in the framework have a natural implementation on top of an *incremental* SAT solver. We evaluate the prototype implementation of a MaxSAT algorithm WMSU1 in this setting, demonstrate the effectiveness of preprocessing, and show overall improvement with respect to non-incremental versions of the algorithm on some classes of problems.

1 Introduction

Maximum Satisfiability (MaxSAT) and its generalization to the case of Satisfiability Modulo Theories (MaxSMT) find a growing number of practical applications [17,19]. For problem instances originating from practical applications, state of the art MaxSAT algorithms rely on iterative calls to a SAT oracle. Moreover, and for a growing number of iterative algorithms, the calls to the SAT oracle are guided by iteratively computed unsatisfiable cores (e.g. [19]).

In practical SAT solving, formula preprocessing has been extensively studied and is now widely accepted to be an often effective, if not crucial, technique. In contrast, formula preprocessing is not used in practical MaxSAT solving. Indeed, it is well-known

---

* This work is partially supported by SFI PI grant BEACON (09/IN.1/I2618), FCT grants ATTEST (CMU-PT/ELE/0009/2009) and POLARIS (PTDC/EIA-CCO/123051/2010), and INESC-IDs multiannual PIDDAC funding PEst-OE/EEI/LA0021/2011.

that resolution and subsumption elimination, which form the core of many effective preprocessors, are unsound for MaxSAT solving [17]. This has been addressed by the development of a resolution calculus specific to MaxSAT [7]. Nevertheless, for practical instances of MaxSAT, dedicated MaxSAT resolution is ineffective.

The application of SAT preprocessing to problems where a SAT oracle is used a number of times has been the subject of recent interest [2]. For iterative MaxSAT solving, SAT preprocessing can be used internally to the SAT solver. However, we are interested in the question of whether an input instance of a MaxSAT problem can be preprocessed *up-front*, i.e. prior to running the MaxSAT solver, rather than (or, in addition to) during each iterative SAT solver call. The key requirement in this setting is that the preprocessing has to be *sound*, i.e. so that the solution can be reconstructed correctly and efficiently after the execution of a MaxSAT algorithm on the preprocessed instance.

In this paper we make the following contributions. First, we establish that certain class of clause elimination procedures, and in particular monotone clause elimination procedures such as blocked clause elimination [14], are sound for MaxSAT. Second, we use a recently proposed labelled-CNF framework [3,2] to re-formulate MaxSAT and its generalizations, and show that within the framework the resolution and subsumption-elimination based preprocessing techniques can be applied soundly. This result complements a similar result with respect to the MUS computation problem presented in [2]. An interesting related result is that MaxSAT algorithms formulated in the labelled-CNF framework can naturally implemented on top of an *incremental* SAT solver (cf. [10]). We evaluate a prototype implementation of a MaxSAT algorithm WMSU1 [11,1,18] in this setting, demonstrate the effectiveness of preprocessing, and show overall improvement with respect to non-incremental versions of this algorithm on weighted partial MaxSAT instances.

2 Preliminaries

We assume the familiarity with propositional logic, its clausal fragment, SAT solving in general, and the assumption-based incremental SAT solving cf. [10]. We focus on formulas in CNF (*formulas*, from hence on), which we treat as (finite) (multi-)sets of clauses. When it is convenient we treat clauses as sets of literals, and hence we assume that clauses do not contain duplicate literals. Given a formula F we denote the set of variables that occur in F by $Var(F)$, and the set of variables that occur in a clause $C \in F$ by $Var(C)$. An *assignment* τ for F is a map $\tau : Var(F) \to \{0, 1\}$. Assignments are extended to formulas according to the semantics of classical propositional logic. If $\tau(F) = 1$, then τ is a *model* of F. If a formula F has (resp. does not have) a model, then F is *satisfiable* (resp. *unsatisfiable*). By SAT (resp. UNSAT) we denote the set of all satisfiable (resp. unsatisfiable) CNF formulas.

MUSes, MSSes, and MCSes. Let F be an unsatisfiable CNF formula. A formula $M \subseteq F$ is a *minimal unsatisfiable subformula (MUS)* of F if (i) $M \in$ UNSAT, and (ii) $\forall C \in M, M \setminus \{C\} \in$ SAT. The set of MUSes of F is denoted by MUS(F). Dually, a formula $S \subseteq F$ is a *maximal satisfiable subformula (MSS)* of F if (i) $S \in$ SAT, and (ii) $\forall C \in F \setminus S, S \cup \{C\} \in$ UNSAT. The set of MSSes of F is denoted by

MSS(F). Finally, a formula $R \subseteq F$ is a *minimal correction subset (MCS), or, co-MSS* of F, if $F \setminus R \in$ MSS(F), or, explicitly, if (i) $F \setminus R \in$ SAT, and (ii) $\forall C \in R$, $(F \setminus R) \cup \{C\} \in$ UNSAT. Again, the set of MCSes of F is denoted by MCS(F). The MUSes, MSSes and MCSes of a given unsatisfiable formula F are connected via so-called *hitting sets duality* theorem, first proved in [20]. The theorem states that M is an MUS of F if and only if M is an irreducible hitting set[1] of the set MCS(F), and vice versa: $R \in$ MCS(F) iff R is an irreducible hitting set of MUS(F).

Maximum Satisfiability. A *weighted clause* is a pair (C, w), where C is a clause, and $w \in \mathbb{N}^+ \cup \{\top\}$ is the cost of falsifying C. The special value $\top$ signifies that C *must* be satisfied, and $(C, \top)$ is then called a *hard* clause, while (C, w) for $w \in \mathbb{N}^+$ is called a *soft* clause. A *weighted CNF (WCNF)* is a set of weighted clauses, $F = F^H \cup F^S$, where F^H is the set of hard clauses, and F^S is the set of soft clauses. The satisfiability, and the related concepts, are defined for weighted CNFs by disregarding the weights. For a given WCNF $F = F^H \cup F^S$, a *MaxSAT model* for F is an assignment τ for F that satisfies F^H. A *cost* of a MaxSAT model τ, $cost(\tau)$, is the sum of the weights of the soft clauses *falsified* by τ. For the rest of this paper, we assume that (i) $F^H \in$ SAT, i.e. F has at least one MaxSAT model, and (ii) $F \in$ UNSAT, i.e. $cost(\tau) > 0$. *(Weighted) (Partial) MaxSAT* is a problem of finding a MaxSAT model of the minimum cost for a given WCNF formula $F = F^H \cup F^S$. The word "weighted" is used when there are soft clauses with weight > 1, while the word "partial" is used when $F^H \neq \emptyset$.

A straightforward, but nevertheless important, observation is that solving a weighted partial MaxSAT problem for WCNF F is equivalent to finding a minimum-cost MCS R_{min} of F, or, alternatively, a minimum-cost hitting set of MUS(F)[2]. The MaxSAT solution is then a model for the corresponding MSS of F, i.e. $F \setminus R_{min}$.

SAT Preprocessing. Given a CNF formula F, the goal of preprocessing for SAT solving is to compute a formula F' that is equisatisfiable with F, and that might be easier to solve. The computation of F' and a model of F from a model of F' in case $F' \in$ SAT, is expected to be fast enough to make it worthwhile for the overall SAT solving. Many SAT preprocessing techniques rely on a combination of resolution-based preprocessing and clause-elimination procedures. Resolution-based preprocessing relies on the application of the resolution rule to *modify* the clauses of the input formula and/or to reduce the total size of the formula. Clause-elimination procedures, on the other hand, do not change the clauses of the input formula, but rather remove some of its clauses, producing a subformula the input formula. SAT preprocessing techniques can be described as non-deterministic procedures that apply atomic preprocessing steps to the, initially input, formula until a fixpoint, or until resource limits are exceeded.

One of the most successful and widely used SAT preprocessors is the SatElite preprocessor presented in [8]. The techniques employed by SatElite are: bounded variable

---

[1] For a given collection $\mathscr{S}$ of arbitrary sets, a set H is called a *hitting set* of $\mathscr{S}$ if for all $S \in \mathscr{S}$, $H \cap S \neq \emptyset$. A hitting set H is *irreducible*, if no $H' \subset H$ is a hitting set of $\mathscr{S}$. Irreducible hitting sets are also known as hypergraph transversals.
[2] For a set of weighted clauses, its cost is the sum of their weights, or $\top$ if any of them is hard.

elimination (BVE), subsumption elimination, self-subsuming resolution (SSR), and, of course, unit propagation (UP). An additional practically relevant preprocessing technique is blocked clause elimination (BCE) [14]. We describe these techniques below, as these will be discussed in this paper in the context of MaxSAT.

Bounded variable elimination (BVE) [8] is a resolution-based preprocessing technique, rooted in the original Davis-Putnam algorithm for SAT. Recall that for two clauses $C_1 = (x \vee A)$ and $C_2 = (\neg x \vee B)$ the *resolvent* $C_1 \otimes_x C_2$ is the clause $(A \vee B)$. For two sets F_x and $F_{\neg x}$ of clauses that all contain the literal x and $\neg x$, resp., define $F_x \otimes_x F_{\neg x} = \{C_1 \otimes_x C_2 \mid C_1 \in F_x, C_2 \in F_{\neg x},$ and $C_1 \otimes_x C_2$ is not a tautology$\}$. The formula $\text{ve}(F, x) = F \setminus (F_x \cup F_{\neg x}) \cup (F_x \otimes_x F_{\neg x})$ is equisatisfiable with F, however, in general, might be quadratic in the size of F. Thus the atomic operation of *bounded* variable elimination is defined as $\text{bve}(F, x) = \textbf{if } (|\text{ve}(F, x)| < |F|) \textbf{ then } \text{ve}(F, x) \textbf{ else } F$. A formula $\text{BVE}(F)$ is obtained by applying $\text{bve}(F, x)$ to all variables in F[3].

Subsumption elimination (SE) is an example of a clause elimination technique. A clause C_1 *subsumes* a clause C_2, if $C_1 \subset C_2$. For $C_1, C_2 \in F$, define $\text{sub}(F, C_1, C_2) = \textbf{if } (C_1 \subset C_2) \textbf{ then } F \setminus \{C_2\} \textbf{ else } F$. The formula $\text{SUB}(F)$ is then obtained by applying $\text{sub}(F, C_1, C_2)$ to all clauses of F.

Notice that *unit propagation (UP)* of a unit clause $(l) \in F$ is just an application of $\text{sub}(F, (l), C)$ until fixpoint (to remove satisfied clauses), followed by $\text{bve}(F, var(l))$ (to remove the clause (l) and the literal $\neg l$ from the remaining clauses), and so we will not discuss UP explicitly.

Self-Subsuming resolution (SSR) uses resolution and subsumption elimination. Given two clauses $C_1 = (l \vee A)$ and $C_2 = (\neg l \vee B)$ in F, such that $A \subset B$, we have $C_1 \otimes_l C_2 = B \subset C_2$, and so C_2 can be replaced with B, or, in other words, $\neg l$ is removed from C_2. Hence, the atomic step of SSR, $\text{ssr}(F, C_1, C_2)$, results in the formula $F \setminus \{C_2\} \cup \{B\}$ if C_1, C_2 are as above, and F, otherwise.

An atomic step of *blocked clause elimination (BCE)* consists of removing one blocked clause — a clause $C \in F$ is *blocked* in F [15], if for some literal $l \in C$, every resolvent of C with $C' \in F$ on l is tautological. A formula $\text{BCE}(F)$ is obtained by applying $\text{bce}(F, C) = \textbf{if } (C \text{ blocked in } F) \textbf{ then } F \setminus \{C\} \textbf{ else } F$ to all clauses of F. Notice, that a clause with a pure literal is blocked (vacuously), and so pure literal elimination is a special case of BCE. BCE possesses an important property called *monotonicity*: for any $F' \subseteq F$, $\text{BCE}(F') \subseteq \text{BCE}(F)$. This holds because if C is blocked w.r.t. to F, it will be also blocked w.r.t to any subset of F. Notice that subsumption elimination is *not* monotone.

3 SAT Preprocessing and MaxSAT

Let F' denote the result of the application of one or more of the SAT preprocessing techniques, such as those discussed in the previous section, to a CNF formula F. The question that we would like to address in this paper is whether it is possible to solve a MaxSAT problem for F', instead of F, in such a way that from any MaxSAT solution of F', a MaxSAT solution of F can be reconstructed feasibly. In a more general setting,

---
[3] Specific implementations often impose additional restrictions on BVE.

F might be a WCNF formula, and F' is the set of weighted clauses obtained by preprocessing the clauses of F, and perhaps, adjusting their weights in some manner. The preprocessing techniques for which the answer to this question is "yes" will be refereed to as *sound for MaxSAT*. To be specific:

Definition 1. *A preprocessing technique* P *is* sound for MaxSAT *if there exist a polytime computable function* α_P *such that for any WCNF formula F and any MaxSAT solution τ of* $P(F)$, $\alpha_P(\tau)$ *is a MaxSAT solution of F.*

This line of research is motivated by the fact that most of the efficient algorithms for industrial MaxSAT problems are based on iterative invocations of a SAT solver. Thus, if F' is indeed easier to solve than F by a SAT solver, it might be the case that it is also easier to solve by a SAT-based MaxSAT solver. To illustrate that the question is not trivial, consider the following example.

Example 1. In the plain MaxSAT setting, let $F = \{C_1, \ldots, C_6\}$, with $C_1 = (p)$, $C_2 = (\neg p)$, $C_3 = (p \vee q)$, $C_4 = (p \vee \neg q)$, $C_5 = (r)$, and $C_6 = (\neg r)$. The clauses C_3 and C_4 are subsumed by C_1, and so $\mathsf{SUB}(F) = \{C_1, C_2, C_5, C_6\}$. $\mathsf{SUB}(F)$ has MaxSAT solutions in which p is assigned to 0, e.g. $\{\langle p, 0\rangle, \langle r, 0\rangle\}$, while F does not. Furthermore, $\mathsf{BVE}(F) = \{\emptyset\}$ — a formula with 8 MaxSAT solutions (w.r.t. to the variables of F) with cost 1. F, on the other hand, has 4 MaxSAT solutions with cost 2.

Thus, even a seemingly benign subsumption elimination already causes problems for MaxSAT. While we do not prove that the technique is not sound for MaxSAT, a strong indication that this might be the case is that SUB might remove clauses that are included in one or more of the MUSes of the input formula F (c.f. Example 1), and thus lose the information required to compute the MaxSAT solution of F. The problems with the application of the resolution rule in the context of MaxSAT has been pointed out already in [17], and where the motivation for the introduction of the so-called *MaxSAT resolution* rule [7] and a complete proof procedure for MaxSAT based on it. However, MaxSAT resolution does not lead to effective preprocessing techniques for industrial MaxSAT since it often introduces a large number of auxiliary "compensation" clauses. Once again, we do not claim that resolution is unsound for MaxSAT, but it is likely to be the case, since for example ve ran to completion on any unsatisfiable formula will always produce a formula $\{\emptyset\}$.

In this paper we propose an alternative solution, which will be discussed shortly. But first, we observe that *monotone* clause elimination procedures *are* sound for MaxSAT.

3.1 Monotone Clause Elimination Procedures

Recall that given a CNF formula F, an application of clause elimination procedure E produces a formula $\mathsf{E}(F) \subseteq F$ equisatisfiable with F. Monotonicity implies that for any $F' \subseteq F$, $\mathsf{E}(F') \subseteq \mathsf{E}(F)$. Some examples of monotone clause elimination procedures include BCE (and as a special case, pure literal elimination), and also *covered clause elimination* introduced in [12].

It was observed already in [16] that if a clause $C \in F$ is blocked in F, then none of the MUSes of F can include C. Thus, $\mathsf{MUS}(\mathsf{BCE}(F)) = \mathsf{MUS}(F)$, and therefore, by the hitting-sets duality, $\mathsf{MCS}(\mathsf{BCE}(F)) = \mathsf{MCS}(F)$. In particular, any minimum-cost

MCS of BCE(F) is also a minimum-cost MCS of F. Thus, the *cost* of any MaxSAT solution τ of BCE(F) is exactly the same as of any MaxSAT solution of F, and moreover, there exist a MaxSAT solution of F that falsifies the exact same set of clauses as τ in BCE(F). The only question is whether a solution of F can be feasibly constructed from τ. A linear time procedure for reconstruction of satisfying assignments after BCE has been described in [13] (Prop. 3). We show that the same procedure can be applied to reconstruct the solutions in the context of MaxSAT. We generalize the discussion to include some of the clause elimination procedures beside BCE.

Definition 2. *A clause elimination procedure* E *is* MUS-preserving *if* MUS(E(F)) = MUS(F).

Theorem 1. *Any MUS-preserving clause elimination procedure is sound for MaxSAT.*

Proof. Let E be an MUS-preserving clause elimination procedure, and let α_E be a feasibly computable function that for any CNF formula G maps a model of E(G) to a model of G when E(G) is satisfiable. Let F be a WCNF formula, and let τ be a MaxSAT solution of the formula E(F). Let E(F) = $R \uplus S^4$, where R (resp. S) is the set of clauses falsified (resp. satisfied) by τ, i.e. R is a minimum-cost MCS of E(F), and S is the corresponding MSS of E(F). Since E is MUS-preserving, MUS(E(F)) = MUS(F), and, by hitting-sets duality, MCS(E(F)) = MCS(F), and so R is also a minimum-cost MCS of F. To show that $\tau' = \alpha_E(\tau)$ satisfies $S' = F \setminus R$, we observe that since $F = R \uplus S'$, E(F) = E($R \uplus S'$) = $R \uplus$ E(S'), because $R \subset$ E(F). Hence $S =$ E(S'), and therefore given any model τ of S, $\alpha_E(\tau)$ is a model of S'. □

Proposition 1. *Any monotone clause elimination procedure is MUS-preserving*[5].

Corollary 1. *Any monotone clause elimination procedure is sound for MaxSAT.*

3.2 Resolution-Based and Subsumption Elimination Based Techniques

To enable sound preprocessing for MaxSAT using resolution-based and subsumption elimination based preprocessing techniques, we propose to recast the MaxSAT problem in the framework of so-called *labelled CNF (LCNF)* formulas. The framework was introduced in [3], and was already used to enable sound preprocessing for MUS extraction in [2]. We briefly review the framework here, and refer the reader to [3,2] for details.

Labelled CNFs. Assume a countable set of labels $Lbls$. A *labelled clause* (L-clause) is a tuple $\langle C, L \rangle$, where C is a clause, and L is a finite (possibly empty) subset of $Lbls$. We denote the label-sets by superscripts, i.e. C^L is the labelled clause $\langle C, L \rangle$. A *labelled CNF (LCNF)* formula is a finite set of labelled clauses. For an LCNF formula Φ[6], let $Cls(\Phi) = \bigcup_{C^L \in \Phi} \{C\}$ be the *clause-set* of Φ, and $Lbls(\Phi) = \bigcup_{C^L \in \Phi} L$ be the

---
[4] The symbol $\uplus$ refers to a *disjoint* union.
[5] All missing proofs are included in the extended version of this paper [4].
[6] We use capital Greek letters to distinguish LCNFs from CNFs.

label-set of Φ. LCNF satisfiability is defined in terms of the satisfiability of the clause-sets of an LCNF formula: Φ is satisfiable if and only if $Cls(\Phi)$ is satisfiable. We will re-use the notation SAT (resp. UNSAT) for the set of satisfiable (resp. unsatisfiable) LCNF formulas[7]. However, the semantics of minimal unsatisfiability and maximal and maximum satisfiability of labelled CNFs are defined in terms of their label-sets via the concept of the *induced subformula*.

Definition 3 (Induced subformula). *Let Φ be an LCNF formula, and let $M \subseteq Lbls(\Phi)$. The subformula of Φ induced by M is the LCNF formula $\Phi|_M = \{C^L \in \Phi \mid L \subseteq M\}$.*

In other words, $\Phi|_M$ consists of those labelled clauses of Φ whose label-sets are included in M, and so $Lbls(\Phi|_M) \subseteq M$, and $Cls(\Phi|_M) \subseteq Cls(\Phi)$. Alternatively, any clause that has at least one label outside of M is removed from Φ. Thus, it is convenient to talk about the *removal* of a label from Φ. Let $l \in Lbls(\Phi)$ be any label. The LCNF formula $\Phi|_{M \setminus \{l\}}$ is said to be obtained by the *removal of label l from Φ*.

To the readers familiar with the assumption-based incremental SAT (c.f. [10]), it might be helpful to think of labels as selector variables attached to clauses of a CNF formula, taking into account the possibility of having multiple, or none at all, selectors for each clause[8]. Then an induced subformula $\Phi|_M$ is obtained by "turning-on" the selectors in M, and "turning-off" the selectors outside of M. An operation of removal of a label l from Φ can be seen as an operation of "turning-off" the selector l.

The concept of induced subformulas allows to adopt all notions related to satisfiability of subsets of CNF formulas to LCNF setting. For example, given an unsatisfiable LCNF Φ, an unsatisfiable core of Φ is any set of labels $C \subseteq Lbls(\Phi)$ such that $\Phi|_C \in$ UNSAT. Note that the selectors that appear in the final conflict clause in the context of assumption-based incremental SAT constitute such a core. Furthermore, given an unsatisfiable LCNF Φ, a set of labels $M \subseteq Lbls(\Phi)$ is an *MUS* of Φ, if (i) $\Phi|_M \in$ UNSAT, and (ii) $\forall l \in M, \Phi|_{M \setminus \{l\}} \in$ SAT. As with CNFs, the set of all MUSes of LCNF Φ is denoted by MUS(Φ). MSSes and MCSes of LCNF formulas can be defined in the similar manner. Specifically, for an unsatisfiable LCNF formula Φ, a set of labels $R \subseteq Lbls(\Phi)$ is an *MCS* of Φ, if (i) $\Phi|_{Lbls(\Phi) \setminus R} \in$ SAT, and (ii) $\forall l \in R$, $\Phi|_{(Lbls(\Phi) \setminus R) \cup \{l\}} \in$ UNSAT. The set of all MCSes of Φ is denoted by MCS(Φ). It was shown in [3] that the hitting-sets duality holds for LCNFs, i.e. for any LCNF Φ, $M \subseteq Lbls(\Phi)$ is an MUS of Φ if and only if M is an irreducible hitting set of MCS(Φ), and vice versa.

Example 2. Let $\Phi = \{(\neg p)^{\emptyset}, (r)^{\emptyset}, (p \vee q)^{\{1\}}, (p \vee \neg q)^{\{1,2\}}, (p)^{\{2\}}, (\neg r)^{\{3\}}\}$. The label-set of a clause is given in the superscript, i.e. $Lbls = \mathbb{N}^+$ and $Lbls(\Phi) = \{1, 2, 3\}$. The subformula induced by the set $S = \{1\}$ is $\Phi|_S = \{(\neg p)^{\emptyset}, (r)^{\emptyset}, (p \vee q)^{\{1\}}\}$. S is an MSS of Φ, as $\Phi|_S \in$ SAT and both formulas $\Phi|_{\{1,2\}}$ and $\Phi|_{\{1,3\}}$ are unsatisfiable. $R = \{2, 3\}$ is the corresponding MCS of Φ.

To clarify the connection between LCNF and CNF formulas further, consider a CNF formula $F = \{C_1, \ldots, C_n\}$. The LCNF formula Φ_F associated with F is con-

---

[7] To avoid overly optimistic complexity results, we will tacitly assume that the sizes of label-sets of the clauses in LCNFs are polynomial in the number of the clauses

[8] Furthermore, notice that clauses with multiple selectors show up exactly when resolution-based preprocessing is applied in the context of incremental SAT.

structed by labelling each clause $C_i \in F$ with a *unique, singleton* labelset $\{i\}$, i.e. $\Phi_F = \{C_i^{\{i\}} \mid C_i \in F\}$. Then, a removal of a label i from Φ_F corresponds to a removal of a clause C_i from F, and so every MUS (resp. MSS/MCS) of Φ_F corresponds to an MUS (resp. MSS/MCS) of F and vice versa.

The resolution rule for labelled clauses is defined as follows [2]: for two labelled clauses $(x \vee A)^{L_1}$ and $(\neg x \vee B)^{L_2}$, the *resolvent* $C_1^{L_1} \otimes_x C_2^{L_2}$ is the labelled clause $(A \vee B)^{L_1 \cup L_2}$. The definition is extended to two sets of labelled clauses Φ_x and $\Phi_{\neg x}$ that contain the literal x and $\neg x$ resp., as with CNFs. Finally, a labelled clause $C_1^{L_1}$ is said to *subsume* $C_2^{L_2}$, in symbols $C_1^{L_1} \subset C_2^{L_2}$, if $C_1 \subset C_2$ and $L_1 \subseteq L_2$. Again, the two definitions become immediate if one thinks of labels as selector variables in the context of incremental SAT.

Resolution and Subsumption Based Preprocessing for LCNFs. Resolution and subsumption based SAT preprocessing techniques discussed in Section 2 can be applied to LCNFs [2], so long as the resolution rule and the definition of subsumption is taken to be as above. Specifically, define $\mathsf{ve}(\Phi, x) = \Phi \setminus (\Phi_x \cup \Phi_{\neg x}) \cup (\Phi_x \otimes_x \Phi_{\neg x})$. Then, an atomic operation of bounded variable elimination for LCNF Φ is defined as $\mathsf{bve}(\Phi, x) = \mathbf{if}\ (|\mathsf{ve}(\Phi, x)| < |\Phi|)\ \mathbf{then}\ \mathsf{ve}(\Phi, x)\ \mathbf{else}\ \Phi$. The size of Φ is just the number of labelled clauses in it. A formula $\mathsf{BVE}(\Phi)$ is obtained by applying $\mathsf{bve}(\Phi, x)$ to all variables in Φ. Similarly, for $C_1^{L_1}, C_2^{L_2} \in F$, define $\mathsf{sub}(\Phi, C_1^{L_1}, C_2^{L_2}) = \mathbf{if}\ (C_1^{L_1} \subset C_2^{L_2})\ \mathbf{then}\ \Phi \setminus \{C_2^{L_2}\}\ \mathbf{else}\ \Phi$. The formula $\mathsf{SUB}(\Phi)$ is then obtained by applying $\mathsf{sub}(\Phi, C_1^{L_1}, C_2^{L_2})$ to all clauses of Φ. Finally, given two labelled clauses $C_1^{L_1} = (l \vee A)^{L_1}$ and $C_2^{L_2} = (\neg l \vee B)^{L_2}$ in Φ, such that $A \subset B$ and $L_1 \subseteq L_2$, the atomic step of self-subsuming resolution, $\mathsf{ssr}(\Phi, C_1^{L_1}, C_2^{L_2})$, results in the formula $\Phi \setminus \{C_2^{L_2}\} \cup \{B^{L_2}\}$. Notice that the operations bve and ssr do not affect the set of *labels* of the LCNF formula, however it might be the case that sub removes some labels from it.

The soundness of the resolution and subsumption based preprocessing for LCNFs with respect to the computation of MUSes has been established in [2] (Theorem 1, Prop. 6 and 7). Specifically, given an LCNF Φ, $\mathsf{MUS}(\mathsf{bve}(\Phi, x)) \subseteq \mathsf{MUS}(\Phi)$, $\mathsf{MUS}(\mathsf{sub}(\Phi, C_1^{L_1}, C_2^{L_2})) \subseteq \mathsf{MUS}(\Phi)$, and $\mathsf{MUS}(\mathsf{ssr}(\Phi, C_1^{L_1}, C_2^{L_2})) \subseteq \mathsf{MUS}(\Phi)$. In this paper we establish stronger statements that, by the hitting-sets duality for LCNFs [3], also imply that the set inclusions $\subseteq$ between the sets $\mathsf{MUS}(\circ)$ are set equalities.

Proposition 2. *For any LCNF formula Φ and variable x,* $\mathsf{MCS}(\mathsf{bve}(\Phi, x)) = \mathsf{MCS}(\Phi)$.

Proposition 3. *For any LCNF formula Φ, and any two clauses $C_1^{L_1}, C_2^{L_2} \in \Phi$,* $\mathsf{MCS}(\mathsf{sub}(\Phi, C_1^{L_1}, C_2^{L_2})) = \mathsf{MCS}(\Phi)$.

Proposition 4. *For any LCNF formula Φ, and any two clauses $C_1^{L_1}, C_2^{L_2} \in \Phi$,* $\mathsf{MCS}(\mathsf{ssr}(\Phi, C_1^{L_1}, C_2^{L_2})) = \mathsf{MCS}(\Phi)$.

To summarize, the three SAT preprocessing techniques discussed in this section, namely bounded variable elimination, subsumption elimination and self-subsuming resolution, preserve MCSes of LCNF formulas. Given that the MaxSAT problem for weighted CNFs can be cast as a problem of finding a minimum-cost MCS (cf. Section 2), we now define the MaxSAT problem for weighted LCNFs, and draw a connection between the two problems.

Maximum Satisfiability for LCNFs. Recall that the maximum satisfiability problem for a given weighted CNF formula $F = F^H \cup F^S$ can be seen as a problem of finding a minimum-cost set of soft clauses R_{min} whose removal from F makes F satisfiable, i.e. a minimum-cost MCS of F. In LCNF framework we do not remove clause directly, but rather via labels associated with them. Thus, a clause labelled with an empty set of labels cannot be removed from an LCNF formula, and can play a role of a hard clause in a WCNF formula. By associating the weights to *labels* of LCNF formula, we can arrive at a concept of a minimum-cost set of labels, and from here at the idea of the maximum satisfiability problem for LCNF formulas.

Thus, we now have *weighted labels* (l, w), with $l \in Lbls$, and $w \in \mathbb{N}^+$ (note that there's no need for the special weight $\top$). A *cost* of a set L of weighted labels is the sum of their weights. A *weighted LCNF formula* is a set of clauses labelled with weighted labels. It is more convenient to define a MaxSAT solution for weighted LCNFs in terms of minimum-cost MCSes, rather that in terms of MaxSAT models. This is due to the fact that given an arbitrary assignment τ that satisfies all clauses labelled with $\emptyset$, the definition of a "set of labels falsified by τ" is not immediate, since in principle a clause might be labelled with more than one label, and, from the MaxSAT point of view, we do not want to remove more labels than necessary.

Definition 4 (MaxSAT solution for weighted LCNF). *Let Φ be a weighted LCNF formula with $\Phi|_\emptyset \in$ SAT. An assignment τ is a MaxSAT solution of Φ if τ is a model of the formula $\Phi|_{Lbls(\Phi) \setminus R_{min}}$ for some minimum-cost MCS R_{min} of Φ. The cost of τ is the cost of R_{min}.*

In other words, a MaxSAT solution τ for a weighted LCNF maximizes the cost of a set $S \subseteq Lbls(\Phi)$, subject to τ satisfying $\Phi|_S$, and the cost of τ is the cost of the set $R = Lbls(\Phi) \setminus S$.

Let $F = F^H \cup F^S$ be a weighted CNF formula. The weighted LCNF formula Φ_F associated with F is constructed similary to the case of plain CNFs: assuming that $F^S = \{C_1, \ldots, C_n\}$, we will use $\{1, \ldots, n\}$ to label the soft clauses, so that a clause C_i gets a unique, singleton labelset $\{i\}$, hard clauses will be labelled with $\emptyset$, and the weight of a label i will be set to be the weight of the soft clause C_i. Formally, $Lbls(\Phi) = \{1, \ldots, |F^S|\} \subset \mathbb{N}^+$, $\Phi_F = (\cup_{C \in F^H} \{C^\emptyset\}) \cup (\cup_{C_i \in F^S} \{C_i^{\{i\}}\})$, and $\forall i \in Lbls(\Phi), w(i) = w(C_i)$.

Let Φ_F be the weighted LCNF formula associated a weighted CNF F. Clearly, every MaxSAT solution of Φ_F is a MaxSAT solution of F, and vice versa. In the previous subsection we showed that the resolution and the subsumption elimination based preprocessing techniques preserve the MCSes of Φ_F. We will show shortly that this leads to the conclusion that the techniques can be applied soundly to Φ_F, and so, assuming the availability of a method for solving MaxSAT problem for Φ_F (Section 4), this allows to use preprocessing, albeit indirectly, for solving MaxSAT problem for F.

Preprocessing and MaxSAT for LCNFs

Theorem 2. *For weighted LCNF formulas, the atomic operations of bounded variable elimination (bve), subsumption elimination (sub), and self-subsuming resolution (ssr) sound for MaxSAT.*

Proof. Let Φ be a weighted LCNF formula. Assume that for some variable x, $\Phi' = \textsf{bve}(\Phi, x)$, and let τ' be a MaxSAT solution of Φ'. Thus, for some minimum-cost MCS R_{min} of Φ', τ' is a model of $\Phi'|_{Lbls(\Phi') \setminus R_{min}}$. By Proposition 2, R_{min} is a minimum-cost MCS of Φ. If x was eliminated, τ' can be transformed in linear time to a model τ of $\Phi|_{Lbls(\Phi) \setminus R_{min}}$ by assigning the truth-value to x (cf. [13]). We conclude that bve is sound for LCNF MaxSAT.

For sub and ssr no reconstruction is required, since the techniques preserve equivalence. The claim of the theorem follows directly from Propositions 3 and 4. □

To conclude this section, lets us summarize the SAT preprocessing "pipeline" for solving the MaxSAT problem for weighted CNFs. Given a WCNF formula F, first apply any MUS-preserving (and so, monotone) clause-elimination technique, such as BCE, to obtain the formula F'. Then, construct an LCNF formula $\Phi|_{F'}$ associated with F', and apply BVE, subsumption elimination and SSR, possibly in an interleaved manner, to $\Phi|_{F'}$ to obtain Φ'. Solve the MaxSAT problem for Φ', and reconstruct the solution to the MaxSAT problem of the original formula F — Theorems 1 and 2 show that it can be done feasibly. The only missing piece is how to solve MaxSAT problem for LCNF formulas — this is the subject of the next section.

We have to point out that the resolution and the subsumption elimination preprocessing techniques in the LCNF framework are not without their limitations. For BVE the label-sets of clauses grow, which may have a negative impact on the performance of SAT solvers if LCNF algorithms are implemented incrementally. Also, two clauses C^{L_1} and C^{L_2} are treated as two different clauses if $L_1 \neq L_2$, while without labels they would be collapsed into one, and thus more variables might be eliminated. Nevertheless, when many hard (i.e. labelled with $\emptyset$) clauses are present, this negative effect is dampened. For subsumption elimination the rule $L_1 \subseteq L_2$ is quite restrictive. In particular, it blocks subsumption completely in the plain MaxSAT setting (though, as we already saw, unrestricted subsumption is dangerous for MaxSAT). However, in partial MaxSAT setting it does enable the removal of any clause (hard or soft) subsumed by a hard clause. In Section 5, we demonstrate that the techniques do lead to performance improvements in practice.

4 Solving MaxSAT Problem for LCNFs

In this section we propose two methods for solving MaxSAT problem for weighted LCNFs. Both methods rely on the connection between the labels in LCNFs and the selector variables.

4.1 Reduction to Weighted Partial MaxSAT

The idea of this method is to encode a given weighted LCNF formula Φ as an WCNF formula F_Φ, mapping the labels of Φ to soft clauses in such a way that a removal of soft clause from F_Φ would emulate the operation of a removal of a corresponding label from Φ. This is done in the following way: for each $l_i \in Lbls(\Phi)$, create a new variable a_i. Then, for each labelled clause C^L create a *hard* clause $C \vee \bigvee_{l_i \in L}(\neg a_i)$. Finally, for each $l_i \in Lbls(\Phi)$, create a *soft* clause (a_i) with a weight equal to the weight of the label l_i.

Example 3. Let $\Phi = \{(\neg p)^{\emptyset}, (r)^{\emptyset}, (p \vee q)^{\{1\}}, (p \vee \neg q)^{\{1,2\}}, (p)^{\{2\}}, (\neg r)^{\{3\}}\}$, and assume that the weights of all labels are 1. Then, $F_\Phi = \{(\neg p, \top), (r, \top), (\neg a_1 \vee p \vee q, \top), (\neg a_1 \vee \neg a_2 \vee p \vee \neg q, \top), (\neg a_2 \vee p, \top), (\neg a_3 \vee \neg r, \top), (a_1, 1), (a_2, 1), (a_3, 1)\}$. Then, removal of $(a_2, 1)$ from the F_Φ leaves $\neg a_2$ pure, and so is equivalent to the removal of all hard clauses clauses that contain a_2, which in turn is equivalent to the removal of the label 2 from Φ.

It is then not difficult to see that any MaxSAT solution of F_Φ is a MaxSAT solution of Φ, and vice versa. The advantage of the indirect method is that any off-the-shelf MaxSAT solver can be turned into a MaxSAT solver for LCNFs. However, it also creates a level of indirection between the selector variables and the clauses they are used in. In our preliminary experiments the indirect method did not perform well.

4.2 Direct Computation

Core-guided MaxSAT algorithms are among the strongest algorithms for industrially-relevant MaxSAT problems. These algorithms iteratively invoke a SAT solver, and for each unsatisfiable outcome, *relax* the clauses that appear in the unsatisfiable core returned by the SAT solver. A clause C_i is *relaxed* by adding a literal r_i to C_i for a fresh *relaxation variable* r_i. Subsequently, a cardinality or a pseudo-Boolean constraint over the relaxation variables r_i is added to the set of the hard clauses of the formula. The exact mechanism is algorithm-dependent — we refer the reader to the recent survey of core-guided MaxSAT algorithms in [19].

The key idea that enables to adapt core-guided MaxSAT algorithms to the LCNF setting is that the "first-class citizen" in the context of LCNF is not a clause, but rather a *label*. In particular, the unsatisfiable core returned by a SAT solver has to be expressed in terms of the labels of the clauses that appear in the core. Furthermore, in the LCNF setting, it is the labels that get relaxed, and not the clauses directly. That is, when a label l_i is relaxed due to the fact that it appeared in an unsatisfiable core, the relaxation variable r_i is added to all clauses whose labelsets include l_i.

To illustrate the idea consider the pseudocode of a core-guided algorithm for solving partial MaxSAT problem due to Fu and Malik [11], presented in Figure 1. And, contrast it with the (unweighted) LCNF-based version of the algorithm, presented in Figure 2. The original algorithm invokes a SAT solver on the, initially input, formula F until the formula is satisfiable. For each unsatisfiable outcome, the soft clauses that appear in the unsatisfiable core $Core$ (assumed to be returned by the SAT solver) are relaxed (lines 5-7), and the CNF representation of the $equals1$ constraint on the sum of relaxation variables is added to the set of the hard clauses of F. The LCNF version of the algorithm proceeds similarly. The only two differences are as follows. When the LCNF formula Φ is unsatisfiable, the unsatisfiable core has to be expressed in terms of the labels, rather than clauses. That is, the algorithm expects to receive a set $L_{core} \subseteq Lbls(\Phi)$ such that $\Phi|_{L_{core}} \in \mathsf{UNSAT}$. Some of the possible ways to obtain such a set of *core labels* are described shortly. The second difference is that a fresh relaxation variable r_i is

Input : $F = F^H \cup F^S$ — a partial MaxSAT formula
Output: τ — a MaxSAT solution for F

1 **while** true **do**
2      $(\text{st}, \tau, Core) = \text{SAT}(F)$
3   **if** st = true **then return** τ
4      $R \leftarrow \emptyset$
      // relax soft clauses in $Core$
5   **foreach** $C_i \in Core \cap F^S$ **do**
6         $R \leftarrow R \cup \{r_i\}$
7   replace C_i with $(r_i \vee C_i)$
8      $F^H \leftarrow F^H \cup \text{CNF}(\sum_{r_i \in R} r_i = 1)$

Fig. 1. Fu and Malik algorithm for partial MaxSAT [11]

Input : Φ — an unweighted LCNF formula
Output: τ — a MaxSAT solution for Φ

1 **while** true **do**
2      $(\text{st}, \tau, L_{core}) = \text{SAT}(\Phi)$
3   **if** st = true **then return** τ
4      $R \leftarrow \emptyset$
      // relax labels in L_{core}
5   **foreach** $l_i \in L_{core}$ **do**
6         $R \leftarrow R \cup \{r_i\}$
7   **foreach** $C^L \in \Phi$ s.t. $l_i \in L$ **do**
8   replace C^L with $(r_i \vee C)^L$
9      $\Phi \leftarrow \Phi \cup \text{CNF}(\sum_{r_i \in R} r_i = 1)^{\emptyset}$

Fig. 2. (Unweighted) LCNF version of Fu and Malik algorithm

associated with each core label l_i, rather than with each clause as in the original algorithm. Each core label l_i is relaxed by replacing each clause C^L such that $l_i \in L$ with $(r_i \vee C)^L$ (lines 7-8). Note that in principle C^L may include more than one core label, and so may receive more than relaxation variable in each iteration of the algorithm. The nested loop on lines 5-8 of the algorithm can be replaced by a single loop iterating over all clauses C^L such that $L \cap L_{core} \neq \emptyset$. Finally, the clauses of the CNF representation of the *equals*1 constraint are labelled with $\emptyset$, and added to Φ.

One of the possible ways to obtain the set of core labels is to use a standard core-producing SAT solver. One can use either a proof-tracing SAT solver, such as PicoSAT [5], that extracts the core from the trace, or an assumption-based SAT solver, that extracts the core from the final conflict clause. Then, to check the satisfiability of Φ, the clause-set $Cls(\Phi)$ of Φ is passed to a SAT solver, and given an unsatisfiable core $Core \subseteq Cls(\Phi)$, the set of core labels is obtained by taking a union of the labels of clauses that appear in $Core$. Regardless of the type of the SAT solver, the solver is invoked in *non-incremental* fashion, i.e. on each iteration of the main loop a new instance of a SAT solver is created, and the clauses $Cls(\Phi)$ are passed to it. It is worth to point out that the majority of SAT-based MaxSAT solvers use SAT solvers in such non-incremental fashion. Also, it is commonly accepted that proof-tracing SAT solvers are superior to the assumption-based in the MaxSAT setting, since a large number of assumption literals tend to slow down SAT solving, while, at the same time, the incremental features of assumption-based solvers are not used.

An alternative to the non-incremental use of SAT solvers in our setting is to take advantage of the incremental features of the assumption-based SAT solvers. While we already explained that labels in LCNFs can be seen naturally as selectors in the assumption-based incremental SAT, the tricky issue is to emulate the operation of relaxing a clause, i.e. adding one or more relaxation variables to it. The only option in the incremental SAT setting is to "remove" the original clause by adding a unit clause $(\neg s)$ to the SAT solver for some selector literal $\neg s$, and add a relaxed version of the clause instead. The key observation here is that since the labels are already represented by selector variables, we can use *these* selector variables to both to remove clauses and to keep track of the core labels. For this, each label $l_i \in Lbls(\Phi)$ is associated with a *sequence* of selector variables $a_i^0, a_i^1, a_i^2, \ldots$. At the beginning, just like in the reduction described in Section 4.1, for each C^L we load a clause $C' = C \vee \bigvee_{l_i \in L}(\neg a_i^0)$ into the SAT solver, and solve under assumptions $\{a_1^0, a_2^0, \ldots\}$. The selectors that appear in the final conflict clause of the SAT solver will map to the set of the core labels L_{core}. Assume now that a label $l_c \in L$ is a core label, i.e. the selector a_c^0 was in the final conflict clause. And, for simplicity, assume that l_c is the only core label in L. Now, to emulate the relaxation of the clause C', we first add a unit clause $(\neg a_c^0)$ to the SAT solver to "remove" C', and then add a clause $C'' = (C' \setminus \{\neg a_c^0\}) \cup \{r, \neg a_c^1\}$, where r is the relaxation variable associated with l_c in this iteration, and a_c^1 is a "new version" of a selector variable for l_c. If on some iteration a_c^1 appears in the final conflict clause, we will know that l_c is a core label that needs to be relaxed, add $(\neg a_c^1)$ to the SAT solver, and create yet another version a_c^2 of a selector variable for the label l_c. For MaxSAT algorithms that relax each clause at most once (e.g. WMSU3 and BCD2, cf. [19]), we only need two versions of selectors for each label.

Note that since, as explained in Section 3, MaxSAT problem for WCNF F can be recast as a MaxSAT problem for the associated LCNF Φ_F, the incremental-SAT based MaxSAT algorithms for LCNFs can be seen as incremental-SAT based MaxSAT algorithm for WCNFs — to our knowledge such algorithms have not been previously described in the literature. The main advantage of using the SAT solver incrementally, beside the saving from re-loading the whole formula in each iteration of a MaxSAT algorithm, is in the possible reuse of the learned clauses between the iterations. While many of the clauses learned from the soft clauses will not be reused (since they would also need to be relaxed, otherwise), the clauses learned from the hard clauses will. In our experiments (see next section) we did observe gains from incrementality on instances of weighted partial MaxSAT problem.

5 Experimental Evaluation

To evaluate the ideas discussed in this paper empirically, we implemented an LCNF-based version of the MaxSAT algorithm WMSU1 [11,1,18], which is an extension of Fu and Malik's algorithm discussed in Section 4.2 to the weighted partial MaxSAT case. Note that none of the important optimizations discussed in [18] were employed. The algorithm was implemented in both the non-incremental and the incremental settings, and was evaluated on the set of industrial benchmarks from the MaxSAT Evaluation 2013[9], a total of 1079 instances. The experiments were performed on an HPC cluster, with quad-core Intel Xeon E5450 3 GHz nodes with 32 GB of memory. All tools were run with a timeout of 1800 seconds and a memory limit of 4 GB per input instance.

In the experiments PicoSAT [5] and Lingeling [6] were used as the underlying SAT solvers. For (pure) MaxSAT benchmarks, we used PicoSAT (v. 935), while for partial and weighted partial MaxSAT instances we used PicoSAT (v. 954) — the difference

---
[9] http://maxsat.ia.udl.cat/

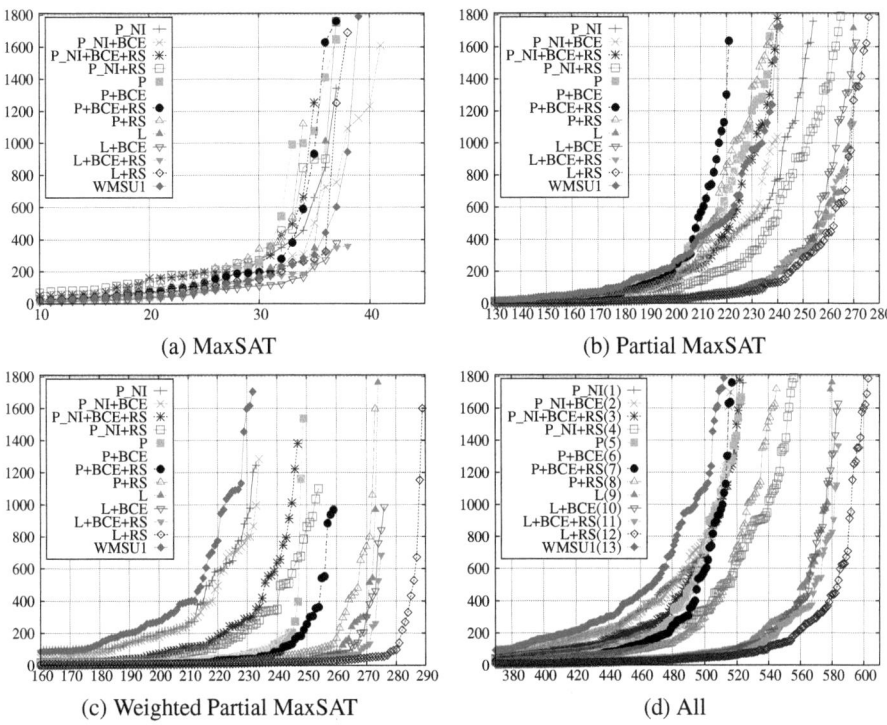

Fig. 3. Cactus plots for the different categories

between versions is due to better performance in the preliminary experiments. Both incremental (P) and non-incremental proof-tracing (P_NI) settings for PicoSAT were tested. For Lingeling (v. ala) the incremental mode (L) was tested.

For the preprocessing, we implemented our own version of Blocked Clause Elimination (BCE), while for Resolution and Subsumption (RS) both SatElite [8] and Lingeling [6] as a preprocessor were used. We have included in the experiments WMSU1 algorithm from MSUnCore [18] in order to establish a reasonable baseline.

Figure 3 shows the results for different classes of industrial MaxSAT instances, while Table 1 complements it by showing the number of solved instances by each configuration/solver, and the average CPU time taken on the solved instances. From the figure and the table, the following conclusions can be drawn. First, we note that the resolution and subsumption elimination based preprocessing (RS) is, in general, quite effective. In fact, for each of the solvers, within the same solver, the configuration that outperforms all others is RS, except for plain MaxSAT instances with PicoSAT. Also L+RS solves the highest number of instances overall, as revealed in Figure 3 (d). Regarding the blocked clause elimination (BCE), the technique is effective for plain MaxSAT instances, however not for other classes of instances. Notice that the combination of BCE+RS never improves over the best of the techniques considered separately, being only equal with Lingeling for (pure) MaxSAT instances.

Table 1. Table of solved instances and average CPU times

	All		MaxSAT		Partial MaxSAT		Weighted Partial MaxSAT	
	#Sol.	A.CPU	#Sol.	A.CPU	#Sol.	A.CPU	#Sol.	A.CPU
Instances	1079		55		627		397	
P_NI	524	144.29	37	172.76	254	152.04	233	131.32
P_NI+BCE	516	115.84	**41**	237.58	241	105.02	234	105.65
P_NI+BCE+RS	522	103.08	35	177.37	240	120.70	247	75.42
P_NI+RS	556	124.48	37	246.68	265	154.84	254	75.00
P	523	91.81	37	236.26	237	132.83	249	31.31
P+BCE	513	57.70	38	180.22	227	70.08	248	27.60
P+BCE+RS	517	67.61	37	209.48	221	85.36	259	32.19
P+RS	545	93.71	34	151.77	238	146.93	273	40.08
L	580	55.93	36	101.92	270	75.45	274	30.64
L+BCE	584	60.84	37	67.88	271	95.89	276	25.49
L+BCE+RS	584	48.03	38	96.02	271	73.90	275	15.90
L+RS	**603**	65.26	38	161.71	**276**	91.15	**289**	27.85
WMSU1	512	157.68	39	165.64	241	149.01	232	165.35

Somewhat surprisingly, our results suggest that, in contrast with standard practice (i.e. most MaxSAT solvers are based on non-incremental SAT), the incremental SAT solving can be effective for some classes of MaxSAT instances. Namely for Weighted Partial MaxSAT instances, where for example PicoSAT incremental (P) solves 16 more instances than PicoSAT non-incremental (P_NI) with a much lower average CPU time on the solved instances.

Finally, comparing the underlying SAT solvers used, it can be seen that in our experiments Lingeling performs significantly better than PicoSAT, which, as our additional experiments suggest, is in turn is much better SAT solver than Minisat [9], for MaxSAT problems.

6 Conclusion

In this paper we investigate the issue of sound application of SAT preprocessing techniques for solving the MaxSAT problem. To our knowledge, this is the first work that addresses this question directly. We showed that monotone clause elimination procedures, such as BCE, can be applied soundly on the input formula. We also showed that the resolution and subsumption elimination based techniques can be applied, although indirectly, through the labelled-CNF framework. Our experimental results suggest that BCE can be effective on (plain) MaxSAT problems, and that the LCNF-based resolution and subsumption elimination leads to performance boost in partial and weighted partial MaxSAT setting. Additionally, we touched on an issue of the incremental use of assumption-based SAT solvers in the MaxSAT setting, and showed encouraging results on weighted partial MaxSAT problems. In the future work we intend to investigate issues related to the sound application of additional SAT preprocessing techniques.

Acknowledgements. We thank the anonymous referees for their comments and suggestions.

References

1. Ansótegui, C., Bonet, M.L., Levy, J.: Solving (weighted) partial maxsat through satisfiability testing. In: Kullmann, O. (ed.) SAT 2009. LNCS, vol. 5584, pp. 427–440. Springer, Heidelberg (2009)
2. Belov, A., Järvisalo, M., Marques-Silva, J.: Formula preprocessing in MUS extraction. In: Piterman, N., Smolka, S.A. (eds.) TACAS 2013 (ETAPS 2013). LNCS, vol. 7795, pp. 108–123. Springer, Heidelberg (2013)
3. Belov, A., Marques-Silva, J.: Generalizing redundancy in propositional logic: Foundations and hitting sets duality. CoRR, abs/1207.1257 (2012)
4. Belov, A., Morgado, A., Marques-Silva, J.: SAT-based preprocessing for MaxSAT (extended version). CoRR, abs/1310.2298 (2013)
5. Biere, A.: Picosat essentials. JSAT 4(2-4), 75–97 (2008)
6. Biere, A.: Lingeling, Plingeling, PicoSAT and PrecoSAT at SAT Race 2010. FMV Report Series Technical Report 10/1, Johannes Kepler University, Linz, Austria (2010)
7. Bonet, M.L., Levy, J., Manyà, F.: Resolution for Max-SAT. Artif. Intell. 171(8-9), 606–618 (2007)
8. Eén, N., Biere, A.: Effective preprocessing in SAT through variable and clause elimination. In: Bacchus, F., Walsh, T. (eds.) SAT 2005. LNCS, vol. 3569, pp. 61–75. Springer, Heidelberg (2005)
9. Eén, N., Sörensson, N.: An extensible sat-solver. In: Giunchiglia, E., Tacchella, A. (eds.) SAT 2003. LNCS, vol. 2919, pp. 502–518. Springer, Heidelberg (2004)
10. Eén, N., Sörensson, N.: Temporal induction by incremental SAT solving. Electr. Notes Theor. Comput. Sci. 89(4), 543–560 (2003)
11. Fu, Z., Malik, S.: On solving the partial max-sat problem. In: Biere, A., Gomes, C.P. (eds.) SAT 2006. LNCS, vol. 4121, pp. 252–265. Springer, Heidelberg (2006)
12. Heule, M., Järvisalo, M., Biere, A.: Covered clause elimination. In: LPAR Short Paper (2010)
13. Järvisalo, M., Biere, A.: Reconstructing solutions after blocked clause elimination. In: Strichman, O., Szeider, S. (eds.) SAT 2010. LNCS, vol. 6175, pp. 340–345. Springer, Heidelberg (2010)
14. Järvisalo, M., Biere, A., Heule, M.: Blocked clause elimination. In: Esparza, J., Majumdar, R. (eds.) TACAS 2010. LNCS, vol. 6015, pp. 129–144. Springer, Heidelberg (2010)
15. Kullmann, O.: On a generalization of extended resolution. Discrete Applied Mathematics 96-97, 149–176 (1999)
16. Kullmann, O., Lynce, I., Marques-Silva, J.: Categorisation of clauses in conjunctive normal forms: Minimally unsatisfiable sub-clause-sets and the lean kernel. In: Biere, A., Gomes, C.P. (eds.) SAT 2006. LNCS, vol. 4121, pp. 22–35. Springer, Heidelberg (2006)
17. Li, C.M., Manya, F.: MaxSAT, hard and soft constraints. In: Biere, A., Heule, M., van Maaren, H., Walsh, T. (eds.) Handbook of Satisfiability. Frontiers in Artificial Intelligence and Applications, vol. 185, pp. 613–631. IOS Press (2009)
18. Manquinho, V., Marques-Silva, J., Planes, J.: Algorithms for weighted boolean optimization. In: Kullmann, O. (ed.) SAT 2009. LNCS, vol. 5584, pp. 495–508. Springer, Heidelberg (2009)
19. Morgado, A., Heras, F., Liffiton, M., Planes, J., Marques-Silva, J.: Iterative and core-guided MaxSAT solving: A survey and assessment. Constraints (2013)
20. Reiter, R.: A theory of diagnosis from first principles. Artif. Intell. 32(1), 57–95 (1987)

Dynamic and Static Symmetry Breaking in Answer Set Programming

Belaïd Benhamou[1,2,*]

[1] Aix-Marseille Université
Laboratoire des Sciences de l'Information et des Systèmes (LSIS)
Domaine universitaire de Saint Jérôme, Avenue Escadrille Normandie Niemen, 13397
MARSEILLE Cedex 20
[2] Centre de Recherche en Informatique de Lens (CRIL)
Université d'Artois, Rue Jean Souvraz, SP 18 F 62307 Lens Cedex
`belaid.benhamou@univ-amu.fr`

Abstract. Many research works had been done in order to define a semantics for logic programs. The well know is the stable model semantics which selects for each program one of its canonical models. The stable models of a logic program are in a certain sens the minimal Herbrand models of its *reduct* programs. On the other hand, the notion of symmetry elimination had been widely studied in constraint programming and shown to be useful to increase the efficiency of the associated solvers. However symmetry in non monotonic reasoning still not well studied in general. For instance Answer Set Programming (ASP) is a very known framework but only few recent works on symmetry breaking are known in this domain. Ignoring symmetry breaking in the answer set systems could make them doing redundant work and lose on their efficiency. Here we study the notion of *local* and *global* symmetry in the framework of answer set programming. We show how *local symmetries* of a logic program can be detected dynamically by means of the automorphisms of its graph representation. We also give some properties that allow to eliminate theses symmetries in SAT-based answer set solvers and show how to integrate this symmetry elimination in these methods in order to enhance their efficiency.

Keywords: symmetry, logic programming, stable model semantics, answer set programming, non-monotonic reasoning.

1 Introduction

The work we propose here to investigate the notion of symmetry in Answer Set Programming (ASP). The (ASP) framework can be considered as a sub-framework of the default logic [37]. One of the main questions in ASP, is to define a semantics to logic programs. A logic program π is a set of first order (formulas) rules of the form $r : concl(r) \leftarrow prem(r)$, where $prem(r)$ is the set of premises of the rule given as a conjunction of literals that could contain negations and negations as failure. The right part $concl(r)$ is the conclusion of the rule r which is generally, a single atom,

---

[*] Actually, I am at CRIL for one year CNRS delagtion position.

or in some cases a disjunction of atoms for logic programs with disjunctions. Some researchers considered $prem(r)$ as the *body* of the rule r and $concl(r)$ as its *head* ($r : head(r) \leftarrow body(r)$). Each logic program π is translated into its equivalent ground logic program $ground(\pi)$ by replacing each rule containing variables by all its ground instances, so that each literal in $ground(\pi)$ is ground. This technique is used to eliminate the variables even when the program contains function symbols and its Herbrand universe is infinite. Among the influential semantics that had been given for these logic programs with negation and negation as failure are the completion semantics [15] and the stable model or the answer set semantics [25]. It is well know that each answer set for a logic program is a model of its completion, but the converse, is in general not true. Fages in his paper [21] showed that both semantics are equivalent for free loops logic programs that are called tight programs. A generalization of Fage's results to logic programs with eventual nested expressions in the bodies of their rules was given in [20]. On the other hand Fangzhen Lin and Yutin Zhao proposed in [31] to add what they called *loop formulas* to the completion of a logic program and showed that the set of models of the extended completion is identical to the program's answer sets even when the program is not tight.

On the other hand, symmetry is by definition a multidisciplinary concept. It appears in many fields ranging from mathematics to Artificial Intelligence, chemistry and physics. It reveals different forms and uses, even inside the same field. In general, it returns to a transformation, which leaves invariant (does not modify its fundamental structure and/or its properties) an object (a figure, a molecule, a physical system, a formula or a constraints network...). For instance, rotating a chessboard up to 180 degrees gives a board that is indistinguishable from the original one. Symmetry is a fundamental property that can be used to study these various objects, to finely analyze these complex systems or to reduce the computational complexity when dealing with combinatorial problems.

As far as we know, the principle of symmetry has been first introduced by Krishnamurthy [29] to improve resolution in propositional logic. Symmetries for Boolean constraints are studied in depth in [5,6]. The authors showed how to detect them and proved that their exploitation is a real improvement for several automated deduction algorithms efficiency. Since that, many research works on symmetry appeared. For instance, the static approach used by James Crawford et al. in [16] for propositional logic theories consists in adding constraints expressing global symmetry of the problem. This technique has been improved in [1] and extended to 0-1 Integer Logic Programming in [2]. The notion of interchangeability in Constraint Satisfaction Problems (CSPs) is introduced in [22] and find a good exploitation in [27], and symmetry for CSPs is studied earlier in [36,4].

Within the framework of the Artificial Intelligence, an important paradigm is to take into account incomplete information (uncertain information, revisable information...). Contrary to the mode of reasoning formalized by a conventional or a classical logic, a result deducible from information (from a knowledge, or from beliefs) is not true but only probable in the sense that it can be invalidated further, and can be revised when adding new information.

To manage the problem of exceptions, several logical approaches in Artificial Intelligence had been introduced. Many non-monotonic formalisms were presented since about thirty years. But, the notion of symmetry within this framework was not well studied. The principle of symmetry had been extended recently in [8,9,11] to non-monotonic reasoning. Symmetry had been defined and studied for three known non-monotonic logics: the preferential logic [13,14,12,28], the X-logic [38] and the default logic [38]. More recently, global symmetry had been studied for the Answer Set Programming framework [18,19]. In the same spirit as what it is done in [16,1,2] for the satisfiability problem, the authors of [18,19] showed how to break the global symmetry statically in a pre-processing phase for the ASP system Clasp[24]. They did that by adding symmetry breaking predicates to the considered logic program. They showed that global symmetry elimination in Clasp improves dramatically its efficiency on several problems. In this work, we investigate dynamic *local symmetry* detection and elimination and static *global symmetry* exploitation in SAT-based answer set programming systems. *Local symmetry* is the symmetry that we can discover at each node of the search tree during search. *Global symmetry* is the particular local symmetry corresponding to the root of the search tree (the symmetry of the initial problem). Almost all of the known works on symmetry are on global symmetry. Only few works on local symmetry [5,6,7,10] are known in the literature. Local symmetry breaking remains a big challenge. As far as we know, local symmetry is not studied yet in ASP.

The rest of the paper is structured as follows: in Section 2, we give some necessary background on answer set programming and permutations. We study the notion of symmetry for answer set programming in Section 3. In Section 4 we show how local symmetry can be detected by means of graph automorphism. We show how both global and local symmetry can be eliminated in Section 5. Section 6 shows how local symmetry elimination is implemented in a SAT-based answer set programming Method. Section 7 investigates the first implementation and experiments. We give a conclusion in Section 8.

2 Background

We summarize in this section some background on both the answer set programming framework and permutation theory.

2.1 Answer Set Programming

A ground general logic program π is a set of rules of the form $r : L_0 \leftarrow L_1, L_2, \ldots, L_m,$ $not L_{m+1}, \ldots, not L_n$, ($0 \leq m < n$) where L_i ($0 \leq i \leq n$) are atoms, and *not* is the symbol expressing negation as failure. The positive body of r is denoted by $body^+(r) = \{L_1, L_2, \ldots, L_m\}$, and the negative body by $body^-(r) = \{L_{m+1}, \ldots, L_n\}$. The word *general* expresses the fact that the rules are more general than Horn clauses, since they contain negations as failure. The sub-rule $r^+ : L_0 \leftarrow L_1, L_2, \ldots, L_m$ expresses the positive projection of the rule r. Intuitively the rule r means "*If we can prove all of* $\{L_1, L_2, \ldots, L_m\}$ *and we can not prove all of* $\{L_{m+1}, \ldots, L_n\}$, *then we deduce* L_0". Given a set of atoms A, we say that a rule r is applicable (active) in A if

$body^+(r) \subseteq A$ and $body^-(r) \cap A = \emptyset$. The reduct of the program π with respect to a given set A of atoms is the positive program π^A where we delete each rule containing an expression $not L_i$ in its negative body such that $L_i \in A$ and where we delete the other expressions $not L_i$ in the bodies of the other rules. More precisely, $\pi^A = \{r^+/r \in \pi, body^-(r) \cap A = \emptyset\}$. The most known semantics for general logic programs is the one of stable models defined in [25] which could be seen as an improvement of the negation as failure of Prolog. A set of atoms A is a stable model (an answer set) of π if and only if A is identical to the minimal Herbrand model of π^A which is called its canonical model (denoted by $CM(\pi^A)$). That is, if only if $A = CM(\pi^A)$. The stable model semantics is based on the closed world assumption, an atom that is not in the stable model A is considered to be false.

An extended logic program is a set of rules as the ones given for general programs which could contain classical negation. The atoms L_i could appear in both positive and negative parity. In other words, the atoms L_i become literals. A logic program is said to be disjunctive when at least one of its rules contains a disjunction of literals in its head part. In the sequel, we will use indifferently the words stable model and answer set to designate a stable model of a general logic program.

2.2 Permutations

Let $\Omega = \{1, 2, \ldots, N\}$ for some integer N, where each integer might represent a propositional variable or an atom. A permutation of Ω is a bijective mapping σ from Ω to Ω that is usually represented as a product of cycles of permutations. We denote by $Perm(\Omega)$ the set of all permutations of Ω and $\circ$ the composition of the permutation of $Perm(\Omega)$. The pair $(Perm(\Omega), \circ)$ forms the permutation group of Ω. That is, $\circ$ is closed and associative, the inverse of a permutation is a permutation and the identity permutation is a neutral element. A pair $(T, \circ)$ forms a sub-group of $(S, \circ)$ iff T is a subset of S and forms a group under the operation $\circ$.

The orbit $\omega^{Perm(\Omega)}$ of an element ω of Ω on which the group $Perm(\Omega)$ acts is $\omega^{Perm(\Omega)} = \{\omega^\sigma : \omega^\sigma = \sigma(\omega), \sigma \in Perm(\Omega)\}$.

A generating set of the group $Perm(\Omega)$ is a subset Gen of $Perm(\Omega)$ such that each element of $Perm(\Omega)$ can be written as a composition of elements of Gen. We write $Perm(\Omega) = <Gen>$. An element of Gen is called a generator. The orbit of $\omega \in \Omega$ can be computed by using only the set of generators Gen.

3 Symmetry in Logic Programs

Since Krishnamurthy's [29] symmetry definition and the one given in [5,6] in propositional logic, several other definitions are given in the CP community.

We will define in the following both semantic and syntactic symmetries in answer set programming and show their relationship. In the sequel π could be the logic program or its completion [15] $Comp(\pi)$, the symmetry definitions and properties remain valuable.

Definition 1. *(semantic symmetry of the logic program)* Let π be a logic program and L_π its complete [1] set of literals. A semantic symmetry of π is a permutation σ defined on L_π such that π and $\sigma(\pi)$ have the same answer sets.

Definition 2. *(semantic symmetry of the completion)* Let $Comp(\pi)$ be the Clark completion of a logic program π and $L_{Comp(\pi)}$ its complete [2] set of literals. A semantic symmetry of $Comp(\pi)$ is a permutation σ defined on $L_{Comp(\pi)}$ such that $Comp(\pi)$ and $\sigma(Comp(\pi))$ have the same answer sets.

In other words a semantic symmetry is a literal permutation that conserves the set of answer sets of the logic program π. We adapt in the following the definition of syntactic symmetry given in [5,6] for satisfiability to logic programs.

Definition 3. *(syntactic symmetry of the logic program)* Let π be a logic program and L_π its complete set of literals. A syntactic symmetry of π is a permutation σ defined on L_π such that the following conditions hold:

1. $\forall \ell \in L_\pi, \sigma(\neg \ell) = \neg \sigma(\ell)$,
2. $\forall \ell \in L_\pi, \sigma(not\, \ell) = not\{\sigma(\ell)\}$,
3. $\sigma(\pi) = \pi$

Definition 4. *(syntactic symmetry of the completion)* Let $Comp(\pi)$ be a logic program and $L_{Comp(\pi)}$ its complete set of literals. A syntactic symmetry of $Comp(\pi)$ is a permutation σ defined on $L_{Comp(\pi)}$ such that the following conditions hold:

1. $\forall \ell \in L_\pi, \sigma(\neg \ell) = \neg \sigma(\ell)$,
2. $\sigma(Comp(\pi)) = Comp(\pi)$

In other words, a syntactical symmetry of a logic program or its completion is a literal permutation that leaves the logic program or the completion invariant. If we denote by $Perm(L_\pi)$ the group of permutations of L_π and by $Sym(L_\pi) \subset Perm(L_\pi)$ the subset of permutations of L_π that are the syntactic symmetries of π, then $Sym(L_\pi)$ is trivially a sub-group of $Perm(L_\pi)$.

Theorem 1. *Each syntactical symmetry of a logic program π is a semantic symmetry of π.*

Proof. It is trivial to see that a syntactic symmetry of a logic program π is always a semantic symmetry of π. Indeed, if σ is a syntactic symmetry of π, then $\sigma(\pi) = \pi$, thus it results that π and $\sigma(\pi)$ have the same set of answer sets.

In a similar way, we can prove the following theorem:

Theorem 2. *Each syntactical symmetry of the completion $Comp(\pi)$ is a semantic symmetry of $Comp(\pi)$.*

---

[1] The set of literals containing each literal of π and its negation as failure.
[2] The set of literals containing each literal of $Comp(\pi)$ and its negation.

Example 1. consider the logic program $\pi = \{d \leftarrow; c \leftarrow; b \leftarrow c, nota; a \leftarrow d, notb\}$ and the permutation $\sigma=(a,b)(c,d)(nota,notb)$ defined on the complete set L_π of literals occurring in π. We can see that σ is a syntactic symmetry of π ($\sigma(\pi)=\pi$).

Remark 1. The converse of each of the previous theorems is not true. That is, it is not true that a semantic symmetry is always a syntactical symmetry.

Now, we give an important property which establishes a relationship between the symmetries of a logic program and its completion.

Proposition 1. *Each syntactical symmetry of a logic program π is a semantic symmetry of its completion $Comp(\pi)$.*

Proof. Let σ be a syntactical symmetry of the program π and I a model of $Comp(\pi)$ which is an answer set of π. We have to prove that $\sigma(I)$ is also a model of $Comp(\pi)$ which is an answer set of π. The permutation σ is a syntactical symmetry of π, thus by Theorem 1 we deduce that σ is also a semantic symmetry of π. It results that $\sigma(I)$ is also an answer set of π. Since each model of a logic program π is also a model of its Clark completion, it follows that $\sigma(I)$ is a model of $Comp(\pi)$ which is in fact an answer set of π.

Remark 2. The previous proposition allows to use the syntactical symmetries of a logic program π in its Clark completion $Comp(\pi)$ in order to detect symmetrical answer sets of π. This gives an important alternative for symmetry detection in SAT-based ASP systems that use the the Clark completion. Indeed, we can just calculate the symmetries of the logic program π instead of calculating those of its completion. This could accelerate the symmetry detection as the size of the program π is generally substantially smaller than the size of its completion.

In the sequel we give some symmetry properties only in the case of logic programs π, but the considered properties are also valid in the case of the completion $Comp(\pi)$.

Definition 5. *Two literals ℓ and ℓ' of a logic π are symmetrical if there exists a symmetry σ of π such that $\sigma(\ell) = \ell'$.*

Definition 6. *Let π be a logic program, the orbit of a literal $\ell \in L_\pi$ on which the group of symmetries $Sym(L_\pi)$ acts is $\ell^{Sym(L_\pi)}=\{\sigma(\ell) : \sigma \in Sym(L_\pi)\}$*

Remark 3. All the literals in the orbit of a literal ℓ are symmetrical two by two.

Example 2. In Example 1, the orbit of the literal a is $a^{Sym(L_\pi)}= \{a,b\}$, the orbit of the literal c is $c^{Sym(L_\pi)}= \{c,d\}$ and the one of the literal $nota$ is $nota^{Sym(L_\pi)}= \{nota, notb\}$ All the literals of a same orbit are all symmetrical.

If I is an answer set of π and σ a syntactic symmetry, we can get another answer set of π by applying σ on the literals which appear in I. Formally we get the following property.

Proposition 2. *I is an answer set of π iff $\sigma(I)$ is an answer set of π.*

Proof. Suppose that I is an answer set of π, then I is a minimal Herbrand model of the reduct π^I. It follows that $\sigma(I)$ is a minimal model of $\sigma(\pi)^{\sigma(I)}$. We can then deduce that $\sigma(I)$ is a minimal model of $\pi^{\sigma(I)}$ since π is invariant under σ. We conclude that $\sigma(I)$ is an answer set of π. The converse can be shown by considering the converse permutation of σ.

For instance, in Example 1 there are two symmetrical answer sets for the logic program π. The fist one is $I = \{d, c, a\}$ and the second is $\sigma(I) = \{d, c, b\}$. These are what we call symmetrical answer sets of π. A symmetry σ transforms each answer set into an answer set and each no-good (not an answer set) into a no-good.

Theorem 3. *Let ℓ and ℓ' be two literals of π that are in the same orbit with respect to the symmetry group $Sym(L_\pi)$, then ℓ participates in an answer set of π iff ℓ' participates in an answer set of π.*

Proof. If ℓ is in the same orbit as ℓ' then it is symmetrical with ℓ' in π. Thus, there exists a symmetry σ of π such that $\sigma(\ell) = \ell'$. If I is an answer set of π then $\sigma(I)$ is also an answer set of $\sigma(\pi) = \pi$, besides if $\ell \in I$ then $\ell' \in \sigma(I)$ which is also an answer set of π. For the converse, consider $\ell = \sigma^{-1}(\ell')$, and make a similar proof.

Corollary 1. *Let ℓ be a literal of π, if ℓ does not participate in any answer set of π, then each literal $\ell' \in orbit^\ell = \ell^{Sym(L_\pi)}$ does not participate in any answer set of π.*

Proof. The proof is a direct consequence of Theorem 3

Corollary 1 expresses an important property that we will use to break local symmetry at each node of the search tree of a SAT-based answer set procedure. That is, if a nogood is detected after assigning the value True to the current literal ℓ, then we compute the orbit of ℓ and assign the value false to each literal in it, since by symmetry the value true will not lead to any answer set of the logic program.

For instance, consider the program of Example 1, and the partial interpretation $I = \{a, b, c\}$ where c is the current literal under assignment. It is trivial that I is not a stable model of the program. By corollary 1, we can deduce that the set $I' = \{a, b, d\}$ is not a stable model of the program too. Indeed, I' is obtained by replacing the current literal c in I by its symmetrical literal d. I is a no-good and by symmetry (without duplication of effort) we infer that I' is a no-good.

4 Symmetry Detection

The most known technique to detect syntactic symmetries for CNF formulas in satisfiability is the one consisting in reducing the considered formula into a graph [16,3,2] whose the automorphism group is identical to the symmetry group of the original formula. We adapt the same approach here to detect the syntactic symmetries of the completion of a program π. That is, we represent the CNF formula corresponding to the completion ($Compl(\pi)$) of the logic program π by a graph G_π that we use to compute the symmetry group of π by means of its automorphism group. When this graph is built, we use a graph automorphism tool like Saucy [3], Nauty [32], AUTOM [35] or the one described in [33] to compute its automorphism group which gives the symmetry group of $Comp(\pi)$. Following the technique used in [16,3,2] to represent CNF formulas, we summarize bellow the construction of the graph which represent the completion of the logic program π. Here we focus on the case of general logic programs, but the technique could be generalized to other classes of logic programs like extended logic programs or disjunctive logic programs. Given the completion of a general logic program π, the associated colored graph $G_\pi(V, E)$ of its completion is defined as follows:

- Each positive literal ℓ_i of $Compl(\pi)$ is represented by a vertex $\ell_i \in V$ of the color 1 in G_π. The negative literal $not\ell_i$ associated with ℓ_i is represented by a vertex $not\ell_i$ of color 1 in G_π. These two literal vertices are connected by an edge of E in the graph G_π.
- Each clause c_i of $Compl(\pi)$ is represented by a vertex $c_i \in V$ (a clause vertex) of color 2 in G_π. An edge connects this vertex c_i to each vertex representing one of its literals.

This technique could be extended to extended and disjunctive logic programs in a natural way.

This is different from the approach which uses a body-atom graph [18]. Since our study is oriented to SAT-based ASP using the completion, we do not need to manage an oriented body-atom graph.

An important property of the graph G_π is that it preserves the syntactic group of symmetries of $Compl(\pi)$. That is, the syntactic symmetry group of the logic program $Compl(\pi)$ is identical to the automorphism group of its graph representation G_π, thus we could use a graph automorphism system like Saucy on G_π to detect the syntactic symmetry group of $Comp(\pi)$. The graph automorphism system returns a set of generators Gen of the symmetry group from which we can deduce each symmetry of $Compl(\pi)$.

5 Symmetry Elimination

There are two ways to break symmetry. The first one is to deal with the global symmetry which is present in the formulation of the given problem. Global symmetry can be eliminated in a static way in a pre-processing phase of an answer set solver by just adding the symmetry predicates. For instance, a method for global symmetry elimination is introduced in [18] for the Clasp ASP system [24]. The second way is the elimination of local symmetry that could appear in the sub-problems corresponding to the different nodes of the search tree of an answer set solver. Global symmetry can be considered as the local symmetry corresponding to the root of the search tree.

Local symmetries have to be detected and eliminated dynamically at some decision node of the search tree. Dynamic symmetry detection in satisfiability had been studied in [5,6] where a local syntactic symmetry search method had been given. However, this method is not complete, it detects only one symmetry σ at each node of the search tree when failing in the assignment of the current literal ℓ. As an alternative to this incomplete symmetry search method, a complete method which uses the tool Saucy [3] had been introduced in [10] to detect and break all the syntactic local symmetries of a constraint satisfaction problem (CSP) [34] during search and local symmetry had been detected and eliminated dynamically in a SAT solver [7].

Consider the completion $Compl(\pi)$ of a logic program π, and a partial assignment I of a SAT-based answer set solver applied to $Compl(\pi)$. Suppose that ℓ is the current literal under assignment. The assignment I simplifies $Compl(\pi)$ into a sub-completion $Compl(\pi)_I$ which defines a state in the search space corresponding to the current node n_I of the search tree. The main idea is to maintain dynamically the graph G_{π_I} of the sub-completion $Compl(\pi)_I$ corresponding to the current node n_I, then color the graph G_{π_I} as shown in the previous section and compute its automorphism group $Aut(\pi_I)$. The sub-completion $Compl(\pi)_I$ can be viewed as the remaining sub-problem corresponding to the unsolved part. By applying an automorphism tool on this colored graph we can get the generator set Gen of the symmetry sub-group existing between literals from which we can compute the orbit of the current literal ℓ that we will use to make the symmetry cut.

After this, we use Corollary 1 to break dynamically the local symmetry and then prune search spaces of tree search answer set methods. Indeed, if the assignment of the current literal ℓ defined at a given node n_I of the search tree is shown to be a failure, then by symmetry, the assignment of each literal in the orbit of ℓ will result in a failure too. Therefore, the negated literal of each literal in the orbit of ℓ has to be assigned in the partial assignment I. Thus, we prune in the search tree, the sub-space which corresponds to the assignment of the literals of the orbit of ℓ. That is what we call the local symmetry cut.

6 Local Symmetry Exploitation in SAT-Based ASP Solvers

The solver ASSAT [31] has some drawbacks: it can compute only one answer set and the formula could blow-up in space. Taking into account these disadvantages of ASSAT and the fact that each answer set of a program π is a model of its completion $Compl(\pi)$, Guinchiglia et al. in [26] do not use SAT solvers as black boxes, but implemented a method which is based on the DLL [17] procedure and where they include a function which checks if a generated model is an answer set or not. This method had been implemented in the Cmodels-2 system [30] and has the following advantages: it performs the search on $Compl(\pi)$ without introducing any extra variable except those used by the clause transformation of $Compl(\pi)$, deals with tight and not tight programs, and works in a polynomial space. Global symmetry breaking do not need any extra-implementation, a SAT-based answer set solver is used as a black box on the completion of the logic program and the generated symmetry breaking predicates. More recently the ASP solvers like the conflict-driven Clasp solver [24] include some materials of modern SAT solvers such as: conflict analysis via the First UIP scheme, no-good recording and deletion, backjumping, restarts, conflict-driven decision heuristics, unit propagation via watched literals, equivalence reasoning and resolution-based pre-processing [23] have shown dramatic improvements in their efficiency and compete with the best SAT solvers.

We give in the following a DLL-based answer set method in which we implement dynamic local symmetry breaking. We used as a baseline method the DLL-based answer set procedure given in [26] to show the implementation of local symmetry eliminations (local symmetry cuts).

If I is an inconsistent partial interpretation in which the assignment of the value $true$ to the current literal ℓ is shown to be a no-good, then, all the literals in the orbit of ℓ computed by using the group $Sym(\pi_I)$ returned by the graph automorphism tool are symmetrical to ℓ. Thus, we assign the value false to each literal in $\ell^{Sym(L_\pi)}$ since the value true is shown to be contradictory, and then we prune the sub-space which corresponds to the value true assignments. The other case of local symmetry cut happen when the assignment I is shown to be a model of $Compl(\pi)$, but is not an answer set of π. In this case, the algorithm makes a backtracking on the last decision literal ℓ in I, then according to corollary 1 assigns the value false to each literal in the orbit $\ell^{Sym(L_\pi)}$ since the value true does not lead to an answer set of π. If $\Gamma = Compl(\pi)$, then the resulting procedure called DLLAnswerSet, is given in Figure 1.

Procedure DLLAnswerSet(Γ, I);
begin
    if $\Gamma = \emptyset$ **then return** $AnswerSetCheck(I, \pi)$
        else return False
    else if Γ contains the empty clause, **then return** False
        else
            if there exists a mono-literal or a monotone literal ℓ **then**
                return DLLAnswerSet($\Gamma_\ell, I \cup \{\ell\}$)
            begin
                Choose an unsigned literal ℓ of Γ
                Gen=AutomorphismTool(Γ_I);
                $\ell^{Sym(L_{\pi_I})}$=orbit(ℓ,Gen)=$\{\ell_1, \ell_2, ..., \ell_n\}$;
                return DLLAnswerSet($\Gamma_\ell, I \cup \{\ell\}$) **or**
                DLLAnswerSet($\Gamma_{\neg\ell \wedge \neg\ell_1 \wedge \neg\ell_2 \wedge ... \wedge \neg\ell_n}$,
                              $I \cup \{\neg\ell, \neg\ell_1, ..., \neg\ell_n\}$)
            end
end

Fig. 1. The DLL-based answer set procedure with local symmetry elimination

The function AutomorphismTool(π_I) is a call to the automorphism tool which return the set of generators in the variable GEN. The function $orbit(\ell, Gen)$ is elementary, it computes the orbit (the symmetrical literals) of the literal ℓ from the set of generators Gen returned by AutomorphismTool(π_I). The set Γ_ℓ is the set of clauses obtained from Γ by removing the clauses to which ℓ belongs, and by removing $\neg\ell$ from the other clauses of Γ.

The function $AnswerSetCheck(I, \pi)$ is also elementary:

- it computes the set $A = I \cap \{head(r) : r \in \pi\}$ of positive literals (atoms) in I and returns $True$ if A is an answer set or π, and
- return $False$, otherwise.

7 Experiments

Now we shall investigate the performances of our search techniques by experimental analysis. We choose for this first implementation the graph coloring problem to show the local symmetry behavior on answer sets search vs the global symmetry. Graph coloring problem is expressed naturally as a set of rules of a general problem. For more details, the reader can refer to the Lparse user's manual given on line on the Cmodels site (http://www.cs.utexas.edu/ tag/cmodels/). Here, we tested and compared on some random graph coloring instances two methods:

1. **Global-sym:** search with global symmetry breaking. This method uses in a pre-processing phase the program SHATTER [1,2] that detects and eliminates the global symmetries of the considered instance by adding to it symmetry breaking clauses, then apply the SAT based answer set solver defined in [26] to the resulting instance. The CPU time of *Global-sym* includes the time that SHATTER spends to compute the global symmetry. A disadvantage of this method is that it could significantly increase the size of the considered instance. Its advantage is that its implementation requires no modification of the solver.
2. **Local-sym:** search with local symmetry breaking. This method implements in the SAT based answer set solver defined in [26] the dynamic local symmetry detection and elimination strategy described in this work. The resulting method is depicted in figure 1 (the DLLAnswerSet procedure). The CPU time of *Local-sym* includes local symmetry search time. A disadvantage of this method is that it could significantly increase the time of execution in the case of instances which contain few local symmetries. Its advantage is that its application does not require any increase in the size of the instance, changing the solver is simple and it detects more symmetries.

The common baseline answer set search method for both previous methods is the one given in [26]. The complexity indicators are the number of nodes of the search tree and the CPU time. Both the time needed for computing local symmetry and global symmetry are added to the total CPU time of search. The source codes are written in C and compiled on a Pentium 4, 2.8 GHZ and 1 Gb of RAM.

7.1 The Results on the Graph Coloring Instances

Random graph coloring problems are generated with respect to the following parameters: (1) n : the number of vertices, (2) $Colors$: the number of colors and (3) d: the density which is a number between 0 and 1 expressed by the ratio : the number of constraints (the number of edges in the graph) to the number of all possible constraints (the number of possible edges in the graph). For each test corresponding to some fixed values of the parameters n, $Colors$ and d, a sample of 100 instances are randomly generated and the measures (CPU time, nodes) are taken on the average.

We reported in Figure 2 the practical results of the methods: *Global-sym*, and *Local-sym*, on the random graph coloring problem where the number of variables is $n = 30$ and where the density is ($d = 0.5$). The curves give the number of nodes respectively the CPU time with respect to the number of colors for each search method.

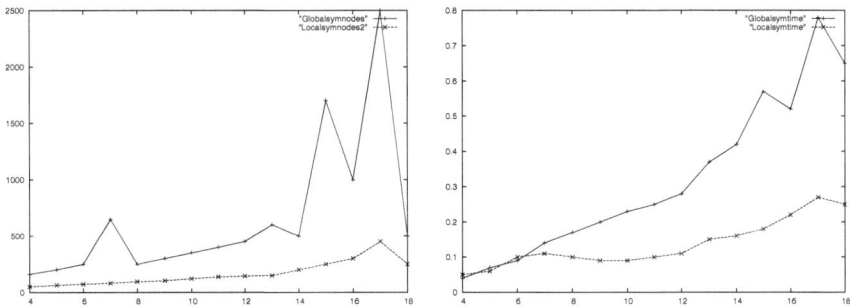

Fig. 2. Node and Time curves of the two symmetry methods on random graph coloring where $n = 30$ and $d = 0.5$

We can see on the node curves (the curves on the left of the figure) that *Local-sym* detects and eliminates more symmetries than the *Global-sym* method and *Global-sym* is not stable for graph coloring. From the CPU time curves (the curves on the right of the figure), we can see that *Local-sym* is in average faster than *Global-sym* even that Saucy is run at each contradictory decision node. Local symmetry elimination is profitable for solving random graph coloring instances and outperforms dramatically global symmetry breaking on these problems.

These are just our first results, our implementation and experiments are still in progress, we need to experiment much more and greater size instances than the ones presented here in order to further confirm the advantage of local symmetry breaking.

8 Conclusion

We studied in this work the notions of global and local symmetry for logic programs in the answer set programing framework . We showed how a logic program or its completion is represented by a colored graph that can be used to compute symmetries. The syntactic symmetry group of the completion is identical to the automorphism group of the corresponding graph. Graph automorphism tools like SAUCY can be naturally used on the obtained graph to detect the syntactic symmetries. Global symmetry is eliminated statically by adding in pre-processing phase the well known lex order symmetry breaking predicates to the program completion and applying as a black box a SAT-based answer set solver on this resulting encoding. We showed how local symmetry can be detected and eliminated dynamically during search. That is, the symmetries of each sub-problem defined at a given contradictory decision node of the search tree and which is derived from the initial problem by considering the partial assignment corresponding to that node. We showed that graph automorphism tools can be adapted to compute this local symmetry by maintaining dynamically the graph of the sub- program or the sub-completion defined at each node of the search tree. We proved some properties that allow us to make symmetry cuts that prune the search tree of a SAT-based answer set method. Finally, we showed how to implement these local symmetry cuts in a DLL-based answer set method.

The proposed local symmetry detection method is implemented and exploited in the tree search method $DLLAnswerSet$ to improve its efficiency. The first experimental results confirmed that local symmetry breaking is profitable for answer set solving and improves global symmetry breaking on the considered problems.

As a future work, we are looking to experiment other problems and combine both the global symmetry and local symmetry eliminations in a DLL-based answer set solver and compare the performances of the obtained methods to existing methods.

Another alternative of symmetry detection that we want to do in the future is to detect symmetries of the logic program by means of a body-atom graph, instead of those of its completion, then use Proposition 1 to make cuts in the search tree of the considered ASP solver. This could accelerated the symmetry detection then get a fastest solver.

We studied the notion of symmetry for the general logic programs, but the study could naturally be generalized for extended logic programs, disjunctive logic programs or other extensions. This is another important point that we are looking to investigate in future.

References

1. Aloul, F.A., Ramani, A., Markov, I.L., Sakallak, K.A.: Solving difficult sat instances in the presence of symmetry. In: DAC, pp. 1117–1137 (2003)
2. Aloul, F.A., Ramani, A., Markov, I.L., Sakallak, K.A.: Symmetry breaking for pseudo-boolean satisfiability. In: ASPDAC 2004, pp. 884–887 (2004)
3. Aloul, F.A., Ramani, A., Markov, I.L., Sakallah, K.A.: Solving difficult SAT instances in the presence of symmetry. In: The Proceedings of the 39th Design Automation Conference (DAC 2002), pp. 731–736. ACM Press (2002)
4. Benhamou, B.: Study of symmetry in constraint satisfaction problems. In: Borning, A. (ed.) PPCP 1994. LNCS, vol. 874, pp. 246–254. Springer, Heidelberg (1994)
5. Benhamou, B., Sais, L.: Theoretical study of symmetries in propositional calculus and application. In: Kapur, D. (ed.) CADE 1992. LNCS, vol. 607, pp. 281–294. Springer, Heidelberg (1992)
6. Benhamou, B., Sais, L.: Tractability through symmetries in propositional calculus. The Journal of Automated Reasoning 12, 89–102 (1994)
7. Benhamou, B., Nabhani, T., Ostrowski, R., Saïdi, M.R.: Dynamic symmetry detection and elimination in the satisfiability problem. In: Proceedings of the 16th International Conference on Logic for Programming, Artificial Intelligence, and Reasoning, LPAR-16, Dakar, Senegal, April 25-May 1 (2010)
8. Benhamou, B., Nabhani, T., Siegel, P.: Reasoning by symmetry in non-monotonic inference. In: The Proceedings of the International Conference on Machine and Web Intelligence (ICMWI 2010), Algiers, Algeria, pp. 264–269 (October 3, 2010)
9. Benhamou, B., Nabhani, T., Siegel, P.: Reasoning by symmetry in non-monotonic logics. In: 13th International Workshop on Non-Monotonic Reasoning (NMR 2010) (May 14, 2010)
10. Benhamou, B., Saïdi, M.R.: Local symmetry breaking during search in cSPs. In: Bessière, C. (ed.) CP 2007. LNCS, vol. 4741, pp. 195–209. Springer, Heidelberg (2007)
11. Benhamou, B., Siegel, P.: Symmetry and non-monotonic inference. In: The Proceedings of Symcon 2008, Sydney, Australia (September 2008)

12. Besnard, P., Siegel, P.: The preferential-models approach in nonmonotonic logics - in nonstandard logic for automated reasoning. In: Smets, P. (ed.) Academic Press, pp. 137–156 (1988)
13. Bossu, G., Siegel, P.: Nonmonotonic reasoning and databases. In: Advances in Database Theory, pp. 239–284 (1982)
14. Bossu, G., Siegel, P.: Saturation, nonmonotonic reasoning and the closed-world assumption. Artif. Intell. 25(1), 13–63 (1985)
15. Clark, K.: Negation as failure. In: Gallaire, H., Minker, J. (eds.) Logic and data bases, pp. 293–322 (1978)
16. Crawford, J., Ginsberg, M.L., Luck, E., Roy, A.: Symmetry-breaking predicates for search problems. In: KR 1996, pp. 148–159 (1996)
17. Davis, M., Logemann, G.W., Loveland, D.W.: A machine program for theorem proving. Journal of Communications of The ACM - CACM 5(7), 394–397 (1962)
18. Drescher, C., Tifrea, O., Walsh, T.: Symmetry-breaking answer set solving. AI Commun. 24(2), 177–194 (2011)
19. Drescher, C., Tifrea, O., Walsh, T.: Symmetry-breaking in answer set solving. In: ICLP 2010 Workshop ASPOCP 2010 (2010)
20. Erdem, E., Lifschitz, V.: Tight logic programs. Thoery and Practice of Logic Programming 3, 499–518 (2003)
21. Fages, F.: Consistency of Clark's completion and existence of stable models. Journal of Methods of Logic Programming in Computer Sciences 1, 51–60 (1994)
22. Freuder, E.: Eliminating interchangeable values in constraints satisfaction problems. In: AAAI 1991, pp. 227–233 (1991)
23. Gebser, M., Kaufmann, B., Neumann, A., Schaub, T.: Advanced pre-processing for answer set solving. In: Proceedings of the 18th European Conference on Artificial Intelligence, pp. 15–19. IOS Press, Amsterdam (2008)
24. Gebser, M., Kaufmann, B., Neumann, A., Schaub, T.: *clasp*: A conflict-driven answer set solver. In: Baral, C., Brewka, G., Schlipf, J. (eds.) LPNMR 2007. LNCS (LNAI), vol. 4483, pp. 260–265. Springer, Heidelberg (2007)
25. Gelfond, M., Lifschitz, V.: The stable model semantics for logic programming. In: Kawalski, R., Bowen, K. (eds.) Logic Programming: Fifth Int'l Conf. and Symp., pp. 1070–1080 (1988)
26. Giunchiglia, E., Lierler, Y., Maratea, M.: Sat-based answer set programming. In: 19th National Conference on Artificial Intelligence, July 25-29. AAAI, San Jose (2004)
27. Haselbck, A.: Exploiting interchangeabilies in constraint satisfaction problems. IJCAI 93, 282–289 (1993)
28. Kraus, S., Lehmann, D.J., Magidor, M.: Nonmonotonic reasoning, preferential models and cumulative logics. Artificial Intelligence 44(1-2), 167–207 (1990)
29. Krishnamurty, B.: Short proofs for tricky formulas. Acta Inf. (22), 253–275 (1985)
30. Lierler, Y., Maratea, M.: Cmodels-2: SAT-based answer set solver enhanced to non-tight programs. In: Lifschitz, V., Niemelä, I. (eds.) LPNMR 2004. LNCS (LNAI), vol. 2923, pp. 346–350. Springer, Heidelberg (2003)
31. Lin, F., Zhao, Y.: Assat: Computing answer sets of a logic program by sat solver. In: Proceedings of AAAI 2002 (2002)
32. McKay, B.: Practical graph isomorphism. Congr. Numer. 30, 45–87 (1981)
33. Mears, C., de la Banda, M.G., Wallace, M.: On implementing symmetry detection. In: Proceedings of SymCon 2006, pp. 1–8 (2006)
34. Montanari, U.: Networks of constraints: Fundamental properties and applications to picture processing. Information Science 7, 95–132 (1974)

35. Puget, J.-F.: Automatic detection of variable and value symmetries. In: van Beek, P. (ed.) CP 2005. LNCS, vol. 3709, pp. 475–489. Springer, Heidelberg (2005)
36. Puget, J.F.: On the satisfiability of symmetrical constrained satisfaction problems. In: Komorowski, J., Raś, Z.W. (eds.) ISMIS 1993. LNCS (LNAI), vol. 689, Springer, Heidelberg (1993)
37. Reiter, R.: A logic for default reasoning. Artificial Intelligence 13, 81–132 (1980)
38. Siegel, P., Forget, L., Risch, V.: Preferential logics are x-logics. Journal of Logic and Computation 11(1), 71–83 (2001)

HOL Based First-Order Modal Logic Provers*

Christoph Benzmüller[1] and Thomas Raths[2]

[1] Dep. of Mathematics and Computer Science, Freie Universität Berlin, Germany
[2] Institute for Computer Science, University of Potsdam, Germany

Abstract. First-order modal logics (FMLs) can be modeled as natural fragments of classical higher-order logic (HOL). The FMLtoHOL tool exploits this fact and it enables the application of off-the-shelf HOL provers and model finders for reasoning within FMLs. The tool bridges between the qmf-syntax for FML and the TPTP thf0-syntax for HOL. It currently supports logics K, K4, D, D4, T, S4, and S5 with respect to constant, varying and cumulative domain semantics. The approach is evaluated in combination with a meta-prover for HOL, which sequentially schedules various HOL reasoners. The resulting system is very competitive.

1 Introduction

First-order modal logics (FMLs) [7] have many applications and these applications motivate the use of automated theorem proving systems for FMLs. Until recently no (correct) ATP systems for FMLs were available.[1] However, good progress has been made in the last two years, and novel provers have recently been implemented and compared [1]. Among these systems is also an approach based on classical higher-order logic (HOL) [3,2]. This HOL approach, which is further improved and evaluated here, is the focus of this paper. The particular contributions include:

(A) The FMLtoHOL tool is presented, which converts problems in FML, formulated in qmf-syntax [13] (which extends the TPTP fol-syntax [15] with operators #box and #dia), into HOL problems in thf0-syntax [16].[2] FMLtoHOL implements a semantic embedding of constant domain FMLs in HOL [3]. The tool has been extended to also support varying and cumulative domains. FMLtoHOL turns any thf0-compliant HOL ATP system into a flexible ATP system for FMLs. At present FMLtoHOL supports modal logics from $L := \{K,K4,D,D4,T,S4,S5\}$. However, its extension to further normal FMLs is straightforward.

(B) The FMLtoHOL tool is exemplarily applied in combination with a meta-prover for HOL, called HOL-P in the remainder. This meta-prover exploits the

---

* Supported by the German Research Foundation (grants BE2501/9-1 & KR858/9-1).
[1] A pioneering prover is GQML [17]. However, GQML has been excluded in recent experiments (in [1] or here) since it returned incorrect results for several formulae.
[2] thf stands for *typed higher-order form* and it refers to family of syntax formats for higher-order logic. So far only the fully developed thf0 format, for simply typed lambda calculus, is in practical use.

SystemOnTPTP infrastructure [15] and sequentially schedules the HOL reasoners LEO-II [4], Satallax [6], Isabelle [10], agsyHOL [9] and Nitpick [5]. HOL-P is evaluated with respect to 580 benchmark problems in the QMLTP library [13]. As a side contribution a complete translation of the QMLTP library (for all logics in L, all different domain conditions, and both options as explained in (C)) into HOL (resp. thf0) is achieved, resulting in $7 \times 3 \times 2 \times 580 = 24360$ problems. The 3480 problems for logic S4 can be download from http://christoph-benzmueller.de/papers/THF-S4-ALL.zip; others can be requested by EMail.

(C) There are different options in the HOL approach for the modeling of logics in L. One is to state the conditions on the accessibility relation R associated with $\Box$ 'semantically', e.g., $\forall x \exists y Rxy$ expresses that R is serial. Exploiting quantification over booleans ($\forall^p$) (cf. [3]) the corresponding 'syntactical' axiom $\forall^p p (\Box p \Rightarrow \Diamond p)$ may instead be postulated. FMLtoHOL so far only supports the 'semantical' approach. A first evaluation of both options is provided in this paper. To enable this the semantical example problems have been converted into their syntactical counterparts by hand.

The structure of the paper is as follows: §2 outlines FML. §3 and §4 describe the theory and implementation of FMLtoHOL. §5 introduces prover HOL-P. Experiments are presented in §6, and §7 concludes the paper.

2 First-Order Modal Logic

The syntax of FML adopted in this paper is: $F, G ::= P(t_1, \ldots, t_n) \mid \neg F \mid F \wedge G \mid F \vee G \mid F \Rightarrow G \mid \Box F \mid \Diamond F \mid \forall x F \mid \exists x F$. The symbols P are n-ary ($n \geq 0$) relation constants which are applied to terms $t_1, \ldots, t_n$. The t_i ($0 \leq i \leq n$) are ordinary first-order terms and they may contain function and constant symbols. The usual precedence rules for logical constants are assumed. The formula E1 := $(\Diamond \exists x P f x \wedge \Box \forall y (\Diamond P y \Rightarrow Q y)) \Rightarrow \Diamond \exists z Q z$ is used as a running example.

Regarding semantics, a Kripke style semantics for FML is adopted [7]. In particular, it is assumed that constants and terms are denoting and rigid, i.e. they always pick an object and this pick is the same object in all worlds. Regarding the universe of discourse constant domain, varying domain and cumulative domain semantics are considered. With respect to these base choices the normal modal logics K, K4, K5, B, D, D4, T, S4, and S5 are studied.

3 Theory of FMLtoHOL

FMLtoHOL exploits the fact that Kripke structures can be elegantly embedded in HOL [3]: FML propositions F are associated with HOL terms F_ρ of predicate type $\rho := \iota \to o$. Type o denotes the set of truth values and type ι is associated with the domain of possible worlds. Thus, the application $(F_\rho w_\iota)$ corresponds to the evaluation of FML proposition F in world w. Consequently, validity is formalized as $vld_{\rho \to o} = \lambda F_\rho \forall w_\iota Fw$. Classical connectives like $\neg$ and $\vee$ are simply lifted to type ρ as follows: $\neg_{\rho \to \rho} = \lambda F_\rho \lambda w_\iota \neg Fw$ and $\vee_{\rho \to \rho \to \rho} =$

$\lambda F_\rho \lambda G_\rho \lambda w_\iota (Fw \vee Gw)$. $\Box$ is modeled as $\Box_{\rho \to \rho} = \lambda F_\rho \lambda w_\iota \forall v_\iota (\neg Rwv \vee Fv)$, where constant symbol $R_{\iota \to \rho}$ denotes the accessibility relation of the $\Box$-operator, which remains unconstrained in logic K. Further logical connectives are defined as usual: $\wedge = \lambda F_\rho \lambda G_\rho \neg(\neg F \vee \neg G)$, $\Rightarrow = \lambda F_\rho \lambda G_\rho (\neg F \vee G)$, $\Diamond = \lambda F_\rho \neg \Box \neg F$.

For individuals a further base type μ is reserved in HOL. Universal quantification $\forall x F$ is introduced as syntactic sugar for $\Pi \lambda x F$, where constant Π is defined as follows: $\Pi_{(\mu \to \rho) \to \rho} = \lambda H_{\mu \to \rho} \lambda w_\iota \forall x_\mu H x w$. For existential quantification, $\Sigma = \lambda H_{\mu \to \rho} \neg \Pi \lambda x_\iota \neg H x$ is introduced. $\exists x F$ is then syntactic sugar for $\Sigma \lambda x F$. n-ary relation symbols P, n-ary function symbols f and individual constants c in FML obtain types $\mu_1 \to \ldots \to \mu_n \to \rho$, $\mu_1 \to \ldots \to \mu_n \to \mu_{n+1}$ (both with $\mu_i = \mu$ for $0 \leq i \leq n+1$) and μ, respectively.

Moreover, universal quantification over propositional variables is added. Similar to above this can be done by introducing a constant Π^p. Π^p and Π are similar and only differ wrt the argument type: $\Pi^p_{(\rho \to \rho) \to \rho} = \lambda H_{\rho \to \rho} \lambda w_\iota \forall p_\rho H p w$. Again, $\forall^p p F$ is introduced as syntactic sugar for $\Pi^p \lambda p F$, etc.

For any FML formula F holds: F is a valid in modal logic K for constant domain semantics if and only if $vld\, F_\rho$ is valid in HOL for Henkin semantics. This correspondence provides the foundation for proof automation of FMLs with HOL-ATP systems. The correspondence is shown in [3].

To extend the above result for logic K to modal logics K4, K5, B, D, D4, T, S4, S5 etc., one may choose between a 'syntactical' and a 'semantical' approach: (**Semantical**) Axioms such as $\forall x R x x$ or $\forall x \forall y \forall z (R x y \wedge R y z \Rightarrow R x z)$ are postulated to ensure that accessibility relation R obeys certain restrictions, here reflexivity and transitivity. (**Syntactical**) Propositional quantification is exploited to postulate corresponding axioms such as $\forall^p p (\Box p \Rightarrow p)$ or $\forall^p p (\Box p \Rightarrow \Box \Box p)$. These axioms characterize R as reflexive and transitive. Similar axioms exist for other FMLs. Respective correspondences between semantical properties of R and respective syntactical axioms are well known.

Arbitrary normal modal logics extending K can be axiomatized this way. There are cases where only the semantical approach is applicable. For example, irreflexivity of accessibility relation R cannot be axiomatized in the syntactic approach. However, it can trivially be modeled in the semantic approach. In other cases the syntactical approach appears more suitable. Examples are non-Stahlquist formulas like the Löb axiom or the McKinsey formula, for which there are no corresponding first-order semantical conditions on R. Note, however, that the HOL approach is not restricted to first-order conditions on R.

The above approach realizes constant domain semantics. For varying domain semantics it is modified: (1) Π is defined as $\Pi = \lambda H_{\mu \to \rho} \lambda w_\iota \forall x_\mu (\texttt{exInW} x w \Rightarrow H x w)$, where relation $\texttt{exInW}_{\mu \to \iota \to o}$ (for 'exists in world') relates individuals with worlds. (2) The non-emptiness axiom $\forall w_\iota \exists x_\mu \texttt{exInW} x w$ for these individual domains is added. (3) For each individual constant symbol c an axiom $\forall w_\iota \texttt{exInW} c w$ is postulated; these axioms enforce the designation of c in the individual domain of each world w. Analogous designation axioms are added for function symbols. For cumulative domains the axiom $\forall x_\mu \forall v_\iota \forall w_\iota (\texttt{exInW} x v \wedge R v w \Rightarrow \texttt{exInW} x w)$

is additionally postulated. It states that the individual domains are increasing along accessibility relation R.

4   Implementation and Functionality of FMLtoHOL

FMLtoHOL is implemented as part of the TPTP2X tool [15], and it is included in the QMLTP—v1.1 package.[3] It is written in Prolog and it can be easily modified and extended.

The tool is invoked as

```
./tptp2X -f thf:<logic>:<domain> <qmf-file>
```

where `<logic>` ∈ {k,k4,d,d4,t,s4,s5} and `<domain>` ∈ {$const, vary, cumul$}.

Assume that file E1.qmf contains example problem E1 in qmf-syntax:

```
qmf(con,conjecture,
    ( ((#dia: ? [X] : p(f(X))) & (#box: ! [Y]: ((#dia: p(Y)) => q(Y))))
    => #dia: ? [Z] : q(Z) )).
```

The command './tptp2X -f thf:d:const E1.qmf' generates a corresponding HOL problem file E1.thf in thf0-syntax[4] [16] for constant domain logic D:

```
%----Include axioms for modal logic D under constant domains
include('Axioms/LCL013^0.ax.const').
include('Axioms/LCL013^2.ax').

%---------------------------------------------------------------
thf(q_type,type,( q: mu > $i > $o )).
thf(p_type,type,( p: mu > $i > $o )).
thf(f_type,type,(f: mu > mu )).

thf(con,conjecture, ( mvalid @
    ( mimplies @
      ( mand @
        ( mdia_d @ ( mexists_ind @ ^ [X: mu] : ( p @ ( f @ X ) ) ) ) @
        ( mbox_d @ ( mforall_ind @ ^ [Y: mu] :
            ( mimplies @ ( mdia_d @ ( p @ Y ) ) @ ( q @ Y ) ) ) ) ) @
      ( mdia_d @ ( mexists_ind @ ^ [Z: mu] : ( q @ Z ) ) ) ) )).
```

mimplies, mand, mbox_d, etc. should be read as 'modal-implies', 'modal-and', 'modal-box-d', respectively. The included axiom files contain the definitions of these connectives as outlined in §2. E.g., the definition for mforall_ind (which realizes Π for constant domain semantics) is given in LCL013^0.ax.const:

---
[3]   The   QMLTP   library   is   available   online   at http://www.iltp.de/qmltp/problems.html

[4] Some explanations: ^ is λ-abstraction and @ an (explicit) application operator. !, ?, ~, |, and => encode universal and existential quantification, negation, disjunction and implication in HOL. mu > $i > $o encodes the HOL type $\mu \to \iota \to o$. mimplies, mforall_ind, and mbox_d are embedded logical connectives as described in §2. Their denotation is fixed by adding definition axioms; see e.g. mforall_ind below.

```
thf(mforall_ind,definition,( mforall_ind =
    ( ^ [Phi: mu > $i > $o, W: $i] : ! [X: mu] : ( Phi @ X @ W ) ) )).
```

File `LCL013^2.ax` contains the definition of the serial □-operator in logic D:

```
thf(mbox_d,definition,( mbox_d =
    ( ^ [Phi: $i > $o,W: $i] :
      ! [V: $i] : ( ~ ( rel_d @ W @ V ) | ( Phi @ V ) ) ) )).

thf(a1,axiom,( mserial @ rel_d )).
```

Similar definitions are provided in the included axiom files for the other logical connectives and for auxiliary terms like `mserial`. For problem `E1.thf` Nitpick finds a countermodel in 8 seconds (when run with a 20s time limit).

When FMLtoHOL is called with option '`-f thf:s5:vary`' a modified file `E1.thf` is created containing a conjecture identical to above except that `mbox_d` is replaced by `mbox_s5` and `rel_d` by `rel_s5`. Moreover, `E1.thf` now includes different axiom files `LCL013^0.ax.vary` and `LCL013^6.ax`. The former contains a modified definition of `mforall_ind`, adds a non-emptiness axiom, and adds further axioms as required (cf. conditions (1)-(3) in §3). Axiom file `LCL013^6.ax` specifies `mbox_s5` as follows:

```
thf(mbox_s5,definition,( mbox_s5 =
    ( ^ [Phi: $i > $o,W: $i] :
      ! [V: $i] : ( ~ ( rel_s5 @ W @ V ) | ( Phi @ V ) ) ) )).

thf(a1,axiom,( mreflexive @ rel_s5 )).
thf(a2,axiom,( mtransitive @ rel_s5 )).
thf(a3,axiom,( msymmetric @ rel_s5 )).
```

The modified problem in file `E1.thf` is proved by Satallax and LEO-II within milliseconds.

The above explanations are all with respect to the adapted `tptp2X` command that comes with the QMLTP package. The included axiom files, like `LCL013^6.ax` etc., are also provided by this package, so that only the QMLTP package is required for installing the FMLtoHOL tool.

5 The Prover HOL-P

In the experiments the following HOL provers were applied: Satallax (2.6) [6], Isabelle (2012) [10], LEO-II [4] (1.5.0), Nitpick (2012) [5] and agsyHOL (1.0) [9]. Isabelle, Satallax, LEO-II and agsyHOL are theorem provers. Nitpick is a (counter-) model finder. Satallax, and to a lesser extend LEO-II, are also capable of finding countermodels. These systems work for Henkin semantics and they support the thf0-syntax as a common input language. Moreover, the SystemOnTPTP infrastructure [15] enables remote calls to instances of these provers at the University of Miami (running on 2.80GHz computers with 1GB memory). Exploiting these features, a simple shell script has been written that bundles these systems into a HOL meta-prover, called HOL-P in the remainder. HOL-P has been employed in the experiments. Using the SystemOnTPTP infrastructure the experiments below can be easily replicated.

6 Evaluation

The QMLTP library [13] is a benchmark library for testing and evaluating ATP systems for FML. It is similar to the TPTP library for classical logic [15] and the ILTP library for intuitionistic logic [14]. Version 1.1 of the QMLTP library includes 600 FML problems divided into 11 problem domains. The problems were taken from different applications, various textbooks, and Gödel's embedding of intuitionistic logic. It also includes 20 problems in multimodal logic. Only the HOL approach is applicable to them do date. Therefore these multimodal logic problems have not been included in our experiments.

HOL-P has been applied in several experiment runs to all 580 monomodal problems in the QMLTP library. The overall time limit of 600s for each problem was equally distributed over the five subprovers of HOL-P. Thus, each subprover was given a 120s time limit per problem. In each experiment run, a different setting with respect to the selected logic (here D and S4) and the domain condition (constant, cumulative, varying) was chosen. The results for HOL-P are presented in Table 1. Moreover, in Table 1 the performance of HOL-P is compared to corresponding results as reported on the QMLTP-website[5] for the provers f2p-MSPASS—3.0 (an instance-based prover which employs MSPASS [8] to prove or refute the propositional formulas it generates), MleanSeP—1.2 (a sequent prover; its calculus extends the classical sequent calculus with specific rules for □ and ◇), MleanTAP—1.3 (a tableaux prover; a classical tableaux calculus is extended by adding and employing prefixes to each formula), and MleanCoP—1.2 (a connection prover based on leanCoP [12,11]; again formula prefixes are employed). Previous results on the HOL provers LEO-II and Satallax (cf. [1]) have not been included in Table 1; they are now subsumed by HOL-P which is significantly stronger than both of them.

The HOL approach has the broadest coverage of logics and domain conditions (and, as mentioned before, it can easily be adapted to support further logics):

ATP system	supported modal logics	supported domain cond.
MleanSeP 1.2	K,K4,D,D4,T,S4	constant,cumulative
MleanTAP 1.3	D,T,S4,S5	constant,cumulative,varying
MleanCoP 1.2	D,T,S4,S5	constant,cumulative,varying
f2p-MSPASS 3.0	K,K4,K5,B,D,T,S4,S5	constant,cumulative
HOL-P	K,K4,K5,B,D,D4,T,S4,S5	constant,cumulative,varying

The experiments show that the HOL approach is very competitive. In particular, with respect to the accumulated numbers of solved problems in each category HOL-P has a slight lead (HOL-P solved 2225 problems, MleanCoP 2129). This

---
[5] Cf. http://www.iltp.de/qmltp/download/QMLTP-v1.1-comparison.txt

Table 1. No. of proved monomodal problems (for constant/cumulative/varying domain semantics, in this order) of the QMLTP library. All provers were run with a 600s time limit. In HOL-P a timeout of 120s was given to each subprover.

	MleanSeP	MleanTAP	f2p-MSPASS	MleanCoP	HOL-P
Logic D: constant/cumulative/varying domains					
Theorem	135/130/–	134/120/100	076/079/–	**217/200/170**	208/184/163
Non-Thm	001/004/–	004/004/004	107/108/–	209/204/243	**250/269/295**
Solved	136/134/–	138/124/104	183/187/–	426/424/413	**458/453/458**
Logic S4: constant/cumulative/varying domains					
Theorem	197/197/–	220/205/169	111/121/–	**352/338/274**	300/278/245
Non-Thm	001/004/–	004/004/004	036/041/–	082/094/119	**132/146/184**
Solved	198/201/–	224/209/173	147/162/–	**434/432**/393	432/424/**429**

Table 2. No. of monomodal problems in the QMLTP library proved or refuted by HOL-P. The timeout was set to 600s. 60s was given to each subprover of HOL-P; each subprover was applied to both the semantical (sem) and the syntactical (syn) variant.

Logic S4	constant domains all (sem/syn)	cumulative domains all (sem/syn)	varying domains all (sem/syn)
Theorem	295 (294/282)	267 (265/256)	241 (238/233)
Non-Theorem	132 (132/132)	146 (146/145)	186 (185/185)
Solved	427 (426/414)	413 (411/401)	427 (423/418)

is due to the excellent performance of the (counter-)model finder Nitpick (which fully subsumes Satallax in the Non-Theorem-category of the experiments and beats MleanCoP by quite a margin). In both categories, Theorems and Non-Theorems, HOL-P solved many problems whose QMLTP status was 'Unsolved'. In terms of theorem proving performance MleanCoP is still the leading system, but its margin of lead over the HOL approach has further decreased (cf. the previous results reported in [1]).

In Table 1 HOL-P has been applied in combination with the semantical encoding of accessibility conditions only. An obvious idea, however, is to test both the semantical and the syntactical encoding. For studying the potential impact of this idea we have conducted further experiments (so far only for S4) in which HOL-P was applied to both versions. Since the overall time limit of 600s per problem was kept, each HOL-P subprover was now given a 60s time limit per problem. Table 2 presents the results of the modified experiment for S4. The first and second numbers in brackets indicate how many problems were solved by the semantical (sem) and the syntactical (syn) approach respectively.

In the Theorem-category the semantical approach performs better. No significant difference can be observed in Non-Theorem-category. The comparison of the overall performance results from Table 2 with those for S4 in Table 1 indi-

Table 3. Individual performances of the subprovers of HOL-P in the Theorem-category with respect to the experiments in Table 2. Results are presented for constant domain (const), cumulative domain (cum) and varying domain (vary) semantics.

Logic S4 Theorem	Isabelle const/cum/vary	LEO-II const/cum/vary	agsyHOL const/cum/vary	Satallax const/cum/vary
syn	177/126/120	213/187/163	231/192/171	**244/233/207**
sem	252/215/192	227/203/183	247/206/183	**257/239/214**
total	1082	1176	1230	1394

Table 4. Individual performances of the subprovers of HOL-P in the Non-Theorem-category with respect to the experiments in Table 2

Logic S4 Non-Theorem	Satallax const/cum/vary	Nitpick const/cum/vary
syn	0/0/0	**132/145/185**
sem	48/56/68	**132/146/185**
total	172	925

cates the following: It makes more sense to run HOL-P in the semantical mode only than to split the time resources and to run HOL-P in both modi (however, what has not been studied yet is the performance of HOL-P when both axiom versions are simply added to one the same problem file).

The individual performances of the subprovers of HOL-P with respect to the experiments in Table 2 are also interesting. They are presented in Table 3. Satallax is the strongest prover in the Theorem-category both in the syntactical and the semantical mode. The weak performance of Isabelle in the syntactic mode is surprising, in particular, since Isabelle has performed strong in recent CASC competitions.

In the Non-Theorem-category Nitpick performs significantly stronger than Satallax. The other HOL-P subprovers didn't solve any problems in this category. Interestingly, Nitpick shows nearly equal performance in both the syntactical and the semantical mode, while Satallax solves problems in this category in the semantical mode only.

As a side-result of our experiments we detected some syntax issues in QMLTP problems which were undetected so far: Identifiers for axioms and conjectures were reused; according to TPTP conventions this is not allowed. Examples include 'substitution_of_equivalents', 'reflexivity' and 'transitivity'. These issues were solved manually in the generated thf0-files.

7 Summary and Outlook

The FMLtoHOL tool enables the application of higher-order automated theorem provers and model finders for solving FML problems encoded in the new qmf-syntax. The tool has been evaluated in combination with the higher-order meta-prover HOL-P on the QMLTP library. The experiments show that the HOL approach to automate FMLs is very competitive. Regarding the combined performance (no. of proved or refuted problems) the HOL approach performed best.

Future work includes optimizations and extensions of HOL-P and FMLtoHOL.

Acknowledgments. We thank Jens Otten, Geoff Sutcliffe, Chad Brown and Jasmin Blanchette for valuable contributions to this work. We also thank the unknown reviewers for several useful comments. The work presented in this paper has been supported by the German Research Foundation DFG under grants BE2501/9-1 and KR858/9-1.

References

1. Benzmüller, C., Otten, J., Raths, T.: Implementing and evaluating provers for first-order modal logics. In: Proc. of ECAI 2012, Montpellier, France (2012)
2. Benzmüller, C., Paulson, L.: Exploring Properties of Normal Multimodal Logics in Simple Type Theory with LEO-II. In: Reasoning in Simple Type Theory: Festschrift in Honour of Peter B. Andrews. Studies in Logic, Mathematical Logic and Foundations, vol. 17, pp. 401–422. College Publications (2008)
3. Benzmüller, C., Paulson, L.C.: Quantified multimodal logics in simple type theory. Logica Universalis (Special Issue on Multimodal Logics) 7(1), 7–20 (2013)
4. Benzmüller, C., Paulson, L.C., Theiss, F., Fietzke, A.: LEO-II - a cooperative automatic theorem prover for higher-order logic. In: Armando, A., Baumgartner, P., Dowek, G. (eds.) IJCAR 2008. LNCS (LNAI), vol. 5195, pp. 162–170. Springer, Heidelberg (2008)
5. Blanchette, J.C., Nipkow, T.: Nitpick: A counterexample generator for higher-order logic based on a relational model finder. In: Kaufmann, M., Paulson, L.C. (eds.) ITP 2010. LNCS, vol. 6172, pp. 131–146. Springer, Heidelberg (2010)
6. Brown, C.E.: Satallax: An automated higher-order prover. In: Gramlich, B., Miller, D., Sattler, U. (eds.) IJCAR 2012. LNCS (LNAI), vol. 7364, pp. 111–117. Springer, Heidelberg (2012)
7. Fitting, M., Mendelsohn, R.L.: First-Order Modal Logic. Kluwer (1998)
8. Hustadt, U., Schmidt, R.: MSPASS: Modal Reasoning by Translation and First-Order Resolution. In: Dyckhoff, R. (ed.) TABLEAUX 2000. LNCS (LNAI), vol. 1847, pp. 67–71. Springer, Heidelberg (2000)
9. Lindblad, F.: agsyHol (2012), https://github.com/frelindb/agsyHOL
10. Nipkow, T., Paulson, L.C., Wenzel, M.T.: Isabelle/HOL. LNCS, vol. 2283. Springer, Heidelberg (2002)
11. Otten, J.: leancop 2.0 and ileancop 1.2: High performance lean theorem proving in classical and intuitionistic logic (system descriptions). In: Armando, A., Baumgartner, P., Dowek, G. (eds.) IJCAR 2008. LNCS (LNAI), vol. 5195, pp. 283–291. Springer, Heidelberg (2008)
12. Otten, J.: Implementing connection calculi for first-order modal logics. In: Schulz, S., Ternovska, E., Korovin, K. (eds.) Intl. WS on the Implementation of Logics (2012)

13. Raths, T., Otten, J.: The QMLTP problem library for first-order modal logics. In: Gramlich, B., Miller, D., Sattler, U. (eds.) IJCAR 2012. LNCS (LNAI), vol. 7364, pp. 454–461. Springer, Heidelberg (2012)
14. Raths, T., Otten, J., Kreitz, C.: The ILTP Problem Library for Intuitionistic Logic - Release v1.1. Journal of Automated Reasoning 38(1-2), 261–271 (2007)
15. Sutcliffe, G.: The TPTP problem library and associated infrastructure. Journal of Automated Reasoning 43(4), 337–362 (2009)
16. Sutcliffe, G., Benzmüller, C.: Automated reasoning in higher-order logic using the TPTP THF infrastructure. Journal of Formalized Reasoning 3(1), 1–27 (2010)
17. Thion, V., Cerrito, S., Cialdea Mayer, M.: A general theorem prover for quantified modal logics. In: Egly, U., Fermüller, C. (eds.) TABLEAUX 2002. LNCS (LNAI), vol. 2381, pp. 266–280. Springer, Heidelberg (2002)

Resourceful Reachability as HORN-LA

Josh Berdine, Nikolaj Bjørner, Samin Ishtiaq,
Jael E. Kriener, and Christoph M. Wintersteiger

Microsoft Research, University of Kent

Abstract. The program verification tool SLAYER uses abstractions during analysis and relies on a solver for reachability to refine spurious counterexamples. In this context, we extract a reachability benchmark suite and evaluate methods for encoding reachability properties with heaps using Horn clauses over linear arithmetic. The benchmarks are particularly challenging and we describe and evaluate pre-processing transformations that are shown to have significant effect.

1 Introduction

When a proof attempt by a static analyzer or model checker fails, an abstract counterexample is commonly produced. The counterexample does not necessarily correspond to a real bug because the analyzer's abstraction could be too coarse. Here we describe and evaluate new techniques to check concrete feasibility of abstract counterexamples produced as failed memory safety proofs by SLAYER, a separation logic–based shape analyzer [3]. The problem addressed in this paper is a particular instance of the more general one of state reachability in "resourceful" abstract transition systems, where the state space is theoretically unbounded, and changes over time, due to behavior such as dynamic allocation of memory.

This poses challenges to reachability tools along two dimensions: scaling search for long counter-examples, and encoding state transformations for heaps in a scalable way. Previous work [2] developed an encoding using bit-vectors and quantifiers and used bounded model checking (BMC). Fig. 1 illustrates that on a representative instance, unfortunately, it exhibits exponential slowdowns as the length of the explored path is increased. To further evaluate tradeoffs we extracted around 100 benchmarks from SLAYER that come from failed proof attempts in analysis of real-world C programs.

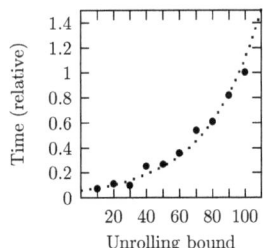

Fig. 1. Average solving time (Sat+Unsat), relative to the solving time of 100 unrollings

We encode reachability into logic as satisfiability of Horn clauses and use two backends of the Z3 SMT-solver for solving such clauses. The *PDR solver* handles Horn clauses over linear arithmetic (HORN-LA). It is compared with a solver based on BMC. (For details on the underlying semantics of the Horn-clause fragment and on the internals of the PDR solver, please see [7]).

Our main methodological contribution is encodings for resourceful reachability into Horn-LA. A basic encoding (§2.2) is refined (§2.3) to use a family of transition relations indexed by "worlds". These limit the state space based on the amount of memory allocated. This refinement allows the solver to explore smaller state spaces over fewer variables, constrained by smaller formulae. Our evaluation shows that this encoding helps the PDR solver on the hard instances, while causing visible overhead on the easy cases. The results (Fig. 6(b)) with the BMC solver are similar, but the overhead is significantly more detrimental. Additionally, we propose and evaluate (Fig. 5) two alternative approaches to shrinking heaps of error states. The evaluation of our methodology establishes that our PDR solver benefits critically from pre-processing transformations that we identify and evaluate (Fig. 7(a),7(b)). This paper is our first thorough experimental evaluation of [7] over arithmetical benchmarks.

2 Resourceful Transition System Reachability

Consider the faulty routine on the right. It contains a memory access error. SLAYER [3] can be used to find such errors. When SLAYER fails in its attempt to establish memory safety, it produces an abstract counterexample in the form of a *Resourceful Transition System* (RTS) – a transition system over states of some resource (memory, in our case). Fig. 2 is an RTS extracted from this example. An RTS is given by $\langle \mathbb{V}, \mathbb{E}, v_0, v_{err}, \nu, \rho \rangle$, where $\mathbb{V}$ and $\mathbb{E}$ are

```
1   void access_error()
2   {
3      int* x0, *x1;
4   
5      x1 = malloc(sizeof(int));
6      if (nondet()) {
7         x0 = malloc(sizeof(int));
8      }
9      while (nondet()) {
10        *x0 = 3;
11     }
12  }
```

sets of vertices and edges respectively, v_0 identifies the root and v_{err} the error vertex, ν labels vertices with states, and ρ labels edges with transition relations. The abstract counterexample is feasible if there is a path $v_0, e_0, v_1, e_1 \ldots, v_n, e_n, v_{err}$ such that the conjunction $\nu(v_0)(\mathbf{s}_0) \wedge \bigwedge \rho(e_i)(\mathbf{s}_i, \mathbf{s}_{i+1})$ is feasible.

2.1 Encoding Resources

To encode resourceful reachability into SMT we adapt a model where states are summarized as a predicate over a store and a heap. The store tracks the values of program variables, $\mathbb{X}$, and the heap tracks memory objects. This representation is given by a triple $(f, \boldsymbol{x}, \mathbf{a})$, where

- $f \in \mathbb{N}$ is a frontier counter, indicating the 'next' free address,
- $\boldsymbol{x} \in \mathbb{D}^{|\mathbb{X}|}$ is the store over values in $\mathbb{D}$ ($\mathbb{D}$ includes $\mathbb{N}$), and
- $\mathbf{a} \in Array\langle \mathbb{N}, \mathbb{B} \times \mathbb{N} \times \mathbb{D} \rangle$ is an array mapping addresses to triples encoding if the address is allocated, the size of the allocated object, and its value.

The state labeling ν is a relation over $(f, \boldsymbol{x}, \mathbf{a})$, where initially f is 0 and $\mathbf{a}$ maps all addresses to an un-allocated state. Similarly, ρ is a relation $\rho(e_i)(f, \boldsymbol{x}, \mathbf{a}, f', \boldsymbol{x}', \mathbf{a}')$.

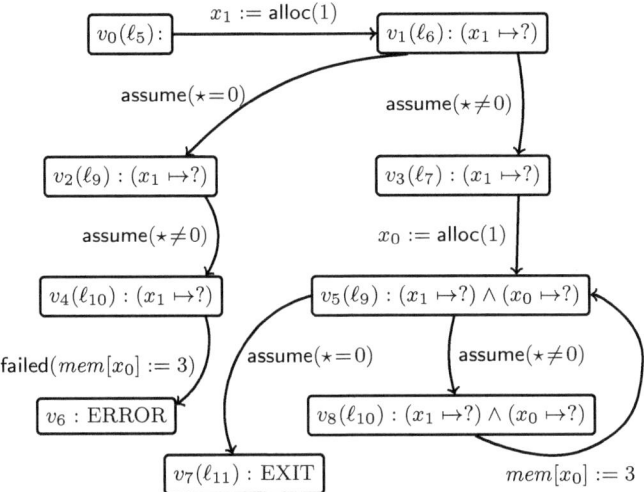

Fig. 2. failed attempt at proving safety for access_error

The unsuccessful transition corresponds to an update into an unallocated memory location, and is marked as failed. An encoding into Horn-LA requires eliminating arrays, so we flatten **a** into a finite tuple of triples. The (preset) size n of this tuple, which is the number of available memory locations and therefore the bound on the resource, plays a crucial role in deciding reachability.

2.2 Resourceful Reachability as SMT - Basic Encoding

Given an RTS $\langle \mathbb{V}, \mathbb{E}, v_0, v_{err}, \nu, \rho \rangle$, and a bound n, reachability can be modeled as a predicate $R(v, f, \boldsymbol{x}, \mathbf{a})$, where $v \in \mathbb{V}$ and $(f, \boldsymbol{x}, \mathbf{a})$ is a state as described above. R is defined by the following set of Horn clauses, where the schema in the second line is repeated for each $e_{ij} \in \mathbb{E}$ s.t. $e_{ij} = (v_i, v_j)$:

$$R(v_0, f, \boldsymbol{x}, \mathbf{a}) \leftarrow \nu(v_0)(f, \boldsymbol{x}, \mathbf{a})$$
$$R(v_j, f', \boldsymbol{x}', \mathbf{a}') \leftarrow R(v_i, f, \boldsymbol{x}, \mathbf{a}) \wedge \rho(e_{ij})(f, \boldsymbol{x}, \mathbf{a}, f', \boldsymbol{x}', \mathbf{a}') \wedge f' \leq n \quad (1)$$
$$\textit{false} \leftarrow R(v_{err}, f, \mathbf{x}, \mathbf{a})$$

The free variables $f, f', \boldsymbol{x}, \mathbf{a}, \boldsymbol{x}', \mathbf{a}'$ are implicitly universally quantified. Reachability corresponds to unsatisfiabilty of these Horn clauses:

Proposition 1 (Bounded Resource Reachability). *For an RTS, there is a feasible path from v_0 to v_{err} allocating at most n resources if and only if the clauses defined by (1) are unsatisfiable.*

Conversely, if the clauses are satisfiable, the error state is unreachable *within a resource of size n*. At this point we see why the bound is crucial: unreachability, i.e. safety, can be proven only relative to a given bound.

Example 1 (RTS encoding). Continuing our running example, below we show the clauses encoding the edges between v_0 and $v_{err} = v_6$ of the ATS in Fig. 2 over a space of four addresses, i.e. $n = 4$.

$$R(0, f, \boldsymbol{x}, \mathbf{a}) \leftarrow f = 0 \wedge \mathbf{a} = \underbrace{(\textit{false}, \_, \_), \ldots, (\textit{false}, \_, \_)}_{4} \quad \text{// initial state}$$

$$R(1, f', y, b) \leftarrow R(0, f, x, a) \land y = \langle x_0, f \rangle \qquad //v_0 \to v_1 : \text{alloc}(x_1, 1)$$
$$f' = f + 1 \land f' \leq 4$$
$$\land \bigwedge_{h=0}^{h<4} b[h] = \big(\text{if } h = f \text{ then } (\text{true}, 1, \_) \text{ else } a[i]\big)$$
$$R(2, f, x, a) \leftarrow R(1, f, x, a) \qquad //v_1 \to v_2 : \text{assume}(\text{nondet}() = 0)$$
$$R(4, f, x, a) \leftarrow R(2, f, x, a) \qquad //v_2 \to v_4 : \text{assume}(\text{nondet}() \neq 0)$$
$$R(6, f, x, a) \leftarrow R(4, f, x, a) \land a[x_0] = (\text{false}, \_, \_) \quad //v_4 \to v_6 : \text{unsuccessfull store}$$
$$\textit{false} \leftarrow R(6, f, x, a)$$

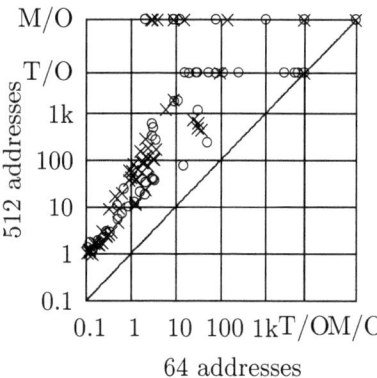

Fig. 3. Slowdown when n increases: BMC ×, PDR ∘

Observe that the value of n, which is fixed prior to encoding, has two effects on the relation R: First, it affects satisfiability of the Horn clauses. Second, it affects, and in fact dominates, the number of parameters of R, which is given by $1+|\mathbb{X}|+3n$. The problems this can cause are demonstrated by the example in Fig. 2. First, suppose the edge (v_0, v_1) was labeled with 'alloc$(x_1, 5)$', allocating 5 words rather than one word. In that case, the corresponding rule would contain a constraint equivalent to $f+5 \leq 4$, and as a result, v_{err} would become unreachable. However, given an $n \geq 5$ it would still be reachable. That is to say, underestimating the size of n required to reach v_{err} may result in a loss of completeness. Second, notice that none of $a[1]$, $a[2]$ nor $a[3]$ are required in a traversal from v_0 to v_{err} here. However, they all contribute to the resulting constraints and become part of the search space during solving. Fig. 3 shows that as n is increased, the runtime and memory-outs increase as well.

2.3 Encoding Reachability - Kripke Style

To reduce the cost of propagation over large predicates, we propose and evaluate a method that introduces a sequence of predicates of increasing arity. The aim is to search over low arity predicates first, and resort to larger arity predicates only when search in the lower arity predicates has been exhausted. If a counterexample trace exists that requires only a part of the available resource, finding it does not require assigning (irrelevant) values to the entire resource. This encoding is inspired by possible-world semantics of programming languages. The idea is that of Kripke models for intuitionistic logics where sets of possible worlds or facts grow monotonically.

The idea is to choose a chain $\mathcal{W} := w_0(= 0) < w_1 < \cdots < w_m = n$, of increasing sizes for the available resource $\mathbf{a}$. From $\mathcal{W}$ we encode a set of predicates $\{R_0, \ldots, R_m\}$, such that R_k has arity $1 + |\mathbb{X}| + 3w_k$. Analogously to the monotonically growing worlds in a Kripke-style program semantics, the predicates R_k

capture the set of reachable states with increasing precision. Each R_k is defined by clauses instantiating the second clause of (1), for each $e \in \mathbb{E}$, s.t. $e_{ij} = (v_i, v_j)$. The first clause of (1) is replaced by the single non-recursive clause, reflecting that initially no resource is allocated:

$$R_0(v_0, \boldsymbol{x}) \leftarrow \nu(v_0)$$

In addition, to allow the solver to access R_l from R_k for all $l > k$, 'world-changing clauses' are introduced at each step instantiating the following schema for all $k < l \le m$, where $|\mathbf{a}| = w_k$ and $|\mathbf{b}| = w_l$:

$$R_l(v_j, f', \boldsymbol{x}', \mathbf{b}') \leftarrow R_k(v_i, f, \boldsymbol{x}, \mathbf{a}) \\
\wedge \rho(e_{ij})(f, \boldsymbol{x}, \mathbf{b}, f', \boldsymbol{x}', \mathbf{b}') \wedge w_{l-1} < f' \le w_l \qquad (2) \\
\wedge \bigwedge_{h=0}^{h<w_l} \mathbf{b}[h] = \bigl(\text{if } h < w_k \text{ then } \mathbf{a}[h] \text{ else } (\text{false}, \_, \_)\bigr)$$

When changing worlds, first the current state of the smaller world $\mathbf{a}$ is 'copied' over to a 'fresh' larger one $\mathbf{b}$, in which the new elements are initialised to be free. In practice, this step is only required for transitions that may actually consume resource (alloc in SLAYER).

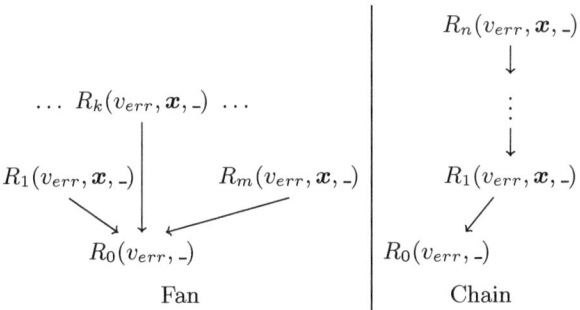

Fig. 4. Schemata for ways of connecting R_0 to R_k in a set of Kripke predicates

Since there are several predicates R_k in this encoding, v_{err} may be reachable in each of them. The purpose of this encoding is to explore smaller R_k before larger ones, hence we will pose the query in R_0 – $R_0(v_{err}, \boldsymbol{x})$ – and let the solver choose a larger one if neccessary. There are several ways of setting up that choice: we could either add m clauses of the form $R_0(v_{err}, \boldsymbol{x}) \leftarrow R_k(v_{err}, \boldsymbol{x}, \mathbf{a})$ (creating a *fan* into R_0, so to speak); or add a *chain* of clauses $R_k(v_{err}, \boldsymbol{x}, \mathbf{a}) \leftarrow R_{k+1}(v_{err}, \boldsymbol{x}, \mathbf{a}')$ for $0 \le k < m$ – see Fig. 4.

2.4 Evaluation

There are now several parameters to an encoding: the size of the maximum available resource n, the set $\mathcal{W}$ of increasing sizes of parts of the resource, and the choice between a fan and a chain of clauses for reaching $R_0(v_{err}, \boldsymbol{x})$.

We considered growing w_k with a linear increase and a log-step increase, i.e. each w_{k+1} is double the size of w_k and settled for the latter encoding for our evaluation. Fig. 5 also suggests that the fanning approach on large heap sizes is better overall, though remarkably chaining handles some hard instances not handled by fanning.

Reducing the sensitivity to the bound n on heap size exhibited by the previous encoding was the motivation for the encoding using Kripke transition relations. This aim is largely achieved when using the PDR backend, as shown in Fig. 6(a). The results show that solving problems encoded using Kripke relations with the PDR backend times out much less frequently, and solves many problems that time out with the single relation encoding.

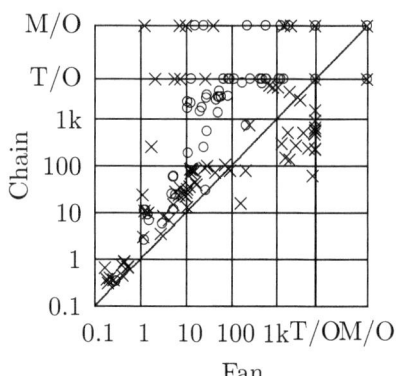

Fig. 5. Fan vs. Chain; PDR ×: 64, ○: 512 addresses

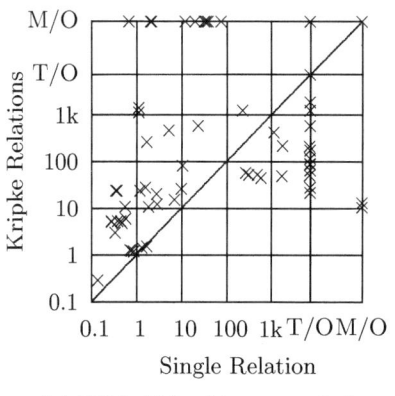

(a) PDR: 512 addresses - chain

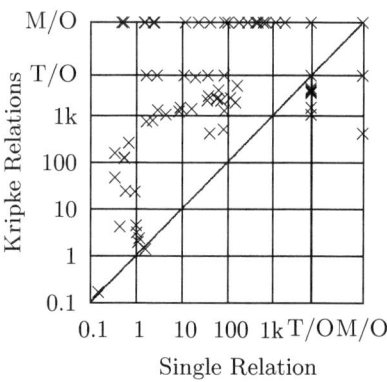

(b) BMC: 512 addresses

Fig. 6. Single vs Kripke Relations

The improvements can be quite dramatic, but the results also indicate that the Kripke predicates encoding imposes a considerable overhead, and a number of problems exhaust memory only with it. Overall, there is a clear improving trend from above to below the break-even line as problems get hard enough that less sensitivity to heap size dominates the overhead. We have observed this effect in both the chaining and the fanning approach.

As shown in Fig. 6(b), the Kripke predicates encoding is, on the other hand, detrimental to the BMC backend. This effect is independent of the chaining or fanning approach. The basic encoding solves many more problems than the Kripke encoding, only a few problems are solved only using the latter. This should not be surprising because BMC effectively causes the largest arity predicate to always be present in the constraints sent to the SMT solving backend.

3 Pre-processing Simplifications

We here evaluate pre-processing simplifications that are key to the performance of our Horn clause solvers. We summarize two transformations on a set of Horn clauses $\mathcal{C}$. The **Inline** transformation replaces two clauses by a single clause in a transformation of the form $\mathcal{C}, \ p(u) \leftarrow B_1 \wedge q(t), \ q(s) \leftarrow B_2 \implies \mathcal{C}, \ (p(u) \leftarrow B_1 \wedge B_2)\theta$, where the head predicate $q(s)$ unifies with $q(t)$ with the substitution θ and there are no other occurences of q in $\mathcal{C}$ that unifies with $q(s)$. The **Unfold** transformation generalizes inlining by replacing m clauses with q in the body and n clauses with q in the head and creating up to $m \times n$ new clauses. It corresponds to an iterative squarring transformation or a Davis Putnam resolution step. Figures 7(a),7(b) demonstrate the significant effect of the exhaustive application of these transformations on PDR and neutral effect on BMC.

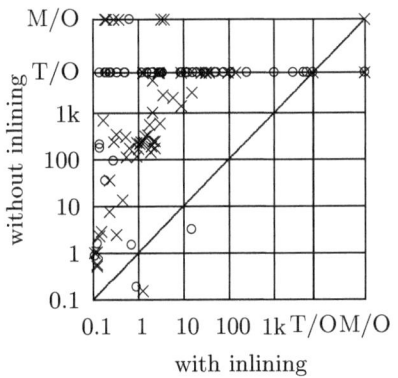
(a) Inlining improves performance for BMC and PDR: BMC: ×, PDR: ○

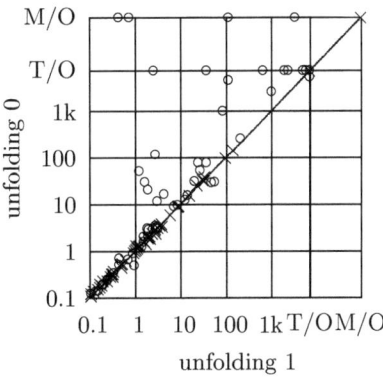
(b) Unfolding is good for PDR and doesn't break BMC: BMC: ×, PDR: ○

Fig. 7. Effects of Inline and Unfold transforms

4 PDR and BMC Backends

We have compared the two backend solvers on our benchmark suite. The results, shown in Fig. 8(a), show that there are instances where each solver succeeds while the other does not. On instances where both succeed, the BMC solver tends to spend less time than the PDR solver. For unsatisfiable instances, there is also a tendency for the BMC solver to succeed only on the very easy ones, while the PDR solver has more success. This effect is more clearly seen when considering smaller heap sizes, see Fig. 8(b). In this configuration we see that the PDR solver dominates for unsatisfiable instances, where the BMC solver usually exhausts resources; while for satisfiable instances, the BMC solver is faster.

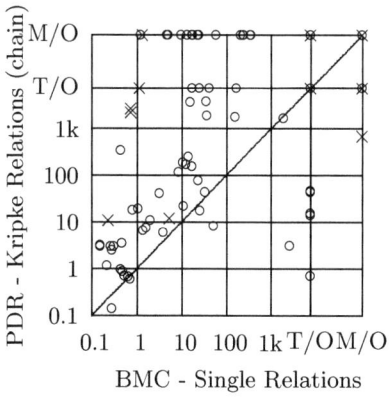 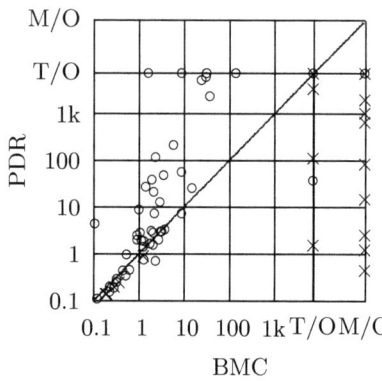

(a) BMC in simple encoding vs PDR in Kripke-style encoding - 256 addresses

(b) BMC vs PDR, both in the simple encoding - 64 addresses

Fig. 8. BMC vs PDR. Reachable ∘, Unreachable ×

5 Comparison with other Solvers

Horn Clause Solvers. Z3 is not the only SMT solver that can check satisfiability of Horn clauses over linear arithmetic. The HSF/QARMC tools [5] check satisfiability of Horn clauses over linear real arithmetic and the Eldarica tool [10] accepts Horn clauses over linear real and integer arithmetic. Furthermore, constraint logic programming systems, such as MAP [1], TRACER [8], and CHiAO [6] support different aspects of Horn clauses over arithmetic. To our knowledge, they don't yet work in a way compatible with the SMT-LIB benchmark suite.

HSF/QARMC solves Horn clauses where constraints are given as a conjunction of literals. It therefore relies on converting constraints in the bodies of Horn clauses into disjunctive normal form (DNF). Given the way memory is encoded in our benchmarks, the DNF transformation is infeasible and therefore the tool times out on all the problems we have produced.

Eldarica uses the SMT solver Princess [9] for handling arithmetical constraints and generating interpolants. It is able to handle Horn clauses with nested constraints and we include a comparison in Figure 9. First of all, we interpret the results to establish these benchmarks as highly challenging for current state-of-the-art Horn clause solvers. We also see the results as a testament to the significance of pre-processing that we described in Section 3.

Bounded Model Checking Tools. We have compared our implementation of BMC on Horn clauses against both the implementation reported in [2] and the well-established, well-tested model checking tool CBMC [4]. The first comparison, shown in Fig. 10(a), indicates that while our BMC backend sometimes outperforms that of [2], when the a priori unrolling depth is chosen well the latter

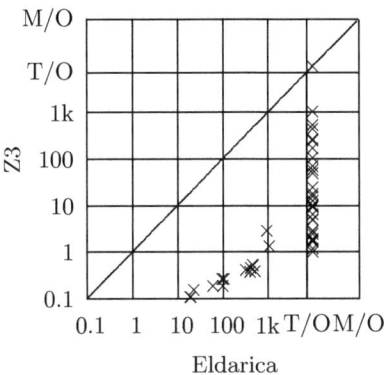
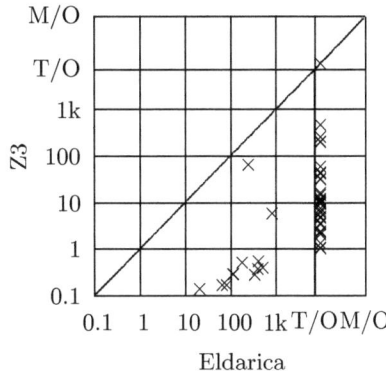

(a) Chaining Encoding (b) Fanning Encoding

Fig. 9. Eldarica vs. Z3

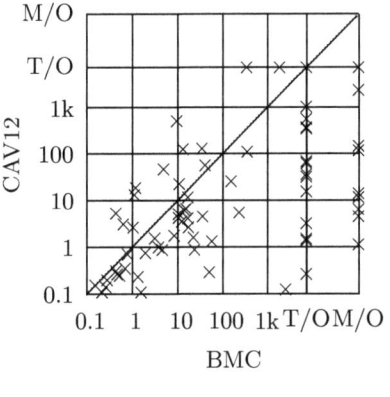
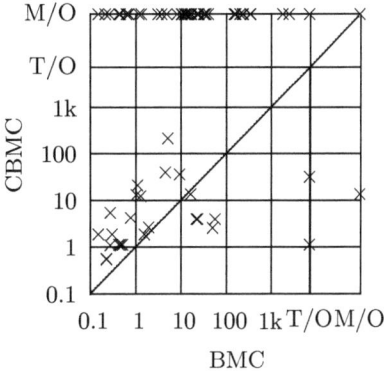

(a) BMC vs CAV12 (b) BMC vs CBMC

Fig. 10. BMC vs. CAV12 and CBMC

performs very well. At present, there is a meaningful price our method pays for the robustness with respect to choice of unrolling bound.

The results of the second comparison, shown in Fig. 10(b), demonstrate that our backend can compete with CBMC on instances of these problems, returning relatively quickly for numerous instances for which CBMC runs out of memory.

There is a significant caveat regarding these results though: our backends operate over the theory of linear real arithmetic, while the other two are over bit-vectors. The benchmarks themselves do not exercise the difference between these theories, so the same high-level problem is being solved here. So the currently best-performing solving method to establish unsafety/reachability is BMC and is based on quantified bit-vectors, while the main available method establishing safety is based on linear arithmetic.

6 Summary

We have presented encodings of resourceful reachability problems into HORN-LA and evaluated these using two engines BMC and PDR. PDR can solve for both reachability and unreachability, wheareas BMC can only determine reachability. We found that BMC is generally faster on the reachable cases, but given significant attention to encoding and pre-processing, our implementation of PDR performs adequately. The raw data from our experiments is available at: http://www.cs.kent.ac.uk/people/rpg/jek26/cex-data.zip.
The experimental data forms the basis of publicly available benchmarks:
https://svn.sosy-lab.org/software/sv-benchmarks/trunk/clauses/LIA/SLayerCF.

Acknowledgements. Matthew Parkinson and Nathan Chong for invaluable feedback on drafts.

References

1. De Angelis, E., Fioravanti, F., Pettorossi, A., Proietti, M.: Verifying programs via iterated specialization. In: PEPM (2013)
2. Berdine, J., Cox, A., Ishtiaq, S., Wintersteiger, C.M.: Diagnosing abstraction failure for separation logic-based analyses. In: Madhusudan, P., Seshia, S.A. (eds.) CAV 2012. LNCS, vol. 7358, pp. 155–173. Springer, Heidelberg (2012)
3. Berdine, J., Cook, B., Ishtiaq, S.: SLAyer: Memory safety for systems-level code. In: Gopalakrishnan, G., Qadeer, S. (eds.) CAV 2011. LNCS, vol. 6806, pp. 178–183. Springer, Heidelberg (2011)
4. Clarke, E., Kroning, D., Lerda, F.: A tool for checking ANSI-C programs. In: Jensen, K., Podelski, A. (eds.) TACAS 2004. LNCS, vol. 2988, pp. 168–176. Springer, Heidelberg (2004)
5. Grebenshchikov, S., Lopes, N.P., Popeea, C., Rybalchenko, A.: Synthesizing software verifiers from proof rules. In: PLDI (2012)
6. Hermenegildo, M.V., Bueno, F., Carro, M., López-García, P., Mera, E., Morales, J.F., Puebla, G.: An overview of Ciao and its design philosophy. TPLP 12(1-2), 219–252 (2012)
7. Hoder, K., Bjørner, N.: Generalized property directed reachability. In: Cimatti, A., Sebastiani, R. (eds.) SAT 2012. LNCS, vol. 7317, pp. 157–171. Springer, Heidelberg (2012)
8. Jaffar, J., Murali, V., Navas, J.A., Santosa, A.E.: TRACER: A symbolic execution tool for verification. In: Madhusudan, P., Seshia, S.A. (eds.) CAV 2012. LNCS, vol. 7358, pp. 758–766. Springer, Heidelberg (2012)
9. Rümmer, P.: A constraint sequent calculus for first-order logic with linear integer arithmetic. In: Cervesato, I., Veith, H., Voronkov, A. (eds.) LPAR 2008. LNCS (LNAI), vol. 5330, pp. 274–289. Springer, Heidelberg (2008)
10. Rümmer, P., Hojjat, H., Kuncak, V.: Disjunctive interpolants for Horn-clause verification. In: Sharygina, N., Veith, H. (eds.) CAV 2013. LNCS, vol. 8044, pp. 347–363. Springer, Heidelberg (2013)

A Seligman-Style Tableau System

Patrick Blackburn[1], Thomas Bolander[2],
Torben Braüner[1], and Klaus Frovin Jørgensen[1]

[1] Roskilde University
[2] The Technical University of Denmark

Abstract. Proof systems for hybrid logic typically use @-operators to access information hidden behind modalities; this labeling approach lies at the heart of most resolution, natural deduction, and tableau systems for hybrid logic. But there is another, less well-known approach, which we have come to believe is conceptually clearer. We call this Seligman-style inference, as it was first introduced and explored by Jerry Seligman in the setting of natural deduction and sequent calculus in the late 1990s. The purpose of this paper is to introduce a Seligman-style tableau system.

The most obvious feature of Seligman-style systems is that they work with arbitrary formulas, not just formulas prefixed by @-operators. To achieve this in a tableau system, we introduce a rule called GoTo which allows us to "jump to a named world" on a tableau branch, thereby creating a local proof context (which we call a *block*) on that branch. To the surprise of some of the authors (who have worked extensively on developing the labeling approach) Seligman-style inference is often clearer: not only is the approach more modular, individual proofs can be more direct. We briefly discuss termination and extensions to richer logics, and relate our system to Seligman's original sequent calculus.

1 Introduction

Hybrid logic is a simple extension of ordinary modal logic in which it is possible to name possible worlds (or computational states, or epistemic states, or locations, or times, or situations, or whatever entities are required for the application at hand). Special propositional symbols called *nominals* are added to the underlying modal language. These symbols are true at exactly one world, thus a nominal i 'names' the unique world it is true at. In addition, a collection of modal operators of the form $@_i$ is added. Such a modality wears its intended interpretation on its sleeve: $@_i\varphi$ is true at any world w iff it is true at the (unique) world named by i. Such expressions are called *satisfaction statements*.

It is relatively straightforward to define proof systems for hybrid logic in a range of reasoning styles (including tableau [26,5,7,11,10], natural deduction [13], and resolution [1,2]). A resolution theorem prover exists (the HyLoRes system [3]) as well as at least two high-performance tableau provers (namely HTab [20,21] and Spartacus [19]). Indeed, even the least practical of all proof styles (the humble Hilbert system) turns out to be well-behaved [9,8]. Moreover, proof systems in different styles can also be given for intuitionistic hybrid logic, which is obtained by replacing the classical base logic by an intuitionistic one; see [13,16,18] for a variety of approaches. In [22], an intuitionistic version of the modal logic S5 extended with @-operators has been proposed as a foundation for distributed functional programming languages; the @-operators are used to reason about the distribution of resources at different locations.

But behind this apparent diversity lies a common strategy, namely *labeling*. Details vary, but in one form or another the basic idea is to use nominals and satisfaction statements to reach behind the modalities and access the information hidden there. Of course, labeled deduction methods are used for many non-classical logics, but the link between labeling and hybrid logic is particularly intimate—*nominals and satisfaction operators provide labeling apparatus built into the object language itself.* So there is a tendency to think that inference in hybrid logic has to be (some form) of labeled deduction. But this is wrong. There is another approach, which we call *Seligman-style* inference, which offers an interesting alternative. The main purpose of this paper is to explore this proof-style in the setting of tableau-based reasoning for hybrid logic.

The difference between label-driven and Seligman-style inference is best introduced by example. Let's consider two ways of formulating the $\Diamond$-elimination rule in a natural deduction framework for hybrid logic. Here's the rule that the label-driven approach naturally leads to:

$$\frac{@_i\Diamond\varphi \qquad \begin{array}{c}[@_i\Diamond j]\ [@_j\varphi]\\ \vdots \\ @_k\psi\end{array}}{@_k\psi}(\Diamond\text{E})$$

This is easy to explain. We make two assumptions: first that at the world named i we can see a world named j (which is what the satisfaction statement $@_i\Diamond j$ says), and second that φ holds at j (which is what the satisfaction statement $@_j\varphi$ says). We assume nothing else about j beyond these two facts: in effect we have said "let j be an arbitrary world accessible from i at which φ is true". Now, if from these two assumptions we can prove some formula $@_k\psi$ (which says that ψ holds at the world named k) then from a proof of an existential statement $@_i\Diamond\varphi$ (which says that at i it is the case that φ holds at some accessible world) then we get a proof of $@_k\psi$.[1]

A little thought will show that this is a sound rule, but note its *form*. In particular, note that *all the formulas used in this rule are satisfaction statements*. Now, satisfaction statements are global. This is easy to see. If φ is indeed true at the world named i, then $@_i\varphi$ is true at *all* worlds. On the other hand, if φ is false at the world named i, then $@_i\varphi$ is false at *all* worlds. Thus satisfaction statements

---

[1] For this rule to be correctly applied, j has to be a fresh nominal different from both i and k, and j must not occur in either φ or ψ or in any non-discharged assumptions of the proof other than those specified. The assumptions $@_i\Diamond j$ and $@_j\varphi$ occurring as assumptions in the sub-proof on the right are discharged in the application of the rule. For more on natural deduction in hybrid logic, see Braüner [13].

embody global information. And this means that the labeled natural-deduction rule just formulated controls the reasoning by adopting a *global* perspective.

Contrast this with Seligman systems. In a Seligman-style natural deduction system the $\Diamond$-elimination rule would look like this:

$$\frac{\Diamond\varphi \quad \begin{array}{c}[\Diamond j]\ [@_j\varphi]\\ \vdots\\ \psi\end{array}}{\psi}\ (\Diamond\mathrm{E})$$

Notice the *local* perspective illustrated by the rule.[2] The premises are not packed inside satisfaction statements. We assume that j is a possible world. We may not know the name of the world where we are currently evaluating formulas; we only know that there is a possible world accessible from it (named j) at which φ holds. Now, if it is possible for us, given this information, to prove some formula ψ (in which j doesn't occur), then we actually have a proof of ψ given a proof of $\Diamond\varphi$. The core of the argument is similar to that used in the labeled rule, but (so to speak) we use naked $\Diamond$ information: we don't wrap it up in the protection of satisfaction statements. In particular, we don't bother to specify a global name for the world in which we are working (which is what the $@_i$ operator does in the labeled version of the rule) and, as it turns out, we don't need to. Moreover, the subtree on the right is a free-floating proof context. It is linked to the world in which we are working only by a simple local claim, namely $\Diamond j$ (that is: there is an accessible world called j).

This is interesting for at least two reasons. The first is that it holds out the promise of more modular proof systems: if we don't have to wrap all our rules in a protective cocoon of satisfaction statements, perhaps we can work directly with the original rules for each connective. This is a possibility worth exploring. The second reason is conceptual. Modal logic is sometimes said to be interesting (see, for example, [8]) because of the *local* perspective it takes on possible worlds. But if hybrid logic relies on label-driven deduction, then it seems that its successes are due to the *global* encodings that satisfaction statements make possible. So it is worth investigating whether the more local approach to inference underlying Seligman-style reasoning adapts naturally to tableau systems.

Little has been written on Seligman-style systems. They were introduced in two papers, both by Jerry Seligman, written in the 1990s, namely the natural deduction based [24] and the Gentzen sequent calculus based [25].[3] The first of these papers gave a natural deduction system for a logic of situations, similar to hybrid logic. A characteristic feature of this system is that it has a proof rule enabling travel to another situation, the performance of some hypothetical

---

[2] The restriction for this rule is that j must not occur in φ, or ψ or in any non-discharged assumptions other than those specified.

[3] Another Gentzen system for hybrid logic that allows arbitrary formulas to occur in derivations can be found in [23]. The latter system makes use of standard Gentzen machinery for the ordinary (non-hybrid) modal logic K, which makes it quite different from the Seligman-style system of [25].

reasoning there, followed by a journey back again (as the reader will see, a similar idea underlies the GoTo rule in our tableau-based approach). This natural deduction system was later modified in Braüner [12] with the aim of obtaining a proof-theoretic property called closure under substitution, which requires keeping more detailed track of hypothetical reasoning. The modified system kept track of hypothetical reasoning, using what are known as *explicit substitutions*, in a modal-logical context. Such explicit substitutions were also used in a natural deduction system for S4 given in [4], and are similar to the "proof boxes" used in linear logic.

The authors of this paper became interested in Seligman-style reasoning because of reasoning problems involving perspective shifts and contextual information. First, Braüner has used his Seligman-style natural deduction system to formalize a well-known false-belief task in cognitive psychology, the Smarties task.[4] To solve such tasks, the subject under investigation has to perform a shift of perspective, either to another person's view of the world, or to the subject's own view at an earlier time. Such shifts lie at the heart of Seligman-style natural deduction, which makes it a natural tool for modeling such problems; see Braüner [14] for further discussion.

More recently, Blackburn and Jørgensen [6] investigated *temporal indexicals*, that is, context-sensitive temporal terms such as *now*, *yesterday*, *today*, and *tomorrow*. They showed they could be modeled in hybrid logic, but did so using a labeled tableau calculus. In the course of adapting their work to other reasoning styles, it became clear that a Seligman-style tableau approach might allow a simpler presentation of the reasoning involved, but no such calculus existed. The present paper arose as an attempt to fill this gap.

2 The Seligman-Style Tableau Calculus ST

Let's get down to details. We work with a basic hybrid language which includes a countable set of propositional symbols, a countable set of nominals, the propositional connectives $\neg$ and $\wedge$, the modal operator $\Diamond$, and for each nominal i an $@_i$-operator. This operator takes any formula φ as argument and (as we have already discussed) $@_i\varphi$ says that at the world named i, φ is true. Formulas are built as follows:

$$\varphi ::= i \mid p \mid \bot \mid \neg\varphi \mid \varphi \wedge \psi \mid \Diamond\varphi \mid @_i\varphi.$$

The other propositional connectives are defined in the usual way, and $\Box\varphi$ is defined to be $\neg\Diamond\neg\varphi$. Note that nominals play a special role in hybrid logic as

---

[4] In one form of the Smarties task, a child is presented with a Smarties tube, the well-known tubes that usually contain the candy-coated chocolate goodies. However this particular tube contains pencils. After the tube is opened, and the context is updated with the knowledge that there are pencils within, the child is asked: *What would your mother think was in the tube if she came in?* This requires a perspective shift to a context in which the Smarties tube is unopened and its real contents undisclosed. Young and autistic children have difficulty with this—they tend to think that mother will say that there are pencils within, something she cannot possibly know.

they can occur either as subscripts to @ ("in operator position") or as formulas in their own right ("in formula position"). We generally use $i, j, k, \ldots$ to denote nominals and $p, q, r, \ldots$ to denote ordinary propositional symbols.

The semantics for the language of basic hybrid logic is given by interpreting formulas in models based on a frame (W, R) together with a valuation function V. Here W is a non-empty set (we call its elements worlds) and R is a binary relation on this set (the accessibility relation). The valuation V distributes information over the frame; that is, V takes atomic formulas to subsets of W and it satisfies the following two conditions:

1. $V(p)$ is a subset of W, when p is an ordinary propositional symbol.
2. $V(i)$ is a *singleton* subset of W, when i is a nominal.

Satisfiability in a model is defined in the usual way as a relation which obtains between a model $\mathfrak{M} = (W, R, V)$, a point W in the model, and a formula φ:

$$
\begin{aligned}
&\mathfrak{M}, w \models \bot && \text{never} \\
&\mathfrak{M}, w \models a && \text{iff } a \text{ is atomic and } w \in V(a) \\
&\mathfrak{M}, w \models \neg\varphi && \text{iff } \mathfrak{M}, w \not\models \varphi \\
&\mathfrak{M}, w \models \varphi \wedge \psi && \text{iff } \mathfrak{M}, w \models \varphi \text{ and } \mathfrak{M}, w \models \psi \\
&\mathfrak{M}, w \models \Diamond\varphi && \text{iff for some } w', \ wRw' \text{ and } \mathfrak{M}, w' \models \varphi \\
&\mathfrak{M}, w \models @_i\varphi && \text{iff } \mathfrak{M}, w' \models \varphi \text{ and } w' \in V(i).
\end{aligned}
$$

A formula φ is *true in* $\mathfrak{M} = (W, R, V)$ when for all worlds $w \in W$ we have that $\mathfrak{M}, w \models \varphi$. A formula is *valid* if it is true in all models.

Now for our tableau system. As we have already mentioned, one of the pleasant properties of Seligman systems is their modularity. So we simply use standard tableau rules for propositional logic as part of our system. The propositional rules we have chosen are shown in Figure 1.

But what are the hybrid logical rules? How are we to get away from the global form of the labeled rules that are standardly used in hybrid tableau systems? (The reader unfamiliar with labeled tableau rules for hybrid logic should consult the Appendix at the end of the paper.) To help us find an answer, let us consider

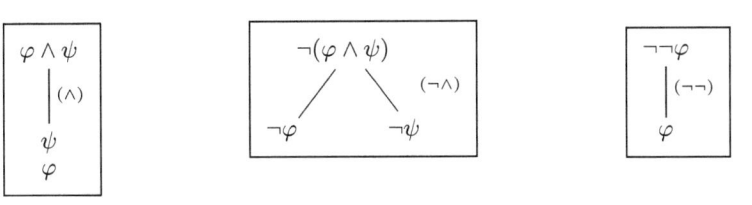

Fig. 1. Module 1: Tableau rules for propositional logic

again the Seligman-style rules for natural deduction discussed earlier. How do the rules of natural deduction deal with the local perspective? Well, in natural deduction, the key idea is to allow for *hypothetical* reasoning. This feature of natural deduction has been utilized in the Seligman-style natural deduction as follows: if from the assumption of being (locally) at some world (about which one has assumed nothing) one can conclude something that holds, then one can delete the assumption of being at that particular world and proceed with the reasoning. Putting it in a nutshell: the key deductive concept in natural deduction is hypothetical reasoning, and the Seligman approach finds a way to embody this concept locally.

So what is the key concept in tableau reasoning? The answer is: *branch expansion*. And how can branch expansion be localized? By means of a process which allows the branch to record *shifting perspectives on worlds*. We do this in our tableau calculus by dividing branches into *blocks*. The general idea here is that a block on a branch is a partial description of the information present at a specific world. The rule that allows us to work with multiple blocks is GoTo. The central idea behind our tableau calculus is that, within a given block, one can work freely with the formulas belonging to the block. But in the course of inference we will often need to make use of information about other worlds. The GoTo rule allows us to temporarily shut down our work in one block and shift to another. The rule opens this new block simply by stating a name for it. On the branch of a tableau, application of the GoTo rule is shown by a horizontal line with a nominal, say j, below the line. This notation means: we have just closed whatever block we were working with before and have shifted our attention to a new world, named j, and are now going to start creating a new block (partial description, proof context) involving this world. In short, just as in any tableau system, the fundamental mechanism is branch expansion. But the division of branches into blocks, and the ability to shift our attention between them that the GoTo rule provides, gives us what we need for Seligman-style reasoning.

So much for intuition. Let's be more precise. Given a branch Θ in a tableau we define a *block* to be one of the following:

1. The *initial block*, consisting of all the formulas on Θ until the first horizontal line (or all formulas if there is no such line on Θ).
2. The *current block*, consisting of all formulas below the last horizontal line (or all formulas if there is no such line).
3. All formulas that occur between a pair of two consecutive horizontal lines.

The crucial rules of the Seligman-style tableau calculus are given in Figure 2 below. The conditions on rule applications are as follows:

- The propositional rules ($\wedge$), ($\neg\wedge$), ($\neg\neg$) as well as ($\Diamond$) and ($\neg\Diamond$) can only be applied to premises that belong to the current block (that is, these connectives, being local, have local rules).
- In the rules (@) and ($\neg$@), the first premise i has to belong to the current block, whereas the second premise $@_i\varphi$ ($\neg@_i\varphi$) can appear anywhere on the

branch (that is, these connectives, being global, transfer information across blocks).
– GoTo and Name can always be applied as they have no premises
– Nom can be applied as described in the rule itself: if φ and i belong to some block distinct from the current block, and i belongs to the current block, then φ can be added to the current block.

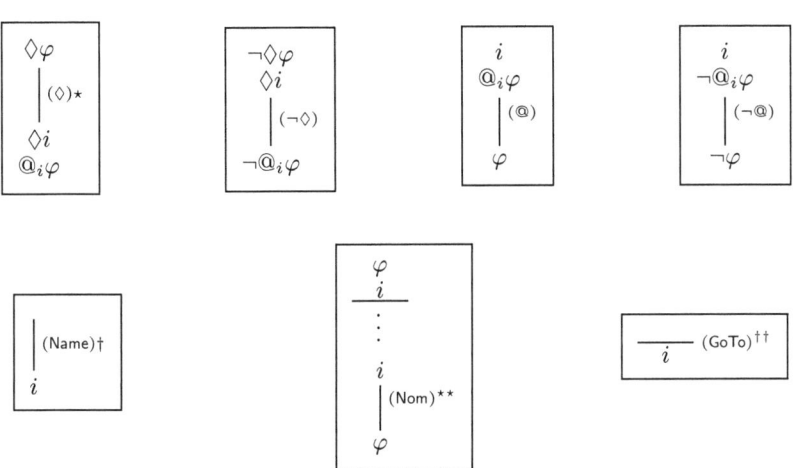

★ The nominal i is fresh and φ is not a nominal.
† The nominal i is fresh.
★★ The horizontal line below the two uppermost premises signifies that these premises belong to a block distinct from the current one, whereas the third premise (the lowermost occurrence of i) belongs to the current block.
†† The nominal i must be on the branch.

Fig. 2. Module 2: Tableau rules for basic hybrid logic

It should be clear that the first four rules are simply the obvious (positive and negative) rules for $\Diamond$ and @. It is the last three rules that really drive the system. The first of these, Name, simply allows us to give a brand new name to a block. This is reminiscent of what GoTo does, and indeed, with a suitable side condition we could have collapsed Name and GoTo into a single rule. But the two rules play rather different roles in our system. Moreover (as we shall see) the role played by Name, though important, is a relatively restricted: as our completeness proof shows, it is never *necessary* to apply Name except possibly to name the initial block. So we prefer to keep the two rules distinct.

What does the Nom rule do? Recall that the GoTo rule enables us to (temporarily) close down a block and create a new one. But in the course of inference we may create multiple blocks, each of which embodies partial information about some world i. We will often need to integrate this information, and Nom lets us do this. Basically, it says that if i and φ occur together in some block, then, if you later find yourself at some bock that also contains i, you are free to recall that φ is true. The point is simply that both i-containing blocks are partial descriptions of the same world, namely the one named by i.

Summing up, our Seligman-style tableau calculus consists of Modules 1 and 2 given in Figure 1 and 2. We call this system ST. Tableaus are built in the expected way, but we should be explicit about our closure condition: a branch *closes* either by having a *local contradiction* φ and $\neg\varphi$ inside a block, or a *global contradiction* between formulas $@_i\varphi$ and $\neg@_i\varphi$ occurring anywhere on the branch.

Let's look at an example, a proof in ST of $\Diamond@_i\varphi \to @_i\varphi$, a formula known as the *Back axiom*. Note that this example closes with a global contradiction.

$$
\begin{array}{rl}
1 & \neg(\Diamond@_i\varphi \to @_i\varphi) \\
  & \quad \big| (\neg\to) \\
2 & \Diamond@_i\varphi \\
3 & \neg@_i\varphi \\
  & \quad \big| (\Diamond) \text{ on } 2 \\
4 & \Diamond j \\
5 & \underline{@_j@_i\varphi} \quad (\text{GoTo}) \\
6 & j \\
  & \quad \big| (@) \text{ on } 5 \text{ and } 6 \\
7 & @_i\varphi \\
  & \otimes \quad \text{on } 3 \text{ and } 7
\end{array}
$$

The argument should be clear: we apply an admissible propositional rule $(\neg\to)$, and then eliminate the $\Diamond$. For the crucial step at line 5 we apply (GoTo) and jump to j; then apply (@) and the branch closes on $@_i\varphi$ and $\neg@_i\varphi$. The reasoning involved is clear and straightforward.

Indeed, it is instructive to compare proofs in our Seligman-style calculus ST with the proofs yielded by the standard labeled calculus LC (see the Appendix). Consider the following proof of $@_ij \wedge @_jk \to @_ik$, a hybrid validity which says that the world-naming relation is transitive. This is a telling example, as it requires equational reasoning about the identity of worlds. The tableau on the left is in the calculus ST, the one on the right in the calculus LC.[5] The Seligman-style approach makes the form of the argument clearer, and hides tedious bookkeeping details.

---

[5] Note that in both tableaus we have skipped the obvious application of the conjunctive rule right after $(\neg\to)$.

```
1    ¬(@_ij ∧ @_jk → @_ik)
     | (¬→)
2    @_ij
3    @_jk
4    ¬@_ik        (GoTo)
5    i
     | (@) on 2 and 5
6    j
     | (@) on 3 and 6
7    k
     | (¬@) on 4 and 5
8    ¬k
     ⊗    on 7 and 8
```

```
1    ¬@_l(@_ij ∧ @_jk → @_ik)
     | (¬→) on 1
2    @_l@_ij
3    @_l@_jk
4    ¬@_l@_ik
     | (@) on 2
5    @_ij
     | (@) on 3
6    @_jk
     | (¬@) on 4
7    ¬@_ik
     | (Ref)
8    @_ii
     | (Nom1) on 5 and 8
9    @_ji
     | (Nom1) on 9 and 6
10   @_ik
     ⊗    on 7 and 10
```

3   Soundness and Completeness

Theorem 1 (Soundness). *If there exists a closed tableau in* ST *having* $\neg\varphi$ *as the root formula, then the formula φ is valid.*

Proof. Let Θ be a branch of a tableau of the calculus ST. Let B be a block on Θ and let $\mathfrak{M} = (W, R, V)$ be a model. We say that B is satisfiable by $\mathfrak{M}$ if and only if there exists a world $w \in W$ such that for any formula ψ in B, it is the case that $\mathfrak{M}, w \models \psi$. Moreover, we say that Θ is block-wise satisfiable by $\mathfrak{M}$ if and only if any block on Θ is satisfiable by $\mathfrak{M}$. We say that Θ is block-wise satisfiable if and only if Θ is block-wise satisfiable by some model $\mathfrak{M}$.

Now, the contrapositive of soundness follows from the observation that if a tableau T of the calculus ST has a branch which is block-wise satisfiable, then the tableau obtained by applying a rule to T also has a branch which is block-wise satisfiable. This can be seen simply by inspecting each rule in ST.   □

We will now prove completeness of ST. We do so by providing a translation from tableaus in the labeled calculus LC into tableaus in ST.[6] The translation allows us to reduce completeness of ST to the completeness result for LC (see [5]). The approach also clarifies the relationship between the Seligman-style and labeling approaches, and yields some extra insights: for example, that the Name rule only needs to be used once in any ST tableau construction.

---

[6] Again, see the Appendix for the definition of LC.

Definition 1. *Let Θ be a tableau branch of the calculus ST. A formula $@_i\varphi$ ($\neg @_i\varphi$) is said to occur as an **induced formula** on Θ if there is a block B on Θ such that $i, \varphi \in B$ ($i, \neg\varphi \in B$).*

Lemma 1. *Let φ be any formula and i any nominal not in φ. Assume T_{LC} is a tableau with root $\neg @_i\varphi$ in the calculus LC. Then there exists a tableau T_{ST} with root $\neg\varphi$ in the calculus ST, and a bijection $b : \{\Theta \mid \Theta \text{ is a branch of } T_{\text{LC}}\} \to \{\Theta' \mid \Theta' \text{ is a branch of } T_{\text{ST}}\}$ such that:*

1. *Given any branch Θ of T_{LC}, all formulas $@_j\psi \in \Theta$ and $\neg @_j\psi \in \Theta$ occur as induced formulas on $b(\Theta)$.*
2. *All nominals that occur on $b(\Theta)$ also occur on Θ.*

Proof. By induction of the number of rule applications made on T_{LC}.

Base case. No rules have been applied and T_{LC} is $\neg @_i\varphi$, where i does not occur in φ. Then let T_{ST} be the following tableau in ST:

T and T' both have a single branch, call them Θ and Θ' respectively. Define b by $b(\Theta) = \Theta'$. The branch Θ only contains the formula $\neg @_i\varphi$ and this occurs as an induced formula on Θ', since the current block of Θ' contains both i and $\neg\varphi$. Hence Condition 1 above holds. Condition 2 holds trivially. This concludes the base case. This is the only place in the translation where we use the Name rule.

Induction step. Assume T_{LC}, T_{ST} and b are given that satisfy the conditions of the lemma, including Conditions 1 and 2. We need to prove that if T_{LC} is extended into T'_{LC} by a single rule application, we can construct a similar extension T'_{ST} of T_{ST} and a new bijection b' so that Conditions 1 and 2 again hold. We prove this by examining each possible case of a rule application building T'_{LC} from T_{LC}.

Case ($\wedge$). Suppose T'_{LC} is obtained from T_{LC} by an application of ($\wedge$) to a premise $@_j(\psi_1 \wedge \psi_2)$ on a branch Θ_{LC} of T_{LC}. In T'_{LC} the branch Θ_{LC} has become extended by formulas $@_j\psi_1$ and $@_j\psi_2$. Call the extended branch Θ'_{LC}. By the induction hypothesis, $b(\Theta_{\text{LC}})$ contains a block B with $j, \psi_1 \wedge \psi_2 \in B$ (since $@_j(\psi_1 \wedge \psi_2)$ occurs as an induced formula on $b(\Theta_{\text{LC}})$ by Condition 1). Note that this block need not be the current one. We can now extend $b(\Theta_{\text{LC}})$ as shown in Figure 3, using GoTo, then Nom, then ($\wedge$). Call this extended branch Θ'_{ST}, and let T'_{ST} denote the tableau in which $b(\Theta_{\text{LC}})$ has been extended into Θ'_{ST}. Now define $b' = (b - \{(\Theta_{\text{LC}}, b(\Theta_{\text{LC}}))\}) \cup \{(\Theta'_{\text{LC}}, \Theta'_{\text{ST}})\}$, and note that b' is a bijection from the branches of T'_{LC} onto the branches of T'_{ST}. It now follows immediately from the induction hypothesis and the construction of the extended tableaus, that Conditions 1 and 2 still hold when T_{LC} is replaced by T'_{LC} and b by b'.

The rest of the cases are similar and are left to the reader. Condition 2 is only used in the case for the rule ($\Diamond$), where we need to show that the same nominal is fresh on T_{ST} as the one chosen when applying ($\Diamond$) on T_{LC}. □

Theorem 2 (Completeness). *If the formula φ is valid, then there exists a closed tableau in ST having $\neg\varphi$ as the root formula.*

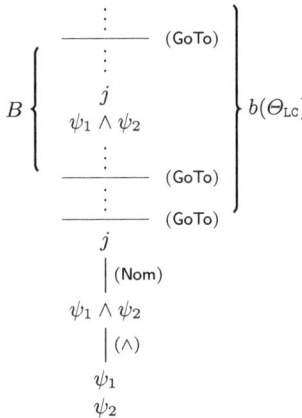

Fig. 3. Case ($\wedge$): The extended branch Θ'_{ST} of T'_{ST}

Proof. Assume φ is valid. As LC is complete [5], there exists a closed LC-tableau T_{LC} with root $\neg @_i \varphi$, where i is a nominal not occurring in φ. By Lemma 1 there is an ST-tableau T_{ST} with root $\neg \varphi$ and a bijection $b : \{\Theta \mid \Theta \text{ is a branch of } T_{\mathsf{LC}}\} \to \{\Theta' \mid \Theta' \text{ is a branch of } T_{\mathsf{ST}}\}$ such that:

1. Given any branch Θ of T_{LC}, all formulas $@_j \psi \in \Theta$ and $\neg @_j \psi \in \Theta$ occur as induced formulas on $b(\Theta)$.
2. All nominals that occur on $b(\Theta)$ also occur on Θ.

We now prove that T_{ST} can be extended into a closed tableau. To this end, let Θ_{ST} denote an arbitrary branch on T_{ST}. By definition, $b^{-1}(\Theta_{\mathsf{ST}})$ is a closed branch, meaning that it contains a pair of formulas $@_j \psi$ and $\neg @_j \psi$. Condition 1 implies that these formulas occur induced on Θ_{ST}. Thus Θ_{ST} contains a pair of blocks B_1, B_2 with $j, \psi \in B_1$ and $j, \neg \psi \in B_2$. We can now extend Θ_{ST} by applying GoTo once to open a new block containing j, and afterwards applying (Nom) twice to get ψ and $\neg \psi$ in the current block. The extended branch is obviously closed, as the current block will then contain a contradiction. Since Θ_{ST} was an arbitrary branch of T_{ST}, this means that every branch of T_{ST} can be extended to a closing branch, so we can close the entire tableau. □

4 Ongoing Work

In this section we briefly discuss ongoing work on termination and extensions to stronger logics. First, we ask whether the system just defined provides a decision procedure for basic hybrid logic. Second, we note that our system can be extended to a complete system for full first-order hybrid logic.

First, can the tableau system just introduced be used as a decision procedure? It is not difficult to see that unrestricted use of the calculus as presented here can lead to non-terminating computations; indeed, repeated applications of GoTo are a trivial way of doing this. Still, our initial investigations suggest that by imposing natural restrictions on the application of rules, we can get a terminating calculus *without* resorting to loop checks (the first loop check free tableau calculus for hybrid logic was provided in [10]). The first step towards a terminating calculus is to adopt the standard rule application restrictions for tableau calculi to our block-based setting. Usually, the following restrictions are imposed (see e.g. [10]):

(R1) A rule is never applied twice to the same set of premises on the same branch.

(R2) A formula is never added to a branch where it already occurs.

The adaptation of these to our block-based setting becomes:

(R1′) A rule is never applied to a pair of premises φ, ψ at the current block B if, for some nominal $i \in B$, there is a block B' with $i, \varphi, \psi \in B'$ at which the rule instance has already been applied.[7]

(R2′) A formula is never added to a block where it already occurs.

The only remaining way a branch can be infinite is if it contains infinitely many blocks initialised with the same nominal (the initialising nominal is the one just below the horisontal line). To avoid this kind of non-termination we need a third restriction (R3′), explicitly limiting the applicability of the GoTo rule. We are currently working on a termination proof based on these ideas.

A second line of work is extending the system to richer logics. One benefit of the Seligman-style approach is its modularity. So, in principle, it should be relatively easy to obtain complete proof system for richer hybrid logics by adding standard rules for the additional connectives involved. This turns out to be the case for hybrid logics equipped with the tense operators F and P, with the universal modality A, and with the $\downarrow$-binder (see [8] for background information). Indeed, we have also obtained a complete system for full first-order hybrid logic; we shall briefly sketch the main ideas involved.

First-order hybrid logic is what you obtain when when you build hybrid logic over first-order logic instead of over propositional logic. There are a number of syntactic and semantic choices to be made about how to do this; for discussions of the various possibilities see [17,15]. We adopted the choices made in [7]. The syntax of our language is:

$$\varphi ::= i \mid t = s \mid P(t_1, \ldots, t_n) \mid \neg\varphi \mid \varphi \wedge \psi \mid \Diamond\varphi \mid @_i\varphi \mid \exists x\varphi.$$

---

[7] For rules taking a single premise, we let $\psi = \varphi$.

Here s, t and $t_1, \ldots, t_n$ are first-order terms. These symbols range over ordinary first-order constants and variables, and also over composite first-order terms of the form $@_i f$. For example, if f is a symbol standing for the "The President of the United States" (such a symbol is called a *non-rigid designator*) then $@_{2013} f$ is a (composite) first-order term denoting President Obama, and $@_{1962} f$ a term denoting President Kennedy. But apart from this, all is standard. Following [7], we assume a *constant domain* semantics.

Now, given that the underlying first-order language (modulo the use of composite terms $@_i f$) is standard, we should expect (if the claims about modularity are correct) to obtain a complete proof system by bolting on a collection of standard first-order logic with equality rules, together with a rule for handling composite terms. And this is exactly what happens. All we need to do is add the following third module:

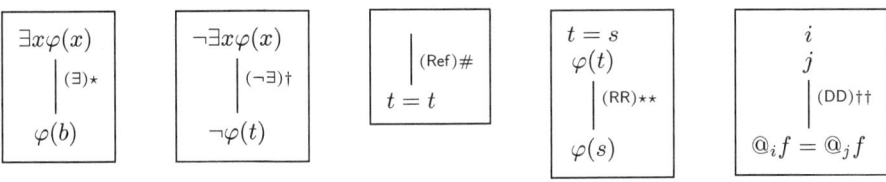

$\star$ $\exists x \varphi(x)$ occurs in the current block and the parameter b is fresh on the branch.
$\dagger$ $\neg \exists x \varphi(x)$ occurs in the current block and the term t occurs on the branch.
$\#$ The term t occurs on the branch.
$\star\star$ $\varphi(t)$ occurs in the current block and $t = s$ is on the branch.
$\dagger\dagger$ The nominals i and j occur together in some block (not necessarily the current one) on the branch and f is a non-rigid symbol occurring on the branch.

Fig. 4. Module 3: First-order tableau rules

All the rules, except the one at the far right should be familiar. And the rule on the far right clearly captures the way our composite terms work: if i and j name the same world (note that the premises are in the same block) then we can safely conclude that $@_i f$ and $@_j f$ both denote the same first-order entity. Completeness can be proved by translation from the labeled system of [7], much as we did in the propositional case, though the proof is longer and more subtle. So instead of giving a proof sketch, we will simply give two example of the system at work. The first shows that if an inequality is true in some world then it is true in any other world; that is, that $@_i(t \neq s) \rightarrow @_j(t \neq s)$ is derivable. The second shows that "equalities are forever".

$$
\begin{array}{ll}
1 & \neg\bigl(@_i(t\neq s)\to @_j(t\neq s)\bigr) \\
 & \;\big|\;(\neg\to)\text{ on }1 \\
2 & @_i(t\neq s) \\
3 & \neg@_j(t\neq s) \\
 & \overline{\qquad\qquad}\;(\mathsf{GoTo}) \\
4 & j \\
 & \;\big|\;(\neg@)\text{ on 3 and 4} \\
5 & \neg t\neq s \\
 & \;\big|\;(\neg\neg)\text{ on 5} \\
6 & t=s \\
 & \overline{\qquad\qquad}\;(\mathsf{GoTo}) \\
7 & i \\
 & \;\big|\;(@)\text{ on 2 and 7} \\
8 & t\neq s \\
 & \otimes \qquad \text{on 6 and 8}
\end{array}
$$

$$
\begin{array}{ll}
1 & \neg\forall x\forall y(x=y\to\Box(x=y)) \\
 & \;\big|\;(\neg\forall)\text{ twice on 1} \\
2 & a=b \\
3 & \neg\Box(a=b) \\
 & \;\big|\;(\neg\Box)\text{ on 3} \\
4 & \Diamond i \\
5 & \neg@_i(a=b) \\
 & \overline{\qquad\qquad}\;(\mathsf{GoTo}) \\
6 & i \\
 & \;\big|\;(\neg@)\text{ on 5 and 6} \\
7 & a\neq b \\
 & \;\big|\;(\mathsf{RR})\text{ on 2 and 7} \\
8 & b\neq b \\
 & \;\big|\;(\mathsf{Ref}) \\
9 & b=b \\
 & \otimes \qquad \text{on 8 and 9}
\end{array}
$$

5 Concluding Remarks

In his most detailed exposition of his approach, Jerry Seligman [25] states his aim clearly: to obtain "a more egalitarian logic in which there are Rules for All" ([25], page 684). The sequent calculus presented there was the starting point for our work, so to conclude this paper we would like to indicate the main similarities and differences.

As should be clear by now, the crucial rules are those that handle the nominals and the @-operator. Seligman uses the following six rules for this purpose; he calls them Nominal Rules (see [25], page 685):

$$
\begin{array}{lll}
{}^{\vee}@L & i,\varphi,\Gamma\longrightarrow\Delta & \Rightarrow\quad i,@_i\varphi,\Gamma\longrightarrow\Delta \\
{}^{\vee}@R & i,\Gamma\longrightarrow\Delta,\varphi & \Rightarrow\quad i,\Gamma\longrightarrow\Delta,@_i\varphi \\
{}^{\wedge}@L & i,@_i\varphi,\Gamma\longrightarrow\Delta & \Rightarrow\quad i,\varphi,\Gamma\longrightarrow\Delta \\
{}^{\wedge}@R & i,\Gamma\longrightarrow\Delta,@_i\varphi & \Rightarrow\quad i,\Gamma\longrightarrow\Delta,\varphi \\
\text{name} & i,\Gamma\longrightarrow\Delta & \Rightarrow\quad \Gamma\longrightarrow\Delta,\text{ if }i\text{ does not occur in }\Gamma,\Delta \\
\text{term} & i,\Gamma\longrightarrow\Delta & \Rightarrow\quad \Gamma\longrightarrow\Delta,\text{ if all formulas in }\Gamma,\Delta\text{ are @-prefixed.}
\end{array}
$$

First the easy part. Tableau rules can often be seen as reversed sequent rules, where the formulas on right of the sequent arrow $\longrightarrow$ are negated. If we read the listed rules this way, our (@) and ($\neg$@) rules are simply his ${}^{\vee}@L$ and ${}^{\vee}@R$ rules, and our Name rule is just Seligman's name.

The divergences stem from the remaining three rules. Our first attempt at a tableau system contained the obvious tableau correlates of Seligman's ${}^{\wedge}@L$ and ${}^{\wedge}@R$ rules. The rules introduced @-prefixes and with these rules we were able to @-prefix whole branches, thereby globalizing the information they contained. Such rules are destructive: they don't simply expand branches, they change them more drastically.

Why did we do this? To try and *directly* capture Seligman's term rule. His term rule is essentially our GoTo rule, but note the side condition: it only lets us jump to a world u if all information is @-prefixed, that is, global. Our first version of GoTo had the same side condition, so proofs in our early systems would typically contain multiple applications of the $^\wedge$@L and $^\wedge$@R rules followed by an application of GoTo. But we were dissatisfied notationally; destructive rules are annoying when using a tableau system by hand. Then we noticed a more serious problem: the @-prefixing permitted by the $^\wedge$@L and $^\wedge$@R rules interacted badly with (our tableau versions of) the rules $^\vee$@L and $^\vee$@R. Often we would prefix an @, only to immediately strip it off, a clear proof redundancy.

These interrelated issues led us to introduce blocks. In essence, by making use of blocks, we avoid having to give explicit tableau rules corresponding to rules $^\wedge$@L and $^\wedge$@R; these rules are absorbed into the concept of a block. This simultaneously eliminates the destructive tableau-rules, and bypasses the proof redundancy just noticed. Moreover, by having GoTo create a local proof context (rather than only be applicable when all the information on the branch has been @-prefixed) we avoid having to impose the side condition.

The drawbacks we discovered in our early tableau systems are *not* present in Seligman's sequent calculus; Seligman's rules and side-conditions elegantly exploit the resources of sequent calculus. But (despite its use of blocks) we believe our system comes close to being a "natural tableau reversal" of Seligman's system. Compare, for example, the sequent derivation of $@_i j \wedge @_j k \rightarrow @_i k$ with the block derivation given earlier:

$$\cfrac{\cfrac{\cfrac{\cfrac{\cfrac{i,j,k \longrightarrow k}{i,j,@_j k \longrightarrow k}\, ^\vee@\text{L}}{i,@_i j,@_j k \longrightarrow k}\, ^\vee@\text{L}}{i,@_i j,@_j k \longrightarrow @_i k}\, ^\vee@\text{R}}{@_i j,@_j k \longrightarrow @_i k}\, \text{term}}{@_i j \wedge @_j k \longrightarrow @_i k}\, (\wedge\text{R})$$

This example also illustrates that the term rule in the sequent system is really more of a GoFrom rule than a GoTo rule. Of course, this reflects the fact that tableau rules are, in a sense, reversed sequent rules.

Finally, we remark that the use of blocks reverses a longstanding trend in hybrid logic (reliance on the labeling apparatus in the object language) in favor of imposing more structure at the metalevel. Dividing branches into blocks *externalizes* (passes up to the metalanguage) some of the work done by the @-operator. The use of induced satisfaction statements in our completeness proofs (which reflects the way that Seligman's $^\wedge$@L and $^\wedge$@R are absorbed into the concept of a block) is a clear reflection of this externalization.

References

1. Areces, C., Heguiabehere, J.: Direct Resolution for Modal-like Logics. In: Proceedings of the 3rd International Workshop on the Implementation of Logics, Tbilisi, Georgia, pp. 3–16 (2002)
2. Areces, C., Gorín, D.: Ordered Resolution with Selection for $\mathcal{H}(@)$. In: Baader, F., Voronkov, A. (eds.) LPAR 2004. LNCS (LNAI), vol. 3452, pp. 125–141. Springer, Heidelberg (2005)
3. Areces, C., Gorín, D.: Resolution with Order and Selection for Hybrid Logics. J. Autom. Reasoning 46(1), 1–42 (2011)
4. Bierman, G., de Paiva, V.: On an Intuitionistic Modal Logic. Studia Logica 65, 383–416 (2000)
5. Blackburn, P.: Internalizing labelled deduction. Journal of Logic and Computation 10(1), 137–168 (2000)
6. Blackburn, P., Jørgensen, K.F.: Indexical Hybrid Tense Logic. In: Bolander, T., Braüner, T., Ghilardi, S., Moss, L. (eds.) Advances in Modal Logic, vol. 9, pp. 144–160 (2012)
7. Blackburn, P., Marx, M.: Tableaux for quantified hybrid logic. In: Egly, U., Fermüller, C. (eds.) TABLEAUX 2002. LNCS (LNAI), vol. 2381, pp. 38–52. Springer, Heidelberg (2002)
8. Blackburn, P., de Rijke, M., Venema, Y.: Modal Logic. Cambridge University Press, Cambridge (2001)
9. Blackburn, P., Tzakova, M.: Hybrid Languages and Temporal Logic. Logic Journal of the IGPL 7(1), 27–54 (1999)
10. Bolander, T., Blackburn, P.: Termination for Hybrid Tableaus. Journal of Logic and Computation 17(3), 517–554 (2007)
11. Bolander, T., Braüner, T.: Tableau-Based Decision Procedures for Hybrid Logic. Journal of Logic and Computation 16, 737–763 (2006)
12. Braüner, T.: Two natural deduction systems for hybrid logic: A comparison. Journal of Logic, Language and Information 13, 1–23 (2004)
13. Braüner, T.: Hybrid Logic and its Proof-Theory. Applied Logic Series, vol. 37. Springer (2011)
14. Braüner, T.: Hybrid-logical Reasoning in False-Belief Tasks. In: Schipper, B. (ed.) Proceedings of Fourteenth Conference on Theoretical Aspects of Rationality and Knowledge (TARK), pp. 186–195 (2013), http://tark.org
15. Braüner, T., Ghilardi, S.: First-order modal logic. In: Handbook of Modal Logic, pp. 549–620. Elsevier (2007)
16. Chadha, R., Macedonio, D., Sassone, V.: A hybrid intuitionistic logic: Semantics and decidability. Journal of Logic and Computation 16, 27–59 (2006)
17. Fitting, M., Mendelsohn, R.: First-Order Modal Logic. Springer (1998)
18. Galmiche, D., Salhi, Y.: Sequent calculi and decidability for intuitionistic hybrid logic. Information and Computation 209, 1447–1463 (2011)
19. Götzmann, D., Kaminski, M., Smolka, G.: Spartacus: A Tableau Prover for Hybrid Logic. Electr. Notes Theor. Comput. Sci. 262, 127–139 (2010)
20. Hoffmann, G., Areces, C.: HTab: A Terminating Tableaux System for Hybrid Logic. In: Proceedings of Methods for Modalities, vol. 5 (November 2007)
21. Hoffmann, G.: Tâches de raisonnement en logiques hybrides. Ph.D. thesis, Université Henri Poincaré - Nancy I (December 2010), http://tel.archives-ouvertes.fr/tel-00541664
22. Jia, L.-m., Walker, D.W.: Modal proofs as distributed programs (extended abstract). In: Schmidt, D. (ed.) ESOP 2004. LNCS, vol. 2986, pp. 219–233. Springer, Heidelberg (2004)

23. Kushida, H., Okada, M.: A Proof-Theoretic Study of the Correspondence of Hybrid Logic and Classical Logic. Journal of Logic, Language and Information 16, 35–61 (2007)
24. Seligman, J.: The Logic of Correct Description. In: de Rijke, M. (ed.) Advances in Intensional Logic. Applied Logic Series, vol. 7, pp. 107–135. Kluwer (1997)
25. Seligman, J.: Internalisation: The Case of Hybrid Logics. Journal of Logic and Computation 11, 671–689 (2001); special Issue on Hybrid Logics. Areces, C., Blackburn, P. (eds.)
26. Tzakova, M.: Tableau Calculi for Hybrid Logics. In: Murray, N.V. (ed.) TABLEAUX 1999. LNCS (LNAI), vol. 1617, pp. 278–292. Springer, Heidelberg (1999)

Appendix: Labeled Tableau Rules for LC

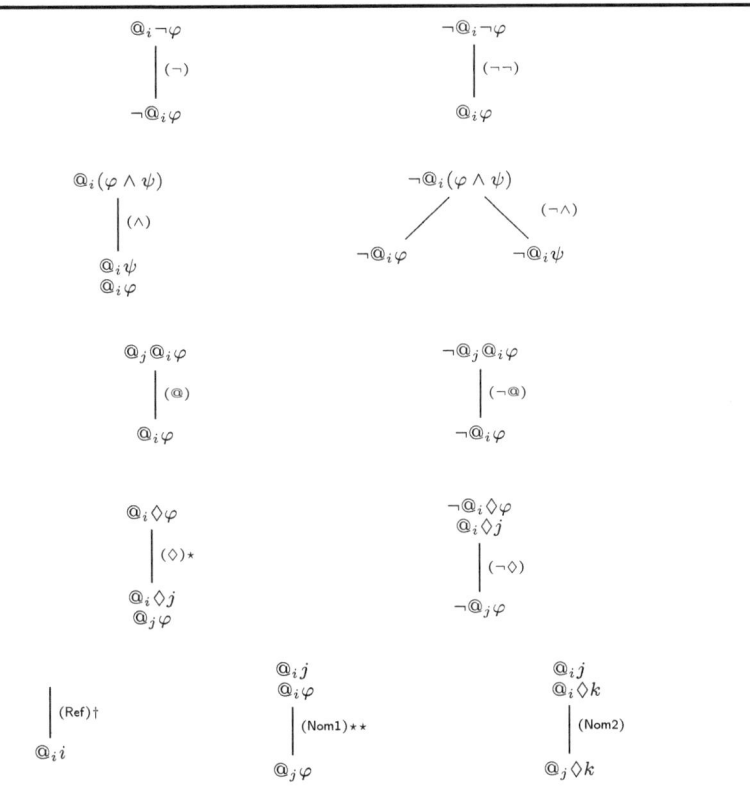

⋆ The nominal j is new and φ is not a nominal.
† The nominal i is on the branch.
⋆⋆ The formula φ is an atomic formula, i.e., ordinary propositional symbol or nominal.

Comparison of LTL to Deterministic Rabin Automata Translators*

František Blahoudek, Mojmír Křetínský, and Jan Strejček

Faculty of Informatics, Masaryk University, Brno, Czech Republic
{xblahoud,kretinsky,strejcek}@fi.muni.cz

Abstract. Increasing interest in control synthesis and probabilistic model checking caused recent development of LTL to deterministic ω-automata translation. The standard approach represented by `ltl2dstar` tool employs Safra's construction to determinize a Büchi automaton produced by some LTL to Büchi automata translator. Since 2012, three new LTL to deterministic Rabin automata translators appeared, namely Rabinizer, LTL3DRA, and Rabinizer 2. They all avoid Safra's construction and work on LTL fragments only. We compare performance and automata produced by the mentioned tools, where `ltl2dstar` is combined with several LTL to Büchi automata translators: besides traditionally used LTL2BA, we also consider LTL->NBA, LTL3BA, and Spot.

1 Introduction

Linear temporal logic (LTL) has proved to be an appropriate formalism for specification of systems behavior with major applications in the area of model checking. Methods for LTL model checking of probabilistic systems [29,5,3] and for LTL synthesis [4,24,19] mostly need to construct, for any given LTL formula, a *deterministic* ω-automaton. As *deterministic Büchi automata (DBA)* cannot express all the properties expressible in LTL, one has to choose deterministic ω-automata with a more complex acceptance condition. The most common choice is the Rabin acceptance.

There are basically two approaches to translation of LTL to deterministic ω-automata. A traditional one translates LTL to *nondeterministic Büchi automata (NBA)* first and then it employs Safra's construction [26] (or some of its variants or alternatives like [23,27]) to obtain a deterministic automaton. This approach is represented by the tool `ltl2dstar` [14] which uses an improved Safra's construction [16,17]. As every LTL formula can be translated into an NBA and Safra's construction can transform any NBA to a *deterministic Rabin automaton (DRA)*, `ltl2dstar` works for the whole LTL. However, the resulting automata are sometimes unnecessarily big.

Since 2012, several translations avoiding Safra's construction have been introduced. The first one is presented in [18] and subsequently implemented in the tool

---

* Authors are supported by The Czech Science Foundation, grant no. P202/10/1469.

Rabinizer [10]. The algorithm builds a *generalized deterministic Rabin automaton (GDRA)* directly from a formula. A DRA is then produced by a degeneralization procedure. Rabinizer often produces smaller automata than ltl2dstar. The main disadvantage is that it works for LTL(F, G) only, i.e. the LTL fragment containing *eventually* (F) and *always* (G) as the only temporal operators. This method has been extended to a semantically larger fragment and reimplemented in the experimental tool Rabinizer 2 [21]. In [1] we present a Safraless translation working with another LTL fragment subsuming LTL(F, G). Our translator LTL3DRA transforms a given formula into a very weak alternating automaton (in the same way as LTL2BA [11]) and then into a *transition-based generalized deterministic Rabin automaton (TGDRA)*. The construction of generalized Rabin pairs of TGDRA is inspired by [18]. A DRA is finally obtained by a degeneralization procedure.

Here we provide a comparison of performance of the LTL to DRA translators ltl2dstar, Rabinizer, Rabinizer 2, and LTL3DRA. The tool ltl2dstar is designed to use an external LTL to NBA translator. To our best knowledge, the last experimental comparison of performance of ltl2dstar with different LTL to NBA translators has been done in 2005 [15]. The comparison shows that with respect to automata sizes, LTL2BA and LTL->NBA [9] "have the lead and were the only programs without failures to calculate the DRA." Since 2005, significant progress has been made in LTL to NBA translation (it can already be seen in the comparison of LTL to NBA translators [25] published in 2007). Hence, we run ltl2dstar with LTL2BA, LTL->NBA, and contemporary translators Spot [6,7] and LTL3BA [2]. The experimental results obtained are briefly interpreted.

2 Compared Tools

Here we describe settings and restrictions of the considered translators.

- ltl2dstar [14] v0.5.1, http://www.ltl2dstar.de/
  We keep the default setting (all optimizations enabled). We use only the option --ltl2nba="<intf>:<tool>[@<params>]" to specify an external <tool> for LTL to NBA translation (<intf> specifies if ltl2dstar communicates with the <tool> via the interface of *lbtt* [28] or *Spin* [13], and <params> are parameters the <tool> is called with). We use four LTL to NBA translators:
  - **LTL->NBA** [9], http://www.ti.informatik.uni-kiel.de/~fritz/
    We call it with --ltl2nba="lbtt:/pathtoLTL->NBA/script4lbtt.py".
  - **LTL2BA** [11] v1.1, http://www.lsv.ens-cachan.fr/~gastin/ltl2ba/
    We call it with --ltl2nba="spin:/pathtoLTL2BA/ltl2ba".
  - **LTL3BA** [2] v1.0.2, http://sourceforge.net/projects/ltl3ba/
    By default, LTL3BA aims to produce small NBAs. With the option -M, it aims to produce potentially larger, but more deterministic automata. We have combined both modes with other optimizations provided by LTL3BA. We have selected two settings with the best results, namely --ltl2nba="spin:/pathtoLTL3BA/ltl3ba" referenced as

LTL3BA and `--ltl2nba="spin:/pathtoLTL3BA/ltl3ba@-M -S"` referenced as LTL3BAd. Option `-S` enables strong fair simulation reduction.
- **Spot** [6,7] v1.1.3, http://spot.lip6.fr/wiki/
  Again, Spot can be set to produce either small or more deterministic Büchi automata. We have combined ltl2dstar with both modes of Spot. The resulting Rabin automata produced with the first mode are usually identical to (and sometimes slightly bigger than) the automata produced with the latter mode. Computation times are also similar. To save some space, we include only the results for the "more deterministic" mode invoked by `--ltl2nba="spin:/pathtoSpot/ltl2tgba@-sD"`.
- **Rabinizer** [10] v0.11, http://crab.in.tum.de/rabinizer/
  Recall that Rabinizer works for LTL(F, G) only.
- **Rabinizer 2** [21],
  http://www.model.in.tum.de/~kretinsk/rabinizer2.html
  Rabinizer 2 works with formulae of a fragment called LTL\GU which uses not only F and G but also *next* (X) and *until* (U) temporal operators. The fragment consists of formulae in the negation normal form (i.e. negations are only in front of atomic propositions) such that no U is in the scope of any G.
- **LTL3DRA** [1] v0.1, http://sourceforge.net/projects/ltl3dra/
  This tool works with formulae of a slightly less expressive fragment than LTL\GU. More precisely, there is one more restriction on the scope of any G: there are no U operators, and X can appear only in front of F or G, i.e. in subformulae of the form XFφ or XGφ. We call this fragment LTL\GUX. The difference is not important for specification formulae of software and asynchronous systems as these usually contain no X operators, but it can play some role in specification formulae of hardware and synchronous systems.

Before we run the translators, we transform input formulae to the expected format (prefix notation for ltl2dstar and negation normal form for Rabinizer 2) using the tool ltlfilt [7]. Note that Rabinizer, Rabinizer 2, and LTL3DRA are called with default settings.

3 Experiments: Benchmarks and Results

All experiments were done on a server with 8 eight-core processors Intel® Xeon® X7560, 2.26GHz, 448 GiB RAM and a 64-bit version of GNU/Linux. All the translators are single-threaded. The timeout limit was set to 2 hours.

We run the tools on three benchmark sets: real specification formulae, parametric formulae, and random formulae. The benchmark sets can be downloaded from the web pages of LTL3DRA.

Real Specification Formulae. We use specification formulae from two sources: BEEM [22] and Spec Patterns [8]. After removing duplicates (typically cases where an atomic proposition a is consistently replaced by its negation or by $a \vee b$), we have 67 formulae. These formulae are divided into three classes: 12

formulae of LTL(F, G), 19 formulae of LTL\GUX not included in LTL(F, G), and 36 formulae outside LTL\GUX. Note that all the considered formulae outside LTL\GUX are also outside LTL\GU.

Unlike standard model checking algorithms, applications requiring deterministic ω-automata usually need automata equivalent to specification formulae and not to their negations. Hence, we do not negate the formulae before translation.

Table 1 presents cummulative results of the considered tools on the three classes of specification formulae. Table 2 provides a cross-comparison of the tools on the same formulae classes.

Parametric Formulae. We consider 8 parametric formulae of [12] and formulae $\theta(n)$ of [11] and $F(n)$ of [18]:

$$E(n) = \bigwedge_{i=1}^{n} \mathsf{F}p_i \qquad\qquad C_1(n) = \bigvee_{i=1}^{n} \mathsf{GF}p_i$$
$$U(n) = (\ldots((p_1 \cup p_2) \cup p_3) \cup \ldots) \cup p_n \qquad C_2(n) = \bigwedge_{i=1}^{n} \mathsf{GF}p_i$$
$$R(n) = \bigwedge_{i=1}^{n} (\mathsf{GF}p_i \vee \mathsf{FG}p_{i+1}) \qquad Q(n) = \bigwedge_{i=1}^{n} (\mathsf{F}p_i \vee \mathsf{G}p_{i+1})$$
$$U_2(n) = p_1 \cup (p_2 \cup (\ldots (p_{n-1} \cup p_n)\ldots)) \qquad S(n) = \bigvee_{i=1}^{n} \mathsf{G}p_i$$

$$\theta(n) = \neg((\bigwedge_{i=1}^{n} \mathsf{GF}p_i) \to \mathsf{G}(q \to \mathsf{F}r)) \qquad F(n) = \bigwedge_{i=1}^{n} (\mathsf{GF}p_i \to \mathsf{GF}q_i)$$

Table 1. For each class of considered real formulae and for each tool, the table shows cummulative numbers of *states*, *edges*, and accepting *pairs* of produced automata. Further, we show the number of *minimal* automata produced by the tool (minimal means that no other considered tool produced an automaton with less states for the same formula). We also provide cummulative computation *time* (in seconds) and maximal and average memory peaks (*mem max* and *mem avg*, measured in MiB) needed for the construction of one automaton. The best results are emphasized.

Class	Measure	ltl2dstar LTL->NBA	LTL2BA	LTL3BA	LTL3BAd	Spot	Rabinizer	Rabinizer 2	LTL3DRA
12 formulae of LTL(F,G)	states	55	49	47	45	52	45	59	**43**
	edges	186	171	158	**151**	167	187	287	161
	pairs	18	18	**17**	**17**	**17**	22	18	21
	minimal	3	7	7	8	3	**10**	7	**10**
	time [s]	0.70	**0.12**	0.14	0.13	0.72	3.08	3.05	**0.12**
	mem max	22.53	**8.02**	18.66	18.69	91.06	240.75	465.09	19.02
	mem avg	19.66	**7.13**	18.57	18.61	86.92	160.03	173.53	18.90
19 more of LTL\GUX	states	180	191	184	167	**132**	—	160	137
	edges	614	699	671	563	**390**	—	827	546
	pairs	43	44	44	44	32	—	**28**	46
	minimal	2	2	2	3	6	—	**11**	**11**
	time [s]	2.83	0.24	0.32	0.30	2.11	—	5.98	**0.19**
	mem max	33.81	**8.72**	18.80	18.83	92.94	—	1013.89	19.50
	mem avg	22.29	**7.44**	18.67	18.72	87.95	—	256.50	19.13
36 more of LTL	states	34 985	135 250	33 927	2 768	**386**	—	—	—
	edges	359 494	1 726 573	416 794	31 287	**1936**	—	—	—
	pairs	100	114	97	83	**49**	—	—	—
	minimal	9	8	9	13	**34**	—	—	—
	time [s]	26.46	102.15	16.86	**1.02**	1.64	—	—	—
	mem max	463.95	1 406.86	345.52	**24.41**	93.69	—	—	—
	mem avg	35.34	65.53	27.77	**18.90**	89.29	—	—	—

Table 2. Cross-comparison of considered tools on the three classes of real specification formulae. The number in row indexed by r and column c represents in how many cases the tool r produced a smaller automaton (in the number of states) than the tool c. The column V shows the sum of these "victories".

#		Tool	12 formulae of LTL(F, G)									19 more of LTL\GUX								36 more of LTL					
			1	2	3	4	5	6	7	8	V	1	2	3	4	5	7	8	V	1	2	3	4	5	V
1	ltl2dstar	LTL->NBA	—	0	0	0	0	1	3	1	5	—	1	1	2	0	4	3	11	—	13	9	3	0	25
2	ltl2dstar	LTL2BA	6	—	0	0	5	1	5	1	18	4	—	0	1	0	4	3	12	12	—	0	2	0	14
3	ltl2dstar	LTL3BA	6	1	—	0	5	1	5	1	19	4	1	—	1	0	4	3	13	14	14	—	4	0	32
4	ltl2dstar	LTL3BAd	6	1	1	—	6	1	5	1	21	4	2	2	—	0	5	4	17	22	17	13	—	2	54
5	ltl2dstar	Spot	1	1	0	0	—	1	4	1	8	12	9	9	8	—	7	6	51	27	28	27	23	—	**105**
6		Rabinizer	8	4	4	3	8	—	5	1	33	—	—	—	—	—	—	—	—	—	—	—	—	—	—
7		Rabinizer 2	6	3	3	3	6	0	—	1	22	15	15	15	14	10	—	4	**73**	—	—	—	—	—	—
8		LTL3DRA	9	4	4	3	9	2	5	—	**36**	14	12	12	11	9	8	—	66	—	—	—	—	—	—

Table 3. For each parametric formula and each tool, the table provides the *size* (number of states) of the automaton for the highest n such that all the considered tools finish the computation within the limit (upper row), and the *max*imal n for which the tool finishes the computation within the limit (lower row). The best values are emphasized.

Formula	size / max	ltl2dstar LTL->NBA	ltl2dstar LTL2BA	ltl2dstar LTL3BA	ltl2dstar LTL3BAd	ltl2dstar Spot	Rabinizer	Rabinizer 2	LTL3DRA
$E(n)$	$n=9$	**512**	**512**	**512**	**512**	**512**	**512**	**512**	**512**
	max n	9	11	11	11	**12**	10	9	10
$U(n)$	$n=5$	**17**	**17**	**17**	**17**	**17**	—	**17**	24
	max n	10	5	6	10	**12**	—	9	9
$R(n)$	$n=3$	375 631	290 046	483 789	2 347	15 980	52	97	**36**
	max n	3	3	3	4	3	4	3	**6**
$U_2(n)$	$n=14$	**15**	**15**	**15**	**15**	**15**	—	**15**	**15**
	max n	15	15	15	15	15	—	**19**	14
$C_1(n)$	$n=7$	129	**2**	**2**	**2**	3	128	128	**2**
	max n	11	23	23	23	22	8	7	**24**
$C_2(n)$	$n=6$	18	17	17	11	13	**7**	384	**7**
	max n	8	11	**17**	**17**	16	8	6	15
$Q(n)$	$n=7$	1 331	1 140	1 140	1 140	736	**578**	**578**	2 790
	max n	7	8	8	8	**9**	8	7	7
$S(n)$	$n=9$	513	513	513	513	513	**512**	**512**	**512**
	max n	**14**	**14**	**14**	**14**	11	9	9	13
$\theta(n)$	$n=5$	21	20	15	5 444	5 444	11	480	**7**
	max n	7	10	**19**	6	6	7	5	14
$F(n)$	$n=2$	13 181	11 324	5 650	302	4 307	20	32	**18**
	max n	2	2	2	2	2	3	2	**4**

The results are shown in Table 3. Note that $U(n)$ and $U_2(n)$ are not in the input fragment of Rabinizer. All the other formulae are from LTL(F, G).

Random Formulae. We use LTL formulae generator `randltl` [7] to get some more formulae of length 15–30 from various fragments. More precisely, we generate 100 formulae from the LTL(F, G) fragment, 100 general formulae with higher occurence of F and G operators, and 100 formulae with uniformly distributed operators. These three sets are generated by the respective commands:

- `randltl -n 100 --tree-size=15..30 --ltl-priorities="ap=1,X=0,\`
  `implies=0,false=0,true=0,R=0,equiv=0,U=0,W=0,M=0,xor=0" a b c d`
- `randltl -n 100 --tree-size=15..30 --ltl-priorities="ap=1,F=2,\`
  `G=2,false=0,true=0,X=1,R=1,U=1,W=0,M=0,xor=0" a b c d`
- `randltl -n 100 --tree-size=15..30 --ltl-priorities="ap=1,\`
  `false=0,true=0,W=0,M=0,xor=0" a b c d`

We removed 10 formulae, out of the 300 generated ones, that were elementary equivalent to *true* or *false*. The remaining formulae are divided into four classes corresponding to the input LTL fragments of the considered tools: we have 97 formulae of LTL(F, G), 29 formulae of LTL\GUX not included in LTL(F, G), 1 formula of LTL\GU not included in LTL\GUX, and 163 formulae not in LTL\GU. Unfortunately, ltl2dstar combined with LTL->NBA produces an error message for one formula of LTL\GUX and two formulae outside LTL\GU. These formulae were removed from the set. Further, there are 19 formulae (none of them in LTL\GU), for which at least one tool does not finish before timeout. These formulae are not included in the cummulative results to make them comparable, but we show the number of timeouts in a separate line. To sum up, Table 4 presents cummulative results for 97 formulae of LTL(F, G), 28 formulae of LTL\GUX not included in LTL(F, G), and 142 formulae outside LTL\GU (plus the numbers of timeouts for another 19 formulae outside LTL\GU). We do not show the results on the single formula of LTL\GU not included in LTL\GUX due to their low statistical significance.

Table 4. The cummulative results on random formulae. Semantics of the table is the same as for Table 1. Moreover, the last line shows the number of *timeouts* of the tools on additional 19 formulae outside LTL\GU.

Class	Measure	ltl2dstar				Spot	Rabinizer	Rabin. 2	LTL3DRA
		LTL->NBA	LTL2BA	LTL3BA	LTL3BAd				
97 formulae of LTL(F, G)	states	107 620	19 470	9 914	6 008	13 940	**511**	741	618
	edges	949 094	165 856	76 827	48 440	137 977	**2222**	4 987	2 666
	pairs	217	204	196	190	164	198	**149**	198
	minimal	18	36	37	44	41	**54**	26	44
	time [s]	743.66	13.47	10.15	3.42	18.09	48.81	79.92	**1.21**
	mem max	6 561.89	151.16	99.75	24.86	94.03	406.66	6 712.00	**22.89**
	mem avg	95.72	**8.90**	19.51	18.77	89.27	205.10	632.62	19.23
28 more of LTL\GUX	states	1 183	6 670	6 375	1 509	633	—	**451**	512
	edges	6 227	39 987	38 591	8 057	3 002	—	**2422**	2 810
	pairs	66	68	69	54	**48**	—	71	70
	minimal	9	14	13	15	17	—	11	**18**
	time [s]	15.86	1.14	1.49	0.76	5.01	—	40.34	**0.50**
	mem max	107.75	45.83	41.53	**19.58**	94.17	—	33 224.44	34.59
	mem avg	39.80	**9.23**	19.63	18.87	89.72	—	1 761.70	20.07
142+19 more of LTL	states	173 156	640 971	157 869	143 436	**11780**	—	—	—
	edges	1 513 621	5 127 962	1 103 410	1 031 393	**85476**	—	—	—
	pairs	523	625	499	438	**354**	—	—	—
	minimal	54	41	57	72	**126**	—	—	—
	time [s]	421.79	384.54	76.33	70.38	**16.80**	—	—	—
	mem max	1 461.08	6 019.14	1 751.94	2 357.64	**99.50**	—	—	—
	mem avg	92.59	96.75	37.61	**35.45**	91.13	—	—	—
	timeouts	8	17	6	2	**1**	—	—	—

Table 5. Cross-comparison of the considered tools on random formulae classes. The table has a similar semantics to Table 2: each number says in how many cases the tool in the corresponding row produces a *better* result than the tool in the corresponding column. An automaton is better than other if it has less states. Any automaton is better than timeout or a tool failure. Timeouts and failures are seen as equivalent results here.

#		Tool	97 formulae of LTL(F, G)									29 more of LTL\GUX								163 more of LTL					
			1	2	3	4	5	6	7	8	V	1	2	3	4	5	7	8	V	1	2	3	4	5	V
1	ltl2dstar	LTL->NBA	—	13	10	6	2	10	35	17	93	—	4	5	4	1	6	6	26	—	79	43	38	16	176
2		LTL2BA	44	—	5	4	9	12	41	22	137	14	—	3	2	0	12	6	37	38	—	13	22	7	80
3		LTL3BA	44	17	—	5	11	13	43	23	156	14	3	—	1	0	11	5	34	68	80	—	30	16	194
4		LTL3BAd	48	24	18	—	15	15	45	28	193	15	6	6	—	2	14	8	51	87	97	73	—	24	281
5		Spot	52	31	26	16	—	19	46	32	222	18	8	9	7	—	15	8	65	106	115	99	74	—	**394**
6		Rabinizer	62	44	43	36	35	—	57	37	314	—	—	—	—	—	—	—	—	—	—	—	—	—	—
7		Rabinizer 2	42	23	19	20	19	2	—	26	151	17	10	10	6	7	—	5	55	—	—	—	—	—	—
8		LTL3DRA	58	43	40	33	35	13	47	—	269	17	11	12	10	9	14	—	**73**	—	—	—	—	—	—

Table 5 contains a cross-comparison of the tools on the same formulae sets. In this case, the formulae previously removed because of a timeout or a tool failure are included.

4 Observations

For each pair of tools, there are some formulae in our benchmarks, for which one tool produces strictly smaller automata than the other (see Table 5). Hence, no tool is fully dominated by another.

All the results for LTL(F, G) fragment show that the Safraless tools (especially Rabinizer and LTL3DRA) usually perform better than ltl2dstar equipped with any of the considered LTL to NBA translators. The best results for formulae of LTL\GUX not included in LTL(F, G) are typically achived by ltl2dstar combined with Spot, and the Safraless tools Rabinizer 2 and LTL3DRA. For formulae outside LTL\GU, the current Safraless tools are not applicable. For these formulae, by far the best results are produced by ltl2dstar combined with Spot.

The results also provide information about particular tools or relations between them. For example, one can immediately see that Rabinizer outperforms Rabinizer 2 on LTL(F, G) formulae. This is explained by an experimental nature of the current version of Rabinizer 2. In particular, the tool misses some optimizations implemented in Rabinizer [20]. Further, one can observe that Rabinizer performs significantly better than the other tools on random formulae of LTL(F, G), while it is just comparable on real specification and parametric formulae of LTL(F, G). We assume that this is due to the fact that Rabinizer builds automata state-spaces according to semantics of LTL formulae rather than their syntax. Thus it does not distinguish between equivalent subformulae which more often appear in random formulae than in formulae written manually.

If we focus on usage of system resources, we observe that LTL3DRA is often the fastest tool. The results also show that ltl2dstar in combination with LTL2BA or LTL3BA has usually the lowest memory consumption.

During our experimentation we found out that ltl2dstar does not check whether an intermediate Büchi automaton is already deterministic or not: it runs Safra's construction in all cases. Running Safra's construction only on nondeterministic BA is profitable for two reasons:

1. Computation of Safra's construction is expensive.
2. Each deterministic BA can be directly converted into a DRA with one Rabin pair without any change in the state space, while Safra's construction typically produces a DRA larger than the intermediate deterministic BA.

For example, given the formula $G(p_1 \to G\neg p_2)$, both Spot and LTL3BAd produce a deterministic BA with two states (and a partial transition function). All considered LTL to DRA translators output DRA with four states (and total transition functions), Rabinizer 2 even yields a DRA with five states. Hence, the automaton produced by Spot or LTL3BAd is smaller even after the addition of one state to make its transition function total.

5 Conclusions

We conclude that the situation with LTL to DRA translation changed substantially since 2005. The former leading combinations of ltl2dstar with LTL->NBA or LTL2BA are now surpassed by Safraless tools (on relevant fragments) and ltl2dstar with Spot. However, there is still a space for further improvements.

Acknowledgements. We would like to thank Alexandre Duret-Lutz for valuable suggestions and comments on a draft of this paper.

References

1. Babiak, T., Blahoudek, F., Křetínský, M., Strejček, J.: Effective translation of LTL to deterministic Rabin automata: Beyond the (F,G)-fragment. In: Van Hung, D., Ogawa, M. (eds.) ATVA 2013. LNCS, vol. 8172, pp. 24–39. Springer, Heidelberg (2013)
2. Babiak, T., Křetínský, M., Řehák, V., Strejček, J.: LTL to Büchi automata translation: Fast and more deterministic. In: Flanagan, C., König, B. (eds.) TACAS 2012. LNCS, vol. 7214, pp. 95–109. Springer, Heidelberg (2012)
3. Baier, C., Katoen, J.-P.: Principles of Model Checking. MIT Press (2008)
4. Church, A.: Logic, arithmetic, and automata. In: ICM 1962, pp. 23–35. Institut Mittag-Leffler (1962)
5. Courcoubetis, C., Yannakakis, M.: The complexity of probabilistic verification. J. ACM 42(4), 857–907 (1995)
6. Duret-Lutz, A.: LTL translation improvements in Spot. In: VECoS 2011, Electronic Workshops in Computing. British Computer Society (2011)
7. Duret-Lutz, A.: Manipulating LTL formulas using Spot 1.0. In: Van Hung, D., Ogawa, M. (eds.) ATVA 2013. LNCS, vol. 8172, pp. 442–445. Springer, Heidelberg (2013)
8. Dwyer, M.B., Avrunin, G.S., Corbett, J.C.: Patterns in property specifications for finite-state verification. In: ICSE 1999, pp. 411–420. IEEE (1999)

9. Fritz, C.: Constructing Büchi automata from linear temporal logic using simulation relations for alternating Büchi automata. In: Ibarra, O.H., Dang, Z. (eds.) CIAA 2003. LNCS, vol. 2759, pp. 35–48. Springer, Heidelberg (2003)
10. Gaiser, A., Křetínský, J., Esparza, J.: Rabinizer: Small deterministic automata for LTL(F,G). In: Chakraborty, S., Mukund, M. (eds.) ATVA 2012. LNCS, vol. 7561, pp. 72–76. Springer, Heidelberg (2012)
11. Gastin, P., Oddoux, D.: Fast LTL to Büchi Automata Translation. In: Berry, G., Comon, H., Finkel, A. (eds.) CAV 2001. LNCS, vol. 2102, pp. 53–65. Springer, Heidelberg (2001)
12. Geldenhuys, J., Hansen, H.: Larger automata and less work for LTL model checking. In: Valmari, A. (ed.) SPIN 2006. LNCS, vol. 3925, pp. 53–70. Springer, Heidelberg (2006)
13. Holzmann, G.: The Spin model checker: primer and reference manual, 1st edn. Addison-Wesley Professional (2003)
14. Klein, J.: ltl2dstar – LTL to deterministic Streett and Rabin automata, http://www.ltl2dstar.de
15. Klein, J.: Linear time logic and deterministic omega-automata. Master's thesis, University of Bonn (2005)
16. Klein, J., Baier, C.: Experiments with deterministic ω-automata for formulas of linear temporal logic. Theor. Comput. Sci. 363(2), 182–195 (2006)
17. Klein, J., Baier, C.: On-the-fly stuttering in the construction of deterministic ω-automata. In: Holub, J., Žďárek, J. (eds.) CIAA 2007. LNCS, vol. 4783, pp. 51–61. Springer, Heidelberg (2007)
18. Křetínský, J., Esparza, J.: Deterministic automata for the (F, G)-fragment of LTL. In: Madhusudan, P., Seshia, S.A. (eds.) CAV 2012. LNCS, vol. 7358, pp. 7–22. Springer, Heidelberg (2012)
19. Kupferman, O.: Recent challenges and ideas in temporal synthesis. In: Bieliková, M., Friedrich, G., Gottlob, G., Katzenbeisser, S., Turán, G. (eds.) SOFSEM 2012. LNCS, vol. 7147, pp. 88–98. Springer, Heidelberg (2012)
20. Křetínský, J.: Personal communication (2013)
21. Křetínský, J., Garza, R.L.: Rabinizer 2: Small deterministic automata for LTL\GU. In: Van Hung, D., Ogawa, M. (eds.) ATVA 2013. LNCS, vol. 8172, pp. 446–450. Springer, Heidelberg (2013)
22. Pelánek, R.: Beem: Benchmarks for explicit model checkers. In: Bošnački, D., Edelkamp, S. (eds.) SPIN 2007. LNCS, vol. 4595, pp. 263–267. Springer, Heidelberg (2007)
23. Piterman, N.: From nondeterministic Büchi and Streett automata to deterministic parity automata. Logical Methods in Computer Science 3(3) (2007)
24. Pnueli, A., Rosner, R.: On the synthesis of an asynchronous reactive module. In: Ronchi Della Rocca, S., Ausiello, G., Dezani-Ciancaglini, M. (eds.) ICALP 1989. LNCS, vol. 372, pp. 652–671. Springer, Heidelberg (1989)
25. Rozier, K.Y., Vardi, M.Y.: LTL Satisfiability Checking. In: Bošnački, D., Edelkamp, S. (eds.) SPIN 2007. LNCS, vol. 4595, pp. 149–167. Springer, Heidelberg (2007)
26. Safra, S.: On the complexity of omega-automata. In: FOCS 1988, pp. 319–327. IEEE Computer Society (1988)
27. Schewe, S.: Tighter bounds for the determinisation of Büchi automata. In: de Alfaro, L. (ed.) FOSSACS 2009. LNCS, vol. 5504, pp. 167–181. Springer, Heidelberg (2009)
28. Tauriainen, H., Heljanko, K.: Testing LTL formula translation into Büchi automata. International Journal on Software Tools for Technology Transfer (STTT) 4(1), 57–70 (2002)
29. Vardi, M.Y.: Automatic verification of probabilistic concurrent finite-state programs. In: FOCS 1985, pp. 327–338. IEEE Computer Society (1985)

Tree Interpolation in Vampire*

Régis Blanc[1], Ashutosh Gupta[2], Laura Kovács[3], and Bernhard Kragl[4]

[1] EPFL
[2] IST Austria
[3] Chalmers
[4] TU Vienna

Abstract. We describe new extensions of the Vampire theorem prover for computing tree interpolants. These extensions generalize Craig interpolation in Vampire, and can also be used to derive sequence interpolants. We evaluated our implementation on a large number of examples over the theory of linear integer arithmetic and integer-indexed arrays, with and without quantifiers. When compared to other methods, our experiments show that some examples could only be solved by our implementation.

1 Introduction

In interpolation-based verification approaches, a Craig interpolant [3] is a logical formula justifying why a program trace is spurious and therefore can be used, for example, to refine the set of predicates for predicate abstraction [10], invariant generation [13], and correctness proofs of programs [8]. As refining a path in the control flow graph of a program requires iterative computations of interpolants for each path location, Craig interpolants have been generalized to sequence interpolants for their use in bounded model checking non-procedural programs [10]. Using sequence interpolants to reason about programs with recursive procedures is however a non-trivial task. The work of [12] introduces the notion of tree interpolants, which can be used for the verification of concurrent [5] and recursive programs [8]. In this context, dependencies between program paths are encoded using a tree data structure, where a tree node represents a formula valid at an intermediate program location. Tree interpolants provide a nested structure for representing formulas, and therefore allow to reason about programs with function/procedure calls.

Similarly to Craig interpolation, the key ingredient in theorem proving based tree interpolation is the computation of special proofs, for example local or split proofs [10,9], with feasible interpolation. Interpolants from such proofs can be constructed in polynomial time in the size of the proof. Current approaches for building Craig/sequence/tree interpolants depend on the existence of such proofs. For example, [14] uses SMT reasoning to derive Craig interpolants in the quantifier-free theory of linear arithmetic and uninterpreted functions. This approach is further generalized in [7] for computing tree interpolants from propositional proofs and in [2,12,5] to derive tree interpolants in the

---

* This research was partly supported by the Austrian National Research Network RiSE (FWF grants S11402-N23 and S11410-N23) and the WWTF PROSEED grant (ICT C-050).

theory of linear arithmetic and uninterpreted functions. Contrary to the above techniques, in [9] Craig interpolants are extracted from first-order local proofs in any sound calculus, without being limited to decidable theories. However, the method of [9] cannot yet be used for deriving tree and sequence interpolants.

In this paper we address the generality of [9] and describe a tool support for extracting tree interpolants in arbitrary first-order theories (Section 4). Our method is implemented in the Vampire theorem prover [11] and extends Vampire with new features for theory reasoning and interpolation. Our implementation adds a general interpolation procedure to Vampire, which can be used for computing Craig interpolants, sequence interpolants and tree interpolants. For doing so, we reduce the problem of tree interpolations to iterative applications of Craig interpolants on tree nodes (Section 3). Our approach is different from [2,7] where tree interpolants are extracted from only one proof, by exploiting propositional reasoning or linear arithmetic properties. Our tool can be used in arbitrary theories and calculus, but comes at the cost of computing different proofs for each tree node. Our implementation can however be optimized when considering specific theories, reducing the burden of iterative proof computations. We tested our tool on challenging examples over arrays, involving reasoning with both quantifiers and theories (Section 5). To the best of our knowledge, our tool is the only approach able to derive tree interpolants with both quantifiers and theory symbols. We also evaluated our implementation on examples coming from the model checking of device drivers, where quantifier-free reasoning over linear integer arithmetic and integer-indexed arrays was required. On these examples our method does not perform as well as theory-specific approaches, e.g. [14]. The strength of our tool comes thus when tree interpolants in full first-order theories are needed. Extending our implementation with proof transformations for various theories is an interesting task for future work.

2 Tree Interpolation

All formulas in this paper are first-order, with standard boolean connectives and quantifiers. The *language* of a formula R, denoted by $\mathcal{L}_R$, is the set of all formulas built from the symbols occurring in R. By a symbol we mean function and predicate symbols; variables are not symbols. Given two formulas R and B such that $R \wedge B$ is unsatisfiable, a formula $I_{R,B}$ is called a *Craig interpolant of R and B* (or simply just an *interpolant*) iff $R \rightarrow I_{R,B}$, $I_{R,B} \wedge B$ is unsatisfiable, and $I_{R,B}$ contains only symbols that occur both in the languages of R and B. A proof of unsatisfiability of $R \wedge B$ is called *local* [9] if every proof step uses symbols either only from R, or only from B.

We describe the problem of tree interpolation, by adapting the notation of [1,12].

Definition 1. *A tree interpolation problem $T = (V, r, P, L)$ is a directed labeled tree, where V is a finite set of nodes, $r \in V$ is the root, $P : (V \setminus \{r\}) \mapsto V$ is a function that maps children nodes to their parents, and $L : V \mapsto \mathbb{F}$ is a labeling function that maps nodes to formulas from a set $\mathbb{F}$ of first-order formulas, such that $\bigwedge_{v \in V} L(v)$ is unsatisfiable.*

Let $T = (V, r, P, L)$ be a tree interpolation problem and P^* be the reflexive transitive closure of P. For $V_0 \subseteq V$ we write $L(V_0)$ to denote the formula $\bigwedge_{v \in V_0} L(v)$. For each

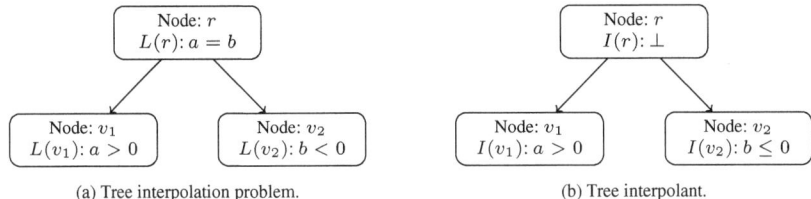

Fig. 1. An example of tree interpolation; a and b are integer-valued constants

$v \in V$ we define $V_{in}(v) = \{c \mid v \in P^*(c)\}$ and $V_{out}(v) = V \setminus V_{in}(v)$. The *problem of tree interpolation* is then to compute a tree interpolant, defined as follows.

Definition 2. *Let* $T = (V, r, P, L)$ *be a tree interpolation problem. A tree interpolant for T is a function* $I : V \mapsto \mathbb{F}$ *satisfying the following conditions:*

(C1) $I(r) = \bot$;
(C2) for each $v \in V$, we have: $\left(\bigwedge_{P(c_i)=v} I(c_i) \wedge L(v) \right) \to I(v)$;
(C3) for each $v \in V$, we have: $\mathcal{L}_{I(v)} \subseteq \mathcal{L}_{L(V_{in}(v))} \cap \mathcal{L}_{L(V_{out}(v))}$.

In the following, we refer to $I(v)$ as a *node interpolant*, or simply just an *interpolant*, of node v. Figure 1(a) gives an example of a tree interpolation problem, and Figure 1(b) shows a correspoding tree interpolant.

3 Tree Interpolation Algorithm

When computing a tree interpolant for a tree interpolation problem T, we need to establish conditions (C1)-(C3) from Definition 2. Since $L(V_{in}(v)) \wedge L(V_{out}(v))$ is unsatisfiable for each $v \in V$, we can compute an interpolant between $L(V_{in}(v))$ and $L(V_{out}(v))$. However, computing all node interpolants $I(v)$ this way may violate condition (C2), as illustrated in Example 1.

Example 1. Consider the tree interpolation problem from Figure 1(a). We compute $I(v_1)$ as an interpolant between $L(v_1)$ and $L(v_2) \wedge L(r)$, and $I(v_2)$ as an interpolant between $L(v_2)$ and $L(v_1) \wedge L(r)$. In this example, we may take $I(v_1) = (a \geq 0)$ and $I(v_2) = (b \leq 0)$. By definition, $I(r) = \bot$. But then $I(v_1) \wedge I(v_2) \wedge L(r)$ is satisfiable, and hence $I(v_1) \wedge I(v_2) \wedge L(r) \to I(r)$ does not hold.

Example 1 shows that node interpolants are logically weaker than node labels. Already computed node interpolants have to be taken into account for computing further node interpolants. Our tree interpolation algorithm is based on this observation and summarized in Algorithm 1.

In line 4 all node interpolants are initialized to ∞, representing undefined. A node interpolant in our algorithm is thus either undefined or a first-order formula. Then we iterate over all nodes of T according to the loop condition in line 6. That is, we always choose an arbitray node v with undefined interpolant, such that the interpolants of its children have already been computed. In lines 7-8 the tree nodes are partitioned into

Algorithm 1. Tree Interpolation.
1: **Input:** Tree interpolation problem $T = (V, r, P, L)$
2: **Output:** Tree interpolant I of T
3: **for** each $v \in V$ **do**
4:     $I(v) = \infty$
5: **end for**
6: **for** each $v \in V$ such that $I(v) = \infty$ and $I(c) \neq \infty$ for each $c \in V$ with $v = P(c)$ **do**
7:     $R_v = S(V_{in}(v), v)$ (call to Alg. 2)
8:     $B_v = S(V_{out}(v), r)$ (call to Alg. 2)
9:     $I(v) = CraigInterpolant(R_v, B_v)$
10: **end for**

Algorithm 2. Interpolant/Label Collection.
1: **Input:** Set of tree nodes $V_0 \subseteq V$ and a node $v \in V$
2: **Output:** Node interpolant of v or conjunction of children interpolants and label of v
3: $S(V_0, v) = \begin{cases} I(v) & \text{if } I(v) \neq \infty \\ \bigwedge_{P(c)=v \wedge c \in V_0} S(V_0, c) \wedge L(v) & \text{otherwise} \end{cases}$

$V_{in}(v)$ and $V_{out}(v)$, which are used to obtain the formulas R_v and B_v, by taking the conjunction of node labels from root to leaves up to the first defined node interpolant (see Algorithm 2). Then $I(v)$ is set to a Craig interpolant of R_v and B_v (line 9). Using induction over the set of nodes, it is now easy to prove that $I(v)$ satisfies the constraints of tree interpolation for every node v, and hence Algorithm 1 computes a tree interpolant I of T. Note that Algorithm 1 does not specify the concrete order in which the nodes are visited. Different feasible orderings lead to different tree interpolants.

4 Implementation in Vampire

We implemented the tree interpolation method of Algorithm 1 in the Vampire theorem prover. To make Vampire able to compute tree interpolants, we had to extend Vampire with new functionalities, including reading tree interpolation problems, deriving tree interpolants, computing interpolants of tree nodes, and theory-specific proof transformation steps for proof localisation. We also extended Vampire with built-in data types for integer-indexed arrays, and added array axioms to the built-in theory reasoning engine of Vampire. All together computing tree interpolants in Vampire required about 5000 lines of C++ code. The architecture of our implementation is given in Figure 2.
Tool Usage. Our implementation is available at http://vprover.org/tree_itp. For using it, one should simply invoke Vampire on the command line as follows:

```
vampire --show_interpolant tree --[vampire/z3] problem
```

The choice of using either `vampire` or `z3` refers to proof generation (see later), whereas the input format of `problem` is as detailed below.
Input. Inputs to our implementation are tree interpolation problems in the SMT-LIB 1.2 format, using the input standard of [1]. Propositional variables are used to denote tree nodes, and logical implication is used to specify parent-child relations between nodes.

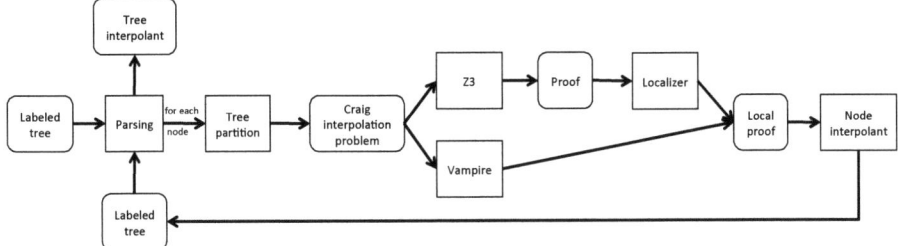

Fig. 2. Tree interpolation in Vampire

Tree Interpolation. We use Algorithm 1 to compute and output a tree interpolant I of T. We explore the tree in a breadth-first manner, starting from the leaves of the tree. At each level, we visit the nodes from left-to-right and compute their interpolants.

Interpolants of Tree Nodes. When computing interpolants for tree nodes, we adapt the Craig interpolation procedure of [9] to our setting of R_v and B_v. We collect the set of symbols occurring only in R_v, respectively in B_v. The set of symbols used in a Craig interpolant of R_v and B_v is then defined as the set of symbols common to both R_v and B_v. With such specification of symbols, our task is to derive a local proof of $R_v \wedge B_v \to \bot$ and compute a Craig interpolant from this proof. We used [9] to construct Craig interpolants from local proofs and computed interpolants that are small both in their number of symbols and quantifiers. For generating local proofs we used the following two directions.

Proof Localization. We generate local proofs either by using Vampire or by localizing an SMT proof generated by the Z3 SMT solver [4]. When using Vampire, the symbol specifications of R_v and B_v are used as Vampire annotations to ensure that the generated Vampire proofs are local. When running Z3, we first obtain a Z3 proof which might not be local. Then, using the symbol specifications of R_v and B_v we try to localize the SMT proof by (i) quantifying away some constant symbols of R_v or B_v as explained in [9] and by (ii) applying proof transformation steps over linear arithmetic and uninterpreted functions (as explained later). For parsing and localising SMT proofs, our implementation extends Vampire with built-in sorts for integer-indexed arrays and adds array reasoning based on the extensionality axioms of the array theory. To use Craig interpolants in further steps of tree interpolation, we also extended Vampire with a parser for converting Vampire formulas into the SMT-LIB format, by considering theory-specific reasoning over linear integer arithmetic and arrays.

Theory-Specific Reasoning for Proof Localization. In some cases, Vampire rewrites the non-local parts of an SMT proof without using the approach of [9] for introducing quantifiers. In [6], we have presented theory-specific proof rewriting rules that localize proofs involving linear arithmetic with uninterpreted function symbols. Vampire uses now some of these rules to recognize patterns of non-local SMT proofs and rewrite them into a local proof in the quantifier-free theory of linear arithmetic and uninterpreted functions. To illustrate how theory-aware SMT proof localisation is performed in our implementation, consider the following example. Let R be $a = b \wedge b = c$ and B the

Table 1. Tree interpolation in Vampire on quantified array problems

Example	Description	Tree Interpolant
Init	set array elements to 0, update one element to 1	all elements 0 or 1
Sorted	sort array in ascending order	ordering between two concrete array elements
Sorted2	sort array in ascending order	ordering for range of array elements
Shift	set array elements to the values of their neighbours	array elements are all equal

formula $c = d \wedge a \neq d$, where a, b, c, d are integer-valued constants. Clearly, R and B is unsatisfiable. A possible SMT proof of unsatisfiability (e.g. by Z3) might involve the following steps: derive $b = d$ from $b = c$ and $c = d$ and derive $a = d$ from $a = b$ and $b = d$, which then contradicts $a \neq d$. Note that $b = d$ yields a non-local proof step as it uses symbols that are not common to R and B. Our proof transformation in Vampire will then reorder this equality derivation. The rewritten proof will then derive $a = c$ from $a = b$ and $b = c$ and infer $a = d$ from $a = c$ and $c = d$; clearly, this proof is local and, unlike [9], uses no quantifiers over b and d.

Optimizations. To reduce the number of local proof computations, we implemented the following heuristic. When extracting the symbols of R_v and B_v for a node v, we also derive whether R_v uses only symbols common to B_v. If this is the case, we take R_v as the interpolant $I_{R_v B_v}$. A similar heuristic is implemented also when B_v contains only symbols common to R_v. In our experiments we observed that these heuristics save expensive theorem proving calls.

Sequence and Craig Interpolants. Our implementation can also be used to compute sequence interpolants. In this case, the sequence structure is represented as a sequence of SMT-LIB assumptions, and no additional propositional variables are used to denote assumptions (i.e. tree nodes). To use Vampire for computing sequence interpolants, one should specify sequence instead of tree in the command run execution of Vampire. Our implementation can also be used to simply compute Craig interpolants of two formulas, by using the approach of [9] and specifying on instead of tree in the command line. Tree interpolation in Vampire hence brings a general interpolation procedure, which can be used for tree, sequence and Craig interpolation.

5 Experiments

We evaluated tree interpolation in Vampire using two benchmark suites. One is a collection of 4 examples where quantified reasoning over the array content is needed. These examples are taken from [13,15] and involve common array operations, such as initialization, copying and sortedness (Table 1). The other one is a collection of 175 problems (Table 2), extracted from the bounded model checking of device drivers [12]. These examples are expressed in the quantifier-free theory of linear integer arithmetic and integer-indexed arrays. All experiments reported here were obtained using a Lenovo X200 machine with 4GB of RAM and Intel Core 2 Duo processor with 2.53GHz, and are available at the url of our tool.

Quantified Array Problems. We computed tree interpolants in the quantified theory of arrays and integer arithmetic for 4 array problems. The examples involved procedure calls implementing array initialization, copy and sorting. We manually converted

Table 2. Tree interpolation in Vampire on quantifier-free array problems

Prover	Nb. Benchmarks	Success	Time
Vampire	175	101	60s
Z3	175	113	60s

Table 3. Tree interpolation in Vampire and iZ3

Tool	Quantified problems		Quantifier-free problems	
	Total	Solved	Total	Solved
Vampire	4	4	175	141
iZ3	4	1	175	175

these problems into corresponding tree interpolation problems, and then run our implementation. Each tree interpolation problem had a tree with 3 nodes. Example 2 shows later one of these benchmark and Table 1 summarizes our experiments. For each example, the table states the name of the example, gives a brief description of the program, and summarizes the tree interpolant. For the examples Init, Sorted2, and Shift, one tree node required the computation of a quantified node interpolant. All examples were solved in less than 1 second. The tree interpolants generated by our method were successfully used to proved quantified safety assertions over arrays.

Quantifier-Free Array Problems. The experiments described in Table 2 involved parsing 738′890 lines of SMT-LIB, with an average of about 90 tree nodes per benchmark. This means, that deriving a tree interpolant required on average computing 90 node interpolants per benchmarks. We distinguish between the use of Z3 or Vampire for computing local proofs of node interpolants – see column 1 of Table 2. Column 2 shows the number of benchmarks used in our experiments. Colum 3 gives the number of problems on which our implementation succeeded to compute tree interpolants, and column 4 list the average time (in seconds) per problem required by our implementation.

When using Vampire for local proof generation, we derived tree interpolants for 101 examples. Since the benchmarks were quantifier-free, the tree interpolants were quantifier-free as well. The 74 examples on which Vampire was not able to compute local proofs required more complex reasoning about arrays, involving both reading and writing to arrays.

When using Z3 for local proof generation, Z3 proved all 175 examples, however the returned proofs were not local. We succeeded to localize proofs, and hence compute tree interpolants, for 113 examples, out of which 14 tree interpolants contained quantifiers. We failed on 62 examples either because (i) proofs could not be localized, or (ii) quantified node interpolants were computed. When using quantified node interpolants in further steps of the tree interpolation, Z3 failed to find proofs in many cases.

Finally we note that some tree interpolation problems could only be solved by either using Vampire or Z3 for local proof generation. In total, we derived tree interpolants for 141 examples. The results of Table 2 suggest that improving theory-specific proof transformations as well as reasoning with both theories and quantifiers would yield better results for tree interpolation in first-order theories.

Experimental Comparison. We compared our tool to the tree interpolation procedure of iZ3 [1]. Table 3 shows that iZ3 performs much better on the quanifier-free examples of Table 2. However, on the quantified array problems, iZ3 succeeded only on the Sorted example where the tree interpolant did not involved quantifiers. Unlike iZ3, we derived tree interpolants for all quantified problems. For the problems where iZ3 failed, we either observed an incorrect interpolant, a segmentation fault or a failed proof attempt by Z3. Example 2 shows an interpolation problem for which iZ3 computes an

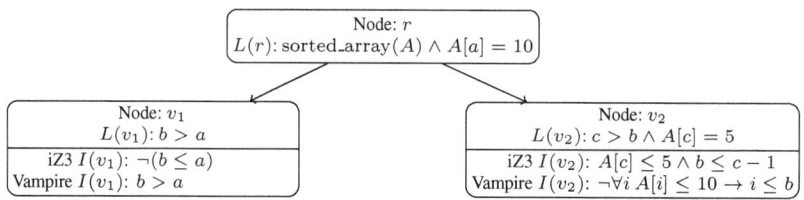

Fig. 3. Tree interpolation on the Sorted2 example from Table 1

incorrect result. Table 3 underlines the advantage of tree interpolation in Vampire: it can be used for quantified reasoning over (arbitrary) first-order theories. To the best of our knowledge, no other approach can compute quantified tree interpolants.

Example 2. The tree structure of Figure 3 shows the tree interpolation problem of the Sorted2 example of Table 1. In this example, a, b, c are integer-valued constants and A is an array of integers. Further, in the root label we have $\text{sorted\_array}(A) \Leftrightarrow (\forall i)(\forall j)\ i < j \rightarrow A[i] < A[j]$. Figure 3 also shows the incorrect tree interpolant computed by iZ3 and the correct tree interpolant computed by Vampire.

6 Conclusion

We described how tree interpolation in Vampire is implemented and can be used. Our implementation extends Vampire with deriving tree interpolants, computing interpolants for tree nodes, theory-specific proof localisations, and built-in data structures for arrays. In addition, tree interpolation in Vampire can be used to compute sequence or Craig interpolants. Our experiments highlight the advantage of our implementation for quantified tree interpolation. Future work includes extending our implementation with better theory reasoning both for proof localisation and proving, and deriving tree interpolants from only one proof of unsatisfiability. We are also interested in evaluating the quality of our tree interpolants in the context of model checking, by using them for proving safety properties of problems.

Acknowledgements. We thank Ken McMillan for the quantifier-free benchmarks.

References

1. iZ3 Documentation, http://research.microsoft.com/en-us/um/redmond/projects/z3/old/iz3documentation.html
2. Albarghouthi, A., Gurfinkel, A., Chechik, M.: Craig Interpretation. In: Miné, A., Schmidt, D. (eds.) SAS 2012. LNCS, vol. 7460, pp. 300–316. Springer, Heidelberg (2012)
3. Craig, W.: Three Uses of the Herbrand-Gentzen Theorem in Relating Model Theory and Proof Theory. J. of Symbolic Logic 22(3), 269–285 (1957)
4. de Moura, L., Bjørner, N.S.: Z3: An Efficient SMT Solver. In: Ramakrishnan, C.R., Rehof, J. (eds.) TACAS 2008. LNCS, vol. 4963, pp. 337–340. Springer, Heidelberg (2008)

5. Gupta, A., Popeea, C., Rybalchenko, A.: Predicate Abstraction and Refinement for Verifying Multi-Threaded Programs. In: Proc. of POPL, pp. 331–344 (2011)
6. Gupta, A., Thevenet-Montagne, A.: Tree Interpolants via Localized Proofs (2012), http://pub.ist.ac.at/~agupta/papers/localize-draft.pdf
7. Gurfinkel, A., Rollini, S.F., Sharygina, N.: Interpolation Properties and SAT-Based Model Checking. In: Van Hung, D., Ogawa, M. (eds.) ATVA 2013. LNCS, vol. 8172, pp. 255–271. Springer, Heidelberg (2013)
8. Heizmann, M., Hoenicke, J., Podelski, A.: Nested Interpolants. In: Proc. of POPL, pp. 471–482 (2010)
9. Hoder, K., Kovács, L., Voronkov, A.: Playing in the Grey Area of Proofs. In: Proc. of POPL, pp. 259–272 (2012)
10. Jhala, R., McMillan, K.L.: A Practical and Complete Approach to Predicate Refinement. In: Hermanns, H., Palsberg, J. (eds.) TACAS 2006. LNCS, vol. 3920, pp. 459–473. Springer, Heidelberg (2006)
11. Kovács, L., Voronkov, A.: First-Order Theorem Proving and VAMPIRE. In: Sharygina, N., Veith, H. (eds.) CAV 2013. LNCS, vol. 8044, pp. 1–35. Springer, Heidelberg (2013)
12. McMillan, K., Rybalchenko, A.: Solving Constrained Horn Clauses using Interpolation. Technical report, MSR (2013)
13. McMillan, K.L.: Quantified invariant generation using an interpolating saturation prover. In: Ramakrishnan, C.R., Rehof, J. (eds.) TACAS 2008. LNCS, vol. 4963, pp. 413–427. Springer, Heidelberg (2008)
14. McMillan, K.L.: Interpolants from Z3 Proofs. In: Proc. of FMCAD, pp. 19–27 (2011)
15. Srivastava, S., Gulwani, S.: Program Verification using Templates over Predicate Abstraction. In: Proc. of PLDI, pp. 223–234 (2009)

Polarizing Double-Negation Translations

Mélanie Boudard[1] and Olivier Hermant[2]

[1] PRiSM, Univ. de Versailles-St-Quentin-en-Yvelines
CNRS, France
melanie.boudard@prism.uvsq.fr
[2] CRI, MINES ParisTech
olivier.hermant@mines-paristech.fr

Abstract. Double-negation translations are used to encode and decode classical proofs in intuitionistic logic. We show that, in the cut-free fragment, we can simplify the translations and introduce fewer negations. To achieve this, we consider the polarization of the formulæ and adapt those translation to the different connectives and quantifiers. We show that the embedding results still hold, using a customized version of the focused classical sequent calculus. We also prove the latter equivalent to more usual versions of the sequent calculus. This polarization process allows lighter embeddings, and sheds some light on the relationship between intuitionistic and classical connectives.

Keywords: classical logic, intuitionnistic logic, double-negation translation, focusing.

1 Introduction

The relationship between different formal systems is a longstanding field of studies, and involves for instance conservativity, relative consistency or independence problems [1]. As for deductive systems, the natural question is to find a conservative encoding of formulæ. By conservative, we mean an encoding of formulæ such that a formula is provable in the first system if and only if its encoding is provable in the second system. This work was pioneered by Kolmogorov [2], Gödel [3] and Gentzen [4] for classical and intuitionistic logics. There exist several classes of sequents that are known to be classically provable if and only if they are intuitionistically provable [5].

In this paper, we refine those translations by removing a large number of unnecessary negations. Instead of focusing on invariant classes as in [5], we consider a translation on all the formulæ. A common point with this work, however, is the use of syntactic transformations. The proof systems we consider are the cut-free intuitionistic and classical sequent calculi [6]. This allows two remarks:

- the left rules of both calculi are identical; therefore it seems natural to translate them by themselves, when possible.

- In the absence of the cut rule, a formula is never active in different sides (both as an hypothesis and as a conclusion) of the turnstyle, having therefore a well-defined *polarity*. This last fact holds for all the rules except the axiom rule, which is easily dealt with, by an η-expansion-like argument, i.e. decomposing the formula by structural rules until we get axioms between atomic formula only.

In summary, we can avoid the introduction of negations on formulæ belonging to the "left" (or hypothesis) side of sequents. We also introduce further refinements, inspired by those of [3,4], to remove even more negations in the translation, based on the observation that some right-rules are also identical in the classical and intuitionistic calculi. To show conservativity by syntactic means without the cut rule, we need to impose a focusing discipline on the right-hand side of the classical sequent calculus, forced by the single-formula condition on the right-hand side of an intuitionistic sequent. We dedicate Section 4 to the study of a customized focused sequent calculus.

The price to pay of an asymmetric translation is that the result misses some modularity since we dismiss the cut rule: given a proof of a A and a proof of $A \Rightarrow B$, we cannot combine them with a cut rule. Both translations of A are not the same and so the translations of the proofs do not compose *directly*. See also the discussion in Section 6.

The paper is organized as follows. In Section 2, we give a brief overview of the background material, in particular the negative translations. In Section 3, we introduce a first polarized refinement of Kolmogorov negative translation, while Section 4 discusses the properties of the focused sequent calculus that we need in Section 5 to show that the polarized refinement of Gentzen-Gödel negative translation still has the same properties than the other translations. Section 6 concludes the paper.

2 Prerequisites

Here, we briefly recall the syntax of first-order logic, sequent calculus and the already known double-negation translations.

2.1 First-Order Logic

We assume that the reader is familiar with one-sorted first-order logic [6]: terms are composed of variables and function symbols applied to terms along their arities, and formulæ are either predicate symbols applied to terms along their arities or composed ones with the help of the conjunction ($\wedge$), disjunction ($\vee$), implication ($\Rightarrow$), negation ($\neg$) connectives and the universal ($\forall$) and existential ($\exists$) quantifiers.

To shorten the statement of our results and their proofs, we also define an operator that removes the trailing negation of formulæ, if any, and otherwise adds it.

Definition 1 (antinegation). *Let A be a formula, we let $\lnot A$ be:*

- *B if A is equal to $\neg B$*
- *$\neg A$ otherwise.*

Note that $\lnot$ is not a connective, it is an operator, similar to Boolean complement in that $\lnot\neg$ is the identity. In particular it has no associated rule in the sequent calculus. For instance $\lnot P(a)$ is the same as $\neg P(a)$ while $\lnot\neg(A \land B)$ is the same as $(A \land B)$.

2.2 Sequent Calculi

Since they will be discussed in details in the next sections, we explicitly give the details of the classical and intuitionistic sequent calculi. A sequent is a pair of two multisets of formulæ, denoted $\Gamma \vdash \Delta$. The comma serves as a shorthand for multi-set union and Γ, A is an overloaded notation for $\Gamma, \{A\}$.

The classical sequent calculus is presented in Figure 1. The formula that is decomposed is called the *active* formula. The intuitionistic sequent calculus differs from the classical in the restriction imposed to the right-hand sides of sequents: it must be either empty, or reduced to one formula. Consequently, the following rules are modified: contr_R disappears; in the first premiss of the $\Rightarrow_L$ rule and the axiom rule, Δ is empty; finally, the $\lor_R$ rule splits to account for the choice of keeping A or B. For clarity, the intuitionistic sequent calculus is presented in Figure 2.

Note that, as announced, we do not consider the cut rule to be part of the calculus; so we reason in cut-free calculi.

2.3 Negative Translations

In this section, we briefly recall four existing translations [7,8]. In 1925, the first translation is published by Kolmogorov [2]. This translation involves adding a double negation in front of every subformula:

$$A^{Ko} \equiv \neg\neg A \text{ for } A \text{ atomic} \quad (\neg A)^{Ko} \equiv \neg\neg(\neg A^{Ko})$$
$$(A \land B)^{Ko} \equiv \neg\neg(A^{Ko} \land B^{Ko}) \quad (\forall x A)^{Ko} \equiv \neg\neg\forall x A^{Ko}$$
$$(A \lor B)^{Ko} \equiv \neg\neg(A^{Ko} \lor B^{Ko}) \quad (\exists x A)^{Ko} \equiv \neg\neg\exists x A^{Ko}$$
$$(A \Rightarrow B)^{Ko} \equiv \neg\neg(A^{Ko} \Rightarrow B^{Ko})$$

With the Kolmogorov's translation, A is provable using classical logic if and only if A^{Ko} is provable using intuitionistic logic.

A few years later, Gödel[3], and independently Gentzen[4], proposed a new translation, where disjunctions and existential quantifiers are replaced by a combination of negation and their De Morgan duals, respectively conjunctions and universal quantifiers:

$$\overline{\Gamma, A \vdash A, \Delta} \text{ ax}$$

$$\frac{\Gamma, A, B \vdash \Delta}{\Gamma, A \wedge B \vdash \Delta} \wedge_L \qquad \frac{\Gamma \vdash A, \Delta \quad \Gamma \vdash B, \Delta}{\Gamma \vdash A \wedge B, \Delta} \wedge_R$$

$$\frac{\Gamma, A \vdash \Delta \quad \Gamma, B \vdash \Delta}{\Gamma, A \vee B \vdash \Delta} \vee_L \qquad \frac{\Gamma \vdash A, B, \Delta}{\Gamma \vdash A \vee B, \Delta} \vee_R$$

$$\frac{\Gamma \vdash A, \Delta \quad \Gamma, B \vdash \Delta}{\Gamma, A \Rightarrow B \vdash \Delta} \Rightarrow_L \qquad \frac{\Gamma, A \vdash B, \Delta}{\Gamma \vdash A \Rightarrow B, \Delta} \Rightarrow_R$$

$$\frac{\Gamma \vdash A, \Delta}{\Gamma, \neg A \vdash \Delta} \neg_L \qquad \frac{\Gamma, A \vdash \Delta}{\Gamma \vdash \neg A, \Delta} \neg_R$$

$$\frac{\Gamma, A[c/x] \vdash \Delta}{\Gamma, \exists x A \vdash \Delta} \exists_L \qquad \frac{\Gamma \vdash A[t/x], \Delta}{\Gamma \vdash \exists x A, \Delta} \exists_R$$

$$\frac{\Gamma, A[t/x] \vdash \Delta}{\Gamma, \forall x A \vdash \Delta} \forall_L \qquad \frac{\Gamma \vdash A[c/x], \Delta}{\Gamma \vdash \forall x A, \Delta} \forall_R$$

$$\frac{\Gamma, A, A \vdash \Delta}{\Gamma, A \vdash \Delta} \text{contr}_L \qquad \frac{\Gamma \vdash A, \Delta}{\Gamma \vdash A, A, \Delta} \text{contr}_R$$

$$\frac{\Gamma \vdash \Delta}{\Gamma, A \vdash \Delta} \text{weak}_L \qquad \frac{\Gamma \vdash \Delta}{\Gamma \vdash A, \Delta} \text{weak}_R$$

where, in $\forall_L$ and $\exists_R$, c is a fresh constant and, in $\forall_R$ and $\exists_L$, t is any term.

Fig. 1. Classical sequent calculus

$$\begin{aligned}
(A^{gg}) &\equiv \neg\neg A \text{ for } A \text{ atomic} & (\neg A)^{gg} &\equiv \neg A^{gg} \\
(A \wedge B)^{gg} &\equiv A^{gg} \wedge B^{gg} & (\forall x A)^{gg} &\equiv \forall x A^{gg} \\
(A \vee B)^{gg} &\equiv \neg(\neg A^{gg} \wedge \neg B^{gg}) & (\exists x A)^{gg} &\equiv \neg\forall x \neg A^{gg} \\
(A \Rightarrow B)^{gg} &\equiv A^{gg} \Rightarrow B^{gg}
\end{aligned}$$

As Kolmogorov's translation, Gödel-Gentzen's translation allows to show that A is provable using classical logic if and only if A^{gg} is provable using intuitionistic logic.

Kuroda [9] defined in 1951 a new translation:
$$\begin{aligned}
A^{Ku} &\equiv A \text{ for } A \text{ atomic} & (\neg A)^{Ku} &\equiv \neg A^{Ku} \\
(A \wedge B)^{Ku} &\equiv A^{Ku} \wedge B^{Ku} & (\forall x A)^{Ku} &\equiv \forall x \neg\neg A^{Ku} \\
(A \vee B)^{Ku} &\equiv A^{Ku} \vee B^{Ku} & (\exists x A)^{Ku} &\equiv \exists x A^{Ku} \\
(A \Rightarrow B)^{Ku} &\equiv A^{Ku} \Rightarrow B^{Ku}
\end{aligned}$$

A is provable classically if and only if $\neg\neg A^{Ku}$ is provable intuitionistically.

More recently, Krivine [10] has introduced a fourth translation:
$$\begin{aligned}
A^{Kr} &\equiv \neg A \text{ for } A \text{ atomic} & (\neg A)^{Kr} &\equiv \neg A^{Kr} \\
(A \wedge B)^{Kr} &\equiv A^{Kr} \vee B^{Kr} & (\forall x A)^{Kr} &\equiv \exists A^{Kr} \\
(A \vee B)^{Kr} &\equiv A^{Kr} \wedge B^{Kr} & (\exists x A)^{Kr} &\equiv \neg\exists x \neg A^{Kr} \\
(A \Rightarrow B)^{Kr} &\equiv \neg A^{Kr} \wedge B^{Kr}
\end{aligned}$$

$$\frac{}{\Gamma, A \vdash A} \text{ ax}$$

$$\frac{\Gamma, A, B \vdash \Delta}{\Gamma, A \land B \vdash \Delta} \land_L \qquad \frac{\Gamma \vdash A \quad \Gamma \vdash B}{\Gamma \vdash A \land B} \land_R$$

$$\frac{\Gamma, A \vdash \Delta \quad \Gamma, B \vdash \Delta}{\Gamma, A \lor B \vdash \Delta} \lor_L \qquad \frac{\Gamma \vdash A}{\Gamma \vdash A \lor B} \lor_{R1} \qquad \frac{\Gamma \vdash B}{\Gamma \vdash A \lor B} \lor_{R2}$$

$$\frac{\Gamma \vdash A \quad \Gamma, B \vdash \Delta}{\Gamma, A \Rightarrow B \vdash \Delta} \Rightarrow_L \qquad \frac{\Gamma, A \vdash B}{\Gamma \vdash A \Rightarrow B} \Rightarrow_R$$

$$\frac{\Gamma \vdash A}{\Gamma, \neg A \vdash \Delta} \neg_L \qquad \frac{\Gamma, A \vdash}{\Gamma \vdash \neg A} \neg_R$$

$$\frac{\Gamma, A[c/x] \vdash \Delta}{\Gamma, \exists x A \vdash \Delta} \exists_L \qquad \frac{\Gamma \vdash A[t/x]}{\Gamma \vdash \exists x A} \exists_R$$

$$\frac{\Gamma, A[t/x] \vdash \Delta}{\Gamma, \forall x A \vdash \Delta} \forall_L \qquad \frac{\Gamma \vdash A[c/x]}{\Gamma \vdash \forall x A} \forall_R$$

$$\frac{\Gamma, A, A \vdash \Delta}{\Gamma, A \vdash \Delta} \text{contr}_L$$

$$\frac{\Gamma \vdash \Delta}{\Gamma, A \vdash \Delta} \text{weak}_L \qquad \frac{\Gamma \vdash}{\Gamma \vdash A} \text{weak}_R$$

where, in $\forall_L$ and $\exists_R$, c is a fresh constant and, in $\forall_R$ and $\exists_L$, t is any term.

Fig. 2. Intuitionistic sequent calculus

A is provable classically if and only if $\neg A^{Kr}$ is provable intuitionistically.

Using these existing translations, in particular Kolmogorov's and Gödel-Gentzen's translations, we propose to simplify them as described below.

3 Polarizing Kolmogorov's Translation

As in Kolmogorov's translation, let us define the polarized Kolmogorov's translation:

Definition 2. *Let A,B,C and D be propositions. An occurrence of A in B is*

- *positive if:*
  - $B = A$.
  - $B = C \land D$ and the occurrence of A is in C or in D and is positive.
  - $B = C \lor D$ and the occurrence of A is in C or in D and is positive.
  - $B = C \Rightarrow D$ and the occurrence of A is in C (resp. in D) and is negative (resp. positive).
  - $B = \neg C$ and the occurrence of A is in C and is negative.
  - $B = \forall x C$ and the occurrence of A is in C and is positive.
  - $B = \exists x C$ and the occurrence of A is in C and is positive.

– negative if:
  - $B = C \wedge D$ and the occurrence of A is in C or in D and is negative.
  - $B = C \vee D$ and the occurrence of A is in C or in D and is negative.
  - $B = C \Rightarrow D$ and the occurrence of A is in C (resp. in D) and is positive (resp. negative).
  - $B = \neg C$ and the occurrence of A is in C and is positive.
  - $B = \forall x C$ and the occurrence of A is in C and is negative.
  - $B = \exists x C$ and the occurrence of A is in C and is negative.

Definition 3. *Let A and B be propositions. We define by induction on the structure of propositions the positive (K^+) and negative translation (K^-):*

$$
\begin{array}{ll}
A^{K^+} \equiv A \text{ if } A \text{ is atomic} & A^{K^-} \equiv A \text{ if } A \text{ is atomic} \\
(A \wedge B)^{K^+} \equiv A^{K^+} \wedge B^{K^+} & (A \wedge B)^{K^-} \equiv \neg\neg A^{K^-} \wedge \neg\neg B^{K^-} \\
(A \vee B)^{K^+} \equiv A^{K^+} \vee B^{K^+} & (A \vee B)^{K^-} \equiv \neg\neg A^{K^-} \vee \neg\neg B^{K^-} \\
(A \Rightarrow B)^{K^+} \equiv \neg\neg A^{K^-} \Rightarrow B^{K^+} & (A \Rightarrow B)^{K^-} \equiv A^{K^+} \Rightarrow \neg\neg B^{K^-} \\
(\neg A)^{K^+} \equiv \neg A^{K^-} & (\neg A)^{K^-} \equiv \neg A^{K^+} \\
(\forall x A)^{K^+} \equiv \forall x A^{K^+} & (\forall x A)^{K^-} \equiv \forall x \neg\neg A^{K^-} \\
(\exists x A)^{K^+} \equiv \exists x A^{K^+} & (\exists x A)^{K^-} \equiv \exists x \neg\neg A^{K^-}
\end{array}
$$

Notice how, compared to Section 2.3, we introduce double negations in front of subformulæ instead of the whole formula. For instance axioms are translated by themselves, and the price to pay is, as for Kuroda's and Krivine's translations, a negation of the whole formula in the following theorem.

Theorem 1. *If the sequent $\Gamma \vdash \Delta$ is provable in the classical sequent calculus then $\Gamma^{K^+}, \neg \Delta^{K^-} \vdash$ is provable in the intuitionistic sequent calculus.*

Proof. By induction on the proof-tree. Since this theorem is not the main result of this paper, and is refined below (Theorem 3), let us process only one case. All other cases follow a similar pattern.

$$
\exists_R \frac{\pi}{\dfrac{\Gamma \vdash \Delta, A[t/x]}{\Gamma \vdash \Delta, \exists x A}} \quad \hookrightarrow \quad \neg_L \dfrac{\neg_R \dfrac{\exists_R \dfrac{\mathrm{IH}(\pi)}{\dfrac{\Gamma^{K^+}, \neg \Delta^{K^-}, \neg A^{K^-}[t/x] \vdash}{\Gamma^{K^+}, \neg \Delta^{K^-} \vdash \neg\neg A^{K^-}[t/x]}}}{\Gamma^{K^+}, \neg \Delta^{K^-} \vdash \exists x \neg\neg A^{K^-}}}{\Gamma^{K^+}, \neg(\exists x \neg\neg A^{K^-}), \neg \Delta^{K^-} \vdash}
$$

where IH(π) denotes, here and later, the proof obtained by the application of the induction hypothesis on π.

We also have the inverse translation.

Theorem 2. *If the sequent $\Gamma^{K^+}, \neg \Delta^{K^-} \vdash D^{K^-}$ is provable in the intuitionistic sequent calculus, then $\Gamma \vdash \Delta, D$ is provable in the classical sequent calculus.*

Proof. By a straightforward induction on the proof-tree.

We now focus on the polarization of the Gödel-Gentzen's translation, which is lighter than the Kolmogorov's translation, again with the idea of getting a simpler translation in both directions.

4   A Focused Sequent Calculus

Gödel-Gentzen negative translation (Definition 2.3 above) removes many negations from translations and the polarization we give in Section 5 will even more. If we want to follow the pattern of Theorem 1 to show equiprovability (in the absence of cut), we can *no longer* systematically move formulæ from the right to the left hand sides, since we lack negation on almost all connectives. Therefore, we must *constrain* our classical sequent calculus to forbid arbitrary proofs, and in particular to impose that once a rule has been applied on some formula of the right-hand side, the next rule must apply on the corresponding subformula of the premiss. Working on the same formula up to some well-chosen point is a discipline of capital importance, since we avoid to eagerly swap formulæ from right to left.

This is why we introduce a focused version of the classical sequent calculus. The resulting constraint is that we must decompose the *stoup* [11,12] formula until it gets removed from the *stoup* position. Only when the stoup becomes empty, can we apply rules on other formulæ.

Definition 4 (Focused sequent). *A focused sequent is a triple, composed of two multisets of formulæ and a distinguished set (the* stoup*) containing zero or one formula. It will be noted* $\Gamma \vdash A; \Delta$ *when the distinguished set contains a formula A, and $\Gamma \vdash .; \Delta$ when it contains no formula.*

The focused sequent calculus we define serves our particular purpose; for instance it is not optimized to maximize the so-called negative and positive phases [13]. Note also that in our paper, negative and positive has a very different meaning. The calculus is presented in Figure 3 and contains a stoup only in the right-hand side, since this is the only problematic side.

Note that all the left rules require an empty stoup, and that two new right rules, `focus` and `release`, respectively place and remove a formula of the right-hand side in the focus.

Only atomic, negated, disjunctive or existentially quantified formulæ can be removed from the stoup:

- Due to the freshness condition of the $\exists$-left and $\forall$-right rule, the $\exists$-right rule is the only rule that cannot be inverted (or equivalently permuted downwards). Therefore existential statements must be removable from the stoup.
- The stoup has only one place, so we cannot allow in it both subformulæ of a disjunction. This choice must be done by a subsequent call to the focus rule. More pragmatically, Gödel-Gentzen's translation introduces negations in this case, enabling the storage of the subformulæ on the left-hand side of the sequent. As an informal translation rule, intuitionistic $\neg_R$ rules will correspond to a lost of focus.
- The same reasoning holds for allowing atomic formulæ to be removed from the stoup. Also, if we do not allow this, the system loses completeness since the stoup becomes stuck forever.

- Allowing to remove negated formulæ from the stoup accounts for the aggressive behavior of the operator ⌋: to keep the statement of Theorem 3 short and close to statements of previous theorems, we must remember that ⌋ removes the negation of negated formulæ, therefore forcing them to move on the left hand side.

As a consequence of the design constraint imposed by our translation, the rule focus cannot act on a formula which has $\exists$, $\neg$ or $\vee$ as main connective and the $\exists_R$, $\neg_R$ and $\vee_R$ rules act on formulæ that are not in the stoup (and, as mentioned, when the stoup itself is empty). The reasons become clear in the proof of Theorem 3.

Lastly, we impose the formula in the axiom rule to be atomic, which boils down to an η-expansion of the usual axiom rule.

To sum up, we consider the connectives $\exists$, $\vee$ and $\neg$, when they appear on the right-hand side of a sequent, to have a "positive phase" in the sense of [13] and the other ones to have a negative phase.

We show that this calculus is equivalent to the usual sequent calculus of Figure 1.

Proposition 1. *Let Γ, Δ be two multisets of formulæ and A be a formula. If the sequent $\Gamma \vdash .; \Delta$ (resp. $\Gamma \vdash A; \Delta$) has a proof in the focused sequent calculus, then it has a proof in the classical sequent calculus.*

Proof. Straightforward by noticing that, forgetting about the stoup (transforming the semicolon into a comma), all focused rules are instances of the classical sequent calculus rules. Both rules *focus* and *release* lose their meaning and are simply erased from the proof-tree. □

The converse is a corollary of the slightly more general following statement. As we see below, it is crucial to have some degree of freedom to decompose arbitrarily Δ' into A and Δ in order to reason properly by induction.

Proposition 2. *Let Γ, Δ' be two multisets of formulæ. Assume that the sequent $\Gamma \vdash \Delta'$ has a proof in the classical sequent calculus. Let A be a set containing either a formula (also named A by abuse of notation) or the empty formula, and let Δ such that $\Delta' = A, \Delta$.*

Then the sequent $\Gamma \vdash A; \Delta$ has a proof in the focused sequent calculus.

Proof. The proof is a little bit more involved, but it appeals only to simple and well-known principles, in particular to Kleene's inversion lemmas [14,15], stating that inferences rules can be permuted and, therefore, gathered.

We give only a sketch of the proof, leaving out the details to the reader, for two reasons. Firstly, giving all the lengthy details would not add any insight on the structure of the proof; in the contrary they would blur the visibility of the main ideas. Secondly, similar completeness results are known for much more constrained focused proof systems; see for instance the one presented in [13].

$$\frac{}{\Gamma, A \vdash .; A, \Delta} \text{ ax}$$

$$\frac{\Gamma, A, B \vdash .; \Delta}{\Gamma, A \wedge B \vdash .; \Delta} \wedge_L \qquad \frac{\Gamma \vdash A; \Delta \quad \Gamma \vdash B; \Delta}{\Gamma \vdash A \wedge B; \Delta} \wedge_R$$

$$\frac{\Gamma, A \vdash .; \Delta \quad \Gamma, B \vdash .; \Delta}{\Gamma, A \vee B \vdash .; \Delta} \vee_L \qquad \frac{\Gamma \vdash .; A, B, \Delta}{\Gamma \vdash .; A \vee B, \Delta} \vee_R$$

$$\frac{\Gamma \vdash A; \Delta \quad \Gamma, B \vdash .; \Delta}{\Gamma, A \Rightarrow B \vdash .; \Delta} \Rightarrow_L \qquad \frac{\Gamma, A \vdash B; \Delta}{\Gamma \vdash A \Rightarrow B; \Delta} \Rightarrow_R$$

$$\frac{\Gamma \vdash A; \Delta}{\Gamma, \neg A \vdash .; \Delta} \neg_L \qquad \frac{\Gamma, A \vdash .; \Delta}{\Gamma \vdash .; \neg A, \Delta} \neg_R$$

$$\frac{\Gamma, A[c/x] \vdash .; \Delta}{\Gamma, \exists x A \vdash .; \Delta} \exists_L \qquad \frac{\Gamma \vdash .; A[t/x], \Delta}{\Gamma \vdash .; \exists x A, \Delta} \exists_R$$

$$\frac{\Gamma, A[t/x] \vdash .; \Delta}{\Gamma, \forall x A \vdash .; \Delta} \forall_L \qquad \frac{\Gamma \vdash A[c/x]; \Delta}{\Gamma \vdash \forall x A; \Delta} \forall_R$$

$$\frac{\Gamma, A, A \vdash .; \Delta}{\Gamma, A \vdash .; \Delta} \text{contr}_L \qquad \frac{\Gamma \vdash .; A, A, \Delta}{\Gamma \vdash .; A, \Delta} \text{contr}_R$$

$$\frac{\Gamma \vdash .; \Delta}{\Gamma, A \vdash .; \Delta} \text{weak}_L \qquad \frac{\Gamma \vdash .; \Delta}{\Gamma \vdash A; \Delta} \text{weak}_R$$

$$\frac{\Gamma \vdash A; \Delta}{\Gamma \vdash .; A, \Delta} \text{focus}$$

$$\frac{\Gamma \vdash .; A, \Delta}{\Gamma \vdash A; \Delta} \text{release}$$

where:
- the axiom rule involves only atomic formulæ,
- in $\forall_L$ and $\exists_R$, c is a fresh constant,
- in $\forall_R$ and $\exists_L$, t is any term,
- in release, A is either atomic or of the form $\exists x B, B \vee C$ or $\neg B$,
- in focus, A is neither atomic nor of the form $\exists x B, B \vee C$ or $\neg B$.

Fig. 3. Focused classical sequent calculus

First of all, we consider a refined version of the classical sequent calculus of Figure 1 where proofs are restricted to use the axiom and weak rules on atomic formulæ. In this way, we know [15] that Kleene's inversion lemmas [14] make the proof height *decrease* strictly. We reason by induction of the *height* of this modified proof-tree π, distinguishing the three following cases:

- A is empty, or A contains an atomic, existential, disjunctive or negated formula that is not the active formula of the last rule r of π. Then we release A, focus on the active formula if necessary, apply rule r, and we get one or two premises, on which we can apply the induction hypothesis. Let us give two instances, where, in the second case, A is empty:

$$\neg L \frac{\pi}{\dfrac{\Gamma \vdash B, A, \Delta}{\Gamma, \neg B \vdash A, \Delta}} \quad \hookrightarrow \quad \dfrac{\dfrac{\dfrac{\mathrm{IH}(\pi)}{\Gamma \vdash B; A, \Delta}}{\Gamma, \neg B \vdash .; A, \Delta} \neg L}{\Gamma, \neg B \vdash A; \Delta} \text{ release}$$

$$\wedge R \frac{\dfrac{\pi_1}{\Gamma \vdash B, \Delta} \quad \dfrac{\pi_2}{\Gamma \vdash C, \Delta}}{\Gamma \vdash B \wedge C, \Delta} \quad \hookrightarrow \quad \dfrac{\dfrac{\dfrac{\mathrm{IH}(\pi_1)}{\Gamma \vdash B; \Delta} \quad \dfrac{\mathrm{IH}(\pi_2)}{\Gamma \vdash C; \Delta}}{\Gamma \vdash B \wedge C; \Delta} \wedge R}{\Gamma \vdash .; B \wedge C, \Delta} \text{ focus}$$

- A contains an atomic, existential, disjunctive or negated formula that is active in the last rule r of π. Then r must be one of the six rules axiom, $\exists_R$, $\vee_R$, $\neg_R$, weak$_R$ or contr$_R$. They are direct and all the remaining cases follow a similar pattern. Here is the case for the $\exists_R$ rule:

$$\exists_R \frac{\pi}{\dfrac{\Gamma \vdash B[t/x], \Delta}{\Gamma \vdash \exists x B, \Delta}} \quad \hookrightarrow \quad \dfrac{\dfrac{\dfrac{\mathrm{IH}(\pi)}{\Gamma \vdash .; B[t/x], \Delta}}{\Gamma \vdash .; \exists x B, \Delta} \exists_R}{\Gamma \vdash \exists x B; \Delta} \text{ release}$$

- If A is not empty and not an atomic, existential, disjunctive or negated formula then, disregarding the last rule of π, we apply Kleene's inversion lemma on A, the induction hypothesis on the premises, since the proof height has decreased, and recompose those premises to get back the corresponding component(s) of A in the stoup. Here is an example of such a rule:

$$\Rightarrow_R \frac{\pi}{\dfrac{\Gamma, B \vdash C, \Delta}{\Gamma \vdash B \Rightarrow C, \Delta}} \quad \hookrightarrow \quad \dfrac{\dfrac{\mathrm{IH}(\pi)}{\Gamma, B \vdash C; \Delta}}{\Gamma \vdash B \Rightarrow C; \Delta} \Rightarrow_R$$

□

5 Polarizing Gödel-Gentzen's Translation

We try to reduce the number of negations. We use the polarization of propositions (Definition 2 above) and replace disjunction and existential quantifiers by conjunction and universal quantifiers, as in Gödel-Gentzen's translation.

Definition 5. *Let A and B be propositions. We define, by induction on the structure of propositions, the positive(^{p}) and negative(^{n}) translations:*

$$\begin{array}{ll} A^p \equiv A \text{ if } A \text{ is atomic} & A^n \equiv \neg\neg A \text{ if } A \text{ is atomic} \\ (A \wedge B)^p \equiv A^p \wedge B^p & (A \wedge B)^n \equiv A^n \wedge B^n \\ (A \vee B)^p \equiv A^p \vee B^p & (A \vee B)^n \equiv \neg(\neg A^n \wedge \neg B^n) \\ (A \Rightarrow B)^p \equiv A^n \Rightarrow B^p & (A \Rightarrow B)^n \equiv A^p \Rightarrow B^n \\ (\neg A)^p \equiv \neg A^n & (\neg A)^n \equiv \neg A^p \\ (\forall x A)^p \equiv \forall x A^p & (\forall x A)^n \equiv \forall x A^n \\ (\exists x A)^p \equiv \exists x A^p & (\exists x A)^n \equiv \neg \forall x \neg A^n \end{array}$$

Theorem 3. *Let Γ, Δ be multisets of formulæ, and A be a set containing zero or one formula. If the sequent $\Gamma \vdash A; \Delta$ has a proof in the (classical) focused sequent calculus, then, in the intuitionistic sequent calculus, the sequent $\Gamma^p, \lrcorner \Delta^n \vdash A^n$ has a proof.*

Notice that $\lrcorner$ removes the trailing negation of Δ in three cases: the negative translations of $\exists$, of $\vee$ and of $\neg$ (this last one more as a side-effect).

Proof. By induction on the proof of $\Gamma \vdash A; \Delta$, considering one by one the 19 cases from Figure 3:

- A left rule. We apply the induction hypothesis on the premises and copy the left rule. For instance, if the rule is $\Rightarrow_L$, then the induction hypothesis gives us proofs of the two sequents $\Gamma^p, \lrcorner \Delta^n \vdash A^n$ (since A is put in the stoup in the $\Rightarrow_L$ rule) and $\Gamma^p, B^p, \lrcorner \Delta^n \vdash$ that can be readily combined with the (intuitionistic) $\Rightarrow_L$ rule to yield a proof of the sequent $\Gamma^p, A^n \Rightarrow B^p, \lrcorner \Delta^n \vdash$. This is what we were looking for, since $(A \Rightarrow B)^p \equiv A^n \Rightarrow B^p$.
- A contr_R rule. It is transformed (after application of the induction hypothesis) into a contr_L rule.
- A weak_R rule. It is transformed into a weak_R rule.
- A release rule. This can occur only if A is atomic or of the form $\exists x B$, $B \vee C$ or $\neg B$. In all cases, we translate it as a $\neg_R$ rule, which removes the trailing negation of A^n, turning it into the formula $\lrcorner A^n$ (see Definition 1), that integrates directly $\lrcorner \Delta^n$, so that we can readily plug the proof obtained by the application of the induction hypothesis.
- A focus rule on $A \in \Delta$. This can occur only if A is neither atomic nor of the form $\exists x B$, $B \vee C$ or $\neg B$. Therefore, $\lrcorner A^n = \neg A^n$, and we apply a $\neg_L$ rule.
- An axiom rule. Since A is restricted to be atomic, we need to build an intuitionistic proof of the sequent $\Gamma^p, A, \lrcorner \neg \neg A, \lrcorner \Delta^n \vdash$ which is a trivial two-step proof since $\lrcorner \neg \neg A$ is $\neg A$.
- A $\neg_R$ rule:

$$\frac{\begin{array}{c} \pi \\ \Gamma, B \vdash .; \Delta \end{array}}{\Gamma \vdash .; \neg B, \Delta}$$

We must find a proof of the sequent $\Gamma^p, \lrcorner \neg B^p, \lrcorner \Delta^n \vdash$. But the formula $\lrcorner \neg B^p$ is identical to B^p, and the induction hypothesis gives us directly a proof of $\Gamma^p, B^p, \lrcorner \Delta^n \vdash$. In other words, $\neg_R$ is not translated, thanks to the operator $\lrcorner$ (that will soon lead us to minor considerations).

- A $\vee_R$ rule:

$$\frac{\begin{array}{c} \pi_1 \\ \Gamma \vdash .; B, C, \Delta \end{array}}{\Gamma \vdash .; B \vee C, \Delta}$$

We must build a proof of the sequent $\Gamma^p, \lrcorner \neg (\neg B^n \wedge \neg C^n), \lrcorner \Delta^n \vdash$, which is equal to $\Gamma^p, \neg B^n \wedge \neg C^n, \lrcorner \Delta^n \vdash$. It is natural to try to apply the $\wedge_L$ rule:

$$\dfrac{\Gamma^p, \neg B^n, \neg C^n, \lrcorner\Delta^n \vdash}{\Gamma^p, \neg B^n \wedge \neg C^n, \lrcorner\Delta^n \vdash}\wedge_L$$

We are committed to find a proof of the premiss, while the induction hypothesis gives us a proof of the following slightly different sequent:

$$\Gamma^p, \lrcorner B^n, \lrcorner C^n, \lrcorner\Delta^n \vdash$$

Therefore we must examine two subcases:

- B is an atom, an existential, disjunctive or negated formula. Then $B^n = \neg D$ for some D, and $\lrcorner B^n = D$. We build the following proof, given the proof obtained by application of the induction hypothesis:

$$\dfrac{\dfrac{\dfrac{\Gamma^p, D, \lrcorner C^n, \lrcorner\Delta^n \vdash}{\Gamma^p, \lrcorner C^n, \lrcorner\Delta^n \vdash \neg D}\neg R}{\Gamma^p, \neg B^n, \lrcorner C^n, \lrcorner\Delta^n \vdash}\neg L}$$

- otherwise $\lrcorner B^n = \neg B^n$, and the induction hypothesis gives us directly a proof of the above sequent.

We do a similar case distinction on C to get from the previous proof a proof of the sequent $\Gamma^p, \neg B^n, \neg C^n, \neg\Delta^n \vdash$, which is now exactly what we were looking for.

- A $\exists_R$ rule:

$$\dfrac{\dfrac{\pi}{\Gamma \vdash .; A[t/x], \Delta}}{\Gamma \vdash .; \exists x A, \Delta}$$

The induction hypothesis gives us a proof of the sequent $\Gamma^p, \lrcorner A[t/x]^n, \lrcorner\Delta^n \vdash$, that we turn, in the same way as in the previous case, into a proof of the sequent $\Gamma^p, \neg A[t/x]^n, \lrcorner\Delta^n \vdash$, to which we apply the $\forall_L$ rule:

$$\forall_L \dfrac{\Gamma^p, \neg A[t/x]^n, \lrcorner\Delta^n \vdash}{\Gamma^p, \forall x\neg A^n, \lrcorner\Delta^n \vdash}$$

the end sequent is also equal to $\Gamma^p, \lrcorner\exists x A^n, \lrcorner\Delta^n \vdash$; so we have exhibited the proof we were looking for.

- A $\wedge_R$, $\Rightarrow_R$ or $\forall_R$ rule. Those three last cases are easy, since we are in the stoup, which corresponds to the right-hand side of the (intuitionistic) sequent. For example, let us consider the case of the $\Rightarrow_R$ rule:

$$\Rightarrow_R \dfrac{\dfrac{\pi}{\Gamma, A \vdash B; \Delta}}{\Gamma \vdash A \Rightarrow B; \Delta} \quad \hookrightarrow \quad \dfrac{\dfrac{IH(\pi)}{\Gamma^p, A^p, \lrcorner\Delta^n \vdash B^n}}{\Gamma^p, \lrcorner\Delta^n \vdash A^p \Rightarrow B^n} \Rightarrow_R$$

□

The reverse translation is expressed with respect to the unfocused sequent calculus, which is more liberal and therefore more convenient for the reverse way. We nevertheless need to slightly generalize the statement.

Theorem 4. *Let $\Gamma, \Delta_1, \Delta_2$ be multisets of formulæ, such that Δ_1 does not contain any negated formula. Let D be at most one formula. If the sequent $\Gamma^p, \neg\Delta_1^n, \neg\Delta_2^n \vdash D^n$ is provable in the intuitionistic sequent calculus, then $\Gamma \vdash \Delta_1, \Delta_2, D$ is provable in the classical sequent calculus.*

Proof. We constraint the intuitionistic proof to have a certain shape before starting the induction. First, we assume that axiom rules are restricted to atoms. It is always possible to expanse the axioms that are not of this form. Second, we also assume that $\neg_L$ rules on atomic formlæ are permuted upwards as far as they can [14], this basically induces that this $\neg_L$ rule becomes glued either to an axiom or to a weakening rule and therefore the axiom case will be integrated to $\neg_L$ case. This way, we avoid the presence of non-double negated axioms on the right-hand side. Unless stated otherwise we do not mention explicitly the application of the induction hypothesis, which is clear from the context.

- A contraction or a weakening on any of the formulæ of $\Gamma^p, \neg\Delta_1^n, \neg\Delta_2^n$ or D^n is turned into the same rule on the corresponding formula of $\Gamma, \Delta_1, \Delta_2$ or D. Below, we now concentrate on connective and quantifier rules.
- A left-rule on Γ^p is turned into the same left-rule on Γ. The potential erasing of D^n in the two cases $\Rightarrow_L$ and $\neg_L$ is handled through a weakening.
- A left-rule on $\neg\Delta_2^n$ can be only a $\neg_L$ rule. It is turned into a weakening on D^n if necessary, since we apply the induction hypothesis on the premiss $\Gamma^p, \neg\Delta_1^n, \neg(\Delta_2')^n \vdash D_2^n$, with $\Delta_2 = \Delta_2', D_2$.
- A right-rule on D^n, assuming the main connective or quantifier of D is $\wedge$, $\Rightarrow$ or $\forall$. The rule is $\wedge_R$, $\Rightarrow_R$ or $\forall_R$, respectively. It is turned into the same right-rule on D.
- A right-rule on D^n, assuming D is an atomic, existentially quantified or disjunctive formula. The rule is $\neg_R$ and the premiss is $\Gamma^p, \neg\Delta_1^n, \neg D^n, \neg\Delta_2^n \vdash$, to which we only need to apply the induction hypothesis.
- A right-rule on D^n assuming D is a negated formula $\neg D'$. In this case, the rule must be $\neg_R$ and the premiss is of the form $\Gamma^p, \neg\Delta_1^n, \neg(D)^n, \neg\Delta_2^n \vdash$. But D is negated, and $\neg D^n = \neg\neg D'^p = D'^p$. So, to apply the induction hypothesis, we consider that the premiss is $\Gamma^p, D'^p, \neg\Delta_1^n, \neg\Delta_2^n \vdash$.
- All possibilities for D have been examined. Notice in particular that a $\vee_R$ or $\exists_R$ rule cannot be applied on D^n, since the negative translation of Definition 5 never introduces this connective (resp. quantifier) in head position.
- A left-rule on $\neg D_1^n \in \neg\Delta_1^n$, assuming D_1 is a disjunctive (resp. existentially quantified) formula. The rule is $\wedge_L$ (resp. $\forall_L$) and is turned in an $\vee_R$ (resp. $\exists_R$) rule on D_1, making the active formula(e) of the premiss(es) move from Δ_1 to Δ_2 if necessary. Let us detail the $\vee$ case. $D_1 = B_1 \vee C_1$, and $\neg D_1^n = \neg B_1^n \wedge \neg C_1^n$. The $\wedge_L$ rule gives us the premiss:

$$\Gamma_1^p, \neg(\Delta_1')^n, \neg B_1^n, \neg C_1^n, \neg\Delta_2^n \vdash D^n$$

We must distinguish according to the shapes of B_1 and C_1. Let us discuss only B_1, the discussion on C_1 being exactly the same:

- B_1 is an atomic, existentially quantified, disjunctive or negated formula. Then $\neg B_1^n$ is different from $\lrcorner B_1^n$, and to apply properly the induction hypothesis, B_1 must be placed into Δ_2.
- Otherwise $\neg B_1^n = \lrcorner B_1^n$ and it is left into Δ_1.
  - A left-rule on $\lrcorner D_1^n \in \lrcorner \Delta_1^n$, assuming that the main connective or quantifier of D_1 is $\Rightarrow$, $\wedge$ or $\forall$. The rule is $\neg_L$ in all cases, and we only need to weaken on D^n if necessary, before applying the induction hypothesis on the premises.
  - A left rule on $\lrcorner D_1^n \in \lrcorner \Delta_1^n$, assuming D_1 is atomic. By assumption, the next rule is a rule on D_1. If it is a weakening, we translate both rules at once by weakening on D_1 and apply the induction hypothesis to the premiss of the weakening rule. Otherwise the next rule is an axiom. The only possibility is that D_1 belongs to Γ^p, and we translate both rules as an axiom.
  - By assumption, D_1 cannot be a negated formula, and therefore all the cases have been considered. □

Corollary 1. *Let Γ, Δ be multisets of formulæ and D be at most one formula. If the sequent $\Gamma^p, \lrcorner \Delta^n \vdash D^n$ is provable in the intuitionistic sequent calculus, then the sequent $\Gamma \vdash \Delta, D$ is provable in the classical sequent calculus.*

Proof. Let $\neg C_1, \cdots, \neg C_n$ be the negated formulæ of Δ and Δ' the other ones. We apply Theorem 4 to a Γ composed of $\Gamma, C_1, \cdots, C_n$, a Δ_1 composed of Δ', an empty Δ_2 and finally a D equal to D, which gives a proof of the sequent:

$$\Gamma, C_1, \cdots, C_n \vdash \Delta', D$$

to which we apply n times the $\neg_R$ rule to get back a proof of the wanted sequent.

6 Conclusion and Further Work

In this paper, we have shown that polarized double-negation translations still are used to navigate between intuitionistic and classical logics. They are lighter in terms of double negation, and let more statements being invariant by translation.

For instance, consider the axiom $(A \wedge B) \Rightarrow (A \vee B)$. Kolmogorov's translation introduces 14 negations: $\neg\neg(\neg\neg(\neg\neg A \wedge \neg\neg B) \Rightarrow \neg\neg(\neg\neg A \vee \neg\neg B))$, while its (positive) polarized variant, only 10 of them: $(\neg\neg(\neg\neg A \wedge \neg\neg B) \Rightarrow (\neg\neg A \vee \neg\neg B)$. Gödel-Gentzen's translation would be $(\neg\neg A \wedge \neg\neg B) \Rightarrow \neg(\neg\neg\neg A \wedge \neg\neg\neg B)$, introducing 11 negations, while its polarized version introduces only 4 of them: $(\neg\neg A \wedge \neg\neg B) \Rightarrow (A \vee B)$. Recent work from Fréderic Gilbert tends to show that it is possible to go further in the removal of double-negations by turning double negations into an operator that analyses the structure of the formula it double-negates. The polarization of Krivine's translation remains also to be examined.

Polarized translations are particularity adapted to cut-free proofs; otherwise the same active formula may appear both in the left and the right hand sides. As the negative and positive translations of a formula usually differ, it is impossible to cut them back. The workaround can be a "manual" elimination of this cut by reductive methods up to the point where both translations become equal, or to loosen the intuitionistic cut rule. We can also decide not to bother with cuts by eliminating them a priori. In all cases, however, we rely on a cut-elimination theorem that does not hold in the general case of the application described below.

Polarized double-negation translations has been primarily designed to fit *polarized deduction modulo* [16], an extension of first-order logic by a congruence on formulæ that is generated by *polarized* rewrite rules that apply only on a given side of the turn-style. It has already led to interesting results [17,18] in automated theorem proving within axiomatic theories. To support this approach, we must ensure the cut-elimination property of the (sequent calculus modulo the polarized) rewrite system.

One canonical way is to first show proof normalization for the natural deduction, and shift this result to the intuitionistic sequent calculus. Then, through a double-negation translation of *the rewrite system* this result can be extended to the classical sequent calculus [19]. In case of polarized rewriting, a polarized translation can be of great help for this last step, in addition to the development of normalization proofs via reducibility candidates. Another way to get cut admissibility would be to develop semantic proofs.

Lastly, it could be interesting to investigate whether, even in absence of cut admissibility as it can be the case, the modularity of our translations can be enforced, or whether cuts between two differently translated left- and right-formulæ can nevertheless be eliminated. We conjecture that this is possible, provided the rewrite relation is confluent and terminating.

Acknowledgments. The authors would like to thank P. Jouvelot for his comments and the choice of the title of this paper.

References

1. Cohen, P.J.: Set Theory and the Continuum Hypothesis. W.A. Benjamin, New York (1966)
2. Kolmogorov, A.: On the principle of the excluded middle. Mat. Sb. 32, 646–667 (1925)
3. Gödel, K.: Zur intuitionistischen arithmetik und zahlentheorie. Ergebnisse Eines Mathematischen Kolloquiums 4, 34–38 (1933)
4. Gentzen, G.: Die widerspruchsfreiheit der reinen zahlentheorie. Mathematische Annalen 112, 493–565 (1936)
5. Schwichtenberg, H., Senjak, C.: Minimal from classical proofs. Annals of Pure and Applied Logic 164, 740–748 (2013)
6. Schwichtenberg, H., Troelstra, A.S.: Basic Proof Theory. Cambridge University Press (1996)
7. Ferreira, G., Oliva, P.: On various negative translations. In: CL&C, pp. 21–33 (2010)
8. Troelstra, A.S., van Dalen, D.: Constructivism in Mathematics, An Introduction. North-Holland (1988)

9. Kuroda, S.: Intuitionistische untersuchungen der formalistischen logik. Nagoya Mathematical Journal 3, 35–47 (1951)
10. Krivine, J.L.: Opérateurs de mise en mémoire et traduction de Gödel. Arch. Math. Logic 30, 241–267 (1990)
11. Girard, J.Y.: On the unity of logic. Ann. Pure Appl. Logic 59, 201–217 (1993)
12. Curien, P.L., Herbelin, H.: The duality of computation. In: Odersky, M., Wadler, P. (eds.) ICFP, pp. 233–243. ACM (2000)
13. Liang, C., Miller, D.: Focusing and polarization in linear, intuitionistic, and classical logics. Theor. Comput. Sci. 410, 4747–4768 (2009)
14. Kleene, S.C.: Permutability of inferences in Gentzen's calculi LK and LJ. Memoirs of the American Mathematical Society 10, 1–26, 27–68 (1952)
15. Hermant, O.: Resolution is cut-free. Journal of Automated Reasoning 44, 245–276 (2010)
16. Dowek, G.: Polarized deduction modulo. In: IFIP Theoretical Computer Science. (2010)
17. Burel, G.: Embedding deduction modulo into a prover. In: Dawar, A., Veith, H. (eds.) CSL 2010. LNCS, vol. 6247, pp. 155–169. Springer, Heidelberg (2010)
18. Burel, G.: Experimenting with deduction modulo. In: Bjørner, N., Sofronie-Stokkermans, V. (eds.) CADE 2011. LNCS, vol. 6803, pp. 162–176. Springer, Heidelberg (2011)
19. Dowek, G., Werner, B.: Proof normalization modulo. The Journal of Symbolic Logic 68, 1289–1316 (2003)

Revisiting the Equivalence of Shininess and Politeness

Filipe Casal[1] and João Rasga[2]

[1] SQIG, Instituto de Telecomunicações, Lisboa, Portugal
filipe.casal@ist.utl.pt
[2] Dep. Matemática, Instituto Superior Técnico, Universidade de Lisboa, Portugal,
and
SQIG, Instituto de Telecomunicações, Lisboa, Portugal
jfr@math.ist.utl.pt

Abstract. The Nelson-Oppen method [4] allows the combination of satisfiability procedures of stably infinite theories with disjoint signatures. Due to its importance, several attempts to extend the method to different and wider classes of theories were made. In 2005, it was shown that shiny [9] and polite [6] theories could be combined with an arbitrary theory (the relationship between these classes was analysed in [6]). Later, a stronger notion of polite theory was proposed, see [3], in order to overcome a subtle issue with a proof in [6]. In this paper, we analyse the relationship between shiny and strongly polite theories in the one-sorted case. We show that a shiny theory with a decidable quantifier-free satisfiability problem is strongly polite and provide two different sufficient conditions for a strongly polite theory to be shiny. Based on these results, we derive a combination method for the union of a polite theory with an arbitrary theory.

Keywords: Nelson-Oppen method, combination of satisfiability procedures, polite theories, strongly polite theories, shiny theories.

1 Introduction

The problem of modularly combining satisfiability procedures of two theories into a satisfiability procedure for their union is of great interest in the area of automated reasoning: for instance, verification systems such as CVC4 [1] and SMTInterpol [2] rely on such a combination procedure.

The first and most well-known method for the combination of satisfiability procedures is due to Nelson and Oppen, [4]. In this seminal paper, the authors provide a combination method to decide the satisfiability of quantifier-free formulas in the union of two theories, provided that both theories have their own procedure for deciding the satisfiability problem of quantifier-free formulas. After a correction, see [5], the two main restrictions of the Nelson-Oppen method are:

- the theories are *stably infinite*,
- their signatures are disjoint.

It is also worth mentioning a correctness proof of the Nelson-Oppen method given by Tinelli and Harandi in [7].

Concerned about the fact that many theories of interest, such as those admitting only finite models, are not stably infinite, Tinelli and Zarba, in [9], showed that the Nelson-Oppen combination procedure still applies when the stable infiniteness condition is replaced by the requirement that all but one of the theories is *shiny*. However, a shiny theory must be equipped with a particular function called mincard, which is inherently hard to compute.

In order to overcome the problem of computing the mincard function and of the shortage of shiny theories, Ranise, Ringeissen and Zarba proposed an alternative requirement, *politeness*, in [6], and analysed its relationship with shininess. A polite theory has to be equipped with a witness function, which was thought to be easier to compute than the mincard function. They show that given a polite theory and an arbitrary one, the Nelson-Oppen combination procedure is still valid when the signatures are disjoint and both theories have their own procedure for deciding the satisfiability problem of quantifier-free formulas. Some time later, in [3], Jovanović and Barrett reported that the politeness notion provided in [6] allowed, after all, witness functions that are not sufficiently strong to prove the combination theorem. In order to solve the problem they provided a seemingly stronger notion of politeness, in the sequel called *strongly politeness*, equipped with a seemingly stronger witness function, s-witness, that allowed to prove the combination theorem. However, the authors left open the relationship between the two notions of politeness and between the strong politeness notion and shininess.

In this paper we investigate the relationship between shiny and strongly polite theories in the one-sorted case. We show that a shiny theory with a decidable quantifier-free satisfiability problem is strongly polite. For the other direction, we provide two different sets of conditions under which a strongly polite theory is shiny (see Figure 1 for a more detailed global view of the results). Moreover, we show that, under some conditions, a polite theory is also strongly polite and so there is a way to transform a witness function into a strong witness function. Given the constructive nature of the proofs we were able to design such a procedure.

1.1 Organization of the Paper

The paper is organized as follows: in Section 2 we recall some relevant definitions. In Section 3 we begin by recalling the definitions of shininess and of (strong) politeness and then we proceed to show the equivalence between these notions. In Section 4 we analyse what was done in the paper and provide directions for further research.

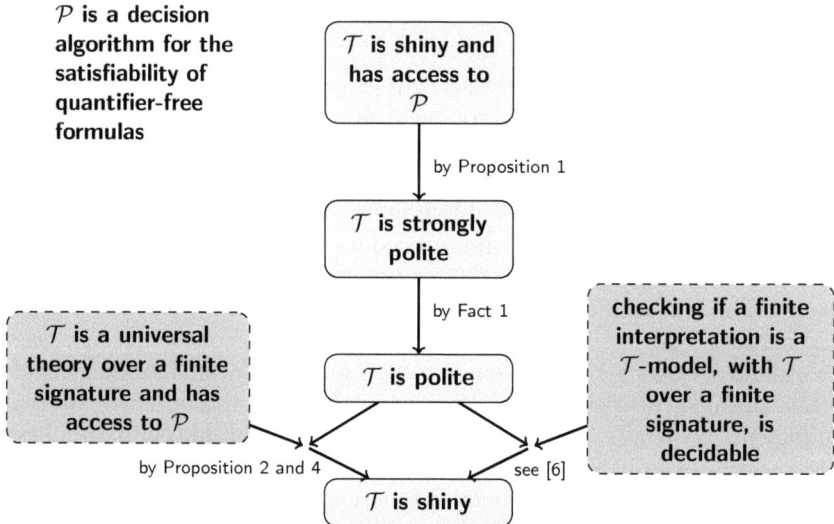

Fig. 1. Schematic representation of the results in the paper

2 Preliminaries

The results in this paper concern first-order logic with equality. We assume given a countably infinite set of variables. We mainly follow the notation in [9].

2.1 Syntax

A *signature* is a tuple $\Sigma = \langle \Sigma^F, \Sigma^P \rangle$ where Σ^F is the set of function symbols and Σ^P is the set of predicate symbols. We use $\cong$ to denote the equality logic symbol and assume the standard definitions of Σ-*atom* and Σ-*term*. A Σ-formula is inductively defined as usual over Σ-atoms and Σ-terms using the connectives $\wedge, \vee, \neg, \rightarrow$ or the quantifiers $\forall$ and $\exists$. We denote by $\mathsf{QF}(\Sigma)$ the set of Σ-formulas with no occurrences of quantifiers and, given a Σ-formula φ, by $\mathsf{vars}(\varphi)$ the set of free variables of φ. We say that a Σ-formula is a Σ-*sentence* if it has no free variables. In the sequel, when there is no ambiguity, we will omit the reference to the signature when referring to atoms, terms, formulas and sentences.

Definition 1 (Arrangement formula). *Given a finite set of variables Y and an equivalence relation $E \subseteq Y^2$, the* arrangement formula *induced by E over Y, denoted by δ_E^Y, is*

$$\bigwedge_{(x,y) \in E} (x \cong y) \wedge \bigwedge_{(x,y) \in Y^2 \setminus E} \neg (x \cong y)$$

In the sequel, we may simply denote δ_E^Y by δ_E if there is no confusion to which variable set the formula refers to.

2.2 Semantics

Given a signature Σ, a Σ-*interpretation* $\mathcal{A}$ with domain A over a set of variables X is a map that interprets each variable $x \in X$ as an element $x^\mathcal{A} \in A$, each function symbol $f \in \Sigma^F$ of arity n as a map $f^\mathcal{A} : A^n \to A$ and each predicate symbol $p \in \Sigma^P$ of arity n as a a subset $P^\mathcal{A}$ of A^n. We denote by $\text{dom}(\mathcal{A})$ the domain of an interpretation $\mathcal{A}$. In the sequel, when there is no ambiguity, we will omit the reference to the signature when referring to interpretations.

Given an interpretation $\mathcal{A}$ and a term t, we denote by $t^\mathcal{A}$ the interpretation of t under $\mathcal{A}$. Similarly, we denote by $\varphi^\mathcal{A}$ the truth value of the formula φ under the interpretation $\mathcal{A}$. Furthermore, given a set Γ of formulas, we denote by $[\![\Gamma]\!]^\mathcal{A}$ the set $\{\varphi^\mathcal{A} : \varphi \in \Gamma\}$, and similarly for a set of terms. We write $\mathcal{A} \Vdash \varphi$ when the formula φ is true under the interpretation $\mathcal{A}$, i.e., $\mathcal{A}$ satisfies φ.

A formula φ is *satisfiable* if it is true under some interpretation, and *unsatisfiable* otherwise.

Given a set of variables Y we say that two interpretations $\mathcal{A}$ and $\mathcal{B}$ over a set X of variables are Y-*equivalent* whenever $\text{dom}(\mathcal{A}) = \text{dom}(\mathcal{B})$, $f^\mathcal{A} = f^\mathcal{B}$ for each function symbol f, $p^\mathcal{A} = p^\mathcal{B}$ for each predicate symbol p, and $x^\mathcal{A} = x^\mathcal{B}$ for each variable x in $X \setminus Y$.

We also say that an *interpretation is finite (infinite)* when its domain is finite (infinite).

2.3 Theories

Given a signature Σ, a Σ-*theory* is a set of Σ-sentences and given a Σ-theory $\mathcal{T}$, a $\mathcal{T}$-*model* is a Σ-interpretation that satisfies all sentences of $\mathcal{T}$. We say that a formula φ is $\mathcal{T}$-*satisfiable* when there is a $\mathcal{T}$-model that satisfies it and say that two formulas are $\mathcal{T}$-*equivalent* if they are interpreted to the same truth value in every $\mathcal{T}$-model. In the sequel, when there is no ambiguity, we will omit the reference to the signature when referring to theories.

Given a Σ_1-theory $\mathcal{T}_1$ and a Σ_2-theory $\mathcal{T}_2$, their union, $\mathcal{T}_1 \oplus \mathcal{T}_2$, is a $\Sigma_1 \cup \Sigma_2$-theory defined by the union of the sentences of $\mathcal{T}_1$ with the sentences of $\mathcal{T}_2$.

The following definitions introduce some of the conditions used in the results presented in this paper.

Definition 2 (Smoothness). *We say that a theory $\mathcal{T}$ is smooth if for every $\mathcal{T}$-satisfiable quantifier-free formula φ, $\mathcal{T}$-model $\mathcal{A}$ satisfying φ and cardinal $\kappa \geq |\mathcal{A}|$ there exists a $\mathcal{T}$-model $\mathcal{B}$ satisfying φ such that $|\mathcal{B}| = \kappa$.*

Definition 3 (Stable finiteness). *We say that a theory $\mathcal{T}$ is stably finite if for every $\mathcal{T}$-satisfiable quantifier-free formula φ there exists a finite $\mathcal{T}$-model of φ.*

Definition 4 (Stable infiniteness). *We say that a theory $\mathcal{T}$ is stably infinite if for every $\mathcal{T}$-satisfiable quantifier-free formula φ there exists an infinite $\mathcal{T}$-model of φ.*

Definition 5 (Finite witnessability, [6]). *We say that a theory $\mathcal{T}$ over a signature Σ is* finitely witnessable *if there exists a computable function* witness : $\mathsf{QF}(\Sigma) \to \mathsf{QF}(\Sigma)$ *such that for every quantifier-free formula φ the following conditions hold:*

- *φ and $\exists \vec{w}$ witness(φ) are $\mathcal{T}$-equivalent, where $\vec{w}$ are the variables in witness(φ) which do not occur in φ;*
- *if witness(φ) is satisfiable in $\mathcal{T}$ then there exists a $\mathcal{T}$-model $\mathcal{A}$ such that $\mathcal{A} \Vdash$ witness(φ) and dom($\mathcal{A}$) = $[\![$vars(witness(φ))$]\!]^{\mathcal{A}}$.*

A function satisfying the above properties is called a *witness function for $\mathcal{T}$*. In [3], a stronger finite witnessability notion was defined in order to clarify an issue found on [6].

Definition 6 (Strong finite witnessability, [3]). *We say that a theory $\mathcal{T}$ over a signature Σ is* strongly finitely witnessable *if there exists a computable function* s-witness : $\mathsf{QF}(\Sigma) \to \mathsf{QF}(\Sigma)$ *such that for every quantifier-free formula φ the following conditions hold:*

- *φ and $\exists \vec{w}$ s-witness(φ) are $\mathcal{T}$-equivalent, where $\vec{w}$ are the variables in the formula s-witness(φ) which do not occur in φ;*
- *for every finite set of variables Y and relation $E \subseteq Y^2$, if s-witness(φ) $\wedge \delta_E^Y$ is satisfiable in $\mathcal{T}$ then there exists a $\mathcal{T}$-model $\mathcal{A}$ such that $\mathcal{A} \Vdash$ s-witness(φ)$\wedge \delta_E^Y$ and dom($\mathcal{A}$) = $[\![$vars(s-witness(φ) $\wedge \delta_E^Y$)$]\!]^{\mathcal{A}}$.*

A function satisfying the above properties is called a *strong witness function for $\mathcal{T}$*. The following notion was introduced by Tinelli and Zarba in [9] and its computability is one of the conditions a theory should satisfy to be shiny.

Definition 7 (mincard function). *Given a theory $\mathcal{T}$ over a signature Σ, let* mincard$_{\mathcal{T}}$ *be the function from $\mathsf{QF}(\Sigma)$ to $\mathbb{N}^+$ such that*

$$\mathsf{mincard}_{\mathcal{T}}(\varphi) = \min\{k : \mathcal{A} \text{ is a } \mathcal{T}\text{-model}, \mathcal{A} \Vdash \varphi \text{ and } |\mathsf{dom}(\mathcal{A})| = k\}$$

if φ is $\mathcal{T}$-satisfiable, otherwise mincard$_{\mathcal{T}}(\varphi)$ *is undefined.*

So, when φ is $\mathcal{T}$-satisfiable the function mincard$_{\mathcal{T}}$ returns the cardinality of the smallest $\mathcal{T}$-model of φ. When there is no ambiguity to which theory the function refers to we will simply write mincard.

3 Shiny and (Strongly) Polite Theories

3.1 Relating Shiny and Strongly Polite Theories

Here we analyse the relationship between shiny and strongly polite theories. We start by showing that a shiny theory is strongly polite when assuming that it has a decidable quantifier-free satisfiability problem, but first we recall what is a shiny theory, see [9], and a strongly polite one, see [3].

Definition 8 (Shininess, [9]). *A theory is* shiny *whenever it is smooth, stably finite and its* mincard *function is computable.*

Several theories were proved to be shiny, such as the theory of equality, the theory of partial orders and the theory of total orders, in [9].

Definition 9 (Strong politeness, [3]). *A theory is* strongly polite *whenever it is smooth and strongly finitely witnessable.*

Proposition 1. *A shiny theory with a decidable quantifier-free satisfiability problem is strongly polite.*

Proof. Let $\mathcal{T}$ be a shiny theory over a signature Σ and $\mathcal{P}$ an algorithm for its quantifier-free satisfiability problem. Since a shiny theory is by definition smooth, we are left to prove that $\mathcal{T}$ is strongly finitely witnessable in order to conclude that $\mathcal{T}$ is strongly polite. In the sequel, given a $\mathcal{T}$-satisfiable quantifier-free formula φ and $E \subseteq \mathsf{vars}(\varphi)^2$ such that $\varphi \wedge \delta_E^{\mathsf{vars}(\varphi)}$ is $\mathcal{T}$-satisfiable, we denote by k_E^φ the result of $\mathsf{mincard}_\mathcal{T}(\varphi \wedge \delta_E^{\mathsf{vars}(\varphi)})$.

Let
$$\text{s-witness} : \mathsf{QF}(\Sigma) \to \mathsf{QF}(\Sigma)$$
be the map such that $\text{s-witness}(\varphi) = \varphi \wedge \Omega$, where Ω is

$$\bigwedge_{\substack{E \subseteq \mathsf{vars}(\varphi)^2 \\ \mathcal{P}(\varphi \wedge \delta_E^{\mathsf{vars}(\varphi)}) = 1}} \left(\delta_E^{\mathsf{vars}(\varphi)} \to \gamma_{k_E^\varphi} \right)$$

and $\gamma_{k_E^\varphi}$ is

$$\bigwedge_{\substack{i,j=1 \\ i \neq j}}^{k_E^\varphi} w_i \not\approx w_j$$

and $w_1, \ldots, w_k$ are distinct variables not occurring in φ and in $\gamma_{k_{E'}^\varphi}$ for all $E' \neq E$ contained in $\mathsf{vars}(\varphi)^2$ with $\mathcal{P}(\varphi \wedge \delta_{E'}^{\mathsf{vars}(\varphi)}) = 1$. It is immediate to conclude that s-witness is computable since:

- there is a finite number of sets E contained in $\mathsf{vars}(\varphi)^2$ since $\mathsf{vars}(\varphi)$ is finite;
- formula $\delta_E^{\mathsf{vars}(\varphi)}$ can be computed in a finite number of steps since E and $\mathsf{vars}(\varphi)$ are finite;
- the value k_E^φ is computable since: (i) the mincard function is computable; (ii) we can decide the satisfiability of $\varphi \wedge \delta_E^{\mathsf{vars}(\varphi)}$ with $\mathcal{P}$; and (iii) $\mathcal{T}$ is stably finite;
- the formula $\gamma_{k_E^\varphi}$ is computable in a finite number of steps because k_E^φ is a natural number.

Let φ be a quantifier free formula. We now show that φ and $\exists \vec{w}\ \text{s-witness}(\varphi)$ are $\mathcal{T}$-equivalent. Let $\mathcal{A}$ be a $\mathcal{T}$-model. Assume that $\mathcal{A} \Vdash \exists \vec{w}\ \text{s-witness}(\varphi)$. Then

$\mathcal{A} \Vdash \varphi \wedge \exists \vec{w}\, \Omega$, and so $\mathcal{A} \Vdash \varphi$. For the other direction, assume $\mathcal{A} \Vdash \varphi$. We need to show that

$$\mathcal{A} \Vdash \exists \vec{w} \bigwedge_{\substack{E \subseteq \mathsf{vars}(\varphi)^2 \\ \mathcal{P}(\varphi \wedge \delta_E^{\mathsf{vars}(\varphi)})=1}} \left(\delta_E^{\mathsf{vars}(\varphi)} \to \gamma_{k_E^\varphi} \right).$$

Let $\mathcal{A}'$ be an interpretation $\vec{w}$-equivalent to $\mathcal{A}$ (and so with the same domain and the same interpretation of functions, predicates and of all variables except possibly $\vec{w}$) such that:

- if their domain is infinite then $w_1^{\mathcal{A}'} \neq w_2^{\mathcal{A}'}$ for every $w_1, w_2 \in \vec{w}$;
- if their domain is finite then for each $E \subseteq \mathsf{vars}(\varphi)^2$ with $\mathcal{P}(\varphi \wedge \delta_E^{\mathsf{vars}(\varphi)}) = 1$:
  - if $k_E^\varphi \leq |\mathsf{dom}(\mathcal{A}')|$ then $w_1^{\mathcal{A}'} \neq w_2^{\mathcal{A}'}$ for every $w_1, w_2 \in \vec{w}$;
  - otherwise, set $w_1^{\mathcal{A}'} = w_2^{\mathcal{A}'}$ for every $w_1, w_2 \in \mathsf{vars}(\gamma_{k_E^\varphi})$.

Then

$$\mathcal{A}' \Vdash \bigwedge_{\substack{E \subseteq \mathsf{vars}(\varphi)^2 \\ \mathcal{P}(\varphi \wedge \delta_E^{\mathsf{vars}(\varphi)})=1}} \left(\delta_E^{\mathsf{vars}(\varphi)} \to \gamma_{k_E^\varphi} \right),$$

since for each $E \subseteq \mathsf{vars}(\varphi)^2$ with $\mathcal{P}(\varphi \wedge \delta_E^{\mathsf{vars}(\varphi)}) = 1$ either

- $\mathcal{A}' \not\Vdash \delta_E^{\mathsf{vars}(\varphi)}$ and so $\mathcal{A}' \Vdash \delta_E^{\mathsf{vars}(\varphi)} \to \gamma_{k_E^\varphi}$; or
- $\mathcal{A}' \Vdash \delta_E^{\mathsf{vars}(\varphi)}$ and so $\mathcal{A}' \Vdash \varphi \wedge \delta_E^{\mathsf{vars}(\varphi)}$ since $\mathcal{A} \Vdash \varphi$ and $\mathcal{A}$ and $\mathcal{A}'$ only differ in the interpretation of the variables in $\vec{w}$ not occurring in φ. Since $\mathcal{A}'$ is a model for $\varphi \wedge \delta_E^{\mathsf{vars}(\varphi)}$, its cardinality has to be greater or equal than $k_E^\varphi = \mathsf{mincard}(\varphi \wedge \delta_E^{\mathsf{vars}(\varphi)})$. Hence $\mathcal{A}' \Vdash \gamma_{k_E^\varphi}$ and so $\mathcal{A}' \Vdash \delta_E^{\mathsf{vars}(\varphi)} \to \gamma_{k_E^\varphi}$.

We now show that given an equivalence relation E' over a finite set of variables Y, if $\varphi \wedge \Omega \wedge \delta_{E'}^Y$ is $\mathcal{T}$-satisfiable, then there exists a $\mathcal{T}$-model $\mathcal{A}$ that satisfies $\varphi \wedge \Omega \wedge \delta_{E'}^Y$ such that $\mathsf{dom}(\mathcal{A}) = [\![\mathsf{vars}(\varphi \wedge \Omega \wedge \delta_{E'}^Y)]\!]^{\mathcal{A}}$. So, let E' be an equivalence relation over a finite set of variables Y such that $\varphi \wedge \Omega \wedge \delta_{E'}^Y$ is $\mathcal{T}$-satisfiable. Let p be a natural number and $Y_1, \ldots, Y_p$ finite pairwise disjoint non-empty sets of variables such that

- $Y = Y_1 \cup \ldots \cup Y_p$; and
- for each $i = 1, \ldots, p$, and $y \in Y_i$,
  - $(y \cong x)$ and $(x \cong y)$ are in $\delta_{E'}^Y$ for each $x \in Y_i$;
  - $\neg(y \cong x)$ and $\neg(x \cong y)$ are in $\delta_{E'}^Y$ for each $x \in Y \setminus Y_i$;

and observe that the variables in Y can be either in $\mathsf{vars}(\varphi)$ or in $\mathsf{vars}(\gamma_{k_E})$ for some E or not in $\mathsf{vars}(\varphi \wedge \Omega)$. Let $\mathcal{A}$ be a $\mathcal{T}$-model that satisfies

$$\varphi \wedge \Omega \wedge \delta_{E'}^Y$$

and let $\delta_{E_\mathcal{A}}^{\mathsf{vars}(\varphi)}$ be the arrangement formula induced by $E_\mathcal{A} = \{(x,y) : x, y \in \mathsf{vars}(\varphi)$ and $x^\mathcal{A} = y^\mathcal{A}\}$. Then, obviously, $\delta_{E_\mathcal{A}}^{\mathsf{vars}(\varphi)}$ is satisfied by $\mathcal{A}$. Moreover, no other formula in $\{\delta_E^{\mathsf{vars}(\varphi)} : E \subseteq \mathsf{vars}(\varphi)^2 \text{ and } \mathcal{P}(\varphi \wedge \delta_E^{\mathsf{vars}(\varphi)}) = 1\}$ is satisfied by $\mathcal{A}$. Since $\varphi \wedge \delta_{E_A}^{\mathsf{vars}(\varphi)}$ is satisfiable we have that the cardinality of its smallest model is $k_{E_A}^{\varphi} = \mathsf{mincard}(\varphi \wedge \delta_{E_A}^{\mathsf{vars}(\varphi)})$. Let $K = \max\{k_{E_A}^{\varphi}, p\}$. By the smoothness of $\mathcal{T}$ and since $\varphi \wedge \delta_{E_A}^{\mathsf{vars}(\varphi)}$ is $\mathcal{T}$-satisfiable, let $\mathcal{B}$ be a $\mathcal{T}$-model such that

$$\mathcal{B} \Vdash \varphi \wedge \delta_{E_A}^{\mathsf{vars}(\varphi)} \quad \text{and} \quad |\mathsf{dom}(\mathcal{B})| = K,$$

and let $d_1, \ldots, d_p$ be distinct elements of $\mathsf{dom}(\mathcal{B})$ such that

$$d_i = y^{\mathcal{B}} \text{ if } Y_i \cap \mathsf{vars}(\varphi) \neq \emptyset \text{ and } y \in Y_i \cap \mathsf{vars}(\varphi)$$

for $i = 1, \ldots, p$, and assuming that the variables of $\gamma_{k_{E_A}^{\varphi}}$ are $w_1 \ldots, w_{k_{E_A}^{\varphi}}$ let $e_1, \ldots, e_{k_{E_A}^{\varphi}}$ be distinct elements of $\mathsf{dom}(\mathcal{B})$ such that

$$e_j = d_i \text{ if } w_j \in Y_i$$

for $j = 1, \ldots, k_{E_A}^{\varphi}$. Observe that distinct variables in $w_1 \ldots, w_{k_{E_A}^{\varphi}}$ are in distinct sets in $Y_1, \ldots, Y_p$ since $\mathcal{A} \Vdash \delta_{E'}^{Y}$ and $\mathcal{A} \Vdash \gamma_{k_{E_A}^{\varphi}}$ taking into account that $\mathcal{A} \Vdash \delta_{E_A}^{\mathsf{vars}(\varphi)}$ and $\mathcal{A} \Vdash \Omega$. Let $\mathcal{B}'$ be the $\mathcal{T}$-model $(\vec{w} \cup (Y \setminus \mathsf{vars}(\varphi)))$-equivalent to $\mathcal{B}$ such that

$$x^{\mathcal{B}'} = \begin{cases} d_i & \text{if } x \in Y_i \text{ for some } i \in \{1, \ldots, p\} \\ e_j & \text{if } x \notin Y \text{ and } x \text{ is } w_j \text{ with } w_j \in \mathsf{vars}(\gamma_{k_{E_A}}) \\ x^{\mathcal{B}} & \text{if } x \notin Y \text{ and } x \notin \mathsf{vars}(\gamma_{k_{E_A}}) \end{cases}$$

for each $x \in \vec{w} \cup (Y \setminus \mathsf{vars}(\varphi))$. Let us now prove that $\mathcal{B}' \Vdash \varphi \wedge \Omega \wedge \delta_{E'}^{Y}$:

(a) $\mathcal{B}' \Vdash \varphi$. This follows immediately taking into account that $\mathcal{B} \Vdash \varphi$ and that $\mathcal{B}$ and $\mathcal{B}'$ may only differ in variables in $\vec{w} \cup (Y \setminus \mathsf{vars}(\varphi))$ not occurring in φ;

(b) $\mathcal{B}' \Vdash \Omega$. Observe that $\mathcal{B}' \Vdash \varphi \wedge \delta_{E_A}^{\mathsf{vars}(\varphi)}$ since $\mathcal{B}$ and $\mathcal{B}'$ may only differ in variables in $\vec{w} \cup (Y \setminus \mathsf{vars}(\varphi))$ not occurring in $\varphi \wedge \delta_{E_A}^{\mathsf{vars}(\varphi)}$. Moreover $\mathcal{B}' \Vdash \gamma_{k_{E_A}}$ and so $\mathcal{B}' \Vdash \delta_{E_A}^{\mathsf{vars}(\varphi)} \to \gamma_{k_{E_A}}$. Since $\mathcal{B}' \Vdash \delta_{E_A}^{\mathsf{vars}(\varphi)}$, we have that $\mathcal{B}' \nVdash \delta_E^{\mathsf{vars}(\varphi)}$ for all $E \neq E_A$ with $E \subseteq \mathsf{vars}(\varphi)^2$. Hence $\mathcal{B}' \Vdash \delta_E^{\mathsf{vars}(\varphi)} \to \gamma_{k_E}$ for all $E \subseteq \mathsf{vars}(\varphi)^2$ and so $\mathcal{B}' \Vdash \Omega$;

(c) $\mathcal{B}' \Vdash \delta_{E'}^{Y}$. We only need to verify that $\mathcal{B}'$ satisfies the equalities and disequalities induced by E'. This holds since by construction, it assigns the same value to variables in the same Y_i set, and assigns different values to variables in different sets.

Finally it remains to show that $\mathsf{dom}(\mathcal{B}') = [\![\mathsf{vars}(\varphi \wedge \Omega \wedge \delta_{E'}^{Y})]\!]^{\mathcal{B}'}$:

($\subseteq$): Let $d \in \mathsf{dom}(\mathcal{B}')$. Then d is either a d_i for some $i = 1, \ldots, p$ or a e_j for some $j = 1, \ldots, k_{E_A}$. In the case that $d = d_i$ then we have that $d = x^{\mathcal{B}'}$ for all $x \in Y_i$. On the other hand, if $d = e_j$ then $d = w_j^{\mathcal{B}'}$ for the w_j variable in $\mathsf{vars}(\gamma_{k_{E_A}})$;

(⊇): From the construction described above we obtain for every $x \in \mathsf{vars}(\varphi \wedge \Omega \wedge \delta^Y_{E'})$ how to define $x^{\mathcal{B}'}$.

Combining the previous items, we obtain that a shiny theory is strongly finitely witnessable, hence strongly polite. □

3.2 Relating Polite and Shiny Theories

In this section, we relate polite and shiny theories using results from [6] and making use of a sufficient condition for the computability of the mincard function [9].

Begin by recalling the notion of *politeness* by Ranise, Ringeissen and Zarba [6].

Definition 10 (Politeness). *We say that a theory is* polite *whenever it is smooth and finitely witnessable.*

We prove that a polite theory is stably infinite, as mentioned in Remark 10 of [6].

Proposition 2. *A polite theory is stably finite.*

Proof. Let $\mathcal{T}$ be a polite theory, witness a witness function for $\mathcal{T}$, and φ a $\mathcal{T}$-satisfiable quantifier-free formula. Hence witness(φ) is $\mathcal{T}$-satisfiable and so there is a $\mathcal{T}$-model $\mathcal{A}$ satisfying witness(φ) with $\mathsf{dom}(\mathcal{A}) = [\![\mathsf{vars}(\mathsf{witness}(\varphi))]\!]^{\mathcal{A}}$. Since the number of variables in witness(φ) is finite we have that $\mathcal{A}$ is a finite model of this formula, and so of φ. Hence $\mathcal{T}$ is stably finite. □

We now recall a proposition by Ranise, Ringeissen and Zarba in [6] that provides conditions under which a polite theory is shiny.

Proposition 3 ([6]). *Let Σ be a finite signature and $\mathcal{T}$ a Σ-theory. Assume that it is decidable to check if a finite Σ-interpretation is a $\mathcal{T}$-model. Then, if $\mathcal{T}$ is polite then $\mathcal{T}$ is shiny and Algorithm 1 computes its* mincard *function.*

Algorithm 1. — mincard$_\mathsf{witness}$ algorithm
Input: φ, where φ is a quantifier-free satisfiable formula
Output: k, where k is the cardinality of the smallest $\mathcal{T}$-model of φ
Requires: access to a witness function witness for $\mathcal{T}$

1: $n = |\mathsf{vars}(\mathsf{witness}(\varphi))|$;
2: **for** $k = 1$ to n
3:     **for** all non-isomorphic $\mathcal{T}$-models $\mathcal{A}$ s.t. $|\mathsf{dom}(\mathcal{A})| = k$ **do**
4:         **if** $\mathcal{A} \Vdash \varphi$ **then return** k
5:     **end for**
6: **end for**

Observe that the conditions on the previous proposition are rather weak – for instance, if a theory $\mathcal{T}$ over Σ is finitely axiomatized then it is decidable to check if a finite Σ-interpretation is indeed a $\mathcal{T}$-model.

On the other hand, even if it is not decidable to check whether a finite interpretation is a $\mathcal{T}$-model, it is still possible to construct the mincard function provided that the theory $\mathcal{T}$ is universal as is stated in the next proposition. This proposition uses a result of Tinelli and Zarba in [9]. Observe that Algorithm 2 makes use of a *simple diagram* of an interpretation. We suggest [9] for this definition.

Proposition 4. *Let Σ be a finite signature and $\mathcal{T}$ a universal Σ-theory with a decidable quantifier-free satisfiability problem. Then, if $\mathcal{T}$ is polite then it is shiny and Algorithm 2 computes its* mincard *function.*

Proof. By Proposition 2 we obtain that $\mathcal{T}$ is stably finite. The thesis follows immediately by Proposition 23 in [9] that establishes that the mincard function of any theory is computable by Algorithm 2, if that theory is stably finite, universal, is over a finite signature, and has a decidable quantifier-free satisfiability problem. □

Algorithm 2. — mincard$_\mathcal{P}$ algorithm, [9]
Input: φ, where φ is a quantifier-free satisfiable formula
Output: k, where k is the cardinality of the smallest $\mathcal{T}$-model of φ
Requires: access to an algorithm $\mathcal{P}$ that decides satisfiability of quantifier-free formulas and where $\Delta(\mathcal{A})$ denotes the simple diagram of $\mathcal{A}$

1: **while** *true* **do**
2:     $k = 1$
3:     **for** all non-isomorphic interpretations $\mathcal{A}$ s.t. $|\text{dom}(\mathcal{A})| = k$ **do**
4:         **if** $\mathcal{P}(\Delta(\mathcal{A}) \wedge \varphi) == 1$ **then return** k
5:     **end for**
6:     $k = k + 1$
7: **end while**

3.3 Relating Polite and Strongly Polite Theories

Finally, we state that a strongly finitely witnessable theory is also finitely witnessable.

Fact 1. *Each strongly finitely witnessable theory is finitely witnessable.*

This fact follows by observing that a strong witness function is also a witness function. Specifically, with respect to the second condition of the finite witnessability, let E and Y to be the empty set and the result follows.

3.4 Relating Shiny, Polite and Strongly Polite Theories

Combining the results in the previous sections, we obtain the equivalence between *strong politeness, shininess* and *politeness*, assuming two sets of different conditions on the theory.

Corollary 1. *Let $\mathcal{T}$ be a theory over a finite signature. If either*

- $\mathcal{T}$ *is universal; or*
- *checking whether a finite interpretation is a $\mathcal{T}$-model is decidable,*

then the following statements are equivalent:

1. $\mathcal{T}$ *is shiny;*
2. $\mathcal{T}$ *is strongly polite;*
3. $\mathcal{T}$ *is polite.*

Proof. (1. → 2.) Follows by Proposition 1.
(2. → 3.) Follows by Fact 1.
(3. → 1.) If $\mathcal{T}$ is universal, follows by Proposition 4, and if checking whether a finite interpretation is a $\mathcal{T}$-model is decidable, follows by Proposition 3. □

Capitalizing on the previous results on the relationship between strong politeness, shininess, and politeness, we now present a new algorithm, Algorithm 3, that computes a strong witness function for a smooth and finitely witnessable theory.

Theorem 1. *Let Σ be a finite signature and $\mathcal{T}$ a polite Σ-theory with a decidable quantifier-free satisfiability problem. Assume that either $\mathcal{T}$ is universal or it is decidable to check if a finite interpretation is a $\mathcal{T}$-model. Then, Algorithm 3 computes a strong witness function for $\mathcal{T}$.*

Proof. We begin by computing the mincard function. If $\mathcal{T}$ is universal, by Proposition 4 we have that the mincard function is computable and that Algorithm 2 is an algorithm for it. In the case that it is decidable to check if a finite Σ-interpretation is a $\mathcal{T}$-model, then by Proposition 3 we have that the mincard function is computed by Algorithm 1. Therefore, $\mathcal{T}$ is shiny. It is immediate to see that Algorithm 3 computes the function shown in the proof of Proposition 1 to be a strong witness function for $\mathcal{T}$, and so the thesis follows. □

Capitalizing on the relationships between the politeness, shininess and strong politeness established in the previous results, we can now establish a combination result very similar to the combination proposition of [3], Proposition 2, but instead of imposing that $\mathcal{T}_2$ is strongly finitely witnessable, imposes that $\mathcal{T}_2$ is

- finitely witnessable;
- either universal or such that checking if a finite Σ_2-interpretation is a model of $\mathcal{T}_2$ is decidable.

Algorithm 3. — Computes a strong witness function for a theory $\mathcal{T}$
Input: φ, where φ is a quantifier-free satisfiable formula
Output: s-witness(φ)
Requires: access to an algorithm $\mathcal{P}$ that decides satisfiability of quantifier-free formulas, and to the function mincard for $\mathcal{T}$

1: **for** $E \subseteq \text{vars}(\varphi)^2$
2:     $\delta_E^{\text{vars}(\varphi)} = \varepsilon$
3:     **for** all pairs $(x, y) \in \text{vars}(\varphi)^2$
4:        **if** $(x, y) \in E$
5:           **then** $\delta_E^{\text{vars}(\varphi)} = \delta_E^{\text{vars}(\varphi)} \wedge (x \cong y)$
6:           **else** $\delta_E^{\text{vars}(\varphi)} = \delta_E^{\text{vars}(\varphi)} \wedge \neg(x \cong y)$
7:        **end if**
8:     **end for**
9:     **if** $\mathcal{P}(\varphi \wedge \delta_E^{\text{vars}(\varphi)}) == 1$
10:        **then** $k_E = \text{mincard}(\varphi \wedge \delta_E^{\text{vars}(\varphi)})$
11:           $\gamma_{k_E} = \varepsilon$
12:           **for** $i, j = 1, i \neq j$ **to** k_E
13:              $\gamma_{k_E} = \gamma_{k_E} \wedge \neg(x_i \cong x_j)$
14:           **end for**
15:           $\varphi = \varphi \wedge (\delta_E^{\text{vars}(\varphi)} \to \gamma_{k_E})$
16:     **end if**
17: **end for**
18: **return** φ

Observe that showing these conditions may be more manageable than proving that $\mathcal{T}_2$ is strongly finitely witnessable, particularly because many theories of interest to SMT applications are either universal or finitely axiomatized.

In other words, these results show that in the one-sorted context, if a theory is either universal or is such that checking whether a finite interpretation is a model is decidable, then we can forget the strong politeness requirement and use the politeness condition by Ranise, Ringeissen and Zarba to construct both a strong witness function and the mincard function. These functions can then be used in the application of the Nelson-Oppen method for the combination of strongly polite theories or shiny theories with an arbitrary theory. The following result formalizes these statements in a Nelson-Oppen combination theorem.

Theorem 2. *Let Σ_2 be a finite signature and $\mathcal{T}_i$ a Σ_i-theory with a decidable quantifier-free satisfiability problem, for $i = 1, 2$, such that $\Sigma_1 \cap \Sigma_2 = \emptyset$. Assume that*

- *$\mathcal{T}_2$ is smooth;*
- *$\mathcal{T}_2$ has a witness function;*
- *either $\mathcal{T}_2$ is universal or checking if a finite Σ_2-interpretation is a model of $\mathcal{T}_2$ is decidable.*

Then, the function mincard$_{\mathcal{T}_2}$ is computable and there is a computable strong witness function, s-witness$_{\mathcal{T}_2}$, for $\mathcal{T}_2$, such that the following statements are equivalent:

1. $\Gamma_1 \wedge \Gamma_2$ is $\mathcal{T}_1 \oplus \mathcal{T}_2$ satisfiable;
2. there exists $E \subseteq Y^2$, where Y is vars(Γ_1) ∩ vars(Γ_2), such that
   - $\Gamma_1 \wedge \delta_E^Y \wedge \gamma_\kappa$ is $\mathcal{T}_1$-satisfiable, where κ is mincard$_{\mathcal{T}_2}(\Gamma_2 \wedge \delta_E^Y)$;
   - $\Gamma_2 \wedge \delta_E^Y$ is $\mathcal{T}_2$-satisfiable;
3. there exists $E \subseteq Y^2$, where Y is vars(s-witness(Γ_2)), such that
   - $\Gamma_1 \wedge \delta_E^Y$ is $\mathcal{T}_1$-satisfiable;
   - s-witness$_{\mathcal{T}_2}(\Gamma_2) \wedge \delta_E^Y$ is $\mathcal{T}_2$-satisfiable;

for every conjunction Γ_1 of Σ_1-literals and Γ_2 of Σ_2-literals.

Proof. Observe that the theory $\mathcal{T}_2$ is polite and that the mincard function of $\mathcal{T}_2$ is computable either by Proposition 3 if it is decidable to check if a finite Σ_2-interpretation is a model of $\mathcal{T}_2$; or by Proposition 4 if $\mathcal{T}_2$ is a universal theory. Moreover $\mathcal{T}_2$ has also a computable strong witness function by Theorem 1. Observe also that $\mathcal{T}_2$ is stably finite by Proposition 2. Then, the equivalence between (1) and (2) follows from the combination theorem in [9], Theorem 18, and the equivalence between (1) and (3) follows from the combination proposition, Proposition 2, in [3]. □

We now provide an example showing an application of the previous theorem.

Example 1. Consider the theories $\mathcal{T}_1$ and $\mathcal{T}_2$ over the empty signature such that $\mathcal{T}_1$ is axiomatized by $\forall x \forall y \, (x \cong y)$ and $\mathcal{T}_2$ is axiomatized by $\exists x \exists y \, \neg (x \cong y)$. Hence every model of $\mathcal{T}_1$ has cardinality at most one and every model of $\mathcal{T}_2$ has cardinality at least 2. Let φ denote the formula $(x \cong x)$.

Observe that, in [3], it was shown that theory $\mathcal{T}_2$ is smooth and that

$$\text{witness}_{\mathcal{T}_2}(\varphi) := \varphi \wedge (w_1 \cong w_1) \wedge (w_2 \cong w_2)$$

is a witness function for $\mathcal{T}_2$. Hence this condition for the application of Theorem 2 is fulfilled. Taking into account that mincard$_{\mathcal{T}_2}(\varphi) = 2$, then by Algorithm 3,

$$\text{s-witness}_{\mathcal{T}_2}(\varphi) = \varphi \wedge (x \cong x) \to \gamma_2$$
$$= \varphi \wedge (x \cong x) \to \neg(z_1 \cong z_2)$$
$$= (x \cong x) \wedge \neg(z_1 \cong z_2).$$

Let Γ_1 be the formula tt, Γ_2 the formula φ and Y the set vars(s-witness(Γ_2)) i.e. $\{x, z_1, z_2\}$. We now would like to check if there is an arrangement of δ_E^Y such that $\Gamma_1 \wedge \delta_E^Y$ is $\mathcal{T}_1$-satisfiable and s-witness(Γ_2)$\wedge \delta_E^Y$ is $\mathcal{T}_2$-satisfiable. Note that the only arrangement satisfied in $\mathcal{T}_1$ is the one induced by $E=\{(x, z_1), (x, z_2), (z_1, z_2)\}$ since all others would require the interpretation to have cardinality greater than one. However, s-witness(Γ_2) $\wedge \delta_E^Y$ is clearly not satisfiable. Hence, by Theorem 2, we conclude that φ is not satisfiable in $\mathcal{T}_1 \oplus \mathcal{T}_2$. In this simple case it is no difficult to see that this was the expected conclusion since there are no models that satisfy the theory resulting from the union of $\mathcal{T}_1$ and $\mathcal{T}_2$.

Observe the importance of Algorithm 3 to define in a computable way the strong witnessable function.

Example 2. One can directly apply Proposition 1 to conclude that the theories of partial orders, total orders and the theory of lattices with top and bottom are strongly polite, since in [9] it is shown that these theories are shiny and have a decidable quantifier-free satisfiability problem. Furthermore, using Algorithm 3 we can construct their s-witness functions.

4 Conclusion and Further Research

In this paper we investigated the relationship between the notions of shininess, politeness and strong politeness. Answering a question left open by Jovanović and Barrett in [3], we showed that a shiny theory with a decidable quantifier-free satisfiability problem is strongly polite, as well as showed that a strongly polite theory is polite. Capitalizing on results relating shiny and polite theories from [6], as well as results regarding the computability of the mincard function from [9], we were able to establish that under two different sets of conditions, the notions of shininess, politeness and strong politeness are equivalent. Moreover, given the constructive nature of the proof showing that a shiny theory with a decidable quantifier-free satisfiability problem is strongly polite, we were able to devise a Nelson-Oppen procedure for the combination of a polite (with an additional restriction) and an arbitrary theory.

We leave as future work the extension of the results presented in this paper to the many-sorted case. This would allow the application of our results to other interesting theories such as the theory of lists and the theory of arrays. We would also like to address the study of the relationship between the complexity of the mincard function (already studied in [9]) and the complexity of a s-witness function. We also hope to investigate the role of shiny, polite and strongly polite theories and their relationships in the context of the union of constraint theories [8].

Acknowledgments. We would like to acknowledge the anonymous reviewers for their helpful comments. This work was partially supported, under the MCL (Meet-Combination of Logics) and PQDR (Probabilistic, Quantum and Differential Reasoning) initiatives of SQIG at IT, by FCT and EU FEDER, namely via the FCT PEst-OE/EEI/LA0008/2013, AMDSC UTAustin/MAT/0057/2008 and ComFormCrypt PTDC/EIA-CCO/113033/2009 projects, as well as by the European Union's Seventh Framework Programme for Research (FP7), namely through project LANDAUER (GA 318287).

References

1. Barrett, C., Conway, C.L., Deters, M., Hadarean, L., Jovanović, D., King, T., Reynolds, A., Tinelli, C.: CVC4. In: CAV 2011. LNCS, vol. 6806, pp. 171–177. Springer, Heidelberg (2011)
2. Christ, J., Hoenicke, J., Nutz, A.: SMTInterpol: An interpolating SMT solver. In: Donaldson, A., Parker, D. (eds.) SPIN 2012. LNCS, vol. 7385, pp. 248–254. Springer, Heidelberg (2012)

3. Jovanović, D., Barrett, C.: Polite theories revisited. In: Fermüller, C.G., Voronkov, A. (eds.) LPAR-17. LNCS, vol. 6397, pp. 402–416. Springer, Heidelberg (2010)
4. Nelson, G., Oppen, D.C.: Simplification by cooperating decision procedures. ACM Transactions on Programming Languages and Systems 1(2), 245–257 (1979)
5. Oppen, D.C.: Complexity, convexity and combinations of theories. Theoretical Computer Science 12, 291–302 (1980)
6. Ranise, S., Ringeissen, C., Zarba, C.G.: Combining data structures with nonstably infinite theories using many-sorted logic. In: Gramlich, B. (ed.) FroCos 2005. LNCS (LNAI), vol. 3717, pp. 48–64. Springer, Heidelberg (2005)
7. Tinelli, C., Harandi, M.T.: A new correctness proof of the Nelson-Oppen combination procedure. In: Proceedings of the First International Workshop on Frontiers of Combining Systems (FroCoS 1996). Applied Logic Series, vol. 3, pp. 103–119 (1996)
8. Tinelli, C., Harandi, M.T.: Constraint logic programming over unions of constraint theories. Journal of Functional and Logic Programming 1998(6) (1998)
9. Tinelli, C., Zarba, C.G.: Combining nonstably infinite theories. Journal of Automated Reasoning 34(3), 209–238 (2005)

Towards Rational Closure for Fuzzy Logic: The Case of Propositional Gödel Logic

Giovanni Casini[1] and Umberto Straccia[2]

[1] Centre for Artificial Intelligence Research, CSIR Meraka Institute and UKZN, South Africa
[2] Istituto di Scienza e Tecnologie dell'Informazione (ISTI - CNR), Pisa, Italy

Abstract. In the field of non-monotonic logics, the notion of *rational closure* is acknowledged as a landmark and we are going to see whether such a construction can be adopted in the context of mathematical fuzzy logic, a so far (apparently) unexplored journey. As a first step, we will characterise rational closure in the context of Propositional Gödel Logic.

1 Introduction and Motivation

A lot of attention has been dedicated to *non-monotonic* (or *defeasible*) reasoning (see, e.g. [11]) to accommodate reasoning patters with exceptions such as "typically, a bird flies, but a penguin is a bird that does not fly". Among of the many proposals, the notion of *rational closure* [18] is acknowledged as a landmark for non-monotonic reasoning due to its firm logical properties.

On the other hand, the main formalism developed for dealing with vague notions is represented by the class of *multi-valued* or *mathematical fuzzy* logics [15,16], allowing to reason with statements involving vague concepts such as "a very young bird does not fly". These logics allow to associate to a statement a truth value that is chosen not only between false and true (*i.e.*, $\{0, 1\}$), but usually from the real interval $[0, 1]$ and, thus, allowing to specify statements of *graded* truth.[1]

Here we propose a first attempt towards the definition of a logical system that combines such two forms of reasoning, namely reasoning about vagueness and defeasible reasoning via rational closure, allowing to cope with reasoning patterns such as

"Typically, a ripe fruit is sweet, but a ripe bitter melon is a ripe fruit that is not sweet." [2]

More specifically, in what follows, we will propose a formalism for reasoning about non-monotonic conditionals involving fuzzy statements as antecedents and consequents, *i.e.* conditionals $C \rightsquigarrow D$ that are read as

(∗) "Typically, if C is true to a positive degree, then D is true to a positive degree too."

---

[1] The previous statement may be graded as a bird may be very young to some degree depending on the birds age.

[2] As the bitter melon ripens, the flesh (rind) becomes tougher, more bitter, and too distasteful to eat.

Note that such an interpretation is different from other ones appeared in the literature, notably *e.g.* [2,3,4,6,7,9,10,20,21].

While one usually distinguishes three different fuzzy logics, namely Gödel, Product and Łukasiewicz logics [16] to interpret graded statements,[3] we start the journey of our investigation with Propositional Gödel Logic, leaving the other two and extensions to (notable fragments of) First-Order Logic for future work.

Related Work. While there have been a non negligible amount of work related to the notion of rational closure in the classical logic setting, very little is know about it in the context of mathematical fuzzy logic. Somewhat related are [2,3,4,6,7,9,10], which rely on a possibilistic logic setting. Specifically, [2] shows that the notion of classical rational closure can be related to possibility distributions: roughly a conditional $C \leadsto D$ is interpreted as $\Pi(C \wedge D) > \Pi(C \wedge \neg D)$, *i.e.* the possibility of classical formula $C \wedge D$ is greater than the possibility of $C \wedge \neg D$. The idea has then be used later on in [4] and related works such as [3,6,10], however, addressing only marginally the fuzzy case as well, by proposing various interpretation of the fuzzy conditional $C \leadsto D$, *e.g.* along the paradigm "the more C the more it is certain that C implies D". This is a different interpretation as the one proposed here and, indeed, seems not to apply to the typical ripe fruits are sweet case. To the best of our knowledge, there has been no attempt so far to combine rational closure in the context of a pure mathematical fuzzy logic setting, which, however, does not mean that an approach based on possibilistic logic may not be viable in the future as well.

In the following, we proceed as follows. After introducing some preliminary notions in the next section, section 3 characterises preferential entailment, section 4 characterises rational monotony, and eventually section 5 concludes and addresses future work.

2 Preliminaries

Syntax. We start with a standard propositional language, defined from a finite set P of atomic propositions and connectives $\{\neg, \wedge, \vee, \supset, \equiv\}$. Let $\mathcal{L}$ be the set of the propositional formulae, which we indicate with $C, D, \ldots$. From $\mathcal{L}$ and the operator $\leadsto$ we define the conditionals $\mathcal{C} = \{C \leadsto D \mid C, D \in \mathcal{L}\}$, where $(*)$ is the intended interpretation of $C \leadsto D$.

A knowledge base $\mathcal{K} = \langle \mathcal{T}, \mathcal{D} \rangle$ consists of a finite set $\mathcal{T}$ of propositions, indicating what the agent considers as fully true, and a finite set of conditionals $\mathcal{D}$, describing defeasible information about what typically holds.

Example 1. The example about ripe fruits being sweet, while a ripe bitter melon isn't, can be encoded as follows:

$$\mathcal{T} = \{rbm \supset (rf \wedge \neg s), rbm \supset bm\}$$
$$\mathcal{D} = \{rf \leadsto s\},$$

where rbm, bm, rf and s encode ripe bitter melon, bitter melon, ripe fruits and sweet, respectively. □

---
[3] The main reason is that any other t-norm, *i.e.*, the function used to interpret conjunction, can be obtained as a combination of these three.

Semantics. At the base of our (preferential) semantics there are the valuations for propositional Gödel logic. A valuation u is a function that maps each atomic proposition in P into $[0,1]$, and u is then extended inductively as follows:

$$u(C \wedge D) = u(C) \otimes u(D)$$
$$u(C \vee D) = u(C) \oplus u(D)$$
$$u(C \supset D) = u(C) \Rightarrow u(D)$$
$$u(\neg C) = \ominus u(C).$$

$C \equiv D$ is, as usual, an abbreviation for $(C \supset D) \wedge (D \supset C)$. In Gödel logic, the semantic operators are defined as:

$$m \otimes n = \min(m,n)$$
$$m \oplus n = \max(m,n)$$
$$m \Rightarrow n = \begin{cases} 1 \text{ if } m \leq n \\ n \text{ otherwise} \end{cases}$$
$$\ominus m = \begin{cases} 1 \text{ if } m = 0 \\ 0 \text{ otherwise} \end{cases}$$

with $m, n \in [0,1]$.

Let $\mathcal{I} = \{u, v, \ldots\}$ be the set of all the valuations for language $\mathcal{L}$. We shall indicate with $\models$ the entailment relation defined on such interpretations, where, given a finite set of propositions Γ, $\Gamma \models D$ iff for every valuation $u \in \mathcal{I}$ that verifies the premises (*i.e.*, s.t. for every proposition $C \in \Gamma$, $u(C) = 1$), it holds that $u(D) = 1$. Note that $\Gamma \models D$ can be decided *e.g.* via the Hilbert style calculi described in [16], or with more practical methods such as [1,14]. However, deciding entailment is a coNP-complete problem [16].

Properties of the Conditionals. The preferential approach to crisp non-monotonic reasoning is characterised by the satisfaction of some desirable properties.

Here we consider the relevant properties w.r.t. the material implication, instead that w.r.t. the consequence relation as usually presented in the crisp propositional case. The properties we take under consideration are *Reflexivity, Left Logical Equivalence, Right Weakening, Cumulative Transitivity (Cut), Monotony,* and *Disjunction in the Premises,* which are illustrated below.

(REF) $C \supset C$

(LLE) $\dfrac{C \supset E \quad C \equiv D}{D \supset E}$ (RW) $\dfrac{C \supset D \quad D \supset E}{C \supset E}$

(CT) $\dfrac{C \wedge D \supset E \quad C \supset D}{C \supset E}$ (MON) $\dfrac{C \supset E}{C \wedge D \supset E}$

(OR) $\dfrac{C \supset E \quad D \supset E}{C \vee D \supset E}$

It is rather straightforward to prove that

Proposition 1. *Propositional Gödel logic satisfies the properties (REF), (LLE), (RW), (CT), (MON), and (OR).*

The properties (REF), (LLE), (RW), (CT), and (OR) are interesting because they represent a set of reasonable and desirable properties for a logic-based reasoning system. On the other hand, (MON) is the property that we want to drop, still keeping a constrained form of monotony that is appropriate for reasoning about typicality. In particular, the first form of constrained monotony that we take under consideration is *Cautious Monotony* (CM). Specifically, the set of properties involving defeasible conditionals we are interested in is the following:

$$
\begin{array}{c}
\text{(REF)}\ C \rightsquigarrow C \\[4pt]
\text{(LLE)}\ \dfrac{C \rightsquigarrow E \quad C \equiv D}{D \rightsquigarrow E} \qquad \text{(RW)}\ \dfrac{C \rightsquigarrow D \quad D \supset E}{C \rightsquigarrow E} \\[10pt]
\text{(CT)}\ \dfrac{C \wedge D \rightsquigarrow E \quad C \rightsquigarrow D}{C \rightsquigarrow E} \qquad \text{(CM)}\ \dfrac{C \rightsquigarrow E \quad C \rightsquigarrow D}{C \wedge D \rightsquigarrow E} \\[10pt]
\text{(OR)}\ \dfrac{C \rightsquigarrow E \quad D \rightsquigarrow E}{C \vee D \rightsquigarrow E}
\end{array}
\qquad (1)
$$

The meaning of (CM) is the following: if in every *typical* situation in which C has a positive degree of truth also D has a positive degree of truth, then a typical situation for $C \wedge D$ will be a typical situation also for C, and whatever typically follows from C (e.g. E) follows also from $C \wedge D$. In classical logic the set of properties above identifies the class of the *preferential conditionals* [17].

Example 2 (Example 1 cont.). Consider Example 1. Let us add the defeasible information "typically, a ripe fruit tastes good" represented via the conditional

$$rf \rightsquigarrow tg,$$

where tg stands for "tastes good". Then, by using (CM) we may infer that

$$rf \wedge tg \rightsquigarrow s,$$

i.e., "typically, a ripe and good tasting fruit is sweet". □

3 Characterising Preferential Entailment

Next, we want to define a very basic non-monotonic connection between the antecedent C and the consequent D according to the interpretation of conditionals given in (∗), that is the conditional $C \rightsquigarrow D$ indicates that in the most typical situations in which C has a positive degree of truth, also D has a positive degree of truth. However, note that Gödel implication is interpreted w.r.t. a specific connection between the truth values of the antecedent and the consequent, that is, the conditional is true if the truth value of the antecedent is at most as high as the truth value of the consequent.

As a consequence, we won't interpret the conditional $C \rightsquigarrow D$ as the truth of $C \supset D$ in the most typical situations in which C has a positive degree of truth, but we shall refer instead to the truth value of $C \supset \neg\neg D$ in the typical situations. As is easy to see from the definition of Gödel negation above, $\neg\neg D$ is true iff D has a positive truth value. Hence, the implication $C \supset \neg\neg D$ is true either if C is totally false, or if D has a positive degree of truth, and that is the kind of connection that we want to model with our conditional.

Note that in propositional Gödel logic the two implications $C \supset \neg\neg D$ and $C \supset \neg\neg\neg\neg D$ are logically equivalent; hence, in order to introduce such an interpretation of our conditional we have to introduce also a new rule (DN) (*Double Negation*), directly connected to the just mentioned logical equivalence.

$$(\text{DN}) \quad \frac{C \rightsquigarrow \neg\neg D}{C \rightsquigarrow D} \; .$$

The first system we are going to take under consideration corresponds to the class of conditionals that is characterised by the preferential properties, specified in the previous section, plus (DN). We shall read such properties as derivation rules, defining a closure operation on the knowledge bases.

More specifically, given a knowledge base $\mathcal{K} = \langle \mathcal{T}, \mathcal{D} \rangle$, we shall indicate with $\models_\mathcal{T}$ the consequence relation obtained from the Gödel consequence relation $\models$ adding the propositions in $\mathcal{T}$ (what the agent considers as strictly true) as extra axioms. Then we shall use the conditionals in $\mathcal{D}$, the consequence relation $\models_\mathcal{T}$ and all the rules in Eq. (1) and rule (DN) to define a closure operation P over the knowledge base. The *closure* $P(\mathcal{K})$ will be the set of defeasible conditionals that is derivable from $\mathcal{D}$ using these rules as derivation rules and $\models_\mathcal{T}$ as the underlying consequence relation. For instance, if $C \rightsquigarrow D$ is in $P(\mathcal{K})$ and $\models_\mathcal{T} D \supset E$, then $C \rightsquigarrow E \in P(\mathcal{K})$ by (RW).

Example 3 (Example 2 cont.). Consider Example 2. Then it can be verified that all conditionals in $\mathcal{D}$ belong to $P(\mathcal{K})$ as well as:

$$rf \wedge tg \rightsquigarrow s$$
$$rf \wedge s \rightsquigarrow tg \; .$$

□

We next are going to completely characterise such an inference relation from the semantics point of view with a specific class of interpretations. The elements of the interpretations we are going to define will be the *belief states* $\mathcal{A}, \mathcal{B}, \ldots$, that are sets of valuations characterising a possible state of affairs that the agent can consider as true. Hence, the set of all the possible belief states will be the power-set $\mathscr{P}(\mathcal{I})$ of all the classical Gödel valuations.

Definition 1 (Belief-state interpretation). *A belief-state interpretation (bs-interpretation, for short) is a pair $M = \langle \mathcal{S}, \prec \rangle$, with $\mathcal{S} \subseteq \mathscr{P}(\mathcal{I})$ and $\prec$ a preferential relation between the states; $\prec$ is asymmetric and transitive and satisfies the property of smoothness (defined below).*

The meaning of $\mathcal{A} \prec \mathcal{B}$ is that the belief state $\mathcal{A}$ describes a situation that is more typical than the belief state $\mathcal{B}$.

In the following, we shall indicate with $\hat{C}$ the *extension* of C in M, that is, the set of belief states in M s.t. each valuation in the belief state associates to C a positive degree of truth, *i.e.*

$$\hat{C} = \{\mathcal{A} \in \mathcal{S} \mid u(C) > 0 \text{ for all } u \in \mathcal{A}\} \; .$$

Next, we define the set of the typical belief states of C, denoted $\overline{C}$, as the set of the preferred states in the extension of C, that is

$$\overline{C} = \min_{\prec}(\hat{C}) = \{\mathcal{A} \in \hat{C} \mid \nexists \mathcal{B} \in \hat{C} \text{ such that } \mathcal{B} \prec \mathcal{A}\}.$$

Now, we will use $\overline{C}$ to define the smoothness condition.

Definition 2 (Smoothness condition). *Given a bs-interpretation $M = \langle \mathcal{S}, \prec \rangle$, the preferential relation $\prec$ satisfies the smoothness condition iff for every $C \in \mathcal{L}$, if $\hat{C} \neq \emptyset$ then $\overline{C} \neq \emptyset$.*

We are now going to use the bs-interpretations to reason about conditionals, that is, we will define a consequence relation that, given a knowledge base $\mathcal{K} = \langle \mathcal{T}, \mathcal{D} \rangle$, gives back new non-monotonic conditionals considered as valid.

Specifically, the notion that a bs-interpretation $M = \langle \mathcal{S}, \prec \rangle$ verifies a proposition C, denoted $M \approx C$, is defined as follows:

$$M \approx C \text{ iff for every } \mathcal{A} \in \mathcal{S}, \text{ for every } u \in \mathcal{A}, u(C) = 1.$$

The notion that $M = \langle \mathcal{S}, \prec \rangle$ verifies a conditional $C \rightsquigarrow D$, denoted $M \approx C \rightsquigarrow D$, is defined as:

$$M \approx C \rightsquigarrow D \text{ iff for every } \mathcal{A} \in \overline{C}, \text{ for every } u \in \mathcal{A}, u \models C \supset \neg\neg D.$$

Hence $C \rightsquigarrow D$ is interpreted as saying that in the most typical belief states in which C has a positive degree of truth also D has a positive degree of truth.

We now move on to the definition of entailment for the conditionals. Given a knowledge base $\mathcal{K} = \langle \mathcal{T}, \mathcal{D} \rangle$, we take under consideration all the bs-interpretations that verify both the propositions in $\mathcal{T}$ and the conditionals in $\mathcal{D}$. So, we say that a bs-interpretation M is a *bs-model* of $\mathcal{K} = \langle \mathcal{T}, \mathcal{D} \rangle$ iff $M \approx E$ for every $E \in \mathcal{T}$ and $M \approx E \rightsquigarrow F$ for every $E \rightsquigarrow F \in \mathcal{D}$.

Definition 3 (Entailment relation $\approx$). *A proposition C is entailed by $\mathcal{K}$, denoted $\mathcal{K} \approx C$, iff for every bs-model M of $\mathcal{K}$, $M \approx C$ holds. A conditional $C \rightsquigarrow D$ is entailed by $\mathcal{K}$, denoted $\mathcal{K} \approx C \rightsquigarrow D$, iff for every bs-model M, $M \approx C \rightsquigarrow D$ holds.*

Now we want to prove that the entailment relation $\approx$ characterises the closure operator P, i.e. given a knowledge base $\mathcal{K} = \langle \mathcal{T}, \mathcal{D} \rangle$, let the closure $P(\mathcal{K})$ be the set of defeasible conditionals that are derivable from $\mathcal{D}$ using all the rules in Eq. (1) and rule (DN), then

$$P(\mathcal{K}) = \{C \rightsquigarrow D \mid \mathcal{K} \approx C \rightsquigarrow D\}.$$

To do so, we next illustrate several interesting properties that follow from the properties of the closure operation P.

Lemma 1. *The conditional $\rightsquigarrow$ satisfies* supraclassicality *(SUPRA):*

$$(\text{SUPRA}) \frac{C \supset D}{C \rightsquigarrow D}.$$

Supraclassicality describes an important property of non-monotonic reasoning, that is, whatever is derivable from $\mathcal{T}$ using propositional Gödel logic is also a defeasible consequence.

Lemma 2. *If a conditional $\leadsto$ satisfies the properties defining the closure operation P, then it satisfies also the following properties:*

$$(EQUIV) \ \frac{C \leadsto D \quad D \leadsto C \quad C \leadsto E}{D \leadsto E} \qquad (AND) \ \frac{C \leadsto D \quad C \leadsto E}{C \leadsto D \wedge E}$$

$$(MPC) \ \frac{C \leadsto D \supset E \quad C \leadsto D}{C \leadsto E} \qquad (1) \ \frac{C \vee D \leadsto C \quad C \leadsto E}{C \vee D \leadsto E}$$

$$(2) \ \frac{C \leadsto E \quad D \leadsto F}{C \vee D \leadsto E \vee F} \qquad (3) \ \frac{C \leadsto D}{C \leadsto \neg\neg D}$$

$$(4) \ \frac{C \vee D \leadsto C \quad D \vee E \leadsto D}{C \vee E \leadsto C}$$

Next, soundness is established.

Proposition 2 (Soundness). *Given a knowledge base $\mathcal{K} = \langle \mathcal{T}, \mathcal{D} \rangle$, if a conditional $C \leadsto D$ is in $P(\mathcal{K})$ then $\mathcal{K} \models C \leadsto D$.*

Now we address the completeness. The proof uses the same general strategy of the proof in [17],[4] based on the notion of *normal valuations* (in [17] called *normal worlds*), but, since the semantic structure is different, the proof is different too.

So, first, let's define the notion of *normal valuation* for a proposition C, that is, a valuation that makes true all the conditionals in $P(\mathcal{K})$ that have C as antecedent.

Definition 4 (Normal valuation). *A valuation u is normal for a proposition C w.r.t a knowledge base $\mathcal{K} = \langle \mathcal{T}, \mathcal{D} \rangle$ iff $u(C) > 0$, for every proposition $E \in \mathcal{T}$ $u(E) = 1$, and for every proposition D s.t. $C \leadsto D \in P(\mathcal{K})$, $u(C \supset \neg\neg D) = 1$ (i.e., $u(\neg\neg D) = 1$).*

Now, we need a main lemma, that states that taking under consideration all the normal valuation for a proposition C we are able to characterise the closure P w.r.t. C.

Lemma 3. *For every proposition D, $C \leadsto D \in P(\mathcal{K})$ iff for every valuation u that is normal for C w.r.t. $\mathcal{K}$, $u(D) > 0$ holds.*

The Lemma above is the main result to prove our completeness. Furthermore, in the following if $C \leadsto D$ and $D \leadsto C$ are both in $P(\mathcal{K})$, then we denote this as $C \sim D \in P(\mathcal{K})$. The following can be shown:

Lemma 4. $C \sim D \in P(\mathcal{K})$ *iff for every proposition E, $C \leadsto E \in P(\mathcal{K})$ iff $D \leadsto E \in P(\mathcal{K})$.*

---

[4] Since the conditionals in [17] are metalinguistic sequents of a non-monotonic consequence relation, there the authors present a representation result. Here, since we consider the non-monotonic conditional as a conditional of the language, we present a completeness result.

From this it follows immediately that if $C \sim D \in P(\mathcal{K})$, a valuation u is normal for C iff it is normal for D.

Given $\mathcal{K}$, we indicate with $C^\sim$ the set of all the propositions that are preferentially equivalent to C w.r.t. $\mathcal{K}$, namely

$$C^\sim = \{D \mid C \sim D \in P(\mathcal{K})\}.$$

Moreover, we indicate with $[C^\sim]$ the belief state containing exactly all the valuations that are normal for the propositions in $C^\sim$. Now we define an ordering of the propositional formulas w.r.t. the conditionals in the preferential closure $P(\mathcal{K})$.

Definition 5. *C is* not less ordinary *than D, denoted $C \leq D$, iff $C \vee D \rightsquigarrow C \in P(\mathcal{K})$. Furthermore, we define $C < D$ iff $C \leq D$ and $D \not\leq C$.*

The following lemma can be shown.

Lemma 5. *If $\rightsquigarrow$ is a preferential conditional, then $<$ is asymmetric and transitive.*

It is easy to see from the definitions of $C^\sim$ and $<$ that if C and D are preferentially equivalent, then they have the same relative position in the ordering $<$, that is:

Lemma 6. *If D is in $C^\sim$, then for every proposition E, $C < E$ iff $D < E$ and $E < C$ iff $E < D$.*

Now we have all the ingredients to define a preferential model $M^\mathcal{K} = \{\mathcal{S}^\mathcal{K}, \prec^\mathcal{K}\}$ satisfying exactly the conditionals in $P(\mathcal{K})$. Specifically, let $\mathcal{S}^\mathcal{K}$ be the set of the belief states that correspond to all the valuations that are normal for some formula w.r.t. $\mathcal{K}$, that is

$$\mathcal{S}^\mathcal{K} = \{[C^\sim] \mid C \in L\}.$$

Let $\prec^\mathcal{K}$ to be defined on $\leq$ in the following way:

$$[C^\sim] \prec^\mathcal{K} [D^\sim] \text{ iff } C < D.$$

Some properties of the interpretation $M^\mathcal{K}$ are easily shown:

Lemma 7. *Given $M^\mathcal{K}$, for every proposition C, $\overline{C} = \{[C^\sim]\}$.*

Lemma 8. *$M^\mathcal{K}$ is a preferential interpretation.*

From these lemmas it is immediate to see that $M^\mathcal{K}$ is a belief-state model that verifies $\mathcal{K}$, and it is exactly the model we need to prove completeness.

Lemma 9. *Given a knowledge base $\mathcal{K}$, for every conditional $C \rightsquigarrow D$, $M^\mathcal{K} \models C \rightsquigarrow D$ implies $C \rightsquigarrow D$ is in $P(\mathcal{K})$.*

Hence, eventually, we have the completeness result.

Proposition 3 (Completeness). *Given a knowledge base $\mathcal{K}$, if a conditional $C \rightsquigarrow D$ is entailed by $\mathcal{K}$, i.e. $\mathcal{K} \models C \rightsquigarrow D$, then $C \rightsquigarrow D$ is in $P(\mathcal{K})$.*

Corollary 1. *Given a knowledge base $\mathcal{K}$, $\mathcal{K} \models C \rightsquigarrow D$ iff $C \rightsquigarrow D \in P(\mathcal{K})$.*

Extended Preferential Entailment. In the following we make one additional step by extending preferential entailment over Gödel logic with the aim to capture a missing property of classical preferential entailment, as the one illustrated below. Specifically, let us note that the following property (S) is derivable from the preferential properties in the classical propositional case:

$$\text{(S)} \quad \frac{C \wedge D \rightsquigarrow E}{C \rightsquigarrow D \supset E} \ .$$

Unfortunately, in the case of Gödel logic we can no longer derive it from our rules.

Example 4 (Example 3 cont.). Consider Example 3. We have seen that we may infer

$$rf \wedge tg \rightsquigarrow s \ .$$

In a classical preferential setting we may infer

$$rf \rightsquigarrow tg \supset s \ ,$$

while under preferential Gödel logic we can not. □

So, we next consider the non-monotonic conditional defined by the previous rules, *i.e.* (REF), (LLE), (RW), (CT), (CM), (OR) and (DN), with the addition of (S). Let us call P' both the set of such rules and the closure operation defined by such a set of rules. Our goal is now to semantically characterise P'.

Luckily, the semantic characterisation of P' is easily obtained as it is sufficient to constrain the previous bs-interpretations to the ones in which the belief sets correspond to singleton sets, *i.e.* single valuations.

Definition 6 (Preferential interpretations). *A* preferential interpretation *is a triple* $M = \langle \mathcal{S}, \ell, \prec \rangle$, *with $\mathcal{S}$ a set of states, $\ell : \mathcal{S} \to \mathcal{I}$ a function that associates to every state s a valuation $u \in \mathcal{I}$, and $\prec$ a preferential relation (asymmetric and transitive), that satisfies the property of smoothness.*

Note that this new class of interpretations is not properly a subclass of the interpretations based on the belief states, since here it is possible to have the same valuation present more than once in a model (we could have that two states $s, t \in \mathcal{S}$ are associated to the same valuation, *i.e.*, $\ell(s) = \ell(t)$), while in the belief-states proposal a subset of $\mathcal{I}$ can appear at most once in a model. Therefore, we have to redefine some previous notions in order to deal with the new kind of models.

To start with, again, $\hat{C}$ will be *extension* of C in M, *i.e.* the set of the states in M that are associated to a valuation verifying a proposition C to a positive degree: that is,

$$\hat{C} = \{s \in \mathcal{S} \mid \ell(s)(C) > 0\} \ .$$

Similarly, $\overline{C}$ is the set of the preferred states in the extension of C, that is

$$\overline{C} = \min_\prec(\hat{C}) = \{s \in \hat{C} \mid \nexists t \in \hat{C} \text{ such that } t \prec s\} \ .$$

We say that M *verifies* a proposition C, denoted $M \mathrel{\vert\approx}' C$, iff for each $s \in \mathcal{S}, \ell(s)(C) = 1$. Moreover, M *verifies* a conditional $C \rightsquigarrow D$, denoted $M \mathrel{\vert\approx}' C \rightsquigarrow D$, iff for every $s \in \overline{C}, \ell(s)(C \supset \neg\neg D) = 1$. We say that M is a *preferential model* of $\mathcal{K} = \langle \mathcal{T}, \mathcal{D} \rangle$ ($M \mathrel{\vert\approx}' \mathcal{K}$) iff $M \mathrel{\vert\approx}' E$ for every $E \in \mathcal{T}$ and $M \mathrel{\vert\approx}' E \rightsquigarrow F$ for every $E \rightsquigarrow F \in \mathcal{D}$. Eventually, we shall indicate with $\mathrel{\vert\approx}'$ the entailment relation defined using preferential models.

Definition 7 (Consequence relation $\approx'$). *A proposition C is* (preferentially) *entailed by $\mathcal{K}$, denoted $\mathcal{K} \approx' C$, iff for every preferential model M of $\mathcal{K}$, $M \approx' C$ holds. A conditional $C \leadsto D$ is* (preferentially) *entailed by $\mathcal{K} = \langle \mathcal{T}, \mathcal{D} \rangle$, denoted $\mathcal{K} \approx' C \leadsto D$, iff for every preferential model M of $\mathcal{K}$, $M \approx' C \leadsto D$ holds.*

Like the previous section, we want again to prove that the closure operation P' is complete w.r.t. the consequence relation $\approx'$, that is

$$P'(\mathcal{K}) = \{C \leadsto D \mid \mathcal{K} \approx' C \leadsto D\}.$$

In this case, the completeness proof follows quite faithfully the representation proof for propositional classical logic in [17]. We have only to consider some contextual changes due to the different underlying monotonic consequence relation (the one defining propositional Gödel logic instead of the one associated to classical propositional logic) and the presence of the two extra-axioms (DN) and (S).

Indeed, we can show that we can obtain a completeness result. The proof being very similar to the one in [17], we omit here the list of its main steps.

Proposition 4. *Given a finite set of conditionals $\mathcal{K}$, a conditional $C \leadsto D$ is in $P'(\mathcal{K})$ iff $\mathcal{K} \approx' C \leadsto D$.*

4 Rational Monotony

Another property that has been deeply investigated in non-monotonic logic is *Rational Monotony* (RM), namely

$$\text{(RM)} \quad \frac{C \leadsto E \quad C \not\leadsto \neg D}{C \wedge D \leadsto E}$$

Rational Monotony is a form of constrained monotony that is stronger than (CM). Intuitively, it states that if typically the truth value of C is connected to the truth value of E, while a typical situation in $\hat{C}$ does not force $\neg D$ to be true, then in a typical situation in which $C \wedge D$ has a positive degree of truth also E is true to a positive degree.

Example 5 (Example 4 cont.). Consider Example 4. According to (RM) we may infer that "typically, a ripe and expensive fruit is sweet", that is, from $rf \leadsto s$ and $rf \not\leadsto \neg e$ (e stands for expensive), we may infer via (RM) that

$$rf \wedge e \leadsto s.$$

This inference is not supported by preferential entailment. □

In order to semantically characterise the property (RM) we have to add a new constraint to the preferential order $\prec$ in the interpretation, that is, *modularity*.

Definition 8 (Modularity). *A partial order $\prec$ on a set $\mathcal{S}$ is modular if for every $x, y, z \in \mathcal{S}$, if $x \prec y$, then either $z \prec y$ or $x \prec z$.*

Informally, a modular order organises the elements of the set into layers, and all the elements of a lower layer are preferred to all the elements laying in higher layers. In our context, we will take under consideration the class of the preferential interpretations that have a modular preference order, that, following [18], we call *ranked* interpretations.

Definition 9 (Ranked Gödel interpretations). *A ranked interpretation is a triple* $M = \langle S, \ell, \prec \rangle$, *with* S *a set of states,* $\ell : S \to \mathcal{I}$ *a function that associates to every state s a valuation* $u \in \mathcal{I}$, *and* $\prec$ *a modular relation, that satisfies the property of smoothness.*

Now, it can be verified that the class of the ranked interpretations satisfy (RM).

Proposition 5 (Soundness). *The properties in P' and (RM) are verified by the class of ranked Gödel interpretations.*

However, we cannot define a form of entailment based on the ranked interpretations as we have done in the preferential case, as it may not give any inferential gain. Indeed, let us say that ranked interpretation M is a *ranked model* of a knowledge base $\mathcal{K} = \langle \mathcal{T}, \mathcal{D} \rangle$ iff $M \approx' C$ for every $C \in \mathcal{T}$ and $M \approx' E \rightsquigarrow F$. Then

Definition 10 (Consequence relation $\approx''$). *A proposition C is* (rationally) *entailed by* $\mathcal{K}$, *denoted* $\mathcal{K} \approx'' C$, *iff for every ranked model M of $\mathcal{K}$, $M \approx' C$ holds. A conditional $C \rightsquigarrow D$ is* (rationally) *entailed by* $\mathcal{K} = \langle \mathcal{T}, \mathcal{D} \rangle$, *denoted* $\mathcal{K} \approx'' C \rightsquigarrow D$, *iff for every ranked model M of $\mathcal{K}$, $M \approx' C \rightsquigarrow D$ holds.*

Then we can prove that such an entailment relation corresponds to the closure operation P'. That is,

Proposition 6. $\mathcal{K} \approx'' C \rightsquigarrow D$ *iff* $C \rightsquigarrow D \in P'(\mathcal{K})$.

Therefore, the entailment relation $\approx''$, does not provide any inferential gain over $\approx'$.

4.1 Rational Closure

Since it is not possible to define a form of non-monotonic reasoning that satisfies the rule (RM) and is based on a classical form of entailment, *i.e.*, defined considering all the ranked models of the knowledge base, Lehmann and Magidor [18] have indicated a form of non-monotonic logical closure of the knowledge base, called *Rational Closure* (RC), that satisfies a series of desiderata and is defined considering only some relevant ranked models of the knowledge base. We shall indicate by $R(\mathcal{K})$ the rational closure of the knowledge base $\mathcal{K}$.

Considering the results in the previous section, it is easy to see that the definition of Lehmann and Magidor's decision procedure is also applicable to our preferential semantics and our conditional. From the semantical point of view, we shall refer to the semantic construction of Rational Closure by Giordano et al. [12] that we find more intuitive than the original formulation by Lehmann and Magidor.

The first step of the procedure is the definition of the notion of *exceptionality*.

Exceptionality. A proposition is exceptional if it is falsified in all the most typical situations that satisfy a knowledge base. That is, a proposition C is exceptional w.r.t. a knowledge base $\mathcal{K}$ iff it is falsified in all the preferential models of the knowledge base, *i.e.*, $\top \rightsquigarrow \neg C \in P'(\mathcal{K})$. The decision whether a proposition is exceptional can be reduced to a fuzzy entailment decision problem. In fact, we interpret every non-monotonic conditional $C \rightsquigarrow D$ as the satisfaction of $C \supset \neg\neg D$ in the most typical situations; we shall indicate with $\mathcal{D}^\supset$ the set of the material implications corresponding to the conditionals in the knowledge base. That is, given a knowledge base $\langle \mathcal{T}, \mathcal{D} \rangle$,

$$\mathcal{D}^\supset := \{C \supset \neg\neg D \mid C \rightsquigarrow D \in \mathcal{D}\}.$$

Such a set will be used to decide exceptionality as a classical decision problem.

Proposition 7. *Given a knowledge base* $\mathcal{K} = \langle \mathcal{T}, \mathcal{D} \rangle$,

$$\top \rightsquigarrow C \in P'(\mathcal{K}) \text{ iff } \mathcal{T} \cup \mathcal{D}^\supset \models \neg\neg C .$$

A conditional $C \rightsquigarrow D$ is exceptional if its antecedent C is exceptional. Hence, we can define a function $\mathcal{E}$ that, given $\langle \mathcal{T}, \mathcal{D} \rangle$, gives back the set of the exceptional conditionals in $\mathcal{D}$, that is,

$$\mathcal{E}(\langle \mathcal{T}, \mathcal{D} \rangle) := \{ C \rightsquigarrow D \in \mathcal{D} \mid \mathcal{T} \cup \mathcal{D}^\supset \models \neg C \} .$$

The construction of the Rational Closure of a knowledge base $\langle \mathcal{T}, \mathcal{D} \rangle$ is then based on the notion of exceptionality by creating a ranking of the conditionals in $\mathcal{D}$ using the function $\mathcal{E}$. To this end, we define a sequence of subsets of $\mathcal{D}$ in the following way:

$$E_0 := \mathcal{D}$$
$$E_{i+1} := \mathcal{E}(\langle \mathcal{T}, E_i \rangle) .$$

Since the set $\mathcal{D}$ is finite, and every application of $\mathcal{E}$ on a set X gives back a subset of X, the procedure ends into an (empty or non-empty) fixed-point of the function $\mathcal{E}$, that we shall call E_∞.

Now, we can partition the set $\mathcal{D}$ in to a sequence $\langle \mathcal{D}_0, \mathcal{D}_1, \ldots, \mathcal{D}_n, \mathcal{D}_\infty \rangle$, where $\mathcal{D}_i := E_i \setminus E_{i+1}$ ($0 \le i \le n$) and $\mathcal{D}_\infty := E_\infty$. Each set $\mathcal{D}_i$ will contain the conditionals that have i as *ranking value*, starting from the conditionals in $\mathcal{D}_0$, describing what is verified only in the most normal situations, up to $\mathcal{D}_\infty$, describing what does not hold even in the most exceptional situations.

Note that, assuming that the cardinality of $\mathcal{D}$ is m, the identification of the partition $\langle \mathcal{D}_0, \mathcal{D}_1, \ldots, \mathcal{D}_n, \mathcal{D}_\infty \rangle$ is definable doing $O(m^2)$ fuzzy entailment tests for propositional Gödel logic, and, for a given knowledge base, once such partition is done, it is done once and for all.

Now we can define the ranking value of every formula in our language using the partition of $\mathcal{D}$ into $\mathcal{D}_0, \ldots, \mathcal{D}_n, \mathcal{D}_\infty$.

Definition 11 (Ranking value). *The ranking value of a proposition C is i, denoted $rank(C) = i$, iff $\mathcal{D}_i$ is the first element of the sequence $\langle \mathcal{D}_0, \mathcal{D}_1, \ldots, \mathcal{D}_n \rangle$ s.t.*

$$\langle \mathcal{T}, \mathcal{D}_i \rangle \not\models' \top \rightsquigarrow \neg C .$$

If there is not such an element, $rank(C) = \infty$. The ranking value of a conditional $C \rightsquigarrow D$, denoted $rank(C \rightsquigarrow D)$, is the ranking value of C, i.e. $rank(C \rightsquigarrow D) = rank(C)$.

Note that, due to Proposition 7, the decision of the ranking value of a formula can be determined in $O(m)$ fuzzy entailment tests.

Following [18], a conditional $C \rightsquigarrow D$ is in the rational closure of the knowledge base $\langle \mathcal{T}, \mathcal{D} \rangle$ if the ranking value of $C \land D$ is lower than the ranking value of $C \land \neg D$, that is, the situation in which $C \land D$ has a positive degree of truth is less exceptional than the situation in which $C \land \neg D$ has a positive degree of truth. That is, we now can formulate the "somewhat typical" definition involving the constraint on ranks (see also the condition on possibility distributions in the introduction)

Definition 12 (Rational Closure). $C \leadsto D \in R(\mathcal{K})$ iff either $rank(C \wedge D) < rank(C \wedge \neg D)$ or $rank(C) = \infty$.

Example 6 (Example 5 cont.). Let's check whether we can infer that

$$rf \wedge e \leadsto s\,.$$

First of all we have to calculate the ranking value of the conditional $rf \leadsto s$. Since $\mathcal{T} \cup \{rf \supset \neg\neg s\} \not\models \neg rf$, $rank(rf \leadsto s) = rank(rf) = 0$ and $\mathcal{D}$ is partitioned into a single set $\mathcal{D}_0 = \mathcal{D}$. Now we have to check the ranking values of

$$rf \wedge e \wedge s \text{ and } rf \wedge e \wedge \neg s\,.$$

We have that $\mathcal{T} \cup \mathcal{D}_0^{\supset} \not\models \neg(rf \wedge e \wedge s)$ and, thus, $rank(rf \wedge e \wedge s) = 0$, while $\mathcal{T} \cup \mathcal{D}_0^{\supset} \models \neg(rf \wedge e \wedge \neg s)$, since $\mathcal{D}_0^{\supset} = \{rf \supset \neg\neg s\}$ and, thus, $rank(rf \wedge e \wedge \neg s) > 0$. From these ranking values, we can conclude that

$$rf \wedge e \leadsto s \in R(\mathcal{K})\,.$$

□

Please observe that, since all computations are based on a polynomially bounded number of fuzzy entailment tests, the computational complexity of the decision procedure for Rational Closure is the same as the entailment problem for propositional Gödel logic and the procedure can be implemented once a decision procedure for fuzzy logic entailment is at hand.

Proposition 8. *Deciding whether $C \leadsto D \in R(\mathcal{K})$ is a coNP-complete problem.*

Semantic characterisation. We now give also a semantic characterisation of the above construction, still referring to the analogous constructions for classical propositional logic. A nice and intuitive characterisation of Rational Closure is given using the *minimal ranked models* introduced in [12]. We apply here a similar definition related to propositional Gödel logic.

The intuitive idea is the following: given a knowledge base $\langle \mathcal{T}, \mathcal{D} \rangle$, we consider all the ranked Gödel interpretations satisfying $\langle \mathcal{T}, \mathcal{D} \rangle$ that are *compatible* with $\langle \mathcal{T}, \mathcal{D} \rangle$, i.e. all the valuations v that verify $\mathcal{T} \cup \{\neg C \mid C \leadsto D \in \mathcal{D}_\infty\}$. Among all such models, we prefer those models in which all the valuations are considered 'as typical as possible', that is, in which the valuations are ranked as low as possible.

First of all we need to define the *height* of a state $s \in \mathcal{S}$ in a ranked interpretation $M = \langle \mathcal{S}, \ell, \prec \rangle$.

Definition 13 (Height k). *Consider a ranked interpretation $M = \langle \mathcal{S}, \ell, \prec \rangle$, with $s \in \mathcal{S}$. The height $k_M(s)$ of s is the length of the shortest chains $s_0 \prec \ldots \prec s$ from a s_0 s.t. for no $s' \in \mathcal{S}$ it holds that $s' \prec s_0$.[5] The height of a formula C, $k_M(C)$, corresponds to the height of the states with the lowest height that do not falsify C, that is, $k_M(C) = k_M(s)$ s.t. $\ell(s)(C) > 0$, and there is no state s' s.t. $s' \prec s$ and $\ell(s')(C) > 0$.*

---
[5] Note that for ranked interpretations, $k_M(s)$ is uniquely determined. See also [13].

Note that it is easy to see that $M \mathrel{|\approx} C \rightsquigarrow D$ iff $k_M(C \wedge D) < k_M(C \wedge \neg D)$ (it is immediate to check that in Gödel logic $v(C) > 0$ iff $v(\neg\neg C) > 0$, for any valuation v and any formula C, and hence $k_M(C \wedge D) = k_M(C \wedge \neg\neg D)$). From now on we consider only ranked models $M = \langle \mathcal{S}, \ell, \prec \rangle$ where $\mathcal{S}$ and ℓ are such that for every valuation v compatible with $\mathcal{K}$ there is a state $s \in \mathcal{S}$ s.t. $\ell(s) = v$.

Definition 14 (Minimal Ranked Models). *Consider two ranked models of $\mathcal{K} = \langle \mathcal{T}, \mathcal{D} \rangle$, $M = \langle \mathcal{S}, \ell, \prec \rangle$ and $M' = \langle \mathcal{S}', \ell', \prec' \rangle$. We say that M is at least as preferred as M' ($M \leq_R M'$) iff $\mathcal{S} = \mathcal{S}'$ and $\ell = \ell'$, and for each $s \in \mathcal{S}$, $k_M(s) \leq k_{M'}(s)$. Let $\mathfrak{M}_\mathcal{K}^R$ be the set of the minimal ranked models of the knowledge base $\mathcal{K}$, that is, $\mathfrak{M}_\mathcal{K}^R = \{M \mid M \mathrel{|\approx}' \mathcal{K} \text{ and } \nexists M' \text{ s.t. } M' \mathrel{|\approx}' \mathcal{K} \text{ and } M' \leq_R M\}$.*

Note that all the minimal ranked interpretations in $\mathfrak{M}_\mathcal{K}^R$ are equivalent w.r.t the verification relation $\mathrel{|\approx}'$, since in each minimal interpretation every pair of states s, s' s.t. $\ell(s) = \ell(s')$ must have the same height. Hence, the elimination of multiple copies of the same valuation is not relevant from the point of view of the formulas verified by the interpretation. Consequently, it is possible to define a smallest minimal ranked interpretation $M_\mathcal{K}^R$, that is obtainable from any element of $\mathfrak{M}_\mathcal{K}^R$ just eliminating the multiple copies of the same valuations. We define *minimal ranked entailment*, denoted $\mathrel{|\approx}_R$, as the entailment relation defined by such a minimal ranked model $M_\mathcal{K}^R$.

Definition 15 (Minimal Ranked Entailment). *A conditional $C \rightsquigarrow D$ is a minimal ranked consequence of a knowledge base $\mathcal{K} = \langle \mathcal{T}, \mathcal{D} \rangle$, denoted $\mathcal{K} \mathrel{|\approx}_R C \rightsquigarrow D$, iff $M_\mathcal{K}^R \mathrel{|\approx}' C \rightsquigarrow D$.*

We can prove that this notion of entailment characterises the closure operation R.

Proposition 9. *Given a knowledge base $\mathcal{K}$, $C \rightsquigarrow D \in R(\mathcal{K})$ iff $\mathcal{K} \mathrel{|\approx}_R C \rightsquigarrow D$.*

The proof of Proposition 9 follows the proof of the analogous result in [12,13], reformulated in order to take into account that we are dealing with Gödel logic, that the conditional $C \rightsquigarrow D$ is interpreted w.r.t. the formula $C \supset \neg\neg D$ and that there are also the rules (DN) and (S) to take into account. Since the closure operation R can be characterised by means of a single ranked model, Proposition 5 guarantees the satisfaction of the property (RM).

5 Conclusions

The notion of rational closure is acknowledged as a landmark for defeasible reasoning, while mathematical fuzzy logic is the reference framework to deal with fuzziness. In this work we have made a first attempt to connect the two, by characterising rational closure in the context of Propositional Gödel Logic, axiomatically, semantically, algorithmically and from a computational complexity point of view.

We plan to continue our investigation along several directions. Specifically, to extend our approach towards other fuzzy logics, such as Łukasiewicz and Product logics, to extend it to notable fragments of First-Order Logic, such as fuzzy Description Logics [19,22] along the line [5], and to investigate about possible connections to a possibilistic logic based approach in line with [2,3,4,6,7,8,10] including as well different interpretations of fuzzy implications as discussed in [9].

References

1. Ansotegui, C., Bofill, M., Manyà, F., Villaret, M.: Building automated theorem provers for infinitely-valued logics with satisfiability modulo theory solvers. In: Proceedings of ISMVL 2012, pp. 25–30. IEEE Computer Society (2012)
2. Benferhat, S., Dubois, D., Prade, H.: Representing default rules in possibilistic logic. In: Proceedings of KR 1992, pp. 673–684. Morgan Kaufman (1992)
3. Benferhat, S., Dubois, D., Prade, H.: Nonmonotonic reasoning, conditional objects and possibility theory. Artificial Intelligence 92(1-2), 259–276 (1997)
4. Benferhat, S., Dubois, D., Prade, H.: Towards fuzzy default reasoning. In: Proceedings of NAFIPS 1999, pp. 23–27. IEEE Computer Society (1999)
5. Casini, G., Straccia, U.: Rational closure for defeasible description logics. In: Janhunen, T., Niemelä, I. (eds.) JELIA 2010. LNCS (LNAI), vol. 6341, pp. 77–90. Springer, Heidelberg (2010)
6. de Dupin Saint-Cyr, F., Prade, H.: Possibilistic handling of uncertain default rules with applications to persistence modeling and fuzzy default reasoning. In: Proceedings of KR 2006, pp. 440–451. AAAI Press (2006)
7. Dubois, D., Prade, H.: Default reasoning and possibility theory. Artificial Intelligence Journal 35(2), 243–257 (1988)
8. Dubois, D., Mengin, J., Prade, H.: Possibilistic uncertainty and fuzzy features in description logic. A preliminary discussion. In: Capturing Intelligence: Fuzzy Logic and the Semantic Web. Elsevier (2006)
9. Dubois, D., Prade, H.: What are fuzzy rules and how to use them. Fuzzy Sets and Systems 84(2), 169–185 (1996)
10. de Dupin Saint-Cyr, F., Prade, H.: Handling uncertainty and defeasibility in a possibilistic logic setting. International Journal of Approximate Reasoning 49(1), 67–82 (2008)
11. Gabbay, D.M., Hogger, C.J., Robinson, J.A. (eds.): Handbook of logic in artificial intelligence and logic programming: nonmonotonic reasoning and uncertain reasoning, vol. 3. Oxford University Press, Inc., New York (1994)
12. Giordano, L., Gliozzi, V., Olivetti, N., Pozzato, G.L.: A minimal model semantics for nonmonotonic reasoning. In: del Cerro, L.F., Herzig, A., Mengin, J. (eds.) JELIA 2012. LNCS, vol. 7519, pp. 228–241. Springer, Heidelberg (2012)
13. Giordano, L., Olivetti, N., Gliozzi, V., Pozzato, G.L.: A minimal model semantics for rational closure. In: Proceedings of NMR 2012 (2012), http://www.dbai.tuwien.ac.at/NMR12/proceedings.html
14. Guller, D.: On the satisfiability and validity problems in the propositional Gödel logic. In: Madani, K., Dourado Correia, A., Rosa, A., Filipe, J. (eds.) Computational Intelligence. SCI, vol. 399, pp. 211–227. Springer, Heidelberg (2012)
15. Hähnle, R.: Advanced many-valued logics. In: Gabbay, D.M., Guenthner, F. (eds.) Handbook of Philosophical Logic, 2nd edn., vol. 2. Kluwer (2001)
16. Hájek, P.: Metamathematics of Fuzzy Logic. Kluwer (1998)
17. Kraus, S., Lehmann, D., Magidor, M.: Nonmonotonic reasoning, preferential models and cumulative logics. Artificial Intelligence 44(1-2), 167–207 (1990)
18. Lehmann, D., Magidor, M.: What does a conditional knowledge base entail? Artificial Intelligence 55(1), 1–60 (1992)
19. Lukasiewicz, T., Straccia, U.: Managing uncertainty and vagueness in description logics for the semantic web. Journal of Web Semantics 6, 291–308 (2008)
20. Raha, S., Hossain, S.: Fuzzy set in default reasoning. In: Pal, N.R., Sugeno, M. (eds.) AFSS 2002. LNCS (LNAI), vol. 2275, pp. 27–33. Springer, Heidelberg (2002)
21. Raha, S., Ray, K.S.: Reasoning with vague default. Fuzzy Sets and Systems 91(3), 327–338 (1997)
22. Straccia, U.: A fuzzy description logic for the semantic web. In: Fuzzy Logic and the Semantic Web, Capturing Intelligence, ch. 4, pp. 73–90. Elsevier (2006)

Multi-objective Discounted Reward Verification in Graphs and MDPs

Krishnendu Chatterjee[1], Vojtěch Forejt[2], and Dominik Wojtczak[3]

[1] IST Austria
[2] Department of Computer Science, University of Oxford, UK
[3] Department of Computer Science, University of Liverpool, UK

Abstract. We study the problem of achieving a given value in Markov decision processes (MDPs) with several independent discounted reward objectives. We consider a generalised version of discounted reward objectives, in which the amount of discounting depends on the states visited and on the objective. This definition extends the usual definition of discounted reward, and allows to capture the systems in which the value of different commodities diminish at different and variable rates.

We establish results for two prominent subclasses of the problem, namely *state-discount models* where the discount factors are only dependent on the state of the MDP (and independent of the objective), and *reward-discount models* where they are only dependent on the objective (but not on the state of the MDP). For the state-discount models we use a straightforward reduction to expected total reward and show that the problem whether a value is achievable can be solved in polynomial time. For the reward-discount model we show that memory and randomisation of the strategies are required, but nevertheless that the problem is decidable and it is sufficient to consider strategies which after a certain number of steps behave in a memoryless way.

For the general case, we show that when restricted to graphs (i.e. MDPs with no randomisation), pure strategies and discount factors of the form $1/n$ where n is an integer, the problem is in PSPACE and finite memory suffices for achieving a given value. We also show that when the discount factors are not of the form $1/n$, the memory required by a strategy can be infinite.

1 Introduction

Dynamic systems with multiple objectives. Graphs are a classical model for dynamical systems with non-deterministic behaviors. Markov decision processes (MDPs) extend the model of graphs by allowing both non-deterministic as well as probabilistic behavior. An MDP is given by a finite number of states and actions, together with a transition function which to a state and an action assigns a probabilistic distribution on (successor) states. Initially, a token is placed in a distinguished initial state, and an action is chosen, possibly in a probabilistic way. The token is then moved to a state determined by the transition function, and the process continues from the beginning, starting from the successor state.

The infinite sequence of states that is produced is called a *run*, and the aim usually is to ensure that the produced runs have certain properties.

Discounted objectives. One of the most fundamental optimization objective for dynamical systems is the discounted reward objective. Given a reward function that assigns a reward to every state, and a discount factor λ which to every state assigns a number strictly smaller than 1, the discounted reward of a run is the sum of the rewards accumulated along the run, where every single reward accumulated is weighted by the product of discounts of states previously visited. The goal is to maximize the expected discounted reward.

Traditionally graphs and MDPs have been studied with the aim to optimize a unique objective. However, in most modeling domains for dynamical systems, there is not a single objective to optimize, but multiple, potentially dependent and conflicting objectives. Hence recently the problem of multi-objective optimization for dynamical systems has become an active area of research. We consider graphs and MDPs with multiple discounted reward objectives (*n*-dimensional discounted sum objectives). In the simplest case (which we call *uniform-discount* model) the discount factor λ is independent of the states as well as the dimension of the objectives. More generally the discount factor can depend on the states of the system (called *state-discount* model, where the discount factor at state s is $\lambda(s)$); or it can depend on the objective (*reward-discount* model, where the discount factor for dimension i is λ_i). In the most general case (*unrestricted model*) the discount factors can depend on the dimension as well as on the state of the system (discount factor for dimension i in state s is $\lambda_i(s)$).

Discounted objectives are intended to capture the fact that the reward gained soon is more valuable than a reward gained in the distant future. For example, in financial applications one often has the opportunity of putting money on a risk-free account with a small interest, and so any reward form (risky) investment needs to be discounted by the value the invested money could gain on the risk-free account. Our notion of discount allow to capture the fact that for different currencies or commodities the interest on the risk-free account can vary (reward-discount model), or that it can change depending on the circumstances (state-discount model). The unrestricted model captures both these phenomena.

Classes of strategies. In case of graphs as well as MDPs strategies are recipes that resolve the non-determinism of the system, i.e. say how actions should be selected. A strategy looks into the current execution of the system, and specifies how to resolve the non-deterministic behavior. The class of strategies can be broadly classified into *randomised* strategies that can specify a probability distribution over the non-deterministic choices, and the special case of *pure* strategies, where for every execution of the system one of the non-deterministic choices is executed (i.e., pure strategies only use Dirac distribution over the choices).

The achievability question. Given a graph or an MDP with n discounted reward objectives, and a vector $(v_1, v_2, \ldots, v_n)$, the achievability question is whether there exists a randomised strategy (resp. pure strategy if restricted to pure strategies) such that for each dimension $1 \leq i \leq n$ the expected discounted reward with respect to ith objective is at least v_i.

Our contributions. While the general problem for graphs and MDPs with multiple discounted sum objectives is challenging, we provide several partial answers. Below we present our contributions and then list some of the key open problems.

1. The decidability of MDPs with multiple discounted reward objectives under randomised strategies under uniform-discount model was established in [6]. We first observe that the problem for state-discount model can be solved by a simple reduction to total reward objectives (solved in [11]). In both the above cases randomised memoryless strategies (that do not depend on the past) are sufficient. We then consider MDPs with randomised strategies under reward-discount model. We show that in contrast to uniform-discount and state-discount model, randomised memoryless strategies are not sufficient, but it is sufficient to consider "eventually memoryless" strategies, i.e. the strategies which behave memorylessly after a fixed-length history-dependent prefix; this helps us in establishing the decidability of the achievability question.
2. For pure strategies, we consider the problem for graphs and establish decidability for the unrestricted model when the discount factors are of the form $1/n$ for natural numbers n. In the above case we show that finite-memory strategies are sufficient, whereas we also show that this is not the case when we lift the restriction on discount factors.

Key open questions: We now list some interesting open questions related to graphs and MDPs with multiple discounted sum objectives: (1) The decidability of MDPs with randomised strategies under the unrestricted model remains open. (2) The decidability of MDPs with pure strategies under the uniform-discount model with discount factors of the form $1/n$ also remains open. (3) Given a graph and a single rational discount factor (independent of the states), the decidability of existence of a pure strategy (i.e. a path) such that the discounted sum is *exactly* zero is another important open question. In fact, (3) can be reformulated in terms of achievability question for two dimensions, with one reward being the negative of the other, such that both are required to be at least zero.

Related work. The study of Markov decision processes with multiple objectives has been an area of research in applied probability theory, where it is known as *constrained MDPs* [14,1]. The attention in the study of constrained MDPs has been focused mainly to restricted classes of MDPs, such as unichain MDPs where all states are visited infinitely often under any strategy. For general finite-state MDPs, [6] studied MDPs with multiple discounted reward functions under the uniform-discount model. It was shown that memoryless randomised strategies suffice, and a polynomial-time algorithm was given to approximate (up to a given relative error) the Pareto curve by reduction to multi-objective linear programming and using the results of [13]. MDPs with multiple qualitative ω-regular specifications were studied in [10]. It was shown that the Pareto curve can be approximated in polynomial time in the size of the model; the algorithm reduces the problem to MDPs with multiple reachability specifications, which can be solved by multi-objective linear programming. In [11,12], the results of [10] were extended to combine ω-regular and expected total reward objectives. MDPs with multiple mean-payoff functions objectives were considered in [4]. Finally, [7,8] study multi-objective verification problem for stochastic games, which is a model extending MDPs with a second kind of nondeterminism [7,8].

2 Preliminaries

We use $\mathbb{N}$, $\mathbb{Z}$, $\mathbb{Q}$, and $\mathbb{R}$ to denote the sets of positive integers, integers, rational numbers, and real numbers, respectively. Given two vectors $\boldsymbol{v}, \boldsymbol{u} \in \mathbb{R}^k$, where $k \in \mathbb{N}$, we write $\boldsymbol{v} \le \boldsymbol{u}$ iff $\boldsymbol{v}_i \le \boldsymbol{u}_i$ for all $1 \le i \le k$, and $\boldsymbol{v} < \boldsymbol{u}$ iff $\boldsymbol{v} \le \boldsymbol{u}$ and $\boldsymbol{v}_i < \boldsymbol{u}_i$ for some $1 \le i \le k$. Given a vector $\boldsymbol{v}$ and a number $t \in \mathbb{R}$ we use $\boldsymbol{v} + t$ for the vector $(\boldsymbol{v}_1 + t, \ldots, \boldsymbol{v}_k + t)$.

A *probability distribution* over a finite or countably infinite set X is a function $f : X \to [0,1]$ such that $\sum_{x \in X} f(x) = 1$. We call f *Dirac* if $f(x) = 1$ for some $x \in X$. The set of all distributions over X is denoted by $dist(X)$, and given two distributions d and d', we define $|d - d'| := \max_{x \in X} |d(x) - d'(x)|$.

Markov Decision Processes. A *Markov decision process* (MDP) is a tuple $M = (S, A, Act, \delta)$ where S is a *finite* set of states, A is a *finite* set of actions, $Act : S \to 2^A \setminus \emptyset$ is an action enabledness function that assigns to each state s the set $Act(s)$ of actions enabled at s, and $\delta : S \times A \to dist(S)$ is a probabilistic transition function that given a state s and an action $a \in Act(s)$ enabled at s gives a probability distribution over the successor states. For simplicity, we assume that every action is enabled in exactly one state, and we denote this state $Src(a)$. Thus, henceforth we will assume that $\delta : A \to dist(S)$. A *graph* is an MDP in which $\delta(a)$ is Dirac for all $a \in A$.

A *run* in M is an infinite alternating sequence of states and actions $\omega = s_1 a_1 s_2 a_2 \ldots$ such that for all $i \ge 1$, $Src(a_i) = s_i$ and $\delta(a_i)(s_{i+1}) > 0$. We denote by Runs_M the set of all runs in M. A *finite path* of length k in M is a finite prefix $w = s_1 a_1 \ldots a_{k-1} s_k$ of a run in M, and we denote by $last(w)$ the last state of w and by $|w| := k$ the number of states in w.

Strategies and Probabilities. Intuitively, a strategy in an MDP M is a "recipe" to choose actions. It is formally defined as a function $\sigma : (SA)^*S \to dist(A)$ that given a finite path w, representing the history of a play, gives a probability distribution over the actions enabled in $last(w)$. In general, a strategy may use infinite memory. According to the use of randomisation, a strategy σ, can be classified as *pure* (or *deterministic*) if $\sigma(w)$ is always Dirac, and *finite-memory* if it can be defined using a finite automaton that reads a history and the choice made by σ is based solely on the state in which the automaton ends. A strategy σ is *eventually memoryless* if there is ℓ such that for all ws and $w's$ where $|ws|, |w's| \ge \ell$ we have $\sigma(ws) = \sigma(w's)$.

Each finite path w in M determines the set $\mathsf{Cone}(w)$ consisting of all runs that start with w. To M, an initial state s and σ we associate the probability space $(\mathsf{Runs}_M, \mathcal{F}, \mathbb{P}^\sigma_{M,s})$, where Runs_M is the set of all runs in M, $\mathcal{F}$ is the σ-field generated by all $\mathsf{Cone}(w)$, and $\mathbb{P}^\sigma_{M,s}$ is the unique probability measure such that $\mathbb{P}^\sigma_{M,s}(\mathsf{Cone}(s_1 a_1 \ldots s_k)) = \mu(s_1) \cdot \prod_{i=1}^{k-1} \sigma(s_1 a_1 \ldots s_i)(a_i) \cdot \delta(a_i)(s_{i+1})$, where $\mu(s_1)$ is 1 if $s_1 = s$ and 0 otherwise. We often omit the M from the subscript.

Rewards. A *(discounted) reward structure* is a tuple (r,λ) where $r : S \to \mathbb{R}$ is a *reward function* and $\lambda : S \to (0,1)$ is a *discount factor*. A discounted reward of a run $\omega = s_1 a_1 s_2 a_2 \ldots$ is defined to be $r(\omega) = \sum_{i=1}^{\infty} r(s_i) \cdot \prod_{j=1}^{i-1} \lambda(s_j)$.

The expected discounted reward under a strategy σ is $\mathbb{E}_s^\sigma[r,\lambda] := \int_{\omega \in \mathsf{Runs}_M} r(\omega)\, d\mathbb{P}_s^\sigma$, and the optimal discounted reward is $\mathbb{E}_s^{opt}[r,\lambda] = \sup_\sigma \mathbb{E}_s^\sigma[r,\lambda]$. We also use $\mathbb{E}_{s,a}^{opt}[r,\lambda]$ to denote the optimal value after taking the action a in s, i.e. $\delta(a)(s') \cdot \mathbb{E}_{s'}^{\sigma'}[r,\lambda]$ where σ' is defined by $\sigma'(w) = \sigma(saw)$ for all w.

In this paper we deal with multi-objective rewards, i.e. we assume that we are given n objectives, each as a tuple (r_i, λ_i), together with a vector $\boldsymbol{v} \in \mathbb{R}^n$. The problem we aim to solve is to decide whether there is a strategy σ such that $\mathbb{E}_s^\sigma[r_i, \lambda_i] \geq \boldsymbol{v}_i$ for every $1 \leq i \leq n$. If the answer is positive, we call the vector $\boldsymbol{v}$ *achievable*. The vectors $\boldsymbol{v}$ such that $\boldsymbol{v} - \tau$ are achievable for all $\tau > 0$, but no $\boldsymbol{u} > \boldsymbol{v}$ is achievable, are called *Pareto-optimal vectors*.

As we have already mentioned, in general this problem appears to be difficult, and hence we study several interesting and useful sub-classes of the general model (which we call the *unrestricted model*).

- *State-discount model*: Here we assume that the discount factor is fully determined by the state, i.e. $\lambda_i(s) = \lambda_j(s)$ for every $1 \leq i, j \leq n$ and $s \in S$.
- *Reward-discount model*: In reward-discount model the discount factor depends only on the objective, i.e. $\lambda_i(s) = \lambda_i(s')$ for all $1 \leq i \leq n$ and $s, s' \in S$. In such case we can write just λ instead of $\lambda(s)$.

Both the above models subsume the restriction studied in [6], where the discount factor is given as one number, independent of the state or the reward. We refer to the model of [6] as the *uniform-discount* model.

3 Results for MDPs and Randomised Strategies

3.1 State-Discount Model

We start with presenting the most direct of our results, which concerns the solution for state-discount model. This result can be obtained by straightforwardly extending a well-known reduction from discounted rewards to total reward. Given a reward function r, the expected total reward of a run $w = s_1 a_1 s_2 \ldots$ is defined to be $\sum_{i=1}^{\infty} r(s_i)$, and the expected value $\mathbb{E}_s^\sigma[r]$ under a strategy σ is defined accordingly.

Theorem 1. *Let us have a state-discount model given by an MDP $M = (S, A, Act, \delta)$ and objectives $(r_1, \lambda), \ldots (r_n, \lambda)$. The problem of deciding whether a point $\boldsymbol{u}$ is achievable can be solved in polynomial time.*

Proof. We create an MDP $M' = (S \cup \{s_\bot\}, A, Act, \delta')$ from M by adding a mandatory transition to dead state $s_\bot$ from $s \in S$ with probability $1 - \lambda(s)$. Formally, for all $s \in S$ we define δ' by $\delta'(s,a)(s') = \lambda(s) \cdot \delta(s,a)(s')$ for all

$s' \neq s_\perp$ and $\delta'(s,a)(s_\perp) = 1 - \lambda(s)$. The state $s_\perp$ has only self-loops available. We also define a reward function r' by $r'(s) = r(s)$ for all $s \in S$, and $r'(s_\perp) = 0$.

It is then easy to show that for any strategy σ we have $\mathbb{E}_s^\sigma[r,\lambda] = \mathbb{E}_s^\sigma[r']$. Thus we can use the results of [11] for multi-objective total reward to obtain the desired result. □

3.2 Reward-Discount Model

We now present the results related to the reward-discount model. We will show that when looking for strategies that achieve a given vector v, it is sufficient to consider randomised history-dependent strategies which are eventually memoryless. To motivate this result, we first give an example where neither memoryless nor deterministic history-dependent strategies suffice. Let us have an MDP (which is in fact a graph) from the following picture:

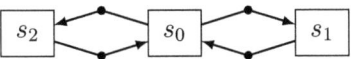

The initial state is s_0, and there are two reward functions, r_1 and r_2, where $r_1(s_1) = r_2(s_2) = 1$ and $r_i(s_j) = 0$ for $i \neq j$. The discount factors are given by $\lambda_1 = 0.25$ and $\lambda_2 = 0.5$.

When the initial state is fixed to s_0, every strategy σ is completely determined by the probabilities $p^\sigma(i)$ of being in the state s_1 after $2 \cdot i + 1$ steps. In addition, we have

$$\mathbb{E}_{s_0}^\sigma[r_1, \lambda_1] = \sum_{i=0}^\infty 0.25^{2 \cdot i + 1} \cdot p^\sigma(i)$$

$$\mathbb{E}_{s_0}^\sigma[r_2, \lambda_2] = \sum_{i=0}^\infty 0.5^{2 \cdot i + 1} \cdot (1 - p^\sigma(i))$$

Consider the strategy σ such that $p^\sigma(0) = 1$, $p^\sigma(1) = 0.5$ and $p^\sigma(i) = 0$ for all $i > 1$. Under such strategy we get $\mathbb{E}_{s_0}^\sigma[r_1, \lambda_1] \approx 0.258$ and $\mathbb{E}_{s_0}^\sigma[r_2, \lambda_2] \approx 0.1$. Obviously, σ must be a history-dependent randomised strategy.

We show that no other strategy performs same as or better than σ. Note that any strategy σ' which satisfies $p^{\sigma'}(i) < 1$ and $p^{\sigma'}(j) > 0$ for $i < j$ can be improved as follows. Let $q = \min\{p^{\sigma'}(j), (1 - p^{\sigma'}(i))/\lambda_1^{2 \cdot (j-i)}\}$. We change the strategy σ' to the strategy σ'' defined by

$$p^{\sigma''}(\ell) = \begin{cases} p^{\sigma'}(\ell) + q \cdot \lambda_1^{2 \cdot (j-i)} & \text{for } \ell = i \\ p^{\sigma'}(\ell) - q & \text{for } \ell = j \\ p^{\sigma'}(\ell) & \text{otherwise} \end{cases}$$

We then get

$$\mathbb{E}_{s_0}^{\sigma''}[r_1, \lambda_1] = q \cdot \lambda_1^{2 \cdot (j-i)} \cdot \lambda_1^{2 \cdot i + 1} - q \cdot \lambda_1^{2 \cdot j + 1} + \mathbb{E}_{s_0}^{\sigma'}[r_1, \lambda_1] = \mathbb{E}_{s_0}^{\sigma'}[r_1, \lambda_1]$$

$$\mathbb{E}_{s_0}^{\sigma''}[r_2, \lambda_2] = -q \cdot \lambda_1^{2 \cdot (j-i)} \cdot \lambda_2^{2 \cdot i + 1} + q \cdot \lambda_2^{2 \cdot j + 1} + \mathbb{E}_{s_0}^{\sigma'}[r_2, \lambda_2] > \mathbb{E}_{s_0}^{\sigma'}[r_2, \lambda_2]$$

so σ'' performs better than σ'. Since this step can be repeated as long as there are $p^{\sigma'}(i) < 1$ and $p^{\sigma'}(j) > 0$ for some $i < j$, we get that any strategy is outperformed by some strategy $\bar{\sigma}$ for which there is ℓ and x satisfying $p^{\bar{\sigma}}(k) = 1$ for $k < \ell$, $p^{\bar{\sigma}}(\ell) = x$ and $p^{\bar{\sigma}}(k) = 0$ for $k > \ell$. However, one can easily see that any such $\bar{\sigma}$, except for σ itself, gives a worse reward than σ in the first or in the second objective, and so in particular no memoryless randomised or history-dependent deterministic strategy can outperform σ.

Now we prove that for the reward-discount model the problem whether a vector $\boldsymbol{v}$ is achievable is decidable. The intuition for the proof is the following. Given discount structures $(r_1, \lambda_1), \ldots, (r_n, \lambda_n)$ where the discount factors are pairwise different, after m steps any future contribution of ith reward will be discounted by λ_i^m. For m being sufficiently large and for $\lambda_i > \lambda_j$ we get that $\lambda_i^m \gg \lambda_j^m$, and so any reward accumulated w.r.t. jth objective becomes comparably negligible and cannot be meaningfully "traded off" for reward accumulated w.r.t. ith objective. This leads to the notion of eventually memoryless strategies, which after certain number of steps don't make any tradeoffs, but instead greedily give the highest priority to the rewards with the higher discount factors.

For the rest of this subsection we fix a reward-discount model given by an MDP $M = (S, A, Act, \delta)$ and reward structures $(r_1, \lambda_1), \ldots, (r_n, \lambda_n)$ such that $\lambda_i \geq \lambda_{i+1}$ for all $1 \leq i \leq n-1$. By U we denote a bound on maximal/minimal value of discounted rewards; for example, we can set $U := \sum_{j=0}^{\infty} \lambda_1^j \cdot r_{\max}$ where $r_{\max} = \max_{1 \leq i \leq n} \max_{s \in S} |r_i(s)|$.

The following two lemmas state some basic properties of the set of achievable points.

Lemma 1. *The set of achievable points for a reward-discount model is convex.*

Proof. When we have two achievable points $\boldsymbol{u}$ and $\boldsymbol{v}$ together with $0 \leq c \leq 1$, the point $c \cdot \boldsymbol{u} + (1-c) \cdot \boldsymbol{v}$ can be achieved by a strategy that in the first step randomly (with probability c and $1-c$) decides whether to mimic the strategy for $\boldsymbol{u}$ or $\boldsymbol{v}$, and sticks to the decision forever. □

Lemma 2. *Pareto-optimal strategies exist for a reward-discount model, i.e. limit of a sequence of achievable points is achievable.*

Proof. Let $\boldsymbol{u}$ be the limit of a sequence of achievable points, and let us have an infinite sequence of strategies $\sigma_0, \sigma_1, \ldots$ such that σ_i achieves the point $\boldsymbol{u} - \frac{1}{i}$. Let Θ_0 denote the set of the strategies in this sequence, and let $w_1, w_2, \ldots$ be the enumeration of all finite paths in the MDP. We construct infinite sets $\Theta_0, \Theta_1 \ldots$ and distributions $d_1, d_2 \ldots$ such that for every $\varepsilon > 0$ the set Θ_i contains a strategy σ that achieves value $\boldsymbol{u} - \varepsilon$, which satisfies $|\sigma(w_j) - d_j| \leq \varepsilon$ for all $j \leq i$.

We then define a strategy σ by $\sigma(w_i) = d_i$ for all $i \geq 1$. We claim that σ achieves the point $\boldsymbol{u}$. Suppose this is not the case, then there must be some ε such that σ does not achieve $\boldsymbol{u} - \varepsilon$, and let k be such that $\lambda_i^k \cdot U \geq \varepsilon/4$ for all $1 \leq i \leq n$. Note that for any strategy $\bar{\sigma}$ we have

$$\mathbb{E}_{s,a}^{\bar{\sigma}}[r_i, \lambda_i] \geq \left(\sum_{w=s_1 a_0 s_1 \ldots s_k} \mathbb{P}_{s,a}^{\bar{\sigma}}[w] \cdot \sum_{\ell=1}^{k} \lambda_i^{\ell-1} \cdot r_i(s_\ell) \right) - \varepsilon/4$$

Let m be an index such that all paths of length at most m are in the sequence $w_1, \ldots, w_m$. There must be a strategy $\sigma' \in \Theta_m$ such that

- $\mathbb{E}^{\sigma'}_{s,a}[r_i, \lambda_i] \geq \boldsymbol{u}_i - \varepsilon/4$
- We have $\prod_{j=0}^{m} |\sigma'(w_j) - d_j| \leq \frac{\varepsilon}{(U+\varepsilon)\cdot 4}$

Fix one such strategy σ', then we get

$$\mathbb{E}^{\sigma}_s[r_i, \lambda_i] \geq \sum_{w=s_0 a_0 s_1 \ldots s_k} \mathbb{P}^{\sigma}_s[w] \cdot \sum_{\ell=0}^{k} \lambda_i^\ell \cdot r_i(s_\ell) - \frac{\varepsilon}{4}$$

$$\geq \sum_{w=s_0 a_0 s_1 \ldots s_k} \left(\mathbb{P}^{\sigma'}_s[w] - \frac{\varepsilon}{(U+\varepsilon)\cdot 4} \right) \cdot \sum_{\ell=0}^{k} \lambda_i^\ell \cdot r_i(s_\ell) - \frac{\varepsilon}{4}$$

$$\geq \sum_{w=s_0 a_0 s_1 \ldots s_k} \left(\mathbb{P}^{\sigma'}_s[w] \cdot \sum_{\ell=0}^{k} \lambda_i^\ell \cdot r_i(s_\ell) - \frac{\varepsilon \cdot \sum_{\ell=0}^{k} \lambda_i^\ell \cdot r_i(s_\ell)}{(U+\varepsilon)\cdot 4} \right) - \frac{\varepsilon}{4}$$

$$\geq \sum_{w=s_0 a_0 s_1 \ldots s_k} \mathbb{P}^{\sigma'}_s[w] \cdot \sum_{\ell=0}^{k} \lambda_i^\ell \cdot r_i(s_\ell) - \frac{\varepsilon}{2}$$

$$\geq \left(\boldsymbol{u} - \frac{\varepsilon}{4}\right) - \frac{\varepsilon}{2} \geq \boldsymbol{u} - \frac{3\cdot\varepsilon}{4}$$

which contradicts that σ does not achieve the value $\boldsymbol{u} - \varepsilon$. $\square$

Theorem 2. *Let let $\boldsymbol{u}$ be a Pareto point for a reward-discount model such that $\boldsymbol{u}$ is not a convex combination of any other Pareto points. Then there is a deterministic eventually memoryless strategy achieving $\boldsymbol{u}$.*

Proof. Since $\boldsymbol{u}$ is not a convex combination of other achievable points and because the set of achievable points is convex by Lemma 1 and downwards closed by definition, by the separating hyperplane theorem [3] there must be a nonnegative vector $\boldsymbol{w}$ and a number d such that for $\boldsymbol{u} \cdot \boldsymbol{w} = d$, but for all achievable points $\boldsymbol{v} \neq \boldsymbol{u}$ we have $\boldsymbol{v} \cdot \boldsymbol{w} < d$.

Note that any strategy σ that satisfies $\sum_{1 \leq i \leq n} w_i \cdot \mathbb{E}^{\sigma}_s[r_i, \lambda_i] \geq d$ also satisfies that $\mathbb{E}^{\sigma}_s[r_i, \lambda_i] \geq \boldsymbol{u}_i$ for all $1 \leq i \leq n$, since otherwise it achieves the point $\boldsymbol{v} := (\mathbb{E}^{\sigma}_s[r_i, \lambda_i])_{1 \leq i \leq n}$ with $\boldsymbol{v} \neq \boldsymbol{u}$ and $\boldsymbol{v} \cdot \boldsymbol{w} \geq d$, which is a contradiction.

Hence, it suffices to show that deterministic eventually memoryless optimal strategies σ suffice for optimising the value of $\sum_{1 \leq i \leq n} w_i \cdot \mathbb{E}^{\sigma}_s[r_i, \lambda_i]$. Before we proceed, we show that we can simplify the problem in several respects. The first observation is that we can restrict to deterministic strategies σ (this can be proved by methods similar to the ones used in by [5], and using properties of single-objective discounted rewards). Further, we can easily preprocess the input to work with the sequence of the discount factors which is strictly decreasing: whenever $\lambda_i = \lambda_{i+1}$, then we can create an objective (r', λ_i) where $r'(s,a) = w_i \cdot r_i(s,a) + w_{i+1} \cdot r_{i+1}(s,a)$, and look for a strategy σ which satisfies $1 \cdot \mathbb{E}^{\sigma}_s[r', \lambda_i] + \sum_{j \neq i} w_j \cdot \mathbb{E}^{\sigma}_s[r_j, \lambda_j] \geq d$. At the same time, whenever some w_i is equal to 0, we can omit the ith reward since it does not affect the value $\sum_{1 \leq i \leq n} w_i \cdot \mathbb{E}^{\sigma}_s[r_i, \lambda_i]$.

Thus, from now on we assume that $\lambda_i > \lambda_{i+1}$ for all i and that all w_i are nonzero.

In what follows we will use the notion of an optimal action subject to taking an action optimal w.r.t. different objectives. For a set $B \subseteq A$ we use $\mathbb{E}^{opt}_{s',B}[r_i, \lambda_i] := \sup_{\sigma \in \Sigma_B} \mathbb{E}^{\sigma}_s[r, \lambda]$ where Σ_B contains the strategies which only assign nonzero probabilities to actions from B. We put $A_0 = A$, and for all $1 \leq i \leq n$ we define A_i to contain the actions of A_{i-1} which give the best value w.r.t. (r_i, λ_i), i.e. $a \in A_i$ iff $a \in A_{i-1}$ and

$$\mathbb{E}^{opt}_{s, A_{i-1}}[r_i, \lambda_i] = r_i(s) + \sum_{s' \in S} \delta(a)(s') \cdot \lambda_i \cdot \mathbb{E}^{opt}_{s', A_{i-1}}[r_i, \lambda_i]$$

where $s = Src(a)$. Note that for every $\sigma \in \Sigma_{A_i}$ we have $\mathbb{E}^{\sigma}_s[r_i, \lambda_i] = \mathbb{E}^{opt}_{s, A_i}[r_i, \lambda_i]$. This is due to the properties of single-objective discounted reward in which taking any optimal action suffices to ensure the optimal values [14]. For every $a \in A_{i-1}(s)$ denote

$$v_{i,s,a} = \left(\mathbb{E}^{opt}_{s, A_{i-1}}[r_i, \lambda_i]\right) - \left(r_i(s) + \sum_{s' \in S} \delta(a)(s') \cdot \lambda_i \cdot \mathbb{E}^{opt}_{s', A_{i-1}}[r_i, \lambda_i]\right)$$

the loss when taking non-optimal optimal action (within $A_{i-1}(s)$) w.r.t. ith objective. We use $\varepsilon := \min\{v_{i,s,a} | v_{i,s,a} > 0\}$ to denote the least positive value among all $v_{i,s,a}$.

Now let k be a number such that for all i we have $w_i \cdot \varepsilon \cdot \lambda_i^k > \sum_{j=i+1}^{n} w_j \cdot U \cdot \lambda_j^k$. Such number certainly exists by the fact that $\lambda_i > \lambda_{i+1}$ and $w_i > 0$ for all i.

By induction in i we show that in order to be optimal, a strategy σ must pick actions from A_i on any path ws where $|ws| = \ell > k$. Suppose we have proved the claim for $i-1$. Note that if the strategy takes an action $a \in A_i$ in ws, then the optimal reward gained after ws is

$$\left(\sum_{j=1}^{i-1} \lambda_j^\ell \cdot w_j \cdot \mathbb{E}^{opt}_{s, A_j}[r_j, \lambda_j]\right) + \lambda_i^\ell \cdot w_i \cdot \mathbb{E}^{opt}_{s, A_i}[r_i, \lambda_i],$$

while if a does not maximise the value, by the choice of k we get that

$$\sum_{i=1}^{n} \lambda_i^\ell \cdot \mathbb{E}^{\sigma}_{ws}[r_i, \lambda_i] \leq \left(\sum_{j=1}^{i-1} \lambda_j^\ell \cdot w_j \cdot \mathbb{E}^{opt}_{s, A_j}[r_j, \lambda_j]\right) + \left(w_i \cdot \lambda_i^\ell \cdot \mathbb{E}^{opt}_{s, A_i}[r_i, \lambda_i] - w_i \cdot \varepsilon \cdot \lambda_i^\ell\right)$$

$$+ \left(\sum_{j=i+1}^{n} w_j \cdot \lambda_j^\ell \cdot \mathbb{E}^{opt}_s[r_j, \lambda_j]\right)$$

$$< \left(\sum_{j=1}^{i-1} \lambda_j^\ell \cdot w_j \cdot \mathbb{E}^{opt}_{s, A_j}[r_j, \lambda_j]\right) + w_i \cdot \lambda_i^\ell \cdot \mathbb{E}^{opt}_{s, A_i}[r_i, \lambda_i]$$

Hence, actions from $A_i(s)$ give better value. Consequently, in order to be optimal, the strategy σ must, for any path ws with $|ws| > \ell$, only take actions from A_n, and as we have argued above, any strategy which takes these actions suffice, meaning that we can pick an arbitrary deterministic eventually memoryless strategy which eventually plays actions from A_n. □

By Carathéodory's theorem [15], for an achievable point u there must be at most $n+1$ achievable points $v_1 \ldots v_{n+1}$ of which u is a convex combination, and for which deterministic eventually memoryless strategies exist. This directly gives an algorithm which for any achievable point u returns "yes", and which does not halt otherwise: Set a step bound m, and try to "guess" n different deterministic strategies which become memoryless after at most m steps and which achieve points of which u (or some larger value) is a convex combination. There is only a finite number of such strategies, so we can guess by exploring all options. If the strategies are found, return that u is achievable. If the appropriate strategies can't be found, increase m and continue from the beginning.

Finally, we give an algorithm that for u which is not achievable returns "no", and does not halt otherwise. If u is not achievable, then by Lemma 2 there is τ such that $u - \tau$ is not achievable. Let us pick m such that $\lambda_i^m \cdot U \leq \tau/3$ for all i. Then any strategy satisfies that within m steps, the reward accumulated w.r.t. ith reward is at most $u_i - 2 \cdot \tau/3$, and we know that from that point on no more than $\tau/3$ can be accumulated. This means that m witnesses that u is not achievable. Hence, our algorithm fixes a number m and verifies whether for all strategies it is the case that there is i such that the reward accumulated up to m steps is at most $u - 2 \cdot \lambda_i^m \cdot U/3$. This problem can be expressed using a formula over reals with addition and multiplication, for which the satisfiability problem is decidable [16]. If we find out that all strategies satisfy the condition, we return that u is not achievable, otherwise we increase m and continue.

The two above algorithms can be run in parallel, giving an algorithm that eventually terminates for any input. This allows us to establish the following corollary.

Corollary 1. *For the reward-discount model, the problem of achievability of a given vector is decidable.*

Remark 1. Our analysis does not yield any upper complexity bound. The limiting factor of our analysis is that in Theorem 1 we don't have any information about the vector w. If we were able to bound the coordinates in of w, then later in the proof we could give a bound on k, and hence establish the upper number of steps after which the strategies start behaving memoryless. Nevertheless, there is no obvious way how to achieve this.

4 Results for Graphs and Pure Strategies

In this section we study the decidability of the problem of achievability of a given vector for graphs. We show decidability of this problem and existence of finite-memory strategies even for the unrestricted model where the discounts depend both on the state as well as the objective function. However, we require all of these discount functions λ_i to be *inverse-integer*, which means that for each i and $s \in S$ there is some $m \in \mathbb{N}$ such that $\lambda_i(s) = 1/m$. Under this restriction, we are able to represent the integer thresholds as periodic sequences, yielding a finite-state system. A similar approach was used in a different setting by [2].

Finally, we show that if not all of the discount reward functions are inverse-integer then any strategy for a given achievable vector may require an infinite amount of memory and we leave the decidability of that case as an open problem.

For the rest of this section, fix a graph $M = (S, A, Act, \delta)$, i.e. $\delta(a)$ is Dirac for all $a \in A$, i.e. $\delta(a)$ is Dirac for all $a \in A$.

Theorem 3. *Let $(r_1, \lambda_1), \ldots (r_n, \lambda_n)$ be discounted reward structures with inverse-integer discount factors and let $\boldsymbol{v} \in \mathbb{Q}^n$ be the bound to be achieved, where n is fixed and all constants are given in unary. The problem whether there exists a pure strategy σ achieving $\boldsymbol{v}$ can be solved in polynomial time.*

Proof. We start by reducing this problem for arbitrary rational rewards functions r_i and lower threshold $\boldsymbol{v}_i$ to integer rewards and thresholds. To do so for each i we multiply the denominator of $\boldsymbol{v}_i$ by the denominators of all rational numbers $r_i(s)$ for every $s \in S$ to obtain some number d_i. We now define $r'_i(s) = d_i \cdot r_i(s)$ and $\boldsymbol{v'}_i = d_i \cdot \boldsymbol{v}_i$. It is easy to see that $r'_i(\omega) = d_i \cdot r_i(\omega)$ for any ω and so for any σ we have $\mathbb{E}^{\sigma}_{s_0}[r_i, \lambda_i] \geq \boldsymbol{v}_i$ iff $\mathbb{E}^{\sigma}_{s_0}[r'_i, \lambda_i] \geq \boldsymbol{v'}_i$. Moreover, notice that all the numbers defining r'_i and $\boldsymbol{v'}_i$ are of polynomial size, because n is fixed.

We first focus on the case $n = 1$. It is well-known that the problem in this setting can be solved in polynomial time even when all the inputs are given in binary by finding a solution to a linear program which gives the optimal value as well as the optimal deterministic strategy for the controller. However, this approach does not generalise to the $n > 1$ case. Instead, we will use automata theory based approach to solve the case $n = 1$ which works in polynomial-time if all the constants are represented in unary, and can be exponential otherwise. The advantage of this approach is that it allows us to solve the general case by using a cross product construction of the automaton generated for each of the reward structure.

Now, let the single inverse-integer reward structure be (r, λ) and the lower threshold bound be v. Also, let $a_{\max} = \lceil \max_{s \in S} r(s)/(1 - \lambda(s)) \rceil$ and $a_{\min} = \lfloor \min_{s \in S} r(s)/(1 - \lambda(s)) \rfloor$. Let $\delta(s)$ be the set of all possible successors of state s, i.e. $\delta(s) = \{s' \in S \mid \exists_{a \in Act(s)} \delta(a)(s') = 1\}$. We construct a deterministic automaton $A = (Q, \Sigma, \Delta)$ with the set of states $Q = S \times \{a_{\min}, a_{\min}+1, \ldots, a_{\max}\} \cup \{\top, \bot\}$, action alphabet $\Sigma = A$ and transition function $\Delta : S \times A \to S$. The initial state of A is (s_0, v). Intuitively, if A is in state (s, x) after reading the k-th letter of the word, then x denotes how big the discounted reward of the tail of this word should be in order for the whole word to satisfy the condition $\geq v$. Formally, we define the transition function Δ as follows. If the current state is (s, x) then notice that $y := (x - r(s))/\lambda(s) \in \mathbb{Z}$, because λ is an inverse-integer discount. Now, if $y \in \{a_{\min}, a_{\min}+1, \ldots, a_{\max}\}$ then the automaton for each action a such that $Src(a) = s$ have a transition to the state $(\delta(a), y)$ which reads letter a. However, if $y > a_{\max}$ then the only transition from (s, x) is to state $\top$ and if $y < a_{\min}$ then the only transition is to $\bot$. Also, from $\top$ the only transition is to $\top$ and from $\bot$ the only transition is to $\bot$. These special transitions can read any action letter.

Lemma 3. *There exists a pure strategy σ such that $\mathbb{E}^\sigma_{s_0}[r, \lambda] \geq v$ iff there exists an infinite word such that the corresponding run of the automaton never reaches $\top$ (a safety accepting condition).*

Proof. ($\Rightarrow$) Let σ be any pure strategy such that $\mathbb{E}^\sigma_{s_0}[r, \lambda] \geq v$ and let it generate a run $\omega = s_1 a_1 s_2 a_2 \ldots$, where $s_1 = s_0$. That is we have $r(\omega) = \mathbb{E}^\sigma_{s_0}[r, \lambda] \geq v$. Let $(s_1, x_1)(s_2, x_2) \ldots$ be the sequence of states visited by A while reading the word $a_1 a_2 \ldots$, where $s_1 = s_0$ and $x_1 = v$. Let us modify this sequence by replacing $\top$ and $\bot$ states by the actual states of the form (s, x) that would have be visited if these special states $\top$ and $\bot$ were not present. In other words, $s_{k+1} = \delta(a_k)$ and $x_{k+1} = (x_k - r(s_k))/\lambda(s_k)$ hold for any k even if $x_k \notin \{a_{\min}, \ldots, a_{\max}\}$. We will show that it cannot be the case that $x_k > a_{\max}$ for some k and as a result $\top$ did not occur in the original sequence.

The proof is by contradiction; let l be the first step for which $x_l > a_{\max} = \max_s r(s)/(1 - \lambda(s))$. It is easy to see that there has to be some constant $\alpha > 1$ such that $x_l \geq \max_s r(s)/(1 - \alpha \cdot \lambda(s))$. In fact, we can pick α to be $\min_s 1/\lambda(s) - r(s)/(\lambda(s) \cdot x_l)$. This is because from the definition of α for any s we would then have $r(s)/(1 - \alpha \cdot \lambda(s)) \leq r(s)/(1 - (1 - r(s)/x_l)) = x_l$. Note that $\alpha > 1$ because from the definition of $a_{\max}$ if $x_l > a_{\max}$ then $(x_l - r(s))/\lambda(s) > x_l$ for all s. Finally, we get $x_{l+1}/x_l = (x_l - r(s_l))/(x_l \cdot \lambda(s_l)) = 1/\lambda(s_l) - r(s_l)/(\lambda(s_l) \cdot x_l) \geq \alpha$. Therefore $x_{l+1} \geq \alpha x_l \geq x_l$, but the expression for α increases as x_l increases and so for any k we have $x_{l+k} \geq \alpha x_{l+k-1} \geq \ldots \geq \alpha^k \cdot x_l$. In conclusion $x_k \to \infty$ as $k \to \infty$.

On the other hand, for any k let us denote the discounted-reward of ω until step k by $r(\omega_k) := \sum_{i=1}^k r(s_i) \cdot \prod_{j=1}^{i-1} \lambda(s_j)$. Notice that $x_1 = v$, $x_2 = (v - r(s_1))/\lambda(s_1) = v/\lambda(s_1) - r(s_1)/\lambda(s_1)$, $x_3 = v/(\lambda(s_1) \cdot \lambda(s_2)) - r(s_1)/(\lambda(s_1) \cdot \lambda(s_2)) - r(s_2)/\lambda(s_2)$, and by induction $x_k = v/\prod_{j=1}^{k-1} \lambda(s_j) - \sum_{i=1}^{k-1} r(s_i)/\prod_{j=i}^{k-1} \lambda(s_j)$. In other words, $x_k \cdot \prod_{j=1}^{k-1} \lambda(s_j) = v - r(\omega_k) \leq r(\omega) - r(\omega_k) = \sum_{i=k+1}^\infty r(s_i) \cdot \prod_{j=1}^{i-1} \lambda(s_j)$, which means $x_k \leq \lambda(s_k) \cdot \sum_{i=k+1}^\infty r(s_i) \cdot \prod_{j=k+1}^{i-1} \lambda(s_j) \leq (\max_s \lambda(s) \cdot \max_s r(s))/(1 - \max_s \lambda(s))$, but the right hand side is a constant while we just showed that $x_k \to \infty$ as $k \to \infty$; a contradiction.

($\Leftarrow$) Let $\omega = a_1 a_2 \ldots$ be any infinite word for which A does not enter state $\top$ and let $(s_1, x_1)(s_2, x_2) \ldots$ be the sequence of states visited by A along this word. If $\bot$ state is in this sequence (and as a result only $\bot$ occurs from that moment on), then note that $(a_{\min} - r(s))/\lambda(s) < a_{\min}$ for any $s \in S$ and so when A is starting at any state (s, x) such that $x < a_{\min}$, no state (s', x') with $x' > a_{\max}$ can be reached. Therefore, $x_k < a_{\max}$ holds for every k in either case. As we will now show, this condition suffices for the word ω to be accepted and so the automaton should accept any word once it enters $\bot$ no matter what the tail of that word is. Again, let us denote the discounted-reward of ω until step k by $r(\omega_k) := \sum_{i=1}^k r(s_i) \cdot \prod_{j=1}^{i-1} \lambda(s_j)$ and notice that $x_k \prod_{j=1}^{k-1} \lambda(s_j) = v - r(\omega_k)$. We know that for any k we have $x_k \leq a_{\max}$ which means that $v - r(\omega_k) \leq a_{\max} \cdot \prod_{j=1}^{k-1} \lambda(s_j)$, and so $v - a_{\max} \cdot \prod_{j=1}^{k-1} \lambda(s_j) \leq r(\omega_k)$. Now taking the limit as $k \to \infty$ we get that $v \leq r(\omega)$, because $a_{\max}$ is a constant, and $\prod_{j=1}^{k-1} \lambda(s_j) \to 0$ and $r(\omega_k) \to r(\omega)$ as $k \to \infty$. □

Now, to deal with more than one reward structures, we will use a cross product of all the automata constructed for each of the reward structures. Let $A_i = (Q_i, \Sigma_i, \Delta_i)$ be the automaton generated using the previous construction for the reward structure (r_i, λ_i). The cross-product automaton A' is defined as follows $A' = (Q', \Sigma', \Delta')$, where the set of states $Q' = \prod_i Q_i$, the letter alphabet $\Sigma' = A$ and the transition function Δ' is defined as follows: $\Delta((s_1, \ldots, s_n), a) = (\Delta_1(s_1, a), \Delta_2(s_2, a), \ldots, \Delta_n(s_n, a))$. The initial state of the automata A' is $s_0' = ((s_0, \boldsymbol{v}_1), (s_0, \boldsymbol{v}_2), \ldots, (s_0, \boldsymbol{v}_n))$. Notice that the size of the automata A' is polynomial in the size of the original graph, because n is fixed. Technically we can further reduce the size of A by noticing that any reachable state $((s_1, \boldsymbol{v}_1), (s_2, \boldsymbol{v}_2), \ldots, (s_n, \boldsymbol{v}_n))$ satisfies $s_1 = s_2 = \ldots = s_n$. A run of A' is accepting if it does not reach the $\top$ state in any of the component automata. This is a safety condition and deciding the existence of a safe run can be done in time linear in the size of the automaton [9]. □

Theorem 4. *Let $(r_1, \lambda_1), \ldots (r_n, \lambda_n)$ be inverse-integer reward structures given in binary, and let $\boldsymbol{v} \in \mathbb{Q}^n$ be a bound. The problem whether there exists a pure strategy σ achieving $\boldsymbol{v}$ can be solved in PSPACE. If such σ exists, then there is also a finite-memory one.*

Proof. We use the same cross-product automaton A' construction as in the proof of Theorem 3. The size of the automata A' is now exponential in the size of the original graph, but every state can be represented using polynomial space, because we just need to remember the current state, (s, x), of each component automaton and the value of x has at most polynomially many bits. Also the number of states of A' can be represented using polynomially many bits. Notice that A' has an accepting run iff there exists a cycle starting s_0' which never reaches a $\top$ state. So a simple NPSPACE (which is =PSPACE) algorithm can be given as follows: we simply simulate the transitions while counting the number of steps made, and we stop and reject if we reach $\top$, and stop and accept if we already made more steps than the number of states in A'. The latter implies that we already formed a cycle and a run that never reaches $\top$ exists. A safe strategy can be reconstructed from the accepting path of our algorithm by looking at the transitions taken, and repeating a pattern based on them forever. Notice that the size of the memory such a strategy requires is at most equal to the number of states in the automaton A'. □

Proposition 1. *There are uniform-discount rewards $(r_1, \lambda), (r_2, \lambda)$ that are not inverse-integer such that for some $\boldsymbol{v} \in \mathbb{Q}^2$: any pure strategy σ which achieves $\boldsymbol{v}$ requires infinite memory.*

Proof. We will show this already for a system with just two states. Let us denote the states by s_1 and s_2 and actions by a_1 and a_2. The uniform discount is set to $\lambda = \frac{2}{3}$. From any state the action a_i leads to state s_i. We set $r_1(s_1) = r_2(s_1) = 0$, $r_1(s_2) = 1$, $r_2(s_2) = -1$, and the thresholds to $\boldsymbol{v}_1 = 3/2$ and $\boldsymbol{v}_2 = -3/2$. Notice that since $r_1(\omega) + r_2(\omega) = 0$ for any infinite path ω, the conditions $\mathbb{E}_{s_0}^\sigma[r_i, \lambda_i] \geq \boldsymbol{v}_i$ are satisfied iff $r_1(\omega) = 3/2$. Because we are only looking at finite-memory pure strategies σ, we can represent the unique run ω it generates by a string $\omega' = b_1 \ldots b_k \cdot (c_1 \ldots c_l)^\omega$, where $k \geq 0$, $l \geq 1$, $b_i, c_i \in \{0, 1\}$ and the j-th position in ω' is 0 iff a_1 is used at the j-th step of the run ω and otherwise it is equal to 1. Notice that we have

$$r_1(\omega) = b_1 + \frac{2}{3}b_2 + \ldots + \left(\frac{2}{3}\right)^{k-1} b_k + \left(\frac{2}{3}\right)^k \frac{1}{1-(\frac{2}{3})^l} \left(c_1 + \frac{2}{3}c_2 + \ldots + \left(\frac{2}{3}\right)^{l-1} c_l\right)$$

and if we multiply both sides by $3^k \cdot (3^l - 2^l)$ the right-hand side will be an integer, but the left-hand side will not be an integer as $r_1(\omega) = 3/2$ and $3^k \cdot (3^l - 2^l)$ is an odd number for $l \geq 1$.

Finally, we just need to show now that there exists an infinite sequence $\omega = b_1 b_2 \ldots$ such that $b_i \in \{0, 1\}$ for all i and

$$r_1(\omega) = b_1 + \frac{2}{3}b_2 + \ldots + \left(\frac{2}{3}\right)^{k-1} b_k + \ldots = \frac{3}{2}. \tag{1}$$

In other words there exists a pure winning strategy σ which uses an infinite amount of memory. We use the following algorithm to generate this sequence ω. We initialise $x := \frac{3}{2}$. At the k-th step, starting with $k := 1$, if $x \geq 1$ then we set $b_k := 1$ and update $x := \frac{3}{2}(x - 1)$, and otherwise set $b_k := 0$ and update $x := \frac{3}{2}x$. We then move to the next step $k := k + 1$. Intuitively the value of x at the k-th step tell us what the value of $\left(\frac{2}{3}\right)^k b_{k+1} + \ldots$ should be in order for the total discount reward to be equal to $\frac{3}{2}$. Also, based on the rules how x gets updated, at any step we have $x \geq 0$ and $x \leq \frac{3}{2}$. From this fact and using similar reasoning to Lemma 3, we can show that this process will generate an infinite sequence $\omega = b_1 b_2 \ldots$ such $b_i \in \{0, 1\}$ for all i and the condition (1) holds.

5 Conclusions

We have studied MDPs with multiple discounted objectives. We have extended the results of [6] by considering a more expressive class of models, which allow to specify discount factors dependent on states and/or objectives.

As we have already mentioned in the introduction, there are several interesting and challenging open questions. Except for these, it is also of interest to obtain a complexity bound for the reward-discound model.

Acknowledgements The authors are grateful to Aisis Šimaitis for his stimulating discussions on the topic. K. Chatterjee is supported by Austrian Science Fund (FWF) Grant No P 23499-N23, FWF NFN Grant No S11407-N23 (RiSE), ERC Start grant (279307: Graph Games), and Microsoft faculty fellows award. V. Forejt is also affiliated with Faculty of Informatics, Masaryk University in Brno, and was supported by a Royal Society Newton Fellowship and EPSRC project EP/J012564/1. D. Wojtczak is supported by the grant EPSRC EP/H046623/1.

References

1. Altman, E.: Constrained Markov Decision Processes (Stochastic Modeling). Chapman & Hall/CRC (1999)
2. Boker, U., Henzinger, T.A.: Determinizing discounted-sum automata. In: CSL, pp. 82–96 (2011)
3. Boyd, S., Vandenberghe, L.: Convex Optimization. Cambridge Univ. Press (2004)
4. Brázdil, T., Brozek, V., Chatterjee, K., Forejt, V., Kucera, A.: Two views on multiple mean-payoff objectives in markov decision processes. In: LICS, pp. 33–42. IEEE Computer Society (2011)
5. Chatterjee, K., Doyen, L., Gimbert, H., Henzinger, T.A.: Randomness for free. In: Hliněný, P., Kučera, A. (eds.) MFCS 2010. LNCS, vol. 6281, pp. 246–257. Springer, Heidelberg (2010)
6. Chatterjee, K., Majumdar, R., Henzinger, T.A.: Markov decision processes with multiple objectives. In: Durand, B., Thomas, W. (eds.) STACS 2006. LNCS, vol. 3884, pp. 325–336. Springer, Heidelberg (2006)
7. Chen, T., Forejt, V., Kwiatkowska, M., Simaitis, A., Wiltsche, C.: On stochastic games with multiple objectives. In: Chatterjee, K., Sgall, J. (eds.) MFCS 2013. LNCS, vol. 8087, pp. 266–277. Springer, Heidelberg (2013)
8. Chen, T., Kwiatkowska, M., Simaitis, A., Wiltsche, C.: Synthesis for multi-objective stochastic games: An application to autonomous urban driving. In: Joshi, K., Siegle, M., Stoelinga, M., D'Argenio, P.R. (eds.) QEST 2013. LNCS, vol. 8054, Springer, Heidelberg (2013)
9. Clarke, E., Grumberg, O., Peled, D.: Model Checking. The MIT Press (1999)
10. Etessami, K., Kwiatkowska, M., Vardi, M., Yannakakis, M.: Multi-objective model checking of Markov decision processes. Logical Methods in Computer Science 4(4), 1–21 (2008)
11. Forejt, V., Kwiatkowska, M., Norman, G., Parker, D., Qu, H.: Quantitative multi-objective verification for probabilistic systems. In: Abdulla, P.A., Leino, K.R.M. (eds.) TACAS 2011. LNCS, vol. 6605, pp. 112–127. Springer, Heidelberg (2011)
12. Forejt, V., Kwiatkowska, M., Parker, D.: Pareto curves for probabilistic model checking. In: Chakraborty, S., Mukund, M. (eds.) ATVA 2012. LNCS, vol. 7561, pp. 317–332. Springer, Heidelberg (2012)
13. Papadimitriou, C.H., Yannakakis, M.: On the approximability of trade-offs and optimal access of web sources. In: FOCS, pp. 86–92. IEEE Computer Society (2000)
14. Puterman, M.: Markov Decision Processes: Discrete Stochastic Dynamic Programming. John Wiley and Sons (1994)
15. Rockafellar, R.: Convex Analysis. Princeton University Press (1997)
16. Tarski, A.: A decision method for elementary algebra and geometry. Rand report. Rand Corporation (1948)

Description Logics, Rules and Multi-context Systems

Luís Cruz-Filipe[1,2,4], Rita Henriques[3], and Isabel Nunes[3,4]

[1] Escola Superior Náutica Infante D. Henrique, Portugal
[2] CMAF, Lisboa, Portugal
[3] Faculdade de Ciências, Universidade de Lisboa
[4] LabMag, Lisboa, Portugal

Abstract. The combination of rules and ontologies has been a fertile topic of research in the last years, with the proposal of several different systems that achieve this goal. In this paper, we look at two of these formalisms, Mdl-programs and multi-context systems, which address different aspects of this combination, and include different, incomparable programming constructs. Despite this, we show that every Mdl-program can be transformed in a multi-context system, and this transformation relates the different semantics for each paradigm in a natural way. As an application, we show how a set of design patterns for multi-context systems can be obtained from previous work on Mdl-programs.

1 Introduction

Several approaches combining rules and ontologies have been proposed in the last years for semantic web reasoning, e.g. [2,8,9,10,12,16] among others. Ontologies are typically expressed through decidable fragments of function-free first-order logic with equality, offering a very good ratio of expressiveness/complexity of reasoning [1]. The addition of some kind of rule capability in order to be able to express more powerful queries together with non-monotonic features (in particular, the negation-as-failure operator not) achieved by joining ontologies and logic programming result in a very powerful framework for semantic web reasoning.

In this paper, we look at two of these systems: Mdl-programs [7], which are a straightforward generalization of the well-known dl-programs [9,10], and multi-context systems (MCSs) [2], which address different aspects of this combination, and include incomparable programming constructs. One of the main differences is the structure of programs – an Mdl-program is essentially a logic program that can query description logic knowledge bases, "feeding" its view of the latter with newly inferred facts; MCSs, on the other hand, consist of several knowledge bases, possibly expressed in different languages, each declaring additional rules that allow communication with the others.

Despite their differences, we show that every Mdl-program can be transformed in a multi-context system in such a way that different semantics for each paradigm are naturally related: answer-set semantics become grounded equilibria, whereas well-founded semantics correspond to well-founded belief sets.

As a consequence, any useful constructions developed within the framework of Mdl-programs may be automatically translated to equivalent constructions in the setting of MCSs. Although the idea behind the syntactic translation is suggested in [3] to justify that MCSs generalize the original dl-programs, even this claim is not substantiated beyond an intuitive perspective. Here, we will not only make this syntactic correspondence precise, but discuss in detail the semantic correspondences it entails, and apply it to obtain a set of design patterns for MCSs based on such a set for Mdl-programs.

The structure of the paper is as follows. Section 2 recalls the syntax and semantics of Mdl-programs. Section 3 introduces the syntax of MCSs and the translation of Mdl-programs into these. Section 4 summarizes the different semantics of MCSs and relates the semantics of an Mdl-program and those of the MCS it generates. Section 5 applies this correspondence to design patterns for Mdl-programs. Section 6 concludes the paper.

2 Mdl-Programs

This section presents multi-description logic programs [7], Mdl-programs for short, which are a straightforward generalization of dl-programs, an already established framework for coupling description logic knowledge bases with rule-based reasoning [9,10]. The main advantage of Mdl-programs, as we will see, is their simplicity. Although they do not possess the level of generality other systems such as HEX-programs [11] or multi-context systems [2] have, Mdl-programs are quite adequate for reasoning within the semantic web, where a lot of effort is being put into developing ontologies, which for the main part are description logic knowledge bases.

2.1 Syntax

The purpose of Mdl-programs is to generalize logic programs with special atoms that communicate with external description logic knowledge bases, which we will refer to henceforth simply as "knowledge bases". The key ingredient of Mdl-programs is the notion of *dl-atom*. A dl-atom relative to a set of knowledge bases $\overline{\Sigma} = \{\Sigma_1, \ldots, \Sigma_n\}$ and a function-free first-order signature Φ is $DL_i[S_1\, op_1\, p_1, \ldots, S_m\, op_m\, p_m; Q](\bar{t})$, where $1 \leq i \leq n$, each S_k is either a concept or role of Σ_i, or a special symbol in $\{=, \neq\}$; $op_i \in \{\uplus, \cup\}$; each p_k is a unary or binary predicate symbol of Φ, according to whether the corresponding S_k is a concept or a role; and $Q(\bar{t})$ is a *dl-query*, that is, it is either a concept inclusion axiom F or its negation $\neg F$, or of the form $C(t)$, $\neg C(t)$, $R(t_1, t_2)$, $\neg R(t_1, t_2)$, $=(t_1, t_2)$, $\neq(t_1, t_2)$, where C is a concept from Σ_i, R is a role from Σ_i, and t, t_1 and t_2 are terms – constants from any Σ_j or Φ, or variables. The sequence $S_1\, op_1\, p_1, \ldots, S_m\, op_m\, p_m$ is the *input context* of the dl-atom; we will use the greek letter χ to denote generic input contexts.

Note that no requirement is made about any relations between the different knowledge bases; in particular, the description logics underlying the Σ_is need not be the same.

A *dl-rule* over $\overline{\Sigma}$ and Φ is a Horn clause that may contain dl-atoms, i.e. it has the form $a \leftarrow b_1, \ldots, b_k, \text{not } b_{k+1}, \ldots, \text{not } b_m$ where a is a logical atom and $b_1, \ldots, b_m$ are either logical atoms or dl-atoms – where the logical atoms are again built using terms from Φ and constants from any Σ_i. The *head* of r is a and the *body* of r is $b_1, \ldots, b_k, \text{not } b_{k+1}, \ldots, \text{not } b_m$. An *Mdl-program* over Φ is a pair $\mathcal{KB} = \langle \overline{\Sigma}, \mathcal{P} \rangle$ where $\overline{\Sigma}$ is as before, each Σ_i is a description logic knowledge base and $\mathcal{P}$ is a finite set of dl-rules over $\overline{\Sigma}$ and Φ (also referred to as a *generalized logic program*). As usual, we will omit referring to Φ explicitly. Note that negation in $\mathcal{P}$ is the usual, closed-world, negation-as-failure, in contrast with the knowledge bases Σ_i, which (being description logic knowledge bases) come with an open-world semantics. An Mdl-program with only one knowledge base ($n = 1$) is a *dl-program* – and this definition coincides with that in [9].

The operators $\uplus$ and $\mathbin{\dot\cup}$ extend Σ_i in the context of the current dl-query. Intuitively, $S_k \uplus p_k$ (resp., $S_k \mathbin{\dot\cup} p_k$) adds to S_k (resp., $\neg S_k$) all instances of (pairs of) terms for which p_k holds – the *extent* of p_k –, before evaluating the query. This only affects $\mathcal{P}$'s current view of Σ_i without changing Σ_i. The components of an Mdl-program are thus kept independent, communicating only through dl-atoms; so, although they function separately, giving Mdl-programs nice modularity properties, there is a bidirectional flow of information via dl-atoms.[1]

We will adopt some notational conventions throughout this paper. Variables are capital letters in math font (e.g. X), while constants and terms are in sans serif. Predicate symbols (from the generalized logic program) begin with a lowercase letter, while concepts and roles (from the knowledge base) are written exactly as they are defined in the source ontologies. We will *not* use different fonts for objects of $\mathcal{P}$ and objects of the Σ_is, since these sets are not necessarily disjoint (the constants of all Σ_is may be used in $\mathcal{P}$); we will however abstain from using the same name for a predicate in $\mathcal{P}$ and a concept or role in Σ_i.

Example 1. We illustrate the syntax of Mdl-programs with a simple example. This program uses two external knowledge bases: Σ_1 is the Travel Ontology travel.owl [13], freely available online, which defines a series of travel-related concepts, including that of (tourist) Destination; and Σ_2 is a freely accessible wine ontology wine.rdf [15], which compiles a substantial amount of information about wines, including the locations of several important wineries around the world; in particular, this ontology contains a concept Region identifying some major wine regions throughout the world. These are combined in an Mdl-program by means of the following generalized logic program $\mathcal{P}$.

$$\text{wineDest}(\text{Tasmania}) \leftarrow \qquad\qquad (r_1)$$
$$\text{wineDest}(\text{Sydney}) \leftarrow \qquad\qquad (r_2)$$
$$\text{wineDest}(X) \leftarrow DL_2[; \text{Region}](X) \qquad\qquad (r_3)$$
$$\text{overnight}(X) \leftarrow DL_1[; \text{hasAccommodation}](X, Y) \qquad\qquad (r_4)$$
$$\text{oneDayTrip}(X) \leftarrow DL_1[\text{Destination} \uplus \text{wineDest}; \text{Destination}](X),$$
$$\text{not overnight}(X) \qquad\qquad (r_5)$$

---

[1] The original definition of dl-programs included a third operator, but it can be defined as an abbreviation of the other two [9], and we follow this methodology.

This program defines a predicate wineDest with two instances, corresponding to two wine regions that are interesting tourist destinations, and a rule (r_3) extending the definition of wineDest with a query to Σ_2, importing all instances of Region in Σ_2. Informally, the goal is that wineDest should be a new subconcept of Destination, but Σ_1 is left unchanged.

Rules (r_4, r_5) identify the destinations only suitable for one-day trips. The possible destinations are selected via (r_5) not only from the information originally in Σ_1, but by (i) extending the concept Destination of Σ_1 with all instances of wineDest in $\mathcal{P}$ and then (ii) querying this extended view of Σ_1 for all instances of Destination. The result is then filtered using the auxiliary predicate overnight defined in (r_4) as the set of destinations for which some accommodation is known. This uses the role hasAccommodation of Σ_1, where hasAccommodation(t_1, t_2) holds whenever t_1 is a Destination and t_2 an accommodation facility located in t_1. The reason for resorting to (r_4) at all is the usual one in logic programming: the operational semantics of negation-as-failure requires all variables in a negated atom to appear in non-negated atoms in the body of the same rule.[2]

An interesting aspect of this example is that Sydney is already an individual of Σ_1 – one of the characteristics of Mdl-programs is precisely that the atoms of $\mathcal{P}$ may use constants of Σ_1 as terms. This is relevant: rule (r_1) adds new constants to the domain of $\mathcal{KB}$, but rule (r_2) adds *information* about an individual already in Σ_1. Note the relevance of the extended query in (r_5): if Destination were not updated with the information from wineDest, we would not be able to infer e.g. oneDayTrip(Tasmania). In the next section we will introduce semantics for dl-programs and show that this is indeed a consequence of $\mathcal{KB}$.

2.2 Semantics

In order to provide semantics for Mdl-programs, we first recall the notion of Herbrand base of a logic program $\mathcal{P}$ over Φ, denoted HB$_\mathcal{P}$ – the set of all ground atoms consisting of predicate symbols and terms from Φ. The Herbrand base of an Mdl-program $\mathcal{KB} = \langle \overline{\Sigma}, \mathcal{P} \rangle$, denoted HB$_{\mathcal{KB}}$, is similarly defined, except that constant symbols may also come from the vocabulary of the Σ_is. An *interpretation* is a subset I of HB$_{\mathcal{KB}}$. We say that I is a *model* of a ground atom or dl-atom a under $\overline{\Sigma}$, or I *satisfies* a under $\overline{\Sigma}$, denoted $I \models_{\overline{\Sigma}} a$, in the following cases:

- if $a \in$ HB$_{\mathcal{KB}}$, then $I \models_{\overline{\Sigma}} a$ iff $a \in I$;
- if a is a ground dl-atom $DL_i[\chi; Q](\bar{t})$ with $\chi = S_1 \, op_1 \, p_1, \ldots, S_m \, op_m \, p_m$, then $I \models_{\overline{\Sigma}} a$ iff $\Sigma_i(I; \chi) \models Q(\bar{t})$, where $\Sigma_i(I; \chi) = \Sigma_i \cup \bigcup_m^{j=1} A_j(I)$ and, for $1 \leq j \leq m$,

$$A_j(I) = \begin{cases} \{S_j(\bar{e}) \mid p_j(\bar{e}) \in I\}, & op_j = \uplus \\ \{\neg S_j(\bar{e}) \mid p_j(\bar{e}) \in I\}, & op_j = \cup\!\!\!\!\!\!\!\!- \end{cases}$$

---
[2] We do not need to extend Destination in this dl-rule because of the structure of Σ_1: the role hasAccommodation is defined as the set of its instances (without any axioms), so changing other concepts or roles has no effect on its semantics.

An interpretation I is a *model* of a ground dl-rule r if $I \models_{\overline{\Sigma}} H(r)$ whenever $I \models_{\overline{\Sigma}} B(r)$, where $H(r)$ and $B(r)$ are the head and body of rule r, respectively. I is a model of $\mathcal{KB}$ if I is a model of all ground instances of all rules of $\mathcal{P}$.

Example 2. Given the dl-program $\mathcal{KB}$ of Example 1, its Herbrand base contains all ground atoms built from applying wineDest, overnight and oneDayTrip not only to the constants of $\mathcal{P}$ – Tasmania and Sydney – but also to all individuals of Σ_1, which include (among others), Canberra and FourSeasons (which is not an instance of Destination), and of Σ_2, which includes e.g. AustralianRegion. Thus, $HB_{\mathcal{KB}}$ contains e.g.

| wineDest(AustralianRegion) | overnight(Tasmania) | oneDayTrip(Canberra) |
| wineDest(FourSeasons) | overnight(Sydney) | oneDayTrip(Sydney),... |

This may seem a bit strange, since e.g. wineDest(FourSeasons) does not fit well with our intended interpretation of wineDest; but this is a well-known side-effect of the absence of types in logic programming.

This program has only one model. To analyze it, one has to know that the only instance of hasAccommodation in Σ_1 has Sydney as its first argument. Thus, this model contains overnight(Sydney), as well as wineDest(Tasmania) and wineDest(Sydney); furthermore, it includes wineDest(t) for every t such that $\Sigma_2 \models \text{Region}(t)$. Finally, for every individual t other than Sydney such that $\Sigma_1 \models \text{Destination}(t)$ or $\Sigma_2 \models \text{Region}(t)$, the model contains oneDayTrip(t).

This model may not seem like a very realistic view of the world, but this is a limitation of the current state of the underlying ontologies.

An Mdl-program $\mathcal{KB} = \langle \overline{\Sigma}, \mathcal{P} \rangle$ is *positive* if the rules in $\mathcal{P}$ do not contain negations. Positive Mdl-programs enjoy the usual properties of positive logic programs, namely they have a unique least model $M_{\mathcal{KB}}$ that can be constructed by computing the least fixed-point of the Herbrand transformation $T_{\mathcal{KB}}$, which is defined as the usual Herbrand transformation for logic programs, resorting to the Σ_is to evaluate dl-atoms. The Mdl-program in Example 1 is not a positive program because of the negation in rule (r_4).

Answer-set semantics. The answer set semantics of (not necessarily positive) Mdl-programs is defined again in analogy to that of logic programs. Given an Mdl-program $\mathcal{KB} = \langle \overline{\Sigma}, \mathcal{P} \rangle$, we can obtain a positive dl-program by replacing $\mathcal{P}$ with its *dl-transform* $s\mathcal{P}^I_{\overline{\Sigma}}$ relative to $\overline{\Sigma}$ and an interpretation I. This is obtained by grounding every rule in $\mathcal{P}$ and then (i) deleting every dl-rule r such that $I \models_{\overline{\Sigma}} a$ for some default negated a in the body of r, and (ii) deleting from each remaining dl-rule the negative body. The informed reader will recognize this to be a generalization of the Gelfond–Lifschitz reduct. Since $\mathcal{KB}^I = \langle \overline{\Sigma}, s\mathcal{P}^I_{\overline{\Sigma}} \rangle$ is a positive Mdl-program, it has a unique least model $M_{\mathcal{KB}^I}$. An *answer set* of $\mathcal{KB}$ is an interpretation I that coincides with $M_{\mathcal{KB}^I}$.

The model of the Mdl-program in the previous example is also an answer set of that program.

Well-founded semantics. Another semantics for Mdl-programs is well-founded semantics, which again generalizes well-founded semantics for logic programs. There are several equivalent ways to define this semantics; for the purpose of this paper, we define the well-founded semantics of an Mdl-program $\mathcal{KB} = \langle \overline{\Sigma}, \mathcal{P} \rangle$ by means of the operator $\gamma_{\mathcal{KB}}$ such that $\gamma_{\mathcal{KB}}(I)$ is the least model of the positive dl-program $\mathcal{KB}^I$ defined earlier. This operator is anti-monotonic, so $\gamma^2_{\mathcal{KB}}$ is monotonic and therefore it has a least and greatest fixpoint, denoted lfp $\left(\gamma^2_{\mathcal{KB}}\right)$ and gfp $\left(\gamma^2_{\mathcal{KB}}\right)$, respectively. An atom $a \in \mathsf{HB}_\mathcal{P}$ is *well-founded* if $a \in \mathsf{lfp}\left(\gamma^2_{\mathcal{KB}}\right)$ and *unfounded* if $a \notin \mathsf{gfp}\left(\gamma^2_{\mathcal{KB}}\right)$; the *well-founded semantics* of $\mathcal{KB}$ is the set containing all well-founded atoms and the negations of all unfounded atoms. Intuitively, well-founded atoms are true in every model of $\mathcal{P}$, whereas unfounded atoms are always false. Note that, unlike answer sets, the well-founded semantics of $\mathcal{KB}$ may not be a model of $\mathcal{KB}$.

The well-founded semantics of the previous example contains all atoms in its models and the negations of all remaining atoms. This is a consequence of there being only one answer set for that Mdl-program (see [9] for details).

2.3 Mdl-Programs with Observers

On top of Mdl-programs, we defined a syntactic construction [7] to extend a concept or role from one of the Σ_is (in $\mathcal{P}$'s view of Σ_i) with all instances of a predicate in $\mathcal{P}$, or reciprocally. An *Mdl-program with observers* is a pair $\langle \mathcal{KB}, \mathcal{O} \rangle$, where $\mathcal{KB} = \langle \overline{\Sigma}, \mathcal{P} \rangle$ is an Mdl-program, $\mathcal{O} = \langle \{\Lambda_1, \ldots, \Lambda_n\}, \{\Psi_1, \ldots, \Psi_n\} \rangle$, the observer sets, where Λ_i is a finite set of pairs $\langle S, p \rangle$ and Ψ_i is a finite set of pairs $\langle p, S \rangle$, in both cases with S a (negated) concept from Σ_i and p a unary predicate from $\mathcal{P}$, or S a (negated) role from Σ_i and p a binary predicate from $\mathcal{P}$.

Intuitively, Λ_i contains the concepts and roles in Σ_i that $\mathcal{P}$ needs to observe, in the sense that $\mathcal{P}$ should be able to detect whenever new facts about them are derived, whereas Ψ_i contains the predicates in $\mathcal{P}$ that Σ_i needs to observe. Note that a specific symbol (be it a predicate, concept or role) may occur in different Ψ_is or Λ_is. An Mdl-program with observers can be transformed in a (standard) Mdl-program by replacing $\mathcal{P}$ with $\mathcal{P}^\mathcal{O}$, obtained from $\mathcal{P}$ by:

– adding rule $p(X) \leftarrow DL_i[; S](X)$ for each $\langle S, p \rangle \in \Lambda_i$, if S is a concept (and its binary counterpart, if S is a role); and
– in each dl-atom $DL_i[\chi; Q](\bar{t})$ (including those added in the previous step), adding $S \uplus p$ to χ for each $\langle p, S \rangle \in \Psi_i$ and $S \mathbin{\rotatebox[origin=c]{180}{$\uplus$}} p$ to χ for each $\langle p, \neg S \rangle \in \Psi_i$.

Example 3. We can rewrite the previous Mdl-program as an Mdl-program with observers by omitting rule (r_3) and taking $\Lambda_2 = \{\langle \mathsf{Region}, \mathsf{wineDest} \rangle\}$.

Having in mind the structure of Σ_1 (see footnote on page 246), we can go a step further, take $\Psi_1 = \{\langle \mathsf{wineDest}, \mathsf{Destination} \rangle\}$ and replace (r_5) with

$$\mathsf{oneDayTrip}(X) \leftarrow DL_1[; \mathsf{Destination}](X), \mathbf{not}\ \mathsf{overnight}(X) \qquad (r'_5)$$

Unfolding this observer now yields a program with the same semantics but where rule (r_4) has been replaced by

$$\mathsf{overnight}(X) \leftarrow DL_1[\mathsf{Destination} \uplus \mathsf{wineDest}; \mathsf{hasAccommodation}](X, Y) \qquad (r'_4)$$

3 From Mdl-Programs to Multi-context Systems

There are other approaches to combining different reasoning and programming paradigms; in particular, rules and ontologies can also be combined within AL-log [8], HEX-programs [11], MKNF [14] and multi-context systems [2,4]. Some of these systems even allow for more general combinations; however, Mdl-programs, being less general, are easier to manipulate and understand.

In this section, we show that Mdl-programs (with observers) can be translated to MCSs. The converse is trivially not true – MCSs are far more general, as their definition shows. Besides being an interesting result by itself, this translation will be used in Section 5 to guide the development of an elementary set of design patterns for MCSs – another useful contribution, since the latter framework is more general than most other existing approaches [4].

Instead of presenting MCSs on their own, this section is organized as follows. We begin by defining their syntax and immediately follow with the definition of the (syntactic) translation from Mdl-programs to MCSs. Then, we introduce the several semantics for MCSs together with the correspondence results that relate the semantics of an Mdl-program and the corresponding MCS. In this way, the constructions and results are more easily appreciated.

Multi-context systems were originally proposed [2] as a way of combining different reasoning paradigms, where information flows among the different logics within the system through bridge rules.

The notion of multi-context system is defined in several layers.

1. A *logic* is as a triple $L = (KB_L, BS_L, ACC_L)$ where KB_L is the set of well-formed knowledge bases of L; BS_L is the set of possible belief sets; and $ACC_L : KB_L \to 2^{BS_L}$ is a function describing the semantics of the logic by assigning to each element of KB_L a set of acceptable sets of beliefs.

   Note that nothing is said about *what* knowledge bases or belief sets are; the former are part of the syntax of the language, their precise definition being left to L, while the latter intuitively represent the sets of syntactical elements representing the beliefs an agent may adopt. Still, this definition is meant to be abstract and general, so part of the purpose of KB_L and BS_L is defining these notions for each logic L.

2. Given a set of logics $\{L_1, \ldots, L_n\}$, an L_k-*bridge rule*, with $1 \leq k \leq n$, has the form

   $$s \leftarrow (r_1 : p_1), \ldots, (r_j : p_j), \mathbf{not}(r_{j+1} : p_{j+1}), \ldots, \mathbf{not}(r_m : p_m)$$

   where $1 \leq r_i \leq n$; each p_i is an element of some belief set of L_{r_i}; and $kb \cup \{s\} \in KB_k$ for each $kb \in KB_k$.

3. A *multi-context system* (MCS) $M = \langle C_1, \ldots, C_n \rangle$ is a collection of contexts $C_i = (L_i, kb_i, br_i)$, where $L_i = (KB_i, BS_i, ACC_i)$ is a logic, $kb_i \in KB_i$ is a knowledge base, and br_i is a set of L_i-bridge rules over $\{L_1, \ldots, L_n\}$.

Given an Mdl-program $\mathcal{KB} = \langle \overline{\Sigma}, \mathcal{P} \rangle$, there are two steps in the process of generating an MCS from $\mathcal{KB}$.

1. We split $\mathcal{P}$ in its purely logical part and its communication part, translating rules that contain dl-atoms into bridge rules.
2. For each distinct input context χ appearing in $\mathcal{P}$, we create a different copy of the knowledge base, corresponding to the view of the knowledge base within the dl-atoms containing χ.

Although the idea behind this syntactic construction is suggested in [4], it is not defined precisely, neither are the semantic implications discussed. Here, we will formalize this syntactic correspondence and analyze its implications at the semantic level.

Definition 1. Let $\mathcal{KB} = \langle \Sigma, \mathcal{P} \rangle$ be an Mdl-program. For each $i = 1, \ldots, n$, let $\chi_1^i, \ldots, \chi_{m_i}^i$ be the input contexts in dl-atoms querying Σ_i. Let ψ be a sequential enumeration of all input contexts in $\mathcal{P}$, i.e. $\psi(i,j)$ is the position of χ_j^i in the sequence of all input contexts in $\mathcal{P}$.

1. The translation $\sigma_{\mathcal{KB}}$ of literals and dl-atoms is defined by

$$\sigma_{\mathcal{KB}}(a) = \begin{cases} (0:L) & \text{if } a \text{ is a literal } L \\ (\psi(i,j):Q(t)) & \text{if } a = DL_i[\chi_j^i;Q](t) \\ \mathbf{not}(\psi(i,j):Q(t)) & \text{if } a = \mathbf{not}\, DL_i[\chi_j^i;Q](t) \end{cases}$$

2. The translation of $\mathcal{P}$ is the context $C_0 = \langle L_0, kb_0, br_0 \rangle$ where:
   - $L_0 = \langle KB_0, BS_0, ACC_0 \rangle$ is the logic underlying $\mathcal{P}$, where KB_0 is the set of all logic programs over $\mathcal{P}$'s signature, BS_0 is the power set of $\mathsf{HB}_\mathcal{P}$, and ACC_0 assigns each program to the set of its models;
   - kb_0 is $\mathcal{P}^-$, the set of rules of $\mathcal{P}$ that do not contain any dl-atoms;
   - br_0 contains $p \leftarrow \sigma_{\mathcal{KB}}(l_1), \ldots, \sigma_{\mathcal{KB}}(l_m)$ for each rule $p \leftarrow l_1, \ldots, l_m$ in $\mathcal{P} \setminus \mathcal{P}^-$.

3. For each input context $\chi_j^i = P_1\, op_1\, p_1, \ldots, P_k\, op_k\, p_k$, the context $C_{\psi(i,j)} = \langle L_i, kb_i, br_{\psi(i,j)} \rangle$ is defined as follows.
   - $L_i = \langle KB_i, BS_i, ACC_i \rangle$ is the description logic underlying Σ_i, with KB_i the set of all knowledge bases over Σ_i's signature; BS_i contains all sets of dl-queries to Σ_i; and ACC_i assigns to each knowledge base the set of dl-queries it satisfies.[3]
   - kb_i is Σ_i.
   - For $j = 1, \ldots, k$, $br_{\psi(i,j)}$ contains $P_j \leftarrow (0:p_j)$, if $op_j = \uplus$, or $\neg P_j \leftarrow (0:p_j)$, if $op_j = \cup\!\!\!\!-$.

   Note that L_i and kb_i are the same for all contexts originating from Σ_i.

4. The MCS generated by $\mathcal{KB}$, $\mathsf{M}(\mathcal{KB})$, contains C_0 and all the $C_{\psi(i,j)}$.

The first context in $\mathsf{M}(\mathcal{KB})$ is a logic program with the same underlying language of $\mathcal{P}$. This implies that any interpretation I of $\mathcal{P}$ is an element of BS_0, and vice-versa. We will use this fact hereafter without mention.

---

[3] Formally, we can define ACC_i as computing the set of logical consequences of the knowledge base and restricting it to those formulas that are dl-queries.

Example 4. Recall the Mdl-program $\mathcal{KB}$ from Example 1. For the purpose of generating an MCS from $\mathcal{KB}$, observe that there are two different input contexts associated with Σ_1, $\chi_1 = \epsilon$ and $\chi_2 =$ Destination $\uplus$ wineDest, and one associated with Σ_2, $\chi_3 = \epsilon$. Rules (r_1) and (r_2) do not include dl-atoms, so they belong to $\mathcal{P}^-$. Rules (r_3), (r_4) and (r_5), which contain dl-atoms, are translated as the following L_0-bridge rules.

$$\text{wineDest}(X) \leftarrow (3 : \text{Region}(X)) \quad (r_3')$$
$$\text{overnight}(X) \leftarrow (1 : \text{hasAccommodation}(X, Y)) \quad (r_4')$$
$$\text{oneDayTrip}(X) \leftarrow (2 : \text{Destination}(X)), \textbf{not}\, \text{overnight}(X) \quad (r_5')$$

The generated multi-context system $\mathsf{M}(\mathcal{KB})$ is thus $\langle C_0, C_1, C_2, C_3 \rangle$, where:

$C_0 = \langle L_0, \{r_1, r_2\}, \{r_3', r_4', r_5'\}\rangle \qquad C_1 = \langle L_1, \Sigma_1, \emptyset \rangle$
$C_2 = \langle L_1, \Sigma_1, \{\text{Destination}(X) \leftarrow (0 : \text{wineDest}(X))\}\rangle \quad C_3 = \langle L_2, \Sigma_2, \emptyset \rangle$

Note that, formally, the syntax of MCSs does not allow variables, so $\mathsf{M}(\mathcal{KB})$ should instead include the ground versions of these rules. However, it is usual to write MCSs with variables for readability and succinctness [4].

An interesting aspect is that we can translate an Mdl-program with observers *directly* to an MCS (without first "unfolding" the observers) as follows.

Definition 2. *Let $\langle \mathcal{KB}, \mathcal{O} \rangle$ be an Mdl-program with observers. The MCS it generates is $\mathsf{M}(\mathcal{KB}, \mathcal{O})$, defined as follows.*

1. *Construct $M = \mathsf{M}(\mathcal{KB})$.*
2. *Without loss of generality, assume that M contains contexts C_{i^*} corresponding to the empty input context for each Σ_i.*
3. *For each $(S, p) \in \Lambda_i$, add the bridge rule $p \leftarrow (i^* : S)$ to br_0.*
4. *For each $(p, S) \in \Psi_i$, add the bridge rule $S \leftarrow (0 : p)$ to each $br_{\psi(i,j)}$, with $j = 1, \ldots, n_i$, and to br_{i^*}.*

This construction captures the intended meaning of the observers.[4]

Theorem 1. *Let $\mathcal{KB} = \langle \overline{\Sigma}, \mathcal{P} \rangle$ be an Mdl-program and $\mathcal{O}$ be observer sets for $\mathcal{KB}$. Then $\mathsf{M}(\mathcal{KB}, \mathcal{O}) = \mathsf{M}\left(\langle \overline{\Sigma}, \mathcal{P}^{\mathcal{O}} \rangle\right)$.*

4 Semantics of Multi-context Systems

There are several different semantics for MCSs, all of which are defined in terms of the semantics for the logics in the individual contexts.

Let $M = \langle C_1, \ldots, C_n \rangle$ be a multi-context system, with $C_i = (L_i, kb_i, br_i)$ for each $1 \leq i \leq n$. A *belief state* for M is a collection $S = \langle S_1, \ldots, S_n \rangle$ of belief sets for each context, i.e. $S_i \in BS_i$ for each $1 \leq i \leq n$.

A bridge rule $s \leftarrow (r_1 : p_1), \ldots, (r_j : p_j), \textbf{not}(r_{j+1} : p_{j+1}), \ldots, \textbf{not}(r_m : p_m)$ is *applicable* in belief state $S = \langle S_1, \ldots, S_n \rangle$ iff $p_i \in S_{r_i}$ for $1 \leq i \leq j$ and $p_k \notin S_{r_k}$

---
[4] The proofs of all results can be found in [6].

for $j+1 \leq k \leq m$. A belief state $S = \langle S_1,\ldots,S_n\rangle$ of M is an *equilibrium* if the condition $S_i \in ACC_i(kb_i \cup \{H(r) \mid r \in br_i$ is applicable in $S\})$ holds for $1 \leq i \leq n$, where $H(r)$ denotes the head of rule r as usual.

In other words, belief states are simply "candidate" models, in the sense that they are acceptable as potential models of each context. Information is transported between different contexts by means of bridge rules, since a bridge rule in one context may refer to other contexts, and the notion of equilibrium guarantees that all belief states are not only models of the local information at each context, but also reflect the relationships imposed by the bridge rules.

Just as we can generate a multi-context system $\mathsf{M}(\mathcal{KB})$ from an Mdl-program $\mathcal{KB}$, we can generate a belief state for $\mathsf{M}(\mathcal{KB})$ from any interpretation of $\mathcal{KB}$.

Definition 3. *Let $\mathcal{KB} = \langle \overline{\Sigma},\mathcal{P}\rangle$ be an Mdl-program and I be an interpretation of $\mathcal{KB}$. The belief state generated by I is $\mathsf{S}_{\mathcal{KB}}(I) = \langle S_0^I, S_1^I,\ldots,S_m^I\rangle$ of $\mathsf{M}(\mathcal{KB})$, where $S_0^I = I$ and $S_{\psi(i,j)}^I$ is the only element of*

$$ACC_i\left(\Sigma_i \cup \{P(t) \mid I \models p(t), P \uplus p \in \chi_j^i\} \cup \{\neg P(t) \mid I \models p(t), P \uplus p \in \chi_j^i\}\right).$$

It is straightforward to verify that $\mathsf{S}_{\mathcal{KB}}(I)$ is a belief state of $\mathsf{M}(\mathcal{KB})$. When there is only one Mdl-program under consideration, we omit the subscript in $\mathsf{S}_{\mathcal{KB}}$.

In the example from the previous section, one can check that its model generates a belief state that is also an equilibrium of $\mathsf{M}(\mathcal{KB})$. This suggests that there are very close connections between I and $\mathsf{S}(I)$, which we now prove formally.

Theorem 2. *Let $\mathcal{KB} = \langle \overline{\Sigma},\mathcal{P}\rangle$ be an Mdl-program.*

1. *If I is a model of $\mathcal{KB}$, then $\mathsf{S}(I)$ is an equilibrium of $\mathsf{M}(\mathcal{KB})$.*
2. *If $S = \langle S_0,\ldots,S_m\rangle$ is an equilibrium of $\mathsf{M}(\mathcal{KB})$, then S_0 is a model of $\mathcal{KB}$.*

Furthermore, since ACC_i always yields a singleton set, equilibria for MCSs generated from an Mdl-program can be uniquely derived from their first component, as expressed by the following corollary.

Corollary 1. *If $S = \langle S_0,\ldots,S_m\rangle$ is an equilibrium of $\mathsf{M}(\mathcal{KB})$, then $\mathsf{S}(S_0) = S$.*

This result allows us to state all future equivalences in terms of models of $\mathcal{P}$.

Minimal equilibria. As is the case in logic programming, there can be too many equilibria for a given multi-context system; for this reason, several particular kinds of equilibria are defined in [2], reflecting different kinds of preferences one may adopt to choose among them. These categories closely follow the usual hierarchy for models of logic programs, as well as of Mdl-programs. The basic concept is that of minimal equilibrium. This is a relative notion, since (as discussed in [2]) it may not make sense to minimize the belief sets for *all* contexts.

Let $M = \langle C_1,\ldots,C_n\rangle$ be a multi-context system and $C^* \subseteq \{C_1,\ldots,C_n\}$ be the set of contexts of M whose models should be minimized. An equilibrium $S = \langle S_1,\ldots,S_n\rangle$ of M is C^*-*minimal* if there is no equilibrium $S' = \langle S_1',\ldots,S_n'\rangle$ of M such that: (1) $S_i' \subseteq S_i$ for all $C_i \in C^*$; (2) $S_i' \subsetneq S_i$ for some $C_i \in C^*$; and

(3) $S'_i = S_i$ for all $C_i \notin C^*$. In this paper, we will always use $C^* = M$ and simply refer to *minimal* equilibria, which the reader should understand to mean M-minimal equilibria.

Since the transformation S from interpretations of Mdl-programs to belief states preserves inclusions, we also have the following relationship.

Theorem 3. *Let $\mathcal{KB} = \langle \overline{\Sigma}, \mathcal{P} \rangle$ be an Mdl-program. Then I is the least model of $\mathcal{KB}$ iff $S(I)$ is a minimal equilibrium of $M(\mathcal{KB})$.*

Minimal equilibria (or even C^*-equilibria) do not necessarily exist. In logic programming, it is shown that least models always exist for positive programs, a result that holds also for dl-programs [9] and Mdl-programs. In MCSs, this class corresponds to that of definite multi-context systems.

A logic L is *monotonic* if $ACC_L(kb)$ is always a singleton set, and $kb \subseteq kb'$ implies that the only element of $ACC_L(kb)$ is a subset of the only element of $ACC_L(kb')$. This coincides with the usual notion of monotonic logic. A logic $L = (KB_L, BS_L, ACC_L)$ is *reducible* if (1) there is $KB_L^* \subseteq KB_L$ such that the restriction of L to KB_L^* is monotonic; and (2) there is a reduction function $\text{red}L : KB_L \times BS_L \to KB_L^*$ such that, for each $k \in KB_L$ and $S, S' \in BS_L$, (2a) $\text{red}_L(k, S) = k$ whenever $k \in KB_L^*$; (2b) $\text{red}L$ is anti-monotonic in the second argument; and (2c) $S \in ACC_L(k)$ iff $ACC_L(\text{red}_L(k, S)) = \{S\}$. A context $C = (L, kb, br)$ is *reducible* if (1) L is reducible; and (2) for all $H \subseteq \{H(r) \mid r \in br\}$ and belief sets S, $\text{red}_L(kb \cup H, S) = \text{red}_L(kb, S) \cup H$. A multi-context system is *reducible* if all of its contexts are reducible.

A *definite* MCS is a reducible MCS in which bridge rules are monotonic (that is, they do not contain **not**) and knowledge bases are in reduced form (that is, $kb_i = \text{red}_{L_i}(kb_i, S)$ for all i and every $S \in BS_i$). Every definite MCS has a unique minimal equilibrium [2], which we will denote by $Eq(M)$.

Grounded equilibria. The semantics of non-definite MCSs is defined via a generalization of the Gelfond–Lifschitz reduct to the multi-context case. If $M = \langle C_1, \ldots, C_n \rangle$ is a reducible MCS and $S = \langle S_1, \ldots, S_n \rangle$ is a belief state of M, then the S-reduct of M is $M^S = \langle C_1^S, \ldots, C_n^S \rangle$, where $C_i^S = (L_i, \text{red}_{L_i}(kb_i, S_i), br_i^S)$ and, for each i, br_i^S is obtained from br_i by (1) deleting every rule with some **not** $(k : p)$ in the body such that $p \in S_k$, and (2) deleting all **not** literals from the bodies of remaining rules. If $S = Eq(M^S)$, then S is a *grounded equilibrium* of M.

Note that this definition only makes sense if M^S is definite; indeed, it has been shown [2] that this is always the case. In particular, if M is a definite MCS, then its minimal equilibrium is its only grounded equilibrium. In other cases, several grounded equilibria (or none) may exist. It is also easy to verify that grounded equilibria of M are indeed equilibria of M.

Answer sets for Mdl-programs correspond to grounded equilibria for MCSs. This should not come as a big surprise: both the dl-transform of Mdl-programs and the reduct of an MCS are generalizations of the Gelfond–Lifschitz transform of ordinary logic programs.

Theorem 4. *I is an answer set for $\mathcal{KB}$ iff $\mathsf{S}(I)$ is a grounded equilibrium of $\mathsf{M}(\mathcal{KB})$.*

Well-founded semantics. The well-founded semantics for reducible MCSs is also defined in [2], based on the operator $\gamma_M(S) = Eq(M^S)$. Since γ_M is antimonotonic, γ_M^2 is monotonic as usual. However, one can only guarantee the existence of its least fixpoint by the Knaster–Tarski theorem if BS_i has a least element for each logic Σ_i in any of M's contexts. If this is the case, then the well-founded semantics of M is $WFS(M) = \mathsf{lfp}\left(\gamma_M^2\right)$.

As with models of logic programs (and of Mdl-programs), $WFS(M)$ is not necessarily an equilibrium: it contains the knowledge that is common to all equilibria, but being an equilibrium is not preserved by intersection.[5]

This definition is very similar to that of well-founded semantics for Mdl-programs. Therefore, the following result should not come as a surprise.

Theorem 5. *I is the well-founded semantics of $\mathcal{KB}$ iff $\mathsf{S}(I)$ is the well-founded equilibrium of $\mathsf{M}(\mathcal{KB})$.*

5 Design Patterns in Multi-context Systems

In real life, a substantial amount of the time required in software development is spent in finding and implementing design solutions for recurrent problems already addressed and for which good solutions already exist. For this reason, an important field in research is that of identifying common scenarios and proposing mechanisms to deal with these scenarios – the so-called *design patterns* for software development. With this in mind, the authors proposed an elementary set of design patterns for Mdl-programs [7].

In this section, we apply the translation from Mdl-programs to MCSs to obtain an initial set of design patterns for MCSs, and discuss how adequate the resulting patterns are. This discussion focuses on the potential usefulness of the translation: we capitalize on the mapping previously defined to port interesting constructions from one formalism to another automatically. As it turns out, we can overcome some of the problems that affected the set described in [7], thereby obtaining a more expressive set of design patterns for MCSs. Also, we take advantage of the intrinsic structure of MCSs to optimize some of the resulting design patterns, a simpler process than developing efficient ones from scratch.

The simplest design pattern is the **Observer Down** pattern, applicable when there is a predicate in $\mathcal{P}$ that should include all instances of a concept or role S in some Σ_i. This pattern is implemented in an Mdl-program with observers simply by adding the pair (S,p) to the appropriate observer set Λ_i. According to Definition 2, this corresponds to adding a bridge rule $p \leftarrow (i^* : S)$ to br_0. Reciprocally, the pattern **Observer Up** allows S to include all instances of p, and is implemented by adding $S \leftarrow (0 : p)$ to all contexts generated from Σ_i.

---

[5] In view of the following result, to obtain an example, pick a dl-program whose well-founded semantics is not a model (see [5]) and apply the translation defined above.

Looking at these constructions from the perspective of MCSs, their implementation follows the same structure: a bridge rule with exactly one literal in its body is added to a context C_i, thereby updating some S_i in C_i's language using input from some S_j in C_j. This mechanism makes sense in general, regardless of whether the MCS is generated from an Mdl-program or not. We thus obtain a general **Observer** design pattern that we can apply in any MCS whenever we want to ensure that some S_i in context C_i is updated every time another S_j in context C_j is changed: simply add the rule $S_i \leftarrow (j : S_j)$ to br_i.

This pattern also captures the **Transversal Observer** pattern of Mdl-programs, applicable when one knowledge base needs to observe another; however, this implementation is simpler than translating this pattern directly, since in MCSs there is in general no need to use an intermediate context. This type of simplification will also be used in other patterns.

A more interesting example arises when one looks at the **Polymorphic Entities** design pattern. The setting is the following: in $\mathcal{P}$, there is a predicate p whose instances are inherited from $Q_1, \ldots, Q_k$, where each Q_j is a concept or role from Σ_j. This pattern is again implemented by adding a number of observers, namely (Q_j, p) to each Λ_j. In the generated MCS, this corresponds to adding bridge rules $p \leftarrow (j^* : Q_j)$ for each j to br_0. This pattern can be applied in a generic MCS whenever we want predicate P from context C_i to inherit all instances of predicates $Q_1, \ldots, Q_k$ where each Q_j is a predicate from a context C_j. This is achieved by adding bridge rules $P \leftarrow (j : Q_j)$ for each j to br_i.

An example where we can substantially simplify the design pattern obtained is adding closed world semantics to a predicate in some context. In the setting of Mdl-programs, where each description logic knowledge base has open-world semantics and the logic program has default negation, this is achieved by the **Closed World** design pattern. To give closed-world semantics to a concept (or role) S in Σ_i, we choose fresh predicate symbols s^+ and s^- in $\mathcal{P}$ and add (S, s^+) to Λ_i, $(s^-, \neg S)$ to Ψ_i and the rule $s^-(X) \leftarrow \mathbf{not}\, s^+(X)$ to $\mathcal{P}$. In the generated MCS, this corresponds to adding $s^+ \leftarrow (i^* : S)$ to br_0, $\neg S \leftarrow (0 : s^-)$ to br_{i^*}, and the rule $s^-(X) \leftarrow \mathbf{not}\, s^+(X)$ to kb_0.

To generalize this pattern, we first observe that adding $s^-(X) \leftarrow \mathbf{not}\, s^+(X)$ to kb_0 is equivalent to adding the bridge rule $s^- \leftarrow \mathbf{not}(0 : s^+)$ to br_0, since the semantics of bridge rules is that of logic programs. As before, the context C_0 is now being used solely as an intermediate for a construction that can be made directly in C_i; therefore, we can implement **Closed-World** in an MCS, giving closed-world semantics to a predicate S_i in context C_i by adding the bridge rule $\neg S_i \leftarrow \mathbf{not}(i : S_i)$ to br_i. Once again, this pattern makes sense in any MCS, regardless of the nature of its components – as long as the context C_i has negation.

The last design pattern we discuss here is **Adapter**, which is applied whenever a component Σ_k is not known or available at the time of implementation of others, yet it is necessary to query it. In an Mdl-program, one adds an empty interface knowledge base Σ_I whose language includes the desired concept and role names, and later connect each concept and role in Σ_I with its counterpart in Σ_k

by means of ***Transversal Observer***. This pattern works without any changes in any MCS; however, the resulting program will be simpler because the application of ***Observer*** yields a simpler MCS than the application of ***Transversal Observer*** in an Mdl-program.

Furthermore, as was observed in [7], in Mdl-programs this pattern does not work well if one needs dl-atoms querying Σ_I which locally extend this knowledge base. In MCSs, this problem does not arise, and thus this implementation of ***Adapter*** is closer to the spirit of this pattern in e.g. object-oriented programming. It is also interesting to notice that this pattern can be modified in a very simple way to implement a proxy: simply add side-conditions to the body of the bridge rules connecting C_I with C_k that restrict the communication between these two contexts. As was observed in [7], it is not clear whether a proxy can be implemented in Mdl-programs.

The ideas in this section constitute an initial approach to the study of design patterns in multi-context systems. We point out that we obtained for free a set of design patterns including all design patterns for Mdl-programs in [7], applicable in a more general setting. Furthermore, several of these patterns were simplified in a systematic way, removing indirections resulting from the need, in Mdl-programs, to go through the logic program in order to establish communication between two different knowledge bases.

6 Conclusions

The basic constructs of Mdl-programs and multi-context systems are based upon different motivations, and are therefore fundamentally different. In this paper, we showed how, even so, an arbitrary Mdl-program can be translated into an MCS, which is equivalent to it in a very precise way – namely, the interpretations of the Mdl-program naturally give rise to belief states for the generated MCS, taking this correspondence to the semantic level. Thus, (minimal) models become (minimal) equilibria, answer sets become grounded equilibria, and well-founded semantics (for Mdl-programs) become well-founded semantics (for MCSs).

An important aspect of this construction is that we can *compute* minimal equilibria and well-founded semantics for MCSs generated from Mdl-programs efficiently, which is not true in general (the definition of minimal equilibrium is a characterization that is not computational, and minimal equilibria cannot usually be constructed in a practical way, except by brute-force testing of all candidates). Also, there is an algorithmic procedure to check whether an equilibrium for an MCS generated from a Mdl-program is grounded, which again is not true in general.

Finally, we showed how this technique can be applied to obtain a start set of design patterns for MCSs. This set was obtained by translating a pre-existing set of design patterns for Mdl-programs and simplifying the result following some general principles motivated by the specificities of MCSs. In some cases, the resulting patterns turned out to be more encompassing than the original ones. We intend to use this work as a first step in a more comprehensive study of design patterns for multi-context systems.

Acknowledgments. The authors wish to thank Graça Gaspar for the fruitful discussions and her insightful comments on a first version of the manuscript.

This work was partially supported by Fundação para a Ciência e Tecnologia under contracts PEst-OE/MAT/UI0209/2011 and PEst-OE/EEI/UI0434/2011.

References

1. Baader, F., Calvanese, D., McGuinness, D.L., Nardi, D., Patel-Schneider, P.F. (eds.): The Description Logic Handbook: Theory, Implementation, and Applications, 2nd edn. Cambridge University Press (2007)
2. Brewka, G., Eiter, T.: Equilibria in heterogeneous nonmonotonic multi-context systems. In: AAAI 2007, pp. 385–390. AAAI Press (2007)
3. Brewka, G., Eiter, T., Fink, M.: Nonmonotonic multi-context systems: A flexible approach for integrating heterogeneous knowledge sources. In: Balduccini, M., Son, T.C. (eds.) Gelfond Festschrift. LNCS, vol. 6565, pp. 233–258. Springer, Heidelberg (2011)
4. Brewka, G., Eiter, T., Fink, M., Weinzierl, A.: Managed multi-context systems. In: Walsh, T. (ed.) IJCAI, pp. 786–791. IJCAI/AAAI (2011)
5. Cruz-Filipe, L., Engrácia, P., Gaspar, G., Nunes, I.: Achieving tightness in dl-programs. Technical Report 2012;03, Faculty of Sciences of the University of Lisbon (July 2012), http://hdl.handle.net/10455/6872
6. Cruz-Filipe, L., Henriques, R., Nunes, I.: Viewing dl-programs as multi-context systems. Technical Report 2013;05, Faculty of Sciences of the University of Lisbon (April 2013), http://hdl.handle.net/10455/6895
7. Cruz-Filipe, L., Nunes, I., Gaspar, G.: Patterns for interfacing between logic programs and multiple ontologies. Proceedings of KEOD 2013 (2013), http://tinyurl.com/itsweb2013-09
8. Donini, F.M., Lenzerini, M., Nardi, D., Schaerf, A.: AL-log: Integrating Datalog and description logics. Int. Inf. Systems (1998)
9. Eiter, T., Ianni, G., Lukasiewicz, T., Schindlauer, R.: Well-founded semantics for description logic programs in the semantic Web. ACM Transactions on Computational Logic 12(2), Article Nr 11 (2011)
10. Eiter, T., Ianni, G., Lukasiewicz, T., Schindlauer, R., Tompits, H.: Combining answer set programming with description logics for the semantic web. Artificial Intelligence 172(12-13), 1495–1539 (2008)
11. Eiter, T., Ianni, G., Schindlauer, R., Tompits, H.: A uniform integration of higher-order reasoning and external evaluations in answer-set programming. In: Kaelbling, L.P., Saffiotti, A. (eds.) IJCAI 2005, pp. 90–96. Professional Book Center (2005)
12. Heymans, S., Eiter, T., Xiao, G.: Tractable reasoning with DL-programs over Datalog-rewritable description logics. In: Coelho, H., Studer, R., Wooldridge, M. (eds.) ECAI 2010. Frontiers in Artificial Intelligence and Applications, vol. 215, pp. 35–40. IOS Press (2010)
13. Knublauch, H.: Travel ontology 1.0, http://protege.cim3.net/file/pub/ontologies/travel/travel.owl
14. Motik, B., Rosati, R.: Reconciling description logics and rules. Journal of the ACM 57, Article Nr 30 (June 2010)
15. The OWL Working Group. Wine ontology, http://www.w3.org/TR/2004/REC-owl-guide-20040210/wine.rdf
16. Rosati, R.: DL+log: Tight integration of description logics and disjunctive Datalog. In: Doherty, P., Mylopoulos, J., Welty, C.A. (eds.) KR 2006, pp. 67–78. AAAI Press (2006)

Complexity Analysis in Presence of Control Operators and Higher-Order Functions*

Ugo Dal Lago and Giulio Pellitta

Università di Bologna & INRIA Sophia Antipolis
{dallago,pellitta}@cs.unibo.it

Abstract. A polarized version of Girard, Scedrov and Scott's Bounded Linear Logic is introduced and its normalization properties studied. Following Laurent [25], the logic naturally gives rise to a type system for the $\lambda\mu$-calculus, whose derivations reveal bounds on the time complexity of the underlying term. This is the first example of a type system for the $\lambda\mu$-calculus guaranteeing time complexity bounds for typable programs.

1 Introduction

Among non-functional properties of programs, bounds on the amount of resources (like computation time and space) programs need when executed are particularly significant. The problem of deriving such bounds is indeed crucial in safety-critical systems, but is undecidable whenever non-trivial programming languages are considered. If the units of measurement become concrete and close to the physical ones, the problem becomes even more complicated and architecture-dependent. A typical example is the one of WCET techniques adopted in real-time systems [29], which not only need to deal with how many machine instructions a program corresponds to, but also with how much time each instruction costs when executed by possibly complex architectures (including caches, pipelining, etc.), a task which is becoming even harder with the current trend towards multicore architectures.

A different approach consists in analysing the *abstract* complexity of programs. As an example, one can take the number of instructions executed by the program as a measure of its execution time. This is of course a less informative metric, which however becomes more accurate if the actual time taken *by each instruction* is kept low. One advantage of this analysis is the independence from the specific hardware platform executing the program at hand: the latter only needs to be analysed once. A variety of *complexity analysis* techniques have been employed in this context, from abstract interpretation [21] to type systems [22] to program logics [10] to interactive theorem proving. Properties of programs written in higher-order functional languages are for various reasons well-suited to be verified by way of type systems. This includes not only safety properties

---

* An extended version of this paper including more details is available [9].

(e.g. well-typed programs do not go wrong), but more complex ones, including resource bounds [22,5,15,7].

In this paper, we delineate a methodology for complexity analysis of higher-order programs *with control operators*. The latter are constructs which are available in most concrete functional programming languages (including Scheme and OCaml), and allow control to flow in non-standard ways. The technique we introduce takes the form of a type system for de Groote's $\lambda\mu$-calculus [12] derived from Girard, Scedrov and Scott's Bounded Linear Logic [19] (BLL in the following). We prove it to be sound: typable programs can indeed be reduced in a number of steps lesser or equal to a (polynomial) bound which can be read from the underlying type derivation. A similar result can be given when the cost model is the one induced by an abstract machine. To the authors' knowledge, this is the first example of a complexity analysis methodology coping well not only with higher-order functions, but also with control operators.

In the rest of this section, we explain the crucial role Linear Logic has in this work, in the meantime delineating its main features.

1.1 Linear Logic and Complexity Analysis

Linear Logic [16] is one of the most successful tools for characterizing complexity classes in a higher-order setting, through the Curry-Howard correspondence. Subsystems of it can indeed be shown to correspond to the polynomial time computable functions [19,18,23] or the logarithmic space computable functions [28]. Many of the introduced fragments can then be turned into type systems for the λ-calculus [5,15], some of them being relatively complete in an intensional sense [7].

The reason for this success lies in the way Linear Logic decomposes intuitionistic implication into linear implication, which has low complexity, and an *exponential modality*, which marks those formulas to which structural rules can be applied. This gives a proper status to proof duplication, without which cut-elimination can be performed in a linear number of steps. By tuning the rules governing the exponential modality, then, one can define logical systems for which cut-elimination can be performed within appropriate resource bounds. Usually, this is coupled with an encoding of all functions in a complexity class $\mathcal{C}$ into the system at hand, which makes the system a *characterization* of $\mathcal{C}$.

Rules governing the exponential modality can be constrained in (at least) two different ways:
- On the one hand, one or more of the rules governing the modality (e.g., dereliction or digging) can be *dropped* or *restricted*. This is what happens, for example, in Light Linear Logic [18] or Soft Linear Logic [23].
- On the other, the logic can be further refined and *enriched* so as to control the number of times structural rules are applied. In other words, rules for the modality are still all there, but in a refined form. This is what happens in Bounded Linear Logic [19]. Similarly, one could control so-called modal impredicativity by a system of levels [4].

The first approach corresponds to cutting the space of proofs with an axe: many proofs, and among them many corresponding to efficient algorithms, will not be part of the system because they require one of the forbidden logical principles. The second approach is milder in terms of the class of good programs that are "left behind": there is strong evidence that with this approach one can obtain a quite expressive logical system [8,7].

Not much is known about whether this approach scales to languages in which not only functions but also first-class continuations and control operators are present. Understanding the impact of these features to the complexity of programs is an interesting research topic, which however has received little attention in the past.

1.2 Linear Logic and Control Operators

On the other hand, more than twenty years have passed since Classical Logic has been shown to be amenable to the Curry-Howard paradigm [20]. And, interestingly enough, classical axioms (e.g. Pierce's law or the law of the Excluded Middle) can be seen as the type of control operators like Scheme's callcc. In the meantime, the various facets of this new form of proofs-as-programs correspondence have been investigated in detail, and many extensions of the λ-calculus for which Classical Logic naturally provides a type discipline have been introduced (e.g. [27,6]).

Moreover, the decomposition provided by Linear Logic is known to scale up to Classical Logic [17]. Actually, Linear Logic was known to admit an involutive notion of negation from its very inception [16]. A satisfying embedding of Classical Logic into Linear Logic, however, requires restricting the latter by way of polarities [24]: this way one is left with a logical system with most of the desirable dynamical properties.

In this paper, we define BLLP, a polarized version of Bounded Linear Logic. The kind of enrichment resource polynomials provide in BLL is shown to cope well with polarization. Following the close relationship between Polarized Linear Logic and the $\lambda\mu$-calculus [25], BLLP gives rise to a type system for the $\lambda\mu$-calculus. Proofs and typable $\lambda\mu$-terms are both shown to be reducible to their cut-free or normal forms in a number of steps bounded by a polynomial weight. Such a result for the former translates to a similar result for the latter, since any reduction step in $\lambda\mu$-terms corresponds to one or more reduction steps in proofs. The analysis is then extended to the reduction of $\lambda\mu$-terms by a Krivine-style abstract machine [13].

2 Bounded Polarized Linear Logic as a Sequent Calculus

In this section, we define BLLP as a sequent calculus. Although this section is self-contained, some familiarity with both Bounded [19] and Polarized [25] Linear Logic would certainly help. Some more details can be found in an extended version of the present paper [9].

2.1 Polynomials and Formulas

A *resource monomial* is any (finite) product of binomial coefficients in the form $\prod_{i=1}^{m} \binom{x_i}{n_i}$, where the x_i are distinct variables and the n_i are non-negative integers. A *resource polynomial* is any finite sum of resource monomials. Given resource polynomials p, q we write $p \sqsubseteq q$ to denote that $q - p$ is a resource polynomial. If $p \sqsubseteq r$ and $q \sqsubseteq s$ then also $q \circ p \sqsubseteq s \circ r$. Resource polynomials are closed by addition, multiplication, bounded sums and composition [19].

A *polarized formula* is a formula (either positive or negative) generated by the following grammar

$$P ::= V \mid P \otimes P \mid 1 \mid !_{x<p}N;$$
$$N ::= V^{\perp} \mid N \mathbin{\text{⅋}} N \mid \perp \mid ?_{x<p}P;$$

where V ranges over a countable sets of atoms. Throughout this paper, formulas (but also terms, contexts, etc.) are considered modulo α-equivalence. Formulas (either positive or negative) are ranged over by metavariables like A, B. Formulas like $V^{\perp}$ are sometimes denoted as X, Y.

In a polarized setting, contraction can be performed on any negative formula. As a consequence, we need the notion of a *labelled formula* $[A]_x^p$, namely the *labelling* of the formula A with respect to x and p. The labelled formula $[N]_x^p$ (resp. $[P]_x^p$) can be thought of roughly as $?_{x<p}N^{\perp}$ (resp. $!_{x<p}P^{\perp}$), i.e., in a sense we can think of labelled formulas as formulas hiding an implicit exponential modality. All occurrences of x in A are bound in $[A]_x^p$. Metavariables for labellings of positive (respectively, negative) formulas are **P, Q, R** (respectively, **N, M, L**). Labelled formulas are sometimes denoted with metavariables **A, B** when their polarity is not essential. Negation, as usual in classical linear systems, can be applied to any (possibly labelled) formula, à la De Morgan. When the resource variable x does not appear in A, then we do not need to mention it when writing $[A]_x^p$, which becomes $[A]^p$. Similarly for $!_{x<p}N$ and $?_{x<p}P$.

Both the space of formulas and the space of labelled formulas can be seen as partial orders by stipulating that two (labelled) formulas can be compared iff they have *exactly* the same skeleton and the polynomials occurring in them can be compared. As an example,

$$!_{x<p}N \sqsubseteq !_{x<q}M \text{ iff } q \sqsubseteq p \wedge N \sqsubseteq M;$$
$$?_{x<p}P \sqsubseteq ?_{x<q}Q \text{ iff } p \sqsubseteq q \wedge P \sqsubseteq Q.$$

In a sense, then, polynomials occurring next to atoms or to the *whynot* operator are in positive position, while those occurring next to the *bang* operator are in negative position. In all the other cases, $\sqsubseteq$ is defined component-wise, in the natural way, e.g. $P \otimes Q \sqsubseteq R \otimes S$ iff both $P \sqsubseteq R$ and $Q \sqsubseteq S$. Finally $[N]_x^p \sqsubseteq [M]_x^q$ iff $N \sqsubseteq M \wedge p \sqsupseteq q$. And dually, $[P]_x^p \sqsubseteq [Q]_x^q$ iff $N \sqsubseteq M \wedge p \sqsubseteq q$.

Certain operators on resource polynomials can be lifted to formulas. As an example, we want to be able to *sum* labelled formulas provided they have a proper form:

$$[N]_x^p \uplus [N\{x/y+p\}]_y^q = [N]_x^{p+q}.$$

We are assuming, of course, that x, y are not free in either p or q. This construction can be generalized to *bounded* sums: suppose that a labelled formula is in the form

$$[M]_y^r = [N\{x/y + \sum_{u<z} r\{z/u\}\}]_y^r,$$

where y and u are not free in N nor in r and z is not free in N. Then the labelled formula $\sum_{z<q}[M]_y^r$ is defined as $[N]_x^{\sum_{z<q} r}$. See [19, §3.3] for more details about the above constructions.

2.2 Sequents and Rules

The easiest way to present BLLP is to give a sequent calculus for it. Actually, proofs will be structurally identical to proofs of Laurent's LLP. Of course, only *some* of LLP proofs are legal BLLP proofs — those giving rise to an exponential blow-up cannot be decorated according to the principles of Bounded Linear Logic.

A *sequent* is an expression in the form $\vdash \Gamma$, where $\Gamma = \mathbf{A}_1, \ldots \mathbf{A}_n$ is a multiset of labelled formulas such that at most one among $\mathbf{A}_1, \ldots, \mathbf{A}_n$ is positive. If Γ only contains (labellings of) negative formulas, we indicate it with metavariables like $\mathcal{N}, \mathcal{M}$. The operator $\uplus$ can be extended to one on multisets of formulas component-wise, so we can write expressions like $\mathcal{N} \uplus \mathcal{M}$: this amounts to sum the polynomials occurring in $\mathcal{N}$ and those occurring in $\mathcal{M}$. Similarly for bounded sums.

The rules of the sequent calculus for BLLP are in Figure 1. Please observe

$$\frac{\mathbf{N} \sqsubseteq \mathbf{M} \qquad \mathbf{M}^\perp \sqsupseteq \mathbf{P}}{\vdash \mathbf{N}, \mathbf{P}}\ \mathsf{Ax} \qquad \frac{\vdash \Gamma, \mathbf{N} \qquad \vdash \mathcal{N}, \mathbf{N}^\perp}{\vdash \Gamma, \mathcal{N}}\ \mathsf{Cut}$$

$$\frac{\vdash \Gamma, [N]_x^p, [M]_x^q \qquad p \sqsubseteq r \quad q \sqsubseteq r}{\vdash \Gamma, [N \parr M]_x^r}\ \parr \qquad \frac{\vdash \mathcal{N}, [P]_x^p \qquad \vdash \mathcal{M}, [Q]_x^q \quad r \sqsubseteq p \quad r \sqsubseteq q}{\vdash \mathcal{N}, \mathcal{M}, [P \otimes Q]_x^r}\ \otimes$$

$$\frac{\vdash \mathcal{N}, [N]_x^p \qquad \mathcal{M} \sqsubseteq \sum_{y<q} \mathcal{N}}{\vdash \mathcal{M}, [!_{x<p} N]_y^q}\ ! \qquad \frac{\vdash \mathcal{N}, [P\{y/0\}]_x^{p\{y/0\}} \qquad \mathbf{N} \sqsubseteq [?_{x<p} P]_y^1}{\vdash \mathcal{N}, \mathbf{N}}\ ?d$$

$$\frac{\vdash \Gamma}{\vdash \Gamma, \mathbf{N}}\ ?w \qquad \frac{\vdash \Gamma, \mathbf{N}, \mathbf{M} \qquad \mathbf{L} \sqsubseteq \mathbf{N} \uplus \mathbf{M}}{\vdash \Gamma, \mathbf{L}}\ ?c \qquad \frac{\vdash \Gamma}{\vdash \Gamma, [\perp]_x^p}\ \perp \qquad \frac{}{\vdash [1]_x^p}\ 1$$

Fig. 1. BLLP, Sequent Calculus Rules

that:

- The relation $\sqsubseteq$ is implicitly applied to both formulas and polynomials whenever possible in such a way that "smaller" formulas can always be derived (see Section 2.3).

- As in LLP, structural rules can act on any negative formula, and not only on exponential ones. Since all formulas occurring in sequents are labelled, however, we can still keep track of how many times formulas are "used", in the spirit of BLL.
- A byproduct of taking sequents as multisets of *labeled* formulas is that multiplicative rules themselves need to deal with labels. As an example, consider rule ⊗: the resource polynomial labelling the conclusion $P \otimes Q$ is anything smaller or equal to the polynomials labeling the two premises.

The sequent calculus we have just introduced could be extended with second-order quantifiers and additive logical connectives. For the sake of simplicity, however, we have kept the language of formulas very simple here. The interested reader can check [24] for a treatment of these connectives in a polarized setting or [9] for more details.

As already mentioned, BLLP proofs can be seen as obtained by decorating proofs from Laurent's LLP [25] with resource polynomials. Given a proof π, $\langle \pi \rangle$ is the LLP proof obtained by erasing all resource polynomials occurring in π. If π and ρ are two BLLP proofs, we write $\pi \sim \rho$ iff $\langle \pi \rangle = \langle \rho \rangle$, i.e., iff π and ρ are two decorations of the same LLP proof.

Even if structural rules can be applied to all negative formulas, only certain proofs will be copied or erased along the cut-elimination process, as we will soon realize. A *box* is any proof which ends with an occurrence of the ! rule. In non-polarized systems, only boxes can be copied or erased, while here the process can be applied to ⊗-*trees*, which are proofs inductively defined as follows:

- Either the last rule in the proof is Ax or ! or 1;
- or the proof is obtained from two ⊗-trees by applying the rule ⊗.

A ⊗-tree is said to be *closed* if it does not contain any axiom nor any box having auxiliary doors (i.e., no formula in the context of the ! rules).

2.3 Malleability

The main reason for the strong (intensional) expressive power of BLL [8] is its *malleability*: the conclusion of any proof π can be modified in many different ways without altering its structure. Malleability is not only crucial to make the system expressive, but also to prove that BLLP enjoys cut-elimination. In this section, we give four different ways of modifying a sequent in such a way as to preserve its derivability. Two of them are anyway expected and also hold in BLL, while the other two only make sense in a polarized setting.

First of all, taking smaller formulas (i.e., more general — cf. [19, §3.3, p. 21]) preserves derivability:

Lemma 1 (Subtyping). *If $\pi \triangleright \vdash \Gamma, \mathbf{A}$ and $\mathbf{A} \sqsupseteq \mathbf{B}$, then there is $\rho \triangleright \vdash \Gamma, \mathbf{B}$ such that $\pi \sim \rho$.*

Substituting resource variables for polynomials itself preserves typability:

Lemma 2 (Substitution). *Let $\pi \triangleright \vdash \Gamma$. Then there is a proof $\pi\{x/p\}$ of $\vdash \Gamma\{x/p\}$. Moreover, $\pi\{x/p\} \sim \pi$.*

Both Lemma 1 and Lemma 2 can be proved by easy inductions on the structure of π.

As we have already mentioned, one of the key differences between Linear Logic and its polarized version is that in the latter, arbitrary proofs can potentially be duplicated (and erased) along the cut-elimination process, while in the former only special ones, namely boxes, can. This is, again, a consequence of the fundamentally different nature of structural rules in the two systems. Since BLLP is a refinement of LLP, this means that the same phenomenon is expected. But beware: in a bounded setting, contraction is not symmetric, i.e., the two copies of the proof π we are duplicating are not identical to π.

What we need to prove, then, is that proofs can indeed be *split* in BLLP:

Lemma 3 (Splitting). *If* $\pi \triangleright \vdash \mathcal{N}, [P]_x^p$ *is a* $\otimes$*-tree and* $p \sqsupseteq r + s$ *then there exist* $\mathcal{M}, \mathcal{O}$ *such that* $\rho \triangleright \vdash \mathcal{M}, [P]_x^r$, $\sigma \triangleright \vdash \mathcal{O}, [P\{x/y + r\}]_y^s$. *Moreover,* $\mathcal{N} \sqsubseteq \mathcal{M} \uplus \mathcal{O}$ *and* $\rho \sim \pi \sim \sigma$.

Observe that not every proof can be split, but only $\otimes$-trees can. The proof of Lemma 3 is not trivial and requires some auxiliary results (see [9] for more details). A parametric version of splitting is also necessary here:

Lemma 4 (Parametric Splitting). *If* $\pi \triangleright \vdash \mathcal{N}, [P]_x^p$, *where* π *is a* $\otimes$*-tree and* $p \sqsupseteq \sum_{x<r} s$, *then there exists* $\rho \triangleright \vdash \mathcal{M}, [P]_x^s$ *where* $\sum_{x<r} \mathcal{M} \sqsupseteq \mathcal{N}$ *and* $\rho \sim \pi$.

While splitting allows to cope with duplication, parametric splitting implies that an arbitrary $\otimes$-tree can be modified so as to be lifted into a box through one of its auxiliary doors. Please observe that p^π continues to be such an upper bound even if any natural number is substituted for any of its free variables, an easy consequence of Lemma 2. The following is useful when dealing with cuts involving the rule $?d$:

Lemma 5. *If* $q \sqsupseteq 1$, *then* $\sum_{z<q} [M]_y^r \sqsubseteq [M]_y^r \{z/0\}$.

3 Cut Elimination

In this section, we give some ideas about how cuts can be eliminated from BLLP proofs.

Logical cuts (i.e., those in which the two immediate subproofs end with a rule introducing the formula involved in the cut) can be reduced as in LLP [24], but exploiting malleability whenever polynomials need to be modified. This defines the reduction relation $\longmapsto$ (see [9] for more details). All instances of the Cut rule which are not logical are said to be *commutative*, and induce an equivalent relation $\cong$ on proofs. In general, not all cuts in a proof are logical, but any cut can be turned into a logical one:

Lemma 6. *Let* π *be any proof containing an occurrence of the rule* Cut. *Then, there are two proofs* ρ *and* σ *such that* $\pi \cong \rho \longmapsto \sigma$, *where* ρ *can be effectively obtained from* π.

The proof of Lemma 6 goes as follows: given any instance of the Cut rule

$$\frac{\pi \triangleright \vdash \Gamma, [N]_x^p \quad \rho \triangleright \vdash \mathcal{N}, [P]_x^p}{\vdash \Gamma, \mathcal{N}} \text{ Cut}$$

consider the path (i.e., the sequence of formula occurrences) starting from $[N]_x^p$ and going upward inside π, and the path starting from $[P]_x^p$ and going upward inside ρ. Both paths end either at an Ax rule or at an instance of a rule introducing the main connective in N or P. The game to play is then to show that these two paths can always be *shortened* by way of commutations, thus exposing the underlying logical cut.

Lemma 6 is implicitly defining a cut-elimination procedure: given any instance of the Cut rule, turn it into a logical cut by the procedure from Lemma 6, then fire it. This way we are implicitly defining another reduction relation $\longrightarrow$. The next question is the following: is this procedure going to terminate for every proof π (i.e., is $\longrightarrow$ strongly, or weakly, normalizing)? How many steps does it take to turn π to its cut-free form?

Actually, $\longrightarrow$ produces reduction sequences of very long length, but is anyway strongly normalizing. A relatively easy way to prove it goes as follows: any BLLP proof π corresponds to a LLP sequent calculus proof $\langle \pi \rangle$, and the latter itself corresponds to a polarized proof net $\langle\!\langle \pi \rangle\!\rangle$ [25]. Moreover, $\pi \longrightarrow \rho$ implies that $\langle\!\langle \pi \rangle\!\rangle \mapsto \langle\!\langle \rho \rangle\!\rangle$, where $\mapsto$ is the canonical cut-elimination relation on polarized proof-nets. Finally, $\langle\!\langle \pi \rangle\!\rangle$ is identical to $\langle\!\langle \rho \rangle\!\rangle$ whenever $\pi \cong \rho$. Since $\mapsto$ is known to be strongly normalizing, $\longrightarrow$ does not admit infinite reduction sequences:

Proposition 1 (Cut-Elimination). *The relation $\longrightarrow$ is strongly normalizing.*

This does not mean that cut-elimination can be performed in (reasonably) bounded time. Already in BLL this can take exponential time: the whole of Elementary Linear Logic [18] can be embedded into it.

3.1 Soundness

To get a soundness result, then, we somehow need to restrict the underlying reduction relation $\longrightarrow$. Following [19], one could indeed define a subset of $\longrightarrow$ just by imposing that in dereliction, contraction, or box cut-elimination steps, the involved $\otimes$-trees are closed. Moreover, we could stipulate that reduction is external, i.e., it cannot take place inside boxes. Closed and external reduction, however, is not enough to simulate head-reduction in the $\lambda\mu$-calculus, and not being able to reduce under the scope of μ-abstractions does not make much sense anyway. We are forced, then, to consider an extension of closed reduction. The fact that this new notion of reduction still guarantees polynomial bounds is technically a remarkable strengthening with respect to BLL's Soundness Theorem [19].

There is a quite natural notion of *downward* path in proofs: from any occurrence of a negative formula **N**, just proceed downward until you either find (the main premise of) a Cut rule, or a conclusion. In the first case, the occurrence of **N** is said to be *active*, in the second it is said to be *passive*. Proofs can then be endowed with a new notion of reduction: all dereliction, contraction or box digging cuts can be fired only if the negative formula occurrences in its rightmost argument are all passive. In the literature, this is sometimes called a *special cut* (e.g. [3]). Moreover, reduction needs to be external, as usual. This notion of reduction, as we will see, is enough to mimic head reduction, and is denoted with $\Longrightarrow$.

The next step consists in associating a weight, in the form of a resource polynomial, to every proof, similarly to what happens in BLL. The *pre-weight* $\pi^\diamond$ of a proof π with conclusion $\vdash \mathbf{A}_1, \ldots, \mathbf{A}_n$ consists in:
- a resource polynomial p^π.
- n disjoints sets of resource variables $S_1^\pi, \ldots, S_n^\pi$, each corresponding to a formula in $\mathbf{A}_1, \ldots, \mathbf{A}_n$; if this does not cause ambiguity, the set of resource variables corresponding to a formula $\mathbf{A}$ will be denoted by $S^\pi(\mathbf{A})$. Similarly for $S^\pi(\Gamma)$, where Γ is a multiset of formulas.

If π has pre-weight $p^\pi, S_1^\pi, \ldots, S_n^\pi$, then the *weight* q^π of π is simply p^π where, however, all the variables in $S_1^\pi, \ldots, S_n^\pi$ are substituted with 0: $p^\pi\{\cup_{i=1}^n S_i^\pi/0\}$. The pre-weight of a proof π is defined by induction on the structure of π (see [9] for more details). The idea is that every occurrence of negative formulas is attributed a fresh variable, which later is instantiated with either 0 (if the formula is passive) or 1 (if it is active). This allows to discriminate between the case in which rules can "produce" time complexity along the cut-elimination, and the case in which they do not. Ultimately, this leads to:

Lemma 7. *If $\pi \cong \rho$, then $q^\pi = q^\rho$. If $\pi \Longrightarrow \rho$, then $q^\pi \sqsupset q^\rho$.*

The main idea behind Lemma 7 is that even if the logical cut we perform when going from π to ρ is "dangerous" (e.g. a contraction) *and* the involved $\otimes$-tree is not closed, the residual negative rules have null weight, because they are passive.

We can conclude that:

Theorem 1 (Polystep Soundness). *For every proof π, if $\pi \Longrightarrow^n \rho$, then $n \leq q^\pi$.*

In a sense, then, the weight of any proof π is a resource polynomial which can be easily computed from π (rules in [9] are anyway inductively defined), but which is also an upper bound on the number of logical cut-elimination steps separating π from its normal form. Please observe that q^π continues to be such an upper bound even if any natural number is substituted for any of its free variables, an easy consequence of Lemma 2.

Why then, are we talking about *polynomial* bounds? In BLL, and as a consequence also in BLLP, one can write programs in such a way that the size of the input is reflected by a resource variable occurring in its type. As an example, the type of (Church encodings of) binary strings of length at most x could be the following in BLLP:

$$(X \multimap^1 X) \multimap^x (X \multimap^1 X) \multimap^x (X \multimap^1 X)$$

(where $N \multimap^p M$ stands for $?_p N^\perp \mathbin{\bindnasrepma} M$). The weight, then, turns out to be a tool to study the behavior of terms seen as functions taking arguments of varying length. A more in-depth discussion about these issues is outside the scope of this paper. Please refer to [19].

4 A Type System for the λμ-Calculus

We describe here a version of the λμ-calculus as introduced by de Groote [11]. Terms are as follows

$$t, u ::= x \mid \lambda x.t \mid \mu\alpha.t \mid [\alpha]t \mid (t)t,$$

where x and α range over two infinite disjoint sets of variables (called λ-variables and μ-variables, respectively). In contrast with the λμ-calculus as originally formulated by Parigot [27], μ-abstraction is not restricted to terms of the form $[\alpha]t$ here.

4.1 Notions of Reduction

The reduction rules we consider are the following ones:

$$(\lambda x.t)u \rightarrow_\beta t[^u/_x]; \qquad (\mu\alpha.t)u \rightarrow_\mu \mu\alpha.t[^{[\alpha](v)u}/_{[\alpha]v}]; \qquad \mu\alpha.[\alpha]t \rightarrow_\theta t;$$

where, as usual, $\rightarrow_\theta$ can be fired only if $\alpha \notin FV(t)$. In the following, $\rightarrow$ is just $\rightarrow_{\beta\mu\theta}$. In so-called *weak reduction*, denoted $\rightarrow_w$, reduction simply cannot take place in the scope of binders, while *head reduction*, denoted $\rightarrow_h$, is a generalization of the same concept from pure λ-calculus [13]. Details are in Figure 2. Please

$$\frac{t \rightarrow u}{t \rightarrow_w u} \qquad \frac{t \rightarrow_w u}{tv \rightarrow_w uv} \qquad \frac{t \rightarrow_w u}{[\alpha]t \rightarrow_w [\alpha]u}$$

$$\frac{t \rightarrow_w u}{t \rightarrow_h u} \qquad \frac{t \rightarrow_h u}{\lambda x.t \rightarrow_h \lambda x.u} \qquad \frac{t \rightarrow_h u}{\mu\alpha.t \rightarrow_h \mu\alpha.u}$$

Fig. 2. Weak and Head Notions of Reduction

notice how in head reduction, redexes can indeed be fired even if they lie in the scope of λ-or-μ-abstractions, which, however, cannot themselves be involved in a redex. This harmless restriction, which corresponds to taking the *outermost* reduction order, is needed for technical reasons that will become apparent soon.

4.2 The Type System

Following Laurent [25], types are just negative formulas. Not all of them can be used as types, however: in particular, $N \bindnasrepma M$ is a legal type only if N is in the form $?_{x<p}O^\perp$, and we use the following abbreviation in this case: $N \multimap_x^p M = (?_{x<p}N^\perp) \bindnasrepma M$. In particular, if M is $\perp$ then $N \multimap_x^p M$ can be abbreviated as $\neg_x^p N$. *Typing formulas* are negative formulas which are either $\perp$, or X, or in the form $N \multimap_x^p M$ (where N and M are typing formulas themselves). A *modal formula* is one in the form $?_{x<p}N^\perp$ (where N is a typing formula). Please

observe that all the constructions from Section 2.1 (including labellings, sums, etc.) easily apply to typing formulas. Finally, we use the following abbreviation for labeled modal formulas: $_y^q[N]_x^p = [?_{y<q}N^\perp]_x^p$.

A *typing judgment* is a statement in the form $\Gamma \vdash t : \mathbf{N} \mid \Delta$, where:
- Γ is a context assigning labelled modal formulas to λ-variables;
- t is a $\lambda\mu$-term;
- $\mathbf{N}$ is a typing formula;
- Δ is a context assigning labelled typing formulas to μ-variables.

The way typing judgments are defined allows to see them as BLLP sequents. This way, again, various concepts from Section 2.2 can be lifted up from sequents to judgments, and this remarkably includes the subtyping relation $\sqsubseteq$.

Typing rules are in Figure 3. The typing rule for applications, in particular,

$$\frac{1 \sqsubseteq p,\, r\{y/0\} \sqsubseteq q,\, M \sqsubseteq N\{y/0\}}{\Gamma, x :{}_z^r[N]_y^p \vdash x : [M]_z^q \mid \Delta} \text{ var} \qquad \frac{\Gamma, x :{}_z^s[N]_y^p \vdash t : [M]_y^q \mid \Delta \qquad r \sqsupseteq q,\, r \sqsupseteq p}{\Gamma \vdash \lambda x.t : [N \multimap_z^s M]_y^r \mid \Delta} \text{ abs}$$

$$\frac{\Theta \vdash t : [N \multimap_x^p M]_y^q \mid \Psi \qquad \Xi \vdash u : [N]_x^p \mid \Phi \qquad \begin{array}{l} h \sqsupseteq q \\ \Gamma \sqsubseteq \Theta \uplus \Upsilon \\ \Delta \sqsubseteq \Psi \uplus \Pi \end{array} \qquad \begin{array}{l} k \sqsupseteq q \\ \Upsilon \sqsubseteq \sum_{b<h} \Xi \\ \Pi \sqsubseteq \sum_{b<h} \Phi \end{array}}{\Gamma \vdash (t)u : [M]_y^k \mid \Delta} \text{ app}$$

$$\frac{\Gamma \vdash t : \mathbf{N} \mid \alpha : \mathbf{M}, \Delta \qquad \mathbf{L} \sqsubseteq \mathbf{N} \uplus \mathbf{M}}{\Gamma \vdash [\alpha]t : [\perp]_z^q \mid \alpha : \mathbf{L}, \Delta} \text{ }\mu\text{-name} \qquad \frac{\Gamma \vdash t : [\perp]_z^q \mid \beta : \mathbf{N}, \Delta}{\Gamma \vdash \mu\beta t : \mathbf{N} \mid \Delta} \text{ }\mu\text{-abs}$$

Fig. 3. Type Assignment Rules

can be seen as overly complicated. In fact, all premises except the first two are there to allow the necessary degree of malleability for contexts, without which even subject reduction would be in danger. Alternatively, one could consider an explicit subtyping rule, the price being the loss of syntax directedness. Indeed, all malleability results from Section 2.3 can be transferred to the just defined type assignment system.

4.3 Subject Reduction and Polystep Soundness

The aim of this section is to show that *head* reduction preserves types, and as a corollary, that the number of reduction steps to normal form is bounded by a polynomial, along the same lines as in Theorem 1. Actually, the latter will easily follow from the former, because so-called Subject Reduction will be formulated (and in a sense proved) with a precise correspondence between type derivations and proofs in mind.

In order to facilitate this task, Subject Reduction is proved on a modified type-assignment system, called $\mathsf{BLLP}_{\lambda\mu}^{\mathsf{mult}}$ which can be proved equivalent to $\mathsf{BLLP}_{\lambda\mu}$. The only fundamental difference between the two systems lies in how structural rules, i.e., contraction and weakening, are reflected into the type system. As we have already noticed, $\mathsf{BLLP}_{\lambda\mu}$ has an *additive* flavour, since structural rules are implicitly applied in binary and 0-ary typing rules. This, in particular, makes the system syntax directed and type derivations more compact. The only problem with this approach is that the correspondence between type derivations and proofs is too weak to be directly lifted to a dynamic level (e.g., one step in $\rightarrow_h$ could correspond to possibly many steps in $\Longrightarrow$). In $\mathsf{BLLP}_{\lambda\mu}^{\mathsf{mult}}$, on the contrary, structural rules are explicit, and turns it into a useful technical tool to prove properties of $\mathsf{BLLP}_{\lambda\mu}$. The rules of $\mathsf{BLLP}_{\lambda\mu}^{\mathsf{mult}}$ are in [9].

Whenever derivability in one of the systems needs to be distinguished from derivability on the other, we will put the system's name in subscript position (e.g. $\Gamma \vdash_{\mathsf{BLLP}_{\lambda\mu}^{\mathsf{mult}}} t : \mathbf{N} \mid \Delta$). Not so surprisingly, $\mathsf{BLLP}_{\lambda\mu}$ and $\mathsf{BLLP}_{\lambda\mu}^{\mathsf{mult}}$ type exactly the same class of terms:

Lemma 8. $\Gamma \vdash_{\mathsf{BLLP}_{\lambda\mu}^{\mathsf{mult}}} t : \mathbf{N} \mid \Delta$ *iff* $\Gamma \vdash_{\mathsf{BLLP}_{\lambda\mu}} t : \mathbf{N} \mid \Delta$

Proof. The left-to-right implication follows from weakening and contraction lemmas for $\mathsf{BLLP}_{\lambda\mu}$, which are easy to prove. The right-to-left implication is more direct, since additive var and app are multiplicatively derivable. □

Given a $\mathsf{BLLP}_{\lambda\mu}^{\mathsf{mult}}$ type derivation π, one can define a BLLP proof π° by induction on the structure of π, closely following Laurent's translation [25]. This way one not only gets some guiding principles for subject-reduction, but can also prove that the underlying transformation process is nothing more than cut-elimination:

Theorem 2 (Subject Reduction). *Let* $\pi \vartriangleright \Gamma \vdash t : \mathbf{N} \mid \Delta$ *and suppose* $t \rightarrow_h u$. *Then there is* $\rho \vartriangleright \Gamma \vdash u : \mathbf{N} \mid \Delta$. *Moreover* $\pi^\circ \Longrightarrow^+ \rho^\circ$.

Observe how performing head reduction corresponds to $\Longrightarrow$, instead of the more permissive $\longrightarrow$. The following, then, is an easy corollary of Theorem 2 and Theorem 1:

Theorem 3 (Polystep Soundness for Terms). *Let* $\pi \vartriangleright \Gamma \vdash t : \mathbf{N} \mid \Delta$ *and let* $t \rightarrow_h^n u$. *Then* $n \leq q^{\pi^\circ}$.

5 Control Operators

In this section, we show that $\mathsf{BLLP}_{\lambda\mu}$ is powerful enough to type (the natural encoding of) two popular control operators, namely Scheme's callcc and Felleisen's $\mathcal{C}$ [2,25].

Control operators change the evaluation context of an expression. This is simulated by the operators μ and $[\cdot]$ which can, respectively, save and restore a stack of arguments to be passed to subterms. This idea, by the way, is the starting point of an extension of Krivine's machine for de Groote's $\lambda\mu$ [13] (see Section 6).

5.1 `callcc`

An encoding of `callcc` into the $\lambda\mu$-calculus could be, e.g.,

$$\kappa = \lambda x.\mu\alpha.[\alpha](x)\lambda y.\mu\beta.[\alpha]y.$$

Does κ have the operational behavior we would expect from `callcc`? First of all, it should satisfy the following property (see [14]): if $k \notin FV(e)$, then $(\kappa)\lambda k.e \to^* e$. Indeed:

$$(\lambda x.\mu\alpha.[\alpha](x)\lambda y.\mu\beta.[\alpha]y)\lambda k.e \to_{\mathsf{h}} \mu\alpha.[\alpha](\lambda k.e)\lambda y.\mu\beta.[\alpha]y \to_{\mathsf{h}} \mu\alpha.[\alpha]e \to_{\mathsf{h}} e,$$

where the second β-reduction step replaces $e\{k/\lambda y.\mu\beta.[\alpha]y\}$ with e since $k \notin FV(e)$ by hypothesis. It is important to observe that the second step replaces a variable for a term with a free μ-variable, hence weak reduction gets stuck. Actually, our notion of weak reduction is even more restrictive than the one proposed by de Groote in [13]. Head reduction, on the contrary, is somehow more liberal. Moreover, it is also straightforward to check that the reduction of `callcc` in [27, §3.4] can be simulated by head reduction on κ.

But is κ typable in $\mathsf{BLLP}_{\lambda\mu}$? The answer is positive: a derivation typing it with (an instance of) Pierce's law is in Figure 4, where π is the obvious derivation of $x : {}^{r}_{v}[(X \multimap^s Y) \multimap^1 X]^1 \vdash x : [(X \multimap^s Y) \multimap^1 X]^r_v \mid \alpha : [X]^0$.

$$
\dfrac{
  \dfrac{
    \pi \qquad
    \dfrac{
      \dfrac{
        \dfrac{
          \dfrac{}{y : {}^{s}[X]^1 \vdash y : [X]^s \mid \alpha : [X]^0, \beta : [Y]^0}\ \mathsf{var}
        }{y : {}^{s}[X]^1 \vdash [\alpha]y : [\bot]^0 \mid \alpha : [X]^s, \beta : [Y]^0}\ \mu\text{-}\mathsf{name}
      }{y : {}^{s}[X]^1 \vdash \mu\beta.[\alpha]y : [Y]^0 \mid \alpha : [X]^s}\ \mu\text{-}\mathsf{abs}
    }{\vdash \lambda y.\mu\beta.[\alpha]y : [X \multimap^s Y]^1 \mid \alpha : [X]^s}\ \mathsf{abs}
  }{x : {}^{r}_{v}[(X \multimap^s Y) \multimap^1 X]^1 \vdash (x)\lambda y.\mu\beta.[\alpha]y : [X]^r_v \mid \alpha : [X]_v^{\sum_{v<r} s}}\ \mathsf{app}
  \qquad
  \begin{array}{l} k \sqsupseteq r + \sum_{v<r} s \\ k \sqsupseteq 1 \end{array}
}{
  \dfrac{
    x : {}^{r}_{v}[(X \multimap^s Y) \multimap^1 X]^1 \vdash [\alpha](x)\lambda y.\mu\beta.[\alpha]y : [\bot]^1 \mid \alpha : [X]^k
  }{
    \dfrac{x : {}^{r}_{v}[(X \multimap^s Y) \multimap^1 X]^1 \vdash \mu\alpha.[\alpha](x)\lambda y.\mu\beta.[\alpha]y : [X]^k \mid}{\vdash \lambda x.\mu\alpha.[\alpha](x)\lambda y.\mu\beta.[\alpha]y : [((X \multimap^s Y) \multimap^1 X) \multimap^r_v X]^k \mid}\ \mathsf{abs}
  }\ \mu\text{-}\mathsf{abs}
}\ \mu\text{-}\mathsf{name}
$$

Fig. 4. A Type Derivation for κ

5.2 Felleisen's $\mathcal{C}$

The canonical way to encode Felleisen's $\mathcal{C}$ as a $\lambda\mu$-term is as the term $\aleph = \lambda f.\mu\alpha.(f)\lambda x.[\alpha]x$. Its behavior should be something like

$$(\aleph)wt_1 \ldots t_k \to (w)\lambda x.(x)t_1 \ldots t_k,$$

$$\frac{\overline{x : {}^r[X]^1 \vdash x : [X]^r}\text{ var}}{\frac{x : {}^r[X]^1 \vdash [\alpha]x : [\bot]^0 \mid \alpha : [X]^r}{\frac{\vdash \lambda x.[\alpha]x : [\neg^r X]^1 \mid \alpha : [X]^r}{\frac{\sigma \quad f : {}^h_v[\neg^1\neg^r X]^1 \vdash (f)\lambda x.[\alpha]x : [\bot]^h_v \mid \alpha : [X]^{\Sigma_{v<h} r}}{\frac{f : {}^h_v[\neg^1\neg^r X]^1 \vdash \mu\alpha.(f)\lambda x.[\alpha]x : [X]^{\Sigma_{v<h} r} \mid}{\vdash \lambda f.\mu\alpha.(f)\lambda x.[\alpha]x : [\neg^1\neg^r X \multimap^h_v X]^k}\text{ abs}}\text{ }\mu\text{-abs}}\text{ app}}\text{ abs}}\text{ }\mu\text{-name}}$$

$$k \sqsupseteq 1 \qquad k \sqsupseteq \Sigma_{v<h} r$$

Fig. 5. A Type Derivation for $\aleph$

where $x \notin FV(t_1, \ldots, t_k)$, i.e., x is a fresh variable. Indeed:

$$(\aleph)wt_1 \ldots t_k \to_h (\mu\alpha.(w)\lambda x.[\alpha](x))t_1 \ldots t_k \to^k_h \mu\alpha.(w)\lambda x.[\alpha](x)t_1 \ldots t_k.$$

A type derivation for $\aleph$ is in Figure 5, where σ is a derivation for

$$f : {}^h_v[\neg^1\neg^r X]^1 \vdash f : [\neg^1\neg^r X]^h_v \mid \alpha : [X]^0.$$

It is worth noting that weak reduction is strong enough to properly simulating the operational behavior of $\mathcal{C}$. It is not possible to type $\mathcal{C}$ in Parigot's $\lambda\mu$, unless an open term is used. Alternatively, a free continuation constant must be used (obtaining yet another calculus [2]). This is one of the reasons why we picked the version of $\lambda\mu$-calculus proposed by de Groote over other calculi. See [12] for a discussion about $\lambda\mu$-and-λ-calculi and Felleisen's $\mathcal{C}$.

6 Abstract Machines

Theorem 3, the main result of this paper so far, tells us that the number of *head-reduction steps* performed by terms typable in $\text{BLLP}_{\lambda\mu}$ is bounded by the weight of the underlying type derivation. One may wonder, however, whether taking the number of reduction steps as a measure of term complexity is sensible or not — substitutions involve arguments which can possibly be much bigger than the original term. Recent work by Accattoli and the first author [1], however, shows that in the case of λ-calculus endowed with head reduction, the unitary cost model is polynomially invariant with respect to Turing machines. We conjecture that those invariance results can be extended to the $\lambda\mu$-calculus.

It can be shown that $\text{BLLP}_{\lambda\mu}$ is polystep sound for another cost model, namely the one induced by de Groote's K, an abstract machine for the $\lambda\mu$-calculus. This is done following a similar proof for PCF typed with linear dependent types [7] and Krivine's Abstract Machine (of which K is a natural extension). The main idea consists in extending BLLP to a type system for K's configurations, this way defining a *weight* for each of them in the form of a resource polynomial. The weight, as expected, can then be shown to decrease at each K's computation step. It is worth noting that the weight defined this way is fundamentally different than the one from Section 3.1. See [9] for some more details.

7 Conclusions

In this paper we have presented some evidence that the enrichment to Intuitionistic Linear Logic provided by Bounded Linear Logic is robust enough to be lifted to Polarized Linear Logic and the $\lambda\mu$-calculus. This paves the way towards a complexity-sensitive type system, which on the one hand guarantees that typable terms can be reduced to their normal forms in a number of reduction steps which can be read from their type derivation, and on the other allows to naturally type useful control operators.

Many questions have been purposely left open here: in particular, the language of programs is the pure, constant-free, $\lambda\mu$-calculus, whereas the structure of types is minimal, not allowing any form of polymorphism. We expect that endowing BLLP with second order quantification or $\text{BLLP}_{\lambda\mu}$ with constants and recursion should not be particularly problematic, although laborious: the same extensions have already been considered in similar settings in the absence of control [19,7]. Actually, a particularly interesting direction would be to turn $\text{BLLP}_{\lambda\mu}$ into a type system for Ong and Stewart's μPCF [26], this way extending the linear dependent paradigm to a language with control. This is of course outside the scope of this paper, whose purpose was only to delineate the basic ingredients of the logic and the underlying type system.

As we stressed in the introduction, we are convinced this work is the first one giving a time complexity analysis methodology for a programming language with higher-order functions *and control*. One could of course object that complexity analysis of $\lambda\mu$-terms could be performed by translating them into equivalent λ-terms, e.g. by way of a suitable CPS-transform [11]. This, however, would force the programmer (or whomever doing complexity analysis) to deal with programs which are structurally different from the original one. And of course, translations could introduce inefficiencies, which are maybe harmless from a purely qualitative viewpoint, but which could make a difference for complexity analysis.

References

1. Accattoli, B., Dal Lago, U.: On the invariance of the unitary cost model for head reduction. In: RTA. LIPIcs, vol. 15, pp. 22–37 (2012)
2. Ariola, Z.M., Herbelin, H.: Minimal classical logic and control operators. In: Baeten, J.C.M., Lenstra, J.K., Parrow, J., Woeginger, G.J. (eds.) ICALP 2003. LNCS, vol. 2719, pp. 871–885. Springer, Heidelberg (2003)
3. Baillot, P., Coppola, P., Dal Lago, U.: Light logics and optimal reduction: Completeness and complexity. Information and Computation 209(2), 118–142 (2011)
4. Baillot, P., Mazza, D.: Linear logic by levels and bounded time complexity. Theoretical Computer Science 411(2), 470–503 (2010)
5. Baillot, P., Terui, K.: Light types for polynomial time computation in lambda-calculus. Information and Computation 207(1), 41–62 (2009)
6. Curien, P.-L., Herbelin, H.: The duality of computation. In: ICFP, pp. 233–243. ACM (2000)
7. Dal Lago, U., Gaboardi, M.: Linear dependent types and relative completeness. Logical Methods in Computer Science 8(4) (2012)

8. Dal Lago, U., Hofmann, M.: Bounded linear logic, revisited. In: Curien, P.-L. (ed.) TLCA 2009. LNCS, vol. 5608, pp. 80–94. Springer, Heidelberg (2009)
9. Dal Lago, U., Pellitta, G.: Complexity analysis in presence of control operators and higher-order functions (long version), http://arxiv.org/abs/1310.1763
10. de Bakker, J.W., de Bruin, A., Zucker, J.: Mathematical theory of program correctness. Prentice-Hall International Series in Computer Science. Prentice Hall (1980)
11. de Groote, P.: A CPS-translation of the $\lambda\mu$-calculus. In: Tison, S. (ed.) CAAP 1994. LNCS, vol. 787, pp. 85–99. Springer, Heidelberg (1994)
12. de Groote, P.: On the relation between the $\lambda\mu$-calculus and the syntactic theory of sequential control. In: Pfenning, F. (ed.) LPAR 1994. LNCS, vol. 822, pp. 31–43. Springer, Heidelberg (1994)
13. de Groote, P.: An environment machine for the $\lambda\mu$-calculus. Mathematical Structures in Computer Science 8(6), 637–669 (1998)
14. Felleisen, M.: On the expressive power of programming languages. In: Jones, N. (ed.) ESOP 1990. LNCS, vol. 432, pp. 134–151. Springer, Heidelberg (1990)
15. Gaboardi, M., Ronchi Della Rocca, S.: A soft type assignment system for *lambda*-calculus. In: Duparc, J., Henzinger, T.A. (eds.) CSL 2007. LNCS, vol. 4646, pp. 253–267. Springer, Heidelberg (2007)
16. Girard, J.-Y.: Linear logic. Theoretical Computer Science 50(1), 1–101 (1987)
17. Girard, J.-Y.: A new constructive logic: Classical logic. Mathematical Structures in Computer Science 1(3), 255–296 (1991)
18. Girard, J.-Y.: Light linear logic. Information and Computation 143(2), 175–204 (1998)
19. Girard, J.-Y., Scedrov, A., Scott, P.: Bounded linear logic: a modular approach to polynomial-time computability. Theoretical Computer Science 97(1), 1–66 (1992)
20. Griffin, T.: A formulae-as-types notion of control. In: POPL, pp. 47–58. ACM Press (1990)
21. Gulwani, S.: Speed: Symbolic complexity bound analysis. In: Bouajjani, A., Maler, O. (eds.) CAV 2009. LNCS, vol. 5643, pp. 51–62. Springer, Heidelberg (2009)
22. Jost, S., Hammond, K., Loidl, H.-W., Hofmann, M.: Static determination of quantitative resource usage for higher-order programs. In: POPL, Madrid, Spain. ACM Press (2010)
23. Lafont, Y.: Soft linear logic and polynomial time. Theoretical Computer Science 318(1), 163–180 (2004)
24. Laurent, O.: Étude de la polarisation en logique. Thèse de doctorat, Université Aix-Marseille II (March 2002)
25. Laurent, O.: Polarized proof-nets and $\lambda\mu$-calculus. Theoretical Computer Science 290(1), 161–188 (2003)
26. Ong, C.-H.L., Stewart, C.A.: A Curry-Howard foundation for functional computation with control. In: POPL, pp. 215–227. ACM Press (1997)
27. Parigot, M.: $\lambda\mu$-calculus: an algorithmic interpretation of classical natural deduction. In: Voronkov, A. (ed.) LPAR 1992. LNCS (LNAI), vol. 624, pp. 190–201. Springer, Heidelberg (1992)
28. Schöpp, U.: Stratified bounded affine logic for logarithmic space. In: LICS, pp. 411–420 (2007)
29. Wilhelm, R., Engblom, J., Ermedahl, A., Holsti, N., Thesing, S., Whalley, D., Bernat, G., Ferdinand, C., Heckmann, R., Mitra, T., Mueller, F., Puaut, I., Puschner, P., Staschulat, J., Stenström, P.: The worst case execution time problem - overview of methods and survey of tools. ACM Transactions on Embedded Computing Systems (2008)

Zenon Modulo: When Achilles Outruns the Tortoise Using Deduction Modulo[*]

David Delahaye[1], Damien Doligez[2], Frédéric Gilbert[2], Pierre Halmagrand[1], and Olivier Hermant[3]

[1] Cedric/Cnam/Inria, Paris, France
David.Delahaye@cnam.fr, Pierre.Halmagrand@inria.fr
[2] Inria, Paris, France
{Damien.Doligez,Frederic.Charles.Gilbert}@inria.fr
[3] CRI, MINES ParisTech, Fontainebleau, France
Olivier.Hermant@mines-paristech.fr

Abstract. We propose an extension of the tableau-based first order automated theorem prover Zenon to deduction modulo. The theory of deduction modulo is an extension of predicate calculus, which allows us to rewrite terms as well as propositions, and which is well suited for proof search in axiomatic theories, as it turns axioms into rewrite rules. We also present a heuristic to perform this latter step automatically, and assess our approach by providing some experimental results obtained on the benchmarks provided by the TPTP library, where this heuristic is able to prove difficult problems in set theory in particular. Finally, we describe an additional backend for Zenon that outputs proof certificates for Dedukti, which is a proof checker based on the $\lambda\Pi$-calculus modulo.

Keywords: Tableaux, Deduction Modulo, Rewriting, Automated Theorem Proving, Proof Checking, Zenon, Dedukti.

1 Introduction

Proof search in axiomatic theories, such as Peano arithmetic and set theory, or decidable fragments (Presburger arithmetic, arrays and pointers, axiomatizations of memory models, etc.) is receiving increasing attention, driven by the applications of formal methods in industrial settings. Leaving axioms wandering among the hypotheses is not a reasonable option, as it induces a combinatorial explosion in the proof search space. Moreover, axioms themselves generally do not bear any specific meaning that could be used by automated theorem provers.

A solution to address this problem is to use a cutting-edge combination of a first order automated theorem proving method (resolution) with theory-specific decision procedures. This approach has drawbacks, namely the need for a specific decision procedure for each given theory. This imposes a decidability constraint on the theories that we can work with, as well as a lack of automatability. As

---

[*] This work is supported by the BWare project [13] (ANR-12-INSE-0010) funded by the INS programme of the French National Research Agency (ANR).

a consequence, we lose genericity over the theories. However, SMT solvers are well-suited for industrial applications, where those problems are not a concern.

Our approach is to make use of the advances of deduction modulo [9], which allows us to transform axioms into rewrite rules. For example, Peano arithmetic or Zermelo set theory can be expressed without axioms. This way, we turn proof search among the axioms into computations, avoiding unnecessary blowups, and we shrink the size of proofs by recording only their meaningful steps. Deduction modulo has already been experimented within first order automated theorem provers. This is the case of iProver Modulo [7], where a resolution-based automated theorem prover has been extended to deduction modulo. This is also the case of Super Zenon [10], which is an extension of the Zenon tableau-based automated theorem prover [4] to superdeduction [5], a variant of deduction modulo.

In this paper, we go further along this path by adapting Zenon to deduction modulo itself, and following some of the ideas of [3]. Compared to the approach of Super Zenon, this new tool, called Zenon Modulo, allows us to capture more computational aspects of theories, since deduction modulo also adds the possibility to rewrite over terms, while superdeduction only considers rewrite rules over propositions. Moreover, it will also allow us to compare this extension with that of iProver Modulo, and assess the impact of the integration of deduction modulo into different proof search techniques (i.e. resolution and tableaux).

Another contribution introduced in this paper is a heuristic that automatically transforms any set of axioms (and therefore any theory) into a set of rewrite rules, which can be used during the proof search step of Zenon. With this heuristic, we observe significant improvements over the pure axiomatic proof search of Zenon, as can be seen in the experimental results obtained on the set of problems provided by the TPTP library [12]. In particular, this heuristic appears to be quite appropriate for set theory, where we are able to prove difficult problems.

It should be noted that in the short term, we also plan to work on the dual approach, which consists in building theories modulo manually. In particular, we aim to consider the set theory of the B method [1], in order to apply Zenon Modulo to the verification of proof obligations coming from industrial applications, which is one of the goals of the BWare project [13].

One of the major interests of Zenon to experiment deduction modulo resides in its certifying approach, i.e. its ability to produce proof certificates that can be skeptically checked by other proof assistants such as Coq or Isabelle. Extending Zenon to deduction modulo means to also provide a backend able to check proofs in deduction modulo. To do so, we have provided Zenon with a backend that outputs proofs for Dedukti [2], a proof checker based on the $\lambda\Pi$-calculus modulo.

This paper is organized as follows: in Sec. 2, we first introduce the principles of deduction modulo; we then present, in Sec. 3, the rules of Zenon for deduction modulo, and describe, in Sec. 4, the corresponding implementation and the experimental results obtained on the benchmarks provided by the TPTP library; finally, in Sec. 5, we provide an overview of the Dedukti backend.

2 From Axioms to Deduction Modulo

Deduction modulo [9] focuses on the computational part of a theory, where axioms are transformed into rewrite rules, which induces a congruence over propositions, and where reasoning is performed modulo this congruence. For example, considering the inclusion in set theory $\forall X, Y \ (X \subseteq Y \Leftrightarrow \forall x \ (x \in X \Rightarrow x \in Y))$, the proof of $A \subseteq A$ in sequent calculus has the following form:

$$\cfrac{\cfrac{\cfrac{\cfrac{\cfrac{\cfrac{\ldots, x \in A \vdash A \subseteq A, x \in A}{\ldots \vdash A \subseteq A, x \in A \Rightarrow x \in A} \text{Ax}}{\ldots \vdash A \subseteq A, \forall x \ (x \in A \Rightarrow x \in A)} \Rightarrow \text{R}}{\ldots, \forall x \ (x \in A \Rightarrow x \in A) \Rightarrow A \subseteq A \vdash A \subseteq A} \forall \text{R} \quad \cfrac{\ldots, A \subseteq A \vdash A \subseteq A}{} \text{Ax}}{A \subseteq A \Leftrightarrow \forall x \ (x \in A \Rightarrow x \in A) \vdash A \subseteq A} \Rightarrow \text{L}}{\forall X, Y \ (X \subseteq Y \Leftrightarrow \forall x \ (x \in X \Rightarrow x \in Y)) \vdash A \subseteq A} \land \text{L}}{} \forall \text{L} \times 2$$

In deduction modulo, the axiom of inclusion can be seen as a computation rule, and therefore replaced by the rewrite rule $X \subseteq Y \longrightarrow \forall x \ (x \in X \Rightarrow x \in Y)$. The previous proof is then transformed as follows:

$$\cfrac{\cfrac{\cfrac{x \in A \vdash x \in A}{\vdash x \in A \Rightarrow x \in A} \Rightarrow \text{R}}{\vdash A \subseteq A} \forall \text{R}, \ A \subseteq A \longrightarrow \forall x \ (x \in A \Rightarrow x \in A)}{} \text{Ax}$$

where it can be seen that computations are interleaved with the deduction rules. It can be noticed that the proof is much simpler than the one completed using sequent calculus. In addition to simplicity, deduction modulo also allows for unbounded proof size reduction [6].

There exist some other approaches, which can be considered as variants of deduction modulo. This is the case of superdeduction [5], the formalism at the origin of **Super Zenon** [10], which proposes to use axioms to enrich the deduction system with new deduction rules (called superdeduction rules). Thus, while deduction modulo integrates some axioms of the theory as computations, superdeduction integrates them as deduction rules, following Prawitz's ideas [11].

However, in contrast with superdeduction, deduction modulo can also capture some computational aspects that are modeled by means of equational axioms. For instance, if we consider an equational sequent calculus with the theory of Peano arithmetic, the proof of $\exists x \ (x + s(0) = s(s(0)))$ is the following without deduction modulo (in the proof context, we only provide the two axioms of Peano arithmetic required to complete the proof, referring to them as $\mathcal{P}$):

$$\cfrac{\cfrac{\cfrac{\cfrac{\mathcal{P}, s(0) + s(0) = s(s(0) + 0) \vdash s(0) + s(0) = s(s(0) + 0)}{\mathcal{P} \vdash s(0) + s(0) = s(s(0) + 0)} \text{Ax}}{\mathcal{P} \vdash s(0) + s(0) = s(s(0))} \forall \text{L} \times 2 \quad \cfrac{\varPi}{} \text{Subst}_{\mathcal{P}}}{\left\{\begin{array}{l} \forall x \ (x + 0 = x) \\ \forall x, y \ (x + s(y) = s(x + y)) \end{array}\right\} \vdash \exists x \ (x + s(0) = s(s(0)))} \exists \text{R}$$

where Π is the proof expressed as follows:

$$\dfrac{\dfrac{\overline{\mathcal{P}, s(0)+0=s(0) \vdash s(0)+0=s(0)}\ \text{Ax}}{\mathcal{P} \vdash s(0)+0=s(0)}\ \forall \text{L} \quad \dfrac{}{\mathcal{P} \vdash s(s(0))=s(s(0))}\ \text{Refl}}{\mathcal{P} \vdash s(s(0)+0)=s(s(0))}\ \text{Subst}_\text{P}$$

In deduction modulo, the two axioms are transformed into computation rules on terms, and therefore replaced by the two rewrite rules $x + 0 \longrightarrow x$ and $x + s(y) \longrightarrow s(x+y)$. The corresponding proof is then the following:

$$\dfrac{\dfrac{}{\vdash s(0)+s(0)=s(s(0))}\ \text{Refl},\ s(0)+s(0) \longrightarrow^* s(s(0))}{\vdash \exists x\ (x+s(0)=s(s(0)))}\ \exists \text{R}$$

As previously, it can be noticed that the proof in deduction modulo is much simpler and shorter than the one obtained using the equational sequent calculus.

3 Deduction Modulo Rules for Zenon

In this section, we provide the adaptation of the proof search rules of Zenon to deduction modulo. This mainly consists in extending the usual rules of Zenon [4] by allowing them to work modulo a congruence relation over propositions induced by a set of rewrite rules over propositions and a set of equational axioms and rewrite rules over terms (this extension is partially inspired by the presentation of tableaux modulo presented in [3]).

In the following, we borrow some of the notations, definitions, and propositions of [9], and we call FV the function that returns the set of free variables of a formula. In particular, we introduce the notion of class rewrite system:

Definition 1 (Class Rewrite System). *A term rewrite rule is a pair of terms denoted by $l \longrightarrow r$, where $\text{FV}(r) \subseteq \text{FV}(l)$. An equational axiom is a pair of terms denoted by $l = r$. A proposition rewrite rule is a pair of propositions denoted by $l \longrightarrow r$, where l is an atomic proposition and r is an arbitrary proposition, and where $\text{FV}(r) \subseteq \text{FV}(l)$.*

A class rewrite system is a pair, denoted by $\mathcal{RE}$, consisting of:

- *$\mathcal{R}$: a set of proposition rewrite rules;*
- *$\mathcal{E}$: a set of term rewrite rules and equational axioms.*

Given a class rewrite system $\mathcal{RE}$, the relations $=_\mathcal{E}$ and $=_{\mathcal{RE}}$ are the congruences generated respectively by the sets $\mathcal{E}$ and $\mathcal{R} \cup \mathcal{E}$. We then define the notion of $\mathcal{RE}$-rewriting. In the definition below, we use the standard concepts of subterm and term replacement: given an occurrence ω in a proposition P, we write $P_{|\omega}$ for the term or proposition at ω, and $P[t]_\omega$ for the proposition obtained by replacing $P_{|\omega}$ by t in P at ω.

Definition 2 ($\mathcal{RE}$-Rewriting). *Given a class rewrite system $\mathcal{RE}$, the proposition P $\mathcal{RE}$-rewrites to P', denoted by $P \longrightarrow_{\mathcal{RE}} P'$, if $P =_\mathcal{E} Q$, $Q_{|\omega} = \sigma(l)$, and $P' =_\mathcal{E} Q[\sigma(r)]_\omega$, for some rule $l \longrightarrow r \in \mathcal{R}$, some proposition Q, some occurrence ω in Q, and some substitution σ.*

The relation $=_{\mathcal{RE}}$ is not decidable in general, but there are some cases where this relation is decidable depending on the class rewrite system $\mathcal{RE}$ and the rewrite relation $\longrightarrow_{\mathcal{RE}}$, as identified by the following proposition:

Proposition 1 (Decidability of $=_{\mathcal{RE}}$). *If the rewrite relation $\longrightarrow_{\mathcal{RE}}$ is confluent and (weakly) terminating, then the relation $=_{\mathcal{RE}}$ is decidable.*

Given a class rewrite system $\mathcal{RE}$, the proof search rules of Zenon adapted to deduction modulo are summarized in Figs. 1 and 2 (for the sake of simplification, the unfolding and extension rules are omitted), where the "|" symbol is used to separate the formulas of two distinct nodes to be created, ϵ is Hilbert's operator ($\epsilon(x).P(x)$ means some x that satisfies $P(x)$, if it exists, and is considered as a term), capital letters are used for metavariables, and R_r, R_s, R_t, and R_{ts} are respectively reflexive, symmetric, transitive, and transitive-symmetric relations (the corresponding rules also apply to equality). As hinted by the use of Hilbert's operator, the δ-rules are handled by means of ϵ-terms rather than using Skolemization. What we call here metavariables are often named free variables in the tableau-related literature. However, metavariables are not used as variables as they are never substituted, and do not even help to generate a global constraint closing all the branches of the tableau at once; metavariables are instead used as clues (through unification attempts) for the "real" instantiation rules $\gamma_{\forall_{inst}}/\gamma_{\neg\exists_{inst}}$. The proof search rules are applied with the usual tableau method: starting from the negation of the goal, apply the rules in a top-down fashion to build a tree. When all branches are closed (i.e. end with a closure rule), the tree is closed, and this closed tree is a proof of the goal. This algorithm is applied in strict depth-first order: we close the current branch before starting working on another branch. Moreover, we work in a non-destructive way: working on a branch will never change the formulas of another branch.

Compared to [9] and [3], it should be noticed that there is no explicit rule of extended narrowing in the proposed deduction modulo rules for Zenon, since the relation $=_{\mathcal{RE}}$ is actually disseminated in all the initial rules of Zenon. However, the extended narrowing rule is not only a rule that allows us to apply rewrite rules, but also a rule that may suggest instantiations for metavariables. The technique used by Zenon to find those instantiations must therefore be extended as well. Initially, Zenon tries to close a branch by looking for two formulas P and $\neg P$ that can be unified by a substitution σ (over metavariables), and this substitution σ is then used in the $\gamma_{\forall_{inst}}/\gamma_{\neg\exists_{inst}}$ rules corresponding to the unified metavariables. In deduction modulo, this method must be extended as follows: we look for two formulas P and Q s.t. $P =_{\mathcal{RE}} P'$, $Q =_{\mathcal{RE}} \neg Q'$, and there exists a substitution σ s.t. $\sigma(P') =_{\mathcal{E}} \sigma(Q')$. To be complete, we must also extend this metavariable instantiation search to any propositional narrowing (even if we are not trying to close a branch): we look for a formula P and a substitution σ s.t. $P =_{\mathcal{RE}} P'$, and there exist $P'_{|\omega}$ and a rule $l \longrightarrow r$ of $\mathcal{R} \cup \mathcal{E}$ s.t. $\sigma(P'_{|\omega}) =_{\mathcal{E}} \sigma(l)$.

Closure and Cut Rules

$$\frac{P \quad \neg Q}{\odot} \odot \text{ if } P =_{\mathcal{RE}} Q \qquad \frac{}{P \mid \neg Q} \text{ cut if } P =_{\mathcal{RE}} Q$$

$$\frac{P}{\odot} \odot_\bot \text{ if } P =_{\mathcal{RE}} \bot \qquad \frac{\neg P}{\odot} \odot_{\neg\top} \text{ if } P =_{\mathcal{RE}} \top$$

$$\frac{\neg P}{\odot} \odot_r \text{ if } P =_{\mathcal{RE}} R_r(t,t) \qquad \frac{P \quad \neg Q}{\odot} \odot_s \text{ if } P =_{\mathcal{RE}} R_s(a,b) \text{ and } Q =_{\mathcal{RE}} R_s(b,a)$$

Analytic Rules

$$\frac{S}{P,Q} \alpha_\wedge \text{ if } S =_{\mathcal{RE}} P \wedge Q \qquad \frac{\neg S}{\neg P \mid \neg Q} \beta_{\neg\wedge} \text{ if } S =_{\mathcal{RE}} P \wedge Q$$

$$\frac{S}{P \mid Q} \beta_\vee \text{ if } S =_{\mathcal{RE}} P \vee Q \qquad \frac{\neg S}{\neg P, \neg Q} \alpha_{\neg\vee} \text{ if } S =_{\mathcal{RE}} P \vee Q$$

$$\frac{S}{\neg P \mid Q} \beta_\Rightarrow \text{ if } S =_{\mathcal{RE}} P \Rightarrow Q \qquad \frac{\neg S}{P, \neg Q} \alpha_{\neg\Rightarrow} \text{ if } S =_{\mathcal{RE}} P \Rightarrow Q$$

$$\frac{S}{\neg P, \neg Q \mid P, Q} \beta_\Leftrightarrow \text{ if } S =_{\mathcal{RE}} P \Leftrightarrow Q \qquad \frac{\neg S}{\neg P, Q \mid P, \neg Q} \beta_{\neg\Leftrightarrow} \text{ if } S =_{\mathcal{RE}} P \Leftrightarrow Q$$

$$\frac{\neg S}{P} \alpha_{\neg\neg} \text{ if } S =_{\mathcal{RE}} \neg P$$

$$\frac{S}{P(\epsilon(x).P(x))} \delta_\exists \text{ if } S =_{\mathcal{RE}} \exists x\, P(x) \qquad \frac{\neg S}{\neg P(\epsilon(x).\neg P(x))} \delta_{\neg\forall} \text{ if } S =_{\mathcal{RE}} \forall x\, P(x)$$

γ-Rules

$$\frac{S}{P(X)} \gamma_{\forall M} \text{ if } S =_{\mathcal{RE}} \forall x\, P(x) \qquad \frac{\neg S}{\neg P(X)} \gamma_{\neg\exists M} \text{ if } S =_{\mathcal{RE}} \exists x\, P(x)$$

$$\frac{S}{P(t)} \gamma_{\forall\text{inst}} \text{ if } S =_{\mathcal{RE}} \forall x\, P(x) \qquad \frac{\neg S}{\neg P(t)} \gamma_{\neg\exists\text{inst}} \text{ if } S =_{\mathcal{RE}} \exists x\, P(x)$$

Fig. 1. Deduction Modulo Rules for Zenon (Part 1)

4 Implementation and Experimental Results

In this section, we present our implementation of the extension of Zenon to deduction modulo, as well as a heuristic to transform an axiomatic theory into a theory modulo automatically. We also discuss the results obtained on the benchmarks provided by the TPTP library, and we detail a problem that is difficult according to the TPTP ranking, and whose proof is found by our extension.

Relational Rules

$$\frac{P(t_1,\ldots,t_n) \qquad \neg Q(s_1,\ldots,s_n)}{t_1 \neq s_1 \mid \ldots \mid t_n \neq s_n} \text{ pred } \begin{array}{l} \text{if } P(t_1,\ldots,t_n) =_{\mathcal{RE}} S(t_1,\ldots,t_n) \\ \text{and } Q(s_1,\ldots,s_n) =_{\mathcal{RE}} S(s_1,\ldots,s_n) \end{array}$$

$$\frac{f(t_1,\ldots,t_n) \neq g(s_1,\ldots,s_n)}{t_1 \neq s_1 \mid \ldots \mid t_n \neq s_n} \text{ fun } \begin{array}{l} \text{if } f(t_1,\ldots,t_n) =_{\mathcal{E}} h(t_1,\ldots,t_n) \\ \text{and } g(s_1,\ldots,s_n) =_{\mathcal{E}} h(s_1,\ldots,s_n) \end{array}$$

$$\frac{P(s,t) \qquad \neg Q(u,v)}{t \neq u \mid s \neq v} \text{ sym } \begin{array}{l} \text{if } P(s,t) =_{\mathcal{RE}} R_s(s,t) \\ \text{and } Q(u,v) =_{\mathcal{RE}} R_s(u,v) \end{array}$$

$$\frac{\neg P(s,t)}{s \neq t} \text{ }\neg\text{refl } \text{ if } P(s,t) =_{\mathcal{RE}} R_r(s,t)$$

$$\frac{P(s,t) \qquad \neg Q(u,v)}{u \neq s, \neg R_t(u,s) \mid t \neq v, \neg R_t(t,v)} \text{ trans } \begin{array}{l} \text{if } P(s,t) =_{\mathcal{RE}} R_t(s,t) \\ \text{and } Q(u,v) =_{\mathcal{RE}} R_t(u,v) \end{array}$$

$$\frac{P(s,t) \qquad \neg Q(u,v)}{v \neq s, \neg R_{ts}(v,s) \mid t \neq u, \neg R_{ts}(t,u)} \text{ transsym } \begin{array}{l} \text{if } P(s,t) =_{\mathcal{RE}} R_{ts}(s,t) \\ \text{and } Q(u,v) =_{\mathcal{RE}} R_{ts}(u,v) \end{array}$$

$$\frac{P(s,t) \qquad \neg Q(u,v)}{u \neq s, \neg R_t(u,s) \mid \neg R_t(u,s), \neg R_t(t,v) \mid t \neq v, \neg R_t(t,v)} \text{ transeq } \begin{array}{l} \text{if } P(s,t) =_{\mathcal{RE}} (s=t) \\ \text{and } Q(u,v) =_{\mathcal{RE}} R_t(u,v) \end{array}$$

$$\frac{P(s,t) \qquad \neg Q(u,v)}{v \neq s, \neg R_{ts}(v,s) \mid \neg R_{ts}(v,s), \neg R_{ts}(t,u) \mid t \neq u, \neg R_{ts}(t,u)} \text{ transeqsym } \begin{array}{l} \text{if } P(s,t) =_{\mathcal{RE}} (s=t) \\ \text{and } Q(u,v) =_{\mathcal{RE}} R_{ts}(u,v) \end{array}$$

Fig. 2. Deduction Modulo Rules for Zenon (Part 2)

4.1 Implementation

The extension of Zenon to deduction modulo described in Sec. 3 has been implemented in a tool called Zenon Modulo[1]. In this implementation, the class rewrite system $\mathcal{RE}$ is assumed to be a pure rewrite system, i.e. there are only rewrite rules and no equational axiom in $\mathcal{E}$. In addition, the rewrite relation $\longrightarrow_{\mathcal{RE}}$ is assumed to be confluent and (weakly) terminating, and the relation $=_{\mathcal{RE}}$ is therefore decidable (see Prop. 1 in Sec. 3). Thus, given two propositions P and Q, it is sufficient to compare their normal forms (w.r.t. $\longrightarrow_{\mathcal{RE}}$) to decide whether $P =_{\mathcal{RE}} Q$. A solution to deal with the relation $=_{\mathcal{RE}}$ is then to normalize all the formulas of the proof search tree. However, this solution is not efficient in general, as it may perform many useless rewritings. To alleviate this problem, we use an alternate (but equivalent) solution, which consists in performing rewriting only if the formula is a literal. In this case, the terms of the formula are normalized, and one step of proposition rewriting is then applied; if the obtained formula is still a literal, the process is reiterated.

---

[1] Available on demand (sending a mail to the authors).

To generate the rewrite system $\mathcal{R} \cup \mathcal{E}$, we have implemented two options. With the first one, the user builds a theory modulo (with axioms and rewrite rules) and provides this theory to Zenon Modulo through an extension of the TPTP input syntax [12], which is one of the input formats used by Zenon, to natively support rewrite rules. With the second option, the user provides a purely axiomatic theory and Zenon Modulo transforms it into a theory modulo automatically. This transformation relies on a heuristic described in Subsec. 4.2.

Zenon Modulo is still in an early stage of development and some features have not been implemented yet. In particular, this is the case of the narrowing for terms and propositions. As a consequence, this leads to incompleteness cases, some of which arise in the benchmarks presented in this paper.

4.2 A Heuristic to Build Theories Modulo

To obtain a theory modulo from an axiomatic theory automatically, we propose a heuristic that generates rewrite rules from axioms based on the shape of the latter. In general, this heuristic does not preserve cut-free completeness. Here are the shapes of axioms that can be handled by our heuristic, as well as the rewrite rules that are generated from them (in the following P is an atomic formula that is not an equation, φ an arbitrary formula, and s and t two terms):

- Axiom of the form $\forall \bar{x}\ (P \Leftrightarrow \varphi)$: the proposition rewrite rule $P \longrightarrow \varphi$ is generated if $\mathrm{FV}(\varphi) \subseteq \mathrm{FV}(P)$, otherwise if φ is a literal and $\mathrm{FV}(P) \subset \mathrm{FV}(\varphi)$ then we apply the heuristic to the formula $\forall \bar{x}\ (\varphi \Leftrightarrow P)$;
- Axiom of the form $\forall \bar{x}\ (\neg P \Leftrightarrow \varphi)$: the proposition rewrite rule $P \longrightarrow \neg \varphi$ is generated if $\mathrm{FV}(\varphi) \subseteq \mathrm{FV}(P)$, otherwise if φ is a literal and $\mathrm{FV}(P) \subset \mathrm{FV}(\varphi)$ then we apply the heuristic to the formula $\forall \bar{x}\ (\varphi \Leftrightarrow \neg P)$;
- Axiom of the form $\forall \bar{x}\ s = t$: the term rewrite rule $s \longrightarrow t$ is generated if $\mathrm{FV}(t) \subseteq \mathrm{FV}(s)$, otherwise the term rewrite rule $t \longrightarrow s$ if $\mathrm{FV}(s) \subset \mathrm{FV}(t)$. In addition, all the axioms expressing the commutativity of a given symbol are excluded from this rule of our heuristic.

In this heuristic, it should be noticed that we exclude the axioms where P is an equation in order to benefit from the equational reasoning of Zenon. To illustrate this heuristic, an example is provided in Subsec. 4.4, where it is shown how a part of the theory is transformed into rewrite rules automatically.

4.3 Experimental Results

We propose a test of our approach on a benchmark drawn from the TPTP library [12] (v.5.5.0), which is a large library of standard benchmark examples for automated theorem proving systems. On this benchmark, we compare Zenon with two different heuristics of Zenon Modulo. The first heuristic consists in only selecting the axioms that can be transformed into proposition rewrite rules (equational axioms that can be transformed into term rewrite rules are ignored), while the second one is a greedy heuristic that transforms every axiom that matches one of the patterns described above, producing both term

Table 1. Experimental Results over the TPTP Library

TPTP Category	Zenon	Zenon Modulo (Prop. Rewriting)		Zenon Modulo (Term & Prop. Rewriting)	
FOF 6,659 problems	1,586	1,626 (2.5%)	+114 (7.2%) -74 (4.7%)	1,616 (1.9%)	+170 (10.7%) -140 (8.8%)
SET 462 problems	149	219 (47%)	+78 (52.3%) -8 (5.4%)	222 (49%)	+86 (57.7%) -13 (8.7%)

and propositional rewrite rules. The results of this experiment (run on an Intel Xeon X5650 2.67GHz computer, with a memory limit of 1GB and a timeout of 300s) are summarized in Tab. 1, where we have considered the first order problems of the whole library (FOF category) and the problems of set theory (SET category). This table has three columns: the first one provides the number of problems proved by Zenon for each category, while the two other columns show the results of Zenon Modulo with each of the heuristics described above. For Zenon Modulo, there are three numbers per category and heuristic: the left-hand side number is the number of problems proved by Zenon Modulo, while the two right-hand side numbers represent, from top to bottom, the number of problems proved by Zenon Modulo but not by Zenon, and the number of problems proved by Zenon but not by Zenon Modulo.

From the results of Tab. 1, we observe that Zenon Modulo always proves more problems than Zenon whatever the considered category and the selected heuristic. If the gain seems to be low for the whole FOF category (less than 3%) in spite of a significant proportion of problems proved by Zenon Modulo but not by Zenon (about 7% and 11% depending on the heuristic), this is essentially due to incompleteness cases of Zenon Modulo, where narrowing is actually required and for which Zenon succeeds in finding a proof (about 5% and 9% of the cases depending the heuristic). Once narrowing will have been implemented, we can reasonably hope to drastically reduce the number of these cases, and obtain a quite higher gain (probably up to about 11% in the best case scenario).

However, even without narrowing, the gain of Zenon Modulo becomes quite significant for the SET category (about 50% for both heuristics). This very promising result in the SET category tends to show that set theory is a good candidate for automated reasoning with deduction modulo, even when using an automated heuristic. Moreover, as said in the introduction, we plan to apply Zenon Modulo in the context of the B method [1], in particular to verify proof obligations coming from industrial applications. This is one of the tasks of the BWare project [13]. As the modeling technique used by the B method relies on a customized set theory, which will have a hand-tailored expression as a rewrite system, we can therefore be quite confident in the effectiveness of our tool in the verification of these proof obligations.

The results of the two instances of Zenon Modulo are close, but the heuristic based on term and proposition rewriting proves more problems that are not proved by Zenon (about 11% for FOF and 58% for SET), and once narrowing will be implemented, this heuristic should therefore be preferred.

It should be also noticed that among the 86 problems of the SET category proved by Zenon Modulo (with the heuristic based on term and proposition rewriting) but not by Zenon, there are 29 difficult problems according to the TPTP ranking, namely 29 with a ranking greater than 0.7^2, 9 with a ranking greater than 0.8, and 1 with a ranking greater than 0.9.

4.4 A Nontrivial Example from the TPTP Library

To show the effectiveness of Zenon Modulo, let us describe the proof found for the problem SET815+4, which has the highest ranking (0.91) among those solved, and which deals with the theory of ordinal numbers. The conjecture states that any ordinal number is equal to the union of the elements of its successor. The axioms used to complete this proof are the following:

$$\forall A, B \quad (A \subseteq B \Leftrightarrow \forall X\ (X \in A \Rightarrow X \in B)) \quad (subset)$$
$$\forall A, B \quad (A =_{set} B \Leftrightarrow A \subseteq B \wedge B \subseteq A) \quad (eqset)$$
$$\forall X, A, B\ (X \in A \cup B \Leftrightarrow X \in A \vee X \in B) \quad (union)$$
$$\forall X, A \quad (X \in \{A\} \Leftrightarrow X = A) \quad (singleton)$$
$$\forall X, A \quad (X \in \bigcup A \Leftrightarrow \exists Y\ (Y \in A \wedge X \in Y)) \quad (sum)$$
$$\forall A \quad (A \in \text{On} \Leftrightarrow \text{set}(A) \wedge \forall X\ (X \in A \Rightarrow X \subseteq A) \wedge \quad (ordinal)$$
$$\text{strict\_wo}(\text{mem\_pred}, A))$$
$$\forall X, A\ (X \in A + 1 \Leftrightarrow X \in A \cup \{A\}) \quad (successor)$$

where set is a predicate that requires the argument to be a set, and where On is the "set" of ordinal numbers, mem_pred the membership relation over ordinal numbers (this relation is related to $\in$ by means of an axiom not shown here as it is not required to complete the proof), and strict_wo a formula encoding the strict well-order relation.

According the rules of the heuristic described in Subsec. 4.2, all these axioms can be turned into proposition rewrite rules (we use the first rule of the heuristic, and each axiom is oriented from left to right). Once this theory modulo has been built, we can then try to prove the conjecture, which is expressed as follows:

$$\forall A\ (A \in \text{On} \Rightarrow \bigcup (A + 1) =_{set} A)$$

When applied to this specification, Zenon Modulo produces the (rather short) proof of Fig. 3. The proof is presented using the rules of Sec. 3, even though these rules are more used for proof search rather than for proof presentation (for that purpose, Zenon actually uses an intermediate format, which is described in

---

[2] It means that at least 70% of the tested automated theorem provers fail in proving the considered problems.

$$\cfrac{\cfrac{\neg(\forall A\ (A\in \text{On}\Rightarrow \bigcup(A+1)=_{\text{set}} A))}{\neg(\bigcup(\tau_1+1)\subset\tau_1\wedge\tau_1\subset\bigcup(\tau_1+1)),\quad \forall X\ (X\in\tau_1\Rightarrow X\subset\tau_1)}l_1}{\cfrac{\neg(\forall X\ (X\in\bigcup(\tau_1+1)\Rightarrow X\in\tau_1))}{\Pi_1}l_3 \quad \cfrac{\neg(\forall X\ (X\in\tau_1\Rightarrow X\in\bigcup(\tau_1+1)))}{\Pi_2}l_4}l_2$$

$$\Pi_1$$

$$\cfrac{\cfrac{\tau_3\in\tau_1\vee\tau_3\in\{\tau_1\},\quad \neg(\tau_2\in\tau_1),\quad \tau_2\in\tau_3}{\cfrac{\tau_3\in\tau_1}{\cfrac{\tau_3\in\tau_1\Rightarrow\tau_3\subset\tau_1}{\cfrac{\forall X\ (X\in\tau_3\Rightarrow X\in\tau_1)}{\cfrac{\tau_2\in\tau_3\Rightarrow\tau_2\in\tau_1}{\cfrac{\neg(\tau_2\in\tau_3)}{\odot}\quad \cfrac{\tau_2\in\tau_1}{\odot}}l_9}l_8}l_7}l_6}\quad \cfrac{\tau_3=\tau_1}{\cfrac{\tau_2\neq\tau_2}{\odot}\odot_r\quad \cfrac{\tau_3\neq\tau_1}{\odot}\odot}l_{10}}l_5$$

$$\cfrac{\neg(\tau_3\in\tau_1)}{\odot}\odot$$

$$\Pi_2$$

$$\cfrac{\neg(\exists Y\ (Y\in(\tau_1+1)\wedge\tau_4\in Y)),\quad \tau_4\in\tau_1}{\cfrac{\neg(\tau_1\in(\tau_1+1)\wedge\tau_4\in\tau_1)}{\cfrac{\tau_1\neq\tau_1}{\odot}\odot_r\quad \cfrac{\neg(\tau_4\in\tau_1)}{\odot}\odot}l_{12}}l_{11}$$

where :
$\tau_1 = \epsilon(A).\neg(A\in\text{On}\Rightarrow \bigcup(A+1)=A)$
$\tau_2 = \epsilon(X).\neg(X\in\bigcup(\tau_1+1)\Rightarrow X\in\tau_1)$
$\tau_3 = \epsilon(Y).(Y\in(\tau_1+1)\wedge\tau_2\in Y)$
$\tau_4 = \epsilon(X).\neg(X\in\tau_1\Rightarrow X\in\bigcup(\tau_1+1))$

$l_1 = \delta_{\neg\forall},\alpha_{\neg\Rightarrow},\text{ordinal, eqset}$
$l_2 = \beta_{\neg\wedge},\text{subset}$
$l_3 = \delta_{\neg\forall},\alpha_{\neg\Rightarrow},\text{sum},\delta_\exists,\alpha_\wedge,\text{successor, union}$
$l_4 = \delta_{\neg\forall},\alpha_{\neg\Rightarrow},\text{sum}$
$l_5 = \beta_\vee,\text{singleton}$
$l_6 = \gamma_{\forall\text{inst}}$
$l_7 = \beta_\Rightarrow,\text{subset}$
$l_8 = \gamma_{\forall\text{inst}}$
$l_9 = \beta_\Rightarrow$
$l_{10} = \text{pred}$
$l_{11} = \gamma_{\neg\exists\text{inst}}$
$l_{12} = \beta_{\neg\wedge},\text{successor, union},\alpha_{\neg\vee},\text{singleton}$

Fig. 3. Proof of Problem SET815+4

detail in [4]). Moreover, to make the presentation more compact, one proof step may consist of several rules. Notice the clever instantiation rule l_6, which cannot be done before the $\delta_\exists$ of l_3.

5 Proof Verification with Dedukti

In this section, we describe the Dedukti backend that has been implemented for Zenon Modulo, and which relies in particular on a proof transformation from classical to constructive logic.

5.1 Dedukti as a Backend for Deduction Modulo

Skeptically checking proof traces produced by an automated theorem prover imposes that the traces contain all the information needed by the proof checker to assert the validity of proofs. A naive way to check proofs performed by Zenon Modulo would be to record rewriting as a special rule, but this method would be very expensive in space, because an arbitrary number of rewrite rules can occur between any consecutive nodes of the proof. To circumvent this problem, the proof checker or the formalization of the proof must not distinguish propositions or terms belonging to the same equivalence class modulo rewriting. The only information needed is the set of rewrite rules, which cannot be bigger than the problem statement itself. Dedukti fits this specific constraint in a simple way: if the set of rewrite rules is translated into Dedukti rewrite rules specified in the header of the proof, any proposition or term used in the proof can be replaced by an equivalent proposition or term modulo rewriting.

Dedukti [2] is a type checker for the $\lambda\Pi$-calculus modulo, which is an extension of the λ-calculus with dependent types and rewrite rules. In order to check proofs of a given logical system, we have to define an embedding of this system into the $\lambda\Pi$-calculus modulo. A logical system is embedded into the $\lambda\Pi$-calculus modulo using declarations of constants and declarations of rewrite rules. As an example, let us consider the implicative fragment of natural deduction and a predicate P. To encode this example, we provide the context of Fig. 4, where the syntax of $\lambda\Pi$-calculus modulo is used. In this context, we can check the trivial proof of $Imp\ P\ P$ by verifying that the term $Intro\ P\ P\ (\lambda t : (Proof\ P).\ t)$ has type $Proof\ (Imp\ P\ P)$. This technique, which consists in defining rules as constants in the $\lambda\Pi$-calculus modulo, is called deep embedding.

However, the $\lambda\Pi$-calculus modulo allows us to define rewrite rules that avoid the definitions of the previous encoding and therefore get shorter proofs. For example, we can replace the *Intro* and *Elim* constants by the rewrite rule $Proof\ (Imp\ A\ B) \longrightarrow (Proof\ A \to Proof\ B)$, where A and B are variables of type *Prop*. The previous term then reduces to $\lambda t : (Proof\ P).t$, which has the same type. This technique, which consists in reusing the language features (here, the $\lambda\Pi$-calculus modulo) is called shallow embedding. In particular, the computations (β-reduction) of the initial system are preserved. Notice how deduction modulo allows us to smoothly go from deep to shallow embedding.

The definition of an output to deduction modulo first consists in providing the declaration of the language (terms, predicates, connectives, etc.), and the

---

$Prop : Type$

$P : Prop$

$Imp : Prop \to Prop \to Prop$

$Proof : Prop \to Type$

$Intro : \Pi A : Prop.\Pi B : Prop.(Proof\ A \to Proof\ B) \to Proof\ (Imp\ A\ B))$

$Elim : \Pi A : Prop.\Pi B : Prop.(Proof\ (Imp\ A\ B)) \to (Proof\ A) \to Proof\ B)$

Fig. 4. Encoding of Natural Deduction in $\lambda\Pi$-Calculus Modulo

shallow embedding of the natural deduction rules that is close to $\lambda\Pi$-calculus. We then proceed to the definition of the rewrite rules for propositions and terms, according to the input set of rewrite rules. Once this encoding has been defined, proofs can be checked in this context. As an example, we can extend the previous encoding with a predicate Q and two axioms $Imp\ Q\ (Imp\ P\ P)$ and $Imp\ (Imp\ P\ P)\ Q$. The heuristic of Sec. 4 will replace these two axioms by a single rewrite rule (these two axioms represent an equivalence), and we just have to declare the rewrite rule $Q \longrightarrow Imp\ P\ P$, modulo which Q admits the same proof as before, i.e. $\lambda t : (Proof\ P).t$.

5.2 From Classical to Constructive Proofs

Zenon's logic is classical and expressed in a formalism very close to sequent calculus [14]. As a consequence, using Dedukti as a backend requires two steps: the first one is to translate classical proofs of Zenon into proofs of constructive sequent calculus with equality, which we discuss here, and the second one is a standard translation from sequent calculus to natural deduction.

The translation from classical to constructive logic relies on an optimized double-negation translation [15], presented in Tab. 2, where other connectives ($\neg$ and $\top$) are defined as usual through $\Rightarrow$ and $\bot$. With these definitions, it is possible to show that a formula A has a classical proof if and only if $\varphi(A)$ has a constructive proof. The purpose of defining the three functions of Tab. 2 is that the algorithm introduces a minimal number of double negations. In particular, we improve over both Kuroda's and Gödel's translations [15] by combining their principles: double negation only after universal quantifiers and double negation only in front of disjunctive and existentially quantified propositions, respectively. At top level, we push double negations as far as possible inside the formula, as Gödel, in front of the first encountered disjunction/existential quantifier (the role of φ); at this point, we stop introducing double negations until, as Kuroda, we meet a universal quantifier, in which case we start again the process (the role of ψ). We refine our translation with the polarity of formulas (i.e. the side of the sequent on which the formula appears): if a formula appears on the left-hand side of a sequent, we do not put a double-negation in front of it (the role of χ).

Furthermore, the algorithm analyses the structure of the classical proof in order to remove more double negations. For instance, a disjunction can be proved constructively even in a classical calculus. As a consequence, the statement of many proofs remains unchanged. This is the case of the TPTP problem SET815+4, discussed in Sec. 4, whose proof certificate (expressed in $\lambda\Pi$-calculus modulo), is given in Figs. 5 and 6 of Appx. A. This algorithm of proof transformation has been implemented for Zenon Modulo to produce Dedukti proof certificates. In particular, Zenon Modulo succeeds in producing a proof certificate for the previous problem SET815+4, which is correctly checked by Dedukti.

Table 2. Translation from Classical to Constructive Logic

	φ	χ	ψ
$A \wedge B$	$\varphi(A) \wedge \varphi(B)$	$\chi(A) \wedge \chi(B)$	$\psi(A) \wedge \psi(B)$
$A \vee B$	$\neg\neg(\psi(A) \vee \psi(B))$	$\chi(A) \vee \chi(B)$	$\psi(A) \vee \psi(B)$
$A \Rightarrow B$	$\chi(A) \Rightarrow \varphi(B)$	$\psi(A) \Rightarrow \chi(B)$	$\chi(A) \Rightarrow \psi(B)$
$\forall x\ A$	$\forall x\ \varphi(A)$	$\forall x\ \chi(A)$	$\forall x\ \varphi(A)$
$\exists x\ A$	$\neg\neg\exists x\ \psi(A)$	$\exists x\ \chi(A)$	$\exists x\ \psi(A)$
$\bot$	$\bot$	$\bot$	$\bot$
Atomic P	$\neg\neg P$	P	P

6 Conclusion

We have proposed an extension of the tableau-based first order automated theorem prover Zenon to deduction modulo. This extension essentially consists in considering a part of a given theory as rewrite rules (over terms and propositions), and integrating these rewrite rules into the proof search rules of Zenon. We have also presented an implementation of this extension, called Zenon Modulo, as well as a heuristic to turn axioms of theories into rewrite rules automatically. This new tool significantly improves the proof search of Zenon, as shown by the experimental results obtained on the benchmarks provided by the TPTP library. In particular, this is the case of the SET category, where Zenon Modulo is able to prove difficult problems according to the TPTP ranking. Finally, we have also described an additional backend for Zenon that outputs proof certificates for Dedukti, which is a proof checker based on the $\lambda\Pi$-calculus modulo.

As future work, we first aim to complete our implementation to deal with narrowing when trying to find instantiations for metavariables. This will allow us to ensure completeness for our extension of Zenon, even though narrowing may paradoxically widen the proof search space in some cases (e.g., in set theory, a metavariable representing a set can be "narrowed" using the major part of rewrite rules defining the set operators). To deal with these cases, we will probably implement a switch that will allow us to activate/deactivate the use of narrowing. It might be also desirable to extend our proof search method to polarized deduction modulo [8], which is a refinement of deduction modulo to deal with theories formed with axioms using implications. This extension would allow us to consider more theories, where a significant part of the axioms are expressed neither by equivalences, nor by equations, but only by implications. Finally, in the framework of the BWare project [13], we plan to apply this tool in the context of the B method [1], with in particular the verification of proof obligations coming from industrial applications. To achieve this task, we have to build a theory modulo for the modeling method of B, which is actually a typed set theory, and we should be able to reuse some ideas of [10], where a B set theory is proposed using superdeduction. Given the very promising results of our tool in the SET category of the TPTP library, we are quite confident in the effectiveness of our tool in the verification of B proof obligations.

Acknowledgement. Many thanks to G. Dowek, F. Irigoin, and P. Jouvelot for their detailed comments on this paper, to G. Burel for helpful discussions, and to the Deducteam Inria research team for the many interactions.

References

1. Abrial, J.-R.: The B-Book, Assigning Programs to Meanings. Cambridge University Press, Cambridge (1996) ISBN 0521496195
2. Boespflug, M., Carbonneaux, Q., Hermant, O.: The $\lambda\Pi$-Calculus Modulo as a Universal Proof Language. In: Pichardie, D., Weber, T. (eds.) Proof Exchange for Theorem Proving (PxTP), Manchester, UK, pp. 28–43 (June 2012)
3. Bonichon, R.: TaMeD: A Tableau Method for Deduction Modulo. In: Basin, D., Rusinowitch, M. (eds.) IJCAR 2004. LNCS (LNAI), vol. 3097, pp. 445–459. Springer, Heidelberg (2004)
4. Bonichon, R., Delahaye, D., Doligez, D.: Zenon: An Extensible Automated Theorem Prover Producing Checkable Proofs. In: Dershowitz, N., Voronkov, A. (eds.) LPAR 2007. LNCS (LNAI), vol. 4790, pp. 151–165. Springer, Heidelberg (2007)
5. Brauner, P., Houtmann, C., Kirchner, C.: Principles of Superdeduction. In: Logic in Computer Science (LICS), Wrocław, Poland, pp. 41–50. IEEE Computer Society Press (July 2007)
6. Burel, G.: Efficiently Simulating Higher-Order Arithmetic by a First-Order Theory Modulo. Logical Methods in Computer Science (LMCS) 7(1), 1–31 (2011)
7. Burel, G.: Experimenting with Deduction Modulo. In: Bjørner, N., Sofronie-Stokkermans, V. (eds.) CADE 2011. LNCS (LNAI), vol. 6803, pp. 162–176. Springer, Heidelberg (2011)
8. Dowek, G.: What is a Theory? In: Alt, H., Ferreira, A. (eds.) STACS 2002. LNCS, vol. 2285, pp. 50–64. Springer, Heidelberg (2002)
9. Dowek, G., Hardin, T., Kirchner, C.: Theorem Proving Modulo. Journal of Automated Reasoning (JAR) 31(1), 33–72 (2003)
10. Jacquel, M., Berkani, K., Delahaye, D., Dubois, C.: Tableaux Modulo Theories using Superdeduction: An Application to the Verification of B Proof Rules with the Zenon Automated Theorem Prover. In: Gramlich, B., Miller, D., Sattler, U. (eds.) IJCAR 2012. LNCS, vol. 7364, pp. 332–338. Springer, Heidelberg (2012)
11. Prawitz, D.: Natural Deduction. A Proof-Theoretical Study. Stockholm Studies in Philosophy 3 (1965)
12. Sutcliffe, G.: The TPTP Problem Library and Associated Infrastructure: The FOF and CNF Parts, v3.5.0. Journal of Automated Reasoning (JAR) 43(4), 337–362 (2009)
13. The BWare Project (2012), http://bware.lri.fr/
14. Troelstra, A.S., Schwichtenberg, H.: Basic Proof Theory. Cambridge University Press, Cambridge (1996) ISBN 0521779111
15. Troelstra, A.S., van Dalen, D.: Constructivism in Mathematics: An Introduction. Elsevier, Amsterdam (1988) ISBN 0444705066

A Proof Certificate for Problem SET815+4 in $\lambda\Pi$-Calculus Modulo

---

Declarations:

$Term, Prop : Type$
$Proof : Prop \to Type$
$\wedge, \vee, \Rightarrow : Prop \to Prop \to Prop$
$\forall, \exists : (Term \to Prop) \to Prop$
$On, mem\_pred : Term$
$+1, \{\ \}, \bigcup : Term \to Term$
$\cup : Term \to Term \to Term$
$set : Term \to Prop$
$=, =_{set}, \in, \subset, strict\_wo : Term \to Term \to Prop$

Rewrite Rules:

$[A, B : Prop] Proof\ (A \wedge B) \longrightarrow \Pi P : Prop.$
  $(Proof\ A \to Proof\ B \to Proof\ P) \to Proof\ P$
$[A, B : Prop] Proof\ (A \vee B) \longrightarrow \Pi P : Prop.(Proof\ A \to Proof\ P) \to$
  $(Proof\ B \to Proof\ P) \to Proof\ P$
$[A, B : Prop] Proof\ (A \Rightarrow B) \longrightarrow Proof\ A \to Proof\ B$
$[A : Term \to Prop] Proof\ (\forall\ A) \longrightarrow \Pi x : Term.Proof\ (A\ x)$
$[A : Term \to Prop] Proof\ (\exists\ A) \longrightarrow \Pi P : Prop.$
  $(\Pi x : Term.Proof\ (A\ x) \to Proof\ P) \to Proof\ P$
$[x, y : Term] Proof\ (x = y) \longrightarrow \Pi P : (Term \to Prop).Proof\ ((P\ x) \Rightarrow (P\ y))$
$[A, B : Term] A \subset B \longrightarrow \forall\ (\lambda X : Term.X \in A \Rightarrow X \in B)$
$[A, B : Term] A =_{set} B \longrightarrow A \subset B \wedge B \subset A$
$[A, B, X : Term] X \in A \cup B \longrightarrow X \in A \vee X \in B$
$[A, X : Term] X \in \{A\} \longrightarrow X = A$
$[A, X : Term] X \in \bigcup(A) \longrightarrow \exists(\lambda Y : Term.Y \in A \wedge X \in Y)$
$[A : Term] A \in On \longrightarrow set(A) \wedge strict\_wo(mem\_pred, A) \wedge$
  $\forall\ (\lambda X : Term.X \in A \Rightarrow X \subset A)$
$[A, X : Term] X \in (A + 1) \longrightarrow X \in A \cup \{A\}$

where $[\cdot]$ is the typing context of a rewrite rule.

Fig. 5. Context of the Proof of Problem SET815+4 in $\lambda\Pi$-Calculus Modulo

Proof (λ-term):

$\lambda A : Term.\lambda H0 : Proof\ (A \in On).H0\ (\bigcup(A + 1) =_{set} A)$
$(\lambda H1 : Proof\ (set(A)).$
  $\lambda H2 : Proof\ (strict\_wo(mem\_pred, A) \wedge$
  $(\forall\ (\lambda X : Term.X \in A \Rightarrow X \subset A))).H2\ (\bigcup(A + 1) =_{set} A)$
  $(\lambda H3 : Proof\ (strict\_wo(mem\_pred, A)).$
  $\lambda H4 : Proof\ \forall\ (\lambda X : Term.(X \in A \Rightarrow X \subset A)).\lambda P0 : Prop.$
  $\lambda H6 : (Proof\ (\bigcup(A + 1) \subset A) \to Proof\ (A \subset \bigcup(A + 1)) \to Proof\ P0).H6$
  $(\lambda B : Term.\lambda H7 : Proof\ (B \in \bigcup(A + 1)).H7\ (B \in A)$
    $(\lambda D : Term.\lambda H8 : Proof\ (D \in (A + 1) \wedge B \in D).H8\ (B \in A)$
      $(\lambda H9 : Proof\ (D \in (A + 1)).\lambda H10 : Proof\ (B \in D).H9\ (B \in A)$
        $(\lambda H11 : Proof\ (D \in A).((((H4\ D)\ H11)\ B)\ H10))$
        $(\lambda H12 : Proof\ (D = A).$
          $(\lambda P1 : (Term \to Prop).\lambda H13 : Proof\ (P1\ B).H13\ (\lambda X : Term.X \in A)$
          $(H12\ (\lambda X : Term.B \in X)\ H10))))))$
  $(\lambda C : Term.\lambda H14 : Proof\ (C \in A).\lambda P2 : Prop.$
  $\lambda H15 : (\Pi Y : Term.Proof\ (Y \in (A + 1) \wedge C \in Y) \to Proof\ P2).H15\ A$
    $(\lambda P3 : Prop.\lambda H16 : (Proof\ (A \in A) \to Proof\ (C \in A) \to Proof\ P3).H16$
      $(\lambda P4 : Prop.\lambda H17 : (Proof\ (A \in A) \to Proof\ P4).$
      $\lambda H18 : (Proof\ (A = A) \to Proof\ P4).H18$
        $(\lambda P5 : (Term \to Prop).\lambda H19 : Proof\ (P5\ A).H19))\ H14))))$

Fig. 6. Proof of Problem SET815+4 in $\lambda \Pi$-Calculus Modulo

Long-Distance Resolution: Proof Generation and Strategy Extraction in Search-Based QBF Solving*

Uwe Egly, Florian Lonsing, and Magdalena Widl

Institute of Information Systems, Vienna University of Technology, Austria
`http://www.kr.tuwien.ac.at/staff/{egly,lonsing,widl}`

Abstract. Strategies (and certificates) for quantified Boolean formulas (QBFs) are of high practical relevance as they facilitate the verification of results returned by QBF solvers and the generation of solutions to problems formulated as QBFs. State of the art approaches to obtain strategies require traversing a Q-resolution proof of a QBF, which for many real-life instances is too large to handle. In this work, we consider the long-distance Q-resolution (LDQ) calculus, which allows particular tautological resolvents. We show that for a family of QBFs using the LDQ-resolution allows for exponentially shorter proofs compared to Q-resolution. We further show that an approach to strategy extraction originally presented for Q-resolution proofs can also be applied to LDQ-resolution proofs. As a practical application, we consider search-based QBF solvers which are able to learn tautological clauses based on resolution and the conflict-driven clause learning method. We prove that the resolution proofs produced by these solvers correspond to proofs in the LDQ calculus and can therefore be used as input for strategy extraction algorithms. Experimental results illustrate the potential of the LDQ calculus in search-based QBF solving.

1 Introduction

The development of decision procedures for quantified Boolean formulas (QBFs) has recently resulted in considerable performance gains. A common approach is search-based QBF solving with conflict-driven clause learning (CDCL) [2,11], which is related to propositional logic (SAT solving) in that it extends the DPLL algorithm [3]. In addition to solving the QBF decision problem, QBF solvers with clause learning are able to produce Q-resolution proofs [7] to certify their answer. These proofs can be used to obtain solutions to problems encoded as QBFs. For instance, if the QBF describes a synthesis problem, then the system to be synthesized can be generated by inspecting the proof [12]. Such solutions can be represented as control strategies [6] expressed by an algorithm that computes assignments to universal variables rendering the QBF false, or as control circuits [1] expressed by Herbrand or Skolem functions. Both approaches can be used for true QBFs as well as false QBFs. In this work, we focus on false QBFs.

Strategies can be extracted from Q-resolution proofs of false QBFs based on a game-theoretic view [6]. A strategy is an assignment to each universal ($\forall$) variable that depends

---
* This work was supported by the Austrian Science Fund (FWF) under grant S11409-N23 and by the Vienna Science and Technology Fund (WWTF) through project ICT10-018.

on assignments to existential ($\exists$) variables with a lower quantification level and maintains the falsity of the QBF. The extraction algorithm is executed for each quantifier block from the left to the right. Certificate extraction [1] constructs solutions in terms of a Herbrand function for each $\forall$ variable from a Q-resolution proof of a false QBF. Replacing each $\forall$ variable by its Herbrand function in the formula and removing the quantifiers yields an unsatisfiable propositional formula. The run time of both extraction algorithms is polynomially related to the size of the proof. It is therefore beneficial to have short proofs in practice. Calculi more powerful than traditional Q-resolution possibly allow for shorter proofs.

A way to strengthen Q-resolution is to admit tautological resolvents under certain conditions. In search-based QBF solving, this approach called *long-distance resolution* is applied to learn tautological clauses in CDCL [15,16]. The idea of generating tautological resolvents is formalized in the *long-distance Q-resolution calculus (LDQ)* [1].

We consider long-distance resolution in search-based QBF solving. First, we show that formulas of a certain family of QBFs [7] have LDQ-resolution proofs of polynomial size in the length of the formula. According to [7], any Q-resolution proof of these formulas is exponential.

Second, we prove that long-distance resolution for clause learning in QBF solvers as presented in [15,16] corresponds to proof steps in the formal LDQ-resolution calculus. This observation is complementary to the correctness proof of learning tautological clauses (i.e. the theorem in [15]) in that we embed this practical clause learning procedure in the formal framework of the LDQ-resolution calculus. Thereby we obtain a generalized view on the practical side and the theoretical side of long-distance resolution in terms of the clause learning procedure and the formal calculus, respectively.

Third, we prove that strategy extraction [6] is applicable to LDQ-resolution proofs in the same way as it is to Q-resolution proofs, which have been its original application.

Our results illustrate that the complete workflow from generating proofs in search-based QBF solving to extracting strategies from these proofs can be based on the LDQ-resolution calculus. We modified the search-based QBF solver DepQBF [9] to learn tautological clauses in CDCL. We report preliminary experimental results which illustrate the potential of the LDQ-resolution calculus in terms of a lower effort in the search process. Since LDQ-resolution proofs can be significantly shorter than Q-resolution proofs, strategy extraction will also benefit from applying LDQ-resolution proofs in practice.

2 Preliminaries

Given a set $\mathcal{V}$ of Boolean variables, the set $L := \mathcal{V} \cup \{\overline{v} \mid v \in \mathcal{V}\}$ of literals contains each variable in its positive and negative polarity. We write $\overline{v}$ for the opposite polarity of v regardless of whether v is positive or negative. A quantified Boolean formula (QBF) in prenex conjunctive normal form (PCNF) over a set $\mathcal{V}$ of variables and the two quantifiers $\exists$ and $\forall$ is of the form $\mathcal{P}.\phi$ where (1) $\mathcal{P} := Q_1 v_1 \dots Q_n v_n$ is the *prefix* with $Q_i \in \{\exists, \forall\}$, $v_i \in \mathcal{V}$ and all v_i are pairwise distinct for $1 \leq i \leq n$, and (2) $\phi \subseteq 2^L$ is a set of clauses called the *matrix*. We write $\square$ for the empty clause and occasionally represent a clause as disjunction of literals. A *quantifier block* of the form QV combines all subsequent variables with the same quantifier Q in set V. A prefix can be alternatively written as sequence $Q_1 V_1 \dots Q_m V_m$ of quantifier blocks where $Q_i \neq Q_{i+1}$ for $1 \leq i \leq m-1$.

We use var(l) to refer to the variable of literal l and vars(ϕ) to refer to the set of variables used in the matrix. A QBF is *closed* if vars(ϕ) = $\{v_i \mid 1 \leq i \leq n\}$, i.e., if all variables used in the matrix are quantified and vice versa. In the following, by QBF we refer to a closed QBF in PCNF. Function lev : $L \to \{1,\ldots,m\}$ refers to the quantification level of a literal and quant : $L \to \{\exists,\forall\}$ refers to the quantifier type of a literal such that for $1 \leq i \leq m$ and any $l \in L$, if var(l) $\in V_i$ then lev(l) := i and quant(l) := Q_i. A literal l is *existential* if quant(l) = $\exists$ and *universal* if quant(l) = $\forall$. We use the same terms for the variable var(l) of l. We write e for an existential variable and x for a universal variable.

Given a QBF $\psi = \mathcal{P}.\phi$, an *assignment* is a mapping of variables in vars(ϕ) to the truth values *true* ($\top$) and *false* ($\bot$). We denote an assignment as a set σ of literals such that if var(l) is assigned to $\top$ then $l \in \sigma$, and if var(l) is assigned to $\bot$ then $\bar{l} \in \sigma$. An assignment is total if for each $v \in$ vars(ϕ) either $v \in \sigma$ or $\bar{v} \in \sigma$, and partial otherwise.

A *clause C under an assignment* σ is denoted by $C_{\lceil \sigma}$ and is defined as follows: $C_{\lceil \sigma} = \top$ if $C \cap \sigma \neq \emptyset$, $C_{\lceil \sigma} = \bot$ if $C \setminus \{v \mid \bar{v} \in \sigma\} = \emptyset$, and $C_{\lceil \sigma} = C \setminus \{v \mid \bar{v} \in \sigma\}$ otherwise. A *QBF* $\psi = \mathcal{P}.\phi$ *under an assignment* σ is denoted by $\psi_{\lceil \sigma}$ and is obtained from ψ by replacing each $C \in \phi$ by $C_{\lceil \sigma}$, eliminating truth constants $\top$ and $\bot$ by standard rewrite rules from Boolean algebra, removing for each literal in σ its variable from the prefix, and removing each quantifier block that does no longer contain any variable.

The QBF $\forall v.\phi$ is true if and only if $\phi_{\lceil \{v\}} = \top$ and $\phi_{\lceil \{\bar{v}\}} = \top$. The QBF $\exists v.\phi$ is true if and only if $\phi_{\lceil \{v\}} = \top$ or $\phi_{\lceil \{\bar{v}\}} = \top$. The QBF $\forall v \mathcal{P}.\phi$ is true if and only if $\mathcal{P}.\phi_{\lceil \{v\}}$ and $\mathcal{P}.\phi_{\lceil \{\bar{v}\}}$ are true. The QBF $\exists v \mathcal{P}.\phi$ is true if and only if $\mathcal{P}.\phi_{\lceil \{v\}}$ or $\mathcal{P}.\phi_{\lceil \{\bar{v}\}}$ is true.

Given a QBF $\psi = \mathcal{P}.\phi$ and a clause $C \in \phi$, *universal reduction* [7] produces the clause $C' :=$ reduce(C) := $C \setminus \{l \mid$ quant(l) = $\forall$ and $\forall e \in C :$ quant(e) = $\exists \to$ lev(e) $<$ lev(l)$\}$ by removing all universal literals from C which have a maximal quantification level. Universal reduction on ψ produces the QBF resulting from ψ by the application of universal reduction to each clause in ϕ.

A clause C is *satisfied* under an assignment σ if $C_{\lceil \sigma} = \top$ and *falsified* under σ and universal reduction if reduce($C_{\lceil \sigma}$) = $\square$.

Clause learning (Section 4) is based on restricted variants of *resolution*, which is defined as follows. Given two clauses C^l and C^r and a *pivot variable* p with $p \in C^l$ and $\bar{p} \in C^r$, resolution produces the *resolvent* $C :=$ resolve(C^l, p, C^r) := $(C^l \setminus \{p\} \cup C^r \setminus \{\bar{p}\})$.

Long-distance (LD) resolution [15] is an application of resolution where the resolvent $C =$ resolve(C^l, p, C^r) is *tautological*, i.e. $\{v, \bar{v}\} \subseteq C$ for some variable v. In contrast to [15], our definition of LD-resolution allows for unrestricted LD-resolution steps. LD-resolution in the context of [15] is restricted and hence sound, whereas its unrestricted variant is unsound, as pointed out in the following example.

Example 1. For the true QBF $\forall x \exists e.(x \lor \bar{e}) \land (\bar{x} \lor e)$, an erroneous LD-refutation is given by $C_1 :=$ resolve($(x \lor \bar{e}), e, (\bar{x} \lor e)$) = $(x \lor \bar{x})$ and $C_2 :=$ reduce(C_1) = $\square$.

Q-resolution [7] is a restriction of resolution. Given two *non-tautological* clauses C^l and C^r and an *existential* pivot variable p, the *Q-resolvent* is defined as follows. Let $C' :=$ resolve(reduce(C^l), p, reduce(C^r)) be the resolvent of the two universally reduced clauses C^l and C^r. If C' is non-tautological then $C :=$ reduce(C') is the Q-resolvent of C^l and C^r. Otherwise no Q-resolvent exists.

The *long-distance Q-resolution (LDQ) calculus* [1] extends Q-resolution by allowing *certain* tautological resolvents. The rules of this calculus amount to a restricted application of LD-resolution. In the following we reproduce the formal rules (LDQ-rules) of the LDQ-calculus [1] using our notation and definitions. We write p for an existential pivot variable, x for a universal variable, and x^* as shorthand for $x \vee \overline{x}$. We call x^* a *merged literal*. Further, X^l and X^r are sets of universal literals (merged or unmerged), such that for each $x \in X^l$ it holds that if x is not a merged literal then either $\overline{x} \in X^r$ or $x^* \in X^r$, and otherwise either of $x \in X^r$ or $\overline{x} \in X^r$ or $x^* \in X^r$. X^r does not contain any additional literals. X^* contains the merged literal of each literal in X^l. Symmetric rules are omitted.

$$[p] \frac{C^l \vee p \quad C^r \vee \overline{p}}{C^l \vee C^r} \quad \text{for all } v \in C^l \text{ it holds that } \overline{v} \notin C^r \tag{r_1}$$

$$[p] \frac{C^l \vee p \vee X^l \quad C^r \vee \overline{p} \vee X^r}{C^l \vee C^r \vee X^*} \quad \begin{array}{l}\text{for all } x \in X^r \text{ it holds that } \mathsf{lev}(p) < \mathsf{lev}(x) \\ \text{for all } v \in C^l \text{ it holds that } \overline{v} \notin C^r\end{array} \tag{r_2}$$

$$[x] \frac{C \vee x'}{C} \quad \begin{array}{l}\text{for } x' \in \{x, \overline{x}, x^*\} \text{ and} \\ \text{for all existential } e \in C \text{ it holds that } \mathsf{lev}(e) < \mathsf{lev}(x')\end{array} \tag{u_1}$$

Rule r_2 is a restricted application of $\mathsf{resolve}(C^l, p, C^r)$ in that a tautological clause can be derived only if literals occurring in both polarities are universal and have a higher quantification level than p. Example u_1 extends universal reduction by removing x^*.

Given a QBF ψ, a *derivation* of a clause C is a sequence of applications of resolution and universal reduction to the clauses in ψ and to derived clauses resulting in C. If either only Q-resolution, only LD-resolution or only the LDQ-calculus is applied, then the derivation is a *(Q,LD,LDQ)-derivation*. A (Q,LD,LDQ)-derivation of the empty clause $\square$ is a *(Q,LD,LDQ)-refutation* or *(Q,LD,LDQ)-proof*. Both Q-resolution and the LDQ-calculus are sound and refutationally complete proof systems for QBFs that do not contain tautological clauses [1,7]. Figure 1 shows an LDQ-refutation.

3 Short LDQ-Proofs for Hard Formulas

We argue that LDQ-resolution has the potential to shorten proofs of false QBFs by showing that the application of LDQ-resolution on QBFs of a particular family [7] results in proofs of polynomial size.

A formula φ_t in this family $(\varphi_t)_{t \geq 1}$ of QBFs has the quantifier prefix

$$\exists d_0 d_1 e_1 \forall x_1 \exists d_2 e_2 \forall x_2 \exists d_3 e_3 ... \forall x_{t-1} \exists d_t e_t \forall x_t \exists f_1 ... f_t$$

and a matrix consisting of the following clauses:

$$\begin{array}{ll}
C_0 = \overline{d_0} & C_1 = d_0 \vee \overline{d_1} \vee \overline{e_1} \\
C_{2j} = d_j \vee \overline{x_j} \vee \overline{d_{j+1}} \vee \overline{e_{j+1}} & C_{2j+1} = e_j \vee x_j \vee \overline{d_{j+1}} \vee \overline{e_{j+1}} \quad \text{for } j=1,...,t-1 \\
C_{2t} = d_t \vee \overline{x_t} \vee \overline{f_1} \vee ... \vee \overline{f_t} & C_{2t+1} = e_t \vee x_t \vee \overline{f_1} \vee ... \vee \overline{f_t} \\
B_{2j-1} = x_j \vee f_j & B_{2j} = \overline{x_j} \vee f_j \quad \text{for } j=1,...,t
\end{array}$$

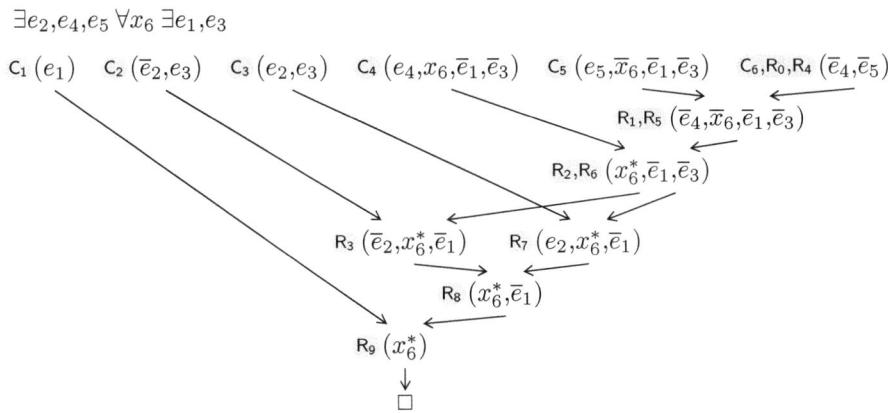

Fig. 1. The LDQ-refutation as a running example. Labels C_1 to C_6, R_1 to R_9 denote the original clauses and the resolvents, respectively. E.g. "R_2,R_6" is shorthand for "$R_2 = R_6$", meaning that the clauses R_2 and R_6 are equal. The derivation and the labels are explained in Examples 2 and 3.

By Theorem 3.2 in [7], any Q-refutation of φ_t for $t \geq 1$ is exponential in t. The formula φ_t has a polynomial size Q-resolution refutation if universal pivot variables are allowed [14]. In the following, we show how to obtain polynomial size LDQ-refutations in the form of a directed acyclic graph (DAG). A straightforward translation of this DAG to a tree results in an exponential blow-up.

Proposition 1. *Any φ_t has an LDQ-refutation of polynomial size in t for $t \geq 1$.*

Proof. An LDQ-refutation with $O(t)$ clauses for $(\varphi_t)_{t \geq 1}$ can be constructed as follows:

1. Derive $d_t \vee \overline{x}_t \vee \bigvee_{i=1}^{t-1} \overline{f}_i$ from B_{2t} and C_{2t}. Derive $e_t \vee x_t \vee \bigvee_{i=1}^{t-1} \overline{f}_i$ similarly.
2. Use both clauses from Step 1 together with $C_{2(t-1)}$ and derive the clause $d_{t-1} \vee \overline{x}_{t-1} \vee \bigvee_{i=1}^{t-1} \overline{f}_i \vee x_t^*$. Observe that the quantification level of d_t and e_t is smaller than the level of x_t. Use $B_{2(t-1)}$ to get $d_{t-1} \vee \overline{x}_{t-1} \vee \bigvee_{i=1}^{t-2} \overline{f}_i \vee x_t^*$. Derive the clause $e_{t-1} \vee x_{t-1} \vee \bigvee_{i=1}^{t-2} \overline{f}_i \vee x_t^*$ in a similar way.
3. Iterate the procedure to derive $d_2 \vee \overline{x}_2 \vee \bigvee_{i=1}^{1} \overline{f}_i \vee \bigvee_{i=3}^{t} x_i^*$ as well as $e_2 \vee x_2 \vee \bigvee_{i=1}^{1} \overline{f}_i \vee \bigvee_{i=3}^{t} x_i^*$.
4. With C_2, derive $d_1 \vee \overline{x}_1 \vee \overline{f}_1 \vee \bigvee_{i=2}^{t} x_i^*$. Use B_2 to obtain $d_1 \vee \overline{x}_1 \vee \bigvee_{i=2}^{t} x_i^*$. Derive $e_1 \vee x_1 \vee \bigvee_{i=2}^{t} x_i^*$ in a similar fashion.
5. Use the two derived clauses together with C_0 and C_1 to obtain $\bigvee_{i=1}^{t} x_i^*$, which can be reduced to the empty clause by universal reduction. □

This result leads to the assumption that QBF solving algorithms can benefit from employing the LDQ-calculus. Next, we discuss how it is integrated in search-based QBF solvers.

4 LDQ-Proof Generation in Search-Based QBF Solving

We consider *search-based QBF solving with conflict-driven clause learning (QCDCL)* as an application of LDQ-resolution. Search-based QBF solving is an extension of the

```
State ld-qcdcl()
  while (true)
    State s = qbcp();                    Assignment analyze_conflict()
    if (s == UNDET)                        i = 0;
      assign_dec_var();                    R_i = find_confl_clause();
    else                                   while (!stop_res(R_i))
      if (s == UNSAT)                        p_i = get_pivot(R_i);
        a = analyze_conflict();              R'_i = get_antecedent(p_i);
      else if (s == SAT)                     R_{i+1} = resolve(R_i,p_i,R'_i);
        a = analyze_solution();              R_{i+1} = reduce(R_{i+1});
      if (a == INVALID)                      i++;
        return s;                          add_to_formula(R_i);
      else                                 return get_retraction(R_i);
        backtrack(a);
```

Fig. 2. Search-based QBF solving with LD-QCDCL [15,16] using long-distance resolution

DPLL algorithm [2,3]. Given a QBF $\psi = \mathcal{P}.\phi$, the idea of QCDCL [4,8,15,16] is to dynamically generate and add derived clauses to the matrix ϕ. If ψ is false, then the empty clause $\square$ will finally be generated. In this case, the sequence of clauses involved in the generation of all the learned clauses forms a Q-refutation of ψ.

We focus on the generation of tautological learned clauses in QCDCL based on long-distance (LD) resolution [15,16]. We call the application of this method in search-based QBF solving *LD-QCDCL*. The soundness proof of LD-QCDCL (Lemma 2 and the theorem in [15]) shows that the learned clauses have certain properties *in the context of LD-QCDCL*. Due to these properties of the learned clauses, LD-resolution is applied in a restricted fashion in LD-QCDCL, which ensures soundness. In general, unrestricted LD-resolution relying on the definition in Section 2 is unsound, as pointed out in Example 1.

We prove that the generation of a (tautological) learned clause by LD-resolution in LD-QCDCL corresponds to a derivation in the LDQ-resolution calculus [1] from Section 2. Hence learning tautological clauses in LD-QCDCL produces LDQ-refutations. With our observation we embed the LD-QCDCL procedure [15,16] in the formal framework of the LDQ-resolution calculus, the soundness of which was proved in [1].

In order to make the presentation of our results self-contained and to emphasize the relevance of long-distance resolution in search-based QBF solving, we describe LD-QCDCL in the following. Figure 2 shows a pseudo code.

In our presentation of LD-QCDCL we use the following terminology. Given a QBF $\psi = \mathcal{P}.\phi$, a clause $C \in \phi$ is *unit* if and only if $C = (l)$ and $\text{quant}(l) = \exists$, where l is a *unit literal*. The operation of *unit literal detection* $UL(C) := \{l\}$ collects the assignment $\{l\}$ from the unit clause $C = (l)$. In this case, clause $C = \text{ante}(l)$ is the *antecedent clause* of the assignment $\{l\}$. Otherwise, if C is not unit then $UL(C) := \{\}$ is the empty assignment. Unit literal detection is extended from clauses to sets of clauses in ψ: $UL(\psi) := \bigcup_{C \in \phi} UL(C)$. Resolution (function resolve) and universal reduction (function reduce) are defined as in Section 2.

The operation of *quantified boolean constraint propagation (QBCP)* extends an assignment σ to $\sigma' \supseteq \sigma$ by iterative applications of unit literal detection and universal reduction until fixpoint[1] and computes ψ under σ', such that for $\psi' := \mathsf{reduce}(\psi_{\lceil\sigma'})$, $QBCP(\psi_{\lceil\sigma}) := \psi'_{\lceil\sigma'}$.

LD-QCDCL successively generates partial assignments to the variables in a given QBF ψ. This process amounts to splitting the goal of proving falsity or truth of a QBF into subgoals by case distinction based on QBF semantics. Similar to [15,16], we assume that all clauses in the original ψ are non-tautological. Initially, the current assignment σ is empty. First, QBCP is applied to $\psi_{\lceil\sigma}$ (function qbcp). If $QBCP(\psi_{\lceil\sigma}) \neq \top$ and $QBCP(\psi_{\lceil\sigma}) \neq \bot$, then the QBF is undetermined under σ (s == UNDET). A variable from the leftmost quantifier block, called *decision variable* or *assumption*, is selected heuristically and assigned a value (function assign_dec_var). Assigning the decision variable extends σ to a new assignment σ' and QBCP is applied again to $\psi_{\lceil\sigma}$ with respect to $\sigma := \sigma'$.

If $QBCP(\psi_{\lceil\sigma}) = \bot$ ($QBCP(\psi_{\lceil\sigma}) = \top$), then the QBF is false (true) under the current assignment σ and the result of the subcase corresponding to σ has been determined (s == SAT or s == UNSAT). The case $QBCP(\psi_{\lceil\sigma}) = \bot$ is called a *conflict* because σ does not satisfy all the clauses in ϕ. Analogously, the case $QBCP(\psi_{\lceil\sigma}) = \top$ is called a *solution* because σ satisfies all clauses in ϕ. Depending on the cases, σ is analyzed. In the following, we focus on the generation of a learned clause from a conflict by function analyze_conflict. Dually to clause learning, LD-QCDCL learns *cubes*, i.e. conjunctions of literals, from solutions by function analyze_solution. We refer to related literature on cube learning [4,5,8,10,16].

Consider the case $QBCP(\psi_{\lceil\sigma}) = \bot$. Function analyze_conflict generates a learned clause as follows. Since $QBCP(\psi_{\lceil\sigma}) = \bot$, there is at least one clause $C \in \phi$ which is falsified, i.e. $\mathsf{reduce}(C_{\lceil\sigma}) = \square$. Function find_confl_clause finds such a clause C and initially sets $R_i := C$ for $i = 0$, where R_i denotes the current resolvent in the derivation of the clause to be learned (while-loop).

In the derivation of the learned clause, the current resolvent R_i is resolved with the antecedent clause $R'_i := \mathsf{ante}(l)$ of an existential variable $p_i = \mathsf{var}(l)$, where $\bar{l} \in R_i$ (functions get_antecedent and resolve). Variable p_i has been assigned by unit literal detection during QBCP and it is the pivot variable of the current resolution step (function get_pivot). According to [16], function get_pivot selects the unique variable p_i as pivot which has been assigned most recently by unit literal detection among the variables in R_i. Hence in the derivation variables are resolved on in reverse assignment ordering. Universal reduction is applied to the resolvent (function reduce).

If the current resolvent R_i satisfies a particular stop criterion (stop_res) then the derivation terminates and R_i is the clause to be learned. The stop criterion according to [16] makes sure that R_i is an *asserting* clause, which amounts to the following property: R_i is unit under a new assignment $\sigma' \subset \sigma$ obtained by retracting certain assignments from the current assignment σ. Function get_retraction computes the assignments to be retracted from σ by backtracking (function backtrack). The learned clause R_i is added to ϕ. QBCP with respect to the new assignment $\sigma := \sigma'$ detects that R_i is unit.

LD-QCDCL determines that ψ is false if and only if the empty clause $\square$ is derived by function analyze_conflict. This case (and similarly for true QBFs and cube

---

[1] For simplicity, we omit *monotone (pure) literal detection* [2], which is typically part of QBCP.

learning) is indicated by r == INVALID, meaning that all subcases have been explored and the truth of ψ has been determined.

Example 2. We illustrate LD-QCDCL by the QBF from Fig. 1. In the following, C_i and R_i, respectively, denote clauses and resolvents as shown in Fig. 1. Equal, multiply derived resolvents are depicted as single resolvents with multiple labels, e.g. "R_2,R_6".

Given the empty assignment $\sigma := \{\}$, QBCP detects the unit clause C_1, records the antecedent clause ante(e_1):=C_1, and collects the assignment $\{e_1\}$: $\sigma := \sigma \cup \{e_1\} = \{e_1\}$. No clause is unit under σ at this point. Assume that variable e_2 is selected as decision variable and assigned to *true*, i.e., $\sigma := \sigma \cup \{e_2\} = \{e_1,e_2\}$. Clause C_2 is unit under σ and $\sigma := \sigma \cup \{e_3\} = \{e_1,e_2,e_3\}$ with ante(e_3):=C_2. Further, clauses C_4 and C_5 are unit under σ and universal reduction, and $\sigma := \sigma \cup \{e_4\} \cup \{e_5\} = \{e_1,e_2,e_3,e_4,e_5\}$ with ante(e_4):=C_4 and ante(e_5):=C_5. Now, clause C_6 is falsified under σ, which constitutes a conflict.

The derivation of the learned clause starts with $R_0 := C_6$. Variable e_5 has been assigned most recently among the variables in R_0 assigned by unit literal detection. Hence R_0 is resolved with ante(e_5) = C_5, which gives R_1. The following pivot variables are selected in similar fashion. Further, R_1 is resolved with ante(e_4) = C_4, which gives R_2. Finally, R_2 is resolved with ante(e_3) = C_2, which gives R_3 to be learned and added to the clause set.

Clause R_3 is unit under $\sigma' \subset \sigma$ and universal reduction, where $\sigma = \{e_1,e_2,e_3,e_4,e_5\}$ and $\sigma' = \{e_1\}$. Hence the assignments in $\sigma \setminus \sigma' = \{e_2,e_3,e_4,e_5\}$ are retracted to obtain the new current assignment $\sigma := \sigma' = \{e_1\}$. Now, QBCP detects the unit clauses R_3 and C_3, and $\sigma := \sigma \cup \{\bar{e}_2,e_3\} = \{e_1,\bar{e}_2,e_3\}$. Like above, the clauses C_4 and C_5 are unit and C_6 is falsified. The assignment obtained finally is $\sigma = \{e_1,\bar{e}_2,e_3,e_4,e_5\}$.

At this point, the empty clause is derived as follows (for readability we continue the numbering of the resolvents R_i at the previously learned clause R_3): like above, starting from $R_4 := C_6 = R_0$, R_4 is resolved with ante(e_5) = C_5 and ante(e_4) = C_4, which gives $R_5 := R_1$ and $R_6 := R_2$, respectively. Further, R_6 is resolved with ante(e_3) = C_3, which gives R_7. Two further resolution steps on ante(e_2) = R_3 and ante(e_1) = C_1 give R_8 and R_9, respectively. Finally $\square$ is obtained from R_9 by universal reduction.

With Proposition 4 below, we prove that every application of universal reduction and resolution (functions resolve and reduce in Fig. 2) corresponds to a rule of the LDQ-resolution calculus [1] from Section 2. We use the following notation. Every resolution step S_i by function resolve in the derivation of a learned clause has the form of a quadruple $S_i = (R_i, p_i, R'_i, R_{i+1})$, where $i \geq 0$, R_i is the previous resolvent, p_i is the existential pivot variable, R'_i = ante(l) is the antecedent clause of a literal $\bar{l} \in R_i$ with var(l)=p_i, and R_{i+1} is the resolvent of R_i and R'_i. Proposition 2 and Proposition 3 hold due to the definition of unit literal detection, because the derivation of a learned clause starts at a falsified clause, and because existential variables assigned as unit literals are selected as pivots.

Proposition 2. *Every clause R_i in function* analyze_conflict *in Fig. 2 is falsified under the current assignment σ and universal reduction.*

Proof. For resolvents returned by function resolve, we argue by induction on the number of resolution steps. Consider the first step S_0 and the clause R_0, which by definition of function find_confl_clause is falsified under σ and universal reduction. If R_0

is tautological by $x^* \in R_0$ then variable x must be unassigned. If it were assigned then either $x \in \sigma$ or $\overline{x} \in \sigma$ and hence R_0 would be satisfied but not falsified under σ and thus R_0 would not be returned by function find_confl_clause. Therefore, the property holds for R_0.

Consider an arbitrary step S_i with $i > 0$ and assume that the property holds for R_i. The clause R_i is resolved with an antecedent clause R'_i of a unit literal. That is, the clause R'_i has been unit under σ and universal reduction, and hence contains exactly one existential literal l such that $l \in \sigma$. If R'_i is tautological by $x^* \in R'_i$ then x must be unassigned by similar arguments as above. Otherwise, R_i would have been satisfied and not unit. The variable $p_i = \text{var}(l)$ has been assigned by unit literal detection and it is selected as pivot of the resolution step S_i. Hence no literal of p_i occurs in the resolvent R_{i+1}. If R_{i+1} is tautological by $x^* \in R_{i+1}$ then x must be unassigned. Otherwise, either R_i or R'_i would be satisfied, which either contradicts the assumption that the property holds for R_i or the fact that R'_i was unit, respectively. Therefore, the property holds for the resolvent R_{i+1}.

The property also holds for clauses returned by function reduce since this function is applied to clauses which have the property and universal reduction only removes literals from clauses. □

Proposition 3. *A tautological clause R_i in function* analyze_conflict *in Fig. 2 is never due to an existential variable e with $e \in R_i$ and $\overline{e} \in R_i$.*

Proof. We argue by induction on the number of resolution steps. Similar to [15,16], we assume that all clauses in the original QBF ψ are non-tautological. Consider the first step S_0 and the clause R_0, which by definition of function find_confl_clause is falsified under σ and universal reduction. By contradiction, assume that $e \in R_0$ and $\overline{e} \in R_0$, hence R_0 is tautological due to an existential variable e. Since R_0 is falsified, either $e \in \sigma$ or $\overline{e} \in \sigma$. In either case R_0 is satisfied but not falsified since both $e \in R_0$ and $\overline{e} \in R_0$. Hence, the property holds for R_0.

Consider an arbitrary step S_i with $i > 0$ and assume that the property holds for R_i. By contradiction, assume that the resolvent R_{i+1} of R_i and R'_i is tautological due to an existential variable e with $e \in R_{i+1}$ and $\overline{e} \in R_{i+1}$. We distinguish three cases how the literals e and $\overline{e}$ have been introduced in R_{i+1}: (1) $e \in R_i$ and $\overline{e} \in R_i$, (2) $e \in R'_i$ and $\overline{e} \in R'_i$, and (3) $e \in R_i$ and $\overline{e} \in R'_i$ (the symmetric case $\overline{e} \in R_i$ and $e \in R'_i$ can be handled similarly). By assumption that the property holds for R_i, case (1) cannot occur. In case (2), R'_i is the antecedent clause of a unit literal $l \in R'_i$. Therefore, either $e \notin R'_i$ or $\overline{e} \notin R'_i$ because otherwise R'_i would not have been found as unit: if e is assigned then R'_i would be satisfied and if e is unassigned then R'_i is not unit by definition of unit literal detection. Hence case (2) cannot occur. For case (3), R'_i is the antecedent clause of a unit literal. Since $\overline{e} \in R'_i$, variable e must be assigned with $e \in \sigma$ because R'_i has been unit. Then R_i is satisfied because $e \in R_i$, which contradicts Proposition 2. Since none of the three cases can occur, the property holds for the resolvent R_{i+1}. □

Proposition 4. *Every application of universal reduction and resolution in the derivation of a learned clause in function* analyze_conflict *in Fig. 2 corresponds to an application of a rule of the LDQ-resolution calculus [1] introduced in Section 2.*

Proof. The following facts about function analyze_conflict conform to the rules of the LDQ-resolution calculus. By assumption similar to the original LD-QCDCL procedure [15,16], all clauses in the given QBF ψ (i.e. not containing learned clauses) are non-tautological. By Proposition 3, all tautological resolvents R_{i+1} by function resolve are due to universal variables in R_{i+1}. Only existential pivot variables are selected by function get_antecedent because universal literals cannot be unit in clauses.

The LDQ-rule u_1 of universal reduction is defined for tautological clauses as well. Therefore, universal reduction by function reduce corresponds to the LDQ-rule u_1.

Consider an arbitrary resolution step $S_i = (R_i, p_i, R'_i, R_{i+1})$ in the derivation of a learned clause. If R_{i+1} is non-tautological then S_i corresponds to the LDQ-rule r_1.

If R_{i+1} is tautological by $x^* \in R_{i+1}$ such that $x^* \in R_i$ or $x^* \in R'_i$ and (1) if $x^* \in R_i$ then $x \notin R'_i$ and $\overline{x} \notin R'_i$, and (2) if $x^* \in R'_i$ then $x \notin R_i$ and $\overline{x} \notin R_i$, then S_i corresponds to the LDQ-rule r_1.

If R_{i+1} is tautological by $x^* \in R_{i+1}$ with $\mathsf{lev}(p_i) < \mathsf{lev}(x)$ then S_i corresponds to the LDQ-rule r_2 because the condition on the levels of the pivot variable p_i and the variable x, which causes the tautology, holds.

In the following, we show that the problematic case where the resolvent R_{i+1} is tautological by $x^* \in R_{i+1}$ with $\mathsf{lev}(x) < \mathsf{lev}(p_i)$, thus violating the level condition, cannot occur.

By contradiction, assume that R_{i+1} is tautological by $x^* \in R_{i+1}$ with $\mathsf{lev}(x) < \mathsf{lev}(p_i)$. Assume that $x \in R_i$ and $\overline{x} \in R'_i$. By Proposition 2, R_i is falsified under the current assignment σ and universal reduction. Hence variable x is unassigned. If it were assigned then we would have $\overline{x} \in \sigma$ because $x \in R_i$, but then the antecedent clause R'_i would be satisfied since $\overline{x} \in R'_i$. Hence R'_i would not have been unit and would not be selected by function get_antecedent. Since $\mathsf{lev}(x) < \mathsf{lev}(p_i)$ and x is unassigned, the antecedent clause R'_i could not have been unit. In this case, a literal $l \in R'_i$ of the pivot variable $p_i = \mathsf{var}(l)$ would prevent universal reduction from reducing the literal $\overline{x} \in R'_i$, which is a contradiction. The same reasoning as above applies to the other cases where $\overline{x} \in R_i$ and $x \in R'_i$, $x^* \in R_i$ and $x \in R'_i$, $x \in R_i$ and $x^* \in R'_i$, and to $x^* \in R_i$ and $x^* \in R'_i$. Hence Proposition 4 holds. □

In the following example, we illustrate Proposition 4 by relating the steps in the LDQ-refutation shown in Fig. 1 to rules in the LDQ-calculus.

Example 3. Referring to the resolvents R_i in Example 2 and to clause labels in Fig. 1, clause "R$_1$,R$_5$" is obtained by Example r_1, clause "R$_2$,R$_6$" by r_2 where $x_6 \in X^l$ and $\overline{x}_6 \in X^r$, clause R$_7$ by r_1, clause R$_3$ by r_1, clause R$_8$ by r_2 where $x_6^* \in X^l$ and $x_6^* \in X^r$, clause R$_9$ by r_1, and clause □ by u_1.

We have modified the search-based QBF solver DepQBF [9] to generate tautological learned clauses by LD-QCDCL as in Fig. 2. This is the variant DepQBF-LDQ implementing the LDQ-resolution calculus, which follows from Proposition 4. Instead of *dependency schemes*, both DepQBF and DepQBF-LDQ applied the variable ordering by the quantification levels in the prefix of a QBF. We considered the solver yQuaffle [15,16] as a reference implementation of LD-QCDCL[2]. The left part of Table 1 shows the number of instances solved in the benchmark set from the QBF evaluation

---

[2] http://www.princeton.edu/~chaff/quaffle.html, last accessed in July 2013.

Table 1. Search-based QBF solvers with (yQuaffle, DepQBF-LDQ) and without LD-resolution (DepQBF) in clause learning on preprocessed instances from QBFEVAL'12. Number of solved instances (left) with a timeout of 900s and detailed statistics (right).

QBFEVAL'12-pre (276 formulas)		115 solved by both:	DepQBF-LDQ	DepQBF
yQuaffle	61 (32 sat, 29 unsat)	Avg. assignments	13.7×10^6	14.4×10^6
DepQBF	120 (62 sat, 58 unsat)	Avg. backtracks	43,676	50,116
DepQBF-LDQ	117 (62 sat, 55 unsat)	Avg. resolutions	573,245	899,931
		Avg. learn.clauses	31,939 (taut: 5,571)	36,854
		Avg. run time	51.77	57.78

2012 (QBFEVAL'12-pre),[3] which was preprocessed by Bloqqer.[4] Compared to DepQBF-LDQ, yQuaffle in total solved fewer instances, among them five instances not solved by DepQBF-LDQ. DepQBF-LDQ solved three instances less than DepQBF and solved two instances not solved by DepQBF. A comparison of the 115 instances solved by both DepQBF-LDQ and DepQBF illustrates the potential of the LDQ-resolution calculus in LD-QCDCL. For DepQBF-LDQ, the average numbers in the right part of Table 1 are smaller than for DepQBF, regarding assignments (-5%), backtracks (-13%), resolution steps (-37%), learned clauses (-14%), and run time (-11%). On average, 17% (5,571) of the learned clauses were tautological.

We computed detailed statistics to measure the effects of tautological learned clauses in DepQBF-LDQ. Thereby we focus on instances which were solved and where tautological clauses were learned. Tautological clauses were learned on 38 of the 117 instances solved by DepQBF-LDQ (32%). Among these 38 instances, 2,714,908 clauses were learned in total, 641,746 of which were tautological clauses (23%). A total of 22,324,295 learned clauses became unit by unit literal detection, among them 903,619 tautological clauses (4%). A total of 1,364,248 learned clauses were used as start points (i.e. clauses returned by function find_confl_clause in Fig. 2) to derive a new learned clause, among them no tautological clauses (0%).

On a different benchmark set from the QBF competition 2010,[3] DepQBF-LDQ solved three instances more than DepQBF and solved five instances not solved by DepQBF. On that set, we observed fewer resolutions (-11%) and smaller run time (-9%) with DepQBF-LDQ, compared to DepQBF. Further, tautological clauses were learned on 25% of the instances solved by DepQBF-LDQ in that set. On these instances, 35% of the learned clauses were tautological. Among the learned clauses which became unit, 8% were tautological. Like for the set QBFEVAL'12-pre, no tautological learned clauses were used as start points to derive new learned clauses.

Additionally, we empirically confirmed Proposition 1. As expected, the refutation size for the family $(\varphi_t)_{t \geq 1}$ produced by yQuaffle and DepQBF-LDQ scales linearly with t. In contrast to that, the refutation size scales exponentially with Q-resolution [7] in DepQBF. Table 2 illustrates the difference in the refutation sizes. Somewhat unexpectedly, yQuaffle times out on formulas of size $t \geq 19$ (and DepQBF times out for $t \geq 21$), whereas DepQBF-LDQ solves formulas of size up to $t = 100$ in about one second of run time (we did not

---

[3] We refer to supplementary material like further experiments, binaries, log files, and an appendix: http://www.kr.tuwien.ac.at/staff/lonsing/lpar13.tar.7z
[4] http://fmv.jku.at/bloqqer/

Table 2. Number of resolution steps (in units of 1,000) in refutations of selected formulas in the family φ_t from Section 3. The solvers yQuaffle and DepQBF-LDQ implement the LDQ-resolution calculus, and DepQBF implements Q-resolution. The timeout (TO) was 900 seconds.

Parameter t	13	14	15	16	17	18	19	20
yQuaffle	0.448	0.524	0.606	0.694	0.788	0.888	TO	TO
DepQBF	118	253	540	1,146	2,424	5,111	10,747	22,544
DepQBF-LDQ	0.287	0.330	0.376	0.425	0.477	0.532	0.590	0.651

test with higher parameter values). As an explanation, we found that the number of *cubes* learned by yQuaffle (i.e. the number of times function analyze_solution in Fig. 2 is called) doubles with each increase of t. The learned cubes do not affect the refutation size but the time to generate the refutation. With DepQBF-LDQ, both the number of learned clauses and learned cubes scales linearly with t.

5 Extracting Strategies from LDQ-Proofs

We show that the method to extract strategies from Q-refutations [6] is also correct when applied to LDQ-refutations. This result enables a complete workflow including QBF solving and strategy extraction based on the LDQ-resolution calculus. A similar workflow could be implemented based on a translation of an LDQ-refutation into a Q-refutation as presented in [1]. However, this translation can cause an exponential blow-up in proof size. By applying strategy extraction directly on LDQ-refutations we avoid this blow-up.

Strategy extraction [6] is described as a game between a universal ($\forall$) player and an existential ($\exists$) player on a Q-refutation of a QBF. The game aims at an assignment to $\forall$ variables that renders the matrix unsatisfiable. It proceeds through the quantifier prefix from the left to the right alternating the two players according to the quantifier blocks. The $\exists$ player arbitrarily chooses an assignment $\sigma_\exists$ to the variables in the current block. Then the proof is modified according to $\sigma_\exists$ using sound derivation rules outside the Q-resolution calculus. This modification results in a smaller derivation of $\square$ with all literals contained in $\sigma_\exists$ and their opposite polarities being removed. Based on this modified proof, an assignment $\sigma_\forall$ to the following quantifier block, a $\forall$ block, is calculated such that applying $\sigma_\forall$ to each clause of the proof and applying some extra derivation rules to the proof results in a derivation of $\square$. In this section we show with an argument similar to [6], that (1) the modification of an LDQ-refutation according to any assignment to $\exists$ variables derives $\square$, and (2) the modification of an LDQ-refutation according to a computed assignment to $\forall$ variables derives $\square$.

The reason why this method works for LDQ-refutations in the same way as for Q-refutations is the following. Consider an LDQ-refutation under an assignment $\sigma_\exists$ to $\exists$ variables of some quantifier block of level ℓ. Then the applications of rule r_2 from Section 2 (LD-steps) on $\forall$ variables with quantification level $\ell + 1$ are always removed. This is the case because an LD-step can result in a merged literal x^* only if the pivot variable p (an $\exists$ variable) has a lower quantification level than x. Thus before the $\forall$ player's turn, the pivot variable of each LD-step that results in merged literals of the respective quantifier block is contained in the partial assignment. Either of the parents in the

Algorithm 1. play

Input : QBF $\mathcal{P}.\psi$, LDQ-refutation Π

1 **foreach** *Quantifier block Q in $\mathcal{P}$ from left to right* **do**
2   **if** *Q is existential* **then**
3        $\sigma \leftarrow$ any assignment to each variable in Q;
4   **else** Q is universal
5        $C \leftarrow$ topologically first clause in Π with no existential literals;
6        $\sigma \leftarrow \{\overline{x} \mid x \in C \wedge \text{var}(x) \in Q\} \cup \{x \mid x \notin C \wedge \overline{x} \notin C \wedge \text{var}(x) \in Q\}$;
7     $\Pi^p \leftarrow \texttt{assign}(\Pi, \sigma)$ *(Π^p is not an LDQ-refutation)*;
8     $\Pi \leftarrow \texttt{transform}(\Pi^p)$ *(Π is an LDQ-refutation)*;

Algorithm 2. assign

Input : LDQ-refutation Π, assignment σ to all variables of outermost block
Output Refutation under assignment σ containing LD-rules and P-rules

1 **foreach** *leaf clause C in Π* **do**
2     $C \leftarrow C_{\lceil \sigma}$;
3 **foreach** *inner clause C topologically in Π* **do**
4   **if** *C is a resolution clause* **then**
5        $C^l, C^r \leftarrow$ parents of C;
6        $p \leftarrow$ pivot of C;
7        $C \leftarrow$ p-resolve(C^l, p, C^r);
8   **else** C is a clause derived by reduction
9        $C^c \leftarrow$ parent of C;
10        $x \leftarrow$ variable reduced from C^c;
11        $C \leftarrow$ p-reduce(C^c, p);
12 **return** Π

LD-step is then set to $\top$, and by fixing the derivation, only one polarity of the $\forall$ variable is left in the derived clause.

The algorithms `play` and `assign` describe the algorithm presented in [6], where `play` implements the alternating turns of the $\forall$ and the $\exists$ player. Each player chooses an assignment to the variables in the current quantifier block (Lines 3 and 6 of `play`). The proof is modified after each assignment (Lines 7 and 8 of `play`) and results in an LDQ-refutation of the QBF under the partial assignment. The modification of the LDQ-refutation Π consists of two steps represented by `assign` and `transform`. The algorithm `assign` applies an assignment to Π. It changes each leaf clause according to the definition of a clause under an assignment in Section 2. Then it adjusts the successor clauses in topological order (from leaves to root) by either applying an LDQ-resolution rules or, in cases where the pivot variable or a reduced variable has been removed from at least one of the parents, by applying one of the additional rules presented in [6,13]. These additional rules (P-rules) are reproduced in the following. Symmetric rules are omitted.

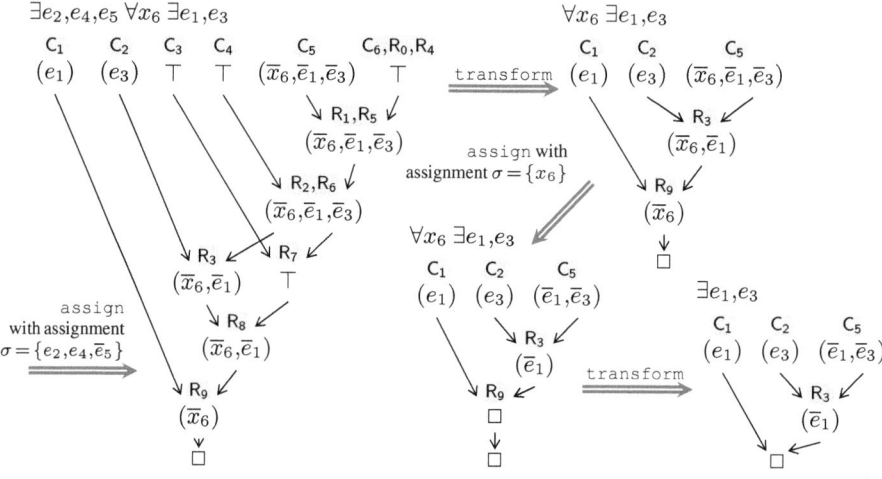

Fig. 3. Two possible iterations of the strategy extraction algorithm play on the example in Fig. 1

$$[p] \frac{C^l \vee p \quad \top}{\top} \quad (r_3) \qquad [x] \frac{C}{C} \quad x \notin C \quad (u_2)$$

$$[p] \frac{C^l \vee p \quad C^r}{C^r} \quad \overline{p} \notin C^r \quad (r_4) \qquad [x] \frac{\top}{\top} \quad (u_3)$$

$$[p] \frac{C^l \quad C^r}{C^l C^r} \quad \overline{p}, p \notin C^l \text{ and } \overline{p}, p \notin C^r \quad (r_5)$$

In rule r_5, narrower(C^l, C^r) returns the clause containing fewer literals. If C^l and C^r contain the same number of literals, C^l is returned. The narrowest clause is $\square$ and $\top$ is defined to contain all literals. In the remainder, we write p-resolve(C^l, p, C^r) for a resolution step over pivot variable p according to rules r_1 to r_5, and p-reduce(C, x) for a reduction step reducing variable x according to rules u_1 to u_3.

After this procedure, the refutation contains applications of P-rules and thus is a proof outside the LDQ-resolution calculus. It is transformed back into an LDQ-refutation by the following procedure. Starting at the leaves of the proof, the algorithm transform(Π^p), where Π^p is a proof that contains clauses derived using LDQ-rules and P-rules, steps through the proof in topological order. Each clause derived by rule r_3, is merged with its parent $\top$. Each clause derived by rule r_4 is merged with its parent C^r. Each clause derived by rule r_5, is merged with its narrower parent. Each clause derived by rules u_1 to u_3 is merged with its parent. When an empty clause $C = \square$ is encountered, the procedure stops and all clauses that are not involved in deriving C are removed. $\top$-clauses are eliminated by applying rule r_4 or by removing clauses when $\square$ is found. The resulting refutation is an LDQ-refutation.

Example 4. Figure 3 depicts a possible execution of the play algorithm on the instance introduced in Fig. 1. First, an arbitrary assignment is chosen for the first existential quantifier block. The leftmost proof shows the result of executing assign on the original proof in Fig. 1. The leaf clauses are changed according to σ. P-rules are applied to the derived clauses "R_1,R_5", "R_2,R_6", R_8 (by rule r_4) and R_7 (by rule r_3). The merged literal x_6^* has disappeared in clause "R_2,R_6" because of the assignment to e_4, which is the pivot variable of the resolution step deriving "R_2,R_6". Before continuing with the $\forall$ player's move, the proof is transformed back to the LDQ-resolution calculus by deleting redundant clauses and edges as depicted in the proof in the right upper corner of Fig. 3. Next, an assignment is calculated for the variable x_6 in following universal quantifier block by inspecting the clause R_9 from which $\bar{x}_6$ is reduced. The proof is then modified according to the computed assignment, which sets R_9 to $\square$ in the middle lower proof. If there were more than one variable in this quantifier block, reducing one after another would result in a subsequent application of universal reduction, eventually deriving $\square$. In the next transformation, a list of redundant clauses containing $\square$ is removed, resulting in the lower right proof. This remaining proof shows unsatisfiability of a propositional formula. The example can be executed similarly for any other assignment to the variables in the existential quantifier blocks.

This algorithm is correct when executed on a Q-resolution proof [6]. We show that it is also correct when executed on an LDQ-resolution proof. To this end, we prove that assign, when called in Line 7 of play, returns a derivation of $\square$ using LDQ-rules and P-rules. Proposition 5 shows that this holds for an arbitrary assignment to all $\exists$ variables in the outermost quantifier block, and Proposition 6 shows the same for the computed assignment to $\forall$ variables.

We start by showing that any clause generated from parent(s) under a partial assignment by applying an LDQ-rule or a P-rule subsumes the clause generated from the original parent(s) under the partial assignment. The proof of the following lemma is based on a case distinction of C^l, C^r, and C containing none, at least one, or only literals also contained in σ. The subset relation is shown separately for each case.[5]

Lemma 1. *(cf. Lemma 2.6 in [13]) Given a QBF $\psi = \exists \mathcal{V} \mathcal{P} \phi$ with $\mathcal{V}$ the set of all variables of the outermost quantifier block, $\mathcal{P}$ the prefix of ψ without $\exists \mathcal{V}$, and ϕ the matrix of ψ, let C, C^l and C^r be clauses of ϕ, and σ an assignment to $\mathcal{V}$. Then it holds that* p-resolve$(C^l_{\lceil \sigma}, p, C^r_{\lceil \sigma}) \subseteq$ p-resolve$(C^l, p, C^r)_{\lceil \sigma}$ *and* p-reduce$(C_{\lceil \sigma}, x) \subseteq$ p-reduce$(C,x)_{\lceil \sigma}$.

With respect to the application of rule r_2 (LD-step), we observe the following from the play algorithm: Let ℓ be the level of an existential quantifier block, p be an existential variable with lev$(p)=\ell$, x be a universal variable with lev$(x)=\ell+1$, $\sigma_\exists$ be an assignment to the variables of the quantifier block with level ℓ, and C be a clause derived by rule r_2 with pivot variable p producing the merged literal x^*. Recall that by the conditions for rule r_2 it must hold that lev$(p) <$ lev(x^*) whenever any merged literal x^* is produced by resolving over a pivot p. The algorithm play iterates over the prefix from the lower to the higher quantification levels. Therefore, $\sigma_\exists$ must contain a literal of p. By modifying the proof according to $\sigma_\exists$, one of C's parents becomes $\top$ and with that, one polarity of

---
[5] We refer to Footnote 3 for an appendix containing a detailed proof of Lemma 1.

the x disappears. By further modifying the proof, the P-rule r_4 must be applied to derive the modified C, which keeps only opposite polarity of x. Therefore, x^* is no longer contained in the proof when its quantifier block is processed.

Lemma 2. *Given a QBF in PCNF $\psi = \exists \mathcal{V}\mathcal{P}\phi$ with $\mathcal{V}$ the set of all variables of the outermost quantifier block, $\mathcal{P}$ the prefix of ψ without $\exists \mathcal{V}$, and ϕ the matrix of ψ, an LDQ-derivation Π of a clause C from ψ, and an assignment $\sigma_\exists$ to $\mathcal{V}$, it holds that $\Pi' = \mathtt{assign}(\Pi, \sigma_\exists)$ derives a clause C' from $\mathcal{P}\phi_{\lceil \sigma_\exists}$ such that $C' \subseteq C_{\lceil \sigma_\exists}$.*

Proof. By induction on the structure of Π using Lemma 1. □

Proposition 5. *Given a QBF in PCNF $\psi = \exists \mathcal{V}\mathcal{P}\phi$ with $\mathcal{V}$ the set of all variables of the outermost quantifier block, $\mathcal{P}$ the prefix of ψ without $\exists \mathcal{V}$, and ϕ the matrix of ψ, an LDQ-refutation Π of ψ, and an assignment $\sigma_\exists$ to $\mathcal{V}$, it holds that $\Pi^p = \mathtt{assign}(\Pi, \sigma_\exists)$ derives $\square$ from $\mathcal{P}\phi_{\lceil \sigma_\exists}$.*

Proof. By Lemma 2, for any clause C derived in Π it holds that Π' derives a clause C' such that $C' \subseteq C_{\lceil \sigma_\exists}$. Therefore, if $C = \square$, then Π' must derive a clause $C' = \square$. □

Proposition 6. *Given a QBF in PCNF $\psi = \forall \mathcal{V}\mathcal{P}\phi$ with $\mathcal{V}$ the set of all variables of the outermost quantifier block, $\mathcal{P}$ the prefix of ψ without $\forall \mathcal{V}$, and ϕ the matrix of ψ, an LDQ-refutation Π of ψ, and an assignment $\sigma_\forall$ to $\mathcal{V}$ as computed in Line 6 of Algorithm 1, $\Pi^p = \mathtt{assign}(\Pi, \sigma_\forall)$ derives $\square$ from $\mathcal{P}\phi_{\lceil \sigma_\forall}$.*

Proof. For any $l \in \sigma_\forall$ it holds that $\mathrm{var}(l)$ is either not reduced at all, or reduced exactly once in Π. If $\mathrm{var}(l)$ is not reduced at all, then it is not involved in Π and therefore its assignment does not alter the proof. Let $R \subseteq \sigma_\forall$ be the set of literals of opposite polarity of those that are reduced exactly once in the proof. Then there is a set $\mathcal{C}$ with $|\mathcal{C}| = |R|$ of clauses such that the clauses in $\mathcal{C}$ are directly following one another, each reducing exactly one literal r in R. The last reduced clause of $\mathcal{C}$ results in $\square$. This is the case because all literals of R are in the outermost quantifier block. The algorithm $\mathtt{assign}\,(\Pi, \sigma_\forall)$ then applies rule u_2 to each clause C, setting each C in $\mathcal{C}$ to $\square$. □

6 Conclusions and Future Work

We have shown that the LDQ-resolution calculus [1] allows for a complete workflow in search-based QBF solving, including the generation of LDQ-refutations in QBF solvers and the extraction of strategies [6] from these LDQ-refutations. The run time of strategy extraction is polynomial in the refutation size. Therefore, a speedup in strategy extraction can be obtained from having short LDQ-refutations, compared to Q-refutations [7].

It is unclear whether Herbrand functions can be efficiently constructed in certificate extraction [1] based on LDQ-refutations. It is possible to build Herbrand functions from truth tables generated by the strategy extraction method in [6]. However, since each possible assignment to the existential variables has to be considered, the run time of this naive method is exponential in the size of the quantifier prefix.

Regarding practice, learning tautological clauses by LD-QCDCL as used in QBF solvers is conceptually simpler than disallowing tautological resolvents. Tautological resolvents can entirely be avoided in clause learning [4]. However, this approach has an exponential worst case [14], in contrast to a more sophisticated polynomial-time procedure [10].

Experimental results for our implementation of LD-QCDCL illustrate the potential of the LDQ-calculus in search-based QBF solving. For instances solved by both methods, one learning only non-tautological clauses and the other learning also tautological clauses, we observed fewer backtracks, resolution steps, and learned clauses for the latter.

Long-distance resolution can also be applied to derive learned *cubes* or *terms*, i.e. conjunctions of literals (Proposition 6 in [16]). Dually to learned clauses, the learned cubes represent a *term-resolution proof* [4] of a true QBF. Our implementation of LD-QCDCL in DepQBF-LDQ includes cube learning as well.

In LD-QCDCL, a tautological clause is satisfied as soon as the variable causing the tautology is assigned either truth value. These clauses cannot become unit *under the current assignment* and hence cannot be used to derive a new learned clause in this context. Therefore, further experiments are necessary to assess the value of learning tautological clauses.

In general, it would be interesting to compare the different clause learning methods [4,10,15,16] in search-based QBF solving to identify their individual strengths.

References

1. Balabanov, V., Jiang, J.-H.R.: Unified QBF Certification and Its Applications. Formal Methods in System Design 41, 45–65 (2012)
2. Cadoli, M., Giovanardi, A., Schaerf, M.: An Algorithm to Evaluate Quantified Boolean Formulae. In: AAAI/IAAI (1998)
3. Davis, M., Logemann, G., Loveland, D.W.: A Machine Program for Theorem-Proving. Communications of the ACM 5(7), 394–397 (1962)
4. Giunchiglia, E., Narizzano, M., Tacchella, A.: Clause/Term Resolution and Learning in the Evaluation of Quantified Boolean Formulas. Journal of Artificial Intelligence Research 26, 371–416 (2006)
5. Goultiaeva, A., Bacchus, F.: Recovering and Utilizing Partial Duality in QBF. In: Järvisalo, M., Van Gelder, A. (eds.) SAT 2013. LNCS, vol. 7962, pp. 83–99. Springer, Heidelberg (2013)
6. Goultiaeva, A., Van Gelder, A., Bacchus, F.: A Uniform Approach for Generating Proofs and Strategies for Both True and False QBF Formulas. In: 22nd International Joint Conference on Artificial Intelligence (IJCAI), pp. 546–553. AAAI Press (2011)
7. Kleine Büning, H., Karpinski, M., Flögel, A.: Resolution for Quantified Boolean Formulas. Information and Computation 117(1), 12–18 (1995)
8. Letz, R.: Lemma and Model Caching in Decision Procedures for Quantified Boolean Formulas. In: Egly, U., Fermüller, C. (eds.) TABLEAUX 2002. LNCS (LNAI), vol. 2381, pp. 160–175. Springer, Heidelberg (2002)
9. Lonsing, F., Biere, A.: DepQBF: A Dependency-Aware QBF Solver (System Description). Journal on Satisfiability, Boolean Modeling and Computation 7, 71–76 (2010)
10. Lonsing, F., Egly, U., Van Gelder, A.: Efficient Clause Learning for Quantified Boolean Formulas via QBF Pseudo Unit Propagation. In: Järvisalo, M., Van Gelder, A. (eds.) SAT 2013. LNCS, vol. 7962, pp. 100–115. Springer, Heidelberg (2013)
11. Marques Silva, J.P., Lynce, I., Malik, S.: Conflict-Driven Clause Learning SAT Solvers. In: Handbook of Satisfiability, pp. 131–153. IOS Press (2009)

12. Staber, S., Bloem, R.: Fault Localization and Correction with QBF. In: Marques-Silva, J., Sakallah, K.A. (eds.) SAT 2007. LNCS, vol. 4501, pp. 355–368. Springer, Heidelberg (2007)
13. Van Gelder, A.: Input Distance and Lower Bounds for Propositional Resolution Proof Length. In: Bacchus, F., Walsh, T. (eds.) SAT 2005. LNCS, vol. 3569, pp. 282–293. Springer, Heidelberg (2005)
14. Van Gelder, A.: Contributions to the Theory of Practical Quantified Boolean Formula Solving. In: Milano, M. (ed.) CP 2012. LNCS, vol. 7514, pp. 647–663. Springer, Heidelberg (2012)
15. Zhang, L., Malik, S.: Conflict Driven Learning in a Quantified Boolean Satisfiability Solver. In: 2002 IEEE/ACM International Conference on Computer-Aided Design, pp. 442–449 (2002)
16. Zhang, L., Malik, S.: Towards a Symmetric Treatment of Satisfaction and Conflicts in Quantified Boolean Formula Evaluation. In: Van Hentenryck, P. (ed.) CP 2002. LNCS, vol. 2470, pp. 200–215. Springer, Heidelberg (2002)

Verifying Temporal Properties in Real Models

Tim French, John McCabe-Dansted, and Mark Reynolds*

School of Computer Science and Software Engineering
University of Western Australia
Crawley, Perth Western Australia 6009
{tim.french,john.mccabe-dansted,mark.reynolds}@uwa.edu.au

Abstract. Based on pioneering work of Läuchli and Leonard in the 1960s, a novel and expressive formal language, Model Expressions, for describing the compositional construction of general linear temporal structures has recently been proposed. A sub-language, Real Model Expressions, is capable of specifying models over the real flow of time but its semantics are subtly different because of the specific properties of the real numbers.

Model checking techniques have been developed for the general linear Model Expressions and it was shown that checking temporal formulas against structures described in the formal language is PSPACE-Complete and linear in the length of the model expression.

In this paper we present a model checker for temporal formulas over real-flowed models. In fact the algorithm, and so its complexity, is the same as for the general linear case.

To show that this is adequate we use a concept of temporal bisimulations and establish that it is respected by the compositional construction method. We can then check the correctness of using the general linear model checking algorithm when applied to real model expressions with their special semantics on real-flowed structures.

1 Introduction

RTL [Rey10a] is the propositional temporal logic with Kamp's Until and Since connectives over structures which have the real numbers as the flow of time. It is the most fundamental continuous time temporal logic, being a basis for practical metric temporal logics [AH91], and so for reasoning about refinement, open and reactive systems, distributed (interleaved) and parallel processes, AI and natural language semantics. The language is as expressive as first-order languages on structures with monadic predicates over the reals.

Although it may not seem as amenable to automated reasoning as discrete time temporal logics, some progress has been made towards reasoning techniques for RTL: decidability was shown in [BG85], complete axiom systems in [GH90,Rey92], and [Rey10a] showed that the complexity, PSPACE, of deciding satisfiability of RTL formulas was the same as that for discrete time.

---
* The work was partially supported by the Australian Research Council.

Model-checking in continuous time is a popular ongoing research area with important practical applications. Up until now it has mostly been concerned with checking properties of discrete-step systems operating against a continuous metric background: see for example the timed automata of [AD94] and recent advances in model-checking in [Be08].

In an alternative, and hopefully eventually complimentary, approach we have built on foundations from [LL66] and [BG85] and have considered truly continuous-time behaviour that might be observed in the environment of a reactive system or from the behaviour of hybrid systems [DN00]. The main contribution [Fe12] has been formal languages for the compositional construction of models of behaviour in both general linear time and specifically over the reals. We were able to use the formal language to prove a *synthesis* result for RTL: any satisfiable RTL formula has a model described in the formal language, and we gave an EXPTIME algorithm to find the model [Fe12].

The formal language we introduced in [Fe12] was that of *Model Expressions*. Using the historical results in [LL66], it followed that any Until and Since formula that is satisfiable in a linear structure has a model described by a Model Expression (ME). We formulated a sub-language called Real Model Expressions (RME) which was adequate to represent a model of any satisfiable RTL formula, i.e. an Until and Since formula that has a model with flow of time being the real numbers under their usual order. For the purposes of the current paper it is important to note that, in order to end up with a real-flowed model, we had to give a subtly different semantics to RMEs than we gave to MEs over general linear time. The reals satisfy some rather idiosyncratic properties which we describe below.

In separate work we have recently proposed model checking algorithms for Until and Since formulas in general linear structures [Fe13d,Fe13c]. These procedures take, as inputs, a temporal formula and an ME. The yes/no output is supposed to tell us whether or not the formula is true at some time in a model described by the ME. It was shown that checking temporal formulas against structures described in the formal language is PSPACE-Complete and linear in the length of the model expression.

Here we want to extend the model-checking approach to RTL. Of course, as RMEs are a subset of MEs we could just supply a formula and the RME directly to the general linear time model checker. The trouble with doing that is that, as we have mentioned above, the semantics for MEs and RMEs are different. In fact, the corresponding structures are not even isomorphic: one having a countable flow, the other uncountable.

So in this paper we show that the difference in semantics is not a problem for the truth of temporal formulas and so not a problem for our model checkers. To prove this we rely on a bisimulation result from [KdR97], where a notion of temporal bisimulations was introduced and shown to respect temporal equivalence. By tracing through such bisimulations through the iterations of the compositional construction method underlying MEs and RMEs we show that the meaning of an RME as an ME is bisimilar to its meaning via the specifically real-flowed semantics for RMEs.

As we have mentioned, the language with Until and Since is expressively complete for the reals [Kam68,GHR94]. There are algorithms via translations to temporal languages, e.g. separation results [GHR93], although they are probably too computationally complex to be usable in practice. Thus, as a by-product, we have a (theoretical) model checking algorithm for first-order monadic formulas over the reals.

Contributions of this paper are as follows: showing that the compositional construction method preserves temporal bisimulations; showing that the different semantics for MEs and RMEs agree on the truth of temporal formulas; a model checking algorithm for any Until and Since formula against any RME; (inherited) complexity results for the algorithm; and a model checking algorithm for any first-order monadic formula against an RME.

This is a shortened conference version of the paper: full details can be found in an online report at [Fe13a].

In section 2 we introduce the two logics USLIN over general linear time and RTL over the reals. Section 3 reminds us of Model Expressions for general linear time. Section 4 summarises the model checking algorithms for MEs. Section 5 introduces the RME sub-language with its different semantics. Section 6 shows that the compositional constructions preserve bisimulation between structures and hence that the two semantics for RMEs and MEs agree on temporal truth. Section 7 tells us how to do model checking of temporal formulas against models described by RMEs. Section 8 translates the results for the first-order monadic logic of the reals order.

2 The Logics

In this section we will introduce the two main logics that we will be considering: USLIN and RTL.

Fix a countable set $\mathcal{L}$ of atoms. Here, frames $(T, <)$, or flows of time, will be irreflexive linear orders. *Structures* $\mathbf{T} = (T, <, h)$ will have a frame $(T, <)$ and a valuation h for the atoms i.e. for each atom $p \in \mathbf{L}$, $h(p) \subseteq T$. Of particular importance will be *real* structures $\mathbf{T} = (\mathbb{R}, <, h)$ which have the real numbers flow (with their usual irreflexive linear ordering). For technical reasons, which we explain briefly later, our definitions here are slightly unusual in that we allow frames and structures to be empty.

The language $L(U, S)$ is generated by the 2-place connectives U and S along with classical $\neg$ and $\wedge$. That is, we define the set of formulas recursively to contain the atoms and for formulas α and β we include $\neg \alpha$, $\alpha \wedge \beta$, $U(\alpha, \beta)$ and $S(\alpha, \beta)$.

Formulas are evaluated at points in structures $\mathbf{T} = (T, <, h)$. We write $\mathbf{T}, x \models \alpha$ when α is true at the point $x \in T$. This is defined recursively as follows. Suppose that we have defined the truth of formulas α and β at all points of $\mathbf{T}$. Then for all points x:

$\mathbf{T}, x \models p$ iff $x \in h(p)$, for p atomic;
$\mathbf{T}, x \models \neg \alpha$ iff $\mathbf{T}, x \not\models \alpha$;
$\mathbf{T}, x \models \alpha \wedge \beta$ iff both $\mathbf{T}, x \models \alpha$ and $\mathbf{T}, x \models \beta$;
$\mathbf{T}, x \models U(\alpha, \beta)$ iff there is $y > x$ in T such that $\mathbf{T}, y \models \alpha$ and for all $z \in T$ such that $x < z < y$ we have $\mathbf{T}, z \models \beta$; and
$\mathbf{T}, x \models S(\alpha, \beta)$ iff there is $y < x$ in T such that $\mathbf{T}, y \models \alpha$ and for all $z \in T$ such that $y < z < x$ we have $\mathbf{T}, z \models \beta$.

We use the following abbreviations in illustrating the logic: $F\alpha = U(\alpha, \top)$, "alpha will be true (sometime in the future)"; $G\alpha = \neg F(\neg \alpha)$, "alpha will always hold (in the future)"; and their mirror images P and H. Particularly for dense time applications we also have: $C^+\alpha = U(\top, \alpha)$, "alpha will be constantly true for a while after now"; and $K^+\alpha = \neg C^+\neg\alpha$, "alpha will be true arbitrarily soon". They have mirror images C^- and K^-.

Note that it is straightforward to show that isomorphisms between structures respect the truth of temporal formulas.

2.1 USLIN

If we use the $L(U, S)$ language over the class LIN of all linear structures then we obtain the logic which we will call USLIN.

A formula ϕ is *USLIN-satisfiable* if it has a linear model: i.e. there is a linear structure $\mathbf{S} = (T, <, h)$ and $x \in T$ such that $\mathbf{S}, x \models \phi$. We say that a formula ϕ is satisfied *in* a structure $\mathbf{S} = (T, <, h)$ iff there is $x \in T$ such that $\mathbf{S}, x \models \phi$. A formula is *USLIN-valid* iff it is true at all points of all linear structures. Of course, a formula is USLIN-valid iff its negation is not USLIN-satisfiable. We will refer to the logic of L(U,S) over real structures as USLIN.

Validity has been axiomatised by Burgess in [Bur82] and shown to be decidable in PSPACE by Reynolds in [Rey10b].

Some interesting formulas satisfiable in USLIN include $G\bot$, $U(\top, \bot)$ and $G(U(\top, \bot) \wedge \neg S(\top, \bot))$.

2.2 RTL

If we work with the L(U,S) language but restrict our attention only to structures which have the reals as a flow of time then we obtain the logic known as RTL.

A formula ϕ is $\mathbb{R}$-*satisfiable* if it has a real model: i.e. there is a real structure $\mathbf{S} = (\mathbb{R}, <, h)$ and $x \in \mathbb{R}$ such that $\mathbf{S}, x \models \phi$. A formula is $\mathbb{R}$-*valid* iff it is true at all points of all real structures. Again a formula is $\mathbb{R}$-valid iff its negation is not $\mathbb{R}$-satisfiable. We will refer to the logic of L(U,S) over real structures as RTL.

Let RTL-SAT be the problem of deciding whether a given formula of L(U,S) is $\mathbb{R}$-satisfiable or not. The main result of [Rey10a] is:

Theorem 1. *RTL-SAT is PSPACE-complete.*

Previously, it was known from [BG85], via Rabin's famous decision procedure for the second-order monadic logic of two successors [Rab69], that RTL was decidable with a non-elementary upper bound on the complexity of RTL-SAT.

There are complete axiom systems for RTL in [GH90] and in [Rey92]: the former using a special rule of inference and the latter just using orthodox rules. The axioms required by RTL above and beyond those needed for linearity generally correspond to specific mathematical properties of the reals that are important for our work below. So we examine a few in detail.

The formulas $GF\top$ and $HP\top$ ensure that there are no endpoints. $U(\top, \bot)$ is a formula which only holds at a point with a discrete successor point so its negation is valid in RTL and ensures density. Alternatively, $Fp \to FFp$ is a formula which can be used as an axiom for density: it is also valid in RTL.

$(C^+p \wedge F\neg p) \to U(\neg p \vee K^+(\neg p), p)$ was used as an axiom for Dedekind completeness (in [Rey92]) and is valid. Recall the following:

Definition 1. *A linear order is Dedekind complete if and only if each non-empty subset which has an upper bound has a least upper bound.*

The formula above says that if p is true constantly for a while but not forever then there is a least upper bound on the interval in which it remains true. This formula is not valid in the temporal logic with until and since over the rational numbers flow of time (but, note that instances can be true in some non-Dedekind complete structures).

One of the most interesting valid formulas of RTL is Hodkinson's axiom "Sep" (see [Rey92]). It is

$$K^+p \wedge \neg K^+(p \wedge U(p, \neg p)) \to K^+(K^+p \wedge K^-p).$$

This can be used in an axiomatic completeness proof to enforce the *separability* of the linear order:

Definition 2. *A linear order is separable iff it has a countable suborder which is spread densely throughout the order: i.e. between every two elements of the order lies an element of the suborder.*

The fact that the rationals are dense in the reals shows that the reals are separable.

Important for us is the following well-known characterisation of the reals. See for example [Ros82], Theorem 2.30 on page 37.

Theorem 2. *If $(T, <)$ is a linear, dense, Dedekind complete, separable order without endpoints then it is isomorphic to the reals.*

3 Model Expressions

In this section we present our formal notation for describing temporal structures over linear time.

It is well-known from the study of linear orders (e.g., see [Ros82,BG85]), that four simple operations allow complex structures to be built up iteratively from simple ones. They are:

1. concatenation of two structures, consisting of one followed by the other;
2. ω repeats of some structure laid end to end towards the past;
3. ω repeats laid end to end towards the future;
4. and making a densely thorough *shuffle* of copies from a finite set of structures.

These four operations were used to define a formal language called *Model Expressions* (MEs) which describe constructions of linear structures [Fe12]:

$$\mathcal{I} ::= a \mid \lambda \mid \mathcal{I} + \mathcal{J} \mid \overleftarrow{\mathcal{I}} \mid \overrightarrow{\mathcal{I}} \mid \langle \mathcal{I}_1, \ldots, \mathcal{I}_n \rangle$$

where $a \in \Sigma = \wp(\mathcal{L})$ so the letter indicates the atoms true at a point. We refer to these operators, respectively, as *a letter, the empty order, concatenation, lead, trail,* and *shuffle*.

To define the semantics of model expressions, that is the way that they represent actual structures, it is best to first remind ourselves of the concept of lexicographic sums of linear structures [BG85].

Definition 3 (Lexicographic Sum).
Suppose $(T, <_T)$ is a (non-empty) linear order and for each $t \in T$, $\mathcal{X}_t = (X_t, <_t, h_t)$ is a linear structure.
Then the lexicographic sum of the $\mathcal{X}_t$ is

$$\Sigma_{(T,<_T)} \mathcal{X}_t = (U, <, h)$$

where $U = \{(t, x) \mid t \in T, x \in X_t\}$, $(t, x) < (t', x')$ iff $t <_T t'$ or $t = t'$ and $x <_t x'$, and $h(p) = \{(t, x) \mid t \in T, x \in h_t(p)\}$.

For stating and proving a few fundamentals for lexicographic sums $\Sigma_{(T,<_T)} \mathcal{X}_t$ over small finite sets T, it is convenient to introduce the following $\oplus$ notation as well. If $T = \{1, 2, \ldots, n\}$ under the usual ordering, and each $\mathcal{X}_t$ is a linear structure, define

$$\mathcal{X}_1 \oplus \cdots \oplus \mathcal{X}_n = \Sigma_{(T,<_T)} \mathcal{X}_t.$$

It is straightforward to prove that lexicographic sum is associative.

Next we assume that we have fixed a particular partition $Q_0, Q_1, \ldots$ of $\mathbb{Q}$ such that for each $i \in \mathbb{N}$, Q_i is dense in $\mathbb{Q}$. These are used to define particular shuffles deterministically as needed by the following constructions.

For the semantics of model expressions we proceed to say when a model expression is the description of a particular structure. We use the term *correspondence* for this relationship.

Definition 4. *[Correspondence] A model expression $\mathcal{I}$ corresponds to a structure as follows:*

- *λ is the empty expression and corresponds to the empty structure $(\emptyset, <, h)$ where $<$ is the empty relation and $h(p) = \emptyset$ for all $p \in \mathcal{L}$.*
- *a corresponds to any single point structure $(\{x\}, <, h)$ where x is any object, $<$ is the empty relation and $h(p) = \{x\}$ if and only if $p \in a$.*

- $\mathcal{I}+\mathcal{J}$ corresponds to any structure isomorphic to $\mathbf{T}\oplus\mathbf{S}$, for some structure $\mathbf{T}$ which corresponds to $\mathcal{I}$ and $\mathbf{S}$ which corresponds to $\mathcal{J}$.
- $\overleftarrow{\mathcal{I}}$ corresponds to any structure isomorphic to $\Sigma_{(\mathbb{N},>)}\mathcal{X}_t$ where, for all $t \in \mathbb{N}$, $\mathcal{X}_t = \mathcal{X}$ is some structure corresponding to $\mathcal{I}$.
- $\overrightarrow{\mathcal{I}}$ corresponds to any structure isomorphic to $\Sigma_{(\mathbb{N},<)}\mathcal{X}_t$ where, for all $t \in \mathbb{N}$, $\mathcal{X}_t = \mathcal{X}$ is some structure corresponding to $\mathcal{I}$.
- For the case of shuffle, say $\mathcal{I} = \langle \mathcal{I}_1, \ldots, \mathcal{I}_n \rangle$, and suppose that for each $i = 1, \ldots, n$, $\mathcal{X}_i$ coresponds to $\mathcal{I}$. Now define $s\colon \mathbb{Q} \to \langle \mathcal{I}_1, \ldots, \mathcal{I}_n \rangle$ by: if $t \in Q_i \subseteq \mathbb{Q}$ then $s(t) = \mathcal{X}_i$; otherwise—if $t \in \mathbb{Q} \setminus \bigcup_{i \leq n} Q_i$—define $s(t) = \mathcal{X}_1$. Then $\mathcal{I}$ corresponds to any structure isomorphic to $\Sigma_{(\mathbb{Q},<)}s(t)$.

We will give an illustration of the non-trivial operations below. The *lead* operation, $\mathcal{I} = \overleftarrow{\mathcal{J}}$ has ω submodels, each corresponding to $\mathcal{J}$, and each preceding the last, as illustrated in Figure 1.

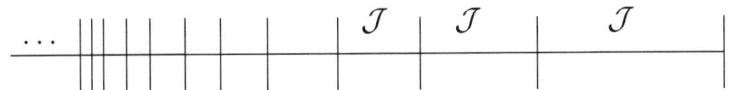

Fig. 1. The lead operation, where $\mathcal{I} = \overleftarrow{\mathcal{J}}$

The *trail* operator is the mirror image of *lead*, whereby $\mathcal{I} = \overrightarrow{\mathcal{J}}$ has ω structures, each corresponding to $\mathcal{J}$ and each proceeding the earlier structures.

The *shuffle* operator is harder to represent with a diagram. The model expression $\mathcal{I} = \langle \mathcal{I}_1, \ldots \mathcal{I}_n \rangle$ corresponds to a dense, thorough mixture of intervals corresponding to $\mathcal{I}_1$, ..., $\mathcal{I}_n$, without endpoints. We define the shuffle operation using the rationals, $\mathbb{Q}$ as they are a convenient order with the required properties.

As an example we might suggest the model expression, and corresponding structure, from Figure 3 for a model of $U(q \wedge K^+p \wedge GS(p, \neg p), \neg U(q, \neg q) \wedge \neg U(q,q))$. Note the three different shuffles that it contains.

A famous result from last century, [LL66,BG85], (which has recently been embellished with a formal notation and efficient discovery algorithm [Fe12,Fe13b]), tells us that such a model expression is capable of describing a model of any satisfiable formula.

Theorem 3. *If ϕ is a satisfiable formula of $USLIN$ then there is an ME $\mathcal{I}$ and a structure $\mathbf{T}$, and point x such that $\mathbf{T}$ corresponds to $\mathcal{I}$, and $\mathbf{T}, x \models \phi$.*

4 Model Checking

We will here give a brief outline of existing results on model checking MEs. We first formally define the model-checking problem.

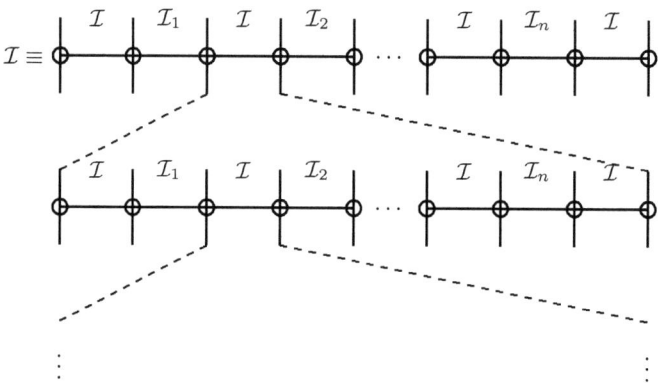

Fig. 2. The shuffle operation, where $\mathcal{I} = \langle \mathcal{I}_1, \ldots, \mathcal{I}_n \rangle$

Definition 5. *We define the* USME*-checking problem as follows: given an ME $\mathcal{I}$ and formula ϕ, determine whether there exists a structure $\mathbf{T} = (T, <, h)$ corresponding to $\mathcal{I}$ and point $x \in T$ such that $\mathbf{T}, x \vDash \phi$.*

The traditional definition of a model checking problem only tests whether a formula is true at a particular point in the model. The definition above is simpler for MEs because we do not need to define a way of identifying points in an ME; note that a letter with a lead, trail or shuffle will appear infinitely often in the ME. If we want to test whether a formula ϕ is true at a particular letter in an ME, we add an atom p_{start} to that letter and model-check the formula $p_{\text{start}} \to \phi$. If the letter to which we add p_{start} does not occur with the scope of a lead, trail or shuffle, it will correspond to only a single point in the structure.

The simplest USME-model checking procedure to understand is the one presented in the paper [Fe13d]. This procedure follows the traditional approach of adding subformulas to the model as atoms. The result of adding a formula α as an atom to an ME $\mathcal{I}$ is "add_atom$_\alpha(\mathcal{I})$" which will be defined later in this section. When adding α as an atom, all sub-formulas of α have already been added

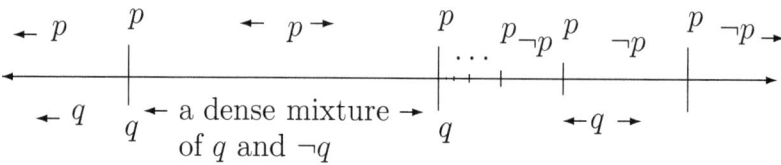

Fig. 3. $\langle\{p,q\}\rangle + \{p,q\} + \langle\{p,q\},\{p\}\rangle + \{p,q\} + \overleftarrow{\{p,q\}} + \langle\{q\}\rangle$

as atoms, so α will be of the form: $p \wedge q$, $\neg p$, $U(p,q)$ or $S(p,q)$. The classical cases are as we would expect, for example add_atom$_{p \wedge q}(\{p,q\}) = \{p, q, p \wedge q\}$.

The difficulty in the model checking procedure comes in adding $U(p,q)$ and $S(p,q)$ as atoms. Note that the truth of $U(p,q)$ at a point cannot be determined from the truth of the atoms at the point. In fact, since we are using strict until operators, the truth of $U(p,q)$ is independent of the truth of the atoms at that point. The truth of $U(p,q)$ is determined solely by the interval following a point. For a fixed formula of the form $U(p,q)$ we define a function pre to represent whether $U(p,q)$ would be true at a point added prior to an interval.

There is a slightly more detailed overview of the procedure in [Fe13a]. Otherwise see [Fe13d] and [MD12] for full details. Another model-checking procedure has been specified that avoids building the ME so that it can run in polynomial space [Fe13c].

In the rest of the paper, we can build our further results on top of any ME model checker, either of the two above or any other similar correct one.

Definition 6. *We assume the* USME*-checking procedure is as follows: given an ME $\mathcal{I}$ and $L(U,S)$ formula ϕ, USME$(\mathcal{I}, \phi)$ will output yes or no to determine correctly whether there exists a structure* $\mathbf{T} = (T, <, h)$ *corresponding to $\mathcal{I}$ and point $x \in T$ such that $\mathbf{T}, x \vDash \phi$.*

5 Real Model Expressions

Model expressions give us a grammar to describe general linear structures. Our particular interest in this paper, though, are frames that are isomorphic to the real numbers. There are two problems that we need to address in order to allow concentration on real-flowed models. First, some model expressions naturally describe linear models which can not be real-flowed; for example, ones with endpoints, with discrete jumps or with obvious Dedekind gaps. Second, the general "correspondence" relationship between model expressions and linear structures, would not necessarily pick out real-flowed structures, even when a suitable one exists—in fact the correspondence relationship as defined above will not match a real-flowed model as it is limited to countable structures.

To address these issues, in [Fe12,Fe13b], we first presented a sublanguage of model expressions, which we called Real Model Expressions, that can describe the reals. Here is the syntax for *real model expressions* (RMEs)[1]:

Definition 7 (Real Model Expressions). *This is a subset of MEs defined inductively as follows. If $a, a_i, x_i, y_i \in \wp(\mathcal{L})$, $m, n \geq 0$ and $\mathcal{K}$ and the $\mathcal{K}_i$ are RMEs, then $\langle a_0, \ldots, a_m, x_1 + \mathcal{K}_1 + y_1, \ldots, x_n + \mathcal{K}_n + y_n \rangle$, $\mathcal{K}_0 + a + \mathcal{K}_1$, $\overleftarrow{a + \mathcal{K}}$ and $\overrightarrow{\mathcal{K} + a}$ are RMEs. (Note that the first case includes the base case when $n = 0$).*

---

[1] Note that here we use the correct version of the RME sublanguage as in [Fe13b]. There was an unfortunate typographical error in the shortened conference exposition [Fe12].

We will see below that the letter a_0 is used as a sort of background filler to help ensure that the shuffle structure is Dedekind complete. The abstract syntax for real model expressions is a direct sub-language of the abstract syntax for general model expressions. We can see that their syntax will always define structures without end points and that the base case of this iteration is a shuffle containing only points. We will see below that such a point shuffle will define a dense, separable linear order with all the letters homogeneously distributed across the linear order.

By the way, the ME in Figure 3 is an RME and it is clear that it can describe a real-flowed structure.

Thus, in our search for model expressions over the reals, we have partially taken care of the first-mentioned problem above: we have eliminated some expressions that obviously can not be dense or Dedekind complete, etc. However, we still need to ensure that the semantics do give us real-flowed structures when they exist.

To define a real-flowed structure from a real model expression, we define a function $\mathcal{R}$ inductively on all model expressions. However, the main use of $\mathcal{R}(\mathcal{K})$ will be when $\mathcal{K}$ is a real model expression.

Definition 8 ($\mathcal{R}(\mathcal{I})$). *Suppose $\mathcal{I}$ is a model expression. We define a particular structure $\mathcal{R}(\mathcal{I})$ inductively and depending on the form of $\mathcal{I}$ as follows.*

- $\mathcal{R}(\lambda) = (\emptyset, \emptyset, h)$, where $h(p) = \emptyset$ for every $p \in \mathcal{L}$.
- For a letter a, $\mathcal{R}(a) = (\{0\}, \emptyset, h)$, where for each $p \in \mathcal{L}$, $h(p) = \{0\}$ if $p \in a$ and $h(p) = \emptyset$ otherwise.
- If $\mathcal{I}_1$ and $\mathcal{I}_2$ are model expressions, then $\mathcal{R}(\mathcal{I}_1 + \mathcal{I}_2) = \mathcal{R}(\mathcal{I}_1) \oplus \mathcal{R}(\mathcal{I}_2)$.
- If $\mathcal{I}$ is a model expression then $\mathcal{R}(\overleftarrow{\mathcal{I}}) = \Sigma_{(\mathbb{N},>)} \mathcal{X}_t$ where $\mathcal{X}_t = \mathcal{R}(\mathcal{I})$ for each $t \in \mathbb{N}$.
- $\mathcal{R}(\overrightarrow{\mathcal{I}})$ is analogously based on $(\mathbb{N}, <)$.
- For the case of shuffle, say $\mathcal{I} = \langle \mathcal{I}_1, \ldots, \mathcal{I}_n \rangle$, define $f \colon \mathbb{R} \to \langle \mathcal{I}_1, \ldots, \mathcal{I}_n \rangle$ by: if $t \in Q_i \subseteq \mathbb{Q}$ then $f(t) = \mathcal{I}_i$; otherwise—if $t \in \mathbb{R} \setminus \bigcup_{i \leq n} Q_i$—define $f(t) = \mathcal{I}_1$. Define $\mathcal{R}(\mathcal{I}) = \Sigma_{(\mathbb{R},<)} \mathcal{R}(f(t))$.

Earlier work in [BG85] used similar refinements of the four [LL66] operations without a formal language of composition of models. They were applied to provide a decidability result for the monadic and temporal theory of the reals. The following lemma (with full proof in [Fe13b]) is implicit in that work. It relies on the above-mentioned characterisation of the reals as dense, Dedekind complete, separable orders without endpoints.

Lemma 1. *For every real model expression $\mathcal{K}$, $\mathcal{R}(\mathcal{K})$ is a structure with a frame that is isomorphic to the reals.*

Definition 9. *We say that a real-flowed structure $(\mathbb{R}, <, h)$ is a compositional real structure (or model) iff it is isomorphic to $R(\mathcal{K})$ for some real model expression $\mathcal{K}$.*

An important result from [BG85,Fe12] is that an RTL formula has a real-flowed model iff it has a compositional real model. In [Fe12,Fe13b], we provided the explicit RME notation that is adequate for representing real structures, we are able to give a finite representation in this notation for a model that supports a given satisfiable L(U,S) formula, and we gave an efficient effective means for finding it.

Theorem 4. *There is an EXPTIME procedure which given a formula ϕ from L(U,S) will decide whether ϕ is $\mathbb{R}$-satisfiable or not and, if so, will provide a real model expression for a compositional model of ϕ.*

6 Correspondence versus $\mathcal{R}$ for an RME

Since the RMEs used to represent real models are a syntactic restriction on the MEs used to represent general linear time, it is possible to simply enter the RME into a model checker for general linear time. Our main theorem below confirms the intuition that it is also correct to do so. The reason that this is not trivial, is, of course, that the relationship between an RME $\mathcal{K}$ and $\mathcal{R}(\mathcal{K})$ is not the same as correspondence between MEs and structures. In this section we investigate these relationships.

First note that for a given RME $\mathcal{K}$, $\mathcal{R}(\mathcal{K})$ is not even isomorphic to any structure which corresponds to $\mathcal{K}$ (as an ME). This is because such a structure would be countable, the iterations in the definition of correspondence all preserve countability. The flow of time of $\mathcal{R}(\mathcal{K})$, however, is of course the uncountable reals.

Fortunately we can use a *bisimulation* result for temporal logic that gives us a way of saying that two structures satisfy the same temporal formulas. This is based on the notion of bisimulation for temporal logics over linear structures defined by [KdR97].

Definition 10 (Bisimulation). *Say $M = (T, <, g)$ and $M' = (T', <', g')$ are bisimilar linear structures.*

A bisimulation between M and M' is a triple $Z = (Z_0, Z_1, Z_2)$ where $Z_0 \subseteq T \times T'$, $Z_1 \subseteq (T^2 \times T'^2)$ and $Z_2 \subseteq (T'^2 \times T^2)$ such that $Z_0 \neq \emptyset$ and the following clauses hold[2]:

B1. *If $x_1 Z_0 x_2$ then x_1 and x_2 satisfy the same proposition letters.*
B2. *If $x_1 Z_0 x_2$ and $x_1 <_1 y_1$, then there exists y_2 in T' with $x_2 <_2 y_2$ such that $y_1 Z_0 y_2$ and $x_1 y_1 Z_1 x_2 y_2$.*
B3. *If $x_1 y_1 Z_1 x_2 y_2$ and there exists z_2 with $x_2 <_2 z_2 <_2 y_2$, then there exists z_1 with $x_1 <_1 z_1 <_1 y_1$ and $z_1 Z_0 z_2$.*
B4. *If $x_1 Z_0 x_2$ and $x_2 <_2 y_2$, then there exists y_1 in T with $x_1 <_1 y_1$ such that $y_1 Z_0 y_2$ and $x_2 y_2 Z_2 x_1 y_1$.*

---
[2] There seemed to be some typos in the original definition. These have been fixed to make the definition consistent with its use in proofs in that paper.

B5. If $x_2y_2Z_2x_1y_1$ and there exists z_1 with $x_1 <_1 z_1 <_1 y_1$, then there exists z_2 with $x_2 <_2 z_2 <_2 y_2$ and $z_1Z_0z_2$.

B6-B9: *Clauses B2 to B5 with $>_1$ ($>_2$) instead of $<_1$ ($<_2$).*

Definition 11 (Bisimilar). *If there is a bisimulation $Z = (Z_0, Z_1, Z_2)$ with $x_1Z_0x_2$ then we say that x_1 and x_2 are bisimilar (notation $x_1 \leftrightarrow x_2$, or $Z: x_1 \leftrightarrow x_2$), and similarly for intervals x_1y_1 and x_2y_2.*

Definition 12 (Bisimilar Structures). *Say $M = (T, <, g)$ is bisimilar to $M' = (T', <', g')$ iff there is a bisimulation $Z = (Z_0, Z_1, Z_2)$ such that Z_0 relates everything in T to something in T' and vice versa. (Also say that a pair of empty structures are bisimilar to each-other.)*

The main result in [KdR97] is that bisimulation implies temporal equivalence.

Lemma 2. *If $T, t \leftrightarrow T', t'$ then t and t' agree on the truth of all US formulas.*

The important result for us that we manage to prove in this section is that the two different ways that we make models out of RMEs give us bisimilar results.

However, we shall approach this result in a more general way that will give us a useful theorem about bisimulations and temporal equivalence being preserved by the compositional construction method.

Lemma 3. *Lexicographic sum preserves bisimulation.*

Proof. Say $\mathcal{U} = (U, <_U, h_U) = \Sigma_{(T, <_T)} \mathcal{X}_t$ with each $\mathcal{X}_t = (X_t, <_t, h_t)$ and $\mathcal{V} = (V, <_V, h_V) = \Sigma_{(T, <_T)} \mathcal{Y}_t$ with each $\mathcal{Y}_t = (Y_t, <_t, h_t)$.

Assume that for each $t \in T$, $\mathcal{X}_t$ is bisimilar to $\mathcal{Y}_t$ via the bisimulation $Z^t = (Z_0^t, Z_1^t, Z_2^t)$.

We will show that $\mathcal{U}$ is bisimilar to $\mathcal{V}$.

We define the triple $Z = (Z_0, Z_1, Z_2)$ as follows.

We simply put $(t, x_1)Z_0(t', x_2)$ iff $t = t'$ and $x_1Z_0^t x_2$.

We put $(s, x_1)(t, y_1)Z_1(s', x_2)(t', y_2)$ iff either 1) $s = t = s' = t'$ and $x_1y_1Z_1^t x_2y_2$, or 2) $s <_T t$, $s = s'$, $t = t'$, $x_1Z_0^s x_2$ and $y_1Z_0^t y_2$.

We put $(s', x_2)(t', y_2)Z_2(s, x_1)(t, y_1)$ iff either 1) $s' = t' = s = t$ and $x_2y_2Z_2^t x_1y_1$, or 2) $s' = s <_T t = t'$, $x_1Z_0^s x_2$ and $y_1Z_0^t y_2$.

Now we show that $Z = (Z_0, Z_1, Z_2)$ is a bisimulation between $\mathcal{U}$ and $\mathcal{V}$.

Note that Z_0 is not empty because none of the Z_0^t are empty and neither is T.

Property B1 holds of Z_0 as it is inherited from the Z_0^t.

To show B2, suppose $(s, x_1)Z_0(s', x_2)$ and $(s, x_1) <_U (t, y_1)$. So $s = s'$ and either $s = t$ and $x_1 <_t y_1$ or $s <_T t$. The first case is easy. In the second case put $t' = t$ and just choose any $y_2 \in Y_t$ such that $y_1Z_0^t y_2$. Thus $(s', x_2) <_V (t', y_2)$, $(t, y_1)Z_0(t', y_2)$ and $(s, x_1)(t, y_1)Z_1(s', x_2)(t', y_2)$. Which is as required.

To show B3, suppose $(s, x_1)(t, y_1)Z_1(s', x_2)(t', y_2)$ and there exists (u', z_2) with $(s', x_2) <_V (u', z_2) <_V (t', y_2)$.

We are to show that there exists (u, z_1) with $(s, x_1) <_U (u, z_1) <_U (t, y_1)$ and $(u, z_1)Z_0(u', z_2)$.

From the definition of Z_1 there are two cases: either 1) $s = t = s' = t'$ and $x_1y_1Z_1^t x_2y_2$, or 2) $s <_T t$, $s = s'$, $t = t'$, $x_1Z_0^s x_2$ and $y_1Z_0^t y_2$.

Consider the first case: $s = t = s' = t'$ and $x_1 y_1 Z_1^s x_2 y_2$. Then B3 for Z^s gives us the desired z_1 to use with $u = s$.

Otherwise, $s <_T t$, $s = s'$, $t = t'$, $x_1 Z_0^s x_2$ and $y_1 Z_0^s y_2$.

As $(s', x_2) <_V (u', z_2) <_V (t', y_2)$ but $s' = s <_T t = t'$, there are three sub-cases: $u' = s$, $u' = t$ or $s <_T u' <_T t$.

Consider the sub-case with $u' = s$. By B4 for Z^s, as $x_1 Z_0^s x_2$ and $x_2 < z_2$, there exists $z_1 \in X_s$ with $x_1 <_s z_1$, $z_1 Z_0^s z_2$ and $x_2 z_2 Z_2^s x_1 z_1$. Now put $u = u' = s$. We have $(s, x_1) <_U (u, z_1) <_U (t, y_1)$ and $(u, z_1) Z_0(u', z_2)$ as required.

The sub-case with $u' = t$ is similar.

Now consider the sub-case with $s <_T u' <_T t$. Put $u = u'$. As Z^u is a bisimulation between $\mathcal{X}_u$ and $\mathcal{Y}_u$ there is some $z_1 \in X_u$ such that $z_1 Z_0^u z_2$. Again we have $(s, x_1) <_U (u, z_1) <_U (t, y_1)$ and $(u, z_1) Z_0(u', z_2)$ as required.

That demonstrates B3.

B4-B9 are similar variations on B2 and B3.

We are done.

One of the main differences between the semantics of MEs and those for RMEs via $\mathcal{R}$ is the exact type of shuffle that is used. For the former it is based on $\mathbb{Q}$ while for the latter it is based on $\mathbb{R}$. This is enough to make structures non-isomorphic, as we have noted.

Fortunately, the notion of a shuffle can be more general than we have used above, and so we can go on to show that any kind of shuffle has the same effect on the truth of temporal formulas.

Definition 13 (General Shuffling). *T is a shuffle of $\{T_1, \ldots, T_n\}$ iff T is isomorphic to $\Sigma_{(Q, <)} T_{f(q)}$ where:*

- *$(Q, <)$ is a dense order without end-points;*
- *$f: Q \to \{1, \ldots, n\}$;*
- *for every $q, q' \in Q$, for every $i \in \{1, \ldots, n\}$, if $q < q'$ then there is $q'' \in Q$ such that $q < q'', < q'$ and $f(q'') = i$.*

Lemma 4. *(General) Shuffling preserves bisimulation. In fact, the respective shuffling methods do not have to match: made precise as follows.*

Suppose $\{S_1, \ldots, S_n\}$ and $\{T_1, \ldots, T_n\}$ are such that each S_i is bisimilar with T_i. Suppose S is a shuffle of $\{S_1, \ldots, S_n\}$ and T is a shuffle of $\{T_1, \ldots, T_n\}$. Then S and T are bisimilar.

The proof of this lemma is similar in form to that of lemma 3, so we omit it from the short version of the paper. See [Fe13a] for full details.

The following lemma then follows.

Lemma 5. *Suppose $\mathcal{K}$ is a Model Expression.*
Then $\mathcal{R}(\mathcal{K})$ is bisimilar to any linear structure which corresponds to $\mathcal{K}$.

Proof. By induction on the construction of $\mathcal{K}$.

Case of λ. Follows by definition of bisimilarity for empty structures.

Case of a. Just use a bisimulation $Z = (Z_0, Z_1, Z_2)$ in which Z_0 relates the two respective singleton objects and Z_1 and Z_2 are empty. Checking the definition of bisimulation is trivial.

Cases of $\mathcal{I} + \mathcal{J}, \overleftrightarrow{(\mathcal{I})}$ **and** $\overrightarrow{(\mathcal{I})}$. Follows directly from Lemma 3.

Case of $\langle \mathcal{I}_1, \ldots, \mathcal{I}_n \rangle$. Follows directly from Lemma 4.

7 Model Checking the Reals

So at last we can prove the main theorem that it is correct just to put RMEs into USME and expect the correct answer regarding truth in the real-flowed model that they determine.

Theorem 5. *Say $\mathcal{K}$ is an RME. Given any RTL formula ϕ, if ϕ is satisfied within $\mathcal{R}(\mathcal{K})$ then USME($\mathcal{K}, \phi$) returns "true" and otherwise returns "false".*

Proof. This follows immediately from the correctness of USME for general linear models, the bisimulation between $\mathcal{R}(\mathcal{K})$ and any model corresponding to $\mathcal{K}$ and the fact that bisimulation implies temporal equivalence.

The complexity of using a USME checker on RMEs is thus the same as for USME applied to MEs, of course. That is, using the best possible algorithms, in PSPACE and linear in the length of the RME.

8 Model Checking FOMLO over the Reals

The first-order monadic language of order, FOMLO, is a first order language which can describe temporal structures and it is useful to translate between it and the temporal language.

Kamp showed in [Kam68] that $L(U, S)$ is expressively complete over $\mathbb{R}$ and over $\mathbb{N}$. This means that each formula of the first-order monadic language of the reals order with one free time variable, has an equivalent expression in the US language, a formula true at exactly the same times in any real-flowed model. The equivalence preserving translations from FOMLO (formulas with one free variable) to temporal formulas (in $L(U, S)$ over the reals) can be extracted from such places as the "separation" proofs in [GHR94]. However, it is considered that any such algorithm may be non-elementarily complex [HR05]. Thus using them is infeasible.

Nevertheless, we have, in theory, for any RME $\mathcal{K}$ a way of model checking any sentence ψ of FOMLO to see whether $\mathcal{R}(\mathcal{K}) \models \psi$ or not. We translate ψ into an equivalent temporal formula and use USME to check whether that holds in $\mathcal{R}(\mathcal{K})$.

References

AD94. Alur, R., Dill, D.: A theory of timed automata. TCS 126, 183–235 (1994)

AH91. Alur, R., Henzinger, T.A.: Logics and models of real time: A survey. In: de Bakker, J.W., Huizing, C., de Roever, W.P., Rozenberg, G. (eds.) REX 1991. LNCS, vol. 600, pp. 74–106. Springer, Heidelberg (1992)

BG85.   Burgess, J.P., Gurevich, Y.: The decision problem for linear temporal logic. Notre Dame J. Formal Logic 26(2), 115–128 (1985)
Be08.   Bouyer, P., Markey, N., Ouaknine, J., Worrell, J.B.: On expressiveness and complexity in real-time model checking. In: Aceto, L., Damgård, I., Goldberg, L.A., Halldórsson, M.M., Ingólfsdóttir, A., Walukiewicz, I. (eds.) ICALP 2008, Part II. LNCS, vol. 5126, pp. 124–135. Springer, Heidelberg (2008)
Bur82. Burgess, J.P.: Axioms for tense logic I: "Since" and "Until". Notre Dame J. Formal Logic 23(2), 367–374 (1982)
DN00.   Davoren, J., Nerode, A.: Logics for hybrid systems. Proc. IEEE (2000)
Fe12.   French, T., McCabe-Dansted, J., Reynolds, M.: Synthesis for temporal logic over the reals. In: AiML, 2012, pp. 217–238. College Pub. (2012)
Fe13a. French, T., McCabe-Dansted, J., Reynolds, M.: Verifying temporal properties in real models (long report version) (2013),
        http://www.csse.uwa.edu.au/~mark/research/Online/vtprm.html
Fe13b. French, T., McCabe-Dansted, J., Reynolds, M.: Synthesis for continuous time: long draft online. Journal Version Submitted,
        http://www.csse.uwa.edu.au/~mark/research/Online/sctm.htm
Fe13c. French, T., McCabe-Dansted, J., Reynolds, M.: Complexity of Model Checking over General Linear Time. In: TIME 2013, pp. 107–116. IEEE CPS (2013)
Fe13d. French, T., McCabe-Dansted, J., Reynolds, M.: Model Checking General Linear Temporal Logic. In: Galmiche, D., Larchey-Wendling, D. (eds.) TABLEAUX 2013. LNCS, vol. 8123, pp. 119–133. Springer, Heidelberg (2013)
GH90.   Gabbay, D., Hodkinson, I.: An axiomatisation of the temporal logic with until and since over the real numbers. JLC 1(2), 229–260 (1990)
GHR93. Gabbay, D.M., Hodkinson, I.M., Reynolds, M.A.: Temporal expressive completeness in the presence of gaps. In: Oikkonen, et al. (eds.) Logic Colloquium 1990. LNL, vol. 2, pp. 89–121. Springer (1993)
GHR94. Gabbay, D., Hodkinson, I., Reynolds, M.: Temporal Logic: Mathematical Foundations and Computational Aspects. OUP (1994)
HR05.   Hodkinson, I., Reynolds, M.: Separation: past, present &future. In: We Will Show Them: Essays in Honour of D. Gabbay, pp. 117–142. Coll. Publ. (2005)
Kam68. Kamp, H.: Tense logic and the theory of linear order. PhD thesis, University of California, Los Angeles (1968)
KdR97. Kurtonina, N., de Rijke, M.: Bisimulations for temporal logic. Journal of Logic, Language and Information 6(4), 403–425 (1997)
LL66.   Läuchli, H., Leonard, J.: On the elementary theory of linear order. Fundamenta Mathematicae 59, 109–116 (1966)
MD12.   Christopher McCabe-Dansted, J.: Model Checker Online (2012),
        http://www.csse.uwa.edu.au/~mark/research/Online/mechecker.html
Rab69. Rabin, M.O.: Decidability of second order theories and automata on infinite trees. American Mathematical Society Transactions 141, 1–35 (1969)
Rey92. Reynolds, M.: An axiomatization for Until and Since over the reals without the IRR rule. Studia Logica 51, 165–193 (1992)
Rey10a. Reynolds, M.: The complexity of the temporal logic over the reals. Annals of Pure and Applied Logic 161(8), 1063–1096 (2010)
Rey10b. Reynolds, M.: The complexity of decision problems for linear temporal logics. Journal of Studies in Logic 3, 19–50 (2010)
Ros82. Rosenstein, J.G.: Linear Orderings. Academic Press, New York (1982)

A Graphical Language for Proof Strategies

Gudmund Grov[1], Aleks Kissinger[2], and Yuhui Lin[1]

[1] School of Mathematical and Computer Sciences, Heriot-Watt University,
Edinburgh, UK
{G.Grov,Y.Lin}@hw.ac.uk
[2] Department of Computer Science, University of Oxford, UK
aleks.kissinger@cs.ox.ac.uk

Abstract. Complex automated proof strategies are often difficult to extract, visualise, modify, and debug. Traditional tactic languages, often based on stack-based goal propagation, make it easy to write proofs that obscure the flow of goals between tactics and are fragile to minor changes in input, proof structure or changes to tactics themselves. Here, we address this by introducing a graphical language called PSGraph for writing proof strategies. Strategies are constructed visually by "wiring together" collections of tactics and evaluated by propagating goal nodes through the diagram via graph rewriting. Tactic nodes can have many output wires, and use a filtering procedure based on goal-types (predicates describing the features of a goal) to decide where best to send newly-generated sub-goals. In addition to making the flow of goal information explicit, the graphical language can fulfil the role of many tacticals using visual idioms like branching, merging, and feedback loops. We argue that this language enables development of more robust proof strategies and provide several examples, along with a prototype implementation in Isabelle.

1 Introduction

Most tactic languages for interactive theorem provers are not designed to distinguish goals in cases where tactics produce multiple sub-goals. Thus when composing tactics, one has no choice but to rely on the order in which goals arrive, thus making them brittle to minor changes. For example, consider a case where we expect three sub-goals from tactic t_1, where the first two are sent to t_2 and the last to t_3. A small improvement of t_1 may result in only two sub-goals. This "improvement" causes t_2 to be applied to the second goal when it should have been t_3. The tactic t_2 may then fail or create unexpected new sub-goals that cause some later tactic to fail.

As a result: (1) it is often difficult to compose tactics in such a way that all sub-goals are sent to the correct target tactic, especially when different goals should be handled differently; (2) when a large tactic fails, it is hard to analyse where the failure occurred; and (3) the reliance of goal order means that machine learning new tactics from existing proofs have not been as successful for tactics as it has been for discovering relevant hypothesis in automated theorem provers.

Moreover, if the structure of a tactic is difficult to understand, often the easiest way for a user to deal with failure is to manually guide the proof until the tactic succeeds (or becomes unnecessary), rather than correcting the weakness of the tactic itself. In this case, the proof is made more complicated and insight from this failure is not carried across to other proofs. Thus, a tactic language where it is easy to diagnose and correct failures will lead to better tactics and simpler, more general proofs.

This can be achieved in part by attempting to find as many errors as possible *statically*. The problem with existing tactic languages is that tactics are essentially untyped: they are essentially functions from a *goal* to a conjunction of *sub-goals*. In many programming languages, types are used statically to rule out many "obvious" errors. For example, in typed functional languages, a type error will occur when one tries to compose two functions which do not have a unifiable type. In an untyped tactic language, this kind of "round-peg-square-hole" situation will not manifest until run-time.

For errors that cannot be found statically, it is very hard to inspect and analyse the failures during debugging. In the above example, if t_2 creates sub-goals that tactics later in the proof do not expect, the error may be reported in a completely different place. Without a clear handle on the flow of goals through the proof, finding the real source of the error could be very difficult indeed.

In this paper, we address these issues by introducing a graphical proof strategy language called *PSGraph*. We argue that this language has three advantages over more traditional tactic languages: (i) it improves robustness of proof strategies with static goal typing and type-safe tactic "wirings"; (ii) it improves the ability to dynamically inspect, analyse, and modify strategies, especially when things go wrong; and (iii) it enables machine learning of new tactics from proofs.

For the sake of this paper, we shall focus on (i) and (ii). A discussion on the use of PSGraph for (iii) can be found in [10], where a form of of *analogous reasoning* through tactic generalisation is developed using PSGraph.

A high-level introduction to PSGraph is given Section 2, followed by a discussion on goal types in Section 3. Section 4 gives a detailed description of the language and evaluation, before combinators and hierarchies are introduced in Section 5. An Isabelle implementation, including experiments, is given in Section 6. We then discuss related work (Section 7) and conclude (Section 8).

2 Proof Strategy Graphs = Tactics + Plumbing

A useful analogy for thinking about designing sophisticated tactics is that of plumbing. Instead of thinking of tactics as functions that compose, think of them as individual components whose inputs and outputs can be connected by various pipes. Each component of the system is a tactic of the underlying theorem prover, and your job in designing a proof strategy is to create a network of tactics by plugging input and output from tactics together.

In a pipe network, pipes comes in all sizes and shapes, and you can only connect the same *type* of pipes together – after all, there is a reason you don't connect the toilet waste water to the mains water. The same is true for tactics:

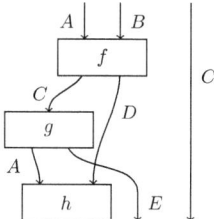

Fig. 1. A string diagram

they only work for certain goals (although for some tactics this range of goals is rather wide). For example, an 'assumption' tactic expects a hypothesis to be unifiable with the goal, and '∀-intro' expects the goal to start with a ∀ quantifier.

Formally, we represent a "pipe network" as a *string diagram* (see Fig. 1) [8], and we represent dynamics, or "goals flowing down pipes" using string diagram rewriting. String diagrams consist of *boxes*, representing processes and typed *wires* that connect them together. Unlike graph edges, wires need not be connected to a box at both ends, but can be left open to represent inputs and outputs. Just like a piece of pipe on its own, a wire that is open at both ends represents the *identity* or "do-nothing" process.

A *string diagram rewrite rule* is a pair of string diagrams L and R sharing the same boundary (i.e. there are type-respecting bijections of the respective inputs and outputs). Typically we write this $L \dashrightarrow R$. In order to apply a rewrite rule, one first finds a *matching* $m : L \to G$, which is an embedding of L into G respecting the type of wires and the input/output arities of boxes. Once a matching is found, the image of m is cut out of G and replaced with R to produce a new graph. The fact that there exists a bijection of the boundary between L and R is crucial to the final step, because it tells us precisely how to "glue" R into the location that L used to be. This agrees with a visual intuition for diagram substitution, and can also be formalised using double-pushout graph rewriting. For details, see [8].

Proof strategy graphs (PSGraphs) are string diagrams whose boxes are labelled with tactics. As with the plumbing analogy, we think the typing information associated with a pipe as a property of the pipe itself. For that reason, we label wires with *goal types*, which are predicates defined on goals. Intuitively, these provide information about some characteristics, such as "shape", of a goal, which are used to influence the path a goal takes as it passes through the strategy graph. To represent a goal being on a wire, we introduce a special *goal* node to the graph. In the diagrams, we draw such nodes as a circle, while a tactic is a rectangle.

One evaluation step works by a single tactic node on a single goal. Here, the goal is consumed from the input wire, the tactic in the tactic node is applied to the goal, and the resulting sub-goals (if any) are sent down the output wires where they match. When all the goal nodes are in the output wires of the graph, i.e. a wire with an open destination, then it has successfully evaluated. If no output type matches a goal, then evaluation fails. For evaluation this improves robustness of the tactic in two ways: (1) since composition is over the *type of goals*, we avoid the brittleness arising from defining composition in terms of the number of sub-goals or order of sub-goals, and (2) if an unexpected sub-goal arises then evaluation will fail at the actual point of failure as it will not fit into any of the output pipes. In general, we allow this evaluation procedure to be non-deterministic by introducing branching whenever a tactic behaves non-deterministically, or a sub-goal produced by a tactic matches more than one output wire. However, with appropriate choice of goal types and evaluation strategy, this branching can be minimised.

An example of a proof strategy which relies on specific properties of a goal is *rippling* [5]. It is a rewriting technique most commonly used on step cases of inductive proofs. It ensures that each 'ripple' step moves the goal towards the induction hypothesis (IH). This step is repeated until the IH can be applied to simplify or fully discharge the goal – a process called 'fertilisation'. The advantage of rippling is that it is guaranteed to terminate, whilst allowing rewriting behaviour that would not otherwise terminate (e.g. allowing a rewrite rule to be applied in both directions). Termination is ensured by checking that a certain *embedding* property holds for the goal being rippled, while a measure is reduced from a previous goal. Collectively, these properties are captured by a goal type, in this cased called '*can-ripple*'. When a goal is fully 'rippled', then 'fertilisation' is applied. Fig. 2 illustrates a variant of "induction with rippling" in PSGraph, where the base case and any resulting goals from the rippling process is sent to the 'simp' tactic.

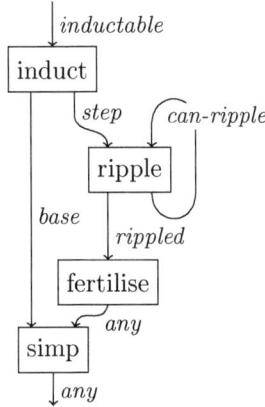

Fig. 2. Rippling

Example 1. Evaluating the top half of the strategy graph given in Fig. 2:

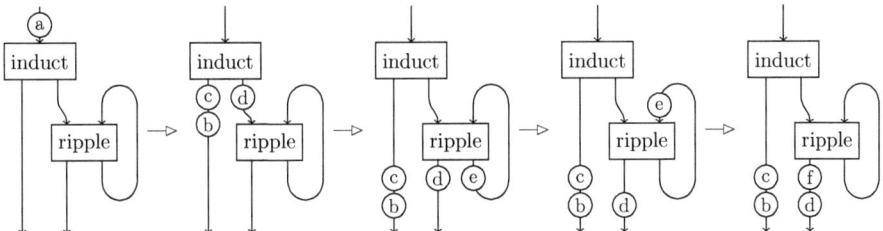

Suppose applying induction to goal a yields two base cases b, c and a step case d. Then, in the first step, a is consumed and b, c are output on the first wire (of type *base*) and d is output on the second wire (of type *step*). Then **ripple** is repeatedly applied until all sub-goals are on the output wires.

Proof strategies can easily become very large and complex. In PSGraph, we can reduce this complexity and size by hiding parts of a graph – achieved by boxing a subgraphs into a single vertex. This box can be evaluated by evaluating

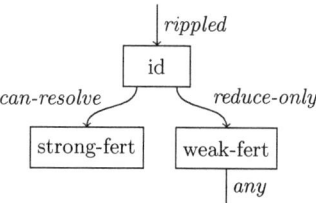

Fig. 3. Fertilisation

the graph it contains, or it may be unfolded in place. One example of such hierarchy, is the 'fertilise' box of Fig. 2, which is shown in Fig. 3. Here, the 'id' tactic simply returns the input goal (e.g. idtac in Coq or all_tac in Isabelle), however it is used to route the input goal to the correct tactic, using the goal types of the output wires. Here, we separate the case where the goal can be resolved directly with the IH (called 'strong fertilisation'), from the case where the IH can only be used to reduce the goal ('weak fertilisation'). Note that the input and output wires of a nested graph must be the same as the node which contains it. It is also possible in the PSGraph language to nest multiple graphs in a single node, which can be used to produce branching OR/ORELSE behaviour, as detailed in Section 5.

3 Goal Types

For a type τ, let $[\tau]$ be the type of finite lists and $\{\tau\}$ be the type of finite sets whose elements are of type τ.

Rather than considering all goals as members of one big type "**goal**", assume that we have a set of goal types $\mathcal{G}$. A particular goal type $\alpha \in \mathcal{G}$ represents all goals with some particular features, which may include local properties like "contains symbol X", proof state properties such as available facts, global properties like shared meta-variables, and relational properties with parent and possible children goals. Others have developed more detailed type theories for tactics (e.g. [17]) which are closely related to our notion of a goal type. However, for our purposes it is sufficient to see a goal type as a predicate defined on goals:

Definition 1. A *goal type* α is a predicate $\alpha : \mathbf{goal} \to \mathbf{bool}$. Two goal types are said to be *orthogonal*, written $\alpha \perp \beta$, if for all goals g, $\neg(\alpha(g) \wedge \beta(g))$.

The focus in this paper is on the use of goal types in the diagrammatic language, and the underlying theory is therefore beyond the scope of the paper. In fact, a PSGraph is generic w.r.t. the underlying goal type as it only relies on predicates as in Definition 1. However, in order to illustrate goal types, we will use the following example of a goal type in the remainder of this paper:

Example 2. The following BNF shows the syntax of a goal type with a description of what it means:

$$\begin{aligned}
GT :=~ & top\_symbol(x_1, \cdots, x_n) && \text{the top symbol of the goal is one of: } x_1, \cdots, x_n \\
 \mid~ & inductable && \text{structural induction is applicable} \\
 \mid~ & hyp\_embeds && \text{hypothesis embeds in the goal} \\
 \mid~ & measure\_reducible && \text{a measure towards a hypothesis is possible to reduce} \\
 \mid~ & hyp\_subst \mid hyp\_bck\_res && \text{hypothesis applicable as rewrite/resolution rule} \\
 \mid~ & GT_1~;~GT_2 \mid or(GT_1 \ldots GT_N) && \text{conjunction and disjunction} \\
 \mid~ & not(GT) \mid any && \text{negation and always succeed}
\end{aligned}$$

Whilst being relatively simple, GT captures a range of properties, including all of the goal types from Figs. 2 and 3:

$$\begin{aligned}
base &= not(hyp\_embeds) \\
step &= can\_ripple = hyp\_embeds;~measure\_reduces \\
rippled &= not(measure\_reducible);~or(hyp\_bck\_res, hyp\_subst) \\
can\_resolve &= hyp\_bck\_res;~hyp\_embeds \\
reduce\_only &= not(hyp\_bck\_res);~hyp\_subst;~hyp\_embeds
\end{aligned}$$

A richer goal type for the PSGraph framework, developed to support goal type generalisation for machine learning new graphs from example proofs, is defined in [10].

The usual notion of a tactic can be treated as a function of the form:

$$\textbf{tac} : \textbf{goal} \to \{[\textbf{goal}]\} \tag{1}$$

That is, it takes a single goal to a set whose elements are lists of sub-goals. Each element of the set represents a branch in the (possibly non-deterministic) tactic evaluation. Note that we assume that internal details such as the production of an LCF justification function or direct modification of the proof state (a la Isabelle [15]), are implicitly handled by the tactic. These details are not necessary to give the semantics of PSGraph evaluation, but shall play a role in the implementation of PSGraph in a particular prover, as discussed in Section 6.

For a list L, we say a list of lists L' is an *ordered partition* if all of the lists are distinct, L' contains the same elements as L and each $l \in L'$ is obtained by deleting zero or more elements of L (i.e. the order of L is preserved).

Definition 2. For goal types $\beta_1, \ldots, \beta_n$ and a list of goals $[g_1, \ldots, g_m]$, a *type-partition* is an ordered partition: $P = [[g_i, g_{i'}, \ldots], [g_j, g_{j'}, \ldots], \ldots]$ such that the k-th list in P contains only goals of type β_k.

In general, there may be more than one way to partition a list of goals. Let $\textbf{part}([\beta_1, \ldots, \beta_n], [g_1, \ldots, g_m])$ be the set of all possible partitions. The set of partitions is empty precisely when there is a goal in L that is not of type β_k for any k. Furthermore, if all of the goal types are orthogonal, this set must either be empty or a singleton.

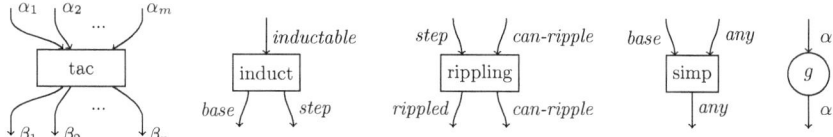

Fig. 4. Left to right: A generic tactic, 3 example tactics and a goal node

4 Evaluation of Proof Strategy Graphs

As already mentioned in section 2, a PSGraph is a string diagram whose wires are labelled with goal types with two kinds of nodes: tactic nodes and goal nodes (Fig. 4). Tactic nodes, represented as boxes, are labelled by the name of a tactic function of the form given in (1) and have at least one input and zero or more outputs. A goal node is represented as a circle with exactly one input and output.

Suppose a goal node g occurs on an input wire of a tactic node labelled 'tac', with output types $\beta_1, \ldots, \beta_n$. The goal node g is propagated through the tactic node via a set of rewrite rules defined as follows:

1. Evaluate $\mathbf{tac}(g)$ to obtain a set of results (lists of sub-goals) from the tactic
2. For each result $R \in \mathbf{tac}(g)$ form a set of type-partitions: $\mathbf{part}([\beta_1, \ldots, \beta_n], R)$
3. For each type-partition $[[h_1, h'_1, \ldots], \ldots, [h_n, h'_n, \ldots]] \in \mathbf{part}([\beta_1, \ldots, \beta_n], R)$, define a rewrite rule where the input goal in the LHS is consumed in the RHS and each sub-goals of $[h_k, h'_k, \ldots]$ are added to the k-th output wire of the RHS:

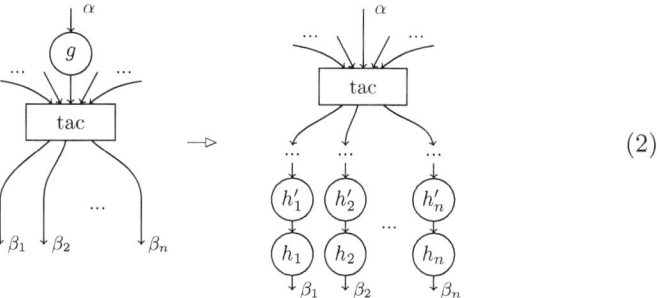

(2)

We shall call this set of rewrite rules $\mathbf{RW}(\mathbf{tac}, [\beta_1, \ldots, \beta_n], g)$. If this set is empty, this corresponds to a failure. If it is a singleton, this corresponds to deterministic evaluation.

Example 3. Suppose a goal $a := even(2*n)$ occurs on an input wire of the **induct** tactic, which applies a two-step induction on the naturals (creating two base cases). To evaluate a, we first compute the ruleset $\mathbf{RW}(\mathbf{induct}, [base, step], a)$ by applying the tactic $\mathbf{induct}(a)$. There is only one possible induction to perform, so the **induct** tactic returns a single list of sub-goals $\{[b, c, d]\}$, where

$$b = even(2*0), \quad c = even(2*1) \quad \text{and} \quad d = even(2*n) \vdash even(2*S(S(n))).$$

Next, the set of partitions **part**($[base, step], [b, c, d]$) is computed. Here, we see that a and b are *base* cases, as there are no hypothesis which can embed in the goal, while d is a step case as the hypothesis does indeed embed in the goal. Thus, a single partition $[[b, c], [d]]$ is created. In the final step, the single rewrite rule (Fig. 5) is created. The result of applying this rule corresponds to the first step of example 1.

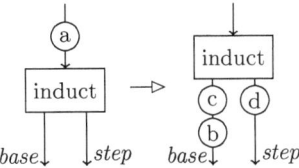

Fig. 5. Evaluation rule from Example 3

To evaluate a goal g over a PSGraph G, we first add g to an input of G with a goal type which g matches, then repeatedly apply rewrites generated by evaluating tactic nodes. By using PSGraph evaluation as a tactic in an LCF-style theorem prover, soundess will be guaranteed by the prover kernel. However, the next theorem states that evaluation is already "as sound as the tactics it uses".

Theorem 1 (Soundness). *During PSGraph evaluation, goal nodes are only produced/consumed by calls to tactics, and never duplicated or lost during evaluation.*

Proof. Every rewrite rule applied during evaluation is the result of a call to the partition function **part** on the output of a tactic, which yields rewrite rules where the input of a tactic is consumed and sub-goals produced by the tactic must each occur on precisely one output wire.

Definition 3. A PSGraph is said to be in *terminal form* if the only goal nodes it contains are on output wires.

Definition 4. Let $\mathcal{T}$ be a tree whose leaves are labelled with PSGraphs or $\bot$. Graph leaves in terminal form in $\mathcal{T}$ are said to be *closed*. Otherwise, they are called *open*. An *evaluation strategy* is a function $S : \mathcal{T} \to \mathcal{T}$ which chooses an open PSGraph G in $\mathcal{T}$ and unfolds it by: (i) selecting a goal g on the input wire of a tactic node **tac** and (ii) adding the children arising from applying each of the rules $r \in \mathbf{RW}(\mathbf{tac}, [\beta_1, \ldots, \beta_n], g)$, or a single child $\bot$ indicating failure, to G in $\mathcal{T}$. We say $\mathcal{T}$ is *terminated* when all graph leaves are closed.

Example 4. A depth-first strategy S_{DF} will select the open PSGraph that was last produced, and within it unfold the goal that was last produced. A more sophisticated strategy S_S may for example select the open PSGraph with the fewest goals and evaluate the goal which is most likely to fail to cut a failed branch as early as possible.

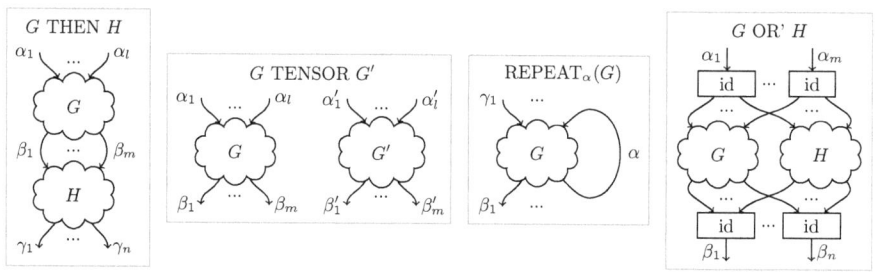

Fig. 6. THEN, TENSOR, REPEAT$_\alpha$, and OR' combinators

5 Combinators and Hierarchies

An interesting feature of graphical languages is that it gives us many techniques for combining strategies. In this section, we will discuss two such techniques: graph *combinators* and graph *hierarchies*.

Graph combinators can be used to syntactically build new strategy graphs from old graphs. Perhaps the simplest graph combinators are the THEN and TENSOR[1] combinators (Fig. 6). THEN takes all the outputs of one graph and connects them to all of the inputs of another graph[2]. TENSOR is at the other extreme: it combines two graphs into one without plugging any wires together. The THEN combinator uses goal types on the wires to figure out which output should be connected to which input, i.e. an output of type β_i in G is always connected to an input of type β_i in H. As a consequence, "G THEN H" is only well-defined when the output types of G match the input types of H and all of the β_i are distinct.

TENSOR can be thought of as a sort of "parallel composition" of strategies. In an expression like "G THEN (H TENSOR H')", H will handle some of the goals produced by G and H' will handle the rest. Which goal goes where is determined by the goal type.

One could imagine many variations on the THEN combinator that perform various more general kinds of wire-pluggings, however, for space reasons, we consider just one more kind of plugging combinator called REPEAT$_\alpha$ (Fig. 6). It connects an output of type α to an input of type α, introducing a feedback loop. As with the THEN combinator, REPEAT$_\alpha$ is not always well-defined. It is defined whenever the graph G has precisely one input and one output of type α. This is not much of a restriction, as input and output types of PSGraphs should typically be distinct to make the most of the goal typing system. Note also that REPEAT$_\alpha$ is close in character to the traditional REPEAT_WHILE tactical, taking α to be the predicate controlling the repeated application.

Branching can be achieved by exploiting non-determinism of tactic node evaluation when faced with non-orthogonal output goal types. This can be seen by

---

[1] We use TENSOR for parallel composition as this is common for graphical languages (see e.g. [16]), and has also been used in tactic languages such as HiTac [2].
[2] This process of plugging one or more inputs and outputs together is defined formally using graph pushouts in [8].

the OR' combinator in Fig. 6, which is a graphical variant of the OR combinator. However, when considering G and H as two distinct alternatives, each graph should really be considered in isolation, but this information is effectively lost by combining them into the same graph. For instance, there is nothing to stop us from adding a wire between them or interleaving evaluation of the two branches. Moreover, we cannot represent other more controlled types of branching, such as an ORELSE combinator.

In Section 2, we saw that we can hide complexities by folding subgraphs into a single node in the graph. This was illustrated by the 'fertilise' node for rippling. We call such a hierarchical node in a PSGraph a *graph tactic*. In addition to hiding complexity, a graph tactic can handle branching in a natural way, and allows us to mark specific subgraphs with different evaluation strategies.

Definition 5. A *graph tactic* N contains a pair $(A, \mathcal{G})$, consisting of a label $A \in \{\text{OR}, \text{ORELSE}\}$ and a non-empty list of pairs $\mathcal{G} = [(G_1, S_1), \ldots, (G_n, S_n)]$, where all of the graphs G_i have the same number and type of inputs/outputs as N and each S_i is an optional evaluation strategy for the graph G_i. A tactic node that is not a graph tactic is called an *atomic tactic*.

For a graph tactic containing $(\text{OR}, [(G_1, S_1), (G_2, S_2)])$, we often omit the evaluation strategy and label this node $\text{OR}[G_1, G_2]$. In other cases we give the node an explicit name, as in e.g. 'fertilise'. The list $\mathcal{G}$ holds the graphs that are nested, and multiple elements in the list correspond to alternation. The label OR/ORELSE is called the *alternation style* of the graph tactic, and the OR and ORELSE combinators can be naturally expressed with these alternation styles. OR is a branching search, attempting to evaluate each graph G_i in turn. On the other hand, ORELSE proceeds sequentially until a *single* graph is evaluated successfully. If $\mathcal{G}$ is a singleton list then the alternation style will have no impact on evaluation.

5.1 Evaluation and Unfolding of Hierarchies

So, it only remains to describe the evaluation of a single element (G_i, S_i) of $\mathcal{G}$ of graph tactic 'tac'. This is achieved in the same way as in Section 4, by generating a set of evaluation rewrite rules. It deviates from evaluation of such atomic tactics by the way the output nodes are generated. Let L be the LHS of the usual evaluation rewrite rule (2), with goal node g be on the j-th input wire of 'tac'. The set of evaluation rules from (S_i, G_i) is then created as follows:

1. Place g on the j-th input wire of the graph G_i, which becomes the root of the singleton search tree $\mathcal{T}$.
2. Let S be S_i if it is defined, if not let it be the evaluation strategy of the parent graph. Use S to evaluate $\mathcal{T}$ until $\mathcal{T}$ has terminated.
3. For each terminal leaf G'_i of $\mathcal{T}$, there will be zero or more goals on each of the output wires. Let R be L with node g removed. For all k, place all of the goals on the k-th output wire of G'_i on to the k-th output wire of tac in R, in the same order. This yields a rewrite rule $L \dashrightarrow R$.

Thus, there will be one rewrite rule for each terminal PSGraph in $\mathcal{T}$. This hierarchical evaluation procedure buys us two things at once. The first is modularity: complex strategies can be broken into multiple graph tactics composed in a high-level strategy graph. The second is fine-grained control over evaluation strategies: different subgraphs can be associated with different evaluation strategies, which can be tailored to the specific task at hand.

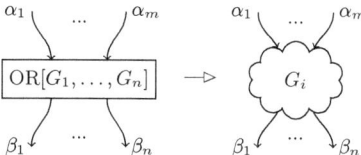

Fig. 7. An "unfolding" rule

It is also worth noting that there is a second, rewriting-based method of expressing this hierarchical evaluation procedure. Since the graphs $G_1, \ldots, G_n$ in a graph tactic node have the same inputs and outputs as the node itself, we can define a rewrite rule for each G_i (Fig. 7). This rule (and its inverse) give us a way to selectively unfold and re-fold parts of the graph. These rules can be used during evaluation to perform an *in situ* version of the hierarchical evaluation procedure described above. Perhaps more interestingly, inspired by [18], they can be used during proof strategy design to refactor a complex strategy graph.

6 Implementation

The PSGraph language is independent of both the underlying theorem prover and the goal types used. This is reflected in our implementation, called PSGraph.[3] It is implemented in Poly/ML and consists of 4 layers:

1. At the bottom is the core of the existing *Quantomatic* graph rewriting system [13], which implements the (string diagram) theory from [8].
2. Then there is the *generic PSGraph language layer*, which implements the features described in Sections 3–5 using Quantomatic.
3. On top of the PSGraph layer, there is the *goal type layer*, where a goal node (wrapping a theorem proving specific sub-goal), a goal type and a matching function between them is defined. The generic layer is then instantiated with these features.
4. At the top is the *theorem prover specific layer*, which instantiates the generic and goal type layers with theorem proving specific features. These include: the underlying proof and tactic representations, term/goal matching functions, and a set of tactics provided by the prover.

The implementation discussed here contains an instantiation of the goal type GT of Section 3 for Isabelle/HOL [15]. The goal type in [10] and limited support for the ProofPower theorem prover[4] has also been implemented (also available from the PSGraph webpage).

[3] The tool is available at https://github.com/ggrov/psgraph/tree/lpar13
[4] See http://www.lemma-one.com/ProofPower/index/

6.1 Proof Representation in Isabelle

Theorem provers typically work by applying a tactic to one of the open sub-goals, which either discharges the sub-goal, or generates new sub-goal which then has to be discharged. This is repeated until there are no more sub-goals. The results of these applications must then be combined to create the actual proof. This step is handled differently between provers: Isabelle combines these steps by having just one goal in which all the remaining "sub-goals" occur as premises, whereas HOL/ProofPower generates a "justification function" to combine sub-goals. Others, such as [2,18,17], have given formal semantics to the relationship between tactics and the proofs produced. In the context of PSGraph, we see this as a theorem prover specific task, and instead only focus on working with the open sub-goals produced. This is reflected by the fact that our key soundness property is the goal property highlighted in Theorem 1. As a result, the proof representation has to be handled by the top layer in our architecture, which instantiates the system for a particular prover.

To prove F in Isabelle, the initial goal (henceforth proof) $F \implies F$ is created, where $\implies$ should be read as logical entailment. If a tactic reduces F to the sub-goals G and H, then the proof becomes $G \implies H \implies F$. A tactic in Isabelle (normally) works on a particular sub-goal, and the index of this sub-goal must be provided. This will produce a set (lazy sequence to be exact) of new proofs, where each element is a branch. For example, let **tac** be a tactic which reduces H to sub-goals I and J. Then '**tac** 2' applied to the above proof will give the (singleton) proof $G \implies I \implies J \implies F$. When there are no sub-goals, and we are left with just F, then the proof is completed.

To handle this "side effect" a tactic has on the proof object, during evaluation we keep track of an Isabelle proof *prf*, paired with a map m from a name to a sub-goal index. Then, for a goal g and a tactic **tac**, the first step in the evaluation of Section 3 becomes:

- Look up the name of g in m to give the index i.
- Apply **tac** i *prf*, which creates a set of new proofs.
- For each new proof: find the new sub-goals starting at position i; update all indices in m to reflect the new sub-goals (e.g. if two sub-goals are created then all indices after i have to be incremented by 1); create a fresh name for each new-sub-goal and update m, and return the new sub-goals with their name.

6.2 Isabelle/Isar Proof Method and GUI

PSGraph has a GUI where users can both draw and, for a given conjecture, inspect the evaluation of a PSGraph. Fig. 8 shows some screen-shots of this GUI, which we will return to below.

Our Isabelle instantiation is encoded as a new theory on top of the 'Main' Isabelle/HOL theory[5]. On top of this we have created a new proof method for Isabelle/Isar called psgraph in order to make usage more Isabelle friendly. Graphs that have been drawn, or implemented (using the combinators), must

---

[5] See https://isabelle.in.tum.de/ for details.

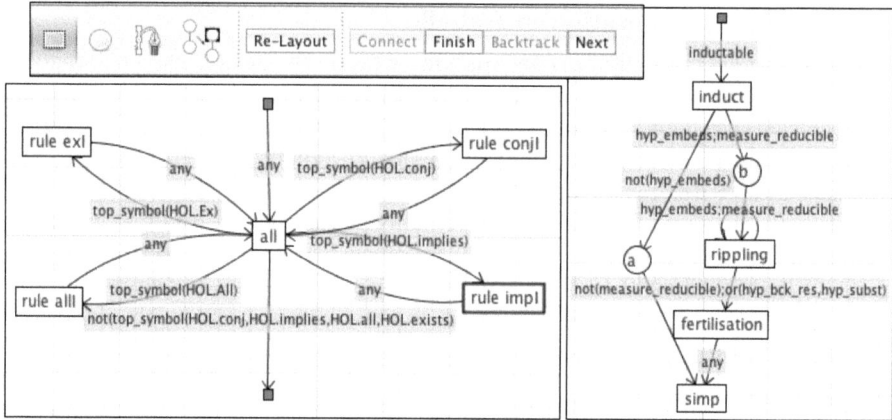

Fig. 8. GUI: navigation bar (top), intro graph (left), rippling evaluation (right)

be explicitly registered in Isabelle with a name in order to use them. They can then be used by the following Isabelle method in the middle of a proof:

apply (psgraph [(interactive)] ⟨graph-name⟩ [searchf: ⟨sname⟩] [goalf: ⟨ename⟩])

⟨graph-name⟩ refers to the name of a registered graph. The optional (interactive) flag enters a 'debugging mode' where the user can use the GUI to step through a proof. The navigation bar in Fig. 8 illustrates how the user can 'Connect' to Isabelle, and step through ('Next') the proof. 'Finish' will return to Isabelle, and all remaining sub-goals become sub-goals in the Isabelle proof. The evaluation strategies can be configured by searchf, with a name of a search strategy, and goalf, which selects which goal to pick first. Finally, note that there is a special 'current' mode for the interactive version, where the graph which is currently open in GUI is used. This option is selected by '**apply** (psgraph (current))', and is useful for testing while strategies are being drawn.

Examples and Tool Evaluation. We have implemented the *rippling* strategy in PSGraph as an adaptation of the version found in IsaPlanner [7]. The right hand side of Fig. 8, illustrates a rippling proof in interactive mode with two open goals (*a* and *b*). We have evaluated our rippling implementation on 35 Peano arithmetic and list examples. These can be seen and tested by downloading the tool[6]. The butterfly-shaped strategy on the left of Fig. 8 is an implementation of the well-known *intro*-tactic as a PSGraph. This strategy supports 'any' input goal, and uses *top_symbol*, *any* and *not GT* predicates. The *all* node uses all_tac, which is Isabelle's version of '*id*', i.e. the tactic that always succeeds and leaves the goal unchanged. It is only used to direct the goal to the correct place using the goal types on the output wires. If a goal starts with an existential/universal quantifier, a conjunction or implication, then it is sent to the relevant tactic, and

---

[6] See https://github.com/ggrov/psgraph/tree/lpar13/src/examples/LPAR13

the process is repeated. If not, it is sent to the output. Note that an output goal from this strategy is guaranteed not to start with any of the above symbols.

Limitations. Currently, the GUI navigation is limited in the sense that the user cannot select specific goals to apply or work with more than one level of graph hierarchy at the same time. Furthermore, nested graph tactics have to be implemented separately before they can be used, whereas ideally, these could be created in place. More generally, we would like to be able to configure tactics more easily in the GUI, both tactics provided by the prover and graph tactics. At the moment only 'breadth-first' and 'depth-first' search are supported, while a variant of 'breadth-first' goal selection is possible. So, we would like to improve on the evaluation and search strategies and make it easier for users to develop and plug-in their own strategies. Finally, we would like to improve the debugging facilities to e.g. enable inspection from a given point in the graph.

7 Related Work

The graphical part of PSGraph is described using *string diagrams*, whose rewrite theory was formalised in [8] using a particular family of typed digraphs called *open-graphs*. We have elided most details of the underlying formalisation, and refer to [8]. We are not claiming to be more expressive compared with tactic languages found in systems such as Isabelle, PVS and Coq. In particular, many syntactic goal type properties can be handled by the matching construct of Coq's Ltac [6]. However, we do believe that the way we handle the flow of goals is more natural, and PSGraphs are easier to debug, and may lead to more robust proof strategies, by making users think more about where goals should go next.

Tactics in common theorem provers are essentially untyped (even in Ltac), meaning there is limited, if any, support for static checking. However, the idea of "types", or goal properties, for tactics, which can be checked statically, is not new. In *proof planning* [4] tactics are given pre-conditions and post-conditions. This entails a significant amount of reasoning just to compose them, thus we have opted for a more light-weight version with our goal types. Moreover, our graphs provide additional flow properties to guide the goals. There have also been more type-theoretical approaches to typed tactics, such as the VeriML language [17]. PSGraph deviates from VeriML by using (goal) types purely to compose tactics and ensure that goals are sent to the correct target. In VeriML, the types include information about the relationship between tactics and the proofs produced. As the goal of PSGraph is to be theorem prover generic, this is assumed to be property of the theorem prover. In that sense, it is closer to proof planning. In fact, PSGraph did initially start as a new version of the IsaPlanner proof planner [7], however this was abandoned for pragmatic reasons. We believe our way of capturing the flow of goals by utilising goal types and essentially treating composition as "piping", is novel for proof (strategy) languages.

When writing proofs, as opposed to proof strategies, one often distinguishes between *procedural* proofs, where a proof is described as a sequence of tactic applications (i.e. function composition), ignoring the goals; and *declarative* or *structured* proofs, where the proof is described in terms of intermediate goals (goal islands), and the actual proof commands are seen more as a side issue. We can view PSGraph as a marriage of these concepts in the sense that the *goal-type* and goals on the wires create a declarative view, while the graph as a whole gives a *procedural* view of how tactics are composed. Autexier and Dietrich [3] have developed *a declarative tactic language on top of a declarative proof language*. Their work is more declarative than PSGraph, whilst our is more general w.r.t. compositions, as they represent a strategy as a *schema* which needs to be instantiated. Similarly, there have been several attempts to create *declarative tactic languages on top of procedural tactic languages* [11,9]. Asperti et al [1] argues that these approaches suffer from two drawbacks: goal selection for multiple sub-goals, and information flow between tactics – both of these are addressed by goal types in PSGraph. HiTac is a tactic language with additional support for hiding complexities using hierarchies [2,18]. Graph tactics have been inspired by this work, however the use of goal types on input wires enables multiple goals as input without introducing non-determinism or relying on goal order, whereas HiTac is restricted to a single input goal.

Finally, it is important to note the difference with the field of *diagrammatic reasoning*, as in e.g. [12] and [14], where diagrams are the objects of interest for reasoning rather than the means of capturing the reasoning process.

8 Conclusion and Future Work

We have presented the PSGraph language together together with an implementation of it in the PSGraph tool. PSGraph's "lifting" of proof strategies to the level of goal-types, rather than the level of goals, enables us to write more robust strategies that no longer rely on the number and order of sub-goals resulting from a tactic application for tactic composition. Moreover, as composition of proof strategies is also at the level of goal-types, we increase type safety and enable better static analysis. Moreover, the problem of goal selection/focus/classification when composing tactics, as highlighted in [1], is significantly improved. Graphs naturally represent the flow of goals, and enable graphical inspection of evaluation to improve debugging of proof strategies.

We have already discussed the current tool's limitations. We are currently working on overcoming some of them by enhancing the GUI and developing new evaluation strategies. One interesting avenue to pursue is to try to implement some existing larger compound tactics such as 'auto' in Isabelle. We suspect that this work will be quite useful in terms developing goal types that are necessary to direct goals in non-trivial strategies. One way to approach this problem is to draw the strategies with all goal types being *any* and use machine learning techniques on a large number of examples to discover the goal type for each wire. We would also like to develop a notion of sub-typing for goal types, e.g. anything should be able to be plugged into an *any* goal type. We are also in the process of starting to use PSGraph to find new proof strategies by data mining existing libraries as well as for *analogical reasoning*. A first attempt on using PSGraph for analogical reasoning can be found in [10]. Finally, as we support multiple theorem provers, it will also be interesting to see if strategies we develop can be carried across theorem provers, thus using PSGraph as a form of proof (strategy) exchange.

Acknowledgements. Several of the ideas behind the language is joint with Lucas Dixon, and Alan Bundy provided valuable comments on a previous version of this paper. Also thanks to Alex Merry, Rod Burstall, Andrius Velykis and Ewen Maclean for suggestions and discussions, and the anonymous reviewers for constructive feedback. This work has been supported by EPSRC grants: EP/H023852, EP/H024204 and EP/J001058, the John Templeton Foundation, and the Office of Navel Research.

References

1. Asperti, A., Ricciotti, W., Sacerdoti, C., Tassi, C.: A new type for tactics. In: PLMMS 2009, pp. 229–232 (2009)
2. Aspinall, D., Denney, E., Lüth, C.: A Tactic Language for Hiproofs. In: Autexier, S., Campbell, J., Rubio, J., Sorge, V., Suzuki, M., Wiedijk, F. (eds.) AISC/Calculemus/MKM 2008. LNCS (LNAI), vol. 5144, pp. 339–354. Springer, Heidelberg (2008)
3. Autexier, S., Dietrich, D.: A Tactic Language for Declarative Proofs. In: Kaufmann, M., Paulson, L.C. (eds.) ITP 2010. LNCS, vol. 6172, pp. 99–114. Springer, Heidelberg (2010)
4. Bundy, A.: A science of reasoning. In: Computational Logic - Essays in Honor of Alan Robinson, pp. 178–198 (1991)
5. Bundy, A., Basin, D., Hutter, D., Ireland, A.: Rippling: Meta-level Guidance for Mathematical Reasoning. Cambridge University Press (2005)
6. Delahaye, D.: A Proof Dedicated Meta-Language. Electr. Notes Theor. Comput. Sci. 70(2), 96–109 (2002)
7. Dixon, L., Fleuriot, J.D.: IsaPlanner: A Prototype Proof Planner in Isabelle. In: Baader, F. (ed.) CADE 2003. LNCS (LNAI), vol. 2741, pp. 279–283. Springer, Heidelberg (2003)
8. Dixon, L., Kissinger, A.: Open Graphs and Monoidal Theories. CoRR, abs/1011.4114 (2010)
9. Giero, M., Wiedijk, F.: MMode, A Mizar Mode for the proof assistant Coq. Technical report (January 7, 2004)
10. Grov, G., Maclean, E.: Towards Automated Proof Strategy Generalisation. CoRR, abs/1303.2975 (2013)
11. Harrison, J.: A Mizar Mode for HOL. In: von Wright, J., Harrison, J., Grundy, J. (eds.) TPHOLs 1996. LNCS, vol. 1125, pp. 203–220. Springer, Heidelberg (1996)
12. Jamnik, M.: Mathematical Reasoning with Diagrams: From Intuition to Automation. CSLI Press, Stanford University (2001)
13. Kissinger, A., Merry, A., Dixon, L., Duncan, R., Soloviev, M., Frot, B.: Quantomatic (2011), https://sites.google.com/site/quantomatic/
14. Kissinger, A.: Pictures of Processes. PhD thesis, University of Oxford (2012)
15. Paulson, L.C.: Isabelle: The Next 700 Theorem Provers. In: Odifreddi, P. (ed.) Logic and Computer Science, pp. 361–386. Academic Press (1990)
16. Selinger, P.: A Survey of Graphical Languages for Monoidal Categories. In: Coecke, B. (ed.) LFCS 1994. Lecture Notes in Physics, vol. 813, pp. 289–355. Springer, Heidelberg (2011)
17. Stampoulis, A., Shao, Z.: VeriML: Typed Computation of Logical Terms inside a Language with Effects. In: ICFP, pp. 333–344. ACM (2010)
18. Whiteside, I., Aspinall, D., Dixon, L., Grov, G.: Towards Formal Proof Script Refactoring. In: Davenport, J.H., Farmer, W.M., Urban, J., Rabe, F. (eds.) Calculemus/MKM 2011. LNCS, vol. 6824, pp. 260–275. Springer, Heidelberg (2011)

A Proof of Strong Normalisation of the Typed Atomic Lambda-Calculus

Tom Gundersen[1], Willem Heijltjes[2], and Michel Parigot[1]

[1] Laboratoire Preuves, Programmes, Systèmes
CNRS & Université Paris Diderot
teg@jklm.no, parigot@pps.univ-paris-diderot.fr
[2] University of Bath
w.b.heijltjes@bath.ac.uk

Abstract. The atomic lambda-calculus is a typed lambda-calculus with explicit sharing, which originates in a Curry-Howard interpretation of a deep-inference system for intuitionistic logic. It has been shown that it allows fully lazy sharing to be reproduced in a typed setting. In this paper we prove strong normalization of the typed atomic lambda-calculus using Tait's reducibility method.

1 Introduction

The *atomic lambda-calculus* is a typeable lambda-calculus with explicit sharing, recently introduced in [13,12], developed as the Curry–Howard interpretation of a deep-inference proof system for intuitionistic logic. The present paper constitutes an important step in the development of its meta-theory, by extending Tait's reducibility method to show strong normalisation of the simply typed atomic lambda-calculus. The primary motivation for establishing this result is to demonstrate that the atomic lambda-calculus is a natural and well-behaved calculus, to which the main standard techniques and results apply.

Sharing is an approach to efficient computation in lambda-calculi whereby duplication of subterms is deferred in favor of reference to a common representation. It is a leading principle behind, among others, explicit substitution calculi [1,18,8,9,15,2], term calculi with strategies or higher-order transformations [14,3], and sharing graphs in the style of Lamping [17,4,21]. The atomic lambda-calculus represents a novel category in this range. As a typeable term calculus it is an alternative to explicit substitution calculi, providing a different perspective on sharing: as in sharing graphs, sharing is evaluated *atomically*, by duplicating individual constructors. A salient property is that the calculus implements *fully lazy sharing* [22,14,5], a degree of sharing that, while standard, had previously been achieved in lambda-calculi only by means of external transformations.

The paper [12] details how the atomic lambda-calculus and its sharing mechanisms are derived from *deep inference* [6], a proof methodology where inferences apply *in context*, reminiscent of term rewriting. Sharing in deep inference is by explicit *contraction* rules, which implement atomic duplication by interacting with individual inferences. By embedding natural deduction within the deep-inference formalism *open deduction* [11], duplication in traditional normalisation is broken up into atomic steps. The atomic lambda-calculus is a direct computational interpretation of the resulting proof system. The paper [12] further establishes the technical properties of full laziness and *PSN*, preservation of strong normalisation with respect to the lambda-calculus.

In the present paper strong normalisation for the typed atomic lambda-calculus will be proven using the Tait-reducibility method [20,10]. Reducibility is an abstract method compatible with higher-order logic, whose application provides a deeper understanding of reduction and its dynamics. The fact that a reducibility proof can be carried out for the atomic lambda-calculus shows the generic character of this extension of the lambda-calculus.

2 The Atomic Lambda-Calculus

The *atomic lambda-calculus* introduced in [12] is a refined lambda-calculus, in which abstraction is split into a linear abstraction and a sharing operation. Duplication and deletion proceeds locally through the evaluation of sharings. The calculus consists of a standard linear lambda-calculus with a sharing construct, extended by a further construction called the *distributor*. The distributor allows to duplicate an abstraction without duplicating its scope: it replaces the abstraction while duplication of its scope is in progress, where the duplicated parts of the scope are stored in a tuple of terms (see also the reduction rules in Section 2.1).

Definition 1. *The* atomic lambda-calculus Λ_A *is defined by the grammars*

$$
\begin{aligned}
s,t,u,v,w &::= x \mid \lambda x.t \mid (t)u \mid t[\gamma] \\
[\gamma],[\delta] &::= [x_1,\ldots,x_n \leftarrow t] \mid [x_1,\ldots,x_n \leftarrow \lambda y.t^n] \\
t^n &::= \langle t_1,\ldots,t_n \rangle \mid t^n[\gamma]
\end{aligned}
$$

where (i) $n \geq 0$, (ii) each variable may occur at most once in a term, (iii) in $\lambda x.t$, x must be free in t and becomes bound, (iv) in $\lambda y.t^n$, y must be free in t^n and becomes bound, (v) in $t[\gamma]$ where $[\gamma]$ is $[x_1,\ldots,x_n \leftarrow u]$ or $[x_1,\ldots,x_n \leftarrow \lambda y.t^n]$, each x_i must be free in t and becomes bound, and (vi) likewise for $t^n[\gamma]$.

Terms t are *atomic lambda-terms*. The *closures* $[\gamma]$ are called respectively *sharing* and *distributor*, and a nullary sharing $[\leftarrow t]$ is a *weakening*. Atomic lambda-terms not containing a distributor are *basic* terms. A sequence of closures $[\gamma_1]\ldots[\gamma_n]$ will be denoted $[\gamma_i]_{i\leq n}$ or $[\Gamma]$. The t^n are *terms of multiplicity n* or *n-terms*, and are of the form $\langle t_1,\ldots,t_n \rangle[\Gamma]$. Where possible, terms and n-terms will not be distinguished, and both denoted t,u,v. A sequence of variables $x_1,\ldots,x_n$ may be abbreviated $\vec{x}$; a sharing is then denoted $[\vec{x} \leftarrow t]$. Standard notions are: $\mathrm{FV}(u)$ is the set of free variables of u, and $u\{t/x\}$ denotes the substitution of t for x in u. A series of substitutions $\{t_1/x_1\}\ldots\{t_n/x_n\}$ is abbreviated $\{t_i/x_i\}_{i\leq n}$.

Atomic lambda terms will be considered up to the congruence ($\sim$) induced by (1) below; note that due to linearity, both terms are only well-defined if both $[\gamma]$ and $[\delta]$ bind only in t.

$$t[\gamma][\delta] \sim t[\delta][\gamma] \tag{1}$$

The functions $(\!|-|\!) : \Lambda \to \Lambda_A$ and $[\![-]\!] : \Lambda_A \to \Lambda$ translate between atomic lambda-terms and standard lambda-terms. The former is defined below. For a formal definition of the function $(\!|-|\!)$ see [12]; intuitively, it replaces each abstraction $\lambda x.-$ in a term by $\lambda x. - [x_1, \ldots, x_n \leftarrow x]$, where $x_1, \ldots, x_n$ replace the occurrences of x, so that $[\![(\!|N|\!)]\!] = N$ for any lambda-term N.

Definition 2. *The functions $[\![-]\!]$ and $\{\!|-|\!\}$ interpret atomic lambda-terms and closures respectively as lambda-terms and substitutions. For a sequence of closures $[\Gamma] = [\gamma][\Gamma']$ with $[\Gamma']$ non-empty, let $\{\!|\Gamma|\!\} = \{\!|\gamma|\!\}\{\!|\Gamma'|\!\}$.*

$$[\![x]\!] = x \qquad [\![\lambda x.t]\!] = \lambda x.[\![t]\!] \qquad [\![(t)u]\!] = ([\![t]\!])[\![u]\!] \qquad [\![t[\gamma]]\!] = [\![t]\!]\{\!|\gamma|\!\}$$

$$\{\!|x_1, \ldots, x_n \leftarrow t|\!\} = \{[\![t]\!]/x_i\}_{i \leq n}$$

$$\{\!|x_1, \ldots, x_n \leftarrow \lambda y.\langle t_1, \ldots, t_n\rangle[\Gamma]|\!\} = \{\lambda y.[\![t_i]\!]\{\!|\Gamma|\!\}/x_i\}_{i \leq n}$$

2.1 Reduction Rules

Reduction in the atomic lambda-calculus, denoted $\rightsquigarrow$, consists of two parts: (i) linear β-reduction, denoted $\rightsquigarrow_\beta$: the usual rule (rule β below) applied linearly; (ii) sharing reductions, denoted $\rightsquigarrow_S$, comprising two kinds of rule: (a) *permutations* taking closures outward (rules 2–6), and (b) local *transformations* that evaluate closures (rules 7–10).

Linear β-Reduction:

$$(\lambda x.u)t \rightsquigarrow_\beta u\{t/x\} \tag{β}$$

Permutations of Closures:

$$\lambda x.t[\gamma] \rightsquigarrow_S (\lambda x.t)[\gamma] \qquad \text{if } x \in \mathsf{FV}(t) \tag{2}$$

$$(u[\gamma])t \rightsquigarrow_S ((u)t)[\gamma] \tag{3}$$

$$(u)t[\gamma] \rightsquigarrow_S ((u)t)[\gamma] \tag{4}$$

$$u[x_1, \ldots, x_n \leftarrow t[\gamma]] \rightsquigarrow_S u[x_1, \ldots, x_n \leftarrow t][\gamma] \tag{5}$$

$$u[x_1, \ldots, x_n \leftarrow \lambda y.t^n[\gamma]] \rightsquigarrow_S u[x_1, \ldots, x_n \leftarrow \lambda y.t^n][\gamma] \qquad \text{if } y \in \mathsf{FV}(t^n) \tag{6}$$

Transformations on Closures:

$$u[\vec{y} \leftarrow y][\vec{x}, y, \vec{z} \leftarrow t] \rightsquigarrow_S u[\vec{x}, \vec{y}, \vec{z} \leftarrow t] \tag{7}$$

$$u[x_1, \ldots, x_n \leftarrow (v)t] \rightsquigarrow_S u\{(y_i)z_i/x_i\}_{i \leq n}[y_1, \ldots, y_n \leftarrow v][z_1, \ldots, z_n \leftarrow t] \tag{8}$$

$$u[x_1, \ldots, x_n \leftarrow \lambda x.t] \rightsquigarrow_S u[x_1, \ldots, x_n \leftarrow \lambda x.\langle y_1, \ldots, y_n\rangle[y_1, \ldots, y_n \leftarrow t]] \tag{9}$$

$$u[x_1, \ldots, x_n \leftarrow \lambda y.\langle t_1, \ldots, t_n\rangle[\vec{z} \leftarrow y]] \rightsquigarrow_S u\{\lambda y_i.t_i[\vec{z}_i \leftarrow y_i]/x_i\}_{i \leq n}$$

$$\text{where } \{\vec{z}_i\} = \{\vec{z}\} \cap \mathsf{FV}(t_i) \text{ for every } i \leq n \tag{10}$$

The fact that a term u reduces to v in exactly n steps will be denoted $u \leadsto^n v$, while an arbitrary number of steps is indicated simply by $\leadsto$. A term u is called *strongly normalisable* if all the reduction sequences starting with u are finite. The set of strongly normalisable terms is denoted $\mathcal{N}$. Reduction in the atomic lambda-calculus commutes 1–1 with substitution, due to the linearity condition on free variables.

Lemma 3. *For atomic lambda-terms u, u', v and v' and variable $x \in \mathsf{FV}(u)$, if $u \leadsto^1 u'$, then $u\{v/x\} \leadsto^1 u'\{v/x\}$; and if $v \leadsto^1 v'$, then $u\{v/x\} \leadsto^1 u\{v'/x\}$.*

2.2 Basic Properties of the Atomic Lambda-Calculus

We collect in this section the main basic properties we are using in the strong normalisation proof. The two main properties are (i) the strong normalisation property of the sharing reduction, and (ii) the decomposition of the computational content of sharings and distributors.

Theorem 4 ([12, Theorem 11]). *The reduction $\leadsto_S$ is strongly normalising and confluent.*

Sharing reductions preserve the denotation $[\![t]\!]$ of a term [12, Prop. 10]. The normal form under $\leadsto_S$ of an atomic lambda-term t is called its *unfolding* $\mathsf{u}(t)$. It is a basic term (i.e., no distributors occur) of the form $u[\Gamma]$, where sharing in u occurs only as $\lambda y.v[\vec{x} \leftarrow y]$, of bound variables immediately within the scope of their binder, and where $[\Gamma]$ are sharings $[\vec{x} \leftarrow y]$ of the free variables y in t that occur in shared subterms [12, Prop. 9]. For closed terms, $\mathsf{u}(t) =_\alpha ([\![t]\!])$.

Definition 5. *The unfolded body $\mathsf{ub}(t)$ of t is the largest subterm of $\mathsf{u}(t)$ not of the form $u[\gamma]$.*

The unfolded body of a term is what is duplicated during reduction. To identify the various copies, let a *variant* of a term t be any term obtained from t by renaming certain (bound or free) variables. A variant is *fresh* if all its variables are fresh, and t^i is the fresh variant of t obtained by replacing each variable x by a fresh variable x^i.

For an n-term $t^n = \langle t_1, \ldots, t_n \rangle[\Gamma]$ let the ith *projection* $\pi_i(t^n)$ be the atomic lambda term $t_i[\Gamma_i]$ where $[\Gamma_i]$ is obtained by removing the binders from $[\Gamma]$ binding in any t_j ($i \neq j$), and iteratively removing binders in s_k when x_k is removed from a distributor $[x_1, \ldots, x_k, \ldots, x_m \leftarrow \lambda y.\langle s_1, \ldots, s_k, \ldots, s_m \rangle[\Gamma']]$.

The following basic facts then characterise ub.

Proposition 6.

$\mathsf{ub}(x) = x$ $\mathsf{ub}(\lambda x.t) = \lambda x.\mathsf{ub}(t)[\vec{x} \leftarrow x]$ $\mathsf{ub}((u)v) = (\mathsf{ub}(u))\mathsf{ub}(v)$

$\mathsf{ub}(u[x_1, \ldots, x_n \leftarrow t]) = \mathsf{ub}(u)\{\mathsf{ub}(t)^i/x_i\}_{i \leq n}$

$\mathsf{ub}(u[x_1, \ldots, x_n \leftarrow \lambda y.t^n]) = \mathsf{ub}(u)\{\mathsf{ub}(\lambda y.\pi_i(t^n))^i/x_i\}_{i \leq n}$

Proposition 7. *For* $t = \langle t_1, \ldots, t_n \rangle[\Gamma]$, $\mathsf{ub}(\pi_i(t)) = \mathsf{ub}(t_i[\leftarrow x_1] \ldots [\leftarrow x_m][\Gamma])$ *where* $x_1, \ldots, x_m$ *are the free variables of all* t_j $(i \neq j)$.

To characterise the effects of duplication on the free variables of a term t or an abstracted n-term $\lambda y.t^n$, let $\mathsf{FV}(t) = \mathsf{FV}(\lambda y.t^n) = \{y_1, \ldots, y_k\}$, and let $\mathsf{FV}(\mathsf{ub}(t)^i) = \mathsf{FV}(\mathsf{ub}(\lambda y.\pi_i(t^n))^i) = \{\vec{y}_1^i, \ldots, \vec{y}_k^i\}$. Define the *renamings* of t and $\lambda y.t^n$ to be the sharings $[\vec{y}_i^1, \ldots, \vec{y}_i^n] \leftarrow y_i]_{i \leq k}$, denoted $[\mathsf{rn}(t) : 1, \ldots, n]$ and $[\mathsf{rn}(\lambda y.t^n) : 1, \ldots, n]$ and abbreviated $[\mathsf{rn}(t)]$ and $[\mathsf{rn}(\lambda y.t^n)]$ where possible. The unfolded body and the renamings give the following key decomposition properties of the computational content of closures.

Lemma 8. $u[x_1, \ldots, x_n \leftarrow t] \rightsquigarrow u\{\mathsf{ub}(t)^i/x_i\}_{i \leq n}[\mathsf{rn}(t)]$

Lemma 9. $u[x_1, \ldots, x_n \leftarrow \lambda y.t^n] \rightsquigarrow u\{\mathsf{ub}(\lambda y.\pi_i(t^n))^i/x_i\}_{i \leq n}[\mathsf{rn}(\lambda y.t^n)]$

3 Typed Atomic Lambda-Calculus

The simply typed atomic lambda-calculus S_a is defined by the following rules (see [13,12]). Terms, including variables, are typed $t : A$ with A a *minimal* formula, one built over $\to$, while n-terms are typed by *conjunctive* formulae, $t^n : A_1 \wedge \cdots \wedge A_n$. With the notation t^* indicating either a term or an n-term, a *judgment* is of the form $x_1 : A_1, \ldots, x_n : A_n \vdash t^* : B$, where $x_1, \ldots, x_n$ are the free variables of t^*. The antecedent $x_1 : A_1, \ldots, x_n : A_n$ of a judgement is treated as a set, denoted Γ, Δ, and abbreviated $(x_i : A_i)_{i \leq n}$, or $\vec{x} : A$ if $A_i = A$ for all i.

Typing Rules of S_a:

$$\frac{\Gamma, x : A \vdash t : B}{\Gamma \vdash \lambda x.t : A \to B}\lambda \qquad \frac{\Gamma \vdash u : A \to B \quad \Delta \vdash v : A}{\Gamma, \Delta \vdash (u)v : B}@$$

$$\frac{}{x : A \vdash x : A}\mathsf{ax} \qquad \frac{\Gamma_1 \vdash t_1 : A_1 \quad \cdots \quad \Gamma_n \vdash t_n : A_n}{\Gamma_1, \ldots, \Gamma_n \vdash \langle t_1, \ldots, t_n \rangle : A_1 \wedge \cdots \wedge A_n}\langle\rangle_n$$

$$\frac{\Gamma, (x_i : B)_{i \leq n} \vdash t^* : A \quad \Delta \vdash u : B}{\Gamma, \Delta \vdash t^*[x_1, \ldots, x_n \leftarrow u] : A}\leftarrow$$

$$\frac{\Gamma, (x_i : A \to B_i)_{i \leq n} \vdash s^* : C \quad \Delta, y : A \vdash t^n : B_1 \wedge \cdots \wedge B_n}{\Gamma, \Delta \vdash s^*[x_1, \ldots, x_n \leftarrow \lambda y.t^n] : C}\leftarrow$$

The type system S_a of the atomic lambda-calculus is a refinement of the simply typed lambda-calculus S: the rules ax, λ, and @ are the rules of S restricted by the linearity condition. The rule for sharing, $\leftarrow$, is a standard cut-rule combined with contraction on the left. Similarly, the rule for the distributor, $\leftarrow$, is a cut-rule, albeit a highly non-standard one. It contracts on A, the antecedent of the implications, but not on their consequent, integrating a limited amount of deepness.

The typed atomic lambda-calculus S_a enjoys the usual properties of typed systems, in particular subject reduction.

Theorem 10 ([13]). *If $\Gamma \vdash u : A$ and $u \rightsquigarrow v$, then $\Gamma \vdash v : A$.*

Moreover, types are preserved in the interpretation of standard lambda-terms as atomic lambda-terms, by inserting sharing-inferences ($\leftarrow$) where required.

Proposition 11. *If $\Gamma \vdash N : A$, then $\Gamma \vdash (\!|N|\!) : A$*

Despite the fact that sharing reductions are strongly normalising, commute with denotation, and preserve typing, preservation of strong normalisation (PSN) is not immediate since infinite reduction may take place within weakenings: consider the denotation $[\![x[\leftarrow t]]\!] = x$ where t is not SN.

4 Proof of Strong Normalisation for Simple Types

In this section we prove the strong normalisation theorem for atomic lambda-terms, typed in the system S_a, using Tait's reducibility method. The proof of the main proposition (Proposition 18) relies on closure properties of the reducibility sets (Lemma 17), which again relies on closure properties on the set of strongly normalisable atomic lambda terms proved in Section 5.

For simplifying the presentation, we consider in the remainder of this paper, that no beta-reduction happens inside n-tuples, that n-tuples are unfolded, and that all their free variables are captured by closures. This property is preserved by reduction and it is natural in the context of sharing calculus. In particular all the useful computation strategies satisfy it, including the one reproducing fully lazy sharing.

Definition 12. *The value $|A|$ of a formula A is defined inductively by:*

$|X| = \mathcal{N}$
$|A \rightarrow B| = \{u \mid u \text{ is a term and, for each term } v \in |A|, (u)v \in |B|\}$

Values are extended to conjunctive formulae by the following clauses, for $n > 0$. We denote by $\mathcal{V}$ the set of variables, and note that $\langle\rangle$ is the empty tuple.

$|A_1 \wedge \ldots \wedge A_n| = \{t^n \mid \text{for each } i \leq n, \pi_i(t) \in |A_i|\}$
$|\top| = \{\langle\rangle[\Gamma] \mid \text{for any } x \in \mathcal{V}, x[\Gamma] \in \mathcal{N}\}$

Values of formulae are called *reducibility sets*. Note that if $t \in |A|$ and t' is a variant of t, then $t' \in |A|$.

Proposition 13. *For each minimal formula A, $\mathcal{V} \subseteq |A| \subseteq \mathcal{N}$*

Proposition 14. *For any formulae $A_1, \ldots, A_n$, $|A_1 \wedge \ldots \wedge A_n| \subseteq \mathcal{N}$.*

Lemma 15. *For any formula A, if $u \in |A|$ and $u \leadsto v$, then $v \in |A|$.*

Proof. Immediate by induction on A. □

Let $\{\cdot\}\overline{w}$ denote a term context consisting of repeated applications, so that $\{u\}\overline{w}$ is $(\ldots(u)w_1\ldots)w_n$.

Lemma 16. *For any formula B, if $u \in |B|$ then $u[\vec{x} \leftarrow y] \in |B|$.*

Proof. By induction on B, if $(u)\overline{w} \in |B|$ then $(u[\vec{x} \leftarrow y])\overline{w} \in |B|$. □

Lemma 17.
 (i) *If $u\{v/x\} \in |B|$ and $x \in \mathsf{FV}(u)$, then $(\lambda x.u)v \in |B|$.*
 (ii) *If $u\{\mathsf{ub}(t)^i/x_i\}_{i\leq n}[\mathsf{rn}(t)] \in |B|$ and $t \in \mathcal{N}$, then $u[x_1,\ldots,x_n \leftarrow t] \in |B|$.*
 (iii) *If $u\{\mathsf{ub}(\lambda y.\pi_i(t^n))^i/x_i\}_{i\leq n}[\mathsf{rn}(\lambda y.t^n)] \in |B|$ and $t^n \in \mathcal{N}$, then $u[x_1,\ldots,x_n \leftarrow \lambda y.t^n] \in |B|$.*

Proof. Each case is proved by induction on B, using context $\{\cdot\}\overline{w}$.

(i) If B is a variable, $|B| = \mathcal{N}$ and the result is given by Lemma 21. Otherwise, let $B = C \to D$. Suppose $(u\{v/x\})\overline{w} \in |C \to D|$ and $x \in \mathsf{FV}(u)$. Let $t \in |C|$. We prove that $(((\lambda x.u)v)\overline{w})t \in |D|$. Because $(u\{v/x\})\overline{w} \in |C \to D|$ and $t \in |C|$, we have $((u\{v/x\})\overline{w})t \in |D|$ and by the induction hypothesis, $(((\lambda x.u)v)\overline{w})t \in |D|$. It follows that $((\lambda x.u)v)\overline{w} \in |C \to D|$.

(ii) If B is a variable, $|B| = \mathcal{N}$ and the result is given by Lemma 24. Otherwise, let $B = C \to D$. Let $u' = (u\{\mathsf{ub}(t)^i/x_i\}_{i\leq n}[\mathsf{rn}(t)])\overline{w} \in |C \to D|$ and $t \in \mathcal{N}$. Let $v \in |C|$. We prove that $((u[x_1,\ldots,x_n \leftarrow t])\overline{w})v \in |D|$. By the definition of $|C \to D|$ we have $(u')v \in |D|$. By the induction hypothesis $((u[x_1,\ldots,x_n \leftarrow t])\overline{w})v \in |D|$. It follows that $(u[x_1,\ldots,x_n \leftarrow t])\overline{w} \in |C \to D|$.

(iii) The proof is similar to that of (ii). □

Proposition 18. *If $(x_i : A_i)_{i\leq n} \vdash u : B$ and $v_i \in |A_i|$, then $u\{v_i/x_i\}_{i\leq n} \in |B|$.*

Proof. We proceed by induction on the derivation of $(x_i : A_i)_{i\leq n} \vdash u : B$.

1. The last rule is ax, with conclusion $x : A \vdash x : A$. For $v \in |A|$ we have $x\{v/x\} = v \in |A|$.

2. The last rule is

$$\frac{(x_i : C_i)_{i\leq n} \vdash t : A \to B \qquad (y_j : D_j)_{j\leq m} \vdash u : A}{(x_i : C_i)_{i\leq n}, (y_j : D_j)_{j\leq m} \vdash (t)u : B} @$$

Let $v_i \in |C_i|$ and $w_j \in |D_j|$ for $i \leq n$ and $j \leq m$. By the induction hypothesis, $t\{v_i/x_i\}_{i\leq n} \in |A \to B|$ and $u\{w_j/y_j\}_{j\leq m} \in |A|$. By the definition of $|-|$,

$$((t)u)\{v_i/x_i\}_{i\leq n}\{w_j/y_j\}_{j\leq m} = (t\{v_i/x_i\}_{i\leq n})u\{w_j/y_j\}_{j\leq m} \in |B|.$$

3. The last rule is
$$\frac{(x_i : C_i)_{i \leq n}, x : A \vdash t : B}{(x_i : C_i)_{i \leq n} \vdash \lambda x.t : A \to B} \lambda$$

Let $v_i \in |C_i|$ for $i \leq n$, and suppose $w \in |A|$. By the induction hypothesis we have $t\{v_i/x_i\}_{i \leq n}\{w/x\} \in |B|$. By Lemma 17, $(\lambda x.t\{v_i/x_i\}_{i \leq n})w \in |B|$. It follows that

$$(\lambda x.t)\{v_i/x_i\}_{i \leq n} = \lambda x.t\{v_i/x_i\}_{i \leq n} \in |A \to B| .$$

4. The last rule is
$$\frac{(y_i : C_i)_{i \leq k}, (x_i : B)_{i \leq n} \vdash u : A \quad (z_i : D_i)_{i \leq m} \vdash t : B}{(y_i : C_i)_{i \leq k}, (z_i : D_i)_{i \leq m} \vdash u[x_1, \ldots, x_n \leftarrow t] : A} \leftarrow$$

Let $v_i \in |C_i|$ and $w_j \in |D_j|$ for $i \leq k$ and $j \leq m$, and let $u' = u\{v_i/y_i\}_{i \leq k}$ and $t' = t\{w_j/z_j\}_{j \leq m}$. We have to prove that the following term is in $|A|$:

$$(u[x_1, \ldots, x_n \leftarrow t])\{v_i/y_i\}_{i \leq k}\{w_j/z_j\}_{j \leq m} = u'[x_1, \ldots, x_n \leftarrow t'] .$$

By the induction hypothesis, $t' \in |B|$; then by Lemma 15 also the unfolded body $\mathsf{ub}(t')$ is in $|B|$. Let $\mathsf{ub}(t')^1, \ldots, \mathsf{ub}(t')^n$ be fresh variants. By the induction hypothesis, $u'\{\mathsf{ub}(t')^i/x_i\}_{i \leq n} \in |A|$, and $u'\{\mathsf{ub}(t')^i/x_i\}_{i \leq n}[\mathsf{rn}(t')] \in |A|$ by Lemma 16. It follows by Lemma 17 that $u'[x_1, \ldots, x_n \leftarrow t'] \in |A|$.

5. The last rule is
$$\frac{(y_i : C_i)_{i \leq k}, (x_i : A \to B)_{i \leq n} \vdash u : C \quad (z_i : D_i)_{i \leq m}, y : A \vdash t^n : B \wedge \cdots \wedge B}{(y_i : C_i)_{i \leq k}, (z_i : D_i)_{i \leq m} \vdash u[x_1, \ldots, x_n \leftarrow \lambda y.t^n] : C} \leftarrow$$

Let $v_i \in |C_i|$ and $w_j \in |D_j|$ for $i \leq k$ and $j \leq m$, and let $u' = u\{v_i/y_i\}_{i \leq k}$ and $t' = t^n\{w_j/z_j\}_{j \leq m}$. We have to prove that the following term is in $|C|$:

$$(u[x_1, \ldots, x_n \leftarrow \lambda y.t^n])\{v_i/y_i\}_{i \leq k}\{w_j/z_j\}_{j \leq m} = u'[x_1, \ldots, x_n \leftarrow \lambda y.t'] .$$

By the induction hypothesis, $t'\{s/y\} \in |B \wedge \cdots \wedge B|$ for each $s \in |A|$, and therefore $\pi_i(t'\{s/y\}) = \pi_i(t')\{s/y\} \in |B|$. Then, for each $s \in |A|$, $(\lambda y.\pi_i(t'))s \in |B|$ by Lemma 17, and by definition of $|-|$, $\lambda y.\pi_i(t') \in |A \to B|$. By Lemma 15 also the unfolding of $\lambda y.\pi_i(t')$ belongs to $|A \to B|$, as does any variant $\mathsf{ub}(\lambda y.\pi_i(t'))^i$. By the induction hypothesis, $u'\{\mathsf{ub}(\lambda y.\pi_i(t'))^i/x_i\}_{i \leq n}$ is in $|C|$, and by Lemma 16, $u'\{\mathsf{ub}(\lambda y.\pi_i(t'))^i/x_i\}_{i \leq n}[\mathsf{rn}(\lambda y.t^n)] \in |C|$. It follows by Lemma 17 that $u'[x_1, \ldots, x_n \leftarrow \lambda y.t'] \in |C|$. □

Theorem 19. *If $(x_i : A_i)_{i \leq n} \vdash u : B$ then $u \in \mathcal{N}$.*

Proof. Suppose $(x_i : A_i)_{i \leq n} \vdash u : B$. By Proposition 13, we have $x_i \in |A_i|$ for $i \leq n$. Therefore by Proposition 18, $u\{x_i/x_i\}_{i \leq n} \in |B|$, i.e. $u \in |B|$, and by Proposition 13 we have $u \in \mathcal{N}$. □

5 Closure Properties of Strongly Normalisable Atomic Lambda Terms

In this section we prove closure properties for the set of strongly normalisable atomic lambda terms which are used in Section 4. To strengthen the induction hypothesis in several lemmata, we define a further context, $\{\cdot\}\overline{w}[\overline{\Delta}]$, which is given by the following grammar.

$$* ::= \{\cdot\} \mid (*)u \mid *[\delta]$$

The terms within a context $\{\cdot\}\overline{w}[\overline{\Delta}]$ are denoted $\overline{w} = w_1, \ldots, w_n$, and the sharings are denoted $[\overline{\Delta}] = [\delta_1], \ldots, [\delta_m]$.

Lemma 20. *If $x \in \mathcal{V}$ and in $\{\cdot\}\overline{w}$ each $w_i \in \mathcal{N}$, then $(x)\overline{w} \in \mathcal{N}$.*

For each term $t \in \mathcal{N}$, we denote by $\mathcal{R}(t)$ the sum of the number of reduction steps in all reduction sequences of t to its normal form. For any term t, we denote by $\mathcal{S}(t)$ the number of sharing-reduction steps in all reduction paths to $\mathsf{u}(t)$.

Lemma 21. *If $(u\{v/x\})\overline{w} \in \mathcal{N}$ and $x \in \mathsf{FV}(u)$, then $((\lambda x.u)v)\overline{w} \in \mathcal{N}$.*

Proof. To obtain a suitable induction hypothesis, the context $\{\cdot\}\overline{w}$ is strengthened to $\{\cdot\}\overline{w}[\overline{\Delta}]$, and further closures are inserted. It will be shown by induction on $(\mathcal{R}(T'), \mathcal{S}(T))$ that if $T' \in \mathcal{N}$ then $T \in \mathcal{N}$, where

$$T = (((\lambda x.u)[\Gamma])v)\overline{w}[\overline{\Delta}] \qquad T' = (u\{v/x\}[\Gamma])\overline{w}[\overline{\Delta}] \ .$$

It will be shown that for any term U reached by a reduction step $T \leadsto^1 U$, there is a term U' reached by a reduction $T' \leadsto U'$, such that the induction hypothesis applies to U and U' and $(\mathcal{R}(U'), \mathcal{S}(U)) < (\mathcal{R}(T'), \mathcal{S}(T))$, giving $U \in \mathcal{N}$. Since this holds for any term U, it follows that $T \in \mathcal{N}$.

The first, special case, is $T' = U$ (with $[\Gamma]$ empty), for which $U \in \mathcal{N}$ is immediate. For the remaining cases, we have to verify that U and U' have the right form, that the measure decreases and that $T' \leadsto U'$, which implies that $U' \in \mathcal{N}$. In the following cases, $\mathcal{R}(U') < \mathcal{R}(T')$.

1. If $T \leadsto^1 U$ is due to $u \leadsto^1 u'$, then U and U' are as follows.

$$U = (((\lambda x.u')[\Gamma])v)\overline{w}[\overline{\Delta}] \qquad U' = (u'\{v/x\}[\Gamma])\overline{w}[\overline{\Delta}]$$

2. If $T \leadsto^1 U$ is due to $v \leadsto^1 v'$, then U and U' are as follows.

$$U = (((\lambda x.u)[\Gamma])v')\overline{w}[\overline{\Delta}] \qquad U' = (u\{v'/x\}[\Gamma])\overline{w}[\overline{\Delta}]$$

3. If $T \leadsto^1 U$ is due to a rewrite step entirely inside $[\Gamma]$ or inside $\overline{w}[\overline{\Delta}]$—which covers any rule except (8) and (10)—then U and U' are as follows.

$$U = (((\lambda x.u)[\Gamma'])v)\overline{w'}[\overline{\Delta'}] \qquad U' = (u\{v/x\}[\Gamma'])\overline{w'}[\overline{\Delta'}]$$

A Proof of Strong Normalisation of the Typed Atomic Lambda-Calculus 349

4. If $T \leadsto^1 U$ is due to an application of rule (8) or (10) to $[\Gamma]$ with substitutions in u, then U and U' are as follows.

$$U = (((\lambda x.u')[\Gamma'])v)\overline{w[\Delta]} \qquad U' = (u'\{v/x\}[\Gamma'])\overline{w[\Delta]}$$

5. If $T \leadsto^1 U$ is due to an application of rule (8) or (10) to $\overline{w[\Delta]}$ with substitutions anywhere in $((\lambda x.u)[\Gamma])v$, then U and U' are as follows.

$$U = (((\lambda x.u')[\Gamma'])v')\overline{w'[\Delta']} \qquad U' = (u'\{v'/x\}[\Gamma'])\overline{w'[\Delta']}$$

For the remaining cases, $\mathcal{R}(U') \leq \mathcal{R}(T')$ and $\mathcal{S}(U) < \mathcal{S}(T)$.

6. If $T \leadsto^1 U$ is an application of permutation rule (2) to $[\gamma]$ in $\lambda x.u'[\gamma]$, where $u = u'[\gamma]$, then U and U' are as follows (note that $T' = U'$).

$$U = (((\lambda x.u')[\gamma][\Gamma])v)\overline{w[\Delta]} \qquad U' = (u'\{v/x\}[\gamma][\Gamma])\overline{w[\Delta]}$$

7. If $T \leadsto^1 U$ is an application of permutation rule (3) to $[\gamma]$ in $((\lambda x.u)[\Gamma'])[\gamma])v$, where $[\Gamma] = [\Gamma'][\gamma]$, then U and U' are as follows (note that $T' = U'$).

$$U = ((((\lambda x.u)[\Gamma'])v)[\gamma])\overline{w[\Delta]} \qquad U' = (u\{v/x\}[\Gamma'][\gamma])\overline{w[\Delta]}$$

8. If $T \leadsto^1 U$ is an application of permutation rule (4) to $[\gamma]$ in $((\lambda x.u)[\Gamma])v'[\gamma]$, where $v = v'[\gamma]$, then U and U' are as below. Note that $T' \leadsto U'$ by permuting $[\gamma]$ outward, from $u\{v'[\gamma]/x\}$ to $u\{v'/x\}[\gamma]$, and $T' = U'$ if $u = x$.

$$U = ((((\lambda x.u)[\Gamma])v')[\gamma])\overline{w[\Delta]} \qquad U' = (u\{v'/x\}[\Gamma][\gamma])\overline{w[\Delta]}$$

□

For the following proofs, we associate with each closure $[\gamma]$ its *body* $\mathsf{b}[\gamma]$ and its *computation* $[\gamma]^c$, defined as follows.

$$\mathsf{b}[\vec{x} \leftarrow t] = t$$
$$\mathsf{b}[\vec{x} \leftarrow \lambda y.t^n] = \lambda y.t^n$$
$$[x_1, \ldots, x_n \leftarrow t]^c = \{\mathsf{ub}(t)^i/x_i\}_{i \leq n}[\mathsf{rn}(t)]$$
$$[x_1, \ldots, x_n \leftarrow \lambda y.t^n]^c = \{\mathsf{ub}(\lambda y.\pi_i(t^n))^i/x_i\}_{i \leq n}[\mathsf{rn}(\lambda y.t^n)]$$

Lemma 22.
1. If z is free in t, then $u[\vec{x} \leftarrow t]^c\{w/z\} \leadsto u[\vec{x} \leftarrow t\{w/z\}]^c$.
2. If z is free in t^n, then $u[\vec{x} \leftarrow \lambda y.t^n]^c\{w/z\} \leadsto u[\vec{x} \leftarrow \lambda y.t\{w/z\}]^c$.

Proof. Immediate from the definitions, Lemma 8, and Lemma 9. □

The notation $[\gamma]^*$ will indicate a either $[\gamma]$ or $[\gamma]^c$. For a sequence of closures $[\Gamma] = [\gamma_1] \ldots [\gamma_p]$, we denote by $[\Gamma]^*$ a *partial computation* $[\gamma_1]^* \ldots [\gamma_p]^*$. Analogously, $\{\cdot\}\overline{w[\Delta]}^*$ denotes a partial computation for a context $\{\cdot\}\overline{w[\Delta]}$.

In order to measure the number of reduction steps in a context $\overline{w[\Delta]}$, we use the notion of *applicative n-term*, defined by the following grammar.

$$T^n \quad ::= \quad \langle t_1, \ldots, t_n \rangle \quad | \quad T^n[\gamma] \quad | \quad (T^n)t$$

Rewrite rules apply to applicative n-terms as normal, but reduction within the tuple is permitted. Then for a term $(u)\overline{w[\Delta]}$, reduction in the context $\overline{w[\Delta]}$ is separated from that in u by considering reduction in the applicative n-term $\langle x_1, \ldots, x_n \rangle \overline{w[\Delta]}$, where $\{x_1, \ldots, x_n\} = \mathsf{FV}(u)$.

Lemma 23. *For any terms t, v, and w, if $t \rightsquigarrow^1 v$ and $t \rightsquigarrow_S w$ then $w \rightsquigarrow \mathsf{u}(v)$.*

Proof. There are two cases.
1. If $t \rightsquigarrow^1_S v$, then $\mathsf{u}(v) = \mathsf{u}(w)$, as sharing reduction is confluent and strongly normalising by Theorem 4.
2. If $t \rightsquigarrow^1_\beta v$, by [12, Lemma 17 and Theorem 18] the unfolding of w beta-reduces (in zero or more beta-steps) to a term w' such that $\mathsf{u}(w') = \mathsf{u}(v)$. □

Lemma 24. *If $(u[\gamma]^c)\overline{w} \in \mathcal{N}$ and $\mathsf{b}[\gamma] \in \mathcal{N}$, then $(u[\gamma])\overline{w} \in \mathcal{N}$.*

Proof. The following stronger statement will be proved: given

$$T = (u)\overline{w[\Delta]} \quad \text{and} \quad T' = (u)\overline{w[\Delta]^*} \,,$$

let T^n be the applicative n-term $\langle x_1, \ldots, x_n \rangle \overline{w[\Delta]}$ where $\mathsf{FV}(u) = \{\vec{x}\}$. If $T' \in \mathcal{N}$ and $T^n \in \mathcal{N}$, then $T \in \mathcal{N}$.

We proceed by induction on the measure $(\mathcal{R}(T'), \mathcal{R}(T^n))$. For each term U reached by a reduction step $T \rightsquigarrow^1 U$ it will be shown that $U \in \mathcal{N}$, proving that $T \in \mathcal{N}$. This will be done by giving a term U' reachable by a reduction $T' \rightsquigarrow U'$, to which the induction hypothesis applies; note that since $T' \in \mathcal{N}$ also $U' \in \mathcal{N}$, but it must also be shown that the corresponding applicative n-term U^n is in $\mathcal{N}$. The induction hypothesis for U and U' then gives $U \in \mathcal{N}$.

1. If the reduction step $T \rightsquigarrow^1 U$ takes place inside u, then U and U' are as follows.
$$U = (u')\overline{w[\Delta]} \qquad U' = (u')\overline{w[\Delta]^*}$$
Then $\mathcal{R}(U') < \mathcal{R}(T')$, and since $\mathsf{FV}(u) = \mathsf{FV}(u')$ we have $U^n = T^n \in \mathcal{N}$.
2. If the reduction step $T \rightsquigarrow^1 U$ takes place inside the context $\overline{w[\Delta]}$, then $\mathcal{R}(U^n) < \mathcal{R}(T^n)$. Let U and U' be
$$U = (u')\overline{w'[\Delta']} \qquad U' = (u')\overline{w'[\Delta']^*}$$
where every closure in $\overline{w'[\Delta']^*}$ is computed. The reduction $T \rightsquigarrow^1 U \rightsquigarrow_S U'$ corresponds 1-1 to a reduction from $T^n = \langle x_1, \ldots, x_n \rangle \overline{w[\Delta]}$ of the form
$$T^n \rightsquigarrow^1 V \rightsquigarrow_S \mathsf{u}(V) \,.$$

A Proof of Strong Normalisation of the Typed Atomic Lambda-Calculus   351

(Given that only unfolded terms are instantiated into the n-tuple in the reduction $V \rightsquigarrow_S \mathsf{u}(V)$, which holds due to the restriction on tuples instated in the beginning of Section 4.) Similarly, for the reduction $T \rightsquigarrow_S T'$ there is a corresponding $T^n \rightsquigarrow_S W$. For these reduction paths, Lemma 23 gives a reduction $W \rightsquigarrow_S \mathsf{u}(V)$. The corresponding reduction path $T' \rightsquigarrow U'$ gives $\mathcal{R}(U') \leq \mathcal{R}(T')$, so that the induction hypothesis applies.

3. If the reduction step $T \rightsquigarrow^1 U$ is a beta-step where $u = \lambda x.u'$ is the function, and the argument v is the first element of the context $\{\cdot\}\overline{w[\Delta]}$, then U and U' are as follows.

$$U = (u'\{v/x\})\overline{w'[\Delta]} \qquad U' = (u'\{v/x\})\overline{w'[\Delta]}^*$$

Here, $\overline{w'[\Delta]}$ is $\overline{w[\Delta]}$ with the first application v removed; it follows that $U^n = \langle \vec{x}, \vec{y} \rangle \overline{w'[\Delta]} \in \mathcal{N}$ because $T^n = (\langle \vec{x} \rangle v)\overline{w'[\Delta]} \in \mathcal{N}$, where $\vec{x}$ and $\vec{y}$ are the free variables of $\lambda x.u'$ and v respectively. The induction hypothesis applies since $\mathcal{R}(U') < \mathcal{R}(T')$.

4. Let the reduction step $T \rightsquigarrow^1 U$ be an application of rule (7), combining two sharings $[\gamma] = [\vec{y} \leftarrow y]$ and $[\delta] = [\vec{x}, y, \vec{z} \leftarrow t]$ into one $[\delta'] = [\vec{x}, \vec{y}, \vec{z} \leftarrow t]$, where $u = u'[\gamma]$ and $[\delta]$ is the first element of the context $\overline{w[\Delta]}$. Then U and U' are as follows.

$$U = u'[\delta']\overline{w[\Delta]} \qquad U' = u'[\delta']^*\overline{w[\Delta]}^*$$

Then $T' = u'[\gamma][\delta]^*\overline{w[\Delta]}^* \rightsquigarrow U'$, and hence $\mathcal{R}(U') < \mathcal{R}(T')$. The difference between T^n and U^n is that between the following n-terms.

$$\langle \vec{x}, y, \vec{z} \rangle [\vec{x}, y, \vec{z} \leftarrow t] \qquad \langle \vec{x}, \vec{y}, \vec{z} \rangle [\vec{x}, \vec{y}, \vec{z} \leftarrow t]$$

While t may be duplicated more times in U^n than in T^n, since no interaction is possible between the elements of a tuple it follows that $U^n \in \mathcal{N}$, so that the induction hypothesis applies.

5. Finally, there is one case where $u = u'[\gamma]$ and a reduction step forces the closure $[\gamma]$ into the context $\overline{w[\Delta]}$. Since the context $\overline{w[\Delta]}$ consists of closures and applications; moving $[\gamma]$ into it means it must be permuted past a closure $[\delta]$ or an application $(\cdot)v$. In the former case, $u'[\gamma][\delta] \sim u'[\delta][\gamma]$ is an equivalence, not a rewrite step; thus the reduction step must be an application of rewrite rule (3). But because of the congruence $\sim$ on terms, the application $(\cdot)v$ need not be the first element of $\overline{w[\Delta]}$: there may be closures $[\Gamma]$ such that $u[\gamma][\Gamma] \sim u[\Gamma][\gamma]$. Then consider the following rewrite step.

$$(u'[\gamma][\Gamma])v \sim (u'[\Gamma][\gamma])v \rightsquigarrow^1 ((u'[\Gamma])v)[\gamma]$$

Then T, T', U and U' are as follows.

$$T = ((u'[\gamma][\Gamma])v)\overline{w'[\Delta']} \qquad T' = ((u'[\gamma][\Gamma]^*)v)\overline{w'[\Delta']}^*$$
$$U = ((u'[\Gamma])v)[\gamma]\overline{w'[\Delta']} \qquad U' = ((u'[\Gamma]^*)v)[\gamma]\overline{w'[\Delta']}^*$$

Here, the context $\{\cdot\}\overline{w[\Delta]} = ((\{\cdot\}[\Gamma])v)\overline{w'[\Delta']}$. Since $T' \leadsto^1 U'$ we have that $\mathcal{R}(T') < \mathcal{R}(U')$. To apply the induction hypothesis to U and U', due to the presence of $[\Gamma]^*$ we are forced to include $[\gamma]$ into the context $\overline{w[\Delta]}$. It must then be shown that the n-term U^n is in $\mathcal{N}$, given that $T^n \in \mathcal{N}$; however, U^n includes $[\gamma]$ where T^n does not:

$$T^n = (((\langle x_1, \ldots, x_n, y_1, \ldots, y_m\rangle [\Gamma])v)\overline{w'[\Delta']}$$

$$U^n = (((\langle x_1, \ldots, x_n, z_1, \ldots, z_k\rangle [\Gamma])v)[\gamma]\overline{w'[\Delta']} \ .$$

Here, $\mathsf{FV}(\mathsf{b}[\gamma]) = \{y_1, \ldots, y_m\}$ and $\mathsf{FV}(u') = \{x_1, \ldots, x_n, z_1, \ldots, z_k\}$, with the z_i bound by $[\gamma]$.

In case $\overline{w'[\Delta']}$ does not bind in $[\gamma]$, it follows that $U^n \in \mathcal{N}$ because $\mathsf{b}[\gamma] \in \mathcal{N}$ (as it is a subterm of $T' \in \mathcal{N}$) and $T^n \in \mathcal{N}$.

Otherwise, let $\overline{w'[\Delta']}$ bind in $[\gamma]$. The n-term B' below is obtained from T' by replacing $u = u'[\gamma]$ by the tuple $\langle x_1, \ldots, x_n, \mathsf{b}[\gamma]\rangle$.

$$B' = (((\langle x_1, \ldots, x_n, \mathsf{b}[\gamma]\rangle [\Gamma]^*)v)\overline{w'[\Delta']}^* \in \mathcal{N}$$

Recall that the x_i are the free variables of u' not bound by $[\gamma]$; then each element of the tuple is a subterm of u. Then since $T' \in \mathcal{N}$, also $B' \in \mathcal{N}$, and since $\overline{w'[\Delta']}$ binds in $[\gamma]$, the computations or closures in $\overline{w'[\Delta']}^*$ binding in $\mathsf{b}[\gamma]$ create reductions in $u[\gamma]$ that have no counterpart in $\langle x_1, \ldots, x_n, \mathsf{b}[\gamma]\rangle$, so that $\mathcal{R}(B') < \mathcal{R}(T')$. Then the induction hypothesis can be applied for B' and the term B below, with $B^n = T^n \in \mathcal{N}$, giving $B \in \mathcal{N}$.

$$B = (((\langle x_1, \ldots, x_n, \mathsf{b}[\gamma]\rangle [\Gamma])v)\overline{w'[\Delta']}$$

From this it follows that $U^n \in \mathcal{N}$, by the following argument. Let $B^1, \ldots, B^m$ be variants of B. Then a reduction step in U^n must do one of three things:
(a) if it duplicates a part of $\mathsf{b}[\gamma]$ from $[\gamma]$ into a y_i, it is a sharing step, of which there are only finitely many until a step of kind (b) or (c) is performed,
(b) if it applies to an x_i or outside the tuple, there is a corresponding step in each B^j,
(c) if it applies to a (part of) $\mathsf{b}[\gamma]^i$ that has been duplicated into the tuple, there is a corresponding step in B^i.

□

6 Conclusions and Further Work

The present result, of strong normalisation for the simply typed atomic lambda-calculus, emphasises how the calculus is a natural and well-behaved formalisation of sharing in the lambda-calculus. Future investigations will expand in three directions: strengthening the current strong normalisation result; adapting the atomic lambda-calculus to address further notions of sharing; and investigating the practical use of the calculus in computation, for instance in compiling or implementing functional programming languages.

The present work strongly suggests two angles for future research. A natural extension would be to characterise the strongly normalisable atomic lambda-terms by an intersection typing discipline [7,19,16], to which the current reducibility proof is expected to extend naturally. In a second direction, it is expected that the type system and strong normalisation proof can be extended to the second-order case—although subject reduction is not immediately obvious.

For the atomic lambda-calculus in general, further work will focus on variations on the calculus that more closely approach the reduction dynamics of sharing graphs, to encompass further degrees of sharing. Another direction would be the inclusion of general recursion in the calculus, and the investigation of its interaction with the sharing constructs, as a prerequisite of making the calculus useful in practice to the implementation of functional programming languages.

References

1. Abadi, M., Cardelli, L., Curien, P.-L., Lévy, J.-J.: Explicit substitutions. Journal of Functional Programming 1(4), 375–416 (1991)
2. Accattoli, B., Kesner, D.: The structural λ-calculus. In: Dawar, A., Veith, H. (eds.) CSL 2010. LNCS, vol. 6247, pp. 381–395. Springer, Heidelberg (2010)
3. Ariola, Z.M., Felleisen, M., Maraist, J., Odersky, M., Wadler, P.: A call-by-need lambda calculus. In: POPL (1995)
4. Asperti, A., Guerrini, S.: The Optimal Implementation of Functional Programming Languages. Cambridge University Press (1998)
5. Balabonski, T.: A unified approach to fully lazy sharing. In: POPL (2012)
6. Brünnler, K., Tiu, A.F.: A local system for classical logic. In: Nieuwenhuis, R., Voronkov, A. (eds.) LPAR 2001. LNCS (LNAI), vol. 2250, pp. 347–361. Springer, Heidelberg (2001)
7. Coppo, M., Dezani-Ciancaglini, M.: An extension of the basic functionality theory for the λ-calculus. Notre Dame Journal of Formal Logic 21(4), 685–693 (1980)
8. David, R., Guillaume, B.: A λ-calculus with explicit weakening and explicit substitution. MSCS 11(1), 169–206 (2001)
9. Cosmo, R.D., Kesner, D., Polonovski, E.: Proof nets and explicit substitutions. In: MSCS (2003)
10. Girard, J.-Y., Lafont, Y., Taylor, P.: Proofs and Types. Cambridge University Press (1989)
11. Guglielmi, A., Gundersen, T., Parigot, M.: A proof calculus which reduces syntactic bureaucracy. In: RTA, pp. 135–150 (2010)
12. Gundersen, T., Heijltjes, W., Parigot, M.: Atomic lambda-calculus: a typed lambda-calculus with explicit sharing. In: LICS (2013)
13. Gundersen, T., Heijltjes, W., Parigot, M.: Un lambda-calcul atomique. Journées Francophones des Langages Applicatifs (2013)
14. Hughes, R.J.M.: Super-combinators: a new implementation method for applicative languages. In: ACM Symposium on Lisp and Functional Programming, pp. 1–10 (1982)

15. Kesner, D., Lengrand, S.: Resource operators for lambda-calculus. Information and Computation 205(4), 419–473 (2007)
16. Krivine, J.-L.: Lambda-calculus types and models. Ellis Horwood, Chichester, UK (1993)
17. Lamping, J.: An algorithm for optimal lambda calculus reduction. In: POPL, pp. 16–30 (1990)
18. Lescanne, P.: From lambda-sigma to lambda-upsilon, a journey through calculi of explicit substitutions. In: POPL (1994)
19. Pottinger, G.: A type assignment for the strongly normalizable λ-terms. In: To H. B. Curry: Essays on Combinatory Logic, Lambda Calculus and Formalism, pp. 561–577. Academic Press, London (1980)
20. Tait, W.W.: Intensional interpretations of functionals of finite type I. The Journal of Symbolic Logic 32(2), 198–212 (1967)
21. van Oostrom, V., van de Looij, K.-J., Zwitserlood, M.: Lambdascope: another optimal implementation of the lambda-calculus. In: Workshop on Algebra and Logic on Programming Systems (2004)
22. Wadsworth, C.P.: Semantics and Pragmatics of the Lambda-Calculus. PhD thesis, University of Oxford (1971)

Relaxing Synchronization Constraints in Behavioral Programs

David Harel, Amir Kantor, and Guy Katz

Dept. of Computer Science and Applied Mathematics,
Weizmann Institute of Science, Rehovot, Israel
{dharel,amir.kantor,guy.katz}@weizmann.ac.il

Abstract. In *behavioral programming*, a program consists of separate modules called *behavior threads*, each representing a part of the system's allowed, necessary or forbidden behavior. An execution of the program is a series of synchronizations between these threads, where at each synchronization point an event is selected to be carried out. As a result, the execution speed is dictated by the slowest thread. We propose an *eager execution* mechanism for such programs, which builds upon the realization that it is often possible to predict the outcome of a synchronization point even without waiting for slower threads to synchronize. This allows faster threads to continue running uninterrupted, whereas slower ones catch up at a later time. Consequently, eager execution brings about increased system performance, better support for the modular design of programs, and the ability to distribute programs across several machines. It also allows to apply behavioral programming to a variety of problems that were previously outside its scope. We illustrate the method by concrete examples, implemented in a behavioral programming framework in C++.

Keywords: behavioral programming, synchronization, eager execution, modular design, distributed design.

1 Introduction

This work is carried out within the framework of *behavioral programming (BP)* [10] — a recently proposed approach for the development of reactive systems, which originated from the language of *live sequence charts* [5,8]. The basis of the approach is the construction of systems from special threads, called *behavior threads (b-threads)*, each of which represents an aspect of the system's behavior which is specified as being allowed, necessary or forbidden. A simultaneous execution of these threads constitutes the combined system behavior.

An execution of the program is comprised of a series of synchronization points between the threads, each of which results in an event being triggered. The choice of the triggered event is performed by a global *coordinator*, which, at every synchronization point, receives input from all the threads before making the choice. This high amount of coordination grants behavioral programs many of their qualities: it eliminates race conditions between the threads, allows for multi-modal, modular and incremental development, and, in general, promotes the development of comprehensible and maintainable code. See [10].

However, extensive synchronization has implications on system performance (see [11]). Since all threads must synchronize before the system can continue to the next synchronization point, the step from one point to another is constrained by the slowest b-thread. In parallel architectures (e.g., multi-core processors), execution resources may stand idle while the system waits for a slow b-thread to finish performing nontrivial computations or time-consuming actions and reach the next synchronization point. Similar situations can also occur in programs that run on a single processor — for instance, if a b-thread is performing lengthy input/output actions that require no processing power, but delay its synchronization.

We introduce a new execution mechanism for behavioral programs, which we term *eager execution*. It allows relaxing the synchronization constraints between b-threads, resulting in a higher level of concurrency when executing the program. At the same time, eager execution maintains all information necessary for triggering events, and thus adheres to BP's semantics and supports its idioms.

Eager execution is made possible by automatically *analyzing* a thread prior to its execution, resulting in an approximation of the thread's behavior. With this information at hand, the eager execution mechanism can sometimes choose events for triggering without waiting for all of the threads to synchronize, thus improving the efficiency of the system's run and avoiding excessive synchronization. We present two analysis methods that lead to more eager execution: one is *static* and considers the thread as a whole, whereas the other is *dynamic* and takes into account the thread's state during the run. Both methods have been implemented and tested in *BPC*, a framework for behavioral programming in C^{++}. The framework itself, along with the examples described in this paper, is available online [1].

Relaxing synchronization is helpful in several contexts. First, it improves system performance and reduces processor idle time. Moreover, it gives rise to better modular design of the system, by grouping together related threads into components, which we call *behavioral modules*, and allowing these to operate independently on different time scales. Finally, the techniques presented in this paper can be leveraged to support a decentralized assimilation of the modules on different machines by distributing BP's execution mechanism. Distributed execution has been implemented and tested in BPC. It is not included in this paper due to space limitations; it is discussed in Appendix I of [2].

The paper is organized as follows. A short description of behavioral programming and the BPC tool appears in Section 2. We define the eager execution mechanism and present the two analysis methods in Section 3. In Section 4, we show how eager execution allows for a modular design of programs. Related work is discussed in Section 5, and we conclude in Section 6. Proofs are included in the appendices to this paper.

2 Behavioral Programming

A behavioral program consists of a set of *behavior threads (b-threads)*, each of which is an independent code module, which implements a certain part of the system's behavior. The threads are interwoven at run time through a series of *synchronization points*, and together produce a cohesive system.

The b-threads are driven by *events*, which are managed by a global *coordinator* that is implemented at the core of the behavioral programming framework. At every synchronization point, each thread BT passes to the coordinator three disjoint sets of events: those *requested* by BT, those for which BT *waits*, and those *blocked* by BT. BT then halts until the coordinator wakes it up.

Once *all* b-threads have reached a synchronization point, the coordinator calculates the set of *enabled events* — events that are requested by at least one b-thread and blocked by none. It then selects one of these events for triggering, say e, and passes it to some of the b-threads, and those then continue their execution until the next synchronization point. More specifically, e is passed to a thread BT if it is either requested or waited-upon by BT; other threads remain at the synchronization point, and their declared event sets are re-considered when the coordinator selects the next event. The model assumes that all inter-b-thread communication is performed through the synchronization mechanism.

Various implementations of reactive systems as behavioral programs have been carried out, using frameworks built on top of high-level programming languages such as Java, Erlang and Blockly; see [10] and references therein. These frameworks allow the user to use the full flexibility offered by the underlying programming language in writing threads. In this paper, we demonstrate our techniques using a BP framework in C++, termed *BPC* [1].

For illustration, we provide an example of a vending machine programmed in BPC. The example is extended in later sections to demonstrate various aspects of our techniques. In this section, we only implement the basic functionality of the machine — collecting coins and dispensing products. The code consists of three b-threads, called *Dispenser*, *KeyPad* and *ProductSlot*; they are depicted in Fig. 1, 2, and 3, respectively. Observe that coin insertions and product selections are inputs from the environment. In the actual application they are implemented using a simple user interface, which is omitted from the code snippets. The same applies to the actual dispensing of the product in the *ProductSlot* thread.

We stress the key fact that the threads' transition from one synchronization point to the next may not be immediate. Since all the threads are required to synchronize in order for the coordinator to trigger an event, the thread that takes the longest to move from one synchronization point to the next dictates the speed of the entire system. This is the issue we address in the paper.

2.1 Behavioral Programming Formalized

While behavioral programming is geared toward natural and intuitive development using programming languages, its underlying infrastructure can be conveniently described and analyzed in terms of transition systems. We present

```
class Dispenser : public BThread {
    void entryPoint() {
        while ( true ) {
            bSync( none, {CoinInserted}, none );
            bSync( none, {ProductChosen}, {CoinInserted} );
            bSync( {ProvideProduct}, none, {CoinInserted} );
}}};
```

Fig. 1. The ***Dispenser*** thread. This thread is responsible for dispensing wares, after the user inserts a coin and selects a desired product. The programmer writes behavioral code by overriding the method entryPoint of class *BThread*. The thread runs in an infinite loop, invoking the synchronization API bSync three times in each iteration; each invocation corresponds to a synchronization point, and includes three sets of events: requested (blue), waited-upon (green) and blocked (red). In the first synchronization point, the thread waits for a coin insertion, signified by a CoinInserted event. In the second, it waits for product selection, signified by a ProdcutChosen event. Finally, in the third, it dispenses the product, by requesting a ProvideProduct event. Since each call suspends the thread until an event that was requested or waited-for is triggered, one product is dispensed per coin; also, it is impossible to obtain the product without inserting a coin. Observe that the thread also blocks CoinInserted events during its last two synchronization points; otherwise, extra coins inserted before a product is provided could be swallowed by the machine.

```
while ( true ) {
    waitForCoinInsertion();
    bSync( {CoinInserted}, none, none );
    waitForProductSelection();
    bSync( {ProductChosen}, none, none );
}
```

Fig. 2. The main method of the ***KeyPad*** thread. This thread is an input "sensor" — a thread responsible for receiving inputs from the environment and translating them into BP events. It waits for the user to insert a coin and then requests a CoinInserted event. Then, it waits for the user to select a product, and requests a ProductChosen event. Coin insertions and product selections are inputs coming from the environment, and are abstracted away inside the functions waitForCoinInsertion and waitForProductSelection. The thread translates these inputs into events that are to be processed by other threads.

an abstract formalization of behavioral programs and their semantics, similarly to [9,11].

In the following definitions we implicitly assume a given set Σ of *events*. A *behavior thread (b-thread) BT* is abstractly defined to be a tuple $BT = \langle Q, q_0, \delta, R, B \rangle$, where Q is a set of *states*, $q_0 \in Q$ is an *initial state*, $\delta : Q \times \Sigma \to Q$ is a *transition function*, $R : Q \to \mathcal{P}(\Sigma)$ assigns for each state a set of *requested events*, and $B : Q \to \mathcal{P}(\Sigma)$ assigns for each state a set of *blocked events*. A *behavioral program P* is defined to be a finite set of b-threads.

Note that in the definitions above, a b-thread's transition rules are given as a *deterministic*, single valued, function δ, assigning the next state given a state and an event trigger in that state. A natural variant in which the transitions are *nondeterministic* is analogously defined; see Appendix II of the supplementary

```
while ( true ) {
    bSync( none, {ProvideProduct}, none );
    provideActualProduct();
}
```

Fig. 3. The main method of the *ProductSlot* thread. This thread is an output "actuator"; it is responsible for translating ProvideProduct events into the dispensing of actual products. Thus, it waits for a ProvideProduct event, and then provides the product by invoking provideActualProduct.

material [2]. The latter is useful for reactive systems, where the next state might also depend on external input. Also note that in the formal definition of a bthread, there is no need to distinguish between events that are waited-upon by the thread, and those that are not. In any of the thread's states, an event that is not waited-upon can be captured by a transition that forms a self-loop; i.e., a transition that does not leave the state.

Semantics. Let $P = \{BT^1, \ldots, BT^n\}$ be a behavioral program, where $n \in \mathbb{N}$ and each $BT^i = \langle Q^i, q_0^i, \delta^i, R^i, B^i \rangle$ is a distinct b-thread. In order to define the semantics of P, we construct a deterministic *labeled transition system (LTS)* [12] denoted by LTS(P), which is defined as follows. LTS(P) = $\langle Q, q_0, \delta \rangle$, where $Q := Q^1 \times \cdots \times Q^n$ is the set of states, $q_0 := \langle q_0^1, \ldots, q_0^n \rangle \in Q$ is the initial state, $\delta : Q \times \Sigma \to 2^Q$ is a deterministic[1] transition function, defined for all $q = \langle q^1, \ldots, q^n \rangle \in Q$ and $a \in \Sigma$, by

$$\delta(\langle q^1, \ldots, q^n \rangle, a) := \begin{cases} \{\langle \delta^1(q^1, a), \ldots, \delta^n(q^n, a) \rangle\} & ; \text{if } a \in E(q) \\ \emptyset & ; \text{otherwise} \end{cases}$$

where $E(q) = \bigcup_{i=1}^n R^i(q^i) \setminus \bigcup_{i=1}^n B^i(q^i)$ is the set of *enabled events* at state q.

An execution of P is an execution of the induced LTS(P). The latter is executed starting from the initial state q_0. In each state $q \in Q$, an enabled event $a \in \Sigma$ is selected for triggering if such exists (i.e., an event $a \in \Sigma$ for which $\delta(q, a) \neq \emptyset$). Then, the system moves to the next state $q' \in \delta(q, a)$, and the execution continues. Such an execution can be formally recorded as a possibly infinite sequence of triggered events, called a *run*. The set of all *complete* runs is denoted by $\mathcal{L}(P) := \mathcal{L}(\text{LTS}(P))$. It contains either infinite runs, or finite ones that terminate in a state in which no event is enabled, called a *terminal state*.

3 The Eager Execution Mechanism

We begin with a general description of our proposed execution mechanism for BP, termed *eager execution*. Let $P = \{BT^1, \ldots, BT^n\}$ be a behavioral program consisting of b-threads $BT^1, \ldots, BT^n$. Assume that at some point in the execution

---

[1] I.e., its range includes only singletons and the empty set.

of P, a subset $P_{\text{sync}} \subseteq P$ of the threads has reached a synchronization point, while the rest are still executing. Further, assume that the coordinator has additional information about the events that the threads in $P \setminus P_{\text{sync}}$ will request and block at the next synchronization point. If, combining the information from threads in P_{sync} with the information about threads in $P \setminus P_{\text{sync}}$, the coordinator can find an event e that will be enabled at the next synchronization point, then e can immediately be chosen for triggering.

The coordinator may then pass e to the threads in P_{sync} to let them continue their execution immediately, without waiting for the remaining threads to synchronize. Once any of these other threads reaches its synchronization point, the coordinator immediately passes it event e, as this event was selected for that particular synchronization point. This is accomplished by having a designated queue for each of the b-threads, of events that are waiting to be passed, and putting e in the queues corresponding to the not-yet synchronized threads. The execution mechanism described is *eager*, in the sense that it uses predetermined information to choose the next event as early as possible.

When a thread BT reaches a synchronization point, if the corresponding queue is nonempty, the coordinator dequeues the next pending event e'. If BT requests or waits for e', it is passed to the thread, which then continues to execute. Otherwise, e' is ignored, and the coordinator continues with the next event pending in the queue. In order to reflect the semantics of BP, from the coordinator's global perspective BT is not considered synchronized as long as it has events pending in the queue. Particularly, the events that are requested or blocked by BT at this point are not considered for the selection of the next event; the coordinator considers only threads that have synchronized and for which there are no pending events (so that they are halted).

Observe that the eager execution mechanism strictly adheres to the semantics of BP, as described in Section 2; at every synchronization point, the triggered event is indeed enabled. Consequently, we get the following result:

Proposition 1. *Given a behavioral program P, the sequence of events triggered by the eager execution mechanism is a valid run (under BP's semantics).*

The key point, however, is that the eager mechanism makes its decisions more quickly, and thus often produces more efficient runs. The eager execution mechanism is formalized in Section 3.3, and Proposition 1 is proved in Appendix A.

It remains to show how the execution mechanism knows which events could be requested and blocked by threads that are yet to synchronize. We propose two approaches: *static analysis* and *dynamic analysis*.

3.1 Static Analysis

In this approach, the coordinator is given in advance a static over-approximation of the events that a thread might block when synchronizing. Explicitly, if a thread has states $s_1, \ldots, s_n$, this over-approximation is $\bigcup_{1 \leq i \leq n} B(s_i)$, where $B(s_i)$ is the set of events blocked in state s_i. The over-approximation is static in the sense that it does not change throughout the run.

When a thread synchronizes, the coordinator checks if there are events that are enabled based on the data gathered so far — namely, events that are requested and not blocked by threads in P_{sync}, and that are never blocked by the other threads, based on their over-approximations. If such an event exists, it can be triggered immediately. Otherwise, the coordinator waits for more threads to synchronize. This generally results in more events becoming enabled, since the actual set of events that are blocked by a thread is always a subset of the over-approximation, and since additional requested events are revealed. As soon as enough information is gathered to deduce that an event is enabled, it is immediately triggered and passed to all synchronized threads. For threads that are yet to synchronize, the event is stored in a designated queue, to be passed to them upon reaching their synchronization point.

Observe that we only discuss over-approximating blocked events but not the approximation of requested events. The reason is that the analogous version would entail using an under-approximation of requested events; and, since threads do not generally request an event in each of their states, these under-approximations are typically empty.

Example: Using Static Analysis. We further evolve the example from Section 2. Suppose that the vending machine's developer wishes to introduce a maintenance mechanism. Once every fixed period of time, the machine is to go into maintenance mode and measure its inner temperature and humidity.

This type of requirement poses a challenge, in the form of integrating different time scales into a behavioral program. If maintenance is to occur every t seconds, a natural approach is adding a thread with the following structure, wrapped in a loop: (a) sleep for t seconds; (b) request an InitiateMaintenance event. Unfortunately, under a traditional BP execution mechanism, this results in the entire system pausing for t seconds at a time; since the thread does not reach the next synchronization point while asleep, the coordinator is unable to trigger an event,

```
while ( true ) {
    sleep( TimeBetweenMaintenancePeriods );
    bSync( {InitiateMaintenance}, none, none );
}
```

Fig. 4. The main method of the *MaintenanceTimer* thread. TimeBetweenMaintenancePeriods is a constant, indicating the desired time between consecutive maintenance cycles. Whenever the thread wakes up it requests an InitiateMaintenance event, and then goes back to sleep. Observe that since the thread neither requests nor waits for any other events, any events that were triggered while it was asleep — such as coin insertions or user selections — are not passed on to it when it awakes. Therefore, it immediately catches up with the execution upon waking up.

In order to tell the coordinator that the *MaintenanceTimer* thread blocks no events, the following line of code is provided as well: `bProgram.addThreadBlockingData( "MaintenanceTimer", none );`

This allows the coordinator to trigger an event even if this thread has not synchronized yet.

and any coin insertions or product requests by the user go unanswered between maintenance phases.

One solution is to have the event which initiates the periodic maintenance be triggered by some external entity — similarly to coin insertions and product selections. This approach, though feasible, means that the system would depend on these external events in order to operate properly; the BP framework does not offer a way to enforce their proper generation.

Instead, we adopt a solution that combines in-line waiting and eager execution. We use the method described above, and declare (or, as we later discuss, find automatically) that the new thread does not block any events; in effect, this tells the coordinator that it should not wait for it at any synchronization point. The system can then progress, and go along serving clients, while the thread is asleep. When the thread awakes and synchronizes, it is informed, one at a time, of the events that have occurred so far, and it can then synchronize and request that maintenance be triggered. The new thread is depicted in Fig. 4.

3.2 Dynamic Analysis

In this approach, the coordinator is given complete *state graphs* of the threads, which are automatically calculated before the program is executed. The labeled vertices of a state graph correspond to the thread's synchronization points and requested/blocked events, while the labeled edges correspond to the program's events (that are not blocked at that state). The graph thus provides a complete description of the thread from the coordinator's point of view — that is, a complete description of the events requested and blocked by the thread, but without any calculations or input/output actions performed by the thread when not synchronized. For more details on these state graphs, see [6].

During runtime, the coordinator keeps track of the threads' positions in the graphs, allowing it to approximate the events they will request and block at the next synchronization point — even before they actually synchronize. This method is dynamic, in the sense that the approximations for a given thread can change during the run, as different states are visited. The fundamental difference between running a thread and simulating its run using its state graph is that in the latter, no additional computations are performed, and consequently transitions can be considered immediate.

Recall that our definition of threads dictates that a thread's transitions be deterministic. Therefore, simulating a thread through its state graph yields precise predictions of its requested and blocked events at each synchronization point. In the nondeterministic model, where threads may depend on coin tosses or inputs from the environment, it may be impossible for the coordinator to determine a thread's exact state until it synchronizes; however, the coordinator can approximate the thread's requested and blocked events by considering all the states to which the nondeterministic transitions might send the thread. If, due to a previous transition, the thread is known to be in one of states $s_1, \ldots, s_n$, then the blocked events may be over-approximated by $\bigcup_{1 \leq i \leq n} B(s_i)$ — similarly to what is done in static analysis. Analogously, the requested events may be under-approximated by $\bigcap_{1\leq i\leq n} R(s_i)$. For more details see Appendix II of the supplementary material [2]. As before, if these approximations leave no enabled events, the coordinator waits for more threads to synchronize.

The other details are as they were in the static analysis scheme. Once an event is triggered, it is immediately sent to all synchronized threads, and is placed in queues for threads that are yet to synchronize.

Example: Using Dynamic Analysis. In Section 3.1, we added a thread that periodically initiates a maintenance process in the vending machine. We now describe this process in greater detail. Suppose that the goal of the maintenance process is to keep the machine's temperature and humidity at a certain level. Maintenance thus includes two phases: measurement and correction, applied once for temperature and once for humidity. For simplicity, assume that both values are always out of the safe range; i.e., that they always require adjusting.

To handle these requirements, we add two new threads to the program — one to do the measurements, and one to do the corrections. The first, the *Measurer*, reads information from the environment through sensors, while the second, the *Corrector*, affects the environment, through air conditioning and humidity control systems. These threads are triggered by the periodic InitiateMaintenance event, as described earlier. Code snippets appear in Fig. 5 and Fig. 6.

```
while ( true ) {
    bSync( none, {InitiateMaintenance}, none );

    if ( temperatureTooHigh() )
        bSync( {DecreaseTemperature}, none, {ProvideProduct} );
    else bSync( {IncreaseTemperature}, none, {ProvideProduct} );
    bSync( none, {TemperatureCorrected}, {ProvideProduct} );

    if ( humidityTooHigh() ) bSync( {DecreaseHumidity}, none, none );
    else bSync( {IncreaseHumidity}, none, none );
    bSync( none, {HumidityCorrected}, none );
}
```

Fig. 5. The main method of the *Measurer* thread. Upon triggering of the InitiateMaintenance event, this thread wakes up, asks for the appropriate temperature correction, and waits for confirmation. Afterwards, an analogous process is performed for the humidity level. Observe that the ProvideProduct event is blocked during the temperature phase, but not during the humidity phase.

Another requirement is that, due to constraints in the machine, it is forbidden to dispense products between temperature measurement and correction, otherwise the correction might be interrupted. Therefore, the *Measurer* thread blocks events of type ProvideProduct during temperature measurement and correction. During humidity measurement, however, this limitation does not apply. As measurement and correction operations take a non-zero amount of time, there is a time window during maintenance in which the dispensing of products is forbidden.

We seek a solution that would prevent dispensing products during the temperature phase, but would permit it during the humidity phase. Static analysis does

```
while ( true ) {
    bSync( none, allEvents(), none );
    if ( lastEvent() == IncreaseTemperature ) {
        increaseTemperature(); bSync( {TemperatureCorrected}, none, none );
    }
    else if ( lastEvent() == DecreaseTemperature ) {
        decreaseTemperature(); bSync( {TemperatureCorrected}, none, none );
    }
    else if ( lastEvent() == IncreaseHumidity ) {
        increaseHumidity(); bSync( {HumidityCorrected}, none, none );
    }
    else if ( lastEvent() == DecreaseHumidity ) {
        decreaseHumidity(); bSync( {HumidityCorrected}, none, none );
    }
}
```

Fig. 6. The main method of the *Corrector* thread. The thread waits for events IncreaseTemperature, DecreaseTemperature, IncreaseHumidity or DecreaseHumidity; if they are triggered, it responds by adjusting the temperature or humidity (this part is abstracted away in the subroutines). Then, the thread requests an event notifying that the request has been handled, and goes back to waiting for new requests. Accessing the last event triggered is performed via the `lastEvent` method.

not suffice: as the *Measurer* thread blocks the ProvideProduct event at some of its states, the over-approximation includes this event — and so ProvideProduct events would not be triggered during humidity measurement and correction. Dynamic analysis, on the other hand, resolves this issue, as it is able to distinguish between the two phases; see Table 1 for performance comparison.

Table 1. Performance of the vending machine program using the different execution mechanisms. The measurements were performed using a customer simulator, purchasing 250 products in random intervals. The table depicts the time the experiment took, the number of maintenance rounds performed during the experiment, and the average delay — the time between making an order and receiving the product. The improvement column measures the reduction in delay compared to the traditional execution mechanism.

Execution	#Servings	Time (min)	#Maintenance	Delay (sec)	Improvement
Traditional	250	15:40	59	1.68	—
Static	250	12:30	50	0.85	50%
Dynamic	250	9:20	37	0.18	90%

We point out that the *Measurer* thread's transitions are not deterministic — as they depend on input from the `temperatureTooHigh` and `humidityTooHigh` subroutines. As previously explained, this does not pose a problem, as the coordinator calculates an over-approximation based on all the successor states of the thread's last known state.

Remark: Recall that dynamic analysis includes spanning the state graphs of threads and integrating these graphs into the program. Manual spanning of state graphs is prone to error, and is rather tedious in large systems with many events.

Consequently, BPC includes an automated tool for performing this spanning without any overhead on the programmer's side.

The spanning is performed by separating the thread under inspection from its siblings, and then iteratively exploring its state graph until all its states and transitions have been found. Starting at the initial state, we check the thread's behavior in response to the triggering of each event that is not blocked by the thread in that state. After the triggering of each event, the thread arrives at a new state (synchronization point) — and, with proper book keeping, it is simple to check if the state was previously visited or not. New states are then added to a queue to be explored themselves, in an iterative BFS-like manner.

Isolating threads is performed using the CxxTest [15] tool, which is able capture and redirect function calls within programs. The thread's calls to the synchronization method bSync are captured, and used to determine the thread's current state; similarly, calls to the lastEvent method are captured and used to fool the thread into believing that a certain event was just triggered. The strength of this method is that the entire process takes place using the original, unmodified program code. Other methods, such as the one used in BPJ [7], include adding dedicated threads for this purpose — a process that might in itself introduce additional errors. Once the state graph has been spanned, it is automatically transformed into a C++ code module and integrated into the program.

3.3 Eager Execution Formalized

We now formally define the the eager execution mechanism. All definitions in this section exclusively consider deterministic b-threads; handling nondeterministic ones is similar (see Appendix II of the supplementary material [2]).

Let $P = \{BT^1, \ldots, BT^n\}$ be a behavioral program, where $n \in \mathbb{N}$ and each BT^i is a distinct b-thread. In order to define the eager execution mechanism, we construct a labeled transition system (LTS) denoted by $\widehat{\text{LTS}}(P) = \langle \widehat{Q}, \widehat{q_0}, \widehat{\delta} \rangle$, which is defined next. We use some of the notation introduced in Section 2.1.

The set of states is given by $\widehat{Q} := (Q^1 \times \Sigma^*) \times \cdots \times (Q^n \times \Sigma^*)$. Each state is thus a tuple consisting for each thread of its state and the contents of its event queue. Let $q = \langle q^i, u^i \rangle_{i=1}^n \in \widehat{Q}$ be a state. We use the standard notation $\delta^i(q^i, u^i)$ to denote the state in Q^i after applying the transition function δ^i of thread BT^i starting from state q^i for each event in the queue u^i. Given q, we denote the tuple comprised of these states by $\bar{q} := \langle \delta^i(q^i, u^i) \rangle_{i=1}^n$; we refer to it as the *indication* of q. Note that $\bar{q}$ naturally corresponds to a state in Q, which is the set of states of $\text{LTS}(P) = \langle Q, q_0, \delta \rangle$ defined in Section 2.1. We slightly abuse notation and write that $\bar{q} \in Q$. Naturally, the initial state is $\widehat{q_0} := \langle (q_0^1, \varepsilon), \ldots, (q_0^n, \varepsilon) \rangle \in \widehat{Q}$.

In each state $q = \langle q^i, u^i \rangle_{i=1}^n \in \widehat{Q}$, eager execution *approximates* the requested and blocked events of each thread. This is indicated by the following sets of events: $\mathcal{R}^i(q) \subseteq \Sigma$, for the requested events of thread BT^i, and $\mathcal{B}^i(q) \subseteq \Sigma$, for the its blocked events. As previously mentioned, eager execution has various forms (depending on the analysis technique that is used); each form is characterized by its specific choice for these approximations. The requirements imposed on them are the following. We require that $\mathcal{R}^i(q)$ is a subset of the events that are requested by thread BT^i at state $\delta^i(q^i, u^i)$, and that $\mathcal{B}^i(q)$ is a superset of the blocked events at that state. That is,

$$\mathcal{R}^i(q) \subseteq R^i(\delta^i(q^i, u^i)) \qquad B^i(\delta^i(q^i, u^i)) \subseteq \mathcal{B}^i(q). \tag{1}$$

Moreover, we require that in case a thread is synchronized, the two approximations are precise. More formally, if $u^i = \varepsilon$ for some $i \in [n]$ (where $[n]$ denotes the set of indices $\{1, \ldots, n\}$), so that in particular $\delta^i(q^i, u^i) = q^i$, then we require

$$\mathcal{R}^i(q) = R^i(q^i) \qquad \mathcal{B}^i(q) = B^i(q^i). \tag{2}$$

These two requirements are sufficient for our purposes. One may easily verify that the eager execution with either static or dynamic analysis technique complies with the requirements. From these, we obtain that the *approximated enabled events*, defined in the following, are contained in the enabled events at the indication state $\bar{q} \in Q$; i.e.,

$$\mathcal{E}(q) := \bigcup_{i=1}^{n} \mathcal{R}^i(q) \setminus \bigcup_{i=1}^{n} \mathcal{B}^i(q) \subseteq E(\bar{q}). \tag{3}$$

In case all threads are synchronized, i.e., $u^i = \varepsilon$ for all $i \in [n]$, we obtain

$$\mathcal{E}(q) = E(\bar{q}). \tag{4}$$

The nondeterministic transition function $\widehat{\delta} : \widehat{Q} \times (\Sigma \dot{\cup} \{\varepsilon\}) \to 2^{\widehat{Q}}$ includes also silent ε-labeled transitions; these ε transitions are not considered part of the runs of the system. $\widehat{\delta}$ is defined for each state $q = \langle q^i, u^i \rangle_{i=1}^n \in \widehat{Q}$, and $\sigma \in \Sigma \cup \{\varepsilon\}$, as:

- If $\sigma = \varepsilon$, then $\widehat{\delta}(q, \varepsilon)$ is defined to be those states $\langle r^i, v^i \rangle_{i=1}^n \in \widehat{Q}$ for which there is $i_0 \in [n]$ and $a \in \Sigma$ such that $u^{i_0} = a\, v^{i_0}$ and $r^{i_0} = \delta^{i_0}(q^{i_0}, a)$, and for all other $i \in [n] \setminus \{i_0\}$ it holds that $r^i = q^i$ and $v^i = u^i$. These transitions correspond to threads with queued events processing these events — they change states, while the other threads do not move.
- If $\sigma \in \Sigma$, and moreover $\sigma \in \mathcal{E}(q)$, then $\widehat{\delta}(q, \sigma)$ is defined to be the singleton $\widehat{\delta}(q, \sigma) = \{\langle q^i, u^i \sigma \rangle_{i=1}^n\}$. These transitions correspond to new events being triggered.
- If $\sigma \in \Sigma$ and $\sigma \notin \mathcal{E}(q)$, we define $\widehat{\delta}(q, \sigma) = \emptyset$. This reflects the fact that events that are not enabled cannot be triggered.

For a rigorous proof of Proposition 1 using these definitions, see Appendix A.

4 Modularity by Eager Execution

Complex systems can generally benefit from being partitioned into several components, each assigned its own execution resources (e.g., a dedicated computer) [13].

An intelligent partitioning of the system into components makes it possible to execute different facets of system behavior independently, and thus improve response time to different tasks. This is particularly crucial when system behavior involves multiple time scales.

The fact that a behavioral program consists of a collection of threads, each addressing part of the system's behavior, suggests a natural way to design program components. We call a collection of b-threads that collectively addresses a certain facet of the system a *behavioral module*. Each such module can be assigned distinct computational resources (e.g., a computer) so as to form an independent component. However, BP's complete stepwise synchronization between the b-threads undermines the benefits expected from such a design. In particular, it would not result in alleviating run-time dependencies between the components.

In order to understand how eager execution affects behavioral modules, we make the following definitions. Consider a behavioral program P consisting of a set behavioral modules $M_1, \ldots, M_k$; thus, the threads in the program are $\bigcup_{i=1}^{k} M_i$. Denote by E_i the set of events that are *controlled* — i.e., requested or blocked — at some synchronization point of a thread of module M_i. Typically, these events are part of the 'vocabulary' corresponding to that facet of the system addressed in module M_i. The modular design of the program is termed *strict* if $E_1, \ldots, E_k$ are pairwise disjoint; i.e., $E_i \cap E_j = \emptyset$ for $i \neq j$. However, any thread can wait for any event. A strict modular design essentially means that while modules may signal one another (by waiting for each other's events), they do *not* control each other's events; i.e., they are assigned sufficiently independent duties.

For a strict modular design, the eager execution mechanism results in an implementation in which the threads in each module never need to wait for a thread in another module to synchronize. Here, static analysis, as described in Section 3.1, is enough. The modules are thus effectively independent and may involve different time scales. This is formalized by the following proposition:

Proposition 2. *Let P be a behavioral program having a strict modular design and executed with the eager execution mechanism. If all b-threads of module M_i are synchronized, then an event $e \in E_i$ is enabled if and only if it will also be enabled upon the arrival of any other thread at its synchronization point.*

The proposition implies that, in a strict design, as soon as a module's threads have synchronized any enabled event that they control may immediately be triggered, without waiting for threads from other modules. See Appendix III of the supplementary material [2] for a rigorous definition of a modular program design and a proof of the proposition.

4.1 Example: A Modular Design

We implement the traveling vehicles example from [11, Section 7]. The example includes several vehicles, each operating as an autonomous component traveling on pre-given cyclic route along an (x, y) grid; in each given time unit during the run, each vehicle can travel north, east, south or west. We assume that all vehicles travel at identical speeds, i.e., cover one unit of distance per time unit.

Using eager execution, this multi-component system can be programmed entirely within the behavioral programming framework, without relying on external means of communication. The threads of each vehicle, v_i, form an independent behavioral module M_i that involves a designated set of events. This results in a strict modular design allowing each vehicle to operate independently of others. A code snippet for the main thread of vehicle v_i is depicted in Fig. 7. If each module has a dedicated processor and event selection is fair, all vehicles are constantly moving — as the coordinator does not wait for vehicle v_i to finish moving and synchronize again before triggering the movement requested by another vehicle.

```
while ( true ) {
    Vector<Event> requestedEvents;
    if ( destinationIsNorth() ) requestedEvents.append( #iMoveNorth );
    if ( destinationIsSouth() ) requestedEvents.append( #iMoveSouth );
    if ( destinationIsEast()  ) requestedEvents.append( #iMoveEast  );
    if ( destinationIsWest()  ) requestedEvents.append( #iMoveWest  );
    bSync( requestedEvents, none, none );
    adjustPositionByLastEvent();
}
```

Fig. 7. The main method of each vehicle thread. The placeholder '#i' is replaced by the number of the vehicle; for instance, for vehicle v_5, the events are 5MoveNorth, 5MoveWest, etc. The thread requests moves in all directions that bring it closer to the destination. When the call to bSync returns, one of these moves was selected by the behavioral execution mechanism. The thread then updates its position (by invoking adjustPositionByLastEvent), and proceeds.

Eager execution allows a light-weight solution if communication between the vehicles is required — e.g., for collision prevention. Each vehicle can be accompanied by an adviser thread that keeps track of other vehicles. Whenever its vehicle is dangerously close to another, the adviser blocks movement in the dangerous direction (for simplicity, deadlocks are ignored). As the modular design remains strict, adding the adviser threads does not impede the vehicles' ability to move independently.

5 Related Work

Within the scope of BP, an alternative approach for supporting modular designs and multiple time scales in behavioral programs is suggested in [11], where a program consists of sub-programs, called *behavior nodes* (*b-nodes*), each with its own pool of (internal) events. Coordination between the b-nodes is carried out by sending *external events* from one to another. Thus, internal events have to be translated into external events and vice versa. The feasibility of this approach is exhibited in [11] by using several examples.

Observing that the b-node approach naturally induces a strict modular design, our approach offers similar benefits but without the need to go beyond the behavioral programming idioms; indeed, no additional layer of external events is needed. Relaxed synchronization also supports more general, non-strict designs, in which behavioral programming idioms are used more liberally. In the case of non-strict designs, eager execution does not ensure that the modules are executed independently. Nevertheless, it avoids unnecessary synchronization between the modules (especially when using dynamic analysis of the threads), which may be sufficient in many situations.

Outside the scope of BP, performance optimization and communication minimization in parallel and distributed settings have been studied extensively. The trade-off between these two goals is discussed in [4,16]. In [14], the author suggests imposing certain limitations on the communication between the components, which allows for execution-time optimization to be performed during compilation.

A method similar to our static analysis appears in [3], where invariants about system components are used for conflict resolution within the BIP framework.

6 Conclusion and Future Work

The contribution of this paper is in the proposed eager execution mechanism, which allows relaxing synchronization in behavioral programs. This scheme generally improves system performance, and allows behavioral programs to be written using a modular design that supports multiple time scales. Our approach is made possible by the realization that, by analyzing a b-thread prior to its execution, it is sometimes possible to accurately predict a valid outcome of a synchronization point without actually waiting for the thread to synchronize.

In this paper we made no assumptions on how the coordinator chooses the next event to be triggered from among the enabled events. In practice, however, such assumptions can sometimes simplify system development. One example is the *prioritized* event selection used in [9]. We believe that our methods can be naturally adapted to such mechanisms too.

The technique discussed in this paper requires that each b-thread communicate with a *global* coordinator at every synchronization point. While this constraint is significantly weaker than stepwise synchronization with all other b-threads, it may limit the applicability of the approach for designing multi-component applications in distributed architectures, in which communication is costly and time-consuming. In Appendix I of [2], we show how a variant of eager execution, called *distributed execution*, can be utilized to reduce these costs. This is done at the expense of not completely refraining from synchronization between threads of different modules, even in a strict modular design, so that Proposition 2 does not hold in that context. Finding ways to reduce communication costs while still upholding Proposition 2 is left for future work.

Acknowledgements. We thank Assaf Marron, Gera Weiss and Guy Wiener for their helpful comments on this work. This work was supported by an Advanced Research Grant to DH from the European Research Council (ERC) under the European Community's 7th Framework Programme (FP7/2007-2013), and by an Israel Science Foundation grant.

References

1. BPC: Behavioral Programming in C^{++},
   http://www.wisdom.weizmann.ac.il/~bprogram/bpc/.
2. Supplementral material,
   http://www.wisdom.weizmann.ac.il/~bprogram/bpc/relaxedSync/
3. Bensalem, S., Bozga, M., Quilbeuf, J., Sifakis, J.: Knowledge-Based Distributed Conflict Resolution for Multiparty Interactions and Priorities. In: Giese, H., Rosu, G. (eds.) FMOODS/FORTE 2012. LNCS, vol. 7273, pp. 118–134. Springer, Heidelberg (2012)
4. Cheng, Y., Robertazii, T.: Distributed Computation with Communication Delay (Distributed Intelligent Sensor Networks). IEEE Transactions on Aerospace and Electronic Systems 24(6), 700–712 (1988)
5. Damm, W., Harel, D.: LSCs: Breathing Life into Message Sequence Charts. J. on Formal Methods in System Design 19(1), 45–80 (2001)
6. Harel, D., Katz, G., Marron, A., Weiss, G.: Non-Intrusive Repair of Reactive Programs. In: Proc. 17th IEEE Int. Conf. on Engineering of Complex Computer Systems (ICECCS), pp. 3–12 (2012)
7. Harel, D., Lampert, R., Marron, A., Weiss, G.: Model-Checking Behavioral Programs. In: Proc. 11th Int. Conf. on Embedded Software (EMSOFT), pp. 279–288 (2011)
8. Harel, D., Marelly, R.: Come, Let's Play: Scenario-Based Programming Using LSCs and the Play-Engine. Springer (2003)
9. Harel, D., Marron, A., Weiss, G.: Programming Coordinated Scenarios in Java. In: D'Hondt, T. (ed.) ECOOP 2010. LNCS, vol. 6183, pp. 250–274. Springer, Heidelberg (2010)
10. Harel, D., Marron, A., Weiss, G.: Behavioral Programming. Comm. Assoc. Comput. Mach. 55(7), 90–100 (2012)
11. Harel, D., Marron, A., Weiss, G., Wiener, G.: Behavioral Programming, Decentralized Control, and Multiple Time Scales. In: Proc. 1st SPLASH Workshop on Programming Systems, Languages, and Applications based on Agents, Actors, and Decentralized Control (AGERE!), pp. 171–182 (2011)
12. Keller, R.: Formal verification of parallel programs. Comm. Assoc. Comput. Mach. 19(7), 371–384 (1976)
13. Parnas, D.: On the Criteria To Be Used in Decomposing Systems into Modules. Comm. Assoc. Comput. Mach. 15(12), 1053–1058 (1972)
14. van Gemund, A.J.: The Importance of Synchronization Structure in Parallel Program Optimization. In: Proc. 11th ACM Int. Conf. on Supercomputing (ICS), pp. 164–171 (1997)
15. Volk, E.: CxxTest: A Unit Testing Framework for C^{++}, http://cxxtest.com/
16. Yook, J.K., Tilbury, D.M., Soparkar, N.R.: Trading Computation for Bandwidth: Reducing Communication in Distributed Control Systems Using State Estimators. IEEE Transactions on Control Systems Technology 10(4), 503–518 (2002)

A Proof of Proposition 1

In this section we formally prove Proposition 1, stating that the runs produced by the eager execution mechanism are valid runs according to BP's original semantics. We consider $\widehat{\mathrm{LTS}}(P)$ from Section 3.3, which captures the execution of program P using the eager execution mechanism, and LTS(P) from Section 2.1, which captures the original semantics. Technically, we claim that each complete run of $\widehat{\text{LTS}}(P)$ is a complete run of LTS(P); i.e., $\mathcal{L}(\widehat{\text{LTS}}(P)) \subseteq \mathcal{L}(\text{LTS}(P))$. This is a consequence of the following lemmata.

When considering $\widehat{\text{LTS}}(P)$, $q \xrightarrow{\sigma} q'$ stands for $q' \in \hat{\delta}(q, \sigma)$, as customary when discussing transition systems (for any states $q, q' \in \hat{Q}$ and a possibly silent event $\sigma \in \Sigma \cup \{\varepsilon\}$). Also, recall that $q \in \hat{Q}$ is a *terminal state* if for all $\sigma \in \Sigma \cup \{\varepsilon\}$ it holds that $\hat{\delta}(q, \sigma) = \emptyset$. Similar notations and terminology apply to LTS(P).

Lemma 1. *Let $q, q' \in \hat{Q}$ and $\sigma \in \Sigma \cup \{\varepsilon\}$ such that $q \xrightarrow{\sigma} q'$ in $\widehat{\text{LTS}}(P)$.*

1. *If $\sigma = \varepsilon$, then $\overline{q'} = \overline{q}$.*
2. *If $\sigma \in \Sigma$, then $\overline{q} \xrightarrow{\sigma} \overline{q'}$ in LTS(P).*

Proof. 1: Denote $q = \langle q^i, u^i \rangle_{i=1}^n \in \hat{Q}$, and suppose that $\sigma = \varepsilon$. By the definition of $\hat{\delta}$, we obtain that $q' = \langle r^i, v^i \rangle_{i=1}^n$, where all the coordinates are the same as in q, except for the one corresponding to $i_0 \in [n]$. In the latter coordinate we get $\delta^{i_0}(r^{i_0}, v^{i_0}) = \delta^{i_0}(\delta^{i_0}(q^{i_0}, a), v^{i_0}) = \delta^{i_0}(q^{i_0}, a\, v^{i_0}) = \delta^{i_0}(q^{i_0}, u^{i_0})$, as needed.

2: Now, suppose $\sigma \in \Sigma$. According to the definition of $\hat{\delta}$, $\sigma \in \mathcal{E}(q)$ and $q' = \langle q^i, u^i\, \sigma \rangle_{i=1}^n$. By (3) (see Section 3.3) and by the definition of δ, we get that in LTS(P) it holds that $\overline{q} \xrightarrow{\sigma} \langle\, \delta^i(\delta^i(q^i, u^i), \sigma)\, \rangle_{i=1}^n = \langle\, \delta^i(q^i, u^i\, \sigma)\, \rangle_{i=1}^n = \overline{q'}$. □

Corollary 1.

1. *Let $r_0 \xrightarrow{\sigma_1} r_1 \xrightarrow{\sigma_2} \cdots \xrightarrow{\sigma_k} r_k$ be a finite execution of $\widehat{\text{LTS}}(P)$ ($k \geq 0$). There exists a finite execution $s_0 \xrightarrow{a_1} s_1 \xrightarrow{a_2} \cdots \xrightarrow{a_t} s_t$ of LTS(P) ($t \geq 0$) such that $\overline{r_k} = s_t$ and $\sigma_1 \sigma_2 \cdots \sigma_k = a_1 a_2 \cdots a_t$.*
2. *Let $r_0 \xrightarrow{\sigma_1} r_1 \xrightarrow{\sigma_2} \cdots$ be an infinite execution of $\widehat{\text{LTS}}(P)$. There exists an execution $s_0 \xrightarrow{a_1} s_1 \xrightarrow{a_2} \cdots$ of LTS(P) such that $\sigma_1 \sigma_2 \cdots = a_1 a_2 \cdots$.*

Proof (sketch). 1: By induction on k. For $k = 0$ the claim follows from the fact that $\overline{q_0} = q_0 \in Q$; the induction step follows from Lemma 1.

2: By an inductive construction of the execution, which similarly follows from Lemma 1. □

Lemma 2.

1. *If $q \in \hat{Q}$ is a terminal state in $\widehat{\text{LTS}}(P)$, then $\overline{q}$ is a terminal state in LTS(P).*
2. *There is no infinite sequence $q \xrightarrow{\varepsilon} q' \xrightarrow{\varepsilon} q'' \xrightarrow{\varepsilon} \cdots$ in $\widehat{\text{LTS}}(P)$.*

Proof. 1: As q is terminal, by the definition of $\hat{\delta}$ it holds that all the queues in q are empty (otherwise, $\hat{\delta}(q, \varepsilon) \neq \emptyset$); i.e., $q = \langle q^i, \varepsilon \rangle_{i=1}^n$. Let $a \in \Sigma$. Because q is terminal, $a \notin \mathcal{E}(q)$. Thus, by (4) (see Section 3.3), $a \notin E(\overline{q})$, and therefore by the definition of δ, $\delta(\overline{q}, a) = \emptyset$.

2: For each state $q = \langle q^i, u^i \rangle_{i=1}^n \in \hat{Q}$, consider the total size of the queues, denoted by $\varphi(q) := \Sigma_{i=1}^n |u^i| \in \mathbb{N}$. Given such an infinite sequence of states, φ is strictly decreasing (by the definition of $\hat{\delta}$), which contradicts the well-foundness of the natural numbers. □

Corollary 2. Let $r_0 \xrightarrow{\sigma_1} r_1 \xrightarrow{\sigma_2} \cdots$ be a complete (finite or infinite) execution of $\widehat{\mathrm{LTS}}(P)$. There exists a complete (finite or infinite, respectively) execution $s_0 \xrightarrow{a_1} s_1 \xrightarrow{a_2} \cdots$ of $\mathrm{LTS}(P)$ such that $\sigma_1 \sigma_2 \cdots = a_1 a_2 \cdots$.

The corollary follows from Corollary 1 and Lemma 2. It is equivalent to $\mathcal{L}(\widehat{\mathrm{LTS}}(P)) \subseteq \mathcal{L}(\mathrm{LTS}(P))$, which is the technical formulation of Proposition 1.

Characterizing Subset Spaces as Bi-topological Structures

Bernhard Heinemann

Faculty of Mathematics and Computer Science,
University of Hagen,
58084 Hagen, Germany
bernhard.heinemann@fernuni-hagen.de

Abstract. Subset spaces constitute a relatively new semantics for bi-modal logic. This semantics admits, in particular, a modern, computer science oriented view of the classic interpretation of the basic modalities in topological spaces à la McKinsey and Tarski. In this paper, we look at the relationship of both semantics from an opposite perspective as it were, by asking for a consideration of subset spaces in terms of topology and topological modal logic, respectively. Indeed, we shall finally obtain a corresponding characterization result. A third semantics of modal logic, namely the standard relational one, and the associated first-order structures, will play an important part in doing so as well.

Keywords: modal logic, topological semantics, subset spaces, knowledge and topological reasoning.

1 Introduction

Nowadays, successful applications of modal logic to computer science are abundant. We focus on a particular system from the realm of formal reasoning here, which may be seen as a cross-disciplinary framework for dealing with spatial as well as epistemic scenarios: the talk is of Moss and Parikh's bi-modal logic of subset spaces; see [12], [5], or Ch. 6 of [2].

We shall now indicate how the interrelation of the underlying ideas, *knowledge* and *spatiality*, is correspondingly revealed. The *epistemic state* of an agent under discussion, i.e., the set of all those states that cannot be distinguished by what the agent topically knows, can be viewed as a *neighborhood U* of the actual state x of the world. Formulas are then interpreted with respect to the resulting pairs x, U called *neighborhood situations*. Thus, both the set of all states and the set of all epistemic states constitute the relevant semantic domains as particular subset structures. The two modalities involved, K and □, quantify over all elements of U and 'downward' over all neighborhoods contained in U, respectively. This means that K captures the notion of knowledge as usual (see [7]), and □ reflects *effort to acquire knowledge* since gaining knowledge goes hand in hand with a shrinkage of the epistemic state. In fact, knowledge acquisition is this way reminiscent of a topological procedure. The appropriate logic for 'real' topological spaces, called *topologic,* was first determined by Georgatos in his thesis [8]. Meanwhile, a lot of work has been done on the development of a modal logical theory of subset spaces and, in particular, topological spaces on this basis; see [2] for a guide to the earlier literature. (To our knowledge, [10], [3], and [13], are the most recent papers in this field, with the last two forging links between subset spaces and *Dynamic Epistemic Logic (DEL);* see [6].)

The topological semantics of modal logic dates back to the late 1930s; see the respective notes in the paper [11]. In recent years, the research into logics based on this semantics has considerably been ramped up to satisfy requirements relating to spatial modelling and reasoning tasks in computer science; the handbook [5] contains lots of references regarding this as well (see, in particular, Ch. 5 and Ch. 10 there). The characteristic feature is the following interpretation of the modal box here: for every formula α, the validity domain of $\Box\alpha$ is defined to be the *interior* of the validity domain of α. With that, the well-known modal system S4 has been proved to be the logic of the class of all topological spaces; see [11] again. – This is all that must be said about topological modal logic for the moment; more facts will be given in Section 3 below.

There is a translation from mono-modal to bi-modal formulas which conveys the already rather transparent connection between the two interpretations in topological spaces just mentioned. Its decisive clause reads $\Box\alpha \mapsto \Diamond\mathsf{K}\alpha$; see [5], Proposition 3.5. This translation even gives rise to an *embedding* of S4 into *topologic;* see [5], Theorem 3.7. Thus, the elder, purely spatial formalism may be retrieved from a more comprehensive framework regarding epistemic issues, too.

Conversely, can subset spaces be identified in a purely topological way? – As it stands, this question is not raised precisely enough. So we must say that we are not looking for a somehow good-natured translation in the other direction here; this issue has already been discussed in [5], Sect. 3.2. Instead, our topic is the following. Subset spaces are closely related to certain bi-modal Kripke models having the same logic; see [5], Sect. 2.3. These structures of course are *bi-topological* since they validate, in particular, two modal logics containing S4. Thus, our initial question is to be specified as follows: can a topological characterization of all those bi-topological structures that originate from a subset space be given and, should the situation arise, up to what extent in terms of topological modal logic? – The goal of this paper is to give an affirmative answer and a corresponding description, respectively.

The present paper grew out of a remark of Anil Nerode at LFCS 2013. It makes a contribution in several respects. First, it clarifies the interplay of the three semantics involved to a greater extent. Second, it facilitates an alternative view of subset spaces. In fact, it is generally very desirable (and common in mathematics) to have at hand different ways of seeing a subject, in order to be able to react on varying problems flexibly. Third, the crucial axiom schema of the logic of subset spaces, called the *Cross Axioms* in [5], is given a topological reading as a certain *cover property* here. And finally, a topological formulation of the properties defining subset spaces as first-order structures is supplied. All this makes this paper a theoretical one on a system being, on the other hand, of practical relevance to the reasoning process. The latter has been taken as a justification to submit the paper to LPAR.

We now proceed to the technical issues. In the following section, we first introduce the language for subset spaces, and we recapitulate the known relationship between subset spaces and Kripke models. Later on in this section, we review the logic arising from that language. Section 3 then deals with the basics of topological modal logic in more detail. In Section 4, the topological effect of the Cross Axioms is illuminated. The final technical section contains the characterization theorem announced above, before the paper is finished by some concluding remarks.

2 The Language and the Logic of Subset Spaces

In this section, we first fix the language for subset spaces, $\mathcal{L}$. After that, we link the semantics of $\mathcal{L}$ with the common relational semantics of modal logic. Finally, we recall some facts on the logic of subset spaces needed subsequently.

To begin with, we define the syntax of $\mathcal{L}$. Let $\mathsf{Prop} = \{p, q, \ldots\}$ be a denumerably infinite set of symbols called *proposition variables* (which should represent the basic facts about the states of the world). Then, the set Form of all $\mathcal{L}$-*formulas*[1] over Prop is defined by the rule $\alpha ::= \top \mid p \mid \neg \alpha \mid \alpha \wedge \alpha \mid \mathsf{K}\alpha \mid \Box \alpha$. The *mono-modal fragment* MF of Form is obtained by disregarding the clause for K in this rule. Later on, the boolean connectives that are missing here are treated as abbreviations, as needed. The dual operators of K and $\Box$ are denoted by L and $\diamond$, respectively; K is called the *knowledge operator* and $\Box$ the *effort operator*.

We now turn to the semantics of $\mathcal{L}$. For a start, we define the relevant domains. We let $\mathcal{P}(X)$ designate the powerset of a given set X.

Definition 1 (Semantic Domains).

1. Let X be a non-empty set (of states) and $\mathcal{O} \subseteq \mathcal{P}(X)$ a set of subsets of X. Then, the pair $\mathcal{S} = (X, \mathcal{O})$ is called a (subset) frame.
2. Let $\mathcal{S} = (X, \mathcal{O})$ be a subset frame. Then the set

$$\mathcal{N}_\mathcal{S} := \{(x, U) \mid x \in U \text{ and } U \in \mathcal{O}\}$$

   is called the set of neighborhood situations of $\mathcal{S}$.
3. Let $\mathcal{S} = (X, \mathcal{O})$ be a subset frame. An $\mathcal{S}$-valuation is a mapping $V : \mathsf{Prop} \to \mathcal{P}(X)$.
4. Let $\mathcal{S} = (X, \mathcal{O})$ be a subset frame and V an $\mathcal{S}$-valuation. Then, $\mathcal{M} := (X, \mathcal{O}, V)$ is called a subset space (based on $\mathcal{S}$).

Note that neighborhood situations denominate the semantic atoms of our bi-modal language. The first component of such a situation indicates the actual state of the world, while the second reflects the uncertainty of the agent in

---
[1] The prefix '$\mathcal{L}$' will be omitted provided there is no risk of confusion.

question about it. Furthermore, Definition 1.3 shows that values of proposition variables depend on states only. This is in accordance with the common practice in epistemic logic; cf. [7].

For a given subset space $\mathcal{M}$, we now define the relation of *satisfaction*, $\models_{\mathcal{M}}$, between neighborhood situations of the underlying frame and formulas from Form. Based on that, we define the notion of *validity* of $\mathcal{L}$-formulas in subset spaces and in subset frames. In the following, neighborhood situations are often written without parentheses.

Definition 2 (Satisfaction and Validity). *Let $\mathcal{S} = (X, \mathcal{O})$ be a subset frame.*

1. *Let $\mathcal{M} = (X, \mathcal{O}, V)$ be a subset space based on $\mathcal{S}$, and let $(x, U) \in \mathcal{N}_{\mathcal{S}}$ be a neighborhood situation. Then*

$$
\begin{aligned}
&x, U \models_{\mathcal{M}} \top && \text{is always true} \\
&x, U \models_{\mathcal{M}} p &:&\iff x \in V(p) \\
&x, U \models_{\mathcal{M}} \neg \alpha &:&\iff x, U \not\models_{\mathcal{M}} \alpha \\
&x, U \models_{\mathcal{M}} \alpha \wedge \beta &:&\iff x, U \models_{\mathcal{M}} \alpha \text{ and } x, U \models_{\mathcal{M}} \beta \\
&x, U \models_{\mathcal{M}} \mathsf{K}\alpha &:&\iff \forall y \in U : y, U \models_{\mathcal{M}} \alpha \\
&x, U \models_{\mathcal{M}} \Box\alpha &:&\iff \forall U' \in \mathcal{O} : [x \in U' \subseteq U \Rightarrow x, U' \models_{\mathcal{M}} \alpha],
\end{aligned}
$$

where $p \in \mathsf{Prop}$ and $\alpha, \beta \in \mathsf{Form}$. In case $x, U \models_{\mathcal{M}} \alpha$ is true we say that α holds in $\mathcal{M}$ at the neighborhood situation x, U.

2. *Let $\mathcal{M} = (X, \mathcal{O}, V)$ be a subset space based on $\mathcal{S}$. An $\mathcal{L}$-formula α is called valid in $\mathcal{M}$ iff it holds in $\mathcal{M}$ at every neighborhood situation of $\mathcal{S}$.*

3. *An $\mathcal{L}$-formula α is called valid in $\mathcal{S}$ iff it is valid in every subset space $\mathcal{M}$ based on $\mathcal{S}$; in this case, we write $\mathcal{S} \models \alpha$.*

Note that the idea of knowledge and effort described in the introduction is made precise by Item 1 of this definition. In particular, knowledge *is defined* as validity at all states that are indistinguishable to the agent; cf. [7].

Obviously, subset spaces are on the same level of language as are Kripke models in common modal logic (whereas subset frames correspond to Kripke frames).

Subset frames and spaces might be considered from a different perspective, as is known since [5] and reviewed in the following. Let a subset frame $\mathcal{S} = (X, \mathcal{O})$ and a subset space $\mathcal{M} = (X, \mathcal{O}, V)$ based on $\mathcal{S}$ be given. Take $W_{\mathcal{S}} := \mathcal{N}_{\mathcal{S}}$ as a set of worlds, and define two accessibility relations $R^{\mathsf{K}}_{\mathcal{S}}$ and $R^{\Box}_{\mathcal{S}}$ on $W_{\mathcal{S}}$ by

$$
\begin{aligned}
(x, U) \, R^{\mathsf{K}}_{\mathcal{S}} \, (x', U') &: \iff U = U' \text{ and} \\
(x, U) \, R^{\Box}_{\mathcal{S}} \, (x', U') &: \iff (x = x' \text{ and } U' \subseteq U),
\end{aligned}
$$

for all $(x, U), (x', U') \in W_{\mathcal{S}}$. Moreover, let $V_{\mathcal{M}}(p) := \{(x, U) \in W_{\mathcal{S}} \mid x \in V(p)\}$, for every $p \in \mathsf{Prop}$. Then, bi-modal Kripke structures $\mathcal{S}_{\mathcal{S}} := \left(W_{\mathcal{S}}, \{R^{\mathsf{K}}_{\mathcal{S}}, R^{\Box}_{\mathcal{S}}\}\right)$ and $\mathcal{M}_{\mathcal{M}} := \left(W_{\mathcal{S}}, \{R^{\mathsf{K}}_{\mathcal{S}}, R^{\Box}_{\mathcal{S}}\}, V_{\mathcal{M}}\right)$ result in such a way that $\mathcal{M}_{\mathcal{M}}$ is equivalent to $\mathcal{M}$ in the following sense.

Proposition 1. *For all $\alpha \in \mathsf{Form}$ and $(x, U) \in W_{\mathcal{S}}$, we have that $x, U \models_{\mathcal{M}} \alpha$ iff $\mathcal{M}_{\mathcal{M}}, (x, U) \models \alpha$.*

Here (and later on as well), the symbol '$\models$' denotes the usual satisfaction relation of modal logic. – The proposition is easily proved by induction on α. We call $S_{\mathcal{S}}$ and $M_{\mathcal{M}}$ the Kripke structures *induced* by $\mathcal{S}$ and $\mathcal{M}$, respectively.

The question to what extent one can go the other way round, i.e., associate subset spaces to suitable Kripke structures so that the latter are the induced ones, will play an important part below. Some significant information on what 'suitable' means in this connection, is provided by looking at the *logic* of subset spaces (referred to as LSS later). Here is a sound and complete axiomatization (cf. [5], Sect. 2.2):

1. All instances of propositional tautologies
2. $\mathsf{K}(\alpha \to \beta) \to (\mathsf{K}\alpha \to \mathsf{K}\beta)$
3. $\mathsf{K}\alpha \to (\alpha \wedge \mathsf{KK}\alpha)$
4. $\mathsf{L}\alpha \to \mathsf{KL}\alpha$
5. $(p \to \Box p) \wedge (\Diamond p \to p)$
6. $\Box(\alpha \to \beta) \to (\Box\alpha \to \Box\beta)$
7. $\Box\alpha \to (\alpha \wedge \Box\Box\alpha)$
8. $\mathsf{K}\Box\alpha \to \Box\mathsf{K}\alpha$,

where $p \in \mathsf{Prop}$ and $\alpha, \beta \in \mathsf{Form}$; note that the last schema represents the aforementioned Cross Axioms. As a result, we obtain that LSS is sound and complete also with respect to the class of all *Kripke* models M such that

- the accessibility relation R of M belonging K is an equivalence (in other words, where K is an S5-modality),
- the accessibility relation R' of M belonging to $\Box$ is reflexive and transitive (i.e., $\Box$ is S4-like),
- the composite relation $R' \circ R$ is contained in $R \circ R'$ (this is usually called the *cross property*), and
- the valuation of M is constant along every R'-path, for all proposition variables.

The most interesting fact is the cross property here, formalizing the interplay between knowledge and effort. Thus, a bi-modal Kripke frame is called a *cross axiom frame*, iff its relations satisfy all these conditions apart from the last one; and a bi-modal Kripke model is called a *cross axiom model*, iff it is based on a cross axiom frame and the final requirement is satisfied, too. Now, it is easy to see that every induced Kripke frame is a cross axiom frame and every induced Kripke model is a cross axiom model. Hence we should find the candidates relating to the above question among these structures.

We are going to change from first-order to topological properties for now. However, we shall return to those later on.

3 Topological Modal Logic

The paper [1] as well as van Benthem and Bezhanishvili's chapter of the handbook [2] (that is, Ch. 5 there) contain all the facts from topological modal logic that are relevant for our purposes; these are freely quoted below.

First in this section, we revisit the topological semantics of modal logic. Let $\mathcal{T} = (X, \tau)$ be a topological space, V a $\mathcal{T}$-valuation in the sense of Definition 1, and $\mathcal{M} := (X, \tau, V)$. Then, the topological satisfaction relation $\models_t$ is defined canonically for $\top$, the proposition variables, and in the boolean cases, whereas the clause for the $\Box$-operator reads

$$\mathcal{M}, x \models_t \Box \alpha :\iff \exists U \in \tau : [x \in U \wedge \forall y \in U : \mathcal{M}, y \models_t \alpha],$$

for all $x \in X$ and every mono-modal formula $\alpha \in \mathsf{MF}$.[2]

We now connect $\models_t$ to the common relational semantics. As is known, a reflexive and transitive binary relation R on a set W is called a *quasi-order* on W. Quasi-ordered non-empty sets (W, R) are also called S4-*frames* since the modal logic S4 is sound and complete with respect to this class of structures. Given an S4-frame (W, R), a subset $U \subseteq W$ is called R-*upward closed* iff $w \in U$ and $w R v$ imply $v \in W$, for all $w, v \in W$. (Correspondingly, R-*downward closed* sets are defined.) The set of all R-upward closed subsets of W is, in fact, a topology on W (with the R-downward closed sets being topologically closed ones). This topology, denoted by τ_R, is *Alexandroff*, i.e., the intersection of arbitrarily many open sets is again open. With that, we obtain the following correlation (which is easy to prove again).

Proposition 2. *Let $M = (W, R, V)$ be an S4-model and $\mathcal{M}_M := (W, \tau_R, V)$ be based on the associated Alexandroff space. Then, for all $\alpha \in \mathsf{MF}$ and $w \in W$, we have that $M, w \models \alpha$ iff $\mathcal{M}_M, w \models_t \alpha$.*

And vice versa, starting from an Alexandroff space $\mathcal{T} = (X, \tau)$ yields an equivalent S4-frame $S_\mathcal{T} := (X, R_\tau)$ by taking the *specialization order* R_τ of τ for the accessibility relation (i.e., $x R_\tau y :\iff x$ belongs to the closure $\overline{\{y\}}$ of $\{y\}$, for all $x, y \in X$); as for the equivalence just asserted, note that we have $\tau = \tau_{R_\tau}$ in this case (while $R = R_{\tau_R}$ is always true).

Restricting the just established one-to-one correspondence to spaces satisfying the separation axiom T_0 additionally (i.e., for any two distinct points there is an open neighborhood of either of them not containing the other one), yields a one-to-one correspondence between partially ordered sets and Alexandroff T_0-spaces; this is recorded for later purposes here.

The next topic to be treated is the topological impact of the modal system S5. It is well-known that the accessibility relation of a Kripke frame validating this logic is an *equivalence*. The topological counterpart of the class of all such frames is given by the next proposition.

Proposition 3. *Let $\mathcal{T} = (X, \tau)$ be a topological space. Then, all S5-sentences are (topologically) valid in $\mathcal{T}$ iff every τ-closed set is open.*

Here, we have used the obvious notion of topological frame validity. A proof of Proposition 3 only making recourse to the satisfaction relation $\models_t$ is given

---

[2] This formulation and the one given in the introduction are easily seen to be equivalent.

in [2], p. 253. However, one can also argue with the aid of the accessibility relation and the specialization order, respectively. For that, note that the R-upward closed sets are precisely the unions of equivalence classes whenever R is an equivalence relation. This implies that every τ_R-closed set is open in this case. On the other hand, the latter demand on τ entails that R_τ is symmetric and thus an equivalence, as can be seen easily.

Finally in this section, we deal with the question of topological completeness, which has been touched upon in the introduction already. Concerning S4, several ways to establish this property can be found in the literature quoted so far.

We focus on our bi-modal setting now, in view of subsequent applications. It turns out that the most straightforward proceeding will do here, at least for the time being.

Definition 3 (Bi-topological Structures).

1. Let X be a non-empty set and σ, τ topologies on X. Then, the tuple $\mathfrak{S} := (X, \sigma, \tau)$ is called a bi-topological space.
2. Let $\mathfrak{S} = (X, \sigma, \tau)$ be a bi-topological space and V an $\mathfrak{S}$-valuation. Then $\mathfrak{M} := (X, \sigma, \tau, V)$ is called a bi-topological model.

Unless stated otherwise, formulas from Form will be interpreted in bi-topological structures by use of the bi-topological satisfaction relation $\models_t$ as from now;[3] the modality K should correspond to σ and the modality $\square$ to τ in doing so.

Proposition 2 has an obvious bi-modal analogue which is formulated for the more special structures we are interested in here.[4]

Proposition 4. *Let $M = (W, \{R, R'\}, V)$ be a Kripke model such that R is an equivalence relation, R' a quasi-order, and, for all proposition variables, V is constant along every R'-path. Moreover, let $\mathfrak{M}_M := (W, \tau_R, \tau_{R'}, V)$. Then, for all $\alpha \in$ Form and $w \in W$, we have that $M, w \models \alpha$ iff $\mathfrak{M}_M, w \models_t \alpha$.*

Let LS denote the bi-modal logic determined by the axiom schemata 1 – 7 from above (and having *modus ponens* as well as the *necessitation rules for both modalities* as proof rules). Then, we obtain the following theorem.

Theorem 1. *The logic LS is sound and complete with respect to the class of all bi-topological models (X, σ, τ, V) satisfying the following requirements.*

1. *Every σ-closed set is open.*
2. *The topology τ is Alexandroff.*
3. *For every point $x \in X$, the valuation V is constant throughout the least τ-open set containing x.*

---

[3] Concerning notations in this regard, we do not distinguish between the common mono-modal case and the bi-modal one considered here; this should not lead to confusion.
[4] Some later auxiliary results too could have been stated in a more general form.

Proof. First note that, for every point $x \in X$, a least τ-open neighborhood of x really exists in case τ is Alexandroff. Now, the soundness of the axioms is clear from the above, except for Axiom 5. However, the validity of Axiom 5 can be established directly (i.e., by using the definition of $\models_t$).

As to completeness, note that the canonical model M_{LS} of the logic LS satisfies all the conditions that are stated for M in Proposition 4. Thus, it suffices to prove that $\mathfrak{M}_{M_{\mathsf{LS}}}$ meets the three requirements given in the theorem. Since the first and the second item are clear from the above again, an argument is needed for the third one only. For it, note that, in general, the least $\tau_{R'}$-open neighborhood of any point x is contained in the union of all R'-paths through x, provided that R' is a quasi-order. The path-constancy of the proposition variables, which is satisfied on the canonical model, therefore implies the validity of the third condition. This completes the proof of the theorem.

Can the preceding theorem be extended (in the correctly understood sense) to the logic LSS? – Among other things, this question will be discussed in the next section.

4 Topological Cross Axiom Spaces

It is not immediately clear how a topological counterpart of the cross property looks like. The 'naïve' LSS-analogue of Theorem 1 should, therefore, apply to the specialization orders of the topologies involved. We state the corresponding result at the beginning of this section. Afterwards, we show that a particular correspondence between topological concepts and the Cross Axioms appears nevertheless. – We need a certain converse of Proposition 4.

Proposition 5. *Let $\mathfrak{M} := (X, \sigma, \tau, V)$ be a bi-topological model, and let $M_{\mathfrak{M}} := (X, \{R_\sigma, R_\tau\}, V)$. Then, for all $\alpha \in$ Form and $x \in X$, we have that $\mathfrak{M}, x \models_t \alpha$ iff $M_{\mathfrak{M}}, x \models \alpha$.*

With that, the just announced theorem can be proved easily.

Theorem 2. *The logic LLS is sound and complete with respect to the class of all bi-topological models (X, σ, τ, V) satisfying the following requirements.*

1. *Every σ-closed set is open.*
2. *The topology τ is Alexandroff.*
3. *The specialization orders R_σ and R_τ satisfy the cross property (i.e., $R_\tau \circ R_\sigma \subseteq R_\sigma \circ R_\tau$).*
4. *For every point $x \in X$, the valuation V is constant throughout the least τ-open set containing x.*

Proof. Only the third item must be considered yet. First, note that the canonical relations of LLS (see [4], Definition 4.18) satisfy the cross property.[5] Hence

---

[5] A direct argument for this is given in [5], Proposition 2.2. Note that a simpler argument would do in case of a normal modal logic, since the Cross Axioms $\mathsf{K}\Box p \to \Box \mathsf{K} p$ with p a proposition variable are Sahlqvist formulas; see [4], Theorem 4.42.

completeness ensues in the same way as in the proof of Theorem 1. On the other hand, the soundness of LLS for the given class of structures follows from Proposition 5. This proves the theorem.

We now introduce a certain cover property for bi-topological spaces. Then we show that this property corresponds to the Cross Axioms in the same way as, for example, the transitivity of the accessibility relation associated with the operator $\Box$ corresponds to the formula schema $\Box\alpha \to \Box\Box\alpha$ (as related to the most basic modal logic).

Definition 4 (Cover Property). *Let $\mathfrak{S} = (X, \sigma, \tau)$ be a bi-topological space. Then, $\mathfrak{S}$ is said to satisfy the* cover *property iff, for all points $x \in X$, every τ-open cover $\mathcal{C}$ of any σ-open neighborhood of x contains a σ-open cover $\mathcal{C}'$ of some τ-open neighborhood of x (to the effect that $\bigcup \mathcal{C} \supseteq \bigcup \mathcal{C}'$).*

The desired correspondence between the cover property and the Cross Axioms is established by the following proposition (cf. Proposition 3).

Proposition 6. *Let $\mathfrak{S} = (X, \sigma, \tau)$ be a bi-topological space. Then, all the Cross Axioms are (topologically) valid in $\mathfrak{S}$ iff $\mathfrak{S}$ satisfies the cover property.*

Proof. First, we prove that every Cross Axiom is valid in $\mathfrak{S}$ whenever $\mathfrak{S}$ satisfies the cover property. To this end, take any bi-topological model $\mathfrak{M} = (X, \sigma, \tau, V)$ based on $\mathfrak{S}$ and any point $x \in X$, and assume that $\mathfrak{M}, x \models_t \mathsf{K}\Box\alpha$ (with $\alpha \in$ Form). Then there exists a σ-open neighborhood U of x such that $\Box\alpha$ holds in $\mathfrak{M}$ throughout U. Thus, for all $y \in U$ there is a τ-open neighborhood U_y of y such that α holds in $\mathfrak{M}$ throughout U_y. Evidently, $\mathcal{C} := \{U_y \mid y \in U\}$ is a τ-open cover of the σ-open neighborhood U of x. According to the cover property, $\mathcal{C}$ contains a σ-open cover $\mathcal{C}'$ of some τ-open neighborhood U_x of x. Take any $z \in U_x$. Then there is a σ-open set $U' \in \mathcal{C}'$ containing z. We have $\mathfrak{M}, z \models_t \mathsf{K}\alpha$ because $U' \subseteq \bigcup \mathcal{C}' \subseteq \bigcup \mathcal{C}$. From that we obtain that $\mathfrak{M}, x \models_t \Box\mathsf{K}\alpha$, as z has been chosen arbitrarily. This shows that $\mathsf{K}\Box\alpha \to \Box\mathsf{K}\alpha$ is valid in $\mathfrak{S}$.

Second, suppose that the cover property is violated in $\mathfrak{S}$. Then there is a point $x \in X$ and a τ-open cover $\mathcal{C}$ of some σ-open neighborhood U of x such that no σ-open cover $\mathcal{C}'$ of any τ-open neighborhood U' of x is contained in $\mathcal{C}$. Define an $\mathfrak{S}$-valuation V as follows. Fix any $p \in$ Prop, let $V(p) := \bigcup \mathcal{C}$, and let V be arbitrary for the proposition variables different from p. Let $\mathfrak{M} := (X, \sigma, \tau, V)$. Then, $\mathfrak{M}, x \models_t \mathsf{K}\Box p$. On the other hand, for all τ-open neighborhoods U' of x there is a point $y \in U'$ such that every σ-open neighborhood U'' of y contains a point $z \notin \bigcup \mathcal{C}$, since otherwise we could construct a good-natured σ-open cover $\mathcal{C}'$ of some τ-open neighborhood of x. This implies that $\mathfrak{M}, x \models_t \Diamond\mathsf{L}\neg p$. It follows that some of the Cross Axioms are invalid in $\mathfrak{S}$.

Note that, in a sense, the just given argument is incompatible with the requirement on the constance of proposition variables as stated, e.g., in the fourth item of Theorem 2.

With a view to canonicity (and to the topological characterization result we have in mind), we now connect the cover property with the cross property (in the fashion of our reasoning after Proposition 3).

Proposition 7. 1. *Let $S = (W, \{R, R'\})$ be a cross axiom frame, and let $\mathfrak{S}_S :=$ $(W, \tau_R, \tau_{R'})$. Then $\mathfrak{S}_S$ satisfies the cover property.*
2. *Let $\mathfrak{S} = (X, \sigma, \tau)$ be a bi-topological space with σ and τ being Alexandroff. Suppose that $\mathfrak{S}$ satisfies the cover property. Then the associated Kripke frame $S_\mathfrak{S} := (X, \{R_\sigma, R_\tau\})$ satisfies the cross property.*

Proof. 1. For every $u \in W$, let $R(u) := \{v \in W \mid u \, R \, v\}$ and $R'(u) := \{v \in W \mid u \, R' \, v\}$. Obviously, $R(u)$ and $R'(u)$ are the least τ_R-open and $\tau_{R'}$-open neighborhoods of u, respectively; moreover, $R(u)$ equals the R-equivalence class of u. Now, let $w \in W$ be any point, and let $\mathcal{C}$ be any $\tau_{R'}$-open cover of some τ_R-open neighborhood U_w of w. Take the $\tau_{R'}$-open neighborhood $R'(w)$ of w and define $\mathcal{C}' := \{R(v) \mid v \in R'(w)\}$. Then, $\mathcal{C}'$ clearly is a τ_R-open cover of $R'(w)$. We argue that $\bigcup \mathcal{C}' \subseteq \bigcup \mathcal{C}$. For this, take any $x \in \bigcup \mathcal{C}'$. Then, $x \in R(v)$ for some $v \in R'(w)$. Thus we have $w \, R' \, v \, R \, x$. Due to the cross property, it follows that $w \, R \, y \, R' \, x$, for some $y \in W$. We obtain $y \in R(w) \subseteq U_w$ because of the minimality of $R(w)$. And we get $x \in R'(y) \subseteq U$ for some $U \in \mathcal{C}$ because of the minimality of $R'(y)$ and the fact that $y \in U_w$. This shows that $x \in \bigcup \mathcal{C}$, as desired.

2. Let $x \, R_\tau \, y \, R_\sigma \, z$ be satisfied for any $x, y, z \in X$. We have $\sigma = \sigma_{R_\sigma}$ and $\tau = \tau_{R_\tau}$, since σ and τ are Alexandroff; this was mentioned right after Proposition 2 above. Thus, it makes sense to speak about the minimal τ-open cover $\mathcal{C}$ of the minimal σ-open neighborhood U_x of the point x on the one hand, on the other hand, we have $U_x = R_\sigma(x)$ and $\mathcal{C} = \{R_\tau(u) \mid u \in U_x\}$. According to the cover property, $\mathcal{C}$ contains a σ-open cover $\tilde{\mathcal{C}}$ of some τ-open neighborhood of x. For reasons of minimality, this means that $\mathcal{C}$ contains the cover $\mathcal{C}'$ of the minimal τ-open neighborhood of x defined in the first part of the proof (here with R_σ instead of R and R_τ instead of R' though) as well. From $x \, R_\tau \, y \, R_\sigma \, z$ we now infer $z \in \bigcup \mathcal{C}'$. Hence $z \in \bigcup \mathcal{C}$. This implies that there exists a point $v \in X$ such that $x \, R_\sigma \, v \, R_\tau \, z$, due to the choice of $\mathcal{C}$. Thus, the cross property is established.

As a consequence, we obtain the following characterization of bi-topological spaces arising from cross axiom frames.

Theorem 3. *Let $\mathfrak{S} = (X, \sigma, \tau)$ be a bi-topological space. Then there is a cross axiom frame $S = (W, \{R, R'\})$ such that $\sigma = \tau_R$ and $\tau = \tau_{R'}$ iff*

1. *every σ-closed set is open,*
2. *the topology τ is Alexandroff, and*
3. *$\mathfrak{S}$ satisfies the cover property.*

Proof. The necessity of the three conditions follows from both Proposition 7.1 and some of the results quoted in Section 3. Now, assume that these conditions are satisfied. Then σ is clearly Alexandroff. By Proposition 7.2, the frame $S_\mathfrak{S} = (X, \{R_\sigma, R_\tau\})$ satisfies the cross property. Moreover, R_σ is an equivalence and R_τ a quasi-order; see Section 3 again. Additionally, we have $\sigma = \tau_{R_\sigma}$ and $\tau = \tau_{R_\tau}$. This proves the theorem.

In the next section, we will prove a similar (but more complex) statement with regard to Kripke structures induced by subset spaces. This will be the main outcome of this paper.

By virtue of Theorem 3, a bi-topological space $\mathfrak{S} = (X, \sigma, \tau)$ is called a *topological cross axiom space* iff those three requirements are satisfied. And a bi-topological model $\mathfrak{M} = (X, \sigma, \tau, V)$ based on a topological cross axiom space is called a *topological cross axiom model* iff, for every point $x \in X$, the valuation V is constant throughout the least τ-open set containing x.

We conclude this section with a version of Theorem 2 having a purely topological reading.

Theorem 4. *The logic* LLS *is sound and complete with respect to the class of all topological cross axiom models.*

Proof. The soundness of LLS with respect to the given class of structures is clear from (the uncritical part of) Proposition 6. Concerning completeness, we must give reasons respecting just the cover property. We proceed as in the proof of Theorem 2 relating to this, and apply Proposition 7.1 additionally.

Theorem 3 and Theorem 4 comprise, in particular, all that we can achieve with regard to our characterization problem on the (modal-)logical side. However, more turns out to be possible on the topological one.

5 The Characterization Theorem

We shall now specify a couple of further requirements for bi-topological Alexandroff spaces to arise from induced cross axiom frames. This puts us in a position to state and prove the main result of this paper subsequently.

Definition 5 (Minimal Basis; Orthogonality).

1. Let $\mathfrak{S} = (X, \sigma, \tau)$ be a bi-topological space such that σ and τ are Alexandroff. For any $x \in X$, let $R_\sigma(x) := \{y \in X \mid x\,R_\sigma\,y\}$ (as above), and let $R_\tau(x)$ be defined analogously. Then, the sets $\mathcal{B}_\sigma := \{R_\sigma(x) \mid x \in X\}$ and $\mathcal{B}_\tau := \{R_\tau(x) \mid x \in X\}$ are called the minimal bases *of σ and τ, respectively.*
2. Let $\mathfrak{S}$, x, and $R_\tau(x)$, be as above. Then we let $R_\tau^{-1}(x) := \{y \in X \mid y\,R_\tau\,x\}$ and $\overline{\mathcal{B}_\tau} := \{R_\tau^{-1}(x) \mid x \in X\}$. The latter set is called the set of minimal τ-closed sets.
3. Let $\mathcal{A}, \mathcal{B} \subseteq \mathcal{P}(X)$ be two sets of subsets of X. These sets are said to be orthogonal *iff any two members $A \in \mathcal{A}$ and $B \in \mathcal{B}$ intersect in at most one point.*

Note that $\mathcal{B}_\sigma$ and $\mathcal{B}_\tau$ are indeed bases of σ and τ, respectively. Moreover, note that, for every $x \in X$, the set $R_\tau^{-1}(x)$ is downward closed (see Section 3) and equals the closure $\overline{\{x\}}$ of $\{x\}$ actually; this justifies the naming in Definition 5.2. Finally, the condition stated in the third item reflects, at least in part, the geometric idea of orthogonality.

We obtain the following criterion resting on the just introduced notations.

Proposition 8. *Let $\mathfrak{S} = (X, \sigma, \tau)$ be a bi-topological space with σ and τ being Alexandroff.*

1. *The minimal bases $\mathcal{B}_\sigma$ and $\mathcal{B}_\tau$ are orthogonal iff, for all $x, y \in X$, there exists at most one R_τ-successor of x inside $R_\sigma(y)$.*
2. *The minimal base $\mathcal{B}_\sigma$ and the set $\overline{\mathcal{B}_\tau}$ of minimal τ-closed sets are orthogonal iff, for all $x, y \in X$, there exists at most one R_τ-predecessor of x inside $R_\sigma(y)$.*

Proof. 1. First, assume that $\mathcal{B}_\sigma$ and $\mathcal{B}_\tau$ are orthogonal. Let x, y be any points of X and suppose that two different R_τ-successors z_1, z_2 of x are contained in $R_\sigma(y)$. Then, however, a contradiction to the orthogonality of the minimal bases immediately results, since both $z_1, z_2 \in R_\tau(x)$. – The sufficiency of the condition can be seen easily as well.
2. This assertion can be proved in a similar manner.

For brevity, we say that a bi-topological space $\mathfrak{S}$ satisfies the *orthogonality properties* iff both conditions stated in Proposition 8 are met.

Our next requirement concerns a certain binary relation $\preccurlyeq_\mathfrak{S}$ on the minimal base $\mathcal{B}_\sigma$ of a bi-topological Alexandroff space $\mathfrak{S} = (X, \sigma, \tau)$. This relation should be a quasi-order and, in a sense, without a gap. The precise definitions follow right away.

Definition 6 ($\preccurlyeq_\mathfrak{S}$; Density Property). *Let $\mathfrak{S} = (X, \sigma, \tau)$ be a bi-topological space with σ and τ being Alexandroff.*

1. *For all $x, y \in X$, put $R_\sigma(x) \preccurlyeq_\mathfrak{S} R_\sigma(y) : \iff$ there are $x' \in R_\sigma(x)$ and $y' \in R_\sigma(y)$ such that $y' \in R_\tau(x')$.*
2. *The just defined relation $\preccurlyeq_\mathfrak{S}$ is said to satisfy the* density property *iff, whenever $R_\sigma(x) \preccurlyeq_\mathfrak{S} R_\sigma(y) \preccurlyeq_\mathfrak{S} R_\sigma(z)$, then, for any $x' \in R_\sigma(x)$ and $z' \in R_\sigma(z)$ such that $z' \in R_\tau(x')$, there exists $y' \in R_\sigma(y)$ satisfying $y' \in R_\tau(x')$ and $z' \in R_\tau(y')$.*

With that, we obtain the following result with the aid of standard arguments from the logic of subset spaces.

Proposition 9. *Let $\mathfrak{S} = (X, \sigma, \tau)$ be a topological cross axiom space. Then, the corresponding relation $\preccurlyeq_\mathfrak{S}$ is*

1. *a quasi-order in any case, and*
2. *even a partial order if, in addition, the relation R_τ is antisymmetric and the minimal bases $\mathcal{B}_\sigma$ and $\mathcal{B}_\tau$ are orthogonal.*

Proof. 1. The reflexivity of $\preccurlyeq_\mathfrak{S}$ is obvious. In order to establish the transitivity of this relation, we take advantage of the cross property, which is satisfied by the frame $\mathcal{S}_\mathfrak{S} = (X, \{R_\sigma, R_\tau\})$ according to Proposition 7.2.
2. This follows from the definitions with the aid of the cross property again.[6]

---
[6] Note that this result can under certain conditions be obtained 'purely logically', by adding a particular axiom schema for tree-like structures; see [9], Proposition 3.5.

Finally, we introduce a condition that may appear somewhat odd to the reader at first glance. However, its significance will become clear from the construction in the proof of Theorem 5 below.

Definition 7 (Tamely Ramified). *Let $\mathfrak{S} = (X, \sigma, \tau)$ be a bi-topological space such that σ and τ are Alexandroff. Moreover, let $\mathcal{B}_\sigma$ and $\mathcal{B}_\tau$ be the minimal bases of σ and τ, respectively. Then we say that $\mathcal{B}_\sigma$ is tamely ramified across $\mathcal{B}_\tau$, iff the following is satisfied for any two $R_\sigma(x), R_\sigma(y) \in \mathcal{B}_\sigma$: if every point of $R_\sigma(y)$ is contained in the symmetric closure, taken with respect to R_τ, of $R_\sigma(x)$, then $R_\sigma(x) \preccurlyeq_\mathfrak{S} R_\sigma(y)$.*

It turns out that tame ramification in the sense of the previous definition is always factual for spaces that are derived from induced Kripke frames.

Proposition 10. *Let $\mathfrak{S} = (X, \sigma, \tau)$ be a bi-topological space and $\mathcal{S} = (X, \mathcal{O})$ a subset frame such that $\sigma = \tau_{R_\mathcal{S}^\mathsf{K}}$ and $\tau = \tau_{R_\mathcal{S}^\square}$. Then $\mathcal{B}_\sigma$ is tamely ramified across $\mathcal{B}_\tau$.*

Proof. Due to the fact that $R_\mathcal{S}^\square$ originates from the containment relation, the correctness of the assertion can be seen rather easily.

The preparatory work towards our main result has been completed by the last proposition. Thus, we are in a position to prove our final theorem now.

Theorem 5. *Let $\mathfrak{S} = (X, \sigma, \tau)$ be a bi-topological space. Then there is a subset frame $\mathcal{S} = (X, \mathcal{O})$ such that $\sigma = \tau_{R_\mathcal{S}^\mathsf{K}}$ and $\tau = \tau_{R_\mathcal{S}^\square}$ iff*

1. *every σ-closed set is open,*
2. *the topology τ is Alexandroff and satisfies the separation property T_0,*
3. *$\mathfrak{S}$ satisfies the cover property,*
4. *$\mathfrak{S}$ satisfies the orthogonality properties,*
5. *the relation $\preccurlyeq_\mathfrak{S}$ is a quasi-order satisfying the density property,*
6. *the minimal basis $\mathcal{B}_\sigma$ of σ is tamely ramified across the minimal basis $\mathcal{B}_\tau$ of τ, and*
7. *every element of the minimal basis $\mathcal{B}_\sigma$ contains a τ-open point.*

Proof. The left-to-right direction is easy to prove. Let $\mathcal{S} = (X, \mathcal{O})$ be a subset frame such that $\sigma = \tau_{R_\mathcal{S}^\mathsf{K}}$ and $\tau = \tau_{R_\mathcal{S}^\square}$. Items 1 and 2 then follow from topological modal logic; see Section 3. Item 3 is clear from Proposition 7.1, since $R_\mathcal{S}^\mathsf{K}$ and $R_\mathcal{S}^\square$ satisfy the cross property; see the end of Section 2. Furthermore, one is quickly convinced that the first-order conditions corresponding to the orthogonality and the density properties are applicable to $R_\mathcal{S}^\mathsf{K}$ and $R_\mathcal{S}^\square$. By Proposition 8, $\mathfrak{S}$ satisfies the orthogonality properties, and by Proposition 9.1, the relation $\preccurlyeq_\mathfrak{S}$ is a quasi-order which, in particular, satisfies the density property. Proposition 10 guarantees that the last but one item is satisfied. For the last one, note that the openness of $\{x\}$ exactly means that x has no R_τ-successor apart from x itself.

For the other direction, assume that the seven requirements are met by $\mathfrak{S}$. It suffices to show that $\mathcal{S}_\mathfrak{S} = (X, \{R_\sigma, R_\tau\})$ is isomorphic to the Kripke frame

$\mathcal{S}_{\mathcal{S}} = (\mathcal{W}_{\mathcal{S}}, \{R_{\mathcal{S}}^{\mathsf{K}}, R_{\mathcal{S}}^{\square}\})$ induced by some subset frame $\mathcal{S} = (Y, \mathcal{O})$, for we will have $\sigma = \tau_{R_\sigma} = \tau_{R_{\mathcal{S}}^{\mathsf{K}}}$ and $\tau = \tau_{R_\tau} = \tau_{R_{\mathcal{S}}^{\square}}$ in this case (after identifying isomorphic structures). – The following is clear from our previous statements and results.

(a) The relation R_σ is an equivalence (see Proposition 3 and the remark thereafter), and the relation R_τ is a partial order (see the remarks after Proposition 2).
(b) $\mathcal{S}_{\mathcal{S}}$ satisfies the cross property (see Proposition 7.2).
(c) For all $x, y \in X$, there exists at most one R_τ-successor of x inside the equivalence class $R_\sigma(y)$ of y, and there exists at most one R_τ-predecessor of x inside $R_\sigma(y)$ (see Proposition 8).
(d) The relation $\preccurlyeq_{\mathfrak{S}}$ is a partial order (see Proposition 9.2).

The set Y will be obtained as a certain set of partial functions on $\mathcal{B}_\sigma$ shortly.[7] For this purpose, let $x, y \in X$ be given and suppose that $R_\sigma(x) \preccurlyeq_{\mathfrak{S}} R_\sigma(y)$. It can be concluded from (b) and (c) that the relation R_τ restricted to $R_\sigma(x)$ in the domain and $R_\sigma(y)$ in the range, is an injective and surjective partial function, say $f_{R_\sigma(x), R_\sigma(y)}$. This function is, in fact, *strictly* partial because of the last condition stated in the theorem. Now, let Y be the set of all partial functions $f : \mathcal{B}_\sigma \to X$ having a domain $\mathrm{dom}(f)$ that is maximal with respect to the following three conditions:

– $f(R_\sigma(x)) \in R_\sigma(x)$, for all $R_\sigma(x) \in \mathrm{dom}(f)$;
– $f(R_\sigma(y)) = f_{R_\sigma(x), R_\sigma(y)} \circ f(R_\sigma(x))$, for all $R_\sigma(x), R_\sigma(y) \in \mathrm{dom}(f)$ satisfying $R_\sigma(x) \preccurlyeq_{\mathfrak{S}} R_\sigma(y)$;
– the range of f is R_τ-*connected*, i.e., for all $x, y \in \mathrm{range}(f)$, $x\, R_\tau^s\, y$ is valid, where R_τ^s denotes the symmetric closure of R_τ.

Note that (d) and the density property imply the coherence of the second condition, whence the process of maximizing the domain is really possible.

For every $x \in X$, let $U_{R_\sigma(x)} := \{f \in Y \mid f(R_\sigma(x)) \text{ exists}\}$, and let $\mathcal{O} := \{U_{R_\sigma(x)} \mid x \in X\}$. Then, $\mathcal{S}_{\mathfrak{S}} \cong \mathcal{S}_{\mathcal{S}}$ is valid for the subset frame $\mathcal{S} := (Y, \mathcal{O})$. To see this, note that a one-to-one mapping h from the set $\mathcal{N}_{\mathcal{S}}$ of all neighborhood situations of $\mathcal{S}$ onto the set of all points of X is mediated by $f, U_{R_\sigma(x)} \mapsto f_{R_\sigma(x)}$, where $f_{R_\sigma(x)} := f(R_\sigma(x))$, in such a way that, for all $f, g \in Y$ and $x, y \in X$ with $f \in U_{R_\sigma(x)}$, we have that

$$g \in U_{R_\sigma(x)} \iff g_{R_\sigma(x)}\, R_\sigma\, f_{R_\sigma(x)}.$$

All this is rather easy to prove, and the claimed isomorphism is established with regard to the K-component thus. As to the $\square$-part, we prove that, for all $f \in Y$ and $x, y \in X$ such that $f \in U_{R_\sigma(x)} \cap U_{R_\sigma(y)}$,

$$U_{R_\sigma(y)} \subseteq U_{R_\sigma(x)} \iff f_{R_\sigma(x)}\, R_\tau\, f_{R_\sigma(y)},$$

showing the compatibility of the containment relation $\subseteq$ with the accessibility relation R_τ. The right-to-left direction is more or less obvious. For the left-to-right direction, assume that $U_{R_\sigma(y)} \subseteq U_{R_\sigma(x)}$. This means that, for all $f \in Y$, if

---

[7] We once more note that $\mathcal{B}_\sigma$ equals the set of all R_σ-equivalence classes.

$f_{R_\sigma(y)}$ is defined, then $f_{R_\sigma(x)}$ is defined as well. According to the way the elements of Y have been obtained, we conclude that every point of $R_\sigma(y)$ is contained in the symmetric closure, taken with respect to R_τ, of $R_\sigma(x)$ from that. Now, the ramification condition applies, ensuring the existence of points $x' \in R_\sigma(x)$ and $y' \in R_\sigma(y)$ which materialize $R_\sigma(x) \preccurlyeq_\mathfrak{S} R_\sigma(y)$. Since $f \in U_{R_\sigma(x)} \cap U_{R_\sigma(y)}$, it follows that $f_{R_\sigma(x)} \, R_\tau \, f_{R_\sigma(y)}$ holds as well, whence the left-to-right direction is proved, too. Consequently, h is an isomorphism, as desired.

The proof of Theorem 5 lights up the relative proximity of the topological and the relational semantics of modal logic once again.

Finally in this section, we fix the analogue of Theorem 5 for bi-topological *models*. In fact, the following corollary is obtained as an immediate consequence of that theorem.

Corollary 1. *A bi-topological model $\mathfrak{M}$ is determined by a subset space in the sense of the preceding theorem, iff*

1. *the bi-topological space underlying $\mathfrak{M}$ satisfies all the conditions stated there, and*
2. *the valuation of $\mathfrak{M}$ meets the constancy property as formulated, e.g., in the third item of Theorem 1.*

6 Concluding Remarks

Investigations into multi-topological structures appear rather unfrequent in topological modal logic; see [2], Sect. 2 and Sect. 3 of Ch. 5, for some hints. The present paper adds a new facet to this field by working out a hitherto undiscovered connection between bi-modal logic and bi-topological spaces. We have, actually, given a bi-modally oriented characterization of bi-topological spaces arising from subset spaces here.

The second contribution of this paper is Theorem 4, stating the soundness and completeness of the logic of subset spaces, LLS, with respect to the class of all topological cross axiom spaces. In this connection, the question arises whether this theorem can also be proved in a 'more topological' way, i.e., by means of the approach to topological canonicity undertaken, e.g., in [1], Sect. 3.1.

Our new approach raises several issues that should be treated by future research. We only mention two of the questions coming up here, in particular, by confining ourselves to the framework of subset spaces. What is the bi-topological effect of those additional schemata that are relevant to the logic of *special classes* of subset spaces? And can notably topological spaces be characterized along the lines followed in this paper? – Here is a concrete starting point towards a possible answer. The *Weak Directedness Axioms* of common modal logic, $\Diamond \Box \alpha \to \Box \Diamond \alpha$, come along with the closure of the open sets under finite intersections in *topologic;* see [5]. In topological modal logic, we have a corresponding class of spaces: the *extremally disconnected* ones (where the closure of each open set is clopen by definition); see [2], Sect. 2.6 of Ch. 5. But we neither know up to now whether the latter property is sufficient for the closure under finite intersections (as related to the subset space semantics), nor how the *Union Axioms* of *topologic* can be captured within the new framework.

References

1. Aiello, M., van Benthem, J., Bezhanishvili, G.: Reasoning about space: The modal way. Journal of Logic and Computation 13(6), 889–920 (2003)
2. Aiello, M., Pratt-Hartmann, I.E., van Benthem, J.F.A.K.: Handbook of Spatial Logics. Springer, Dordrecht (2007)
3. Balbiani, P., van Ditmarsch, H., Kudinov, A.: Subset space logic with arbitrary announcements. In: Lodaya, K. (ed.) ICLA 2013. LNCS (LNAI), vol. 7750, pp. 233–244. Springer, Heidelberg (2013)
4. Blackburn, P., de Rijke, M., Venema, Y.: Modal Logic, Cambridge Tracts in Theoretical Computer Science, vol. 53. Cambridge University Press, Cambridge (2001)
5. Dabrowski, A., Moss, L.S., Parikh, R.: Topological reasoning and the logic of knowledge. Annals of Pure and Applied Logic 78, 73–110 (1996)
6. van Ditmarsch, H., van der Hoek, W., Kooi, B.: Dynamic Epistemic Logic, Synthese Library, vol. 337. Springer, Dordrecht (2007)
7. Fagin, R., Halpern, J.Y., Moses, Y., Vardi, M.Y.: Reasoning about Knowledge. MIT Press, Cambridge (1995)
8. Georgatos, K.: Modal Logics of Topological Spaces. Ph.D. thesis, City University of New York (May 1993)
9. Georgatos, K.: Knowledge on treelike spaces. Studia Logica 59, 271–301 (1997)
10. Heinemann, B.: Subset space vs relational semantics of bimodal logic: Bringing out the difference. In: Artemov, S., Nerode, A. (eds.) LFCS 2013. LNCS, vol. 7734, pp. 219–233. Springer, Heidelberg (2013)
11. McKinsey, J.C.C.: A solution to the decision problem for the Lewis systems S2 and S4, with an application to topology. Journal of Symbolic Logic 6(3), 117–141 (1941)
12. Moss, L.S., Parikh, R.: Topological reasoning and the logic of knowledge. In: Moses, Y. (ed.) Theoretical Aspects of Reasoning about Knowledge (TARK 1992), pp. 95–105. Morgan Kaufmann, Los Altos (1992)
13. Wáng, Y.N., Ågotnes, T.: Subset space public announcement logic. In: Lodaya, K. (ed.) Logic and Its Applications. LNCS, vol. 7750, pp. 245–257. Springer, Heidelberg (2013)

Proof-Pattern Recognition and Lemma Discovery in ACL2*

Jónathan Heras[1], Ekaterina Komendantskaya[1],
Moa Johansson[2], and Ewen Maclean[3]

[1] School of Computing, University of Dundee, UK
[2] Dept. of Computer Science and Engineering, Chalmers University, Sweden
[3] School of Informatics, University of Edinburgh, UK
{jonathanheras,katya}@computing.dundee.ac.uk, moa.johansson@chalmers.se,
E.Maclean@ed.ac.uk

Abstract. We present a novel technique for combining statistical machine learning for proof-pattern recognition with symbolic methods for lemma discovery. The resulting tool, **ACL2(ml)**, gathers proof statistics and uses statistical pattern-recognition to pre-processes data from libraries, and then suggests auxiliary lemmas in new proofs by analogy with already seen examples. This paper presents the implementation of ACL2(ml) alongside theoretical descriptions of the proof-pattern recognition and lemma discovery methods involved in it.

Keywords: Theorem Proving, Statistical Machine-Learning, Pattern Recognition, Lemma Discovery, Analogy.

1 Introduction

Over the last few decades, theorem proving has seen major developments. *Automated (first-order) theorem provers (ATPs)* (e.g. E, Vampire, SPASS) and SAT/SMT solvers (e.g. CVC3, Yices, Z3) are becoming increasingly fast and efficient. *Interactive (higher-order) theorem provers (ITPs)* (e.g. Coq, Isabelle/HOL, Agda, Mizar) have been enriched with dependent types, (co)inductive types, type classes and provide rich programming environments.

The main conceptual difference between ATPs and ITPs lies in the styles of proof development. For ATPs, the proof process is primarily an automatically performed *proof search* in a *first-order* language. In ITPs, the proof is guided by *the user* who specifies which tactics to apply. ITPs often work with *higher-order* logic and type theory.

Communities working on development, implementation and applications of ATPs and ITPs have accumulated big corpora of electronic proof libraries. However, the size of the libraries, as well as their technical and notational sophistication often stand in the way of efficient knowledge re-use. Very often, it is easier

---

* The work was supported by EPSRC grants EP/J014222/1[1], EP/H024204/1[3] and a VINNMER Marie Curie Fellowship[2].

to start a new library from scratch rather than search the existing proof libraries for potentially common heuristics and techniques.

Pattern-recognition [2] is an area of machine-learning that develops statistical methods for discovering patterns in data. In the statistical sense, a pattern is a correlation of several numeric features, by which the data is represented. For instance, the correlation between the theorem statement and the auxiliary lemmas required in its proof can be data-mined to improve automation of premise selection in ATPs [7, 8, 18, 22, 23]. The history of successful and unsuccessful proof attempts and proof steps can also be used to inform interactive proof development in ITPs [9, 17].

Statistical machine-learning methods are well-suited for fast processing of big proof libraries, adapt well to proofs of varied sizes and complexities (first- or higher-order); and are generally tolerant to noise. However, they have very weak capacities for conceptualisation. For instance, ML4PG [17] only displays the families of related proofs to the Coq user, and can tell the correlation of which features formed the pattern, but it neither explains why this happens nor formulates any conceptual proof hints.

While statistical methods focus on extracting information from existing large theory libraries, many symbolic methods are instead concerned with automating the discovery of lemmas in new theories [4, 6, 11, 13, 20, 21], while relying on existing proof strategies, e.g. proof-planning and rippling [1]. These systems are naturally more deterministic and algorithmic than statistical AI.

IsaCoSy [13] and IsaScheme [21] are two term synthesis systems built on top of Isabelle. They generate candidate conjectures which are filtered through a counter-example checker. Surviving conjectures are passed to an automated prover and those proven are added to the theory. The systems differ in their heuristics for term generation: IsaCoSy only generates irreducible terms, while IsaScheme uses *schemes* [3] to specify the shapes of candidate theorems. A similar system is QuickSpec and its extension HipSpec [4,5], which generates equational theorems about Haskell programs, using congruence closure for conjecture generation. MATHsAiD [20] generates theories by forward reasoning from a given set of axioms, applying various 'interestingness' heuristics.

Symbolic methods have limits: they can be slow on large inputs due to the increase in the search space, rely on having access to good counter-example finders for filtering of candidate conjectures and require existing proof strategies for proving those remaining.

In this paper, we show that it is possible to combine statistical and symbolic methods to get the best of both worlds: statistical pattern-recognition methods are well-suited for finding families of similar proofs; symbolic tools can use this data for more efficient lemma discovery. Feeding outputs of one algorithm to the other leads to a very natural proof-pattern recognition system, see Figure 1. To realise this general thesis about the synthesis of the two styles of proof-pattern recognition, we have made the following methodological choices:

1) We chose the ACL2 prover for our experiments: it is based on first-order logic and has features of both ITPs and ATPs. ACL2 will try to prove given

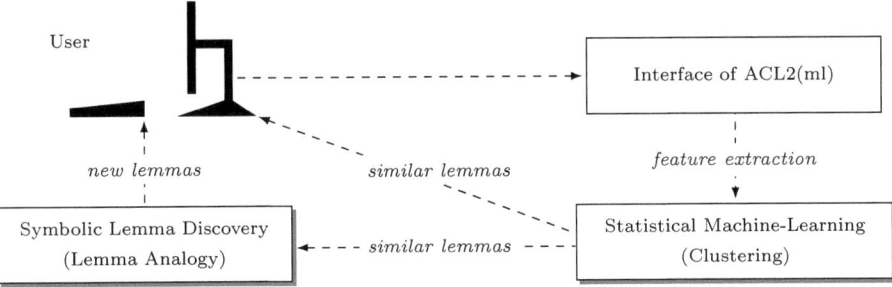

Fig. 1. *Architecture of proof-pattern recognition methods in ACL2(ml).* The Emacs interface for ACL2 extracts important features from ACL2 theorems, connects to machine-learning software, clusters the theorems there, and sends the result (families of similar theorems) to the screen. In addition, for an unproved theorem T, it sends the cluster C of T to the Lemma Analogy tool, which in its turn generates an auxiliary lemma by analogy with auxiliary lemmas of the theorems in C.

conjectures automatically, but strongly relies on the user having supplied the auxiliary lemmas required for rewriting. Thus, the user must often intervene and advance the proof by adding new lemmas, much like in ITPs. Section 2 gives a brief introduction to ACL2.

2) On the machine-learning side, we chose to adapt the ML4PG [17] design of *interactive* proof-pattern recognition; cf. Figure 1. We extended this work with a new feature extraction algorithm for ACL2(ml), based on term trees and recurrent clustering. Much like in ML4PG, we discover families of related lemmas, rather than premise hierarchies like in [18,22,23]. Unlike [18,22,23], we use clustering instead of supervised learning; and do not use sparse methods. Section 3 explains our new method in detail.

3) On the symbolic side, we develop a novel lemma generation approach which uses the statistical suggestions to reduce the search space. Speculating the correct lemma in a proof can often be the *eureka* moment which allows a proof to succeed. It is these eureka lemmas which we would like to reproduce automatically. We propose an analogy driven approach where the term structure of an example *source lemma* is analysed to produce an analogous *target lemma* for a given target problem. In the context of ITP, the user is then presented with an auxiliary lemma suggestion which is customised to the particular problem on which he is working. Section 4 is devoted to this subject.

We implement the above choices in the ACL2 extension ACL2(ml), available at [10]. Finally, we conclude with evaluation of this method in Section 5. The results we obtain with ACL2 have a wider significance, as methodology we develop here would apply to a wide range of first-order theorem provers.

2 Background

ACL2 [14, 16] (standing for *A Computational Logic for an Applicative Common Lisp*) is a programming language, a logic, and a theorem prover supporting

```
;; Factorial
1 (defun fact (n) (if (zp n) 1 (* n (fact (- n 1)))))

2 (defun helper-fact (n a) (if (zp n) a (helper-fact (- n 1) (* a n))))

3 (defun fact-tail (n) (helper-fact n 1))

4 (defthm fact-fact-tail (implies (natp n) (equal (fact-tail n) (fact n))))
;; 2^n
1 (defun power (n) (if (zp n) 1 (* 2 (power (- n 1)))))

2 (defun helper-power (n a) (if (zp n) a (helper-power (- n 1) (+ a a))))

3 (defun power-tail (n) (helper-power n 1))

4 (defthm power-power-tail (implies (natp n) (equal (power-tail n) (power n))))
;; Fibonacci
1 (defun fib (n) (if (zp n) 0 (if (equal n 1) 1 (+ (fib (- n 1)) (fib (- n 2))))))

2 (defun helper-fib (n j k) (if (zp n) j (if (equal n 1) k (helper-fib (- n 1) k (+ j k)))))

3 (defun fib-tail (n) (helper-fib n 0 1))

4 (defthm fib-fib-tail (implies (natp n) (equal (fib-tail n) (fib n))))
```

Fig. 2. *ACL2 definitions and theorems.* 1: recursive arithmetic functions. 2: helpers of tail-recursive arithmetic functions. 3: tail-recursive arithmetic functions. 4: Equivalence theorems of recursive and tail-recursive functions.

reasoning in the logic. The ACL2 programming language is an extension of an applicative subset of Common Lisp. The ACL2 logic is an untyped first-order logic with equality, used for specifying properties and reasoning about the functions defined in the programming language. All the variables in the formulas allowed by the ACL2 system are implicitly universally quantified. The syntax of its terms and formulas is that of Common Lisp.

Example 1. Given the recursive and tail-recursive functions to compute factorial, 2^n and Fibonacci, the ACL2 user can specify the equivalence between the functions as shown in Figure 2 with theorems fact-fact-tail, power-power-tail and fib-fib-tail. Note the similarity between these lemmas.

ACL2 has both automatic and interactive features. It is automatic in the sense that once a defthm command is submitted, the user can no longer interact with the system (the ACL2 proof engine applies a collection of automatic tactics until either the conjecture is proven or none of the tactics is applicable). Often, non-trivial results cannot be proven on the first attempt. The user then has to interact with the prover by supplying a suitable collection of definitions and auxiliary lemmas, used in subsequent proofs as rewriting rules. These lemmas are suggested by a preconceived hand proof or by inspection of failed proofs; this kind of interaction is referred to as *The Method* [14].

Example 2. ACL2's first attempt at proving the conjecture `fact-fact-tail` of Example 1 fails, and the user needs to introduce a lemma (inspired by the failed proof of `fact-fact-tail`), which is automatically proven by ACL2:

```
(defthm fact-fact-tail-helper (implies (and (natp n) (natp a))
      (equal (helper-fact n a) (* a (fact n)))))
```

ACL2 can now automatically prove the conjecture `fact-fact-tail`, using this auxiliary result. In later sections, we will show how ACL2(ml) automatically detects similar theorems and generates auxiliary lemmas for them.

The proofs of equivalence between the recursive and tail-recursive functions in Figure 2 follow a common pattern: the equivalence theorems are not proven by ACL2 in the first attempt, and the user must introduce auxiliary lemmas about the `helper` functions. In general, the detection of common patterns and the generation of new lemmas from those patterns is based on user's experience and can be challenging. The ACL2 distribution consists of several libraries containing hundreds of theorems, developed by several users with their own notations. It can be a challenge to detect patterns across different users, notations and libraries. Moreover, given two similar theorems T_1 and T_2, the lemmas used to prove T_1 can be substantially different to the ones needed for T_2 (e.g. different function symbols, different lemma structures, additional conditions, new concepts).

In the next sections, we describe how these challenges can be addressed automatically. We consider two running examples. The first one is the JVM library developed in [12]. This library contains the correctness proofs of the Java bytecode associated with several arithmetic programs such as multiplication, factorial and Fibonacci, including the theorems of Figure 2. As a second running example, we consider the *Lists* library presented in [15]. From this library, we consider three functions that will appear later in the paper: `sort` (that sorts a list of natural numbers), `rev` (which reverses a list), and `int` (which takes two lists as arguments and returns the list of elements that appear in both); and three theorems about these functions.

```
(defthm sortsort (implies (nat-listp x) (equal (sort (sort x)) (sort x))))
(defthm revrev (implies (true-listp x) (equal (rev (rev x)) x)))
(defthm int-x-x (implies (true-listp x) (equal (int x x) x)))
```

3 Statistical Proof-Pattern Recognition with ACL2(ml)

We present a statistical proof-pattern recognition extension to ACL2, called **ACL2(ml)**. Its implementation design follows the ML4PG tool for Coq [17]: this Emacs-based machine-learning extension works on the background of the theorem prover, gathers statistics of proof features, and then, on user's request, connects to a machine-learning toolbox (MATLAB or Weka); groups the proofs using *clustering* algorithms, and displays families of related proofs to the user. This approach allows real-time interaction between the user, the prover, and the machine-learning systems; as [17] explains in detail.

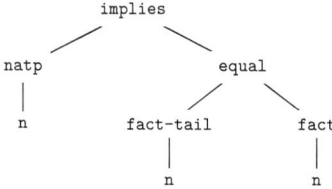

	impl	natp	equal	fact-t.	fact	n	n'	n"
impl	0	1	1	0	0	0	0	0
natp	0	0	0	0	0	1	0	0
equal	0	0	0	1	1	0	0	0
fact-t.	0	0	0	0	0	0	1	0
fact	0	0	0	0	0	0	0	1
n	0	0	0	0	0	0	0	0
n'	0	0	0	0	0	0	0	0
n"	0	0	0	0	0	0	0	0

Fig. 3. Term tree and adjacency matrix for Theorem `fact-fact-tail`; assuming the root-to-leaf direction of edges

Here, we concentrate only on original components of ACL2(ml) as compared to ML4PG. There are two such features: a novel algorithm for term tree feature extraction and the method of *recurrent clustering*.

Term Tree Feature Extraction in ACL2(ml). The discovery of statistically significant features in data is a research area of its own in machine learning, known as *feature extraction* [2]. Irrespective of the particular algorithm used, most pattern-recognition tools will require that the features have numeric values; and the number of selected features is limited and fixed (sparse methods, like the ones applied in e.g. [18,22,23], are the exception to the latter rule). The feature extraction algorithm implemented in ML4PG was based on correlation between the goal shapes, the tactics and tactic parameters within a few steps of the interactive proof. As ACL2 is not a tactic-driven language, we need to extract features from the ACL2 terms directly. Feature extraction from terms or *term trees* is common to most feature-extraction algorithms implemented in automated theorem provers: see e.g. [18,22,23].

Definition 1 (Term tree). *A variable or a constant is represented by a tree consisting of one single node, labelled by the variable or the constant itself. A function application $f(t_1, \ldots, t_n)$ is represented by the tree with the root node labelled by f, and its immediate subtrees given by trees representing $t_1, \ldots, t_n$.*

Example 3. Theorem `fact-fact-tail` from Example 1 can be represented by the term tree of Figure 3.

A variety of methods exists to represent trees as matrices, for instance using *adjacency matrices* and *incidence matrices*, with the former shown in Figure 3. The adjacency matrix and the various previous methods of term tree feature extraction (e.g. [18,22,23]) share the following common properties: different tree nodes are represented by distinct matrix entries (*features*); the matrix entries (*feature values*) are binary; and the size of the matrix depend on the tree size. For big libraries, such matrices can grow very large (up to 10^6 in some experiments) and at the same time very sparse, which implies the use of *sparse* machine-learning in [18,22,23].

In ACL2(ml), we implement a more compact feature extraction, where a total number of features is fixed for all libraries at 49, and the average density of matrices is 20%. The smaller and denser feature vectors can be used to data-mine

Table 1. *Left. Dense term tree feature extraction matrix for theorem* `fact-fact-tail`. *Right. Dense term tree feature extraction matrix for definition* `fact`. *The operator* "::" *indicates the concatenation of values (e.g. 4::5=45).*

	variables	arity 0	arity 1	arity 2
td0	0	0	0	[implies]
td1	0	0	[natp]	[equal]
td2	[n]	0	[fact-tail]::[fact]	0
td3	[n]::[n]	0	0	0

	variables	arity 0	arity 1	arity 2	arity 3
td0	0	0	0	0	[if]
td1	0	[1]	[zp]	[*]	0
td2	[n]::[n]	0	[fact]	0	0
td3	0	0	0	[-]	0
td4	[n]	[1]	0	0	0

both big and small data sets. Large and sparse feature vectors would require to use big data sets of proofs, where the size of the example data set is comparable to the number of features. In our interactive setting, it is crucial that the ACL2(ml) tool works equally well with both big and small proof libraries; and that the user can interact with it at any stage of the proof development.

We develop a method to overcome the problem of having to track a large (potentially unlimited) number of ACL2 symbols by a finite number of features, as follows. The ACL2 symbols are represented by distinct feature values given by rational numbers. The feature values are computed dynamically by *recurrent clustering* algorithm, thus reflecting the recursive nature of the ACL2 functions and proofs. The *features* are given by the finite number of properties common to all possible term trees: the term arity and the term tree depth; see Table 1. This is formalised in the following definitions.

Definition 2 (Term tree depth level). *Given a term tree T, the depth of the node t in T, denoted by depth(t), is defined as follows:*
- *depth(t) = 0, if t is a root node;*
- *depth(t) = $n + 1$, where n is the depth of the parent node of t.*

Definition 3 (ACL2(ml) term tree matrices). *Given a term tree T for a term with signature Σ, and a function $[.] : \Sigma \to \mathbb{Q}$, the ACL2(ml) term tree matrix M_T is a 7×7 matrix that satisfies the following conditions:*
- *the $(0, j)$-th entry of M_T is a number $[t]$, such that t is a node in T, t is a variable and depth(t) = j.*
- *the (i, j)-th entry of M_T ($i \neq 0$) is a number $[t]$, such that t is a node in T, t has arity $i + 1$ and depth(t) = j.*

We deliberately specify [.] only by its type in Definition 3. In ACL2(ml), this function is dynamically re-defined for every library and every given proof stage, as we are going to describe shortly in Definition 4. In practice, there will be a set of such functions computed in every session of ACL2(ml).

To make the feature extraction uniform across all ACL2 terms appearing in the library, the matrices are extended to cover terms up to arity n and tree-depth m. The parameters n and m can vary slightly; for all libraries considered in the paper $n = 5$ and $m = 7$ were sufficient, giving a feature vector size of 49 – a small size compared to sizes up to 10^6 in sparse approaches [18, 22, 23]. Having a clustering algorithm working for small sets of examples is crucial for the technique of recurrent clustering we implement for ACL2(ml).

Recurrent Clustering. As discussed above, the function [.] influences results of ACL2(ml) proof-pattern recognition; and the computation of [.] needs to be sensitive to the similarities that exist between the symbols appearing in the proofs. As ACL2 is a functional language, every entry in a term tree is necessarily itself defined in ACL2. This symbol definition can itself be clustered against other definitions used by the library; and the process can be repeated recursively to include all the necessary standard library definitions. This is how the feature extraction becomes a part of **recurrent clustering** in ACL2(ml).

We first define some essential clustering parameters. ACL2(ml) connects automatically to clustering [2] algorithms available in Weka (K-means, FarthestFirst and E.M.). Clustering techniques divide data into n groups of similar objects (*clusters*), where the value of n is a learning parameter provided by the user. Increasing the value of n makes the algorithm separate objects into more classes, and, as a consequence, each cluster will contain fewer examples. There is a number of heuristics to determine the optimal value of n; ACL2(ml) has its own function to dynamically adjust n for every run of clustering using an auxiliary *granularity* parameter. Granularity can be varied by the user; and ranges between 1 and 5, low granularity produces big and general clusters while high granularity produces small and precise clusters (see the top row of Table 2). Given a granularity value g, the number of clusters n is given by the formula

$$n = \lfloor \frac{\text{objects to cluster}}{10 - g} \rfloor.$$

The clustering algorithm assigns a *proximity value* to every term in a cluster. This ranges from 0 to 1, and indicates the certainty of the given example belonging to the cluster. ACL2(ml) shares with ML4PG some additional heuristics to ensure output quality, e.g., all experiments are run 200 times and only the ones with high frequencies are displayed to the user.

The choice of clustering algorithm, granularity and ACL2 libraries are accommodated in ACL2(ml) through a menu included in the Emacs interface. On user's demand, the ACL2(ml) interface displays families of related theorems; we call this process *Theorem Clustering*. In addition, ACL2(ml) clusters all the library definitions in the background every time a new definition is introduced. We call this process *Definition Clustering*.

The main reason for distinguishing theorem clustering and definition clustering is as follows. Theorem clustering is the ultimate goal of the proof mining here, but the feature tables for the theorems depend on the numeric representation of the symbols appearing in the theorems (see Definition 3 and Table 1). These symbols are normally defined within the libraries one uses, or else imported from CLISP. The following definition proceeds inductively on the type of symbols appearing in ACL2 definitions.

Definition 4 (Function [.]). *Given the nth term definition of the library (call the term t), a function [.] is inductively defined for every symbol s in t as follows:*
− [s] = i, if s is the ith distinct variable in t (note that all formulas are implicitly universally quantified in ACL2);
− [s] = −[m], if t is a recursive definition defining the function s with measure function m automatically assigned by the ACL2;

* Type recognisers ($r = \{$symbolp, characterp, stringp, consp, acl2-numberp, integerp, rationalp, complex-rationalp$\}$): $[r_i] = 1 + \sum_{j=1}^{i} \frac{1}{10 \times 2^{j-1}}$ (where r_i is the ith element of r).
* Constructors ($c = \{$cons, complex$\}$): $[c_i] = 2 + \sum_{j=1}^{i} \frac{1}{10 \times 2^{j-1}}$.
* Accessors ($a^1 = \{$car, cdr$\}$, $a^2 = \{$denominator, numerator$\}$, $a^3 = \{$realpart, imagpart$\}$): $[a_i^j] = 3 + \frac{1}{10 \times j} + \frac{i-1}{100}$.
* Operations on numbers ($o = \{$unary$-/$, unary$--$, binary$-+$, binary$-*\}$): $[o_i] = 4 + \sum_{j=1}^{i} \frac{1}{10 \times 2^{j-1}}$.
* Integers and rational numbers: $[0] = 4.3$, $[n] = 4.3 + \frac{|n|}{10}$ (with $n \neq 0$ and $|n| < 1$) and $[n] = 4.3 + \frac{1}{100 * |n|}$ (with $n \neq 0$ and $|n| \geq 1$).
* Boolean operations ($b = \{$equal, if, $<\}$): $[b_i] = 5 + \sum_{j=1}^{i} \frac{1}{10 \times 2^{j-1}}$.

Fig. 4. Formulas to compute the value of function [.] for the ACL2 functions imported from CLISP. The above formulas serve to assign closer values to the functions within each of the six above groups, and more distant numbers across the groups – thus distinguishing the groups unambiguously.

– $[s] = k$, if s is a function imported from CLISP; and $[s] = k$ in Figure 4;
– $[s] = 5 + 2 \times j + p$, where C_j is a cluster obtained as a result of definition clustering with granularity 3 for library definitions 1 to $n-1$, $s \in C_j$ and p is the proximity value of s in C_j. (Note that a cluster in definition clustering is given by a set of terms; and the default granularity 3 generally provides a good balance between the size of clusters and their precision.)

Note the recurrent nature of clustering in Definition 4, with symbol numbering for the nth term depending on the clustering results for previous $n-1$ terms. As the above definition implies, the function [.] is adaptive, and is recomputed automatically when new definitions (and hence new symbols) are introduced. The motivation behind the various parameters of Definition 4 is as follows:
– *Variables.* The variable encoding reflects the number and order of unique variables appearing in the term, note its correspondence to the De Bruijn indexes.
– *Recursive case.* For every recursive function s, ACL2 assigns a termination measure function m. So, m necessarily exists for all recursive definitions and implicitly contains some "type" information (e.g. the measure for the function rev is the length of its input and the measure for fact is the value of its input). It has a negative value in order for feature values to distinguish the occurrence of the inductive symbol being currently defined from occurrence of any external functions invoked in the body of the term. The value $-[m]$ identifies all inductively defined symbols with the same ACL2 termination measure function.
– Finally, the formula $5+2\times j+p$ assigns $[s]$ a value within $[5+2\times j, 5+2\times j+1]$, depending on their statistical proximity p for that cluster – p always lies within $[0, 1]$. Thus, elements of the same cluster have closer values comparing to the values assigned to elements of other clusters or to the imported CLISP functions.

We finish this section with some examples of ACL2(ml) clustering. All examples are run with several clustering functions and a choice of statistical parameters, allowing us to evaluate whether the feature extraction method we present here is robust across a range of algorithms, see Table 2.

Table 2. *Results of Clustering experiments in ACL2(ml) for a choice of algorithms and granularities.* When granularity g is chosen by the user, ACL2(ml) dynamically calculates the number n of clusters; the table shows the size of one most relevant cluster that ACL2(ml) displays to the user in each case. **Top table**. Experiments for Theorem `fib-fib-tail` using JVM library (150 lemmas). We mark if the cluster contains (in addition to Theorem `fib-fib-tail`): a) Theorem `fact-fact-tail`, b) Theorem `power-power-tail`, c) other theorems related to the equivalence of recursive and tail-recursive functions. **Bottom table**. Experiments for Theorem `revrev` using Lists library (100 lemmas). All the clusters contain theorems d) `sortsort` and e) `int-x-x` (in addition to `revrev`). Note the stable performance of our feature extraction algorithm across several algorithms and parameters.

	Algorithm:	$g=1$ ($n=16$)	$g=2$ ($n=18$)	$g=3$ ($n=21$)	$g=4$ ($n=25$)	$g=5$ ($n=30$)
fib-fib-tail experiments (one relevant cluster)	K-means	$9^{a,b,c}$	$4^{a,b,c}$	$3^{a,c}$	2^a	2^a
	E.M.	$16^{a,b,c}$	$16^{a,b,c}$	$9^{a,b,c}$	$4^{a,b,c}$	$4^{a,b,c}$
	FarthestFirst	$12^{a,b,c}$	$12^{a,b,c}$	$10^{a,b,c}$	$5^{a,b,c}$	$4^{a,b,c}$
	Algorithm:	$g=1$ ($n=11$)	$g=2$ ($n=12$)	$g=3$ ($n=14$)	$g=4$ ($n=16$)	$g=5$ ($n=20$)
revrev experiments (one relevant cluster)	K-means	$22^{d,e}$	$22^{d,e}$	$20^{d,e}$	$11^{d,e}$	$3^{d,e}$
	E.M.	$29^{d,e}$	$25^{d,e}$	$25^{d,e}$	$23^{d,e}$	$19^{d,e}$
	FarthestFirst	$45^{d,e}$	$34^{d,e}$	$30^{d,e}$	$26^{d,e}$	$15^{d,e}$

Example 4. Using the *JVM* library, ACL2(ml) detects lemmas similar to theorem `fib-fib-tail` (see Figure 2). Table 2 shows the sizes of clusters that ACL2(ml) will display for this theorem for various clustering algorithms and granularities. In Table 2, we can see a clear pattern: `fib-fib-tail` is consistently grouped with other theorems related to the equivalence of recursive and tail-recursive functions – this is done with all variations of learning algorithms and granularities, albeit with varied degree of precision. For this set of examples and this stage of the proof, the feature extraction function [.] returned values:
[`fact`] $= 12.974$, [`power`] $= 12.973$, [`fib`] $= 12.618$.
[`helper-fact`] $= 16.961$, [`helper-power`] $= 16.967$, [`helper-fib`] $= 16.431$.
[`fact-tail`] $= 18.970$, [`power-tail`] $= 18.969$, [`fib-tail`] $= 18.735$.
Note that the numbers above correspond to our intuitive grouping in Figure 2.

Table 2 also shows the lemmas of library *Lists* that are similar to `revrev`. In this case, the most precise cluster is detected by K-means with $g=5$, but we can notice that `revrev` is always clustered with theorems `sortsort` and `int-x-x`.

4 Lemma Discovery in ACL2(ml)

One of the motivations of this research is to provide the ACL2 users with an efficient interactive lemma suggestion mechanism when automated proof search fails. The symbolic side of ACL2(ml) uses analogical reasoning to efficiently produce lemmas which are relevant to the current conjecture. In particular, it automatically attempts to suggest lemmas which are characterised as *eureka lemmas* – i.e. ones whose invention is mathematically creative and difficult to automate. In Section 3, we described how ACL2(ml) employs statistical machine-learning

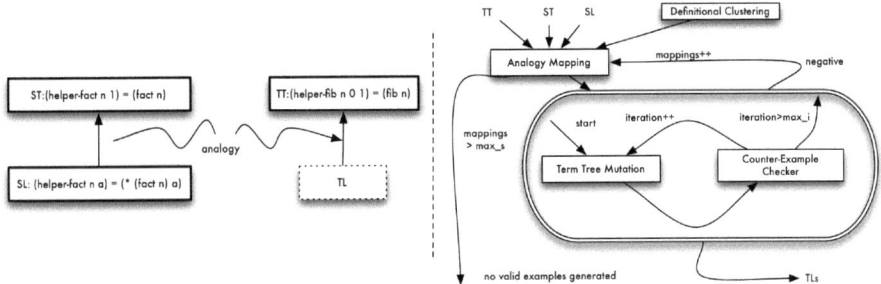

Fig. 5. Left: The source theorem and lemma along with the target theorem for which we seek an analogous lemma. Right: overview of the process of generating analogical lemmas. Here the label `iteration` is the iteration step and `mappings` is a count of the number of analogy mappings.

to determine similarity of theorem statements based on the term structure. In this section, we show how ACL2(ml) uses this information to construct analogous lemmas – this greatly reduces the search space for lemma discovery.

We introduce the following terminology: A *Target Theorem (TT)* is a theorem currently being attempted in ACL2, but requiring user's intervention. A *Source Theorem (ST)* is a theorem which has been suggested as similar to the TT by the statistical ACL2(ml). A *Source Lemma (SL)* is a user-supplied lemma required for proving the source theorem. The symbolic side of ACL2(ml) groups (potentially multiple) statistical suggestions into ST and SL pairs, each being evaluated in turn. The process then outputs some *Target Lemmas (TLs)* — these lemmas are analogical to some SL and not falsified by counter-example checking.

Example 5. Let us consider the case shown by Figure 5, where a user of ACL2 wants to prove the TT[1]: (helper-fib n 0 1) = (fib n). As described in Section 3 and Table 2, ACL2(ml) suggests the closest analogy to be:
(helper-fact n 1) = (fact n). Only one user-defined auxiliary lemma is used in the proof of this ST: (helper-fact n a) = (* a (fact n)). The job of the lemma analogy process is to construct the corresponding TL for the `fibonacci` example, this will be our running example throughout this section.

The overall process for lemma analogy is shown in Figure 5. It has two main components: *Analogy Mapping* and *Term Tree Mutation*. Analogy Mapping calculates which symbols could be analogical to each other using the definition clustering techniques from Section 3. Term Tree Mutation then uses this information to construct candidate target lemmas analogical to a given SL. Symbols belonging to the background theory, i.e. symbols shared between the source and target, are not changed by Analogy Mapping.

---

[1] To ease readability, we use infix notation instead of ACL2 notation, e.g. t1 = t2 instead of (equal t1 t2).

Definition 5 (Analogy Mapping $\mathcal{A}$). *For all symbols $s_1, \ldots, s_n$ occurring in the current ST, the set of admissible analogy mappings is the set of all mappings $\mathcal{A}$ such that*
- *$\mathcal{A}(s_i) = s_i$ for all shared background symbols; otherwise:*
- *$\mathcal{A}(s_i) = s_j$ for all combinations of $i, j \in 1 \ldots n$, such that s_i and s_j belong to the same cluster in the last iteration of definition clustering.*

Example 6. For our running example, the shared background theory includes symbols {+, *,-, 1, 0}. We thus get a mapping:
$\mathcal{A} = \{$fact $\mapsto$ fib, helper-fact $\mapsto$ helper-fib, + $\mapsto$ +, 1 $\mapsto$ 1 ... $\}$

Term Tree Mutation. Given an analogy mapping, candidate lemmas are constructed by mutating the term tree of the SL. IsaScheme [21] works similarly, by defining *schemes* which determine the shape of a generated term. Here, we extend this idea by iteratively allowing larger perturbations on this shape if no suitable candidate lemma has been found. We refer to this as *mutation*, an overview of the process is shown in Figure 5. The algorithm proceeds down three levels of increasing term tree mutation. After each iteration, we test the validity of the set of generated equations using a counter-example checker. If no candidate conjecture survives counter-example checking, mutation proceeds to the next iteration. The Term Tree Mutation algorithm for the case of equational lemmas is shown in Figure 6, however note that each sub-routine work on arbitrary terms and the mutation algorithm can thus trivially be generalised. The first iteration, *Tree Reconstruction*, replaces symbols in the SL with their analogical counterparts. The second iteration, *Node Expansion* further mutates the term, by synthesising small terms (max depth 2) in place of variables. Finally, the last iteration, *Term Tree Expansion* similarly adds new term structure, but on the top-level of the term.

Iteration 1 – Tree Reconstruction. The first iteration recursively replaces symbols in the source term by their analogical counterpart specified by $\mathcal{A}$. If the analogous function has fewer arguments than the source, we simply ignore excess arguments. If it has more arguments, we insert variables in the free positions.

Example 7. The running example has SL (helper-fact n a) = (* a (fact n)) with $\mathcal{A}$ as in Example 6. TreeRec performs the replacements to produce sets of candidate left- and right-hand sides, including for instance, the potential left-hand side (helper-fib n n1 a) and the right-hand sides (* a (fib n)) and (* n1 (fib a)) – as well as other variants with variables in different order. Note that we introduce a new variable n1 as helper-fib has one more argument than its analogical counterpart helper-fact. In this case, no combination of left- and right-hand sides yield an equational theorem.

Iteration 2 – Node Expansion. If Tree Reconstruction fails to produce any conjecture passing counter-example testing, the second iteration synthesises terms which are allowed to replace variables, thus growing the term tree from the leaves. These synthesised terms are however limited to depth 2 and built from the shared function symbols, to keep the search space tractable.

```
TTMutation
Input:   An analogy mapping A, a set of shared symbols F, and an equational source
         term tl = tr.

  1. Compute Tree Reconstructions giving sets of candidate left- and right hand sides.
L1 = TreeRec(A, tl)
R1 = TreeRec(A, tr)

  Counter-example check all pairs of terms as candidate equations.
Res = TestAllEqs(L1, R1)
if not(Res = []) then return Res
  If no candidate lemma found, continue to next iteration.
else

  2. Compute Node Expansions
L2 = map (NodeExp F) L1
R2 = map (NodeExp F) L2

  Counter-example check all pairs of terms generated so far as candidate equations.
Res = TestAllEqs(L1++L2, R1++R2)
. . .

  3. Compute Tree Expansions
L3 = (TreeExp F) L2
R3 = (TreeExp F) R2

return TestAllEqs (L1++L2++L3, R1++R2++R3)
```

Fig. 6. Term Tree Mutation. The algorithm proceeds through three iterations of increasingly mutating the source term. This work is performed by the functions TreeRec, NodeExp and TreeExp. The left- and right hand sides of the original equation are mutated separately and after each step all combinations of equalities are counter-example tested (by the function TestAllEqs).

Example 8. In our running example, we look at the new terms generated from the right-hand side of the SL. Suppose we start from one candidate from the previous iteration: (* n1 (fib a)). Node Expansion will consider all possible ways of replacing the variables a and/or n1 by terms built from shared background theory functions {+, *, -}, applied to available variables, {a, n, n1}, and constants, {1, 0}. The set of potential right-hand sides will now include terms such as (* n1 (fib (- n 1))) (having replaced a by (- n 1)), as well as many more similar alternatives.

Iteration 3 – Term Tree Expansion. As opposed to Iteration 2, which introduced new term structure at the leaves, this phase allows for insertion of term structure at the top level. Term Tree Expansion considers all terms synthesised so far and explores how they can be used as arguments to shared background theory functions.

Example 9. For the running example, we consider the whole set of candidate terms for the right-hand side. We consider all terms that can be built giving some combination of these as arguments to the background theory functions {+, *, -}. For instance, one of the new terms that is built in this iteration is (+ (* n (fib (- n1 1))) (* a (fib n1)), having added a top-level +. The counter-example checker does not find a counter-example for the conjecture (helper-fib n n1 a) = (+ (* n (fib (- n1 1))) (* a (fib n1)). Hence, the result is shown to the user as a suggestion of an auxiliary lemma to employ in the current proof.

5 Evaluation and Conclusions

We have presented ACL2(ml), an ACL2 extension combining statistical machine learning, to detect proof patterns, with symbolic techniques for generating new auxiliary lemmas. All software and extensive evaluation results are available from [10]. Both sides of ACL2(ml) are original techniques on their own. However, comparing ACL2(ml) with other alternative tools, two of its features distinguish it from all other approaches: its methods of generating the proof-hints *interactively* and in real-time, in response to the user's call; and secondly, its flexible environment for integration of statistical and symbolic techniques. We finish with an evaluation of the system.

Scalability. The ACL2 proofs libraries can grow very big, especially in industrial scenarios. The statistical ACL2(ml) tool works well with libraries of varied sizes and complexities; and does not need any fine-tuning when the user adds more libraries. To illustrate this, we increased by 6.64 times the data set used in Example 4 and Table 2 (by adding as noise lemmas coming from standard ACL2 libraries; and also the ones presented in [19] – the data set contains 996 theorems). Table 3 shows that ACL2(ml) still finds precise clusters; e.g., it still finds a cluster containing exactly the three theorems proving equivalence of recursive and tail-recursive functions similar to `fib-fib-tail`. Similar results are shown with respect to other functions from e.g. JVM library, see [10].

Table 3. *Results of Clustering experiments in ACL2(ml) for k−means clustering algorithm and a choice of granularities. Experiments for Theorem* `fib-fib-tail`*. We mark if the cluster contains (in addition to Theorem* `fib-fib-tail`*): a) Theorem* `fact-fact-tail`*, b) Theorem* `power-power-tail`*, c) theorems related to the equivalence of recursive and tail-recursive functions. The size of the data set is 996 theorems coming from the JVM library [12], the standard ACL2 libraries: Lists, powerlists and sorting; and a library related to the formalisation of a computer algebra system presented in [19].*

	$g=1$ $(n=110)$	$g=2$ $(n=124)$	$g=3$ $(n=142)$	$g=4$ $(n=166)$	$g=5$ $(n=199)$
fib-fib-tail	$57^{a,b,c}$	$50^{a,b,c}$	$25^{a,b,c}$	$8^{a,b,c}$	$4^{a,b,c}$

Usability of Statistical Suggestions. The statistical side of ACL2(ml) is not deterministic; but it is possible to empirically evaluate the usability of the statistical results produced by ACL2(ml). Using the data set containing 996 theorems presented in Table 3, and considering the clusters obtained with granularity 5, we notice that: 37% of clusters identified by ACL2(ml) can be directly used by the Lemma Analogy tool of ACL2(ml) to mutate lemmas. Additionally, 15%

of clusters contain theorems that use the same lemmas in their proofs, another 15% of clusters consist of theorems that are used in the proofs of other theorems of the same cluster, and about 19% of clusters contain basic theorems whose proofs are similar, but based on simplification, and hence unsuitable for Lemma Analogy application. Only 14% of clusters do not show a clear correlation that could be reused.

Modularity. ACL2(ml) provides a flexible environment for integrating statistical and symbolic machine-learning methods. The statistical parameters can be easily tuned to provide a better input for the Analogy tool.

Example 10. Consider the generation of auxiliary lemmas for `fib-fib-tail` and `revrev`. The auxiliary lemma for `fib-fib-tail` is generated from the lemma marked with either *a* or *b* in Table 2. Other lemmas in this cluster can be considered as noise. In this case, the granularity and algorithm choice are not particularly relevant because the auxiliary lemma can be created from all the clusters and the search space is small. However, the correct auxiliary lemma is generated faster when increasing the granularity parameter.

In the case of `revrev`, the relevant clusters are bigger than in the case of `fib-fib-tail` and the relevant lemma for `revrev` is only generated from theorem `sortsort`. Then, the noise can be reduced by setting ACL2(ml) to the highest granularity 5 with K-means algorithm, which reduces the cluster to 3 lemmas.

All our running examples were based on the cases when the proofs of the theorems required introduction of only one user-defined auxiliary lemma; and hence the analogy tool concentrated only on them. However, in the general case, the similar theorems found by statistical ACL2(ml) can rely on several auxiliary lemmas. To help the Analogy tool decide which of them should be used for new lemma generation, the statistical tool can be applied recursively to cluster these auxiliary lemmas; and thus find those more likely to result in a good analogy.

Lemma Discovery. The Analogy algorithm is designed to be fast and reduce the combinatorial explosion introduced by typical theory exploration techniques. By starting from an exemplar source lemma, we use mutation to perturb the term. We compare our tool with QuickSpec [5] – a state of the art system for generating equational conjectures about Haskell programs. While QuickSpec is designed to suggest a number of conjectures about a given set of symbols, the lemma analogy system aims at just discovering a few lemmas relevant to some particular proof attempt.

The ACL2(ml) approach is more suitable for integration into an ITP, as analogy can reduce the search space, making lemma discovery tractable in theories where QuickSpec runs out of memory. QuickSpec works by generating all terms up to a given depth (default is 3) and then use testing to evaluate the terms and divide them into equivalence classes. These represent a large number of equations so the set is pruned before displaying it to the user in an attempt to only show a small set of interesting equations. Table 4 shows the results of all combinations of source and target theorems from the examples used on the natural numbers examples introduced into ACL2(ml). QuickSpec takes as input only the function

Table 4. Results of lemma analogy in comparison with QuickSpec. $\checkmark_n$ denotes a success with n returned lemmas, and $(\checkmark_n)$ denotes a valid generated lemma which is not applicable to the TT. × denote failure to find exactly the desired lemma, while OoM denotes that the system ran out of memory. The numbers correspond to the number of formulae generated by QuickSpec

		Target							QuickSpec		
		$fact$	$power$	$expt$	sum	sum_sq	$mult$	fib	Lemma	Valid	Invalid
Source	$fact$	-	$\checkmark_1$	$\checkmark_1$	$\checkmark_1$	$\checkmark_1$	$\checkmark_2$	$\checkmark_1$	×	10	5
	$power$	$\checkmark_1$	-	$\checkmark_1$	$\checkmark_1$	$\checkmark_1$	$\checkmark_2$	$\checkmark_1$	×	17	4
	$expt$	$\checkmark_1$	$\checkmark_1$	-	$\checkmark_1$	$\checkmark_1$	$\checkmark_2$	$\checkmark_1$	×	OoM	OoM
	sum	$\checkmark_1$	$\checkmark_1$	$\checkmark_1$	-	$\checkmark_1$	$\checkmark_2$	$\checkmark_1$	×	7	2
	sum_sq	$\checkmark_1$	$\checkmark_1$	$\checkmark_1$	$\checkmark_1$	-	$\checkmark_2$	$\checkmark_1$	×	7	1
	$mult$	$\checkmark_1$	$\checkmark_1$	$\checkmark_1$	$\checkmark_1$	$\checkmark_1$	-	$\checkmark_1$	×	200	20
	fib	$(\checkmark_2)$	$(\checkmark_2)$	×	×	×	×	-	×	OoM	OoM

symbols from the target theorems for each run. Both systems produce results instantly, except in the cases where QuickSpec runs into exponential blowups. The Analogy tool usually returns one lemma relevant to the TT, whereas QuickSpec may return a very large number of results (some of which are not valid), which is not ideal for displaying to a user of an interactive system. It also runs out of memory on examples involving functions with many arguments and a higher degree of commutativity, such as the tail recursive version of multiplication (as the number of terms within its depth limit increases). These kind of theories are generally problematic for any theory exploration system relying merely on term generation, e.g. [4,13,21]. Despite their heuristics, the search space grows too big. The integration in an ITP allows us to use information about the current proof attempt, and thus navigate these theories.

Like proof-critics [1], which is a technique for lemma discovery in automated provers, we use information from the current proof-attempt to guide the search for auxiliary lemmas. However, while proof-critics only analyses the current proof attempt, ACL2(ml) also learns from all previous proofs. Some proof-critics are also closely reliant on particular proof-techniques, such as rippling, while ACL2(ml) is independent of this.

Limitations and Further Work. Below, we summarise the limitations of the system and indicate directions of further work. Although the statistical side of ACL2(ml) can process and cluster any proof and lemma shape, the symbolic analogy tool cannot handle all possible analogical cases (and no algorithmic approach could do that in principle).

Different patterns. Statistical ACL2(ml) groups in the same clusters theorems revrev, and int-x-x; however, the lemmas used in revrev cannot be mutated to generate any of the lemmas needed in the proof of int-x-x.

Smaller lemmas. The lemma analogy tool currently only adds term structure; therefore, it cannot generate smaller lemmas. E.g. Lemmas fact-fact-tail and fib-fib-tail are in the same cluster (see Table 2); the analogy tool succeeds in generating the lemma fib-fib-tail given the source lemma fact-fact-tail, but fails to go the other way around. This would require removing term structure, i.e. the inverse operation of Term Tree Expansion (see Section 4).

Conditional lemmas. Apart from type recogniser conditions (e.g. `natp` is the type recogniser for natural numbers), several ACL2 lemmas need additional conditions, which, at the moment, are not generated by the symbolic ACL2(ml). Discovering appropriate conditions for generated lemmas is a difficult problem for theory exploration systems.

New definitions. Another big challenge in lemma discovery is invention of new concepts. The proof of Lemma `int-x-x` needs a new concept called `subp` which is the recogniser for subsets of lists – `(subp x y)` returns `true` or `false` according to whether every element of `x` is an element of `y`.

References

1. Basin, D., Bundy, A., Hutter, D., Ireland, A.: Rippling: Meta-level Guidance for Mathematical Reasoning. Cambridge University Press (2005)
2. Bishop, C.: Pattern Recognition and Machine Learning. Springer (2006)
3. Buchberger, B., et al.: Theorema: towards computer-aided mathematical theory exploration. Journal of Applied Logic 4(4), 470–504 (2006)
4. Claessen, K., Johansson, M., Rosén, D., Smallbone, N.: Automating inductive proofs using theory exploration. In: Bonacina, M.P. (ed.) CADE 2013. LNCS, vol. 7898, pp. 392–406. Springer, Heidelberg (2013)
5. Claessen, K., Smallbone, N., Hughes, J.: QuickSpec: Guessing formal specifications using testing. In: Fraser, G., Gargantini, A. (eds.) TAP 2010. LNCS, vol. 6143, pp. 6–21. Springer, Heidelberg (2010)
6. Colton, S.: The HR Program for Theorem Generation. In: Voronkov, A. (ed.) CADE 2002. LNCS (LNAI), vol. 2392, pp. 285–289. Springer, Heidelberg (2002)
7. Denzinger, J., Fuchs, M., Goller, C., Schulz, S.: Learning from previous proof experience: A survey. Technical report, Technische Universitat Munchen (1999)
8. Denzinger, J., Schulz, S.: Automatic Acquisition of Search Control Knowledge from Multiple Proof Attempts. Inform. and Comput. 162(1-2), 59–79 (2000)
9. Duncan, H.: The use of Data-Mining for the Automatic Formation of Tactics. PhD thesis, University of Edinburgh (2002)
10. Heras, J., et al.: ACL2(ml): downloadable programs, manual, examples (2013), http://staff.computing.dundee.ac.uk/jheras/acl2ml
11. Hetzl, S., Leitsch, A., Weller, D.: Towards algorithm cut-introduction. In: Bjørner, N., Voronkov, A. (eds.) LPAR-18 2012. LNCS, vol. 7180, pp. 228–242. Springer, Heidelberg (2012)
12. Moore, J.: Proving theorems about Java and the JVM with ACL2. In: Models, Algebras and Logic of Engineering Software, pp. 227–290. IOS Press (2003)
13. Johansson, M., Dixon, L., Bundy, A.: Conjecture synthesis for inductive theories. JAR 47(3), 251–289 (2011)
14. Kaufmann, M., Manolios, P., Moore, J.S.: Computer-Aided Reasoning: An Approach. Kluwer Academic Publishers (2000)
15. Kaufmann, M., Moore, J.S.: How to Prove Theorems Formally (2005), http://www.cs.utexas.edu/users/moore/publications/how-to-prove-thms/main.ps
16. Kaufmann, M., Moore, J.S.: ACL2 version 6.2 (2013), http://www.cs.utexas.edu/users/moore/acl2/

17. Komendantskaya, E., Heras, J., Grov, G.: Machine Learning for Proof General: interfacing interfaces. ENTCS 118, 15–41 (2013)
18. Kühlwein, D., et al.: Overview and evaluation of premise selection techniques for large theory mathematics. In: Gramlich, B., Miller, D., Sattler, U. (eds.) IJCAR 2012. LNCS, vol. 7364, pp. 378–392. Springer, Heidelberg (2012)
19. Martín-Mateos, F.J., et al.: ACL2 verification of simplicial degeneracy programs in the Kenzo system. In: Carette, J., Dixon, L., Coen, C.S., Watt, S.M. (eds.) Calculemus/MKM 2009. LNCS (LNAI), vol. 5625, pp. 106–121. Springer, Heidelberg (2009)
20. McCasland, R.L., Bundy, A., Smith, P.F.: Ascertaining mathematical theorems. ENTCS 151(1), 21–38 (2006)
21. Montano-Rivas, O., et al.: Scheme-based theorem discovery and concept invention. Expert Syst. Appl. 39(2), 1637–1646 (2012)
22. Tsivtsivadze, E., Urban, J., Geuvers, H., Heskes, T.: Semantic graph kernels for automated reasoning. In: SDM 2011, pp. 795–803 (2011)
23. Urban, J., et al.: Malarea sg1- machine learner for automated reasoning with semantic guidance. In: Armando, A., Baumgartner, P., Dowek, G. (eds.) IJCAR 2008. LNCS (LNAI), vol. 5195, pp. 441–456. Springer, Heidelberg (2008)

Semantic A-translations and Super-Consistency Entail Classical Cut Elimination

Lisa Allali[1] and Olivier Hermant[2]

[1] École Polytechnique, INRIA & Région Ile de France
allali@lix.polytechnique.fr
[2] CRI, MINES ParisTech
olivier.hermant@mines-paristech.fr

Abstract. We show that if a theory R defined by a rewrite system is super-consistent, the classical sequent calculus modulo R enjoys the cut elimination property, which was an open question. For such theories it was already known that proofs strongly normalize in natural deduction modulo R, and that cut elimination holds in the intuitionistic sequent calculus modulo R.

We first define a syntactic and a semantic version of Friedman's A-translation, showing that it preserves the structure of pseudo-Heyting algebra, our semantic framework. Then we relate the interpretation of a theory in the A-translated algebra and its A-translation in the original algebra. This allows to show the stability of the super-consistency criterion and the cut elimination theorem.

Keywords: Deduction modulo, cut elimination, A-translation, pseudo-Heyting algebra, super-consistency.

1 Introduction

Deduction Modulo is a formalism that aims at separating computation from reasoning in proofs by making inferences *modulo* some congruence. This congruence is generated by rewrite rules on terms and on propositions, and, assuming confluence and termination, it is decidable by blind computation (normalization).

Rewrite rules on propositions is a key feature, allowing to express in a first-order setting *without* any axiom theories such as higher-order logic [8,10] or arithmetic [11]. Reasoning without axioms turns out to be a critical advantage for automated theorem provers [18,2,3,5] to not get lost during proof-search.

As a counterpart, fundamental properties such as cut elimination become a hard challenge. At the same time it is needed at both theoretical (consistency issues, e.g.) and practical levels, for instance to ensure the completeness of the proof-search algorithm of the aforementioned theorem provers. In the general case, it does not hold and this is why new techniques have been developed in order to ensure cut elimination for the widest possible range of rewrite systems.

Anticipating the definitions of Section 2, let us give two examples (see also Section 4.3) to illustrate the failure of cut elimination and/or normalization in general. For terminating (and confluent) examples, see [16]. The congruence generated by the rewrite system $P \to P \Rightarrow Q$ enables to prove the sequent $\vdash Q$ with a cut and this proof is neither normalizable in Natural deduction (the λ-term $(\lambda x.x\ x)\ (\lambda x.x\ x)$, that represents the aforementioned proof is typable) nor admits cut [10]. Instantiating Q by P yields the rewrite system $P \to P \Rightarrow P$. This allows for the same non-normalizing proof, while $\vdash A$ becomes provable in only two steps and without cut ; more generally, semantic means [16] show that in this case cut is admissible, showing the independence of normalization and cut elimination. All those questions are undecidable [6].

A first path to solve this problem, investigated in [10], is to show that a congruence has a reducibility candidate-valued model. Then any proof normalizes in natural deduction modulo this congruence. This propagates to cut elimination in intuitionistic sequent calculus modulo, but fails to directly extend to classical sequent calculus modulo. To fix this, a second derived criterion is proposed.

A second way is *super-consistency*, a notion developed in [7] that is a semantic criterion independent from reducibility candidates. It assumes the existence, for a given congruence, of a model for *any* pseudo-Heyting algebra. Since the reducibility candidates model of [10] is an instance of pseudo-Heyting algebra, this criterion implies that of [10], and all of its normalization / cut elimination corollaries. So this suffers the same drawback. A recent work [4] has also extended the criterion to the classical case, but still requires a modification of the criterion - specifically, pseudo-Heyting algebras become pre-Boolean algebras.

The beauty of super-consistency is that it is not hardwired for a particular deduction system. That is why it should indifferently prove cut elimination for the natural deduction, the intuitionistic as well as the classical sequent calculus. This is exactly what show here: cut-elimination for the classical sequent calculus modulo a given congruence, assuming the *unmodified* congruence has the *unmodified* super-consistency property.

After giving the definitions one would need to keep the paper as much self contained as possible, we introduce shortly the deduction modulo, relying on a basic knowledge first-order logic. Then we present the A-translation of propositions and rewrite systems [10], inspired by Friedman's A-translation [12], a refinement of double-negation translations, that bridges the intuitionistic and the classical worlds.

The core of the paper resides in the lifting of this translation on pseudo-Heyting algebras, at the semantic level. After verifying that all properties are preserved, we show that super-consistency is stable by A-translation: the rewrite system has a model in the translated algebra, so the translated rewrite system has a model in the original algebra.

Those results allow us to deduce that super-consistency is sufficient to prove cut-elimination in classical sequent calculus, propagating the normalization property of natural deduction modulo to cut elimination in intuitionistic and eventually classical sequent calculus, following [10].

2 Definitions

2.1 Pseudo-Heyting Algebra

Definition 1 (pseudo-Heyting algebra (pHA, [7])). *Let $\mathcal{B}$ be a set and $\leq$ a relation on it, $\mathcal{A}$ and $\mathcal{E}$ be subsets of $\wp(\mathcal{B})$, $\tilde{\top}$ and $\tilde{\bot}$ be elements of $\mathcal{B}$, $\tilde{\Rightarrow}$, $\tilde{\wedge}$, and $\tilde{\vee}$ be functions from $\mathcal{B} \times \mathcal{B}$ to $\mathcal{B}$, $\tilde{\forall}$ be a function from $\mathcal{A}$ to $\mathcal{B}$ and $\tilde{\exists}$ be a function from $\mathcal{E}$ to $\mathcal{B}$. The structure $\tilde{\mathcal{B}} = \langle \mathcal{B}, \leq, \mathcal{A}, \mathcal{E}, \tilde{\top}, \tilde{\bot}, \tilde{\Rightarrow}, \tilde{\wedge}, \tilde{\vee}, \tilde{\forall}, \tilde{\exists} \rangle$ is said to be a* pseudo-Heyting algebra *if for all a, b, c in $\mathcal{B}$, A in $\mathcal{A}$ and E in $\mathcal{E}$:*

1. *$a \leq a$ and if $a \leq b$, $b \leq c$ then $a \leq c$ ($\leq$ is a pre-order),*
2. *$a \leq \tilde{\top}$ and $\tilde{\bot} \leq a$ (maximum and minimum element),*
3. *$a \tilde{\wedge} b \leq a$, $a \tilde{\wedge} b \leq b$ and if $c \leq a$, $c \leq b$ then $c \leq a \tilde{\wedge} b$,*
4. *$a \leq a \tilde{\vee} b$, $b \leq a \tilde{\vee} b$ and if $a \leq c$, $b \leq c$ then $a \tilde{\vee} b \leq c$,*
5. *for any $x \in A$, $\tilde{\forall} A \leq x$ and if for any $x \in A$, $b \leq x$ then $b \leq \tilde{\forall} A$,*
6. *for any $x \in E$, $x \leq \tilde{\exists} E$ and if for any $x \in E$, $x \leq b$ then $\tilde{\exists} E \leq b$,*
7. *$a \leq b \tilde{\Rightarrow} c$ iff $a \tilde{\wedge} b \leq c$.*

Axioms for $\tilde{\wedge}$ and $\tilde{\forall}$ (resp. $\tilde{\vee}$ and $\tilde{\exists}$) confer them the property of a greatest lower bound (resp. lowest upper bound), while the unicity of the latters is not guaranteed, since $\leq$ is not anntisymmetric. Another guise of pHAs are Truth Value Algebras [7]. Also, $\tilde{\wedge}$ and $\tilde{\vee}$ are easily shown to be pre-commutative ($a \tilde{\wedge} b \leq \geq b \tilde{\wedge} a$) and pre-associative.

Definition 2 (Full [7]). *A pseudo-Heyting algebra is said to be* full *if $\mathcal{A} = \mathcal{E} = \wp(\mathcal{B})$, i.e. if $\tilde{\forall} A$ and $\tilde{\exists} A$ are defined for all $A \subset \mathcal{B}$.*

In this paper, all the pHA considered are full. When the pre-order is antisymmetric, then a full pHA is exactly a complete HA, in the terminology of [20]. In this paper, complete refers to the order $\sqsubseteq$ described below.

Definition 3 (Ordered pseudo-Heyting algebra). *A pseudo-Heyting algebra $\tilde{\mathcal{B}}$ is called* ordered *if it is equipped with an additional order relation $\sqsubseteq$ on $\mathcal{B}$ such that*

- *$\sqsubseteq$ is a refinement of $\leq$, i.e. if $a \sqsubseteq b$ then $a \leq b$,*
- *$\tilde{\top}$ is a maximal element,*
- *$\tilde{\wedge}$, $\tilde{\vee}$, $\tilde{\forall}$ and $\tilde{\exists}$ are monotonous, $\tilde{\Rightarrow}$ is left anti-monotonous and right monotonous.*

Definition 3 is an adapation to pHA of the corresponding definition of [7]. The "refinement condition" is shown in [7] to be a derived property (Proposition 4), but it is in fact trivially equivalent to the closure condition of $\tilde{\mathcal{B}}^+$.

Definition 4 (Complete ordered pseudo-Heyting algebra [7]). *An ordered pseudo-Heyting algebra $\tilde{\mathcal{B}}$ is said to be* complete *if every subset of $\mathcal{B}$ has a greatest lower bound for $\sqsubseteq$. Notice that this implies that every subset also has a least upper bound. We write $glb(a, b)$ and $lub(a, b)$ the greatest lower bound and the least upper bound of a and b for the order $\sqsubseteq$.*

The order relation $\sqsubseteq$ does not define a Heyting algebra order and, if by chance it does, the Heyting algebra operations may be different from those of $\tilde{\mathcal{B}}$.

2.2 Rewrite System

We work in usual predicate logic. Terms are variables and applied function symbols along their arity. Propositions are atoms (applied predicate symbols along their arity), and compound propositions with the help of connectives $\wedge, \vee, \Rightarrow, \top, \bot$ and quantifiers $\forall, \exists$. α-equivalent propositions are identified. To avoid parenthesis, $\Rightarrow$ and $\tilde{\Rightarrow}$ are considered to be *left* associative, therefore $A \Rightarrow B \Rightarrow B$ reads $(A \Rightarrow B) \Rightarrow B$. Negation is not a primitive connective, and is defined by $A \Rightarrow \bot$.

Definition 5 (Proposition rewrite rule). *We call* proposition rewrite rule *any rule $P \to A$ rewriting atomic propositions P into an arbitrary proposition A such that $\mathcal{FV}(A) \subseteq \mathcal{FV}(P)$.*

Definition 6 (Proposition rewrite system). *We define a* proposition rewrite system *as an orthogonal [19], hence confluent, set of proposition rewrite rules. The congruence generated by this rewrite system is noted $\equiv$.*

2.3 Interpretation

Definition 7 ($\tilde{\mathcal{B}}$-valued structure [7]). *Let $\mathcal{L} = \langle f_i, P_j \rangle$ be a language in predicate logic and $\tilde{\mathcal{B}}$ be a pHA, a $\tilde{\mathcal{B}}$-valued structure $\mathcal{M} = \langle \mathcal{M}, \tilde{\mathcal{B}}, \hat{f}_i, \hat{P}_j \rangle$ for the language $\mathcal{L}$ is a structure such that $\hat{f}_i$ is a function from $\mathcal{M}^n$ to $\mathcal{M}$ where n is the arity of the symbol f_i and $\hat{P}_j$ is a function from $\mathcal{M}^n$ to $\mathcal{B}$, the domain of $\tilde{\mathcal{B}}$, where n is the arity of the symbol P_i.*

Definition 8 (Denotation [7]). *Let $\tilde{\mathcal{B}}$ be a pHA, $\mathcal{M}$ be a $\tilde{\mathcal{B}}$-valued structure and ϕ be an assignment, i.e. a function associating elements of $\mathcal{M}$ to variables. The denotation in $\mathcal{M}$ of a proposition A or of a term t is defined as:*

- $[\![x]\!]_\phi = \phi(x)$,
- $[\![f(t_1, ..., t_n)]\!]_\phi = \hat{f}([\![t_1]\!]_\phi, ..., [\![t_n]\!]_\phi)$,
- $[\![P(t_1, ..., t_n)]\!]_\phi = \hat{P}([\![t_1]\!]_\phi, ..., [\![t_n]\!]_\phi)$,
- $[\![\top]\!]_\phi = \tilde{\top}$,
- $[\![\bot]\!]_\phi = \tilde{\bot}$,
- $[\![A \Rightarrow B]\!]_\phi = [\![A]\!]_\phi \tilde{\Rightarrow} [\![B]\!]_\phi$,
- $[\![A \wedge B]\!]_\phi = [\![A]\!]_\phi \tilde{\wedge} [\![B]\!]_\phi$,
- $[\![A \vee B]\!]_\phi = [\![A]\!]_\phi \tilde{\vee} [\![B]\!]_\phi$,
- $[\![\forall x\, A]\!]_\phi = \tilde{\forall}\, \{[\![A]\!]_{\phi + \langle x, e \rangle} \mid e \in \mathcal{M}\}$,
- $[\![\exists x\, A]\!]_\phi = \tilde{\exists}\, \{[\![A]\!]_{\phi + \langle x, e \rangle} \mid e \in \mathcal{M}\}$.

The denotation of a proposition containing quantifiers is always defined if the pHA is full, otherwise it may be undefined.

Definition 9 (Model [7]). *The $\tilde{\mathcal{B}}$-valued structure $\mathcal{M}$ is said to be a model of a rewrite system R if for any two propositions A, B such that $A \equiv B$, $[\![A]\!] = [\![B]\!]$.*

Soundness and completeness hold [7]: the sequent $\Gamma \vdash B$ is provable if and only if $[\![\Gamma]\!] \leq [\![B]\!]$ for any pseudo-Heyting algebra $\tilde{\mathcal{B}}$ and any model interpretation for R in $\tilde{\mathcal{B}}$. The direct way is an usual induction [7], while the converse is a direct consequence of the completeness theorem with respect to Heyting algebra. For instance one can construct the Lindenbaum algebra [7], or a context-based algebra [17].

2.4 Classical Sequent Calculus Modulo

Figure 1 recalls the classical sequent calculus modulo. It depends on a congruence $\equiv$ determined by a fixed rewrite system R. If R is empty $\equiv$ boils down to syntactic equality and we get usual sequent calculus. The intuitionistic sequent calculus modulo has the same rules, except that the right-hand sides of sequents contain at most *one* proposition. Two rules are impacted: $\vee$-r splits into two rules $\vee_1$ and $\vee_2$, and, in the right premiss of the $\Rightarrow$-left rule, Δ is overwritten by A.

$$
\begin{array}{c}
\textbf{identity group} \\[4pt]
\text{axiom, } A \equiv B \quad \dfrac{}{A \vdash B} \qquad \dfrac{\Gamma \vdash A, \Delta \quad \Gamma, B \vdash \Delta}{\Gamma \vdash \Delta} \text{ cut, } A \equiv B \\[10pt]
\textbf{logical group} \\[4pt]
\wedge\text{-l, } C \equiv A \wedge B \ \dfrac{\Gamma, A, B \vdash \Delta}{\Gamma, C \vdash \Delta} \qquad \dfrac{\Gamma \vdash A, \Delta \quad \Gamma \vdash B, \Delta}{\Gamma \vdash C, \Delta} \wedge\text{-r, } C \equiv A \wedge B \\[10pt]
\vee\text{-l, } C \equiv A \vee B \ \dfrac{\Gamma, A \vdash \Delta \quad \Gamma, B \vdash \Delta}{\Gamma, C \vdash \Delta} \qquad \dfrac{\Gamma \vdash A, B, \Delta}{\Gamma \vdash C, \Delta} \vee\text{-r, } C \equiv A \vee B \\[10pt]
\Rightarrow\text{-l, } C \equiv A \Rightarrow B \ \dfrac{\Gamma, B \vdash \Delta \quad \Gamma \vdash A, \Delta}{\Gamma, C \vdash \Delta} \qquad \dfrac{\Gamma, A \vdash B, \Delta}{\Gamma \vdash C, \Delta} \Rightarrow\text{-r, } C \equiv A \Rightarrow B \\[10pt]
\bot\text{-l, } A \equiv \bot \ \dfrac{}{A \vdash} \qquad \dfrac{}{\vdash A} \text{ T-r, } A \equiv \top \\[10pt]
\forall\text{-l, } B \equiv \forall x A \ \dfrac{\Gamma, \{t/x\}A \vdash \Delta}{\Gamma, B \vdash \Delta} \qquad \dfrac{\Gamma \vdash A, \Delta}{\Gamma \vdash B, \Delta} \forall\text{-r, } B \equiv \forall x A, \ x \text{ fresh} \\[10pt]
\exists\text{-l, } B \equiv \exists x A, \ x \text{ fresh} \ \dfrac{\Gamma, A \vdash \Delta}{\Gamma, B \vdash \Delta} \qquad \dfrac{\Gamma \vdash \{t/x\}A, \Delta}{\Gamma \vdash B, \Delta} \exists\text{-r, } B \equiv \exists x A \\[10pt]
\textbf{structural group} \\[4pt]
\text{contr-l, } A \equiv B_1 \equiv B_2 \ \dfrac{\Gamma, B_1, B_2 \vdash \Delta}{\Gamma, A \vdash \Delta} \qquad \dfrac{\Gamma \vdash B_1, B_2, \Delta}{\Gamma \vdash A, \Delta} \text{ contr-r, } A \equiv B_1 \equiv B_2 \\[10pt]
\text{weak-l } \dfrac{\Gamma \vdash \Delta}{\Gamma, A \vdash \Delta} \qquad \dfrac{\Gamma \vdash \Delta}{\Gamma \vdash A, \Delta} \text{ weak-r}
\end{array}
$$

Fig. 1. Classical sequent calculus modulo

2.5 Super-Consistency

Definition 10 (Super-consistency [7]). *A rewrite system R (a congruence $\equiv$) in deduction modulo is* super-consistent *if it has a $\tilde{\mathcal{B}}$-valued model for all full, ordered and complete pseudo-Heyting algebra $\tilde{\mathcal{B}}$.*

Super-consistency is akin to consistency with respect to *all* pHA. Note that the choice of the structure (Definition 7) is open. Considering only HA is not enough, as the rewrite system $P \to P \Rightarrow P$ devised in Section 1, as well as the one of Section 4.3 would then be super-consistent but not normalizing.

3 A-translations

Instead of first performing a negative translation [10] and then the proper A-translation, as in the original work of Friedman [12], we consider a variant of the composition of both.

3.1 Syntactic Translation of a Proposition

Definition 11 (A-translation of a proposition).
Let B be a proposition. Let A be a proposition in which free variables are not bound by quantifiers in B. A is said B-unbound. We let B^A be:

- $B^A = B$ if B is atomic,
- $\top^A = \top$,
- $\bot^A = \bot$,
- $(B \Rightarrow C)^A = (B^A \Rightarrow A \Rightarrow A) \Rightarrow (C^A \Rightarrow A \Rightarrow A)$,
- $(B \wedge C)^A = (B^A \Rightarrow A \Rightarrow A) \wedge (C^A \Rightarrow A \Rightarrow A)$,
- $(B \vee C)^A = (B^A \Rightarrow A \Rightarrow A) \vee (C^A \Rightarrow A \Rightarrow A)$,
- $(\forall x\ B)^A = \forall x\ (B^A \Rightarrow A \Rightarrow A)$,
- $(\exists x\ B)^A = \exists x\ (B^A \Rightarrow A \Rightarrow A)$.

Remark 1. Kolmogorov's double negation translation [10] of B is $\neg\neg B^\bot$. As well as this translation has been simplified by Gödel, Gentzen and others [14,13,20], we can also simplify Definition 11 so that it introduces less A.

Definition 12 (A-translation of a rewrite system). *Let $R = \{P_i \to A_i\}$ be a proposition rewrite system and A be a formula that is A_i-unbound for all i. We define its A-translation, written R^A, as $\{P_i \to A_i^A\}$.*

3.2 Semantic a-translation of a pHA

We now lift the A-translation process at the semantic level.

Definition 13 (Semantic a-translation). *Let $\tilde{\mathcal{B}}$ be the full pseudo-Heyting algebra $\langle \mathcal{B}, \leq, \wp(\mathcal{B}), \wp(\mathcal{B}), \tilde{\top}, \tilde{\bot}, \tilde{\Rightarrow}, \tilde{\wedge}, \tilde{\vee}, \tilde{\forall}, \tilde{\exists} \rangle$ and let $a \in \mathcal{B}$.*
We let $\tilde{\mathcal{B}}^a$ be the structure $\langle \mathcal{B}, \overset{a}{\leq}, \wp(\mathcal{B}), \wp(\mathcal{B}), \overset{a}{\top}, \overset{a}{\bot}, \overset{a}{\Rightarrow}, \overset{a}{\wedge}, \overset{a}{\vee}, \overset{a}{\forall}, \overset{a}{\exists} \rangle$, that we call the a-translation of $\tilde{\mathcal{B}}$, where:

- $b \stackrel{a}{\leq} c$ iff $b \stackrel{.}{\Rightarrow} a \stackrel{.}{\Rightarrow} a \leq c \stackrel{.}{\Rightarrow} a \stackrel{.}{\Rightarrow} a$,
- $\stackrel{a}{\top} \triangleq \tilde{\top}$,
- $\stackrel{a}{\bot} \triangleq \tilde{\bot}$,
- $b \stackrel{a}{\Rightarrow} c \triangleq ((b \stackrel{.}{\Rightarrow} a \stackrel{.}{\Rightarrow} a) \stackrel{.}{\Rightarrow} (c \stackrel{.}{\Rightarrow} a \stackrel{.}{\Rightarrow} a))$,
- $b \stackrel{a}{\wedge} c \triangleq ((b \stackrel{.}{\Rightarrow} a \stackrel{.}{\Rightarrow} a) \tilde{\wedge} (c \stackrel{.}{\Rightarrow} a \stackrel{.}{\Rightarrow} a))$,
- $b \stackrel{a}{\vee} c \triangleq ((b \stackrel{.}{\Rightarrow} a \stackrel{.}{\Rightarrow} a) \tilde{\vee} (c \stackrel{.}{\Rightarrow} a \stackrel{.}{\Rightarrow} a))$,
- $\stackrel{a}{\forall} A \triangleq (\tilde{\forall} \, (A \stackrel{.}{\Rightarrow} a \stackrel{.}{\Rightarrow} a))$,
- $\stackrel{a}{\exists} A \triangleq (\tilde{\exists} \, (A \stackrel{.}{\Rightarrow} a \stackrel{.}{\Rightarrow} a))$.

with the convention that, for any $A \subseteq \mathcal{B}$, $A \stackrel{.}{\Rightarrow} a \stackrel{.}{\Rightarrow} a = \{b \stackrel{.}{\Rightarrow} a \stackrel{.}{\Rightarrow} a \mid b \in A\}$.

We may straightforwardly check that $\langle \mathcal{B}, \stackrel{a}{\leq}, \wp(\mathcal{B}), \wp(\mathcal{B}), \stackrel{a}{\top}, \stackrel{a}{\bot}, \stackrel{a}{\Rightarrow}, \stackrel{a}{\wedge}, \stackrel{a}{\vee}, \stackrel{a}{\forall}, \stackrel{a}{\exists} \rangle$ is a valid *structure*, in the sense that $\stackrel{a}{\leq}$ operators are well-defined; in particular $\stackrel{a}{\forall}$ and $\stackrel{a}{\exists}$ are defined for any subset of $\mathcal{B}$. We show below that it is also a full, ordered and complete pHA.

4 Results

4.1 On the a-translation of a pHA

We recall some useful facts about the semantic implication that hold in pseudo-Heyting algebras:

Proposition 1. *Let $\mathcal{B}$ be a pHA and $a, b, c \in \tilde{\mathcal{B}}$ such that $b \leq c$. Then:*

$$b \leq a \stackrel{.}{\Rightarrow} b \tag{1}$$
$$a \stackrel{.}{\Rightarrow} b \tilde{\wedge} a \leq b \tag{2}$$
$$b \leq b \stackrel{.}{\Rightarrow} a \stackrel{.}{\Rightarrow} a \tag{3}$$
$$a \stackrel{.}{\Rightarrow} b \leq a \stackrel{.}{\Rightarrow} c \tag{4}$$
$$c \stackrel{.}{\Rightarrow} a \leq b \stackrel{.}{\Rightarrow} a \tag{5}$$
$$b \stackrel{.}{\Rightarrow} a \stackrel{.}{\Rightarrow} a \leq c \stackrel{.}{\Rightarrow} a \stackrel{.}{\Rightarrow} a \tag{6}$$
$$b \stackrel{.}{\Rightarrow} a \stackrel{.}{\Rightarrow} a \stackrel{.}{\Rightarrow} a \leq b \stackrel{.}{\Rightarrow} a \tag{7}$$

Proof. Standard, using the definition of $\stackrel{.}{\Rightarrow}$. Let us show 7: by 3 $b \leq b \stackrel{.}{\Rightarrow} a \stackrel{.}{\Rightarrow} a \leq b \stackrel{.}{\Rightarrow} a \stackrel{.}{\Rightarrow} a \stackrel{.}{\Rightarrow} a \stackrel{.}{\Rightarrow} a$. Then by definition of $\stackrel{.}{\Rightarrow}$ we get first $(b \stackrel{.}{\Rightarrow} a \stackrel{.}{\Rightarrow} a \stackrel{.}{\Rightarrow} a) \tilde{\wedge} b \leq a$ and then $b \stackrel{.}{\Rightarrow} a \stackrel{.}{\Rightarrow} a \stackrel{.}{\Rightarrow} a \leq b \stackrel{.}{\Rightarrow} a$. □

Proposition 2. *If $\tilde{\mathcal{B}}$ is a full pHA then its a-translation $\stackrel{a}{\mathcal{B}}$ is a full pHA.*

Proof. We check one by one all the points of Definition 1 and Definition 2:

- $\stackrel{a}{\leq}$ is a pre-order: inherited from $\leq$
- $b \stackrel{a}{\leq} \stackrel{a}{\top}$ since $b \stackrel{.}{\Rightarrow} a \stackrel{.}{\Rightarrow} a \leq \tilde{\top} \stackrel{.}{\Rightarrow} a \stackrel{.}{\Rightarrow} a$ (by 6). Similarly for $\stackrel{a}{\bot}$.
- $b \stackrel{a}{\wedge} c$ is a lower bound of b and c. Let us show $b \stackrel{a}{\wedge} c \stackrel{a}{\leq} b$. By definition of $\stackrel{a}{\wedge}$ and of $\tilde{\wedge}$, $b \stackrel{a}{\wedge} c \leq b \stackrel{.}{\Rightarrow} a \stackrel{.}{\Rightarrow} a$. By 6 $(b \stackrel{a}{\wedge} c) \stackrel{.}{\Rightarrow} a \stackrel{.}{\Rightarrow} a \leq b \stackrel{.}{\Rightarrow} a \stackrel{.}{\Rightarrow} a \stackrel{.}{\Rightarrow} a \stackrel{.}{\Rightarrow} a$ and by 7 of Proposition 1 $b \stackrel{.}{\Rightarrow} a \stackrel{.}{\Rightarrow} a \stackrel{.}{\Rightarrow} a \stackrel{.}{\Rightarrow} a \leq b \stackrel{.}{\Rightarrow} a \stackrel{.}{\Rightarrow} a$ which allows us to conclude. Similar arguments show that $b \stackrel{a}{\wedge} c \stackrel{a}{\leq} c$.

- $b \stackrel{a}{\wedge} c$ is a greatest lower bound of b and c: let d such that $d \stackrel{a}{\leq} b$ and $d \stackrel{a}{\leq} c$. By definition of $\tilde{\wedge}$, $\stackrel{a}{\wedge}$ and of $\stackrel{a}{\leq}$, $d \tilde{\Rightarrow} a \tilde{\Rightarrow} a \leq b \stackrel{a}{\wedge} c$ and by 3 of Proposition 1, $b \stackrel{a}{\wedge} c \leq (b \stackrel{a}{\wedge} c) \tilde{\Rightarrow} a \tilde{\Rightarrow} a$ which allows us to conclude.
- $b \stackrel{a}{\vee} c$ is an upper bound of b and c. Let us show $b \stackrel{a}{\leq} b \stackrel{a}{\vee} c$. By definition of $\tilde{\vee}$ and of $\stackrel{a}{\vee}$, $b \tilde{\Rightarrow} a \tilde{\Rightarrow} a \stackrel{\tilde{}}{\leq} b \stackrel{a}{\vee} c$. We conclude by 3 of Proposition 1. Similar arguments show that $c \stackrel{a}{\leq} b \stackrel{a}{\vee} c$.
- $b \stackrel{a}{\vee} c$ is a least upper bound of b and c. Let d such that $b \stackrel{a}{\leq} d$ and $c \stackrel{a}{\leq} d$. Then, $(b \tilde{\Rightarrow} a \tilde{\Rightarrow} a) \tilde{\vee} (c \tilde{\Rightarrow} a \tilde{\Rightarrow} a) \leq d \tilde{\Rightarrow} a \tilde{\Rightarrow} a$ and by 6 of Proposition 1, $((b \tilde{\Rightarrow} a \tilde{\Rightarrow} a) \tilde{\vee} (c \tilde{\Rightarrow} a \tilde{\Rightarrow} a)) \tilde{\Rightarrow} a \tilde{\Rightarrow} a \leq d \tilde{\Rightarrow} a \tilde{\Rightarrow} a \tilde{\Rightarrow} a \tilde{\Rightarrow} a$. By applying 7, $d \tilde{\Rightarrow} a \tilde{\Rightarrow} a \tilde{\Rightarrow} a \tilde{\Rightarrow} a \leq d \tilde{\Rightarrow} a \tilde{\Rightarrow} a$, which allows us to conclude.
- $\stackrel{a}{\forall} A$ is a lower bound of A. Let $x \in A$. Then $\stackrel{a}{\forall} A \leq x \tilde{\Rightarrow} a \tilde{\Rightarrow} a$ by definition of $\stackrel{a}{\forall}$ and $\tilde{\forall}$. Using Proposition 1, by 6 $(\stackrel{a}{\forall} A) \tilde{\Rightarrow} a \tilde{\Rightarrow} a \leq x \tilde{\Rightarrow} a \tilde{\Rightarrow} a \tilde{\Rightarrow} a \tilde{\Rightarrow} a$ and by 7 $x \tilde{\Rightarrow} a \tilde{\Rightarrow} a \tilde{\Rightarrow} a \tilde{\Rightarrow} a \leq x \tilde{\Rightarrow} a \tilde{\Rightarrow} a$, which allows us to conclude.
- $\stackrel{a}{\forall} A$ is a greatest lower bound of A. Let b such that for any $x \in A$, $b \stackrel{a}{\leq} x$. Then $b \tilde{\Rightarrow} a \tilde{\Rightarrow} a \leq x \tilde{\Rightarrow} a \tilde{\Rightarrow} a$ and by definition of $\tilde{\forall}$, $b \tilde{\Rightarrow} a \tilde{\Rightarrow} a \leq \tilde{\forall}(A \tilde{\Rightarrow} a \tilde{\Rightarrow} a) = \stackrel{a}{\forall} A$. By 3 of Proposition 1, $\stackrel{a}{\forall} A \leq (\stackrel{a}{\forall} A) \tilde{\Rightarrow} a \tilde{\Rightarrow} a$, which allows us to conclude.
- $\stackrel{a}{\exists} A$ is an upper bound of A. Let $x \in A$. Then $x \tilde{\Rightarrow} a \tilde{\Rightarrow} a \leq \stackrel{a}{\exists} A$ by definition of $\stackrel{a}{\exists}$ and $\tilde{\exists}$. By 3 $\stackrel{a}{\exists} A \leq (\stackrel{a}{\exists} A) \tilde{\Rightarrow} a \tilde{\Rightarrow} a$, which allows us to conclude.
- $\stackrel{a}{\exists} A$ is a least upper bound of A. Let b such that for any $x \in A$, $x \stackrel{a}{\leq} b$. Then $x \tilde{\Rightarrow} a \tilde{\Rightarrow} a \leq b \tilde{\Rightarrow} a \tilde{\Rightarrow} a$ and by definition of $\tilde{\exists}$, $\stackrel{a}{\exists} A = \tilde{\exists}(A \tilde{\Rightarrow} a \tilde{\Rightarrow} a) \leq b \tilde{\Rightarrow} a \tilde{\Rightarrow} a$. By Proposition 1 we derive $(\stackrel{a}{\exists} A) \tilde{\Rightarrow} a \tilde{\Rightarrow} a \leq b \tilde{\Rightarrow} a \tilde{\Rightarrow} a \tilde{\Rightarrow} a \tilde{\Rightarrow} a$ and $b \tilde{\Rightarrow} a \tilde{\Rightarrow} a \tilde{\Rightarrow} a \tilde{\Rightarrow} a \leq b \tilde{\Rightarrow} a \tilde{\Rightarrow} a$, which allows us to conclude.
- direct way of the implication property. Assume $b \stackrel{a}{\leq} c \stackrel{a}{\Rightarrow} d$, that is to say $b \tilde{\Rightarrow} a \tilde{\Rightarrow} a \leq ((c \tilde{\Rightarrow} a \tilde{\Rightarrow} a) \tilde{\Rightarrow} (d \tilde{\Rightarrow} a \tilde{\Rightarrow} a)) \tilde{\Rightarrow} a \tilde{\Rightarrow} a$. As an intermediate result we claim that for any x, y and z, $(x \tilde{\Rightarrow} (y \tilde{\Rightarrow} z)) \tilde{\Rightarrow} z \tilde{\Rightarrow} a \leq x \tilde{\Rightarrow} (y \tilde{\Rightarrow} a)$.

$$
\begin{array}{ll}
x \tilde{\Rightarrow} (y \tilde{\Rightarrow} z) \leq x \tilde{\Rightarrow} (y \tilde{\Rightarrow} z) & \text{(reflexivity)} \\
(x \tilde{\Rightarrow} (y \tilde{\Rightarrow} z)) \tilde{\wedge} x \tilde{\wedge} y \leq z & \text{(Definition of } \tilde{\Rightarrow}) \\
x \tilde{\wedge} y \leq x \tilde{\Rightarrow} (y \tilde{\Rightarrow} z) \tilde{\Rightarrow} z & \text{(Definition of } \tilde{\Rightarrow}) \\
x \tilde{\wedge} y \leq [x \tilde{\Rightarrow} (y \tilde{\Rightarrow} z) \tilde{\Rightarrow} z] \tilde{\Rightarrow} a \tilde{\Rightarrow} a & \text{(Proposition 1)} \\
[x \tilde{\Rightarrow} (y \tilde{\Rightarrow} z) \tilde{\Rightarrow} z \tilde{\Rightarrow} a] \tilde{\wedge} x \tilde{\wedge} y \leq a & \text{(Definition of } \tilde{\Rightarrow}) \\
x \tilde{\Rightarrow} (y \tilde{\Rightarrow} z) \tilde{\Rightarrow} z \tilde{\Rightarrow} a \leq x \tilde{\Rightarrow} (y \tilde{\Rightarrow} a) & \text{(Definition of } \tilde{\Rightarrow})
\end{array}
$$

  If we replace in this last inequality x by $c \tilde{\Rightarrow} a \tilde{\Rightarrow} a$, y by $d \tilde{\Rightarrow} a$ and z by a, we get $((c \tilde{\Rightarrow} a \tilde{\Rightarrow} a) \tilde{\Rightarrow} (d \tilde{\Rightarrow} a \tilde{\Rightarrow} a)) \tilde{\Rightarrow} a \tilde{\Rightarrow} a \leq ((c \tilde{\Rightarrow} a \tilde{\Rightarrow} a) \tilde{\Rightarrow} (d \tilde{\Rightarrow} a \tilde{\Rightarrow} a))$ so that we derive $b \tilde{\Rightarrow} a \tilde{\Rightarrow} a \leq (c \tilde{\Rightarrow} a \tilde{\Rightarrow} a) \tilde{\Rightarrow} (d \tilde{\Rightarrow} a \tilde{\Rightarrow} a)$, or said otherwise $(b \tilde{\Rightarrow} a \tilde{\Rightarrow} a) \tilde{\wedge} (c \tilde{\Rightarrow} a \tilde{\Rightarrow} a) \leq d \tilde{\Rightarrow} a \tilde{\Rightarrow} a$. By Proposition 1 we get the inequality $((b \tilde{\Rightarrow} a \tilde{\Rightarrow} a) \tilde{\wedge} (c \tilde{\Rightarrow} a \tilde{\Rightarrow} a)) \tilde{\Rightarrow} a \tilde{\Rightarrow} a \leq d \tilde{\Rightarrow} a \tilde{\Rightarrow} a \tilde{\Rightarrow} a \tilde{\Rightarrow} a \leq d \tilde{\Rightarrow} a \tilde{\Rightarrow} a$, which is exactly $b \stackrel{a}{\wedge} c \stackrel{a}{\leq} d$.
- conversely, assume $b \stackrel{a}{\wedge} c \stackrel{a}{\leq} d$, i.e. $((b \tilde{\Rightarrow} a \tilde{\Rightarrow} a) \tilde{\wedge} (c \tilde{\Rightarrow} a \tilde{\Rightarrow} a)) \tilde{\Rightarrow} a \tilde{\Rightarrow} a \leq d \tilde{\Rightarrow} a \tilde{\Rightarrow} a$. By 6 of Proposition 1 we get that $((b \tilde{\Rightarrow} a \tilde{\Rightarrow} a) \tilde{\wedge} (c \tilde{\Rightarrow} a \tilde{\Rightarrow} a)) \leq ((b \tilde{\Rightarrow} a \tilde{\Rightarrow} a) \tilde{\wedge} (c \tilde{\Rightarrow} a \tilde{\Rightarrow} a)) \tilde{\Rightarrow} a \tilde{\Rightarrow} a$, so $b \tilde{\Rightarrow} a \tilde{\Rightarrow} a \leq (c \tilde{\Rightarrow} a \tilde{\Rightarrow} a) \tilde{\Rightarrow} (d \tilde{\Rightarrow} a \tilde{\Rightarrow} a)$ by definition of $\tilde{\Rightarrow}$. And by 3 we get that $(c \tilde{\Rightarrow} a \tilde{\Rightarrow} a) \tilde{\Rightarrow} (d \tilde{\Rightarrow} a \tilde{\Rightarrow} a) \leq ((c \tilde{\Rightarrow} a \tilde{\Rightarrow} a) \tilde{\Rightarrow} (d \tilde{\Rightarrow} a \tilde{\Rightarrow} a)) \tilde{\Rightarrow} a \tilde{\Rightarrow} a$, which allows us to conclude. □

Proposition 3. *Let $\mathcal{B}$ be a full and ordered pHA, with respect to $\sqsubseteq$. Let $a \in \tilde{\mathcal{B}}$. The a-translation $\mathcal{B}^a$ of $\mathcal{B}$ is a full and ordered pHA with respect to $\sqsubseteq$.*

Proof. By Proposition 2, $\mathcal{B}^a$ is a full pHA. We check Definition 3:

- $\sqsubseteq$ is by definition an order relation on $\mathcal{B}$, which is also the domain of $\tilde{\mathcal{B}}^a$.
- $\top^a$ (resp. $\bot^a$) is maximal (resp. minimal) for the same reason.
- assume $b \sqsubseteq c$. Then $b \leq c$ and by Proposition 1 $b \stackrel{a}{\leq} c$.
- $\stackrel{a}{\wedge}$ is monotonous. Let b, c, d be elements of the algebra, and assume $b \sqsubseteq c$. By left-antimonotonousity of $\sqsubseteq$ with respect to $\Rightarrow$, $b \Rightarrow a \Rightarrow a \sqsubseteq c \Rightarrow a \Rightarrow a$, so $b \stackrel{a}{\wedge} d = (b \Rightarrow a \Rightarrow a) \tilde{\wedge} (d \Rightarrow a \Rightarrow a) \sqsubseteq (c \Rightarrow a \Rightarrow a) \tilde{\wedge} (d \Rightarrow a \Rightarrow a) = c \stackrel{a}{\wedge} d$ by monotonicity of $\sqsubseteq$ with respect to $\tilde{\wedge}$.
- the other properties with respect to $\stackrel{a}{\vee}, \stackrel{a}{\Rightarrow}, \stackrel{a}{\forall}$ and $\stackrel{a}{\exists}$ are shown in the same way: first notice that $b \Rightarrow a \Rightarrow a \sqsubseteq c \Rightarrow a \Rightarrow a$ and then use the corresponding property of $\sqsubseteq$ with respect to the original connective. Remember that, for A, A' sets of elements of $\tilde{\mathcal{B}}^a$, $A \sqsubseteq A'$ means that, for any $x \in A$, there exists $y \in A'$ such that $x \sqsubseteq y$. $\square$

Proposition 4. *If $\mathcal{B}$ is a full, ordered and complete pHA, then its a-translation $\mathcal{B}^a$ is a full, ordered and complete pHA.*

Proof. From Proposition 3, $\tilde{\mathcal{B}}^a$ is full and ordered. The greatest lower and lowest upper bounds of any A subset of $\mathcal{B}$ (the domain of $\tilde{\mathcal{B}}^a$) for $\sqsubseteq$ are members of $\mathcal{B}$ because $\tilde{\mathcal{B}}$ is complete. The condition of Definition 4 is fulfilled. $\square$

4.2 Relating Interpretations

Proposition 5. *Let $\mathcal{B}$ be a full, ordered and complete pHA. Consider a $\tilde{\mathcal{B}}$-valued structure $\mathcal{M}$ and note $[\![.]\!]$ the denotation $\mathcal{M}$ generates in $\tilde{\mathcal{B}}$. Let A be a closed proposition and let $B^{[\![A]\!]}$ be the $[\![A]\!]$-translation of $\mathcal{B}$:*

1. *$\mathcal{M}$ is also a $\tilde{\mathcal{B}}^{[\![A]\!]}$-valued structure. Let $[\![.]\!]^{[\![A]\!]}$ be the denotation it generates in $\tilde{\mathcal{B}}^{[\![A]\!]}$.*
2. *for any term t, any assignment ϕ, $[\![t]\!]_\phi = [\![t]\!]_\phi^{[\![A]\!]}$.*
3. *For any proposition B, any assignment ϕ, $[\![B^A]\!]_\phi = [\![B]\!]_\phi^{[\![A]\!]}$.*

A is chosen to be closed, otherwise we would need to consider $[\![A]\!]_{\phi_0}$ for a fixed ϕ_0 and consider only formulæ B such that A is B-unbound. We rather avoid those complications.

Proof. $\mathcal{M}$ is obviously a $\tilde{\mathcal{B}}^{[\![A]\!]}$-valued structure (see Definition 7) since the domain of both pHAs is the same and $\mathcal{M}$ assigns values only to atomic constructs. The second claim is also obvious, since the domain for terms does not change. We prove the last claim by an easy induction on the structure of B, where we omit the valuation ϕ, which plays no role. We note $a = [\![A]\!]$ in the definition of the operators of $\tilde{\mathcal{B}}^{[\![A]\!]}$.

- if B is an atomic formula $P(t_1, \cdots, t_n)$, then by construction and definition of the A-translation:

$$[\![B^A]\!] = [\![B]\!] = \hat{P}([\![t_1]\!], \cdots, [\![t_n]\!]) = \hat{P}([\![t_1]\!]^{[\![A]\!]}, \cdots, [\![t_n]\!]^{[\![A]\!]}) = [\![B]\!]^{[\![A]\!]}$$

- $[\![\top^A]\!] = \tilde{\top} = [\![\top]\!]^{[\![A]\!]}$, similarly for $\bot$.
- $[\![(B \Rightarrow C)^A]\!] = ([\![B^A]\!] \tilde{\Rightarrow} [\![A]\!] \tilde{\Rightarrow} [\![A]\!]) \tilde{\Rightarrow} ([\![C^A]\!] \tilde{\Rightarrow} [\![A]\!] \tilde{\Rightarrow} [\![A]\!]) = [\![B^A]\!] \stackrel{a}{\Rightarrow} [\![C^A]\!]$
  which, by induction hypothesis is equal to $[\![B]\!]^{[\![A]\!]} \stackrel{a}{\Rightarrow} [\![C]\!]^{[\![A]\!]} = [\![B \Rightarrow C]\!]^{[\![A]\!]}$.
- similarily for $\wedge$ and $\vee$.
- $[\![\forall x B^A]\!] = \tilde{\forall}\{[\![B^A]\!]_{\langle x,d \rangle} \tilde{\Rightarrow} [\![A]\!] \tilde{\Rightarrow} [\![A]\!] \mid d \in \mathcal{M}\}$ and by induction hypothesis and the notation of Definition 13, this is equal to $\tilde{\forall}\{[\![B]\!]^{[\![A]\!]}_{\langle x,d \rangle} \mid d \in \mathcal{M}\} \tilde{\Rightarrow} [\![A]\!] \tilde{\Rightarrow} [\![A]\!] = \tilde{\forall}\{[\![B]\!]^{[\![A]\!]}_{\langle x,d \rangle} \mid d \in \mathcal{M}\} = [\![\forall x B]\!]^{[\![A]\!]}$.
- similarly for $\exists$. □

4.3 Stability of Super-Consistency

In this section we show that the super-consistency property of a rewrite system is preserved by A-translation under certain conditions.

First, notice that the general statement is not true because nasty interferences can happen if the A-translation is done with respect to a A containing propositions of the rewrite system. In particular, we can lose the normalization property, which is implied by super-consistency, and so, super-consistency itself. To illustrate this, consider the following rewrite system consisting of the sole rule $P \to \top \wedge \top$. Super-consistency comes out easily: given a pHA $\tilde{\mathcal{B}}$, we let $\hat{P} = \tilde{\top} \tilde{\wedge} \tilde{\top}$. But super-consistency fails for its P-translated rewrite system:

$$P \to (\top \Rightarrow P \Rightarrow P) \wedge (\top \Rightarrow P \Rightarrow P)$$

$$\frac{\Gamma \vdash \pi_1 : A \quad \Gamma \vdash \pi_2 : B}{\Gamma \vdash \langle \pi_1, \pi_2 \rangle : C} \wedge_i, A \wedge B \equiv C \qquad \frac{\Gamma, x : A \vdash \pi : B}{\Gamma \vdash \lambda x.\pi : C} \Rightarrow_i, C \equiv A \Rightarrow B$$

$$\frac{\Gamma \vdash \pi : C}{\Gamma \vdash fst(\pi) : A} \wedge_{e1}, C \equiv A \wedge B \qquad \frac{\Gamma \vdash \pi_1 : C \quad \Gamma \vdash \pi_2 : A}{\Gamma \vdash \pi_1 \, \pi_2 : B} \Rightarrow_e, C \equiv A \Rightarrow B$$

$$fst\langle \pi_1, \pi_2 \rangle \triangleright \pi_1 \qquad (\lambda x.\pi_1) \, \pi_2 \triangleright \{\pi_2/x\}\pi_1$$

Fig. 2. Some typing and reduction rules of natural deduction modulo [10]

As we will see, in natural deduction we can define a proof-term that is not normalizing. Adopting the syntax and typing rules of [10], shown in Figure 2, we let t_1 and t_2 be the following λ-terms, I being the constant corresponding to the $\top$-intro rule:[1]

---

[1] At the price of readability, I and $\top$ can be everywhere safely replaced by $\lambda y.y$ and $B \Rightarrow B$, respectively.

$$t_1 = \lambda x.[fst(x\ I)\ (\lambda z.(x\ I))]$$
$$t_2 = \lambda z.\langle t_1, t_1 \rangle$$

Those terms can be typed respectively by $\top \Rightarrow P \Rightarrow P$ and by $\top \Rightarrow (\top \Rightarrow P \Rightarrow P \wedge \top \Rightarrow P \Rightarrow P)$ or, using the congruence, by $\top \Rightarrow P$: both bound z can be assigned the type $\top$, while x has the type $\top \Rightarrow P \equiv \top \Rightarrow (\langle\langle(\top \Rightarrow P) \Rightarrow P), (\top \Rightarrow P) \Rightarrow P\rangle\rangle$, this last type identification being the source of the problems. With those terms, we form the following looping reduction sequence:

$$t_1\ t_2 \triangleright fst(t_2\ I)\ (\lambda z.(t_2\ I))$$
$$\triangleright fst(\langle t_1, t_1\rangle)\ (\lambda z.\langle t_1, t_1\rangle)$$
$$\triangleright t_1\ t_2$$

Since we do not have normalization, we cannot have super-consistency. This is why restricting A is the key to Theorem 1.

Definition 14 (R-compatibility). *Let R be a rewriting system. A proposition A is said to be R-compatible if and only if does not contain any predicate or function symbol appearing in R.*

Proposition 6. *Let R be a rewrite system, and A be a closed proposition. Let $\tilde{\mathcal{B}}$ be a pHA and consider a $\tilde{\mathcal{B}}$-valued structure $\mathcal{M}$, generating an interpretation $[\![\_]\!]$. Let $\tilde{\mathcal{B}}^{[\![A]\!]}$ be the $[\![A]\!]$-translation of $\tilde{\mathcal{B}}$ and R^A be the A-translation of R.*

If the interpretation $[\![\_]\!]^{[\![A]\!]}$ generated by $\mathcal{M}$ in $\tilde{\mathcal{B}}^{[\![A]\!]}$ is a model of R then R^A has a $\mathcal{B}$-model.

Proof. Let $P \to F^A \in R^A$. By hypothesis, $P \to F \in R$ and $[\![P]\!]^{[\![A]\!]} = [\![F]\!]^{[\![A]\!]}$. We conclude by noticing that, by definition, $[\![P]\!]^{[\![A]\!]} = [\![P]\!]$ and that, by Proposition 5, $[\![F]\!]^{[\![A]\!]} = [\![F^A]\!]$. □

The main requirement of Proposition 6 is that $[\![\_]\!]^{[\![A]\!]}$ must be a model of R. The choice of $[\![\_]\!]$ is here a degree of freedom, but this is not sufficient, even assuming super-consistency. Indeed, the example of the beginning of the section shows that this is impossible if A is not R-compatible. We must go through the following definition lemma.

Lemma 1 (Relative grafting of structures). *Let $\tilde{\mathcal{B}}$ be a pHA and $\mathcal{M}_0$ and $\mathcal{M}_1$ be two $\tilde{\mathcal{B}}$-valued structures. Let A be a proposition. We define $\mathcal{M}_2$, the A-grafting of $\mathcal{M}_0$ onto $\mathcal{M}_1$ as the following $\tilde{\mathcal{B}}$-structure:*

- *for any function symbol f, $\hat{f} = \hat{f}_0$ (the value assigned by $\mathcal{M}_0$) if f syntactically appears in A and $\hat{f} = \hat{f}_1$ (the value assigned by $\mathcal{M}_1$) otherwise.*
- *for any predicate symbol P, $\hat{P} = \hat{P}_0$ (the value assigned by $\mathcal{M}_0$) if P syntactically appears in A and $\hat{P} = \hat{P}_1$ (the value assigned by $\mathcal{M}_1$) otherwise.*

Let $\llbracket \_ \rrbracket_i$ be the interpretation generated by $\mathcal{M}_i$ for $i = 0, 1, 2$. Then, for any proposition B:

- if B contains only predicate and function symbols appearing in A, (remind that $\top$ and $\bot$ are connectives), $\llbracket B \rrbracket_2 = \llbracket B \rrbracket_0$
- if B contains no predicate or function symbol appearing in A, $\llbracket B \rrbracket_2 = \llbracket B \rrbracket_1$

Proof. Easy induction on the structure of B. The base case is guaranteed by the definition and it propagates readily. □

Theorem 1. *Let R be a super-consistent rewrite system and let A be a closed R-compatible proposition. R^A is super-consistent.*

Proof. Let $\tilde{\mathcal{B}}$ be a pHA. Let $\mathcal{M}_0$ be any $\tilde{\mathcal{B}}$-valued structure, and $\llbracket \_ \rrbracket_0$ the interpretation it generates. Let $a = \llbracket A \rrbracket_0$.

R has a $\tilde{\mathcal{B}}^a$-model because it is super-consistent. Let $\llbracket \_ \rrbracket_1^a$ be the interpretation and $\mathcal{M}_1$ the associated $\tilde{\mathcal{B}}^a$-valued structure. $\mathcal{M}_1$ is as well a $\tilde{\mathcal{B}}$-valued structure, so let $\mathcal{M}_2$ be the A-grafting of $\mathcal{M}_0$ onto $\mathcal{M}_1$, as in Lemma 1. Let $\llbracket \_ \rrbracket_2$ and $\llbracket \_ \rrbracket_2^a$ be the interpretations generated in $\tilde{\mathcal{B}}$ and $\tilde{\mathcal{B}}^a$, respectively. From Lemma 1 we derive:

- $\llbracket A \rrbracket_2 = \llbracket A \rrbracket_0$
- for any rewrite rule in R, $P \to F$, $\llbracket P \rrbracket_2^a = \llbracket P \rrbracket_1^a$ and $\llbracket F \rrbracket_2^a = \llbracket F \rrbracket_1^a$

In particular, $\llbracket \_ \rrbracket_2^a$ inherits from $\llbracket \_ \rrbracket_1^a$ the property to be a model of the rewrite system R. We have fulfilled the requirements of Proposition 6: the pHA is $\tilde{\mathcal{B}}$, the structure is $\mathcal{M}_2$, $\llbracket \_ \rrbracket_2^a$ is a model of R in $\tilde{\mathcal{B}}^a = \tilde{\mathcal{B}}^{\llbracket A \rrbracket_2}$, since $\llbracket A \rrbracket_2 = \llbracket A \rrbracket_0 = a$.

Therefore R^A has a $\tilde{\mathcal{B}}$-model for any $\tilde{\mathcal{B}}$-model, and it is super-consistent. □

5 Super-Consistency and Classical Sequent Calculus

5.1 From Intuitionistic to Classical Deduction Modulo

We adapt results of [10] to the settings of A-translation that shift cut-elimination in the intuitionistic calculus to the classical calculus. In the sequel we let R be a rewrite system and A be a closed R-compatible proposition.

Proposition 7. *Let B, C be propositions. If $B \to_R C$ then $B^A \to_{R^A} C^A$. If $B \equiv_R C$ then $B^A \equiv_{R^A} C^A$.*

Proof. By induction on the structure of B for the first point, and on the derivation of $B \equiv_R C$ for the second point. □

Proposition 8. *Assume that A is R-compatible. If R is a terminating and confluent rewrite system[19] then so is R^A.*

Proof. Consider a rewriting sequence $A_1 \to_{R^A} \cdots \to_{R^A} A_n$. A is R-compatible, so no proposition or term appearing in A can be rewritten. Thus we can define the rewriting sequence $A'_1 \to_R \cdots \to_R A'_n$, starting at $A'_1 = A_1$ by applying the same rules. This sequence must be finite.

As for confluence, consider a critical pair $C \leftarrow_{R^A} B \to_{R^A} D$, with B atomic. We know that B can be rewritten by the corresponding "antecedent" rules of R: $C_0 \leftarrow_R B \to_R D_0$, with $C_0^A = C$ and $D_0^A = D$. Since R is confluent, there exists some proposition E_0 such that $C_0 \to_R^* E_0 \leftarrow_R^* D_0$. We also have $C \to_R^* E_0^A \leftarrow_R^* D$ by Proposition 7, and R^A has the diamond property [19]. Since it is terminating, it is confluent. □

Lemma 2. *The rules* $\dfrac{\Gamma, C \vdash A}{\Gamma, C \Rightarrow A \Rightarrow A \vdash A}$ *and* $\dfrac{\Gamma \vdash C}{\Gamma, C \Rightarrow A \vdash A}$ *are derivable in intuitionistic sequent calculus modulo.*

Proof. Direct combination of $\Rightarrow$-l, $\Rightarrow$-r and axiom rules. □

Proposition 9. *If the sequent $\Gamma \vdash \Delta$ has a proof (with cuts) in the classical sequent calculus modulo R then $\Gamma^A, (\Delta^A) \Rightarrow A \vdash A$ has a proof (with cuts) in the intuitionistic sequent calculus modulo R^A.*

Proof. By an immediate induction we copy the structure of the proof of $\Gamma \vdash \Delta$, using Proposition 7 to rewrite propositions and the admissible rules of Lemma 2 to remove the tail As. This is the only hurdle to get back a sequent of a shape that allows us to apply the induction hypothesis.

Notice that, in the ∨-r case, we must apply once the ∨$_1$ rule and once the ∨$_2$, which requires a contraction on the left-hand side. □

Definition 15. *Let $\Gamma \vdash \Delta; A$ be an intuitionistic sequent. Δ contains at most one proposition and $\Delta; A$ stands for A if Δ is empty and Δ otherwise.*

$\Gamma \vdash \Delta; A$ is said to represent a classical sequent $A_1, \cdots, A_n \vdash B_1, \cdots, B_p$ if there exists a one-to-one correspondence ξ between $A_1, \cdots, A_n, B_1, \cdots B_p$ and Γ, Δ:

- *if $\xi(A_i) \in \Gamma$ then $\xi(A_i) = A_i^A$ or $\xi(A_i) = A_i^A \Rightarrow A \Rightarrow A$*
- *if $\xi(A_i) \in \Delta$ then $\xi(A_i) = A_i^A \Rightarrow A$*
- *if $\xi(B_i) \in \Gamma$ then $\xi(B_i) = B_i^A \Rightarrow A$*
- *if $\xi(B_i) \in \Delta$ then $\xi(B_i) = B_i^A$ or $\xi(B_i) = B_i^A \Rightarrow A \Rightarrow A$*

Lemma 3. *Let B be a proposition. Then B^A cannot be of the forms A, $X \Rightarrow A$ and $X \Rightarrow A \Rightarrow A$.*

Proof. A mere check of Definition 11 according to the structure of B. □

Proposition 10. *Let A be a proposition. Let $\Gamma \vdash \Delta; A$ be a sequent that represents $A_1, \cdots, A_n \vdash B_1, \cdots, B_p$. If this sequent has a cut-free proof in the intuitionistic sequent calculus modulo R^A, and no right-rule other than axiom apply on A then the sequent $A_1, \cdots, A_n \vdash_R B_1, \cdots, B_p$ has a cut-free proof in the classical sequent calculus modulo R.*

Proof. By induction on the intuitionistic proof of the sequent $\Gamma \vdash \Delta; A$, using Proposition 7:

- if the last rule is a logical rule applied to a proposition of the form A_i^A or B_i^A, we copy this rule and apply the induction hypothesis.
- If the last rule is a logical rule applied to a proposition of another form, it must be an $\Rightarrow$-l or a $\Rightarrow$-r rule. The sequent in the principal premiss is also a representation of the sequent $A_1, \cdots, A_n \vdash_R B_1, \cdots, B_p$ - potentially weakened by one proposition if Δ is not empty and a $\Rightarrow$-l rule was applied. So we just need to apply the induction hypothesis, potentially introducing a weak-r if necessary.
- if the last rule is an axiom, we copy it. Copying an axiom rule is possible because, by Lemma 3, the axiom rule can be only applied between propositions of the same nature, with no, a single, or two implications with A at the head and the same A-translated proposition at the base.
- if the last rule is a structural rule, we copy it on the side required by ξ and apply induction hypothesis. □

It is essential to assume that no rule apply on A other than axiom, otherwise the result fails; for instance the sequent $\vdash; C \Rightarrow C$ is intuitionistically provable while the empty sequent is not classically provable.

5.2 Cut Elimination in Classical Sequent Calculus Modulo

Theorem 2. *If a rewrite system R is super-consistent the classical sequent calculus modulo R has the cut elimination property.*

Proof. Let $\Gamma \vdash \Delta$ be a provable sequent in the classical sequent calculus modulo R. Let A be a proposition not containing any predicate or function symbol of R. The sequent $\Gamma^A, \Delta^A \Rightarrow A \vdash A$ has a proof in the intuitionistic sequent calculus modulo R^A by Proposition 9 above. By Theorem 1, R^A is super-consistent. Therefore, by Corollary 4.1 of Proposition 4.1 of, $\Gamma^A, \Delta^A \Rightarrow A \vdash A$ has a cut-free proof in the intuitionistic sequent calculus.

Moreover, no rule on A other than axiom is introduced: Proposition 9 introduces only axioms, that are translated into axioms in natural deduction, and the structure of A is therefore not exposed to any introduction or elimination rules. Another argument is that we can "freeze" A and view it as an atomic formula in all the discussion above. So the proof cannot use any information on A, since it is a generic parameter of the theorem.

Consequently, by Proposition 10 the sequent $\Gamma \vdash \Delta$ has a cut-free proof. □

Note that the argument appeals to a normalization procedure of the proof-terms of Natural deduction modulo, considering commutative cuts (Section 3.6 of [10]). Other cut elimination methods for Natural deduction modulo (as the one of [9]) do not apply since they do not get rid of commutative cuts.

6 Conclusion

In [10] $R^\perp$ had to be assumed to have a pre-model in order to show cut elimination for the classical sequent calculus modulo R (Theorem 4.1 of [10]). [7] shows that it is sufficient to show $R^\perp$ to be super-consistent. We have shown here that we can instead discuss the super-consistency of R directly.

Our result is a priori more restrictive, since by instantiating A by $\perp$ we get the super-consistency of $R^\perp$ that in turn implies the existence of a pre-model for $R^\perp$. It is currently unknown whether all those criteria are equivalent or not: can we, for instance, find a rewrite system and a proposition A, such that R^A is super-consistent while R is not super consistent ? Does the existence of a pre-model for R entail super-consistency ? On the good side, our criterion works directly on R and avoids a duplication of arguments: we now in one pass have normalization for natural deduction modulo R ([7,10]) and cut elimination for the classical sequent calculus, and bypass the need of two separate pre-model (or super-consistency arguments) for R and $R^\perp$. Moreover, super-consistency, by abstracting over reducibility candidates, provides a certain ease of use.

We have also shown a general result, by A-translating rewrite systems and semantics frameworks, instead of $\perp$-translating them. For the proof of cut elimination, we believe that the latter, better known as double-negation translation, would have been sufficient, as in [10]. But the work on A-translation bears a more general character, that can be used for other applications.

Super-consistency appears to be the right criterion to deal with when one wants to know about the cut elimination property of a deduction modulo theory, as the property holds whatever the syntactic calculus is. It would be interesting to see how the super-consistency criterion extends to other first-order framework, like the calculus of structures [15] or $\lambda\Pi$-calculus modulo, that is at the root of the Dedukti proof-checker [1].

Whether we can widen the criterion and replace pseudo-Heyting algebras by Heyting algebras in Definition 10, the idea being to use *cut-admissibility* (through semantic completeness, in the mood of [17] for instance) instead of normalization in the proof of Theorem 2 is a conjecture. Analyzing [4,9] closely shows that cut-admissibility results crucially depend on finding in the interpretation of the atoms P a syntactical version of P in the model formed out of contexts/propositions. Super-consistency does not *directly* allows this, due to the abstract construction of a generic model. This appeals to a more informative structure, in both papers algebras of sequents were introduced which happens to be only pseudo-Heyting algebras.

References

1. Boespflug, M., Carbonneaux, Q., Hermant, O.: The $\lambda\Pi$-Calculus Modulo as a Universal Proof Language. In: Proof Exchange for Theorem Proving (PxTP), Manchester, UK, pp. 28–43 (June 2012)
2. Bonichon, R.: TaMeD: A tableau method for deduction modulo. In: Basin, D., Rusinowitch, M. (eds.) IJCAR 2004. LNCS (LNAI), vol. 3097, pp. 445–459. Springer, Heidelberg (2004)

3. Bonichon, R., Hermant, O.: A Semantic Completeness Proof for TaMeD. In: Hermann, M., Voronkov, A. (eds.) LPAR 2006. LNCS (LNAI), vol. 4246, pp. 167–181. Springer, Heidelberg (2006)
4. Brunel, A., Hermant, O., Houtmann, C.: Orthogonality and boolean algebras for deduction modulo. In: Ong, L. (ed.) TLCA 2011. LNCS, vol. 6690, pp. 76–90. Springer, Heidelberg (2011)
5. Burel, G.: Embedding Deduction Modulo into a Prover. In: Dawar, A., Veith, H. (eds.) CSL 2010. LNCS, vol. 6247, pp. 155–169. Springer, Heidelberg (2010)
6. Burel, G., Kirchner, C.: Regaining cut admissibility in deduction modulo using abstract completion. Inf. Comput. 208(2), 140–164 (2010)
7. Dowek, G.: Truth values algebras and proof normalization. In: Altenkirch, T., McBride, C. (eds.) TYPES 2006. LNCS, vol. 4502, pp. 110–124. Springer, Heidelberg (2007)
8. Dowek, G., Hardin, T., Kirchner, C.: HOL-$\lambda\sigma$ an intentional first-order expression of higher-order logic. Mathematical Structures in Computer Science 11(1), 21–45 (2001)
9. Dowek, G., Hermant, O.: A simple proof that super-consistency implies cut elimination. Notre-Dame Journal of Formal Logic 53(4), 439–456 (2012)
10. Dowek, G., Werner, B.: Proof normalization modulo. The Journal of Symbolic Logic 68(4), 1289–1316 (2003)
11. Dowek, G., Werner, B.: Arithmetic as a theory modulo. In: Giesl, J. (ed.) RTA 2005. LNCS, vol. 3467, pp. 423–437. Springer, Heidelberg (2005)
12. Friedman, H.: Classically and intuitionistically provably recursive functions. In: Müller, G.H., Scott, D.S. (eds.) MPC 1992. Lecture Notes in Mathematics, vol. 669, pp. 21–27. Springer, Heidelberg (1978)
13. Gentzen, G.: Die widerspruchsfreiheit der reinen zahlentheorie. Mathematische Annalen 112, 493–565 (1936)
14. Gödel, K.: Zur intuitionistischen arithmetik und zahlentheorie. Ergebnisse Eines Mathematischen Kolloquiums 4, 34–38 (1933)
15. Guglielmi, A.: A system of interaction and structure. ACM Trans. Comput. Log. 8(1), 1–64 (2007)
16. Hermant, O.: Semantic cut elimination in the intuitionistic sequent calculus. In: Urzyczyn, P. (ed.) TLCA 2005. LNCS, vol. 3461, pp. 221–233. Springer, Heidelberg (2005)
17. Hermant, O., Lipton, J.: A constructive semantic approach to cut elimination in type theories with axioms. In: Kaminski, M., Martini, S. (eds.) CSL 2008. LNCS, vol. 5213, pp. 169–183. Springer, Heidelberg (2008)
18. Jacquel, M., Berkani, K., Delahaye, D., Dubois, C.: Tableaux Modulo Theories using Superdeduction: An Application to the Verification of B Proof Rules with the Zenon Automated Theorem Prover. In: Gramlich, B., Miller, D., Sattler, U. (eds.) IJCAR 2012. LNCS, vol. 7364, pp. 332–338. Springer, Heidelberg (2012)
19. TeReSe. Term Rewriting Systems. Cambridge Tracts in Theoretical Computer Science, vol. 55. Cambridge University Press (2003)
20. Troelstra, A.S., van Dalen, D.: Constructivism in Mathematics, An Introduction. North-Holland (1988)

Blocked Clause Decomposition

Marijn J.H. Heule* and Armin Biere**

The University of Texas at Austin and Johannes Kepler University Linz

Abstract. We demonstrate that it is fairly easy to decompose any propositional formula into two subsets such that both can be solved by blocked clause elimination. Such a blocked clause decomposition is useful to cheaply detect backbone variables and equivalent literals. Blocked clause decompositions are especially useful when they are unbalanced, i.e., one subset is much larger in size than the other one. We present algorithms and heuristics to obtain unbalanced decompositions efficiently. Our techniques have been implemented in the state-of-the-art solver Lingeling. Experiments show that the performance of Lingeling is clearly improved due to these techniques on application benchmarks of the SAT Competition 2013.

1 Introduction

Random simulation is a useful technique to find patterns in Boolean circuits, such as equivalent gates and gates that are always true or false [1]. It works as follows: random values are assigned to the input gates and propagated through a given Boolean circuit. In case two gates always have the same value in many simulations, they are potentially equivalent. SAT sweeping [2] can be used to determine whether a potentially equivalent pair is indeed equivalent.

We want to lift random simulation to the domain of Boolean formulas. Yet even computing a single solution is hard for most interesting Boolean formulas. Therefore we focus on computing solutions for a satisfiable subset of a Boolean formula. The main question that arises is: which subset? If the subset is too large, then solving the formula is still hard. Hence, computing many solutions to observe patterns is too costly. On the other hand, if the subset is too small, the patterns get obscured and therefore hard to detect.

We propose to obtain a useful subset by *blocked clause decomposition*. A set of clauses is called *blocked* if and only if *blocked clause elimination* (BCE) [3] is able to remove it completely. We show that any Boolean formula can be decomposed in polynomial time into two blocked sets such that one subset is maximal. On average, the maximal subset contains about 90% of the clauses of a given formula. A major advantage of our approach is that multiple solutions for blocked sets can be computed using a linear number of steps in the size of the set. We conjecture that *all* solutions of a blocked set can be computed in a time polynomial in the number of solutions.

---

* Supported by DARPA contract number N66001-10-2-4087.
** Supported by Austrian Science Foundation (FWF) NFN Grant S11408-N23 (RiSE).

We want to find *backbone variables* [4] and *implied binary equivalences*. To detect these patterns, we decompose a formula into two blocked sets of which one is maximal. Afterwards, many solutions for the large subset are obtained by applying a linear time algorithm. These solutions partition the literals of the formula into equivalence classes. Literals in the same class are potentially equivalent. SAT sweeping is used to compute the backbone and equivalences of the large subset which are used to simplify the original formula. Experimental results show that this approach helps to solve hard application benchmarks.

Detection of these patterns has been studied in earlier work as well. Instead of using a subset of a formula to detect backbone variables, [5] proposes to use local minima computed by a local search solver. However, local search solvers perform poorly on most hard real-world SAT problems. For random formulas, the backbone of a formula is fragile [6]: i.e., removal of a few clauses reduces the size of the backbone. *Hyper binary resolution* (HBR) can be used to detect binary equivalences [7]. Yet HBR can only find "easy" equivalences, i.e., those that can be detected by unit propagation.

The remainder of this paper is structured as follows: first we briefly discuss the preliminaries in Section 2 and some definitions is Section 3. Section 4 deals with the theoretical results regarding blocked clause decompositions. We present in Section 5 heuristics and optimizations for decomposition algorithms. Section 6 explains how decompositions can be used to find backbone variables and binary equivalences. Experimental results are shown in Section 7 and we draw some conclusions in Section 8.

2 Preliminaries

In this section we review necessary background concepts: conjunctive normal form level Boolean satisfiability, resolution and blocked clause elimination.

CNF. For a Boolean variable x, there are two *literals*, the positive literal, denoted by x, and the negative literal, denoted by $\bar{x}$. A *clause* is a disjunction of literals and a conjunctive normal form (CNF) formula a conjunction of clauses. A clause can be seen as a finite set of literals and a CNF formula as a finite set of clauses. A *unit clause* contains exactly one literal. A clause is a *tautology* if it contains both x and $\bar{x}$ for some x. The sets of variables and literals occurring in a formula F are denoted by $\mathsf{vars}(F)$ and $\mathsf{lits}(F)$, respectively. A literal l is *pure* within a formula F if and only if $\bar{l} \notin \mathsf{lits}(F)$.

A truth assignment for a CNF formula F is a function τ that maps variables in F to $\{1, 0\}$. If $\tau(x) = v$, then $\tau(\bar{x}) = \neg v$, where $\neg 1 = 0$ and $\neg 0 = 1$. A clause C is satisfied by τ if $\tau(l) = 1$ for some $l \in C$. An assignment satisfies F if it satisfies every clause in F. An assignment falsifies a clause C if it assigns all literals that occur in C to 0. Formulas are *logically equivalent* if they have the same set of satisfying assignments over the common variables.

A variable is said to be in the *backbone* of a formula if it is assigned to the same truth value in all satisfying assignments.

Resolution and Blocked Clauses. The *resolution rule* states that, given two clauses $C_1 = (l \vee a_1 \vee \ldots \vee a_n)$ and $C_2 = (\bar{l} \vee b_1 \vee \ldots \vee b_m)$, the clause $C = (a_1 \vee \ldots \vee a_n \vee b_1 \vee \ldots \vee b_m)$, called the *resolvent* of C_1 and C_2, can be inferred by *resolving* on the literal l. This is denoted by $C = C_1 \otimes_l C_2$.

Given a CNF formula F, a clause C, and a literal $l \in C$, l blocks C w.r.t. F if (i) for each clause $C' \in F$ with $\bar{l} \in C'$, $C \otimes_l C'$ is a tautology, or (ii) $\bar{l} \in C$, i.e., C is itself a tautology[1]. A pure literal blocks the clauses in which it occurs. *Pure literal elimination* removes clauses with pure literals until fixpoint.

A clause C is *blocked* w.r.t. a given formula F if there is a literal that blocks C w.r.t. F. Removal of blocked clauses preserves satisfiability [8]. For a CNF formula F, *blocked clause elimination* (BCE) repeats the following until fixpoint:

If there is a blocked clause $C \in F$ w.r.t. F, let $F := F \setminus \{C\}$.

BCE is confluent and does not preserve logical equivalence [9]. The CNF formula resulting from applying BCE on F is denoted by $\text{BCE}(F)$. We say that BCE can *solve* a formula F if and only if $\text{BCE}(F) = \emptyset$. Also note the following *monotonicity* property, which immediately follows from the definitions (also see Lemma 1 in [3]). It is a crucial observation for the rest of the paper.

Proposition 1. *If $G \subseteq F$ and C is blocked w.r.t. F, then C is blocked w.r.t. G.*

3 Definitions

Let F be a formula in CNF represented as a set of clauses. A subset $G \subseteq F$ is called a *satisfiable subset* (SS) of F, if it satisfiable. If in addition G is maximal, i.e., there is no other SS H with $G \subset H \subseteq F$, then G is called a *maximal satisfiable subset* (MSS) of F.

Note that maximality of G does not require that G is an SS of F with the largest cardinality (a solution to the MaxSAT problem). Actually if G is an MSS then the complement $F \setminus G$ is a minimal correcting subset (MCS). See [10] for more details on the relation between the notions of MSS, MCS, as well as the minimal unsatisfiable subset (MUS), and the MaxSAT problem. Similar to these standard definitions we propose the following new characterizations.

Definition 1. *Let $G \subseteq F$ be a subset of F for which $\text{BCE}(G) = \emptyset$. Then G is called a* Blocked Subset (BS) *of F.*

Definition 2. *Let $\mathcal{BS}$ be the set of all formulas that can be solved by* BCE.

Hence all blocked subsets of any formula occur in $\mathcal{BS}$. Lemma 1 in [3] can be reformulated as follows.

---
[1] Here $\bar{l} \in C$ is included in order to handle the special case that for any tautological binary clause $(l \vee \bar{l})$, both l and $\bar{l}$ block the clause. Notice that, even without this addition, every *non-binary* tautological clause contains at least one literal that blocks the clause.

Proposition 2 ($\mathcal{BS}$ monotonicity). *If $F \in \mathcal{BS}$ and $G \subseteq F$ then $G \in \mathcal{BS}$.*

If $G \in \mathcal{BS}$, $G \subseteq F$, and maximal then G is called a *maximal blocked subset* (MBS) of F. Obviously an MBS is also an MSS, but there are of course MSSs, which are not an MBS, since all satisfiable formulas have itself as MSS, but in general can not be solved by BCE. For example, consider the CNF formula $F = (a \vee \bar{b}) \wedge (b \vee \bar{c}) \wedge (c \vee \bar{a})$. F is satisfiable, but cannot be solved by BCE. We define MaxBS of a given CNF formula F to be the problem of finding an MBS of F with the largest cardinality.

4 Decompositions

One key observation in this paper is that every CNF formula can be decomposed into two subsets that both can be solved by BCE. Throughout the paper we will present procedures how to compute such decompositions. We will use the symbols L and R to denote the two subsets. Set L refers to the *left* or *large* subset as some algorithms aim to make one subset as large as possible. Set R refers to the *right* or *remainder* subset.

4.1 Symmetric Decompositions

A blocked clause decomposition of a CNF formula F is called *symmetric* if both subsets can be solved by BCE. A decomposition is *asymmetric* if only one of the subsets can be solved by BCE. It is easy to compute a symmetric decomposition for a given formula.

Consider the *PureDecompose* algorithm shown in Fig. 1. When this algorithm terminates, L and $R := F \setminus L$ can be solved by pure literal elimination and hence both L and R are blocked subsets of F. Note, that BCE simulates pure literal elimination [3]. Following the construction method, $|L| \geq |R|$. The runtime of *PureDecompose* can be made linear in the size of F using a standard implementation of occurrence lists.

Lemma 1. *The PureDecompose algorithm will produce a symmetric blocked clause decomposition for any CNF formula.*

```
       PureDecompose (formula F)
PD1       let L := ∅
PD2       while F not empty do
PD3          select a variable x ∈ vars(F)
PD4          if |F_x| ≥ |F_x̄| then L := L ∪ F_x
PD5          else L := L ∪ F_x̄
PD6          F := F \ (F_x ∪ F_x̄)
PD7       return L
```

Fig. 1. Pseudo-code of *PureDecompose* algorithm, with F_l the set of clauses with l

Proof. Follows from the observation that L and $F \setminus L$ are blocked sets of F. □

Theorem 1. *Any CNF formula F can be decomposed into two subsets $L, R \subseteq F$ such that $F = L \cup R$ and $L, R \in \mathcal{BS}$, in a time linear in the size of F.*

Proof. Follows from the observation that the *PureDecompose* algorithm produces a symmetric blocked clause decomposition in linear time. □

The *PureDecompose* algorithm can be made more unbalanced (i.e., produce a larger L) by applying BCE on F in between lines PD2 and PD3 and move eliminated clauses to L. We decided against this "optimization" in the remainder of this paper, after observing that it is too costly for some huge formulas. As *post-processing*, after *PureDecompose* terminates, one can increase unbalancedness by looping over the clauses $C \in F \setminus L$ and add C to L if C is blocked with respect to L. Notice that blockedness of C has to be checked with the latest L.

4.2 Maximal Blocked Sets

This subsection discusses two favorable properties of maximal blocked sets. First, given an MBS M of a formula F, both F and M contain the same set of variables. Second, given a formula F one can compute an MBS of F in polynomial time.

Lemma 2. *Given a CNF formula F and an MBS M of F, $\mathsf{vars}(F) = \mathsf{vars}(M)$.*

Proof. Assume that $\mathsf{vars}(F) \neq \mathsf{vars}(M)$. There must be a clause $C \in F \setminus M$ containing a literal l corresponding to a variable $x \in \mathsf{vars}(F) \setminus \mathsf{vars}(M)$. Because $\bar{l}$ does not occur in $\mathsf{lits}(M)$, C is blocked on l w.r.t. M. Hence, $M \cup C$ is a blocked subset of F. However this contradicts that M is a maximal blocked subset. □

Consider the *ConstructiveDecompose* algorithm shown in Fig. 2 which moves clauses from F to L using BCE. The number of BCE calls is at most $|F|$ and each of those calls has a polynomial runtime in the size of F.

ConstructiveDecompose (formula F)
CD1   let $L := \emptyset$
CD2   **forall** $C \in F$ **do**
CD3   **if** $\mathrm{BCE}(L \cup \{C\}) = \emptyset$ **then** $L := L \cup \{C\}$
CD4   **return** L

Fig. 2. Pseudo-code of the *ConstructiveDecompose* algorithm

Lemma 3. *ConstructiveDecompose returns an MBS for a CNF formula F.*

Proof. Given a CNF formula F and the blocked subset M returned by the algorithm *ConstructiveDecompose*. Assume that M is not an MBS of M. In other words, there exists a clause $C \in F \setminus M$ such that $\text{BCE}(M \cup C) = \emptyset$. This is not possible because when C was evaluated in the algorithm, the current L of ConstructiveDecompose must have been a subset of M. If $\text{BCE}(M \cup C) = \emptyset$, then due to monotonicity of BCE for all $L \subseteq M$ it holds that $\text{BCE}(L \cup C) = \emptyset$. Hence, C should have been in M. □

Theorem 2. *Computing a maximal blocked subset of a given CNF formula F can be realized in a time polynomial in the size of F.*

Proof. Follows from the observations that ConstructiveDecompose produces an MBS for a given formula F and requires polynomial time in the size of F. □

Lemma 4. *There exists a CNF formula for which the ConstructiveDecompose algorithm produces an asymmetric decomposition.*

Proof. Consider the following formula:

$$A := (a \vee \bar{b}) \wedge (\bar{a} \vee b) \wedge (b \vee \bar{c}) \wedge (\bar{b} \vee c) \wedge (c \vee \bar{d}) \wedge (\bar{c} \vee d) \wedge (d \vee \bar{e}) \wedge (\bar{d} \vee e) \wedge$$
$$(\bar{a} \vee c) \wedge (a \vee \bar{e}) \wedge (\bar{c} \vee e)$$

Assume that the ConstructiveDecompose algorithm adds the clauses to L in the order in which they occur in A. This means the first eight clauses, lets call them A', are added to L because A' is a blocked set. However, BCE cannot solve any $A' \cup C$ with $C \in A \setminus A'$. Additionally, $A \setminus A'$ is not a blocked set. Hence, ConstructiveDecompose produces an asymmetric decomposition of A. □

We can obtain an algorithm that produces a symmetric maximal blocked clause decomposition by combining the PureDecompose and ConstructiveDecompose algorithms. Instead of $L := \emptyset$ in ConstructiveDecompose, change the initialization to $L := $ PureDecompose (F).

An alternative approach is a *destructive* algorithm. Initially all clauses are in the large set and one by one a clause is eliminated. Algorithm 3 shows this approach for BS extraction. On the notion of "destructive" and "constructive" minimization algorithms, particularly in the context of minimal unsatisfiable subset (MUS) extraction, see [11].

In contrast to the ConstructiveDecompose algorithm, the DestructiveDecompose algorithm might not produce an MBS.

Lemma 5. *There is a CNF formula for which the DestructiveDecompose algorithm produces an asymmetric decomposition and a non-maximal blocked set.*

DestructiveDecompose (formula F)
DD1   let $L := F$
DD2   **while** $\text{BCE}(L)$ is not empty **do**
DD3   remove a clause $C \in \text{BCE}(L)$ from L
DD4   **return** L

Fig. 3. Pseudo-code of the DestructiveDecompose algorithm

Proof. Consider the following formula:

$$D := (a \vee b) \wedge (a \vee \bar{b}) \wedge (\bar{a} \vee b) \wedge (\bar{a} \vee \bar{b}) \wedge (a \vee c) \wedge (\bar{a} \vee c) \wedge (b \vee \bar{c}) \wedge (\bar{b} \vee \bar{c})$$

Let's assume that the *DestructiveDecompose* algorithm removes clauses based on their order in D. This means that first the clauses $(a \vee b), (a \vee \bar{b}), (\bar{a} \vee b)$, and $(\bar{a} \vee \bar{b})$ will be removed, because BCE cannot eliminate any clause from D before that point. Now $F \setminus L$ is unsatisfiable and hence cannot be solved by BCE. In contrast, *PureDecompose* will produce a symmetric decomposition of D resulting in $L = (a \vee b), (a \vee \bar{b}), (a \vee c), (b \vee c)$ and $R := F \setminus L = (\bar{a} \vee b), (\bar{a} \vee \bar{b}), (\bar{a} \vee c), (\bar{b} \vee \bar{c})$.

DestructiveDecompose produces $L = (\bar{a} \vee c), (b \vee \bar{c}), (\bar{b} \vee \bar{c})$ which is not an MBS of F, because $(\bar{a} \vee b), (\bar{a} \vee \bar{b}) \in D$ are blocked w.r.t. L. □

Theorem 3. *The* MaxBS *problem is NP-hard.*

Proof. We show that the theorem holds by converting the NP-complete problem of Maximum Independent Set into MaxBS. The conversion works as follows. Given a graph $G = (V, E)$, we construct a CNF formula that contains Boolean variables v for each vertex $v \in V$. For each vertex $v \in V$, the formula contains the unit clause (v), while for each edge $uv \in E$ the formula contains the binary clause $(\bar{u} \vee \bar{v})$.

$$F_{\mathrm{MIS}} := \bigwedge_{v \in V} (v) \wedge \bigwedge_{uv \in E} (\bar{u} \vee \bar{v})$$

Now we will show that a graph $G = (V, E)$ has an independent set of size k if and only if the corresponding F_{MIS} contains a blocking set of size $k + |E|$.

($\Rightarrow$) Let $S \subseteq V$ be an independent set of size k of G. The formula F' containing all binary clauses of F_{MIS} and unit clauses (v) for $v \in S$ is a blocking set of size $k + |E|$. To see that BCE can solve F', notice that all binary clauses are blocked on the literals $\bar{u}$ for $u \in V \setminus S$. After eliminating all these binary clauses, the unit clauses (v) for $v \in S$ have become blocked (pure literals).

($\Leftarrow$) Given a blocked subset B of F_{MIS} of size $k + |E|$. If B contains all the binary clauses in F_{MIS}, then the independent set is represented by the unit clauses in B: since B contains all binary clauses, it cannot contain both vertices of an edge because the clauses $(u), (v), (\bar{u} \vee \bar{v})$ together are unsatisfiable and hence not solvable by BCE.

If B does not contain all binary clauses, we will make another blocked subset B' of F_{MIS} that contains all binary clauses of F_{MIS} by exchanging unit clauses in B with the missing binary clauses. Let $(\bar{u} \vee \bar{v})$ be a missing binary clause in $F_{\mathrm{MIS}} \setminus B$. In case $(\bar{u} \vee \bar{v})$ is blocked w.r.t. B, simply add $(\bar{u} \vee \bar{v})$ to B and remove an arbitrary unit clause from B. In case $(\bar{u} \vee \bar{v})$ is *not* blocked w.r.t. B, then both $(u), (v) \in B$. Now, add $(\bar{u} \vee \bar{v})$ and remove either (u) or (v) from B. By removing (u) or (v) from B, $(\bar{u} \vee \bar{v})$ becomes blocked on $\bar{u}$ or $\bar{v}$, respectively. □

4.3 Computing Solutions in Polynomial Time

Given a blocked set B, one can compute a solution for B in polynomial time [3]. A procedure to obtain a solution uses the *reconstruction stack*. This stack is a sorted list of the clauses in B based on the order in which BCE can eliminate them. Given a reconstruction stack S of B, one can compute a solution as follows. Generate a random truth assignment τ of the variables in B. Pop the clauses from S one by one. If τ falsifies a clause C with blocking literal l, flip the truth value of l in τ to 1. Fig. 4 shows how to compute a reconstruction stack and demonstrates how to use the stack to obtain satisfying assignments.

ReconstructionStack (blocked set B)
- RS1 let S be an empty stack
- RS2 **while** B not empty **do**
- RS3   let $C \in B$ be a clause that is blocked w.r.t. B
- RS4 $B := B \setminus C$
- RS5 $S.push(C)$
- RS6 **return** S

GetSolution (blocked set B)
- GS1 let τ be a random truth assignment of the variables in B
- GS2 $S := \mathsf{ReconstructionStack}\ (B)$
- GS3 **while** S not empty **do**
- GS4 $C := S.pop()$ and let $l \in C$ be the blocking literal
- GS5   **if** τ falsifies C **then** $\tau(l) = 1$
- GS6 **return** τ

GetMultipleSolutions (blocked set B, bit-width w)
- GMS1 let T be a set of assignments of random bit-vectors with width w for $x \in \mathrm{vars}(B)$
- GMS2 $S := \mathsf{ReconstructionStack}\ (B)$
- GMS3 **while** S not empty **do**
- GMS4 $C := S.pop()$
- GMS5   let b be an all zero bit-vector of width w
- GMS6   **forall** $l \in C$ **do** $b := b$ OR $T(l)$
- GMS7   let $l' \in C$ be the blocking literal w.r.t. B
- GMS8 $T(l') := T(l')$ XOR NOT(b)
- GMS9 **return** T // set of w satisfying assignments

Fig. 4. Pseudo-code ReconstructionStack, GetSolution, GetMultipleSolutions algorithms

One can use the reconstruction set to compute multiple solutions in linear time of the size of the blocked set using bit-vectors. The bottom part of Fig. 4 shows the algorithm. Each variable is assigned a random bit-vector of width w. Positive literals have the bit-vector assignment of the corresponding variable, while negative literals have a bit-vector assignment which complements the one of the corresponding variable. For each clause C that is popped from the stack, a bit-vector b is obtained by computing the logical OR of all the bit-vectors of the literals $l \in C$. If b contains zeros, then those bits are flipped in the bit-vector assignment of the literal that blocks C. The result of the algorithm is a set of w satisfying assignments — some of them might be equivalent.

The complexity of computing *all* solutions of a blocked set is unknown, but we conjecture below that they can be computed in polynomial time in the number of solutions. It is not clear whether one can use the reconstruction stack to enumerate the solutions of blocked sets.

Conjecture 1. Given a blocked set B with k satisfying assignments. Computing all satisfying assignments of B requires at most k polynomial-time computations.

Below some intuition why we believe that the conjecture might hold. Consider a Boolean circuit BC with unrestricted output gates and a CNF formula F_{BC} being the Tseitin translation of BC. Let n be the number of input gates of BC. The number of solutions of F_{BC} is 2^n – exactly one solution for each assignment to the input gates. We showed that BCE can eliminate all clauses from a Boolean circuit for which the output gates are not restricted [3]. Hence F_{BC} is a blocked set. The variables in F_{BC} corresponding to the input gates occur in the last clauses that BCE will eliminate. Assigning variables in the reverse order that BCE eliminates them, will enumerate the solutions of F_{BC}. We observed this for other blocked sets as well, although we also found some counter-examples. We expect that a more sophisticated procedure could work for any blocked set.

In case the conjecture holds, blocked sets are useful when they have few and many solutions. Given a maximal blocked set M of a CNF formula F, F is satisfiable if and only if a solution of M exists which satisfies F — because M is a subset of F and $\mathsf{vars}(F) = \mathsf{vars}(M)$. So in case M has few solutions we can compute them all in polynomial time to solve F. If M has many solutions, then we can generate a lot of them in linear time to search for patterns.

5 Heuristics and Efficiency

For the applications of blocked clause decomposition that we have in mind, one wants to have the decomposition as unbalanced as possible. Ideally, one subset contains only one clause while the large subset contains all the other clauses. In this section we discuss heuristics to obtain unbalanced decompositions.

In order to make a decomposition useful, one must be able to compute it efficiently. This section offers several ideas we came up with to improve the performance. A fast implementation of BCE is crucial for all the algorithms. An important optimization is a literal-based priority queue. Details about this and other BCE optimizations are presented in Section 10 of [3].

The QuickDecompose Algorithm. If a formula is partitioned arbitrarily it is not unlikely that one of its part can be solved by BCE. In this case we can add all its clauses to the MBS, which we want to construct. Otherwise, the partition should be refined. This idea leads to the *QuickDecompose* algorithm shown in Fig. 5, which is similar in spirit to the *QuickXplain* algorithm [12].

QuickDecompose is a more efficient variant of *ConstructiveDecompose*. Hence, it will always produce a maximal blocked set (Lemma 3), but decompositions can be asymmetric (for example on the CNF formula A in Lemma 4). In order to make all decompositions symmetric, the initialization at line QD1 should be changed to $L := \mathit{PureDecompose}\ (F)$.

The advantage of this algorithm is that it only needs $\mathcal{O}(\log|F|)$ calls to BCE to zero in on an MBS, if the formula F has exactly one MSB, which in addition also is assumed to contain a single clause. We conjecture that $\mathcal{O}(m + \log|F|)$ calls are needed in general, where m is the maximum size of an MBS of F. Thus this algorithm is particularly useful if m is small. However, for practically all benchmarks from the SAT competitions, we observed that m is close to $|F|$.

	$\mathit{QuickDecomposeRecursive}$ (formula F)
QDR1	**if** $\mathrm{BCE}(L \cup F) = \emptyset$ **then** $L := L \cup F$
QDR2	**else if** $|F| \neq 1$ **then** // partition F in non-empty sets G and H
QDR3	let $F = G \cup H$ with $G, H \neq \emptyset$ and $G \cap H = \emptyset$
QDR4	$\mathit{QuickDecomposeRecursive}\ (G)$
QDR5	$\mathit{QuickDecomposeRecursive}\ (H)$
	$\mathit{QuickDecompose}$ (formula F)
QD1	let $L := \emptyset$ // visible in $\mathit{QuickDecomposeRecursive}$
QD2	$\mathit{QuickDecomposeRecursive}\ (F)$
QD3	**return** L

Fig. 5. Pseudo-code of the $\mathit{QuickDecompose}$ algorithm

Optimizations. The most important optimization is to replace the recursive simple depth-first search by a prioritized search, where larger subsets are tried first. Further, many instances are encodings from circuit SAT problems [3], where the circuit is encoded via Tseitin encoding and zero/one constraints on circuit nodes and outputs are added as additional unit clauses. In this situation, removing the units from the CNF results in a blocked set. Thus we added a pre-processing algorithm, which removes N from F, where $N \subseteq F$ is the set of non-unit clauses of F, and then initializes L to N, if $\mathrm{BCE}(N) = \emptyset$.

We also observed that it can be useful to check whether removing at most 50% of the longest clauses would result in a blocked set. If this is the case we proceed with the shorter clauses and initialize L accordingly.

Finally, redundant BCE calls might occur, for which it has already determined previously that the formula is not solvable through BCE. Thus we maintain a cache of formulas F for which $\mathrm{BCE}(F)$ was not successful and produced a non-empty set as result. Thus the call to the BCE procedure at line QDR1 would first check whether its argument is not already in the cache.

Results. We developed two decomposition tools. The first tool, called BCDD, implements *PureDecompose*. BCDD comes in two variants: the one shown in Fig. 1 (default) and one with the optimization discussed in the last sentences of Section 4.1 (post-processing). The second tool, called SBLITTER, implements *QuickDecompose* and includes the optimizations described above. The results are shown in Table 1. Observe that the tools can help each other by providing the symmetric decomposition of BCDD to SBLITTER. Although the runtime of SBLITTER is polynomial in the size of its input, it was not able to finish (obtain a maximal blocked set) on most benchmarks within 100 seconds.

Table 1. Comparing the decomposition tools on 299 benchmarks from the SAT Competition 2013 application track. We removed a huge instance (esawn_uw3.debugged) with 54 million clauses which caused a memory out. Column 'A' shows the *average* fraction of the large subset. The sum of the sizes of the *blocked* subset L is shown in column 'B', the sum of the *remaining* clauses in 'R', both in millions of clauses. The number of benchmarks with exactly *one* remaining clause is listed in column 'O'. Then the sum of the time taken follows in column 'T'. The number of times the time-out of 100 seconds was hit for SBLITTER and 10 seconds for BCDD is shown in column 'TO'. In those $81 = 299 - 218$ cases where SBLITTER (actually all versions) finished before the time-out an MBS was found. The last column 'M' lists the sum of the maximum memory used in all the runs in GB.

tool	mode	A	B	R	O	T	TO	M
BCDD|SBLITTER	post-processing	85%	371	69	55	25	218	71
BCDD|SBLITTER	default	84%	367	73	55	25	218	71
BCDD	post-processing	82%	358	82	0	2	44	41
BCDD	default	80%	349	91	0	2	21	39
SBLITTER	default	33%	143	298	55	24	218	72

6 SAT Sweeping, Equivalence Checking and Extraction

SAT sweeping is a well-known and very effective preprocessing technique for satisfiability problems represented as circuits. It is based on techniques used in formal equivalence checking of circuits. See [2,13] for a complete list of references, and further the independently derived results in [14,15]. Similar techniques have been used in the context of computing backbones, see for instance [16]. Related approaches for sequential equivalence checking [17] are used for preprocessing model checking problems and resemble refinement techniques in fast algorithms for minimizing automata [18].

One variant of SAT sweeping starts by assigning random bit-vectors to the input gates of a given circuit. Afterwards, these values are propagated. Gates with the same bit-vector value are potentially equivalent. Next, a pair of potentially equivalent gates is selected and a SAT formula is generated stating that these gates are not equivalent. In case the formula is satisfiable, the set of potentially equivalent gates is refined. Otherwise, the two gates are merged. This process continues until there are no potentially equivalent gates left.

SAT sweeping might also be a useful preprocessing technique for SAT solving. However, porting this technique to SAT solving is not trivial. Unlike a circuit, a SAT formula has no input gates. Consequently, assigning variables to random values followed by propagation will typically result in a conflict. Hence, it is much harder to obtain a list of potentially backbone or equivalent variables.

In order to use SAT sweeping as preprocessing technique for a CNF formula F, we need to compute a large satisfiable subset L of F, which is easy to satisfy. This is exactly what blocked clause decomposition gives us. Further, it is easy to find a solution for a blocked set, i.e., linear in the size of the subset. This gives a fast way to initialize the partition of potentially equivalent literals. We used the *GetMultipleSolutions* algorithm in Fig. 4 to efficiently generate many random solutions in linear time. Variables with the same bit-vector value are potentially equivalent, while potential backbone variables have either all true or all false bit-vectors.

EquivalenceExtraction (satisfiable set L)
EE1   let τ be a solution for L, hence $\tau(L) = 1$
EE2   let $P = \{\{l \in \text{lits}(L) \mid \tau(l) = 1\}\}$ // partition of potentially equivalent literals
EE3   let $E = \emptyset$ // set of determined equivalences
EE4   **while** exists a class $C \in P$ with $l, k \in C$ and $l \neq k$ **do**
EE5   **if** $\text{SAT}(L \cup \{(l)\} \cup \{(\bar{k})\})$ **then** refine P by returned solution τ
EE6   **else if** $\text{SAT}(L \cup \{(\bar{l})\} \cup \{(k)\})$ **then** refine P by returned solution τ
EE7   **else** add equivalence $l = k$ to E and remove k from C
EE8   **return** E

Fig. 6. Pseudo-code of the *EquivalenceExtraction* algorithm

Given a *satisfiable* formula L, SAT sweeping can be implemented as shown in the algorithm in Fig. 6. As result it produces the strongest set of equivalences E, modulo transitivity and equivalent literal substitution, with $L \models E$. If one of the SAT calls in line EE5 or EE6 returns a solution τ then $\tau(l) \neq \tau(k)$ and thus the partition P is refined by splitting class C into $C_0 = \{l \in C \mid \tau(l) = 0\}$ and $C_1 = \{l \in C \mid \tau(l) = 1\}$. The result of the refinement is $(P \setminus \{C\}) \cup \{C_0, C_1\}$.

In practice, several important optimizations are required (see also [13]). First, incremental SAT solving [19] should be used, adding L as fixed formula permanently, but treating the two unit clauses added in line EE5 and EE6 as assumptions [19]. This allows to reuse learned facts from one SAT call to the next, which is particularly important for learned equivalences: If both queries to the SAT solver in line EE5 and EE6 are unsatisfiable, the SAT solver will in essence learn the two clauses $(\bar{l} \vee k)$ and $(l \vee \bar{k})$, which implicitly record equivalence of l and k in the SAT solver as well.

The second most important optimization is to bound the time spent in each SAT solver call, by for instance posing a limit on the number of conflicts. Third, it is useful to simplify L by SAT based preprocessing. Note, however, that unrestricted satisfiability preserving preprocessing, such as unrestricted BCE, will just turn L into an empty CNF, which then will not have any equivalences. We propose to restrict preprocessing to those cases, where solutions to L projected on the common variables between L and $R = F \setminus L$ do not change. More concretely blocked clause addition is disabled, and common variables are "frozen", which means they can not be eliminated nor used as blocking literal etc. This technique will of course not preserve internal equivalences within L, but still proved to be useful in practice.

Regarding heuristics for choosing the pair of literals l and k in line EE4, which are tried to be merged next, we suggest to alternate between randomly picking literals, favoring large equivalence classes, and then for every second candidate pair pick two random literals from the next equivalence class in a round-robin fashion, smallest classes first.

The extraction algorithm will implicitly also produce many learned unit clauses of the backbone of the blocked set. In our current implementation we remove them immediately from the partition P. If at least one unit is kept in P our algorithm will actually produce the backbone of the blocked set. It can then be seen as an extension of the iterative backbone extraction algorithm in [16].

7 Results

The algorithms presented above have been implemented. Source code and the log files of the experiments are available at http://fmv.jku.at/bcd.

We evaluated the effectiveness of SAT sweeping on CNF formulas on some instances from the application track of the SAT Competition 2013 using an improved version of the SAT solver Lingeling [20], the winner of this track.

We observed that our equivalence extraction tool was only useful for those benchmarks for which our decompose tools were able to compute a maximal blocked subset. Therefore, we selected all 81 instances of the application track for which BCDD | SBLITTER (with post-processing) was able to compute an MBS in 100 seconds (see Table 1 for details). Our equivalence extraction tool outputs the backbone variables and equivalences or a subset in case the time limit of 2000 seconds was hit. The simplified CNF is finally given to Lingeling. The total running time is limited to 5000 seconds, both for the sequence of blocked clause decomposition, equivalence extraction and then Lingeling, as well as for plain SAT solving by Lingeling. This is the same time limit as used in the competition but on Intel Q9550 2.83GHz instead of Intel E5440 2.83 GHz processors.

For 16 out of 81 instances with an MBS, the extract part runs into the time limit of 2000 seconds. For the other 65 instances, extract was able to reduce all equivalence classes of the partition P to singletons. Altogether, the MBSs of all 81 instances consist of 10 355 344 clauses, from which 3 313 948 (32%) were still active (non-singletons) after SAT based preprocessing. From those active variables the tool removed 66 267 backbone variables (2%) and found 343 716 equivalences (10%), due to succeeding implication checks at lines EE5 and EE6 in *EquivalenceExtraction*. Out of 397 228 SAT solver calls, 48 912 produced a solution (12%), while 241 790 were unsatisfiable (61%), and 106 526 calls (27%)

used up the budget of 100 conflicts. The *GetMultipleSolutions* algorithm was called 52 834 times in an interleaved fashion with the main equivalence extraction loop, right after the SAT calls in line EE5 and EE6, scheduled with a frequency of approximately every 4th SAT solver call. Each time it used bit-vectors of width 512 and produced altogether 27 051 008 solutions. These solutions were used to split 2 164 294 classes (90%), while the single solutions from the SAT solver calls in lines EE5 or EE6 returning a solution only split 237 943 classes (10%).

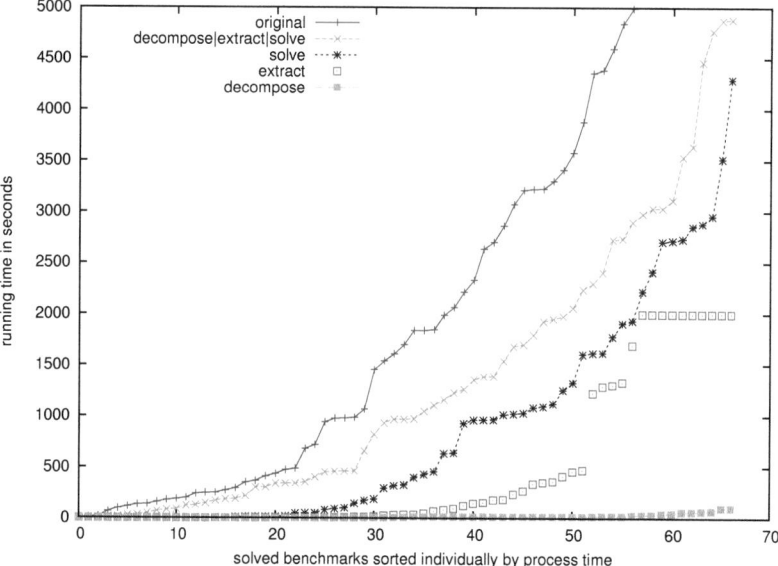

Fig. 7. Running plain SAT solving (original) and our new approach (decompose | extract | solve) on the 81 application track instances from the SAT Competition 2013 for which our decompose tools can compute a maximal blocked subset within 100 seconds. The total time limit is 5000 seconds (also used during the competition). For the anytime algorithms decompose and extract a fixed time budget was allowed of at most 100 and 2000 seconds, respectively. The rest of the time is used for solving (solve).

Fig. 7 shows the results of our experiments. Notice that Lingeling contains many advanced equivalence reasoning engines which were enabled during all runs. Our new approach is able to solve ten instances more than plain SAT solving. It requires at most 100 seconds to determine whether a formula would benefit from our approach, i.e., whether decompose can compute an MBS. If we take this time into account on the other 218 instances, Lingeling solves one instance less. So the total gain on the whole suite is nine benchmarks. Although the new approach is faster, quite some time is spent on equivalence extraction. We expect that a faster implementation of extract can further improve the results by bringing the decompose | extract | solve line closer to the solve line. Furthermore, by speeding up decompose, we can compute MBSs for more formulas thereby enlarging the number of benchmarks for which our approach is expected to be useful.

8 Conclusions

We introduced the concept of *blocked clause decompositions* and showed that any CNF formula can be decomposed into two blocked sets in polynomial time. Additionally, we showed how to obtain a maximal blocked set in polynomial time. The problem of finding a maximal blocked set with the largest cardinality is NP-hard. We presented several algorithms to obtain decompositions as well as heuristics and optimizations to make the procedures effective and efficient.

We implemented blocked clause decomposition and SAT sweeping for CNF formulas in Lingeling, winner of the application track of the SAT Competition 2013. We evaluated the proposed techniques on the benchmarks of this track. Lingeling with the new techniques was able to solve ten more instances for which our tools were able to compute a maximal blocked set within 100 seconds.

Future work will focus on improving the efficiency of our tools. In case we can obtain maximal blocked sets faster, SAT sweeping is expected to be useful for more benchmarks. Additionally, by reducing the costs of SAT sweeping, we can increase the benefit of this preprocessing technique. Finally, SAT sweeping can be implemented more effectively via inprocessing [21] — by interleaving detection of backbone variables and binary equivalences with conflict-driven search.

References

1. Krohm, F., Kuchlmann, A., Mets, A.: The use of random simulation in formal verification. In: Proceedings of the 1996 IEEE International Conference on Computer Design: VLSI in Computers and Processors, ICCD 1996, pp. 371–376 (1996)
2. Kuehlmann, A.: Dynamic transition relation simplification for bounded property checking. In: ICCAD, pp. 50–57 (2004)
3. Järvisalo, M., Biere, A., Heule, M.J.H.: Simulating circuit-level simplifications on cnf. Journal of Automated Reasoning 49(4), 583–619 (2012)
4. Parkes, A.J.: Clustering at the phase transition. In: Proceedings of AAAI 1997, pp. 340–345. AAAI Press (1997)
5. Zhang, W., Rangan, A., Looks, M.: Backbone guided local search for maximum satisfiability. In: Proceedings of IJCAI 2003, pp. 1179–1184. Morgan Kaufmann Publishers Inc., San Francisco (2003)
6. Singer, J., Gent, I.P., Smaill, A.: Backbone fragility and the local search cost peak. Journal of Artificial Intelligence Research 12, 235–270 (2000)
7. Heule, M.J.H., Järvisalo, M., Biere, A.: Revisiting hyper binary resolution. In: Gomes, C., Sellmann, M. (eds.) CPAIOR 2013. LNCS, vol. 7874, pp. 77–93. Springer, Heidelberg (2013)
8. Kullmann, O.: On a generalization of extended resolution. Discrete Applied Mathematics 96-97, 149–176 (1999)

9. Järvisalo, M., Biere, A., Heule, M.J.H.: Blocked clause elimination. In: Esparza, J., Majumdar, R. (eds.) TACAS 2010. LNCS, vol. 6015, pp. 129–144. Springer, Heidelberg (2010)
10. Liffiton, M., Sakallah, K.: Algorithms for computing minimal unsatisfiable subsets of constraints. Journal of Automated Reasoning 40(1), 1–33 (2008)
11. Belov, A., Lynce, I., Marques-Silva, J.: Towards efficient MUS extraction. AI Commun. 25(2), 97–116 (2012)
12. Junker, U.: Quickxplain: Preferred explanations and relaxations for overconstrained problems. In: AAAI, pp. 167–172 (2004)
13. Khasidashvili, Z., Nadel, A.: Implicative simultaneous satisfiability and applications. In: Eder, K., Lourenço, J., Shehory, O. (eds.) HVC 2011. LNCS, vol. 7261, pp. 66–79. Springer, Heidelberg (2012)
14. Codish, M., Fekete, Y., Metodi, A.: Compiling finite domain constraints to SAT with BEE. In: POS (2013)
15. Metodi, A., Codish, M., Stuckey, P.J.: Boolean equi-propagation for concise and efficient SAT encodings of combinatorial problems. JAIR 46, 303–341 (2013)
16. Janota, M., Lynce, I., Marques-Silva, J.: Experimental analysis of backbone computation algorithms. In: International Workshop on Experimental Evaluation of Algorithms for Solving Problems with Combinatorial Explosion, RCRA (2012)
17. van Eijk, C.A.J.: Sequential equivalence checking based on structural similarities. IEEE Trans. on CAD of Integrated Circuits and Systems 19(7), 814–819 (2000)
18. Hopcroft, J.E.: An n log n algorithm for minimizing states in a finite automaton. Technical report, Stanford, CA, USA (1971)
19. Eén, N., Sörensson, N.: An extensible sat-solver. In: Giunchiglia, E., Tacchella, A. (eds.) SAT 2003. LNCS, vol. 2919, pp. 502–518. Springer, Heidelberg (2004)
20. Biere, A.: Lingeling, Plingeling and Treengeling entering the SAT competition 2013. In: Proceedings of SAT Competition 2013 (2013)
21. Järvisalo, M., Heule, M.J.H., Biere, A.: Inprocessing rules. In: Gramlich, B., Miller, D., Sattler, U. (eds.) IJCAR 2012. LNCS (LNAI), vol. 7364, pp. 355–370. Springer, Heidelberg (2012)

Maximal Falsifiability:
Definitions, Algorithms, and Applications

Alexey Ignatiev[1,4], Antonio Morgado[1], Jordi Planes[3], and Joao Marques-Silva[1,2]

[1] IST/INESC-ID, Lisbon, Portugal
[2] University College Dublin, Ireland
[3] Universitat de Lleida, Spain
[4] ISDCT SB RAS, Irkutsk, Russia
{aign,ajrm}@sat.inesc-id.pt, jplanes@diei.udl.cat, jpms@ucd.ie

Abstract. Similarly to Maximum Satisfiability (MaxSAT), Minimum Satisfiability (MinSAT) is an optimization extension of the Boolean Satisfiability (SAT) decision problem. In recent years, both problems have been studied in terms of exact and approximation algorithms. In addition, the MaxSAT problem has been characterized in terms of Maximal Satisfiable Subsets (MSSes) and Minimal Correction Subsets (MCSes), as well as Minimal Unsatisfiable Subsets (MUSes) and minimal hitting set dualization. However, and in contrast with MaxSAT, no such characterizations exist for MinSAT. This paper addresses this issue by casting the MinSAT problem in a more general framework. The paper studies *Maximal Falsifiability*, the problem of computing a subset-maximal set of clauses that can be simultaneously falsified, and shows that MinSAT corresponds to the complement of a largest subset-maximal set of simultaneously falsifiable clauses, i.e. the solution of the *Maximum Falsifiability* (MaxFalse) problem. Additional contributions of the paper include novel algorithms for Maximum and Maximal Falsifiability, as well as minimal hitting set dualization results for the MaxFalse problem. Moreover, the proposed algorithms are validated on practical instances.

1 Introduction

Maximum and Minimum Satisfiability (resp. MaxSAT and MinSAT) are two well-known optimization extensions of Boolean Satisfiability (SAT) (e.g. [30,34,39]). While the goal of MaxSAT is to compute an assignment that *maximizes* the number of satisfied clauses, the goal of MinSAT is to compute an assignment that *minimizes* the number of satisfied clauses. Besides the plain versions, where all clauses are *soft* and so relaxable, both MaxSAT and MinSAT admit weighted versions as well as the existence of hard clauses, i.e. clauses that *must* be satisfied. MinSAT has been studied since the mid 90s [8,9,27,37], with the original focus being on the computational complexity of the problem and on approximation algorithms. In recent years there has been a renewed interest in MinSAT, with the focus being on branch-and-bound and iterative algorithms, but also on encodings of MinSAT to MaxSAT [5,6,21,28,31,33,34,45].

Like MaxSAT, MinSAT finds a growing number of practical applications (e.g. [13, 14,16,19,23,26]), and it has also been used in complexity characterizations of other problems (e.g. [2,15,18,20]). More importantly, given a MaxSAT problem where the soft clauses are all unit, complementing the soft clauses gives a MinSAT problem. As shown in recent work (e.g. [6, 34] among others), the resulting optimization problems can be fairly different, and so reducing MaxSAT to MinSAT can in some settings produce problem instances that are easier to solve. As a result, one can expect the integration of MinSAT algorithms in portfolios of MaxSAT algorithms in the near future.

MaxSAT has been extensively studied in the context of reasoning about inconsistent sets of constraints. It is well-known that each MaxSAT solution represents a largest Maximal Satisfiable Subset (MSS) [12, 36]. The complement of an MSS is a Minimal Correction Subset (MCS), i.e. a subset-minimal relaxation of a formula that renders the formula satisfiable. Moreover, another well-known result is that each MCS is a minimal hitting set of the Minimal Unsatisfiable Subsets (MUSes), and each MUS is a minimal hitting set of the MCSes [10, 12, 36, 43]. In contrast, and despite the vast body of work on MinSAT, similar results for the case of MinSAT are non-existent.

This paper addresses this issue and conducts a more comprehensive characterization of the MinSAT problem. The main contributions of the paper can be summarized as follows. First, the paper introduces *Maximal Falsifiability*, which represents the problem of computing subset-maximal sets of simultaneously falsifiable clauses. Second, the paper addresses MinSAT from the perspective of the largest maximal falsifiable solution based on the connection between MinSAT solutions and the so-called *Maximum Falsifiability* (MaxFalse) solutions. Third, the paper develops algorithms for Maximal and Maximum Falsifiability, thereby indirectly developing novel algorithms for the MinSAT problem. Moreover, and for the case of plain maximal falsifiability, the paper shows that it can be reduced to the maximal independent set problem. Thus, well-known linear time algorithms for maximal independent set [25] can be used for computing a single maximal falsifiability solution. Similarly, algorithms for the enumeration of maximal independent set [24, 29] can be used for enumerating maximal falsifiability solutions. In addition, the paper also shows that a minimal hitting set relationship, which for the case of maximal satisfiability relates MCSes and MUSes [10, 12, 36, 43], also exists for the case of maximal falsifiability. Thus, enumeration problems related with Maximal Falsifiability can be tackled by hitting set dualization, similarly to what has been done in the context of maximal satisfiability [10, 36]. Finally, the paper presents some preliminary results on both Maximal and Maximum Falsifiability algorithms.

The paper is organized as follows. Section 2 introduces the basic definitions and notation used throughout the paper. Section 3 introduces the Maximal and Maximum Falsifiability problems as well as related computational problems. Section 4 develops algorithms for Maximal Falsifiability, whereas Section 5 develops algorithms for Maximum Falsifiability (and so for MinSAT). Theoretical results for enumeration problems and minimal hitting sets are presented in Section 6. Section 7 provides experimental results for Maximal and Maximum Falsifiability, and Section 8 concludes the paper. Appendix A presents a list of acronyms used in the paper followed by Appendix B containing pseudo-codes of some of the algorithms proposed in the paper.

2 Preliminaries

This section briefly introduces the definitions used throughout. Additional standard definitions can be found elsewhere (e.g. [11]). Boolean formulas are represented in calligraphic font, $\mathcal{F}, \mathcal{M}, \mathcal{S}, \mathcal{T}, \mathcal{U}, \mathcal{W}, \mathcal{F}', \ldots$ A Boolean formula in conjunctive normal form (CNF) is defined as a finite set of finite sets of literals. Where appropriate, a CNF formula will also be understood as a conjunction of disjunctions of literals, where each disjunction represents a *clause* and a literal is a variable or its complement. The variables of formula $\mathcal{F}$ are denoted by $\text{var}(\mathcal{F})$. Variables are represented by $X = \{x, y, z, x_1, y_1, z_1, \ldots\}$ and literals by $\{l, l_1, l_2, \ldots\}$. The clauses of a formula are represented by $\{c, c_1, c_2, \ldots\}$. A literal l is called *pure* in formula $\mathcal{F}$ if there is a clause in formula $\mathcal{F}$ containing l but no clause in $\mathcal{F}$ that contains a complementary literal $\neg l$. An assignment is a map $\mathcal{A} : \text{var}(\mathcal{F}) \mapsto \{0, 1\}$. A clause is satisfied by an assignment if one of its literals is assigned value 1. A model of $\mathcal{F}$ is an assignment that satisfies all clauses in $\mathcal{F}$.

The standard definitions of MaxSAT are assumed (e.g. [30]). Moreover, the following definitions also apply. Given a CNF formula $\mathcal{F}$, sets of clauses $\mathcal{S}$, $\mathcal{S} \subseteq \mathcal{F}$, and $\mathcal{C}$, $\mathcal{C} = \mathcal{F} \setminus \mathcal{S}$, are called a *Maximal Satisfiable Subset* (MSS) and a *Minimal Correction Subset* (MCS), respectively, if $\mathcal{S}$ is satisfiable and $\forall_{c \in \mathcal{C}}$ set $\mathcal{S} \cup \{c\}$ is unsatisfiable. A set of clauses $\mathcal{U}$, $\mathcal{U} \subseteq \mathcal{F}$, is called a *Minimal Unsatisfiable Subset* (MUS) if $\mathcal{U}$ is unsatisfiable and $\forall_{c \in \mathcal{U}}$ set $\mathcal{U} \setminus \{c\}$ is satisfiable. The reader is referred to [12, 36] for further details. In the context of MaxSAT and MinSAT, a formula $\mathcal{F}$ is viewed as a 2-tuple $(\mathcal{H}, \mathcal{R})$, where $\mathcal{H}$ denotes the *hard* clauses, which must be satisfied, and $\mathcal{R}$ denotes the *soft* (or *relaxable*) clauses. A weight can be associated with each clause, such that hard clauses have a special weight $\top$. Hence, the weight function is a map $w : \mathcal{H} \cup \mathcal{R} \rightarrow \{\top\} \cup \mathbb{N}$, such that $\forall_{c \in \mathcal{H}} w(c) = \top$ and $\sum_{c \in \mathcal{R}} w(c) < \top$. If no weight function is specified, it is assumed that $\forall_{c \in \mathcal{R}} w(c) = 1$.

The paper also considers a number of optimization problems in graphs. Given an undirected graph $\mathcal{G} = (V, E)$, an *Independent Set* (IS) is a set $I \subseteq V$ such that $\forall_{u,v \in I}, (u, v) \notin E$. A *vertex cover* is a set $C \subseteq V$ such that $\forall_{(u,v) \in E}, u \in C \vee v \in C$. Finally, a *clique* (or complete subgraph) is a set $L \subseteq V$ such that $\forall_{u,v \in L}, u \neq v \Rightarrow (u, v) \in E$. Given an independent set $I \subseteq V$, a well-known result is that $V \setminus I$ is a vertex cover of $\mathcal{G}$ and I is a clique of $\mathcal{G}^C$, the complemented graph. The *Maximum Independent Set* (MIS) problem consists in computing an IS of largest size. The *Maximal Independent Set* (MxIS) problem consists in computing a subset-maximal IS. Both problems can be generalized to the case when a weight is associated with each vertex. More importantly, given the above relationships between ISes, VCes and cliques, solutions of the MIS and MxIS problems also represent, respectively, solutions for the *Minimum Vertex Cover* (MVC) and a *Minimal Vertex Cover* (MnVC) of graph of a graph $\mathcal{G}$, as well as a *Maximum Clique* (MaxClique) and a *Maximal Clique* (MxClique) of the complemented graph $\mathcal{G}^C$. A well-known result is that a maximal independent set can be computed in linear time [25]. The topic of enumeration of maximal independent sets has also been extensively studied (e.g. [1, 24, 29, 44]).

3 Maximal and Maximum Falsifiability

This section starts by introducing the plain maximal and maximum falsifiability problems. In this case, $\mathcal{H} = \emptyset$ and so $\mathcal{F} = \mathcal{R}$, i.e. all clauses are soft (and so relaxable) and their cost is 1. Generalizations of the basic problems are considered later in this section.

Definition 1 (All-Falsifiable). *A set of clauses $\mathcal{U}$ is* All-Falsifiable *if there exists a truth assignment $\mathcal{A}$ such that $\mathcal{A}$ falsifies all clauses in $\mathcal{U}$.*

Proposition 1. *A set of clauses $\mathcal{U}$ is all-falsifiable iff all the literals of $\mathcal{U}$ are pure.*

Proof. Let $\mathcal{U}$ be all-falsifiable. Assume, that not all the literals of $\mathcal{U}$ are pure. This means that there exist a literal l and clauses c_i and c_j in $\mathcal{U}$ such that $l \in c_i$ and $\neg l \in c_j$. But every complete truth assignment $\mathcal{A}$ satisfies at least one of these clauses, because literals l and $\neg l$ cannot be falsified simultaneously. Hence, our initial assumption — that not all the literals of $\mathcal{U}$ are pure — must be false.

Let all the literals of $\mathcal{U}$ be pure. And let us choose a complete assignment $\mathcal{A}$ in the following way: $\mathcal{A}(\text{var}(l)) = \neg l$, $\forall_{l \in \mathcal{U}}$. Then assignment $\mathcal{A}$ falsifies all clauses of $\mathcal{U}$, i.e. $\mathcal{U}$ is all-falsifiable. □

Definition 2 (MFS). *Given a formula $\mathcal{F}$, a Maximal Falsifiable Subset (MFS) of $\mathcal{F}$ is a subset $\mathcal{M} \subseteq \mathcal{F}$ such that:*
1. *$\mathcal{M}$ is all-falsifiable.*
2. *For any subformula $\mathcal{P}$, $\mathcal{F} \supseteq \mathcal{P} \supsetneq \mathcal{M}$, $\mathcal{P}$ is not all-falsifiable.*

Definition 3 (Maximum Falsifiability). *Given a formula $\mathcal{F}$, Maximum Falsifiability (MaxFalse) denotes the problem of computing the largest (in terms of the number of clauses) MFS of $\mathcal{F}$.*

Definition 4 (Minimum Satisfiability). *Given a formula $\mathcal{F}$, Minimum Satisfiability (MinSAT) is the problem of computing the smallest number of simultaneously satisfied clauses of $\mathcal{F}$ (while the other clauses of $\mathcal{F}$ are falsified).*

Proposition 2. *$\mathcal{M}$ represents a MaxFalse solution iff $\mathcal{F} \setminus \mathcal{M}$ represents a MinSAT solution.*

Notice that the proof of Proposition 2 is quite trivial and, thus, is omitted here. Nevertheless, Proposition 2 indicates that, in addition to recent algorithms for MinSAT [5, 28, 31, 33, 34], possible alternatives include dedicated algorithms for the MaxFalse problem, and also solutions based on the enumeration of MFSes.

Besides MFSes, additional minimal sets are of interest. One example is a minimal set of clauses which, if removed from $\mathcal{F}$, yield an all-falsifiable set of clauses.

Definition 5 (MCFS). *Given a formula $\mathcal{F}$, a Minimal Correction (for Falsifiability) Subset (MCFS) is a set $\mathcal{C} \subseteq \mathcal{F}$ such that:*
1. *$\mathcal{F} \setminus \mathcal{C}$ is all-falsifiable.*
2. *$\forall_{c \in \mathcal{C}}, \mathcal{F} \setminus (\mathcal{C} \setminus \{c\})$ is not all-falsifiable.*

Definition 6 (MNFS). *Given a formula $\mathcal{F}$, a Minimal Non-Falsifiable Subset (MNFS) is a set $\mathcal{N} \subseteq \mathcal{F}$ such that:*
1. *$\mathcal{N}$ is not all-falsifiable.*
2. *$\forall_{c \in \mathcal{N}}, \mathcal{N} \setminus \{c\}$ is all-falsifiable.*

Example 1. Consider the following formula:

$$F \triangleq \underset{c_1}{(x_1)} \wedge \underset{c_2}{(\bar{x}_1)} \wedge \underset{c_3}{(\bar{x}_1 \vee x_2)} \wedge \underset{c_4}{(\bar{x}_2)} \wedge \underset{c_5}{(x_3)}$$

The sets $\{c_2, c_3, c_5\}$, $\{c_1, c_4\}$, and $\{c_1, c_2\}$ denote, respectively, examples of an MFS, an MCFS and an MNFS.

A relevant result is the relationship between plain maximal falsifiability and maximal independent sets. Given $\mathcal{F}$, let $\mathcal{G} = (V, E)$ be an undirected graph such each clause of $\mathcal{F}$ is represented by a vertex of $\mathcal{G}$. Moreover, there exists an edge between two vertices iff the corresponding clauses have complemented literals. Clearly (see Proposition 1) clauses with complemented literals *cannot* be simultaneously falsified. Hence, an MFS of $\mathcal{F}$ represents a MxIS of $\mathcal{G}$ and a MxClique of the complemented graph. Moreover, an MCFS corresponds to an MnVC of $\mathcal{G}$. Thus, for plain maximal falsifiability, an MFS can be computed in linear time [25].

The relationship between MFSes and MxISes yields a somewhat straightforward hitting set relationship. For any maximal independent set I, $V \setminus I$ represents a minimal vertex cover. An immediate observation is:

Proposition 3. *Given a graph $\mathcal{G} = (V, E)$ with a set of MnVCes $\mathbb{C}$, the minimal hitting sets of $\mathbb{C}$ are the edges of $\mathcal{G}$ and the minimal hitting sets of the edges of $\mathcal{G}$ are the MnVCes $\mathbb{C}$ of $\mathcal{G}$.*

As a result, for the case of plain maximal falsifiability the following holds:

Proposition 4. *Let $\mathcal{F}$ be a set of soft clauses. Then:*
- *The MNFSes of $\mathcal{F}$ are the minimal hitting sets of the MCFSes $\mathcal{F}$ and vice-versa.*
- *Each MNFS of $\mathcal{F}$ consists of exactly two clauses and represents an edge in the graph $\mathcal{G}$ defined above.*
- *The number of MNFSes of $\mathcal{F}$ is $\mathcal{O}(m^2)$, where m denotes the number of clauses in $\mathcal{F}$.*

Reductions of MaxClique to MaxSAT and MinSAT are well-known (e.g. [32]). For example, such reductions also allow solving MIS, MVC, with MaxSAT (and MinSAT) algorithms. A *new* encoding of MIS into MinSAT can be devised, which does not use hard clauses. Given an undirected graph $\mathcal{G} = (V, E)$, one can construct a set of clauses $\mathcal{F}$ such that each vertex $v_i \in V$ is represented by a clause $c_i \in \mathcal{F}$. For each edge $e = (v_i, v_j)$ a new variable x_e is introduced in $\mathcal{F}$ such that $x_e \in c_i$ and $\neg x_e \in c_j$.

Example 2. Consider the graph $\mathcal{G} = (V, E)$, with $V = \{v_1, v_2, v_3, v_4\}$ and $E = \{(v_1, v_2), (v_1, v_3), (v_2, v_3), (v_2, v_4)\}$, shown in Figure 1a. Each vertex v_i is represented by a clause c_i and for each edge (v_i, v_j) a new variable x_{v_i, v_j} is introduced. The graph can be represented by a set of clauses $\mathcal{F}$ (Figure 1b) in the following way: $c_1 = x_{v_1,v_2} \vee x_{v_1,v_3}$, $c_2 = \neg x_{v_1,v_2} \vee x_{v_2,v_3} \vee x_{v_2,v_4}$, $c_3 = \neg x_{v_1,v_3} \vee \neg x_{v_2,v_3}$, $c_4 = \neg x_{v_2,v_4}$. A maximal independent set of $\mathcal{G}$ corresponds to an MFS of $\mathcal{F}$.

We now consider other formulations of maximal falsifiability, where $\mathcal{H} \neq \emptyset$ and where each soft clause c is associated a non-unit weight. As a result, a weight is also associated with each MFS, MCFS and MNFS.

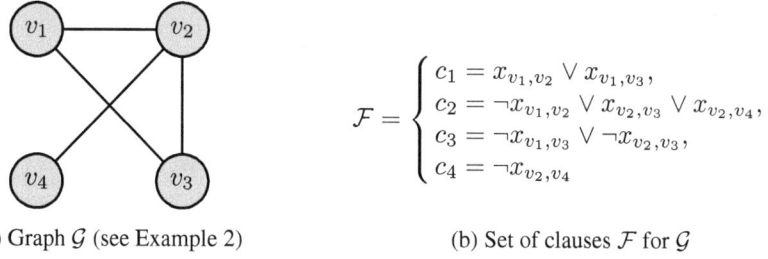

(a) Graph $\mathcal{G}$ (see Example 2)   (b) Set of clauses $\mathcal{F}$ for $\mathcal{G}$

Fig. 1. From maximal independent set to maximal falsifiability

Similar to the MaxSAT case, the problems considered for MaxFalse/MinSAT are plain ($\mathcal{H} = \emptyset$ and unit weights), partial ($\mathcal{H} \neq \emptyset$ and unit weights), weighted ($\mathcal{H} = \emptyset$ and arbitrary weights), and partial weighted ($\mathcal{H} \neq \emptyset$ and arbitrary weights) Max-False/MinSAT. Observe that these definitions follow earlier work for the concrete case of MinSAT (e.g. [34]).

MFSes for (partial) (weighted) maximal falsifiability problems are defined similarly to plain case, but $\mathcal{H}$ is required to be satisfied for the truth assignment that identifies the MFS. Moreover, the weighted versions of the MaxFalse and MinSAT problems are defined as follows.

Definition 7 (Partial Weighted Maximum Falsifiability). *Given a formula $\mathcal{F}$, with hard clauses $\mathcal{H}$, $\mathcal{H}$ is satisfiable, and soft clauses $\mathcal{R}$, Maximum Falsifiability (Max-False) denotes the problem of computing the MFS of $\mathcal{F}$ with the largest weight.*

Definition 8 (Partial Weighted Minimum Satisfiability). *Given a formula $\mathcal{F}$, with hard clauses $\mathcal{H}$ and soft clauses $\mathcal{R}$, Minimum Satisfiability (MinSAT) is the problem of computing a subset of clauses of $\mathcal{R}$ with the smallest weight, that together with $\mathcal{H}$ are simultaneously satisfiable (while the other clauses of $\mathcal{R}$ are falsified).*

A simple observation is that although weights can be associated with MFSes, MCFSes and MNFSes, their number is independent of the weight function (e.g. [41]).

For the cases where $\mathcal{H} \neq \emptyset$, the problems of computing MFSes and MxISes are no longer equivalent. Observe that, when $\mathcal{H} \neq \emptyset$, finding an MFS becomes NP-hard. A proof is immediate, since we can reduce SAT to MaxFalse: $\mathcal{H}$ corresponds to the original clauses and there are no soft clauses. Section 6 revisits the difference between MFSes and MxISes in the case $\mathcal{H} \neq \emptyset$, and also general minimal hitting results.

4 Algorithms for Maximal Falsifiability

As indicated in Section 3, there are linear time algorithms for plain maximal falsifiability, while the general case of the problem is NP-hard. Since there are several encodings of MinSAT into MaxSAT (e.g. [21,31,45]), these encodings can be also used for solving the maximal falsifiability problem. One of the most effective encodings of MinSAT is the so-called $\top$-encoding[1]. It consists in negating each soft clause c of the formula,

---

[1] The reader is referred to [21] for the details of $\top$-encoding.

Algorithm 1. Basic linear search (BLS)

```
 1  Function BLS(F = H ∪ R)
 2   │  (st, A) ← SAT(H)                      # initial SAT call
 3   │  if st = false then
 4   │   └  return (false, ∅)
 5   │  C ← R
 6   │  FilterFalsifiedClauses(H, C, A)
 7   │  foreach c ∈ C do                      # trying to falsify each clause
 8   │   │  (st, A) ← SAT(H ∪ {¬c})
 9   │   │  if st = true then
10   │   │   │  H ← H ∪ {¬c}
11   │   │   │  C ← C \ {c}
12   │   │   └  FilterFalsifiedClauses(H, C, A)
13   └  return (true, R \ C)
```

which results in constructing a group of unit clauses $g = \{\neg c\}$. Group g is then relaxed by a relaxation variable r and made hard, while the clause $\neg r$ is added to the soft part of the formula.

Let $\mathcal{F}$ be a CNF formula, and $\mathsf{T}\text{-Enc}(\mathcal{F})$ be its T-encoding into MaxSAT. Observe that there is a one to one correspondence between an MFS of $\mathcal{F}$ and an MSS of $\mathsf{T}\text{-Enc}(\mathcal{F})$, an MCFS of $\mathcal{F}$ and an MCS of $\mathsf{T}\text{-Enc}(\mathcal{F})$ and, finally, an MNFS of $\mathcal{F}$ and an MUS of $\mathsf{T}\text{-Enc}(\mathcal{F})$. Moreover, the size of an MFS of $\mathcal{F}$ equals the size of the corresponding MSS of $\mathsf{T}\text{-Enc}(\mathcal{F})$, and similarly for MCFSes/MCSes and MNFSes/MUSes of $\mathcal{F}$ and $\mathsf{T}\text{-Enc}(\mathcal{F})$, respectively. Thus, one approach for finding an MFS of formula $\mathcal{F}$ is to find an MSS (or its complement — MCS) of $\mathsf{T}\text{-Enc}(\mathcal{F})$, e.g. with recently proposed algorithms for computing MCSes [38, 42]. Nevertheless, this paper proposes instead *native* algorithms for both maximal and maximum falsifiability.

Let $\mathcal{H}$ and $\mathcal{R}$ denote the hard and soft clauses of $\mathcal{F}$, respectively. To find an MFS of $\mathcal{F}$, one needs to determine a subset of $\mathcal{R}$ that is a maximally all-falsifiable set, subject to the models of $\mathcal{H}$. Therefore, during the search it is necessary to call a SAT oracle.

Algorithm 1 shows the pseudo-code of the *Basic Linear Search* (*BLS*) algorithm for the general case of maximal falsifiability, inspired on algorithms for MCSes [38, 42]. Given a $\mathcal{H}$ and $\mathcal{R}$, denoting the hard and soft clauses of $\mathcal{F}$, the algorithm finds an MFS $\mathcal{M}$, $\mathcal{M} \subseteq \mathcal{R}$, of formula $\mathcal{F}$. Algorithm 1 is based on the connection between MinSAT and MaxFalse and at first finds a solution of the minimal satisfiability problem for $\mathcal{F}$, i.e. an MCFS $\mathcal{C}$, $\mathcal{C} \subset \mathcal{R}$, and then uses it to compute the complementary MFS $\mathcal{M} = \mathcal{R} \setminus \mathcal{C}$. First, Algorithm 1 checks whether the hard part of the formula is satisfiable or not (see line 3). If it is not, the BLS algorithm returns an empty MFS. Otherwise, it initializes the correction set $\mathcal{C}$ to be equal to $\mathcal{R}$ (line 5). At each iteration of the main loop (lines 7–12) Algorithm 1 tries to reduce $\mathcal{C}$ by removing a single clause $c \in \mathcal{C}$. This is done by checking whether clause c can be falsified together with

Algorithm 2. MaxFalse Binary Search (MFBS)

1 **Function** MFBS($\mathcal{F} = \mathcal{H} \cup \mathcal{R}$)
2     $(\mathcal{F}_w, R, W) \leftarrow (\mathcal{H}, array[\mathcal{R}.\text{size}()], array[\mathcal{R}.\text{size}()])$
3   **foreach** $(c_i, w_i) \in \mathcal{R}$ **do**
4        $(R[i], W[i]) \leftarrow (r_i, w_i)$ # r_i fresh relaxation variable
5   **foreach** $l_{i_j} \in c_i$ **do** $\mathcal{F}_w \leftarrow \mathcal{F}_w \cup \{(\neg l_{i_j} \vee r_i)\}$
6     $(\lambda, \mu, last\mathcal{A}) \leftarrow (\text{ComputeLB}(\mathcal{R}), \text{ComputeUB}(\mathcal{F}_w), \emptyset)$
7   **while** $\lambda \neq \mu$ **do**
8        $\kappa \leftarrow \lfloor \frac{\lambda + \mu}{2} \rfloor$
9        $(\text{st}, \mathcal{A}) \leftarrow \text{SAT}(\mathcal{F}_w \cup \text{CNF}(\sum_{i=0}^{\mathcal{R}.size()-1} W[i] \times R[i] \leq \kappa))$
10   **if** st = true **then** $(last\mathcal{A}, \mu) \leftarrow (\mathcal{A}, \text{GetSolution}(\mathcal{R}, \mathcal{A}))$
11   **else** $\lambda \leftarrow \text{SubSetSum}(W, \kappa)$
12   **return** Falsified($\mathcal{R}, last\mathcal{A}$)

clauses that were falsified at previous iterations (line 8). A possible improvement of the BLS algorithm is that instead of removing just one clause c from $\mathcal{C}$ per iteration, one can filter all clauses from $\mathcal{C}$ that were falsified by each SAT call. This is done by calling a function FilterFalsifiedClauses($\mathcal{H}, \mathcal{C}, \mathcal{A}$) (line 6 and line 12), where $\mathcal{A}$ is a model of $\mathcal{H} \cup \{\neg c\}$ returned by the oracle. Every clause falsified by $\mathcal{A}$ is removed from $\mathcal{C}$, and its negation is then made hard (added to $\mathcal{H}$). Note that calling the function FilterFalsifiedClauses($\mathcal{H}, \mathcal{C}, \mathcal{A}$) can significantly reduce the number of SAT calls.

5 Algorithms for Maximum Falsifiability

A solution to the MaxFalse problem can be obtained by computing a solution to the MinSAT problem (Proposition 2). On the other hand, and as mentioned in Section 4 several encodings have been proposed to translate MinSAT into MaxSAT. Thus, the MaxFalse problem can be computed by encoding the problem into MaxSAT. This paper proposes instead *native* algorithms for the MaxFalse problem.

The three algorithms proposed are based on iteratively calling a SAT solver, to determine if a subset of the soft clauses with a maximum current cost exists. The idea is similar to the classical iterative SAT-based MaxSAT solvers. Initially each soft clause is relaxed by associating to the clause a relaxation variable (a fresh Boolean variable). This process of relaxing a soft clause, guarantees that whenever a soft clause is satisfied by an assignment, then its associated relaxation variable is assigned true. In each iteration a constraint is added to the formula sent to the SAT solver, in order to force a current maximum cost on the set of relaxation variables assigned true. The current cost of each iteration depends on the bounds being refined, either a lower bound, an upper bound or both. The three algorithms proposed correspond to the three types of search possible (to refine the bounds): Binary search (MFBS) (which refines both an upper and a lower bound); Linear search starting from a lower bound (named Linear search UNSAT-SAT,

MFLSUS); and Linear search starting from an upper bound (named Linear search SAT-UNSAT, MFLSSU). In the following the pseudo-code of the Binary search algorithm is presented and described, while the pseudo-codes of the Linear search algorithms are presented in appendix B.

Algorithm 2 shows the pseudo-code of the *MaxFalse Binary Search (MFBS)* algorithm for maximum falsifiability. First, Algorithm 2 obtains a working formula $\mathcal{F}_w$ by relaxing all the soft clauses in $\mathcal{R}$ together with all the hard clauses. In this case, the relaxation of the soft clauses is not the usual relaxation as in MaxSAT. Instead, the algorithm follows the relaxation of soft clauses as in the Model-Guided algorithm [21] for MinSAT. A fresh relaxation variable is associated with the original soft clause, and a set of binary clauses is added to the working formula, each containing the negation of a literal of the soft clause, and the associated relaxation variable (line 5).

The algorithm proceeds by computing an initial lower and upper bound in line 6. The upper bound is computed by calling the SAT solver on the working formula with preferences set for the relaxation variables, that is the relaxation variables are prefered to be falsified. Then the sum of weights of the relaxation variables set to true corresponds to the upper bound.

The lower bound is computed by a greedy heuristic. Each variable is associated with two sums: the sum of weights of the soft clauses where the variable appears as a positive literal, and the sum of weights of the soft clauses where the variable appears as a negative literal. The minimum value of the two sums is obtained, and associated with the variable, as the minimum weight necessary to satisfy due to an assignment to the variable. Then the maximum among all variables is computed and added to the lower bound. Afterwards the clauses associated to the variable with the maximum value are processed by deleting all clauses associated to the minimum sum. The process is repeated until there are no more variables.

Lines 7-11 present the main loop of the MFBS algorithm. In each iteration the algorithm computes a value κ in the middle of the bounds, and makes a call to the SAT solver with the working formula $\mathcal{F}_w$ together with a constraint (encoded into CNF) enforcing the maximum allowed cost to be at most κ. If the SAT solver returns true, then the satisfying assignment is recorded and the upper bound μ is updated accordingly. If the SAT solver returns false, then the lower bound is updated to the next allowed weight considering the set of weights. Such weight is obtained by the SubSetSum() function similar to [3].

The algorithm iterates until both bounds are the same (line 7), and returns a set of soft clauses falsified by the last assignment with function Falsified() in line 12.

6 Minimal Hitting Sets and Enumeration Problems

One of the most important practical applications of the Maximal Satisfiability problem is enumeration of MUSes of a CNF formula. The idea of the method is based on the well-known relationship of minimal hitting set duality between MCSes and MUSes: each MCS (MUS) of a CNF formula is a minimal hitting set (or a *minimal set cover*) of the complete set of MUSes (MCSes) of the formula. The corresponding theoretical results were considered in [12, 43]. Enumeration of MUSes based on enumerating MCSes was done in [10, 36, 42]. The duality relationship between MCSes and MUSes was also used for solving the SMUS problem in [22, 35]. The approach did not consist in enumerating all MCSes and MUSes — instead, in order to get a lower bound on the size of the smallest MUS, only some MCSes were computed.

This section proves that the relationship of a minimal hitting set duality also exists for the case of Maximal Falsifiability, i. e. between MCFSes and MNFSes. The corresponding assertions are presented in the form of theorems. Two auxiliary propositions are used in the proofs. Hereinafter, letters $\mathcal{M}$, $\mathcal{N}$, and $\mathcal{C}$ are used to denote an MFS, an MNFS, and an MCFS of a CNF formula, respectively. The complete sets of MFSes, MNFSes and MCFSes of a CNF formula $\mathcal{F}$ are denoted by $\mathbb{M}(\mathcal{F})$, $\mathbb{N}(\mathcal{F})$, and $\mathbb{C}(\mathcal{F})$.

Proposition 5. *Formula $\mathcal{F}$ is not all-falsifiable iff it contains at least one MNFS.*

Proof. Such an MNFS can be constructed by a simple algorithm that finds a pair of clauses in $\mathcal{F}$ that contain a complemented literal. The opposite is trivial. □

Proposition 6. *A set of clauses $\mathcal{U}$, $\mathcal{U} \subseteq \mathcal{F}$, is all-falsifiable iff there is an MCFS $\mathcal{C}$ such that $\mathcal{U} \cap \mathcal{C} = \emptyset$.*

Proof. It follows from the fact that for any all-falsifiable subset $\mathcal{U}$, $\mathcal{U} \subseteq \mathcal{F}$, there is an MFS $\mathcal{M}$ such that $\mathcal{U} \subseteq \mathcal{M} \subseteq \mathcal{F}$. By definition, for any MFS $\mathcal{M}$ there exists a complementary MCFS $\mathcal{C} = \mathcal{F} \setminus \mathcal{M}$. It is not hard to see that $\mathcal{U} \cap \mathcal{C} = \emptyset$. □

Theorem 1. *Subformula $\mathcal{C}$, $\mathcal{C} \subset \mathcal{F}$, is an MCFS iff $\mathcal{C}$ is a minimal hitting set of $\mathbb{N}(\mathcal{F})$.*

Proof. Proposition 5 implies that subformula $\mathcal{C}$ is a hitting set of $\mathbb{N}(\mathcal{F})$ iff the complementary subformula $\mathcal{M} = \mathcal{F} \setminus \mathcal{C}$ is all-falsifiable (otherwise, $\mathcal{M}$ contains at least one MNFS that is not hit by $\mathcal{C}$).

Let $\mathcal{C} \subset \mathcal{F}$ be a *minimal* hitting set of $\mathbb{N}(\mathcal{F})$. This means that $\mathcal{M}$ is all-falsifiable, and $\forall_{c \in \mathcal{C}}$ formula $\mathcal{C} \setminus \{c\}$ is not a hitting set of $\mathbb{N}(\mathcal{F})$. Assume, that $\mathcal{M}$ is not an MFS of $\mathcal{F}$, i. e. $\exists_{c \in \mathcal{C}}$ such that $\mathcal{M} \cup \{c\}$ is still all-falsifiable. This implies that $\mathcal{C} \setminus \{c\}$ is a hitting set of $\mathbb{N}(\mathcal{F})$ — contradiction. Hence, $\mathcal{M}$ is an MFS and $\mathcal{C}$ is MCFS of $\mathcal{F}$.

Let $\mathcal{C} \subset \mathcal{F}$ be an MCFS of formula $\mathcal{F}$. Then the complementary subformula $\mathcal{M}$ is an MFS, and $\mathcal{C}$ is a hitting set of $\mathbb{N}(\mathcal{F})$. Assume, that $\mathcal{C}$ is not a minimal hitting set of $\mathbb{N}(\mathcal{F})$. Then $\exists_{c \in \mathcal{C}}$ such that $\mathcal{C} \setminus \{c\}$ is still a hitting set of $\mathbb{N}(\mathcal{F})$. This means that its complementary subformula $\mathcal{M} \cup \{c\}$ is all-falsifiable. However, this contradicts the fact that $\mathcal{M}$ is an MFS of $\mathcal{F}$. Therefore, $\mathcal{C}$ is a minimal hitting set of $\mathbb{N}(\mathcal{F})$. □

Theorem 2. *Subformula $\mathcal{N}$, $\mathcal{N} \subseteq \mathcal{F}$, is an MNFS iff $\mathcal{N}$ is a minimal hitting set of $\mathbb{C}(\mathcal{F})$.*

Proof. Proposition 6 implies that subformula $\mathcal{N}$ is not all-falsifiable iff $\mathcal{N}$ has a nonempty intersection with all the MCFSes of $\mathcal{F}$, i. e. $\mathcal{N}$ is a hitting set of $\mathbb{C}(\mathcal{F})$.

Let $\mathcal{N}$ be an MNFS of formula $\mathcal{F}$. Irreducibility of $\mathcal{N}$ ensures that any subformula $\mathcal{N}'$, $\mathcal{N}' \subset \mathcal{N}$, is an all-falsifiable formula. Hence, by Proposition 6, $\mathcal{N}'$ does not *hit* all the MCFSes of $\mathcal{F}$. Thus, $\mathcal{N}$ is a minimal hitting set of $\mathbb{C}(\mathcal{F})$.

Let $\mathcal{N}$ be a minimal hitting set of $\mathbb{C}(\mathcal{F})$. This means that $\forall_{c \in \mathcal{N}}$ formula $\mathcal{N} \setminus \{c\}$ does not hit all the MCFSes of $\mathcal{F}$, i. e. there is an MCFS $\mathcal{C}$ such that $\mathcal{N} \setminus \{c\} \cap \mathcal{C} = \emptyset$. Hence, $\mathcal{N} \setminus \{c\}$ is a subset of MFS $\mathcal{M} = \mathcal{F} \setminus \mathcal{C}$, and, therefore, is all-falsifiable. By definition, subformula $\mathcal{N}$ is an MNFS of $\mathcal{F}$. □

Observe that the proofs of the propositions presented above make use only of the general definitions of an MFS, MCFS, and MNFS described in Section 3. Therefore, the propositions hold for both plain and partial maximal falsifiability.

It should be noted that in contrast to Maximal Satisfiability, for the case of Maximal Falsifiability it can be more helpful to enumerate MNFSes instead of MCFSes. A set of MNFSes can give us a lower bound on the size of each MCFS and, hence, an upper bound on the optimal value for MaxFalse. Therefore, this can be used to bootstrap algorithms that refine an upper bound (see Section 5).

Observe that there is no correspondence between computing MFSes and MxISes for the case $\mathcal{H} \neq \emptyset$ because of the different interpretations of the hard constraints. Although the maximal independent set problem does not consider a concept of a hard constraint (in this sense computing an MFS is a more general problem than computing an MxIS), one can consider the *weighted* version of the problem. While for the case of partial maximal falsifiability each clause $c \in \mathcal{H}$ must be *satisfied*, vertices with a high weight in the weighted maximal independent set problem are preferable to be *independent*. Hence, there is no translation from one problem into another similar to the one described[2] in Section 3.

Nevertheless, it is trivial that an MNFS of a partial formula cannot contain more than two clauses. And, in contrast to the plain case, formulas with hard clauses may have MNFSes that contain just one clause. This fact is shown below.

Proposition 7. *Let $\mathcal{F}$ be a pair of sets of clauses $(\mathcal{H}, \mathcal{R})$, where clauses of $\mathcal{H}$ are hard while clauses of $\mathcal{R}$ are soft (relaxable). Then if there exists a subset of clauses $\mathcal{W} \subseteq \mathcal{R}$ such that $\mathcal{H} \models \mathcal{W}$, then $\mathcal{W}$ is included into all MCFSes of $\mathcal{F}$.*

Proof. Proof by contradiction. Let $\mathcal{W}$ be a subset of $\mathcal{R}$ such that $\mathcal{H} \models \mathcal{W}$. Assume, that there exists MCFS $\mathcal{C}$ such that $\mathcal{W} \not\subseteq \mathcal{C}$. This means that an MFS $\mathcal{M} = \mathcal{R} \setminus \mathcal{C}$ intersects $\mathcal{W}$, i.e. $\mathcal{M} \cap \mathcal{W} \neq \emptyset$. Entailment $\mathcal{H} \models \mathcal{W}$ means that each clause $c \in \mathcal{W}$ is satisfied by all models of $\mathcal{H}$. By definition, all clauses of $\mathcal{M}$ can be falsified simultaneously by some model of $\mathcal{H}$, Therefore, $\mathcal{M} \cap \mathcal{W} = \emptyset$ — contradiction. □

Corollary 1. *Let $\mathcal{F}$ be a pair of sets of clauses $(\mathcal{H}, \mathcal{R})$, where clauses of $\mathcal{H}$ are hard while clauses of $\mathcal{R}$ are soft (relaxable). Then if there exists a subset of clauses $\mathcal{W} \subseteq \mathcal{R}$ such that $\mathcal{H} \models \mathcal{W}$, then for any clause $c_i \in \mathcal{W}$ set $\{c_i\}$ is an MNFS of $\mathcal{F}$.*

Proof. Implied by Proposition 7 and Theorem 2. □

Now we can extend Proposition 4 to the case of partial maximal falsifiability, i.e. the number of all MNFSes of $\mathcal{F} = \mathcal{H} \cup \mathcal{R}$ is $\mathcal{O}(m^2)$, where m is the number of clauses of $\mathcal{R}$. This implies that enumeration of MNFSes can be feasible and, thus, reasonable for both enumerating MCFSes and bootstrapping the algorithms for MaxFalse that refine an upper bound.

Proposition 8. *For partial maximal falsifiability, the number of all MNFSes of a formula is less than m^2, where m is the number of soft clauses of the formula.*

---
[2] Recall that the connection between plain maximal falsifiability and maximal independent set in Section 3 established the correspondence between *independent* vertices and clauses that can be *simultaneously falsified*.

Proof. It is trivial that the number of all MNFSes is bounded by the number of all pairs of soft clauses since each MNFS of the formula contains at most 2 clauses. □

7 Experimental Results

This section describes the experimental results obtained for Maximal Falsifiability as well as for Maximum Falsifiability. The first section shows a comparison on the quality of the solution obtained for Maximal Falsifiability. Then section two presents a study on the performance of the algorithms proposed for Maximum Falsifiability.

The algorithms described in this paper were implemented in C++ using incremental SAT solvers. The experiments were performed on an HPC cluster, with quad-core Intel Xeon E5450 3 GHz nodes with 32 GB of memory. In order to evaluate the performance of the algorithms in *real* industrial problems (not random nor crafted problems), all the Industrial Partial MaxSAT and Industrial Weighted Partial benchmarks from the MaxSAT Evaluation 2013[3] were collected. The collected MaxSAT benchmarks were transformed into MaxFalse instances by selecting the ones that only contained unit soft clauses and by negating the unit literals on those instances. A total of 935 MaxFalse instances were obtained.

As explained in Section 4, a different alternative to Maximal/Maximum Falsifiability consists in transforming the MaxFalse instance by encoding it into MaxSAT via for example the $\top-$encoding, and then computing a MCS/MaxSAT of the resulting MaxSAT instance. In our experiments, whenever we compare with this encoding approach, since the original instances only contain unit soft clauses, then no aditional variables or clauses are added, and this corresponds to solving MaxSAT on the original instances obtained from the MaxSAT Evaluation.

7.1 Maximal Falsifiability

The BLS Algorithm 1 of Section 4 was implemented in a tool *mxlFalse*. The underlying SAT solver of the maximumFalse tool is the Minisat 2.2 [17].

This section studies the quality of the solutions obtained. The cost of the MCFSes obtained with mxlFalse is compared against the value of the upper bound heuristic of Section 5, as well as against the cost of the MCSes obtained by mcsls2 [38] (an efficient MCS extractor) after transforming the instance into MaxSAT.

In the experiments both the mxlFalse and mcsls2 were set to enumerate MCFSes and MCFS (respectively) for 3 min, whereupon the minimum cost MCFS/MCS was obtained. The results obtained were then divided by the optimum cost, and the values were plotted in the scatter plots of Figure 2. Figure 2 (a) compares the value of mxlFalse (divided by the optimum cost) and the value obtained by the upper bound (divided by the optimum cost). It can be seen from the scatter plot that in the vast majority of cases the value of mxlFalse is closer to 1 (thus, closer to the optimum) than the value of the upper bound (UB). In particular all the instances in the left hand side of the plot.

Figure 2 (b) compares the value of mxlFalse (divided by the optimum cost) and the value obtained by mcsls2 (divided by the optimum cost). In this case, mcsls2 produces

---
[3] http://maxsat.ia.udl.cat/

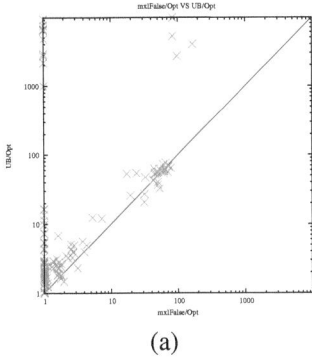 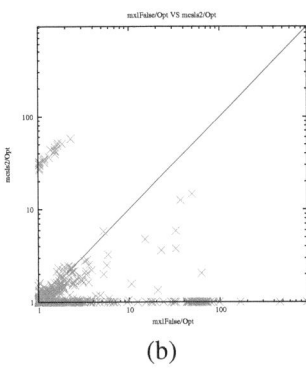

Fig. 2. (a) scatter plot between mxlfalse and ub (b) scatter plot between mxlfalse and mcsls2

solutions closer to the optimum, but nevertheless there are instances that mcsls2 is 10 times over the optimum while mxlFalse is very close. In such situations, it would be worthwhile to additionally consider running mxlFalse.

7.2 Maximum Falsifiability

The Maximum False algorithms proposed in Section 5 were implemented in a tool called *maximumFalse*. Namely, the following algorithms were implemented: binary search (maximumFalse-b), linear search unsat-sat (maximumFalse-lsus) and linear search sat-unsat (maximumFalse-lssu). This section presents results on the performance of the previous algorithms running for 1800 seconds with 4GB of memory limit. The underlying SAT solver of the maximumFalse tool is the Glucose SAT solver [7].

Figure 3 presents a cactus plot for the previous algorithms on the MaxFalse benchmarks considered. From the figure it can be seen that binary search (maximumFalse-b) is much better than the linear search approaches (maximumFalse-lsus/-lssu), while the linear search unsat-sat outperforms (slighty) the linear search sat-unsat.

Figure 3 also shows the running times for two core-guided MaxSAT algorithms running on the original MaxSAT instances. Namely, we consider bcd2 [40] and wpm1 [4] (2012 version). As expected, the core-guided MaxSAT approaches outperform maximumFalse algorithms. Note that the MaxSAT algorithms result from over a decade of research, while in this paper we are proposing a more general framework for MaxFalse. Also, it is unknown in the literature how to take advantage of core-guided algorithms natively in MaxFalse algorithms, whether if it is even possible.

Nevertheless, we considered the use of virtual best solvers (VBS) between the maximumFalse solvers and the core-guided algorithms. Interestingly, the VBSes considering maximumFalse solvers consistently outperform their counterpart without the maximumFalse solvers. For example, vbs-wpm1-maximumFalse is able to solver over 100 more instances than wpm1 alone.

Such results indicate that porfolio approaches for MaxSAT solver can benefit from the inclusion of maximumFalse solvers.

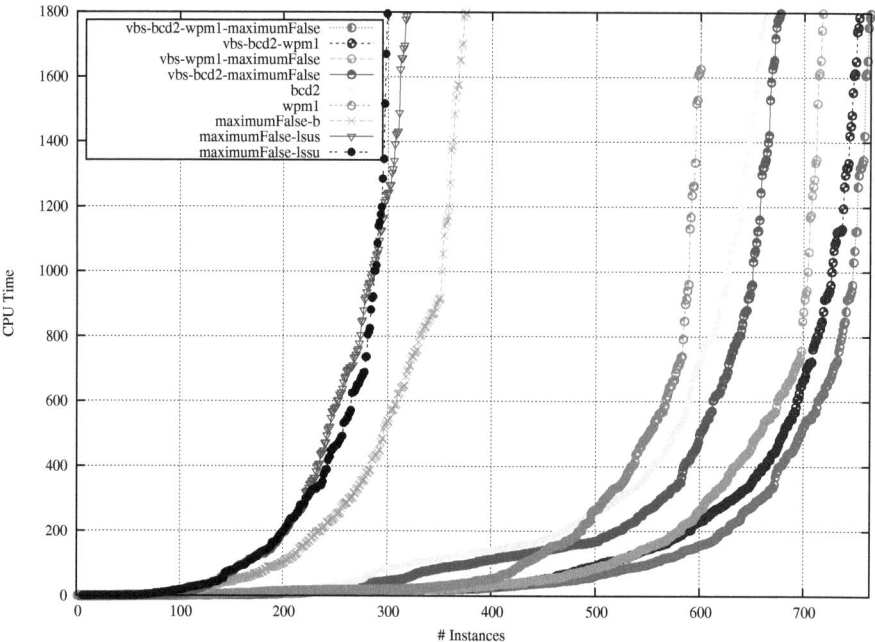

Fig. 3. Cactus plot

8 Conclusions

Motivated by the recent interest in MinSAT, this paper develops a comprehensive characterization of this problem, which follows the one developed earlier for MaxSAT. To achieve this goal, the paper introduces the problems of maximum and maximal falsifiability. The case of plain maximal falsifiability is shown to correspond to the computation of a maximal independent set in an undirected graph. Also, the paper develops a reduction of maximal independent set into maximal falsifiability (and so to minimal satisfiability), which does not involve hard clauses. Moreover, as pointed out, maximal falsifiability can be viewed as a more general formulation (with respect to maximal independent set), as it allows hard clauses to be considered. Maximal falsifiability is also used to introduce a number of new concepts: maximal falsifiable subsets (MSFes), minimal correction for falsifiability subsets (MCFSes), and minimal non-falsifiability subsets (MNFSes). In addition, the paper develops native algorithms for both maximal and maximum falsifiability, namely algorithms for computing one MFS and for solving the MaxFalse problem, and shows how these problems can be solved by reduction to MaxSAT. Finally, minimal hitting set duality between MCFSes and MNCSes is proven for the general (partial) case. The experimental results are interesting in that algorithms for maximal/maximum falsifiability show promise to be used in portfolios of algorithms for maximal/maximum satisfiability.

The work described in the paper opens a significant number of research directions. Concrete examples include additional algorithms for computing MFSes and for MaxFalse, the integration of MaxFalse algorithms in portfolios of MaxSAT algorithms, among others.

Acknowledgments. This work is partially supported by SFI PI grant BEACON (09-/IN.1/I2618), FCT grants ATTEST (CMU-PT/ELE/0009/2009) and POLARIS (PTDC-/EIA-CCO/123051/2010), INESC-ID's multiannual PIDDAC funding PEst-OE/EE-I/LA0021/2011, and by Spanish MICINN Project ARINF (TIN2009-14704-C03-01).

References

1. Akkoyunlu, E.A.: The enumeration of maximal cliques of large graphs. SIAM J. Comput. 2(1), 1–6 (1973)
2. Angel, E., Bampis, E., Gourvès, L.: On the minimum hitting set of bundles problem. Theor. Comput. Sci. 410(45), 4534–4542 (2009)
3. Ansótegui, C., Bonet, M.L., Levy, J.: A new algorithm for weighted partial maxsat. In: AAAI (2010)
4. Ansótegui, C., Bonet, M.L., Levy, J.: Sat-based maxsat algorithms. Artif. Intell. 196, 77–105 (2013)
5. Ansotegui, C., Li, C.M., Manya, F., Zhu, Z.: A SAT-based approach to MinSAT. In: CCIA, pp. 185–189 (2012)
6. Argelich, J., Li, C.-M., Manyà, F., Zhu, Z.: MinSAT versus MaxSAT for optimization problems. In: Schulte, C. (ed.) CP 2013. LNCS, vol. 8124, pp. 133–142. Springer, Heidelberg (2013)
7. Audemard, G., Simon, L.: Predicting learnt clauses quality in modern sat solvers. In: IJCAI, pp. 399–404 (2009)
8. Avidor, A., Zwick, U.: Approximating MIN k-SAT. In: Bose, P., Morin, P. (eds.) ISAAC 2002. LNCS, vol. 2518, pp. 465–475. Springer, Heidelberg (2002)
9. Avidor, A., Zwick, U.: Approximating MIN 2-SAT and MIN 3-SAT. Theory Comput. Syst. 38(3), 329–345 (2005)
10. Bailey, J., Stuckey, P.J.: Discovery of minimal unsatisfiable subsets of constraints using hitting set dualization. In: Hermenegildo, M.V., Cabeza, D. (eds.) PADL 2004. LNCS, vol. 3350, pp. 174–186. Springer, Heidelberg (2005)
11. Biere, A., Heule, M., van Maaren, H., Walsh, T. (eds.): Handbook of Satisfiability, Frontiers in Artificial Intelligence and Applications, vol. 185. IOS Press (2009)
12. Birnbaum, E., Lozinskii, E.L.: Consistent subsets of inconsistent systems: structure and behaviour. J. Exp. Theor. Artif. Intell. 15(1), 25–46 (2003)
13. Bourke, C., Deng, K., Scott, S.D., Schapire, R.E., Vinodchandran, N.V.: On reoptimizing multi-class classifiers. Machine Learning 71(2-3), 219–242 (2008)
14. Brihaye, T., Bruyère, V., Doyen, L., Ducobu, M., Raskin, J.-F.: Antichain-based QBF solving. In: Bultan, T., Hsiung, P.-A. (eds.) ATVA 2011. LNCS, vol. 6996, pp. 183–197. Springer, Heidelberg (2011)
15. Butman, A., Hermelin, D., Lewenstein, M., Rawitz, D.: Optimization problems in multiple-interval graphs. ACM Transactions on Algorithms 6(2) (2010)
16. Chen, T., Filkov, V., Skiena, S.: Identifying gene regulatory networks from experimental data. Parallel Computing 27(1-2), 141–162 (2001)

17. Eén, N., Sörensson, N.: An Extensible SAT-solver. In: Giunchiglia, E., Tacchella, A. (eds.) SAT 2003. LNCS, vol. 2919, pp. 502–518. Springer, Heidelberg (2004)
18. Gate, J., Stewart, I.A.: Frameworks for logically classifying polynomial-time optimisation problems. In: Ablayev, F., Mayr, E.W. (eds.) CSR 2010. LNCS, vol. 6072, pp. 120–131. Springer, Heidelberg (2010)
19. Goldstein, A., Kolman, P., Zheng, J.: Minimum common string partition problem: Hardness and approximations. Electr. J. Comb. 12 (2005)
20. Hassin, R., Monnot, J., Segev, D.: Approximation algorithms and hardness results for labeled connectivity problems. J. Comb. Optim. 14(4), 437–453 (2007)
21. Heras, F., Morgado, A., Planes, J., Marques-Silva, J.: Iterative SAT solving for minimum satisfiability. In: ICTAI, pp. 922–927 (2012)
22. Ignatiev, A., Janota, M., Marques-Silva, J.: Quantified maximum satisfiability: A core-guided approach. In: Järvisalo, M., Van Gelder, A. (eds.) SAT 2013. LNCS, vol. 7962, pp. 250–266. Springer, Heidelberg (2013)
23. Interian, Y., Corvera, G., Selman, B., Williams, R.: Finding small unsatisfiable cores to prove unsatisfiability of QBFs. In: ISAIM (2006)
24. Johnson, D.S., Papadimitriou, C.H., Yannakakis, M.: On generating all maximal independent sets. Inf. Process. Lett. 27(3), 119–123 (1988)
25. Karp, R.M., Wigderson, A.: A fast parallel algorithm for the maximal independent set problem. J. ACM 32(4), 762–773 (1985)
26. Kohli, R., Krishnamurti, R., Jedidi, K.: Subset-conjunctive rules for breast cancer diagnosis. Discrete Applied Mathematics 154(7), 1100–1112 (2006)
27. Kohli, R., Krishnamurti, R., Mirchandani, P.: The minimum satisfiability problem. SIAM J. Discrete Math. 7(2), 275–283 (1994)
28. Kügel, A.: Natural Max-SAT encoding of Min-SAT. In: Hamadi, Y., Schoenauer, M. (eds.) LION 6 2012. LNCS, vol. 7219, pp. 431–436. Springer, Heidelberg (2012)
29. Lawler, E.L., Lenstra, J.K., Kan, A.H.G.R.: Generating all maximal independent sets: NP-hardness and polynomial-time algorithms. SIAM J. Comput. 9(3), 558–565 (1980)
30. Li, C.M., Manya, F.: MaxSAT, hard and soft constraints. In: Biere, et al. (eds.) [11], pp. 613–631
31. Li, C.M., Manyà, F., Quan, Z., Zhu, Z.: Exact MinSAT solving. In: Strichman, O., Szeider, S. (eds.) SAT 2010. LNCS, vol. 6175, pp. 363–368. Springer, Heidelberg (2010)
32. Li, C.M., Quan, Z.: Combining graph structure exploitation and propositional reasoning for the maximum clique problem. In: ICTAI, pp. 344–351 (2010)
33. Li, C.M., Zhu, Z., Manya, F., Simon, L.: Minimum satisfiability and its applications. In: IJCAI, pp. 605–610 (2011)
34. Li, C.M., Zhu, Z., Manya, F., Simon, L.: Optimizing with minimum satisfiability. Artif. Intell. 190, 32–44 (2012)
35. Liffiton, M.H., Mneimneh, M.N., Lynce, I., Andraus, Z.S., Marques-Silva, J., Sakallah, K.A.: A branch and bound algorithm for extracting smallest minimal unsatisfiable subformulas. Constraints 14(4), 415–442 (2009)
36. Liffiton, M.H., Sakallah, K.A.: Algorithms for computing minimal unsatisfiable subsets of constraints. J. Autom. Reasoning 40(1), 1–33 (2008)
37. Marathe, M.V., Ravi, S.S.: On approximation algorithms for the minimum satisfiability problem. Inf. Process. Lett. 58(1), 23–29 (1996)
38. Marques-Silva, J., Heras, F., Janota, M., Previti, A., Belov, A.: On computing minimal correction subsets. In: IJCAI (to appear 2013)
39. Morgado, A., Heras, F., Liffiton, M.H., Planes, J., Marques-Silva, J.: Iterative and core-guided maxsat solving: A survey and assessment. Constraints 18(4), 478–534 (2013)

40. Morgado, A., Heras, F., Marques-Silva, J.: Improvements to core-guided binary search for maxsat. In: Cimatti, A., Sebastiani, R. (eds.) SAT 2012. LNCS, vol. 7317, pp. 284–297. Springer, Heidelberg (2012)
41. Morgado, A., Liffiton, M., Marques-Silva, J.: MaxSAT-based MCS enumeration. In: Biere, A., Nahir, A., Vos, T. (eds.) HVC. LNCS, vol. 7857, pp. 86–101. Springer, Heidelberg (2013)
42. Nöhrer, A., Biere, A., Egyed, A.: Managing SAT inconsistencies with HUMUS. In: VaMoS, pp. 83–91 (2012)
43. Reiter, R.: A theory of diagnosis from first principles. Artif. Intell. 32(1), 57–95 (1987)
44. Tsukiyama, S., Ide, M., Ariyoshi, H., Shirakawa, I.: A new algorithm for generating all the maximal independent sets. SIAM J. Comput. 6(3), 505–517 (1977)
45. Zhu, Z., Li, C.-M., Manyà, F., Argelich, J.: A new encoding from MinSAT into MaxSAT. In: Milano, M. (ed.) CP 2012. LNCS, vol. 7514, pp. 455–463. Springer, Heidelberg (2012)

A List of Acronyms

CNF Conjunctive Normal Form
SAT Boolean Satisfiability
IS Independent Set
MIS Maximum Independent Set
MxIS Maximal Independent Set
MaxClique Maximum Clique
MxClique Maximal Clique
MnVC Minimal Vertex Cover
MVC Minimum Vertex Cover
VC Vertex Cover

MaxSAT Maximum Satisfiability
MCS Minimal Correction Subset
MSS Maximal Satisfiable Subset
MUS Minimal Unsatisfiable Subset
MaxFalse Maximum Falsifiability
MCFS Minimal Correction (for Falsifiability) Subset
MFS Maximal Falsifiable Subset
MinSAT Minimum Satisfiability
MNFS Minimal Non-Falsifiable Subset

B Linear Search Algorithms for Maximum Falsifiability

Algorithm 3. MaxFalse Linear Search SAT-UNSAT(MFLSSU)

1 **Function** MFLSSU($\mathcal{F} = \mathcal{H} \cup \mathcal{R}$)
2 $\quad (\mathcal{F}_w, R, W) \leftarrow (\mathcal{H}, array[\mathcal{R}.\text{size}()], array[\mathcal{R}.\text{size}()])$
3 $\quad$ **foreach** $(c_i, w_i) \in \mathcal{R}$ **do**
4 $\quad\quad (R[i], W[i]) \leftarrow (r_i, w_i)$ $\quad\quad$ # r_i fresh relaxation variable
5 $\quad\quad$ **foreach** $l_{i_j} \in c_i$ **do** $\mathcal{F}_w \leftarrow \mathcal{F}_w \cup \{(\neg l_{i_j} \vee r_i)\}$
6 $\quad (\text{st}, \mu, lastA) \leftarrow (\text{true}, \text{ComputeUB}(\mathcal{F}_w), \emptyset)$
7 $\quad$ **while** st = true **do**
8 $\quad\quad (\text{st}, \mathcal{A}) \leftarrow \text{SAT}(\mathcal{F}_w \cup \text{CNF}(\sum_{i=0}^{\mathcal{R}.size()-1} W[i] \times R[i] < \mu))$
9 $\quad\quad$ **if** st = true **then** $(lastA, \mu) \leftarrow (A, \text{GetSolution}(\mathcal{R}, \mathcal{A}))$
10 $\quad$ **return** Falsified($\mathcal{R}, lastA$)

Algorithm 4. MaxFalse Linear Search UNSAT-SAT(MFLSUS)

1 **Function** MFLSUS($\mathcal{F} = \mathcal{H} \cup \mathcal{R}$)
2     $(\mathcal{F}_w, R, W) \leftarrow (\mathcal{H}, array[\mathcal{R}.\text{size}()], array[\mathcal{R}.\text{size}()])$
3   **foreach** $(c_i, w_i) \in \mathcal{R}$ **do**
4        $(R[i], W[i]) \leftarrow (r_i, w_i)$ # r_i fresh relaxation variable
5   **foreach** $l_{i_j} \in c_i$ **do** $\mathcal{F}_w \leftarrow \mathcal{F}_w \cup \{(\neg l_{i_j} \vee r_i)\}$
6     $(\text{st}, \lambda, last\mathcal{A}) \leftarrow (\text{false}, \texttt{ComputeLB}(\mathcal{R}), \emptyset)$
7   **while** st = false **do**
8        $(\text{st}, \mathcal{A}) \leftarrow \texttt{SAT}(\mathcal{F}_w \cup \texttt{CNF}(\sum_{i=0}^{\mathcal{R}.size()-1} W[i] \times R[i] \leq \lambda))$
9   **if** st = false **then** $\lambda \leftarrow \texttt{SubSetSum}(W, \lambda)$
10   **else** $last\mathcal{A} \leftarrow \mathcal{A}$
11   **return** Falsified($\mathcal{R}, last\mathcal{A}$)

Solving Geometry Problems Using a Combination of Symbolic and Numerical Reasoning

Shachar Itzhaky[1], Sumit Gulwani[2], Neil Immerman[3], and Mooly Sagiv[1]

[1] Tel Aviv University, Israel
[2] Microsoft Research, Redmond, WA, USA
[3] University of Massachusetts, Amherst, MA, USA

Abstract. We describe a framework that combines deductive, numeric, and inductive reasoning to solve geometric problems. Applications include the generation of geometric models and animations, as well as problem solving in the context of intelligent tutoring systems.

Our novel methodology uses (i) deductive reasoning to generate a partial program from logical constraints, (ii) numerical methods to evaluate the partial program, thus creating geometric models which are solutions to the original problem, and (iii) inductive synthesis to read off new constraints that are then applied to one more round of deductive reasoning leading to the desired deterministic program. By the combination of methods we were able to solve problems that each of the methods was not able to solve by itself.

The number of nondeterministic choices in a partial program provides a measure of how close a problem is to being solved and can thus be used in the educational context for grading and providing hints.

We have successfully evaluated our methodology on 18 Scholastic Aptitude Test geometry problems, and 11 ruler/compass-based geometry construction problems. Our tool solved these problems using an average of a few seconds per problem.

Keywords: geometry, reasoning, synthesis.

1 Introduction

We describe a framework for solving geometry problems, which are specified as a tuple of inputs, outputs, and constraints between them. The perfect solution to a geometry problem consists of a constructive model generation procedure along with a proof of its correctness. The synthesized procedure can allow models to be constructed in real time, within an interactive environment, as the input points are moved — this has applications in both dynamic geometry environments [WCY05] and animations.

This class of problems is a subset of CLP(R) [JMSY92] — Constraint Logic Programming with Real variables. Current implementation of CLP(R) in Prolog has limited support for non-linear constraints [swi]. Gröbner bases suggest a technique for solving ruler-and-compass construction problems, but this technique relies on expressing the constraints using polynomials [Buc98]. This is insufficient for our target domain, since problems typically contain numerical data in the form of both angles and length, requiring some use of trigonometry.

Our solver starts out by constructing a model of inputs and outputs that satisfy the constraints using a combination of symbolic and numeric reasoning. To bridge the gap between the two techniques, we use the notion of *partial programs*. A partial program is one that contains "choice" statements, meaning that certain output objects need to be chosen nondeterministically from certain loci. To evaluate these programs in practice, we use numerical methods for minimizing a non-negative function that has the value 0 iff the relevant constraints are met. These methods typically perform well when the number of dimensions is low (up to 2), so a considerable effort is invested in decreasing the search dimension. More specifically, the solver has a built-in knowledge base of geometric theorems, written as a set of Datalog rules. Given an input problem specification, the algorithm tries to identify small search spaces and splits the problem into individual search invocations of low dimension. Once all the output objects are found we have a solution to the given problem. Constructing the instance suffices to solve geometry problems from SAT exams, etc. (This typically requires computing the value of some quantity such as length, angle, area, etc, which can be read off from the model).

Perhaps more interestingly, the solver goes beyond the construction of the model in the following two ways. First, if numeric reasoning was required to constructing the model, then the solver attempts to eliminate this need in an attempt to decrease running time. The procedure works as follows: it constructs a second model for another instance of the problem in which the positions of the inputs have been perturbed. The solver next searches for equalities between distances and angles that occur in both of the constructed models, but were not mentioned in the input specification. According to theorems shown in [Hon86,GKT11], the probability that such equalities are incidental approaches zero. The solver adds these new equalities to the input constraints and solves the new problem. This elimination of numeric search produces a more efficient program, making future evaluations of instance of the same problem much faster. By an *instance* of a given problem we mean the same constraints with different values for the inputs (e.g. different lengths of segments or positions of points). Furthermore, the resulting program provides a complete, constructive solution rather than a numeric approximation. Second, once a deterministic program has been synthesized, our solver generates a proof that the program always constructs a model satisfying the constraints. Thus the correctness of the construction is automatically proved. We view a total program as a perfect solution for a given geometric problem, whereas a partial program searches for the answer. The dimension of the search spaces provides an estimation for the run-time cost of the search.

In the future we plan to use our geometric solver as a helper and tutor for geometry students. The above metric for partial programs will be useful for measuring how far a student is from a solution, and gauging the "size of hints" that students need to help them solve a given problem.

The main contributions of this paper are the following:

1. Our solver for geometric programs shows how we can combine the complementary strengths of symbolic, numeric, and inductive reasoning.
2. We introduce a non-deterministic language of partial programs for capturing partial insights about geometric constructions. Such programs have an underlying cost corresponding to the size and number of loci that must be searched numerically. This language is useful both as an intermediate data-structure for our solver, and for the user to communicate insights.
3. We provide a substantial experimental evaluation that demonstrates the efficacy of our solver. Out of the 21 questions in SAT practice tests we found freely available on the Internet, we were able to automatically solve 18. The only questions we were not able to solve are those when the size of the problem is part of the input or output (e.g. when the user is asked to determine the number of sides a given polygon has). In 6 of the problems we tested it on, the solver was able to eliminate all of the numeric search steps, thus synthesizing a very efficient program that solves a general version of the given problem.

In the following we define the format of geometry problems that we consider. We present our solver in detail. Finally we report on our experimental results.

2   Geometric Construction Problems

We begin by describing how a geometric construction problem is specified. We also define the three components of the solution to that problem, namely the model, the drawing program, and the proof that the program is correct.

The same formalism also applies to another subclass of problems, which we refer to as *measurement* problems, where a student is required to calculate some value, for example, an angle or an area.

Problem Specification; A geometry construction problem is a CSP — constraint satisfaction problem — consisting of a set $\mathcal{V}$ of variables and a set $\mathcal{C}$ of constraints. Each variable, $v \in \mathcal{V}$, denotes a real number, point, line, or circle. For pure construction problems, the variables are partitioned into input variables $\mathcal{I}$ (thought of as given with the problem) and output variables $\mathcal{O}$ (to be constructed).

For measurement problems, the distinction between inputs and outputs is not significant; instead, a set of query expressions $\mathcal{Q}$ is given, and the output is a numeric value for each such term.

Solution; The solution consists of a **model**, a **drawing program**, and a **proof of correctness**. The model is an assignment to the variables that satisfies all of the constraints $\mathcal{C}$. The drawing program is a sequence of computations. The program is proved correct for all inputs that satisfy their constraints.

3 Partial Programs

We now describe the language of partial programs, which combines imperative and declarative constructs. The solver's first main step will be to construct a partial program that is used to build the desired model.

A partial program is a sequence of instructions. Some of the construction steps require numeric search to find the relevant objects. The language of partial programs is defined by the BNF grammar shown in Figure 1. The scheme is generic, in the sense that it allows for domain-specific predicate and function symbols, denoted by P and F respectively in the grammar.

$$
\begin{aligned}
\text{Program } S &::= A_1; \ldots; A_n; \\
\text{Statement } A &::= v := F(v_1, \ldots, v_n) \mid p :\in R \mid \texttt{Assert } \varphi \\
\text{Range } R &::= G(v_1, \ldots, v_n) \mid R_1 \cap R_2 \\
\text{Constraint } \varphi &::= \gamma_1 \wedge \ldots \wedge \gamma_n \\
\text{Atom } \gamma &::= P(v_1, \ldots, v_n)
\end{aligned}
$$

Fig. 1. A language for partial programs

For geometry, We used the set of symbols shown in Table 1. These predicates and functions are very natural for two-dimensional Euclidean geometry. The functions $\texttt{line}(\ell)$, $\texttt{ray}(p, u)$, $\texttt{segment}(a, b)$, $\texttt{circle}(p, r)$, and $\texttt{disc}(p, r)$ are *primitive*, in the sense they are internally recognized by the system; the others are just names to use in logical inference rules (see 4.1 below). To re-target the framework to another domain, such as three-dimensional space, a designer may introduce other symbols, but the discussion of this goes beyond the scope of this paper.

Intuitively, the reader may find it useful to think of a partial program as a representation of partial insight into the problem, an algorithm for solving it but with a few "holes".

Example 1. A simple partial program.
1: $a := \langle 0, 0 \rangle$ // a is the origin
2: $b :\in \texttt{circle}(a, 10)$ // b is on circle of given center, radius
3: $c := \textsc{Middle}(a, b)$ // c is midpoint of segment $\overline{ab}$
4: $\texttt{Assert } c.y = 4$ // the y value of c is 4

This program looks for a point b of distance 10 from the origin, such that the midpoint of the line segment from the origin to b has height 4 above the x axis.

The first three statements specify a range of possible values for the objects to be found (in this case, the three points a, b, and c), and the assertion specifies a constraint. An assertion is different from an assignment, in the sense that it constrains properties of objects that have already been assigned.

To evaluate this program, one should search across points on the circle of radius 10 around the origin, for a point b such that $c.y = 4$ holds.

Program variables and functions are typed, and assignments must be properly typed. Thus, in a statement $v := F(v_1, \ldots, v_n)$, if the type of v is T, then F should be a function returning an object of type T, and in a statement $v :\in G(v_1, \ldots, v_n)$, G should return a set $S \subseteq T$. E.g., if v is a point ($T = R^2$), we require that $G(v_1, \ldots, v_n) \subseteq R^2$.

The Assert φ statement initiates a numeric search over variables provided in ranges above, but not yet fixed. A successful completion of the search assigns fixed values to some of these variables. Each constraint is translated to the numeric requirement that some necessarily non-negative value be minimized. For example, the constraint $c.y = 4$ is translated to "minimize $(c.y - 4)^2$".

Table 1. Notation for function and predicate symbols used for geometry

circle(O,r)	the circle centered at O with radius r
linetru(A,B)	the line through A and B
raythru(A,B)	the ray whose origin is A and goes through B
ray(A,u)	the ray whose origin is A with direction u
segment(A,B)	the line segment connecting A and B
DIST(A,B)	distance between points A and b
∠(A,B,C)	the (smaller) angle ∠ABC
∠$_{ccw}$(A,B,C)	the angle ∠ABC, measured counterclockwise
MIDDLE(A,B)	the mid-point of the segment AB
CIRCUMF(R)	the circumference of the circle R
ARCDIST(O,A,B)	the length of the arc $\widehat{AB}$ on the circle centered at O
DIAMETER(R,AB)	**true** iff AB is a diameter in circle R
INTERSECTSEGMENTS(A,B,C,D)	**true** iff AB intersects CD
COLINEAR(A,B,C)	**true** iff A, B, and C are on the same line

Running Example, Part I. Partial program to generate a regular hexagon.

The following partial program generates a regular hexagon *abcdef* given side *ab*. It first chooses a point *o* on the perpedicular bisector of *ab*. Next it draws *c* such that *cob* makes the same angle as *aob* and *oc = ob*. Next draw *d* such that *dob* makes the same angle as *aob* and *od = ob*, and so on, until point *f* is drawn. The user then asserts that ∠*foa* = ∠*aob*.

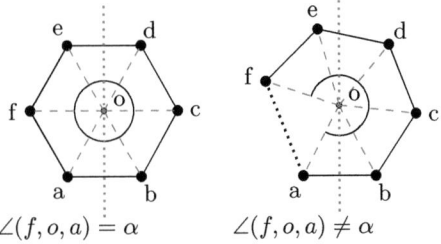

Fig. 2. A hexagon — drawn around its circumcenter; A different choice of *o* leads to a sub-optimal run

1: $o :\in \text{PERP-BISECT}(a, b)$
2: $r := |\overline{ob}|$
3: $\alpha := \angle(a, o, b)$
4: $c :\in \texttt{circle}(o, r) \cap \texttt{ray}(o, \text{ROTATE}(b - o, \alpha))$
5: $d :\in \texttt{circle}(o, r) \cap \texttt{ray}(o, \text{ROTATE}(c - o, \alpha))$
6: $e :\in \texttt{circle}(o, r) \cap \texttt{ray}(o, \text{ROTATE}(d - o, \alpha))$
7: $f :\in \texttt{circle}(o, r) \cap \texttt{ray}(o, \text{ROTATE}(e - o, \alpha))$
8: $\texttt{Assert } \angle(f, o, a) = \alpha$

This partial program relies on the insight that all sides subtend the same angle with the circumcenter of the regular hexagon, as illustrated by Figure 2. Other insights, e.g. that triangle $\triangle abo$ is equilateral, would generate simpler partial programs (see part V of this running example).

3.1 Operational Semantics

The partial program interpreter visits each non-deterministic assignment ($p :\in R$) and attempts to choose a value for p that satisfies the assertions.

To be able to use numeric methods, we interpret each assertion as a non-negative expression that is zero iff the assertion is true. We then choose those points that minimize the sum of these expressions.

For example, the assertion that two real scalar values x, y are equal is translated to the expression $(x - y)^2$ and the assertion that two vectors $\mathbf{u}, \mathbf{v} \in \mathbb{R}^2$ are perpendicular is translated to the square of their inner product, $(\mathbf{u} \cdot \mathbf{v})^2$.

Example 2. Consider the following partial program:
1: $a := (0, 10)$
2: $b := (40, 0)$
3: $c :\in \texttt{segment}(a, b)$
4: $\texttt{Assert } |\overline{ac}| = 2|\overline{bc}|$

In the assertion, $|\overline{xy}|$ denotes the distance function. We use a standard hill-climbing algorithm to find the value of c in the segment ab that minimizes the expression $|\overline{ac}| - 2|\overline{bc}|$.

Our hill-climbing procedure discretizes the search space. It partitions it into a finite number of sub-spaces and minimizes the expression among the division points. It then recursively descends to the chosen sub-space. The coarser the discretization factor, the faster the search, but the greater the chances of the search getting stuck in non-optimal local minima and thus requiring random restarts.

The interpreter is implemented using a sequential pass that keeps track of the variables that are not yet determined. It processes each Assert statement in turn by invoking numeric search. If the dimension of the combined search space is 1 at that point (space is isomorphic to $\mathbb{R}$), numeric search is done by hill-climbing. If it is 2 or more, we use nested hill-climbing, such that for every value of the first variable that has to be evaluated, we perform hill-climbing on the second variable and determine an optimum with respect to the value set for the first variable.

The model generation algorithm uses a heuristic for avoiding multi-dimensional search where possible: it iterates the variables (in the order they are defined in the program), fixing them one by one to the minimum obtained from hill-climbing. If at some point, however, the procedure encounters a non-model (the minimum of the target function is not 0), it back-tracks and try different minima for variables that have already been set.

3.2 Cost Metric for Partial Programs

We define a metric to approximate performance of partial programs. The deductive algorithm that creates the partial program tries to construct a minimal one via this metric. As part of this effort, we will consider 3 compile-time criteria:
- Combined dimension of loci being searched;
- Number of choice statements ($v :\in R$) in the program;
- Distance from a choice to its corresponding Assert.

A program with smaller dimension will always be preferred over higher dimensions. The statement counts are considered less important.

Definition 1. *The cost of a choice statement $v :\in R$ is defined in terms of a set of symbolic parameters, which represent the cost of searching various kinds of spaces (that is, there is some partial ordering between them).*
- S – if R is a segment.
- C – if R is a circle.
- Y – if R is a ray.
- S · C – if R is a disc.
- L – if R is a line.

For an R that is any finite number of points, the cost is 1.

We partition the partial program into *blocks*, where a block is a sequence of statements between two assertions.

Definition 2. *For each assertion, its* cost *is the cost of the block between it and the assertion before it (or the beginning of the program, if this is the first assertion).*

Definition 3. *The cost of a block is the product of the costs of all the choice statements in it, and the number of variables controlled by the choice statements in the block. It is a **polynomial** in the symbolic parameters.*

Definition 4. *A variable v is said to be* controlled *by a choice statement iff:*
- *It is on the left-hand side of a choice statement, $v :\in R$; or*
- *It is assigned via $v := F(v_1, \ldots, v_n)$, and there is some v_i which is itself controlled by a choice statement.*

Definition 5. *The cost of a partial program is the sum of the costs of all the* Assert *statements occurring in it.*

When we later say *dimension*, it means the degree of the cost polynomial.

Example 3. The cost of the program in Example 2 is S, because the search is over a segment, and only one variable is controlled by the choice statement.

Running Example, Part II. Consider the partial program from part I.

The choice of o is over the perpendicular bisector of the segment ab (written PERP-BISECT(a, b)) which is a line. The choices for c, d, e, f are then over the intersections of a circle in a ray, which are at most 2 each – so they are assigned a cost of 1. The set of choice-controlled variables in the block is $\{o, c, d, e, f, r, \alpha\}$. The cost is therefore 7L.

4 Solution Generation

Figure 3 shows the phases that our geometry solver follows. The first pass of deductive reasoning produces an initial partial program. This program is run with some inputs to build a model or two. If the partial program is nondeterministic, then the models produced are studied to induce additional constraints. These constraints are then used in a second pass of deductive synthesis to construct a (lower cost) program.

Most of the computational effort goes into identifying implied constraints. Part of them are identified symbolically (4.1) and some numerically (4.3).

4.1 Deductive Reasoning

Our deductive reasoning involves standard application of logic programming with Datalog (e.g., see [AHV95,GMUW09]), which is too weak by itself to solve the problem we are targeting. Later on, we combine deductive with inductive reasoning to make the method more effective. The deductive reasoning procedure builds the partial program, by first doing a single step of preprocessing and encoding, and then running inference in a loop.

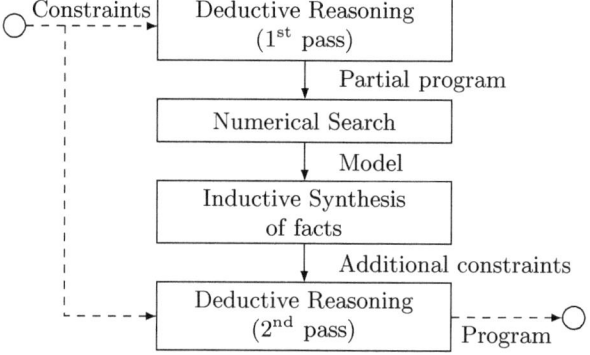

Fig. 3. Architectural diagram

Preprocessing and Encoding. Each geometric axiom in our knowledge base is originally given in the form $\varphi(\boldsymbol{U}) \to \psi(\boldsymbol{U})$ where φ and ψ are conjunctions of literals with free variables $\boldsymbol{U}$. The problem specification is a conjunction of ground literals.

The main gap between the language of geometric axioms and Datalog is the presence of function symbols. From both axioms and ground facts, we replace function symbols f of arity k via relation symbols $\tilde{f}$ of arity $k+1$. In particular, we replace each term $f(t_1, t_2, \ldots, t_k)$ by a new symbol α and we assert $\tilde{f}(t_1, t_2, \ldots, t_k, \alpha)$. If the term is a ground term then α is a constant, otherwise it is a variable. As a by-product we loose the information that α is unique, but we will see that this will not keep us from proving the required properties.

This translation may introduce variables in the head of a rule that do not occur in the body. In Datalog terminology, such a rule is *unsafe*. In the next subsection we will explain how our deductions are evaluated. We will point out that since our axioms are "acyclic", deduction remains tractable and in fact bounded, even with these unsafe rules.

We must ensure that each such unsafe variable occurs in exactly one atom. We do this by rewriting each relevant conjunction as a new invented predicate symbol and adding a new rule to define it.

Inference. Datalog programs can be efficiently evaluated using seminaïve evaluation as described in [AHV95,GMUW09]. A small extension of this method is needed when instantiating an unsafe rule, e.g., if the variable X_i occurs in the head but not the body of the rule $r(X_1, X_2, \ldots) \leftarrow \varphi$ [KR11].

We instantiate such rules, with *fresh constant symbols* for the unsafe variables. Furthermore, if a constant symbol c already exists such that the corresponding head is already in the generated set, then this instance of the rule is superfluous, so it is not instantiated.

Recall that by construction each such unsafe variable occurs in exactly one atom. This ensures that the derived atom with its fresh constant symbol exactly captures the meaning of the implicit existential quantifier.

Note that the introduction of fresh constant symbols above has the effect of introducing new objects into our system. Our current set of geometry axioms is acyclic meaning that for any input problem only a bounded number of new objects can be created.

Table 2. Axioms for explaining the running example

1 $\lvert\overline{PQ}\rvert = X \to Q \in \text{circle}(P, X)$
2 $\lvert\overline{PQ}\rvert = \lvert\overline{SQ}\rvert \to Q \in \text{Perp-Bisect}(P, S)$
3 $\angle(P, Q, S) = Y \to S \in \text{ray}(Q, \text{Rotate}(P - Q, Y))$

Running Example, Part III. We will show how the partial program from part I might be constructed automatically using this technique.

Assume we have the following declarative specification of the regular hexagon:

$$|\overline{ao}| = |\overline{bo}| = |\overline{co}| = |\overline{do}| = |\overline{eo}| = |\overline{fo}|$$
$$\angle(a,o,b) = \angle(b,o,c) = \angle(c,o,d) = \angle(d,o,e)$$
$$= \angle(e,o,f) = \angle(f,o,a)$$

Our inference system contains the axioms shown in Table 2 (For the sake of this example only, there is an underlying assumption that $\angle$ denotes a counterclockwise angle and ROTATE performs a counterclockwise rotation. This is done to keep the example simple. In practice, we use a richer set of axioms). It produces the following atoms (among others):

$$o \in \text{PERP-BISECT}(a,b);$$
$$c,d,e,f \in \texttt{circle}(o, |\overline{ao}|)$$
$$c \in \texttt{ray}(o, \text{ROTATE}(b-o, \angle(a,o,b)))$$

4.2 Query Planning

Query planning mediates deductive reasoning and numerical search: it attempts to associate a search space with variables that have not been inferred. To this end, the query planner may choose a set of input variables $\mathcal{I}'$. Note that in the case of construction problems, after the second pass it must be that $\mathcal{I}' = \mathcal{I}$ so there is no freedom, but for the first pass we are free to choose any subset.

Locus Assignment. Let P be the Datalog program representing the axioms, and $\mathbf{I}$ the set of tuples from the specification. $P(\mathbf{I})$ is the result of inference, expressed as sets of ground atoms, e.g., $r(c_1, \ldots, c_k) \in P(\mathbf{I})$.

During this phase of the computation, three relation symbols become important: $\neq$ (disequality), $\in$ (set membership), and known (indicates already-computed values).

To disambiguate these symbols occurring in derived ground atoms from their common mathematical use, we surround such atoms in quotes.

Initially, known $= \mathcal{I}'$. The 'known's are then propagated according to assignments that have been inferred. For each **output symbol** s such that 'known(s)' $\notin P(\mathbf{I})$, look for the following potential search spaces:

1. l, s.t. l is a constant and '$s \in l$', 'known(l)' $\in P(\mathbf{I})$
2. $l_1 \cap l_2$ s.t. '$l_1 \neq l_2$' $\in P(\mathbf{I})$ and

$$'s \in l_1\text{'}, 's \in l_2\text{'}, '\text{known}(l_1)\text{'}, '\text{known}(l_2)' \in P(\mathbf{I})$$

We choose the "best" locus based on the cost metric of 3.2. The best locus over all symbols is chosen and an assignment of the form '$s :\in R$' is emitted to the program. Then s is marked as known by adding 'known(s)' to $\mathbf{I}$. This process is repeated until all output symbols s have 'known(s)' $\in P(\mathbf{I})$.

Running Example, Part IV. We are given one side of the hexagon, ab. We therefore introduce 'known(a)', 'known(b)'. From these we infer (by way of deduction) that 'known(PERP-BISECT(a, b)))', and the procedure will emit the choice statement '$o :\in$ PERP-BISECT(a, b)'.

As a consequence, 'known(o)' is introduced, which makes two more objects known: $o_1 =$ 'circle$(o, |\overline{ao}|)$' and $y_1 =$ 'ray$(o,$ ROTATE$(b - o, \angle(a, o, b)))$'. Now — because both $c \in o_1$ and $c \in y_1$ are present, it will also emit:
'$c :\in$ circle$(o, |\overline{ao}|) \cup$ ray$(o,$ ROTATE$(b - o, \angle(a, o, b)))$'

The other points are traced similarly leading to the program in part I.

Assertion Assignment. The assigned search spaces define an over-approximation of the input–output relation. In order to generate a correct partial program, we need to add Assert statements. To this end, we go back to the specification, breaking it down into individual constraints. For each constraint, we identify the earliest point in the partial program at which it can be tested, that is, when all of the constraint's arguments have already been defined.

Example 4. If the locus assignment generated the associations in (a) below, and if the specification has the atoms: $|\overline{ab}| = 10$ $|\overline{ac}| = 20$ $|\overline{bc}| = 15$, then knowing only a, none of the constraints can be checked. Knowing a and b allows us to check the first constraint, so an Assert statement is inserted after line 2. Knowing a, b, and c provides the means to check the other two constraints, so another Assert is added after line 3 (see (b) below).

1: $a := (10, 0)$
2: $b :\in$ ray$(a, (1, 1)))$
3: $c :\in$ circle$(a, 20)$

(a)

1: $a := (10, 0)$
2: $b :\in$ ray$(a, (1, 1)))$
3: Assert $|ab| = 20$
4: $c :\in$ circle$(a, 20)$
5: Assert $|ac| = 20 \wedge |bc| = 15$

(b)

4.3 Inductive Synthesis

In the next phase, we try to improve the efficiency of the program generated by the first pass of deductive reasoning. To do that, we attempt to learn facts that our deductive reasoning technique fell short of inferring by reading them off the model generated by the previous phase. There is an underlying assumption that since the model contains real numbers, then if we perform computations on the values and uncover an equality — with very high probability [Hon86] this equality is not coincidental, but is in fact logically implied by the partial program (hence, by the specification) that created the model in the first place.

The new facts we reveal may then be used by the same deductive reasoning mechanism, as if they were originally given as part of the specifications. Because we now have more information, there is a chance that the second run will yield a lower-cost partial program.

Running Example, Part V. Consider the partial program for drawing the hexagon from part I. The generated model contains 7 points: 6 vertices of the hexagon (a, b, c, d, e, f) and one circumcenter (o). Among the facts learnable from the model are $|\overline{ao}| = |\overline{ab}|$ and $|\overline{bo}| = |\overline{ab}|$. Given these two facts, the deductive reasoning engine is now able to produce the following code fragment to compute the coordinates of the point o more efficiently:

1: $o :\in$ `circle`$(a, |\overline{ab}|) \cap$ `circle`$(b, |\overline{ab}|)$

Replacing line 1 of the original program with this statement would then yield a program with search dimension 0 (because there are only two points in the intersection of the two circles) instead of dimension 1 (an infinite number of points lying on the perpendicular bisector).

Note. section 4 of the technical report [IGIS12] provides a much more detailed study of this example.

5 Evaluation

We consider two kinds of benchmark examples.
- Questions found in SAT practice tests.
- Construction problems, when some elements are given and you are required to draw a new shape: a regular polygon of n sides, given one of them, a square inside a given square, a rectangle inside a given square, a square inside a given triangle, a right triangle, given its circumcircle, an equilateral triangle touching 3 given parallel lines

Appendix A contains a partial listing of SAT benchmarks. A full listing of our benchmarks can be found in [IGIS12].

5.1 Generation of Partial Programs

We show that our partial program generation scheme is very effective. We evaluate this by comparing statistics about model generation for the following cases:
- Without a partial program
- Using deductive synthesis.
- Using a combination of deductive + inductive synthesis.

Table 3 contains the statistics of time taken to generate a model and the total number of dimensions that were searched (For example, the number of dimensions for a completely unknown point is 2, while the number of dimensions for an unknown point that lies on a circle is 1). The column "O" shows the original dimension of the problem, if we were to apply numerical methods to it directly.

On the first pass, the symbolic part generates a partial program (as described in 4.1, 4.2), and the numeric part generates a model via hill-climbing search based on the partial program. The running time (in seconds) of each part is provided in columns "S" (symbolic) and "N" (numeric) below "1st pass". The resulting dimension is shown in column "R", and "k" is the maximal dimension of the individual search space associated with each `Assert` (see 3.2). Where k is lower than the total dimension, it means that the multi-dimensional search has been decomposed into several searches of lower dimension, improving performance considerably.

Table 3. Benchmark measurements

#	|O|R	k^*	1st pass Time (s) S	N	Dim. R	k^*	2nd pass Time (s) S	N
1	4|1	1	0.16	0.54	0	0	0.98	0.00
2	2|0	0	0.04	0.00	0	0		
3	4|1	1	0.14	0.35	1	1	0.13	0.36
4	6|1	1	0.22	0.12	0	0	0.40	0.00
5	8|4	1	0.35	0.24	1	1	5.19	0.11
6	6|1	1	0.38	0.84	1	1	3.23	1.63
7	4|1	1	0.09	0.02	1	1	0.12	0.02
8	4|2	1	0.38	0.02	2	1	0.42	0.02
9	8|2	2	0.64	38.13	1	1	1.86	0.62
10	14|1	1	0.73	0.53	1	1	21.16	0.54
11	12|2	1	0.63	0.86	0	0	12.17	0.01
12	8|1	1	0.22	0.02	1	1	0.59	0.02
13	4|1	1	0.18	0.06	1	1	0.18	0.06
14	6|1	1	0.06	0.03	1	1	0.10	0.03
15	10|2	1	0.29	1.20	2	1	11.93	0.98
16	7|1	1	0.53	0.01	1	1	1.41	0.02
17	8|2	1	0.27	0.47	2	1	0.54	0.46
18	10|1	1	0.20	0.04	1	1	0.70	0.03
19	6|2	1	0.23	0.08	2	1	0.31	0.08
20	8|0	0	0.14	0.00	0	0		
21	11|2	1	0.11	0.26	1	1	0.85	0.03
22	4|1	1	0.08	0.01	1	1	0.09	0.01
23	6|0	0	0.56	0.00	0	0		
24	10|2	1	0.18	0.04	2	1	0.95	0.04
25	4|1	1	0.22	0.10	1	1	0.24	0.09
26	10|2	1	0.35	0.19	2	1	0.49	0.19
27	10|2	1	0.32	0.04	2	1	1.13	0.35
28	8|3	1	0.37	0.48	3	1	0.37	0.46
29	6|1	1	0.47	0.03	1	1	0.75	0.03

* k (the *rank*) is the maximal dimension of the search space as defined in 3.2

The results of the second pass show the effect of incorporating results of inductive synthesis, that is, facts learned by querying the model generated by the first pass. In 6 of the cases, the values in the columns of "2nd pass" exhibit lower dimensions compared to the first pass. The running time of the symbolic reasoning part is higher, due to the increase in the number of formulas to process. In most cases, however, this effort is worthwhile as it leads to a faster program, reducing the running time of the numeric part.

5.2 Proof Statistics

With the deductive inference mechanism shown earlier, the average number of steps effectively used to generate the program (not including tried and failed paths) was 51.7. We had 47 axioms; each axiom was used 31.9 times on average. The average number of statements per partial program generated was 8.2.

6 Related Work

Geometry constraint solving is a long studied problem, where the goal is to find a configuration for a set of geometric objects that satisfy a given set of constraints between the geometric elements [BFH+95]. A variety of techniques have been proposed including logical inference and term rewriting [Ald88], numerical methods [Nel85], algebraic methods [Kon92], and graph based constraint solving [BFH+95]. These techniques either require some symbolic reasoning or some form of search. Our work is different from these works in two regards. First, we combine **both** symbolic reasoning and numerical search for model generation. Second, we deal with the more sophisticated problem of **constructive** model generation. While essentially an instance of CLP(R) [JMSY92], geometry has its own properties, which we use to create a specialized solver.

This paper is most closely related to some recent work in the area [GKT11]. Our methodology of program generation followed by model generation is similar and relies on the same theoretical result about geometry property testing. We add to it the incorporation of symbolic deduction, and the additional artifact of the partial program, which provides a more general answer to a given problem and also conveys some insight about the solution.

Our notion of partial programs, which combine imperative and declarative constructs for geometry constructions is similar to a recent proposal on doing so for a general purpose programming language [SL08]. Our interpretation of a partial program is based on use of numerical methods unlike use of SMT solvers [KKS12]. More significantly, we also automate the construction of a partial program from fully declarative specifications using deductive reasoning, and also refine a partial program into one that is more constructive using inductive synthesis techniques.

7 Conclusion and Future Work

We have presented a system that constructs geometric figures. It also allows insights from the user in the form of partial programs. In the case of end-users, this interactivity allows humans and machines to work together to solve complicated problems. In the educational domain, this interactivity allows students to express partial insights about a geometry construction problem, which the system can then extend to a complete solution, following the student's hint. In the future we will perform user studies both in the end-user setting and the classroom setting. We believe that the methodology we have introduced, combining deductive and inductive synthesis via partial programs, will find uses in many other domains.

References

AHV95. Abiteboul, S., Hull, R., Vianu, V.: Foundations of Databases. Addison-Wesley (1995)

Ald88. Aldefeld, B.: Variation of geometries based on a geometric-reasoning method. Computer Aided Design 20(3), 117–126 (1988)

BFH^+95. Bouma, W., Fudos, I., Hoffmann, C.M., Cai, J., Paige, R.: Geometric constraint solver. Computer-Aided Design 27(6), 487–501 (1995)

Buc98. Buchberger, B.: Applications of Gröbner bases in non-linear computational geometry. In: Janßen, R. (ed.) Trends in Computer Algebra. LNCS, vol. 296, pp. 52–80. Springer, Heidelberg (1988)

GKT11. Gulwani, S., Korthikanti, V., Tiwari, A.: Synthesizing geometry constructions. In: Programming Language Design and Implementation, PLDI (2011)

GMUW09. Garcia-Molina, H., Ullman, J.D., Widom, J.: Database systems - the complete book, 2nd edn. Pearson Education (2009)

Hon86. Hong, J.: Proving by example and gap theorems. In: FOCS, pp. 107–116. IEEE Computer Society (1986)

IGIS12. Itzhaky, S., Gulwani, S., Immerman, N., Sagiv, M.: Solving geometry problems using a combination of symbolic and numerical reasoning. Technical Report MSR-TR-2012-8, Microsoft Research (January 2012), http://www.cs.tau.ac.il/~shachar/dl/tr-2012.pdf

JMSY92. Jaffar, J., Michaylov, S., Stuckey, P.J., Yap, R.H.C.: The CLP(R) language and system. ACM Trans. Program. Lang. Syst. 14(3), 339–395 (1992)

KKS12. Köksal, A.S., Kuncak, V., Suter, P.: Constraints as control. In: ACM SIGPLAN Symposium on Principles of Programming Languages, POPL (2012)

Kon92. Kondo, K.: Algebraic method for manipulation of dimensional relationships in geometric models. Computer-Aided Design 24(3), 141–147 (1992)

KR11. Krötzsch, M., Rudolph, S.: Extending decidable existential rules by joining acyclicity and guardedness. In: Walsh, T. (ed.) IJCAI, pp. 963–968. IJCAI/AAAI (2011)

Nel85. Nelson, G.: Juno, a constraint-based graphics system. In: SIGGRAPH, pp. 235–243 (1985)

SL08. Solar-Lezama, A.: Program Synthesis by Sketching. PhD thesis, University of California, Berkeley (2008)

swi. http://www.swi-prolog.org/man/clpqr.html

WCY05. Wong, W.-K., Chan, B.-Y., Yin, S.-K.: A dynamic geometry environment for learning theorem proving. In: Proceedings of the 5th IEEE International Conference on Advanced Learning Technologies, ICALT 2005, Kaohsiung, Taiwan, July 05-08, pp. 15–17. IEEE Computer Society (2005)

A Examples of Benchmarks

This is a partial listing. The full list can be found in the Technical Report [IGIS12].

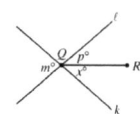

Note: Figure not drawn to scale.

4. In the figure above, lines ℓ and k intersect at point Q. If $m = 40$ and $p = 25$, what is the value of x?

(A) 15
(B) 20
(C) 25
(D) 40
(E) 65

```
dist(Q, A) = 100
dist(Q, R) = 100      Q ≠ B
Q ≠ L                 ∠ccw(B, Q, A) = 40
∠ccw(R, Q, L) = 25    middle(L, A) = Q
middle(K, B) = Q      known(Q)
known(B)              ?(A, R, L, K)
```

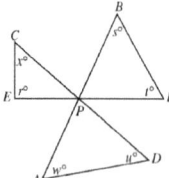

Note: Figure not drawn to scale.

7. In the figure above, $\overline{AB}$, $\overline{CD}$, and $\overline{EF}$ intersect at P. If $r = 90$, $s = 50$, $t = 60$, $u = 45$, and $w = 50$, what is the value of x?

(A) 45
(B) 50
(C) 65
(D) 75
(E) It cannot be determined from the information given.

```
∠ccw(D, A, B) = 50    ∠ccw(C, D, A) = 45
∠ccw(A, B, F) = 50    ∠ccw(B, F, E) = 60
∠ccw(F, E, C) = 90    segment(A, B) = AB
segment(C, D) = CD    P ∈ AB
P ∈ CD                segment(E, F) = EF
P ∈ EF                known(A)
known(B)              ?(C, D, E, F, P)
```

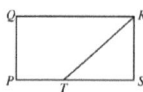

18. In the figure above, $PQRS$ is a rectangle. The area of $\triangle RST$ is 7 and $PT = \frac{2}{5} PS$. What is the area of $PQRS$?

```
∠(P, S, R) = :90:    segment(P, S) = PS
∠(S, R, Q) = :90:    T ∈ PS
∠(R, Q, P) = :90:    dist(P, S) = d
∠(Q, P, S) = :90:    dist(P, T) = k
5 · r = 2            r · d = k
known(P)             known(S)
?(R, Q, T)
```

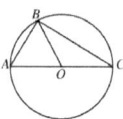

5. In the figure above, triangle ABC is inscribed in the circle with center O and diameter $\overline{AC}$. If $AB = AO$, what is the degree measure of $\angle ABO$?

(A) 15°
(B) 30°
(C) 45°
(D) 60°
(E) 90°

```
circle(O, 75) = R
A ∈ R                    A ≠ B
B ∈ R                    A ≠ C
C ∈ R                    B ≠ C
segment(A, C) = AC  O ∈ AC
dist(B, O) = d           dist(A, B) = d
known(O)                 ?(A, B, C, R)
```

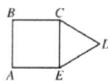

4. In the figure above, CDE is an equilateral triangle and $ABCE$ is a square with an area of 1. What is the perimeter of polygon $ABCDE$?

(A) 4
(B) 5
(C) 6
(D) 7
(E) 8

```
square(A, B, C, D)
dist(B, E) = e           known(A)
dist(C, E) = e           known(B)
dist(B, C) = e           ?(C, D, E)
```

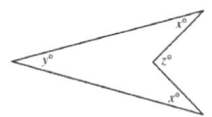

Note: Figure not drawn to scale.

12. If $x = 20$ and $y = 30$ in the figure above, what is the value of z?

(A) 60
(B) 70
(C) 80
(D) 90
(E) 100

```
∠ccw(A, B, C) = 30  known(A)
∠ccw(B, C, D) = 20  known(B)
∠ccw(D, A, B) = 20  ?(C, D)
¬colinear(A, C, D)
```

On QBF Proofs and Preprocessing

Mikoláš Janota[1], Radu Grigore[3], and Joao Marques-Silva[1,2]

[1] INESC-ID, Lisbon, Portugal
[2] University College Dublin, Ireland
[3] University of Oxford, UK

Abstract. QBFs (quantified boolean formulas), which are a superset of propositional formulas, provide a canonical representation for PSPACE problems. To overcome the inherent complexity of QBF, significant effort has been invested in developing QBF solvers as well as the underlying proof systems. At the same time, formula preprocessing is crucial for the application of QBF solvers. This paper focuses on a missing link in currently-available technology: How to obtain a certificate (e.g. proof) for a formula that had been preprocessed before it was given to a solver? The paper targets a suite of commonly-used preprocessing techniques and shows how to reconstruct certificates for them. On the negative side, the paper discusses certain limitations of the currently-used proof systems in the light of preprocessing. The presented techniques were implemented and evaluated in the state-of-the-art QBF preprocessor bloqqer.

1 Introduction

Preprocessing [24,47,46,9] and certificate generation [5,6,35,23,39,40] are both active areas of research related to QBF solving. Preprocessing makes it possible to solve many more problem instances. Certification ensures results are correct, and certificates are themselves useful in applications. In this paper we show how to generate certificates while preprocessing is used. Hence, it is now possible to certify the answers for many more problem instances than before.

QBF solvers are practical tools that address the standard PSPACE-complete problem: given a closed QBF, decide whether it is true. In principle, such solvers can be applied to any PSPACE problem, of which there are many; for example, model checking in first-order logic [50], satisfiability of word equations [43], the decision problem of the existential theory of the reals [18], satisfiability for many rank-1 modal logics [48], and so on [23,7,34]. Unlike SAT solvers (for NP problems), QBF solvers are not yet routinely used in practice to solve PSPACE problems: they need to improve.

Fortunately, QBF solvers do improve rapidly [44]. One of the main findings is that a two-phase approach increases considerably the number of instances that can be solved in practice: in the first phase, *preprocessing*, a range of fast techniques is used to simplify the formula; in the second phase, actual solving, a complete search is performed. Another recent improvement is that QBF solvers now produce *certificates*, which include the true/false answer together with a

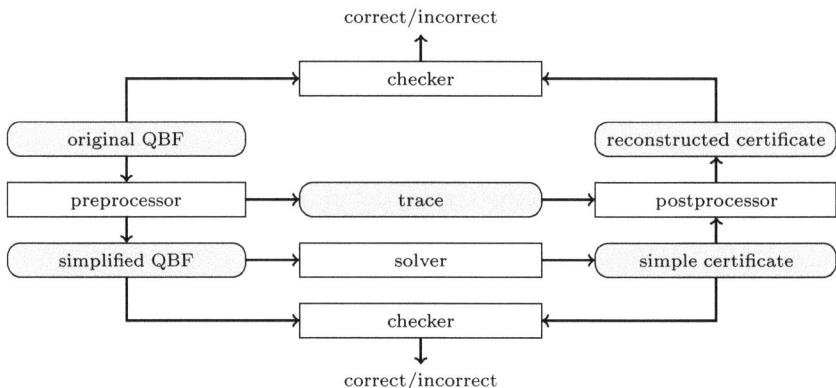

Fig. 1. Architecture

justification for it. Such a justification can be for example in the form of a proof of the given formula. Certificates ensure that answers are correct, and are sometimes necessary for other reasons. For example, certificates are used to suggest repairs in QBF-based diagnosis [25,49,45].

Clearly, both preprocessing and certificate generation are desirable. Alas, no tool-chain supports both preprocessing and certificate generation at the same time. This paper shows how to reconstruct certificates in the presence of a wide range of preprocessing techniques. In our setup (Figure 1), the preprocessor produces a simplified formula together with a *trace*. After solving, we add a postprocessing step, which uses the trace to reconstruct a certificate for the original formula out of a certificate for the simplified formula.

The contributions of this paper are the following:

- a review of many preprocessing techniques used in practice (Section 3)
- a negative result about the reconstruction of term resolution-based certificates (Section 4)
- certificate reconstruction techniques, corresponding to a wide range of formula preprocessing techniques (Section 5)
- an efficient implementation, and its experimental evaluation (Section 7)

2 Preliminaries

A *literal* is a Boolean variable or its negation. For a literal l, we write $\bar{l}$ to denote the literal *complementary* to l, i.e. $\bar{x} = \neg x$ and $\overline{\neg x} = x$; we write $\mathsf{var}(l)$ for x. A *clause* is a disjunction of literals. A formula in *conjunctive normal form* (CNF) is a conjunction of clauses. Whenever convenient, a clause is treated as a set of literals, and a CNF formula as a set of sets of clauses. Dually to a clause, a *term* is a conjunction of literals. A formula in *disjunctive normal form* (DNF) is a conjunction of terms.

For a set of variables X, an *assignment* τ is a function from X to the constants 0 and 1. We say that τ is *complete* for X if the function is total.

Substitutions are denoted as $\psi_1/x_1,\ldots,\psi_n/x_n$, with $x_i \neq x_j$ for $i \neq j$. An application of a substitution is denoted as $\phi[\psi_1/x_1,\ldots,\psi_n/x_n]$ meaning that variables x_i are simultaneously substituted with corresponding formula ψ_i in ϕ.

Quantified Boolean Formulas (QBFs) [14] extend propositional logic with quantifiers that have the standard semantics: $\forall x.\Psi$ is satisfied by the same truth assignments as $\Psi[0/x] \wedge \Psi[1/x]$, and $\exists x.\Psi$ as $\Psi[0/x] \vee \Psi[1/x]$. Unless specified otherwise, QBFs are in *closed prenex* form, i.e. in the form $\mathcal{Q}_1 x_1 \ldots \mathcal{Q}_k x_k.\phi$, where x_i form a nonrepeating sequence of variables and $\mathcal{Q}_i \in \{\exists,\forall\}$; the formula ϕ is over the variables $\{x_1,\ldots,x_k\}$. The propositional part ϕ is called the *matrix* and the rest the *prefix*. If additionally the matrix is in CNF, we say that the formula is in QCNF. A prefix $\mathcal{P}$ induces *ordering on literals* [13]: for literals l_1, l_2 we write $l_1 < l_2$ and say that l_1 is *less than* l_2 if $\mathsf{var}(l_1)$ appears before $\mathsf{var}(l_2)$ in $\mathcal{P}$.

A closed QBF is *false* (resp. *true*), iff it is semantically equivalent to the constant 0 (resp. 1). If a variable is universally quantified, we say that the variable is *universal*. For a literal l and a universal variable x such that $\mathsf{var}(l) = x$, we say that l is *universal*. Existential variable and literal are defined analogously.

2.1 QU-Resolution

QU-resolution [52] is a calculus for showing that a QCNF is false. It comprises two operations, *resolution* and *∀-reduction*. Resolution is defined for two clauses $C_1 \vee x$ and $C_2 \vee \bar{x}$ such that $C_1 \cup C_2$ does not contain complementary literals nor any of the literals x, $\bar{x}$. The *QU-resolvent* (or simply resolvent) of such clauses is the clause $C_1 \vee C_2$. The *∀-reduction* operation removes from a clause C all universal literals l for which there is *no* existential literal $k \in C$ s.t. $l < k$.

For a QCNF $\mathcal{P}.\phi$, a *QU-resolution proof* of a clause C is a finite sequence of clauses $C_1,\ldots,C_n$ where $C_n = C$ and any C_i in the sequence is part of the given matrix ϕ; or it is a QU-resolvent for some pair of the preceding clauses; or it was obtained from one of the preceding clauses by ∀-reduction. A QU-resolution proof is called a *refutation* iff C is the empty clause.

QU-resolution is a slight extension of Q-resolution [15]. Unlike QU-resolution, Q-resolution does *not* enable resolving on universal literals. While Q-resolution is on its own refutationally complete for QCNF, resolutions on universal literals are useful in certain situations (see also [21]).

2.2 Term-Resolution and Model Generation

Term-resolution is analogous to Q-resolution with the difference that it operates on terms and its purpose is to prove that a QBF is true [22]. Resolution is defined for two terms $T_1 \wedge x$ and $T_1 \wedge \bar{x}$ where $T_1 \cup T_2$ do not contain any complementary literals nor any of the literals x, $\bar{x}$; the resolvent is the term $T_1 \wedge T_2$. The *∃-reduction* operation removes from a term T all existential literals l such that there is *no* universal literal $k \in T$ with $l < k$.

Since term-resolution is defined on terms, i.e. on DNF, the *model generation* rule is introduced in order to enable generation of terms from a CNF matrix. For a QCNF $\Phi = \mathcal{P}.\phi$, a term T is generated by the model generation rule if for each clause C there is a literal l s.t. $l \in C$ and $l \in T$. Then, a *term-resolution proof* of the term T_m from Φ a is a finite sequence $T_1, \ldots, T_m$ of terms such that each term T_i was generated by the model generation rule; or it was obtained from the previous terms by ∃-reduction or term-resolution. Such proof *proves* $\mathcal{P}.\phi$ iff T_m is the empty term. (Terms are often referred to as 'cubes', especially in the context of DPLL QBF solvers that apply cube learning.) In the remainder of the article, whenever we talk about term-resolution proofs for QCNF, we mean the application of the model generation and term-resolution rule. A QCNF formula is true iff it has a term-resolution proof [22].

In this paper, both term-resolution and QU-resolution proofs are treated as connected directed acyclic graphs so that the each clause/term in the proof corresponds to some node labeled with that clause/term.

2.3 QBF as Games

The semantics of QBF can be stated as a game between an *universal* and an *existential player* [1]. The universal player assigns values to universal variables and analogously the existential player assigns values to the existential variables. A player assigns a value to a variable if and only if all variables preceding it in the prefix were assigned a value. The universal player wins if under the complete resulting assignment the underlying matrix evaluates to false and the existential player wins if the underlying matrix evaluates to true. A formula is true iff there exists a winning strategy for the existential player. The notion of strategy was formalized into *models of QBF* [16].

Definition 1 (Strategy and Model). *Let $\Phi = \mathcal{P}.\phi$ be QBF with the universal variables $u_1, \ldots, u_n$ and with the existential variables $e_1, \ldots, e_m$. A strategy M is a sequence of propositional formulas $\psi_{e_1}, \ldots, \psi_{e_m}$ such that each ψ_{e_i} is over the universal variables preceding e_i in the quantification order. We refer to the formula ψ_x as the definition of x in M.*

A strategy M is a model of Φ if and only if the following formula is true

$$\forall u_1, \ldots, u_n. \phi[\psi_{e_1}/e_1, \ldots, \psi_{e_m}/e_m]$$

i.e., $\phi[\psi_{e_1}/e_1, \ldots, \psi_{e_m}/e_m]$ is a tautology.

Notation. *Let $\Phi = \mathcal{P}.\phi$ be a QBF as in Definition 1 and $M = (\psi_{e_1}, \ldots, \psi_{e_m})$ be a strategy. For a formula ξ we write $M(\xi)$ for the formula $\xi[\psi_{e_1}/e_1, \ldots, \psi_{e_m}/e_m]$. For a total assignment τ to the universal variables $U = u_1, \ldots, u_n$, we write $M(\xi, \tau)$ for $M(\xi)[\tau(u_1)/u_1, \ldots, \tau(u_n)/u_n]$. Intuitively, $M(\xi, \tau)$ is the result of the game under strategy M and the moves τ. Hence, if ξ is over the variables of Φ, then $M(\xi)$ is over U and $M(\xi, \tau)$ yields the constant which results from evaluating ξ under the strategy M and assignment τ. In particular, M is a model of Φ iff $M(\xi, \tau) = 1$ for any τ.*

Example 1. For a QCNF $\forall u \exists e. (\bar{u} \vee e) \wedge (u \vee \bar{e})$, the strategy $M = (\phi_e)$, where $\phi_e = u$ is a model. Observe that $M(\bar{u} \vee e) = M(u \vee \bar{e}) = u \vee \bar{u}$ are tautologies.

A formula QCNF is true if and only if it has a model [16, Lemma 1]; deciding whether a strategy is a model of a formula is coNP-complete [16, Lemma 3]. We should note that here we follow the definition of model by Büning *et. al.*, which has a syntactic nature. However, semantic-based definitions of the same concept appear in literature [35,4].

3 QBF Preprocessing Techniques

For the following overview of preprocessing techniques we consider a QCNF $\mathcal{P}.\phi$ for some quantifier prefix $\mathcal{P}$ and a CNF matrix ϕ. All the techniques are validity-preserving.

Let $C \in \phi$ be a clause comprising a single existential literal l. *Unit propagation* is the operation of removing from ϕ all clauses that contain l, and removing the literal $\bar{l}$ from clauses containing it.

A clause $C \in \phi$ is *subsumed* by a different clause $D \in \phi$ if $D \subseteq C$; *subsumption removal* consists in removing clause C.

Consider clauses $C, D \in \phi$ together with their resolvent R. If R subsumes C, then we say that C is *strengthened* by *self-subsumption* using D. *Self-subsumption strengthening* consists in replacing C with R [20].

A literal l is *pure* in Φ if $\bar{l}$ does not appear in ϕ. If l is pure and universal, then the *pure literal rule* (PRL) [17] consists in removing all occurrences of l. If l is pure and existential, then the PLR removes all the clauses containing the literal l.

The technique of *blocked clause elimination* (BCE) [36,9] hinges on the definition of a *blocked literal*. An existential literal l is blocked in a clause C if for any clause $D \in \phi$ s.t. $\bar{l} \in D$ there is a literal $k \in C$ with $k < l$ and $\bar{k} \in D$. A clause is blocked if it contains a blocked literal. BCE consists in removing blocked clauses from the matrix.

Variable elimination (VE) [42,24] replaces all clauses containing a certain variable with all their possible resolvents on that variable. In QBF, to ensure soundness, the technique is carried out only if a certain side-condition is satisfied. For an existential variable x, let us partition ϕ into $\phi_x \cup \phi_{\bar{x}} \cup \xi$ where ϕ_x has all clauses containing the literal x, and $\phi_{\bar{x}}$ has all clauses containing the literal $\bar{x}$. For any clause $C \in \phi_x$ that contains some literal k s.t. $x < k$ and any clause $D \in \phi_{\bar{x}}$, there is a literal $z < x$ s.t. $z \in C$ and $\bar{z} \in D$. Variable elimination consists in replacing $\phi_x \cup \phi_{\bar{x}}$ with the set of resolvents between the pairs of clauses of ϕ_x and $\phi_{\bar{x}}$ for which the resolution is defined.

The *binary implication graph* (e.g. [28]) G_ϕ is constructed by generating for each binary clause $l_1 \vee l_2 \in \phi$ two edges: $\bar{l}_1 \to l_2$ and $\bar{l}_2 \to l_1$. If two literals appear in the same strongly connected component of G_ϕ, then they must be equivalent. *Equivalent literal substitution* (ELS) consists in replacing literals appearing in the same strongly connected component S by one of the literals from S; this literal is called the *representative*. The representative is then substituted in place of the other literals of S. While in plain SAT preprocessing a representative can be chosen arbitrarily, in QBF it must be done with care. First, three conditions are checked: (1) S contains two distinct universal literals (also covers complementary universal literals); (2) S contains an existential literal l_e and a universal literal l_u such that $l_e < l_u$; (3) S contains two complementary existential literals. If either of the conditions (1), (2), or (3) is satisfied, then the whole formula is false (cf. [2]), and ELS stops. Otherwise, ELS picks as representative the literal that is the outermost with respect to the considered prefix. Observe that if the component contains exactly one universal literal, it will be chosen as the representative. All clauses that become tautologous due to the substitution, are removed from the matrix (this includes the binary clauses that were used to construct the strongly connected components).

4 Limitations

In this section we focus on the limitations of currently-available calculi from the perspective of preprocessing. In particular, we show that term-resolution+model-generation proofs cannot be tractably reconstructed for blocked clause elimination and variable elimination. For a given parameter $n \in \mathbb{N}^+$ construct the following true QCNF with $2n$ variables and $2n$ clauses.

$$\forall u_1 \exists e_1 \ldots \forall u_n \exists e_n. \bigwedge_{1 \le i \le n} (\bar{u}_i \vee e_i) \wedge (u_i \vee \bar{e}_i) \qquad (1)$$

Proposition 1. *Any term-resolution proof of* (1) *has size exponential in* n.

Proof. Pick an arbitrary assignment τ to the universal variables $u_1, \ldots, u_n$. We say that a term T *agrees* with an assignment τ iff there is no literal l such that $\bar{l} \in T$ and $\tau(l) = 1$. Given a term-resolution proof π for (1), we show that π must have a leaf that agrees with τ by constructing a path from the root to some leaf such that each node on that path agrees with τ. The root of π agrees with τ because it does not contain any literals. If a term T agrees with τ, and T is obtained from T' by $\exists$-reduction, then T' also agrees with τ since τ assigns only to universal variables. If T agrees with τ and is obtained from T_0 and T_1 by term-resolution on some variable y, then $y \in T_k$ and $\bar{y} \in T_{1-k}$ for some $k \in \{0, 1\}$. Hence, at least one of the terms T_0 and T_1 agrees with τ.

Recall that each leaf T of π must be obtained by the model-generation rule; i.e., for each clause C of (1) there is a literal l s.t. $l \in C$ and $l \in T$. Hence, for each pair of clauses $(\bar{u}_i \vee e_i) \wedge (u_i \vee \bar{e}_i)$ either $\bar{u}_i, \bar{e}_i \in T$ or $u_i, e_i \in T$. Consequently, each leaf of π has n universal literals.

For each of the 2^n possible assignments τ, the proof π must contain a leaf T_τ that agrees with τ. Since T_τ contains n universal literals, for a different assignment τ' there must be another leaf $T_{\tau'}$ that agrees with it. Overall, π must must contain at least 2^n different terms.

Proposition 2. *Both blocked clause elimination and variable elimination reduce the matrix of* (1) *to the empty set of clauses in polynomial time.*

Proof. Immediate from definitions of blocked clause and variable elimination.

Corollary 1. *If blocked clause elimination or variable elimination are used for preprocessing, then reconstructing a term-resolution proof takes exponentially more time than preprocessing, in the worst case.*

In the remainder of the paper we do not consider term-resolution+model-generation proofs for certification since Corollary 1 shows that, in the context of preprocessing, this calculus is not appropriate. Rather than term-resolution, we will use models to certify true formulas. We should note, however, that for such we are paying a price of higher complexity for certificate verification. While term-resolution+model-generation proofs can be verified in polynomial time, verification of models is coNP-complete. (For false formulas, QU-resolution is used for certification, which is still verifiable in polynomial time.)

In a similar spirit, we do not consider the preprocessing technique of universal-expansion [12], which is based on the identity $\forall x. \Phi = \Phi[1/x] \wedge \Phi[0/x]$. While there is no hard evidence that there is no tractable algorithm for reconstructing QU-resolution proofs for universal-expansion, recent work hints in this direction [30]. Hence, only the techniques described in Section 3 are considered.

5 Certificate Reconstruction

This section shows how to produce certificates in the context of preprocessing. In particular, we focus on two types of certificates: QU-resolution refutations (Section 2.1) for false formulas and models (Definition 1) for true formulas. We consider each of the techniques presented in Section 3 and we show how a certificate is *reconstructed* from the certificate of the preprocessed formula. This means that reconstruction produces a model (resp. refutation) for a formula Φ from a model (resp. refutation) for a formula Φ', which resulted from Φ by the considered technique. For nontrivial reconstructions we also provide a proof of why the reconstruction is correct.

Having a reconstruction for each of the preprocessing techniques individually enables us to reconstruct a certificate for the whole preprocessing process. The preprocessing process produces a sequence of formulas $\Phi_0, \ldots, \Phi_n$ where Φ_0 is the input formula, Φ_n is the final result, and each formula Φ_{i+1} is obtained from Φ_i by *one* preprocessing technique. For the purpose of the reconstruction, we are given a certificate $\mathcal{C}_n$ for the formula Φ_n. This final certificate $\mathcal{C}_n$ is in practice obtained by a QBF solver. The reconstruction for the whole processing process works backwards through the sequence of formulas $\Phi_0, \ldots, \Phi_n$. Using $\mathcal{C}_n$, it reconstructs a certificate $\mathcal{C}_{n-1}$ for the formula Φ_{n-1}, then for Φ_{n-2} and so on until it produces a certificate $\mathcal{C}_0$ for the input formula. The reminder of the section describes these individual reconstructions for the considered techniques.

We begin by two simple observations. If a transformation removes a clause, then reconstruction of a QU-resolution proof does not need to do anything. Analogously, reconstruction of models is trivial for transformations adding new clauses.

Observation 1. *Consider a QCNF $\Phi = \mathcal{P}.\phi$ and a clause $C \in \phi$. Any QU-resolution proof of $\Phi' = \mathcal{P}.\phi \smallsetminus \{C\}$ is also a QU-resolution proof of Φ.*

Observation 2. *Consider a QCNF $\Phi = \mathcal{P}.\phi$ and a clause C over the variables of Φ. Any model of $\Phi' = \mathcal{P}.\phi \cup \{C\}$ is a model of Φ.*

5.1 Subsumption, Self-Subsumption, and Unit Propagation

In the case of subsumption, a QCNF $\Phi = \mathcal{P}.\phi$ is transformed into $\Phi' = \mathcal{P}.\phi \smallsetminus \{C\}$ for a clause C for which that there is another clause $D \in \phi$ such that $D \subseteq C$. For reconstructing QU-resolution nothing needs to be done due to Observation 1. For any model M' of Φ', the formula $M'(\phi \smallsetminus \{C\})$ is a tautology and in particular $M'(D)$ is a tautology and therefore necessarily $M'(C)$ is a tautology because C is weaker than D. Hence, $M'(\phi)$ is a tautology and M' is also a model of Φ.

In order to reconstruct unit propagation and self-subsumption we first show how to reconstruct resolution steps. For such, consider the transformation of a QCNF $\Phi = \mathcal{P}.\phi$ into the formula $\Phi' = \mathcal{P}.\phi \cup \{C\}$ where C is a resolvent of some clauses $D_1, D_2 \in \phi$. Any QU-resolution proof π' of Φ' where C appears as a leaf of π' is transformed into a QU-resolution proof of Φ by prepending this leaf with the resolution step of D_1 and D_2. Any M' model of Φ' is also a model of Φ due to Observation 2.

Each self-subsumption strengthening consists of two steps: resolution and subsumption. Unit propagation consists of resolution steps, subsumption, and the pure literal rule (see Section 5.3). Hence, certificates are reconstructed accordingly. Note that in self-subsumption strengthening, resolution steps may be carried out on universal literals while in unit propagation this would not be meaningful because the moment the matrix contains a unit clause where the literal is universal, the whole formula is trivially false due to universal reduction.

5.2 Variable Elimination (VE)

To eliminate a variable x from $\mathcal{P}.\phi$, VE partitions the matrix ϕ into the sets of clauses ϕ_x, $\phi_{\bar{x}}$, and ξ as described in Section 3. Subsequently, ϕ_x and $\phi_{\bar{x}}$ are replaced by the set $\phi_x \otimes \phi_{\bar{x}}$, which is defined as the set of all possible resolvents on x of clauses that do not contain another complementary literal. Recall that VE can be only carried out if the side-condition specified in Section 3 is fulfilled.

To reconstruct a QU-resolution proof we observe that VE can be split into operations already covered. The newly added clauses are results of resolution on existing clauses, which was already covered in Section 5.1. Clauses containing x are removed, which does not incur any reconstruction due to Observation 1.

To reconstruct models we observe that any given formula Φ can be written as $\Phi = \mathcal{P}_1 \exists x \mathcal{P}_2. (x \lor \phi_1) \land (\bar{x} \lor \phi_2) \land \xi$ for CNF formulas ϕ_1, ϕ_2, and ξ that do not contain x. Then, VE consists in transforming Φ into the formula $\Phi' = \mathcal{P}_1 \mathcal{P}_2. (\phi_1 \lor \phi_2) \land \xi$ (note that $\phi_1 \lor \phi_2$ corresponds to $(x \lor \phi_1) \otimes (\bar{x} \lor \phi_2)$). VE's side-condition specifies that any clause $C \in \phi_1$ that contains some literal k

such that $k > x$ and any clause $D \in \phi_2$, there is a literal $z < x$ such that $z \in C$ and $\bar{z} \in D$.

In order to construct a model for the original formula Φ from a model M' of Φ', we aim to add to M' a definition for x which sets x to 1 when ϕ_1 becomes 0 and it sets it to 1 when ϕ_2 becomes 0. Since M' is a model of Φ', the strategy M' satisfies one of the ϕ_1, ϕ_2 for any game. The difficulty lies in the fact that ϕ_1 and ϕ_2 may contain variables that are on the right from x in the quantifier prefix (those in $\mathcal{P}_2$) and these must not appear in the definition of x. Hence, we cannot use ϕ_1 and ϕ_2 to define x as they are. Instead, we construct a formula ϕ'_2 by removing from ϕ_2 all unsuitable literals, i.e. literals k for which $x < k$. Then, we set the definition for x to $M'(\phi'_2)$. Now whenever ϕ'_2 evaluates to 1, so do ϕ_2 and $(x \vee \phi_1) \wedge (\bar{x} \vee \phi_2)$, because x is set to 1. If, however, ϕ'_2 evaluates to 0, then ϕ_2 might not necessarily evaluate to 0, but x is set to 0 by our strategy regardless. Due to the side-condition, in such cases ϕ_1 must evaluate to 1 and therefore our strategy is safe. This is formalized by the following proposition.

Proposition 3. *Let $\Phi = \mathcal{P}_1 \exists x \mathcal{P}_2 . (x \vee \phi_1) \wedge (\bar{x} \vee \phi_2) \wedge \xi$ with ϕ_1 and ϕ_2 not containing x; let $\Phi' = \mathcal{P}_1 \mathcal{P}_2 . (\phi_1 \vee \phi_2) \wedge \xi$, as above. Define ϕ'_2 to be ϕ_2 with all the literals not less than x deleted; i.e., $\phi'_2 = \{\{l \mid l \in C, l < x\} \mid C \in \phi_2\}$. If M' is a model for Φ', then $M = M' \cup \{\psi_x\}$ is a model for Φ, where $\psi_x = M'(\phi'_2)$.*

Proof. The functions of M form a well-defined strategy since M' is a well-defined strategy and ψ_x does not contain any literals k with $k > x$. To show that M is a model of Φ, consider any complete assignment τ to the universal variables of Φ. Now we wish to show that the matrix of Φ evaluates to 1 under M and τ. Since M' is a model of Φ', and ξ does not contain x, it holds that $M(\xi, \tau) = M'(\xi, \tau) = 1$. So it is left to be shown that the subformula $(x \vee \phi_1) \wedge (\bar{x} \vee \phi_2)$ is true under M and τ.

Because ϕ_1, ϕ_2 do not contain x we have $M(\phi_1) = M'(\phi_1)$, $M(\phi_2) = M'(\phi_2)$, $M(\phi'_2) = M'(\phi'_2)$, and $M(\phi_1 \vee \phi_2, \tau) = M'(\phi_1 \vee \phi_2, \tau) = 1$. Split on the following cases (distinguishing between the values of x under τ and M).

If $M(x, \tau) = M'(\phi'_2, \tau) = 1$. Because ϕ'_2 is stronger than ϕ_2, i.e. $M(\phi'_2) \to M(\phi_2)$, also $M(\phi_2, \tau) = 1$. Hence $M((x \vee \phi_1) \wedge (\bar{x} \vee \phi_2), \tau) = 1$.

If $M(x, \tau) = M'(\phi'_2, \tau) = 0$. There must be a clause $C' \in \phi'_2$ s.t. $M'(C', \tau) = 0$, i.e. for all literals $l \in C'$, $M'(l, \tau) = 0$. Let $C \in \phi_2$ be a clause from which C' resulted by removing some literals (possibly none), i.e. $C' = \{l \mid l \in C, l < x\}$. Now consider two sub-cases depending on whether $C = C'$ or $C \neq C'$. If $C = C'$, $M'(C, \tau) = 0$ and $M'(\phi_2, \tau) = 0$, from which $M'(\phi_1, \tau) = 1$ because $M'(\phi_1 \vee \phi_2, \tau) = 1$. Hence $M((x \vee \phi_1) \wedge (\bar{x} \vee \phi_2)) = 1$. If $C \neq C'$, due to the side-condition, C contains for each clause $D \in \phi_1$ a literal l_D s.t. $\bar{l}_D \in D$ and $l_D < x$. Since each literal l_D is less than x, it is also in C'. Since $M(C', \tau) = 0$, each $M(l_D, \tau) = 0$ and $M(\bar{l}_D, \tau) = 1$. From which $M(\phi_1, \tau) = 1$ and $M((x \vee \phi_1) \wedge (\bar{x} \vee \phi_2), \tau) = 1$. □

5.3 Pure Literal Rule (PLR)

PLR for existential literals is a special case of both variable elimination and blocked clause elimination. (An existential pure literal is a blocked literal in any clause.) Hence, certificate reconstruction for existential PLR is done accordingly.

For a universal literal l with $\mathsf{var}(l) = y$, a QCNF $\varPhi = \mathcal{P}_1 \forall y \, \mathcal{P}_2 \,.\, \phi$ is translated into the QCNF formula $\varPhi' = \mathcal{P}_1 \mathcal{P}_2 \,.\, \phi'$ by removing l from all clauses where it appears. To obtain a QU-resolution proof π for $\varPhi$ from a QU-resolution proof π' one inserts l in any of the leafs $C' \in \phi'$ of π' s.t. there exists $C \in \phi$ with $C' = C \smallsetminus \{l\}$. Then, $\forall$-reductions of l are added to π' whenever possible. Note that the addition of l cannot lead to tautologous resolvents since only l is inserted and never $\bar{l}$. The newly added universal literals must be necessarily $\forall$-reduced as π' eventually resolves away all existential literals. Since l is universal, any model of $\varPhi'$ is also a model of $\varPhi$.

5.4 Blocked Clause Elimination (BCE)

For a QCNF $\varPhi = \mathcal{P} \,.\, \phi$, BCE identifies a blocked clause $C \in \phi$ and a blocked existential literal $l \in C$, and removes C from ϕ. Recall that for a blocked literal it holds that for any $D \in \phi$ such that $\bar{l} \in D$ there exists a literal $k \in C$ such that $\bar{k} \in D$ and $k < l$.

To reconstruct QU-resolution proofs, nothing needs to be done due to Observation 1. To show how to reconstruct models, let M' be a model for $\varPhi' = \mathcal{P} \,.\, \phi \smallsetminus \{C\}$. Let W be the set of literals that serve as witnesses for l being blocked, i.e. $W = \{k \in C \mid k \neq l \text{ and there exists a } D \in \phi \text{ s.t. } \bar{k}, \bar{l} \in D \text{ and } k < l\}$.

The intuition for constructing a model for $\mathcal{P} \,.\, \phi$ is to play the same as M' except for the case when the literals W are all 0, then make sure that l evaluates to 1. This is formalized by the following proposition.

Proposition 4. *Let $\varPhi$, $\varPhi'$, M', and W be defined as above. Let $x = \mathsf{var}(l)$ and $\psi'_x \in M'$ be the definition for x. Define $\psi_x = \psi'_x \vee M'(\bigwedge_{k \in W} \bar{k})$ if $l = x$ and $\psi_x = \psi'_x \wedge M'(\bigvee_{k \in W} k)$ if $l = \bar{x}$. Finally, define $M = M' \smallsetminus \{\psi'_x\} \cup \{\psi_x\}$. Then M is a model of $\varPhi$. (Note that universal literals of W are untouched by M'.)*

Proof. Strategy M is well-defined because literals in W are all less than l and therefore definitions for those literals also contains literals less than l. Let us consider some total assignment τ to the universal variables of $\varPhi$ under which all literals in W are 0 under M (for other assignments M behaves as M' and C is true). Now let us split the clauses of ϕ into 3 groups. Clauses that do not contain $\bar{l}$ nor l; clauses that contain l; and those that contain $\bar{l}$. For any clause $D \in \phi$ not containing l nor $\bar{l}$, $M(D, \tau) = 1$ since $M(D, \tau) = M'(D, \tau)$ and M' is a model of $\varPhi'$. For any clause $D \in \phi$ containing l, $M(D, \tau) = 1$ since $M(l, \tau) = 1$; this includes the clause C. Due to the sidecondition, any clause $D \in \phi$ that contains $\bar{l}$ also contains a literal k s.t. $\bar{k} \in W$. Since for $M(\bar{k}, \tau) = 0$, i.e. $M(k, \tau) = 1$, it holds that $M(D, \tau) = 1$. □

5.5 Equivalent Literal Substitution (ELS)

For a formula $\Phi = \mathcal{P}.\phi$, ELS constructs strongly connected components of the binary implication graph G of ϕ. Once a strongly connected component S of the graph is constructed, ELS checks whether S yields falsity. If it does, ELS produces a QU-resolution proof for such. The following discusses scenarios of falsity that may arise. First recall that if there is a path in G from a literal l_1 to l_k then there is a set of clauses $(\bar{l}_1 \vee l_2), (\bar{l}_2 \vee l_3), \ldots, (\bar{l}_{k-1} \vee l_k)$, which through a series of QU-resolution steps enables us to derive the clause $\bar{l}_1 \vee l_k$. Also recall that whenever there is a path from l_1 to l_k in some component S_1, there is also a path from $\bar{l}_1$ to $\bar{l}_k$ in the component S_2, obtained from S_1 by negating all literals and reversing all edges. These observations are repeatedly used in the following text.

(1) If S contains two universal literals l_1 and l_2, derive the clause $\bar{l}_1 \vee l_2$, which is then $\forall$-reduced to the empty clause. (Note that this also covers $l_2 = \bar{l}_1$.)

(2) If S contains an existential literal l_e and an universal literal l_u such that $l_e < l_u$, derive the clause $\bar{l}_e \vee l_u$ from which $\forall$-reduction gives $\bar{l}_e$. Derive l_e analogously. Finally resolve $\bar{l}_e$ and l_e to obtain the empty clause.

(3) If S contains two literals e and $\bar{e}$ for some existential variable e, derive the unit clauses e and $\bar{e}$ and resolve them into the empty clause.

If none of the three conditions above are satisfied, all literals in S are substituted by a representative literal r, which is the smallest literal from S w.r.t. the literal ordering $<$. This yields a formula $\Phi' = \mathcal{P}'.\phi'$, where $\mathcal{P}'$ resulted from $\mathcal{P}$ by removing all variables that appear in S except for $\text{var}(r)$. A certificate is reconstructed as follows.

If a QU-resolution proof π' for Φ' relies on a clause $C' \in \phi'$ that resulted from some cause $C \in \phi$ by replacing a $l \in S$ by r, construct the clause $\bar{l} \vee r$ and resolve it with C to obtain C'. Analogously, if C' resulted from C by replacing $\bar{l} \in S$ with $\bar{r}$, construct the clause $l \vee \bar{r}$ and resolve it with C to obtain C'.

If M' is a model of Φ' and r is existential, then S does not contain any universal literals and M' defines the value for r by some formula $\psi_r = M'(r)$. In such case ψ_r is over universal variables that are less than all the literals in S because r was chosen to be the outermost literal. If $x \in S$ for some existential variable x, set ψ_x as ψ_r; if $\bar{x} \in S$ for some existential variable x, set ψ_x as $\neg\psi_r$. If r is universal, all the other literals in S are existential and so for $x \in S \setminus \{r\}$ we set $\psi_x = r$; for $\bar{x} \in S \setminus \{r\}$, we set $\psi_x = \bar{r}$.

6 Related Work

Local simplifications based on identities such as $0x = 0$ appear in number of instances of automated reasoning (c.f. [27]). In SAT solving, it was early recognized that going beyond such local simplifications leads to significant performance gains. A notable technique is variable elimination (VE), which originates in the Davis&Putnam procedure (DP). While DP is itself complete, it suffers from unwieldy memory consumption. It has been shown that applying VE *only* if it does not lead to increase of the formula's size, gives an incomplete yet powerful technique [51]. The preprocessor SatELite [20] boosts VE by subsumption, self-subsumption, and unit propagation.

Nowadays, preprocessors (and SAT solvers themselves) contain a number of preprocessing techniques such as *blocked clauses elimination* [36,41,32], *hyper binary resolution* [3] and others (cf. [28]). Reconstructing solutions in SAT is generally easier than in QBF, but it has also been investigated [31].

Many SAT preprocessing techniques were generalized for QBF [8,47,24,11,9]; application thereof is crucial for QBF solving [44]. QBF leads to a number of specifics in the techniques. VE can be only performed under a certain side-condition (Section 3); Van Gelder [52] further generalizes this side-condition. A technique specific to QBF is *universal-variable expansion* [12,11] where a universal quantifier $\forall x. \Phi$ is expanded into $\Phi[0/x] \wedge \Phi[1/x]$ and then brought into the prenex form by variable renaming. (Expansion can be used to obtain a complete solver [5,8,37,29].) In his recent work, Van Gelder provides some initial insights into reconstruction of variable elimination and expansion [53]. There, however, he only shows how to reconstruct an individual leaf of a term-resolution proof, but does not show how to construct the proofs themselves.

A number of works focus on the certification of QBF solvers (e.g. [6,35,39,26]) motivated by error prevention [10], but also because the certificates themselves can be useful (e.g. [25,49,45,4,33]).

7 Experimental Evaluation

We test five scenarios, corresponding to different settings for preprocessing (**f**ull, **s**imple, or **n**one) and for solving (with a **q**dag dependency manager, or **s**imple). Table 1 defines and names the scenarios that we tested—the last letter indicates whether certificate generation was enabled (**y**es or **n**o). The scenario *nsy* represents the state-of-the-art in QBF solving *with* certificate generation, and is the scenario we set out to improve. The scenario *ssy* represents our contribution to QBF solving with certificate generation. We use the QBC format for certificates [35]: the size of models is the number of $\wedge$-gates used, the size of refutations is the number of resolution steps used. (See online[1] for the exact testing environment being used.)

Results and Discussion. Figure 2 shows the overall performance of five scenarios on the QBFEVAL 2012 benchmark. There is a clear gap between scenarios that use preprocessing (fqn, ssn, ssy) and scenarios that do not use preprocessing (nsn, nsy)—preprocessing is clearly beneficial. The gap nsy–nsn shows that enabling tracing in depqbf deteriorates its performance. The gap ssy–ssn is smaller than the gap nsy–nsn, indicating that enabling tracing in bloqqer+depqbf deteriorates performance *less* than it does for depqbf alone. The gap fqn–ssn should be reduced by future work. The most important observation to make on

---
[1] http://sat.inesc-id.pt/~mikolas/lpar13-prepro/

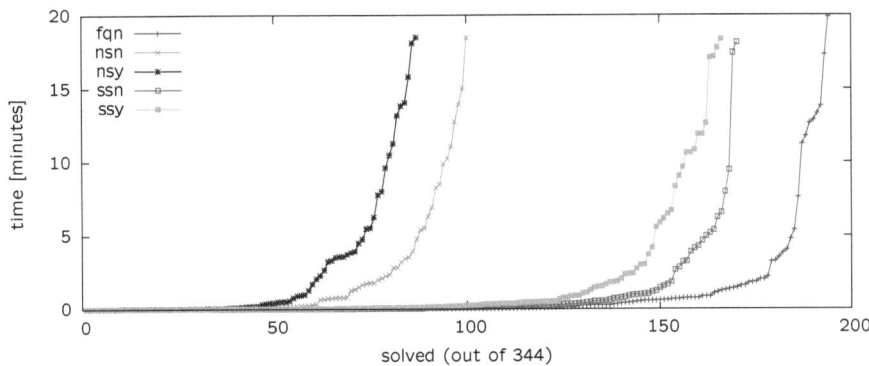

Fig. 2. Overall performance on the QBFEVAL 2012 benchmark

Table 1. Number of solved instances out of 344, for several scenarios

Scenario				True/SAT		False/UNSAT		
Name	Preprocessing	Solving	Tracing	Unchecked	Checked	Unchecked	Checked	Total
fqn	full	qdag	no	99	n/a	94	n/a	194
nsn	none	simple	no	42	n/a	58	n/a	100
nsy	none	simple	yes	7	25	0	55	87
ssn	simple	simple	no	80	n/a	90	n/a	170
ssy	simple	simple	yes	8	69	0	89	166

Figure 2 is that our proposed scenario (ssy) significantly improves the state-of-the-art in QBF solving with certificate generation (nsy). Table 1 gives the total number of solved instances for each scenario, thus it corresponds to the rightmost points in Figure 2. The generated certificates (in scenarios nsy, ssy) were not all checked: Those instances on which the certificate checker timed out are listed in the unchecked column. (Recall that checking strategies is coNP-complete.) The 7 unchecked certificates in the nsy scenario are largely disjoint from the 8 unchecked certificates in the ssy scenario—the overlap is exactly one instance.

Figure 3 shows that preprocessing is beneficial mostly for hard instances. Figure 3a depicts certificate size with preprocessing (ssy) versus certificate size without preprocessing (nsy). There is a clear threshold around 10^5: above it preprocessing helps, below it preprocessing is detrimental. Figure 3b depicts time spent in the solver versus total solving time (which includes preprocessing and postprocessing) for the three scenarios that use preprocessing. There is a clear threshold around 2 minutes: above it, scenarios that do not generate certificates (fqn, ssn) have negligible overhead.

The correlation between certificate size and total running time is only moderate (≈ 0.6). As an example of the high variance, for the 10 instances that were solved in 64-to-128 seconds, the average certificate size was 4.7×10^5, with a standard deviation of 4.8×10^5.

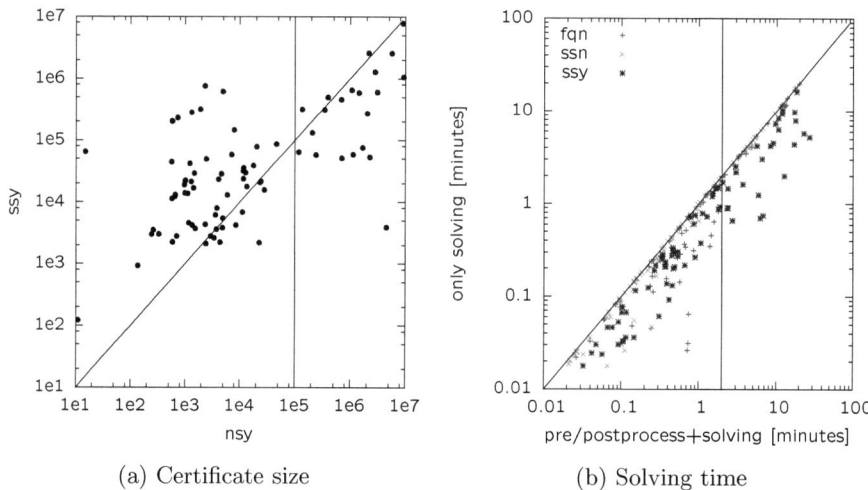

Fig. 3. The effect of pre/postprocessing on certificate size and on solving time

Table 2. Time spent in solver as a percent of the total solving time

Scenario	min [%]	med [%]	geom avg [%]	max [%]
fqn	4	91	66	100
ssn	19	98	86	100
ssy	11	57	50	92

8 Conclusions and Future Work

This paper brings together two different facets of QBF solving: preprocessing and certification. Certification is important for practical applications of QBF and preprocessing is crucial for performance of nowadays QBF solvers. Both of the facets were extensively investigated [22,52,40,8,47,9,24] but there is no available toolchain combining the two. However, the need for such technology has been recognized by others [44]. This paper addresses exactly this deficiency. For a number of representative preprocessing techniques, the paper shows how certificates can be reconstructed from a certificate of a preprocessed formula. Experimental evaluation of the implemented prototype demonstrates that the proposed techniques enable QBF solving *with* certification that is performance-wise very close to a state-of-the-art QBF solving *without* certification. Hence, the contribution of the paper is not only theoretical but also practical since the implemented tool will be useful to the QBF community.

On the negative side, the paper demonstrates that current methods of QBF certification are insufficient for full-fledged preprocessing in the case of true formulas. Namely, term-resolution+model-generation proofs incur worst-case exponential blowup in blocked clause elimination and variable elimination. This is an important drawback because term-resolution proofs can be checked in polynomial time, which is not the case for model-based certification (used in the paper). This drawback delimits one direction for future work: Can we produce polynomially-verifiable certificates for true QBFs in the context of preprocessing? Another item of future work is narrowing the performance gap between solving with and without certificate generation. In this regard, methods for certifying universal-variable expansion should be developed [12] and other techniques, such as hyper-binary resolution, must be certified.

Last but not least, methods for solving QBF were generalized to domains such as SMT or verification [19,38]. We may expect that the contributions made by this paper will also be helpful for these works.

Acknowledgments. We thank Armin Biere and Allen Van Gelder for helpful conversations on QBF and preprocessing. This work is partially supported by SFI PI grant BEACON (09/IN.1/I2618), FCT grants ATTEST (CMU-PT/ELE/0009/2009), POLARIS (PTDC/EIA-CCO/123051/2010), and INESC-ID's multiannual PIDDAC funding PEst-OE/EEI/LA0021/2011. Grigore was supported by the EPSRC Programme Grant 'Resource Reasoning' (EP/H008373/2).

References

1. Arora, S., Barak, B.: Computational Complexity — A Modern Approach. Cambridge University Press (2009)
2. Aspvall, B., Plass, M.F., Tarjan, R.E.: A linear-time algorithm for testing the truth of certain quantified Boolean formulas. Inf. Process. Lett. 8(3) (1979)
3. Bacchus, F., Winter, J.: Effective preprocessing with hyper-resolution and equality reduction. In: Giunchiglia, E., Tacchella, A. (eds.) SAT 2003. LNCS, vol. 2919, pp. 341–355. Springer, Heidelberg (2004)
4. Balabanov, V., Jiang, J.H.R.: Unified QBF certification and its applications. Formal Methods in System Design 41(1) (2012)
5. Benedetti, M.: Evaluating QBFs via symbolic Skolemization. In: Baader, F., Voronkov, A. (eds.) LPAR 2004. LNCS (LNAI), vol. 3452, pp. 285–300. Springer, Heidelberg (2005)
6. Benedetti, M.: sKizzo: a suite to evaluate and certify QBFs. In: Nieuwenhuis, R. (ed.) CADE 2005. LNCS (LNAI), vol. 3632, pp. 369–376. Springer, Heidelberg (2005)
7. Benedetti, M., Mangassarian, H.: QBF-based formal verification: Experience and perspectives. JSAT 5(1-4) (2008)
8. Biere, A.: Resolve and expand. In: Hoos, H.H., Mitchell, D.G. (eds.) SAT 2004. LNCS, vol. 3542, pp. 59–70. Springer, Heidelberg (2005)
9. Biere, A., Lonsing, F., Seidl, M.: Blocked clause elimination for QBF. In: Bjørner, N., Sofronie-Stokkermans, V. (eds.) CADE 2011. LNCS (LNAI), vol. 6803, pp. 101–115. Springer, Heidelberg (2011)
10. Brummayer, R., Lonsing, F., Biere, A.: Automated testing and debugging of SAT and QBF solvers. In: Strichman, O., Szeider, S. (eds.) SAT 2010. LNCS, vol. 6175, pp. 44–57. Springer, Heidelberg (2010)
11. Bubeck, U.: Model-based transformations for quantified Boolean formulas. Ph.D. thesis, University of Paderborn (2010)

12. Bubeck, U., Kleine Büning, H.: Bounded universal expansion for preprocessing QBF. In: Marques-Silva, J., Sakallah, K.A. (eds.) SAT 2007. LNCS, vol. 4501, pp. 244–257. Springer, Heidelberg (2007)
13. Buning, H.K., Letterman, T.: Propositional Logic: Deduction and Algorithms. Cambridge University Press, New York (1999)
14. Büning, H.K., Bubeck, U.: Theory of quantified boolean formulas. In: Handbook of Satisfiability. IOS Press (2009)
15. Büning, H.K., Karpinski, M., Flögel, A.: Resolution for quantified Boolean formulas. Inf. Comput. 117(1) (1995)
16. Büning, H.K., Subramani, K., Zhao, X.: Boolean functions as models for quantified Boolean formulas. J. Autom. Reasoning 39(1) (2007)
17. Cadoli, M., Schaerf, M., Giovanardi, A., Giovanardi, M.: An algorithm to evaluate quantified Boolean formulae and its experimental evaluation. J. Autom. Reasoning 28(2) (2002)
18. Canny, J.F.: Some algebraic and geometric computations in PSPACE. In: STOC (1988)
19. Cheng, C.H., Shankar, N., Ruess, H., Bensalem, S.: EFSMT: A logical framework for cyber-physical systems (2013), http://arxiv.org/abs/1306.3456
20. Eén, N., Biere, A.: Effective preprocessing in SAT through variable and clause elimination. In: Bacchus, F., Walsh, T. (eds.) SAT 2005. LNCS, vol. 3569, pp. 61–75. Springer, Heidelberg (2005)
21. Egly, U., Widl, M.: Solution extraction from long-distance resolution proofs (July 2013), http://fmv.jku.at/qbf2013/reportQBFWS13.pdf
22. Giunchiglia, E., Narizzano, M., Tacchella, A.: Clause/term resolution and learning in the evaluation of quantified Boolean formulas. JAIR 26(1) (2006)
23. Giunchiglia, E., Marin, P., Narizzano, M.: Reasoning with quantified boolean formulas. In: Handbook of Satisfiability. IOS Press (2009)
24. Giunchiglia, E., Marin, P., Narizzano, M.: sQueezeBF: An effective preprocessor for QBFs based on equivalence reasoning. In: Strichman, O., Szeider, S. (eds.) SAT 2010. LNCS, vol. 6175, pp. 85–98. Springer, Heidelberg (2010)
25. Gorogiannis, N.: Computing Minimal Changes of Models of Systems. Ph.D. thesis, University of Birmingham (2003)
26. Goultiaeva, A., Van Gelder, A., Bacchus, F.: A uniform approach for generating proofs and strategies for both true and false QBF formulas. In: IJCAI, pp. 546–553. IJCAI/AAAI (2011)
27. Harrison, J.: Handbook of Practical Logic and Automated Reasoning. Cambridge University Press (2009)
28. Heule, M., Järvisalo, M., Biere, A.: Clause elimination procedures for CNF formulas. In: Fermüller, C.G., Voronkov, A. (eds.) LPAR-17. LNCS, vol. 6397, pp. 357–371. Springer, Heidelberg (2010)
29. Janota, M., Klieber, W., Marques-Silva, J., Clarke, E.: Solving QBF with counterexample guided refinement. In: Cimatti, A., Sebastiani, R. (eds.) SAT 2012. LNCS, vol. 7317, pp. 114–128. Springer, Heidelberg (2012)
30. Janota, M., Marques-Silva, J.: On propositional QBF expansions and Q-resolution. In: Järvisalo, M., Van Gelder, A. (eds.) SAT 2013. LNCS, vol. 7962, pp. 67–82. Springer, Heidelberg (2013)
31. Järvisalo, M., Biere, A.: Reconstructing solutions after blocked clause elimination. In: Strichman, O., Szeider, S. (eds.) SAT 2010. LNCS, vol. 6175, pp. 340–345. Springer, Heidelberg (2010)
32. Järvisalo, M., Biere, A., Heule, M.: Simulating circuit-level simplifications on CNF. J. Autom. Reasoning 49(4) (2012)

33. Jordan, C., Kaiser, L.: Experiments with reduction finding. In: Järvisalo, M., Van Gelder, A. (eds.) SAT 2013. LNCS, vol. 7962, pp. 192–207. Springer, Heidelberg (2013)
34. Jussila, T., Biere, A.: Compressing BMC encodings with QBF. Electr. Notes Theor. Comput. Sci. 174(3) (2007)
35. Jussila, T., Biere, A., Sinz, C., Kroning, D., Wintersteiger, C.M.: A first step towards a unified proof checker for QBF. In: Marques-Silva, J., Sakallah, K.A. (eds.) SAT 2007. LNCS, vol. 4501, pp. 201–214. Springer, Heidelberg (2007)
36. Kullmann, O.: New methods for 3-SAT decision and worst-case analysis. Theor. Comput. Sci. 223(1-2) (1999)
37. Lonsing, F., Biere, A.: Nenofex: Expanding NNF for QBF solving. In: Kleine Büning, H., Zhao, X. (eds.) SAT 2008. LNCS, vol. 4996, pp. 196–210. Springer, Heidelberg (2008)
38. Morgenstern, A., Gesell, M., Schneider, K.: Solving games using incremental induction. In: Johnsen, E.B., Petre, L. (eds.) IFM 2013. LNCS, vol. 7940, pp. 177–191. Springer, Heidelberg (2013)
39. Narizzano, M., Peschiera, C., Pulina, L., Tacchella, A.: Evaluating and certifying QBFs: A comparison of state-of-the-art tools. AI Commun. 22(4) (2009)
40. Niemetz, A., Preiner, M., Lonsing, F., Seidl, M., Biere, A.: Resolution-based certificate extraction for QBF. In: Cimatti, A., Sebastiani, R. (eds.) SAT 2012. LNCS, vol. 7317, pp. 430–435. Springer, Heidelberg (2012)
41. Ostrowski, R., Grégoire, É., Mazure, B., Saïs, L.: Recovering and exploiting structural knowledge from CNF formulas. In: Van Hentenryck, P. (ed.) CP 2002. LNCS, vol. 2470, pp. 185–199. Springer, Heidelberg (2002)
42. Pan, G., Vardi, M.Y.: Symbolic decision procedures for QBF. In: Wallace, M. (ed.) CP 2004. LNCS, vol. 3258, pp. 453–467. Springer, Heidelberg (2004)
43. Plandowski, W.: Satisfiability of word equations with constants is in PSPACE. J. ACM 51(3) (2004)
44. QBF gallery (2013), http://www.kr.tuwien.ac.at/events/qbfgallery2013/
45. Samanta, R., Deshmukh, J.V., Emerson, E.A.: Automatic generation of local repairs for Boolean programs. In: FMCAD (2008)
46. Samulowitz, H., Bacchus, F.: Binary clause reasoning in QBF. In: Biere, A., Gomes, C.P. (eds.) SAT 2006. LNCS, vol. 4121, pp. 353–367. Springer, Heidelberg (2006)
47. Samulowitz, H., Davies, J., Bacchus, F.: Preprocessing QBF. In: Benhamou, F. (ed.) CP 2006. LNCS, vol. 4204, pp. 514–529. Springer, Heidelberg (2006)
48. Schröder, L., Pattinson, D.: PSPACE bounds for rank-1 modal logics. ACM Trans. Comput. Log. 10(2) (2009)
49. Staber, S., Bloem, R.: Fault localization and correction with QBF. In: Marques-Silva, J., Sakallah, K.A. (eds.) SAT 2007. LNCS, vol. 4501, pp. 355–368. Springer, Heidelberg (2007)
50. Stockmeyer, L.J.: The complexity of decision problems in automata theory and logic. Ph.D. thesis, Massachusetts Institute of Technology (1974)
51. Subbarayan, S., Pradhan, D.K.: NiVER: Non increasing variable elimination resolution for preprocessing SAT instances. In: Hoos, H.H., Mitchell, D.G. (eds.) SAT 2004. LNCS, vol. 3542, pp. 276–291. Springer, Heidelberg (2005)
52. Van Gelder, A.: Contributions to the theory of practical quantified Boolean formula solving. In: Milano, M. (ed.) CP 2012. LNCS, vol. 7514, pp. 647–663. Springer, Heidelberg (2012)
53. Van Gelder, A.: Certificate extraction from variable-elimination QBF preprocessors (July 2013), http://fmv.jku.at/qbf2013/reportQBFWS13.pdf

Partial Backtracking in CDCL Solvers

Chuan Jiang and Ting Zhang

Iowa State University, Ames IA 50011, USA
{cjiang,tingz}@iastate.edu

Abstract. Backtracking is a basic technique of search-based satisfiability (SAT) solvers. In order to backtrack, a SAT solver uses conflict analysis to compute a backtracking level and discards all the variable assignments made between the conflicting level and the backtracking level. We observed that, due to the branching heuristics, the solver may repeat lots of previous decisions and propagations later. In this paper, we present a new backtracking strategy, which we refer to as partial backtracking. We implemented this strategy in our solver Nigma. Using this strategy, Nigma amends the variable assignments instead of discarding them completely so that it does not backtrack as many levels as the classic strategy. Our experiments show that Nigma solves 5% more instances than the version without partial backtracking.

Keywords: satisfiability, backtracking, conflict-driven conflict learning.

1 Introduction

Most modern SAT solvers are based on *conflict-driven clause learning* (CDCL). As a basic technique of CDCL solvers, *backtracking* helps the solver jump out of a local search space where no solution could ever be found [1]. In CDCL solvers, backtracking is non-chronological and guided by conflict analysis to determine how far the solver would jump back. The first non-chronological backtracking strategy was introduced in GRASP [1]. When GRASP meets a conflict, it keeps the current level and flips the value of the most recent decision variable. Backtracking only occurs if the flipping still leads to a conflict. Later, *random backtracking* was proposed to introduce randomness into selecting the backtracking level [2,3]. Essentially, the learnt clause is used for randomly deciding which variable is to be flipped. Nowadays, most solvers utilize a non-randomized backtracking strategy [4], which is referred to as *classic backtracking* in this paper. This strategy is more aggressive than that used in GRASP, since backtracking is always carried out after each conflict, making the resulting assignment trail always look like the one obtained when the learnt clause has already been included in the formula.

No matter what kind of backtracking a solver takes, it is observed that sometimes the solver backtracks quite far, which is almost equivalent to a restart. However, due to the wide adoption of VSIDS [4] and phase saving [5], the solver may make similar decisions as the ones before backtracking and hence repeat some propagations. In this paper, we present a new backtracking strategy, referred to as *partial backtracking*. We implemented this strategy in our solver Nigma. Using this strategy, Nigma amends the variable assignments between the conflicting level and the assertion level instead of discarding them completely. Nigma still backtracks after each conflict, but it does not have to backtrack as many levels as those solvers using classic backtracking. Our experiments show that Nigma backtracks 10% ~ 60% fewer levels than the version with classic backtracking.

This paper is organized as follows. Section 2 introduces the basic notions in SAT solving and CDCL solvers. Section 3 analyzes the classic backtracking strategy and the phenomenon of repeated propagation. Section 4 presents the implementation details of the partial backtracking strategy. Several optimizations on the implementation are discussed in Section 5. Section 6 presents the experiment results, showing the performance of our solver Nigma is improved after adopting the partial backtracking strategy. Section 7 concludes with some discussion on the future work.

2 Preliminaries

In this section, we introduce the basic notations and terminology on SAT solving and CDCL solvers.

A *literal* is either a Boolean variable x or its negation $\neg x$, and a *clause* is a disjunction of literals. A formula is said in *conjunction normal form* (CNF) if it is a conjunction of clauses. The *satisfiability* problem is to determine if there exists an assignment that evaluates a given Boolean formula to TRUE.

We say a variable or literal is *free* if it is unassigned and a clause is *unit* if it only contains one free literal and all other literals have been assigned FALSE. A unit clause essentially asserts that the sole free literal must be assigned TRUE. We call this assertion an *implication*, written as $l@dl$, indicating that the literal l is implied to be TRUE at the decision level dl (the definition of decision level is given below).

CDCL solvers check the satisfiability of Boolean formulas through *Boolean constraint propagation* (BCP) and conflict analysis. BCP is an iterative process of searching for unit clauses and obtaining implications until reaching a fixed point or encountering a conflict, that is, a clause whose literals are all assigned FALSE. We call the clause with all literals being assigned FALSE a *conflicting clause*. Most solvers store implications in the *implication queue* and propagate them one by one in FIFO manner. Algorithm 1 shows the propagation of an implication with two watched literals [4] and Algorithm 2 shows the iterative process of propagation.

If BCP terminates with a conflict, then the solver extracts the reason as a clause and adds it into the Boolean formula to avoid recurrence of the same conflict in the future. This process is called *conflict analysis* or *learning* and the new added clause is called a *learnt clause*. It is always desirable for a learnt clause to become unit after backtracking to some level.

Algorithm 1. $Propagate(l@dl)$

1: $wl_1 \leftarrow \neg l$
2: **for all** clause c where wl_1 is watched **do**
3:    Search for a non-FALSE unwatched literal l' in c
4:    **if** Exists l' **then**
5:       Unwatch wl_1
6:       Watch l'
7:    **else**
8:       $wl_2 \leftarrow$ the other watched literal in c
9:       **if** wl_2 is FALSE **then**
10:          $ImplicationQueue.Clear()$
11:          $ConflictAnalysis()$
12:          **return**
13:       **else if** wl_2 is TRUE **then**
14:          continue
15:       **else**
16:          $ImplicationQueue.Push(wl_2@dl_{curr})$ {dl_{curr} is the current level}
17:       **end if**
18:    **end if**
19: **end for**

Algorithm 2. $BCP()$

1: **while** $ImplicationQueue$ is not empty **do**
2:    $l@dl \leftarrow ImplicationQueue.Pop()$
3:    $Propagate(l@dl)$
4: **end while**

If BCP terminates without conflicts, then the solver selects a free variable and gives it a value heuristically. This variable assignment is referred to as a *decision* and pushed into a stack. A *decision level* is associated with each decision to denote the its depth in that stack.

We refer the readers to [6] for more information on SAT solving and CDCL solvers.

3 Classic Backtracking

In this section, we present the classic backtracking and identify the phenomenon of *repeated propagation*.

According to the classic backtracking, the solver resolves conflicts by backtracking to the *assertion level* dl_{asrt}, which is the second highest level among the literals in the learnt clause (we say a level dl_1 is higher than dl_2 if $dl_1 > dl_2$), and hence erasing all the variable assignments between dl_{asrt} and the *conflicting level* dl_{conf}, which is the level where the conflict occurs. After backtracking, the learnt clause becomes unit and the solver invokes BCP. This kind of backtracking unavoidably discards all the propagations between dl_{asrt} and dl_{conf}.

(a) Clauses:

$\neg x_1 \vee x_2$
$\neg x_3 \vee \neg x_4$
$\neg x_1 \vee x_4 \vee x_5 \vee x_6$
$x_5 \vee x_{13}$
$\neg x_7 \vee x_8$
$\neg x_7 \vee x_9$
$\neg x_2 \vee \neg x_8 \vee x_{10}$
$\boxed{\neg x_8 \vee \neg x_9 \vee \neg x_{10}}$
$x_4 \vee x_7 \vee \neg x_{11}$
$x_7 \vee x_{11} \vee x_{12}$
$x_6 \vee x_{11}$

(b) Variables:

Variable	Activity Score	Last Value
x_1	10	TRUE
x_3	8.1	TRUE
x_2	7.2	TRUE
x_5	6.4	FALSE
x_{12}	6	FALSE
x_7	5.5	TRUE
x_6	3.7	FALSE
x_{13}	2.5	TRUE
x_{10}	2.2	TRUE
x_8	1.5	TRUE
x_4	0.5	FALSE
x_9	0	FALSE
x_{11}	0	FALSE

(c) Assignments:

Level	Assignments
1	x_1, x_2
2	$x_3, \neg x_4$
3	$\neg x_5, x_6, x_{13}$
4	$\neg x_{12}$
5	x_7, x_8, x_9, x_{10}

Fig. 1. The status before backtracking

Peter van der Tak et al. observed that CDCL solvers may reassign the same variables to the same Boolean values after a restart, and proposed the *partial restart* strategy [7]. One important reason of reassignments is the wide adoption of VSIDS [4] and phase saving [5]. We observed that backtracking exhibits a similar phenomenon, which we refer to as *repeated propagation* (note that a restart is a special form of backtracking). We give an example to illustrate this phenomenon.

Consider the clauses and variable assignments in Figure 1a and Figure 1b. Since the solver tends to select the most active free variables and their last values as decisions, we have the resulting assignment trail shown in Figure 1c. Then the solver encounters a conflict while propagating x_8 at the level 5 (the conflicting clause is framed in Figure 1a). The clause $\neg x_7 \vee \neg x_2$ is learnt by 1-UIP [8] and thus $dl_{asrt} = 1$. According to VSIDS, the solver will only increase the activity scores (assuming the increment is 1) of the variables involving in the conflict, namely, $\{x_2, x_7, x_8, x_9, x_{10}\}$. Therefore, the activity scores of the variables assigned between dl_{conf} and dl_{asrt}, $\{x_3, x_4, x_5, x_6, x_{12}, x_{13}\}$, remain the same. As shown in Figure 2c, in the decision immediately after backtracking to dl_{asrt}, x_3 will be chosen and assigned TRUE again at the level 2. Note that the resulting set of variable assignments at the level 2 is a superset of that before backtracking. The set of variable assignments at the level 3 is also similar to that before backtracking, except that x_6 has been "lifted" to the level 2.

(a) Clauses:

$\neg x_1 \vee x_2$
$\neg x_3 \vee \neg x_4$
$\neg x_1 \vee x_4 \vee x_5 \vee x_6$
$x_5 \vee x_{13}$
$\neg x_7 \vee x_8$
$\neg x_7 \vee x_9$
$\neg x_2 \vee \neg x_8 \vee x_{10}$
$\neg x_8 \vee \neg x_9 \vee \neg x_{10}$
$x_4 \vee x_7 \vee \neg x_{11}$
$x_7 \vee x_{11} \vee x_{12}$
$x_6 \vee x_{11}$
$\neg \mathbf{x_7} \vee \neg \mathbf{x_2}$

(b) Variables:

Variable	Activity Score	Last Values
x_1	10	TRUE
x_2	**8.2**	TRUE
x_3	8.1	TRUE
x_7	**6.5**	TRUE
x_5	6.4	FALSE
x_{12}	6	FALSE
x_6	3.7	**TRUE**
x_{10}	**3.2**	TRUE
x_8	**2.5**	TRUE
x_{13}	2.5	TRUE
x_9	1	**TRUE**
x_4	0.5	FALSE
x_{11}	0	FALSE

(c) Assignments:

Level	Assignments
1	$x_1, x_2, \neg x_7$
2	$x_3, \neg x_4, \neg x_{11}, x_{12}, x_6$
3	$\neg x_5, x_{13}$
4	x_{10}
5	$x_8, \neg x_9$

Fig. 2. The status after backtracking

By comparing the variable assignments before and after each backtracking, we have Figure 3 that shows the percentage of discarded variable assignments that are chosen as decisions or propagated again before the next backtracking. It is interesting to see that the solver tends to either enter a totally different search space or stubbornly stick to its previous choices. But for a majority of backtrackings, a large proportion of discarded variable assignments are repeated. Note that we only consider those backtrackings that go back more than 10 levels and do not take account of restarts. Also, the variable assignments on the conflicting level are not counted in computing this percentage.

4 Partial Backtracking

In this section, we present the partial backtracking strategy that allows the solver to backtrack to some level dl_{back} such that $dl_{conf} > dl_{back} \geq dl_{asrt}$, therefore saving the propagations between dl_{back} and dl_{asrt}.

There are two reasons that classic backtracking prefers to use the assertion level as the backtracking level. First, after each backtracking, the learnt clause becomes unit and hence BCP can be invoked. Second, the succeeding BCP will not cause any consistency issue. To adopt the partial backtracking strategy, we need to update BCP procedure so that the two conditions are still met.

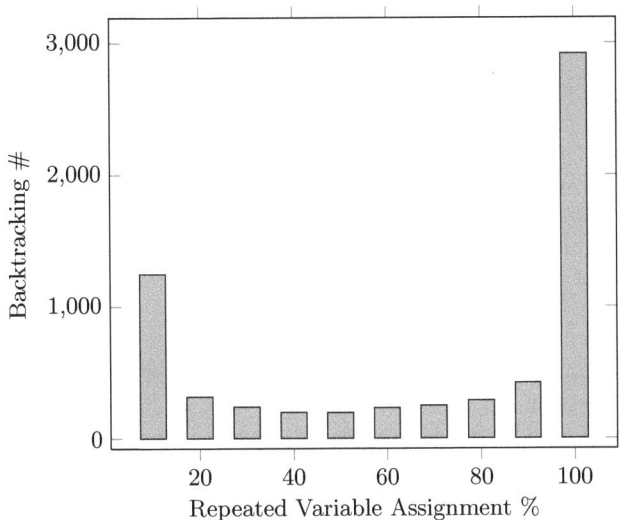

Fig. 3. Repeated variable assignment percentage while solving ACG-15-5p1.cnf from SAT Challenge 2012

The first condition can be easily satisfied by backtracking to any level lower than dl_{conf} but higher than or equal to dl_{asrt}. We note that the assertion level is the lowest level that the solver can backtrack to while keeping the learnt clause unit. The main complications come from maintaining the second condition. There are four kinds of issues BCP may encounter after backtracking to a level higher than dl_{asrt}. In Section 4.1, we will discuss these issues and give the corresponding solutions at clause level. The complete solution will be given in Section 4.2.

4.1 Complications and Solutions for Partial Backtracking

Unusual Implication. Classic backtracking guarantees that the solver always obtains implications at the current level dl_{curr}, that is, for any implication $l@dl$ in the implication queue, $dl = dl_{curr}$ (see Algorithm 1). However, this is not true for partial backtracking. A simple counterexample is the implication obtained from the learnt clause. This implication is at dl_{asrt}, which is lower than or equal to dl_{curr} after backtracking partially ($dl_{curr} = dl_{back} \geq dl_{asrt}$). Moreover, this implication may result in more implications, which can be scattered at any level between dl_{asrt} and dl_{curr}.

To the best of our knowledge, no existing solver exploits this guarantee in any essential way. In the implementation of Nigma, we simply relax this restriction.

Inappropriate Watched Literal. Generally, if a clause becomes unit and its sole free literal gets assigned according to this implication, its watched literals are certainly assigned at the highest decision level among all its literals. This condition may be violated after backtracking partially.

Consider a clause $x_1 \vee \neg x_2 \vee x_3$. Suppose x_3 is assigned FALSE at the level 10, and x_1 and x_2 are free. So x_1 and $\neg x_2$ are watched for this clause. During BCP after backtracking partially, x_1 may be assigned FALSE at the level 6. In this case, it is inappropriate to still watch x_1. Since the level of x_3 is higher than the level of x_1, x_3 should be watched instead.

In order to solve this issue, we use the following procedure, where $\delta(l)$ is a function that returns the decision level where the literal l gets assigned.

- *AdjustWatchedLiteral(wl, c)*
  Pre-condition: The literal wl is watched in the clause c; All the unwatched literals in c are FALSE.
  Description: Search for an unwatched literal l in c such that $\delta(l) > \delta(wl)$ and for any unwatched literal l' in c, $\delta(l) \geq \delta(l')$. If successful, unwatch wl, watch l and return l. Otherwise, return wl.

Spurious Conflict. As we noted before, BCP may lead to conflicts. A standard conflict has the following implicit feature: the two FALSE literals with the highest levels in the conflicting clause are assigned at the same level. However, during BCP after backtracking partially, the solver might encounter a *spurious conflict* where these two literals are assigned at different levels.

We give a simple example to illustrate the spurious conflict. Consider a clause $x_1 \vee \neg x_2$. After backtracking partially, we may have two implications $\neg x_1@10$ and $x_2@15$ at the same time. This is a conflict (as all the literals are FALSE), but it is different from the standard one.

The spurious conflict cannot be resolved by the standard learning procedure. From another perspective, the spurious conflict essentially implies that the FALSE literal with the highest level should have been implied at the second highest level among the literals in the conflicting clause. In other words, without learning, we can immediately obtain an implication by simply backtracking to a level between the highest level and the second highest level in the conflicting clause. That level can also be but not necessary the second highest level because we are able to handle the unusual implication now. We have the following procedure to resolve spurious conflicts.

- *ResolveSpuriousConflict(c)*
  Pre-condition: All the literals in the clause c are FALSE; The literals wl_1 and wl_2 are watched in c; $\delta(wl_1) \neq \delta(wl_2)$.
  Description: If $\delta(wl_1) > \delta(wl_2)$, backtrack to the level $\delta(wl_1) - 1$ and push the implication $wl_1@\delta(wl_2)$ into the implication queue. If $\delta(wl_1) < \delta(wl_2)$, backtrack to the level $\delta(wl_2) - 1$ and push the implication $wl_2@\delta(wl_1)$ into the implication queue.

Wrong Decision Level. After backtracking partially, some assigned variables need to update their decision levels. For example, consider a clause $x_1 \vee x_2$.

Initially, x_1 is assigned TRUE at the level 18 and x_2 is free. Suppose at the level 20, a conflict is identified and the solver backtracks to the level 19 while $dl_{asrt} = 5$. Further suppose that the succeeding BCP induces the implication $\neg x_2 @ 15$. As a result, the decision level of x_1 should be modified to 15. The issue can be solved by backtracking to the level 17 and get the implication $x_1 @ 15$. The following procedure is used for this purpose.

– $ResolveWrongDecisionLevel(c)$
  Pre-condition: All the unwatched literals in the clause c are FALSE; c has a TRUE watched literal wl_{true} and a FALSE watched literal wl_{false}; $\delta(wl_{true}) > \delta(wl_{false})$.
  Description: Backtrack to the level $\delta(wl_{true}) - 1$ and push the implication $wl_{true} @ \delta(wl_{false})$ into the implication queue.

Both processes of resolving spurious conflict and wrong decision level might trigger further backtracking. A helper procedure, $ClearInvalidImplications$, is defined to adjust the implication queue accordingly.

– $ClearInvalidImplications()$
  Description: Remove invalid implications from the implication queue. An implication $l@dl$ is *invalid* if $dl > dl_{curr}$.

In spite of the possible chained backtracking, whenever BCP terminates, the current decision level is always higher than or equal to the assertion level.

4.2 BCP after Partial Backtracking

As mentioned before, the standard BCP needs an adjustment if the solver takes a partial backtracking. Algorithm 3 shows the procedure *PropagateAmending* that is a special propagating procedure to be used after backtracking partially. Algorithm 4 shows the procedure *BCPAmending* that replaces the standard BCP procedure.

Let us revisit the example in Section 3. At this time, when the conflict occurs at the level 5, the solver takes a partial backtracking to the level 4 (see Figure 4a). While propagating the implication $\neg x_7 @ 1$, the solver obtains $\neg x_{11} @ 2$ (unusual implication) (see Figure 4b) due to $x_4 \vee x_7 \vee \neg x_{11}$. In the next iteration of propagation, the solver identifies a spurious conflict ($x_7 \vee x_{11} \vee x_{12}$) and has to go back one level to resolve it (see Figure 4c). Due to the existence of $x_6 \vee x_{11}$, x_6 should have been implied at the level 2 (wrong decision level), so the solver goes back one level again (see Figure 4d). Then BCP terminates because no more implication or conflict can be found. It is clearly seen that the solver amends the existing assignment trail conservatively, not simply discarding a significant portion of it. We note that under this strategy, it is possible that the solver enters a search space which is quite different from the one resulting from the classic backtracking.

We shall point out that, when the implication to be propagated happens to be at the current level, the effect of *PropagateAmending* is exactly the same as

Algorithm 3. $PropagateAmending(l@dl)$

1: $wl_1 \leftarrow \neg l$
2: **for all** clause c where wl_1 is watched **do**
3:    Search for a non-FALSE unwatched literal l' in c
4:    **if** Exists l' **then**
5:       Unwatch wl_1
6:       Watch l'
7:    **else**
8:       $wl_1 \leftarrow AdjustWatchedLiteral(wl_1, c)$
9:       $wl_2 \leftarrow$ the other watched literal in c
10:      **if** wl_2 is FALSE **then**
11:         **if** $\delta(wl_1) > \delta(wl_2)$ **then**
12:            $wl_2 \leftarrow AdjustWatchedLiteral(wl_2, c)$
13:         **end if**
14:         **if** $\delta(wl_1) == \delta(wl_2)$ **then**
15:            Backtrack to $\delta(wl_1)$
16:            $ConflictAnalysis()$ {Standard conflict}
17:            $ClearInvalidImplications()$
18:            **return**
19:         **else**
20:            $ResolveSpuriousConflict(c)$ {Spurious conflict}
21:            $ClearInvalidImplications()$
22:         **end if**
23:      **else if** wl_2 is TRUE **then**
24:         **if** $\delta(wl_2) > \delta(wl_1)$ **then**
25:            $ResolveWrongDecisionLevel(c)$ {Wrong decision level}
26:            $ClearInvalidImplications()$
27:         **end if**
28:      **else**
29:         $ImplicationQueue.Push(wl_2@\delta(wl_1))$
30:      **end if**
31:    **end if**
32: **end for**

Algorithm 4. $BCPAmending()$

1: **while** $ImplicationQueue$ is not empty **do**
2:    $l@dl \leftarrow ImplicationQueue.pop()$
3:    $PropagateAmending(l@dl)$
4: **end while**

Level	Assignments
1	$x_1, x_2, \neg x_7$
2	$x_3, \neg x_4$
3	$\neg x_5, x_6, x_{13}$
4	$\neg x_{12}$

(a)

Level	Assignments
1	$x_1, x_2, \neg x_7$
2	$x_3, \neg x_4, \neg x_{11}$
3	$\neg x_5, x_6, x_{13}$
4	$\neg x_{12}$

(b)

Level	Assignments
1	$x_1, x_2, \neg x_7$
2	$x_3, \neg x_4, \neg x_{11}, x_{12}$
3	$\neg x_5, x_6, x_{13}$
4	

(c)

Level	Assignments
1	$x_1, x_2, \neg x_7$
2	$x_3, \neg x_4, \neg x_{11}, x_{12}, x_6$
3	
4	

(d)

Fig. 4. The status after backtracking partially

Propagate. This indicates that *PropagateAmending* is essentially a generalization of *Propagate*.

5 Optimization

In this section, we discuss optimizations applicable to *PropagateAmending* and *BCPAmending*.

First, the implication queue can be constructed as a priority queue. As we described before, most CDCL solvers organize implications in a queue and propagates them in FIFO manner. However, since the implications in the queue can be scattered on different levels, unnecessary propagations can be avoided by giving higher priority to the implication at the lowest level in the queue. The intuition is that propagation may induce backtracking due to spurious conflict and wrong decision level, making some implications invalid and removed from the queue. For example, suppose that we have the implications $x_1@10$ and $\neg x_2@20$ in the implication queue. If propagating $x_1@10$ incurs a backtracking to some level lower than 20, $\neg x_2@20$ becomes invalid and the solver needs not propagate it.

Second, even if encountering a standard conflict in *PropagateAmending*, it is possible to postpone the conflict analysis. Suppose, while propagating $x_1@10$, the solver meets a standard conflict at the level 20. If the solver does not analyse the conflict immediately but continues propagating, it may backtrack to some level lower than 20 later due to spurious conflict or wrong decision level, making that conflict disappear automatically.

Third, it is unnecessary to call *PropagateAmending* in each iteration of *BCPAmending*. As mentioned before, *PropagateAmending* is a generalization of *Propagate* and it is more expensive than *Propagate*. If the implication to be propagated happens to be at the current level, calling *Propagate* directly instead of *PropagateAmending* will not cause any issue.

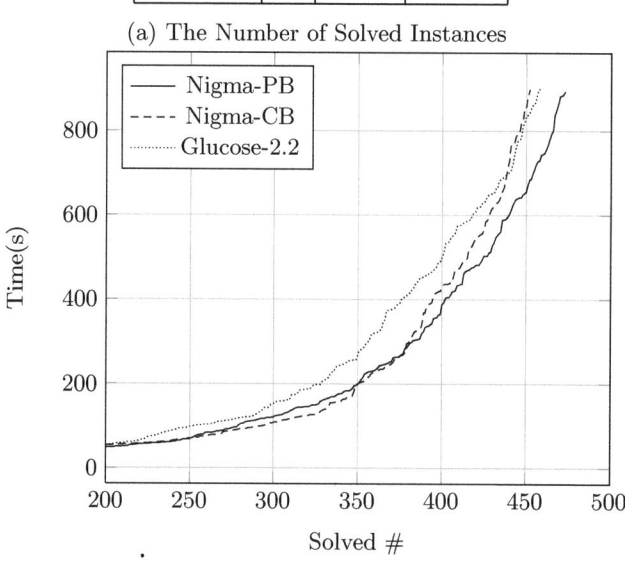

Fig. 5. Experiment results of Nigma-PB, Nigma-CB and Glucose 2.2 on the benchmark suite from the application track of SAT Challenge 2012

Fourth, it is also unnecessary to backtrack partially every time a conflict occurs. The motivation of partial backtracking is to save propagations. Thus this strategy should be more efficient if a large number of propagations are going to be discarded or repeated. In Nigma, we measure the saving by the number of levels the solver would go back by classic backtracking, namely, $dl_{conf} - dl_{asrt}$. According to our experiments, when we set the triggering condition to $dl_{conf} - dl_{asrt} > 10$, around 5% ~ 30% of conflicts will trigger partial backtracking.

6 Experiment Results

In this section, we present experiment results using our solver Nigma, which is a CDCL solver based on MiniSat 2.2 [9]. The benchmark suite consists of the 600 instances from the application track of SAT Challenge 2012 [10]. We conducted experiments on a 3.40GHz × 8 Intel Core i7-2600K processor with 900 second timeout and 7GB memory limit per instance.

The versions of Nigma with partial backtracking and with classic backtracking are denoted by Nigma-PB and Nigma-CB, respectively. Nigma-PB is configured as follows: if $dl_{conf} - dl_{asrt} \leq 10$, the solver simply follows the classic backtracking

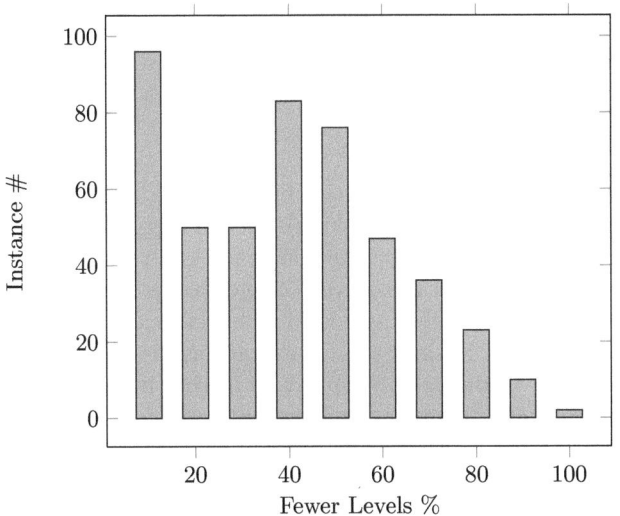

Fig. 6. Nigma backtracks fewer levels with partial backtracking

strategy; otherwise, the solver backtracks only one level, that is, it backtracks to the level $dl_{conf} - 1$. We use Glucose 2.2 [11] as an additional reference.

Figure 5a shows the number of instances solved by the three solvers and Figure 5b is the cactus plot of the results. It is clearly seen that when applying partial backtracking, Nigma-PB solved 21 more instances than Nigma-CB, and it also performs better than Glucose 2.2.

An in-depth view of the effect of partial backtracking is given in Figure 6, showing the percentage of fewer levels the solver backtracks for each solved instance. We note that, for a majority of instances, when the solver takes a partial backtracking, it backtracks 10% ∼ 60% fewer levels finally, compared with classic backtracking.

We also compare two additional metrics in the experiment, in order to explain the performance improvement by partial backtracking from a different perspective. The first metric is the number of decisions to solve an instance. Generally speaking, fewer decisions indicate the solver explores the search space in a better way [8]. According to the experiment, among the 439 instances solved by both Nigma-PB and Nigma-CB, 317 instances are solved by Nigma-PB with fewer decisions than by Nigma-CB.

The second metric is the number of decisions per conflict for a solved instance. We are interested in this metric because the power of CDCL solvers stems from identifying and learning from conflicts. The number of decisions per conflict reflects how frequently the solver identifies a conflict. The smaller this number is, the more often the solver detects and corrects its fault in making decisions. Partial backtracking has the potential to reduce this number as the solver might detect a standard conflict at a level higher than dl_{asrt} (see Line 14-18 in Algorithm 3) while retaining the ability to detect a standard conflict at

dl_{asrt}. The experiment result confirms our conjecture: 387 instances are solved by Nigma-PB with fewer decisions per conflict than by Nigma-CB.

7 Conclusions

In this paper, we presented the partial backtracking strategy which is essentially an extension of classic backtracking. This strategy amends the assignment trail instead of simply discarding a portion of it. As a result, some propagations need not to be repeated and the solver can go deeper in certain search space. Our experiments show that this new kind of backtracking improves the performance of CDCL solvers. Besides the optimizations mentioned in Section 5, we are investigating the following two aspects to further improve its efficiency.

First, in our current implementation, the solver backtracks to $dl_{asrt} - 1$ first. In fact, any level higher than dl_{asrt} can be used for the initial backtracking, as going back to that level still keeps the learnt clause unit. We are interested in designing a better heuristic to select the initial backtracking level.

Second, we would explore other criteria to trigger a partial backtracking. A promising candidate is the number of variable assignments the solver would discard by taking a classic backtracking.

References

1. Marques-Silva, J.P., Sakallah, K.A.: Grasp: A search algorithm for propositional satisfiability. IEEE Transactions on Computers 48(5), 506–521 (1999)
2. Lynce, I., Baptista, L., Marques-Silva, J.P.: Stochastic systematic search algorithms for satisfiability. Electronic Notes in Discrete Mathematics 9, 190–204 (2001)
3. Lynce, I., Marques-Silva, J.P.: Random backtracking in backtrack search algorithms for satisfiability. Discrete Applied Mathematics 155(12), 1604–1612 (2007)
4. Moskewicz, M.W., Madigan, C.F., Zhao, Y., Zhang, L., Malik, S.: Chaff: Engineering an efficient sat solver. In: Proceedings of the 38th Conference on Design Automation, New York, USA, pp. 530–535 (2001)
5. Pipatsrisawat, K., Darwiche, A.: A lightweight component caching scheme for satisfiability solvers. In: Marques-Silva, J., Sakallah, K.A. (eds.) SAT 2007. LNCS, vol. 4501, pp. 294–299. Springer, Heidelberg (2007)
6. Marques-Silva, J.P., Lynce, I., Malik, S.: Conflict-driven clause learning sat solvers. In: Handbook of Satisfiability, pp. 131–154 (2009)
7. van der Tak, P., Ramos, A., Heule, M.: Reusing the assignment trail in cdcl solvers. Journal on Satisfiability, Boolean Modeling and Computation 7, 133–138 (2011)
8. Zhang, L., Madigan, C.F., Moskewicz, M.H., Malik, S.: Efficient conflict driven learning in a boolean satisfiability solver. In: Proceedings of the 2001 IEEE/ACM International Conference on Computer-Aided Design, pp. 279–285. IEEE Press (2001)
9. Eén, N., Sörensson, N.: Minisat 2.2, http://minisat.se/
10. Balint, A., Belov, A., Järvisalo, M., Sinz, C.: Sat challenge (2012), http://baldur.iti.kit.edu/SAT-Challenge-2012/index.html
11. Audemard, G., Simon, L.: Glucose 2.2, https://www.lri.fr/~simon/?page=glucose

Lemma Mining over **HOL Light**

Cezary Kaliszyk and Josef Urban

[1] University of Innsbruck, Austria
[2] Radboud University, Nijmegen

Abstract. Large formal mathematical libraries consist of millions of atomic inference steps that give rise to a corresponding number of proved statements (lemmas). Analogously to the informal mathematical practice, only a tiny fraction of such statements is named and re-used in later proofs by formal mathematicians. In this work, we suggest and implement criteria defining the estimated usefulness of the HOL Light lemmas for proving further theorems. We use these criteria to mine the large inference graph of all lemmas in the core HOL Light library, adding thousands of the best lemmas to the pool of named statements that can be re-used in later proofs. The usefulness of the new lemmas is then evaluated by comparing the performance of automated proving of the core HOL Light theorems with and without such added lemmas.

1 Introduction

In the last decade, large formal mathematical corpora such as the Mizar Mathematical Library [5] (MML), Isabelle/HOL [33] and HOL Light [7]/Flyspeck [6] have been translated to formats that allow easy experiments with external automated theorem provers (ATPs) and AI systems [10, 17, 26]. Several AI/ATP methods for reasoning in the context of a large number of related theorems and proofs have been suggested and tried already, including: (i) methods (often external to the core ATP algorithms) that select relevant premises (facts) from the thousands of theorems available in such corpora [8,15], (ii) methods for internal guidance of ATP systems when reasoning in the large-theory setting [31], (iii) methods that automatically evolve more and more efficient ATP strategies for the clusters of related problems from such corpora [28], and (iv) methods that learn which of such specialized strategies to use for a new problem [14].

In this work, we start to complement the first set of methods – ATP-external premise selection – with *lemma mining* from the large corpora. The main idea of this approach is to enrich the pool of human-defined main (top-level) theorems in the large libraries with the most useful/interesting lemmas extracted from the proofs in these libraries. Such lemmas are then eligible together with (or instead of) the main library theorems as the premises that are given to the ATPs to attack new conjectures formulated over the large libraries.

This high-level idea is straightforward, but there are a number of possible approaches involving a number of issues to be solved, starting with a reasonable definition of a *useful/interesting lemma*, and with making such definitions efficient over corpora that contain millions to billions of candidate lemmas. These issues are discussed in Sections 4 and 5, after motivating and explaining the overall approach for using lemmas in large theories in Section 2 and giving an overview of the recent related work in Section 3.

As in any AI discipline dealing with large amount of data, research in the large-theory field is driven by rigorous experimental evaluations of the proposed methods over the existing corpora. For the first experiments with lemma mining we use the HOL Light system, together with its core library and the Flyspeck library. The various evaluation scenarios are defined and discussed in Section 6, and the implemented methods are evaluated in Section 7. Section 8 discusses the various future directions and concludes.

2 Using Lemmas for Theorem Proving in Large Theories

The main task in the Automated Reasoning in Large Theories (ARLT) domain is to prove new conjectures with the knowledge of a large body of previously proved theorems and their proofs. This setting reasonably corresponds to how large ITP libraries are constructed, and hopefully also emulates how human mathematicians work more faithfully than the classical scenario of a single hard problem consisting of isolated axioms and a conjecture [30]. The pool of previously proved theorems ranges from thousands in large-theory ATP benchmarks such as MPTP2078 [1], to tens of thousands when working with the whole ITP libraries.[1]

The strongest existing ARLT systems combine variously parametrized premise-selection techniques (often based on machine learning from previous proofs) with ATP systems and their strategies that are called with varied numbers of the most promising premises. These techniques can go quite far already: when using 14-fold parallelization and 30s wall-clock time, the HOL(y)Hammer system [10,11] can today prove 47% of the 14185 Flyspeck theorems [12]. This is measured in a scenario[2] in which the Flyspeck theorems are ordered *chronologically* using the loading sequence of the Flyspeck library, and presented in this order to HOL(y)Hammer as conjectures. After each theorem is attempted, its human-designed HOL Light proof is fed to the HOL(y)Hammer's learning components, together with the (possibly several) ATP proofs found by HOL(y)Hammer itself. This means that for each Flyspeck theorem, all human-written HOL Light proofs of all previous theorems are assumed to be known, together with all their ATP proofs found already by HOL(y)Hammer, but nothing is known about the current conjecture and the following parts of the library (they do not exist yet).

So far, systems like HOL(y)Hammer (similar systems include Sledgehammer/-MaSh [13] and MaLARea [29]) have only used the set of *named library theorems* for proving new conjectures and thus also for the premise-selection learning. This is usually a reasonable set of theorems to start with, because the human mathematicians have years of experience with structuring the formal libraries. On the

---

[1] 14185 theorems are in the HOL/Flyspeck library, about 20000 are in the Isabelle/HOL library, and about 50000 theorems are in the Mizar library.

[2] A similar scenario has been introduced in 2013 also for the CASC LTB competition.

other hand, there is no guarantee that this set is in any sense optimal, both for the human mathematicians and for the ATPs. The following three observations indicate that the set of human-named theorems may be suboptimal:

Proofs of different length: The human-named theorems may differ considerably in the length of their proofs. The human naming is based on a number of (possibly traditional/esthetical) criteria that may sometimes have little to do with a good structuring of the library.

Duplicate and weak theorems: The large collaboratively-build libraries are hard to manually guard against duplications and naming of weak versions of various statements. The experiments with the MoMM system over the Mizar library [27] and with the recording of the Flyspeck library [9] have shown that there are a number of subsumed and duplicated theorems, and that some unnamed strong lemmas are proved over and over again.

Short alternative proofs: The experiments with AI-assisted ATP over the Mizar and Flyspeck libraries [2,10] have shown that the combined AI/ATP systems may sometimes find alternative proofs that are much shorter and very different from the human proofs, again turning some "hard" named theorems into easy corollaries.

Suboptimal naming may obviously influence the performance of the current large-theory systems. If many important lemmas are omitted by the human naming, the ATPs will have to find them over and over when proving the conjectures that depend on such lemmas. On the other hand, if many similar variants of one theorem are named, the current premise-selection methods might focus too much on those variants, and fail to select the complementary theorems that are also necessary for proving a particular conjecture.[3]

To various extent, this problem might be remedied by the alternative learning/guidance methods (ii) and (iii) mentioned in the introduction: Learning of internal ATP guidance using for example Veroff's hint technique [32], and learning of suitable ATP strategies using systems like BliStr [28]. But these methods are so far much more experimental in the large-theory setting than premise selection.[4] That is why we propose the following lemma-mining approach:

1. Considering (efficiently) the detailed graph of all atomic inferences contained in the ITP libraries. Such a graph has millions of nodes for the core HOL Light corpus, and hundreds of millions of nodes for the whole Flyspeck.
2. Defining over such large proof graphs efficient criteria that select a smaller set of the strongest and most orthogonal lemmas from the corpora.
3. Using such lemmas together with (or instead of) the human-named theorems for proving new conjectures over the corpora.

---

[3] This behavior obviously depends on the premise-selection algorithm. It is likely to occur when the premise selection is mainly based on symbolic similarity of the premises to the conjecture. It is less likely to occur when complementary semantic selection criteria are additionally used as, e.g., in SRASS [25] and MaLARea [29].

[4] In particular, several initial experiments done so far with Veroff's hints over the MPTPChallenge and MPTP2078 benchmarks were so far unsuccessful.

3 Overview of Related Work and Ideas

A number of ways how to measure the quality of lemmas and how to use them for further reasoning have been proposed already, particularly in the context of ATP systems and proofs. Below we summarize recent approaches and tools that initially seemed most relevant to our work.

Lemmas are an essential part of various ATP algorithms. State-of-the-art ATPs such as Vampire [21], E [23] and Prover9 [16] implement various variants of the ANL loop [34], resulting in hundreds to billions of lemmas inferred during the prover runs. This gave rise to a number of efficient ATP indexing techniques, redundancy control techniques such as subsumption, and also fast ATP heuristics (based on weight, age, conjecture-similarity, etc.) for choosing the best lemmas for the next inferences. Several ATP methods and tools work with such ATP lemmas. Veroff's *hint technique* [32] extracts the best lemmas from the proofs produced by successful Prover9 runs and uses them for directing the proof search in Prover9 on related problems. A similar lemma-extracting, generalizing and proof-guiding technique (called *E Knowledge Base – EKB*) was implemented by Schulz in E prover as a part of his PhD thesis [22].

Schulz also implemented the *epcllemma* tool that estimates the best lemmas in an arbitrary DAG (directed acyclic graph) of inferences. Unlike the hint-extracting/guiding methods, this tool works not just on the handful of lemmas involved in the final refutational proof, but on the typically very large number of lemmas produced during the (possibly unfinished) ATP runs. The epcllemma's criteria for selecting the next best lemma from the inference DAG are: (i) the size of the lemma's inference subgraph based at the nodes that are either axioms or already chosen (better) lemmas, and (ii) the weight of the lemma. This lemma-selection process may be run recursively, until a stopping criterion (minimal lemma quality, required number of lemmas, etc.) is reached. Our algorithm for HOL Light (Section 5) is quite similar to this.

AGIntRater [20] is a tool that computes various characteristics of the lemmas that are part of the final refutational ATP proof and aggregates them into an overall *interestingness* rating. These characteristics include: obviousness, complexity, intensity, surprisingness, adaptivity, focus, weight, and usefulness, see [20] for details. AGIntRater so far was not directly usable on our data for various reasons (particularly the size of our graph), but we might re-use and try to efficiently implement some of its ideas later.

Pudlák [19] has conducted experiments over several datasets with automated re-use of lemmas from many existing ATP proofs in order to find smaller proofs and also to attack unsolved problems. This is similar to the hints technique, however more automated and closer to our large-theory setting (hints have so far been successfully applied mainly in small algebraic domains). To interreduce the large number of such lemmas with respect to subsumption he used the E-based *CSSCPA* [24] subsumption tool by Schulz and Sutcliffe. *MoMM* [27] adds a number of large-theory features to CSSCPA. It was used for (i) fast interreduction of million of lemmas extracted (generalized) from the proofs in the Mizar library, and (ii) as an early ATP-for-ITP hammer-style tool for completing proofs in Mizar with the help of the whole Mizar library. All library lemmas can be loaded, indexed and considered for each query, however the price for this breadth of coverage is that the inference process is limited to subsumption extended with Mizar-style dependent types.

AGIntRater and epcllemma use a lemma's position in the inference graph as one of the lemma's characteristics that contribute to its importance. There are also purely graph-based algorithms that try to estimate a relative importance of nodes in a graph. In particular, research of large graphs became popular with the appearance of the World Wide Web and social networks. Algorithms such as *PageRank* [18] (eigenvector centrality) have today fast approximative implementations that easily scale to billions of nodes.

4 The Proof Data

We initially consider two corpora: the core HOL Light corpus (SVN version 146) and the Flyspeck corpus (SVN version 2886). The core HOL Light corpus consists of 1,984 named theorems, while the Flyspeck corpus contains 14,185 named theorems. There are 97,714,465 lemmas in Flyspeck when exact duplicates are removed, and 420,253,109 lemmas when counting duplicates. When removing duplicates only within the proof of each named theorem, the final number of lemmas is 146,120,269. For core HOL Light the number of non-duplicate lemmas is 1,987,781. When counting duplicates it is 6,963,294, and when removing duplicates only inside the proof of each named theorem it is 2,697,212 . To obtain the full inference graph for Flyspeck we run the proof-recording version of HOL Light [9]. This takes 14 hours of CPU time and 42 GB of RAM on an Intel Xeon 2.6 GHz machine. This time and memory consumption are much lower when working only with the core HOL Light, hence many of the experiments were so far done only on the smaller corpus.

There are 140,534,426 inference edges between the unique Flyspeck lemmas, each of them corresponding to one of the LCF-style kernel inferences done by HOL Light [9]. During the proof recording we additionally export the information about the symbol weight (size) of each lemma, and its normalized form that serially numbers bound and free variables and tags them with their types. This information is later used for external postprocessing, together with the information about which theorems where originally named. Below is a commented example of the initial segment of the Flyspeck proof trace, the full trace (1.5G in size) is available online[5], as well as the numbers of the original named Flyspeck theorems.[6]

```
F13        #1, Definition (size 13): T <=> (\A0. A0) = (\A0. A0)
R9         #2, Reflexivity (size 9): (\A0. A0) = (\A0. A0)
R5         #3, Reflexivity (size 5): T <=> T
R5         #4, Reflexivity (size 5): (<=>) = (<=>)
C17 4 1    #5, Application(4,1):    (<=>) T = (<=>) ((\A0. A0) = (\A0. A0))
C21 5 3    #6, Application(5,3):    (T <=> T) <=> (\A0. A0) = (\A0. A0) <=> T
E13 6 3    #7, EQ_MP(6,3) (size 13): (\A0. A0) = (\A0. A0) <=> T
```

---

[5] http://mizar.cs.ualberta.ca/~mptp/lemma_mining/proof.trace.old.gz
[6] http://mizar.cs.ualberta.ca/~mptp/lemma_mining/facts.trace.old.gz

4.1 Initial Post-processing and Optimization of the Proof Data

During the proof recording, only exact duplicates are easy to detect. Due to various implementational issues, it is simpler to always limit the duplication detection to the lemmas derived within a proof of each named theorem, hence this is our default initial dataset. HOL Light does not natively use de Bruijn indices for representing variables, i.e., two alpha-convertible versions of the same theorems will be kept in the proof trace if they differ in variable names. Checking for alpha convertibility during the proof recording is nontrivial, because in the HOL Light's LCF-style approach alpha conversion itself results in multiple kernel inferences. That is why we keep the original proof trace untouched, and implement its further optimizations as external postprocessing of the trace.

In particular, to merge alpha convertible lemmas in a proof trace T, we just use the above mentioned normalized-variable representation of the lemmas as an input to an external program that produces a new version of the proof trace T'. This program goes through the trace T and replaces references to each lemma by a reference to the earliest lemma in T with the same normalized-variable representation. The proofs of the later named alpha variants of the lemmas in T are however still kept in the new trace T', because such proofs are important when computing the usage and dependency statistics over the normalized lemmas. So far we have done this postprocessing only for the core HOL Light 2,697,212 lemmas,[7] because printing out of the variable-normalized version of the 146,120,269 partially de-duplicated Flyspeck lemmas would produce more than 100G of data. From the 2,697,212 partially de-duplicated core HOL Light lemmas 1,076,995 are left after this stronger normalization. It is clear that such post-processing operations can be implemented different ways. In this case, some original information about the proof graph is lost, while some information (proofs of duplicate lemmas) is still kept, even though it could be also pruned from the graph, producing a differently normalized version.

The ATP experiments described below use only the two versions of the proof trace described above, but we have also explored some other normalizations. A particularly interesting optimization from the ATP point of view is the removal of subsumed lemmas. An initial measurement with the (slightly modified) MoMM system done on the clausified first-order versions of about 200,000 core HOL Light lemmas has shown that about 33% of the clauses generated from the lemmas are subsumed. But again, ATP operations like subsumption interact with the level of inferences recorded by the HOL Light kernel in nontrivial ways. It is an interesting task to define exactly how the original proof graph should be transformed with respect to such operations, and how to perform such proof graph transformations efficiently over the whole Flyspeck.

5 Selecting Good Lemmas

Several approaches to defining the notion of a useful/interesting lemma are mentioned in Section 3. There are a number of ideas that can be explored and

---
[7] http://mizar.cs.ualberta.ca/~mptp/lemma_mining/human.gz

combined together in various ways, but the more complex methods (such as those used by AGIntRater) are not yet directly usable on the large ITP datasets that we have. So far, we have experimented mainly with the following techniques:

1. A direct OCAML implementation of lemma quality metrics based on the HOL Light proof-recording data structures.
2. Schulz's epcllemma and its minor modifications.
3. PageRank, applied in various ways to the proof trace.

5.1 Direct Computation of Lemma Quality

The advantage of the direct OCAML implementation is that no export to external tools is necessary and all the information collected about the lemmas by the HOL Light proof recording is directly available. The basic factors that we use so far for defining the quality of a lemma i are its: (i) set of direct proof dependencies $d(i)$ given by the proof trace, (ii) number of recursive dependencies $D(i)$, (iii) number of recursive uses $U(i)$, and (iv) number of HOL symbols (HOL weight) $S(i)$. When recursively defining $U(i)$ and $D(i)$ we assume that in general some lemmas may already be named ($k \in Named$) and some lemmas are just axioms ($k \in Axioms$). Note that in HOL Light there are many lemmas that have no dependencies, but formally they are still derived using for example the reflexivity inference rule (i.e., we do not count them among the HOL Light axioms). The recursion when defining D thus stops at axioms, named lemmas, and lemmas with no dependencies. The recursion when defining U stops at named lemmas and unused lemmas. Formally:

Definition 1 (Recursive dependencies and uses).

$$D(i) = \begin{cases} 1 & \text{if } i \in Named \vee i \in Axioms, \\ \sum_{j \in d(i)} D(j) & \text{otherwise.} \end{cases}$$

$$U(i) = \begin{cases} 1 & \text{if } i \in Named, \\ \sum_{i \in d(j)} U(j) & \text{otherwise.} \end{cases}$$

In particular, this means that

$$D(i) = 0 \iff d(i) = \emptyset \wedge \neg(i \in Axioms)$$

and also that

$$U(i) = 0 \iff \forall j \neg(i \in d(j))$$

These basic characteristics are combined into the following lemma quality metrics $Q_1(i)$, $Q_2(i)$, and $Q_3(i)$. $Q_1^r(i)$ is a generalized version of $Q_1(i)$, which we (apart from Q_1) test for $r \in \{0, 0.5, 1.5, 2\}$:

Definition 2 (Lemma quality).

$$Q_1(i) = \frac{U(i) * D(i)}{S(i)} \qquad Q_1^r(i) = \frac{U(i)^r * D(i)^{2-r}}{S(i)}$$

$$Q_2(i) = \frac{U(i) * D(i)}{S(i)^2} \qquad Q_3(i) = \frac{U(i) * D(i)}{1.1^{S(i)}}$$

The justification behind these definitions are the following heuristics:

1. The higher is $D(i)$, the more necessary it is to remember the lemma i, because it will be harder to infer with an ATP when needed.
2. The higher is $U(i)$, the more useful the lemma i is for proving other desired conjectures.
3. The higher is $S(i)$, the more complicated the lemma i is in comparison to other lemmas. In particular, doubled size may often mean in HOL Light that i is just a conjunction of two other lemmas.[8]

5.2 Lemma Quality via Epcllemma

Lemma quality in epcllemma is defined on clause inferences recorded using E's native PCL protocol. The lemma quality computation also takes into account the lemmas that have been already named, and with minor implementational variations it can be expressed using D and S as follows:

$$EQ_1(i) = \frac{D(i)}{S(i)}$$

The difference to $Q_1(i)$ is that $U(i)$ is not used, i.e., only the cumulative effort needed to prove the lemma counts, together with its size (this is also very close to $Q_1^r(i)$ with $r = 0$). The main advantage of using epcllemma is its fast and robust implementation using the E code base. This allowed us to load in reasonable time (about one hour) the whole Flyspeck proof trace into epcllemma, taking 67 GB of RAM. Unfortunately, this experiment showed that epcllemma assumes that D is always an integer. This is likely not a problem for epcllemma's typical use, but on the Flyspeck graph this quickly leads to integer overflows and wrong results. To a smaller extent this shows already on the core HOL Light proof graph. A simple way how to prevent the overflows was to modify epcllemma to use instead of D the longest chain of inferences L:

$$L(i) = \begin{cases} 1 & \text{if } i \in Named \vee i \in Axioms, \\ max_{j \in d(i)}(1 + L(j)) & \text{otherwise.} \end{cases}$$

---

[8] The possibility to create conjunctions is quite a significant difference to the clausal setting handled by the existing tools. A longer clause is typically weaker, while longer conjunctions are stronger. A dependence on a longer conjunction should ideally be treated by the evaluating heuristics as a dependence on the multiple conjuncts.

This leads to:
$$EQ_2(i) = \frac{L(i)}{S(i)}$$

Apart from this modification, only minor changes were needed to make epcllemma work on the HOL Light data. The HOL proof trace was expressed as a PCL proof (renaming the HOL inferences into E inferences), and artificial TPTP clauses of the corresponding size were used instead of the original HOL clauses.

5.3 Lemma Quality via PageRank

PageRank (eigenvector centrality of a graph) is a method that assigns weights to the nodes in an arbitrary directed graph (not just DAG) based on the weights of the neighboring nodes ("incoming links"). In more detail, the weights are computed as the dominant eigenvector of the following set of equations:

$$PR_1(i) = \frac{1-f}{N} + f \sum_{i \in d(j)} \frac{PR_1(j)}{|d(j)|}$$

where N is the total number of nodes and f is a damping factor, typically set to 0.85. The advantage of using PageRank is that there are fast approximative implementations that can process the whole Flyspeck proof graph in about 10 minutes using about 21 GB RAM, and the weights of all nodes are computed simultaneously in this time.

This is however also a disadvantage in comparison to the previous algorithms: PageRank does not take into account the lemmas that have already been selected (named). The closer a lemma i is to an important lemma j, the more important i will be. Modifications that use the initial PageRank scores for more advanced clustering exist [3] and perhaps could be used to mitigate this problem while still keeping the overall processing reasonably fast. Another disadvantage of PageRank is its ignorance of the lemma size, which results in greater weights for the large conjunctions that are used quite often in HOL Light. PR_2 tries to counter that:

$$PR_2(i) = \frac{PR_1(i)}{S(i)}$$

PR_1 and PR_2 are based on the idea that a lemma is important if it is needed to prove many other important lemmas. This can be again turned around: we can define that a lemma is important if it depends on many important lemmas. This is equivalent to computing the reverse PageRank and its size-normalized version:

$$PR_3(i) = \frac{1-f}{N} + f \sum_{i \in u(j)} \frac{PR_3(j)}{|u(j)|} \qquad PR_4(i) = \frac{PR_3(i)}{S(i)}$$

where $u(j)$ are the direct uses of the lemma j, i.e., $i \in u(j) \iff j \in d(i)$. The two ideas can again be combined (note that the sum of the PageRanks of all

nodes is always 1):
$$PR_5(i) = \frac{PR_1(i) + PR_3(i)}{S(i)}$$

5.4 Selecting Many Lemmas

From the methods described above, only the various variants of PageRank (PR_i) produce the final ranking of all lemmas in one run. Both epcllemma (EQ_i) and our custom methods (Q_i) are parametrized by the set of lemmas ($Named$) that have already been named. When the task is to choose a predefined number of the best lemmas, this naturally leads to the following recursive lemma-selection algorithm (used also by epcllemma):

Algorithm 1. Best lemmas

Input a lemma-quality metric Q, set of lemmas $Lemmas$, an initial set of named lemmas $Named_0 \subset Lemmas$, and a required number of lemmas M
Output set $Named$ of M best lemmas according to Q
1: $Named \leftarrow Named_0$
2: $m \leftarrow 0$
3: **while** $m < M$ **do**
4:    **for** $i \in Lemmas$ **do**
5:       CALCULATE($Q_{Named}(i)$)
6:    **end for**
7:    $j \leftarrow argmax\{Q_{Named}(i) : i \in Lemmas \setminus Named\}$
8:    $Named \leftarrow Named \cup \{j\}$
9:    $m \leftarrow m + 1$
10: **end while**
11: RETURN($Named$)

There are two possible choices of $Named_0$: either the empty set, or the set of all human-named theorems. This choice depends on whether we want reorganize the library from scratch, or whether we just want to select good lemmas that complement the human-named theorems. Below we experiment with both approaches. Note that this algorithm is currently quite expensive: the fast epcllemma implementation takes 65 seconds to update the lemma qualities over the whole Flyspeck graph after each change of the $Named$ set. This means that producing the first 10000 Flyspeck lemmas takes 180 CPU hours. That is why most of the experiments are limited to the core HOL Light graph where this takes about 1 second and 3 hours respectively.

6 Evaluation Scenarios and Issues

To assess and develop the lemma-mining methods we define several evaluation scenarios that vary in speed, informativeness and rigor. The simplest and least rigorous is the *expert-evaluation* scenario: We use our knowledge of the formal corpora to quickly see if the top-ranked lemmas produced by a particular method look plausible. Because of its size, this is the only evaluation done for the whole Flyspeck corpus so far.

The *cheating ATP* scenario uses the full proof graph of a corpus to compute the set of the (typically 10,000) best lemmas (*BestLemmas*) for the whole corpus. Then the set of newly named theorems (*NewThms*) is defined as the union of *BestLemmas* with the set of originally named theorems (*OrigThms*): $NewThms := BestLemmas \cup OrigThms$. The derived graph $G_{NewThms}$ of direct dependencies among the elements of *NewThms* is used for ATP evaluation, which may be done in two ways: with human selection and with AI selection. When using human selection, we try to prove each lemma from its parents in $G_{NewThms}$. When using AI selection, we use the chronological order (see Section 2) of *NewThms* to incrementally train and evaluate the k-NN machine learner [12] on the direct dependencies from $G_{NewThms}$. This produces for each new theorem an ATP problem with premises advised by the learner trained on the $G_{NewThms}$ dependencies of the preceding new theorems. This scenario may do a lot of cheating, because when measuring the ATP success on *OrigThms*, a particular theorem i might be proved with the use of lemmas from *NewThms* that have been stated for the first time only in the original proof of i (we call such lemmas *directly preceding*). In other words, such lemmas did not exist before the original proof of i was started, so they could not possibly be suggested by lemma-quality metrics for proving i. Such directly preceding lemmas could also be very close to i, and thus equally hard to prove.

The *almost-honest ATP* scenario is like the *cheating ATP* scenario, however directly preceding new lemmas are replaced by their closest *OrigThms* ancestors. This scenario is still not fully honest, because the lemmas are computed according to their lemma quality measured on the full proof graph. In particular, when proving an early theorem i from *OrigThms*, the newly used parents of i are lemmas whose quality was clear only after taking into account the theorems that were proved later than i. These theorems and their proofs however did not exist at the time of proving i. Still, we consider this scenario sufficiently honest for most of the ATP evaluations done with over the whole core HOL Light dataset.

The *fully-honest ATP* scenario removes this last objection, at the price of using considerably more resources for a single evaluation. For each originally named theorem j we limit the proof graph used for computing *BestLemmas* to the proofs that preceded j. Since computing *BestLemmas* for the whole core HOL Light takes at least three hours for the Q_i and EQ_i methods, the full evaluation on all 1,984 core HOL Light theorems would take about 2,000 CPU hours. That is why we further scale down this evaluation by doing it only for every tenth theorem in core HOL Light.

The *chained-conjecturing ATP* scenario is similar to the cheating scenario, but with limits imposed on the directly preceding lemmas. In $chain_1$-*conjecturing*, any (possibly directly preceding) lemma used to prove a theorem i must itself have an ATP proof using only *OrigThms*. In other words, it is allowed to guess good lemmas that still do not exist, but such lemmas must not be hard to prove from $OrigThms$. Analogously for $chain_2$-conjecturing (resp. $chain_N$), where lemmas provable from $chain_1$-lemmas (resp. $chain_{N-1}$) are allowed to be guessed. To some extent, this scenario measures the theoretical ATP improvement obtainable with guessing of good intermediate lemmas.

7 Experiments

The ATP experiments are done on the same hardware and using the same setup that was used for the earlier evaluations described in [10, 12]: All systems are run with 30s time limit on a 48-core server with AMD Opteron 6174 2.2 GHz CPUs, 320 GB RAM, and 0.5 MB L2 cache per CPU. When using only the original theorems, the success rate of the 14 most complementary AI/ATP methods run with 30s time limit each and restricted to the 1954 core HOL Light theorems is 65.2% (1275 theorems) and the union of all methods solves 65.4% (1278 theorems).

In the very optimistic *cheating* scenario (limited only to the Q_i metrics), this numbers go up to 76.5% (1496 theorems) resp. 77.9% (1523 theorems). As mentioned in Section 6, many proofs in this scenario may however be too simple because a close directly preceding lemma was used by the lemma-mining/machine-learning/ATP stack. This became easy to see already when using the *almost-honest* scenario, where the 14 best methods (including also EQ_i and PR_i) solve together only 66.3% (1296 theorems) and the union of all methods solves 68.9% (1347 theorems). The resource-intensive *fully-honest* evaluation is limited to a relatively small subset of the core HOL Light theorems, however it confirms the *almost-honest* results. While the original success rate was 61.7% (less than 14 methods are needed to reach it), the success rate with lemma mining went up to 64.8% (again, less than 14 methods are needed). This means that the non-cheating lemma-mining approaches so far improve the overall performance of the AI/ATP methods over core HOL Light by about 5%. The best method in the *fully-honest* evaluation is Q_2 which solves 46.2% of the original problems when using 512 premises, followed by EQ_2 (using the longest inference chain instead of D), which solves 44.6 problems also with 512 premises. The best PageRank-based method is PR_2 (PageRank divided by size), solving 41.4% problems with 128 premises.

An interesting middle-way between the cheating and non-cheating scenarios is the *chained-conjecturing* evaluation, which indicates the possible improvement when guessing good lemmas that are "in the middle" of long proofs. Since this is also quite expensive, only the best lemma-mining method (Q_2) was evaluated so far. Q_2 itself solves (altogether, using different numbers of premises) 54.5% (1066) of the problems. This goes up to 61.4% (1200 theorems) when using only $chain_1$-conjecturing and to 63.8% (1247 theorems) when allowing also $chain_2$ and $chain_3$-conjecturing. These are 12.6% and 17.0% improvements respectively.

Finally, since regular lemma-mining/machine-learning/ATP evaluations over the whole Flyspeck corpus are still outside our resources, we present below several best lemmas computed by epcllemma's EQ_2 method over the 97,714,465-node-large proof graph of all Flyspeck lemmas:[9]

```
|- a + c + d = c + a + d
|- x * (y + z) = x * y + x * z
|- (a + b) + c = a + b + c
|- &1 > &0
|- a ==> b <=> ~a \/ b
|- BIT1 m + BIT0 n = BIT1 (m + n)
```

8 Future Work and Conclusion

We have proposed, implemented and evaluated several approaches that try to efficiently find the best lemmas and re-organize a large corpus of computer-understandable human mathematical ideas, using the millions of logical dependencies between the corpus' atomic elements. We believe that such conceptual re-organization is a very interesting AI topic that is best studied in the context of large, fully semantic corpora such as HOL Light and Flyspeck. The byproduct of this work are the exporting and post-processing techniques resulting in the publicly available proof graphs that can serve as a basis for further research.

The most conservative improvement in the strength of automated reasoning obtained so far over the core HOL Light thanks to lemma mining is about 5%. There are potential large improvements if the guessing of lemmas is improved. The benefits from lemma-mining should be larger when proving over larger corpora and when proving larger steps, but a number of implementational issues need to be addressed to scale the lemma-mining methods to very large corpora such as Flyspeck.

There are many further directions for this work. The lemma-mining methods can be made faster and more incremental, so that the lemma quality is not completely recomputed after a lemma is named. Fast PageRank-based clustering should be efficiently implemented and possibly combined with the other methods used. ATP-style normalizations such as subsumption need to be correctly merged with the detailed level of inferences used by the HOL Light proof graph. The whole approach could also be implemented on a higher level of inferences, using for example the granularity corresponding to time-limited MESON ATP steps. Guessing of good intermediate lemmas for proving harder theorems is an obvious next step, the value of which has already been established to a certain extent in this work.

Acknowledgments. We would like to thank Stephan Schulz for help with running epcllemma, Yury Puzis and Geoff Sutcliffe for their help with the Agint tool and Jiří Vyskočil and Petr Pudlák for many discussions about extracting interesting lemmas from proofs.

---

[9] http://mizar.cs.ualberta.ca/~mptp/lemma_mining/proofs.grf1.lm.flfull

References

1. Alama, J., Heskes, T., Kühlwein, D., Tsivtsivadze, E., Urban, J.: Premise selection for mathematics by corpus analysis and kernel methods. Journal of Automated Reasoning (2013), http://dx.doi.org/10.1007/s10817-013-9286-5
2. Alama, J., Kühlwein, D., Urban, J.: Automated and Human Proofs in General Mathematics: An Initial Comparison. In: Bjørner, N., Voronkov, A. (eds.) LPAR-18 2012. LNCS, vol. 7180, pp. 37–45. Springer, Heidelberg (2012)
3. Avrachenkov, K., Dobrynin, V., Nemirovsky, D., Pham, S.K., Smirnova, E.: Pagerank based clustering of hypertext document collections. In: Myaeng, S.-H., Oard, D.W., Sebastiani, F., Chua, T.-S., Leong, M.-K. (eds.) SIGIR, pp. 873–874. ACM (2008)
4. Blazy, S., Paulin-Mohring, C., Pichardie, D. (eds.): ITP 2013. LNCS, vol. 7998. Springer, Heidelberg (2013)
5. Grabowski, A., Korniłowicz, A., Naumowicz, A.: Mizar in a nutshell. Journal of Formalized Reasoning 3(2), 153–245 (2010)
6. Hales, T.C.: Introduction to the Flyspeck project. In: Coquand, T., Lombardi, H., Roy, M.-F. (eds.) Dagstuhl Seminar Proceedings, vol. 05021. Internationales Begegnungs- und Forschungszentrum für Informatik (IBFI), Schloss Dagstuhl (2005)
7. Harrison, J.: HOL Light: A tutorial introduction. In: Srivas, M., Camilleri, A. (eds.) FMCAD 1996. LNCS, vol. 1166, pp. 265–269. Springer, Heidelberg (1996)
8. Hoder, K., Voronkov, A.: Sine qua non for large theory reasoning. In: Bjørner, N., Sofronie-Stokkermans, V. (eds.) CADE 2011. LNCS (LNAI), vol. 6803, pp. 299–314. Springer, Heidelberg (2011)
9. Kaliszyk, C., Krauss, A.: Scalable LCF-style proof translation. In: Blazy, et al. (eds.) [4], pp. 51–66
10. Kaliszyk, C., Urban, J.: Learning-assisted automated reasoning with Flyspeck. CoRR, abs/1211.7012 (2012)
11. Kaliszyk, C., Urban, J.: Automated reasoning service for HOL Light. In: Carette, J., Aspinall, D., Lange, C., Sojka, P., Windsteiger, W. (eds.) CICM 2013. LNCS (LNAI), vol. 7961, pp. 120–135. Springer, Heidelberg (2013)
12. Kaliszyk, C., Urban, J.: Stronger automation for Flyspeck by feature weighting and strategy evolution. In: Blanchette, J.C., Urban, J. (eds.) PxTP 2013. EPiC Series, vol. 14, pp. 87–95. EasyChair (2013)
13. Kühlwein, D., Blanchette, J.C., Kaliszyk, C., Urban, J.: MaSh: Machine learning for Sledgehammer. In: Blazy, et al. (eds.) [4], pp. 35–50
14. Kühlwein, D., Schulz, S., Urban, J.: E-MaLeS 1.1. In: Bonacina, M.P. (ed.) CADE 2013. LNCS (LNAI), vol. 7898, pp. 407–413. Springer, Heidelberg (2013)
15. Kühlwein, D., van Laarhoven, T., Tsivtsivadze, E., Urban, J., Heskes, T.: Overview and evaluation of premise selection techniques for large theory mathematics. In: Gramlich, B., Miller, D., Sattler, U. (eds.) IJCAR 2012. LNCS (LNAI), vol. 7364, pp. 378–392. Springer, Heidelberg (2012)
16. McCune, W.: Prover9 and Mace4. 2005–2010, http://www.cs.unm.edu/~mccune/prover9/
17. Meng, J., Paulson, L.C.: Translating higher-order clauses to first-order clauses. J. Autom. Reasoning 40(1), 35–60 (2008)
18. Page, L., Brin, S., Motwani, R., Winograd, T.: The PageRank citation ranking: Bringing order to the Web. Technical report, Stanford Digital Library Technologies Project (1998)

19. Pudlák, P.: Search for faster and shorter proofs using machine generated lemmas. In: Sutcliffe, G., Schmidt, R., Schulz, S. (eds.) 3rd International Joint Conference on Automated Reasoning, Proceedings of the FLoC 2006 Workshop on Empirically Successful Computerized Reasoning. CEUR Workshop Proceedings, vol. 192, pp. 34–52 (2006)
20. Puzis, Y., Gao, Y., Sutcliffe, G.: Automated generation of interesting theorems. In: Sutcliffe, G., Goebel, R. (eds.) FLAIRS Conference, pp. 49–54. AAAI Press (2006)
21. Riazanov, A., Voronkov, A.: The design and implementation of VAMPIRE. AI Commun. 15(2-3), 91–110 (2002)
22. Schulz, S.: Learning search control knowledge for equational deduction. DISKI, vol. 230. Infix Akademische Verlagsgesellschaft (2000)
23. Schulz, S.: E - A Brainiac Theorem Prover. AI Commun. 15(2-3), 111–126 (2002)
24. Sutcliffe, G.: The Design and Implementation of a Compositional Competition-Cooperation Parallel ATP System. In: de Nivelle, H., Schulz, S. (eds.) Proceedings of the 2nd International Workshop on the Implementation of Logics, pp. 92–102. MPI-I-2001-2-006 in Max-Planck-Institut für Informatik. Research Report (2001)
25. Sutcliffe, G., Puzis, Y.: SRASS - a semantic relevance axiom selection system. In: Pfenning, F. (ed.) CADE 2007. LNCS (LNAI), vol. 4603, pp. 295–310. Springer, Heidelberg (2007)
26. Urban, J.: MPTP - Motivation, Implementation, First Experiments. Journal of Automated Reasoning 33(3-4), 319–339 (2004)
27. Urban, J.: MoMM - fast interreduction and retrieval in large libraries of formalized mathematics. Int. J. on Artificial Intelligence Tools 15(1), 109–130 (2006)
28. Urban, J.: BliStr: The Blind Strategymaker. CoRR, abs/1301.2683 (2013)
29. Urban, J., Sutcliffe, G., Pudlák, P., Vyskočil, J.: MaLARea SG1 - Machine Learner for Automated Reasoning with Semantic Guidance. In: Armando, A., Baumgartner, P., Dowek, G. (eds.) IJCAR 2008. LNCS (LNAI), vol. 5195, pp. 441–456. Springer, Heidelberg (2008)
30. Urban, J., Vyskočil, J.: Theorem proving in large formal mathematics as an emerging AI field. In: Bonacina, M.P., Stickel, M.E. (eds.) McCune Festschrift. LNCS (LNAI), vol. 7788, pp. 240–257. Springer, Heidelberg (2013)
31. Urban, J., Vyskočil, J., Štěpánek, P.: MaLeCoP: Machine learning connection prover. In: Brünnler, K., Metcalfe, G. (eds.) TABLEAUX 2011. LNCS (LNAI), vol. 6793, pp. 263–277. Springer, Heidelberg (2011)
32. Veroff, R.: Using hints to increase the effectiveness of an automated reasoning program: Case studies. J. Autom. Reasoning 16(3), 223–239 (1996)
33. Wenzel, M., Paulson, L.C., Nipkow, T.: The Isabelle framework. In: Mohamed, O.A., Muñoz, C., Tahar, S. (eds.) TPHOLs 2008. LNCS, vol. 5170, pp. 33–38. Springer, Heidelberg (2008)
34. Wos, L., Overbeek, R., Lusk, E.L., Boyle, J.: Automated Reasoning: Introduction and Applications. Prentice-Hall (1984)

On Module-Based Abstraction and Repair of Behavioral Programs

Guy Katz

Dept. of Computer Science and Applied Mathematics,
Weizmann Institute of Science, Rehovot, Israel
guy.katz@weizmann.ac.il

Abstract. The number of states a program has tends to grow exponentially in the size of the code. This phenomenon, known as *state explosion*, hinders the verification and repair of large programs. A key technique for coping with state explosion is using *abstractions*, where one substitutes a program's state graph with smaller over-approximations thereof. We show how module-based abstraction-refinement strategies can be applied to the verification of programs written in the recently proposed framework of *Behavioral Programming*. Further, we demonstrate how — by using a sought-after repair as a means of refining existing abstractions — these techniques can improve the scalability of existing program repair algorithms. Our findings are supported by a proof-of-concept tool.

Keywords: Abstraction-refinement, program repair, behavioral programming.

1 Introduction

Explicit model-checking algorithms operate by spanning a program's state graph and comparing it to a given specification. This method becomes infeasible for large systems, as the state graphs tend to grow exponentially in the size of the program (the *state explosion* problem). Abstraction techniques [11] are among the most important methods for coping with state explosion and increasing the scalability of model-checking algorithms.

The key idea underlying abstraction techniques is to replace the concrete system model (i.e., the program's state graph) with a smaller abstraction thereof. Typically, the abstraction constitutes an *over-approximation* — it includes the behaviors of the concrete system, and may also include other behaviors. In the case of model-checking, proving that a given property holds for the abstract model implies that it holds for the concrete model as well. Since the abstract model is more succinct, the state explosion problem is hopefully mitigated.

We study the application of abstraction techniques to the recently proposed programming framework of *Behavioral Programming* (*BP*) [17]. In BP, programs consist of *behavioral threads* — threads of code that run in parallel, each designed to affect a specific behavior of the system. In the first part of our work, we present a formulation of BP's semantics that supports the notion of *modules*, which are logically related threads grouped together, and discuss abstracting these modules. We then demonstrate how the composition of module abstractions yields an over-approximation of the entire behavioral program.

In the second part of our work we discuss model-checking abstract behavioral programs, and propose a *counterexample guided abstraction refinement (CEGAR)* [10] scheme for BP. When model-checking over-approximations, counterexamples found by the model-checker may prove *spurious*, i.e. nonexistent in the concrete system. In CEGAR, one validates each counterexample against the concrete system and, if it is spurious, refines the abstract model in a way that eliminates it. The process is then repeated iteratively until the property is proven or a genuine counterexample is found. Based on our module-based abstraction of behavioral programs, we propose a two layer abstraction-refinement scheme, similar to that of [9], in which spurious counterexamples of the composed system are used to refine module abstractions. In our setting, module interdependencies make it impossible to resolve spurious counterexamples by examining modules individually; our algorithm compensates by considering these interdependencies and refining multiple modules simultaneously when needed.

In the third part of the paper, we combine our abstraction techniques with a program repair algorithm. In [15] we demonstrated how safety violations can be eliminated from behavioral programs by adding separate, non-intrusive behavioral threads to the program. Since that repair technique included spanning the program's concrete state graph, it was susceptible to the state explosion problem. Here, we modify the technique to work on abstract state graphs instead of concrete ones, without affecting the algorithm's correctness and soundness. We observe that a given abstraction might not allow finding a correct repair even if one exists, in which case we use the desired repair as a means for refining the abstraction further. We believe that similar repair-driven refinement techniques may also be applicable to other frameworks, besides BP.

The rest of this paper is organized as follows. We define behavioral programming and its semantics in Section 2, followed by a discussion on abstracting behavioral programs in Section 3. We then discuss applying CEGAR to BP in Section 4, and suggest an abstraction-based repair algorithm in Section 5. Our experimental results appear in Section 6. Discussion of related and future work appears in Section 7.

2 Behavioral Programming

2.1 Overview

Behavioral Programming (BP) is a programming approach that extends and generalizes scenario-based programming. It was introduced with the language of Live Sequence Charts (*LSC*s) [12,16], and is now implemented also in a variety of programming languages, such as Java, C^{++}, Erlang and others; see [17] and references therein.

A behavioral program consists of independent threads of behavior that are interwoven at run time. Each *behavior thread* (abbr. *b-thread*) repeatedly performs local computations, and then synchronizes with its counterparts. At every synchronization point, each b-thread declares sets of events to be considered for triggering (*requested events*) and events whose triggering it forbids (*blocked events*). The thread then pauses until the synchronization point is resolved.

Events that have been requested by at least one b-thread and blocked by none are termed *enabled*. In each synchronization point, an *event selection mechanism* triggers one of these events and notifies all b-threads, allowing them to resume. B-threads may react to triggered events that they did not request, in which case they are said to be *waiting for* these events. The model disallows inter b-thread communication except through the synchronization mechanism.

The motivation behind BP is that it facilitates incremental non-intrusive development, as demonstrated in the example of Fig. 1, borrowed from [15]. This trait also plays a role in our repair algorithm in Section 5.

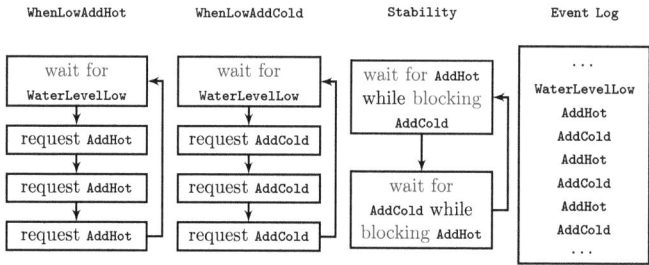

Fig. 1. (From [15]) An example of the incremental development of a system for controlling water level in a tank with hot and cold water sources. At first, b-thread WhenLowAddHot is created; it repeatedly waits for WaterLevelLow events and requests three times the event AddHot. It is then discovered that adding just three water quantities for every sensor reading is insufficient, and b-thread WhenLowAddCold is added. It performs a similar action to that of WhenLowAddHot, but with event AddCold. Then, when WhenLowAddHot and WhenLowAddCold are executed simultaneously, the run may include three consecutive AddHot events followed by three AddCold events. A new requirement is thus introduced, to the effect that water temperature should be kept stable. We add the b-thread Stability to enforce the interleaving of AddHot and AddCold events.

2.2 Semantics

Since b-threads communicate strictly through the synchronization mechanism, a thread is considered "at state" only when at a synchronization point. Thus, local actions performed between synchronization points can be modeled and verified locally for each thread, and are omitted from the BP model.

We formally define a b-thread BT over event set Σ and atomic proposition set AP by a tuple $BT = \langle Q, \delta, q_0, R, B, L \rangle$, where Q is a set of states (one for each synchronization point), q_0 is the initial state, $R : Q \to 2^{\Sigma}$ and $B : Q \to 2^{\Sigma}$ map states to events requested and blocked at these states (respectively), $L : Q \to 2^{AP}$ is a labeling function, and $\delta : Q \times \Sigma \to 2^Q$ is a transition function.

We stipulate that for every $q \in Q$, $R(q) \cap B(q) = \emptyset$. Further, we require that for every state $q \in Q$, if $e \in \Sigma - B(q)$ then $\delta(q,e) \neq \emptyset$; i.e., there is a transition for every event that is not blocked in state q, though it may be a self loop. If $|\delta(q,e)| \leq 1$ for every q and e, we say that BT is *deterministic*.

The construction of a program from b-threads is performed using the *composition* and *finalization* operators. The parallel composition of threads $BT^1 = \langle Q^1, \delta^1, q_0^1, R^1, B^1, L^1 \rangle$ and $BT^2 = \langle Q^2, \delta^2, q_0^2, R^2, B^2, L^2 \rangle$, both over the same Σ and AP, yields the b-thread defined by

$$BT^1 \parallel BT^2 = \langle Q^1 \times Q^2, \delta, \langle q_0^1, q_0^2 \rangle, (R^1 \cup R^2) - (B^1 \cup B^2), B^1 \cup B^2, L^1 \cup L^2 \rangle$$

where $\langle \tilde{q}^1, \tilde{q}^2 \rangle \in \delta(\langle q^1, q^2 \rangle, e)$ if and only if $\tilde{q}^1 \in \delta^1(q^1, e)$ and $\tilde{q}^2 \in \delta^2(q^2, e)$. The union and subtraction of labeling functions are defined in the natural way, i.e. $e \in ((R^1 \cup R^2) - (B^1 \cup B^2))(\langle q^1, q^2 \rangle)$ if and only if $e \in R^1(q^1) \cup R^2(q^2)$ and $e \notin B^1(q^1) \cup B^2(q^2)$. Observe that if an event is blocked in one thread and requested in the other, it becomes blocked in the composed thread, in consistence with the fact that a blocked event cannot be triggered even if requested. It is straightforward to verify that the requested and blocked events in every state remain disjoint, and that in every state there exists a transition for every non-blocked event. Hence, $BT^1 \parallel BT^2$ is a valid b-thread.

A composition of b-threads is also termed a *module*, which is of course a b-thread in its own. Intuitively, a module is a set of threads that have yet to be plugged into a specific behavioral program, and so it still contains the relevant request and block data. Only once all the modules in a program are composed with each other can this data be discarded, through the *finalization* operator.

The finalization operator, denoted $[\cdot]$, transforms a b-thread into a labeled transition system (LTS) over Σ and AP. Formally, $[\langle Q, \delta, q_0, R, B, L \rangle] = \langle Q, \delta', q_0, L \rangle$ where Q, q_0 and L remain the same, and the transition function $\delta' : Q \times \Sigma \to 2^Q$ is given by

$$\tilde{q} \in \delta'(q, e) \iff \tilde{q} \in \delta(q, e) \bigwedge e \in R(q)$$

Observe that R and B are omitted, as they are already taken into consideration through the definition of δ'. The output of the finalization operator thus represents a general (as opposed to a behavioral) program.

Formally, we define the *behavioral program* P, comprised of b-threads $BT^1, BT^2, \ldots, BT^n$ to be the LTS defined by $P = [BT^1 \parallel \ldots \parallel BT^n]$. An execution of P is an execution of this LTS: it starts from q_0, and in each state $q \in Q$ an event is chosen for triggering if such an event exists (i.e., an event $e \in \Sigma$ for which $\delta(q,e) \neq \emptyset$). Then, the execution moves to state $\tilde{q} \in \delta(q,e)$, and so on. An execution can thus be formally recorded as a (possibly infinite) sequence of states and triggered events, $\epsilon = q_0 \xrightarrow{e_1} q_1 \xrightarrow{e_2} \cdots$. The matching set of events, without states, is called a *run*. The set of all runs of the program is denoted by $\mathfrak{L}(P)$. Each execution ϵ of the system defines a *trace* $\text{Tr}(\epsilon) = L(q_0)L(q_1)\ldots$, which is the sequence of sets of atomic propositions associated with the states visited along the execution. The traces of the system are defined as the traces of its executions, i.e. $\text{Tr}(P) = \{\text{Tr}(\epsilon) \mid \epsilon \text{ is an execution of } P\}$.

The above semantics for BP differ from those used previously (e.g., in [15]), as they offer better support of the notion of modules. An equivalence between these two versions is established in Appendix I of the supplementary material [2].

The BP semantics can be extended to better describe open systems. One variant is obtained by marking some of the threads and events as controlled by the environment ("external"), as is done in [15]. Another is to use concurrent game structures and alternating-time temporal logic [3]. While our techniques can be adapted to these extensions, we leave the details for future work.

3 Abstractions for Behavioral Programming

Given behavioral programs P and $\overline{P}$, we say that $\overline{P}$ is an over-approximation of P if and only if $\text{Tr}(P) \subseteq \text{Tr}(\overline{P})$. Thus, for any LTL formula Φ over AP, $\text{Tr}(\overline{P}) \vDash \Phi$ implies $\text{Tr}(P) \vDash \Phi$, and so verifying that $\text{Tr}(\overline{P}) \vDash \Phi$ shows that the original program is correct (for an introduction to LTL see, e.g., [6]). In this section we focus on constructing a suitable program $\overline{P}$ that is smaller than P, so that checking whether $\text{Tr}(\overline{P}) \vDash \Phi$ is easier than checking whether $\text{Tr}(P) \vDash \Phi$.

3.1 Abstracting a Behavioral Thread

We begin by defining abstractions of b-threads. Let $BT = \langle Q, \delta, q_0, R, B, L \rangle$ be a thread over events Σ and propositions AP, and let π be a AP-preserving partition of Q, i.e., $q_1 \equiv_\pi q_2 \implies L(q_1) = L(q_2)$. Let $\eta_\pi : Q \to Q/\pi$, termed the abstraction function induced by π, be a function that maps each state to its equivalence class under π. η_π gives rise to a b-thread $\overline{BT} = \langle \overline{Q}, \overline{\delta}, \overline{q_0}, \overline{R}, \overline{B}, \overline{L} \rangle$, called the abstraction thread of BT induced by π, defined in the following manner. The states of $\overline{BT}$ are the equivalence classes $\overline{Q} = Q/\pi$, and its initial state is $\overline{q_0} = \eta_\pi(q_0)$. For every state $\overline{q} \in \overline{Q}$, the mapping functions are given by $\overline{R}(\overline{q}) = \bigcup_{q \in \eta_\pi^{-1}(\overline{q})} R(q)$, $\overline{B}(\overline{q}) = \bigcap_{q \in \eta_\pi^{-1}(\overline{q})} B(q)$ and $\overline{L}(\overline{q}) = L(q)$ for (every) $q \in \eta_\pi^{-1}(\overline{q})$. The transitions relation $\overline{\delta}$ is derived from δ by:

$$\frac{q \xrightarrow{e} \tilde{q}}{\eta_\pi(q) \xrightarrow{e} \eta_\pi(\tilde{q})}$$

Note that for every $\overline{q}$, $\overline{R}(\overline{q}) \cap \overline{B}(\overline{q}) = \emptyset$, and that $\overline{q}$ has a transition for every $e \notin \overline{B}(\overline{q})$. Hence, $\overline{BT}$ is a valid b-thread. The definition is designed to make $\overline{BT}$ *more permissive* than BT — that is, to ensure that replacing BT with $\overline{BT}$ within a given program results in an over-approximation of that program. In particular, the abstraction preserves atomic proposition of states, and abstract states request at least as much and block no more than their matching concrete states. Formally, we present the following Lemma, proven in Appendix II of the supplementary material [2]:

Lemma 1. *Let $P = [BT^1 \parallel \ldots \parallel BT^n]$ be a behavioral program. Let π be an AP-preserving partition of the states of BT^1, and let $\overline{BT^1}$ be the abstraction of BT^1 induced by π. Finally, let $\overline{P} = [\overline{BT^1} \parallel BT^2 \parallel \ldots \parallel BT^n]$. Then $\text{Tr}(P) \subseteq \text{Tr}(\overline{P})$.*

By definition, a thread's abstraction is determined by the AP-preserving partition π in use. Clearly, an abstraction of a minimal number of states is achieved when π is the AP-partition itself, i.e. $q_1 \equiv_\pi q_2 \iff L(q_1) = L(q_2)$. As our goal is to minimize the number of states of the composed program, this partition is of special interest. We refer to this abstraction as the coarsest abstraction of BT, and denote it by $\widehat{BT}$.

3.2 Abstracting a Behavioral Program

Due to BP's composite nature — where sets of composed threads are threads themselves — thread abstraction can be applied at various points throughout the composition process. In choosing when to apply it, our goal is to end up with an over-approximation that is neither too concrete (to mitigate state explosion), nor too abstract (so that it is meaningful). In our experiments, the best results were achieved by first grouping threads that are logically related and composing them into modules. Intuitively, this entails clustering threads that assign similar atomic propositions to their states into the same module. Each module is then abstracted individually, effectively ignoring threads that deal with other atomic propositions. Finally the abstractions are composed, generating the desired over-approximation. In this section we provide motivation for this approach, and propose an automated way for grouping together logically related threads.

To illustrate the benefits of using modules, we first discuss two of the more natural alternatives. One approach is to apply abstraction at the last step of the composition process: i.e., to compute $BT = BT^1 \parallel \ldots \parallel BT^n$ and then set $\overline{P} = [\widehat{BT}]$. While this method produces meaningful abstractions, it entails calculating the very large b-thread BT, which has at least as many states as P. Hence, this technique suffers from the state explosion problem that we have been trying to avoid. Another natural approach is to abstract each of the basic threads, i.e. calculate $\overline{P} = [\widehat{BT^1} \parallel \ldots \parallel \widehat{BT^n}]$. While this method does indeed circumvent the state explosion problem, our experiments show that the abstractions it tends to produce are too coarse to be of any practical use. Specifically, behavioral programming promotes writing threads that are small and specific, and tend to contain a single atomic proposition. Thus, early abstraction usually collapses the threads into a couple of states each, abstracting away most implementation details. Later, during verification tasks, multiple rounds of refinement are needed until a meaningful model is obtained.

The module based method can be seen as a middle ground between these two extreme alternatives. On one hand, as abstraction is applied during the early phases of the composition process, the state explosion problem is averted. On the other hand, as it is applied to threads that are sufficiently complex, the resulting over approximation is more likely to be meaningful.

The rationale behind grouping together logically related threads, as opposed to just using an arbitrary partitioning of the threads, is the desire to generate small modules: logically related threads tend to share atomic propositions, and request and block similar events. Consequently, the resulting abstractions tend to contain fewer states, and the approximation labeling functions $\overline{R}$ and $\overline{B}$ tend to be tighter, reducing the number of edges in the final over-approximation.

We conclude this section by discussing an automated method for grouping together logically related threads. As the above discussion suggests, such threads tend to share atomic propositions and requested/blocked events, and indeed this is how we attempt to group them. Let BT be a thread with states $q_1, \ldots, q_m$, and let $ap \in AP$. We define the correlation between BT and ap as:

$$cor(BT, ap) = \frac{|\{i \mid ap \in L(q_i)\}|}{m}$$

A thread's correlation to an atomic proposition is thus the fraction of states to which the labeling function assigns the proposition. Intuitively, threads that have high correlation to the same atomic proposition may be logically related. Setting a threshold M, say 0.5, induces a partitioning of the threads into modules, denoted $\equiv_M$. At first each thread is considered to reside in a separate module, and then pairs of modules are iteratively joined by the rule:

$$cor(BT^i, ap) \geq M \bigwedge cor(BT^j, ap) \geq M \implies BT^i \equiv_M BT^j$$

Analogous correlation can be defined between threads and events, by considering the fraction of states in which a thread requires or blocks the event. These correlations are easy to compute using static analysis of the threads, and are supported by the BPC framework.

Further information that can be taken into account when looking for related threads includes various string distance metrics applied to their respective names and locations in the directory structure — as programmers tend to group similar threads together and give them similar names. These measures are also straightforward to compute using automated methods. Finally, any or all of the above measures can be combined into a single metric, yielding the desired partition into logically related modules.

We summarize the resulting module-based abstraction algorithm:

Algorithm 1. Module-Based Abstraction

1: Partition the threads into modules $BT^{M_1}, \ldots, BT^{M_m}$
2: For each module BT^{M_i}, calculate $\widehat{BT^{M_i}}$
3: **return** $\overline{P} = [\widehat{BT^{M_1}} \parallel \ldots \parallel \widehat{BT^{M_m}}]$

By iteratively applying Lemma 1, we get the following corollary:

Corollary 1. *Let $BT^1, \ldots, BT^n$ be threads over event set Σ and atomic propositions AP. Let $P = [BT^1 \parallel \ldots \parallel BT^n]$, and let $\overline{P}$ be the program returned by algorithm 1. Then $\text{Tr}(P) \subseteq \text{Tr}(\overline{P})$.*

4 Counterexample Guided Abstraction-Refinement

Given a behavioral program P and an LTL property Φ, we attempt to prove that $P \vDash \Phi$ by calculating an over-approximation $\overline{P}$ and proving that $\overline{P} \vDash \Phi$. However, it may be the case that $P \vDash \Phi$ but $\overline{P} \nvDash \Phi$, because $\overline{P}$ is too abstract (see an illustration in Fig. 2). Model checking $\overline{P}$ then results in a *spurious* counterexample, i.e. one that exists in $\overline{P}$ but not in P. A standard technique for handling this problem, known as *counterexample guided abstraction refinement* (*CEGAR*) [10], uses such spurious counterexamples in order to refine $\overline{P}$ in a way that eliminates them. The process is repeated until a genuine counterexample is found, or until the property is shown to hold.

In this section, we describe an implementation of CEGAR in the context of BP. The two main phases of the technique — determining whether a counterexample is spurious or genuine and refining the abstraction in order to eliminate spurious executions — are discussed in Sections 4.1 and 4.2, respectively.

For simplicity, we limit the discussion to safety properties, for which counterexamples are finite executions. The method can be extended to liveness properties and the associated loop counterexamples through *loop unwinding*; see [10].

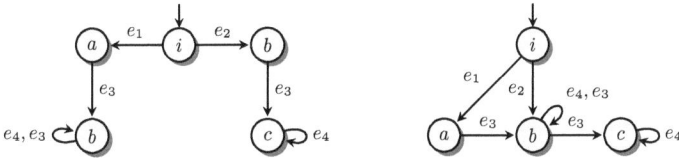

Fig. 2. A concrete state graph (on the left), and a matching abstraction (on the right). The atomic proposition labeling appears inside the states. The two states with identical labeling (b) are abstracted into a single state. The abstract state graph contains fewer states, but it also allows spurious executions. While some properties, such as $G(a \rightarrow X \neg a)$, hold for both graphs, the property $G(a \rightarrow G \neg c)$ holds in the concrete case but not in the abstract one, because of the spurious execution fragment $i \xrightarrow{e_1} a \xrightarrow{e_3} b \xrightarrow{e_3} c$.

4.1 Determining If an Execution Is Spurious

Suppose that on checking whether $\overline{P} \vDash \Phi$, the model-checker replies in the negative, providing a finite counterexample $\overline{\epsilon}$. We wish to determine whether $\overline{\epsilon}$ is a valid execution of the original system. The idea, based on [10], is to simulate $\overline{\epsilon}$ on the concrete program in order to check if it constitutes a genuine execution. During this simulation, we must take into account the two layer structure of our abstraction scheme, as well as the role of *requested* and *blocked* events, in determining whether runs are valid.

Let $\overline{P} = [\widehat{BT^{M_1}} \parallel \ldots \parallel \widehat{BT^{M_m}}]$ be an abstract program, composed of m abstract modules, and let $\overline{\epsilon} = \overline{q_0} \xrightarrow{e_1} \overline{q_1} \xrightarrow{e_2} \ldots \xrightarrow{e_n} \overline{q_n}$ be a finite execution of $\overline{P}$. It is tempting to say that $\overline{\epsilon}$ is a valid execution of the concrete system if and only if its projections onto the modules form valid executions of the modules;

indeed, a similar technique is used in [9]. However, in our context, this approach does not suffice. Consider, for instance, the case where the transition labeled e_1 in $\bar{e}$ exists in each of the concrete modules, but that none of them requests event e_1. In this case, looking at each module separately, we would have no way of knowing whether event e_1 is indeed enabled on the program level. Thus, our scheme must take into account the mutual effect modules have on each other.

We begin with some notation. For a set of states S, we denote by $R(S, e)$ the subset of states of S in which event e is requested. We use $\text{Post}(S, e)$ to denote the set of successors of states in S when event e is triggered. Finally, let $\overline{q} = \langle \overline{q^1}, \overline{q^2}, \ldots, \overline{q^m} \rangle$ denote an abstract state, and let η_j denote the abstraction function of module BT^{M_j}. We use η to denote the global abstraction function, i.e. $\eta(\langle q^1, \ldots, q^m \rangle) = \langle \eta_1(q^1), \ldots, \eta_m(q^m) \rangle$. This function and its inverse function are not stored explicitly, as doing so for every state in $\overline{P}$ would entail enumerating all states of P — negating the advantages offered by our two layered approach. Instead, η is only computed locally for specific states, on demand, by invoking the module abstraction functions.

Our technique follows the idea of [10], and defines a series of sets $\{S_i\}$, representing the concrete states the system can actually reach in each step of $\bar{e}$. These sets are computed by using the concrete module state graphs. The definition of S_i is given by $S_0 = \{\langle q_0^1, q_0^2, \ldots, q_0^m \rangle\}$ for the concrete initial states and $S_i = \text{Post}(R(S_{i-1}, e_i), e_i) \cap \eta^{-1}(\overline{q_i})$ for $1 \leq i \leq n$.

The idea behind this definition is to walk on the abstract graph according to the execution, and for each abstract state identify the concrete states that are truly reachable along this specific execution, using the S_i sets. As we later prove, a run is genuine if and only if it corresponds to a series of non-empty sets. Each set is derived from its predecessor by looking only at states in which the next event is requested, and calculating their successor states. Out of these successors we only keep those that are abstracted to the next state of the abstract execution, as expressed by intersecting with $\eta^{-1}(\overline{q_i})$.

The actual algorithm for checking whether an execution is spurious is thus:

Algorithm 2. Check If Spurious

1: **for** $i := 0$ to n **do**
2:   Calculate S_i; if it is empty, **return** *True*
3: **return** *False*

The algorithm's correctness is established via Lemma 2, proven in Appendix III of the supplementary material [2]:

Lemma 2. *Let $\bar{e}$ be an execution of $\overline{P}$. Then $\bar{e}$ is spurious, i.e. is not a valid execution of P, if and only if algorithm 2 returns* True.

Observe that computing the S_i sets is performed using the concrete state graphs of the modules, and does not entail constructing the explicit state graph of P. Every state $q \in S_i$ is stored as the set of module states to which it corresponds. The sets $R(q, e)$ and $\text{Post}(R(q, e), e)$ can be computed locally from these states. Further, there is no need to actually compute $\eta^{-1}(\overline{q_i})$, which is costly; instead, for every $q \in \text{Post}(R(S_{i-1}, e_i), e_i)$, we check whether $\eta(q) = \overline{q_i}$ by applying the module abstraction functions to its components, which is substantially cheaper.

4.2 Refining in Order to Eliminate a Spurious Execution

We now discuss refining $\overline{P}$ in order to eliminate a spurious counterexample, thus allowing another round of model-checking. The iteration on which algorithm 2 halted indicates where the refinement should occur. Indeed, this is where the abstract and concrete graphs diverge, and so splitting the previous abstract state into multiple states could render the spurious execution invalid.

Suppose that the *Check If Spurious* algorithm stopped because $S_{i+1} = \emptyset$. This indicates a problem with transition $\overline{q_i} \xrightarrow{e_{i+1}} \overline{q_{i+1}}$ of the execution: either the concrete system can only reach states that are not mapped to abstract state $\overline{q_{i+1}}$, or event e_{i+1} is not even enabled in the concrete program — although it is enabled in the abstract one. Each case is characterized and handled differently:

Case 1. For all concrete states in S_i, transitions labeled e_{i+1} do not lead to abstract state $\overline{q_{i+1}}$, i.e. $\text{Post}(S_i, e_{i+1}) \cap \eta^{-1}(\overline{q_{i+1}}) = \emptyset$. In this case, we split $\overline{q_i}$ into 2 abstract states: state $\overline{q_i'}$ that corresponds to the concrete states S_i, and state $\overline{q_i''}$ that corresponds to the remaining states, $\eta^{-1}(\overline{q_i}) - S_i$. By definition, execution $\overline{\epsilon}$ would visit abstract state $\overline{q_i'}$ instead of $\overline{q_i}$, from which there would be no transitions to $\overline{q_{i+1}}$. Thus, $\overline{\epsilon}$ would no longer be a valid execution of the abstract program. This case corresponds to the technique used in [10].

Case 2. There exists a state $q \in S_i$ such that $\text{Post}(q, e_{i+1}) \in \eta^{-1}(\overline{q_{i+1}})$. However, $e_{i+1} \notin R(q)$; if that were not so, we would get $S_{i+1} \neq \emptyset$. In this case, state q is *waiting* for event e_{i+1} without requesting it. The request for e_{i+1} is made by a different state in $\eta^{-1}(\overline{q_i})$. As both states are mapped into the same abstract state, the outcome is the edge $\overline{q_i} \xrightarrow{e_{i+1}} \overline{q_{i+1}}$.

In this case, performing refinement as in Case 1 might not suffice, as the state requesting event e_{i+1} might also be in S_i. We thus resort to two rounds of refinement: first, we split state $\overline{q_i}$ into $\overline{q_i'}$ and $\overline{q_i''}$, as before. Then, we further refine state $\overline{q_i'}$, in order to separate states requesting event e_{i+1} from those that do not. Formally, we split $\overline{q_i'}$ into state $\overline{q_i^R}$ corresponding to concrete states $q \in S_i$ such that $e_{i+1} \in R(q)$, and state $\overline{q_i^{NR}}$ corresponding to concrete states $q \in S_i$ such that $e_{i+1} \notin R(q)$. By definition, execution $\overline{\epsilon}$ would visit abstract state $\overline{q_i^{NR}}$ instead of $\overline{q_i}$, from which there would be no transitions to $\overline{q_{i+1}}$, making it an invalid execution of the abstract program.

The following Lemma immediately follows from the above discussion:

Lemma 3. *Let $\overline{\epsilon}$ be a spurious execution of $\overline{P}$, and let $\overline{P'}$ be the refined program obtained by the above refinement step. Then $\overline{\epsilon}$ is not a valid execution of $\overline{P'}$.*

Observe that the iterative verification process entails explicitly computing $\eta^{-1}(\overline{q})$ once per each refinement step. While this step is expensive, hopefully the number of iterations is small. Reducing the number of iterations is part of our motivation for using logically related modules — see discussion in Section 3.2.

We note that the resulting refinement is defined in terms of a global abstract state that should be split into smaller states. However, as η is not stored explicitly, this refinement cannot be applied directly. Constrained by our two layered setting, we may only perform refinements on the module abstraction functions $\eta_1, \ldots, \eta_m$, indirectly refining η. Thus, a set of refinements for the $\eta_1, \ldots, \eta_m$ functions needs to be derived from the desired η refinement. This can be performed by separating (within the modules) any pair of concrete states that do not always appear simultaneously in the new global abstract states. However, as not every refinement of η can be expressed as refinements of $\eta_1, \ldots, \eta_m$, the resulting global refinement may be finer (i.e., produce more states) than the desired one.

5 Repair Using Abstractions

In this section, we propose a way of dealing with violated safety properties, using a program repair algorithm. For completeness, we begin with a brief review of the work in [15], which the present section extends.

Software maintenance is a difficult and error prone task. As bugs are discovered and requirements are added or changed, developers must modify existing code. This is tedious work; and as programmers are often constrained by limited knowledge of module interdependencies, they may wind up introducing new errors. Research on automated program repair aims to address these challenges.

Our scope includes fixing safety violations in existing programs. Finding these violations can be reduced to invariant checking [6]. Thus, without loss of generality, a program is correct if its state graph has no reachable "bad" states. This, along with the event blocking idiom of BP, enables an elegant method of repair by trimming: correcting the program by removing edges from its state graph using the blocking idiom, so that bad states become unreachable. This technique resembles the Supervisory Control model [23], where one seeks a supervisor that controls a plant by disabling transitions in the plant's state graph.

The repair is non-intrusive, i.e. performed strictly by adding new threads to the program (termed "wait-block patches"), and without modifying existing code. The patch threads are passive, in the sense that they never request any events or assign any atomic propositions to states, thus keeping the repaired program as close to the original as possible. Only when the execution gets dangerously close to a bad state does the patch block events that would cause a violation, forcing the system to choose a different execution path. In [15] it is shown that, for programs with deterministic threads, this method does not eliminate correct executions, as events are blocked only when they are guaranteed to lead to a violation. Further, no deadlocks are created as a result of such patching.

This repair technique is adequate for systems that are capable of generating the desired ("good") behavior but may, in some scenarios, produce erroneous output. For instance, patching may be applied to a variety of bugs resulting from race conditions between parallel components — fixing them by temporarily blocking one of the components, forcing it to yield to its counterpart. However, not all systems can be repaired in this way, and the repair algorithm fails gracefully in this case. A soundness result shows that if a correct patch exists, it will indeed be found by the repair algorithm.

The algorithm operates by analyzing a program's state graph and looking for the smallest fixpoint set of states that can be removed from the graph in order to render q_b, the single bad state, unreachable. Specifically, the algorithm backtracks from q_b, attempting to isolate it by trimming edges without creating deadlocks. Whenever all the successors of a state are bad, it is marked as bad itself; see Fig. 3. Below is the repair algorithm's pseudo-code; *Pre* denotes the predecessor states of a given set of states.

Algorithm 3. Concrete Safety Patching

1: $BAD \leftarrow \{q_b\}$, $PRE \leftarrow Pre(BAD)$
2: **while** $\exists q \in PRE$ such that $\forall e, \text{Post}(q,e) \in BAD$ **do**
3:    Move q from PRE to BAD
4:    **if** q is the initial state **then return** $Failure$
5:    $PRE \leftarrow Pre(BAD)$
6: **return** a patch that blocks edges from PRE to BAD

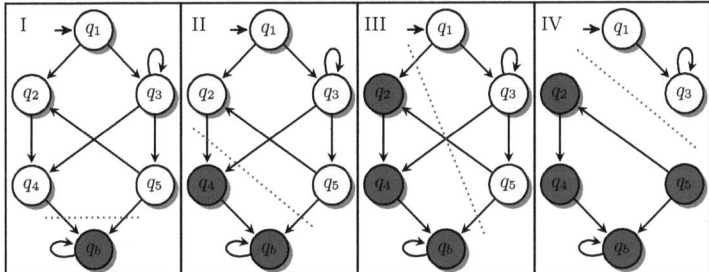

Fig. 3. The algorithm for trimming the concrete state graph of a program in order to correct a safety violation. Graph I depicts the initial configuration, with the only bad state, q_b, marked in red. The edges from states in PRE to states in BAD cross the dotted red line, and are candidates for blocking. In the first iteration, blocking these edges would cause a deadlocked in state q_4. Thus, in graph II state q_4 is also marked as bad, and q_2 joins PRE. Unfortunately, now a deadlock would be caused in state q_2, and the algorithm iterates again, putting q_2 in BAD. The next iteration puts q_5 in BAD. Only then, in graph IV, can edges crossing the dotted line be safely removed without causing deadlocks. The states in BAD are thus rendered unreachable, fixing the safety violation.

As this algorithm uses the program's concrete state graph, it does not scale to large programs. We thus seek to adjust it so it can use an over-approximation instead. Unfortunately, directly applying the concrete patching algorithm to an abstract graph yields erroneous results. In particular, the algorithm might fail

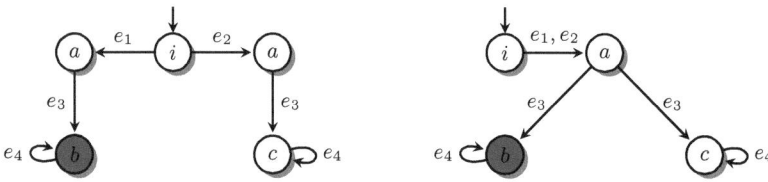

Fig. 4. A concrete state graph on the left, and its abstraction on the right. The atomic propositions appear inside the states. The safety property in question is the invariant $G\neg b$, which is violated when the states in red are reached. In the concrete graph, a simple patch can fix the problem: by blocking e_1 in the initial state, the red state is made unreachable, and no deadlocks are caused. On the abstract graph, however, no repair is possible without causing a deadlock somewhere in the program. As a result of the nondeterminism in state a, where two edges correspond to the same event, we are unable to block one edge while leaving the other enabled.

when a correct answer exists, or the resulting patches might also eliminate good executions — traits that did not exist in the concrete version. See Fig. 4.

Intuitively, the reason for these failures is the fact that *patch-incompatible* concrete states are abstracted into the same abstract states. By patch-incompatible, we mean that the concrete algorithm would block a different set of events in each of the concrete states. In the abstract graph, however, such blocking becomes impossible, resulting in the algorithm's undesired behavior. In order to overcome this difficulty, we incorporate a refinement phase into the repair algorithm; however, instead of using counterexamples as means of guiding the refinement, the driving force is the need to create abstract states that correspond only to patch-compatible concrete states.

The algorithm uses an over-approximation of the state graph, in which $\overline{q_b}$ is the single abstract bad state, corresponding to q_b. As in the concrete case, we assume the concrete b-threads are deterministic. Here is the pseudo-code:

Algorithm 4. Abstract Safety Patching

1: $BAD \leftarrow \{\overline{q_b}\}$
2: **while** $True$ **do**
3:     $PRE \leftarrow Pre(BAD)$
4:     **if** $\exists \overline{q} \in PRE$ such that $NeedToRefine(\overline{q})$ **then**
5:         $Refine(\overline{q})$
6:     **else if** $\exists \overline{q} \in PRE$ such that $\forall e, \text{Post}(\overline{q}, e) \subseteq BAD$ **then**
7:         Move $\overline{q}$ from PRE to BAD
8:         **if** $\overline{q}$ is the initial state **then return** $Failure$
9:     **else**
10:         **return** a patch that blocks edges from PRE to BAD

The core of the algorithm remains the same as in the concrete case: we start at the bad state $\overline{q_b}$, backtracking and marking states that only lead to bad states as bad themselves. Once we reach a setting in which all states in PRE also have edges leading to good states (as to not create deadlocks), we return a patch trimming the edges from PRE to the bad states. The refinement phase prevents good executions from being likewise trimmed:

Algorithm 5. NeedToRefine($\overline{q}$)

1: $E \leftarrow \{e \in \Sigma \mid \text{Post}(\overline{q}, e) \cap BAD \neq \emptyset\}$
2: **if** exists $q \in \eta^{-1}(\overline{q}), e \in E$ such that $e \in R(q)$ and $\eta(\text{Post}(q, e)) \notin BAD$ **then**
3:     **return** $True$
4: **if** exists $q \in \eta^{-1}(\overline{q})$ such that $R(q) \subseteq E$ **then**
5:     **return** $True$
6: **return** $False$

In order to determine if an abstract state $\overline{q}$ needs to be refined, we look at the events that we would like to block in it (set E). If there exists a concrete state in $\eta^{-1}(\overline{q})$ for which $e \in E$ is requested and leads to a good state, refinement is needed to prevent good executions from being eliminated. Similarly if there exists a state in $\eta^{-1}(\overline{q})$ that has no requested events that would remain unblocked, refinement is needed in order to avoid causing a deadlock. The actual refinement is performed as follows:

Algorithm 6. Refine($\overline{q}$)

1: For every $q \in \eta^{-1}(\overline{q})$ calculate $\mathfrak{B}(q) = \{e \in R(q) \mid \eta(\text{Post}(q, e)) \in BAD\}$
2: Form a partition $\eta^{-1}(\overline{q}) = C_1 \uplus C_2 \uplus \ldots \uplus C_k \uplus C_{deadlock}$ such that if $\mathfrak{B}(q) = R(q)$, then $q \in C_{deadlock}$; else, $q_1, q_2 \in C_i \iff \mathfrak{B}(q_1) = \mathfrak{B}(q_2)$.
3: Split abstract state $\overline{q}$ into $k+1$ new states $\overline{q_1}, \ldots, \overline{q_{k+1}}$ such that $\eta^{-1}(\overline{q_i}) = C_i$ for $1 \leq i \leq k$, and $\eta^{-1}(\overline{q_{k+1}}) = C_{deadlock}$.

Set $\mathfrak{B}(q)$ contains the events to be blocked in q. The refinement splits the problematic abstract state into multiple abstract states, each representing concrete states in which the same events need to be blocked. Observe that state $\overline{q_{k+1}}$, in which the necessary blocking will introduce a deadlock, will be put in BAD in one of the following iterations of the main algorithm.

For correctness and soundness, we present the following theorem, proven in Appendix IV of the supplementary material [2]. This result is analogous to the one for the concrete algorithm presented in [15]; hence, it demonstrates that the improved scalability does not come at the expense of the concrete version's desirable qualities.

Theorem 1. *For a behavioral program P and a violated safety property Φ,*

1. A patch returned by algorithm 4 eliminates all bad executions of the program, does not eliminate good executions, and does not create deadlocks.
2. If there exists a wait-block patch that corrects P with respect to Φ, such a patch will be found by algorithm 4. Otherwise, the algorithm will issue a Failure notice.

In this algorithm, the inverse global abstraction $\eta^{-1}(\overline{q})$ is computed multiple times; indeed, this is an expensive step. However, for programs that are "close to being correct", the repair algorithm may only need to perform a few refinements, hopefully terminating in reasonable time. As discussed in Section 4.2, not every refinement is obtainable in our two layered structure; see discussion therein.

6 Experimental Results

For our experiments we used the *BPC* framework for BP in C^{++}, available online [1]. We implemented the algorithms presented in the previous sections, namely thread abstraction, partitioning into modules, CEGAR verification and abstraction based patching, as a proof-of-concept tool on top of BPC. Since our goal was to show the improved scalability offered by the abstraction techniques, we also implemented concrete versions of the same algorithms in BPC. All implementations are explicit; symbolic implementation is left for future work.

We tested our algorithms on a BP based web-server application. The server, a work in progress, implements basic TCP and HTTP protocol stacks and is compatible with the Firefox browser. Due to the server's size of several million states, BPC ran out of memory when attempting to verify it concretely.

In contrast, the abstraction based methods were able to produce an initial abstraction of the system within 22 seconds. The automated module partitioning algorithm successfully divided the threads into logically related modules along the lines of the TCP and HTTP layers, grouping the HTTP threads into a single module and dividing the TCP threads between a few modules. The resulting over-approximation contained 800 states and some 12500 transitions.

We then used this over-approximation to identify and repair a bug where the TCP stack would, under certain conditions, acknowledge a FIN message for already closed connections. Identifying this bug using the CEGAR-based verification algorithm took 9.5 minutes, and included 3 refinement phases, at the end of which a genuine counterexample was produced. Producing a patch that fixes the bug using algorithm 4 then took 38 minutes.

Our experiments were run on a 2.66 GHz T500 laptop. The model and some of the properties used for our tests are available from [2].

7 Related Work and Conclusion

The main contribution of our work is in applying abstraction techniques to behavioral programming. In particular, we propose a technique for efficiently generating over-approximations of programs, which can later be used in analysis algorithms. We demonstrate two such algorithms: a CEGAR based method for model-checking behavioral programs, and an abstraction based algorithm for the repair of safety violations. We regard this research as a step in the direction of developing more scalable methodologies and tools for formal analysis of BP.

Another contribution of our work is in the field of program repair, where we show an abstraction based algorithm that uses repair-guided refinement. Program repair is closely related to the synthesis problem, where various abstraction-refinement schemes have been proposed (e.g., [13, 18]); thus, we feel that this is a useful concept that could potentially improve the scalability of existing repair methods, not necessarily restricted to BP.

The use of abstraction-refinement based techniques to expedite model-checking has been extensively studied (e.g., [4, 10, 11, 22]) and has been implemented in several frameworks, such as SLAM [7] and BLAST [19]. Among these, the work most closely related to ours is the MAGIC framework [8, 9]. There, the authors similarly propose a two layer CEGAR approach, in which modules are abstracted separately and their abstractions then composed. However, the setting of [8, 9] allows spurious counterexamples to be checked against each module separately — whereas in the setting of BP, checking involves all modules simultaneously. Analogously, refinements may not be confined to a single module.

In the area of program repair, recent work has focused on locating faulty components and then using synthesis to alter or replace them. In [20, 24], the authors seek corrections in the form of strategies that may be implemented without introducing new states (memoryless strategies), in order to alter the original program as little as possible. We address the same need by only adding code, leaving the original program unmodified. The work of [14] discusses repairing boolean programs by using abstractions of these programs. This approach is similar to ours, but does not include a refinement phase in case spurious executions in the abstract program prevent finding a repair. In [21], the authors tackle state explosion by maintaining an under-approximation of a repair candidate, at each iteration adding more constraints that it must fulfill. New constraints are produced by checking the candidate against the concrete faulty system. This technique appears orthogonal to our own, in which the program is abstracted and the repair candidate is calculated explicitly. Attempting to combine the two methods seems promising, and is left for future work.

A different repair approach includes using genetic and co-evolutionary programming [5, 25], where a set of candidate programs is iteratively evaluated against the specification. Programs with high *fitness* survive, and are *mutated* to produce the next iteration's candidates, until a correct program is obtained. This approach handles more general bugs than ours (as it is not limited to trimming), but may extensively alter the original program's code.

In the future, we plan to extend our abstraction-based repair algorithm to handle violated liveness properties, as well safety ones. Indeed, some preliminary work we have done shows promising results. Another direction we hope to pursue is improving the performance of BPC by enhancing it with symbolic capabilities. Finally, another interesting line of work is strengthening our module-partitioning algorithm: we feel the programmer-created b-threads contain currently untapped meta data about the structure of the system, which could be utilized in making "smarter" partitions. We hope that tapping this meta data will also prove useful in the context of automated compositional verification.

Acknowledgments. We thank D. Harel for his guidance and support, O. Kupferman for her insightful remarks on this work, and the anonymous reviewers for their valuable and thorough comments. This work was supported by an Advanced Research Grant to D. Harel from the European Research Council (ERC) under the European Community's 7th Framework Programme (FP7/2007-2013), and by an Israel Science Foundation grant.

References

1. BPC: Behavioral Programming in C^{++}, http://www.wisdom.weizmann.ac.il/~bprogram/bpc/
2. Supplementral material, http://www.wisdom.weizmann.ac.il/~bprogram/bpc/module_based_abstraction/
3. Alur, R., Henzinger, T.A., Kupferman, O.: Alternating-Time Temporal Logic. Journal of the ACM 49(5), 672–713 (2002)
4. Amla, N., McMillan, K.L.: Combining Abstraction Refinement and SAT-Based Model Checking. In: Grumberg, O., Huth, M. (eds.) TACAS 2007. LNCS, vol. 4424, pp. 405–419. Springer, Heidelberg (2007)
5. Arcuri, A., Yao, X.: A Novel Co-evolutionary Approach to Automatic Software Bug Fixing. In: Proc. 10th IEEE Congress on Evolutionary Computation (CEC), pp. 162–168 (2008)
6. Baier, C., Katoen, J.-P.: Principles of Model Checking. The MIT Press (2008)
7. Ball, T., Rajamani, S.K.: Automatically Validating Temporal Safety Properties of Interfaces. In: Dwyer, M.B. (ed.) SPIN 2001. LNCS, vol. 2057, pp. 103–122. Springer, Heidelberg (2001)
8. Chaki, S., Clarke, E., Groce, A., Jha, S., Veith, H.: Modular Verification of Software Components in C. IEEE Transactions on Software Engineering, 385–395 (2004)
9. Clarke, E., Groce, A., Ouaknine, J., Strichman, O., Yorav, K.: Efficient Verification of Sequential and Concurrent C Programs. Formal Methods in System Design 25(2-3), 129–166 (2004)
10. Clarke, E., Grumberg, O., Jha, S., Lu, Y., Veith, H.: Counterexample-guided Abstraction Refinement. In: Proc. 12th Int. Conf. on Computer Aided Verification (CAV), pp. 154–169 (2000)
11. Clarke, E., Grumberg, O., Long, D.E.: Model Checking and Abstraction. In: Proc. 19th. Symposium on Principles of Programming Languages (POPL), pp. 343–354 (1992)
12. Damm, W., Harel, D.: LSCs: Breathing Life into Message Sequence Charts. J. on Formal Methods in System Design 19(1), 45–80 (2001)
13. de Alfaro, L., Roy, P.: Solving Games via Three-Valued Abstraction Refinement. In: Caires, L., Vasconcelos, V.T. (eds.) CONCUR 2007. LNCS, vol. 4703, pp. 74–89. Springer, Heidelberg (2007)
14. Griesmayer, A., Staber, S., Bloem, R.: Automated fault localization for c programs. In: Proc. 18th Int. Conf. on Computer Aided Verification (CAV), pp. 82–99 (2006)

15. Harel, D., Katz, G., Marron, A., Weiss, G.: Non-Intrusive Repair of Reactive Programs. In: Proc. 17th IEEE Int. Conf. on Engineering of Complex Computer Systems (ICECCS), pp. 3–12 (2012)
16. Harel, D., Marelly, R.: Come, Let's Play: Scenario-Based Programming Using LSCs and the Play-Engine. Springer (2003)
17. Harel, D., Marron, A., Weiss, G.: Behavioral Programming. Communications of the ACM 55(7), 90–100 (2012)
18. Henzinger, T.A., Jhala, R., Majumdar, R.: Counterexample-guided Control. In: Baeten, J.C.M., Lenstra, J.K., Parrow, J., Woeginger, G.J. (eds.) ICALP 2003. LNCS, vol. 2719, pp. 886–902. Springer, Heidelberg (2003)
19. Henzinger, T.A., Jhala, R., Majumdar, R., Sutre, G.: Software Verification with BLAST. In: Ball, T., Rajamani, S.K. (eds.) SPIN 2003. LNCS, vol. 2648, pp. 235–239. Springer, Heidelberg (2003)
20. Jobstmann, B., Griesmayer, A., Bloem, R.: Program Repair as a Game. In: Etessami, K., Rajamani, S.K. (eds.) CAV 2005. LNCS, vol. 3576, pp. 226–238. Springer, Heidelberg (2005)
21. Könighofer, R., Bloem, R.: Repair with On-The-Fly Program Analysis. In: Biere, A., Nahir, A., Vos, T. (eds.) HVC. LNCS, vol. 7857, pp. 56–71. Springer, Heidelberg (2013)
22. McMillan, K.L., Zuck, L.D.: Abstract Counterexamples for Non-disjunctive Abstractions. In: Bournez, O., Potapov, I. (eds.) RP 2009. LNCS, vol. 5797, pp. 176–188. Springer, Heidelberg (2009)
23. Ramadge, P., Wonham, W.: Supervisory Control of a Class of Discrete Event Processes. SIAM J. on Control and Optimization 25(1), 206–230 (1987)
24. Staber, S., Jobstmann, B., Bloem, R.: Diagnosis is Repair. In: Proc. 16th Int. Workshop on Principles of Diagnosis (DX), pp. 169–174 (2005)
25. Weimer, W., Forrest, S., Le Goues, C., Nguyen, T.: Automatic Program Repair with Evolutionary Computation. Communications of the ACM 53, 109–116 (2010)

Prediction and Explanation over DL-*Lite* Data Streams

Szymon Klarman and Thomas Meyer

Centre for Artificial Intelligence Research,
CSIR Meraka and University of KwaZulu-Natal, South Africa
{sklarman,tmeyer}@csir.co.za

Abstract. Stream reasoning is an emerging research area focusing on the development of reasoning techniques applicable to streams of rapidly changing, semantically enhanced data. In this paper, we consider data represented in Description Logics from the popular DL-*Lite* family, and study the logic foundations of prediction and explanation over DL-*Lite* data streams, i.e., reasoning from finite segments of streaming data to conjectures about the content of the streams in the future or in the past. We propose a novel formalization of the problem based on temporal "past-future" rules, grounded in Temporal Query Language. Such rules can naturally accommodate complex data association patterns, which are typically discovered through data mining processes, with logical and temporal constraints of varying expressiveness. Further, we analyse the computational complexity of reasoning with rules expressed in different fragments of the temporal language. As a result, we draw precise demarcation lines between NP-, DP- and PSPACE-complete variants of our setting and, consequently, suggest relevant restrictions rendering prediction and explanation more feasible in practice.

1 Introduction

A data stream is a temporally ordered collection of data, representing the flow of information through a certain channel over time [1]. Semantic applications generating and consuming such streams of rapidly changing data are becoming increasingly common, with domains ranging through scientific, medical, financial, urban, and many others. As has been argued by many authors, the shift of the paradigm from traditional, static data to streaming information requires deep revisions and advancements in the area of automated reasoning. On the one hand, the capacity and velocity of data streams present a serious technological challenge for the existing reasoning systems, tailored towards static data models and softer latency requirements. On the other one, the real-time and real-world nature of streaming information encourages investigations into novel forms of reasoning, going beyond the basic, deductive query answering — forms, which could support the construction of versatile analytical tools for enhancing the understanding and utilization of knowledge conveyed in data streams [2,3]. This latter research agenda motivates directly our presented work.

In this paper, we study the logic foundations of two non-deductive types of inference over data streams: *prediction* and *explanation*, i.e., reasoning from finite segments of streaming data to conjectures about the content of the streams in the future and in the past. Thus defined notions of prediction and explanation are variations of their well-established analogs in philosophy of science, where they are often related to the classical problem of causality.[1] There, to predict is to identify the expected effects of existing causes, while to explain — inversely — to find possible causes of the observed effects [4]. In systems managing real-time information, prediction is of major importance as an inference guiding decision making processes based on the currently available data. Meanwhile, explanation is pivotal to comprehending the situation which underlies and justifies the observed data, which often requires procuring the relevant chain of circumstances leading to it or abstracting the data into higher-level knowledge. Both modes of inference are essential for achieving situation awareness in a real-time information system [5]. Although prediction (and to a lesser degree explanation) has been addressed in the context of streaming data, the focus of the relevant work lies predominantly on the data mining level, i.e., on the methodology of learning the association patterns occurring in the data and extrapolating them via statistical techniques to yet unobserved data [3,6]. On the contrary, virtually no attention has been given to predictive and explanatory reasoning in its strictly logical sense, as a symbolic inference, on the knowledge representation level. This is a critical gap whenever streams of semantically rich data are considered, as in such scenarios bridging the statistical and semantic view on the data is instrumental to designing robust reasoning techniques. To the best of our knowledge, in this work we present the first insights and results on logical and computational aspects of prediction and explanation over semantic data streams.

Following the popular paradigm of ontology-based data access, we consider data expressed as Description Logic (DL) axioms, accessed through an ontological layer expressed in DLs from the popular DL-*Lite* family [7]. Further, we define a special type of temporal "past-future" rules, grounded in Temporal Query Language [8]. Such rules can naturally accommodate complex data association patterns, identified in the data mining phase, with logical and temporal constraints of varying expressiveness. Based on this foundation, we propose a novel formalization of the two studied types of inference, as abduction of a data sequence satisfying the consequent or, respectively, the antecedent of a temporal rule. We analyse the computational complexity of such tasks over rules expressed in different fragments of the temporal language, and as a result, we draw precise demarcation lines between NP-, DP- and PSPACE-complete variants of the problem. Building on these findings, we discuss relevant restrictions to the prediction and explanation tasks which can render the reasoning feasible in practice.

The paper is organized as follows. In the next section, we recap preliminaries of DLs and conjunctive query answering. In Section 3, we systematically introduce all temporal components of the framework, including data streams, Temporal Query Language and temporal rules. Then, in Section 4, we define prediction and

---

[1] See http://plato.stanford.edu/entries/scientific-explanation/

explanation and motivate our proposal. In Section 5, we present the complexity results and, further, discuss their consequences on the main problem. The proofs of the results are included in the full technical report [9]. An overview of related work and concluding remarks are presented in the last two sections.

2   Preliminaries

A *Description Logic* (DL) language is given by a vocabulary $\Sigma = (\mathsf{N_I}, \mathsf{N_C}, \mathsf{N_R})$ and a set of logical constructors [10]. The vocabulary consists of countably infinite sets of individual names ($\mathsf{N_I}$), concept names ($\mathsf{N_C}$) and role names ($\mathsf{N_R}$). An ABox $\mathcal{A}$ is a finite set of assertions $A(a)$ and $r(a,b)$, for $a, b \in \mathsf{N_I}$, $A \in \mathsf{N_C}$ and $r \in \mathsf{N_R}$. A TBox $\mathcal{T}$ is a finite set of terminological axioms, e.g., concept and role inclusions, whose precise syntax is determined by the given DL. The semantics is given in terms of DL interpretations $\mathcal{I} = (\Delta^\mathcal{I}, \cdot^\mathcal{I})$, defined as usual [10]. An interpretation $\mathcal{I}$ is a model of $\mathcal{T}$ and $\mathcal{A}$, denoted as $\mathcal{I} \models \mathcal{T}, \mathcal{A}$, iff it satisfies every axiom in $\mathcal{T}$ and $\mathcal{A}$. If $\mathcal{T}$ and $\mathcal{A}$ have a common model they are said to be consistent.

Abiding by the nomenclature of ontology-based data access paradigm, we consider the ABox as *data* and the TBox as the *ontology*, which provides an additional semantic layer over the data, thus enriching the querying capabilities. A *conjunctive query* (CQ) over a DL vocabulary Σ is a first-order formula $\exists \boldsymbol{y}.\varphi(\boldsymbol{x}, \boldsymbol{y})$, where $\boldsymbol{x}, \boldsymbol{y}$ are sequences of variables, from a countably infinite set of variables $\mathsf{N_V}$. The sequence $\boldsymbol{x}$ denotes the free (answer) variables in the query, while $\boldsymbol{y}$ the quantified ones. The formula φ is a conjunction of atoms over $\mathsf{N_C}, \mathsf{N_R}$ of the form $A(u), r(u,v)$, where $u, v \in \mathsf{N_V} \cup \mathsf{N_I}$ are called terms. By $\mathsf{term}(q)$ we denote the set of all terms occurring in a CQ q and by $\mathsf{avar}(q)$ the set of all its answer variables. We call q grounded whenever $\mathsf{avar}(q) = \emptyset$. A grounded CQ q is satisfied in $\mathcal{I}$ iff there exists a mapping $\mu : \mathsf{term}(q) \mapsto \Delta^\mathcal{I}$, with $\mu(a) = a^\mathcal{I}$ for every $a \in \mathsf{N_I}$, such that for every $A(u)$ and $r(u,v)$ in q it is the case that $\mu(u) \in A^\mathcal{I}$ and $(\mu(u), \mu(v)) \in r^\mathcal{I}$. We say that q is entailed by a TBox $\mathcal{T}$ and an ABox $\mathcal{A}$, denoted as $\mathcal{T}, \mathcal{A} \models q$ iff q is satisfied in every model of $\mathcal{T}$ and $\mathcal{A}$. An *answer* to q is a mapping σ such that $\sigma : \mathsf{avar}(q) \mapsto \mathsf{N_I}$. By $\sigma(q)$ we denote the result of uniformly substituting every occurrence of x in q with $\sigma(x)$, for every $x \in \mathsf{avar}(q)$. An answer σ is called *certain* over $\mathcal{T}, \mathcal{A}$ iff $\mathcal{T}, \mathcal{A} \models \sigma(q)$. The set of all certain answers to q over $\mathcal{T}, \mathcal{A}$ is denoted by $\mathsf{cert}(\mathsf{q}, \mathcal{T}, \mathcal{A})$. By $\mathcal{Q}_\Sigma$ we denote the class of all conjunctive queries over the vocabulary Σ.

In this paper, we focus on logics from the DL-*Lite* family [7], such as DL-*Lite*$_\mathcal{R}$, DL-*Lite*$_\mathcal{F}$ or DL-*Lite*$_\mathcal{A}$, underlying the OWL 2 QL ontology language profile [2], for which CQs enjoy the so-called first-order rewritability property, defined as follows.

Definition 1 (FO rewritability [7]). *For every CQ $q \in \mathcal{Q}_\Sigma$ and a TBox $\mathcal{T}$, there exists a FO formula $q^\mathcal{T}$ such that for every ABox $\mathcal{A}$ and answer σ to q, it holds that $\sigma \in \mathsf{cert}(\mathsf{q}, \mathcal{T}, \mathcal{A})$ iff $\mathsf{db}(\mathcal{A}) \Vdash \sigma(q^\mathcal{T})$, where $\mathsf{db}(\mathcal{A})$ denotes $\mathcal{A}$ considered as a database/FO interpretation and $\Vdash$ is the FO satisfaction relation.*

---
[2] See http://www.w3.org/TR/owl2-profiles/

Recall, that given $\mathcal{T}$ in any of such DLs and a grounded q, the FO rewriting $q^{\mathcal{T}}$ of q is a union of possibly exponentially many CQs, including q. The number of these CQs is bounded by $\ell(\mathcal{T})^{\ell(q)}$, where $\ell(\dagger)$ denotes the size of the input $\dagger$ measured in the total number of symbols used. Every CQ q' in $q^{\mathcal{T}}$ is of the size linear in $\ell(q)$ and is such that $\mathcal{T} \cup \{q'\} \models q$. The query entailment problem is NP-complete in the combined complexity, even when the TBox is empty, while checking consistency of $\mathcal{T}, \mathcal{A}$ is in PTIME [7].

Regardless of this default focus, many of the results presented here can be naturally extended to other DLs exhibiting similar characteristics, such as other members of the DL-*Lite* family or logics in the $\mathcal{EL}$ family [11].

3 Temporal Data and Queries

We consider a discrete, linear *flow of time* $(\mathbb{Z}, <)$, with integers representing *time instants* ordered by the smaller-than relation. An *interval* over $\mathbb{Z}$ is a set $I = [I^-, I^+] = \{i \in \mathbb{Z} \mid I^- \leq i \leq I^+\}$, where $I^- \leq I^+ \in \mathbb{Z} \cup \{-\infty, +\infty\}$ denote the beginning and the end of I, respectively. We assume that $\mathbb{N} = [0, +\infty]$.

Definition 2 (A-sequence). *An A-sequence $\mathfrak{A} = (\mathcal{A}_i)_{i \in I}$ is a sequence of ABoxes, for some interval I over $\mathbb{Z}$.*

A-sequences represent collections of datasets ordered temporally w.r.t. the underlying time flow. The ordering of the ABoxes follows the smaller-than ordering of their indices. An A-sequence $\mathfrak{A}$ is said to be consistent with a TBox $\mathcal{T}$ if every ABox in it is consistent with $\mathcal{T}$. Consider A-sequences $\mathfrak{A} = (\mathcal{A}_i)_{i \in I}$ and $\mathfrak{B} = (\mathcal{B}_i)_{i \in J}$. We use the following notation:

- $\mathfrak{A} \subseteq \mathfrak{B}$ ($\mathfrak{A} = \mathfrak{B}$) *iff* $I \subseteq J$ ($I = J$) and $\mathcal{A}_i = \mathcal{B}_i$ for every $i \in I$,
- $\mathcal{T}, \mathfrak{A} \models \mathfrak{B}$ ($\mathfrak{A} \models \mathfrak{B}$) *iff* $J \subseteq I$ and $\mathcal{T}, \mathcal{A}_i \models \mathcal{B}_i$ ($\mathcal{A}_i \models \mathcal{B}_i$) for every $i \in J$,
- $\mathfrak{A} \rightharpoonup \mathfrak{B}$ *iff* there exists a mapping $f: I \mapsto J$, such that:
  - $i < j$ *iff* $f(i) < f(j)$, for every $i, j \in I$,
  - $\mathcal{A}_i = \mathcal{B}_{f(i)}$, for every $i \in I$,
- $\mathfrak{A} \uplus \mathfrak{B}$, whenever $I \cap J \neq \emptyset$, to denote the A-sequence $(\mathcal{C}_i)_{i \in I \cup J}$ such that:
  - $\mathcal{C}_i = \mathcal{A}_i$, for every $i \in I \setminus J$,
  - $\mathcal{C}_i = \mathcal{B}_i$, for every $i \in J \setminus I$,
  - $\mathcal{C}_i = \mathcal{A}_i \cup \mathcal{B}_i$, for every $i \in I \cap J$,
- $\mathfrak{A}_{\leq n}$ ($\mathfrak{A}_{\geq n}$), for $n \in I$, to denote the A-sequence $(\mathcal{A}_i)_{i \in I'} \subseteq \mathfrak{A}$, such that $I' = [I^-, n]$ ($I' = [n, I^+]$).

The notion of data stream adopted here specializes that of ontology stream, as introduced in [12], by considering temporal variability only on the data (ABox) level, while prohibiting changes on the ontology (TBox) level.

Definition 3 (Data stream). *A* data stream *under a TBox $\mathcal{T}$ is an A-sequence $\mathfrak{A} = (\mathcal{A}_i)_{i \in \mathbb{Z}}$ consistent with $\mathcal{T}$, with a designated subsequence $\mathfrak{A}_\omega \subseteq \mathfrak{A}$, called the* recorded segment *of $\mathfrak{A}$, where ω is a finite interval over $\mathbb{Z}$. For the current time $n \in \mathbb{Z}$, we call $\mathfrak{A}_{\leq n}$ the* past, *and $\mathfrak{A}_{\geq n}$ the* future *of $\mathfrak{A}$.*

In full generality, a data stream is then an infinite sequence of datasets consistent with a fixed TBox. Obviously, in practical scenarios, one can effectively know and manage only a finite fragment of the past of a given stream, while remaining agnostic about its future. What we call above the recorded segment of $\mathfrak{A}$ is precisely this finite, accessible portion of the stream.

Next, we recall a variant of Temporal Query Language, proposed in [8], to be used for accessing data streams. It is a lightweight combination of Linear Temporal Logic (LTL) [13] with CQs, where CQs are embedded in the temporal language using the epistemic semantics.

Definition 4 (Temporal Query Language). *The* temporal query language *(TQL) over a class of conjunctive queries $\mathcal{Q}_\Sigma$ is the smallest set of formulas induced by the grammar:*

$$\phi ::= [q] \mid \neg \phi \mid \phi \wedge \phi \mid \phi \mathsf{U} \phi \mid \phi \mathsf{S} \phi$$

where $q \in \mathcal{Q}_\Sigma$. By $\mathsf{avar}(\phi)$ we denote the set of free variables in ϕ. A TQL formula ϕ is called grounded *whenever $\mathsf{avar}(\phi) = \emptyset$. The entailment relation for grounded TQL formulas w.r.t. an A-sequence $\mathfrak{A} = (\mathcal{A}_i)_{i \in I}$ under a TBox $\mathcal{T}$ in time $i \in I$ is defined inductively as follows:*

$\mathcal{T}, \mathfrak{A}, i \models [q]$ iff $\mathcal{T}, \mathcal{A}_i \models q$,
$\mathcal{T}, \mathfrak{A}, i \models \neg \phi$ iff $\mathcal{T}, \mathfrak{A}, i \not\models \phi$,
$\mathcal{T}, \mathfrak{A}, i \models \phi \wedge \psi$ iff $\mathcal{T}, \mathfrak{A}, i \models \phi$ and $\mathcal{T}, \mathfrak{A}, i \models \psi$,
$\mathcal{T}, \mathfrak{A}, i \models \phi \mathsf{U} \psi$ iff   there exists $j \in I$ with $j > i$ such that $\mathcal{T}, \mathfrak{A}, j \models \psi$ and $\mathcal{T}, \mathfrak{A}, k \models \phi$ for every $k \in I$ with $i < k < j$,
$\mathcal{T}, \mathfrak{A}, i \models \phi \mathsf{S} \psi$ iff   there exists $j \in I$ with $j < i$ such that $\mathcal{T}, \mathfrak{A}, j \models \psi$ and $\mathcal{T}, \mathfrak{A}, k \models \phi$ for every $k \in I$ with $i > k > j$.

An answer to a TQL formula ϕ is a mapping $\sigma : \mathsf{avar}(\phi) \mapsto \mathsf{N_I}$. By $\sigma(\phi)$ we denote the result of uniformly substituting every occurrence of x in ϕ with $\sigma(x)$, for every $x \in \mathsf{avar}(\phi)$. An answer σ is called certain over $\mathcal{T}, \mathfrak{A}$ at $i \in I$ iff $\mathcal{T}, \mathfrak{A}, i \models \sigma(\phi)$. The set of all such answers is denoted by $\mathsf{cert}_i(\phi, \mathcal{T}, \mathfrak{A})$.

Observe that given the epistemic interpretation of the embedded CQs, $[q]$ reads as "*q is entailed in the given time instant*", for a grounded CQ q. We can immediately paraphrase this interpretation by invoking FO rewriting of q, in the sense of Definition 1. Note that the following correspondences immediately hold:

$$\mathcal{T}, \mathfrak{A}, i \models [q] \quad \text{iff} \quad \mathcal{T}, \mathcal{A}_i \models q \quad \text{iff} \quad db(\mathcal{A}_i) \Vdash q^{\mathcal{T}}.$$

Consequently, the negation $\neg[q]$ is naturally interpreted as negation-as-failure, reading "*it is not true that q is entailed in the given time instant*". This warrants the following equivalences:

$$\mathcal{T}, \mathfrak{A}, i \models \neg[q] \quad \text{iff} \quad \mathcal{T}, \mathcal{A}_i \not\models q \quad \text{iff} \quad db(\mathcal{A}_i) \not\Vdash q^{\mathcal{T}}.$$

These observations are critical for the work presented in this paper, as they allow to study satisfaction of TQL formulas by decoupling the temporal component of the problem from the CQ component, and addressing the latter, without loss of correctness, by applying the standard FO rewriting techniques and results, recalled in Section 2. Importantly, such lightweight combination of languages allows also for a modular reuse of existing temporal reasoners and highly optimized, efficient query answering engines [8].

LTL with operators U and S, standing for (strict) *until* and *since*, which captures precisely the temporal component of TQL, is known to be expressively complete over $(\mathbb{Z}, <)$ [14]. Apart from the full TQL, in what follows we consider also some of its strict subsets. By $TQL^\exists$ we denote the fragment in which the syntax of U- and S-formulas is restricted to the form $\top U\phi$ and $\top S\phi$, where $\top$ is a constant symbol denoting the logical truth. This restriction corresponds to LTL with operators *sometime in the future* and *sometime in the past*, in place of U and S. Further, with TQL^+ we refer to the positive fragment of TQL, i.e., TQL without the negation operator. Finally, by $TQL^{\exists,+}$, we denote the intersection of $TQL^\exists$ and TQL^+.

Following the temporal separation approach of Gabbay [14], we consider TQL formulas belonging to two disjoint categories:

- **past-present**: formulas without the operators of type U,
- **future-present**: formulas without the operators of type S.

By the semantics of TQL, it follows that for any TQL formula ϕ, TBox $\mathcal{T}$, A-sequence $\mathfrak{A} = (\mathcal{A}_i)_{i \in I}$, and time point $n \in I$, the equivalences below hold:

- $\mathsf{cert}_n(\phi, \mathcal{T}, \mathfrak{A}) = \mathsf{cert}_n(\phi, \mathcal{T}, \mathfrak{A}_{\leq n})$, whenever ϕ is past-present,
- $\mathsf{cert}_n(\phi, \mathcal{T}, \mathfrak{A}) = \mathsf{cert}_n(\phi, \mathcal{T}, \mathfrak{A}_{\geq n})$, whenever ϕ is future-present.

Given the distinction above, we define the notion of temporal rules, which is closely related to Gabbay's concept of executable temporal logic [14]. Temporal rules straightforwardly embody the *"declarative past–imperative future"* pattern over TQL.

Definition 5 (Temporal rules). *A temporal rule in TQL is an expression of the form:*

$$\psi \Rightarrow \phi$$

where ψ, ϕ are TQL formulas such that ψ is past-present and ϕ is future-present. The rule $\psi \Rightarrow \phi$ is satisfied for a substitution $\varrho = \sigma \cup \sigma'$, for some $\sigma : \mathsf{avar}(\psi) \mapsto \mathsf{N}_\mathsf{I}$ and $\sigma' : \mathsf{avar}(\phi) \mapsto \mathsf{N}_\mathsf{I}$ agreeing on $\mathsf{avar}(\psi) \cap \mathsf{avar}(\phi)$, over a TBox $\mathcal{T}$ and an A-sequence $\mathfrak{A} = (\mathcal{A}_i)_{i \in I}$, at time $n \in I$ iff $\sigma \in \mathsf{cert}_n(\psi, \mathcal{T}, \mathfrak{A})$ implies $\sigma' \in \mathsf{cert}_n(\phi, \mathcal{T}, \mathfrak{A})$.

Temporal rules are equipped with well-defined semantics and allow for relatively easy control of the expressiveness-complexity trade-off, due to their close relationship with LTL. They are also a natural formalism for expressing association rules discoverable in time series data by means of various data mining techniques. This sort of association rules typically combine diverse data patterns with logical and temporal constraints [15]. Although lacking some essential probabilistic and real-time features, not present in the basic variants of LTL, temporal rules can arguably provide a robust logic foundation for target learning languages over streaming DL-*Lite* data. As an example, we present a prototypical temporal association rule used in a climate application predicting droughts in certain regions of India [16]

Climate application example: Consider a temporal rule $\psi \Rightarrow \phi$ encoding a correlation between several measurements and weather phenomena occurring in specific geographic locations, in a specific order, known to be a good predictor of drought. The rule is defined by the TQL formulas:

$$\psi = (\neg[\exists y.(\mathit{HeavyRainIn}(y) \wedge \mathit{locIn}(y, \mathit{north}))] \;\mathsf{S}\; [\exists y, z.(\mathit{SST}(y, \mathit{low}) \wedge \mathit{NAO}(z, \mathit{high})])$$
$$\wedge \, [\mathit{locIn}(x, \mathit{northeast})]$$
$$\phi = \top \;\mathsf{U}\; ([\mathit{DroughtIn}(x)] \wedge ([\mathit{DroughtIn}(x)] \;\mathsf{U}\; [\mathit{SevereDroughtIn}(x)]))$$

It states that if at some point in the past the SST (sea surface temperature) was found out to be low, the NAO (North Atlantic Oscillation) was high, and since then there has been no heavy rain recorded in North province, then at some point in the future there will be drought in x, whenever x is located in Northeast, which will persist until severe drought occurs in x. □

4 Prediction and Explanation

By adopting temporal rules as the language of association patterns in streaming data, we are able to formulate very intuitive and clear-cut definitions of prediction and explanation over data streams: *a prediction (explanation) is a possible future (past) of the data stream, which entails the consequent (antecedent) of a temporal rule, given its antecedent (consequent) is entailed by the recorded segment*. This meaning of the two types of inference is schematically depicted in Figure 1 and further made precise in the following two definitions. We consider a data stream $\mathfrak{A}$ under a TBox $\mathcal{T}$, with the recorded segment $\mathfrak{A}_\omega \subseteq \mathfrak{A}$, where ω is a finite interval over $\mathbb{Z}$.

Definition 6 (Prediction). *Let $\psi \Rightarrow \phi$ be a temporal rule and $\sigma \in \mathsf{cert}_n(\psi, \mathcal{T}, \mathfrak{A}_\omega)$, for a time $n \in \omega$. A prediction at n from $\psi \Rightarrow \phi$ and σ over $\mathcal{T}, \mathfrak{A}_\omega$ is an A-sequence $\mathfrak{D} = (\mathcal{D}_i)_{i \in [n,+\infty]}$ such that $\sigma' \in \mathsf{cert}_n(\phi, \mathcal{T}, \mathfrak{A}_\omega \uplus \mathfrak{D})$, for some σ' agreeing with σ on $\mathsf{avar}(\psi) \cap \mathsf{avar}(\phi)$.*

Definition 7 (Explanation). *Let $\psi \Rightarrow \phi$ be a temporal rule and $\sigma \in \mathsf{cert}_n(\phi, \mathcal{T}, \mathfrak{A}_\omega)$, for a time $n \in \omega$. An explanation of σ at n based on $\psi \Rightarrow \phi$ is an A-sequence $\mathfrak{D} = (\mathcal{D}_i)_{i \in [-\infty,n]}$ such that $\sigma' \in \mathsf{cert}_n(\psi, \mathcal{T}, \mathfrak{A}_\omega \uplus \mathfrak{D})$ for some σ' agreeing with σ on $\mathsf{avar}(\psi) \cap \mathsf{avar}(\phi)$.*

From a high-level perspective, prediction and explanation are classifiable as strictly different types of inference in that the former is deductive (following from

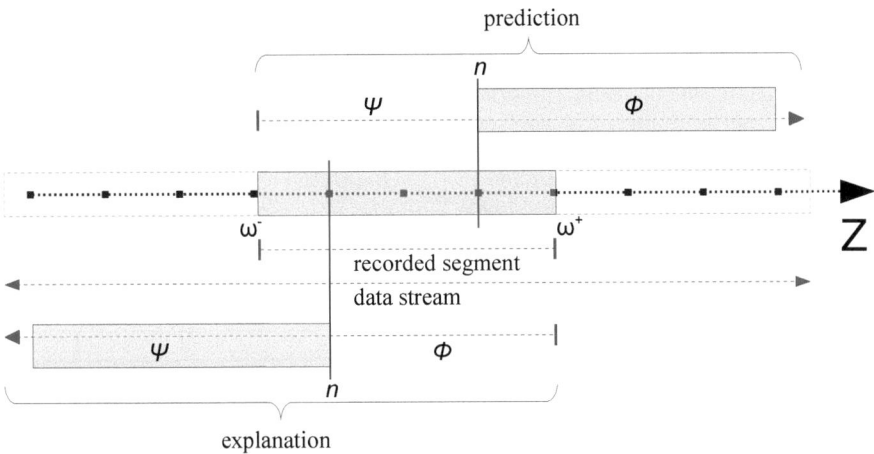

Fig. 1. Prediction and explanation over data streams

the antecedent to the consequent), while the latter abductive (from the consequent to the antecedent) [4]. Technically, however, it is strikingly apparent that the gist of both inferences is essentially the same and comes down to solving two identical subproblems: 1) verifying that a certain TQL formula (ψ in prediction and ϕ in explanantion) is entailed by the recorded segment, thus triggering the particular inference, and 2) finding an A-sequence which entails the second TQL formula in the temporal rule (ϕ in prediction and ψ in explanantion). As far as the former task, reducible to deductive entailment, is relatively well-understood, and hence is only shortly addressed in the next section, the latter has not yet been formulated in the literature, and is the central problem studied in the remainder of this paper. The problem has a strongly abductive flavour and is conceptualized here based on the nomenclature coined in [17,18,19].

Definition 8 (A-sequence abduction). *An A-sequence abduction problem is a tuple $(\mathcal{T}, \mathfrak{A}, \phi)$, where $\mathcal{T}$ is a TBox, $\mathfrak{A} = (\mathcal{A}_i)_{i \in I}$ is an A-sequence, for some $I^-, I^+ \in \mathbb{Z}$, and ϕ is a grounded future-present (resp. past-present) TQL formula. A solution to $(\mathcal{T}, \mathfrak{A}, \phi)$ is an A-sequence $\mathfrak{D} = (\mathcal{D}_i)_{i \in J}$ with $J = [I^-, +\infty]$ (resp. $J = [-\infty, I^+]$), such that $\mathfrak{A} \uplus \mathfrak{D}$ is consistent with $\mathcal{T}$, and $\mathcal{T}, \mathfrak{A} \uplus \mathfrak{D}, 0 \models \phi$. The solution $\mathfrak{D}$ is called:*

- *$\preceq_e$-**minimal** iff for every solution $\mathfrak{D}'$, if $\mathfrak{D} \models \mathfrak{D}'$ then $\mathfrak{D}' \models \mathfrak{D}$,*
- *$\preceq_b$-**minimal** iff for every solution $\mathfrak{D}'$, if $\mathcal{T}, \mathfrak{A} \uplus \mathfrak{D} \models \mathfrak{D}'$ then $\mathcal{T}, \mathfrak{A} \uplus \mathfrak{D}' \models \mathfrak{D}$,*
- *$\preceq_s$-**minimal** iff for every solution $\mathfrak{D}'$, if $\mathfrak{D}' \rightharpoonup \mathfrak{D}$ then $\mathfrak{D} = \mathfrak{D}'$.*

As usually in the context of abductive reasoning, we employ several minimality criteria which help to reduce the solution space to a computationally manageable level. The first two are generalizations of criteria known in the classical, atemporal abduction. Intuitively, $\preceq_e$-minimality (for entailment) places the

Table 1. Data stream in the climate application example

...	-2	-1	0	1	...
	$locIn(l_1, north)$	$locIn(l_1, north)$	$locIn(l_1, north)$	$locIn(l_1, north)$	
	$locIn(l_2, northeast)$	$locIn(l_2, northeast)$	$locIn(l_2, northeast)$	$locIn(l_2, northeast)$	
		$DroughtIn(l_2)$	$SevereDroughtIn(l_2)$		
		$SST(m_1, low)$	$RainIn(l_1)$		
		$NAO(m_2, high)$			

Table 2. Predictions (up) and explanations (down) in the climate application example

	1	2	3	4	...
$\mathfrak{D}_1$:		$DroughtIn(l_2)$	$SevereDroughtIn(l_2)$		
$\mathfrak{D}_2$:	$RainIn(l_1)$	$DroughtIn(l_2)$	$SevereDroughtIn(l_2)$		
$\mathfrak{D}_3$:		$SevereDroughtIn(l_2)$	$SevereDroughtIn(l_2)$		
$\mathfrak{D}_4$:		$DroughtIn(l_2)$	$DroughtIn(l_2)$	$SevereDroughtIn(l_2)$	

	...	-5	-4	-3	-2
$\mathfrak{D}_5$:				$SST(m_1, low)$ $NAO(m_2, high)$	
$\mathfrak{D}_6$:				$SST(m_1, low)$ $NAO(m_2, high)$	$locIn(l_2, northeast)$
$\mathfrak{D}_7$:			$SST(m_1, low)$ $NAO(m_2, high)$		

precedence over solutions which are logically weakest — they assume the least possible data in every given state — irrespectively of the background knowledge. The $\preceq_b$-minimality (for entailment w.r.t. background knowledge) takes also into account the assumed TBox and ABox. Observe that $\preceq_b$-minimality is strictly stronger than $\preceq_e$-minimality, i.e., whenever a solution $\mathcal{D}$ is $\preceq_b$-minimal it must be $\preceq_e$-minimal, while the converse does not hold in general. Note that whenever a problem has a solution at all, it must have a $\preceq_b$-minimal (and thus an $\preceq_e$-minimal) solution. The $\preceq_s$-minimality criterion (for *structure*) is a novel one, tailored specifically for abduction problems, whose solutions are sequential structures. It ensures the identified sequence $\mathfrak{D}$ has no redundant subsequences. To rephrase it, $\mathfrak{D}$ is not minimal in the sense of $\preceq_s$ whenever one can obtain a solution distinct from $\mathfrak{D}$ simply by removing some ABoxes from $\mathfrak{D}$.

The minimality criteria, discussed above, are consequently applied to predictions and explanations. In fact, the abductive procedures developed in the next section are complete for $\preceq_s$- and $\preceq_e$-minimal solutions, and in practice, we also tend to favor $\preceq_b$-minimal solutions, as more basic. For a more intuitive illustration of the two tasks and the minimality criteria we elaborate further on the climate application scenario, introduced in the previous section.

Climate application example cntd.: Let $\psi \Rightarrow \phi$ be the temporal rule as before, grounded with the substitution $\sigma = \{x \mapsto l_2\}$. Consider TBox $\mathcal{T} =$

{$SevereDroughtIn \sqsubseteq DraughtIn$, $HeavyRainIn \sqsubseteq RainIn$} and data stream $\mathfrak{A}$ with the recorded segment $\mathfrak{A}_\omega \subseteq \mathfrak{A}$, where $\omega = [-2,1]$, defined as in Table 1. Table 2 presents several predictions from $\psi \Rightarrow \phi$ and σ, at time 1 ($\mathfrak{D}_1$-$\mathfrak{D}_4$) and explanations of σ based on $\psi \Rightarrow \phi$, at time -2 ($\mathfrak{D}_5$-$\mathfrak{D}_7$). To put equivalently, these are possible solutions to the A-sequence abduction problems $(\mathcal{T}, \mathcal{A}_1, \phi)$ and $(\mathcal{T}, \mathcal{A}_{-2}, \psi)$, respectively. Note, that all empty and hidden cells in the table are empty ABoxes. Observe that $\mathfrak{D}_1$ and $\mathfrak{D}_5$ are both $\preceq_s$- and $\preceq_b$-minimal. Equivalently, Solutions $\mathfrak{D}_2$ and $\mathfrak{D}_6$ are still $\preceq_s$-minimal but not $\preceq_e$-minimal, and hence not $\preceq_b$-minimal either. In the case of $\mathfrak{D}_2$ axiom $RainIn(l_1) \in \mathcal{D}_1$, although not undermining the prediction, is not necessary for the solution to hold. In $\mathfrak{D}_6$, axiom $locIn(l_2, northeast) \in \mathcal{D}_{-2}$ is simply redundant, as it is already present in the data stream. Prediction $\mathfrak{D}_3$ is $\preceq_s$-minimal and $\preceq_e$-minimal, yet not $\preceq_b$-minimal. Note that considering the background knowledge constraint $SevereDroughtIn \sqsubseteq DraughtIn$, axiom $DraughtIn(l_2)$ is logically weaker than the assumed $SevereDroughtIn(l_2) \in \mathcal{D}_2$, and could be possibly used to replace the latter in the solution. Finally, $\mathfrak{D}_4$ and $\mathfrak{D}_7$ are $\preceq_b$-minimal but not $\preceq_s$-minimal, as both can be turned into distinct solutions by subtracting the state $\mathcal{D}_2$ from the former and either of the empty states $\mathcal{D}_{-3}$ or $\mathcal{D}_{-2}$ from the latter.

5 Complexity of Reasoning

In this section, we study the combined complexity of reasoning problems comprising different variants of prediction and explanation tasks. The proofs are included in the full technical report [9]. Note that a "recognition" result with respect to a minimality criterion signals that the underlying decision procedure is complete but not necessarily sound, i.e. the identified solutions might require an additional check for being minimal in the given sense. A "computation" result implies soundness as well [19].

We start by considering ABox abduction, i.e., the task of abducing a minimal ABox ensuring entailment and non-entailment of selected CQs, which is later generalized to sequences of such problems.

Definition 9 (ABox abduction). *An ABox abduction problem is a tuple $\Omega = (\mathcal{T}, \mathcal{A}, P, N)$, where $\mathcal{T}$ is a TBox, $\mathcal{A}$ an ABox, and $P, N \subseteq \mathcal{Q}_\Sigma$ are sets of grounded CQs. An ABox $\mathcal{D}$ is called a solution to problem Ω iff $\mathcal{A} \cup \mathcal{D}$ is consistent with $\mathcal{T}$ and:*

1. $\mathcal{T}, \mathcal{A} \cup \mathcal{D} \models [q]$, *for every* $q \in P$,
2. $\mathcal{T}, \mathcal{A} \cup \mathcal{D} \models \neg[q]$, *for every* $q \in N$.

Note, that $\preceq_e$- and $\preceq_b$-minimality criteria transfer immediately from Definition 8, on considering a single ABox as an A-sequence with exactly one element. The $\preceq_s$-minimality does not apply in the context of ABox abduction. The results obtained here rest on and extend some of those presented in [19].

Lemma 1 (Solving ABox abduction problems). *Let Ω be an ABox abduction problem and $\mathcal{D}$ an $\preceq_e$-minimal solution to Ω. Then:*

1. computing $\mathcal{D}$ for $\Omega = (\mathcal{T}, \emptyset, P, \emptyset)$ is in PTIME, if $\mathcal{T} = \emptyset$ or $\mathcal{D}$ is $\preceq_b$-minimal,
2. recognizing $\mathcal{D}$ for $\Omega = (\mathcal{T}, \mathcal{A}, P, \emptyset)$ is NP-complete, if $\mathcal{T} \neq \emptyset$ or $\mathcal{A} \neq \emptyset$,
3. computing $\mathcal{D}$ for $\Omega = (\mathcal{T}, \mathcal{A}, P, N)$ is DP-complete, if $P \neq \emptyset$ and $N \neq \emptyset$, even when $\mathcal{A} = \emptyset$ and irrespective of deciding $\preceq_b$-minimality,

where $\mathfrak{D}$ is fixed up to renaming individuals in the included ABoxes.

The PTIME result in the first case follows by observing that the addressed ABox abduction problems can be solved immediately by grounding the conjuncts of the CQs. Solving the second type of problems might involve NP-complete CQ entailment checks and/or a nondeterministic choice from an exponential number of queries in the FO rewriting of a CQ. For the last case, recall that DP denotes the intersection of the classes of NP and CONP problems. The result is due to the simultaneous presence of positive and negative CQs, which requires entailment and non-entailment checks, with the latter in CONP.

Next we focus on solving A-sequence abduction problems in TQL. Since technically abduction for future-present formulas is symmetric to abduction for past-present formulas, we only study the former setting, noting that all results transfer automatically to the latter. The central challenge to be addressed is that solutions to such problems are in principle of infinite length, which makes their computation generally impossible in finite time. However, we are able to identify certain finite structures which can be unambiguously unfolded into the corresponding A-sequences. Thus, rather than searching for A-sequences directly, we focus on finding their finite representations, called *A-structures*.

Definition 10 (A-structures). *An A-structure is a tuple* $\mathfrak{S} = (S, \mathcal{S}_0, \rightarrow)$, *where S is a finite set of ABoxes, $\mathcal{S}_0 \in S$ is the initial ABox, and $\rightarrow: S \mapsto S$ is a transition function. The* unfolding *of $\mathfrak{S}$ is an A-sequence $\mathcal{S}_0, \ldots, \mathcal{S}_i, \mathcal{S}_{i+1}, \ldots$, where for every $i \in \mathbb{N}$, $\mathcal{S}_i \in S$ and $\mathcal{S}_i \rightarrow \mathcal{S}_{i+1}$.*

The key to the abductive algorithms we develop here is ensuring existence of an upper bound on the size of the A-structures that are to be found. Technically, the proofs rest on the construction of so-called *quasimodels*, which link A-structures with the input abductive problems. Intuitively, a quasimodel $s = (s_i)_{i \in \mathbb{N}}$ is an abstraction of an infinite sequence of temporal states entailing a given A-sequence. Each s_i-th element $(t_i, \mathcal{A}(t_i))$ in that sequence consists of the set t_i of subformulas of ϕ that must be entailed in i and the minimal ABox $\mathcal{A}(t_i)$ that must hold at i for ϕ to be true at time 0. Particularly instrumental are special quasimodels called ultimately periodic, which consist of a finite initial sequence called the head, followed by an infinite repetition of some terminal subsequence of the head, called the period. We show that every $\preceq_e$- and $\preceq_s$-minimal solution to an A-sequence abduction problem corresponds to an ultimately periodic quasimodel, which can be further associated with an A-structure of a particular size, linear in the length of the head of the quasimodel.

For A-sequence abduction over full TQL formulas the relevant A-structures are consist of at most exponentially many states in the size of the given abduction problem. This resonates closely with the "small model" property of LTL, which rests on similarly defined bounds [13]. Recall that by $\ell(\dagger)$ we denote the total size of the input $\dagger$.

Lemma 2 (A-sequence vs. A-structure). *Let $\mathfrak{D}$ be an $\preceq_e$- and $\preceq_s$-minimal solution to an A-sequence abduction problem $\Omega = (\mathcal{T}, \mathfrak{A}, \phi)$, where $\mathfrak{A} = (\mathcal{A}_i)_{i \in I}$ and ϕ is a TQL formula. Then there exists an A-structure $\mathfrak{S} = (S, \mathcal{S}_0, \to)$ whose unfolding is $\mathfrak{D}$, such that $|S| = f(\ell(\Omega))$, for some function $f(x) \in O(2^x)$.*

The basic algorithm which recognizes $\preceq_e$- and $\preceq_s$-minimal solutions to A-sequence abduction problems is an adaptation of Sistla and Clarke's decision procedure for LTL [13]. In principle, the underlying computation model has to be changed from finite-state automata to finite-state transducers, i.e., Turing machines using additional write-only output tapes, as a recognized solution needs to be effectively presented. This revision, however, does not affect the complexity of the algorithm, which remains PSPACE-complete, irrespectively of the possibly exponential size of solutions.

Theorem 1 (Recognizing A-sequence solutions). *Recognizing an $\preceq_e$- and $\preceq_s$-minimal solution to an A-sequence abduction problem $\Omega = (\mathcal{T}, \mathfrak{A}, \phi)$, where ϕ is a TQL formula, is PSPACE-complete.*

In case of $\text{TQL}^\exists$ and TQL^+ we are able to show that the upper bound on the size of the relevant A-structures is smaller — in fact, linear in the size of the input.

Lemma 3 (A-sequence vs. A-structure for $\text{TQL}^\exists, \text{TQL}^+$). *Let $\mathfrak{D}$ be an $\preceq_e$- and $\preceq_s$-minimal solution to an A-sequence abduction problem $\Omega = (\mathcal{T}, \mathfrak{A}, \phi)$, where $\mathfrak{A} = (\mathcal{A}_i)_{i \in I}$ and ϕ is a $\text{TQL}^\exists$ or TQL^+ formula. Then there exists an A-structure $\mathfrak{S} = (S, \mathcal{S}_0, \to)$ whose unfolding is $\mathfrak{D}$, such that $|S| \leq f(\ell(\phi))$, for some $f(x) \in O(x)$.*

Given the linear size of the solutions, the worst case complexity of recognizing A-sequence solutions for $\text{TQL}^\exists$ drops to DB. In this case, it is sufficient to guess a linearly long head of a candidate quasimodel and verify it satisfies all the necessary structural conditions. As states in the quasimodel can contain positive and negative occurrences of CQs, the abduction of the respective minimal ABoxes is DB-complete.

Theorem 2 (Recognizing A-sequence solutions for $\text{TQL}^\exists$). *Recognizing an $\preceq_e$- and $\preceq_s$-minimal solution to an A-sequence abduction problem $(\mathcal{T}, \mathfrak{A}, \phi)$, where ϕ is a $\text{TQL}^\exists$ formula, is DB-complete.*

In case of TQL^+, the complexity of abductive reasoning is even smaller, in fact NP-complete, as no negative CQs have to be considered. Reducing the TQL language further down to $\text{TQL}^{\exists,+}$ does not yield any additional gain, even when $\preceq_b$-minimality is considered. This is a consequence of the non-determinism involved in choosing the order in which U-formulas are fulfilled in the consecutive states. In the worst case, all permutations must be considered, which enables reduction from the NP-hard Hamiltonian path problem.

Lemma 4 (Recognizing A-sequence solutions for $\text{TQL}^+, \text{TQL}^{\exists,+}$). *Recognizing a $\preceq_e$- and $\preceq_s$-minimal solution to an A-sequence abduction problem $\Omega = (\mathcal{T}, \mathfrak{A}, \phi)$, where ϕ is a TQL^+ or $\text{TQL}^{\exists,+}$ formula, is NP-complete. The result holds even for $\preceq_b$-minimal solutions and when $\mathfrak{A} = \emptyset$.*

Note that in most cases computing A-sequence solutions, as opposed to recognizing them, is bound to be of a higher complexity due to the necessity of conducting pairwise comparisons between exponentially many alternatives.

As the last task considered in this section, we address entailment of TQL formulas by finite A-sequences. As explained in Section 4, this problem corresponds to deciding whether the antecedent of a temporal rule, in case of prediction, or its consequent, in explanation, is entailed by a given fragment of the recorded segment. In the following theorem, we show that the problem is DP-complete in general or NP-complete in a special case, where the difference is determined by the presence of lack of negative CQ occurrences.

Theorem 3 (Entailment by finite A-sequences). *Let $\mathcal{T}$ be a TBox and $\mathfrak{A} = (\mathcal{A}_i)_{i \in I}$ an A-sequence, where I is a finite interval over $\mathbb{Z}$. Deciding $\mathcal{T}, \mathfrak{A}, n \models \phi$, for some $n \in \mathbb{Z}$, is DP-complete iff ϕ is a grounded TQL or $\text{TQL}^\exists$ formula, and NP-complete iff ϕ is a grounded $\text{TQL}^{\exists,+}$ formula.*

The analysis above shows that prediction and explanation are computationally hard in general, but can be made easier by progressively simplifying the assumed setting. Notably, by restricting the expressiveness of temporal operators and eliminating negation from the underlying TQL, the complexity of reasoning can be reduced from PSPACE- to NP-complete. The remaining non-determinism, warranting NP-hardness, can be mostly attributed to the size of FO rewritings of CQs and the number of alternative orders in which U/S-subformulas are to be fulfilled over time. Can these too be tamed granting an even lower complexity? Most likely, yes. We suspect that by considering $\preceq_b$-minimal solutions and allowing only formulas whose structure unambiguously determines the order of fulfilment of U/S-subformulas, the combined complexity of prediction and explanation should drop further to PTIME. Less assumptive predictions and explanations (such as based on the $\preceq_b$-minimality criterion) and a simpler language for learning temporal association rules might moreover offer conjectures of a higher likelihood, thus offering another reward for the lost expressiveness.

6 Related Work

To the best of our knowledge, prediction and explanation in the conceptual and technical sense considered here have not been addressed in the literature. Lecue and Pan study prediction over ontology streams in [3], but clearly follow the data mining approach to the problem, focusing on detection of statistical correlations in data and their future projections. Such a perspective is orthogonal to ours, as here we deal exclusively with the knowledge representation and reasoning level, assuming that relevant association rules are already given and symbolically expressed as temporal rules. In the report [5], Thirunarayan et al. propose to use abductive logic programming for generating explanations, understood as abstractions of quantitative data into qualitative descriptions, as an integral component of a situation awareness framework over the Semantic Sensor Web. Although the preliminary nature of this proposal does not allow for a detailed comparison with ours, it clearly follows a similar motivation and formal direction.

Other types of reasoning services over semantic streaming data, not of immediate relevance to this work, have been considered in a number of papers, e.g., [1,12,2]. Yet more remotely related work deals with prediction and temporal association rule mining in the field of relational databases [6,15], aspects of abductive reasoning in temporal logics [20], logics for causal reasoning [21], and prediction and explanation in other AI contexts [4].

7 Conclusions and Outlook

In this paper, we have introduced a novel formalization of predictive and explanatory reasoning over DL-*Lite* data streams, and delivered a number of results characterizing the computational complexity of both tasks using different variants of the underlying temporal rule formalism. We believe that the approach we propose, which allows for studying prediction and explanation from the purely logical and computational perspective, is vital for the development of robust stream reasoning techniques applicable to semantically rich data, as it introduces a symbolic layer which can usefully mediate between the semantic and statistical view on the data.

An especially promising direction of advancing this work further is to investigate the use of other temporal logics for expressing temporal rules, in particular those offering real-time and probabilistic features, e.g., PCTL [22]. Arguably, such rules could be tighter aligned with typical models of causal reasoning [21] and the practice of temporal association rule learning [15]. As an alternative to the probabilistic approach, a qualitative one, based on defeasible semantics [23], could be also potentially useful. Considering the implementation prospects, a natural and technically feasible approach is likely to be found in combining temporal databases, recently supported via SQL:2011 [24], with existing reasoning tools enabling execution of temporal logic programs, such as METATEM [25].

References

1. Valle, E.D., Ceri, S., van Harmelen, F., Fensel, D.: It's a streaming world! reasoning upon rapidly changing information. IEEE Intelligent Systems 24(6) (2009)
2. Barbieri, D.F., Braga, D., Ceri, S., Valle, E.D., Huang, Y., Tresp, V., Rettinger, A., Wermser, H.: Deductive and inductive stream reasoning for semantic social media analytics. IEEE Intelligent Systems 25(6), 32–41 (2010)
3. Lecue, F., Pan, J.Z.: Predicting Knowledge in An Ontology Stream. In: Proc. of the International Joint Conference on Artificial Intelligence, IJCAI 2013 (2013)
4. Shanahan, M.: Prediction is deduction but explanation is abduction. In: Proc. of the International Joint Conference on Artificial Intelligence, IJCAI 1989 (1989)

5. Thirunarayan, K., Henson, C.A., Sheth, A.P.: Situation awareness via abductive reasoning from semantic sensor data: A preliminary report. In: Proc. of the International Symposium on Collaborative Technologies and Systems, CTS 2009 (2009)
6. Akdere, M., Çetintemel, U., Upfal, E.: Database-support for continuous prediction queries over streaming data. In: Proc. of the International Conference on Very Large Data Bases, VLDB 2010 (2010)
7. Calvanese, D., De Giacomo, G., Lembo, D., Lenzerini, M., Rosati, R.: Tractable reasoning and efficient query answering in description logics: The DL-Lite family. J. of Automated Reasoning 39(3), 385–429 (2007)
8. Gutiérrez-Basulto, V., Klarman, S.: Towards a unifying approach to representing and querying temporal data in description logics. In: Krötzsch, M., Straccia, U. (eds.) RR 2012. LNCS, vol. 7497, pp. 90–105. Springer, Heidelberg (2012)
9. Klarman, S., Meyer, T.: Prediction and explanation over DL-Lite data streams. Technical report, Centre for Artificial Intelligence Research, CSIR Meraka and University of KwaZulu-Natal (2013),
http://klarman.synthasite.com/resources/KlaMeyLPAR13.pdf
10. Baader, F., Calvanese, D., Mcguinness, D.L., Nardi, D., Patel-Schneider, P.F.: The description logic handbook: theory, implementation, and applications. Cambridge University Press (2003)
11. Lutz, C., Toman, D., Wolter, F.: Conjunctive query answering in the description logic EL using a relational database system. In: Proc. of the International Joint Conference on Artifical Intelligence, IJCAI 2009 (2009)
12. Ren, Y., Pan, J.Z.: Optimising ontology stream reasoning with truth maintenance system. In: Proc. of the ACM Conference on Information and Knowledge Management, CIKM 2011 (2011)
13. Sistla, A.P., Clarke, E.M.: The complexity of propositional linear temporal logics. Journal of ACM 32(3), 733–749 (1985)
14. Gabbay, D.: The declarative past and imperative future: Executable temporal logic for interactive systems. In: Proc. of the Conference on Temporal Logic in Specification, TLS 1987 (1987)
15. Guillame-Bert, M., Crowley, J.L.: Learning temporal association rules on symbolic time sequences. Journal of Machine Learning Research - Proceedings Track 25, 159–174 (2012)
16. Dhanya, C.T., Kumar, D.N.: Data mining for evolution of association rules for droughts and floods in India using climate inputs. Journal of Geophysical Research 114 (2009)
17. Elsenbroich, C., Kutz, O., Sattler, U.: A case for abductive reasoning over ontologies. In: Proc. of the International Workshop on OWL: Experiences and Directions, OWLED 2006 (2006)
18. Klarman, S., Endriss, U., Schlobach, S.: Abox abduction in the description logic $\mathcal{ALC}$. Journal of Automated Reasoning 46, 43–80 (2011)
19. Calvanese, D., Ortiz, M., Simkus, M., Stefanoni, G.: The complexity of explaining negative query answers in DL-Lite. In: Proc. of the International Conference on the Principles of Knowledge Representation and Reasoning, KR 2012 (2012)
20. Ribeiro, C., Porto, A.: Abduction in temporal reasoning. In: Gabbay, D.M., Ohlbach, H.J. (eds.) ICTL 1994. LNCS (LNAI), vol. 827, pp. 349–364. Springer, Heidelberg (1994)
21. Kleinberg, S., Mishra, B.: The temporal logic of causal structures. In: Proc. of the Conference on Uncertainty in Artificial Intelligence, UAI 2009 (2009)

22. Hansson, H., Jonsson, B.: A logic for reasoning about time and reliability. Formal Aspects of Computing 6, 102–111 (1994)
23. Governatori, G., Terenziani, P.: Temporal extensions to defeasible logic. In: Proc. of the Australian Conference on Advances in Artificial Intelligence (2007)
24. Kulkarni, K., Michels, J.E.: Temporal features in SQL: 2011. SIGMOD Rec. 41(3) (2012)
25. Barringer, H., Fisher, M., Gabbay, D., Gough, G., Owens, R.: METATEM: AN INTRODUCTION. FORMAL ASPECTS OF COMPUTING 7(5), 533–549 (1995)

Forgetting Concept and Role Symbols in $\mathcal{ALCH}$-Ontologies

Patrick Koopmann and Renate A. Schmidt

The University of Manchester, UK
{koopmanp,schmidt}@cs.man.ac.uk

Abstract. We develop a resolution-based method for forgetting concept and role symbols in $\mathcal{ALCH}$ ontologies, or for computing uniform interpolants in $\mathcal{ALCH}$. Uniform interpolants use only a restricted set of symbols, while preserving logical consequences of the original ontology involving these symbols. While recent work towards practical methods for uniform interpolation in expressive description logics limits attention to forgetting concept symbols, we believe most applications would benefit from the possibility to forget both role and concept symbols. We focus on the description logic $\mathcal{ALCH}$, which allows for the formalisation of role hierarchies. Our approach is based on a recently developed resolution-based calculus for forgetting concept symbols in $\mathcal{ALC}$ ontologies, which we extend by redundancy elimination techniques to make it practical for larger ontologies. Experiments on $\mathcal{ALCH}$ fragments of real life ontologies suggest that our method is applicable in a lot of real-life applications.

1 Introduction

Ontologies model a domain of interest using description logics by describing the vocabulary of this domain in terms of roles and concepts. Reflecting the different applications and contexts in which ontologies are used, ontologies are modelled using different description logics that vary in expressivity and complexities of common reasoning tasks. In the development of complex ontologies, it is often desirable to restrict the vocabulary of an ontology to a smaller set of symbols. Uniform interpolation, also known as forgetting, establishes this by constructing a new ontology that only uses a predefined set of symbols, such that all logical consequences of the original ontology using these symbols are preserved. Examples where this is useful are: (i) *Ontology Reuse*. When constructing larger ontologies, it can be useful to reuse parts from existing ontologies. Using uniform interpolation, one can restrict the vocabulary of the reused ontology to the symbols that are known and interesting for the new application. (ii) *Predicate Hiding*. When publishing or sharing an ontology, it is often desirable to hide confidential parts from the ontology, without affecting the intended meaning of the remaining vocabulary [5]. (iii) *Exhibiting Hidden Relations*. Relations between symbols are often stated indirectly in an ontology and only become visible through the use of reasoners. With increased complexity of the ontology, this makes it hard to get a deeper understanding of the ontology and to maintain ontology changes.

The uniform interpolant over a set of symbols makes the relations between these symbols explicit. (iv) *Logical difference.* In the development of evolving ontologies, it is important for ontology engineers to ensure that modifications do not interfere with the meaning of existing terms. This can be achieved by computing the uniform interpolants of two versions of an ontology over the common set of used symbols, or over a set of symbols under consideration, and checking whether the resulting ontologies are equivalent [12].

Uniform interpolation has been extensively investigated for simpler description logics such as $\mathcal{EL}$ or DL-Lite [8,22,15,13]. Recently, practical algorithms for forgetting concept symbols in the more expressive description logic $\mathcal{ALC}$ have been developed [12,11]. In this paper, we investigate forgetting of role symbols as well, and supplement earlier presented work with optimisation techniques to make it practical on larger ontologies. Since roles play a larger role in this context, we focus on the description logic $\mathcal{ALCH}$, which extends $\mathcal{ALC}$ with role hierarchies. It is known that already in the description logic $\mathcal{ALC}$ uniform interpolants cannot be finitely expressed in the language of the logic [14]. This also applies to $\mathcal{ALCH}$. For this reason our method computes uniform interpolants for the target language $\mathcal{ALCH}\mu$, which extends $\mathcal{ALCH}$ with fixpoint operators, thus enabling us to always compute finite representations. If fixpoints are used in the uniform interpolant, it is possible to represent it in $\mathcal{ALCH}$ by extending the signature of the interpolant.

Our work is based on a recently developed method for forgetting concept symbols in $\mathcal{ALC}$-ontologies [11]. The method is based on a resolution-based decision procedure for $\mathcal{ALCH}$. In order to analyse the practicality of our approach, we undertake an experimental evaluation on $\mathcal{ALCH}$-fragments of a set of real-life ontologies. The results suggest that uniform interpolation can be used for the presented applications in a lot of real-life situations.

Proofs of all theorems can be found in the accompanying technical report [9].

2 Preliminaries

Let N_c, N_r be two disjoint sets of *concept symbols* and *role symbols*. Concepts in $\mathcal{ALCH}$ are of the following form:

$$\bot \mid \top \mid A \mid \neg C \mid C \sqcup D \mid C \sqcap D \mid \exists r.C \mid \forall r.C,$$

where $A \in N_c$, $r \in N_r$ and C and D are arbitrary concepts. $\top$, $C \sqcap D$ and $\forall r.C$ are defined as abbreviations: $\top$ stands for $\neg\bot$, $C \sqcap D$ for $\neg(\neg C \sqcup \neg D)$ and $\forall r.C$ for $\neg\exists r.\neg C$.

A TBox is a set of *concept axioms* of the forms $C \sqsubseteq D$ (*concept inclusion*) and $C \equiv D$ (*concept equivalence*), where C and D are concepts. An RBox is a set of *role axioms* of the form $r \sqsubseteq s$ (*role inclusion*) and $r \equiv s$ (*role equivalence*), where r and s are role symbols. $C \equiv D$ is a short-hand for the two concept axioms $C \sqsubseteq D$ and $D \sqsubseteq C$, and $r \equiv s$ is a short-hand for the two role axioms $r \sqsubseteq s$ and $s \sqsubseteq r$. We assume an ontology consists of a TBox and an

RBox. Given an ontology $\mathcal{O}$, we define $\sqsubseteq_{\mathcal{O}}$ to be the reflexive transitive closure of the role inclusions in $\mathcal{O}$.

The semantics of $\mathcal{ALCH}$ is defined as follows. An *interpretation* is a pair $\mathcal{I} = \langle \Delta^{\mathcal{I}}, \cdot^{\mathcal{I}} \rangle$, where the *domain* $\Delta^{\mathcal{I}}$ is a nonempty set and the *interpretation function* $\cdot^{\mathcal{I}}$ assigns to each concept symbol $A \in N_c$ a subset of $\Delta^{\mathcal{I}}$ and to each role symbol $r \in N_r$ a subset of $\Delta^{\mathcal{I}} \times \Delta^{\mathcal{I}}$. The interpretation function is extended to concepts as follows.

$$\bot^{\mathcal{I}} := \emptyset \quad (\neg C)^{\mathcal{I}} := \Delta^{\mathcal{I}} \setminus C^{\mathcal{I}} \quad (C \sqcup D)^{\mathcal{I}} := C^{\mathcal{I}} \cup D^{\mathcal{I}}$$
$$(\exists r.C)^{\mathcal{I}} := \{x \in \Delta^{\mathcal{I}} \mid \exists y : (x,y) \in r^{\mathcal{I}} \wedge y \in C^{\mathcal{I}}\}$$

A concept inclusion $C \sqsubseteq D$ is *true* in an interpretation $\mathcal{I}$ iff $C^{\mathcal{I}} \subseteq D^{\mathcal{I}}$. $\mathcal{I}$ is model of a TBox $\mathcal{T}$ if all concept inclusions in $\mathcal{T}$ are true in $\mathcal{I}$. A TBox $\mathcal{T}$ is *satisfiable* if there exists a model for $\mathcal{T}$, otherwise it is *unsatisfiable*. $\mathcal{T} \models C \sqsubseteq D$ holds iff in every model of $\mathcal{T}$ we have $C^{\mathcal{I}} \subseteq D^{\mathcal{I}}$. Two TBoxes $\mathcal{T}_1$ and $\mathcal{T}_2$ are *equi-satisfiable* if every model of $\mathcal{T}_1$ can be extended to a model of $\mathcal{T}_2$, and vice versa. The definitions of truth, model, satisfiability and equi-satisfiability extend to roles, RBoxes and ontologies in a similar way. Observe that $\mathcal{O} \models r \sqsubseteq s$ iff $r \sqsubseteq_{\mathcal{O}} s$.

In order to define $\mathcal{ALCH}\mu$, we extend the language with a set N_v of *concept variables*. $\mathcal{ALCH}\mu$ extends $\mathcal{ALCH}$ with concepts of the form $\mu X.C$ and $\nu X.C$, where $X \in N_v$, and C is a concept in which X occurs as a concept symbol only positively (under an even number of negations). $\mu X.C$ denotes the *least fixpoint* of C on X and $\nu X.C$ the *greatest fixpoint*.

A concept variable X is *bound* if it occurs in the scope C of a fixpoint expression $\mu X.C$ or $\nu X.C$. Otherwise it is *free*. A concept is *closed* if it does not contain any free variables. Axioms in $\mathcal{ALCH}\mu$ are of the form $C \sqsubseteq D$ and $C \equiv D$, where C and D are closed concepts.

Following [2], we define the semantics of fixpoint expressions. Let $\mathcal{V}$ be an *assignment function* that maps concept variables to subsets of $\Delta^{\mathcal{I}}$. $\mathcal{V}[X \mapsto W]$ denotes $\mathcal{V}$ modified by setting $\mathcal{V}(X) = W$. $C^{\mathcal{I},\mathcal{V}}$ is the interpretation of C taking into account this assignment, and when $\mathcal{V}$ is defined for all variables in C, $C^{\mathcal{I},\mathcal{V}} = C^{\mathcal{I}}$. The semantics of fixpoint concepts is defined as follows:

$$(\mu X.C)^{\mathcal{I},\mathcal{V}} := \bigcap \{W \subseteq \Delta^{\mathcal{I}} \mid C^{\mathcal{I},\mathcal{V}[X \mapsto W]} \subseteq W\}$$
$$(\nu X.C)^{\mathcal{I},\mathcal{V}} := \bigcup \{W \subseteq \Delta^{\mathcal{I}} \mid W \subseteq C^{\mathcal{I},\mathcal{V}[X \mapsto W]}\}.$$

The *size* of an ($\mathcal{ALCH}$- or $\mathcal{ALCH}\mu$-)axiom is defined recursively as follows: $size(A) = 1$, where A is a concept symbol, $size(\neg C) = size(C) + 1$, $size(\exists r.C) = size(\forall r.C) = size(C) + 2$, $size(C \sqcup D) = size(C \sqcap D) = size(C) + size(D) + 1$, $size(\mu X.C) = size(\nu X.C) = size(C) + 2$ and $size(C \sqsubseteq D) = size(C \equiv D) = size(C) + size(D) + 1$.

A *signature* Σ is a subset of $N_c \cup N_r$. $sig(E)$ denotes the concept and role symbols occurring in E, where E ranges over concept descriptions, axioms, TBoxes, RBoxes and ontologies. Given two ontologies $\mathcal{O}_1$ and $\mathcal{O}_2$ and a signature Σ, we say $\mathcal{O}_1$ and $\mathcal{O}_2$ are *Σ-inseparable*, in symbols $\mathcal{O}_1 \equiv_\Sigma \mathcal{O}_2$, iff for every concept or role inclusion α with $sig(\alpha) \subseteq \Sigma$, $\mathcal{O}_1 \models \alpha$ implies $\mathcal{O}_2 \models \alpha$, and vice versa. Given an ontology $\mathcal{O}$ and a signature Σ, $\mathcal{O}'$ is a *uniform interpolant of $\mathcal{O}$* if $sig(\mathcal{O}') \subseteq \Sigma$ and $\mathcal{O} \equiv_\Sigma \mathcal{O}'$. From this definition, it follows that uniform interpolants for a given ontology and signature are unique modulo logical equivalence. For a given ontology $\mathcal{O}$ and signature Σ, we will therefore speak of *the* uniform interpolant and denote it by $\mathcal{O}^\Sigma$. Given an ontology $\mathcal{O}$ and a concept or role symbol σ, the result of *forgetting σ in $\mathcal{O}$*, denoted by $\mathcal{O}^{-\sigma}$, is the uniform interpolant $\mathcal{O}^\Sigma$, where $\Sigma = sig(\mathcal{O}) \setminus \{\sigma\}$.

3 Overview of the Method

We reduce the problem of computing uniform interpolants to the problem of forgetting single symbols. In order to compute the uniform interpolant for any signature Σ, we forget each symbol in $sig(\mathcal{O}) \setminus \Sigma$ one by one. The method for computing $\mathcal{O}^{-\sigma}$, where σ is either a role or a concept symbol, consists of three phases:

Phase 1: Eliminate the symbol using a resolution-based calculus, obtaining $\mathcal{O}' = \mathcal{F}^\sigma_{\mathcal{ALCH}}(\mathcal{O})$.
Phase 2: Eliminate the newly introduced symbols, obtaining $\mathcal{O}^{-\sigma} = \mathcal{F}_D(\mathcal{O}')$.
Phase 3: Apply simplifications and represent clauses as proper concept inclusions.

Central to the method is a new resolution-based calculus which works on a structural transformation based normal form. The calculus is described in Section 4. Depending on whether the symbol to be forgotten is a role or a concept symbol, in Phase 1 a different method based on this resolution calculus is used to derive consequences on the selected symbol. This is described in Section 5. The result is a finitely bounded set N of axioms such that $\sigma \notin sig(N)$ and $N \equiv_\Sigma \mathcal{O}$ for $\Sigma = sig(\mathcal{O}) \setminus \{\sigma\}$, but N may use new symbols due to structural transformation. These symbols, called definers, all occur in a form that allows for elimination in a simple and uniform way, following a known principle first presented in [16]. This is performed in Phase 2 and described in Section 6. Depending on whether the aim is to compute a representation in $\mathcal{ALCH}\mu$ or in $\mathcal{ALCH}$, the result may involve fixpoint operators or extend the signature of the original ontology.

After Phase 2, the uniform interpolant is already computed, but we add a third phase that makes the resulting ontology more accessible by applying several equivalence-preserving transformations. The following main theorem of this paper states the correctness of the method.

Theorem 1. *For any $\mathcal{ALCH}$-ontology $\mathcal{O}$ and any symbol σ, our method terminates and returns the uniform interpolant of $\mathcal{O}$ over $sig(\mathcal{O}) \setminus \{\sigma\}$ in $\mathcal{ALCH}\mu$. If the result does not make use of a fixpoint operator, it is the uniform interpolant of $\mathcal{O}$ over $sig(\mathcal{O}) \setminus \{\sigma\}$ in $\mathcal{ALCH}$.*

4 The Underlying Calculus

Our method for forgetting concept and role symbols is based on a resolution calculus $\mathcal{R}_{\mathcal{ALCH}}$ which provides a decision procedure for $\mathcal{ALCH}$-ontology satisfiability. The calculus extends a calculus introduced in [11] by incorporating the role hierarchy. In order to make our method practical for larger ontologies, we extend $\mathcal{R}_{\mathcal{ALCH}}$ with redundancy elimination techniques, resulting in the calculus $\mathcal{R}^s_{\mathcal{ALCH}}$.

Both calculi operate on sets of clauses, which are defined as follows. Let $N_D \subseteq N_c$ be a set of *definer symbols* or *definers*, which do not occur in any input ontology.

Definition 1. *An $\mathcal{ALCH}$-literal is a concept description of the form A, $\neg A$, $\forall r.D$ or $\exists r.D$, where A is a concept symbol, r a role symbol and D is a definer.*

A TBox is in $\mathcal{ALCH}$-conjunctive normal form if every axiom is of the form $\top \sqsubseteq L_1 \sqcup ... \sqcup L_n$, where each L_i is an $\mathcal{ALCH}$-literal. The right part of such a concept inclusion is called $\mathcal{ALCH}$-clause. In the following we assume $\mathcal{ALCH}$-clauses are represented as sets of literals (this means no clause contains the same literal more than once and the order of the literals does not matter). The empty clause is denoted by $\bot$ and represents a contradiction.

For our method it is crucial that any $\mathcal{ALCH}$-TBox is transformed into an equisatisfiable TBox in $\mathcal{ALCH}$-conjunctive normal form using structural transformation as follows. First the input TBox is transformed into negation normal form. Then every concept C that occurs immediately below a role restriction is replaced by a definer D, and we add the axiom $D \sqsubseteq C$ for each such subconcept. The resulting TBox does not contain any nested role restrictions and can be brought into $\mathcal{ALCH}$-conjunctive normal form by applying standard CNF-transformation techniques. For an ontology $\mathcal{O}$, let $clauses(\mathcal{O})$ refer to the set of clauses generated in this way from the TBox of $\mathcal{O}$.

The calculus $\mathcal{R}_{\mathcal{ALCH}}$ uses the rules shown in Figure 1. Since the normal form has to be preserved, the role propagation rule may require the introduction of a new definer symbol D_3 representing the conjunction of the definers D_1 and D_2 occurring in the premises. This is done by adding new clauses $\neg D_3 \sqcup D_1$ and $\neg D_3 \sqcup D_2$ to the clause set. Observe that the resolution rule also applies to definer literals. This way for each pair of clauses $\neg D_1 \sqcup C_1$ and $\neg D_2 \sqcup C_2$ we derive the clauses $\neg D_3 \sqcup C_1$ and $\neg D_3 \sqcup C_2$, for which the side conditions of the rules are satisfied.

In order to ensure termination, it is necessary to reuse definers whenever possible. For this we define an identification function for introduced definers, that identifies definers with the context from which they have been created, and whose range is finitely bounded. The function $id(D)$ is defined as follows. (i) If D is introduced by the initial normal form transformation, then $id(D) = \{D\}$. (ii) If D is required by the role propagation rule and the respective role restrictions are $\forall s.D_1$ and $\mathsf{Q}r.D_2$, then $id(D) = id(D_1) \cup id(D_2)$.

If the role propagation rule requires a new definer D, we first check whether a definer D' with $id(D) = id(D')$ is already present, and reuse it in this case.

Resolution:

$$\frac{C_1 \sqcup A \quad C_2 \sqcup \neg A}{C_1 \sqcup C_2}$$

provided $C_1 \sqcup C_2$ does not contain more than one negative definer literal.

Role Propagation:

$$\frac{C_1 \sqcup \forall s.D_1 \quad C_2 \sqcup \mathsf{Q}r.D_2}{C_1 \sqcup C_2 \sqcup \mathsf{Q}r.D_3} \quad r \sqsubseteq_\mathcal{O} s$$

where $\mathsf{Q} \in \{\exists, \forall\}$ and D_3 is a (possibly new) definer representing $D_1 \sqcap D_2$, provided $C_1 \sqcup C_2$ does not contain more than one negative definer literal.

Existential Role Restriction Elimination:

$$\frac{C \sqcup \exists r.D \quad \neg D}{C}$$

Fig. 1. Rules of the calculus $\mathcal{R}_{\mathcal{ALCH}}$

Otherwise we introduce a new definer in the way described above. Observe that the domain of id is bounded by 2^n, where n is the number of definers introduced by the initial normal form transformation. Therefore the number of clauses that can possibly be derived is limited by a double-exponential bound. We can prove:

Theorem 2. $\mathcal{R}_{\mathcal{ALCH}}$ *is sound and refutationally complete, and provides a decision procedure for $\mathcal{ALCH}$-ontology satisfiability.*

As in traditional resolution-based decision procedures, it is possible to extend the method with redundancy elimination and further simplification techniques. For this purpose, it is possible to exploit the structure imposed by the introduced definers. Note that new definers are introduced by adding clauses of the form $\neg D_1 \sqcup D_2$. $\neg D_1 \sqcup D_2$ is equivalent to the concept inclusion $D_1 \sqsubseteq D_2$. This concept inclusion can be transferred to subsumption between existential and universal role restrictions, and to subsumption between clauses.

Definition 2. *A literal l_1 is subsumed by a literal l_2 ($l_1 \sqsubseteq_l l_2$) if either $l_1 = l_2$ or if $l_1 = \mathsf{Q}r.D_1$ and $l_2 = \mathsf{Q}r.D_2$ for $\mathsf{Q} \in \{\exists, \forall\}$ and there is a clause $\neg D_1 \sqcup D_2$ in the current clause set. A clause C_1 is subsumed by a clause C_2 ($C_1 \sqsubseteq_c C_2$) if every literal $l_1 \in C_1$ is subsumed by a literal $l_2 \in C_2$. A clause C is redundant with respect to a clause set N, if N contains a clause C' with $C' \sqsubseteq_c C$. The reduction of a clause C, $red(C)$, is obtained from C by removing every literal that is subsumed by another literal in C.*

Example 1 (Subsumption and reduction). Assume D_3 represents $D_1 \sqcap D_2$, which means we have the clauses $\neg D_3 \sqcup D_1$ and $\neg D_3 \sqcup D_2$. Then $\neg A \sqcup B$ is subsumed by

Tautology deletion:	$\dfrac{N \cup \{C \sqcup A \sqcup \neg A\}}{N}$	
Subsumption deletion:	$\dfrac{N \cup \{C, D\}}{N \cup \{C\}}$	provided $C \sqsubseteq_c D$
Reduction:	$\dfrac{N \cup \{C\}}{N \cup \{red(C)\}}$	

Fig. 2. Simplification rules

$\neg A \sqcup B \sqcup C$, $\exists r.D_3$ is subsumed by $\exists r.D_1$, $\forall r.D_3 \sqcup B$ is subsumed by $\forall r.D_1 \sqcup A \sqcup B$ and $red(A \sqcup \exists r.D_3 \sqcup \exists r.D_2) = A \sqcup \exists r.D_2$.

In addition to subsumption and reduction, we also detect tautological clauses which contain pairs of contradictory literals. This leads to a set of simplification rules shown in Figure 2. We denote the calculus $\mathcal{R}_{\mathcal{ALCH}}$ extended with these rules by $\mathcal{R}^s_{\mathcal{ALCH}}$. It can be shown that these rules preserve soundness and refutational completeness, as stated by the following theorem.

Theorem 3. $\mathcal{R}^s_{\mathcal{ALCH}}$ *is sound and refutationally complete and provides a decision procedure for* $\mathcal{ALCH}$*-ontology satisfiability.*

5 Forgetting Concept and Role Symbols

In this section, we describe the methods $\mathcal{F}^A_{\mathcal{ALCH}}$ and $\mathcal{F}^r_{\mathcal{ALCH}}$ for forgetting respectively concept symbols and role symbols. Both methods are based on $\mathcal{R}^s_{\mathcal{ALCH}}$.

For any definer D, we say D is *connected to* A, if D either co-occurs with A in a clause or if D co-occurs in a clause with another definer D' that is connected to A. If the aim is to forget a concept symbol, we restrict the rules of $\mathcal{R}^s_{\mathcal{ALCH}}$ by adding the following conditions:

Resolution: A is the symbol we want to forget or a definer.
Role Propagation: D_1 and D_2 are connected to the symbol we want to forget.

For a concept symbol A, $\mathcal{F}^A_{\mathcal{ALCH}}$ denotes the calculus $\mathcal{R}^s_{\mathcal{ALCH}}$ with these modifications for A. For any ontology $\mathcal{O}$, $\mathcal{F}^A_{\mathcal{ALCH}}(\mathcal{O})$ denotes the ontology consisting of the RBox of $\mathcal{O}$ and the TBox represented by $clauses(\mathcal{O})$ saturated using the rules of $\mathcal{F}^A_{\mathcal{ALCH}}$, after removing all clauses containing A or positive definer literals that are not role restrictions.

Theorem 4. *Given an ontology* $\mathcal{O}$*,* $\mathcal{F}^A_{\mathcal{ALCH}}(\mathcal{O})$ *is a clausal representation of* $\mathcal{O}^{-A}$*, that is,* $\mathcal{F}^A_{\mathcal{ALCH}}(\mathcal{O}) \equiv_\Sigma \mathcal{O}$*, where* $\Sigma = sig(\mathcal{T}) \setminus \{A\}$*, and every symbol in* $\mathcal{F}^A_{\mathcal{ALCH}}(\mathcal{O})$ *is either a definer or in* Σ*.*

Role hierarchy:
$$\frac{s \sqsubseteq r \quad r \sqsubseteq t}{s \sqsubseteq t}$$

Universal role restriction monotonicity:
$$\frac{C \sqcup \forall r.D}{C \sqcup \forall s.D} \quad s \sqsubseteq r \in \mathcal{O}$$

Existential role restriction monotonicity:
$$\frac{C \sqcup \exists r.D}{C \sqcup \exists s.D} \quad r \sqsubseteq s \in \mathcal{O}$$

Role restriction resolution:
$$\frac{C_0 \sqcup \forall r.D_0 \quad \ldots \quad C_n \sqcup \forall r.D_n \quad C \sqcup \exists r.D}{C_0 \sqcup \ldots \sqcup C_n \sqcup C} \quad \mathcal{O} \models D_0 \sqcap \ldots \sqcap D_n \sqcap D \sqsubseteq \bot$$

provided (i) there is no role s with $r \sqsubseteq s \in \mathcal{O}$ and (ii) $C_0 \sqcup \ldots \sqcup C_n \sqcup C$ does not contain more than one negative definer literal.

Fig. 3. Rules for forgetting role symbol r

The method $\mathcal{F}^A_{\mathcal{ALCH}}$ provides a focused way to forget the concept symbol A. In order to forget role symbols, a few modifications have to be made. Since role symbols also occur in the RBox of an ontology, the RBox has to be processed as well. Additionally, we need rules that compute all derivations on a selected role symbol in a focused way.

The rules in Figure 3, together with the rules of $\mathcal{R}_{\mathcal{ALCH}}$, where the resolution rule is restricted to only resolve on definer literals, constitute the method $\mathcal{F}^r_{\mathcal{ALCH}}$, where r is the role symbol to be forgotten. The role hierarchy rule is the only rule applied on the RBox of the input ontology, and makes implicit role inclusions around the role symbol to be forgotten explicit. The universal and existential role monotonicity rules compute inferences on the basis of clauses and RBox axioms. If there is no role inclusion $s \sqsubseteq r$, the universal role monotonicity rule cannot be applied and we have to apply role propagation on that role exhaustively in order to preserve all consequences when forgetting r.

If there is no role inclusion $r \sqsubseteq s$, we can neither apply the existential role restriction monotonicity rule nor role propagation. Instead we use the role restriction resolution rule in this case, which is similarly motivated as the resolution rule, but works on larger sets of clauses. This rule is formulated to allow the use of an external reasoner to check satisfiability of concepts (even though in theory $\mathcal{R}_{\mathcal{ALCH}}$ can be used for this as well).

Non-cyclic definer elimination:

$$\frac{\mathcal{T} \cup \{D \sqsubseteq C\}}{\mathcal{T}^{[D \mapsto C]}} \quad \text{provided } D \notin \mathit{sig}(C)$$

Definer purification:

$$\frac{\mathcal{T}}{\mathcal{T}^{[D \mapsto \top]}} \quad \text{provided } D \text{ occurs only positively in } \mathcal{T}$$

Cyclic definer elimination:

$$\frac{\mathcal{T} \cup \{D \sqsubseteq C[D]\}}{\mathcal{T}^{[D \mapsto \nu X. C[X]]}} \quad \text{provided } D \in \mathit{sig}(C[D])$$

Fig. 4. Rules for eliminating definer concept symbols

For any ontology $\mathcal{O}$, we define $\mathcal{F}^r_{\mathcal{ALCH}}(\mathcal{O})$ as the ontology consisting of the RBox of $\mathcal{O}$ and the TBox represented by $\mathit{clauses}(\mathcal{O})$ saturated using the rules of $\mathcal{F}^r_{\mathcal{ALCH}}$, after removing all the axioms and clauses that use the symbol r or contain a positive definer literal that is not a role restriction.

Theorem 5. *For any ontology $\mathcal{O}$, $\mathcal{F}^r_{\mathcal{ALCH}}(\mathcal{O})$ is a clausal representation of $\mathcal{O}^{-r}$.*

6 Definer Elimination

In Phase 2, the symbols introduced by the normal form transformation or the role propagation rule are eliminated. Note that we only derive clauses that contain at most one negative definer literal in Phase 1. This means we can for each definer D group the clauses of the form $\neg D \sqcup C_i$, $0 \leq i \leq n$, into a single axiom of the form $D \sqsubseteq \bigsqcap_{0 \leq i \leq n} C_i$ that can be seen as a *definition* of the definer. This definition can be used to undo the structural transformation and eliminate the remaining definers. If a definition is cyclic, we use a fixpoint operator in the result. Figure 4 shows the rules for definer elimination. The rules are justified by Ackermann's Lemma and its generalisation to the fixpoint case [1,16].

If the output of the algorithm contains fixpoints, we can represent it in $\mathcal{ALCH}$ by extending the desired signature Σ by the cyclic definers. This is done by omitting the cyclic definer elimination rule.

7 Examples

To illustrate the presented method this section includes two examples of respectively forgetting concept and role symbols.

Example 2 (Forgetting Concept Symbols). Let $\mathcal{O}_1$ be the following ontology.

$$A \sqsubseteq B \sqcup C \qquad B \sqsubseteq \exists r.B \qquad C \sqsubseteq \forall s. \neg B \qquad r \sqsubseteq s$$

We want to compute $\mathcal{O}_1^{-B}$. We obtain the following clause set $clauses(\mathcal{O}_1)$.

1. $\neg A \sqcup B \sqcup C$ 2. $\neg B \sqcup \exists r.D_1$ 3. $\neg D_1 \sqcup B$
4. $\neg C \sqcup \forall s.D_2$ 5. $\neg D_2 \sqcup \neg B$

We first apply the resolution rule.

6. $\neg A \sqcup C \sqcup \exists r.D_1$ (resolution on 2 and 1)
7. $\neg D_1 \sqcup \exists r.D_1$ (resolution on 2 and 3)
8. $\neg D_2 \sqcup \neg A \sqcup C$ (resolution on 5 and 1)

We cannot resolve on clauses 3 and 5, since the conclusion would contain more than one negative definer literal. We can however apply role propagation on clauses 2 and 4, which makes further applications of the resolution rule possible.

~~9.~~ $\neg B \sqcup \neg C \sqcup \exists r.D_3$ (role propagation on 2 and 4, $id(D_3) = \{D_1, D_2\}$)
~~10.~~ $\neg D_3 \sqcup D_1$
~~11.~~ $\neg D_3 \sqcup D_2$
~~12.~~ $\neg D_3 \sqcup B$ (resolution on 10 and 3)
~~13.~~ $\neg D_3 \sqcup \neg B$ (resolution on 11 and 5)
14. $\neg D_3$ (resolution on 12 and 13)

Clause 14 makes clauses 10–13 become redundant, and existential role restriction elimination on Clause 9 possible.

15. $\neg B \sqcup \neg C$ (exist. role restr. elimination on 9 and 14)

Clause 15 makes Clause 9 become redundant. We saturate the remaining clauses.

~~16.~~ $\neg A \sqcup C \sqcup \neg C$ (resolution on 15 and 1, tautology)
17. $\neg D_1 \sqcup \neg C$ (resolution on 15 and 3)

Only clauses that do not contain B or a positive definer are included in $\mathcal{F}_{\mathcal{ALCH}}^B(\mathcal{O}_1)$. These are the clauses 4, 6, 7, 8, 14 and 17. Eliminating the definers and expressing clauses as concept inclusions (Phases 2 and 3) results in the following ontology $\mathcal{O}_1^{-B}$:

$$A \sqsubseteq C \sqcup \exists r.\nu X.(\neg C \sqcap \exists r.X) \qquad C \sqsubseteq \forall s.(\neg A \sqcup C)$$

Example 3 (Forgetting Role Symbols). Let $\mathcal{O}_2$ contain the following axioms. We want to compute $\mathcal{O}_2^{-r}$.

$$A \sqsubseteq \exists r.(A \sqcup B) \qquad B \sqsubseteq \forall r.\neg A$$
$$C \sqsubseteq \forall r.\neg B \qquad s \sqsubseteq r$$

We obtain the following clausal representation $clauses(\mathcal{O}_2)$:

1. $\neg A \sqcup \exists r.D_1$ 2. $\neg D_1 \sqcup A \sqcup B$
3. $\neg B \sqcup \forall r.D_2$ 4. $\neg D_2 \sqcup \neg A$
5. $\neg C \sqcup \forall r.D_3$ 6. $\neg D_3 \sqcup \neg B$

We observe that there is no role r' with $r \sqsubseteq r'$ and that $D_1 \sqcap D_2 \sqcap D_3$ is unsatisfiable, which means we can apply role restriction resolution on 1, 3 and 5:

7. $\neg A \sqcup \neg B \sqcup \neg C$ (*role restriction resolution on 1, 3 and 5*)

Furthermore, we do have a role r' with $r' \sqsubseteq r$, namely s which means we can apply universal role restriction monotonicity:

8. $\neg B \sqcup \forall s.D_2$ (*universal role restriction monotonicity on 3*)
9. $\neg C \sqcup \forall s.D_3$ (*universal role restriction monotonicity on 5*)

Omitting all clauses containing r and applying Phases 2 and 3 leads to the uniform interpolant $\mathcal{O}_2^{-r}$ consisting of the following axioms:

$$A \sqcap B \sqcap C \sqsubseteq \bot \qquad B \sqsubseteq \forall s.\neg A \qquad C \sqsubseteq \forall s.\neg B$$

8 Experimental Evaluation

In order to investigate the practicality of our approach, we implemented our method in Scala[1] using the OWL-API[2] and evaluated it on $\mathcal{ALCH}$-fragments of ontologies from the NCBO Bioportal ontology repository.[3] The ontologies of this corpus are known to have diverse complexity, size and structure [7]. For the role restriction resolution rule, we made use of the HermiT reasoner Version 1.3.6 [18] for checking satisfiability of conjunctions of definer concepts.

It turns out that several additional optimisations are necessary to make the method perform well on larger ontologies. Especially the role propagation rule creates a lot of unnecessary derivations when applied in its unrestricted form. This can be reduced by analysing the structure of the clause set before applying the rule to see in which cases it actually leads to new derivations on the symbol we want to forget. We further used module extraction in order to reduce the size of the input ontologies. Given an ontology $\mathcal{O}$, the $\top\bot*$-module of $\mathcal{O}$ over Σ contains a subset of the axioms of $\mathcal{O}$ that preserves all consequences of $\mathcal{O}$ in Σ, given $\mathcal{O}$ is consistent [17]. In order to compute $\mathcal{O}^\Sigma$, it is therefore sufficient to apply our method on the $\top\bot*$-module of $\mathcal{O}$ over Σ. In order to keep the clauses small, we further apply structural transformation to replace every subconcept C in the TBox that does not contain the symbol we want to forget by a new symbol X, which reduces the number of clauses a lot [12]. These symbols are replaced by the original subconcepts in the final result. For a complete overview of optimisations used we refer to the paper [10] on practical aspects of computing uniform interpolants in $\mathcal{ALC}$.

The corpus for our experiments was created as follows. From the NCBO Bioportal repository, we selected those ontologies that contain role hierarchies, and for which parsing and module extraction using the OWL-API was possible. We then restricted the selected ontologies to $\mathcal{ALCH}$ by removing all axioms that are

---
[1] http://www.scala-lang.org
[2] http://owlapi.sourceforge.net
[3] http://bioportal.bioontology.org

not expressible in $\mathcal{ALCH}$ using simple reformulations. This led to a corpus of 115 ontologies, on which we ran our experiments.

The experiments were conducted on an Intel Core i5-2400 CPU with four cores running at 3.10 GHz and 8 GB of RAM. Since our implementation does not make use of multi-threading (except for computations of the HermiT reasoner), we ran several experiments in parallel, taking care that experiments do not affect each other due to use of resources.

We started with a series of experiments to evaluate the perfomance of forgetting small sets of symbols, which may for example be interesting for predicate hiding or for computing logical differences between ontology versions, as mentioned in the Introduction. First, we evaluated the performance of concept forgetting. For this, we randomly selected samples of 5, 50, 100 and 150 concept symbols for each ontology and computed the result of forgetting these, with a timeout set to 100 seconds. In 4.5% of the cases, our implementation was not able to compute the uniform interpolant in the given time limit, and in 16.7% of the remaining cases, fixpoints where used in the result. Even though it known that uniform interpolants can be of size triple exponential of the size of the input ontology [14], in our experiments uniform interpolants were much smaller. In fact, in 62.8% of the cases where a uniform interpolant could be computed, the uniform interpolant was smaller than the input ontology. In the worst case however, the uniform interpolant was 104 times bigger than the input ontology. The difference also becomes more apparent when looking at the axiom size.

On average, the average axiom size of the uniform interpolant was 1.8 times bigger than in the input ontology, and the largest axiom size 10.3 times bigger. This effect was to be expected since more information about the role structure of the ontology and indirect concept relations has to be presented in the definitions of fewer concepts. Considering that in the input ontologies the average axiom size was only 3.48, and the average maximal axiom size was 15.21, this still means most axioms were not overly complex. However, in the worst case, the computed uniform interpolant contained an axiom that was 1,406 times bigger than the largest one in the input.

Next we evaluated forgetting of role symbols. Since the role restriction resolution rule makes use of an external reasoner, and can have more than two clauses as premises, one could expect that forgetting role symbols is much more expensive than forgetting concept symbols. On the other hand, since most ontologies have much fewer role symbols than concept symbols, it seems reasonable to conduct the experiments with smaller sets of symbols to be forgotten. We therefore compared how forgetting 5 role symbols performed in comparison with forgetting 5 concept symbols, again with a timeout of 100 seconds. Forgetting role symbols could be performed in 86.6% of the cases in the given time frame, whereas forgetting concept symbols succeeded in 99.8% of the cases. The impact on the ontology size was on the other hand less apparent. In only 3.8% of the cases the uniform interpolant was actually bigger than the input ontology (10.5% for concept symbols), and on average the interpolant was 93% of the size of the input ontology (97% for concept symbols). The largest axiom per ontology was on

Table 1. Results for computing uniform interpolants

$\|\Sigma\|$	Timeouts	Fixpoints	Interpolant Size	Axiom Size	Max. Axiom Size	Average Duration
50	15.12%	6.99%	22.50%	799.37%	1,053.68%	24.2 sec.
100	18.38%	11.57%	45.21%	646.32%	847.36%	21.0 sec.
150	22.25%	13.58%	76.55%	837.66%	5,657.87%	23.7 sec.
All	18.38%	10.44%	45.74%	757.69%	2,309.08%	23.0 sec.

average 1.58 times larger than in the input ontology (1.18 for concept symbols), and in the worst case 51.1 times larger (360.3 for concept symbols). One might suspect that this result is partly due to the exploitation of role hierarchies using the role restriction monotonicity rules. But it turned out that when ignoring the RBox, the results were nearly unchanged, and even slightly better.

To evaluate our complete method, we computed uniform interpolants for small signatures of size 50, 100 and 150. This corresponds to the applications exhibiting hidden relations and ontology reuse mentioned in the Introduction, as well as predicate hiding, if only a small part of the ontology is to be published.

For these uniform interpolants, usually a large number of symbols, including both role and concept symbols, had to be forgotten from the input ontology, even though module extraction already performs part of the job. For this reason we set a higher timeout of 1,000 seconds. The results are summarised in Table 1. It shows the percentage of experimental runs where a timeout occured, the percentage in the remaining set where fixpoints were used in the result, the ontology size, average axiom size and maximal axiom size of each uniform interpolant compared to the respective values of the input ontologies, and the average duration. In 18.38% of the cases the uniform interpolant could not be computed in 1,000 seconds, and in only 10.44% of the remaining cases, it made use of fixpoint operators. Despite the relatively high number of timeouts, the average duration was only 23 seconds, and the cumulative distribution of durations shows (Figure 5), that around 1,600 out of 2,911 runs (more than half of them) could be performed in less than a second. This suggests that computing uniform interpolants is in most cases a cheap operation.

It is known that uniform interpolants of $\mathcal{ALC}$-ontologies can be in the worst case be triple exponential in the size of the input ontology [14]. When fixpoints are used, the worst case complexity is better, but still double exponential. This bound was not at all reflected in the empirical results, where the average interpolant is less than half the size of the input ontology. In only 6.05% of the cases the uniform interpolant was bigger (see also Figure 5). The axioms in the uniform interpolant were usually around 8–10 times larger than in the input ontology, which is still a reasonable size for ontology analysis considering that in the input ontologies the average axiom size was less than 4.

It should be noted that randomly drawn samples of signatures not neccessarily reflect realistic use cases. One might assume that it is most often desirable to forget or preserve symbols that are closer related to each other, whereas

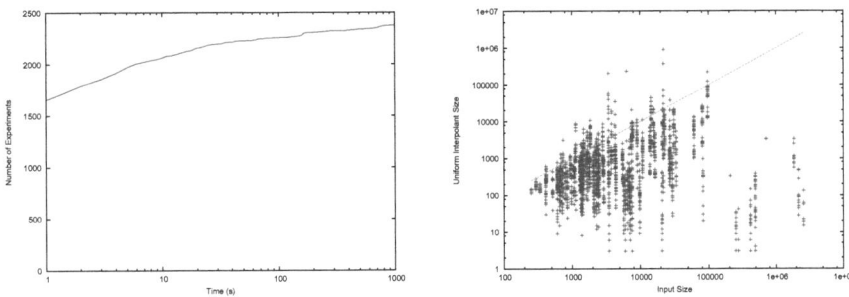

Fig. 5. Cumulative distribution of durations of experimental runs and sizes of the computed uniform interpolants

randomly selected symbols are more likely to be randomly distributed along the whole ontology, which can contain thousands of symbols. We therefore believe that our method would perform even better in realistic use cases.

9 Related Work

Most previous work has focused on uniform interpolation in simpler description logics like $\mathcal{EL}$ and DL-Lite (see for example [8,22,15,13]). In [21,20], one of the first approaches for a more expressive description logic, namely $\mathcal{ALC}$, is presented. Their method uses a tableaux-reasoner to add inferences from the input ontology in an incremental way. Regular checking for TBox-equivalence is used to decide whether the uniform interpolant is computed and the process can stop. By using tableaux-reasoning as a basis, the authors hope to make their method easily extendable with known techniques from existing tableau-reasoners. Its less focused way of deriving inferences make it however unfeasible for large ontologies. In [14], it was discovered that the method is incomplete. The solution offered can be seen as an extension of the original method, even though tableau-reasoning is not stated explicitly. The resulting method can be used to compute all uniform interpolants that can be finitely represented in $\mathcal{ALC}$, but offers no solutions for ontologies where the interpolant cannot be represented without fixpoints.

A more practical approach for forgetting concept symbols in $\mathcal{ALC}$ is presented in [12]. A resolution-based method influenced by [6] is used to derive consequences on the selected concept symbol in a focused way. Experiments on modified ontologies from the NCBO Bioportal ontology show the practicality of this approach under certain restrictions. Since their approach does not use structural transformation, a calculus based on meta-rules is used to make resolutions on nested concepts expressions possible. A disadvantage is that the method does not terminate if infinite chains of nested role-restrictions are derivable. The solution offered is to approximate interpolants by a given (lower) bound instead.

A method using fixpoints for the description logic $\mathcal{EL}$ was presented in [15]. This method aims at forgetting concept symbols, and computes derivation graphs for least common subsumers and most general subsumees of the concept to be eliminated. This graph is analysed to decide whether fixpoint operators are necessary in the result or not. In [13], an automata based representation is used to make finite representations of uniform interpolants possible. The computed automata can be used to decide whether a finite representation in pure $\mathcal{EL}$ is possible and can be translated into corresponding $\mathcal{EL}$-TBoxes in this case.

The method presented in this paper is an extension of a recently introduced method for forgetting concept symbols in $\mathcal{ALC}$-ontologies [11], which is evaluated in [10]. Both methods take ideas from second-order quantifier elimination techniques presented in [4], especially from the resolution-based method SCAN [3] and a method based on a generalised version of Ackermann's Lemma [16]. The latter technique has first been applied for description logics in [19]. Like the methods presented in [12] and [15], the method presented in [11] focuses on forgetting concept symbols. Our current method adds redundancy elimination techniques and is the first practical algorithm for forgetting role symbols from ontologies in expressive description logics.

10 Conclusion and Future Work

We presented a method for forgetting concept and role symbols from $\mathcal{ALCH}$-ontologies, or for computing uniform interpolants of $\mathcal{ALCH}$-ontologies. Since uniform interpolants cannot always be represented in a finite way, the resulting ontology may use fixpoint operators, which can be simulated in $\mathcal{ALCH}$ by extending the signature of the interpolant. Our experimental results suggest that the method is already applicable in a lot of real life situations.

An open point regards the use of fixpoints. One can construct easy examples where our method computes an interpolant with fixpoints, even though the uniform interpolant can be represented in $\mathcal{ALCH}$. Reasons for this are interactions between different fixpoint expressions in the ontology and indirect knowledge encoded in the remaining part of the ontology. For example, it is possible that the cyclic relation expressed by a fixpoint expression is already covered by a set of axioms that was not touched by the method, or that the fixpoint can be represented in a finite way due to entailments from the remaining ontology. Of course this leaves also the question on whether optimal use of fixpoint is actually practical on large ontologies, since an approach focused solely on the symbols we want to forget would not be sufficient here.

References

1. Ackermann, W.: Untersuchungen über das Eliminationsproblem der mathematischen Logik. Mathematische Annalen 110(1), 390–413 (1935)
2. Calvanese, D., Giacomo, G.D., Lenzerini, M.: Reasoning in expressive description logics with fixpoints based on automata on infinite trees. In: Proc. IJCAI 1999, pp. 84–89. Morgan Kaufmann (1999)

3. Gabbay, D., Ohlbach, H.J.: Quantifier elimination in second-order predicate logic. In: Proc. KR 1992, pp. 425–435. Morgan Kaufmann (1992)
4. Gabbay, D.M., Schmidt, R.A., Szalas, A.: Second Order Quantifier Elimination: Foundations, Computational Aspects and Applications. College Publ. (2008)
5. Grau, B.C., Motik, B.: Reasoning over ontologies with hidden content: The import-by-query approach. J. Artificial Intelligence Research 45, 197–255 (2012)
6. Herzig, A., Mengin, J.: Uniform interpolation by resolution in modal logic. In: Hölldobler, S., Lutz, C., Wansing, H. (eds.) JELIA 2008. LNCS (LNAI), vol. 5293, pp. 219–231. Springer, Heidelberg (2008)
7. Horridge, M., Parsia, B., Sattler, U.: The state of bio-medical ontologies. Bio-Ontologies 2011 (2011)
8. Konev, B., Walther, D., Wolter, F.: Forgetting and uniform interpolation in large-scale description logic terminologies. In: Proc. IJCAI 2009, pp. 830–835 (2009)
9. Koopmann, P., Schmidt, R.A.: Forgetting concept and role symbols in $\mathcal{ALCH}$-ontologies. Technical Report (2013), http://www.cs.man.ac.uk/~koopmanp
10. Koopmann, P., Schmidt, R.A.: Implementation and evaluation of forgetting in $\mathcal{ALC}$-ontologies. In: Proc. WoMO 2013. CEUR-WS.org (2013)
11. Koopmann, P., Schmidt, R.A.: Uniform interpolation of $\mathcal{ALC}$-ontologies using fixpoints. In: Fontaine, P., Ringeissen, C., Schmidt, R.A. (eds.) FroCoS 2013. LNCS (LNAI), vol. 8152, pp. 87–102. Springer, Heidelberg (2013)
12. Ludwig, M., Konev, B.: Towards practical uniform interpolation and forgetting for $\mathcal{ALC}$ TBoxes. In: Proc. DL 2013, pp. 377–389. CEUR-WS.org (2013)
13. Lutz, C., Seylan, I., Wolter, F.: An automata-theoretic approach to uniform interpolation and approximation in the description logic $\mathcal{EL}$. In: Proc. KR 2012. AAAI Press (2012)
14. Lutz, C., Wolter, F.: Foundations for uniform interpolation and forgetting in expressive description logics. In: Proc. IJCAI 2011, pp. 989–995. AAAI Press (2011)
15. Nikitina, N.: Forgetting in general $\mathcal{EL}$ terminologies. In: Proc. DL 2011. CEUR-WS.org (2011)
16. Nonnengart, A., Szałas, A.: A fixpoint approach to second-order quantifier elimination with applications to correspondence theory. In: Logic at Work, pp. 307–328. Springer (1999)
17. Sattler, U., Schneider, T., Zakharyaschev, M.: Which kind of module should I extract? In: Proc. DL 2009. CEUR-WS.org (2009)
18. Shearer, R., Motik, B., Horrocks, I.: HermiT: A highly-efficient OWL reasoner. In: Proc. OWLED 2008, pp. 26–27. CEUR-WS.org (2008)
19. Szałas, A.: Second-order reasoning in description logics. J. Appl. Non-Classical Logics 16(3-4), 517–530 (2006)
20. Wang, K., Wang, Z., Topor, R., Pan, J.Z., Antoniou, G.: Eliminating concepts and roles from ontologies in expressive descriptive logics. Computational Intelligence (2012)
21. Wang, Z., Wang, K., Topor, R., Zhang, X.: Tableau-based forgetting in $\mathcal{ALC}$ ontologies. In: Proc. ECAI 2010, pp. 47–52. IOS Press (2010)
22. Wang, Z., Wang, K., Topor, R.W., Pan, J.Z.: Forgetting for knowledge bases in DL-Lite. Ann. Math. Artif. Intell. 58(1-2), 117–151 (2010)

Simulating Parity Reasoning

Tero Laitinen, Tommi Junttila, and Ilkka Niemelä

Aalto University
Department of Information and Computer Science
PO Box 15400, FI-00076 Aalto, Finland
{Tero.Laitinen,Tommi.Junttila,Ilkka.Niemela}@aalto.fi

Abstract. Propositional satisfiability (SAT) solvers, which typically operate using conjunctive normal form (CNF), have been successfully applied in many domains. However, in some application areas such as circuit verification, bounded model checking, and logical cryptanalysis, instances can have many parity (xor) constraints which may not be handled efficiently if translated to CNF. Thus, extensions to the CNF-driven search with various parity reasoning engines ranging from equivalence reasoning to incremental Gaussian elimination have been proposed. This paper studies how stronger parity reasoning techniques in the DPLL(XOR) framework can be simulated by simpler systems: resolution, unit propagation, and parity explanations. Such simulations are interesting, for example, for developing the next generation SAT solvers capable of handling parity constraints efficiently.

1 Introduction

Propositional satisfiability (SAT) solver technology has developed rapidly providing a powerful solution technique in many industrial application domains (see e.g. [1]). The efficiency of SAT solvers is partly due to efficient data structures and algorithms that allow very efficient Boolean constraint propagation and conflict-driven clause learning in conjunctive normal form (CNF). Straightforward Tseitin-translation [2] of a problem instance to CNF may result in poor performance, especially in the case of parity (xor) constraints, that can be abundant in applications such as circuit verification, bounded model checking, and logical cryptanalysis. Although pure parity constraints (linear arithmetic modulo two) can be efficiently solved with Gaussian elimination, they can be very difficult for resolution [3] and thus for state-of-the-art conflict-driven clause learning (CDCL) satisfiability solvers as their underlying proof system is equivalent to resolution [4]. Due to this inherent hardness of parity constraints, several approaches to combining CNF-level and xor-constraint reasoning have been proposed [5,6,7,8,9,10,11,12,13,14,15,16,17,18] (see [19] for an alternative state-based approach). In these approaches, CNF-driven search has been extended with various parity reasoning techniques, ranging from plain unit propagation via equivalence reasoning to Gaussian elimination. Stronger parity reasoning may prune the search space effectively but often at the expense of high computational overhead, so resorting to simpler but more efficiently implementable systems, e.g. unit propagation, may lead to better performance.

In this paper, we study to what extent such simpler systems can simulate stronger parity reasoning engines in the DPLL(XOR) framework [13]. The DPLL(XOR), similar to the DPLL(T) approach [20] to Satisfiability Modulo Theories, is a framework to integrate a parity reasoning engine to a CDCL SAT solver. The aim is to offer generalizable results that provide a foundation for developing techniques to handle xor-constraints in next generation SAT solvers. Instead of developing yet another propagation engine and assessing it through an experimental comparison we believe that useful insights can be acquired by considering unanswered questions on how some existing propagation engines and proof systems relate to each other on a more fundamental level. Several experimental studies have already shown that SAT solvers extended with different parity reasoning engines can outperform unmodified solvers on some instance families, so we focus on more general results on the relationships between resolution, unit propagation, equivalence reasoning, parity explanations, and Gauss-Jordan elimination, which is a complete parity reasoning technique.

We show that resolution can simulate equivalence reasoning efficiently, which raises a question whether significant reductions in solving time can be gained by integrating specialized equivalence reasoning in a SAT solver since in theory it does not strengthen the underlying proof system of the SAT solver. In practice, though, the performance of the SAT solver is largely governed by variable selection and other heuristics that are likely to be non-optimal, which may justify the pragmatic use of equivalence reasoning.

Although equivalence reasoning alone is not enough to cross the "exponential gap" between resolution and Gauss-Jordan elimination, another light-weight parity reasoning technique comes intriguingly close at simulating complete parity reasoning. We show that parity explanations, an efficiently implementable conflict explanation technique, on nondeterministic unit propagation derivations can simulate Gauss-Jordan elimination on a restricted yet practically relevant class of xor-constraint conjunctions. Choosing assumptions and unit propagation steps nondeterministically may not be possible in an actual implementation with greedy propagation strategies. However, we present further experimental results indicating that the simulation may still work in an actual implementation to some degree provided that parity explanations are stored as learned xor-constraints as described in [16].

Additional xor-constraints can also be added to the formula in a preprocessing step in order to enable unit propagation to deduce more implied literals, which has the benefit of not requiring modifications to the SAT solver. We present a translation that enables unit propagation to simulate parity reasoning systems stronger than equivalence reasoning through the use of additional xor-constraints on auxiliary variables. The translation takes into account the structure of the original conjunction of xor-constraints and can produce compact formulas for sparsely connected instances. Using the translation to simulate full Gauss-Jordan elimination with plain unit propagation requires an exponential number of additional xor-constraints in the worst case. Recently, it has been shown in [21] that a conjunction of xor-constraints does not have a polynomial-size "arc consistent" CNF-representation, which implies it is not feasible to simulate Gauss-Jordan elimination by unit propagation in the general case. On many instances, though, better solver performance can be obtained by simulating a weaker parity reasoning system as it reduces the size of the translation substantially. By applying our previous results on detecting whether unit propagation or equivalence reasoning is enough to deduce all implied literals, the size of the translation can be optimized further. The experimental evaluation on a challenging benchmark set suggests that the translation can lead to significant reduction in the solving time for some instances.

2 Preliminaries

Let $\mathbb{B} = \{\bot, \top\}$ be the set of truth values "false" and "true". A literal is a Boolean variable x or its negation $\neg x$ (as usual, $\neg\neg x$ will mean x), and a clause is a disjunction of literals. If ϕ is any kind of formula or equation, (i) vars(ϕ) is the set of variables occurring in it, (ii) lits(ϕ) = $\{x, \neg x \mid x \in \text{vars}(\phi)\}$ is the set of literals over vars(ϕ), and (iii) a truth assignment for ϕ is a, possibly partial, function $\tau : \text{vars}(\phi) \to \mathbb{B}$. A truth assignment satisfies (i) a variable x if $\tau(x) = \top$, (ii) a literal $\neg x$ if $\tau(x) = \bot$, and (iii) a clause $(l_1 \vee .. \vee l_k)$ if it satisfies at least one literal l_i in the clause.

Resolution. Given two clauses, $x \vee C$ and $\neg x \vee D$ for arbitrary disjunctions of literals C and D, their resolvent is $C \vee D$. Given a CNF formula ϕ, a resolution derivation on ϕ is a finite sequence $\pi = \hat{C}_1\hat{C}_2...\hat{C}_m$ of clauses such that for all $1 \leq i \leq m$ it holds that either (i) $\hat{C}_i$ is a clause in ϕ, or (ii) $\hat{C}_i$ is the resolvent of two clauses, $\hat{C}_j$ and $\hat{C}_k$, in π with $1 \leq j, k < i$. A clause C is resolution derivable from ϕ if there is resolution derivation on ϕ including C. The formula ϕ is unsatisfiable if and only if the empty clause is resolution derivable from ϕ.

Xor-constraints. An *xor-constraint* is an equation of the form $x_1 \oplus ... \oplus x_k \equiv p$, where the x_is are Boolean variables and $p \in \mathbb{B}$ is the parity.[1] We implicitly assume that duplicate variables are always removed from the equations, e.g. $x_1 \oplus x_2 \oplus x_1 \oplus x_3 \equiv \top$ is always simplified into $x_2 \oplus x_3 \equiv \top$. If the left hand side does not have variables, then it equals to $\bot$; the equation $\bot \equiv \top$ is a contradiction and $\bot \equiv \bot$ a tautology. We identify the xor-constraint $x \equiv \top$ with the literal x, $x \equiv \bot$ with $\neg x$, $\bot \equiv \bot$ with $\top$, and $\top \equiv \bot$ with $\bot$. A truth assignment τ satisfies an xor-constraint $x_1 \oplus ... \oplus x_k \equiv p$ if $\tau(x_1) \oplus ... \oplus \tau(x_k) = p$. We use $D[x/Y]$ to denote the xor-constraint obtained from D by substituting the variable x in it with Y. For instance, $(x_1 \oplus x_2 \oplus x_3 \equiv \top)[x_1/x_2 \oplus \top] = x_2 \oplus \top \oplus x_2 \oplus x_3 \equiv \top = x_3 \equiv \bot$. The straightforward CNF translation of an xor-constraint D is denoted by cnf(D); for instance, cnf($x_1 \oplus x_2 \oplus x_3 \equiv \bot$) = $(\neg x_1 \vee \neg x_2 \vee \neg x_3) \wedge (\neg x_1 \vee x_2 \vee x_3) \wedge (x_1 \vee \neg x_2 \vee x_3) \wedge (x_1 \vee x_2 \vee \neg x_3)$. We define the linear combination of two xor-constraints, $D = (x_1 \oplus ... \oplus x_k \equiv p)$ and $E = (y_1 \oplus ... \oplus y_l \equiv q)$, by $D + E = (x_1 \oplus ... \oplus x_k \oplus y_1 \oplus ... \oplus y_l \equiv p \oplus q)$. An xor-constraint $E = (x_1 \oplus ... \oplus x_k \equiv p)$ with $k \geq 1$ is a *prime implicate* of a satisfiable xor-constraint conjunction ϕ_{xor} if (i) $\phi_{\text{xor}} \models E$ but (ii) $\phi_{\text{xor}} \not\models E'$ for all xor-constraints E' for which vars(E') is a proper subset of vars(E).

A *cnf-xor formula* is a conjunction $\phi_{\text{or}} \wedge \phi_{\text{xor}}$, where ϕ_{or} is a conjunction of clauses and ϕ_{xor} is a conjunction of xor-constraints. A truth assignment satisfies $\phi_{\text{or}} \wedge \phi_{\text{xor}}$ if it satisfies every clause and xor-constraint in it.

---

[1] The correspondence of xor-constraints to the "xor-clause" representation used e.g. in [13,15,16] is straightforward: $x_1 \oplus ... \oplus x_k \equiv \top$ corresponds to the xor-clause $(x_1 \oplus ... \oplus x_k)$ and $x_1 \oplus ... \oplus x_k \equiv \bot$ to $(x_1 \oplus ... \oplus x_k \oplus \top)$.

2.1 DPLL(XOR) and Xor-Reasoning Modules

We are interested in solving the satisfiability of cnf-xor formulas of the form $\phi_{or} \wedge \phi_{xor}$ defined above. Similarly to the DPLL(T) approach for Satisfiability Modulo Theories, see e.g. [20,22], the DPLL(XOR) approach [13] for solving cnf-xor formulas consists of (i) a conflict-driven clause learning (CDCL) SAT solver that takes care of solving the CNF-part ϕ_{or}, and (ii) an *xor-reasoning module* that handles the xor-part ϕ_{xor}. The CDCL solver is the master process, responsible of guessing values for the variables according to some heuristics ("branching"), performing propagation in the CNF-part, conflict analysis, restarts etc. The xor-reasoning module receives variable values, called xor-assumptions, from the CDCL solver and checks (i) whether the xor-part can still be satisfied under the xor-assumptions, and (ii) whether some variable values, called xor-implied literals, are implied by the xor-part and the xor-assumptions. These checks can be incomplete, like in [13,15] for the satisfiability and in [13,15,12] for the implication checks, as long as the satisfiability check is complete when all the variables have values. The very basic interface for an xor-reasoning module can consist of the following methods:

- init(ϕ_{xor}) initializes the module with ϕ_{xor}. It may return "unsat" if it finds ϕ_{xor} unsatisfiable, or a set of *xor-implied literals*, i.e. literals $\hat{l}$ such that $\phi_{xor} \models \hat{l}$ holds.
- assume(l) is used to communicate a new variable value l deduced in the CNF solver part to the xor-reasoning module. This value, called *xor-assumption* literal l, is added to the list of current xor-assumptions. If $[l_1, ..., l_k]$ are the current xor-assumptions, the module then tries to (i) deduce whether $\phi_{xor} \wedge l_1 \wedge ... \wedge l_k$ became unsatisfiable, i.e. whether an *xor-conflict* was encountered, and if this was not the case, (ii) find *xor-implied literals*, i.e. literals $\hat{l}$ for which $\phi_{xor} \wedge l_1 \wedge ... \wedge l_k \models \hat{l}$ holds. The xor-conflict or the xor-implied literals are then returned to the CNF solver part so that it can start conflict analysis (in the case of xor-conflict) or extend its current partial truth assignment with the xor-implied literals.

  In order to facilitate conflict-driven backjumping and clause learning in the CNF solver part, the xor-reasoning module has to provide a clausal *explanation* for each xor-conflict and xor-implied literal it reports. That is,

  - if $\phi_{xor} \wedge l_1 \wedge ... \wedge l_k$ is deduced to be unsatisfiable, then the module must report a (possibly empty) clause $(\neg l'_1 \vee ... \vee \neg l'_m)$ such that (i) each l'_i is an xor-assumption or an xor-implied literal, and (ii) $\phi_{xor} \wedge l'_1 \wedge ... \wedge l'_m$ is unsatisfiable (i.e. $\phi_{xor} \models (\neg l'_1 \vee ... \vee \neg l'_m)$); and
  - if it was deduced that $\phi_{xor} \wedge l_1 \wedge ... \wedge l_k \models \hat{l}$ for some $\hat{l}$, then the module must report a clause $(\neg l'_1 \vee ... \vee \neg l'_m \vee \hat{l})$ such that (i) each l'_i is an xor-assumption or an xor-implied literal reported earlier, and (ii) $\phi_{xor} \wedge l'_1 \wedge ... \wedge l'_m \models \hat{l}$, i.e. $\phi_{xor} \models (\neg l'_1 \vee ... \vee \neg l'_m \vee \hat{l})$.

- backtrack() retracts the latest xor-assumption and all the xor-implied literals deduced after it.

Naturally, variants of this interface are easily conceivable. For instance, a larger set of xor-assumptions can be given with the assume method at once instead of only one.

For xor-reasoning modules based on equivalence reasoning, see [13,15]. The Gaussian and Gauss-Jordan elimination processes in [12,14,23,18] can also be easily seen as xor-reasoning modules.

$$\frac{x \equiv \top \quad D}{D\,[x/\top]}\qquad \frac{x \equiv \bot \quad D}{D\,[x/\bot]}\qquad \frac{x \oplus y \equiv \bot \quad D}{D\,[x/y]}\qquad \frac{x \oplus y \equiv \top \quad D}{D\,[x/y \oplus \top]}$$
$$\oplus\text{-Unit}^{+} \qquad\qquad \oplus\text{-Unit}^{-} \qquad\qquad \oplus\text{-Eqv}^{+} \qquad\qquad \oplus\text{-Eqv}^{-}$$

Fig. 1. Inference rules of Subst; x and y are variables, D is an xor-constraint, and x occurs in D

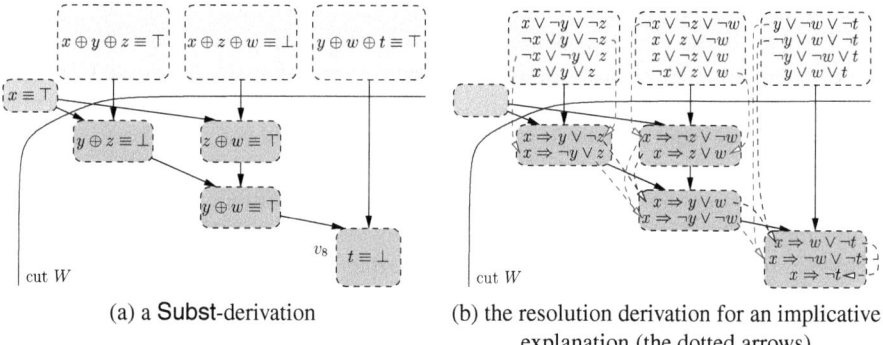

(a) a Subst-derivation

(b) the resolution derivation for an implicative explanation (the dotted arrows)

Fig. 2. Subst-derivations and resolution

3 Equivalence Reasoning and Resolution

We know that there exist infinite families of xor-constraint conjunctions ϕ_{xor} whose CNF translations $\bigwedge_{D \in \phi_{\text{xor}}} \text{cnf}(D)$ have no polynomial size resolution proofs [3]. On the other hand, Gaussian elimination [14] can solve the satisfiability of xor-constraint conjunctions in polynomial time (and Gauss-Jordan [23,18] can detect all xor-implied literals as well). As these elimination procedures can be computationally heavy, more light-weight "equivalence reasoning" systems have been proposed [6,10,13,15].

Here we study how the equivalence reasoning systems Subst [13] and EC [15] relate to resolution. These systems are equally powerful in detecting unsatisfiability and xor-implied literals (we'll use Subst due to its notational simplicity); they are more powerful than unit propagation but weaker than Gaussian/Gauss-Jordan elimination.

The Subst deduction system consists of the inference rules in Fig. 1. Given a conjunction ψ of xor-constraints, a Subst-*derivation* on it is a vertex-labeled directed acyclic graph $G = \langle V, E, L \rangle$ such that for each vertex $v \in V$ it holds that (i) if v has no incoming edges, then $L(v)$ is an xor-constraint in ψ, and (ii) otherwise v has two incoming edges, say from v' and v'', and $L(v)$ is obtained from $L(v')$ and $L(v'')$ by applying one of the inference rules. As an example, Fig. 2(a) shows a Subst-derivation on $(x \oplus y \oplus z \equiv \top) \wedge (x \oplus z \oplus w \equiv \bot) \wedge (y \oplus w \oplus t \equiv \top) \wedge (x)$, please ignore the "Cut W" line for now.

If we can derive an xor-constraint D with Subst, we can derive (in the CNF translated instance) a CNF translation of D with resolution relatively compactly:

Theorem 1. *Assume a* Subst-*derivation* $G = \langle V, E, L \rangle$ *on a conjunction* ψ *of xor-constraints. There is a resolution derivation* π *on* $\bigwedge_{D \in \psi} \text{cnf}(D)$ *such that (i) if* $v \in V$

and $L(v) \neq \top$, then the clauses $\mathrm{cnf}(L(v))$ occur in π, and (ii) π has at most $|V|2^{m-1}$ clauses, where m is the number of variables in the largest xor-constraint in ψ.

A similar result is already observed in [6] when restricted on binary and ternary xor-constraints. Recalling that for each xor-constraint D the CNF translation $\mathrm{cnf}(D)$ is exponentially large in the number of variables in D, we can say that resolution simulates Subst-derivations "pseudo-linearly". Furthermore, the natural encodings in many application domains (e.g. logical cryptanalysis) seem to employ xor-constraints with only few (typically 3) variables only.

3.1 Implicative Explanations

In the DPLL(XOR) framework, the clausal explanations for the xor-implied literals and xor-conflicts are vital for the CDCL solver when it performs its conflict analysis and clause learning. We next show that the implicative explanation procedure described in [13] can also be simulated with resolution, and discuss the consequence of this result.

Like the conflict resolution methods in modern CNF-level CDCL solvers, the explanation method is based on taking certain cuts in derivations. Assume a Subst-derivation $G = \langle V, E, L \rangle$ on $\phi_{\mathrm{xor}} \wedge l_1 \wedge ... \wedge l_k$, where ϕ_{xor} is a conjunction of xor-constraints and $l_1, ..., l_k$ are some xor-assumption literals. For a non-input vertex $v \in V$, a *cut for v* is a partitioning $(V_\mathrm{a}, V_\mathrm{b})$ of V such that (i) $v \in V_\mathrm{b}$, and (ii) if $v' \in V$ is an input vertex and there is a path from v' to v, then $v' \in V_\mathrm{a}$. As an example, the line "cut W" shows a cut for the vertex v_8 in Fig. 2(a). The *implicative explanation* of the vertex v under the cut W is the conjunction $Expl(v, W) = f_W(v)$, there f_W is recursively defined as:

E1 If u is an input vertex with $L(u) \in \phi_{\mathrm{xor}}$, then $f_W(u) = \top$.
E2 If u is an input vertex with $L(u) \in \{l_1, ..., l_k\}$, then $f_W(u) = L(u)$.
E3 If u is a non-input vertex in V_a, then $f_W(u) = L(u)$.
E4 If u is a non-input vertex in V_b, then $f_W(u) = f_W(u_1) \wedge f_W(u_2)$, where u_1 and u_2 are the source vertices of the two edges incoming to u.

If the cut is *cnf-compatible*, meaning that all the vertices in V_a having an edge to a vertex in V_b are either (i) xor-constraints in ϕ_{xor} or (ii) unary xor-constraints, then the explanation $Expl(v, W)$ is a conjunction of literals and the clausal explanation of the xor-implied literal $L(v)$ returned to the CDCL part is $Expl(v, W) \Rightarrow L(v)$. As an example, for the vertex v_8 and cnf-compatible cut W in Fig. 2(a), we have $Expl(v_8, W) = (x)$ and the clausal explanation is thus $x \Rightarrow \neg t$, i.e., $(\neg x \vee \neg t)$.

We now prove that all such clausal explanations can in fact be derived with resolution from the CNF translation of the original xor-constraints ϕ_{xor} only, without the use of xor-assumptions. To illustrate some parts of the construction, Fig. 2(b) shows how the clausal explanation $x \Rightarrow \neg t$ above can be derived.

Theorem 2. *Assume a Subst-derivation $G = \langle V, E, L \rangle$ on $\phi_{\mathrm{xor}} \wedge l_1 \wedge \cdots \wedge l_k$ and a cnf-compatible cut $W = (V_\mathrm{a}, V_\mathrm{b})$. There is a resolution derivation π on $\bigwedge_{D \in \phi_{\mathrm{xor}}} \mathrm{cnf}(D)$ such that (i) for each vertex $v \in V_\mathrm{b}$ with $L(v) \neq \top$, π includes all the clauses in $\{Expl(v, W) \Rightarrow C \mid C \in \mathrm{cnf}(L(v))\}$, and (ii) π has at most $|V|2^{m-1}$ clauses, where m is the number of variables in the largest xor-constraint in ϕ_{xor}.*

As modern CDCL solvers can be seen as resolution proof producing engines [24,25], a DPLL(XOR) solver with Subst or EC as the xor-reasoning module can thus also be seen as such engine: the clausal explanations used by the CDCL part can be first obtained with resolution and then treated as normal clauses when producing the resolution proof corresponding to the execution of the CDCL part. And, recalling that modern CDCL solvers can polynomially simulate resolution [4], we have the following:

Corollary 1. *For cnf-xor instances with fixed width xor-constraints, the underlying proof system of a DPLL(XOR) solver using Subst or EC as the xor-reasoning module is polynomially equivalent to resolution.*

4 Parity Explanations and Gauss-Jordan Elimination

A key observation made in [16] was that the inference rules in Fig. 1 (and some others, as explained in [16]) could not only be read as "the premises imply the consequence" but also as "the linear combination of premises equals the consequence". This led to the introduction of an improved explanation method, called parity explanations, which can produce (i) smaller clausal explanations, and (ii) new xor-constraints that are logical consequences of the original ones. As shown in [16], even when applied on a very weak deduction system UP, which only uses the unit propagation rules $\oplus$-Unit$^+$ and $\oplus$-Unit$^-$ in Fig. 1, the parity explanation method can quickly detect the unsatisfiability of some instances whose CNF translations have no polynomial size resolution refutations [3]. We now strengthen this result and prove that parity explanations on UP-derivations can in fact produce xor-constraints corresponding to the explanations produced by Gauss-Jordan elimination, provided that one can make the xor-assumptions suitably and each variable in the xor-constraint conjunction occurs at most three times (Thm. 3 below).

Formally, assume a UP-derivation $G = \langle V, E, L \rangle$ for $\phi_{\text{xor}} \wedge l_1 \wedge ... \wedge l_k$. For each non-input vertex v of G, and each cut $W = (V_a, V_b)$ of G for v, the *parity explanation* of v under W is $\text{Expl}_\oplus(v, W) = f_W(v)$, there f_W is recursively defined as earlier for $\text{Expl}(v, W)$ except that the case "E4" is replaced by

E4 If u is a non-input node in V_b, then $f_W(u) = f_W(u_1) + f_W(u_2)$, where u_1 and u_2 are the source nodes of the two edges incoming to u.

As shown in [16], $\phi_{\text{xor}} \models \text{Expl}_\oplus(v, W) + L(v)$ and the clausal explanation for $L(v)$ can be obtained from $\text{cnf}(\text{Expl}_\oplus(v, W) + L(v))$. As an example, the parity explanation $\text{Expl}_\oplus(v_8, W)$ of the vertex v_8 in Fig. 2(a) is $(\bot \equiv \bot)$, i.e. $\top$, and indeed $(x \oplus y \oplus z \equiv \top) \wedge (x \oplus z \oplus w \equiv \bot) \wedge (y \oplus w \oplus t \equiv \top) \models (\bot \equiv \bot) + L(v_8) = (t \equiv \bot)$. Note that x does not occur in the parity explanation or in the clausal explanation ($\neg t$) returned.

For instances in which each variable occurs at most three times we can prove that, by selecting the xor-assumptions appropriately, parity explanations can in fact produce all prime implicate xor-constraints:

Theorem 3. *Let ϕ_{xor} be a conjunction of xor-constraints such that each variable occurs in at most three xor-constraints.*

If ϕ_{xor} is unsatisfiable, then there is a UP-derivation on $\phi_{\text{xor}} \wedge y_1 \wedge ... \wedge y_m$ with some $y_1, ..., y_m \in \text{vars}(\phi_{\text{xor}})$, a vertex v with $L(v) = (\bot \equiv \top)$ in it, and a cut W for v such that $\text{Expl}_\oplus(v, W) = (\bot \equiv \bot)$ and thus $\text{Expl}_\oplus(v, W) + L(v) = (\bot \equiv \top)$.

If ϕ_{xor} is satisfiable and $\phi_{\text{xor}} \models (x_1 \oplus ... \oplus x_k \equiv p)$, then there is a UP-derivation on $\phi_{\text{xor}} \wedge (x_1 \equiv p_1) \wedge ... \wedge (x_k \equiv p_k) \wedge y_1 \wedge ... \wedge y_m$ with some $y_1, ..., y_m \in \text{vars}(\phi_{\text{xor}}) \setminus \{x_1, ..., x_k\}$, a vertex v with $L(v) = (\bot \equiv \top)$ in it, and a cut W for v such that $\text{Expl}_\oplus(v, W) + L(v) = (x'_1 \oplus ... \oplus x'_l \equiv p')$ for some $\{x'_1, ..., x'_l\} \subseteq \{x_1, ..., x_k\}$ and $p' \in \{\bot, \top\}$ such that $\phi_{\text{xor}} \models (x'_1 \oplus ... \oplus x'_l \equiv p')$.

Now observe that the clausal explanations provided by the complete Gauss-Jordan elimination propagation engine of [18] are based on prime implicate xor-constraints (this follows from the fact that reduced row-echelon form matrices are used and the explanations are derived from the rows of such matrices). As a consequence, for instances in which each variable occurs at most three times, parity explanations on UP-derivations can in theory simulate the complete Gauss-Jordan elimination propagation engine [18] in the DPLL(XOR) framework if we allow unlimited restarts in the CDCL part and xor-constraint learning [16]: we can first learn all the linear combinations that the Gauss-Jordan engine would use to detect xor-implied literals and conflicts.

4.1 Experimental Evaluation

To evaluate the practical applicability of parity explanations further and to compare it to the xor-reasoning module using incremental Gauss-Jordan elimination presented in [18], we used our prototype solver based on minisat [26] (version 2.0 core) extended with four different xor-reasoning modules: (i) UP deduction system with implicative explanations, (ii) UP with parity explanations (UP+PEXP), (iii) UP with parity explanations and xor-constraint learning (UP+PEXP+learn) as described in [16], and (iv) incremental Gauss-Jordan elimination with biconnected component decomposition (UP+Gauss-Jordan) as described in [18]. We ran the solver configurations on two benchmark sets. The first benchmark set consists of instances in "crafted" and "industrial/application" categories of the SAT Competitions 2005, 2007, and 2009 as well as all the instances in the SAT Competition 2011 (see http://www.satcompetition.org/). We applied the xor-constraint extraction algorithm described in [14] to these CNF instances and found a large number of instances with xor-constraints. To get rid of some "trivial" xor-constraints, we eliminated unary clauses and binary xor-constraints from each instance by unit propagation and substitution, respectively. After this easy preprocessing, 474 instances (with some duplicates due to overlap in the competitions) having xor-constraints remained. In the second benchmark set we focus on the domain of logical cryptanalysis by modeling a "known cipher stream" attack on stream cipher Hitag2. The task is to recover the full key when a small number of cipher stream bits (33-38 bits, 51 instances / stream length) are given. In the attack, the IV and a number of cipher stream bits are given. There are only a few more generated cipher stream bits than key bits, so a number of keys probably produce the same prefix of the cipher stream.

The results for the SAT Competition benchmarks are shown in Fig. 3 and the results for Hitag2 in Fig. 4. The number of solved instances is shown in Fig. 5. For both benchmark sets, parity explanations without learning do not seem to reduce the number of decisions nor the solving time. However, storing parity explanations as learned xor-constraints results in a significant reduction in the number of decisions and this

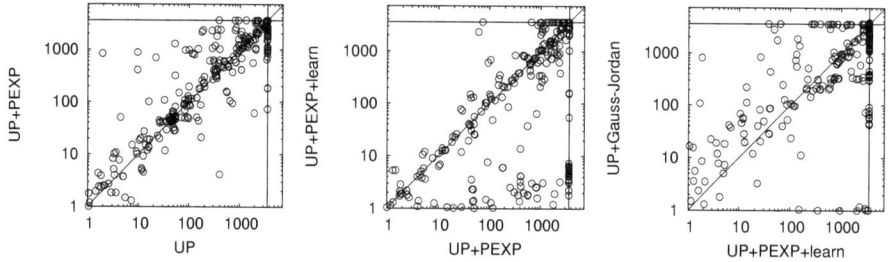

Fig. 3. Comparing parity explanations and Gauss-Jordan elimination on SAT 05-11 instances

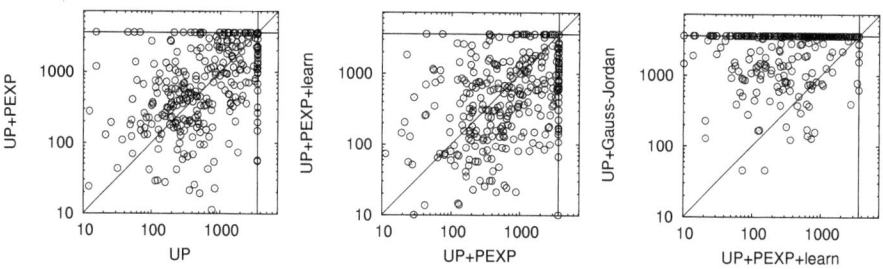

Fig. 4. Comparing parity explanations and Gauss-Jordan elimination on Hitag2 instances

is also reflected in the solving time. Most variables have at most three occurrences (98% of variables in Hitag2, and 97% in SAT instances), so in most cases a parity explanation that is equivalent to the "Gauss-Jordan explanation" could be found using nondeterministic unit propagation. The SAT competition benchmarks has 64 instances consisting entirely of parity constraints which were of course solved without branching by Gauss-Jordan elimination. The results of the other instances that require searching on the CNF part illustrate that when parity explanations are learned, many instances can be solved much faster than with Gauss-Jordan elimination. It remains open whether the theoretical power of parity explanations could be exploited to an even higher degree by employing different propagation heuristics.

	SAT Competition					Hitag2	Grain	A5/1	Trivium
	2005	2007	2009	2011	all				
instances	123	100	140	111	474	301	357	640	1020
UP	79	66	82	41	268	264	**305**	605	879
UP+PEXP	78	**70**	85	**48**	281	257	301	610	867
UP+PEXP+learn	96	69	**88**	**48**	**301**	**274**	257	635	**909**
UP+Gauss-Jordan	**97**	61	82	39	279	115	84	**640**	880

Fig. 5. Number of instances solved within the time limit (3600s)

We also evaluated the performance of the four xor-reasoning modules on three other ciphers, Grain, A5/1, and Trivium, by encoding a similar "known cipher stream" attack as with Hitag2 above. For Grain, the simplest method, plain unit propagation, works the best. Gauss-Jordan elimination does not reduce the number of decisions enough to compensate for the computational overhead of complete parity reasoning. Parity explanations reduce the number of decisions slightly, but the small computational overhead is still too much. For A5/1, the solver using Gauss-Jordan elimination works the best. The solvers using parity explanations perform better than plain unit propagation, too, but not as well as the solver with Gauss-Jordan elimination. For Trivium, the solver using parity explanations with learning solves the most instances.

5 Simulating Stronger Parity Reasoning with Unit Propagation

An efficient translation for simulating equivalence reasoning with unit propagation has been presented in our earlier work [17]. We now present a translation that adds redundant xor-constraints and auxiliary variables in the problem guaranteeing that unit propagation is enough to always deduce all xor-implied literals in the resulting xor-constraint conjunction. The translation thus effectively simulates a complete parity reasoning engine based on incremental Gauss-Jordan elimination presented in [18,23]. The translation can be seen as an arc-consistent encoding of the xor-reasoning theory (also compare to the eager approach to SMT [22]). The translation is based on ensuring that each relevant linear combination of original variables has a corresponding "alias" variable, and adding xor-constraints that enable unit propagation to infer values of "alias" variables when corresponding linear combinations are implied. The translation, which is exponential in the worst-case, can be made polynomial by bounding the length of linear combinations to consider. While unit propagation may not be able then to deduce all xor-implied literals, the overall performance can be improved greatly.

The redundant xor-constraint conjunction, called a *GE-simulation formula* ψ, added to ϕ_{xor} by the translation should satisfy the following: (i) the satisfying truth assignments of ϕ_{xor} are exactly the ones of $\phi_{\text{xor}} \wedge \psi$ when projected to $\text{vars}(\phi_{\text{xor}})$, and (ii) if ϕ_{xor} is satisfiable and $\phi_{\text{xor}} \wedge l_1 \wedge \cdots \wedge l_k \models \hat{l}$, then $\hat{l}$ is UP-derivable from $(\phi_{\text{xor}} \wedge \psi) \wedge l_1 \wedge \cdots \wedge l_k$, and (iii) if ϕ_{xor} is unsatisfiable, then $(\phi_{\text{xor}} \wedge \psi) \vdash_{\text{UP}} (\bot \equiv \top)$.

The translation k-Ge, presented in Fig. 7, where k stands for the maximum length of linear combinations to consider, "eliminates" each variable of the xor-constraint conjunction ϕ_{xor} at a time and adds xor-constraints produced by the subroutine translation ptable, presented in Fig. 6. Although the choice of variable to eliminate does not affect the correctness of the translation, we employ a greedy heuristic to pick a variable that shares xor-constraints with the fewest variables because the number of xor-constraints produced in the subroutine ptable is then the smallest. The translation $\text{ptable}(Y, \psi, k)$ adds "alias" variables and at most $O(2^{2k}) + |\phi_{\text{xor}}|$ xor-constraints to ψ with the aim to simulate Gauss-Jordan row operations involving at most k variables in the xor-constraints of the eliminated variable (the set Y) and no other variables. Provided that the maximum length of linear combinations to consider, the parameter k, is high enough, the resulting xor-constraint conjunction $\psi \wedge \text{ptable}(Y, \psi, k)$ has a UP-*propagation table* for the set of variables $Y \subseteq \text{vars}(\phi_{\text{xor}})$, meaning that the following conditions hold for all $Y', Y_1, Y_2 \subseteq Y$:

ptable(Y, ϕ_{xor}, k): start with $\phi'_{\text{xor}} = \phi_{\text{xor}}$
1.   for each $Y' \subseteq Y$ such that $|Y'| \leq k$ and $Y' \neq \emptyset$
2.   if there is no $a \in \text{vars}(\phi'_{\text{xor}})$ such that $(a \oplus Y' \equiv \bot)$ is in ϕ'_{xor}
3. $\phi'_{\text{xor}} \leftarrow \phi'_{\text{xor}} \wedge (a \oplus Y' \equiv \bot)$ where a is a new "alias" variable for Y'
4.   if $(Y' \equiv p)$ is in ϕ'_{xor} and $(a \equiv p)$ is not in ϕ'_{xor} where $p \in \{\bot, \top\}$
5. $\phi'_{\text{xor}} \leftarrow \phi'_{\text{xor}} \wedge (a \equiv p)$
6.   for each pair of subsets $Y_1, Y_2 \subseteq Y$ such that $|Y_1| \leq k$, $|Y_2| \leq k$, and $Y_1 \neq Y_2$
7.   if there is an "alias" variable $a_3 \in \text{vars}(\phi'_{\text{xor}})$ such that $(a_3 \oplus (Y_1 \oplus Y_2) \equiv \bot)$ is in ϕ'_{xor}
8. $a_1 \leftarrow$ the "alias" variable v such that $(v \oplus Y_1 \equiv \bot)$ is in ϕ'_{xor}
9. $a_2 \leftarrow$ the "alias" variable v such that $(v \oplus Y_2 \equiv \bot)$ is in ϕ'_{xor}
10.   if $(a_1 \oplus a_2 \oplus a_3 \equiv \bot)$ is not in ϕ'_{xor}
11. $\phi'_{\text{xor}} \leftarrow \phi'_{\text{xor}} \wedge (a_1 \oplus a_2 \oplus a_3 \equiv \bot)$
12. return $\phi'_{\text{xor}} \setminus \phi_{\text{xor}}$

Fig. 6. The ptable translation

k-Ge(ϕ_{xor}): start with $\phi'_{\text{xor}} = \phi_{\text{xor}}$ and $V = \text{vars}(\phi_{\text{xor}})$
1.   while $(V \neq \emptyset)$:
2.   Let clauses$(x, \phi'_{\text{xor}}) = \{D \mid D \text{ in } \phi'_{\text{xor}} \text{ and } x \in \text{vars}(D)\}$
3.   Let x be a variable in V minimizing $|\text{vars}(\text{clauses}(x, \phi'_{\text{xor}})) \cap V|$
4. $\phi'_{\text{xor}} \leftarrow \phi'_{\text{xor}} \wedge \text{ptable}(\text{vars}(\text{clauses}(x, \phi'_{\text{xor}})) \cap V, \phi'_{\text{xor}}, k)$
5.   Remove x from V
6.   return $\phi'_{\text{xor}} \setminus \phi_{\text{xor}}$

Fig. 7. The k-Ge translation

PT1: There is an "alias" variable for every non-empty subset of Y: if Y' is a non-empty subset of Y, then there is a variable $a \in \text{vars}(\psi)$ such that $(a \oplus Y' \equiv \bot)$ is in ψ, where $(a \oplus Y' \equiv \bot)$ for $Y' = \{y'_1, \dots, y'_n\}$ means $(a \oplus y'_1 \oplus \cdots \oplus y'_n \equiv \bot)$.
PT2: There is an xor-constraint for propagating the symmetric difference of any two subsets of Y: if $Y_1 \subseteq Y$ and $Y_2 \subseteq Y$, then there are variables $a_1, a_2, a_3 \in \text{vars}(\psi)$ such that $(a_1 \oplus Y_1 \equiv \bot), (a_2 \oplus Y_2 \equiv \bot), (a_3 \oplus (Y_1 \oplus Y_2) \equiv \bot)$, and $(a_1 \oplus a_2 \oplus a_3 \equiv \bot)$ are in ψ.
PT3: Alias variables of original xor-constraints having only variables of Y are assigned: if $(Y' \equiv p)$ is an xor-constraint in ψ such that $Y' \subseteq Y$, then there is a variable $a \in \text{vars}(\psi)$ such that $(a \oplus Y' \equiv \bot)$ it holds that $(a \equiv p)$ is in ψ

A UP-propagation table for a set of variables Y in ψ guarantees that if some alias variables $a_1, \dots, a_n \in \text{vars}(\psi)$ binding the variable sets $Y_1, \dots, Y_n \subseteq Y$ are assigned, the alias variable $a \in \text{vars}(\psi)$ bound to the linear combination $(Y_1 \oplus \cdots \oplus Y_n)$ is UP-deducible: $\psi \wedge (a_1 \equiv p_1) \wedge \cdots \wedge (a_n \equiv p_n) \vdash_{\text{UP}} (a \equiv p_1 \oplus \cdots \oplus p_n)$.

Provided that sufficiently long linear combinations are considered (the parameter k), UP-propagation tables added by the k-Ge enable unit propagation to always deduce all xor-implied literals, and thus simulate a complete Gauss-Jordan propagation engine:

Theorem 4. *If ϕ_{xor} is an xor-constraint conjunction, then k-Ge(ϕ_{xor}) is a GE-simulation formula for ϕ_{xor} provided that $k = |\text{vars}(\phi_{\text{xor}})|$.*

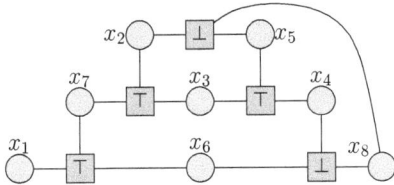

Fig. 8. Constraint graph of an xor-constraint conjunction

Example 1. Consider the xor-constraint conjunction $\phi_{\text{xor}}^{(0)} = (x_1 \oplus x_6 \oplus x_7 \equiv \top) \wedge (x_2 \oplus x_3 \oplus x_7 \equiv \top) \wedge (x_2 \oplus x_5 \oplus x_8 \equiv \bot) \wedge (x_3 \oplus x_4 \oplus x_5 \equiv \top) \wedge (x_4 \oplus x_6 \oplus x_8 \equiv \bot)$ illustrated in Fig. 8. It is clear that $\phi_{\text{xor}} \models (x_1 \equiv \top)$ and $\phi_{\text{xor}} \not\models_{\text{UP}} (x_1 \equiv \top)$.

With the elimination order $(x_1, x_7, x_4, x_5, x_2, x_3, x_6, x_8)$ and $k = 4$, the translation k-Ge first extends ϕ_{xor} to $\phi_{\text{xor}}^{(1)}$ with the xor-constraints in ptable($\{x_1, x_6, x_7\}, \phi_{\text{xor}}, k$). These include (i) the "alias binding constraints" $a_1 \oplus x_1 \equiv \bot$, $a_{6,7} \oplus x_6 \oplus x_7 \equiv \bot$, $a_{1,6,7} \oplus x_1 \oplus x_6 \oplus x_7 \equiv \bot$, (ii) the "linear combination constraint" $a_1 \oplus a_{6,7} \oplus a_{1,6,7} \equiv \bot$, and (iii) the "original constraint binder" $a_{1,6,7} \equiv \top$, where $a_{i,...}$ is the alias for the subset $\{x_i, ...\}$ of the original variables. After unit propagation, these constraints imply the binary constraint $a_1 \oplus a_{6,7} \equiv \top$ allowing us to deduce x_1 from the parity $a_{6,7}$ of x_6 and x_7.

The translation next "eliminates" x_7 and adds ptable($\{x_2, x_3, x_6, x_7\}, \phi_{\text{xor}}^{(1)}, k$) including the linear combination constraint $a_{6,7} \oplus a_{2,3,7} \oplus a_{2,3,6} \equiv \bot$ and the original constraint binder $a_{2,3,7} \equiv \top$, propagating the binary constraint $a_{6,7} \oplus a_{2,3,6} \equiv \top$ allowing us to deduce the parity of $\{x_6, x_7\}$ from the parity of $\{x_2, x_3, x_6\}$.

Eliminating x_4 adds ptable($\{x_3, x_4, x_5, x_6, x_8\}, \phi_{\text{xor}}^{(2)}, k$), including the constraints $a_{3,4,5} \oplus a_{4,6,8} \oplus a_{3,5,6,8} \equiv \bot$, $a_{3,4,5} \equiv \top$, and $a_{4,6,8} \equiv \top$, propagating $a_{3,5,6,8} \equiv \top$.

Eliminating x_5 adds ptable($\{x_2, x_3, x_5, x_6, x_8\}, \phi_{\text{xor}}^{(3)}, k$) (observe that x_6 is in the set as it occurs in the constraint $a_{3,5,6,8} \oplus x_3 \oplus x_5 \oplus x_6 \oplus x_8 \equiv \bot$ added in the previous step), including $a_{2,5,8} \oplus a_{2,3,6} \oplus a_{3,5,6,8} \equiv \bot$ and $a_{2,5,8} \equiv \bot$.

At this point we could already unit propagate $x_1 \equiv \top$ (from $a_{3,5,6,8} \equiv \top$, $a_{2,5,8} \equiv \bot$, and $a_{2,5,8} \oplus a_{2,3,6} \oplus a_{3,5,6,8} \equiv \bot$ we get $a_{2,3,6} \equiv \top$ and from this then $a_{6,7} \equiv \bot$ and finally $a_1 \equiv \top$, i.e. $x_1 \equiv \top$).

Note that the translation 3-Ge(ϕ_{xor}) is not a GE-simulation formula for ϕ_{xor} because ptable does not add "alias" variables for any 4-subset of original variables and the linear combination of any two original xor-constraints has at least four variables.

The translation ptable as presented in 6 for illustration purposes adds new "alias" variables for all relevant linear combinations involving at most k original variables. However, in an actual implementation, the original variables of the xor-constraint conjunction can be used as "alias" variables. For example, the variable x_1 in the xor-constraint $(x_1 \oplus x_2 \oplus x_3 \equiv \top)$ can be used as an "alias" variable for $(x_2 \oplus x_3 \equiv \bot)$.

The translation k-Ge is a generalization of the translation Eq^*, which simulates equivalence reasoning with unit propagation, presented in [17]. Provided that original variables are treated as "alias" variables as above and all xor-constraints have at most three variables, the translation 2-Ge, that considers only (in)equivalences between pairs of variables, enables unit propagation to simulate equivalence reasoning.

The size of the GE-simulation formula for ϕ_{xor} may be reduced considerably if ϕ_{xor} is partitioned into disjoint xor-constraint conjunctions $\phi^1_{\text{xor}} \wedge \cdots \wedge \phi^n_{\text{xor}}$ according to the connected components of the xor-constraint graph, and then combining the component-wise GE-simulation formulas k_1-Ge$(\phi^1_{\text{xor}}) \wedge \cdots \wedge k_n$-Ge$(\phi^n_{\text{xor}})$. Efficient structural tests for deciding whether unit propagation or equivalence reasoning is enough to achieve full propagation in an xor-constraint conjunction, presented in [17], can indicate appropriate values for some of the parameters $k_1, \ldots, k_n$.

5.1 Propagation-Preserving Xor-Simplification

Some of the xor-constraints added by k-Ge can be redundant regarding unit propagation. We now present a simplification method that preserves literals that can be implied by unit propagation. There are two simplification rules, given a pair of xor-constraint conjunctions $\langle \phi_a, \phi_b \rangle$ (initially $\langle \phi_{\text{xor}}, \emptyset \rangle$): [S1] an xor-constraint D in ϕ_a can be moved to ϕ_b, resulting in $\langle \phi_a \setminus \{D\}, \phi_b \cup \{D\} \rangle$, and [S2] an xor-constraint D in ϕ_a can be simplified with an xor-constraint D' in ϕ_b to $(D + D')$ provided that $|\text{vars}(D') \cap \text{vars}(D)| \geq |\text{vars}(D')| - 1$, resulting in $\langle (\phi_a \setminus \{D\}) \cup \{D + D'\}, \phi_b \rangle$.

Theorem 5. *If $\langle \phi'_a, \phi'_b \rangle$ is the result of applying one of the simplification rules to $\langle \phi_a, \phi_b \rangle$ and $\phi_a \wedge \phi_b \wedge l_1 \wedge \cdots \wedge l_k \vdash_{\text{UP}} \hat{l}$, then $\phi'_a \wedge \phi'_b \wedge l_1 \wedge \cdots \wedge l_k \vdash_{\text{UP}} \hat{l}$.*

Example 2. The conjunction 3-Ge$((x_1 \oplus x_2 \oplus x_3 \oplus x_4 \equiv \bot))$ contains the alias binding constraints $D_1 := (a_{1,2,3,4} \oplus x_1 \oplus x_2 \oplus x_3 \oplus x_4 \equiv \bot)$, $D_2 := (a_{1,2} \oplus x_1 \oplus x_2 \equiv \bot)$, $D_3 := (a_{3,4} \oplus x_3 \oplus x_4 \equiv \bot)$, as well as the linear combination constraint $D_4 := (a_{1,2} \oplus a_{3,4} \oplus a_{1,2,3,4} \equiv \bot)$. The alias binding constraint D_1 can in fact be eliminated by first applying the rule S1 to the xor-constraints D_2, D_3, and D_4. Then, by using the rule S2, the xor-constraint D_1 is simplified first with D_2 to $(a_{1,2,3,4} \oplus a_{1,2} \oplus x_3 \oplus x_4 \equiv \bot)$ and then with D_3 to $(a_{1,2,3,4} \oplus a_{1,2} \oplus a_{3,4} \equiv \bot)$, and finally with D_4 to $(\bot \equiv \bot)$.

5.2 Experimental Evaluation

To evaluate the translation k-Ge, we studied the benchmark instances in "crafted" and "industrial/application" categories of the SAT Competitions 2005, 2007, 2009, and 2011. We ran cryptominisat 2.9.6, glucose 2.3, and zenn 0.1.0 on the same 474 SAT Competition cnf-xor instances as in Section 4.1 with the translations k-Ge and $Eq^\star$. It is intractable to simulate full Gauss-Jordan elimination for these instances, so we adjusted the k-value of each call to the subroutine ptable(Y, ψ, k) to limit the number of additional xor-constraints. The translation was computed for each connected component separately. We found good performance by (i) stopping when $|Y| > 66$, (ii) setting $k = 1$ when it was detected that unit propagation deduces all xor-implied literals, (iii) setting $k = 2$ when $|Y| \in [10, 66]$ or when $|Y| < 10$ and it was detected that equivalence reasoning deduces all xor-implied literals, (iv) setting $k = 3$ when $|Y| \in [6, 9]$, and (v) setting $k = |Y|$ when $|Y| \leq 5$. With these parameters, the worst-case number of xor-constraints added by the subroutine ptable is 2145. Figure 9 shows the increase

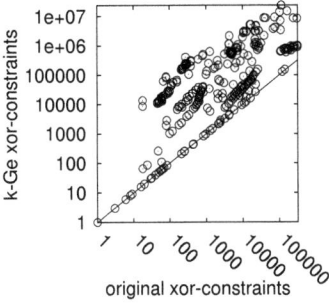

Fig. 9. Xor-constraints in SAT 05-11 instances

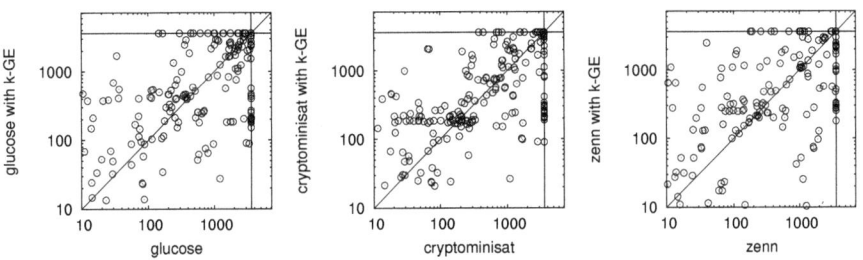

Fig. 10. Comparison on solving time between the unmodified instance and k-Ge using **glucose**, **cryptominisat**, and **zenn**

	SAT Competition				
	2005	2007	2009	2011	all
instances	123	100	140	111	474
glucose	63	**64**	88	54	269
glucose, $Eq^\star$	64	59	89	52	264
glucose, $Eq^\star$, simp	**66**	63	90	52	271
glucose, k-Ge	61	50	86	45	242
glucose, k-Ge, simp	64	60	**95**	**58**	**277**
cryptominisat	74	**70**	92	52	288
cryptominisat, $Eq^\star$	73	65	91	49	278
cryptominisat, $Eq^\star$, simp	**76**	68	91	51	286
cryptominisat, k-Ge	68	53	83	46	250
cryptominisat, k-Ge, simp	71	65	**94**	**64**	**294**
zenn	62	62	91	49	264
zenn, $Eq^\star$	62	62	90	49	263
zenn, $Eq^\star$, simp	**68**	**64**	92	48	272
zenn, k-Ge	61	59	89	52	261
zenn, k-Ge, simp	65	61	**93**	**54**	**273**

Fig. 11. Number of instances solved within the time limit of 3600s

in formula size by the translation k-Ge. Propagation-preserving xor-simplification was used to simplify the instances reducing the formula size in 404 instances with the median reduction being 16%. The translation Eq^* was computed in a similar way. The results are shown in Fig. 11, including the time spent in computing the translations. Using xor-simplification increases the number of solved instances for both translations. The detailed solving time comparison in Fig. 10 shows that that the translation k-Ge can incur some overhead, but also allows great speedupds, enabling the three solvers to solve the highest number of instances for the whole benchmark set.

6 Conclusions

We have studied how stronger parity reasoning techniques in the DPLL(XOR) framework can be simulated by simpler systems. We have shown that resolution simulates equivalence reasoning efficiently. We have proven that parity explanations on nondeterministic unit propagation derivations can simulate Gauss-Jordan elimination on a restricted yet practically relevant class of instances. We have shown that Gauss-Jordan elimination can be simulated by unit propagation by adding additional xor-constraints.

Acknowledgments. This work has been financially supported by the Academy of Finland under the Finnish Centre of Excellence in Computational Inference (COIN). We acknowledge the computational resources provided by Aalto Science-IT project.

References

1. Marques-Silva, J., Lynce, I., Malik, S.: Conflict-driven clause learning SAT solvers. In: Handbook of Satisfiability. IOS Press (2009)
2. Tseitin, G.S.: On the complexity of derivations in the propositional calculus. Studies in Mathematics and Mathematical Logic Part II, 115–125 (1968)
3. Urquhart, A.: Hard examples for resolution. Journal of the ACM 34(1), 209–219 (1987)
4. Pipatsrisawat, K., Darwiche, A.: On the power of clause-learning SAT solvers as resolution engines. Artificial Intelligence 175(2), 512–525 (2011)
5. Li, C.M.: Integrating equivalency reasoning into Davis-Putnam procedure. In: Proc. AAAI/IAAI 2000, pp. 291–296. AAAI Press (2000)
6. Li, C.M.: Equivalency reasoning to solve a class of hard SAT problems. Information Processing Letters 76(1-2), 75–81 (2000)
7. Baumgartner, P., Massacci, F.: The taming of the (X)OR. In: Palamidessi, C., et al. (eds.) CL 2000. LNCS (LNAI), vol. 1861, pp. 508–522. Springer, Heidelberg (2000)
8. Li, C.M.: Equivalent literal propagation in the DLL procedure. Discrete Applied Mathematics 130(2), 251–276 (2003)
9. Heule, M., van Maaren, H.: Aligning CNF- and equivalence-reasoning. In: Hoos, H.H., Mitchell, D.G. (eds.) SAT 2004. LNCS, vol. 3542, pp. 145–156. Springer, Heidelberg (2005)
10. Heule, M., Dufour, M., van Zwieten, J., van Maaren, H.: March_eq: Implementing additional reasoning into an efficient look-ahead SAT solver. In: Hoos, H.H., Mitchell, D.G. (eds.) SAT 2004. LNCS, vol. 3542, pp. 345–359. Springer, Heidelberg (2005)
11. Chen, J.: Building a hybrid SAT solver via conflict-driven, look-ahead and XOR reasoning techniques. In: Kullmann, O. (ed.) SAT 2009. LNCS, vol. 5584, pp. 298–311. Springer, Heidelberg (2009)

12. Soos, M., Nohl, K., Castelluccia, C.: Extending SAT solvers to cryptographic problems. In: Kullmann, O. (ed.) SAT 2009. LNCS, vol. 5584, pp. 244–257. Springer, Heidelberg (2009)
13. Laitinen, T., Junttila, T., Niemelä, I.: Extending clause learning DPLL with parity reasoning. In: Proc. ECAI 2010, pp. 21–26. IOS Press (2010)
14. Soos, M.: Enhanced gaussian elimination in DPLL-based SAT solvers. In: Pragmatics of SAT, Edinburgh, Scotland, GB, p. 1 (July 2010)
15. Laitinen, T., Junttila, T., Niemelä, I.: Equivalence class based parity reasoning with DPLL(XOR). In: IEEE Proc. ICTAI 2011, pp. 649–658 (2011)
16. Laitinen, T., Junttila, T., Niemelä, I.: Conflict-driven XOR-clause learning. In: Cimatti, A., Sebastiani, R. (eds.) SAT 2012. LNCS, vol. 7317, pp. 383–396. Springer, Heidelberg (2012)
17. Laitinen, T., Junttila, T., Niemelä, I.: Classifying and propagating parity constraints. In: Milano, M. (ed.) CP 2012. LNCS, vol. 7514, pp. 357–372. Springer, Heidelberg (2012)
18. Laitinen, T., Junttila, T., Niemelä, I.: Extending clause learning SAT solvers with complete parity reasoning. In: IEEE Proc. ICTAI 2012 (2012)
19. Weaver, S.A.: Satisfiability advancements enabled by state machines. PhD thesis, Cincinnati, OH, USA, AAI3554401 (2012)
20. Nieuwenhuis, R., Oliveras, A., Tinelli, C.: Solving SAT and SAT modulo theories: From an abstract Davis-Putnam-Logemann-Loveland procedure to DPLL(T). Journal of the ACM 53(6), 937–977 (2006)
21. Gwynne, M., Kullmann, O.: On SAT representations of XOR constraints. arXiv document arXiv:1309.3060 (cs.CC) (2013)
22. Barrett, C., Sebastiani, R., Seshia, S.A., Tinelli, C.: Satisfiability modulo theories. In: Handbook of Satisfiability. IOS Press (2009)
23. Han, C.-S., Jiang, J.-H.R.: When boolean satisfiability meets gaussian elimination in a simplex way. In: Madhusudan, P., Seshia, S.A. (eds.) CAV 2012. LNCS, vol. 7358, pp. 410–426. Springer, Heidelberg (2012)
24. Zhang, L., Malik, S.: Validating SAT solvers using an independent resolution-based checker: Practical implementations and other applications. In: IEEE Proc. DATE 2003, pp. 880–885 (2003)
25. Beame, P., Kautz, H., Sabharwal, A.: Towards understanding and harnessing the potential of clause learning. Journal of Artificial Intelligence Research 22, 319–351 (2004)
26. Eén, N., Sörensson, N.: An extensible SAT solver. In: Giunchiglia, E., Tacchella, A. (eds.) SAT 2003. LNCS, vol. 2919, pp. 502–518. Springer, Heidelberg (2004)

Herbrand Theorems for Substructural Logics

Petr Cintula[1,*] and George Metcalfe[2,**]

[1] Institute of Computer Science, Academy of Sciences, Prague, Czech Republic
cintula@cs.cas.cz
[2] Mathematical Institute, University of Bern, Switzerland
george.metcalfe@math.unibe.ch

Abstract. Herbrand and Skolemization theorems are obtained for a broad family of first-order substructural logics. These logics typically lack equivalent prenex forms, a deduction theorem, and reductions of semantic consequence to satisfiability. The Herbrand and Skolemization theorems therefore take various forms, applying either to the left or right of the consequence relation, and to restricted classes of formulas.

1 Introduction

The aim of this paper is to provide Herbrand and Skolemization theorems for a broad family of first-order substructural logics that encompasses first-order fuzzy logics, intermediate logics, exponential-free linear logic, relevance logics, and logics without contraction (see, e.g., [11,15,8,19,9]). Such logics are often undecidable, but their (decidable) fragments provide the foundations for knowledge representation and reasoning methods such as non-classical logic programming and description logics (see, e.g., [21,14,12,10]). One motivation for the work reported here is to avoid a duplication of research effort by providing a general approach to the development of automated reasoning techniques for first-order substructural logics. Herbrand and Skolemization theorems play a pivotal role in this development, reducing first-order problems to propositional problems. These theorems are also helpful for addressing theoretical problems in particular cases such as first-order Łukasiewicz logic.

In classical first-order logic, questions of validity and semantic consequence reduce to the satisfiability of a set of sentences; Skolemization and Herbrand theorems then reduce these questions further to the satisfiability of a set of propositional formulas (see, e.g., [5]). In first-order substructural logics, semantic consequence does not (typically) reduce to satisfiability and in the absence of quantifier shifts and a deduction theorem, non-prenex formulas should be considered on both sides of the consequence relation. The general Skolemization and Herbrand theorems obtained here therefore take various forms, applying either to the left or right of the consequence relation, and to restricted sets of formulas.

---

[*] Supported by RVO 67985807 and Czech Science Foundation grant P202/10/1826.
[**] Supported by Swiss National Science Foundation grant 200021_146748 and Marie Curie Reintegration Grant PIRG06-GA-2009-256492.

The theorems cover first-order intuitionistic logic and t-norm based fuzzy logics, studied already in [16,2,1,3], and other logics not previously considered.[1] We also obtain a new (topology-free) proof of the approximate Herbrand theorem for first-order Łukasiewicz logic (see [4]) via a Herbrand theorem for satisfiability that may hold when the Herbrand theorems for consequence fail.

The logics investigated in this paper are defined based on arbitrary classes of complete FL_e-algebras and include logics defined as extensions of (multiple-conclusion and hypersequent variants of) the full Lambek calculus with exchange augmented with quantifier rules (see [9,18,17]). Herbrand and Skolemization theorems may often be established for such logics proof-theoretically (see [15]) via mid(hyper)sequent theorems proved using permutations of rules tailored to the case at hand. By contrast, the uniform approach described in this paper is purely algebraic and applies also to many cases where no calculus has yet been defined.

2 Preliminaries

In first-order classical logic, predicates are interpreted as relations on a universe S, or, equivalently, as functions from S to the two element Boolean algebra **2**. In the logics defined below, other algebras may take the place of **2**. That is, a predicate may take one of many values, which might represent, for example, degrees of truth, belief, or confidence. For convenience, we restrict our attention here to FL_e-algebras (algebras for the full Lambek calculus with exchange and multiplicative additive intuitionistic linear logic without additive constants). Broadening the scope to non-commutative (or even non-associative) algebras or algebras with different operation symbols would lead to similar results, but complicate the presentation without adding greatly to our stock of useful examples.

Definition 1. *An* FL_e-*algebra is an algebra* $\mathbf{A} = \langle A, \&, \to, \wedge, \vee, \bar{0}, \bar{1} \rangle$ *such that:*

(a) $\langle A, \wedge, \vee \rangle$ *is a lattice with an order defined by* $x \leq y$ *iff* $x \wedge y = x$.
(b) $\langle A, \&, \bar{1} \rangle$ *is a commutative monoid.*
(c) $\to$ *is the residuum of* $\&$; *i.e., for all* $x, y, z \in A$: $x \& y \leq z$ *iff* $x \leq y \to z$.

The algebra $\mathbf{A}$ *is* complete *if for all* $X \subseteq A$, *both* $\bigvee X$ *and* $\bigwedge X$ *exists in* A, *and* $\mathbf{A}$ *is an* FL_e-*chain if for all* $x, y \in A$, *either* $x \leq y$ *or* $y \leq x$.

Example 1. Significant FL_e-chains include the real unit interval $[0,1]$ with the usual order, $\bar{0} = 0$ and $\bar{1} = 1$, and the monoidal operation & interpreted as the Łukasiewicz t-norm $\max(x+y-1, 0)$, the Gödel t-norm $\min(x,y)$, or the product t-norm $x \cdot y$. More generally, let $*$ be any residuated uninorm: an associative and commutative binary function $*$ on $[0,1]$ that is increasing in both arguments and

---

[1] After submitting this paper, we discovered that Terui has independently obtained related results for Herbrand theorems in substructural logics [20]. However, his approach is narrower and more algebraic in scope (e.g., Skolemization is not really considered); his main result shows rather that algebras for a broad class of logics admit suitable completions and that therefore these logics have a Herbrand theorem.

has a unit e_* and residuum $\to_*$. Then $\langle [0,1], *, \to_*, \min, \max, d, e_* \rangle$ is an FL_e-chain for any $d \in [0,1]$. Other examples of FL_e-chains include the lattice-ordered groups formed by the integers, rationals, or reals with the usual order, addition as the monoidal operation (with subtraction as its residuum), and $\overline{0} = \overline{1} = 0$.

Example 2. The class $\mathbb{FL}_e$ of FL_e-algebras forms a variety and its subvarieties provide algebraic semantics for a broad spectrum of substructural logics: in particular, extensions of the sequent calculus FL_e. For example, FL_{ew}-algebras for FL_e with weakening are FL_e-algebras satisfying $\overline{0} \le x \le \overline{1}$, while FL_{ewc}-algebras for intuitionistic logic (term-equivalent to Heyting algebras) are FL_{ew}-algebras satisfying $x\&x = x$. Other varieties consist of "involutive" FL_e-algebras satisfying $(x \to \overline{0}) \to \overline{0} = x$ (corresponding to multiple-conclusion sequent calculi) and "semilinear" FL_e-algebras satisfying $((x \to y) \wedge \overline{1}) \vee ((y \to x) \wedge \overline{1}) = \overline{1}$ (corresponding to hypersequent calculi). In particular, semilinear FL_e-algebras, FL_{ew}-algebras, and FL_{ewc}-algebras provide algebraic semantics for, respectively, uninorm logic, monoidal t-norm logic, and Gödel logic (see [7,9,15,6]).

Varieties of FL_e-algebras may enjoy a useful property that allows us to restrict attention to their complete members. Let $\mathbf{A}, \mathbf{B}$ be FL_e-algebras. An embedding $f: \mathbf{A} \to \mathbf{B}$ is *regular* if $f(\bigvee C) = \bigvee f[C]$ (whenever $\bigvee C$ exists) and $f(\bigwedge D) = \bigwedge f[D]$ (whenever $\bigwedge D$ exists) for all $C, D \subseteq A$. A class $\mathbb{K}$ of FL_e-algebras *admits regular completions* if each $\mathbf{A} \in \mathbb{K}$ regularly embeds into some complete $\mathbf{B} \in \mathbb{K}$.

Example 3. A family of varieties of FL_e-algebras (including, e.g., the varieties of FL_e-algebras, FL_{ew}-algebras, and FL_{ewc}-algebras) is described in [6] that admit regular completions if a corresponding sequent calculus admits a strong form of cut elimination. It is not known, however, whether a proof system (of some specified form) must always exist for classes of FL_e-algebras admitting regular completions. Varieties of FL_e-algebras satisfying the prelinearity law do not in general admit regular completions, but this may still be true for the class of chains of such varieties. In particular, if a variety of FL_e-algebras admits regular completions, then the class of chains of this variety (which generates the variety of semilinear members of the variety) also admits regular completions.

A *(countable) predicate language* $\mathcal{P}$ is a triple $\langle \mathbf{P}, \mathbf{F}, \mathbf{ar} \rangle$ where $\mathbf{P}$ and $\mathbf{F}$ are non-empty countable sets of predicate and function symbols, respectively, and $\mathbf{ar}$ is a function assigning to each predicate and function symbol $\star$ an *arity* $\mathbf{ar}(\star) = n \in \mathbb{N}$ ($\star$ is called n-ary). The function symbols f for which $\mathbf{ar}(f) = 0$ are called *object constants* and we will assume without loss of generality in this paper that every predicate language has at least one object constant. For convenience, we also call predicate symbols P for which $\mathbf{ar}(P) = 0$, *propositional atoms*, and a language $\mathcal{P}$ containing only propositional atoms, *propositional*.

Given a fixed countably infinite set OV of *object variables* $x, y, \ldots$, $\mathcal{P}$-*terms* $s, t, \ldots$, and *(atomic)* $\mathcal{P}$-*formulas* $\varphi, \psi, \chi, \ldots$ are defined as in classical logic using quantifiers $\forall$ and $\exists$, but with binary connectives $\&, \to, \wedge, \vee$, logical constants $\overline{0}, \overline{1}$, and derived connectives $\neg\varphi$ defined as $\varphi \to \overline{0}$ and $\varphi \leftrightarrow \psi$ as $(\varphi \to \psi) \wedge (\psi \to \varphi)$.

The notions of bound and free variables, closed terms, sentences, and substitutability are also defined in the standard way. Instead of $\xi_1, \ldots, \xi_n$ (where

ξ_i's are terms or formulas and n is arbitrary or fixed by the context) we will sometimes write just $\boldsymbol{\xi}$. Unless stated otherwise, by the notation $\varphi(\boldsymbol{z})$ we signify that *all* free variables of φ are among those in the list of pairwise different object variables $\boldsymbol{z}$. If $\varphi(x_1,\ldots,x_n,\boldsymbol{z})$ is a formula and we replace all free occurrences of x_i's in φ by terms t_i, we denote the resulting formula in the context simply by $\varphi(t_1,\ldots,t_n,\boldsymbol{z})$. We write $\chi[\varphi]$ for a formula χ with a distinguished subformula φ and understand $\chi[\psi]$ as the result of replacing φ in χ with the formula ψ. A $\mathcal{P}$-theory T is just a set of $\mathcal{P}$-formulas.

The usual classical notions of structure, evaluation, and truth definition may be generalized relative to a complete FL_e-algebra $\boldsymbol{A}$ as follows, assuming from now on that $\mathbb{K}$ is an arbitrary class of complete FL_e-algebras.[2] As usual for substructural logics, a formula φ will be "true" in a structure based on an FL_e-algebra $\boldsymbol{A}$ if it always takes value greater than or equal to $\overline{1}^{\boldsymbol{A}}$.

Definition 2. *A $\mathcal{P}$-structure $\mathfrak{S} = \langle \boldsymbol{A}, \boldsymbol{S} \rangle$ consists of a complete FL_e-algebra $\boldsymbol{A}$ and a triple $\boldsymbol{S} = \langle S, \langle P^{\boldsymbol{S}} \rangle_{P \in \boldsymbol{P}}, \langle f^{\boldsymbol{S}} \rangle_{f \in \boldsymbol{F}} \rangle$ where S is a non-empty set, $P^{\boldsymbol{S}}$ is a function $S^n \to A$ for each n-ary predicate symbol $P \in \boldsymbol{P}$, and $f^{\boldsymbol{S}} \colon S^n \to S$ is a function for each n-ary function symbol $f \in \boldsymbol{F}$. An $\mathfrak{S}$-evaluation is a mapping $\mathrm{v} \colon OV \to S$. By $\mathrm{v}[x \to a]$ we denote the $\mathfrak{S}$-evaluation where $\mathrm{v}[x \to a](x) = a$ and $\mathrm{v}[x \to a](y) = \mathrm{v}(y)$ for each object variable $y \neq x$.*

We interpret terms and evaluate formulas in $\mathfrak{S}$ as follows:

$$\|x\|_{\mathrm{v}}^{\mathfrak{S}} = \mathrm{v}(x)$$
$$\|f(t_1,\ldots,t_n)\|_{\mathrm{v}}^{\mathfrak{S}} = f^{\boldsymbol{S}}(\|t_1\|_{\mathrm{v}}^{\mathfrak{S}}, \ldots, \|t_n\|_{\mathrm{v}}^{\mathfrak{S}}) \quad \text{for } f \in \boldsymbol{F}$$
$$\|P(t_1,\ldots,t_n)\|_{\mathrm{v}}^{\mathfrak{S}} = P^{\boldsymbol{S}}(\|t_1\|_{\mathrm{v}}^{\mathfrak{S}}, \ldots, \|t_n\|_{\mathrm{v}}^{\mathfrak{S}}) \quad \text{for } P \in \boldsymbol{P}$$
$$\|\varphi \circ \psi\|_{\mathrm{v}}^{\mathfrak{S}} = \|\varphi\|_{\mathrm{v}}^{\mathfrak{S}} \circ^{\boldsymbol{A}} \|\psi\|_{\mathrm{v}}^{\mathfrak{S}} \quad \text{for } \circ \in \{\&, \to, \wedge, \vee\}$$
$$\|c\|_{\mathrm{v}}^{\mathfrak{S}} = c^{\boldsymbol{A}} \quad \text{for } c \in \{\overline{0}, \overline{1}\}$$
$$\|(\forall x)\varphi\|_{\mathrm{v}}^{\mathfrak{S}} = \inf\nolimits_{\leq_{\boldsymbol{A}}} \{\|\varphi\|_{\mathrm{v}[x \to a]}^{\mathfrak{S}} \mid a \in S\}$$
$$\|(\exists x)\varphi\|_{\mathrm{v}}^{\mathfrak{S}} = \sup\nolimits_{\leq_{\boldsymbol{A}}} \{\|\varphi\|_{\mathrm{v}[x \to a]}^{\mathfrak{S}} \mid a \in S\}.$$

A $\mathcal{P}$-structure $\mathfrak{M} = \langle \boldsymbol{A}, \boldsymbol{M} \rangle$ is a $\mathcal{P}$-$\mathbb{K}$-model of a $\mathcal{P}$-theory T, written $\mathfrak{M} \models T$, if $\boldsymbol{A} \in \mathbb{K}$ and for each $\varphi \in T$ and $\mathfrak{M}$-evaluation v, $\|\varphi\|_{\mathrm{v}}^{\mathfrak{M}} \geq \overline{1}^{\boldsymbol{A}}$.

To simplify notation, for a formula $\varphi(x_1,\ldots,x_n)$ and an $\mathfrak{S}$-evaluation v with $\mathrm{v}(x_i) = a_i$, we write $\|\varphi(a_1,\ldots,a_n)\|^{\mathfrak{S}}$ instead of $\|\varphi(x_1,\ldots,x_n)\|_{\mathrm{v}}^{\mathfrak{S}}$. Note that, as

---

[2] First-order logics can be defined based on arbitrary classes of FL_e-algebras by requiring only that necessary suprema and infima exist for a particular structure. Indeed, this more general semantics is needed for certain axiomatization results: e.g., for first-order logics based on the classes of all MV-chains or BL-chains [11,8] (interestingly, axiomatizability is lost if we restrict to complete MV-chains or complete BL-chains). On the other hand, for classes of algebras admitting regular completions (see Example 3), the general definition gives exactly the consequence relation for the complete members of the class, and we can use the mentioned axiomatization results. Moreover, since our Skolemization and Herbrand theorems apply only to these classes, we may simplify our presentation here without limiting its scope.

in classical logic, the truth value of a sentence does not depend on an evaluation. Also, $\mathfrak{M} \models \varphi \to \psi$ iff for each evaluation v, $\|\varphi\|_v^{\mathfrak{M}} \leq \|\psi\|_v^{\mathfrak{M}}$, and $\mathfrak{M} \models \varphi \leftrightarrow \psi$ iff for each evaluation v, $\|\varphi\|_v^{\mathfrak{M}} = \|\psi\|_v^{\mathfrak{M}}$.

Definition 3. *A $\mathcal{P}$-formula φ is a* semantic consequence *of a $\mathcal{P}$-theory T in $\mathbb{K}$, written $T \models_{\mathbb{K}}^{\mathcal{P}} \varphi$, if for each $\mathcal{P}$-$\mathbb{K}$-model $\mathfrak{M}$ of T, also $\mathfrak{M} \models \varphi$.*

Both in the definition of model and semantic consequence, the language plays a minor role. Indeed, for any $\mathcal{P}$-theory $T \cup \{\varphi\}$, $T \models_{\mathbb{K}}^{\mathcal{P}} \varphi$ iff $T \models_{\mathbb{K}}^{\mathcal{P}'} \varphi$ for any $\mathcal{P}' \supseteq \mathcal{P}$. We omit the prefixes for the class $\mathbb{K}$ or language $\mathcal{P}$ when known from the context.

The next lemma collects together some useful facts for FL_e-algebras.

Lemma 1 ([8,15,18]). *Given formulas φ, ψ, χ, a variable x not free in χ, and a term t substitutable for x in φ:*

1. $\models_{\mathbb{K}} (\forall x)\varphi(x) \to \varphi(t)$
2. $\models_{\mathbb{K}} \varphi(t) \to (\exists x)\varphi(x)$
3. $\models_{\mathbb{K}} (\forall x)(\chi \to \varphi) \leftrightarrow (\chi \to (\forall x)\varphi)$
4. $\models_{\mathbb{K}} (\forall x)(\varphi \to \chi) \leftrightarrow ((\exists x)\varphi \to \chi)$
5. $\{\varphi, \varphi \to \psi\} \models_{\mathbb{K}} \psi$
6. $\{\varphi\} \models_{\mathbb{K}} (\forall x)\varphi$
7. $\models_{\mathbb{K}} (\exists x)(\chi \to \varphi) \to (\chi \to (\exists x)\varphi)$
8. $\models_{\mathbb{K}} (\exists x)(\varphi \to \chi) \to ((\forall x)\varphi \to \chi)$
9. $\models_{\mathbb{K}} (\chi \mathbin{\&} (\exists x)\varphi) \leftrightarrow (\exists x)(\chi \mathbin{\&} \varphi)$
10. $\models_{\mathbb{K}} (\chi \mathbin{\&} (\forall x)\varphi) \to (\forall x)(\chi \mathbin{\&} \varphi)$
11. $\models_{\mathbb{K}} (\exists x)(\varphi \vee \psi) \leftrightarrow ((\exists x)\varphi \vee (\exists x)\psi)$
12. $\models_{\mathbb{K}} (\chi \vee (\forall x)\varphi) \to (\forall x)(\chi \vee \varphi)$
13. $\models_{\mathbb{K}} ((\forall x)\varphi \wedge (\forall x)\psi) \leftrightarrow (\forall x)(\varphi \wedge \psi)$
14. $\models_{\mathbb{K}} (\exists x)(\chi \wedge \varphi) \to (\chi \wedge (\exists x)\varphi)$.

Moreover, if $\mathbb{K}$ is a class of complete FL_e-chains:

15. $\models_{\mathbb{K}} (\forall x)(\chi \vee \varphi) \leftrightarrow \chi \vee (\forall x)\varphi$
16. $\models_{\mathbb{K}} (\exists x)(\chi \wedge \varphi) \leftrightarrow \chi \wedge (\exists x)\varphi$.

Notice that certain quantifier shifts (7–14) are available for every choice of $\mathbb{K}$, and two more (15–16) if $\mathbb{K}$ consists of FL_e-chains, but that, in general, the formulas $(\chi \to (\exists x)\varphi) \to (\exists x)(\chi \to \varphi)$, $((\forall x)\varphi \to \chi) \to (\exists x)(\varphi \to \chi)$, and $(\forall x)(\chi \mathbin{\&} \varphi) \to (\chi \mathbin{\&} (\forall x)\varphi)$ (where x is not free in χ) are not valid (see e.g. [8]).

A description of *propositional* substructural logics is implicit in our definitions. Let $\mathcal{P}_0$ be a propositional language (in the sense described above) consisting of countably infinitely many propositional atoms. Then clearly any $\mathcal{P}_0$-formula ψ is equivalent to a quantifier-free formula ψ'; i.e., $\models_{\mathbb{K}} \psi \leftrightarrow \psi'$. Hence we can identify $\models_{\mathbb{K}}^{\mathcal{P}_0}$ with the propositional logic of $\mathbb{K}$. In particular, the propositional logic of all complete FL_e-algebras is the finitely axiomatizable logic FL_e and other well-known propositional substructural logics are axiomatized by adding finitely many additional (propositional) axioms.

Consider a variety $\mathbb{V}$ of FL_e-algebras and suppose that either $\mathbb{V}$ or the class of chains in $\mathbb{V}$ admits regular completions. Let $\mathbb{K}$ be the class of complete members of $\mathbb{V}$ or the class of complete chains of $\mathbb{V}$, respectively. Then the first-order logic $\models_{\mathbb{K}}^{\mathcal{P}}$ is axiomatized by extending an axiomatization of $\models_{\mathbb{K}}^{\mathcal{P}_0}$ (where all propositional atoms are replaced by arbitrary $\mathcal{P}$-formulas) with the deduction rules 5 and 6 of modus ponens and generalization and axioms 1–4 plus axiom 15 if $\mathbb{K}$ consists only of FL_e-chains (see [8]).

3 Skolemization

In this section, we provide two quite general Skolemization theorems for first-order substructural logics. Unlike first-order classical logic, we cannot assume the existence of equivalent prenex formulas or reductions of semantic consequence to satisfiability. We therefore obtain separate Skolemization theorems for formulas of a restricted form on the right and left of the consequence relation, where the latter is established only for certain cases.

Recall that $\mathbb{K}$ is an arbitrary class of complete FL_e-algebras.

Theorem 1 (Skolemization Right). *For each $\mathcal{P}$-theory $T \cup \{\varphi(x, y), \psi\}$ and function symbols $f_\varphi \notin \mathcal{P}$ of the same arity as y:*

$$T \models_\mathbb{K} \psi \to (\exists y)(\forall x)\varphi(x, y) \quad \textit{iff} \quad T \models_\mathbb{K} \psi \to (\exists y)\varphi(f_\varphi(y), y)$$

$$T \models_\mathbb{K} (\forall y)(\exists x)\varphi(x, y) \to \psi \quad \textit{iff} \quad T \models_\mathbb{K} (\forall y)\varphi(f_\varphi(y), y) \to \psi.$$

Proof. The left-to-right directions of both claims are straightforward; just note that $\models_\mathbb{K} (\forall x)\varphi(x, y) \to \varphi(f_\varphi(y), y)$ and $\models_\mathbb{K} \varphi(f_\varphi(y), y) \to (\exists x)\varphi(x, y)$.

We prove the right-to-left directions contrapositively, assuming without loss of generality (see Lemma 1) that $T \cup \{\psi\}$ consists of $\mathcal{P}$-sentences. Let us consider just the first equivalence, the proof of the second being very similar. Suppose that $T \not\models_\mathbb{K} \psi \to (\exists y)(\forall x)\varphi(x, y)$. So there is a model $\mathfrak{M} = \langle A, M \rangle$ of T such that $V = \|(\exists y)(\forall x)\varphi(x, y)\|^\mathfrak{M} \not\geq \|\psi\|^\mathfrak{M}$. I.e., $V < V \vee \|\psi\|^\mathfrak{M}$. Clearly, for each $m \in M$, $\|(\forall x)\varphi(x, m)\| \leq V$. We show that there exists $r \in A$ satisfying $V \leq r < V \vee \|\psi\|^\mathfrak{M}$ such that for each $m \in M$, there is a $d \in M$ satisfying $\|\varphi(d, m)\|^\mathfrak{M} \leq r$. This is obviously the case if there exists $r \in A$ such that $V < r < V \vee \|\psi\|^\mathfrak{M}$. Otherwise, we can take $r = V$: in this case, $\|(\forall x)\varphi(x, m)\| \leq V$ implies that there exists $d \in M$ such that $\|\varphi(d, m)\|^\mathfrak{M} \leq V$. Finally, define (using the axiom of choice) $f_\varphi(m) = d$ with $\|\varphi(d, m)\|^\mathfrak{M} \leq r$ and note that $\|(\exists y)\varphi(f_\varphi(y), y)\|^\mathfrak{M} \leq r < V \vee \|\psi\|^\mathfrak{M}$. Thus $\|(\exists y)\varphi(f_\varphi(y), y)\|^\mathfrak{M} \not\geq \|\psi\|^\mathfrak{M}$. □

Theorem 2 (Skolemization Left). *Suppose that one of the following holds:*

(a) $\mathbb{K}$ *is the class of complete members of a variety of* FL_{ewc}*-algebras (Heyting algebras) admitting regular completions.*

(b) $\mathbb{K}$ *is the class of complete chains of a variety of* FL_e*-algebras whose class of chains admits regular completions.*

(c) $\max\{V \in A \mid V < \overline{1}^A\}$ *exists for all $A \in \mathbb{K}$ (e.g., if each $A \in \mathbb{K}$ is finite).*

(d) $\mathbb{K}$ *consists of the standard Łukasiewicz algebra $[0, 1]_Ł$ (see Example 1).*

Then for each $\mathcal{P}$-theory $T \cup \{\varphi(x, y), \psi\}$ and any function symbol $f_\varphi \notin \mathcal{P}$ of the same arity as y:

$$T \cup \{(\forall y)(\exists x)\varphi(x, y)\} \models_\mathbb{K} \psi \quad \textit{iff} \quad T \cup \{(\forall y)\varphi(f_\varphi(y), y)\} \models_\mathbb{K} \psi.$$

Proof. We consider just the right-to-left direction of the above equivalence. The other direction always holds, using $\models_\mathbb{K} \varphi(f_\varphi(y), y) \to (\exists x)\varphi(x, y)$.

For (a), note first that $\models_\mathbb{K}$ can be axiomatized as an axiomatic extension of first-order intuitionistic logic and therefore admits the deduction theorem. Hence $T \cup \{(\forall \boldsymbol{y})(\exists x)\varphi(x,\boldsymbol{y})\} \models_\mathbb{K} \psi$ implies $T \models_\mathbb{K} (\forall \boldsymbol{y})(\exists x)\varphi(x,\boldsymbol{y}) \to \psi$ and then, by Theorem 1, $T \models_\mathbb{K} (\forall \boldsymbol{y})\varphi(f_\varphi(\boldsymbol{y}),\boldsymbol{y}) \to \psi$. So by the deduction theorem again, $T \cup \{(\forall \boldsymbol{y})\varphi(f_\varphi(\boldsymbol{y}),\boldsymbol{y})\} \models_\mathbb{K} \psi$.

For (b), we apply [8, Theorem 4.5.7] which establishes that the above equivalence holds if it holds in the special case where $\boldsymbol{y}$ is empty. Suppose then that $T \cup \{(\exists x)\varphi(x)\} \models_\mathbb{K} \psi$. By the local deduction theorem for first-order substructural logics (see [15, Theorem 8.9]), $T \models_\mathbb{K} (((\exists x)\varphi(x)) \wedge \overline{1})^n \to \psi$ for some $n \in \mathbb{N}$ (where $\chi^0 = \overline{1}$ and $\chi^{n+1} = \chi^n \mathbin{\&} \chi$ for $n \in \mathbb{N}$). Because $\mathbb{K}$ consists of chains, also $T \models_\mathbb{K} (\exists x)(\varphi(x) \wedge \overline{1})^n \to \psi$ for some $n \in \mathbb{N}$ (see [8, Proposition 4.3.2]). But then, by Theorem 1, $T \models_\mathbb{K} (\varphi(c_\varphi) \wedge \overline{1})^n \to \psi$ for some $n \in \mathbb{N}$ and new constant c_φ. So finally, by the local deduction theorem again, $T \cup \{\varphi(c_\varphi)\} \models_\mathbb{K} \psi$.

For (c) and (d), we prove that the Skolemization property is implied by the following condition: whenever $T \not\models_\mathbb{K} \varphi$, there is a $\mathbb{K}$-model $\mathfrak{M} = \langle \boldsymbol{A}, \boldsymbol{M} \rangle$ of T such that $\mathfrak{M} \not\models \varphi$ and for each formula $(\exists x)\chi(x,\boldsymbol{y})$ and $\boldsymbol{a} \in M$, $\|(\exists x)\chi(x,\boldsymbol{a})\|^\mathfrak{M} \geq \overline{1}^{\boldsymbol{A}}$ implies $\|\chi(w,\boldsymbol{a})\|^\mathfrak{M} \geq \overline{1}^{\boldsymbol{A}}$ for some $w \in M$.

Suppose that $T \cup \{(\forall \boldsymbol{y})(\exists x)\varphi(x,\boldsymbol{y})\} \not\models_\mathbb{K} \psi$. By assumption, there is a model $\mathfrak{M}$ of $T \cup \{(\forall \boldsymbol{y})(\exists x)\varphi(x,\boldsymbol{y})\}$ such that $\mathfrak{M} \not\models \psi$ and for each $\boldsymbol{a} \in M$, since $\|(\exists x)\varphi(x,\boldsymbol{a})\|^\mathfrak{M} \geq \overline{1}$, there is $w \in M$ such that $\|\varphi(w,\boldsymbol{a})\|^\mathfrak{M} \geq \overline{1}$. But then (by the axiom of choice), we can define a function f_φ and expand the model $\mathfrak{M}$ into a model $\mathfrak{M}'$ such that $\|\varphi(f_\varphi(\boldsymbol{a}),\boldsymbol{a})\|^{\mathfrak{M}'} \geq \overline{1}$ and $\|\chi(\boldsymbol{b})\|^\mathfrak{M} = \|\chi(\boldsymbol{b})\|^{\mathfrak{M}'}$ for each $\mathcal{P}$-formula χ and $\boldsymbol{b} \in M$. So $\mathfrak{M}'$ is a model of $T \cup \{(\forall \boldsymbol{y})\varphi(f_\varphi(\boldsymbol{y}),\boldsymbol{y})\}$ and $\mathfrak{M}' \not\models \psi$.

(c) follows almost immediately. For (d), assume that $T \not\models_{[0,1]_Ł} \varphi$ and let $\mathfrak{M}$ be a $[0,1]_Ł$-model of T such that $T \not\models \varphi$. Without loss of generality, we may assume that $T \cup \{\varphi\}$ consists of sentences. Then using [12, Lemma 3] we obtain a $[0,1]_Ł$-model $\mathfrak{M}'$ satisfying: (1) there is an embedding $f \colon [0,1]_Ł \to [0,1]_Ł$ such that for each sentence χ: $f(\|\chi\|^\mathfrak{M}) = \|\chi\|^{\mathfrak{M}'}$; (2) for each formula $\chi(x,\boldsymbol{y})$ and $\boldsymbol{a} \in M'$, there is $w \in M'$ such that $\|(\exists x)\chi(x,\boldsymbol{a})\|^{\mathfrak{M}'} = \|\chi(w,\boldsymbol{a})\|^{\mathfrak{M}'}$. Clearly this is the desired model. □

The Skolemization left property described in Theorem 2 fails for many other choices of $\mathbb{K}$, even when $\boldsymbol{y}$ is empty. For example, let $\mathbb{K}$ be the class of complete FL_e-algebras and consider a language $\mathcal{P}$ with a single unary relation symbol P, extended with a new constant symbol c. Clearly $\{P(c)\} \models_\mathbb{K} P(c) \mathbin{\&} P(c)$, so

$$\{P(c)\} \models_\mathbb{K} (\exists x)(P(x) \mathbin{\&} P(x)).$$

Consider, however, an FL_e-algebra $\boldsymbol{A}$ with $A = \{0, a_1, a_2, 1\}$, $0 < a_1, a_2 < 1$, a_1 and a_2 incomparable, $1 \mathbin{\&} x = x \mathbin{\&} 1 = x$, and $x \mathbin{\&} y = 0$ for $x, y \in \{0, a, b\}$, and let $\mathfrak{M} = \langle \boldsymbol{A}, \boldsymbol{M} \rangle$ be a model with $M = \{d_1, d_2\}$ and $\|P(d_i)\|^\mathfrak{M} = a_i$ for $i = 1, 2$. Then $\mathfrak{M}$ is a model of $(\exists x)P(x)$, but not of $(\exists x)(P(x) \mathbin{\&} P(x))$, so

$$\{(\exists x)P(x)\} \not\models_\mathbb{K} (\exists x)(P(x) \mathbin{\&} P(x)).$$

4 An Expansion Lemma

A standard semantic proof of the Herbrand theorem for first-order classical logic consists of two steps. First it is shown that a universal formula is satisfiable iff the (typically infinite) set of its ground instances is satisfiable. Then by compactness, this set of ground instances is satisfiable iff each of its finite subsets is satisfiable. In this section, we establish an analogue of the first step for all first-order substructural logics considered in this paper: an "expansion lemma" that replaces universally quantified formulas on the left of the consequence relation with their instances. We then extend applications of this lemma to a wider class of semantic consequences.

In first-order classical logic, it can be assumed (using Skolemization and quantifier shifts) that only universal formulas appear on the left and existential formulas on the right of the consequence relation. Indeed we may even consider, using the deduction theorem, only existential formulas on the right, or, using also the double negation law, only universal formulas on the left. In general, for first-order substructural logics, formulas are not equivalent to prenex formulas and the deduction theorem and double negation law fail. Nevertheless, we can establish Herbrand theorems of the same scope using formulas that are *classically* equivalent to universal and existential formulas. Such formulas are defined using BNF as follows, denoting quantifier-free formulas (for a given language) by Δ_0:

g-universal formulas $\quad P ::= \Delta_0 \mid P \wedge P \mid P \vee P \mid P \mathbin{\&} P \mid (\forall x)P \mid N \to P$

g-existential formulas $\quad N ::= \Delta_0 \mid N \wedge N \mid N \vee N \mid N \mathbin{\&} N \mid (\exists x)N \mid P \to N$.

We refer to theories containing only (g-)universal and (g-)existential formulas as (g-)-universal and (g-)existential theories, respectively.

The key ingredient for the expansion lemma is the behaviour of g-universal and g-existential sentences under taking substructures.

Definition 4. *A $\mathcal{P}$-structure $\mathfrak{M}_1 = \langle \mathbf{A}, \mathbf{M}_1 \rangle$ is a substructure of a $\mathcal{P}$-structure $\mathfrak{M}_2 = \langle \mathbf{A}, \mathbf{M}_2 \rangle$ if $M_1 \subseteq M_2$ and $*^{\mathfrak{M}_1}(\mathbf{a}) = *^{\mathfrak{M}_2}(\mathbf{a})$ for each predicate and function symbol $*$ of $\mathcal{P}$ and each $\mathbf{a} \in M_1$.*

Proposition 1. *For any substructure $\mathfrak{M}'$ of a $\mathcal{P}$-structure $\mathfrak{M}$:*

1. *$\mathfrak{M} \models \varphi$ iff $\mathfrak{M}' \models \varphi$ whenever φ is a quantifier-free $\mathcal{P}$-sentence.*
2. *$\mathfrak{M} \models \varphi$ implies $\mathfrak{M}' \models \varphi$ whenever φ is a g-universal $\mathcal{P}$-formula.*
3. *$\mathfrak{M}' \models \varphi$ implies $\mathfrak{M} \models \varphi$ whenever φ is g-existential $\mathcal{P}$-formula.*

Proof. The proposition is an easy corollary of the following two claims, proved jointly for any $\mathfrak{M}'$-evaluation e by induction on the definition of χ:

(i) $\|\chi\|_e^{\mathfrak{M}'} \geq \|\chi\|_e^{\mathfrak{M}}$ for any g-universal $\mathcal{P}$-formula χ

(ii) $\|\chi\|_e^{\mathfrak{M}'} \leq \|\chi\|_e^{\mathfrak{M}}$ for any g-existential $\mathcal{P}$-formula χ.

If χ is quantifier-free, then clearly $\|\chi\|_e^{\mathfrak{M}'} = \|\chi\|_e^{\mathfrak{M}}$. For the induction step we prove two cases, other cases being very similar. If $\chi = (\forall x)\varphi$ for some g-universal formula φ, then for each $a \in M$:

$$\|\varphi\|_{e[x\to a]}^{\mathfrak{M}'} \geq \|\varphi\|_{e[x\to a]}^{\mathfrak{M}} \geq \inf\{\|\varphi\|_{e[x\to b]}^{\mathfrak{M}} \mid b \in M\} = \|(\forall x)\varphi\|_e^{\mathfrak{M}}.$$

Thus also

$$\|(\forall x)\varphi\|_e^{\mathfrak{M}} \leq \inf\{\|\varphi\|_{e[x\to a]}^{\mathfrak{M}'} \mid a \in M'\} = \|(\forall x)\varphi\|_e^{\mathfrak{M}'}.$$

If $\chi = \varphi \to \psi$ for some g-existential formula φ and g-universal formula ψ, then by the induction hypothesis:

$$\|\varphi\|_e^{\mathfrak{M}'} \leq \|\varphi\|_e^{\mathfrak{M}} \quad \text{and} \quad \|\psi\|_e^{\mathfrak{M}'} \geq \|\psi\|_e^{\mathfrak{M}}.$$

So by the monotonicity of the operations and the definition of truth:

$$\|\varphi \to \psi\|_e^{\mathfrak{M}} = \|\varphi\|_e^{\mathfrak{M}} \to \|\psi\|_e^{\mathfrak{M}} \leq \|\varphi\|_e^{\mathfrak{M}'} \to \|\psi\|_e^{\mathfrak{M}}$$
$$\leq \|\varphi\|_e^{\mathfrak{M}'} \to \|\psi\|_e^{\mathfrak{M}'}$$
$$= \|\varphi \to \psi\|_e^{\mathfrak{M}'}. \qquad \square$$

For any predicate language $\mathcal{P}$, the *Herbrand universe* $\mathcal{U}(\mathcal{P})$ is the set of closed $\mathcal{P}$-terms, recalling that, by assumption, every predicate language contains at least one object constant and hence $\mathcal{U}(\mathcal{P}) \neq \emptyset$.

Lemma 2 (Expansion Lemma). *For each g-existential $\mathcal{P}$-formula ψ and each g-universal $\mathcal{P}$-theory $T \cup R$:*

$$T \cup \{(\forall \boldsymbol{x})\varphi(\boldsymbol{x}) \mid \varphi(\boldsymbol{x}) \in R\} \models_{\mathbb{K}} \psi \quad \text{iff} \quad T \cup \{\varphi(\boldsymbol{t}) \mid \varphi(\boldsymbol{x}) \in R, \boldsymbol{t} \in \mathcal{U}(\mathcal{P})\} \models_{\mathbb{K}} \psi.$$

Proof. The right-to-left direction is straightforward since $\models_{\mathbb{K}} (\forall \boldsymbol{x})\varphi(\boldsymbol{x}) \to \varphi(\boldsymbol{t})$. We prove the converse direction contrapositively. Let $S = T \cup \{\varphi(\boldsymbol{t}) \mid \varphi(\boldsymbol{x}) \in R, \boldsymbol{t} \in \mathcal{U}(\mathcal{P})\}$ and suppose that there is a model $\mathfrak{M} = \langle \boldsymbol{A}, \mathbf{M} \rangle$ of S such that $\mathfrak{M} \not\models \psi$. Consider the substructure $\mathfrak{M}' = \langle \boldsymbol{A}, \mathbf{M}' \rangle$ with domain $M' = \{\|t\|^{\mathfrak{M}} \mid t \in \mathcal{U}(\mathcal{P})\}$. Then by Proposition 1, $\mathfrak{M}'$ is a model of S such that $\mathfrak{M}' \not\models \psi$. Consider $\varphi(\boldsymbol{x}) \in R$. For each $\boldsymbol{b} \in M'$ there is $\boldsymbol{t} \in \mathcal{U}(\mathcal{P})$ such that $\boldsymbol{b} = \boldsymbol{t}^{\mathfrak{M}}$ and we have $\mathfrak{M}' \models \varphi(\boldsymbol{t})$. So $\mathfrak{M}' \models (\forall \boldsymbol{x})\varphi_i$. Hence $T \cup \{(\forall \boldsymbol{x})\varphi(\boldsymbol{x}) \mid \varphi(\boldsymbol{x}) \in R\} \not\models_{\mathbb{K}} \psi$. $\square$

In the remainder of this section, we show that the expansion lemma applies to a wider class of consequences. We show (in Corollary 1 and Lemma 5) that although g-universal and g-existential formulas are not equivalent to universal and existential formulas, checking semantic consequence between g-universal formulas on the left and g-existential formulas on the right may be reduced to checking semantic consequence between universal formulas on the left and existential formulas on the right. To prove this we first state two technical lemmata: one concerning montonicity properties for g-universal and g-existential formulas and the other concerning predicate substitutions.

Lemma 3.

1. $\{\varphi \to \psi\} \models_\mathbb{K} \chi[\varphi] \to \chi[\psi]$ for any g-universal formula $\chi[(\forall x)\alpha]$.
2. $\{\varphi \to \psi\} \models_\mathbb{K} \chi[\psi] \to \chi[\varphi]$ for any g-existential formula $\chi[(\forall x)\alpha]$.
3. $\{\varphi \to \psi\} \models_\mathbb{K} \chi[\psi] \to \chi[\varphi]$ for any g-universal formula $\chi[(\exists x)\alpha]$.
4. $\{\varphi \to \psi\} \models_\mathbb{K} \chi[\varphi] \to \chi[\psi]$ for any g-existential formula $\chi[(\exists x)\alpha]$.

Proof. We prove 1 and 2 together by induction on the definition of the g-universal or g-existential formula $\chi[(\forall x)\alpha]$; the proofs of 3 and 4 are analogous. The base case where $\chi = (\forall x)\alpha$ or $(\forall x)\alpha$ does not occur in χ is immediate (note that the first option could not happen in case 2). For the induction step, we have one of the following cases:

- $\chi = \chi_1[(\forall x)\alpha] \circ \chi_2$ or $\chi = \chi_1 \circ \chi_2[(\forall x)\alpha]$ for $\circ \in \{\wedge, \vee, \&\}$.
- $\chi = \chi_1[(\forall x)\alpha] \to \chi_2$ or $\chi = \chi_1 \to \chi_2[(\forall x)\alpha]$.
- $\chi = (\forall y)\chi_1[(\forall x)\alpha]$ or $\chi = (\exists y)\chi_1[(\forall x)\alpha]$.

In the first two cases we use the induction hypothesis and derivability of useful consequences. For example, suppose that $\chi = \chi_1[(\forall x)\alpha] \to \chi_2$. If χ is a g-universal formula, then $\chi_1[(\forall x)\alpha]$ is a g-existential formula and by the induction hypothesis $\{\varphi \to \psi\} \models_\mathbb{K} \chi_1[\psi] \to \chi_1[\varphi]$ and so

$$\{\varphi \to \psi\} \models_\mathbb{K} (\chi_1[\varphi] \to \chi_2) \to (\chi_1[\psi] \to \chi_2).$$

If χ is a g-existential formula, then $\chi_1[(\forall x)\alpha]$ is a g-universal formula and by the induction hypothesis: $\{\varphi \to \psi\} \models_\mathbb{K} \chi_1[\varphi] \to \chi_1[\psi]$ and so

$$\{\varphi \to \psi\} \models_\mathbb{K} (\chi_1[\psi] \to \chi_2) \to (\chi_1[\varphi] \to \chi_2).$$

For the last case, suppose that $\chi = (\forall y)\chi_1[(\forall x)\alpha]$. By the induction hypothesis

$$\{\varphi \to \psi\} \models_\mathbb{K} \chi_1[\varphi] \to \chi_1[\psi]$$

and the result follows using properties of $\models_\mathbb{K}$ given in Lemma 1. □

Lemma 4. *A predicate substitution σ is any mapping assigning to each n-ary predicate symbol $P \in \mathcal{P}$ a $\mathcal{P}$-formula $\sigma(P)$ of n free variables. The substitution is extended to arbitrary $\mathcal{P}$-formulas by substituting each atomic predicate $P(\mathbf{t})$ with a $\mathcal{P}$-formula $\sigma(P)(\mathbf{t})$. Then for any $\mathcal{P}$-theory $T \cup \{\varphi\}$:*

$$T \models_\mathbb{K} \varphi \quad \text{implies} \quad \sigma[T] \models_\mathbb{K} \sigma(\varphi).$$

Moreover, the converse direction holds when the only predicates in $T \cup \{\varphi\}$ are propositional atoms and σ restricted to the set of propositional atoms is a one-one mapping into the set of closed atomic formulas.

Proof. We proceed by contraposition. If $\sigma[T] \not\models_\mathbb{K} \sigma(\varphi)$, then there is a model $\mathfrak{M}'$ with of $\sigma[T]$ such that $\mathfrak{M}' \not\models \sigma(\varphi)$. We construct a model $\mathfrak{M}$ with the same domain as $\mathfrak{M}'$ where $f^\mathfrak{M} = f^{\mathfrak{M}'}$ and $P^\mathfrak{M}(\boldsymbol{a}) = \|\sigma(P)(\boldsymbol{a})\|^{\mathfrak{M}'}$. Thus for every formula ψ we can easily show by induction:

$$\|\psi(\boldsymbol{a})\|^\mathfrak{M} = \|\sigma(\psi)(\boldsymbol{a})\|^{\mathfrak{M}'}.$$

Then $\mathfrak{M}$ is indeed a model of T such that $\mathfrak{M}' \not\models \varphi$.

For the converse direction, we can assume without loss of generality that there are no quantifiers in $T \cup \{\varphi\}$. Assume further that we have a model $\mathfrak{M} = \langle \boldsymbol{A}, \mathbf{M} \rangle$ of T such that $\mathfrak{M} \not\models \varphi$. We define a model $\mathfrak{M}' = \langle \boldsymbol{A}, \mathbf{M}' \rangle$ with the domain consisting of closed terms, functional symbols interpreted in the obvious way, and predicate symbols interpreted by:

$$P^{\mathfrak{M}'}(\boldsymbol{t}) = \begin{cases} \|P\|^\mathfrak{M} & \text{if there is some prop. atom } P \in \mathcal{P} \text{ such that } \sigma P = P(\boldsymbol{t}) \\ \overline{1}^{\boldsymbol{A}} & \text{otherwise.} \end{cases}$$

Note that the definition is sound because σ is a one-one mapping. To complete the proof we observe that for each $\chi \in T \cup \{\varphi\}$, we have $\|\sigma\chi\|^{\mathfrak{M}'} = \|\chi\|^\mathfrak{M}$. □

Corollary 1. *Let T be a $\mathcal{P}$-theory, φ a $\mathcal{P}$-sentence, and $P \notin \mathcal{P}$. Then*

$$T \models_\mathbb{K} \varphi \quad \text{iff} \quad T \cup \{\varphi \to P\} \models_\mathbb{K} P.$$

Proof. Immediate, using the previous lemma for the right-to-left direction and the soundness of modus ponens for the left-to-right direction. □

Lemma 5. *For any g-universal formula φ, there is a finite set $F(\varphi)$ of universal sentences such that for each theory $T \cup \{\chi\}$:*

$$T \cup \{\varphi\} \models_\mathbb{K} \chi \quad \text{iff} \quad T \cup F(\varphi) \models_\mathbb{K} \chi.$$

Proof. We prove the claim by induction on the number of quantifiers in φ. The base case, where φ is already a universal formula, is immediate; we just let $F(\varphi)$ consist of the universal closure of φ. Suppose that φ has a proper universal subformula; i.e., $\varphi = \varphi[(\forall \boldsymbol{x})\psi(\boldsymbol{x}, \boldsymbol{y})]$ for some quantifier-free formula $\psi(\boldsymbol{x}, \boldsymbol{y})$. Given a new predicate symbol P_ψ of an appropriate arity (the length of $\boldsymbol{y}$), it suffice to show that

$$T \cup \{\varphi\} \models_\mathbb{K} \chi \quad \text{iff} \quad T \cup \{(\forall \boldsymbol{x})(\forall \boldsymbol{y})(P_\psi(\boldsymbol{y}) \to \psi(\boldsymbol{x}, \boldsymbol{y})), \varphi[P_\psi(\boldsymbol{y})]\} \models_\mathbb{K} \chi,$$

since then we can apply the induction hypothesis. The left-to-right direction follows using Lemma 3 to obtain $\{P_\psi(\boldsymbol{y}) \to (\forall \boldsymbol{x})\psi(\boldsymbol{x}, \boldsymbol{y})\} \models_\mathbb{K} \varphi[P_\psi(\boldsymbol{y})] \to \varphi$ and then Lemma 1. The converse direction follows from Lemma 4 using a substitution σ that is the identity except for $\sigma(P_\psi) = (\forall \boldsymbol{x})\psi(\boldsymbol{x}, \boldsymbol{y})$. The case where φ has an existential subformula is very similar. □

5 Herbrand Theorems

The expansion lemma reduces semantic consequence involving certain first-order formulas to propositional consequence. To obtain Herbrand theorems involving finite sets of formulas, we require a further crucial ingredient. Let us say that $\mathbb{K}$ is *finitary* if for each *propositional* language $\mathcal{P}$ and $\mathcal{P}$-theory $T \cup \{\varphi\}$:

$$T \models_{\mathbb{K}}^{\mathcal{P}} \varphi \quad \text{iff} \quad \text{there is a finite } T' \subseteq T \text{ such that } T' \models_{\mathbb{K}}^{\mathcal{P}} \varphi.$$

In particular, any class $\mathbb{K}$ satisfying one of the following conditions is finitary (this follows from the fact that in these cases there is a finitary axiomatization of $\models_{\mathbb{K}}^{\mathcal{P}}$ for every propositional language $\mathcal{P}$; see the end of Section 2):

- The class of complete algebras of a variety admitting regular completions; this is the case, e.g., if the variety is axiomatized relative to the class of FL_e by so-called N_2 identities (see [6]).
- The class of complete chains of a variety whose class of chains admits regular completions; this is the case, e.g., if the variety is axiomatized relative to the class of FL_{ew} by so-called P_3 identities.
- A finite class of finite algebras.

The next lemma shows that finitarity at the propositional level extends to a more general first-order setting (even without axiomatization results).

Lemma 6. *If $\mathbb{K}$ is finitary, then for each g-universal $\mathcal{P}$-theory T and g-existential $\mathcal{P}$-formula χ:*

$$T \models_{\mathbb{K}} \chi \quad \text{iff} \quad \text{there is a finite } T' \subseteq T \text{ such that } T' \models_{\mathbb{K}} \chi.$$

Proof. Note that we may assume without loss of generality that $T \cup \{\chi\}$ consists of sentences. We show first that it is sufficient to give the proof for the case where χ is a propositional atom. If $T \models_{\mathbb{K}} \chi$, then by Corollary 1, $T \cup \{\chi \to P\} \models_{\mathbb{K}} P$ for some new propositional atom P. But then if $T' \cup \{\chi \to P\} \models_{\mathbb{K}} P$ for some finite $T' \subseteq T$, by Corollary 1 again, $T' \models_{\mathbb{K}} \chi$.

Suppose now that $T \models_{\mathbb{K}} P$. Using Lemma 5, we obtain for each $\varphi \in T$, a finite universal theory $F(\varphi)$ such that

$$\bigcup_{\varphi \in T} F(\varphi) \models_{\mathbb{K}} P.$$

Using Lemma 2 we obtain

$$\bigcup_{\varphi \in T} \{\psi(\boldsymbol{t}) \mid (\forall \boldsymbol{x})\psi(\boldsymbol{x}) \in F(\varphi) \text{ and } \boldsymbol{t} \in \mathcal{U}(\mathcal{P})\} \models_{\mathbb{K}} P.$$

All the formulas in this semantic consequence are quantifier-free sentences. Hence using Lemma 4 and the finitarity of $\mathbb{K}$, for some finite $T' \subseteq T$

$$\bigcup_{\varphi \in T'} \{\psi(\boldsymbol{t}) \mid (\forall \boldsymbol{x})\psi(\boldsymbol{x}) \in F(\varphi) \text{ and } \boldsymbol{t} \in \mathcal{U}(\mathcal{P})\} \models_{\mathbb{K}} P.$$

But then by Lemma 2, $\bigcup_{\varphi \in T'} F(\varphi) \models_{\mathbb{K}} P$, and Lemma 5 completes the proof. □

Now putting together the expansion lemma and Lemma 6, we obtain:

Corollary 2. *If $\mathbb{K}$ is finitary, then for each g-universal $\mathcal{P}$-theory $T\cup\{(\forall \boldsymbol{x})\varphi(\boldsymbol{x})\}$ and g-existential $\mathcal{P}$-formula ψ:*

$$T\cup\{(\forall \boldsymbol{x})\varphi(\boldsymbol{x})\} \models_{\mathbb{K}} \psi \quad \text{iff} \quad T\cup\{\varphi(\boldsymbol{t}) \mid \boldsymbol{t} \in H\} \models_{\mathbb{K}} \psi \text{ for some finite } H \subseteq \mathcal{U}(\mathcal{P}).$$

We now extend Corollary 2 to obtain Herbrand theorems on both sides of the consequence relation with g-universal formulas on the left and a g-existential formula on the right. The $\mathcal{P}$-Herbrand expansion $E(\varphi)$ of a $\mathcal{P}$-formula φ consists of all formulas obtained by applying the following two steps repeatedly, starting with φ, until no quantifiers remain:

I Replace $\psi[(\forall \boldsymbol{x})\chi(\boldsymbol{x}, \boldsymbol{y})]$ where χ is quantifier-free with $\psi[\bigwedge_{\boldsymbol{t} \in H} \chi(\boldsymbol{t}, \boldsymbol{y})]$ for some finite $H \subseteq \mathcal{U}(\mathcal{P})$.

II Replace $\psi[(\exists \boldsymbol{x})\chi(\boldsymbol{x}, \boldsymbol{y})]$ where χ is quantifier-free with $\psi[\bigvee_{\boldsymbol{t} \in H} \chi(\boldsymbol{t}, \boldsymbol{y})]$ for some finite $H \subseteq \mathcal{U}(\mathcal{P})$.

Notice that if φ is a sentence, then so are all formulas in $E(\varphi)$. Moreover, a simple induction making use of Lemma 3 together with $\models_{\mathbb{K}} (\forall \boldsymbol{x})\chi(\boldsymbol{x}, \boldsymbol{y}) \to \bigwedge_{\boldsymbol{t} \in H} \chi(\boldsymbol{t}, \boldsymbol{y})$ and $\models_{\mathbb{K}} \bigvee_{\boldsymbol{t} \in H} \chi(\boldsymbol{t}, \boldsymbol{y}) \to (\exists \boldsymbol{x})\chi(\boldsymbol{x}, \boldsymbol{y})$ establishes:

Lemma 7. *Let φ be a $\mathcal{P}$-formula and $\varphi' \in E(\varphi)$. Then $\models_{\mathbb{K}} \varphi \to \varphi'$ if φ is g-universal, and $\models_{\mathbb{K}} \varphi' \to \varphi$ if φ is g-existential.*

We are now able to establish Herbrand theorems for the left and right sides of the consequence relation, obtaining an equivalence for the left side.

Theorem 3 (Herbrand Left). *The following are equivalent:*

(1) $\mathbb{K}$ *is finitary.*

(2) *For every g-universal theory $T \cup \{\varphi\}$ and g-existential $\mathcal{P}$-formula χ:*

$$T \cup \{\varphi\} \models_{\mathbb{K}} \chi \quad \text{iff} \quad \text{there exists } \varphi' \in E(\varphi) \text{ such that } T \cup \{\varphi'\} \models_{\mathbb{K}} \chi.$$

Proof. (1) $\Rightarrow$ (2) The right-to-left direction follows directly using Lemma 7. For the left-to-right direction, it is sufficient to use Lemma 5 to obtain a finite set of universal formulas $F(\varphi)$ and then apply Corollary 2. However, to see that we obtain exactly the formulas we need, we consider again the induction step of the proof of Lemma 5.

Recall that we proceed by induction on the number of quantifiers in φ. For the induction step, we suppose that φ has a proper universal subformula $(\forall \boldsymbol{x})\psi(\boldsymbol{x}, \boldsymbol{y})$ i.e., $\varphi = \varphi[(\forall \boldsymbol{x})\psi(\boldsymbol{x}, \boldsymbol{y})]$ (if it has no such subformula, then φ has an existential subformula $(\exists \boldsymbol{x})\psi(\boldsymbol{x}, \boldsymbol{y})$ and the proof is analogous). Recall that a new predicate symbol P_ψ of an appropriate arity (the length of $\boldsymbol{y}$) is introduced such that

$$T \cup \{\varphi[P_\psi(\boldsymbol{y})]\} \cup \{(\forall \boldsymbol{x})(\forall \boldsymbol{y})(P_\psi(\boldsymbol{y}) \to \psi(\boldsymbol{x}, \boldsymbol{y}))\} \models_{\mathbb{K}} \chi.$$

Now we can use Corollary 2 for $T \cup \{\varphi[P_\psi(\boldsymbol{y})]\}$ and $(\forall \boldsymbol{x})(\forall \boldsymbol{y})(P_\psi(\boldsymbol{y}) \to \psi(\boldsymbol{x}, \boldsymbol{y}))$ to obtain a finite $H \subseteq \mathcal{U}(\mathcal{P})$ such that

$$T \cup \{\varphi[P_\psi(\boldsymbol{y})]\} \cup \{(\forall \boldsymbol{y})(P_\psi(\boldsymbol{y}) \to \psi(\boldsymbol{t}, \boldsymbol{y})) \mid \boldsymbol{t} \in H\} \models_\mathbb{K} \chi.$$

So also using the properties of $\wedge$:

$$T \cup \{\varphi[P_\psi(\boldsymbol{y})], (\forall \boldsymbol{y})(P_\psi(\boldsymbol{y}) \to \bigwedge_{\boldsymbol{t} \in H} \psi(\boldsymbol{t}, \boldsymbol{y}))\} \models_\mathbb{K} \chi.$$

By Lemma 4, using a substitution σ that satisfies $\sigma(P_\psi) = \bigwedge_{\boldsymbol{t} \in H} \psi(\boldsymbol{t}, \boldsymbol{y})$ and is the identity otherwise:

$$T \cup \{\sigma(\varphi[P_\psi(\boldsymbol{y})])\} \models_\mathbb{K} \chi.$$

To complete the proof, note that the induction hypothesis can be applied to $\sigma(\varphi[P_\psi(\boldsymbol{y})]) = \varphi[\bigwedge_{\boldsymbol{t} \in H} \psi(\boldsymbol{t}, \boldsymbol{y})]$. Crucially, by repeating this process until we obtain a quantifier-free formula, we obtain the appropriate element of $E(\varphi)$.

(2) $\Rightarrow$ (1) Let $\mathcal{P}_0$ be a propositional language and $\mathcal{P}$ a predicate language with a unary predicate symbol P such that $\mathcal{U}(\mathcal{P})$ is countably infinite. We enumerate the elements of $\mathcal{U}(\mathcal{P})$ as t_i ($n \in \mathbb{N}$), and the elements of $\mathcal{P}_0$ as P_i (without loss of generality we can assume that $\mathcal{P}_0$ is also infinite). Let $\{\varphi_i \mid i \in \mathbb{N}\} \cup \{\psi\}$ be a set of propositional formulas such that

$$\{\varphi_i \mid i \in \mathbb{N}\} \models_\mathbb{K}^{\mathcal{P}_0} \psi.$$

Then because $\{(\forall x)P(x), P(t_i) \to \varphi_i\} \models_\mathbb{K} \varphi_i$, we obtain

$$\{(\forall x)P(x)\} \cup \{P(t_i) \to \varphi_i \mid i \in \mathbb{N}\} \models_\mathbb{K} \psi.$$

Then by (2), without loss of generality, we obtain for some $n \in \mathbb{N}$:

$$\{\bigwedge_{i \leq n} P(t_i)\} \cup \{P(t_i) \to \varphi_i \mid i \in \mathbb{N}\} \models_\mathbb{K} \psi.$$

We define a $\mathcal{P}_0 \cup \mathcal{P}$-substitution σ that satisfies $\sigma P_{2k} = P(t_k)$ and $\sigma P_{2k+1} = P_k$ and is the identity otherwise, and, using the second part of Lemma 4, obtain

$$\{\bigwedge_{i \leq n} P_{2i}\} \cup \{P_{2i} \to \bar{\varphi}_i \mid i \leq n\} \models_\mathbb{K} \psi,$$

where $\bar{\varphi}_i$ is the formula resulting from φ_i by replacing propositional atoms P_k by P_{2k+1}. Finally, we use the first part of Lemma 4 and the substitution $\sigma P_{2k} = \varphi_k$ and $\sigma P_{2k+1} = P_k$ to obtain $\{\varphi_i \mid i \leq n\} \models_\mathbb{K} \psi$. Hence $\{\varphi_i \mid i \leq n\} \models_\mathbb{K}^{\mathcal{P}_0} \psi$. □

Theorem 4 (Herbrand Right). *If $\mathbb{K}$ is finitary, then for every g-universal $\mathcal{P}$-theory T and g-existential $\mathcal{P}$-formula ψ:*

$$T \models_\mathbb{K} \psi \quad \text{iff} \quad \text{there is } \psi' \in E(\psi) \text{ such that } T \models_\mathbb{K} \psi'.$$

Proof. The left-to-right direction follows directly using Lemma 7. For the right-to-left direction, we use Corollary 1 to obtain $T \cup \{\psi \to P\} \models_\mathbb{K} P$ (for a new propositional atom P). Using Theorem 3, we obtain $\psi' \in E(\psi)$ such that $T \cup \{\psi' \to P\} \models_\mathbb{K} P$, and we use Corollary 1 again to complete the proof. □

We show finally that finitarity and the Herbrand theorems fail for any logic admitting quantifier shifts that is defined by a class of FL_e-algebras with arbitrarily large chains (for example, logics based on classes of finite FL_e-algebras containing chains of increasing size).

Proposition 2. *Suppose that:*

(a) $\{(\forall x)\varphi \to \psi\} \models_\mathbb{K} (\exists x)(\varphi \to \psi)$ *where x is not free in ψ.*
(b) *For each $n \in \mathbb{N}$, there is an FL_e-chain $\boldsymbol{A} \in \mathbb{K}$ such that $|A| \geq n$.*

Then $\mathbb{K}$ is not finitary and $\models_\mathbb{K}$ does not admit the left or right Herbrand theorem.

Proof. Consider a language with a unary predicate symbol P and a constant symbol c. Since $\models_\mathbb{K} (\forall x)P(x) \to (\forall y)P(y)$, by (a) and Lemma 1, also $\models_\mathbb{K} (\exists x)(\forall y)(P(x) \to P(y))$. So by Theorem 2, $\models_\mathbb{K} (\exists x)(P(x) \to P(f(x)))$. Suppose that the right Herband theorem holds, noting that this is implied by the left Herbrand theorem or finitarity. Then we have $\models_\mathbb{K} \bigvee_{i \leq n}(P(f^i(c)) \to P(f^{i+1}(c)))$ for some $n \in \mathbb{N}$. Consider, however, a model $\mathfrak{M}$ over the chain $\boldsymbol{A}$ with a descending sequence of elements $a_1, \ldots, a_{n+1}$ whose domain is the Herbrand universe and predicate P defined such that $P^\mathfrak{M}(f^i(c)) = a_i$ for $i \leq n+1$ and $P^\mathfrak{M}(t) = a_1$ otherwise. Then $\|P(f^i(c)) \to P(f^{i+1}(c))\|^\mathfrak{M} = a_i \to a_{i+1} < \bar{1}^{\boldsymbol{A}}$ and so $\mathfrak{M} \not\models \bigvee_{i \leq n}(P(f^i(c)) \to P(f^{i+1}(c)))$, a contradiction. □

6 A Herbrand Theorem for Satisfiability

The Herbrand theorem for first-order classical logic may be stated in terms of satisfiability rather than semantic consequence. As remarked already, this is not generally the case for first-order substructural logics. Indeed there are cases where $\mathbb{K}$ is not finitary and the left and right Herbrand theorems fail, but a Herbrand theorem for satisfiability holds.

A $\mathcal{P}$-theory T is $\mathbb{K}$-*satisfiable* if it has a $\mathcal{P}$-$\mathbb{K}$-model. Let us say that $\mathbb{K}$ is *compact* if for each propositional language $\mathcal{P}$: a $\mathcal{P}$-theory T is $\mathbb{K}$-satisfiable iff each finite $T' \subseteq T$ is $\mathbb{K}$-satisfiable. Then by adjusting the proof of Theorem 3 (and corresponding necessary lemmata) to deal with satisfiability rather than consequence and using compactness rather than finitarity, we obtain:

Theorem 5. *If $\mathbb{K}$ is compact, then for every g-universal theory $T \cup \{\varphi\}$:*

$T \cup \{\varphi\}$ *is $\mathbb{K}$-satisfiable iff $T \cup \{\varphi'\}$ is $\mathbb{K}$-satisfiable for every $\varphi' \in E(\varphi)$.*

For example, the classes consisting of just the standard algebra of Łukasiewicz logic or product logic (see Example 1) are compact but not finitary. For product logic, satisfiability coincides with classical satisfiability. For Łukasiewicz logic, compactness is proved in [11, Theorem 5.4.24] and the failure of finitarity is folklore, see e.g. [11, Remark 3.2.15]. Indeed, the failure of finitarity and the left and right Herbrand theorems for this logic also follow from Proposition 2.

We show that the previous theorem can be used to obtain a new topology-free proof of an "approximate" Herbrand theorem treated in a slightly weaker form in [4]. First we introduce a useful notion of approximate validity for $[0,1]_Ł$, defining for each $r \in [0,1] \cap \mathbb{Q}$:

$$T \models_Ł r < \psi \quad \text{iff} \quad \text{for every } [0,1]_Ł\text{-model } \mathfrak{M} \text{ of } T, r < \|\psi\|^\mathfrak{M}.$$

Lemma 8. *For any $r \in [0,1] \cap \mathbb{Q}$, there exists a quantifier-free formula χ_r^P containing just one propositional atom P such that for any theory $T \cup \{\psi\}$ in which P does not occur:*

$$T \models_Ł r < \psi \quad \text{iff} \quad T \cup \{\psi \to \chi_r^P\} \text{ is } [0,1]_Ł\text{-unsatisfiable.}$$

In particular, let $r = \frac{n}{n+1}$ for $n \in \mathbb{N}$. Then $\chi_r^P = (P \wedge \neg P^n)$ has this property.

Proof. By McNaughton's theorem [13], for each $r \in [0,1] \cap \mathbb{Q}$, there is a propositional formula χ_r of one variable p such that $\chi_r(\frac{1}{2}) = r$ and $\chi_r(d) \leq r$ for all $d \in [0,1]$. We define χ_r^P to be the result of replacing p with a nullary predicate symbol P in χ_r. To prove the above claim, we proceed contrapositively. Suppose that $T \not\models_Ł r < \psi$. Then there is a $[0,1]_Ł$-model $\mathfrak{M}$ of T such that $\|\psi\|^\mathfrak{M} \leq r$. Expand this model by setting $\|P\|^\mathfrak{M} = \frac{1}{2}$ and we obtain a $[0,1]_Ł$-model of $\psi \to \chi_r^P$. I.e., $T \cup \{\psi \to \chi_r^P\}$ is $[0,1]_Ł$-satisfiable. Conversely, suppose that $\mathfrak{M}$ is a $[0,1]_Ł$-model of $T \cup \{\psi \to \chi_r^P\}$. Then $\|\psi\|^\mathfrak{M} \leq \|\chi_r^P\|^\mathfrak{M} \leq r$ as required. □

It follows that the approximate consequence relation for $r \in [0,1] \cap \mathbb{N}$ can be defined in terms of the standard consequence relation $\models_{[0,1]_Ł}$.

The following proposition and approximate Herbrand theorem for Łukasiewicz logic are now immediate consequences of Lemma 8 and Theorem 5.

Proposition 3. *For each g-universal theory $T \cup \{\varphi\}$, g-existential formula ψ, and $r \in [0,1] \cap \mathbb{Q}$:*

$$T \models_Ł r < \psi \quad \text{iff} \quad T \models_Ł r < \psi' \text{ for some } \psi' \in E(\psi)$$
$$T \cup \{\varphi\} \models_Ł r < \psi \quad \text{iff} \quad T \cup \{\varphi'\} \models_Ł r < \psi \text{ for some } \varphi' \in E(\varphi).$$

Theorem 6. *For each g-universal theory $T \cup \{\varphi\}$ and g-existential formula ψ:*

$$T \models_{[0,1]_Ł} \psi \quad \text{iff for all } n \in \mathbb{N},\ T \models_Ł \tfrac{n}{n+1} < \psi' \text{ for some } \psi' \in E(\psi)$$
$$T \cup \{\varphi\} \models_{[0,1]_Ł} \psi \quad \text{iff for all } n \in \mathbb{N},\ T \cup \{\varphi'\} \models_Ł \tfrac{n}{n+1} < \psi \text{ for some } \varphi' \in E(\varphi).$$

References

1. Baaz, M., Ciabattoni, A., Fermüller, C.: Herbrand theorem for prenex Gödel logic and its consequences for theorem proving. In: Nieuwenhuis, R., Voronkov, A. (eds.) LPAR 2001. LNCS (LNAI), vol. 2250, pp. 201–216. Springer, Heidelberg (2001)

2. Baaz, M., Iemhoff, R.: On Skolemization in constructive theories. Journal of Symbolic Logic 73(3), 969–998 (2008)
3. Baaz, M., Metcalfe, G.: Herbrand Theorems and Skolemization for Prenex Fuzzy Logics. In: Beckmann, A., Dimitracopoulos, C., Löwe, B. (eds.) CiE 2008. LNCS, vol. 5028, pp. 22–31. Springer, Heidelberg (2008)
4. Baaz, M., Metcalfe, G.: Herbrand's theorem, Skolemization, and proof systems for first-order Łukasiewicz logic. Journal of Logic and Computation 20(1), 35–54 (2010)
5. Buss, S. (ed.): Handbook of Proof Theory. Kluwer (1998)
6. Ciabattoni, A., Galatos, N., Terui, K.: Algebraic proof theory for substructural logics: Cut-elimination and completions. Annals of Pure and Applied Logic 163(3), 266–290 (2012)
7. Cintula, P., Hájek, P., Noguera, C. (eds.): Handbook of Mathematical Fuzzy Logic (in 2 volumes). College Publications, London (2011)
8. Cintula, P., Noguera, C.: A general framework for mathematical fuzzy logic. In: Cintula, P., Hájek, P., Noguera, C. (eds.) Handbook of Mathematical Fuzzy Logic, vol. 1, pp. 103–207. College Publications (2011)
9. Galatos, N., Jipsen, P., Kowalski, T., Ono, H.: *Residuated Lattices: An Algebraic Glimpse at Substructural Logics*. Studies in Logic and the Foundations of Mathematics, vol. 151. Elsevier, Amsterdam (2007)
10. García-Cerdaña, À., Armengol, E., Esteva, F.: Fuzzy description logics and t-norm based fuzzy logics. International Journal of Approximate Reasoning 51(6), 632–655 (2010)
11. Hájek, P.: *Metamathematics of Fuzzy Logic*. Trends in Logic, vol. 4. Kluwer, Dordrecht (1998)
12. Hájek, P.: Making fuzzy description logic more general. Fuzzy Sets and Systems 154(1), 1–15 (2005)
13. McNaughton, R.: A theorem about infinite-valued sentential logic. Journal of Symbolic Logic 16(1), 1–13 (1951)
14. Meghini, C., Sebastiani, F., Straccia, U.: A model of multimedia information retrieval. Journal of the ACM 48(5), 909–970 (2001)
15. Metcalfe, G., Olivetti, N., Gabbay, D.M.: Proof Theory for Fuzzy Logics. Applied Logic Series, vol. 36. Springer (2008)
16. Minc, G.E.: The Skolem method in intuitionistic calculi. Proceedings of the Steklov Institute of Mathematics 121, 73–109 (1974)
17. Ono, H.: Algebraic semantics for predicate logics and their completeness. In: Orlowska, E. (ed.) Logic at Work. Essays Dedicated to the Memory of Helena Rasiowa, pp. 637–650. Physica Verlag, Heidelberg (1999)
18. Ono, H.: Crawley completions of residuated lattices and algebraic completeness of substructural predicate logics. Studia Logica 100(1-2), 339–359 (2012)
19. Restall, G.: An Introduction to Substructural Logics. Routledge, New York (2000)
20. Terui, K.: Herbrand's theorem via hypercanonical extensions (manuscript)
21. Vojtáš, P.: Fuzzy logic programming. Fuzzy Sets and Systems 124(3), 361–370 (2001)

On Promptness in Parity Games*

Fabio Mogavero, Aniello Murano, and Loredana Sorrentino

Università degli Studi di Napoli Federico II

Abstract. *Parity games* are a powerful formalism for the automatic synthesis and verification of reactive systems. They are closely related to alternating ω-automata and emerge as a natural method for the solution of the μ-calculus model checking problem. Due to these strict connections, parity games are a well-established environment to describe *liveness properties* such as "every request that occurs infinitely often is eventually responded". Unfortunately, the classical form of such a condition suffers from the strong drawback that there is no bound on the effective time that separates a request from its response, i.e., responses are *not promptly* provided. Recently, to overcome this limitation, several parity game variants have been proposed, in which quantitative requirements are added to the classic qualitative ones.

In this paper, we make a general study of the concept of promptness in parity games that allows to put under a unique theoretical framework several of the cited variants along with new ones. Also, we describe simple polynomial reductions from all these conditions to either Büchi or parity games, which simplify all previous known procedures. In particular, they improve the complexity results of *cost* and *bounded-cost parity games*. Indeed, we provide solution algorithms showing that determining the winner of these games lies in UPTIME ∩ CoUPTIME.

1 Introduction

Parity games [13,24] are abstract infinite-duration two-player turn-based games, which represent a powerful mathematical framework to analyze several problems in computer science and mathematics. Their importance is deeply related to the strict connection with other games of infinite duration, in particular, *mean, discounted* payoff, *stochastic* and *multi-agent* games [6,7,9,10]. In the basic setting, parity games are played on directed graphs whose nodes are labeled with priorities (namely, *colors*) and players have perfect information about the adversary moves. The two players, player ∃ and player ∀, move in turns a token along the edges of the graph starting from a designated initial node. Thus, a play induces an infinite path and player ∃ wins the play if the greatest priority that is visited infinitely often is even, otherwise, player ∀ wins the play. The problem of finding a

---

* Partially supported by FP7 European Union project 600958-SHERPA, InDAM 2013 project "Logiche di Gioco Estese", Embedded System Cup Project, B25B09090100007 (POR Campania FSE 2007/2013, asse IV e asse V), Italian Ministry of University and Research, and EU under the PON OR.C.HE.S.T.R.A. project.

winning strategy in parity games is in UPTIME ∩ COUPTIME [16] and the question whether or not a polynomial time solution exists is a long-standing open one.

In formal system design and verification [11,12,21,23], parity games arise as a natural evaluation machinery for the automatic synthesis and verification of distributed and reactive systems [3–5, 20]. Specifically, in model-checking, one can check the correctness of a system with respect to a desired behavior, by checking whether a model of the system, that is, a *Kripke structure*, is correct with respect to a formal specification of its behavior, usually described in terms of a modal logic formula. In case the specification is given as a μ-calculus formula [17], the model checking question can be polynomially rephrased as a parity game [13].

Parity games can express several important system requirements such as *safety* and *liveness* properties. Along an infinite play, safety requirements are used to ensure that nothing "bad" will ever happen, while liveness properties ensure that something "good" eventually happens [2]. Often, safety and liveness properties alone are simple to satisfy, while it becomes a very challenging task when properties of this kind need to be satisfied simultaneously. As an example, assume we want to check the correctness of a printer scheduler that serves two users in which it is required that, whenever a user sends a job to the printer, it is eventually printed out (liveness property) and that two jobs are never printed simultaneously (safety property). The above liveness property can be written as the LTL [22] formula $\mathtt{G}(req \to \mathtt{F}grant)$, where $\mathtt{G}$ and $\mathtt{F}$ stand for the classic temporal operators "always" and "eventually", respectively. This kind of question is also known in literature as a *request-response condition* [15]. As explained above, in a parity game, this requirement is interpreted over an infinite path generated by the interplay of the two players. From a theoretical viewpoint, on checking whether a request is eventually granted, there is no bound on the "waiting time", namely the time elapsed until the job is printed out. In other words, it is enough to check that the system "can" grant the request, while we do not care when it happens. In a real industry scenario, instead, the request is more concrete, that is, the job must be printed in a reasonable time bound.

Lately, several works have focused on the above timing aspect in system specification. In [19], it has been addressed by forcing LTL to express "prompt" requirements, by means of a *prompt* operator $\mathtt{F}_p$ added to the logic. In [1] the automata-theoretic counterpart of the $\mathtt{F}_p$ operator has been studied. In particular, *prompt-Büchi* automata are introduced and it has been showed that their intersection with ω-regular languages is equivalent to co-Büchi. Successively, the prompt semantics has been lifted to ω-regular games, under the parity winning condition [8], by introducing finitary parity games. There, the concept of "*distance*" between positions in a play has been introduced and referred as the number of edges traversed to reach a node from a given one. Then, winning positions of the game are restricted to those occurring bounded. To give few more details, first consider that, as in classic parity games, arenas have vertexes equipped with natural number priorities and in a play every odd number met is seen as a pending "*request*" that, to be satisfied, requires to meet a bigger even number afterwards along the play, which is therefore seen as a *"response"*. Then, player ∃ wins the game if almost all requests are responded within a bounded distance. It has been shown in [8] that the problem of determining the winner in a finitary parity game is in PTIME.

Recently, the work [8] has been generalized in [14] to deal with more involved prompt parity conditions. For this reason, arenas are further equipped with two kinds of edges, *i-edges* and *ϵ-edges*, which indicate whether there is or not a time-unit consumption while traversing an edge, respectively. Then, the cost of a path is determined by the number of its *i*-edges. In some way, the cost of traversing a path can be seen as the consumption of resources. Therefore, in such a game, player ∃ aims to achieve its goal with a bounded resource, while player ∀ tries to avoid it. In particular, player ∃ wins a play if there is a bound b such that all requests, except at most a finite number, have a cost bounded by b and all requests, except at most a finite number, are responded. Since we now have an explicit cost associated to every path, the corresponding condition has been named *cost parity* (CP). Note that in cost parity games a finite number of unanswered requests with unbounded cost is also allowed. By disallowing this, in [14], a strengthening of the cost parity condition has been introduced and named *bounded-cost parity* (BCP) condition. There, it has been shown that the winner of both cost parity and bounded-cost parity can be decided in NPTIME ∩ CoNPTIME.

In this article we keep working on two-player parity games, under the prompt semantics, over colored (vertexes) arenas with or without weights over edges. In the sequel, we refer to the latter as *colored arenas* and to the former as *weighted arenas*. Our aim is twofold. On one side, we give a clear picture of all different extended parity conditions introduced in the literature working under the prompt assumption. In particular, we analyze their main intrinsic peculiarities and possibly improve the complexity results related to the game solutions. On the other side, we introduce new parity conditions to work on both colored and weighted arenas and study their relation with the known ones. For a complete list of all the conditions we address in the sequel of this article, see Table 1.

In order to make our reasoning more clear, we first introduce the concept of *non-full*, *semi-full* and *full* acceptance parity condition. To understand their meaning, first consider again the cost parity condition. By definition, it is a conjunction of two properties and in both of them a finite number of requests (possibly different) can be ignored. For this reason, we call this condition "non-full". Consider now the bounded-cost parity condition. By definition, it is still a conjunction of two properties, but now only in one of them a finite number of requests can be ignored. For this reason, we call this condition "semi-full". Finally, a parity condition is named "full" if none of the requests can be ignored. Note that the full concept has been already addressed in [8] on classic arenas. We also refer to [8] for further motivations and examples.

As a main contribution in this work, we introduce and study three new parity conditions named *full parity* (FP), *prompt parity* (PP) and *full-prompt parity* (FPP), respectively. The full parity condition is defined over colored arenas and, in accordance to the full semantics, it simply requires that all requests must be responded. Clearly, it has no meaning to talk about a semi-full parity condition, since there is just one property to verify. Also, the non-full parity condition corresponds to the classic parity one. See Table 2 for a schematic view of this argument. We prove that the complexity of checking whether player ∃ wins under the full parity condition is in PTIME. This result is obtained by a quadratic translation to classic Büchi games. The prompt parity condition, which we consider on both colored and weighted arenas, requires that almost all requests are responded within a bounded cost, which we name here *delay*. The full-prompt parity condition is defined accordingly. Observe that the main difference between the cost parity and the prompt parity conditions is that the former is a conjunction of two properties, in each of which a possibly different set of finite requests can be ignored, while in the latter we indicate only one set of finite requests to be used in two different properties. Nevertheless, since the quantifications of the winning conditions range on co-finite sets, we are able to prove that prompt and cost parity conditions are semantically equivalent. We also prove that the complexity of checking whether player ∃ wins the game under the prompt parity condition is UPTIME ∩ COUPTIME, in the case of weighted arenas. So, the same result holds for cost parity games and this improves the previously known results. The statement is obtained by a quartic translation to classic parity games. Our algorithm always reduces the original problem to a unique parity game, which is the core of how we gain a better result w.r.t. the time complexity point of view. Obviously, this is different from what is done in [14] as the algorithm there performs several calls to a parity game solver. Observe that, on colored arenas prompt and full-prompt parity conditions correspond to the finitary and bounded-finitary parity conditions [8], respectively. Hence, both the corresponding games can be decided in PTIME. We prove that for full-prompt parity games the PTIME complexity holds even in the case the arenas are weighted. Finally, by means of a cubic translation to classic parity games, we prove that bounded-cost parity over weighted arenas is in UPTIME ∩ COUPTIME, which also improves the previously known result about this condition.

Due to the lack of space, proofs are omitted and reported in the full version.

2   Preliminaries

In this section, we give the concepts of two-player turn-based arena, payoff-arena, and game. As they are common definitions, an expert reader can skip this part.

Arenas. An *arena* is a tuple $\mathcal{A} \triangleq \langle \mathrm{Ps}_\exists, \mathrm{Ps}_\forall, Mv \rangle$, where $\mathrm{Ps}_\exists$ and $\mathrm{Ps}_\forall$ are the disjoint sets of *existential* and *universal* positions and $Mv \subseteq \mathrm{Ps} \times \mathrm{Ps}$ is the left-total *move relation* on $\mathrm{Ps} \triangleq \mathrm{Ps}_\exists \cup \mathrm{Ps}_\forall$. The *order* of $\mathcal{A}$ is the number $|\mathcal{A}| \triangleq |\mathrm{Ps}|$ of its positions. An arena is *finite* iff it has finite order. A *path* (resp., *history*) in $\mathcal{A}$ is an infinite (resp., finite non-empty) sequence of vertexes $\pi \in \mathrm{Pth} \subseteq \mathrm{Ps}^\omega$ (resp., $\rho \in \mathrm{Hst} \subseteq \mathrm{Ps}^+$) compatible with the move relation, *i.e.*, $(\pi_i, \pi_{i+1}) \in Mv$ (resp., $(\rho_i, \rho_{i+1}) \in Mv$), for all $i \in \mathbb{N}$ (resp., $i \in [0, |\rho| - 1[$), where Pth (resp., Hst) denotes the set of all paths (resp., histories). Intuitively, histories and paths are legal sequences of reachable positions that can be seen, respectively, as partial and complete descriptions of possible outcomes obtainable by following the rules of the game modeled by the arena. An *existential* (resp., *universal*) *history* in $\mathcal{A}$ is just a history $\rho \in \mathsf{Hst}_\exists \subseteq \mathsf{Hst}$ (resp., $\rho \in \mathsf{Hst}_\forall \subseteq \mathsf{Hst}$) ending in an existential (resp., universal) position, *i.e.*, $\mathsf{lst}(\rho) \in \mathsf{Ps}_\exists$ (resp., $\mathsf{lst}(\rho) \in \mathsf{Ps}_\forall$). An *existential* (resp., *universal*) *strategy* on $\mathcal{A}$ is a function $\sigma_\exists \in \mathsf{Str}_\exists \subseteq \mathsf{Hst}_\exists \to \mathsf{Ps}$ (resp., $\sigma_\forall \in \mathsf{Str}_\forall \subseteq \mathsf{Hst}_\forall \to \mathsf{Ps}$) mapping each existential (resp., universal) history $\rho \in \mathsf{Hst}_\exists$ (resp., $\rho \in \mathsf{Hst}_\forall$) to a position compatible with the move relation, *i.e.*, $(\mathsf{lst}(\rho), \sigma_\exists(\rho)) \in Mv$ (resp., $(\mathsf{lst}(\rho), \sigma_\forall(\rho)) \in Mv$), where $\mathsf{Str}_\exists$ (resp., $\mathsf{Str}_\forall$) denotes the set of all existential (resp., universal) strategies. Intuitively, a strategy is a high-level plan for a player to achieve his own goal, which contains the choice of moves as a function of the histories of the current outcome. A path $\pi \in \mathsf{Pth}(v)$ starting at a position $v \in \mathsf{Ps}$ is the *play* in $\mathcal{A}$ w.r.t. a pair of strategies $(\sigma_\exists, \sigma_\forall) \in \mathsf{Str}_\exists \times \mathsf{Str}_\forall$ $(((\sigma_\exists, \sigma_\forall), v)$-*play*, for short) iff, for all $i \in \mathbb{N}$, it holds that if $\pi_i \in \mathsf{Ps}_\exists$ then $\pi_{i+1} = \sigma_\exists(\pi_{\leq i})$ else $\pi_{i+1} = \sigma_\forall(\pi_{\leq i})$. Intuitively, a play is the unique outcome of the game given by the player strategies. The *play function* play : $\mathsf{Ps} \times (\mathsf{Str}_\exists \times \mathsf{Str}_\forall) \to \mathsf{Pth}$ returns, for each position $v \in \mathsf{Ps}$ and pair of strategies $(\sigma_\exists, \sigma_\forall) \in \mathsf{Str}_\exists \times \mathsf{Str}_\forall$, the $((\sigma_\exists, \sigma_\forall), v)$-play play$(v, (\sigma_\exists, \sigma_\forall))$.

Payoff Arenas. A *payoff arena* is a tuple $\widehat{\mathcal{A}} \triangleq \langle \mathcal{A}, \mathsf{Pf}, \mathsf{pf} \rangle$, where $\mathcal{A}$ is the underlying arena, Pf is the non-empty set of *payoff values*, and pf : $\mathsf{Pth} \to \mathsf{Pf}$ is the *payoff function* mapping each path to a value. The *order* of $\widehat{\mathcal{A}}$ is the order of its underlying arena $\mathcal{A}$. A payoff arena is *finite* iff it has finite order. The overloading of the payoff function pf from the set of paths to the sets of positions and pairs of existential and universal strategies induces the function pf : $\mathsf{Ps} \times (\mathsf{Str}_\exists \times \mathsf{Str}_\forall) \to \mathsf{Pf}$ mapping each position $v \in \mathsf{Ps}$ and pair of strategies $(\sigma_\exists, \sigma_\forall) \in \mathsf{Str}_\exists \times \mathsf{Str}_\forall$ to the payoff value $\mathsf{pf}(v, (\sigma_\exists, \sigma_\forall)) \triangleq \mathsf{pf}(\mathsf{play}(v, (\sigma_\exists, \sigma_\forall)))$ of the corresponding $((\sigma_\exists, \sigma_\forall), v)$-play.

Games. A *(extensive-form) game* is a tuple $\partial \triangleq \langle \widehat{\mathcal{A}}, \mathsf{Wn}, v_\mathsf{o} \rangle$, where $\widehat{\mathcal{A}} = \langle \mathcal{A}, \mathsf{Pf}, \mathsf{pf} \rangle$ is the underlying payoff arena, $\mathsf{Wn} \subseteq \mathsf{Pf}$ is the *winning payoff set*, and $v_\mathsf{o} \in \mathsf{Ps}$ is the designated *initial position*. The *order* of $\mathcal{G}$ is the order of its underlying payoff arena $\widehat{\mathcal{A}}$. A game is *finite* iff it has finite order. The *existential* (resp., *universal*) *player* $\exists$ (resp., $\forall$) wins the game ∂ iff there exists an existential (resp., universal) strategy $\sigma_\exists \in \mathsf{Str}_\exists$ (resp., $\sigma_\forall \in \mathsf{Str}_\forall$) such that, for all universal (resp., existential) strategies $\sigma_\forall \in \mathsf{Str}_\forall$ (resp., $\sigma_\exists \in \mathsf{Str}_\exists$), it holds that $\mathsf{pf}(\sigma_\exists, \sigma_\forall) \in \mathsf{Wn}$ (resp., $\mathsf{pf}(\sigma_\exists, \sigma_\forall) \notin \mathsf{Wn}$).

3 Parity Conditions

In this section, we give an overview about all different parity conditions we consider in this article, which are variants of classical parity games that will be investigated over both classic colored arenas (*i.e.*, with unweighted edges) and weighted arenas. Specifically, along with the known Parity (P), Cost Parity (CP), and Bounded-Cost Parity (BCP) conditions, we introduce three new winning conditions, namely Full Parity (FP), Prompt Parity (PP), and Full-Prompt Parity (FPP).

Before continuing, we introduce some notation to formally define all addressed winning conditions. A *colored arena* is a tuple $\widetilde{\mathcal{A}} \triangleq \langle \mathcal{A}, \mathrm{Cl}, \mathsf{cl}\rangle$, where $\mathcal{A}$ is the underlying arena, $\mathrm{Cl} \subseteq \mathbb{N}$ is the non-empty sets of *colors*, and $\mathsf{cl} : \mathrm{Ps} \to \mathrm{Cl}$ is the *coloring function* mapping each position to a color. Similarly, a *(colored) weighted arena* is a tuple $\overline{\mathcal{A}} \triangleq \langle \mathcal{A}, \mathrm{Cl}, \mathsf{cl}, \mathrm{Wg}, \mathsf{wg}\rangle$, where $\langle \mathcal{A}, \mathrm{Cl}, \mathsf{cl}\rangle$ is the underlying colored arena, $\mathrm{Wg} \subseteq \mathbb{N}$ is the non-empty sets of *weights*, and $\mathsf{wg} : \mathrm{Mv} \to \mathrm{Wg}$ is the *weighting functions* mapping each move to a weight. The overloading of the coloring (resp., weighting) function from the set of positions (resp., moves) to the set of paths induces the function $\mathsf{cl} : \mathrm{Pth} \to \mathrm{Cl}^\omega$ (resp., $\mathsf{wg} : \mathrm{Pth} \to \mathrm{Wg}^\omega$) mapping each path $\pi \in \mathrm{Pth}$ to the infinite sequence of colors $\mathsf{cl}(\pi) \in \mathrm{Cl}^\omega$ (resp. weights $\mathsf{wg}(\pi) \in \mathrm{Wg}^\omega$) such that $(\mathsf{cl}(\pi))_i = \mathsf{cl}(\pi_i)$ (resp., $(\mathsf{wg}(\pi))_i = \mathsf{wg}((\pi_i, \pi_{i+1}))$), for all $i \in \mathbb{N}$. Every colored (resp., weighted) arena $\widetilde{\mathcal{A}} \triangleq \langle \mathcal{A}, \mathrm{Cl}, \mathsf{cl}\rangle$ (resp., $\overline{\mathcal{A}} \triangleq \langle \mathcal{A}, \mathrm{Cl}, \mathsf{cl}, \mathrm{Wg}, \mathsf{wg}\rangle$) induces a canonical payoff arena $\widehat{\mathcal{A}} \triangleq \langle \mathcal{A}, \mathrm{Pf}, \mathsf{pf}\rangle$, where $\mathrm{Pf} \triangleq \mathrm{Cl}^\omega$ (resp., $\mathrm{Pf} \triangleq \mathrm{Cl}^\omega \times \mathrm{Wg}^\omega$) and $\mathsf{pf}(\pi) \triangleq \mathsf{cl}(\pi)$ (resp., $\mathsf{pf}(\pi) \triangleq (\mathsf{cl}(\pi), \mathsf{wg}(\pi))$).

Along a play, we interpret the occurrence of an odd priority as a "*request*" and the occurrence of the first bigger even priority at a later position as a "*response*". Then, we distinguish between *prompt* and *not-prompt* requests. In the not-prompt case, a request is responded independently from the elapsed time between its occurrence and response. Conversely, in the prompt case, the time within a request is responded has an important role. It is for this reason that we consider weighted arenas. So, a *delay* over a play is the sum of the weights over of all the edges crossed from a request to its response. We now formalize these concepts. Let $c \in \mathrm{Cl}^\omega$ be an infinite sequence of colors. Then, $\mathrm{Rq}(c) \triangleq \{i \in \mathbb{N} : c_i \equiv 1 \pmod 2\}$ denotes the set of all *requests* in c and $\mathrm{rs}(c, i) \triangleq \min\{j \in \mathbb{N} : i \leq j \wedge c_i \leq c_j \wedge c_j \equiv 0 \pmod 2\}$ represents the *response* to the requests $i \in \mathrm{Rs}$, where by convention we set $\min \emptyset \triangleq \omega$. Moreover, $\mathrm{Rs}(c) \triangleq \{i \in \mathrm{Rq}(c) : \mathrm{rs}(c, i) < \omega\}$ denotes the subset of all requests for which a response is provided. Now, let $w \in \mathrm{Wg}^\omega$ be an infinite sequence of weights. Then, $\mathrm{dl}((c, w), i) \triangleq \sum_{k=i}^{\mathrm{rs}(c,i)-1} w_k$ denotes the *delay* w.r.t. w with which a request $i \in \mathrm{Rq}(c)$ is responded. Also, $\mathrm{dl}((c, w), \mathrm{R}) \triangleq \sup_{i \in \mathrm{R}} \mathrm{dl}((c, w), i)$ is the supremum of all delays of the requests contained in $\mathrm{R} \subseteq \mathrm{Rq}(c)$.

As usual, all conditions we consider are given on infinite plays. Then, the winning of the game can be defined with respect to how often the characterizing properties of the winning condition are satisfied along each play. For example, we may require that *all* requests have to be responded along a play, which we denote as a *full* behavior of the acceptance condition. Also, we may require that the condition (given as a unique or a *conjunction* of properties) holds almost everywhere along the play (*i.e.*, a finite number of places along the play can be ignored), which we denote as a *not-full* behavior of the acceptance

Table 1. Prompt/non-prompt conditions under the full/semi-full/non-full constraints

	Non-Prompt	Prompt
Non-Full	Parity (P)	Prompt Parity (PP) ≡ Cost Parity (CP)
Semi-Full	–	Bounded Cost Parity (BCP)
Full	Full Parity (FP)	Full Prompt Parity (FPP)

condition. More in general, we may have conditions, given as a *conjunction* of several properties, to be satisfied in a mixed way, that is, some of them have to be satisfied almost everywhere and the remaining ones, over all the play. We denote the latter as a *semi-full* behavior of the acceptance condition. Table 1 reports the combination of the full, not-full, and semi-full behaviors with the known conditions of parity, cost-parity and bounded cost-parity and the new condition of prompt-parity we introduce. As it will be clear in the following, bounded cost-parity has intrinsically a semi-full behavior on weighted arenas, but it has no meaning on (unweighted) colored arenas. Also, over colored arenas, the parity condition has an intrinsic not-full behavior. Note that, as far as we known, some of these combinations have never been studied previously on colored arenas (full parity) and weighted arenas (prompt parity and full-prompt parity).

3.1 Non-prompt Conditions

The non-prompt conditions relate only to the satisfaction of a request (*i.e.*, its response), without taking into account the elapsing of time before the response is provided (*i.e.*, its delay). As reported in Table 1, here we consider as non-prompt conditions, those ones of parity and full parity. To do this, let $\eth \triangleq \langle \widehat{\mathcal{A}}, \text{Wn}, v_o \rangle$ be a game, where the payoff arena $\widehat{\mathcal{A}}$ is induced by a colored arena $\widetilde{\mathcal{A}} = \langle \mathcal{A}, \text{Cl}, \text{cl} \rangle$.

Parity condition (P) $\eth$ is a *parity game* iff it is played under a parity condition, which requires that all requests, except at most a finite number, are responded. Formally, for all $c = \text{Cl}^\omega$, we have that $c \in \text{Wn}$ iff there exists a finite set $\text{R} \subseteq \text{Rq}(c)$ such that $\text{Rq}(c) \setminus \text{R} \subseteq \text{Rs}(c)$, *i.e.*, c is a winning payoff iff almost all requests in $\text{Rq}(c)$ are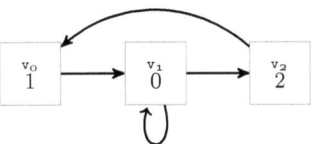

Fig. 1. Colored Arena $\widetilde{\mathcal{A}}_1$

responded. Consider for example the colored arena $\widetilde{\mathcal{A}}_1$ depicted in Figure 1, where all positions are universal, and let $\alpha + \beta$ be the regular expression describing all possible plays starting at v_0, where $\alpha = (v_0 \cdot v_1^* \cdot v_2) \cdot v_0 \cdot v_1^\omega$ and $\beta = (v_0 \cdot v_1^* \cdot v_2)^\omega$. Now, keep a path $\pi \in \alpha$ and let $c_\alpha \triangleq \text{pf}(\pi) \in (1 \cdot 0^* \cdot 2) \cdot 1 \cdot 0^\omega$ be its payoff. Then, $c_\pi \in \text{Wn}$, since the parity condition is satisfied by putting in R the last index in which the color 1 occurs in c_π. Again, keep a path $\pi \in \beta$ and let $c_\pi \triangleq \text{pf}(\pi) \in (1 \cdot 0^* \cdot 2)^\omega$ be its payoff. Then, $c_\pi \in \text{Wn}$, since the parity condition is satisfied by simply choosing $\text{R} \triangleq \emptyset$. In the following, as a special case, we also consider parity games played over arenas colored only with the two priorities 1 and 2, to which we refer as *Büchi games* (B).

Full Parity condition (FP) $\eth$ is a *full parity game* iff it is played under a full parity condition, which requires that all requests are responded. Formally, for all $c \in \text{Cl}^\omega$, we have that $c \in \text{Wn}$ iff $\text{Rq}(c) = \text{Rs}(c)$ *i.e.*, c is a winning payoff iff all requests in $\text{Rq}(c)$ are responded. Consider for example the colored arena $\widetilde{\mathcal{A}}_2$ in Figure 2, where all positions are

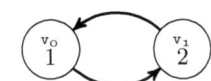

Fig. 2. Colored Arena $\widetilde{\mathcal{A}}_2$

existential. There is a unique path $\pi = (v_0 \cdot v_1)^\omega$ starting at v_0 having payoff $c_\pi \triangleq \mathsf{pf}(\pi) = (1 \cdot 2)^\omega$ and set of requests $\mathsf{Rq}(c_\pi) = \{2n : n \in \mathbb{N}\}$. Then, $c_\pi \in \mathsf{Wn}$, since the full parity condition is satisfied as all requests are responded by the color 2 at the odd indexes.

3.2 Prompt Conditions

The prompt conditions take into account, in addition to the satisfaction of a request, also the delay before it occurs. As reported in Table 1, here we consider as prompt conditions, those ones of prompt parity, full-prompt parity, cost parity, and bounded-cost parity. To do this, let $\eth \triangleq \langle \widehat{\mathcal{A}}, \mathsf{Wn}, v_0 \rangle$ be a game, where the payoff arena $\widehat{\mathcal{A}}$ is induced by a (colored) weighted arena $\overline{\mathcal{A}} = \langle \mathcal{A}, \mathsf{Cl}, \mathsf{cl}, \mathsf{Wg}, \mathsf{wg} \rangle$.

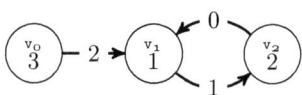

Fig. 3. Weighted Arena $\overline{\mathcal{A}_3}$

Prompt Parity condition (PP) $\eth$ is a *prompt parity game* iff it is played under a prompt parity condition, which requires that all requests, except at most a finite number of them, are responded with a bounded delay. Formally, for all $(c, w) \in \mathsf{Cl}^\omega \times \mathsf{Wg}^\omega$, we have that $(c, w) \in \mathsf{Wn}$ iff there exists a finite set $\mathsf{R} \subseteq \mathsf{Rq}(c)$ such that $\mathsf{Rq}(c) \setminus \mathsf{R} \subseteq \mathsf{Rs}(c)$ and there exists a bound $b \in \mathbb{N}$ for which $\mathsf{dl}((c, w), \mathsf{Rq}(c) \setminus \mathsf{R}) \leq b$ holds, i.e., (c, w) is a winning payoff iff almost all requests in $\mathsf{Rq}(c)$ are responded with a delay bounded by an a priori number b. Consider for example the weighted arena $\overline{\mathcal{A}_3}$ depicted in Figure 3. There is a unique path $\pi = v_0 \cdot (v_1 \cdot v_2)^\omega$ starting at v_0 having payoff $c_\pi \triangleq \mathsf{pf}(\pi) = (c, w)$, where $c = 3 \cdot (1 \cdot 2)^\omega$ and $w = 2 \cdot (1 \cdot 0)^\omega$, and set of requests $\mathsf{Rq}(c) = \{0\} \cup \{2n+1 : n \in \mathbb{N}\}$. Then, $c_\pi \in \mathsf{Wn}$, since the prompt parity condition is satisfied by choosing $\mathsf{R} = \{0\}$ and $b = 1$.

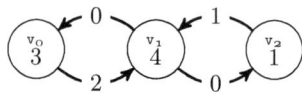

Fig. 4. Weighted Arena $\overline{\mathcal{A}_4}$

Full-Prompt Parity condition (FPP) $\eth$ is a *full-prompt parity game* iff it is played under a full-prompt parity condition, which requires that all requests are responded with a bounded delay. Formally, for all $(c, w) \in \mathsf{Cl}^\omega \times \mathsf{Wg}^\omega$, we have that $(c, w) \in \mathsf{Wn}$ iff $\mathsf{Rq}(c) = \mathsf{Rs}(c)$ and there exists a bound $b \in \mathbb{N}$ for which $\mathsf{dl}((c, w), \mathsf{Rq}(c)) \leq b$ holds, i.e., (c, w) is a winning payoff iff all requests in $\mathsf{Rq}(c)$ are responded with a delay bounded by an a priori number b. Consider for example the weighted arena $\overline{\mathcal{A}_4}$ depicted in Figure 4. Now, take a path $\pi \in v_0 \cdot v_1 \cdot ((v_0 \cdot v_1)^* \cdot (v_2 \cdot v_1)^*)^\omega$ starting at v_0 and let $c_\pi \triangleq \mathsf{pf}(\pi) = (c, w)$ be its payoff, with $c \in 3 \cdot 4 \cdot ((3 \cdot 4)^* \cdot (1 \cdot 4)^*)^\omega$ and $w \in 2 \cdot ((0 \cdot 2)^* \cdot (0 \cdot 1)^*)^\omega$. Then, $c_\pi \in \mathsf{Wn}$, since the full-prompt parity condition is satisfied as all requests are responded by color 4 with a delay bound $b = 2$.

Remark 1. As a special case, the prompt and the full-prompt parity conditions can be analyzed on simply colored arenas, by considering each edge as having weight 1. Then, the above two cases just analyzed correspond to the finitary parity and bounded parity conditions studied in [8].

Cost Parity condition (CP) [14] ⊇ is a *cost parity game* iff it is played under a cost parity condition, which requires that all requests, except at most a finite number of them, are responded and all requests, except at most a finite number of them (possibly different from the previous ones) have a bounded delay. Formally, for all $(c, w) \in Cl^\omega \times Wg^\omega$, we have that $(c, w) \in Wn$ iff there is a finite set $R \subseteq Rq(c)$ such that $Rq(c) \setminus R \subseteq Rs(c)$ and there exist a finite set $R' \subseteq Rq(c)$ and a bound $b \in \mathbb{N}$ for which $dl((c, w), Rq(c)\setminus R') \leq b$ holds, i.e., (c, w) is a winning payoff iff almost all requests in $Rq(c)$ are responded and almost all have a delay bounded by an a priori number b. Consider for example the weighted arena $\overline{\mathcal{A}_5}$ in Figure 5. There is a unique path $\pi = v_0 \cdot v_1^\omega$ starting at v_0 having payoff $c_\pi \triangleq pf(\pi) = (c, w)$, where $c = 1 \cdot 0^\omega$ and $w = 0 \cdot 1^\omega$, and set of requests $Rq(c) = \{0\}$. Then, $c_\pi \in Wn$, since the prompt parity condition is satisfied with $R = R' = \{0\}$ and $b = 0$.

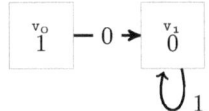

Fig. 5. Weighted Arena $\overline{\mathcal{A}_5}$

Bounded-Cost Parity condition (BCP) [14] ⊇ is a *bounded-cost parity game* iff it is played under a bounded-cost parity condition, which requires that all requests, except at most a finite number, are responded and all have a bounded delay. Formally, for all $(c, w) \in Cl^\omega \times Wg^\omega$, we have that $(c, w) \in Wn$ iff there exists a finite set $R \subseteq Rq(c)$ such that $Rq(c) \setminus R \subseteq Rs(c)$ and there exists a bound $b \in \mathbb{N}$ for which $dl((c, w), Rq(c)) \leq b$ holds, i.e., (c, w) is a winning payoff iff almost all requests in $Rq(c)$ are responded and all have a delay bounded by an a priori number b. Consider for example the weighted arena $\overline{\mathcal{A}_6}$ depicted in Figure 6. There is a unique path $\pi = v_0 \cdot v_1^\omega$ starting at v_0 having payoff $c_\pi \triangleq pf(\pi) = (c, w)$, where $c = 1 \cdot 0^\omega$, and set of requests $Rq(c) = \{0\}$. Then, $c_\pi \in Wn$, since the prompt parity condition is satisfied with $R = \{0\}$ and $b = 1$.

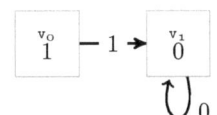

Fig. 6. Weighted Arena $\overline{\mathcal{A}_6}$

Table 2. Summary of all winning condition (Wn) definitions

Wn		Formal definitions	
P	$\forall c \in Cl^\omega . c \in Wn$ iff	$\exists R \subseteq Rq(c), \|R\| < \omega.$	$Rq(c) \setminus R \subseteq Rs(c)$
FP			$Rq(c) = Rs(c)$
PP	$\forall (c, w) \in Cl^\omega \times Wg^\omega.$ $(c, w) \in Wn$ iff	$\exists R \subseteq Rq(c), \|R\| < \omega.$	$Rq(c) \setminus R \subseteq Rs(c) \wedge$ $\exists b \in \mathbb{N} . dl((c, w), Rq(c) \setminus R) \leq b$
FPP			$Rq(c) = Rs(c) \wedge$ $\exists b \in \mathbb{N} . dl((c, w), Rq(c)) \leq b$
CP		$\exists R \subseteq Rq(c), \|R\| < \omega.$ $\exists R' \subseteq Rq(c), \|R'\| < \omega.$	$Rq(c) \setminus R \subseteq Rs(c) \wedge$ $\exists b \in \mathbb{N} . dl((c, w), Rq(c) \setminus R') \leq b$
BCP		$\exists R \subseteq Rq(c), \|R\| < \omega.$	$Rq(c) \setminus R \subseteq Rs(c) \wedge$ $\exists b \in \mathbb{N} . dl((c, w), Rq(c)) \leq b$

In Table 2, we list all winning conditions (Wn) introduced above, along with their respective formal definitions. For the sake of readability, given a game

$\Game = \langle \widehat{\mathcal{A}}, \mathrm{Wn}, v_o \rangle$, we sometimes use the winning condition acronym name in place of Wn, as well as we refer to $\Game$ as a Wn game. For example, if $\Game$ is a parity game, we also say that it is a P game, as well as write $\Game = \langle \widehat{\mathcal{A}}, \mathrm{P}, v_o \rangle$.

4 Equivalences and Implications

We now study the relationships among all parity conditions given above.

4.1 Positive Relationships

We now prove all positive relationships among the given conditions and report them in Figure 7, where an arrow from a condition Wn_1 to another one Wn_2 means that the former implies the latter. Namely, if player $\exists$ wins a game under Wn_1 condition, then it also wins the game under the one Wn_2, over the same

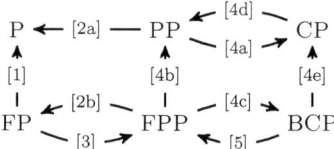

Fig. 7. Implication Schema

arena. The label on the edges indicates next theorem's item in which the result is proved. In particular, we show that prompt parity and cost parity are semantically equivalent. The same holds for full parity and full-prompt parity over finite arenas and for full-prompt parity and bounded-cost parity on positive weighted arenas. Also, as one may expect, fullness implies not-fullness under every condition and all conditions imply the parity one. Observe that, in the following, we refer to $\widehat{\mathcal{A}}, \widetilde{\mathcal{A}}, \overline{\mathcal{A}}$ indicating, respectively the payoff, colored and weighted arenas.

Theorem 1. Let $\Game_1 = \langle \widehat{\mathcal{A}_1}, \mathrm{Wn}_1, v_o \rangle$ and $\Game_2 = \langle \widehat{\mathcal{A}_2}, \mathrm{Wn}_2, v_o \rangle$ be two games defined on arenas $\widehat{\mathcal{A}_1}$ and $\widehat{\mathcal{A}_2}$ having the same underlying arena $\mathcal{A}$. Then, player $\exists$ wins $\Game_2$ if it wins $\Game_1$ under the following constraints:

1. $\widehat{\mathcal{A}_1} = \widehat{\mathcal{A}_2}$ are induced by an arena $\widetilde{\mathcal{A}} = \langle \mathcal{A}, \mathrm{Cl}, \mathrm{cl} \rangle$ and $(\mathrm{Wn}_1, \mathrm{Wn}_2) = (\mathrm{FP}, \mathrm{P})$;
2. $\widehat{\mathcal{A}_1}$ and $\widehat{\mathcal{A}_2}$ are induced, respectively, by an arena $\overline{\mathcal{A}} = \langle \mathcal{A}, \mathrm{Cl}, \mathrm{cl}, \mathrm{Wg}, \mathrm{wg} \rangle$ and its underlying arena $\widetilde{\mathcal{A}} = \langle \mathcal{A}, \mathrm{Cl}, \mathrm{cl} \rangle$ and one among (a) $(\mathrm{Wn}_1, \mathrm{Wn}_2) = (\mathrm{PP}, \mathrm{P})$ and (b) $(\mathrm{Wn}_1, \mathrm{Wn}_2) = (\mathrm{FPP}, \mathrm{FP})$ hold.
3. $\widehat{\mathcal{A}_2}$ and $\widehat{\mathcal{A}_1}$ are finite and induced, respectively, by an arena $\overline{\mathcal{A}} = \langle \mathcal{A}, \mathrm{Cl}, \mathrm{cl}, \mathrm{Wg}, \mathrm{wg} \rangle$ and its underlying arena $\widetilde{\mathcal{A}} = \langle \mathcal{A}, \mathrm{Cl}, \mathrm{cl} \rangle$ and $(\mathrm{Wn}_1, \mathrm{Wn}_2) = (\mathrm{FP}, \mathrm{FPP})$;
4. $\widehat{\mathcal{A}_1} = \widehat{\mathcal{A}_2}$ are induced by an arena $\overline{\mathcal{A}} = \langle \mathcal{A}, \mathrm{Cl}, \mathrm{cl}, \mathrm{Wg}, \mathrm{wg} \rangle$ and one among (a) $(\mathrm{Wn}_1, \mathrm{Wn}_2) = (\mathrm{PP}, \mathrm{CP})$, (b) $(\mathrm{Wn}_1, \mathrm{Wn}_2) = (\mathrm{FPP}, \mathrm{PP})$, (c) $(\mathrm{Wn}_1, \mathrm{Wn}_2) = (\mathrm{FPP}, \mathrm{BCP})$, (d) $(\mathrm{Wn}_1, \mathrm{Wn}_2) = (\mathrm{CP}, \mathrm{PP})$, (e) $(\mathrm{Wn}_1, \mathrm{Wn}_2) = (\mathrm{BCP}, \mathrm{CP})$ hold.
5. $\widehat{\mathcal{A}_1} = \widehat{\mathcal{A}_2}$ are induced by an arena $\overline{\mathcal{A}} = \langle \mathcal{A}, \mathrm{Cl}, \mathrm{cl}, \mathrm{Wg}, \mathrm{wg} \rangle$, with $\mathrm{wg}(v) > 0$ for all $v \in \mathrm{Ps}$, and $(\mathrm{Wn}_1, \mathrm{Wn}_2) = (\mathrm{BCP}, \mathrm{FPP})$.

The following three corollaries follow as immediate consequences of, respectively, Items 2b and 3, 4a and 4d, and 4c and 5 of the previous theorem.

Corollary 1. *Let $\partial_{FPP} = \langle \widehat{\mathcal{A}_{FPP}}, FPP, v_o \rangle$ be an FPP game and $\partial_{FP} = \langle \widehat{\mathcal{A}_{FP}}, FP, v_o \rangle$ an FP one defined on the two finite arenas $\widehat{\mathcal{A}_{FPP}}$ and $\widehat{\mathcal{A}_{FP}}$ induced, respectively, by an arena $\overline{\mathcal{A}} = \langle \mathcal{A}, Cl, cl, Wg, wg \rangle$ and its underlying arena $\widetilde{\mathcal{A}} = \langle \mathcal{A}, Cl, cl \rangle$. Then, player $\exists$ wins ∂_{FPP} if it wins ∂_{FP}.*

Corollary 2. *Let $\partial_{CP} = \langle \widehat{\mathcal{A}}, CP, v_o \rangle$ be a CP game and $\partial_{PP} = \langle \widehat{\mathcal{A}}, PP, v_o \rangle$ a PP one defined on the arena $\widehat{\mathcal{A}}$ induced by an arena $\overline{\mathcal{A}} = \langle \mathcal{A}, Cl, cl, Wg, wg \rangle$. Then, player $\exists$ wins ∂_{CP} if it wins ∂_{PP}.*

Corollary 3. *Let $\partial_{BCP} = \langle \widehat{\mathcal{A}}, BCP, v_o \rangle$ be a BCP game and $\partial_{FPP} = \langle \widehat{\mathcal{A}}, FPP, v_o \rangle$ an FPP one defined on the arena $\widehat{\mathcal{A}}$ induced by an arena $\overline{\mathcal{A}} = \langle \mathcal{A}, Cl, cl, Wg, wg \rangle$, where $wg(v) > 0$, for all $v \in Ps$. Then, player $\exists$ wins ∂_{BCP} if it wins ∂_{FPP}.*

4.2 Negative Relationships

We, now, show a list of counterexamples to point out that some winning conditions are not equivalent to other ones and report the corresponding results in Figure 8, where an arrow from a condition Wn_1 to another condition Wn_2 means that there is an arena on which player $\exists$ wins a Wn_1 game while it loses a Wn_2

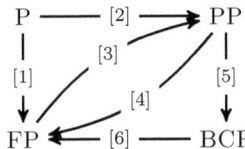

Fig. 8. Counterexample Schema

one. The label on the edges indicates the item of the next theorem in which the result is proved. Moreover, the following list of counter-implications, non reported in the figure, can be simply obtained by the listed ones together with the implication results of Theorem 1: (P, FPP), (P, CP), (P, BCP), (FP, FPP), (FP, CP), (FP, BCP), (PP, FPP), (CP, FP), (CP, FPP), (CP, BCP), and (BCP, FPP).

Theorem 2. *There exist two games $\partial_1 = \langle \widehat{\mathcal{A}_1}, Wn_1, v_o \rangle$ and $\partial_2 = \langle \widehat{\mathcal{A}_2}, Wn_2, v_o \rangle$, defined on the two arenas $\widehat{\mathcal{A}_1}$ and $\widehat{\mathcal{A}_2}$ having the same underlying arena $\mathcal{A}$, such that player $\exists$ wins ∂_1 while it loses ∂_2 under the following constraints:*

1. *$\widehat{\mathcal{A}_1} = \widehat{\mathcal{A}_2}$ are induced by an arena $\widetilde{\mathcal{A}} = \langle \mathcal{A}, Cl, cl \rangle$ and $(Wn_1, Wn_2) = (P, FP)$;*
2. *$\widehat{\mathcal{A}_2}$ and $\widehat{\mathcal{A}_1}$ are induced, respectively, by an arena $\overline{\mathcal{A}} = \langle \mathcal{A}, Cl, cl, Wg, wg \rangle$ and its underlying arena $\widetilde{\mathcal{A}} = \langle \mathcal{A}, Cl, cl \rangle$ and $(Wn_1, Wn_2) = (P, PP)$;*
3. *$\widehat{\mathcal{A}_2}$ and $\widehat{\mathcal{A}_1}$ are infinite and induced, respectively, by $\overline{\mathcal{A}} = \langle \mathcal{A}, Cl, cl, Wg, wg \rangle$ and its underlying arena $\widetilde{\mathcal{A}} = \langle \mathcal{A}, Cl, cl \rangle$ and $(Wn_1, Wn_2) = (FP, PP)$;*
4. *$\widehat{\mathcal{A}_1}$ and $\widehat{\mathcal{A}_2}$ are induced, respectively, by an arena $\overline{\mathcal{A}} = \langle \mathcal{A}, Cl, cl, Wg, wg \rangle$ and its underlying arena $\widetilde{\mathcal{A}} = \langle \mathcal{A}, Cl, cl \rangle$ and $(Wn_1, Wn_2) = (PP, FP)$;*
5. *$\widehat{\mathcal{A}_1} = \widehat{\mathcal{A}_2}$ are induced by $\overline{\mathcal{A}} = \langle \mathcal{A}, Cl, cl, Wg, wg \rangle$ and $(Wn_1, Wn_2) = (PP, BCP)$;*
6. *$\widehat{\mathcal{A}_1}$ and $\widehat{\mathcal{A}_2}$ are induced, resp., by $\overline{\mathcal{A}} = \langle \mathcal{A}, Cl, cl, Wg, wg \rangle$, with $wg(v) = 0$, for $v \in Ps$, and its underlying arena $\widetilde{\mathcal{A}} = \langle \mathcal{A}, Cl, cl \rangle$ and $(Wn_1, Wn_2) = (BCP, FP)$.*

5 Polynomial Reductions

In this section, we face the computational complexity of solving FP, PP, and BCP games. Then, due to the relationships among the winning conditions described above, we extend the achieved results to the other conditions as well. The technique we adopt is to solve a given game through the construction of a new game over an enriched arena, on which we play with a simpler winning condition. Intuitively, the built game encapsulates in the states of its arena some information regarding the satisfaction of the original condition. To this aim, we introduce the concepts of *transition table* and its *product* with an arena. A transition table is an automaton without acceptance condition. It is used to represent the information of the winning condition mentioned above. Then, the product operation allows to pass this information to the new arena. In general, our constructions are pseudo-polynomial, but if we restrict to the case of having only 0 and 1 as weights over the edges, then they become polynomial, due to the fact that the threshold is bounded by the number of edges in the arena. Moreover, since a game with arbitrary weights can be easily transformed into one with weights 0 and 1, we overall get a polynomial reduction for all the cases. Note that to check whether a value is positive or zero can be done in linear time in the number of its bits and, therefore, it is linear in the description of its weights.

In the following, for a given set of colors $Cl \subseteq \mathbb{N}$, we assume $\bot < i$, for all $i \in Cl$. Intuitively, $\bot$ is a special symbol that can be seen as lower bound over color priorities. Moreover, we define $R \triangleq \{c \in Cl : c \equiv 1 \pmod{2}\}$ to be the set of all possible request values in Cl with $R_\bot \triangleq \{\bot\} \cup R$.

5.1 Transition Tables

A *transition table* is a tuple $\mathcal{T} \triangleq \langle Sm, St_D, St_\exists, tr \rangle$, where Sm is the set of *symbols*, St_D and $St_\exists$ with $St \triangleq St_D \cup St_\exists$ are disjoint sets of *deterministic* and *existential states*, and $tr : (St_D \times Sm \to St) \cup (St_\exists \to 2^{St})$ is the *transition function* mapping either pairs of deterministic states and symbols to states or existential states to sets of states. The *order* (resp., *size*) of $\mathcal{T}$ is $|\mathcal{T}| \triangleq |St|$ (resp., $\|\mathcal{T}\| \triangleq |tr|$). A transition table is *finite* iff it has finite order.

Let $\widetilde{\mathcal{A}} = \langle \mathcal{A}, Cl, cl \rangle$ be a colored arena with $\mathcal{A} = \langle Ps_\exists, Ps_\forall, Mv \rangle$ and $\mathcal{T} \triangleq \langle Cl, St_D, St_\exists, tr \rangle$ a transition table. Then, $\widetilde{Ar} \otimes \mathcal{T} \triangleq \langle Ps_\exists^\star, Ps_\forall^\star, Mv^\star \rangle$ is the *product arena* defined as follows:

- $Ps_\exists^\star \triangleq Ps_\exists \times St_D \cup Ps \times St_\exists$ and $Ps_\forall^\star \triangleq Ps_\forall \times St_D$;
- for $(v_1, v_2) \in Mv$ and $s \in St_D$, it holds that $((v_1, s), (v_2, tr(s, cl(v_1)))) \in Mv^\star$;
- for $v \in Ps$, $s_1 \in St_\exists$, and $s_2 \in St$, then, $((v, s_1), (v, s_2)) \in Mv^\star$ iff $s_2 \in tr(s_1)$.

Similarly, let $\overline{\mathcal{A}} = \langle \mathcal{A}, Cl, cl, Wg, wg \rangle$ be a weighted arena with $\mathcal{A} = \langle Ps_\exists, Ps_\forall, Mv \rangle$ and $\mathcal{T} \triangleq \langle Cl \times Wg, St_D, St_\exists, tr \rangle$ a transition table. Then, $\overline{Ar} \otimes \mathcal{T} \triangleq \langle Ps_\exists^\star, Ps_\forall^\star, Mv^\star \rangle$ is the *product arena* as before, except for all moves $(v_1, v_2) \in Mv$ and states $s \in St_D$, where we have that $((v_1, s), (v_2, tr(s, (cl(v_1), wg((v_1, v_2)))))) \in Mv^\star$.

5.2 From Full Parity to Büchi

In this section, we show a reduction from full parity games to Büchi ones. This is done by constructing an ad-hoc transition table $\mathcal{T}$ that maintains basic informations of the parity condition. Then, the Büchi game uses as an arena an enriched version of the original one, which is obtained as its product with $\mathcal{T}$. Intuitively, $\mathcal{T}$ keeps track, along every play, the value of the biggest unanswered request. When such a request is satisfied, this value is set to the special symbol $\bot$. To this aim, $\mathcal{T}$ uses as states $\bot$ and all possible request values, and its transition function is defined as follows: if a request is satisfied, then $\mathcal{T}$ moves to state $\bot$, otherwise, it moves to the state representing the maximum between the new request it reads and the previous memorized one (kept into the current state).

Consider now the arena $\mathcal{A}^\star$ built as the product of the original arena with $\mathcal{T}$ and use as colors the values 1 and 2, assigned as follows: if a position contains $\bot$, color it with 2, otherwise, color it with 1. By definition of full parity and Büchi games, we have that a Büchi game is won over $\mathcal{A}^\star$ if and only if the full parity game is won over the original arena. Indeed, over a play of $\mathcal{A}^\star$, meeting $\bot$ infinitely often means that all requests found over the corresponding play of the old arena are satisfied. The formal construction of $\mathcal{T}$ and the $\mathcal{A}^\star$ follow. For a given FP game $\widehat{\eth} \triangleq \langle \widetilde{\mathcal{A}}, \mathrm{FP}, v_\mathrm{o}\rangle$ induced by a colored arena $\widetilde{\mathcal{A}} = \langle \mathcal{A}, \mathrm{Cl}, \mathrm{cl}\rangle$, we construct a deterministic transition table $\mathcal{T} \triangleq \langle \mathrm{Cl}, \mathrm{St}, \mathrm{tr}\rangle$, with set of states $\mathrm{St} \triangleq \mathrm{R}_\bot$ and transition function defined as follows:

- $\mathrm{tr}(r, c) \triangleq \begin{cases} \bot, & \text{if } r < c \text{ and } c \equiv 0 \pmod{2}; \\ \max\{r, c\}, & \text{otherwise.} \end{cases}$

Now, let $\mathcal{A}^\star = \widetilde{\mathcal{A}} \otimes \mathcal{T}$ be the product arena of $\widetilde{\mathcal{A}}$ and $\mathcal{T}$ and consider the colored arena $\widetilde{\mathcal{A}^\star} \triangleq \langle \mathcal{A}^\star, \{1, 2\}, \mathrm{cl}^\star\rangle$ such that, for all positions $(v, r) \in \mathrm{Ps}^\star$, if $r = \bot$ then $\mathrm{cl}^\star((v, r)) = 2$ else $\mathrm{cl}^\star((v, r)) = 1$. Then, the B game $\eth^\star = \langle \widetilde{\mathcal{A}^\star}, \mathrm{B}, (v_\mathrm{o}, \bot)\rangle$ induced by $\widetilde{\mathcal{A}^\star}$ is such that player $\exists$ wins $\eth$ iff it wins $\eth^\star$.

Theorem 3. *For every* FP *game* $\eth$ *with* $k \in \mathbb{N}$ *priorities, there is a* B *game* $\eth^\star$, *with order* $|\eth^\star| = \mathrm{O}(|\eth| \cdot k)$, *such that player* $\exists$ *wins* $\eth$ *iff it wins* $\eth^\star$.

5.3 From Bounded-Cost Parity to Parity

We now show a construction that allows to reduce a bounded-cost parity game to a parity game. The approach we propose extends the one given in the previous section by further equipping the transition table $\mathcal{T}$ with a counter that keeps track of the delay accumulated since an unanswered request has been issued. Such a counter is bounded in the sense that if the delay exceeds the sum of weights of all moves in the original arena, then it is set to the special symbol $\divideontimes$. The idea is that if in a game such a bound has been exceeded then the adversarial player has taken at least twice a move with a positive weight. So, he can do this an arbitrary number of times and delay longer and longer the satisfaction of a request that therefore becomes not prompt. Thus, we use as states in $\mathcal{T}$, together with $\divideontimes$, a finite set of pairs of numbers, where the first component, as above, represents a finite request, while the second one is its delay. As first state component we also allow ⊥ and (⊥, 0) indicates that there are not unanswered requests up to the current position. Then, the transition function of $\mathcal{T}$ is defined as follows. If a request is not satisfied within a bounded delay, then it goes and remains forever in state ✶. Otherwise, if the request is satisfied, then it goes to (⊥, 0), else it moves to a state that contains, as first component, the maximum between the last request not responded and the read color and, as second component, the one present in the current state plus the weight of the traversed edge.

Now, consider the product arena $\mathcal{A}^\star$ of $\mathcal{T}$ with the original arena and color its positions as follows: unanswered request positions, with delay exceeding the bound, are colored with 1, while the remaining ones are colored as in the original arena. Clearly, in $\mathcal{A}^\star$, a parity game is won if and only if the bounded-cost parity game is won on the original arena. The formal construction of $\mathcal{T}$ and $\mathcal{A}^\star$ follow.

For a given BCP game $\eth \triangleq \langle \widehat{\mathcal{A}}, \mathrm{BCP}, v_\mathrm{o} \rangle$ induced by a weighted arena $\overline{\mathcal{A}} = \langle \mathcal{A}, \mathrm{Cl}, \mathrm{cl}, \mathrm{Wg}, \mathrm{wg} \rangle$, we construct a deterministic transition table $\mathcal{T} \triangleq \langle \mathrm{Cl} \times \mathrm{Wg}, \mathrm{St}, \mathrm{tr} \rangle$, with set of states $\mathrm{St} \triangleq \{✶\} \cup \mathrm{R}_\bot \times [0, s]$, where we assume $s \triangleq \sum_{m \in Mv} \mathrm{wg}(m)$ to be the sum of all weights of moves in $\overline{\mathcal{A}}$, and transition function defined as follows: $\mathrm{tr}(✶, (c, w)) \triangleq ✶$ and, additionally,

$$- \mathrm{tr}((r, k), (c, w)) \triangleq \begin{cases} (\bot, 0), & \text{if } r < c \text{ and } c \equiv 0 \,(\mathrm{mod}\ 2); \\ ✶, & \text{if } k + w > s; \\ (\max\{r, c\}, k + w), & \text{otherwise.} \end{cases}$$

Let $\mathcal{A}^\star = \widetilde{\mathcal{A}} \otimes \mathcal{T}$ be the product arena of $\widetilde{\mathcal{A}}$ and $\mathcal{T}$ and $\widetilde{\mathcal{A}^\star} \triangleq \langle \mathcal{A}^\star, \mathrm{Cl}, \mathrm{cl}^\star \rangle$ be the colored arena such that ✶ is colored with 1, and all other states are colored as in the original arena (w.r.t. the first component). Then, the P game $\eth^\star = \langle \widetilde{\mathcal{A}^\star}, \mathrm{P}, (v_\mathrm{o}, (\bot, 0)) \rangle$ induced by $\widetilde{\mathcal{A}^\star}$ is such that player ∃ wins $\eth$ iff it wins $\eth^\star$.

Theorem 4. *For every BCP game $\eth$ with $k \in \mathbb{N}$ priorities and sum of weights $s \in \mathbb{N}$, there is a P game $\eth^\star$, with order $|\eth^\star| = \mathrm{O}(|\eth| \cdot k \cdot s)$, such that player ∃ wins $\eth$ iff it wins $\eth^\star$.*

5.4 From Prompt Parity to Parity and Büchi

Finally, we show a construction that reduces a prompt parity game to a parity game. In particular, when the underlying weighted arena of the original game has only positive weights, then the construction returns a Büchi game. Our approach extends the one proposed for the above BCP case, by further allowing the transition table $\mathcal{T}$ to guess a request value that is not meet anymore along a play. This is done to accomplish the second part of the prompt parity condition, in which a finite number of requests can be excluded from the delay computation. To do this, first we allow $\mathcal{T}$ to be nondeterministic and label its states with a flag $\alpha \in \{D, \exists\}$ to identify, respectively, deterministic and existential states. Then, we enrich the states by means of a new component $d \in [0, h]$, where

$h \triangleq |\{v \in \text{Ps} : \text{cl}(v) \equiv 1 \,(\text{mod } 2)\}|$ is the maximum number of positions having odd priorities. So, d represents the counter of the forgotten priority and it is used to later check the guess states. As first state we have the tuple $((\bot, 0, D), 0))$ indicating that there are not unanswered and forgotten requests up to the current deterministic position. The transition function over a deterministic state is defined as follows. If a request is not satisfied in a bounded delay, then it goes and remains forever in state $*$; if the request is satisfied then it goes to $((\bot, d, D), 0)$; otherwise it moves to an existential state that contains, as first component, the triple having the maximum between the last request not responded and the read color, the counter of forgotten priority, and a flag indicating that the state is existential. Moreover, as a second component, there is a number that is the one present in the current state plus the weight of the traversed edge. The transition function over an existential state is defined as follows. If d is equal to the maximum allowable number of positions having an odd priority (h), then the computation remains in the same (deterministic) state; otherwise, the computation moves to a state in which the second component is incremented by 1. Note that the guess part is similar to that one performed to translate a nonderministic co-Büchi automaton into a Büchi one [18]. Finally, we color the obtained arena as we did for the above BCP case. In case the weighted arena of the original game has only positive weights, then one can exclude a priory the fact that there are unanswered requests with bounded delays. So, all these kind of requests can be forgotten in order to win the game. Thus, in this case, it is enough to satisfy only the remaining ones, which corresponds to visit infinitely often a position containing as second component the symbol $\bot$. So it is enough to color these positions with 2, all the remaining ones with 1, and play on this arena a Büchi condition. The formal construction of the transition table and the enriched arena follow.

For a PP game $\partial \triangleq \langle \widehat{\mathcal{A}}, \text{PP}, v_o \rangle$ induced by an arena $\overline{\mathcal{A}} = \langle \mathcal{A}, \text{Cl}, \text{cl}, \text{Wg}, \text{wg} \rangle$, we build a transition table $\mathcal{T} \triangleq \langle \text{Cl} \times \text{Wg}, \text{St}_D, \text{St}_\exists, \text{tr} \rangle$, with sets of states $\text{St}_D \triangleq \{*\} \cup Z_D \times [0, s]$ and $\text{St}_\exists \triangleq Z_\exists \times [0, s]$ (where we assume $s \triangleq \sum_{m \in Mv} \text{wg}(m)$ to be the sum of all weights of moves in the original arena and $Z_\alpha \triangleq R_\bot \times [0, h] \times \alpha$) and its transition function defined as follows: $\text{tr}(*, (c, w)) \triangleq *$ and, additionally:

$$- \text{tr}(((r, d, D), k), (c, w)) \triangleq \begin{cases} ((\bot, d, D), 0), & \text{if } r < c \land c \equiv 0 \,(\text{mod } 2); \\ *, & \text{if } k + w > s; \\ ((\max\{r, c\}, d, \exists), k + w), & \text{otherwise.} \end{cases}$$

$$- \text{tr}(((r, d, \exists), k)) \triangleq \begin{cases} \{((r, d, D), k)\}, & \text{if } d = h; \\ \{((r, d, D), k), ((\bot, d+1, D), 0)\}, & \text{otherwise.} \end{cases}$$

Observe that, the set Z_α is the Cartesian product of the biggest unanswered request, the counter of the forgotten priority and, a flag indicating whether the state is deterministic or existential.

Let $\mathcal{A}^* = \overline{\mathcal{A}} \otimes \mathcal{T}$ be the product arena of $\overline{\mathcal{A}}$ and $\mathcal{T}$ and consider the colored arena $\widetilde{\mathcal{A}^*} \triangleq \langle \mathcal{A}^*, \text{Cl}, \text{cl}^* \rangle$ such that, for all positions $(v, t) \in \text{Ps}^*$, if $t = *$

then $\text{cl}^\star((v,t)) = 1$ else $\text{cl}^\star((v,t)) = \text{cl}(v)$. Then, the P game $\eth^\star = \langle \widehat{\mathcal{A}^\star}, \text{P}, (v_\text{o}, ((\bot, 0, D), 0)) \rangle$ induced by $\widetilde{\mathcal{A}^\star}$ is such that player $\exists$ wins $\eth$ iff it wins $\eth^\star$.

Theorem 5. *For every* PP *game* $\eth$ *with* $k \in \mathbb{N}$ *priorities and sum of weights* $s \in \mathbb{N}$, *there is a* P *game* $\eth^\star$, *with order* $|\eth^\star| = \text{O}(|\eth|^2 \cdot k \cdot s)$, *such that player* $\exists$ *wins* $\eth$ *iff it wins* $\eth^\star$.

Observe that the estimation on the size of $\eth^\star$ is quite coarse since several type of states can not be reached by the initial position.

In case the weighted arena $\overline{\mathcal{A}}$ is positive, i.e., $\text{wg}(v) > 0$ for all $v \in \text{Ps}$, we can improve the above construction as follows. Consider the colored arena $\widetilde{\mathcal{A}^\star} \triangleq \langle \mathcal{A}^\star, \{1, 2\}, \text{cl}^\star \rangle$ such that, for all positions $(v, t) \in \text{Ps}^\star$, if $t = ((\bot, d, D), 0)$ for some $d \in [0, h]$ then $\text{cl}^\star((v,t)) = 2$ else $\text{cl}^\star((v,t)) = 1$. Then, the B game $\eth^\star = \langle \widehat{\mathcal{A}^\star}, \text{B}, (v_\text{o}, ((\bot, 0, D), 0)) \rangle$ induced by $\widetilde{\mathcal{A}^\star}$ is such that player $\exists$ wins $\eth$ iff it wins $\eth^\star$.

Theorem 6. *For every* PP *game* $\eth$ *with* $k \in \mathbb{N}$ *priorities and sum of weights* $s \in \mathbb{N}$ *defined on a positive weighted arena, there is a* B *game* $\eth^\star$, *with order* $|\eth^\star| = \text{O}(|\eth|^2 \cdot k \cdot s)$, *such that player* $\exists$ *wins* $\eth$ *iff it wins* $\eth^\star$.

6 Conclusion

Recently, promptness reasonings have received large attention in system design and verification. This is due to the fact that, while from a theoretical point of view questions like "a specific state is eventually reached in a computation" have a clear meaning and application in formal verification, in a practical scenario, such a question results useless if there is no bound over the time the required state occurs. This is the case, for example, when we deal with liveness and safety properties. The question becomes even more involved in the case of reactive systems, well modeled as two-player games, in which the response can be procrastinated later and later due to an adversarial behavior.

In this work, we studied several variants of two-player parity games working under a prompt semantics. In particular, we gave a general and clean setting to formally describe and unify most of such games introduced in the literature, as well as to address new ones. Our framework helped us to investigate peculiarities and relationships among the addressed games. In particular, it helped us to come up with solution algorithms that have as core engine and main complexity the solution of a parity or a Büchi game. This makes the proposed algorithms very efficient.

As games already addressed in literature, we studied cost parity and bounded-cost parity and, for both of them, we provided algorithms that improve their known complexity. As new parity games, we investigated full parity, full-prompt parity, and prompt parity. We showed that full parity is in PTIME, prompt parity and cost parity are equivalent and both in UPTIME ∩ COUPTIME. The latter improves the known complexity result to solve cost parity games because our algorithm reduce the original problem to a unique parity game while their one performs "several calls" to a parity games solver. Tables 1 and 2 report the formal definition of all conditions addressed in the paper along with the full/not-full/semi-full behavior. Tables 3 summarizes the achieved results. In particular, we use the special arrow ↩ to indicate that the result is trivial or an easy consequence of another one.

Table 3. Summary of all winning condition complexities

Conditions	Colored Arena	(Colored) Weighted arena
Parity (P)	UPTIME ∩ COUPTIME [16]	↩
Full Parity (FP)	PTIME [Thm 3]	↩
Prompt Parity (PP)	PTIME [Thm 6]	UPTIME ∩ COUPTIME [Thm 5]
Full Prompt Parity (FPP)	↩	PTIME [FP + Cor 1]
Cost Parity (CP)	PTIME [PP + Cor 2]	UPTIME ∩ COUPTIME [PP + Cor 2]
Bounded Cost Parity (BCP)	PTIME [FPP + Cor 3]	UPTIME ∩ COUPTIME [Thm 4]

References

1. Almagor, S., Hirshfeld, Y., Kupferman, O.: Promptness in omega-Regular Automata. In: Bouajjani, A., Chin, W.-N. (eds.) ATVA 2010. LNCS, vol. 6252, pp. 22–36. Springer, Heidelberg (2010)
2. Alur, R., Henzinger, T.A.: Finitary fairness. ACM Trans. Program. Lang. Syst. 20(6) (1998)
3. Aminof, B., Mogavero, F., Murano, A.: Synthesis of hierarchical systems. In: Arbab, F., Ölveczky, P.C. (eds.) FACS 2011. LNCS, vol. 7253, pp. 42–60. Springer, Heidelberg (2012)
4. Aminof, B., Mogavero, F., Murano, A.: Synthesis of hierarchical systems. Science of Comp. Program (2013), doi: http://dx.doi.org/10.1016/j.scico.2013.07.001
5. Aminof, B., Kupferman, O., Murano, A.: Improved model checking of hierarchical systems. Inf. Comput. 210, 68–86 (2012)
6. Berwanger, D.: Admissibility in infinite games. In: Thomas, W., Weil, P. (eds.) STACS 2007. LNCS, vol. 4393, pp. 188–199. Springer, Heidelberg (2007)
7. Chatterjee, K., Doyen, L., Henzinger, T.A., Raskin, J.-F.: Generalized mean-payoff and energy games. In: FSTTCS 2010. LIPIcs, vol. 8, pp. 505–516 (2010)
8. Chatterjee, K., Henzinger, T.A., Horn, F.: Finitary winning in ω-regular games. ACM Trans. Comput. Logic 11(1) (2009)
9. Chatterjee, K., Henzinger, T.A., Jurdzinski, M.: Mean-payoff parity games. In: LICS 2005, pp. 178–187 (2005)
10. Chatterjee, K., Jurdzinski, M., Henzinger, T.A.: Quantitative stochastic parity games. In: SODA 2004, pp. 121–130 (2004)
11. Clarke, E.M., Emerson, E.A.: Design and Synthesis of Synchronization Skeletons Using Branching-Time Temporal Logic. In: LP 1981. LNCS, vol. 131, pp. 52–71 (1981)
12. Clarke, E.M., Grumberg, O., Peled, D.A.: Model Checking. MIT Press (2002)
13. Emerson, E.A., Jutla, C.: Tree automata, μ-calculus and determinacy. In: FOCS 1991, pp. 368–377 (1991)
14. Fijalkow, N., Zimmermann, M.: Cost-parity and cost-streett games. In: FSTTCS 2012, pp. 124–135 (2012)

15. Horn, F., Thomas, W., Wallmeier, N.: Optimal strategy synthesis in request-response games. In: Cha, S(S.), Choi, J.-Y., Kim, M., Lee, I., Viswanathan, M. (eds.) ATVA 2008. LNCS, vol. 5311, pp. 361–373. Springer, Heidelberg (2008)
16. Jurdzinski, M.: Deciding the winner in parity games is in up ∩ co-up. Inf. Process. Lett. 68(3), 119–124 (1998)
17. Kozen, D.: Results on the Propositional mu-Calculus. TCS 27(3), 333–354 (1983)
18. Kupferman, O., Morgenstern, G., Murano, A.: Typeness for omega-regular automata. Int. J. Found. Comput. Sci. 17(4), 869–884 (2006)
19. Kupferman, O., Piterman, N., Vardi, M.Y.: From liveness to promptness. Formal Methods in System Design 34(2), 83–103 (2009)
20. Kupferman, O., Vardi, M., Wolper, P.: Module Checking. IC 164(2), 322–344 (2001)
21. Kupferman, O., Vardi, M.Y., Wolper, P.: An Automata Theoretic Approach to Branching-Time Model Checking. JACM 47(2), 312–360 (2000)
22. Pnueli, A.: The Temporal Logic of Programs. In: FOCS 1977, pp. 46–57 (1977)
23. Queille, J.P., Sifakis, J.: Specification and Verification of Concurrent Programs in Cesar. In: Dezani-Ciancaglini, M., Montanari, U. (eds.) SP 1981. LNCS, vol. 137, pp. 337–351. Springer, Heidelberg (1981)
24. Zielonka, W.: Infinite games on finitely coloured graphs with applications to automata on infinite trees. Theor. Comput. Sci. 200(1-2), 135–183 (1998)

Defining Privacy Is Supposed to Be Easy*

Sebastian A. Mödersheim[1], Thomas Groß[2], and Luca Viganò[3]

[1] DTU Compute, Lyngby, Denmark
[2] School of Computing Science, Newcastle University, UK
[3] Department of Informatics, King's College London, UK

Abstract. Formally specifying privacy goals is not trivial. The most widely used approach in formal methods is based on the static equivalence of frames in the applied *pi*-calculus, basically asking whether or not the intruder is able to distinguish two given worlds. A subtle question is how we can be sure that we have specified all pairs of worlds to properly reflect our intuitive privacy goal. To address this problem, we introduce in this paper a novel and declarative way to specify privacy goals, called α-β privacy, and relate it to static equivalence. This new approach is based on specifying two formulae α and β in first-order logic with Herbrand universes, where α reflects the intentionally released information and β includes the actual cryptographic ("technical") messages the intruder can see. Then α-β privacy means that the intruder cannot derive any "non-technical" statement from β that he cannot derive from α already. We describe by a variety of examples how this notion can be used in practice. Even though α-β privacy does not directly contain a notion of distinguishing between worlds, there is a close relationship to static equivalence of frames that we investigate formally. This allows us to justify (and criticize) the specifications that are currently used in verification tools, and obtain partial tool support for α-β privacy.

1 Introduction

Context and Motivation. Several formal notions of privacy have been proposed over the last decade, e.g., [1, 3, 5–7, 9, 13, 17]. Although these notions are quite different, we can probably agree that defining privacy is actually quite subtle and not as easy as it is supposed to be. One of the main reasons is that classical secrecy notions do not apply for data that are not themselves secrets, e.g., a vote is not itself a secret value like a private key. Rather, the information we would like to protect is the *relation* between the (usually non-secret) values, e.g., which voter has cast what vote.

For this reason, the vast majority of the popular approaches to formalizing privacy is based not on the question of what the intruder can deduce from a set of

---

* This work was partially supported by the EU FP7 Projects no. 318424, "FutureID: Shaping the Future of Electronic Identity" (futureid.eu), and no. 257876, "SPaCIoS: Secure Provision and Consumption in the Internet of Services" (spacios.eu) and the PRIN 2010-11 project "Security Horizons". Much of this work was carried out while L. Viganò was at Dipartimento di Informatica, Università di Verona, Italy.

known messages, but rather whether he can *distinguish* two different worlds.[1] An interesting follow-up question is thus: what is the "right" set of distinguishability questions to define privacy? For instance, in a voting protocol where each user can just vote yes or no, we may check that the intruder cannot distinguish the world where a given voter voted yes from the one where this voter voted no. However, this is not enough: even if the intruder cannot determine the votes, he should also not be able to tell whether two voters have voted the same.

When we look at privacy-friendly identity management, we have even more different kinds of data and possible relations between them, such as date of birth, home address, or different uses of the same credentials. So, how can we ever be confident that a given set of distinguishability questions is sufficient for privacy, i.e., that we have not overlooked some possible connection the intruder could make that we prefer him not to be able to make?

Contributions. In this paper, we take a step back and approach the problem from a different angle. Our main goal is to find a formal description that reflects the idea of privacy in a "natural" and less technical way and that can then be related to the existing privacy notions, supporting or criticizing them. In fact, ultimately we want to use the existing results in this field, but we take the scientific liberty to first think in a slightly different direction.

More specifically, in this paper, we introduce a novel, simple and declarative approach to specify privacy goals, called α-β *privacy*, which is based on specifying two formulae α and β in First-Order Logic with Herbrand Universes [12].

α formalizes the intentionally released information, i.e., the information that we can legitimately give to the intruder, which we also refer to as *payload*. For instance, in a privacy-friendly zero-knowledge credential system (such as IBM's *Idemix* [13]) a user may prove that she is a female older than 18 years (according to an electronic passport she owns), without releasing any more information, such as her name or the precise date of birth. Hence, we have an immediate specification of the data that the user deliberately released, i.e., the statement proved in the zero-knowledge proof, and it is intuitive that we then have a violation of privacy whenever the server who verified the zero-knowledge proof can derive more about the user than the user deliberately released by the proof. Of course, we must exclude from this definition everything that is already entailed by the proved statement, e.g., the fact that the user is also over 15 years old is entailed by the proved statement, so that is not a violation of privacy, but if the server is able to derive that the user is actually over 21 years, then there is a violation. It is thus quite natural to formalize such statements as formulae in some logic and to define privacy as the inability of the intruder to derive statements that are not entailed by what the users have released.

As a counterpart to the "ideal knowledge" provided by the payload α, we also need the *technical information* β, which represents the "actual knowledge"

---

[1] This is not unlike the earlier paradigm shift in cryptographic definitions from deducibility questions (such as: can the intruder obtain the plaintext of an encrypted message?) to distinguishability questions (such as: can the intruder distinguish the encryption of different chosen values?).

that the intruder has, describing the information (e.g., names, keys ...) that he initially knows, which actual cryptographic messages he has observed and what he knows about these messages. For instance, he may be unable to decrypt a message but anyway know that it has a certain format and contains certain (protected) information, like a vote.

α-β privacy then means that the intruder cannot derive any "non-technical" statement from β that he cannot derive from α already. We believe that this is indeed a simple way to define privacy, and is a more declarative way to talk about privacy than distinguishability of frames. Essentially, the modeler should not think about what technical information the intruder could exploit, but rather what information he is fine to release (α) and what messages are actually exchanged (β).

Another interesting and very declarative feature of our approach is that it is straightforward to model what happens when two intruders collaborate and share their knowledge. α-β privacy allows us to formalize this simply by taking the logical conjunction of the formulae describing the knowledge that the two intruders have, reflecting in a natural way what we can ask the system to provide: The best technology cannot prevent dishonest agents from pooling all the information that they were intentionally given and deriving all possible conclusions from that—but we can ask that they cannot derive more than that.

We describe by a variety of examples how α-β-privacy can be used in practice, and define transition systems based on it. Even though α-β privacy does not directly contain a notion of distinguishing between worlds, there is a close relationship to static equivalence of frames that we investigate formally. This allows us to justify (and criticize) the specifications that are currently used in verification tools and obtain partial tool support for α-β privacy (but we do not discuss these two issues in full detail in this paper). We also prove several results that help in reasoning about α-β privacy in general and give a decision procedure for a fragment of it.

Organization. §2 provides the basis for our approach: we discuss First-Order Logic with Herbrand Universes, messages and frames. In §3, we formalize α-β-privacy and consider some concrete examples. In §4, we discuss automation and the relation of α-β privacy to static equivalence and in §5, we draw conclusions. In the accompanying technical report [14], we provide additional examples of how α-β privacy may be employed to model randomized and deterministic encryption, non-determinism, strong secrecy, guessing attacks, anonymous credential systems and pooling of knowledge.

We introduce primitives of our new α-β privacy approach step by step, where Table 1 gives an overview of where they are introduced.

2 Preliminaries

2.1 Herbrand Logic

To formalize our approach, we need to choose an appropriate logic. An obvious candidate is *first-order logic (FOL)*, but this has one difficulty when it comes

Table 1. Roadmap of the primitives introduced

$\Sigma, \mathcal{V},$	§2.1/p.621	Finite alphabet, disjoint set of variables, and terms of our Herbrand Logic (FOL with Herbrand Universes)
$\mathcal{T}_\Sigma(\mathcal{V})$		
F_i	§2.3/p.625	Frame (as in static equivalence), adapted to Herbrand Logic
m_i	§2.3/p.625	Memory location i, storing a piece of intruder knowledge
α	§3/p.626	*Payload*, information that the intruder may legitimately obtain, over $\mathcal{V}_0 \subseteq \mathcal{V}$ and $\Sigma_0 \subseteq \Sigma$
β	§3/p.626	*Technical information* of and about observed protocol messages, over $\mathcal{V}$ and Σ
$concr$	§2.3/p.625	Encoding of concrete intruder knowledge, ground terms from $\mathcal{T}_\Sigma$
$eval$	§3.2/p.628	Encoding of structural intruder knowledge, terms from $\mathcal{T}_\Sigma(\mathcal{V})$
ϕ_{axiom}	Table 3	Axioms for generable terms, concrete and structural knowledge

to the interpretation of the constants and the cryptographic operators. As it is standard in security protocol verification, we would like to interpret these operators either in the free algebra or in the initial algebra induced by a set of algebraic equations; we also call this the *Herbrand Universe*.[2] In general, we cannot enforce the desired interpretation by axioms in FOL (see, e.g., Example 2). There are some work-arounds for this, e.g., [4, 11, 16, 18] use first-order Horn theories that are inconsistent (in standard FOL) iff there is an attack in the least Herbrand model, but this construction is not possible for our work because we want to talk about deductions that hold in all Herbrand models of a formula (which does not necessarily have a unique least Herbrand model).

As proposed in [12], FOL with Herbrand universes, or *Herbrand Logic* for short, can be seen as a logic in its own right—as justified, e.g., by Example 2 below. We define *Herbrand Logic* as follows (discussing differences with respect to the definition of [12] below).

Definition 1 (Syntax of Herbrand Logic). *Let* $\Sigma = \Sigma_f \uplus \Sigma_i \uplus \Sigma_r$ *be an alphabet that consists of a set* Σ_f *of free function symbols, a set* Σ_i *of interpreted function symbols and a set* Σ_r *of relation symbols, all with their arities.*

We write $f(t_1, \ldots, t_n)$ *when* $f \in \Sigma_f$ *and* $f[t_1, \ldots, t_n]$ *when* $f \in \Sigma_i$, *and we denote the set of considered cryptographic operators by the subset* $\Sigma_{op} \subseteq \Sigma_f$. *Constants are the special case of free function symbols with arity 0.*

Let $\mathcal{V}$ *be a countable set of* variable symbols, *disjoint from* Σ. *We denote with* $\mathcal{T}_\Sigma(\mathcal{V})$ *the set of all* terms *that can be built from the function symbols in* Σ *and the variables in* $\mathcal{V}$. *We simply write* $\mathcal{T}_\Sigma$ *when* $\mathcal{V} = \emptyset$, *and call its elements* ground terms *(over signature* Σ*).*

We define the set $\mathcal{L}_\Sigma(\mathcal{V})$ *of* formulae *over the alphabet* Σ *and the variables* $\mathcal{V}$ *as usual: relations and equality of terms are atomic formulae, and composed formulae are built using conjunction* $\wedge$, *negation* $\neg$, *and existential quantification* $\exists$.

---

[2] Note that it is common to define the Herbrand Universe as the free term algebra but for our purposes it is crucial to also include algebraic properties of the operators, as illustrated in Example 1.

We employ the standard syntactic sugar and write, for example, $\forall x.\phi$ for $\neg \exists x. \neg \phi$. We also write $x \in \{t_1, \ldots, t_n\}$ to abbreviate $x = t_1 \vee \ldots \vee x = t_n$. The function fv returns the set of *free variables* of a formula as expected.

Definition 2 (Herbrand Universe and Algebra). *Formulae in Herbrand logic are always interpreted with respect to a given fixed set Σ_f of free symbols (since this set may contain symbols that do not occur in the formulae) and a congruence relation $\approx$ on $\mathcal{T}_{\Sigma_f}$. We may annotate all notions of the semantics with Σ_f and $\approx$ when it is not clear from the context.*

We write $[t]_\approx = \{t' \in \mathcal{T}_{\Sigma_f} \mid t \approx t'\}$ to denote the equivalence class of a term $t \in \mathcal{T}_{\Sigma_f}$ with respect to $\approx$. Further, let $U = \{[t]_\approx \mid t \in \mathcal{T}_{\Sigma_f}\}$ be the set of all equivalence classes. We call U the Herbrand universe *(since it is freely generated by the function symbols of Σ_f modulo $\approx$). Based on U, we define a Σ_f-algebra $\mathcal{A}$ that interprets every n-ary function symbol $f \in \Sigma_f$ as a function $f^\mathcal{A} : U^n \to U$ in the following standard way. $f^\mathcal{A}([t_1]_\approx, \ldots, [t_n]_\approx) = [f(t_1, \ldots, t_n)]_\approx$, where the choice of the representatives $t_1, \ldots, t_n$ of the equivalence classes is irrelevant because $\approx$ is congruent. $\mathcal{A}$ is sometimes also called the* quotient algebra *(in the literature sometimes denoted with $\mathcal{T}_{\Sigma_f}/\approx$).*

Example 1. As an example, suppose the congruence relation $\approx$ is given by a set of equations like $\forall x, y.\, x+y \approx y+x$ for some binary function symbols $+$ and $-$ in Σ_f. Then we have in the quotient algebra $5+3 \approx 3+5$ but still $3+5 \not\approx (7-4)+5$. Thus, the quotient algebra is the *finest* (or "free-est") interpretation still compatible with the given algebraic properties. □

Definition 3 (Semantics of Herbrand Logic). *An interpretation $\mathcal{I}$ maps every interpreted function symbol $f \in \Sigma_i$ of arity n to a function $\mathcal{I}(f) : U^n \to U$ on the Herbrand universe, every relation symbol $r \in \Sigma_r$ of arity n to a relation $\mathcal{I}(r) \subseteq U^n$ on the Herbrand universe, and every variable $x \in \mathcal{V}$ to an element of U.*

We extend $\mathcal{I}$ to a function on $\mathcal{T}_\Sigma(\mathcal{V}) : \mathcal{I}(f(t_1, \ldots, t_n)) = f^\mathcal{A}(\mathcal{I}(t_1), \ldots, \mathcal{I}(t_n))$ for $f \in \Sigma_f$ and $\mathcal{I}(f[t_1, \ldots, t_n]) = \mathcal{I}(f)(\mathcal{I}(t_1), \ldots, \mathcal{I}(t_n))$.

We define that $\mathcal{I}$ is a model of formula ϕ, *in symbols $\mathcal{I} \models \phi$, as follows:*

$\mathcal{I} \models s = t$ iff $\mathcal{I}(s) = \mathcal{I}(t)$
$\mathcal{I} \models r(t_1, \ldots, t_n)$ iff $(\mathcal{I}(t_1), \ldots, \mathcal{I}(t_n)) \in \mathcal{I}(r)$
$\mathcal{I} \models \phi \wedge \psi$ iff $\mathcal{I} \models \phi$ and $\mathcal{I} \models \psi$
$\mathcal{I} \models \neg \phi$ iff not $\mathcal{I} \models \phi$
$\mathcal{I} \models \exists x. \phi$ iff there is a $c \in U$ such that $\mathcal{I}[x \mapsto c] \models \phi$

where $\mathcal{I}[x \mapsto c]$ denotes the interpretation that is identical to $\mathcal{I}$ except that x is mapped to c. Entailment $\phi \models \psi$ *is defined as $\mathcal{I} \models \phi$ implies $\mathcal{I} \models \psi$ for all interpretations $\mathcal{I}$. We write $\phi \equiv \psi$ when both $\phi \models \psi$ and $\psi \models \phi$. We also use $\equiv$ in the definitions of formulae.*

Example 2. Similar to [12], we can axiomatize arithmetic in Herbrand logic; simply let $\Sigma_f = \{z/0, s/1\}$, representing 0 and (+1), let $\approx$ be syntactic equality on $\mathcal{T}_{\Sigma_f}$, and let $\Sigma_i = \{add/2, mult/2\}$ and $\Sigma_r = \{<\}$ with the following formula:

Table 2. Example set Σ_{op}: standard cryptographic constructors, destructors, verifiers

Constructors	Destructors	Verifiers	Meaning
$\mathsf{crypt}(k,r,t)$	$\mathsf{dcrypt}(k,t)$	$\mathsf{vcrypt}(k,t)$	Asymmetric encryption of t with public key k and randomness r. Decryption with private key k.
$\mathsf{scrypt}(k,r,t)$	$\mathsf{dscrypt}(k,t)$	$\mathsf{vscrypt}(k,t)$	Symmetric encryption of t with secret key k and randomness r.
$\mathsf{sign}(k,t)$	$\mathsf{retrieve}(t)$	$\mathsf{vsig}(k,t)$	Signature of t with private key k; verification with public key k.
$\mathsf{pub}(s), \mathsf{priv}(s)$			Asymmetric key pair generated from seed s.
$\mathsf{pair}(t_1, t_2)$	$\mathsf{proj}_i(t)$	$\mathsf{vpair}(t)$	Concatenation of messages t_1 and t_2.
$\mathsf{h}(t)$			Hash of message t.

$\phi \equiv \forall x, y.\; \mathsf{add}[\mathsf{z}, y] = y \;\wedge\; \mathsf{add}[\mathsf{s}(x), y] = \mathsf{add}[x, \mathsf{s}(y)] \;\wedge\; \mathsf{mult}[\mathsf{z}, y] = \mathsf{z} \;\wedge\; \mathsf{mult}[\mathsf{s}(x), y] = \mathsf{add}[y, \mathsf{mult}[x, y]] \;\wedge\; x < \mathsf{s}(x) \;\wedge\; x < y \implies x < \mathsf{s}(y)$. Then $\phi \models \psi$ iff ψ is a true arithmetic statement. It is well-known that (as a consequence of Löwenheim-Skolem's theorem or of Gödel's incompleteness theorem, see [10]) an equivalent axiomatization cannot be achieved in standard FOL. □

We note the following three differences with respect to the definition of Herbrand logic in [12]. First, in [12] and as is standard, the Herbrand universe is the free term algebra, forbidding one to model algebraic properties of the free operators. Our definition is a generalization to equivalence classes modulo the $\approx$ relation (and $\approx$ can simply be set to be the syntactic equality on $\mathcal{T}_{\Sigma_f}$ to get the free algebra). Second, the logic in [12] treats free variables as implicitly universally quantified, which is quite non-standard. In our definition, an interpretation of a formula includes the interpretation of the free variables as is standard. This is, of course, without loss of expressiveness since one can quantify variables when this is what one wants to express. Third, the logic in [12] does not have interpreted functions and, in fact, these are syntactic sugar: an interpreted n-ary function symbol f can be modeled by an $n+1$-ary relation R_f symbol with the axiom $\forall x_1, \ldots, x_n. \exists y.\, R_f(x_1, \ldots, x_n, y) \wedge \forall y'.\, R_f(x_1, \ldots, x_n, y') \implies y = y'$.

2.2 Messages, Operators and Algebraic Properties

We adopt the common black-box ("Dolev-Yao style" [8]) algebraic model of the cryptographic operations. We consider, in this paper, the example set Σ_{op} of standard operators given, together with their intuitive meanings, in Table 2. Let $\approx$ be the smallest relation so that for all terms s, r, t, t_1, t_2 in $\mathcal{T}_{\Sigma_f}$ and for $i \in \{1, 2\}$:

$\mathsf{dcrypt}(\mathsf{priv}(s), \mathsf{crypt}(\mathsf{pub}(s), r, t)) \approx t$ $\qquad \mathsf{vcrypt}(\mathsf{priv}(s), \mathsf{crypt}(\mathsf{pub}(s), r, t)) \approx \mathsf{yes}$
$\mathsf{retrieve}(\mathsf{sign}(\mathsf{priv}(s), t)) \approx t$ $\qquad \mathsf{vsig}(\mathsf{pub}(s), \mathsf{sign}(\mathsf{priv}(s), t)) \approx \mathsf{yes}$
$\mathsf{dscrypt}(k, \mathsf{scrypt}(k, r, t)) \approx t$ $\qquad \mathsf{vscrypt}(k, \mathsf{scrypt}(k, r, t)) \approx \mathsf{yes}$
$\mathsf{proj}_i(\mathsf{pair}(t_1, t_2)) \approx t_i$ $\qquad \mathsf{vpair}(\mathsf{pair}(t_1, t_2)) \approx \mathsf{yes}$

The equations induce a *congruence relation* $\approx$ on terms, and we interpret all functions in the Herbrand universe modulo this congruence as explained above, i.e., two terms are equal iff that is a consequence of $\approx$ with respect to Σ_{op}.

2.3 Frames

Frames and the notion of their static equivalence are a standard way to formalize privacy goals in formal methods, e.g., [5–7]. We define them here in a slightly non-standard way that is more convenient to directly formalize them in Herbrand logic and later relate them to our concept of α-β privacy (we point the reader to [14] for a detailed discussion on the differences between the standard definition of frames and the one we consider here). *Frames* are written as

$$F = \{\mathsf{m}_1 \mapsto t_1, \ldots, \mathsf{m}_l \mapsto t_l\}$$

where the m_i are distinguished constants and the t_i are ground terms that do not contain any m_i. This frame represents that the intruder *knows* l messages $t_1, \ldots, t_l$ that he can "refer to" as $\mathsf{m}_1, \ldots, \mathsf{m}_l$. In contrast to the standard Dolev-Yao intruders, we thus do not model the intruder knowledge by a set of messages $\{t_1, \ldots, t_l\}$, but we give each message a unique label m_i. This allows us to talk about checks that the intruder can make, e.g., whether hashing the value at m_1 gives the same value as the one stored at m_2. We may thus refer to the m_i as *memory locations* in the intruder's memory.

We define *the terms that the intruder can generate from his knowledge* as the least set that contains $\mathsf{m}_1, \ldots, \mathsf{m}_l$ and is closed under all the cryptographic operators that the intruder can employ. For the example operators of Σ_{op} shown in Table 2, we can formalize this in Herbrand Logic with a formula $\phi_{gen}(l)$, which uses a new predicate $gen(t)$ to represent that the intruder can generate t. Hence, in contrast to the standard Dolev-Yao definition, the intruder does not directly compose the terms he knows but rather he builds what is sometimes called *recipes* by applying operators to the memory locations he has.

The axiom $\phi_{gen}(l)$ is shown in Table 3, together with the other axioms that we will employ in α-β privacy. For a different set Σ_{op} of cryptographic operators the definition is analogous: using semi-formal notation, $\phi_{gen}(l)$ would have the form

$$\phi_{gen}(l) \equiv \forall x.\ gen(x) \iff (x \in \{\mathsf{m}_1, \ldots, \mathsf{m}_l\} \vee \bigvee_{\mathsf{f} \in \Sigma_{op}} \exists x_1 \ldots x_n.\ x = \mathsf{f}(x_1, \ldots, x_n) \wedge gen(x_1) \ldots gen(x_n))$$

The axiom $\phi_{Fr}(F)$ in Table 3 allows us to encode the frame $F = \{\mathsf{m}_1 \mapsto t_1, \ldots, \mathsf{m}_l \mapsto t_l\}$ into Herbrand logic using an interpreted function symbol $concr[\cdot]$ that yields the concrete message stored for a memory location, and the axiom ϕ_{concr} extends the definition of $concr[\cdot]$ congruently for the application of cryptographic operators, so that $concr[t]$ is determined for all terms t that the intruder can generate.

In the following, we use examples with two frames F_0 and F_1, both with the same length l. We use functions $concr_0[t]$ and $concr_1[t]$ for their respective encodings (and denote the above axiom as ϕ_{concr_0} and ϕ_{concr_1} as expected).

Table 3. Axioms used in α-β privacy (for the example set Σ_{op})

$$\phi_{gen}(l) \equiv \forall x.\ gen(x) \iff (x \in \{m_1, \ldots, m_l\} \vee$$
$$(\exists x_1, x_2, x_3.\ x = \mathsf{crypt}(x_1, x_2, x_3) \wedge gen(x_1) \wedge gen(x_2) \wedge gen(x_3)) \vee$$
$$(\exists x_1, x_2.\ x = \mathsf{dcrypt}(x_1, x_2) \wedge gen(x_1) \wedge gen(x_2)) \vee \ldots \vee$$
$$(\exists x_1.\ x = \mathsf{h}(x_1) \wedge gen(x_1))) \quad \text{for a length } l$$

$\phi_{Fr}(F) \equiv concr[m_1] = t_1 \wedge \ldots \wedge concr[m_l] = t_l$ for a frame F of length l

$\phi_{concr} \equiv \forall x_1, x_2, x_3, y_1, y_2, y_3.\ (concr[x_1] = y_1 \wedge concr[x_2] = y_2 \wedge concr[x_3] = y_3) \implies$
$(concr[\mathsf{crypt}(x_1, x_2, x_3)] = \mathsf{crypt}(y_1, y_2, y_3) \wedge$
$concr[\mathsf{dcrypt}(x_1, x_2)] = \mathsf{dcrypt}(y_1, y_2) \wedge \ldots \wedge concr[\mathsf{h}(x_1)] = \mathsf{h}(y_1))$

$\phi_{eval} \equiv \forall x_1, x_2, x_3, y_1, y_2, y_3.\ (eval[x_1] = y_1 \wedge eval[x_2] = y_2 \wedge eval[x_3] = y_3) \implies$
$(eval[\mathsf{crypt}(x_1, x_2, x_3)] = \mathsf{crypt}(y_1, y_2, y_3) \wedge$
$eval[\mathsf{dcrypt}(x_1, x_2)] = \mathsf{dcrypt}(y_1, y_2) \wedge \ldots \wedge eval[\mathsf{h}(x_1)] = \mathsf{h}(y_1))$

$\phi_{struct} \equiv \forall x, y.\ (concr[x] = concr[y] \iff eval[x] = eval[y])$

Example 3. Consider the frame (from [6]): $F_0 = \{m_1 \mapsto \mathsf{scrypt}(k, r_1, n_1), m_2 \mapsto \mathsf{pair}(n_1, n_2), m_3 \mapsto k\}$. We have, for instance, that the intruder can obtain n_1. Let $\Phi \equiv \phi_{Fr}(F_0) \wedge \phi_{concr_0} \wedge \phi_{gen}(3)$. Then we have, e.g., $\Phi \models gen(\mathsf{dscrypt}(m_3, m_1)) \wedge concr_0[\mathsf{dscrypt}(m_3, m_1)] = n_1$. Note that we have $\Phi \models concr_0[\mathsf{dscrypt}(m_3, m_1)] = concr_0[\mathsf{proj}_1(m_2)]$, i.e., the intruder can check that the decrypted term is equal to the first component of m_2. □

Definition 4 (Static Equivalence of Frames). *Two frames F_0 and F_1 of the same length l are* statically equivalent *(in symbols, $F_0 \sim F_1$) iff for any pair of generable terms either both frames give the same result or both frames give a different result. Formally, $F_0 \sim F_1$ iff*

$$\phi_{gen}(l) \wedge \phi_{Fr}(F_0) \wedge \phi_{Fr}(F_1) \wedge \phi_{concr_0} \wedge \phi_{concr_1} \models$$
$$\forall x, y.\ (gen(x) \wedge gen(y)) \implies (concr_0[x] = concr_0[y] \iff concr_1[x] = concr_1[y])$$

Example 4. We can distinguish F_0 of Example 3 from the frame $F_1 = \{m_1 \mapsto \mathsf{scrypt}(k, r_1, n_3), m_2 \mapsto \mathsf{pair}(n_1, n_2), m_3 \mapsto k\}$ since the check $concr_1[\mathsf{dscrypt}(m_3, m_1)] = concr_1[\mathsf{proj}_1(m_2)]$ fails, whereas it succeeds for $concr_0$. □

3 A New Privacy Model: α-β Privacy

We introduce α-β privacy step by step. In §3.1 we introduce the distinction between payload formulae α and technical formulae β as well as the notion of *interesting* derivation from β. In §3.2, we establish the methodology to reason over such formulae, introducing a further function $eval[\cdot]$ similar to $concr[\cdot]$ that represents the structural information the intruder has about his knowledge. In §3.3 we extend the privacy notion to transition systems, and, finally, in §3.4 we discuss further examples of α-β privacy.

3.1 Payload and Technical Information

Our model is inspired by zero-knowledge proofs for privacy (as they are used, e.g., in IBM's Idemix [13]). The following points are characteristic for such proofs:

- The prover (intentionally) conveys some information to the verifier, i.e., the statement being proved to the verifier. We call this statement the *payload* α.
- The participants also (inevitably) convey some cryptographic information (e.g., commitments, challenges, and responses) that, if the scheme is secure, do *not* reveal anything "interesting" besides α; this, of course, is the very reason why such a scheme is called zero-knowledge. We call this kind of information the *technical information* β.

Here the term "interesting" is often defined in the cryptographic world by the fact that it is computationally easy to produce a fake transcript of zero-knowledge proofs that is statistically indistinguishable from a real transcript. Hence, whatever information could possibly be obtained from β one may have created oneself. This kind of definition is, however, quite unhandy in logical reasoning, and it applies only to (some types of) zero-knowledge proofs.

We show that it is fortunately possible to define the term "interesting" on a logical basis that makes sense for many actual situations in which we want to talk about privacy. The key idea is that the payload α may be formulated over a restricted alphabet $\Sigma_0 \subsetneq \Sigma$, whereas the technical information β may talk about the full alphabet Σ (e.g., all cryptographic operators are part of $\Sigma \setminus \Sigma_0$).

Definition 5. *Let $\Sigma_0 \subsetneq \Sigma$. Given a payload formula $\alpha \in \mathcal{L}_{\Sigma_0}(\mathcal{V})$ and a technical formula $\beta \in \mathcal{L}_\Sigma(\mathcal{V})$, where $\beta \models \alpha$ and $fv(\alpha) = fv(\beta)$ and both α and β are consistent, we say that a statement $\alpha' \in \mathcal{L}_{\Sigma_0}(fv(\alpha))$ is an* interesting derivation *from β (with respect to α) if $\beta \models \alpha'$ but $\alpha \not\models \alpha'$. We say that β* respects *the privacy of α if the intruder cannot derive any interesting statement from β, and that β* violates *the privacy of α otherwise.*

We have defined the notion of an interesting derivation α' as anything the intruder may be able to derive from his observations β as long as it is a non-technical statement (i.e., of $\mathcal{L}_{\Sigma_0}$) and it does not follow from α alone, i.e., from what he is permitted to know anyway. This allows us to capture that the intruder may well see a few technical details, e.g., that two messages come from the same IP address, but that in itself is not very interesting as long as he cannot tie that to a relevant information α'.

Another aspect of this definition is that by the information α that we gave out, also all information that can be derived from α is given out, because the best cryptographic systems cannot protect us from the intruder drawing conclusions. In general, the weaker α is (i.e., the less information we deliberately release to the intruder) and the stronger β is (i.e., the more information we assume the intruder might actually have), the stronger is the notion of privacy. So, as a rule of thumb, when a modeler is in doubt, one should be restrictive on α and generous on β.

3.2 Privacy on Messages

We look at a fixed state of a complex system and ask whether the intruder can violate privacy in this state. Let us start with an example:

Example 5. Let the payload alphabet be $\Sigma_0 = \{a, b, c\}$ and let us model that users choose values x from Σ_0. This is the only information we want to give the intruder. Suppose there is a protocol in place where each user sends out a message $h(pair(n, x))$ that the intruder can observe, that is, a hash of the choice x and a fixed number n (that is a secret from $\Sigma \setminus \Sigma_0$). Obviously, using such a fixed number, even though secret from the intruder, is a risk for "guessing attacks". Suppose further that the intruder has previously observed the message $h(pair(n, a))$ and thus that he knows that the choice in this case was a. Let us finally assume that a user has chosen $x = b$ and thus sent out $h(pair(n, b))$. □

We want to reflect that, in this example, the intruder knows not only the concrete message $h(pair(n, b))$, but also the *structural information* that this message has the form $h(pair(n, x))$ where x is the choice we are interested in.

For this reason, we use the *concr* function as before to represent concrete knowledge and further introduce, as a fundamental part of α-β privacy, an interpreted unary function symbol *eval* that works similar to *concr* and *maps memory locations to the structural information that the intruder has about the terms in his knowledge.* Here is one possible way to model Example 5 in Herbrand logic:

$\alpha \equiv x \in \{a, b, c\}$
$\beta \equiv \alpha \land \phi_{gen}(5) \land \phi_{concr} \land \phi_{eval} \land \phi_{struct} \land concr[m_1] = eval[m_1] = a \land$
$\quad concr[m_2] = eval[m_2] = b \land concr[m_3] = eval[m_3] = c \land$
$\quad concr[m_4] = eval[m_4] = h(pair(n, a)) \land concr[m_5] = h(pair(n, b)) \land$
$\quad eval[m_5] = h(pair(n, x))$

where the axioms ϕ_{eval} and ϕ_{struct} are as defined in Table 3 (we will explain them in detail below).

For most part, the structural information is identical to the concrete information, only for the field m_5 we have a difference between *eval* and *concr*. This is indeed a major point for our model: for the choice $x = b$ (i.e., "what really happened"), and only for this choice, we have that $concr[m_5] = eval[m_5]$ but the intruder a priori has no way to check that. However, the axiom ϕ_{eval} allows him to derive the structure of terms he can generate, and most importantly ϕ_{struct} tells us that two generable terms have the same concrete value iff they have the same structure. In this example, we can exploit ϕ_{struct}: from $concr[m_4] \neq concr[m_5]$ (recall that all terms are interpreted in the Herbrand universe) we have $eval[m_4] \neq eval[m_5]$, so that $h(pair(n, a)) \neq h(pair(n, x))$ and thus $x \neq a$ (again since terms are interpreted in the Herbrand universe). Hence, the intruder can derive from β the Σ_0-formula $\alpha' \equiv x \in \{b, c\}$ that does not follow from α. Thus, in this example, β does not respect the privacy of α. Note that the intruder cannot derive more, which is—very declaratively—because β has both a model in which $x = b$, and one where $x = c$, so the intruder was not even able to determine the choice x, he was only able to exclude one interpretation, namely $x = \mathsf{a}$.

Message Analysis. The form of α and β that we have used for Example 5 is at the core of many specifications, namely, when the intruder has observed a set of messages and knows their structure. For this reason, we define a particular fragment of α-β privacy (for which we give some decidability results in §4.2) that deals only with *combinatoric* α and only with the analysis of messages similar to the previous example.[3]

Definition 6. *We call $\alpha \in \mathcal{L}_{\Sigma_0}(\mathcal{V})$ combinatoric if Σ_0 is finite and consists only of free constants. Let α be combinatoric and σ a substitution of the free variables of α to elements of Σ_0 so that $\sigma(\alpha)$ is consistent. We say that β is a message-analysis problem (with respect to α and σ) iff there are $t_1, \ldots, t_l \in \mathcal{T}_\Sigma(fv(\alpha))$ such that*

$$\beta \equiv \alpha \wedge \phi_{gen}(l) \wedge \phi_{concr} \wedge \phi_{eval} \wedge \phi_{struct} \wedge \bigwedge_{i=1}^{l} concr[\mathsf{m}_i] = \sigma(t_i) \wedge eval[\mathsf{m}_i] = t_i$$

In general, such a β allows us to model a system where messages t_i have been exchanged that depend on some payload values $fv(\alpha)$ and the intruder has seen the concrete instantiations $\sigma(t_i)$ of these messages. Typically, the intruder knowledge will contain all the values of Σ_0 but he does not know the substitution σ, i.e., how the payload variables were actually chosen from Σ_0. What he knows, however, is the structure of the terms, i.e., where these variables occur in the t_i, because this structural information is usually part of a publicly available protocol description. He can try to exploit comparisons (ϕ_{struct}) with the actual terms $\sigma(t_i)$ and their compositions (ϕ_{concr} and ϕ_{eval}).

Some Variants of Example 5. One may, of course, consider a similar use of variables for non-payload secrets, like the value n in Example 5. However, since we require that α and β have the same set of free variables, one would then existentially quantify that value; for instance, for Example 5:

$$\beta \equiv \exists y. \ldots concr[\mathsf{m}_4] = \mathsf{h}(\mathsf{pair}(\mathsf{n}, \mathsf{a})) \wedge eval[\mathsf{m}_4] = \mathsf{h}(\mathsf{pair}(y, \mathsf{a})) \wedge$$
$$concr[\mathsf{m}_5] = \mathsf{h}(\mathsf{pair}(\mathsf{n}, \mathsf{b})) \wedge eval[\mathsf{m}_5] = \mathsf{h}(\mathsf{pair}(y, x))$$

Without the existential quantifier (if y were left free), the intruder could derive, e.g., that $y \neq \mathsf{a}$ (by generating $\mathsf{h}(\mathsf{pair}(\mathsf{m}_1, \mathsf{m}_1))$ and comparing the result with m_4). The $\exists$ thus intuitively says that we are not interested in the concrete value of y—the goal is not the protection of the nonces in the hash-values, so if they are found out, then it is *not* in itself a violation of privacy (but may lead to one).

Let us briefly also consider three variants of the example. First, if the intruder also knows n, say, $concr[\mathsf{m}_6] = eval[\mathsf{m}_6] = \mathsf{n}$, then he can indeed derive $x = \mathsf{b}$, because he can verify that $\mathsf{h}(\mathsf{pair}(\mathsf{m}_6, \mathsf{m}_2))$ gives the same concrete value as m_4.

---

[3] We could consider other forms of "combinatoric" α, e.g., such that Σ_0 may contain infinitely many free constants and function symbols as long as α admits only finitely many models (up to isomorphism). We leave a detailed investigation to future work.

Second, if users use different nonces that the intruder does not know, i.e., $\beta \equiv \ldots concr[\mathsf{m}_4] = eval[\mathsf{m}_4] = \mathsf{h}(\mathsf{pair}(\mathsf{n}_1, \mathsf{a})) \wedge concr[\mathsf{m}_5] = \mathsf{h}(\mathsf{pair}(\mathsf{n}_2, \mathsf{b})) \wedge eval[\mathsf{m}_5] = \mathsf{h}(\mathsf{pair}(\mathsf{n}_2, x))$, then β indeed preserves the privacy of α. To see this, note that β has models with $x = \mathsf{a}$, with $x = \mathsf{b}$, and with $x = \mathsf{c}$. Thus, every Σ_0-formula α' that follows β also follows from α.

Third, we have so far seen the message in m_4 as a message that was sent previously by some agent and we are not interested in protecting that, and, in fact, we had assumed that the intruder already knows that it contained the choice a. We can now also model that we are interested in protecting both choices as follows:

$$\alpha \equiv x_1 \in \{\mathsf{a},\mathsf{b},\mathsf{c}\} \wedge x_2 \in \{\mathsf{a},\mathsf{b},\mathsf{c}\}$$
$$\beta \equiv \ldots concr[\mathsf{m}_4] = \mathsf{h}(\mathsf{pair}(\mathsf{n}_1,\mathsf{a})) \wedge eval[\mathsf{m}_4] = \mathsf{h}(\mathsf{pair}(\mathsf{n}_1,x_1)) \wedge$$
$$concr[\mathsf{m}_5] = \mathsf{h}(\mathsf{pair}(\mathsf{n}_2,\mathsf{b})) \wedge eval[\mathsf{m}_5] = \mathsf{h}(\mathsf{pair}(\mathsf{n}_2,x_2))$$

Here again β respects the privacy of α because we can find a model for each combination of values for $x_1, x_2 \in \{\mathsf{a},\mathsf{b},\mathsf{c}\}$. In contrast, if we had used the same nonce (replacing both n_1 and n_2 with n), we would have that $concr[\mathsf{m}_4] \neq concr[\mathsf{m}_5]$ and thus $x_1 \neq x_2$, which does not follow from α. Again the intruder does not find out x_1 or x_2 but only that the two users voted differently. The crucial point here (and the strength of α-β privacy) is that we do not have to specify checks for all the different things that the intruder may be able to figure out, or even think about them, but simply just specify a formula α that describes what he is cleared to know and a formula β containing all information that may be available to him.

3.3 α-β-Privacy in Transition Systems

We now show how we can extend α-β-privacy to transition systems. The key idea is that we can define an α-β state as the pair (α, β) of formulae and privacy as reachability in the resulting transition system. Formally, with Σ, $\Sigma_0 \subseteq \Sigma$, $\mathcal{V}$ and $\approx$ as before:

Definition 7. *An α-β state is a pair (α, β) of formulae where $\alpha \in \mathcal{L}_{\Sigma_0}(\mathcal{V})$ and $\beta \in \mathcal{L}_\Sigma(\mathcal{V})$. Let $\mathcal{S}$ denote the set of all α-β-states. An α-β transition system is a pair (I, R) where $I \in \mathcal{S}$ and $R \subseteq \mathcal{S} \times \mathcal{S}$. As is standard, the set of reachable states is the smallest set that contains I and that is closed under R, i.e.: if S is reachable and $(S, S') \in R$, then also S' is reachable. We say that an α-β-transition system satisfies privacy iff in every reachable state (α, β), β respects the privacy of α.*

As an example of privacy as reachability, consider a simple transition system with an initial state that has no information, and four successor states $S_{i,j}$ with $i, j \in \{0, 1\}$ depending on two independent choices i and j of the user. In all four states, we have $\alpha \equiv x \in \{0, 1\}$. Let now $\beta_{i,j} \equiv \alpha \wedge \phi_{gen}(2) \wedge \phi_{concr} \wedge \phi_{eval} \wedge \phi_{struct} \wedge concr[\mathsf{m}_1] = \mathsf{scrypt}(\mathsf{k}_j, \mathsf{r}_j, i) \wedge eval[\mathsf{m}_1] = \mathsf{scrypt}(\mathsf{k}_j, \mathsf{r}_j, x) \wedge concr[\mathsf{m}_2] = eval[\mathsf{m}_2] = \mathsf{k}_1$, where k_j and r_j are new constants. In the states with $j = 0$, the intruder cannot deduce anything interesting as he does not have the key needed for decryption, but in the states with $j = 1$ we have $\beta_{i,0} \models x = i$. So, there are reachable states in which the intruder can find out more than he is supposed to.

3.4 Modeling Further Example Scenarios

We chose the following three major areas to model further examples of α-β privacy, which are discussed in [14]: randomized vs. non-randomized encryption including non-determinism and the notion of strong secrecy, guessing attacks (in which we discuss different approaches to encode passwords and guessing in α-β privacy and show unique features of our logic), and privacy-friendly identity management including pooling of knowledge.

In particular, in [14], we discuss in detail an example of how to model anonymous credential systems, which highlights two interesting aspects of our approach: (i) we can have formulae α that talk also about relations between data (e.g., $y < 1996$ to specify that a user if at least 18 years old), and (ii) we can easily model that two dishonest agents collaborate and pool their knowledge. To that end, suppose we have individual privacy specifications α_1 and α_2 (i.e., the information that was deliberately given to the two agents individually) and their actual knowledge is β_1 and β_2, respectively, where we further assume that all free variables that occur in both α_1 and α_2 actually refer to the same values. Then, in α-β privacy, we simply use logical *conjunction* and ask whether $\beta_1 \wedge \beta_2$ respects the privacy of $\alpha_1 \wedge \alpha_2$. The rationale is that two agents can always pool their actual knowledge and draw conclusions from it, i.e., we should consider $\beta_1 \wedge \beta_2$ to be available to them, and even the best credential system cannot prevent that they can derive everything that can be derived from what we gave them individually, i.e., we have to at least allow them to derive $\alpha_1 \wedge \alpha_2$.

4 Automation and the Relation to Static Equivalence

The concept of α-β-privacy is very expressive, because Herbrand logic is. Considering Example 2, we recall that we can axiomatize arithmetic (of natural numbers) by a Herbrand formula α so that $\alpha \models \gamma$ iff γ is a true sentence of arithmetic. Let *valid* be a further nullary relation symbol in Σ_0 and $\beta \equiv \alpha \wedge (\gamma \implies valid)$; then β respects the privacy of α iff γ is a true sentence of arithmetic. Thus, in general, α-β privacy (or its complement) is not even semi-decidable.

We see this expressive power as a feature, because it allows us to think about privacy without the tight corset imposed by automated methods. In this section, we explore a decidable fragment and the relation to static equivalence of frames for which many decidability results already exist. Because of its expressive power, it is no surprise that α-β-privacy subsumes static equivalence of frames:

Theorem 1. *Let F_0 and F_1 be two frames, Σ_0 consist of the nullary relation symbol neq, $\alpha \equiv \mathrm{true}$ and $\beta \equiv \alpha \wedge \phi_{gen}(l) \wedge \phi_{Fr}(F_0) \wedge \phi_{Fr}(F_1) \wedge \phi_{concr_0} \wedge \phi_{concr_1} \wedge (\neg neq \implies (\forall x, y.\ (gen(x) \wedge gen(y)) \implies (concr_0[x] = concr_0[y] \iff concr_1[x] = concr_1[y])))$. Then, β respects the privacy of α iff $F_0 \sim F_1$.*

Proof. From the definition of $\sim$ in Herbrand logic it follows that neq is derivable from β iff the frames are not statically equivalent. If neq is not derivable, there is no Σ_0-formula that follows from β and not from α. □

The simple argument of this theorem may seem a bit unfair towards static equivalence of frames, since we are not truly using α for the high-level payload information available to the intruder, but rather considering everything as technical, and then just exploit the expressive power of Herbrand logic. In addition, we show in [14] that a large fragment of the static-equivalence problem for frames can be encoded into the message-analysis fragment of α-β privacy (cf. Def. 6).

Let's look deeper at the two concepts. Static equivalence of frames is essentially the question whether the intruder can distinguish two concrete worlds. For instance, the frames F_0 and F_1 in Examples 3 and 4 represent two concrete worlds that the intruder can distinguish: $F_0 \not\sim F_1$. In contrast, α-β privacy expresses with α all possible worlds (there may be more than two) and with β one concrete world, asking whether the intruder can exclude some of the worlds of α. This, in particular, requires a distinction between high-level payload information and low-level technical information that frames do not have.

4.1 Limiting the Interesting Derivations

In order to show that many α-β-privacy problems can indeed be reduced to static equivalence of frames, we need to overcome one obstacle: α-β-privacy asks for *any* Σ_0-formula α' that can be derived from β but not from α. In general, there is a (countably) infinite choice for α' to consider. Recall that we call α *combinatoric* if Σ_0 is a finite set of free constants. Then the Herbrand Universe for α is finite and so there are finitely many possible different interpretations of the free variables of α. We can use this to limit the number of α' we need to consider:

Theorem 2. *Consider an (α, β) pair where α is combinatoric and consistent. Then, there is a finite number $n > 0$ of satisfying interpretations of the free variables of α, and we can give $N = 2^n - 2$ formulae $\alpha'_1, \ldots, \alpha'_N \in \mathcal{L}_{\Sigma_0}(fv(\alpha))$ such that $\alpha \not\models \alpha'_i$ for all $i \in \{1, \ldots, N\}$ and β violates the privacy of α iff $\beta \models \alpha'_i$ for some $i \in \{1, \ldots, N\}$.*

Before we prove Theorem 2, let us recall that when α is combinatoric, then Σ_0 is a finite set of free constants, so that the Herbrand Universe for α is finite and thus there are finitely many possible different interpretations of the free variables of α. The key observation is that we can use this to limit the number of α' we need to consider. For example, if $\alpha \equiv x \in \{0, 1, 2\}$ then it obviously suffices to check the following six candidates for α': $\alpha'_1 \equiv x = 0$, $\alpha'_2 \equiv x = 1$, $\alpha'_3 \equiv x = 2$, $\alpha'_4 \equiv x \in \{0, 1\}$, $\alpha'_5 \equiv x \in \{0, 2\}$ and $\alpha'_6 \equiv x \in \{1, 2\}$.

In other words, any of the proper, non-empty subsets of the original choice $\{0, 1, 2\}$ are candidates to check—the empty set is excluded because x must be one of the values, and the whole choice $\{0, 1, 2\}$ is excluded because that already follows from α. In fact, all other possible α' that one could come up with (with the same set of free variables) must be equivalent to one of the above candidates, e.g., $\alpha' \equiv x \in \{0,1\} \implies x \notin \{0\}$ is equivalent to α'_6.

Proof (Theorem 2). The Herbrand universe for α is simply Σ_0, so every model of α must map the free variables of α to elements of Σ_0, which gives us a finite set of choices since Σ_0 is finite. In fact, this set of choices can be effectively be computed, since α can only consists of variables, constants of Σ_0, equality, Boolean connectives and quantifiers (so, basically, Quantified Boolean Logic). We can effectively write each model in the form $\gamma \equiv x_1 = c_{i_1} \land \ldots \land x_k = c_{i_k}$. Let $G = \{\gamma_1, \ldots, \gamma_n\}$ be the set of all possible models that satisfy α, i.e., $\alpha \equiv \gamma_1 \lor \ldots \lor \gamma_n$. Consider the set $G_P = \{G_0 \mid \emptyset \not\subset G_0 \subsetneq G\}$ of proper, non-empty subsets of G. G_P has $N = 2^n - 2$ elements $\{g_1, \ldots, g_N\}$. Define now the α'_i to be the disjunction of all formulae in g_i for each $i \in \{1, \ldots, N\}$, i.e., $\alpha'_i = \bigvee_{\phi \in g_i} g_i$. For any $i \in \{1, \ldots, N\}$, $\alpha \not\models \alpha'_i$ since one of the possible valuations of the free variables of α is not satisfied (since we chose only *proper* subsets of G; note that we could exclude the empty set as at least one valuation will true).

Suppose now that β violates the privacy of α. Then, there is a formula $\alpha' \in \mathcal{L}_{\Sigma_0}(fv(\alpha))$ such that $\beta \models \alpha'$ and $\alpha \not\models \alpha'$. From Definition 5, it follows that $fv(\alpha') \subseteq fv(\beta)$: suppose $x \in fv(\alpha') \setminus fv(\beta)$, then $\beta \models \forall x. \alpha'$ and still $\alpha \not\models \forall x. \alpha'$. Since $\alpha \not\models \alpha'$ there is a valuation γ_i of the free variables of α so that $\gamma_i \models \alpha$ but $\gamma_i \not\models \alpha'$. Also there must be some γ_j with $\gamma_j \models \alpha$ and, since $\beta \models \gamma$, also $\gamma_j \models \alpha'$. Thus, the set of models of α' is a proper, non-empty subset of the G, so some $g_i \in G_P$ describes exactly the models of α', and therefore, finally, $\alpha'_i \equiv \alpha'$. □

4.2 Reduction to Frames and Decidability

We now reduce message-analysis problems (cf. Def. 6) to finitely many static equivalence problems of frames. Note that α in a message-analysis problem is by definition combinatoric, and thus, by Theorem 2, there are finitely many satisfying interpretations of the free variables of α (and nothing else is to interpret since Σ_0 does not contain non-constant function or relation symbols). We denote these models simply as substitutions σ_i (that map from $fv(\alpha)$ to Σ_0).

Theorem 3. *Consider (α, β) in the message-analysis problem fragment of α-β privacy (i.e., according to Def. 6), with terms $t_1, \ldots, t_l$. Let $\{\sigma_1, \ldots, \sigma_n\}$ be the models of α, and define $F_i = \{m_1 \mapsto \sigma_i(t_1), \ldots, m_l \mapsto \sigma_i(t_l)\}$. Then, β respects the privacy of α iff $F_1 \sim F_2 \sim \ldots \sim F_n$.*

Proof. We prove that β respects the privacy of α iff $\forall i. F_i \sim F_1$, which is equivalent as $\sim$ is an equivalence relation. Let $eq([x_1 \mapsto t_1, \ldots, x_j \mapsto t_j])$ for some j denote the formula $x_1 = t_1 \land \ldots \land x_j = t_j$. Then $\alpha \equiv \bigvee_{i=1}^n eq(\sigma_i)$. Let $\alpha' \equiv \bigvee_{\{i \mid F_i \sim F_1\}} eq(\sigma_i)$, and $\alpha_i \equiv eq(\sigma_i) \lor eq(\sigma_1)$, i.e., the restriction of α to the choice between σ_1 and σ_i. It follows, for every $i \in \{1, \ldots, n\}$, that $F_i \sim F_1$ iff β respects the privacy of α_i (see [14] for a proof of this claim). Therefore, $\beta \models \alpha'$. The conjunction of α' has at least one element, since $\phi_i \sim \phi_1$ at least for $i = 1$. There are then two possible cases: (i) If there is also at least one $i \in \{2, \ldots, n\}$ such that $F_i \not\sim F_1$, then $\alpha \not\models \alpha'$, and thus β violates the privacy of α. (ii) Otherwise (note: trivially $\alpha \models \alpha'$ in this case), by Theorem 2, there is no α' that follows from β but not from α, thus β respects the privacy of α. □

Since this result is independent of the considered set Σ_{op} of cryptographic operations and algebraic theory, we immediately have that if we can decide static equivalence for a given theory (e.g., [2, 5]), then we can decide the message-analysis problem fragment of α-β privacy for that theory.

Note that, instead of relying on static equivalence, we could have also given a direct decision procedure for our example theory, without an enumeration of all models. In a nutshell, the key idea of such a proof is that in the restricted form of α and β considered in the message-analysis problem, we can find a violation of α-β privacy iff we can make use of the axiom $concr[s] = concr[t] \iff eval[s] = eval[t]$. Then, we can show that there is a violation of α-β privacy iff β has a *witness*, i.e., there are terms $s, t \in \mathcal{T}_\Sigma$ such that $concr$ and $eval$ are defined for s and t, and $concr[s] = concr[t]$ while $eval[s] \neq eval[t]$. Then, we can remove all analysis steps (i.e., decryptions and decompositions) from β by encoding them in additional memory positions. The resulting β' preserves the privacy of α iff β does, and has a witness iff it has one in the free algebra, for which it is straightforward to find witness or to prove their absence, and thus conclude the proof. This argument is, of course, similar to what one does to decide static equivalence in frames. However, static equivalence looks at the more basic problem to compare a pair of frames, while α-β privacy asks to look at all models of α (as did the above reduction).

5 Concluding Remarks

We have introduced α-β privacy as, we believe, a simple and declarative way to specify privacy goals: the intruder should not be able to derive any "non-technical" statement from the technical information β that he cannot derive from the intentionally released information α already. We have given a variety of examples that describe how α-β privacy can be used in practice and investigated formally its close relationship to static equivalence of frames, which allows to use existing methods for deciding a fragment of α-β privacy.

α-β privacy bears some similarities with the non-interference approach (e.g., [15]) since it also distinguishes (at least) two levels of information, usually low-level and high-variables. These are, however, fundamentally different from our payload α and technical information β since they are formulae that express relations between values (rather than directly being public or private values). We actually do not mind that the intruder gets hold of (some) technical information as long as he cannot use it to obtain anything interesting besides the payload.

There are also privacy notions building on database abstractions. The two predominant notions are the *k-anonymity* family [17], asking whether an intruder is unable to reduce the anonymity set below a threshold of k users, and *differential privacy* [9], asking whether an intruder can detect significant changes in a probability distribution on statistical data released by a curator on data sets differing in one element. For k-anonymity, we observe that the property that α has at least k models, and that the intruder cannot deduce an α' with less choices, is encodable in α-β privacy and will be part of future work. As differential privacy is a property established on the information release function of the curator, a relation to our notion is not straightforward.

We have mentioned above and in the previous sections a few directions for future work. In addition to these, we have already started to consider further examples, to formalize a language for specifying α-β transition systems, and to generalize our decidability results to larger fragments of α-β privacy.

References

1. Abadi, M.: Private authentication. In: Dingledine, R., Syverson, P.F. (eds.) PET 2002. LNCS, vol. 2482, pp. 27–40. Springer, Heidelberg (2003)
2. Abadi, M., Cortier, V.: Deciding knowledge in security protocols under (many more) equational theories. In: CSFW, pp. 62–76. IEEE CS (2005)
3. Abadi, M., Fournet, C.: Mobile values, new names, and secure communication. In: POPL, pp. 104–115. ACM Press (2001)
4. Blanchet, B.: An efficient cryptographic protocol verifier based on prolog rules. In: CSFW, pp. 82–96. IEEE CS (2001)
5. Blanchet, B., Abadi, M., Fournet, C.: Automated verification of selected equivalences for security protocols. JLAP 75(1), 3–51 (2008)
6. Cortier, V., Rusinowitch, M., Zalinescu, E.: Relating two standard notions of secrecy. Logical Methods in Computer Science 3(3) (2007)
7. Delaune, S., Ryan, M., Smyth, B.: Automatic verification of privacy properties in the applied pi-calculus. In: Karabulut, Y., Mitchell, J., Herrmann, P., Jensen, C.D. (eds.) Trust Management II. IFIP, vol. 263, pp. 263–278. Springer, Boston (2008)
8. Dolev, D., Yao, A.: On the security of public key protocols. IEEE Transactions on Information Theory 29(2), 198–208 (1983)
9. Dwork, C.: Differential Privacy: A Survey of Results. In: Agrawal, M., Du, D.-Z., Duan, Z., Li, A. (eds.) TAMC 2008. LNCS, vol. 4978, pp. 1–19. Springer, Heidelberg (2008)
10. Ebbinghaus, H.-D., Flum, J., Thomas, W.: Mathematical logic. Springer (1994)
11. Goubault-Larrecq, J.: Finite models for formal security proofs. J. Comput. Secur. 18(6), 1247–1299 (2010)
12. Hinrichs, T., Genesereth, M.: Herbrand logic. Technical Report LG-2006-02, Stanford Univ., USA (2006), http://logic.stanford.edu/reports/LG-2006-02.pdf
13. IBM Research – Zurich. Specification of the identity mixer cryptographic library. version 2.3.4. Technical report, IBM Research (2012)
14. Mödersheim, S., Groß, T., Viganò, L.: Defining Privacy is Supposed to be Easy (Extended Version). Technical Report 2013-21, DTU Compute, Denmark (2013)
15. Ryan, P., Schneider, S.: Process algebra and non-interference. In: CSFW. IEEE CS (1999)
16. Selinger, P.: Models for an Adversary-Centric Protocol Logic. ENTCS 55 (2003)
17. Sweeney, L.: k-anonymity: A model for protecting privacy. International Journal of Uncertainty, Fuzziness and Knowledge-Based Systems 10(5), 557–570 (2002)
18. Weidenbach, C.: Towards an Automatic Analysis of Security Protocols in First-Order Logic. In: Ganzinger, H. (ed.) CADE 1999. LNCS (LNAI), vol. 1632, pp. 314–328. Springer, Heidelberg (1999)

Reachability Modules for the Description Logic $\mathcal{SRIQ}$

Riku Nortje, Katarina Britz, and Thomas Meyer

Center for Artificial Intelligence Research, University of KwaZulu-Natal and CSIR
Meraka Institute, South Africa
{rnortje,abritz,tmeyer}@csir.co.za

Abstract. In this paper we investigate module extraction for the Description Logic $\mathcal{SRIQ}$. We formulate modules in terms of the reachability problem for directed hypergraphs. Using inseparability relations, we investigate the module-theoretic properties of reachability modules and show by means of an empirical evaluation that these modules have the potential of being substantially smaller than syntactic locality modules.

1 Introduction

Description Logics (DLs) are widely used in ontological modeling. They form a family of knowledge representation languages that are mostly decidable fragments of first-order logic. Their formal semantics not only allow for the exchange of DL ontologies but provide support for reasoning — the computation of additional logical inferences from the facts stated explicitly in an ontology.

There are many different DLs, each differing in the expressivity of the language and the complexity of reasoning. In general, the more expressive a DL the more complex the reasoning associated with it. This allows the ontology modeller to choose, for the intended application, the best balance between language expressivity on the one hand and reasoning complexity on the other. The DL $\mathcal{SRIQ}$ is an expressive language and is a subset $\mathcal{SROIQ}$, the W3C OWL DL Web Ontology language.

Modularization plays an important part in the design and maintenance of large scale ontologies. Modules are loosely defined as subsets of ontologies that cover some topic of interest, where the topic of interest is defined by a set of symbols. Extracting minimal modules is computationally expensive and even undecidable for expressive DLs [4,5]. Therefore, the use of approximation techniques and heuristics play an important role in the efficient design of algorithms.

Syntactic locality [4,5], because of its excellent model-theoretic properties, has become an ideal heuristic and is widely used in a diverse set of algorithms [19,3,6]. Suntisrivaraporn [19] showed that, for the DL $\mathcal{EL}^+$, $\bot$-locality module extraction is equivalent to the reachability problem in directed hypergraphs. Nortjé et al. [14,15] extended the reachability problem to include $\top$-locality and introduced bidirectional reachability modules as a subset of $\bot\top^*$-locality modules. This work was further extended to the DL $\mathcal{SROIQ}$ by Nortje et al. [16]

who showed that extracting $\bot\top^*$-reachability modules is equivalent to extracting frontier graphs in hypergraphs. Reachability modules are not only of importance in hypergraph-based reasoning support for CBoxes [16], but are potentially smaller than syntactic locality modules.

In this paper we investigate the module-theoretic properties of reachability modules for the DL $\mathcal{SRIQ}$. We show that these modules are not self-contained or depleting but they are robust under vocabulary restrictions, vocabulary extensions, replacement and joins. By showing that reachability modules preserve all justifications for entailments, we show that depleting modules are sufficient for preserving all justifications but not necessary. This paper is an extended version of the paper presented at DL2013 [17].

In Section 2 we give a brief introduction to the DL $\mathcal{SRIQ}$, hypergraphs and modularization as defined by inseparability relations. Section 3 introduces a normal form for $\mathcal{SRIQ}$ CBoxes as well as the rules necessary to transform any such CBox to normal form. In Section 4 we introduce both $\bot$- and $\top$-reachability modules and investigate all their module theoretic properties in terms of inseparability relations. In Section 5 we show the results of an empirical evaluation of these modules. Lastly in Section 6 we conclude this paper with a short summary of the results.

2 Background

In Section 2.1 we give a brief introduction to DLs and modularization with specific focus on the DL $\mathcal{SRIQ}$ [9]. In Section 2.2 we give a brief introduction to modules and module theoretic properties.

2.1 The DL $\mathcal{SRIQ}$

The syntax and semantics of $\mathcal{SRIQ}$ is listed in Table 1. N_C and N_R denote disjoint sets of atomic concept names and role names. The set N_R includes the universal role whilst N_C excludes the $\top$ and $\bot$ concepts. For a complete definition of $\mathcal{SRIQ}$, refer to Horrocks et al. [9], and for Description Logics refer to [2].

In order to ensure decidability in $\mathcal{SRIQ}$ there are some restrictions on the use of roles. $R_1 \circ \ldots \circ R_n \sqsubseteq R$, where $n \geqslant 1$ and $R_i, R \in N_R$, is a *role inclusion axiom* (RIA). A *role hierarchy* is a finite set of RIAs. Here $R_1 \circ \ldots \circ R_n$ denotes a composition of roles where R, R_i may also be an *inverse role* R^-. A role R is *simple* if (i) it does not appear on the right-hand side of a RIA, or (ii) is the inverse of a simple role, or (iii) appears on the right-hand side of a RIA only if the left-hand side is a simple role. $Ref(R)$, $Irr(R)$ and $Dis(R,S)$, where R, S are roles other than U, are role assertions. A set of role assertions is simple w.r.t. a role-hierarchy H if each assertion $Irr(R)$ and $Dis(R,S)$ uses only simple roles w.r.t. H.

A strict partial order $\prec$ on N_R is a *regular order* if, and only if, for all roles R and S: $S \prec R$ iff $S^- \prec R$. Let $\prec$ be a regular order on roles. A RIA $w \sqsubseteq R$ is

Table 1. Syntax and semantics of $\mathcal{SRIQ}$

Constructs	Syntax	Semantics
atomic concept	C	$C^{\mathcal{I}} \in \Delta^{\mathcal{I}}, C \in N_C$
role	R	$R^{\mathcal{I}} \subseteq \Delta^{\mathcal{I}} \times \Delta^{\mathcal{I}}, R \in N_R$
inverse role	R^-	$R^{-\mathcal{I}} = \{(y,x) \mid (x,y) \in R^{\mathcal{I}}\}, R \in N_R$
universal role	U	$U^{\mathcal{I}} = \Delta^{\mathcal{I}} \times \Delta^{\mathcal{I}}$
role composition	$R_1 \circ \ldots \circ R_n$	$\{(x,z) \mid (x,y_1) \in R_1^{\mathcal{I}} \wedge (y_1, y_2) \in R_2^{\mathcal{I}} \wedge \ldots$
		$\wedge (y_n, z) \in R_n^{\mathcal{I}}, n \geq 2, R_i \in N_R\}$
top	$\top$	$\top^{\mathcal{I}} = \Delta^{\mathcal{I}}$
bottom	$\bot$	$\bot^{\mathcal{I}} = \emptyset$
negation	$\neg C$	$(\neg C)^{\mathcal{I}} = \Delta^{\mathcal{I}} \setminus C^{\mathcal{I}}$
conjunction	$C_1 \sqcap C_2$	$(C_1 \sqcap C_2)^{\mathcal{I}} = C_1^{\mathcal{I}} \cap C_2^{\mathcal{I}}$
disjunction	$C_1 \sqcup C_2$	$(C_1 \sqcup C_2)^{\mathcal{I}} = C_1^{\mathcal{I}} \cup C_2^{\mathcal{I}}$
exist restriction	$\exists R.C$	$\{x \mid (\exists y)[(x,y) \in R^{\mathcal{I}} \wedge y \in C^{\mathcal{I}}]\}$
value restriction	$\forall R.C$	$\{x \mid (\forall y)[(x,y) \in R^{\mathcal{I}} \to y \in C^{\mathcal{I}}]\}$
self restriction	$\exists R.Self$	$\{x \mid (x,x) \in R^{\mathcal{I}}\}$
atmost restriction	$\leqslant nR.C$	$\{x \mid \#\{y \mid (x,y) \in R^{\mathcal{I}} \wedge y \in C^{\mathcal{I}}\} \leqslant n\}$
atleast restriction	$\geqslant nR.C$	$\{x \mid \#\{y \mid (x,y) \in R^{\mathcal{I}} \wedge y \in C^{\mathcal{I}}\} \geqslant n\}$
Axiom	**Syntax**	**Semantics**
concept inclusion	$C_1 \sqsubseteq C_2$	$C_1^{\mathcal{I}} \subseteq C_2^{\mathcal{I}}$
role inclusion	$R_1 \circ \ldots \circ R_n \sqsubseteq R_{n+1}$	$(R_1 \circ \ldots \circ R_n)^{\mathcal{I}} \subseteq R^{\mathcal{I}}, n \geq 1$
reflexivity	$Ref(R)$	$\{(x,x) \mid x \in \Delta^{\mathcal{I}}\} \subseteq R^{\mathcal{I}}$
irreflexivity	$Irr(R)$	$\{(x,x) \mid x \in \Delta^{\mathcal{I}}\} \cap R^{\mathcal{I}} = \emptyset$
disjointness	$Dis(R,S)$	$S^{\mathcal{I}} \cap R^{\mathcal{I}} = \emptyset$

$\prec$-regular if, and only if, $R \in N_R$ and w has one of the following forms: $R \circ R$; R^-; $S_1 \circ \ldots \circ S_n$, where each $S_i \prec R$; $R \circ S_1 \circ \ldots \circ S_n$, where each $S_i \prec R$ or $S_1 \circ \ldots \circ S_n \circ R$, where each $S_i \prec R$. A role hierarchy H is *regular* if there exists a regular order $\prec$ such that each RIA in H is $\prec$-regular. An *RBox* is a finite, regular role hierarchy H together with a finite set of role assertions simple w.r.t. H.

The set of $\mathcal{SRIQ}$ *concept descriptions* is the smallest set such that:

1. $\bot, \top$, and each $C \in N_C$ is a concept description.
2. If C is a concept description, then $\neg C$ is a concept description.
3. If C and D are concept descriptions, R is a role, S is a simple role, and n is a non-negative integer, then the following are all concept descriptions:

$$(C \sqcap D), \quad (C \sqcup D), \quad \exists R.C, \quad \forall R.C, \quad \leqslant nS.C, \quad \geqslant nS.C, \quad \exists S.Self$$

If C and D are concept description then $C \sqsubseteq D$ is a *general concept inclusion* (GCI) axiom. A *TBox* is a finite set of GCIs. If C is a concept description, $a, B \in N_I$, $R, S \in N_R$ with S a simple role, then $C(a)$, $R(a,b)$, $\neg S(a,b)$, and $a \neq b$, are individual assertions. An $\mathcal{SRIQ}$ *ABox* is a finite set of individual assertions. All GCIs, RIAs, role assertions, and individual assertions are referred to as axioms. A $\mathcal{SRIQ}$-KB base is the union of a TBox, RBox and ABox. Given a $\mathcal{SRIQ}$ TBox $\mathcal{T}$ and RBox $\mathcal{R}$ we define a $\mathcal{SRIQ}$ CBox $\mathcal{C}$ as $\mathcal{T} \cup \mathcal{R}$.

2.2 Modules and Their Properties

Module extraction is the process of extracting subsets of axioms from CBoxes that are self contained with respect to some criteria. These sets of axioms, called *modules*, may be used for various purposes such as reuse, optimization and error pinpointing amongst others [5,19].

Definition 1. (Module for the arbitrary DL $\mathcal{L}$ [11,12]) *Let $\mathcal{L}$ be an arbitrary description language, $\mathcal{O}$ an $\mathcal{L}$ ontology, and σ a statement formulated in $\mathcal{L}$. Then, $\mathcal{O}' \subseteq \mathcal{O}$ is a module for σ in $\mathcal{O}$ (a σ-module in $\mathcal{O}$) whenever: $\mathcal{O} \models \sigma$ if and only if $\mathcal{O}' \models \sigma$.*

Definition 1 is sufficiently general so that any subset of an ontology preserving a statement of interest is considered a module, the entire ontology is therefore a module in itself.

Different use cases usually result in different notions of what the definition and characteristics of a module should be. Modules are often defined via the notion of conservative extensions. Given some signature (a set of concept and role names) and a set of axioms, a conservative extension of this set is simply one that implies all the same consequences over the signature. More formally:

Definition 2. (Conservative extension [1,7]) *Let $\mathcal{C}$ and $\mathcal{C}_1$ be two CBoxes such that $\mathcal{C}_1 \subseteq \mathcal{C}$, and let Σ be a signature. Then*

- *$\mathcal{C}$ is a Σ-conservative extension of $\mathcal{C}_1$ if, for every α with $Sig(\alpha) \subseteq \Sigma$, we have $\mathcal{C} \models \alpha$ iff $\mathcal{C}_1 \models \alpha$.*
- *$\mathcal{C}$ is a conservative extension of $\mathcal{C}_1$ if $\mathcal{C}$ is a Σ-conservative extension of $\mathcal{C}_1$ for $\Sigma = Sig(\mathcal{C}_1)$.*

Given that both sets of axioms imply the same consequences for a given signature we may then use the smaller set whenever we wish to reason over this signature. A closely related notion to conservative extensions is that of *inseparability*.

Definition 3. *[18] $\mathcal{C}_1$ and $\mathcal{C}_2$ are Σ-concept name inseparable, written $\mathcal{C}_1 \equiv_\Sigma^c \mathcal{C}_2$, if for all Σ- concept names C, D, it holds that $\mathcal{C}_1 \models C \sqsubseteq D$ if and only if $\mathcal{C}_2 \models C \sqsubseteq D$.*

Definition 4. *[18] $\mathcal{C}_1$ and $\mathcal{C}_2$ are Σ-subsumption inseparable, written $\mathcal{C}_1 \equiv_\Sigma^s \mathcal{C}_2$, if for all terms X, Y that are concepts or roles over Σ, it holds that $\mathcal{C}_1 \models X \sqsubseteq Y$ if and only if $\mathcal{C}_2 \models X \sqsubseteq Y$.*

Definition 5. *[11,12,18] Let $\mathcal{C}$ be a CBox, $\mathcal{M} \subseteq \mathcal{C}$, S an inseparability relation and Σ a signature. We call $\mathcal{M}$*

- *an S_Σ-module of T if $\mathcal{M} \equiv_\Sigma^S \mathcal{C}$.*
- *a self-contained S_Σ-module of $\mathcal{C}$ if $\mathcal{M} \equiv_{\Sigma \cup Sig(\mathcal{M})}^S \mathcal{C}$.*
- *a depleting S_Σ-module of $\mathcal{C}$ if $\emptyset \equiv_{\Sigma \cup Sig(\mathcal{M})}^S \mathcal{C} \setminus \mathcal{M}$.*

Modules may therefore be characterized by some inseparability criteria. It is of interest how modules defined this way would behave under different use case scenarios. For this purpose, several properties of inseparability relations [10] have been investigated in the literature, which allows us to compare different definitions of modules. Given a CBox $\mathcal{C}$ and a module $\mathcal{M} \subseteq \mathcal{C}$ for a signature Σ, we are interested in the following inseparability properties:

- *Robustness under vocabulary restrictions* implies that when we wish to restrict the symbols from Σ further we do not need to import a different module and may continue to use $\mathcal{M}$.
- *Robustness under vocabulary extension* implies that should we wish to add new symbols to Σ that do not appear in $\mathcal{C}$ we do not need to use a different module but may use $\mathcal{M}$.
- *Robustness under replacement* ensures that the result of importing $\mathcal{M}$ into a CBox $\mathcal{C}_1$ is a module of the result of importing $\mathcal{C}$ into $\mathcal{C}_1$. This is also called module coverage and refers to the fact that importing a module does not affect its property of being a module.
- *Robustness under joins* implies that if $\mathcal{C}$ and $\mathcal{C}_1$ are inseparable w.r.t. Σ and all the terms they share are from Σ, then each of them are inseparable with their union w.r.t. Σ.

More formally:

Definition 6. *[10,11,12] The inseparability relation S is called*

- *robust under vocabulary restrictions if, for all CBoxes $\mathcal{C}_1$, $\mathcal{C}_2$ and all signatures Σ, Σ' with $\Sigma \subseteq \Sigma'$, the following holds: if $\mathcal{C}_1 \equiv^S_{\Sigma'} \mathcal{C}_2$, then $\mathcal{C}_1 \equiv^S_{\Sigma} \mathcal{C}_2$.*
- *robust under vocabulary extensions if, for all CBoxes $\mathcal{C}_1$, $\mathcal{C}_2$ and all signatures Σ, Σ' with $\Sigma' \cap (Sig(\mathcal{C}_1) \cup Sig(\mathcal{C}_2)) \subseteq \Sigma$, the following holds: if $\mathcal{C}_1 \equiv^S_{\Sigma} \mathcal{C}_2$, then $\mathcal{C}_1 \equiv^S_{\Sigma'} \mathcal{C}_2$.*
- *robust under replacement if, for all CBoxes $\mathcal{C}_1$, $\mathcal{C}_2$ and all signatures Σ and every CBox $\mathcal{C}$ with $Sig(\mathcal{C}) \cap (Sig(\mathcal{C}_1) \cup Sig(\mathcal{C}_2)) \subseteq \Sigma$, the following holds: if $\mathcal{C}_1 \equiv^S_{\Sigma} \mathcal{C}_2$ then $\mathcal{C}_1 \cup \mathcal{C} \equiv^S_{\Sigma} \mathcal{C}_2 \cup \mathcal{C}$.*
- *robust under joins if, for all CBoxes $\mathcal{C}_1$, $\mathcal{C}_2$ and all signatures Σ with $Sig(\mathcal{C}) \cap Sig(\mathcal{C}_2) \subseteq \Sigma$, if $\mathcal{C}_1 \equiv^S_{\Sigma} \mathcal{C}_2$ then $\mathcal{C}_i \equiv^S_{\Sigma} \mathcal{C}_1 \cup \mathcal{C}_2$, for $i = 1, 2$.*

Deciding conservative extensions has been shown to be computationally expensive or even undecidable for relatively inexpressive DLs. Therefore, an approximation of these modules, based on syntax, called syntactic locality modules has been introduced [5]. Syntactic locality modules possess all the module-theoretic properties discussed in this section and have become one of the most widely used definitions of modules. We will give a definition of a normalized version of syntactic locality once we have introduced a normal form for $\mathcal{SRIQ}$.

3 Normal Form

In this section we introduce a normal form for $\mathcal{SRIQ}$ CBoxes. We utilize normalization in order to simplify the definitions, to ease the understanding of the work that follows, as well as to simplify the presentation of proofs.

Definition 7. *Given $B_i \in (N_C \cup \{\top\})$, $C_i \in (N_C \cup \{\bot\})$, $D \in \{\exists R.B, \geq nR.B, \exists R.Self\}$, with R, S, R_i, S_i role names from N_R or their inverses and $n \geq 1$, a $\mathcal{SRIQ}$ CBox $\mathcal{C}$ is in **normal form** if every axiom $\alpha \in \mathcal{C}$ is in one of the following forms:*

$\alpha_1: B_1 \sqcap \ldots \sqcap B_n \sqsubseteq C_1 \sqcup \ldots \sqcup C_m$	$\alpha_2: D \sqsubseteq C_1 \sqcup \ldots \sqcup C_m$
$\alpha_3: B_1 \sqcap \ldots \sqcap B_n \sqsubseteq D$	$\alpha_4: R_1 \circ \ldots \circ R_n \sqsubseteq R_{n+1}$
$\alpha_5: R_1 \sqsubseteq R_2$	$\alpha_6: D_1 \sqsubseteq D_2$
$\alpha_7: Dis(R_1, R_2)$	

In order to normalize a $\mathcal{SRIQ}$ CBox $\mathcal{C}$ we repeatedly apply the normalization rules from Table 2. Each application of a rule rewrites an axiom into its equivalent normal form. It is easy to see that the application of every rule ensures that the normalized CBox is a conservative extension of the original. We note that the $\mathcal{SRIQ}$ axiom $Ref(R)$ is represented by its equivalent $\top \sqsubseteq \exists R.Self$ and $Irr(R)$ by $\exists R.Self \sqsubseteq \bot$ [2].

Table 2. $\mathcal{SRIQ}$ normalization rules

NR1	$\hat{B} \sqcap \neg \hat{C}_2 \sqsubseteq \hat{C}_1 \rightsquigarrow \hat{B} \sqsubseteq \hat{C}_1 \sqcup \hat{C}_2$
NR2	$\hat{B}_1 \sqsubseteq \hat{C} \sqcup \neg \hat{B}_2 \rightsquigarrow \hat{B}_1 \sqcap \hat{B}_2 \sqsubseteq \hat{C}$
NR3	$\hat{B} \sqcap \hat{D} \sqsubseteq \hat{C} \rightsquigarrow \hat{B} \sqcap A \sqsubseteq \hat{C}, \hat{D} \sqsubseteq A, A \sqsubseteq \hat{D}$
NR4	$\hat{B} \sqsubseteq \hat{C} \sqcup \hat{D} \rightsquigarrow \hat{B} \sqsubseteq \hat{C} \sqcup A, \hat{D} \sqsubseteq A, A \sqsubseteq \hat{D}$
NR5	$\hat{B} \sqsubseteq \hat{C}_1 \sqcap \hat{C}_2 \rightsquigarrow \hat{B} \sqsubseteq \hat{C}_1, \hat{B} \sqsubseteq \hat{C}_2$
NR6	$\hat{B}_1 \sqcup \hat{B}_2 \sqsubseteq \hat{C} \rightsquigarrow \hat{B}_1 \sqsubseteq \hat{C}, \hat{B}_2 \sqsubseteq \hat{C}$
NR7	$\ldots \forall R.\hat{C} \ldots \rightsquigarrow \ldots \neg \exists R.A \ldots, A \sqcap \hat{C} \sqsubseteq \bot, \top \sqsubseteq A \sqcup \hat{C}$
NR8	$\ldots \exists R.\hat{D} \ldots \rightsquigarrow \ldots \exists R.A \ldots, \hat{D} \sqsubseteq A, A \sqsubseteq \hat{D}$
NR9	$\ldots \geq nR.\hat{D} \ldots \rightsquigarrow \ldots \geq nR.A \ldots, \hat{D} \sqsubseteq A, A \sqsubseteq \hat{D}$
NR10	$\ldots \leq nR.\hat{C} \ldots \rightsquigarrow \ldots \neg (\geq (n+1)R.\hat{C}) \ldots$
NR11	$\hat{B} \equiv \hat{C} \rightsquigarrow \hat{B} \sqsubseteq \hat{C}, \hat{C} \sqsubseteq \hat{B}$
NR12	$\geq 0R.B \sqsubseteq \hat{C} \rightsquigarrow \top \sqsubseteq \hat{C}$
NR13	$\hat{B} \sqsubseteq \exists R.\bot \rightsquigarrow \hat{B} \sqsubseteq \bot$
NR14	$\hat{B} \sqsubseteq \geq nR.\bot \rightsquigarrow \hat{B} \sqsubseteq \bot$
NR15	$\hat{B} \sqsubseteq \geq 0R.B \rightsquigarrow$
NR16	$\geq nR.\bot \sqsubseteq \hat{C} \rightsquigarrow$
NR17	$\exists R.\bot \sqsubseteq \hat{C} \rightsquigarrow$
NR18	$\hat{B} \sqcap \bot \sqsubseteq \hat{C} \rightsquigarrow$
NR19	$\bot \sqsubseteq \hat{C} \rightsquigarrow$
NR20	$\hat{B} \sqsubseteq \hat{C} \sqcup \top \rightsquigarrow$
NR21	$\hat{B} \sqsubseteq \top \rightsquigarrow$

Above A is a new concept name not in N_C, $\hat{B}_i$ and $\hat{C}_i$ are possibly complex concept descriptions and $\hat{D}$ a complex concept description. $R \in N_R$ or it's inverse, $n \geq 0$

Theorem 1. *Exhaustively applying the rules from Table 2 to any $\mathcal{SRIQ}$ CBox $\mathcal{C}$ results in a $\mathcal{SRIQ}$ CBox $\mathcal{C}'$ in normal form. The normalization process can be completed in linear time in the number of axioms.*

Proof Sketch: We show that normalization is linear in the number of axioms by applying normalization rules in the following order: $\equiv$-elimination (NR11), $\forall$-elimination (NR7), $\leqslant$-elimination (NR10), Complex role-filler elimination (NR8, NR9), $\neg$-elimination and simplification by iteration of rules NR1, NR3, NR6 and NR2, NR4, NR5. Lastly rules NR12 through NR21 are applied. □

Example 1. Let $\alpha_1 = B \sqsubseteq \neg C$, and $\alpha_2 = \neg A \sqsubseteq B$. Then, α_1 may be normalized by application of rule NR2 to $\alpha_1^N = B \sqcap C \sqsubseteq \bot$ since $\neg C = \neg C \sqcup \bot$. α_2 may be normalized by application of rule NR1 to $\alpha_2^N = \top \sqsubseteq B \sqcup A$ since $\neg A = \neg A \sqcap \top$.

We will discuss the importance of normalization in the context of this paper in more detail in the next section.

4 Reachability Modules

Syntactic locality is a widely used approximation to deciding conservative extensions. Given a normalized CBox $\mathcal{C}$, the definition of syntactic locality can be simplified to the following:

Definition 8. (Normalized Syntactic Locality) *Let Σ be a signature and $\mathcal{C}$ a normalized $\mathcal{SRIQ}$ CBox. An axiom α is $\bot$-local w.r.t. Σ ($\top$-local w.r.t Σ) if $\alpha \in Ax(\Sigma)^\bot$ ($\alpha \in Ax(\Sigma)^\top$), as defined in the grammar:*

$\bot$-*Locality*

$\mathbf{Ax(\Sigma)^\bot}$ ::= $C^\bot \sqsubseteq C \mid w^\bot \sqsubseteq R \mid Dis(S^\bot, S) \mid Dis(S, S^\bot)$
$\mathbf{Con^\bot(\Sigma)}$ ::= $A^\bot \mid C^\bot \sqcap C \mid C \sqcap C^\bot \mid \exists R^\bot.C \mid \exists R.C^\bot \mid \exists R^\bot.Self \mid$
$\quad \geqslant nR^\bot.C \mid \geqslant nR.C^\bot$

$\top$-*Locality*

$\mathbf{Ax(\Sigma)^\top}$ ::= $C \sqsubseteq C^\top \mid w \sqsubseteq R^\top$
$\mathbf{Con^\top(\Sigma)}$ ::= $A^\top \mid C^\top \sqcup C \mid C \sqcup C^\top \mid \exists R^\top.C^\top \mid \geqslant nR^\top.C^\top \mid$
$\quad \exists R^\top.Self$

In the grammar, we have that $A^\bot, A^\top \notin \Sigma$ is an atomic concept, $R^\bot$ (resp. $S^\bot$) is either an atomic role (resp. a simple atomic role) not in Σ or the inverse of an atomic role (resp. of a simple atomic role) not in Σ, C is any concept, R is any role, S is any simple role, and $C^\bot \in \mathbf{Con^\bot(\Sigma)}$, $C^\top \in \mathbf{Con^\top(\Sigma)}$. We also denote by $w^\bot$ a role chain $w = R_1 \circ \ldots \circ R_n$ such that for some i with $1 \leq i \leq n$, we have that R_i is (possibly inverse of) an atomic role not in Σ. A CBox $\mathcal{C}$ is $\bot$-local ($\top$-local) w.r.t. Σ if α is $\bot$-local ($\top$-local) w.r.t. Σ for all $\alpha \in \mathcal{C}$.

For a complete overview of locality modules as well as algorithms for extracting such we refer the interested reader to Cuenca Grau et al [5].

A variant of $\bot$-syntactic locality modules called $\bot$-reachability based modules [19] is based on the reachability problem in directed hypergraphs. Hypergraphs [13,20] are a generalization of graphs and have been studied extensively since the 1970s as a powerful tool for modeling many problems in Discrete Mathematics.

We extend the work done by Nortje et al.[15] and define reachability for $\mathcal{SRIQ}$ CBoxes. We then continue to show that these modules share all the robustness properties of locality modules and therefore is well suited to be used in the ontology reuse scenario.

Definition 9. ($\perp$-Reachability) *Let $\mathcal{C}$ be a $\mathcal{SRIQ}$ CBox in normal form and $\Sigma \subseteq Sig(\mathcal{C})$ a signature. The set of $\perp$-reachable names in $\mathcal{C}$ w.r.t. Σ, denoted by $\Sigma_{\mathcal{C}}^{\leftarrow\perp}$, is defined inductively as follows:*

- *For every $x \in (\Sigma \cup \{\top\})$ we have $x \in \Sigma_{\mathcal{C}}^{\leftarrow\perp}$.*
- *For every inclusion axiom $(\alpha_L \sqsubseteq \alpha_R) \in \mathcal{C}$, if $Sig(\alpha_L) \subseteq \Sigma_{\mathcal{C}}^{\leftarrow\perp}$ then every $y \in Sig(\alpha_R)$ is also in $\Sigma_{\mathcal{C}}^{\leftarrow\perp}$.*

Every axiom $\alpha := \alpha_L \sqsubseteq \alpha_R$ such that $Sig(\alpha_L) \subseteq \Sigma_{\mathcal{C}}^{\leftarrow\perp}$ we call $\Sigma_{\mathcal{C}}^{\leftarrow\perp}$-reachable. Axioms of the form $Dis(R,S) \in \mathcal{C}$ are $\Sigma_{\mathcal{C}}^{\leftarrow\perp}$-reachable whenever $\{R,S\} \subseteq \Sigma_{\mathcal{C}}^{\leftarrow\perp}$. The set of all $\Sigma_{\mathcal{C}}^{\leftarrow\perp}$-reachable axioms is denoted by $\mathcal{C}_{\Sigma}^{\leftarrow\perp}$ and is called the $\perp$-reachability module for $\mathcal{C}$ over Σ.

It is self-evident from Definition 8 that an axiom is $\perp$-reachable w.r.t Σ exactly when it is not $\perp$-local w.r.t. Σ. Similarly we define an axiom to be $\top$-reachable exactly when it is not $\top$-local.

Definition 10. ($\top$-Reachability) *Let $\mathcal{C}$ be a $\mathcal{SRIQ}$ CBox in normal form and $\Sigma \subseteq Sig(\mathcal{C})$ a signature. The set of $\top$-reachable names in $\mathcal{C}$ w.r.t. Σ, denoted by $\Sigma_{\mathcal{C}}^{\leftarrow\top}$, is defined inductively as follows:*

- *For every $x \in (\Sigma \cup \{\perp\})$ we have that $x \in \Sigma_{\mathcal{C}}^{\leftarrow\top}$.*
- *For all inclusion axioms $(\alpha_L \sqsubseteq \alpha_R) \in \mathcal{C}$, if*
  - *$\alpha_R = \perp$, or*
  - *α_R is of the form $A_1 \sqcup \ldots \sqcup A_n$ and all $A_i \in \Sigma_{\mathcal{C}}^{\leftarrow\top}$, or*
  - *α_R has any other form and there exists some $x \in Sig(\alpha_R) \cap \Sigma_{\mathcal{C}}^{\leftarrow\top}$*

  then every $y \in Sig(\alpha_L)$ is also in $\Sigma_{\mathcal{C}}^{\leftarrow\top}$.

Every axiom $\alpha := \alpha_L \sqsubseteq \alpha_R$ such that, $\alpha_R = \perp$, or α_R is of the form $A_1 \sqcup \ldots \sqcup A_n$ and all $A_i \in \Sigma_{\mathcal{C}}^{\leftarrow\top}$, or α_R has any other form and there exists some $x \in Sig(\alpha_R) \cap \Sigma_{\mathcal{C}}^{\leftarrow\top}$, we call $\Sigma_{\mathcal{C}}^{\leftarrow\top}$-reachable. All axioms of the form $Dis(R,S) \in \mathcal{C}$ are always $\Sigma_{\mathcal{C}}^{\leftarrow\top}$-reachable and $\{R,S\} \subseteq \Sigma_{\mathcal{C}}^{\leftarrow\top}$. The set of all $\Sigma_{\mathcal{C}}^{\leftarrow\top}$-reachable axioms is denoted by $\mathcal{C}_{\Sigma}^{\leftarrow\top}$ and is called the $\top$-reachability module for $\mathcal{C}$ over Σ.

Given the appropriate mapping of axioms to hyperedges [16], $\perp$-Reachability can be shown to be equivalent to B-reachability in hypergraphs and $\top$-reachability to hypergraph F-reachability. The $\perp$-reachability module for a signature S is equivalent to the set of all B-hyperpaths for the set of nodes corresponding to S and the $\top$-reachability module equivalent to the set of all F-hyperpaths.

It is easy to show that $\perp$-reachability modules are equivalent to $\perp$-locality modules. However, by the definition of $\top$-reachability we observe that these are not equivalent to $\top$-locality modules.

Example 2. Let $\mathcal{C}$ be a CBox such that $\mathcal{C} = \{\alpha_1, \alpha_2, \alpha_3, \alpha_4\}$, with $\alpha_1 := A \sqsubseteq \exists r.D_1, \alpha_2 := B \sqsubseteq\geq 3r.D_2, \alpha_3 := \exists r.\top \sqsubseteq C, \alpha_4 := D_1 \sqsubseteq D_2$ and let $\Sigma = \{C\}$. Then $\mathcal{C}_\Sigma^{\leftarrow\top} = \{\alpha_1, \alpha_2, \alpha_3\}$ but the $\top$-locality module for $\mathcal{C}$ w.r.t. Σ is $\{\alpha_1, \alpha_2, \alpha_3, \alpha_4\}$.

The difference stems from the fact that in α_1 and α_2 the $\top$-reachability of r does not ensure the $\top$-reachability of D_1 and D_2 respectively. This occurs because, given an axiom $\alpha = \alpha_L \sqsubseteq \alpha_R$, $\top$-locality ensure that if α is $\top$-local then so are all of the symbols in $Sig(\alpha)$, whereas $\top$-reachability is defined such that the $\top$-reachability of α only guarantees that all symbols of α_L and only some symbols of α_R will be $\top$-reachable. Thus $\top$-reachability based modules are at most the size of $\top$-locality modules but in general could be substantially smaller. Similar to $\bot\top^*$-locality modules we note that reachability module extraction may also be alternated until a fixpoint is reached. These modules are denoted by $\mathcal{C}_\Sigma^{\leftarrow\bot\top^*}$.

Normalization plays an important role in the definition of reachability as the algorithm for determining $\top$-reachability of an axiom is different from the algorithm for determining $\top$-locality of an axiom. Not only does normalization simplify the definition of reachability considerably, it also allows us to determine exactly which symbols to exclude from our signature when adding new $\top$-reachable axioms. This can be seen in Example 2 where the symbol D_2 is excluded when adding $Sig(\alpha)$ to our signature. We note that a separate normalization phase is not strictly necessary, and that on-the-fly normalization can be done on an axiom during a reachability check. It is also possible to denormalize a normalized ontology by adding extra bookkeeping and labeling to the normalization process.

In order to investigate the module-theoretic properties of reachability modules, we follow a similar approach to Sattler et al. [18] and define inseparability different from that of conservative extensions. We say that $\mathcal{C}_1$ and $\mathcal{C}_2$ are inseparable if their modules are equivalent, that is, a module extraction algorithm returns the same output for each of them. We define the following inseparability relations for reachability modules:

Definition 11. *Let $\mathcal{C}_1$ and $\mathcal{C}_2$ be CBoxes and Σ a signature. Then $\mathcal{C}_1$ and $\mathcal{C}_2$ are:*

- *$\Sigma - \top$ reachability inseparable, denoted by $\mathcal{C}_1 \equiv_\Sigma^\top \mathcal{C}_2$, if $\mathcal{C}_{1\Sigma}^{\leftarrow\top} = \mathcal{C}_{2\Sigma}^{\leftarrow\top}$;*
- *$\Sigma - \bot$ reachability inseparable, denoted by $\mathcal{C}_1 \equiv_\Sigma^\bot \mathcal{C}_2$, if $\mathcal{C}_{1\Sigma}^{\leftarrow\bot} = \mathcal{C}_{2\Sigma}^{\leftarrow\bot}$;*
- *$\Sigma - \bot\top^*$ reachability inseparable, denoted by $\mathcal{C}_1 \equiv_\Sigma^{\bot\top^*} \mathcal{C}_2$, if $\mathcal{C}_{1\Sigma}^{\leftarrow\bot\top^*} = \mathcal{C}_{2\Sigma}^{\leftarrow\bot\top^*}$.*

Firstly we show that $\top$-reachability modules are subsumption inseparable. Concept inseparability follows as a special case of subsumption inseparability.

Lemma 1. *Let $\mathcal{C}$ be a $\mathcal{SRIQ}$ CBox, and $\Sigma \subseteq Sig(\mathcal{C})$ a signature. Let C, D be arbitrary $\mathcal{SRIQ}$ concept descriptions such that $Sig(C) \cup Sig(D) \subseteq \Sigma$. Then $\mathcal{C} \models C \sqsubseteq D$ if and only if $\mathcal{C}_\Sigma^{\leftarrow\top} \models C \sqsubseteq D$.*

Proof: We have to prove two parts. First: If $\mathcal{C}_\Sigma^{\leftarrow \top} \models C \sqsubseteq D$ then $\mathcal{C} \models C \sqsubseteq D$. This follows directly from the fact that $\mathcal{C}_\Sigma^{\leftarrow \top} \subseteq \mathcal{C}$ and that $\mathcal{SRIQ}$ is monotonic.

Conversely, we show that, if $\mathcal{C} \models C \sqsubseteq D$ then $\mathcal{C}_\Sigma^{\leftarrow \top} \models C \sqsubseteq D$. Assume $\mathcal{C} \not\models C \sqsubseteq D$ with $\mathcal{I}_1$ a model for $\mathcal{C}$. Then there must exist an interpretation $\mathcal{I}$ such that $|\Delta^\mathcal{I}| \geq |\Delta^{\mathcal{I}_1}|$ and an individual $w \in \Delta^\mathcal{I}$ such that $\mathcal{I}$ is a model of $\mathcal{C}_\Sigma^{\leftarrow \top}$ and $w \in C^\mathcal{I} \setminus D^\mathcal{I}$. Modify $\mathcal{I}$ to $\mathcal{I}'$ by setting $x^{\mathcal{I}'} := \Delta^\mathcal{I}$ for all concept names $x \in Sig(\mathcal{C}) \setminus \Sigma_\mathcal{C}^{\leftarrow \top}$, and $r^{\mathcal{I}'} := \Delta^\mathcal{I} \times \Delta^\mathcal{I}$ for all roles names $r \in Sig(\mathcal{C}) \setminus \Sigma_\mathcal{C}^{\leftarrow \top}$ and leaving everything else unchanged. We show that $\mathcal{I}'$ is a model of $\mathcal{C}_\Sigma^{\leftarrow \top}$. For all $\alpha := \alpha_L \sqsubseteq \alpha_R$, with $\alpha \in \mathcal{C}_\Sigma^{\leftarrow \top}$, we have that:

- If α_R is such that $Sig(\alpha_R) \subseteq \Sigma_\mathcal{C}^{\leftarrow \top}$ we have that $(\alpha_R)^\mathcal{I} = (\alpha_R)^{\mathcal{I}'}$ since it does not change the interpretation of any symbols.
- If α_R is an existential restriction of the form $\exists r.A$ with $y \in Sig(\alpha_R) \setminus \Sigma_\mathcal{C}^{\leftarrow \top}$, then $(y)^{\mathcal{I}'} = \Delta^\mathcal{I}$ or $(y)^{\mathcal{I}'} = \Delta^\mathcal{I} \times \Delta^\mathcal{I}$ depending on whether y is a role or concept name. In both cases we have that $(\alpha_R)^\mathcal{I} \subseteq (\alpha_R)^{\mathcal{I}'}$.
- If α_R is an at-least restriction of the form $\geq nr.A$ with $y \in Sig(\alpha_R) \setminus \Sigma_\mathcal{C}^{\leftarrow \top}$, then $(y)^{\mathcal{I}'} = \Delta^\mathcal{I}$ or $(y)^{\mathcal{I}'} = \Delta^\mathcal{I} \times \Delta^\mathcal{I}$ depending on whether y is a role or concept name. In both cases we have that $(\alpha_R)^\mathcal{I} \subseteq (\alpha_R)^{\mathcal{I}'}$.
- If α_R is of the form $\exists R.Self$ with $R \in \Sigma_\mathcal{C}^{\leftarrow \top}$ we have that $(\alpha_R)^\mathcal{I} = (\alpha_R)^{\mathcal{I}'}$ since it does not change the interpretation of the symbol R.
- If α is of the form $Dis(R, S)$ then by definition it is always in $\mathcal{C}_\Sigma^{\leftarrow \top}$, thus $R, S \in \Sigma_\mathcal{C}^{\leftarrow \top}$. Therefore, the interpretation of alpha does not change.

In all cases $(\alpha_L)^\mathcal{I} = (\alpha_L)^{\mathcal{I}'}$ since $\alpha \in \mathcal{C}_\Sigma^{\leftarrow \top}$ and $Sig(\alpha_L) \subseteq \Sigma_\mathcal{C}^{\leftarrow \top}$ and thus $(\alpha_L)^{\mathcal{I}'} \subseteq (\alpha_R)^{\mathcal{I}'}$. Thus, $\mathcal{I}'$ is a model for $\mathcal{C}_\Sigma^{\leftarrow \top}$. Now for every $\alpha = (\alpha_L \sqsubseteq \alpha_R) \in \mathcal{C} \setminus \mathcal{C}_\Sigma^{\leftarrow \top}$ we have:

- α_R is a concept name and $\alpha_R^{\mathcal{I}'} = \Delta^\mathcal{I}$, or
- α_R is a role name and $\alpha_R^{\mathcal{I}'} = \Delta^\mathcal{I} \times \Delta^\mathcal{I}$, or
- α_R is a disjunction of the form $A_1 \sqcup \ldots \sqcup A_n$ with at least one $A_i \notin \Sigma_\mathcal{C}^{\leftarrow \top}$, thus $A_i^{\mathcal{I}'} = \Delta^\mathcal{I}$ and $\alpha_R^{\mathcal{I}'} = A_1^\mathcal{I} \cup \ldots \cup \Delta^\mathcal{I} \cup \ldots \cup A_n^\mathcal{I} = \Delta^\mathcal{I}$, or
- α_R is an existential restriction $\exists r.A_1$, thus $r^{\mathcal{I}'} = \Delta^\mathcal{I} \times \Delta^\mathcal{I}$ and $A_1^{\mathcal{I}'} = \Delta^\mathcal{I}$ so that $(\exists r.A_1)^{\mathcal{I}'} = \Delta^\mathcal{I}$, or
- α_R is $\exists r.Self$, thus $r^{\mathcal{I}'} = \Delta^\mathcal{I} \times \Delta^\mathcal{I}$ so that $(\exists r.Self)^{\mathcal{I}'} = \Delta^\mathcal{I}$, or
- α_R is an atleast restriction $\geq nr.A_2$, thus $r^{\mathcal{I}'} = \Delta^\mathcal{I} \times \Delta^\mathcal{I}$, $A_2^{\mathcal{I}'} = \Delta^\mathcal{I}$ and $|\Delta^\mathcal{I}| \geq n$ so that $(\geq nr.A_2)^{\mathcal{I}'} = \Delta^\mathcal{I}$. This follows from the fact that $|\Delta^\mathcal{I}| \geq |\Delta^{\mathcal{I}_1}|$ and for any concept description $\geq nr.A$, $|\Delta^\mathcal{I}| \geq |(r.A)^\mathcal{I}| \geq n$ for it to be satisfiable.

Since for all cases $\alpha_L^{\mathcal{I}'} \subseteq \alpha_R^{\mathcal{I}'}$, we conclude that $\mathcal{I}'$ is a model for $\mathcal{C}$. But $\mathcal{I}$ and $\mathcal{I}'$ correspond on all symbols $y \in (Sig(D) \cup Sig(C)) \subseteq \Sigma \subseteq \Sigma_\mathcal{C}^{\leftarrow \top}$ and therefore $D^{\mathcal{I}'} = D^\mathcal{I}$ and $C^{\mathcal{I}'} = C^\mathcal{I}$. Now since $C^\mathcal{I} = C^{\mathcal{I}'}$ and $w \in C^\mathcal{I}$ we have that $w \in C^{\mathcal{I}'} \setminus D^{\mathcal{I}'}$ and hence $\mathcal{C} \not\models C \sqsubseteq D$, contradicting the assumption. □

Corollary 1. *Let $\mathcal{C}$ be a normalized $\mathcal{SRIQ}$ CBox, $\Sigma \subseteq Sig(\mathcal{C})$ a signature and S an inseparability relation from Definitions 3 and 4. Then $\mathcal{C}_\Sigma^{\leftarrow \top} \equiv_\Sigma^S \mathcal{C}$. $\mathcal{C}_\Sigma^{\leftarrow \top}$ is therefore a S_Σ-module of $\mathcal{C}$.*

We show by way of counter example that $\mathcal{C}_\Sigma^{\leftarrow\top}$ is not a self-contained or depleting S_Σ module of $\mathcal{C}$ when $\Sigma_\mathcal{C}^{\leftarrow\top} \neq Sig(\mathcal{C}_\Sigma^{\leftarrow\top})$.

Example 3. Let $\mathcal{C}$ be a CBox such that $\mathcal{C} = \{\alpha_1 = A \sqsubseteq \exists r.D_1, \alpha_2 = B \sqsubseteq \geq nr.D_2, \alpha_3 = \exists r.\top \sqsubseteq C, \alpha_4 = D_1 \sqsubseteq D_2\}$, and let $\Sigma = \{C\}$. Then $\mathcal{C}_\Sigma^{\leftarrow\top} = \{\alpha_1, \alpha_2, \alpha_3\}$, $\delta = \Sigma \cup Sig(\mathcal{C}_\Sigma^{\leftarrow\top}) = \{A, B, C, r, D_1, D_2\} \neq \Sigma_\mathcal{C}^{\leftarrow\top}$. But $\mathcal{C} \models D_1 \sqsubseteq D_2$ and $\mathcal{C}_\Sigma^{\leftarrow\top} \not\models D_1 \sqsubseteq D_2$. Therefore $\mathcal{C}_\Sigma^{\leftarrow\top}$ is not a self-contained c_Σ-module of $\mathcal{C}$. Similarly, $\mathcal{C} \setminus \mathcal{C}_\Sigma^{\leftarrow\top} \models \alpha_4 \neq \emptyset$ with $\Sigma = D_1, D_2$ and $D_1, D_2 \in \delta$. Therefore, $\mathcal{C}_\Sigma^{\leftarrow\top}$ is not a depleting c_Σ-module of $\mathcal{C}$.

Before investigating the robustness properties of reachability modules we introduce some lemmas to aid us in the proofs that follow.

Lemma 2. *Let α be an axiom, Σ and Σ' be signatures, $x \in \{\top, \bot\}$ and $\mathcal{C}$ a SRIQ CBox. Then:*

1. *If $\Sigma \subseteq \Sigma'$ and α is not $\Sigma'^{\leftarrow x}_\mathcal{C}$ reachable, then α is not $\Sigma^{\leftarrow x}_\mathcal{C}$ reachable.*
2. *If $\Sigma' \cap Sig(\alpha) \subseteq \Sigma$ and α is not Σ reachable then α is not Σ' reachable.*

Proof:

1. By the inductive definition of x-reachability if $\Sigma \subseteq \Sigma'$ then $\Sigma^{\leftarrow x}_\mathcal{C} \subseteq \Sigma'^{\leftarrow x}_\mathcal{C}$. Thus if α is not $\Sigma'^{\leftarrow x}_\mathcal{C}$ reachable it can also not be $\Sigma^{\leftarrow x}_\mathcal{C}$-reachable.
2. Assume that α is not Σ reachable but it is Σ' reachable. Then there is at least one symbol $y \in Sig(\alpha)$ such that $y \notin \Sigma$ and α is $\Sigma \cup \{y\}$ reachable. α is Σ' reachable so it must be the case that $y \in \Sigma'$. But this contradicts our assumption that $\Sigma' \cap Sig(\alpha) \subseteq \Sigma$. Thus, α is not Σ' reachable.

Lemma 3. *Let α be an axiom, Σ and Σ' be signatures, $x \in \{\top, \bot\}$ and $\mathcal{C}, \mathcal{C}'$ SRIQ CBoxes. Then:*

1. *Given $\mathcal{C}_1 = \mathcal{C}_{\Sigma'}^{\leftarrow x}$, if $\Sigma \subseteq \Sigma'$ then $\mathcal{C}_\Sigma^{\leftarrow x} = \mathcal{C}_{1\Sigma}^{\leftarrow x}$. In particular $\mathcal{C}_\Sigma^{\leftarrow x} \subseteq \mathcal{C}_{\Sigma'}^{\leftarrow x}$.*
2. *If $\Sigma' \cap Sig(\mathcal{C}) \subseteq \Sigma$, then $\mathcal{C}_{\Sigma'}^{\leftarrow x} \subseteq \mathcal{C}_\Sigma^{\leftarrow x}$.*
3. *If $\mathcal{C} \subseteq \mathcal{C}'$, then $\mathcal{C}_\Sigma^{\leftarrow x} \subseteq \mathcal{C}'^{\leftarrow x}_\Sigma$.*

Proof:

1. Assume that there is some axiom $\alpha \in \mathcal{C}_\Sigma^{\leftarrow x}$ such that $\alpha \notin \mathcal{C}_{\Sigma'}^{\leftarrow x}$. Therefore, we have that α is not $\Sigma'^{\leftarrow x}_\mathcal{C}$ reachable but that it is $\Sigma^{\leftarrow x}_\mathcal{C}$ reachable. But this is a contradiction by Lemma 2.1 since $\Sigma \subseteq \Sigma'$. Thus, $\mathcal{C}_\Sigma^{\leftarrow x} \subseteq \mathcal{C}_{\Sigma'}^{\leftarrow x}$. A similar argument is used to show that $\mathcal{C}_\Sigma^{\leftarrow x} \subseteq \mathcal{C}_{1\Sigma}^{\leftarrow x}$ and $\mathcal{C}_{1\Sigma}^{\leftarrow x} \subseteq \mathcal{C}_\Sigma^{\leftarrow x}$.
2. For every $\alpha \in \mathcal{C}$ we have that $\Sigma' \cap Sig(\alpha) \subseteq \Sigma$. Therefore, from Lemma 2.2 we have that whenever $\alpha \in \mathcal{C}$ is not Σ reachable it is also not Σ' reachable and we have that $\mathcal{C}_{\Sigma'}^{\leftarrow x}$ contains at most all those axioms in $\mathcal{C}_\Sigma^{\leftarrow x}$. Thus, $\mathcal{C}_{\Sigma'}^{\leftarrow x} \subseteq \mathcal{C}_\Sigma^{\leftarrow x}$.
3. Let $\delta = \Sigma_\mathcal{C}^{\leftarrow x}$, $\delta' = \Sigma_{\mathcal{C}_1}^{\leftarrow x}$ and $\alpha \in (\mathcal{C} \cap \mathcal{C}_1)$. Assume α is δ reachable but not δ' reachable. Since $\mathcal{C} \subseteq \mathcal{C}_1$ and $Sig(\mathcal{C}) \subseteq Sig(\mathcal{C}_1)$ we have by the inductive definition of x reachability that $\delta \subseteq \delta'$. But by Lemma 2.1 we have that whenever α is not δ' reachable then it is also not δ reachable. Therefore, $\mathcal{C}_\Sigma^{\leftarrow x}$ contains at most all those axioms in $\mathcal{C}_{1\Sigma}^{\leftarrow x}$. Thus, $\mathcal{C}_\Sigma^{\leftarrow x} \subseteq \mathcal{C}_{1\Sigma}^{\leftarrow x}$.

Lemma 4. *Let Σ be a signature, $\mathcal{C}_1$ and $\mathcal{C}_2$ be $\mathcal{SRIQ}$ CBoxes with $Sig(\mathcal{C}_1) \cap Sig(\mathcal{C}_2) \subseteq \Sigma$ and $x \in \{\top, \bot\}$. Then $(\mathcal{C}_1 \cup \mathcal{C}_2)_\Sigma^{\leftarrow x} = \mathcal{C}_{1\Sigma}^{\leftarrow x} \cup \mathcal{C}_{2\Sigma}^{\leftarrow x}$.*

Proof: Let $\mathcal{M} = (\mathcal{C}_1 \cup \mathcal{C}_2)_\Sigma^{\leftarrow x}$, $\mathcal{M}_1 = \mathcal{C}_{1\Sigma}^{\leftarrow x}$, $\mathcal{M}_2 = \mathcal{C}_{2\Sigma}^{\leftarrow x}$. Now $\mathcal{C}_1 \subseteq \mathcal{C}_1 \cup \mathcal{C}_2$ thus by Lemma 3.3 we have that $\mathcal{M}_1 \subseteq \mathcal{M}$. Similarly $\mathcal{M}_2 \subseteq \mathcal{M}$ and thus $\mathcal{M}_1 \cup \mathcal{M}_2 \subseteq \mathcal{M} \cup \mathcal{M}$ which gives us $\mathcal{M}_1 \cup \mathcal{M}_2 \subseteq \mathcal{M}$. Let $\Sigma' = \Sigma \cup \Sigma_{\mathcal{C}_1}^{\leftarrow x} \cup \Sigma_{\mathcal{C}_2}^{\leftarrow x}$. To show that $\mathcal{M} \subseteq \mathcal{M}_1 \cup \mathcal{M}_2$ we note that, when extracting these modules, the order in which axioms are extracted are irrelevant. We therefore assume that any algorithm first extracts axioms in $\mathcal{M}_1 \cup \mathcal{M}_2$ then tests all other axioms for $\Sigma'_{\mathcal{C}_1 \cup \mathcal{C}_2}^{\leftarrow x}$-reachability. Consider any axiom $\alpha \in (\mathcal{C}_1 \cup \mathcal{C}_2) \setminus (\mathcal{M}_1 \cup \mathcal{M}_2)$. If $\alpha \in \mathcal{C}_1$ then $\alpha \in \mathcal{C}_1 \setminus \mathcal{M}_1$ and α is not $\Sigma_{\mathcal{C}_1}^{\leftarrow x} \cup \Sigma$ reachable. Now precondition $Sig(\mathcal{C}_2) \cap Sig(\mathcal{C}_1) \subseteq \Sigma$ implies $\Sigma_{\mathcal{C}_2}^{\leftarrow x} \cap Sig(\alpha) \subseteq \Sigma$, taken that α is not $\Sigma_{\mathcal{C}_1}^{\leftarrow x} \cup \Sigma$ reachable we manipulate this statement to derive $(\Sigma \cup \Sigma_{\mathcal{C}_2}^{\leftarrow x} \cup \Sigma_{\mathcal{C}_1}^{\leftarrow x}) \cap Sig(\alpha) \subseteq \Sigma \cup \Sigma_{\mathcal{C}_1}^{\leftarrow x}$. Thus by Lemma 2.2 we have that α is not $\Sigma \cup \Sigma_{\mathcal{C}_2}^{\leftarrow x} \cup \Sigma_{\mathcal{C}_1}^{\leftarrow x}$ reachable. The case where $\alpha \in \mathcal{C}_2$ is treated analogously. □

Proposition 1. *For $x \in \{\top, \bot\}$, x-reachability is robust under replacement.*

Proposition 2. *For $x \in \{\top, \bot\}$, x-reachability is robust under vocabulary extensions.*

Proposition 3. *For $x \in \{\top, \bot\}$, x-reachability is robust under vocabulary restrictions.*

Proposition 4. *For $x \in \{\top, \bot\}$, x-reachability is robust under joins.*

The proofs to show that reachability modules including $\mathcal{C}_\Sigma^{\leftarrow \bot \top^*}$ modules share all the robustness properties of locality modules follow from the above lemmas and follow the proofs for locality modules by Sattler, et al. [18].

Reachability modules therefore share all the robustness properties listed. However, we have seen that these modules are neither depleting nor self-contained modules. Amongst other things, the depleting and self-contained nature of modules are utilised in order to find all justifications for an entailment [8].

Definition 12. *Let $\mathcal{C}$ be a $\mathcal{SRIQ}$ CBox and $\mathcal{M} \subseteq \mathcal{C}$. $\mathcal{M}$ is a justification for $\mathcal{C} \models C \sqsubseteq D$ if $\mathcal{M} \models C \sqsubseteq D$ and there exists no $\mathcal{M}_1 \subset \mathcal{M}$ such that $\mathcal{M}_1 \models C \sqsubseteq D$.*

We show that although our modules do not share these properties they do contain all justifications for a given signature.

Theorem 2. *Let $\mathcal{C}$ be a normalized $\mathcal{SRIQ}$ CBox and Σ a signature such that $\Sigma \subseteq Sig(\mathcal{C})$. Then for arbitrary concept descriptions C, D, such that $\mathcal{C} \models C \sqsubseteq D$ and $Sig(C) \cup Sig(D) \subseteq \Sigma_\mathcal{C}^{\leftarrow \top}$ we have that $\mathcal{C}_\Sigma^{\leftarrow \top}$ contains all justifications for $\mathcal{C} \models C \sqsubseteq D$.*

Proof: Assume that $\mathcal{C} \models C \sqsubseteq D$ for some $Sig(C) \cup Sig(D) \subseteq \Sigma_\mathcal{C}^{\leftarrow \top}$, but there is a justification $\mathcal{M}$ for $\mathcal{C} \models C \sqsubseteq D$ that is not contained in $\mathcal{C}_\Sigma^{\leftarrow \top}$. If $C \sqsubseteq D$ is a tautology then $\mathcal{M}$ must be empty with $\mathcal{M} \subseteq \mathcal{C}_\Sigma^{\leftarrow \top}$. Thus, we assume that $C \sqsubseteq D$

is not a tautology. Since $\mathcal{M} \not\subseteq \mathcal{C}_\Sigma^{\leftarrow \top}$, there must be an axiom $\alpha \in \mathcal{M} \setminus \mathcal{C}_\Sigma^{\leftarrow \top}$. Define $\mathcal{M}_1 := \mathcal{M} \cap \mathcal{C}_\Sigma^{\leftarrow \top}$. $\mathcal{M}_1$ is a strict subset of $\mathcal{M}$ since $\alpha \notin \mathcal{M}_1$. There are two cases, either $\mathcal{M}_1 = \emptyset$ or it contains at least one axiom.

In the case where $\mathcal{M}_1 = \emptyset$, define $\mathcal{C}_1 = \mathcal{C} \setminus \mathcal{C}_\Sigma^{\leftarrow \top}$ with $\mathcal{M} \subseteq \mathcal{C}_1$. Now since $\mathcal{M} \models C \sqsubseteq D$ we have by monotinocity that $\mathcal{C}_1 \models C \sqsubseteq D$. Since $\mathcal{C}_1 \subseteq \mathcal{C}$ we have by Lemma 3.3 that $\mathcal{C}_{1\Sigma}^{\leftarrow \top} \subseteq \mathcal{C}_\Sigma^{\leftarrow \top}$ and thus that $\mathcal{C}_{1\Sigma}^{\leftarrow \top} = \emptyset$. But by Lemma 1 we have that $\mathcal{C}_{1\Sigma}^{\leftarrow \top} \models C \sqsubseteq D$ if, and only if, $\mathcal{C}_1 \models C \sqsubseteq D$. Since $C \sqsubseteq D$ is not a tautology we have that $\mathcal{C}_{1\Sigma}^{\leftarrow \top} \not\models C \sqsubseteq D$ and thus that $\mathcal{M} \not\models C \sqsubseteq D$.

In the case where $\mathcal{M}_1 \neq \emptyset$ we claim that $\mathcal{M}_1 \models C \sqsubseteq D$, which contradicts the fact that $\mathcal{M}$ is a justification for $\mathcal{C} \models C \sqsubseteq D$.

We use proof by contraposition to show this. Assume that $\mathcal{M}_1 \not\models C \sqsubseteq D$, i.e., there is a model $\mathcal{I}_1$ of $\mathcal{M}_1$ such that $C^{\mathcal{I}_1} \not\subseteq D^{\mathcal{I}_1}$. We modify $\mathcal{I}_1$ to $\mathcal{I}$ by setting $y^{\mathcal{I}} := \Delta^{\mathcal{I}_1}$ for all concept names $y \in Sig(\mathcal{C}) \setminus \Sigma_\mathcal{C}^{\leftarrow \top}$, and $r^{\mathcal{I}} := \Delta^{\mathcal{I}_1} \times \Delta^{\mathcal{I}_1}$ for all roles names $r \in Sig(\mathcal{C}) \setminus \Sigma_\mathcal{C}^{\leftarrow \top}$. We have $D^{\mathcal{I}} = D^{\mathcal{I}_1}$ since $Sig(D) \subseteq \Sigma_\mathcal{C}^{\leftarrow \top}$, and $C^{\mathcal{I}} = C^{\mathcal{I}_1}$ since $Sig(C) \subseteq \Sigma_\mathcal{C}^{\leftarrow \top}$. It follows that $C^{\mathcal{I}} \not\subseteq D^{\mathcal{I}}$. It remains to be shown that $\mathcal{I}$ is indeed a model of $\mathcal{M}$, and therefore satisfies all axioms $\beta = (\beta_L \sqsubseteq \beta_R)$ in $\mathcal{M}$, including α. If $\beta = Dis(R_r, R_2)$ then by definition $Sig(\beta) \subseteq \Sigma_\mathcal{C}^{\leftarrow \top}$ so that $(\beta)^{\mathcal{I}} = (\beta)^{\mathcal{I}^1}$. Otherwise there are two possibilities:

- $\beta \in \mathcal{M}_1$. Since $\mathcal{M}_1 \subseteq \mathcal{C}_\Sigma^{\leftarrow \top}$, all symbols in $Sig(\beta_L)$ are also in $\Sigma_\mathcal{C}^{\leftarrow \top}$ and possibly some symbols of $\text{Sig}(\beta_R)$ may not be in $\Sigma_\mathcal{C}^{\leftarrow \top}$. Consequently, $\mathcal{I}_1$ and $\mathcal{I}$ coincide on the names occurring in β_L and since $\mathcal{I}_1$ is a model of $\mathcal{M}_1$, we have that $(\beta_L)^{\mathcal{I}} = (\beta_L)^{\mathcal{I}_1}$ and $(\beta_R)^{\mathcal{I}_1} \subseteq (\beta_R)^{\mathcal{I}}$. Therefore $(\beta_L)^{\mathcal{I}} \subseteq (\beta_R)^{\mathcal{I}}$.
- $\beta \notin \mathcal{M}_1$. Since $\beta \in \mathcal{M}$, we have that $\beta \notin \mathcal{C}_\Sigma^{\leftarrow \top}$, and hence β is not $\Sigma_\mathcal{C}^{\leftarrow \top}$-reachable. Thus,
  - β_R is a concept name and $\beta_R^{\mathcal{I}'} = \Delta^{\mathcal{I}}$, or
  - β_R is a role name and $\beta_R^{\mathcal{I}'} = \Delta^{\mathcal{I}} \times \Delta^{\mathcal{I}}$, or
  - β_R is a disjunction of the form $A_1 \sqcup \ldots \sqcup A_n$ with at least one $A_i \notin \Sigma_\mathcal{C}^{\leftarrow \top}$, thus $A_i^{\mathcal{I}'} = \Delta^{\mathcal{I}}$ and $\beta_R^{\mathcal{I}'} = A_1^{\mathcal{I}} \cup \ldots \cup \Delta^{\mathcal{I}} \cup \ldots \cup A_n^{\mathcal{I}} = \Delta^{\mathcal{I}}$, or
  - β_R is an existential restriction $\exists r.A_1$, thus $r^{\mathcal{I}'} = \Delta^{\mathcal{I}} \times \Delta^{\mathcal{I}}$ and $A_1^{\mathcal{I}'} = \Delta^{\mathcal{I}}$ so that $(\exists r.A_1)^{\mathcal{I}'} = \Delta^{\mathcal{I}}$, or
  - β_R is $\exists r.Self$, thus $r^{\mathcal{I}'} = \Delta^{\mathcal{I}} \times \Delta^{\mathcal{I}}$ so that $(\exists r.Self)^{\mathcal{I}'} = \Delta^{\mathcal{I}}$, or
  - β_R is an atleast restriction $\geq nr.A_2$, thus $r^{\mathcal{I}'} = \Delta^{\mathcal{I}} \times \Delta^{\mathcal{I}}$, $A_2^{\mathcal{I}'} = \Delta^{\mathcal{I}}$ and $|\Delta^{\mathcal{I}}| \geq n$ so that $(\geq nr.A_2)^{\mathcal{I}'} = \Delta^{\mathcal{I}}$. This follows from the fact that for any concept description $\geq nr.A$, $|\Delta^{\mathcal{I}}| \geq |(r.A)^{\mathcal{I}}| \geq n$ for it to be satisfiable.

  By definition of $\mathcal{I}$, $(\beta_R)^{\mathcal{I}} = \Delta^{\mathcal{I}_1}$. Hence $(\beta_L)^{\mathcal{I}} \subseteq (\beta_R)^{\mathcal{I}}$.

Therefore $\mathcal{I}$ is a model for $\mathcal{M}$. But since $C^{\mathcal{I}} \not\subseteq D^{\mathcal{I}}$ we have that $\mathcal{M} \not\models C \sqsubseteq D$ proving the contrapositive. □

5 Empirical Evaluation

From Example 2 we see that reachability modules have the potential of being smaller than locality modules. In this section we show the results of tests conducted to determine the extent of the difference in size between reachability and locality modules across a range of real world ontologies. The criteria used to select the target ontologies were size and expressivity. In terms of size we tried to find ontologies that range from a few thousand to tens of thousands of CBox axioms. In terms of expressivity we chose ontologies that range from the relatively inexpressive DL $\mathcal{EL}$ up to and including $\mathcal{SRIQ}$. For ontologies containing nominals we simple removed all axioms containing nominals from the test ontology. In Table 3 we provide a non-exhaustive list of DL metrics for each of the ontologies[1] in the test set.

Table 3. DL Metrics

	Chebi	Fly_Anatomy	Gene	GeoSkills	Galen	cton	so-xp	Software
Expressivity	$\mathcal{EL}^{++}$	$\mathcal{EL}^{++}$	$\mathcal{EL}^{++}$	$\mathcal{ALCHOIN}(\mathcal{D})$	$\mathcal{ALEHF}^+$	$\mathcal{SHF}$	$\mathcal{SHI}$	$\mathcal{ALCHIQ}(\mathcal{D})$
Axioms	34387	10471	42656	14861	4735	33203	1943	3347
Concepts	19360	6222	26225	603	2748	17033	1660	735
Roles	8	2	4	23	413	43	22	15
$C \sqsubseteq D$	34387	10467	42650	686	3237	33062	1709	2077
$C \equiv D$	0	2	0	6	0	86	198	7
$C \sqcap D \sqsubseteq \bot$	0	0	2	19	0	8	21	0
$Trans(R)$	0	2	1	0	26	18	5	0
$R \sqsubseteq S$	0	0	2	4	416	25	6	1
R^-	0	0	0	1	207	0	0	3
$Ran(R)$	0	0	0	15	0	0	0	4
$Dom(R)$	0	0	0	16	0	0	0	3
$Sym(R)$	0	0	0	1	0	0	4	0

Test were structured in such a way that we could determine the difference in module sizes across a range of different input signature sizes. For each of the test ontologies $\mathcal{O}_i$ we chose a random signature as a percentage of $Sig(\mathcal{O}_i)$. The input signature size was divided into eight groups namely 0.1%, 0.2%, 0.5%, 1.0%, 2.0%, 5.0%, 10.0% and 20.0% of $Sig(\mathcal{O}_i)$. For each of these input sizes we extracted one thousand $\bot\top^*$-reachability and locality modules, each module based on a random selection of symbols from $Sig(\mathcal{O}_i)$ to act as input signature $\mathcal{S}$. The average difference in size between reachability and locality modules were then calculated by the formula $\mathtt{Avg}((\mathtt{Local_j(S_j)} - \mathtt{Reach_j(S_j)}) * 100 / (\mathtt{Local_j(S_j)}))$ for $1 \leq j \leq 1000$.

Figure 1 represents the reduction in size of reachability modules versus locality modules. The x-axis represents the signature size whereas the y-axis represents percentage reduction of reachability modules over that of locality modules. From

---
[1] Obtained from the TONES repository 15 July 2013
(http://owl.cs.manchester.ac.uk/repository/browser).

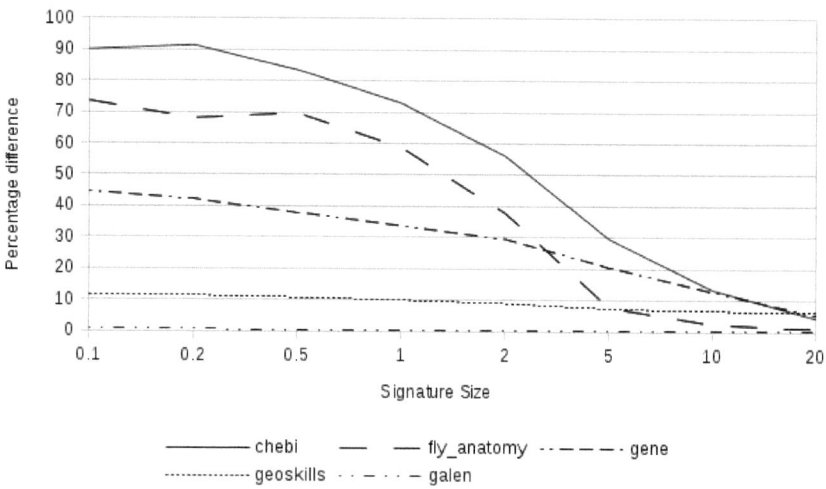

Fig. 1. Reachability v.s. Locality Modules

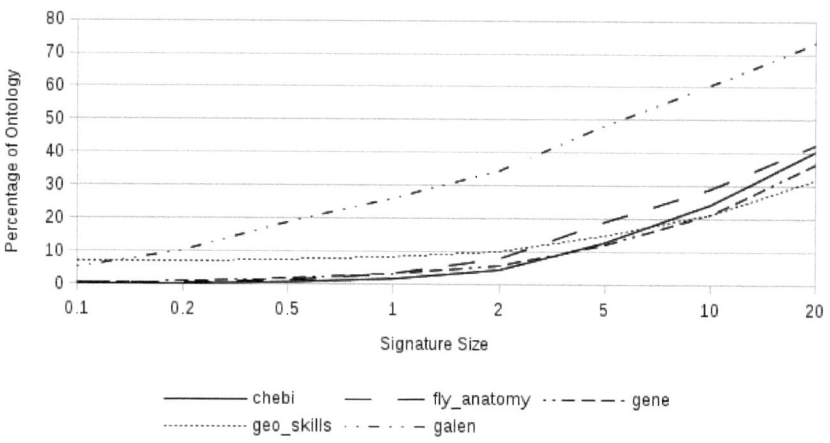

Fig. 2. Reachability module v.s. Ontology

this graph we see that there is a drastic difference between the results for different ontologies. For relatively small signature sizes in the Chebi ontology reachability modules can be up to 90% smaller than locality modules for the same input signature, whereas for the galen ontology there is less than 1% difference. For the so-xp, cton and software ontologies, not listed here, the results are very similar to that of galen.

Figure 2 represents the ratio between the size of the reachability module v.s. the size of the whole ontology. The x-axes represents the signature size and the y-axis represents the reachability module size as a percentage of the ontology size.

From the results we see that reachability modules are potentially smaller than locality modules. The drastic difference in the results further demonstrate that reachability modules may be of better use where the input signature is relatively small. For the current set of results we have not attempted to deduce the reasons why certain ontologies perform better than others.

6 Conclusion

We have investigated the module-theoretic properties of reachability modules for $\mathcal{SRIQ}$ CBoxes. Reachability modules differ from syntactic locality modules in that they are not self-contained or depleting. One application of the self-contained and depleting nature of locality modules is to find all justifications for entailments. However, in terms of finding justifications, by showing that reachability modules do preserve all justifications for entailments, we have shown that these properties are sufficient but that they are not necessary.

We did an empirical evaluation into the size difference between locality and reachability modules. We extracted a random sample of 1000 modules from each of the ontologies listed in Table 3. Reachability modules were between 0% and 90% smaller than locality modules with a relatively small input signature. This difference diminishes when the signature size reaches over 20% of the signature size of the ontology.

Our focus for future research is to extend these results to $\mathcal{SROIQ}$ and to investigate the relationship between other hypergraph based problems and DL reasoning problems more closely.

Acknowledgments. This work is based upon research supported in part by the National Research Foundation of South Africa (UID 85482, IFR2011032700018).

References

1. Antoniou, G., Kehagias, A.: A note on the refinement of ontologies. International Journal of Intelligent Systems 15, 623–632 (2000)
2. Baader, F., Calvanese, D., McGuinness, D.L., Nardi, D., Patel-Schneider, P.F. (eds.): The description logic handbook: theory, implementation, and applications. Cambridge University Press, New York (2003)
3. Cuenca Grau, B., Halaschek-Wiener, C., Kazakov, Y., Suntisrivaraporn, B.: Incremental Classification of Description Logic Ontologies. Tech. rep. (2012)
4. Cuenca Grau, B., Horrocks, I., Kazakov, Y., Sattler, U.: Just the right amount: extracting modules from ontologies. In: Williamson, C., Zurko, M. (eds.) Proceedings of the 16th International Conference on World Wide Web (WWW 2007), pp. 717–726. ACM, New York (2007)

5. Cuenca Grau, B., Horrocks, I., Kazakov, Y., Sattler, U.: Modular Reuse of Ontologies: Theory and Practice. Journal of Artificial Intelligence Research (JAIR) 31, 273–318 (2008)
6. Del Vescovo, C., Parsia, B., Sattler, U., Schneider, T.: The modular structure of an ontology: atomic decomposition and module count. In: Kutz, O., Schneider, T. (eds.) Proc. of WoMO 2011. Frontiers in AI and Appl., vol. 230, pp. 25–39. IOS Press (2011)
7. Ghilardi, S., Lutz, C., Wolter, F.: Did I damage my ontology? A case for conservative extensions in description logics. In: Doherty, P., Mylopoulos, J., Welty, C. (eds.) Proceedings of the Tenth International Conference on Principles of Knowledge Representation and Reasoning (KR 2006), pp. 187–197. AAAI Press (2006)
8. Horridge, M., Parsia, B., Sattler, U.: Laconic and precise justifications in OWL. In: Sheth, A.P., Staab, S., Dean, M., Paolucci, M., Maynard, D., Finin, T., Thirunarayan, K. (eds.) ISWC 2008. LNCS, vol. 5318, pp. 323–338. Springer, Heidelberg (2008)
9. Horrocks, I., Kutz, O., Sattler, U.: The irresistible $\mathcal{SRIQ}$. In: Proc. of OWL: Experiences and Directions (2005)
10. Konev, B., Lutz, C., Walther, D., Wolter, F.: Formal properties of modularisation. In: Stuckenschmidt, H., Parent, C., Spaccapietra, S. (eds.) Modular Ontologies. LNCS, vol. 5445, pp. 25–66. Springer, Heidelberg (2009)
11. Kontchakov, R., Pulina, L., Sattler, U., Schneider, T., Selmer, P., Wolter, F.: Minimal module extraction from DL-Lite ontologies using qbf solvers. In: Boutilier, C. (ed.) IJCAI, pp. 836–841 (2009)
12. Kontchakov, R., Wolter, F., Zakharyaschev, M.: Logic-based ontology comparison and module extraction, with an application to dl-lite. Artificial Intellighence 174(15), 1093–1141 (2010)
13. Nguyen, S., Pretolani, D., Markenzon, L.: On some path problems on oriented hypergraphs. Theoretical Informatics and Applications 32(1-2-3), 1–20 (1998)
14. Nortjé, R.: Module extraction for inexpressive description logics. Master's thesis, University of South Africa (2011)
15. Nortjé, R., Britz, K., Meyer, T.: Bidirectional reachability-based modules. In: Proceedings of the 2011 International Workshop on Description Logics (DL 2011). CEUR Workshop Proceedings, CEUR-WS (2011), http://ceur-ws.org
16. Nortjé, R., Britz, K., Meyer, T.: A normal form for hypergraph-based module extraction for $\mathcal{SROIQ}$. In: Gerber, A., Taylor, K., Meyer, T., Orgun, M. (eds.) Australasian Ontology Workshop 2009 (AOW 2012). Ceur-ws, vol. 969, pp. 40–51. CEUR, Melbourne (2012), http://ceur-ws.org/Vol-969/proceedings.pdf
17. Nortjé, R., Britz, K., Meyer, T.: Module-theoretic properties of reachability modules for $\mathcal{SRIQ}$. In: Description Logic Workshop 2013 (DL 2013). CEUR-WS, CEUR, Ulm, Germany (2013)
18. Sattler, U., Schneider, T., Zakharyaschev, M.: Which kind of module should I extract? In: Grau, B.C., Horrocks, I., Motik, B., Sattler, U. (eds.) Description Logics. CEUR Workshop Proceedings, vol. 477, CEUR-WS.org (2009)
19. Suntisrivaraporn, B.: Polynomial-Time Reasoning Support for Design and Maintenance of Large-Scale Biomedical Ontologies. Ph.D. thesis, Technical University of Dresden (2009)
20. Thakur, M., Tripathi, R.: Complexity of Linear Connectivity Problems in Directed Hypergraphs. In: Linear Connectivity Conference, pp. 1–12 (2001)

An Event Structure Model for Probabilistic Concurrent Kleene Algebra

Annabelle McIver[1], Tahiry Rabehaja[1,2], and Georg Struth[2]

[1] Department of Computing*
Macquarie University, Sydney, Australia
{annabelle.mciver,tahiry.rabehaja}@mq.edu.au
[2] Department of Computer Science
University of Sheffield, United Kingdom
g.struth@dcs.shef.ac.uk

Abstract. We give a new true-concurrent model for probabilistic concurrent Kleene algebra. The model is based on probabilistic event structures, which combines ideas from Katoen's work on probabilistic concurrency and Varacca's probabilistic prime event structures. The event structures are compared with a true-concurrent version of Segala's probabilistic simulation. Finally, the algebraic properties of the model are summarised to the extent that they can be used to derive techniques such as probabilistic rely/guarantee inference rules.

1 Introduction

The use of probability in concurrent systems has provided solutions to many problems where non-probabilistic techniques would fail [1]. However, the combination of probability and concurrency increases the complexity of any formal tool powerful enough to ensure the correctness of a system involving both features. It is then imperative that such a framework should be as simple as possible and the use of algebras in formal verifications is indeed a step in that direction. In this paper, we follow an algebraic approach in the style of Hoare et al's concurrent Kleene algebra (CKA) that is sound under a true-concurrent interpretation [2]. The algebraic laws model the interactions between probability, nondeterminism, concurrency and finite iteration operators. The structure produces an algebra which is an important mathematical tool for carrying out complex verification tasks and can be used to give robust proofs of concurrent systems, and in particular for verification techniques such as Jones rely/guarantee rules [2,3].

We have previously developed an interleaving model for probabilistic concurrent Kleene algebra (pCKA) that aims to combine probability and concurrency in a single algebraic setting [4]. Starting from the same set of axioms, we present a novel true-concurrent model based on bundle event structures (BES) [5,6]. Our motivation is that the concurrency operator of event structures provides a

---

* This research has been supported by the Australia Research Council Discovery Grant DP1092464 and the iMQRS Grant from Macquarie University.

more faithful interpretation of concurrency found in physical systems. In contrast, the parallel composition of automata fails to capture some fundamental properties such as refinement of actions [7]. Indeed, we show that our semantics distinguishes processes that are equal in the interleaving case. Event structures were introduced by Winskel [8] and have been studied extensively by others [5,6,9,10], refined to bundle event structures by Langerak [6] and extended to account for probabilistic specifications by Katoen [5]. Katoen concentrated on event structures for probabilistic process algebras but did not provide the framework needed to compare different event structures. In contrast, Varacca studied the semantics of probabilistic prime event structures (pPES) using valuations on the set of configurations [11]. It is well known that prime event structures are not rich enough to express the right factorisation of sequential composition through nondeterminism. Our true-concurrent model for pCKA requires a bundle event structure framework extended with probabilistic simulations over the "configuration-trees".

Our main contribution is the development of a new model for pCKA endowed with a true-concurrent version of Segala's probabilistic simulation [12]. To the best of our knowledge, this is the first extension of probabilistic simulation to the true-concurrent setting though non probabilistic versions do exist in the literature [13,14]. We also define an adequate weakening of Katoen's techniques for pBES so that they reduce to Varacca's definitions for PES.

The paper is organised as follows. In Section 2, we provide the necessary background for bundle event structures. The algebraic operators are defined in Section 3 where a particular care is needed for the construction of the binary Kleene star. Without probability, we argue that bundle event structures endowed with these operators and quotiented with the pomset language equivalence forms a concrete model for CKA. In Section 4, we set out the necessary tools for constructing pBES. In Section 5, we define the notion of probabilistic simulation on pBES. Section 6 is devoted to showing that the set of pBES endowed with the defined algebraic operators modulo probabilistic simulation satisfies the axioms of pCKA. All incomplete proofs are given in complete version of this paper [15].

2 Bundle Event Structures

Event structures provide a truly concurrent denotation for processes where an event is labelled by an action from a set Σ. An event e may enable another event f, that is, f cannot happen unless e has already happened. This relation, denoted by $\mapsto$, is useful for sequential dependency. It is also possible that two events cannot happen simultaneously in a single run which usually occurs when there is a nondeterministic choice of events. This second relation is denoted by $\#$ and is extended to sets of events $x, y \subseteq E$ such that $x \# y$ iff for all $e \in x$ and $f \in y$, if $e \neq f$ then $e \# f$. Formally, we have the following definition.

Definition 1 ([6]). *A bundle event structure $\mathcal{E}$ is a tuple $(E, \#, \mapsto, \lambda, \Phi)$ such that E is a set of events, $\# \subseteq E \times E$ is an irreflexive and symmetric binary relation (the conflict relation), $\mapsto \subseteq \mathcal{P}(E) \times E$ is called a bundle relation where*

$$\forall x \subseteq E \; \forall e \in E : x \mapsto e \Rightarrow x \# x,$$

$\lambda : E \to \Sigma$ is a labelling (partial) function and $\Phi \subseteq E$ is a set of events such that $\Phi \# \Phi$. Elements of Φ are called final events and $\mathcal{P}(E)$ is the powerset of E.

In the bundle $x \mapsto e$, x is referred to as a bundle set and the event e is pointed by x. Since $x \# x$ holds for every x such that $x \mapsto e$, it follows that exactly one event in x must enable e and such a unique event is required for each bundle set pointing to e before it can happen. Given a set of events $x \subseteq E$, we denote by $\mathbf{cfl}(x) = \{e \in E \mid \exists e' \in x : e \# e'\}$ the set of events that are in conflict with some event in x. A set x is called *conflict free* if $\mathbf{cfl}(x) \cap x = \emptyset$. Unlabelled events happen without any noticeable internal nor external observable outputs. They are only used as "delimiters".

A (finite) sequence of events $e_1 e_2 \cdots e_n$ from E is called an *event trace* if for every $i \geq 1$ and every bundle relation $y \mapsto e_i$, there exists $j < i$ such that $e_j \in y$ and $e_i \notin \mathbf{cfl}(\{e_1, \ldots, e_{i-1}\}) \cup \{e_1, \ldots, e_{i-1}\}$.

Definition 2 ([6]). *A configuration is a subset $x \subseteq E$ such that $x = \{e_1, \ldots, e_n\}$ for some event trace $e_1 \cdots e_n$ referred to as a linearisation of x. The set of all configurations (reps. traces) of $\mathcal{E}$ is denoted by $\mathcal{C}(\mathcal{E})$ (resp. $\mathcal{T}(\mathcal{E})$).*

In the sequel we will need to describe the causal dependencies between events in more detail. To do this we associate a partial order with each configuration.

A *labelled partial order* (lposet) is a tuple $(x, \preceq, \lambda)$ where $(x, \preceq)$ is a poset and $\lambda : x \to \Sigma$. Unlabelled events of a lposet $u = (x, \preceq, \lambda)$ can be removed to obtain the sub-lposet $\hat{u} = (\hat{x}, \preceq|_{\hat{x}}, \lambda|_{\hat{x}})$ such that $\hat{x} = \{e \in x \mid \lambda(e) \text{ is defined}\}$ and where $\preceq|_{\hat{x}}$ and $\lambda|_{\hat{x}}$ are the respective restrictions of $\preceq$ and λ to the set $\hat{x}$. A lposet $u = (x, \preceq_x, \lambda_x)$ *implements* another lposet $v = (y, \preceq_y, \lambda_y)$ if there exists a label-preserving monotonic bijection $f : \hat{y} \to \hat{x}$ and we write $u \sqsubseteq_s v$ or simply $x \sqsubseteq_s y$ if no confusion arises (s stands for subsumption [16]).

Given an event trace $e_1 \cdots e_n$ of a BES $\mathcal{E}$, we denote by $\preceq_{e_1 \cdots e_n}$ the reflexive transitive closure of the order $\preceq$ of events in that sequence i.e. $e_1 \preceq e_2, e_2 \preceq e_3, \ldots, e_{n-1} \preceq e_n$. The tuple $(\{e_1, \ldots, e_n\}, \preceq_{e_1 \cdots e_n}, \lambda|_{\{e_1, \ldots, e_n\}})$ is a lposet. Let $x \in \mathcal{C}(\mathcal{E})$. We generate a lposet $(x, \preceq, \lambda)$ where

$$\preceq = \bigcap_{x=\{e_1,\ldots,e_n\} \wedge e_1 \cdots e_n \in \mathcal{T}(\mathcal{E})} \preceq_{e_1 \cdots e_n}$$

and λ is restricted to x. Intuitively, two events are incomparable iff neither has to happen before the other.

The set of lposets of $\mathcal{E}$ is denoted $\mathcal{L}(\mathcal{E})$, that is, $\mathcal{L}(\mathcal{E}) = \{(x, \preceq, \lambda) \mid x \in \mathcal{C}(\mathcal{E})\}$. Given two bundle event structures $\mathcal{E}$ and $\mathcal{F}$, it is well known that $\mathcal{C}(\mathcal{E}) = \mathcal{C}(\mathcal{F})$ iff $\mathcal{T}(\mathcal{E}) = \mathcal{T}(\mathcal{F})$ iff $\mathcal{L}(\mathcal{E}) = \mathcal{L}(\mathcal{F})$ [5,6]. We say that $(x, \preceq_x, \lambda_x)$ is a *prefix* of $(y, \preceq_y, \lambda_y)$, written $(x, \preceq_x, \lambda_x) \trianglelefteq (y, \preceq_y, \lambda_y)$, if $x \subseteq y$ and $\lambda_y|_x = \lambda_x$ and $e \preceq_y e' \wedge e' \in x \Rightarrow e \in x \wedge e \preceq_x e'$. The next proposition shows that configurations inclusion characterises prefixing.

Proposition 1. *Let $\mathcal{E}$ be a BES. If $x, y \in \mathcal{C}(\mathcal{E})$ and $x \subseteq y$ then $(x, \preceq_x, \lambda_x) \trianglelefteq (y, \preceq_y, \lambda_y)$.*

3 Basic Operations on Bundle Event Structures

A concurrent quantale is a particular kind of concurrent Kleene algebra [2]. It is composed of two quantales that interact via the interchange law (21). In this section, we show that the set **BES** of bundle event structures endowed with the following operators and partial order forms a concurrent quantale. This model is extended to capture probability in Section 4.

Basic BES: we start by defining the basic BES corresponding to Deadlock, Skip and one step action.

- Deadlock is denoted by 0 and is associated with the BES $(\emptyset, \emptyset, \emptyset, \emptyset, \emptyset)$.
- Skip is denoted by 1 and is associated with $(\{e\}, \emptyset, \emptyset, \emptyset, \{e\})$.
- Each $a \in \Sigma$ is associated with $(\{e_a\}, \emptyset, \emptyset, \lambda(e_a) = a, \{e_a\})$, denoted by a.

We fix two BES $\mathcal{E} = (E, \#_\mathcal{E}, \mapsto_\mathcal{E}, \lambda_\mathcal{E}, \Phi_\mathcal{E})$ and $\mathcal{F} = (F, \#_\mathcal{F}, \mapsto_\mathcal{F}, \lambda_\mathcal{F}, \Phi_\mathcal{F})$ such that $E \cap F = \emptyset$. This ensures that the disjoint union of two labelling functions is again a function. We define the set $\mathbf{in}(\mathcal{E}) \subseteq E$ such that $e \in \mathbf{in}(\mathcal{E})$ iff there is no $x \subseteq E$ such that $x \mapsto e$. Events in $\mathbf{in}(\mathcal{E})$ are called initial events.

Concurrency, sequential composition and nondeterminism [5] are defined in Fig. 1. The concurrent composition $\mathcal{E} \| \mathcal{F}$ is the disjoint union of $\mathcal{E}$ and $\mathcal{F}$ delimited by fresh ineffectual events. Notice there is no synchronisation in $\|$, this is because we are mainly interested in lock-free concurrencies in the style of [2,3,17,18]. A special event can however be introduced to force synchronisation [5,7] and most of the algebraic laws remain valid. For the sequential composition, new bundles of the form $\Phi_\mathcal{E} \mapsto e$ for every $e \in \mathbf{in}(\mathcal{F})$ are added to make sure that all events of $\mathcal{E}$ precede all events of $\mathcal{F}$. For nondeterminism, the property $\mathbf{in}(\mathcal{E}) \# \mathbf{in}(\mathcal{F})$ is imposed so that the occurrence of any initial event of $\mathcal{E}$ will block every events of $\mathcal{F}$ from happening (and symmetrically). The choice is resolved as soon as one event from $\mathcal{E}$ or $\mathcal{F}$ happens.

The Kleene star is defined by constructing a complete partial order on the set of BES. We define the order $\mathcal{E} \trianglelefteq \mathcal{F}$, which is the sub-BES relation, such that

$$E \subseteq F$$
$$\#_\mathcal{E} = \#_\mathcal{F} \cap (E \times E)$$
$$\mapsto_\mathcal{E} \subseteq \mapsto_\mathcal{F}$$
$$x \mapsto_\mathcal{F} e \land e \in E \Rightarrow x \subseteq E \land x \mapsto_\mathcal{E} e$$
$$\lambda_\mathcal{E} = \lambda_\mathcal{F}|_E$$
$$\Phi_\mathcal{E} = \Phi_\mathcal{F} \cap E$$

Concurrency $\mathcal{E}\|\mathcal{F}$:

- set of events: $E \cup F \cup \{e, f\}$,
- conflicts: $\#_\mathcal{E} \cup \#_\mathcal{F}$,
- bundles: $\mapsto_\mathcal{E} \cup \mapsto_\mathcal{F} \cup \{\{e\} \mapsto e' \mid e' \in \mathbf{in}(\mathcal{E}) \cup \mathbf{in}(\mathcal{F})\} \cup \{\Phi_\mathcal{E} \mapsto f, \Phi_\mathcal{F} \mapsto f\}$,
- labelling: $\lambda \cup \lambda'$,
- final events: $\Phi_{\mathcal{E}\|\mathcal{F}} = \{f\}$.

where $e, f \notin E \cup F$.

Sequential composition $\mathcal{E} \cdot \mathcal{F}$:

- set of events: $E \cup F$,
- conflicts: $\#_\mathcal{E} \cup \#_\mathcal{F}$,
- bundles: $\mapsto_\mathcal{E} \cup \mapsto_\mathcal{F} \cup \{\Phi_\mathcal{E} \mapsto e \mid e \in \mathbf{in}(\mathcal{F})\}$,
- labelling : $\lambda \cup \lambda'$,
- final events: $\Phi_{\mathcal{E}\cdot\mathcal{F}} = \Phi_\mathcal{F}$.

Nondeterminism $\mathcal{E} + \mathcal{F}$:

- set of events: $E \cup F$,
- conflicts: $\#_\mathcal{E} \cup \#_\mathcal{F} \cup \mathrm{sym}(\mathbf{in}(\mathcal{E}) \times \mathbf{in}(\mathcal{F})) \cup \mathrm{sym}(\Phi_\mathcal{E} \times \Phi_\mathcal{F})$,
- bundles: $\mapsto_\mathcal{E} \cup \mapsto_\mathcal{F}$,
- labelling: $\lambda \cup \lambda'$,
- final events: $\Phi_{\mathcal{E}+\mathcal{F}} = \Phi_\mathcal{E} \cup \Phi_\mathcal{F}$.

where $\mathrm{sym}(x \times y) = (x \times y) \cup (y \times x)$ is the symmetric closure.

Fig. 1. Definitions of $\mathcal{E}\|\mathcal{F}$, $\mathcal{E} \cdot \mathcal{F}$ and $\mathcal{E} + \mathcal{F}$

We use the following binding precedence: $*, \cdot, \|, +$. The probabilistic choice $\oplus_\alpha$ (defined later) and $+$ are unordered and are parsed using brackets.

Proposition 2. $(\mathbf{BES}, \trianglelefteq)$ *is an ω-complete partially ordered set, that is, any countable ascending chain has a least upper bound in* $\mathbf{BES}$.

Proof (Sketch). The proof that $\trianglelefteq$ is a partial order amounts to checking reflexivity, antisymmetry and transitivity which is clear. As for ω-completeness, given a countable increasing sequence of BES $\mathcal{E}_0 \trianglelefteq \mathcal{E}_1 \trianglelefteq \mathcal{E}_2 \trianglelefteq \cdots$, we construct a BES $\mathcal{E} = (\cup_i E_i, \cup_i \#_i, \cup_i \mapsto_i, \cup_i \lambda_i, \cup \Phi_i)$. We can show that $\mathcal{E}$ is indeed the least upper bound w.r.t $\trianglelefteq$ of the countable sequence $(\mathcal{E}_i)_i$. $\square$

Let $\mathcal{E}, \mathcal{F}$ be two BES. The Kleene product of $\mathcal{E}$ by $\mathcal{F}$, denoted by $\mathcal{E} * \mathcal{F}$, is the limit of the $\trianglelefteq$-increasing sequence of BES

$$\mathcal{F} \trianglelefteq \mathcal{F} + \mathcal{E} \cdot \mathcal{F} \trianglelefteq \mathcal{F} + \mathcal{E} \cdot (\mathcal{F} + \mathcal{E} \cdot \mathcal{F}) \trianglelefteq \cdots$$

where adequate events renaming are needed to ensure that the sequence of BES are syntactically similar (see Fig. 2 for a concrete example). Equivalently, $\mathcal{E} * \mathcal{F}$ is the least fixed point of $\lambda X.\mathcal{F} + \mathcal{E} \cdot X$ in $(\mathbf{BES}, \trianglelefteq)$. The unary Kleene star is obtained as usual by $\mathcal{E}^* = \mathcal{E} * \mathbf{1}$. The main reason behind the use of the binary Kleene star [19] is that the unary version introduces unwanted sequential compositions. For instance, in normal Kleene algebras, a while loop with body $\mathcal{E}$ is encoded as $(e_g \cdot \mathcal{E})^* \cdot e_{\neg g}$ where e_g (resp. $e_{\neg g}$) is the event associated with the guard. Hence by the interchange law (21), $((e_g \cdot \mathcal{E})^* \cdot e_{\neg g})\|a$ can behave as

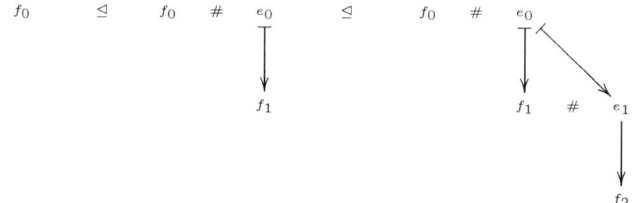

An arrow $\mapsto$ denotes a bundle relation and $\#$ is the conflict relation. The events f_i are labelled by b while the e_is are labelled by a.

Fig. 2. The first three terms in the construction of $a * b$

$(e_g \cdot \mathcal{E})^* \cdot a \cdot e_{\neg g}$ but we would assume that each e_g and the corresponding $e_{\neg g}$ are checked simultaneously. Hence, we interpret a while loop as $(e_g \cdot \mathcal{E}) * e_{\neg g}$.

For convenience, we denote each component of the above sequence by $\mathcal{E} *_{\leq 0} \mathcal{F} = \mathcal{F}$, $\mathcal{E} *_{\leq 1} \mathcal{F} = \mathcal{F} + \mathcal{E} \cdot \mathcal{F}$, $\mathcal{E} *_{\leq 2} \mathcal{F} = \mathcal{F} + \mathcal{E} \cdot (\mathcal{F} + \mathcal{E} \cdot \mathcal{F}), \dots$ The following proposition ensures that these operators are well defined.

Proposition 3. *Let $\mathcal{E}, \mathcal{F}$ be BES. Then for every $\bullet \in \{+, \cdot, \|, *\}$ $\Phi_{\mathcal{E} \bullet \mathcal{F}} \# \Phi_{\mathcal{E} \bullet \mathcal{F}}$.*

Proof. We have $\Phi_{\mathcal{E} + \mathcal{F}} = \Phi_{\mathcal{E}} \cup \Phi_{\mathcal{F}}$ and since $\Phi_{\mathcal{E}} \times \Phi_{\mathcal{F}} \subseteq \#_{\mathcal{E} + \mathcal{F}}$, it follows that $\Phi_{\mathcal{E} + \mathcal{F}} \#_{\mathcal{E} + \mathcal{F}} \Phi_{\mathcal{E} + \mathcal{F}}$. The result is clear for the case of $\mathcal{E} \cdot \mathcal{F}$ and $\mathcal{E} \| \mathcal{F}$ because $\Phi_{\mathcal{E} \cdot \mathcal{F}} = \Phi_{\mathcal{F}}$ and $\Phi_{\mathcal{E} \| \mathcal{F}} = \{f\}$ where f is the fresh final event in the construction of $\mathcal{E} \| \mathcal{F}$. For the Kleene star, we have $\Phi_{\mathcal{E} * \mathcal{F}} = \cup_i \Phi_{\mathcal{E} *_{\leq i} \mathcal{F}}$ (increasing union). Therefore, any pair of events $(e, e') \in \Phi_{\mathcal{E} *_{\leq i} \mathcal{F}} \times \Phi_{\mathcal{E} *_{\leq j} \mathcal{F}}$ are mutually conflicting with respect to the conflict relation of $\mathcal{E} *_{\leq \max(i,j)} \mathcal{F}$. □

We end this section by observing that $(\mathbf{BES}, +, \cdot, \|, 0, 1)$ is a concurrent quantale where the operator $\bullet \in \{\cdot, \|\}$ is redefined so that $\mathcal{E} \bullet 0 = 0 \bullet \mathcal{E} = 0$. Following Gischer [16], we define an order relation based on pomset language subsumption. Recall that a *pomset* is an equivalence class of lposets w.r.t the equivalence relation generated by $\sqsubseteq_s$. For finite lposets u and v, we have $u \sqsubseteq_s v$ and $v \sqsubseteq_s u$ iff $\hat{u}$ is isomorphic to $\hat{v}$; hence our definition coincides with Gischer's. The equivalence class of a lposet u is denoted by the totally labelled lposet $\hat{u}$. The pomset language of a BES $\mathcal{E}$ is defined by

$$\{\hat{v} \mid \exists u \in \mathcal{L}(\mathcal{E}) : v \sqsubseteq_s u \wedge v \text{ is a lposet}\}.$$

When a BES is considered modulo pomset language equivalence, we show that $(\mathbf{BES}, +, \cdot, 0, 1)$ and $(\mathbf{BES}, +, \|, 0, 1)$ are quantales, i.e., each structure is an idempotent semiring, a complete lattice under the natural order $\mathcal{E} \leq \mathcal{E}$ iff $\mathcal{E} + \mathcal{F} = \mathcal{F}$ and the operator $\bullet \in \{\cdot, \|\}$ distributes over arbitrary suprema and infinima. The interchange law (21) is ensured by the subsumption property. The following proposition essentially follows from Gischer's results [16]. In fact, Gischer proves that the axioms of CKA without the Kleene star completely axiomatise the pomset language equivalence.

Proposition 4. *For each $\bullet \in \{\cdot, \|\}$, the structure $(\mathbf{BES}, +, \bullet, 0, 1)$ is a quantale under the pomset language equivalence.*

4 Probabilistic Bundle Event Structures

In this section, we adapt Katoen's and Varacca's works on probabilistic event structures [5,11]. In particular, we refine the notions of *cluster* and *confusion freeness* which are necessary for the definition of probabilistic bundle event structures (pBES). We use the standard transformation of prime event structures into BES to ensure that our definitions properly generalise Varacca's.

4.1 Immediate Conflict, Clusters and Confusion Free BES

The key idea of probabilistic event structures is to use probability as a mechanism to resolve conflicts. However, not all conflicts can be resolved probabilistically [5]. The cases where this occurs are referred to as confusions. A typical example of confusion is depicted by the first three events e_1, e_2 and e_3 of Fig 3 where $e_1 \# e_2$, $e_2 \# e_3$ and $\neg e_1 \# e_3$ hold allowing e_1 and e_3 to occur simultaneously in a single configuration. However, if the conflict $e_1 \# e_2$ is resolved with a coin flip and if the result is e_2, then $e_2 \# e_3$ cannot be resolved probabilistically because it may produce e_3. Following Varacca [11], we start by characterising conflicts that may be resolved probabilistically.

Definition 3. *Given a BES $\mathcal{E}$, two events $e, e' \in E$ are in immediate conflict if $e \# e'$ and there exists a configuration x such that $x \cup \{e\}$ and $x \cup \{e'\}$ are again configurations. We write $e \#_\mu e'$ when e and e' are in immediate conflict.*

Example 1. In the BES of Fig. 3, e_4 and e_5 are in immediate conflict because $\{e_1, e_3, e_4\}$ and $\{e_1, e_3, e_5\}$ are configurations. In fact, every conflicts in that BES are immediate. Notice that the conflict $e_4 \# e_5$ is resolved when e_2 occurs.

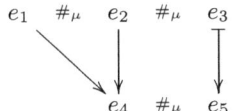

In this BES, the bundles are $\{e_1, e_2\} \mapsto e_4$ and $\{e_3\} \mapsto e_5$. The conflict relation is $e_1 \# e_2$ and $e_2 \# e_3$. Therefore, e_1 and e_3 are concurrent. An arrow $\rightarrow$ represents some part of a bundle (i.e. $\{e_1, e_2\} \mapsto e_4$ is the completed bundle) and $\mapsto$ represents a bundle.

Fig. 3. Immediate conflict in a BES

Events can be grouped into clusters of events that are pairwise in immediate conflict. More precisely, we define a cluster as follow.

Definition 4. *A partial cluster is a set of events $K \subseteq E$ satisfying*

$$\forall e, e' \in K : e \neq e' \Rightarrow e \#_\mu e' \quad \text{and}$$
$$\forall e, e' \in K, x \subseteq E : x \mapsto e \Rightarrow x \mapsto e'$$

A cluster is a maximal partial cluster (w.r.t inclusion).

Given an event $e \in E$, the singleton $\{e\}$ is a partial cluster. Therefore, there is always at least one cluster (i.e. maximal) containing e and we write $\langle e \rangle$ the intersection of all clusters containing e.

Example 2. In Fig. 3, $\{e_1, e_2\}$ and $\{e_2, e_3\}$ are clusters and $\langle e_2 \rangle = \{e_2\}$.

Proposition 5. *A partial cluster K is maximal (i.e. a cluster) iff*

$$\forall e \in E : (\forall e' \in K : e \#_\mu e' \ \land \ \forall x \subseteq E : x \mapsto e \Leftrightarrow x \mapsto e') \Rightarrow e \in K$$

Proof. The forward implication follows from Definition 4 and maximality of K. Conversely, assume that K is a partial cluster satisfying the above property. Let H be a partial cluster such that $K \subseteq H$ and $e \in H$. Then, for all $e' \in K$, $e \#_\mu e'$ and

$$\forall z \subseteq E : x \mapsto e \Leftrightarrow x \mapsto e'$$

because H is a partial cluster. By the hypothesis, $e \in K$ and hence $H = K$. $\square$

As in Katoen's and Varacca's works, clusters are used to carry probability and they can be intuitively seen as providing a choice between events where the chosen event happens instantaneously. Notice that our notion of cluster is weaker than Katoen's original definition [5]: the BES in Fig. 4 contains three clusters $\{e_1, e_2\}$, $\{e_3\}$ and $\{e_4, e_5\}$ and only $\{e_1, e_2\}$ satisfies Katoen's definition.

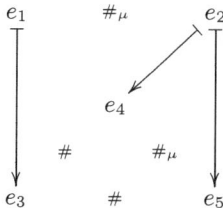

Fig. 4. A BES where $\{e_1, e_2\}$, $\{e_3\}$ and $\{e_4, e_5\}$ are clusters

Definition 5. *A BES $\mathcal{E}$ is confusion free if for all events $e, e' \in E$,*

- *if $e \#_\mu e'$ then $e \in \langle e' \rangle$, and*
- *if $\langle e \rangle \cap x = \emptyset$ and $x \cup \{e\} \in \mathcal{C}(\mathcal{E})$ for some configuration $x \in \mathcal{C}(\mathcal{E})$, then $x \cup \{e''\} \in \mathcal{C}(\mathcal{E})$ for all events $e'' \in \langle e \rangle$.*

The first property implies that $\langle e \rangle$ contains all events in immediate conflict with e and hence the confusion introduced by e_1, e_2 and e_3 in Fig. 3 is avoided. The second property says that once one event in $\langle e \rangle$ is enabled then all events in $\langle e \rangle$ are also enabled. Hence, confusion freeness ensures that all conflicts in $\langle e \rangle$ can be resolved probabilistically regardless of the history. The proof of the following proposition is the same as for prime event structures [11].

Proposition 6. *For a confusion free BES $\mathcal{E}$, the set $\{\langle e \rangle \mid e \in E\}$ defines a partition of E. That is, the reflexive closure of $\#_\mu$ is an equivalence relation and the equivalence classes are of the form $\langle e \rangle$.*

The second property of Definition 5 is usually hard to check. We give a static and simpler sufficient condition for confusion freeness.

Proposition 7. *If a BES $\mathcal{E}$ satisfies*

$$\forall e, e' \in E : (e \#_\mu e' \Rightarrow e \in \langle e' \rangle) \wedge (\langle e \rangle \cap \mathbf{cfl}(e') \neq \emptyset \Rightarrow \langle e \rangle \subseteq \mathbf{cfl}(e'))$$

then it is confusion free.

The second argument of the conjunction says that if some event in $\langle e \rangle$ is in conflict with an event e' then all events in $\langle e \rangle$ are in conflict with e'.

Proof. Let $e \in E$ and $x \in \mathcal{C}(\mathcal{E})$ such that $\langle e \rangle \cap x = \emptyset$ and $x \cup \{e\} \in \mathcal{C}(\mathcal{E})$. Let $e' \in \langle e \rangle$ and $z \mapsto e'$ be a bundle of $\mathcal{E}$. We need to show that $x \cup \{e'\} \in \mathcal{C}(\mathcal{E})$. By Definition 4, $z \mapsto e$ is also a bundle and since x and $x \cup \{e\}$ are configurations, $e_1 \cdots e_n e$ is again a linearisation of $x \cup \{e\}$ for every linearisation $e_1 \cdots e_n$ of x. Therefore, $z \cap \{e_1, \ldots, e_n\} \neq \emptyset$. If $e' \in \mathbf{cfl}(e_i)$ for some i, then $\langle e \rangle \subseteq \mathbf{cfl}(e_i)$ by the hypothesis and hence $e \in \mathbf{cfl}(e_i)$, which is impossible because $x \cup \{e\}$ is a configuration. Hence $e_1 \cdots e_n e'$ is an event trace, that is, $x \cup \{e'\} \in \mathcal{C}(\mathcal{E})$. □

Example 3. Fig. 4 depicts a confusion free BES that satisfies Proposition 7.

With confusion freeness, we are now able to define probability distributions supported by clusters. Recall that a probability distribution on the set E is a function $p : E \to [0, 1]$ such that $\sum_{e \in E} p.e = 1$. We say that p is a *probability distribution on $\mathcal{E}$* if $\mathrm{supp}(p) \subseteq \langle e \rangle$ for some event e.

Definition 6. *A probabilistic BES is a tuple $(\mathcal{E}, \pi)$ where $\mathcal{E}$ is a confusion free BES and π is a set of probability distribution on $\mathcal{E}$ such that for every $e \in E$, there exists $p \in \pi$ such that $e \in \mathrm{supp}(p)$.*

The intuition behind this definition is simple: if there is no $p \in \pi$ such that $e \in \mathrm{supp}(p)$ then e is an impossible event and it can be removed (this may affect any event e' such that $e \preceq_x e'$ for some $x \in \mathcal{C}(\mathcal{E})$). Our approach differs from both Varacca's [11] and Katoen's [5] in that nondeterminism is modelled concretely as a set of probabilistic choices. This approach will mainly contribute to the definition of the probabilistic choice operator $\oplus_\alpha$ of Section 6. For instance, the expression $a + (b \oplus_\alpha c)$ does not have any meaning in Katoen's pBES, however, it will have a precise semantics in our case.

5 Probabilistic Simulation on pBES

The weakest interpretation of $\sqsubseteq$ on pBES is the configuration distribution equivalence [11]. However, as in the interleaving case, that is not a congruence [12].

We use probabilistic simulations which are based on the notion of lifting from [20]. We denote by $\mathbb{D}(X)$ the set of (discrete) probability distributions over the set X. Given $x \in X$, we denote by δ_x the point distribution concentrated at x.

Let $S \subseteq X \times \mathbb{D}(Y)$ be a relation. The lifting of S is a relation $\overline{S} \subseteq \mathbb{D}(X) \times \mathbb{D}(Y)$ such that $(\Delta, \Theta) \in \overline{S}$ iff

- $\Delta = \sum_i \alpha_i \delta_{x_i}$ where $\sum_i \alpha_i = 1$,
- for every x_i, there exists $\Theta_i \in \mathbb{D}(Y)$ such that $(x_i, \Theta_i) \in S$,
- $\Theta = \sum_i \alpha_i \Theta_i$.

Notice that the decomposition of Δ may not be unique. The main properties of lifting are summarised in the following proposition.

Proposition 8 ([20]). *Let $S \subseteq X \times \mathbb{D}(Y)$ be a relation and $\sum_i \alpha_i = 1$. We have*

- *if $(\Delta_i, \Theta_i) \in \overline{S}$ then $(\sum_i \alpha_i \Delta_i, \sum_i \alpha_i \Theta_i) \in \overline{S}$,*
- *if $(\sum_i \alpha_i \Delta_i, \Theta) \in \overline{S}$ then there exists a collection of distributions Θ_i such that $(\Delta_i, \Theta_i) \in \overline{S}$ and $\Theta = \sum_i \alpha_i \Theta_i$.*

Since the notion of configuration for a pBES $(\mathcal{E}, \pi)$ is independent of π, we keep the notation $\mathcal{C}(\mathcal{E})$ for the set of all finite configurations. An example of relation on $\mathcal{C}(\mathcal{E}) \times \mathbb{D}(\mathcal{C}(\mathcal{E}))$ is given by the probabilistic prefixing. We say that $x \in \mathcal{C}(\mathcal{E})$ is a *prefix* of $\Delta \in \mathbb{D}(\mathcal{C}(\mathcal{E}))$, denoted (again) by $x \trianglelefteq \Delta$, if there exists $p \in \pi$ such that $\mathrm{supp}(p) \cap x = \emptyset$ and $\Delta = \sum_{e \in \mathrm{supp}(p)} (p.e) \delta_{x \cup \{e\}}$. In particular, if $\langle e \rangle = \{e\}$, $e \notin x$ and $x \cup \{e\} \in \mathcal{C}(\mathcal{E})$ then $x \trianglelefteq \delta_{x \cup \{e\}}$.

The relation $\trianglelefteq$ is lifted to $\overline{\trianglelefteq} \subseteq \mathbb{D}(\mathcal{C}(\mathcal{E})) \times \mathbb{D}(\mathcal{C}(\mathcal{E}))$ and the reflexive transitive closure of the lifted relation is denoted by $\overline{\trianglelefteq}^*$. Probabilistic prefixing allows us to construct a *configuration-tree* for every pBES. An example is depicted in Fig. 5.

To simplify the presentation, we restrict ourselves to BES satisfying $\Phi \cap x = \emptyset$ for every bundle $x \mapsto e$, that is, no event is enabled by a final event. This allows a simpler presentation of the preservation of final events by a simulation. Notice that all BES constructed from the operators defined in this paper satisfy that property.

Definition 7. *A (probabilistic) simulation from $(\mathcal{E}, \pi)$ to $(\mathcal{F}, \rho)$ is a relation $S \subseteq \mathcal{C}(\mathcal{E}) \times \mathbb{D}(\mathcal{C}(\mathcal{F}))$ such that*

- $(\emptyset, \delta_\emptyset) \in S$,
- *if $(x, \Theta) \in S$ then for every $y \in \mathrm{supp}(\Theta)$, $x \sqsubseteq_s y$,*
- *if $(x, \Theta) \in S$ and $x \trianglelefteq \Delta'$ then there exists $\Theta' \in \mathbb{D}(\mathcal{C}(\mathcal{F}))$ such that $\Theta \overline{\trianglelefteq}^* \Theta'$ and $(\Delta', \Theta') \in \overline{S}$.*
- *if $(x, \Theta) \in S$ and $x \cap \Phi_\mathcal{E} \neq \emptyset$ then for every $y \in \mathrm{supp}(\Theta)$ we have $y \cap \Phi_\mathcal{F} \neq \emptyset$.*

We write $(\mathcal{E}, \pi) \sqsubseteq (\mathcal{F}, \rho)$ if there is a simulation from $(\mathcal{E}, \pi)$ to $(\mathcal{F}, \rho)$.

Indeed, Definition 7 is akin to probabilistic forward simulation on automata. The main difference is the use of the implementation relation $x \sqsubseteq_s y$ which holds iff

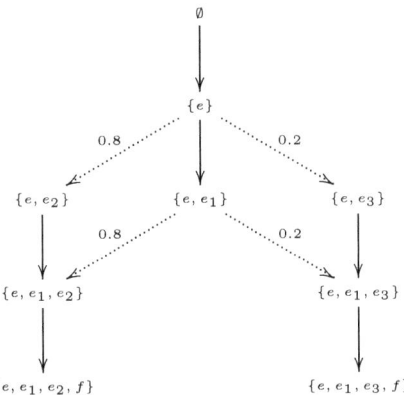

The dotted arrows with common source are parts of a probabilistic prefix relation (e.g. $\{e\} \trianglelefteq 0.8\delta_{\{e,e_2\}} + 0.2\delta_{\{e,e_3\}}$). The events e, f are the delimiters introduced by $\|$.

Fig. 5. The configurations-tree of the pBES $e_1 \| (e_2 \oplus_{0.2} e_3)$ ($\oplus_{0.2}$ is defined later)

there exists a label preserving monotonic bijection from $(\hat{y}, \preceq_y, \lambda_y)$ to $(\hat{x}, \preceq_x, \lambda_x)$. The implementation relation compares partially ordered configurations rather than totally ordered traces, hence, interferences between incomparable or concurrent events are allowed. Another consequence of this definition is that concurrent events can be linearised while preserving simulation.

Proposition 9. $\sqsubseteq$ *is a preorder.*

The proof is the same as in [20], hence, we provide only a sketch.

Proof (Sketch). Reflexivity is clear by considering the relation $\{(x, \delta_x) \mid x \in \mathcal{C}(\mathcal{E})\}$ which is indeed a simulation. If R, S are probabilistic simulations from $(\mathcal{E}, \pi)$ to $(\mathcal{F}, \rho)$ and $(\mathcal{F}, \rho)$ to $(\mathcal{G}, r)$ respectively then we can show, using Proposition 8 and a similar proof as in the interleaving case, that $R \circ \overline{S}$ is a probabilistic simulation from $(\mathcal{E}, \pi)$ to $(\mathcal{G}, r)$. □

A major difference from our previous work [4] is that the event structure approach provides a truly concurrent interpretation of pCKA. The most notable benefit of using a true-concurrent model is substitution [7,16] where a single step event can be refined with another event structure after a concurrency operator has been applied. In the automata model, such a substitution must occur before the application of the concurrency operator to obtain the correct behaviour. Moreover, in interleaving, concurrency is related to the nondeterministic choice whereas here the two operators are orthogonal.

Example 4. In Fig. 6, it is shown that $a \cdot b + b \cdot a \sqsubseteq a \| b$ but the converse does not hold.

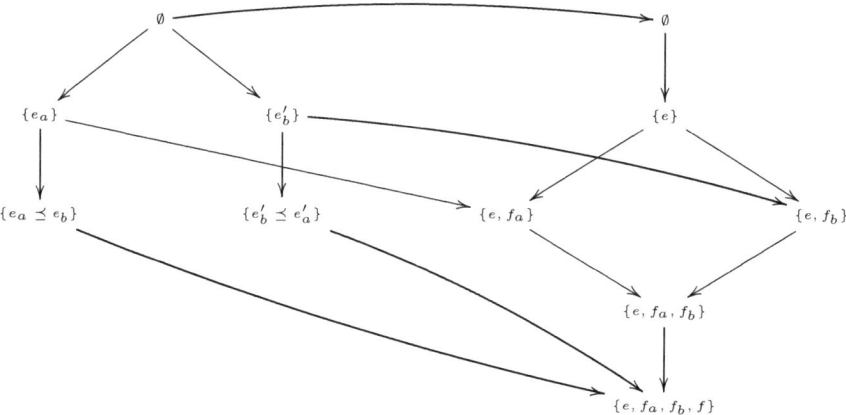

Since $\{e, f_a, f_b, f\} \not\preceq_s \{e_a \preceq e_b\}$ nor $\{e, f_a, f_b, f\} \not\preceq_s \{e'_b \preceq e'_a\}$, it is impossible to find a simulation from $a\|b$ to $a \cdot b + b \cdot a$. In the configuration tree on the left, the order $\preceq$ is made explicit and primes are introduced for disjointness.

Fig. 6. A simulation from $a \cdot b + b \cdot a$ to $a\|b$

6 Probabilistic Concurrent Kleene Algebra

In this section, we show that the set **pBES** endowed with a nondeterministic choice ($+$), a probabilistic choice ($\oplus_\alpha$), a sequential composition ($\cdot$), a concurrent composition ($\|$) and the binary Kleene star ($*$) satisfy the axioms of Fig. 7. These axioms are a combination of the basic algebraic laws of CKA [2] and pKA [21].

We generate the pBES $(0, \emptyset), (1, \{\delta_e\})$ and $(a, \{\delta_{e_a}\})$ from the basic BES. To simplify the notations, these basic pBES are again denoted by $0, 1$ and a. The other operators are defined as follows:

$$(\mathcal{E}, \pi) + (\mathcal{F}, \rho) = (\mathcal{E} + \mathcal{F}, \pi \cup \rho)$$
$$(\mathcal{E}, \pi) \cdot (\mathcal{F}, \rho) = (\mathcal{E} \cdot \mathcal{F}, \pi \cup \rho)$$
$$(\mathcal{E}, \pi)\|(\mathcal{F}, \rho) = (\mathcal{E}\|\mathcal{F}, \pi \cup \rho \cup \{\delta_e, \delta_f\})$$

where e and f are the fresh events delimiting $\mathcal{E}\|\mathcal{F}$. Recall that $\mathcal{E}$ and $\mathcal{F}$ are assumed to be disjoint in these definitions. The probabilistic choice that chooses $\mathcal{E}$ with probability $1 - \alpha$ and $\mathcal{F}$ with probability α is

$$(\mathcal{E}, \pi) \oplus_\alpha (\mathcal{F}, \rho) = (\mathcal{E} + \mathcal{F}, \pi \oplus_\alpha \rho)$$

where $r \in \pi \oplus_\alpha \rho$ iff:

- if $\text{supp}(r) \subseteq \mathbf{in}(\mathcal{E}) \cup \mathbf{in}(\mathcal{F})$ then $r = (1-\alpha)p + \alpha q$ for some $p \in \pi$ and $q \in \rho$,
- else $r \in \pi \cup \rho$.

Intuitively, nondeterminism is resolved first by choosing a probability distribution, then a probabilistic choice is resolved based on that distribution. Indeed, the nondeterministic and probabilisic choices introduce clusters.

$$\mathcal{E} + \mathcal{E} \equiv \mathcal{E} \qquad (1)$$
$$\mathcal{E} + \mathcal{F} \equiv \mathcal{F} + \mathcal{E} \qquad (2)$$
$$\mathcal{E} + (\mathcal{F} + \mathcal{G}) \equiv (\mathcal{E} + \mathcal{F}) + \mathcal{G} \qquad (3)$$
$$\mathcal{E} + 0 \equiv \mathcal{E} \qquad (4)$$

$$\mathcal{E} \equiv \mathcal{E} \oplus_\alpha \mathcal{E} \qquad (5)$$
$$\mathcal{E} \oplus_\alpha \mathcal{F} \equiv \mathcal{F} \oplus_{1-\alpha} \mathcal{E} \qquad (6)$$
$$\mathcal{E} \oplus_\alpha (\mathcal{F} \oplus_\beta \mathcal{G}) \equiv (\mathcal{E} \oplus_{\frac{\alpha(1-\beta)}{1-\alpha\beta}} \mathcal{F}) \oplus_{\alpha\beta} \mathcal{G} \qquad (7)$$
$$(\mathcal{E} \oplus_\alpha \mathcal{F}) \cdot \mathcal{G} \equiv \mathcal{E} \cdot \mathcal{G} \oplus_\alpha \mathcal{F} \cdot \mathcal{G} \qquad (8)$$

$$\mathcal{E} \cdot (\mathcal{F} \cdot \mathcal{G}) \equiv (\mathcal{E} \cdot \mathcal{F}) \cdot \mathcal{G} \qquad (9)$$
$$\mathcal{E} \cdot 1 \equiv \mathcal{E} \qquad (10)$$
$$1 \cdot \mathcal{E} \equiv \mathcal{E} \qquad (11)$$
$$0 \cdot \mathcal{E} \equiv 0 \qquad (12)$$

$$1 \| \mathcal{E} \equiv \mathcal{E} \qquad (13)$$
$$\mathcal{E} \| \mathcal{F} \equiv \mathcal{F} \| \mathcal{E} \qquad (14)$$
$$\mathcal{E} \| (\mathcal{F} \| \mathcal{G}) \equiv (\mathcal{E} \| \mathcal{F}) \| \mathcal{G} \qquad (15)$$

$$(\mathcal{E} + \mathcal{F}) \cdot \mathcal{G} \equiv \mathcal{E} \cdot \mathcal{G} + \mathcal{F} \cdot \mathcal{G} \qquad (16)$$
$$\mathcal{E} \cdot \mathcal{F} + \mathcal{E} \cdot \mathcal{G} \sqsubseteq \mathcal{E} \cdot (\mathcal{F} + \mathcal{G}) \qquad (17)$$
$$\mathcal{E} \cdot (\mathcal{F} \oplus_\alpha \mathcal{G}) \sqsubseteq \mathcal{E} \cdot \mathcal{F} \oplus_\alpha \mathcal{E} \cdot \mathcal{G} \qquad (18)$$

$$\mathcal{E} \| \mathcal{F} + \mathcal{E} \| \mathcal{G} \sqsubseteq \mathcal{E} \| (\mathcal{F} + \mathcal{G}) \qquad (19)$$
$$\mathcal{E} \| (\mathcal{F} \oplus_\alpha \mathcal{G}) \sqsubseteq \mathcal{E} \| \mathcal{F} \oplus_\alpha \mathcal{E} \| \mathcal{G} \qquad (20)$$
$$(\mathcal{E} \| \mathcal{F}) \cdot (\mathcal{E}' \| \mathcal{F}') \sqsubseteq (\mathcal{E} \cdot \mathcal{E}') \| (\mathcal{F} \cdot \mathcal{F}') \qquad (21)$$

$$\mathcal{F} + \mathcal{E} \cdot (\mathcal{E} * \mathcal{F}) \equiv (\mathcal{E} * \mathcal{F}) \qquad (22)$$
$$\mathcal{G} + \mathcal{E} \cdot \mathcal{F} \sqsubseteq \mathcal{F} \Rightarrow \mathcal{E} * \mathcal{G} \sqsubseteq \mathcal{F} \qquad (23)$$

Fig. 7. Axioms of pCKA satisfied by **pBES** modulo probabilistic simulation. Here, we write a pBES simply with $\mathcal{E}$ instead of the tuple $(\mathcal{E}, \pi)$ and $\alpha\beta < 1$ in Equation (7) (the case $\alpha\beta = 1$ being a simplification of the left hand side).

Example 5. The BES $a \| (b \oplus_{0.2} c)$ contains four clusters $\langle e \rangle, \langle e_b, e_c \rangle, \langle e_a \rangle$ and $\langle f \rangle$ where e, f are the delimiter events. It has a set of probability distributions $\{0.8\delta_{e_b} + 0.2\delta_{e_c}, \delta_{e_a}, \delta_e, \delta_f\}$. In contrast, the event structure $a + (b \oplus_{0.2} c)$ has a single cluster $\langle e_a, e_b, e_c \rangle$ with set of probability distributions $\{0.8\delta_{e_b} + 0.2\delta_{e_c}, \delta_{e_a}\}$.

To construct the binary Kleene star, we need the following partial order

$$(\mathcal{E}, \pi) \trianglelefteq (\mathcal{F}, \rho) \quad \text{iff} \quad \mathcal{E} \trianglelefteq \mathcal{F} \wedge \pi = \{p \in \rho \mid \mathrm{supp}(p) \subseteq E\}.$$

The proof that $\trianglelefteq$ is indeed ω-complete is essentially the same as in the standard case (Section 3). Hence the Kleene product $(\mathcal{E}, \pi) * (\mathcal{F}, \rho)$ is again the limit of the increasing sequence of pBES:

$$(\mathcal{F}, \rho) \trianglelefteq (\mathcal{F}, \rho) + (\mathcal{E}, \pi) \cdot (\mathcal{F}, \rho) \trianglelefteq (\mathcal{F}, \rho) + (\mathcal{E}, \pi) \cdot ((\mathcal{F}, \rho) + (\mathcal{E}, \pi)) \trianglelefteq \cdots.$$

More precisely, $(\mathcal{E}, \pi) * (\mathcal{F}, \rho) = (\mathcal{E} * \mathcal{F}, \pi * \rho)$ where $\pi * \rho = \cup_i \pi *_{\leq i} \rho$ and each set $\pi *_{\leq i} \rho$ is obtained from the construction of $\mathcal{E} *_{\leq i} \mathcal{F}$.

A BES is *regular* if it is inductively defined with the operators of Section 3.

Proposition 10. *A Regular BES is confusion free.*

Proof (Sketch). By induction on the structure of the BES.

Proposition 11. *The order $\sqsubseteq$ is a precongruence i.e. for every pBES $(\mathcal{E}, \pi)$, $(\mathcal{F}, \rho)$ and $(\mathcal{G}, \eta)$, if $(\mathcal{E}, \pi) \sqsubseteq (\mathcal{F}, \rho)$ then $(\mathcal{E}, \pi) \bullet (\mathcal{G}, \eta) \sqsubseteq (\mathcal{F}, \rho) \bullet (\mathcal{G}, \eta)$ (and symmetrically) for every $\bullet \in \{+, \cdot, \|, *\}$.*

Proof (Sketch). Let $(\mathcal{E}, \pi) \sqsubseteq (\mathcal{F}, \rho)$ be witnessed by a simulation $S \subseteq \mathcal{C}(\mathcal{E}) \times \mathbb{D}(\mathcal{C}(\mathcal{F}))$ and $(\mathcal{G}, \eta)$ be any pBES. The congruence properties are proven by extending the simulation S to the events of $\mathcal{G}$. For instance, That $(\mathcal{E}, \pi) + (\mathcal{G}, \eta) \sqsubseteq (\mathcal{F}, \rho) + (\mathcal{G}, \eta)$ is deduced by showing that $S \cup \{(x, \delta_x) \mid x \in \mathcal{C}(\mathcal{G})\}$ is indeed a simulation. □

The axioms (1-12) and (14-16) are proven using simulations akin to the interleaving case [4,20]. The existence of simulations that establishes axiom (13) is clear from the definition of $\|$ and 1. It follows from the axioms of $+$ and Proposition 11 that $(\mathcal{E}, \pi) \sqsubseteq (\mathcal{F}, \rho)$ if and only if $(\mathcal{E}, \pi) + (\mathcal{F}, \rho) \equiv (\mathcal{F}, \rho)$.

Proposition 12. *The axioms (17,18) and (19,20) and the interchange law (21) hold on* **pBES** *modulo probabilistic simulation.*

Proof (Sketch). These equations are proven by the usual simulation constructions. □

Proposition 13. *The binary Kleene star satisfies the axioms (22) and (23).*

Proof (Sketch). The first equation is proven using the standard simulation construction. For the second one, let $S \subseteq \mathcal{C}(\mathcal{E} \cdot \mathcal{F}) \times \mathbb{D}(\mathcal{C}(\mathcal{F}))$ be a probabilistic simulation from $(\mathcal{E}, \pi) \cdot (\mathcal{F}, \rho)$ to $(\mathcal{F}, \pi)$. By monotonicity of $\cdot$ and $+$, there exists a simulation $S^{(i)} \subseteq \mathcal{C}(\mathcal{E} *_{\leq i} \mathcal{F}) \times \mathbb{D}(\mathcal{C}(\mathcal{F}))$ from $(\mathcal{E}, \pi) *_{\leq i} (\mathcal{F}, \rho)$ to $(\mathcal{F}, \rho)$, for every $i \in \mathbb{N}$. Moreover, we can find a family of simulations such that $S^{(i-1)}$ is the restriction of $S^{(i)}$ to $(\mathcal{E}, \pi) *_{\leq i-1} (\mathcal{F}, \rho)$. Thus, we can consider the reunion $S = \cup_i S^{(i)}$ and show that it is indeed a simulation from $(\mathcal{E}, \pi) * (\mathcal{F}, \rho)$ to $(\mathcal{F}, \rho)$. Hence, Equation (23) holds. □

Theorem 1. *The set* **pBES** *modulo probabilistic simulation forms a probabilistic concurrent Kleene algebra with a binary Kleene star.*

7 Conclusion

We have constructed a truly concurrent model for probabilistic concurrent Kleene algebra using pBES. In the process, we also set out a notion of probabilistic simulation for these event structures. The semantics of pBES was defined by constructing the configuration-trees using prefixing and probabilistic simulations are exhibited when possible. Since the simulation distinguishes between concurrency and interleaving, we believe that it provides a suitable combination of nondeterminism, probability and true-concurrency.

Our main result is the soundness of pCKA axioms. The completeness of such an axiom system is still open. We believe that other axioms such as guarded tail recursion are needed to achieve a complete characterisation as in [22]. Another interesting specialisation of this work is the labelling of events with one-step probabilistic programs. These however require further studies.

References

1. Rabin, M.O.: Probabilistic Algorithms. Technical Report RC 6164 (#26545), IBM Research Division, San Jose, Yorktown, Zurich (August 1976)
2. Hoare, T., Möller, B., Struth, G., Wehrman, I.: Concurrent Kleene algebra and its foundations. J. Log. Algebr. Program. 80(6), 266–296 (2011)
3. Hayes, I.J., Jones, C.B., Colvin, R.J.: Refining rely-guarantee thinking. Technical report, Newcastle University, United Kingdom (2012)
4. McIver, A.K., Rabehaja, T.M., Struth, G.: Probabilistic concurrent kleene algebra. In: Bortolussi, L., Wiklicky, H. (eds.) QAPL. EPTCS, vol. 117, pp. 97–115 (2013)
5. Katoen, J.P.: Quantitative and qualitative extensions of event structures. PhD thesis, University of Twente (1996)
6. Langerak, R.: Bundle event structures: a non-interleaving semantics for LOTOS. Memoranda informatica. University of Twente (1992)
7. Rensink, A., Gorrieri, R.: Action refinement for vertical implementation. In: Wolisz, A., Schieferdecker, I., Rennoch, A. (eds.) FBT. GMD-Studien., vol. 315, pp. 69–78. GMD-Forschungszentrum Informationstechnik GmbH (1997)
8. Winskel, G.: Event structures. In: Brauer, W., Reisig, W., Rozenberg, G. (eds.) APN 1985. LNCS, vol. 222, pp. 325–392. Springer, Heidelberg (1986)
9. van Glabbeek, R.J., Vaandrager, F.W.: Bundle event structures and CCSP. In: Amadio, R.M., Lugiez, D. (eds.) CONCUR 2003. LNCS, vol. 2761, pp. 57–71. Springer, Heidelberg (2003)
10. van Glabbeek, R.J., Plotkin, G.D.: Configuration structures, event structures and petri nets. Theor. Comput. Sci. 410(41), 4111–4159 (2009)
11. Varacca, D.: Probability, nondeterminism and concurrency: two denotational models for probabilistic computation. PhD thesis, University of Aarhus (2003)
12. Segala, R.: A compositional trace-based semantics for probabilistic automata. In: Lee, I., Smolka, S.A. (eds.) CONCUR 1995. LNCS, vol. 962, pp. 234–248. Springer, Heidelberg (1995)
13. Cherief, F.: Back and forth bisimulations on prime event structures. In: Etiemble, D., Syre, J.-C. (eds.) PARLE 1992. LNCS, vol. 605, pp. 843–858. Springer, Heidelberg (1992)
14. Majster-Cederbaum, M., Roggenbach, M.: Transition systems from event structures revisited. Info. Proc. Letters 67(3), 119–124 (1998)
15. McIver, A.K., Rabehaja, T.M., Struth, G.: An event structure model for probabilistic concurrent kleene algebra. CoRR abs/1310.2320 (2013)
16. Gischer, J.L.: The equational theory of pomsets. Theor. Comput. Sci. 61(23), 199–224 (1988)
17. Jones, C.B.: Development Methods for Computer Programs including a Notion of Interference. PhD thesis, Oxford University (June 1981)
18. Dingel, J.: A refinement calculus for shared-variable parallel and distributed programming. Formal Asp. Comput. 14(2), 123–197 (2002)
19. Fokkink, W., Zantema, H.: Basic process algebra with iteration: Completeness of its equational axioms. Comput. J. 37(4), 259–268 (1994)
20. Deng, Y., van Glabbeek, R.J., Hennessy, M., Morgan, C., Zhang, C.: Remarks on testing probabilistic processes. ENTCS 172, 359–397 (2007)
21. McIver, A.K., Weber, T.: Towards automated proof support for probabilistic distributed systems. In: Sutcliffe, G., Voronkov, A. (eds.) LPAR 2005. LNCS (LNAI), vol. 3835, pp. 534–548. Springer, Heidelberg (2005)
22. Parma, A., Segala, R.: Axiomatization of trace semantics for stochastic nondeterministic processes. In: Franceschinis, G., Haverkort, B.R., Katoen, J.P., Woodside, M. (eds.) QEST, pp. 294–303. IEEE Computer Society (2004)

Three SCC-Based Emptiness Checks for Generalized Büchi Automata

Etienne Renault[1,2], Alexandre Duret-Lutz[1],
Fabrice Kordon[2], and Denis Poitrenaud[2,3]

[1] LRDE, EPITA, Kremlin-Bicêtre, France
[2] LIP6/MoVe, Université Pierre & Marie Curie, Paris, France
[3] Université Paris Descartes, Paris, France

Abstract. The automata-theoretic approach for the verification of linear time properties involves checking the emptiness of a Büchi automaton. However generalized Büchi automata, with multiple acceptance sets, are preferred when verifying under weak fairness hypotheses. Existing emptiness checks for which the complexity is independent of the number of acceptance sets are all based on the enumeration of Strongly Connected Components (SCCs).

In this paper, we review the state of the art SCC enumeration algorithms to study how they can be turned into emptiness checks. This leads us to define two new emptiness check algorithms (one of them based on the Union-Find data structure), introduce new optimizations, and show that one of these can be of benefit to a classic SCCs enumeration algorithm. We have implemented all these variants to compare their relative performances and the overhead induced by the emptiness check compared to the corresponding SCCs enumeration algorithm. Our experiments shows that these three algorithms are comparable.

1 Introduction

The automata-theoretic approach to explicit LTL model checking explores the product between two ω-automata: one automaton that represents the system, and the other that represents (the negation of) the property to check on this system. This product corresponds to the intersection between the executions of the system and the behaviors disallowed by the property. The property is verified by the system if this product is empty.

Usually, a Büchi automaton is used to represent the property, and a Kripke structure represents the model. However, it is possible to use generalized Büchi automata (with several acceptance sets) to represent the property in a more concise way, and such generalized acceptance condition can also be used on the model to express weak fairness hypotheses on the system. In this work, we further generalize the above approach using Transition-based Generalized Büchi Automata (TGBA).

An emptiness check is an algorithm deciding whether such an automaton is empty. A Büchi automaton is non-empty if it accepts an infinite word, i.e., if it contains a lasso-shaped run: a finite prefix followed by an accepting cycle. Most explicit emptiness checks are based on a DFS exploration of the automaton; they can be classified in two families. *Nested Depth First Search* algorithms [3] use a second DFS to detect the accepting cycle: if the automaton has multiple acceptance sets, this approach requires either a degeneralization, or multiple nested DFS. The second family are algorithms based on the enumeration of *Strongly Connected Components* (SCC), to find SCCs that contain accepting cycles. In these algorithms the number of times a state or transitions is visited is independent on the number of acceptance sets.

In this paper, we review the existing SCC enumeration algorithms to study how they can be adapted to become emptiness checks. To be of practical use in a model checker, we would like such emptiness checks to:
- support generalized Büchi acceptance [5, 12] (without requiring a degeneralization, or multiple passes on the automaton),
- support an on-the-fly construction of the automaton so that we do not need to construct unexplored parts of the product,
- be compatible with the bit-state hashing [15] and state-space caching [13] techniques to deal cases where memory is a critical resource.

We focus on three SCC algorithms which we shall refer to as Tarjan [19], Dijkstra [6], Gabow [8]. Tarjan is the most well-known algorithm to compute SCC and it has been extended by Geldenhuys and Valmari [11] to check the emptiness of (non-generalized) Büchi automata. Dijkstra's SCC-enumeration algorithm is a little less known, but has served as the base for several generalized emptiness checks [12, 5, 1, 10]. Essentially, both these algorithms partition the set of states according to the SCCs, and have a complexity that is linear with respect to the size of the graph. An efficient data structure to deal with the construction of a partition is the *Union-Find* [20] and Gabow [8] has suggested an algorithm to label the SCCs of a graph using such a data structure; in this context the number of Union-Find operations is linear in the size of the graph, and the amortized time-complexity of these operations is quasi-constant (related to the inverse of the Ackermann function) in the worst case. To our knowledge, this suggested algorithm, which we call Gabow[1], has never been experimented to compute SCCs, let alone to perform an emptiness check.

Our contributions are as follows. (1) We show how to adapt Tarjan's algorithm to perform a generalized emptiness check. (2) We suggest an optimization of Dijkstra's algorithm that also benefits all the emptiness checks based on this algorithm. (3) We extend Gabow's idea to implement a Union-Find-based emptiness check. (4) Moreover we show how to adjust all these algorithms to support bit-state hashing and state-space caching.

While our experiments shows that there is no algorithm that clearly outperforms the others, we believe that having the choice between these three differents schemes might prove useful to devise new extensions (such as parallel model checking).

---

[1] Beware! The main algorithm of Gabow's paper [8] is a reinvention of Dijkstra's algorithm. Cf. http://www.cs.colorado.edu/~hal/Papers/DFS/pbDFShistory.html. What we call Gabow's algorithm here is the idea evoked on page 109 of that paper.

This paper is organized as follows. Section 2 defines TGBAs and introduces our notations. Sections 3–5 successively present Tarjan's, Dijkstra's, and Gabow's algorithms and discuss how that can be extended to perform emptiness checks. Section 6 discusses the compatibility of these algorithms with the bit-state hashing and state-space caching techniques. Finally Section 7 provides experimental data to compare all these algorithms.

2 Preliminaries

Let $G = \langle Q, q^0, \delta \rangle$ be a directed graph with Q the set of states, q^0 the initial state, and $\delta \subseteq Q \times Q$ the set of transitions.

A *path* of length $n \geq 1$ between two states $q, q' \in Q$ is a finite sequence of edges $\rho = (s_1, s_2)(s_2, s_3) \ldots (s_n, s_{n+1})$ with $s_1 = q$ and $s_{n+1} = q'$. We denote the existence of such a path by $q \rightsquigarrow q'$. When $q = q'$ the path is a *cycle*.

A non-empty set $S \subseteq Q$ is a Strongly Connected Component (SCC) iff $\forall s, s' \in S$, $s \neq s' \Rightarrow s \rightsquigarrow s'$ and S is maximal w.r.t. inclusion. A *trivial SCC* is a state without self-loop.

A *TGBA* is a tuple $A = \langle Q, q^0, \delta, \mathcal{F}, f \rangle$ where $\mathcal{F}$ is a finite set of acceptance marks and $f : \delta \mapsto 2^\mathcal{F}$ labels each transition of the directed graph $\langle Q, q^0, \delta \rangle$ by a set of acceptance marks. Let us note that in a real model checker, transitions (or states) of the automata would be labeled by atomic propositions, but we omit this information as it is not pertinent to emptiness check algorithms.

A *degeneralization* process can transform any TGBA with n states and m acceptances marks into an equivalent TGBA with one acceptance mark and at most nm states.

An SCC $S \subseteq Q$ is *accepting* iff $\bigcup_{t \in (S \times S) \cap \delta} \{f(t)\} = \mathcal{F}$. A TGBA is non-empty iff there is a path from q^0 to an accepting SCC.

All the algorithms we consider are based on a DFS of a TGBA and we can present them by specializing the generic DFS algorithm of Algo. 1. This algorithm is slightly more complex than the average DFS, as we will use it in various settings. The *dfs* variable is the stack of the DFS algorithm and stores: a set *acc* of acceptance marks labeling the transition leading to the state *pos*, and set *succ* of the unexplored successors of this state. The state *pos* is actually represented by a *Position*, which shall be defined differently in each algorithm.

Each state is either LIVE, DEAD, or UNKNOWN. A state is UNKNOWN until it has been explored by the DFS, then it becomes LIVE. A state may only become DEAD after all the successors of the SCC it belongs to have been visited. Maintaining this status will be done by each algorithm by implementing the following methods:

- GET_STATUS: returns the status of a state;
- PUSH: called for any newly visited state, it should mark that state as LIVE;
- UPDATE: called every time a *back-edge* (i.e., a transition leading to a LIVE state) is found, this function detects a transition closing a cycle;
- POP: called every time the DFS backtracks a state. When the last state of an SCC is being popped, all the states in its SCC must be marked as DEAD

Algorithm 1. Generic DFS

1 **Input**: A TGBA $A = \langle Q, q^0, \delta, \mathcal{F}, f \rangle$

2 **struct** *Step* {*acc*: $2^{\mathcal{F}}$, *pos*: *Position*, *succ*: 2^{δ}}
3 **struct** *Transition* {*src*: Q, *dst*: Q}
4 *dfs*: **stack** of $\langle Step \rangle$

5 *Position pos* ← PUSH(q^0)
6 *dfs*.push($\langle \emptyset,\ pos,\ \texttt{successors}(q^0) \rangle$)
7 **while** ¬ *dfs*.isEmpty()
8   *Step step* ← *dfs*.top()
9   **if** *step.succ* ≠ ∅
10   *Transition t* ← pick one from *step.succ*
11   **switch** GET_STATUS(*t.dst*) **do**
12   **case** DEAD
13   skip
14   **case** LIVE
15   UPDATE($f(t)$, *t.dst*)
16   **case** UNKNOWN
17   *pos* ← PUSH(*t.dst*)
18   *dfs*.push($\langle f(t),\ pos,\ \texttt{successors}(t.dst) \rangle$)

19   **else**
20   *dfs*.pop()
21   POP(*step*)

by POP. We call such a last state the *root* of the SCC (notice that this root may depend on the order in which the transitions are visited).

3 Tarjan-Based Algorithm

3.1 SCC Computation

In Tarjan's original algorithm [19], each state is associated to two numbers: a DFS number (indicating the order in which the states has been visited by the DFS), and a *lowlink*. Initially, this *lowlink* is equal to the DFS number, but each time a transition is backtracked (i.e., during UPDATE or POP) the *lowlink* of the source is updated to the DFS number (for UPDATE) or to the *lowlink* (for POP) of the destination if it is smaller. An SCC root is detected during POP as a state whose *lowlink* is equal to the DFS number.

A usual optimization of POP is based on the fact that when a root is popped, the (outside) states that are successors of this SCC have already been marked as DEAD. Consequently, if the set of LIVE states is stored as a stack, then all the states of the current SCC are on this stack between the position of the *root*

Algorithm 2. Tarjan's Algorithm.

```
 1  struct P {lowlink: int; acc: 2^F}           20  PUSH(q ∈ Q) → Position
 2  live: hstack of ⟨Q⟩                         21  │  Position p ← live.size()
 3  dead: store of ⟨Q⟩                          22  │  live.push(⟨q⟩)
 4  dstack: stack of ⟨P⟩                        23  │  dstack.push(⟨p, ∅⟩)
                                                24  └  return p
 5  GET_STATUS(q ∈ Q) → Status
 6  │  if live.get(q) ≠ -1                      25  POP(s ∈ Step)
 7  │  └  return LIVE                           26  │  ⟨ll, acc⟩ ← dstack.pop()
 8  │  else if dead.has(q)                      27  │  if ll = s.pos
 9  │  └  return DEAD                           28  │  │  // An SCC has been found.
10  │  else                                     29  │  │  while live.size() > s.pos
11  └  └  return UNKNOWN                        30  │  │  │  ⟨q⟩ ← live.pop()
                                                31  │  │  └  dead.add(q)
12  UPDATE(acc ∈ 2^F, d ∈ Q)
13  │  dstack.top().lowlink ←                   32  │  else
14  │     min(dstack.top().lowlink,             33  │  │  dstack.top().lowlink ←
15  │     live.get(d))                          34  │  │     min(dstack.top().lowlink, ll)
16  │  dstack.top().acc ← acc ∪                 35  │  │  dstack.top().acc ← s.acc ∪
17  │        dstack.top().acc                   36  │  │     dstack.top().acc ∪ acc
18  │  if dstack.top().acc = F                  37  │  │  if dstack.top().acc = F
19  └  └  report counterexample found           38  └  └  └  report counterexample found
```

and the top of the stack. They can therefore be marked as DEAD by unwinding this stack, without exploring the graph.

Because a *lowlink* is only useful for states on *dfs*, it seems judicious to store it into a dedicated stack denoted *dstack*. This stack stores elements of the form ⟨*lowlink*, *acc*⟩ where *acc* is only useful when doing an emptiness check.

As the states on *dfs* are LIVE, they are simply identified by their position on *live*. We use this position instead of the DFS number when initializing *lowlink*.

To implement this *live* stack, we introduce a data structure **hstack** that stores all LIVE states and can be manipulated like a stack (with **push** and **pop**). To find the status of a state, we need to check whether it belongs to this **hstack**, therefore this structure is equipped with a **get** method that looks up a hash table to return the position associated to a given state, or −1 for missing states.

The set of DEAD states are represented by a separate data structure that support the following two operations: **add** and **has** with obvious semantics. As we shall discuss in Section 6, bit-state hashing and state-space caching can be implemented by redefining these operations.

Algorithm 2 presents our refactoring of the original Tarjan's algorithm to fit in the framework of Algorithm 1. The blue dashed boxes should be ignored on first read: they represent the parts to add to turn this SCC-enumeration algorithm into an emptiness check for TGBA.

Because LIVE and DEAD states are respectively stored in *live* and *dead*, GET_STATUS can easily report all other states as UNKNOWN.

As explained previously, the lowlinks are updated everytime a transition is backtracked, i.e., at lines 12–15 when backtracking a back-edge, and at 32–34 when backtracking a forward-edge inside an SCC. When POP detects the root of an SCC (line 27), it simply unwind *live* to mark all the SCC's states as DEAD.

3.2 Emptiness Check

Adding the blue dashed boxes will turn the SCC enumeration algorithm into an emptiness check algorithm. Each LIVE state on *dfs* is now associated to an empty set of acceptance mark at line 1. This set is updated each time an edge intern to an SCC is backtracked, at lines 16–17 and 35–36. These backtracking updates will ultimately propagate to the root, the set of all acceptance marks present in the SCC. Therefore, in the worse case, an accepting SCC will be detected when the root is popped, but it may happens earlier if one of the intermediate set is equal to $\mathcal{F}$ (hence the tests on lines 18 and 38).

To our knowledge, the only existing emptiness check based on Tarjan's algorithm has been proposed by Geldenhuys and Valmari [11]. Their algorithm targets only degeneralized Büchi automata (one acceptance mark), so they may have to explore a larger automaton that we do. However their algorithm works quite differently from this one: they maintain the *lowlink* for each LIVE state and a stack of LIVE accepting states (it would work for transition-based acceptance too) and they are therefore able to report a counterexample as soon as they close an accepting cycle, while our algorithm would have to wait for an accepting transition to be popped. This detection could be done earlier by associating an acceptance set to each element of *live*. As we target memory efficiency this solution has not been retained.

4 Dijkstra-Based Algorithms

4.1 SCC Computation

Intuitively, Dijkstra's algorithm [6] maintains a stack of SCCs of the subgraph that has been explored. Everytime a back-edge is found, closing a cycle, the SCCs forming that cycle are merged.

In practice, Algorithm 3 (without the green dotted boxes) actually manages three stacks: *live*, the set of LIVE states; *dfs*, the subset of *live* that are on the DFS search path, represented—as in the previous section—by a stack of positions in *live*; and *roots*, the stack of SCC roots, stored as positions in the *dfs* stack. When given two consecutive roots, $roots[i]$ and $roots[i+1]$, the set of states belonging to the SCC rooted in $roots[i]$, are the states at positions $dfs[roots[i]].pos, \ldots, dfs[roots[i+1]].pos - 1$ in *live*. This representation makes several operations efficient. Merging consecutive SCCs can be done by simply removing elements from *roots* (lines 18 and 21). Also, it possible to decide whether

Algorithm 3. Dijkstra's Algorithm.	**Algorithm 4.** Gabow's Algorithm.

```
 1  live: hstack of ⟨Q⟩                          1  uf: union find of
 2  dead: store of ⟨Q⟩                              ⟨Q ∪ {DeadState}⟩
 3  roots: rstack of ⟨root: int, acc: 2^F⟩       2  roots: rstack of ⟨root: int, acc: 2^F⟩
                                                  3  uf.make_set(DeadState)
 4  GET_STATUS(q ∈ Q) → Status
 5   if live.get(q) ≠ -1                         4  GET_STATUS(q ∈ Q) → Status
 6    ⌊ return LIVE                              5   if uf.ufcontains(q)
 7   else if dead.has(q)                         6    if uf.same_set(q, DeadState)
 8    ⌊ return DEAD                              7     ⌊ return DEAD
 9   else                                        8    else
10    ⌊ return UNKNOWN                           9     ⌊ return LIVE
                                                 10   else
                                                 11    ⌊ return UNKNOWN
11  PUSH(q ∈ Q) → Position
12   Position p ← live.size()                   12  PUSH(q ∈ Q) → Position
13   live.push(q)                                13   uf.make_set(q)
14   roots.push_trivial(dfs.size())              14   roots.push_trivial(dfs.size())
15   ⌊ return p                                  15   ⌊ return q

16  UPDATE(acc ∈ 2^F, d ∈ Q)                     16  UPDATE(acc ∈ 2^F, d ∈ Q)
17   dpos ← live.get(d)                          17   ⟨r, a ⟩ ← roots.pop()
18   ⟨r, a ⟩ ← roots.pop()                       18   a ← a ∪ acc
19   a ← a ∪ acc                                 19   while ¬uf.same_set(dfs[r].pos, d)
20   while dpos < dfs[r].pos                     20    uf.unite(dfs[r].pos, d)
21    ⟨r, la ⟩ ← roots.pop()                     21    ⟨r, la ⟩ ← roots.pop()
22    a ← a ∪ dfs[r].acc ∪ la                    22    a ← a ∪ dfs[r].acc ∪ la
23   roots.push_non_trivial( a , r,              23   roots.push_non_trivial( a , r,
24                           dfs.size() - 1)     24                            dfs.size() - 1)
25   if a = F                                    25   if a = F
26    ⌊ report counterexample found              26    ⌊ report counterexample found

27  POP(s ∈ Step)                                27  POP(s ∈ Step)
28   if dfs.size() = roots.top_root()            28   if dfs.size() = roots.top_root()
29    // An SCC has been found.                  29    // An SCC has been found.
30    roots.pop()                                30    roots.pop()
31    while live.size() > s.pos                  31    ⌊ uf.unite(s.pos, DeadState)
32     q ← live.pop()
33     ⌊ dead.add(q)
```

a state is a root of an SCC during POP: when the position pointed to by the top of the *roots* stack is equal to the size of *dfs* (line 28) it means the state that has already been popped by the main DFS algorithm was a root.

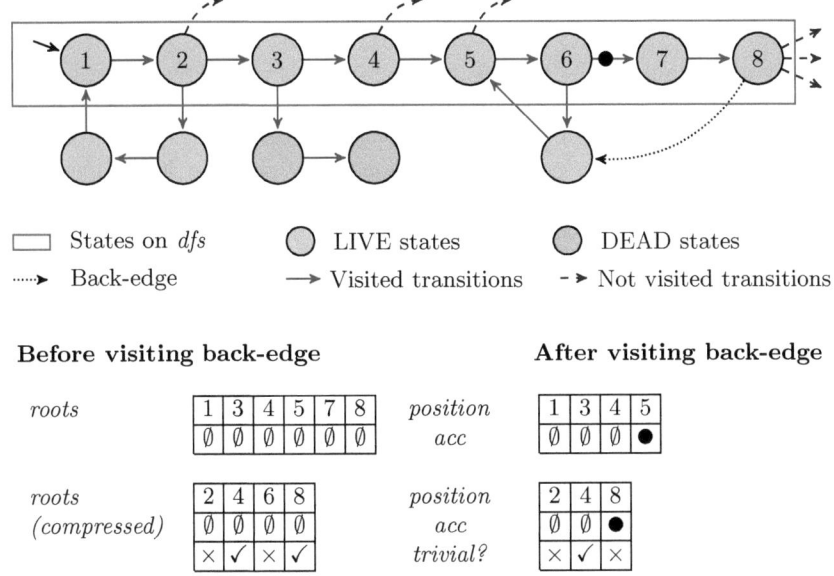

Fig. 1. Stack compression in action where numbers corresponds to DFS positions

The *roots* stack is implemented with a structure called **rstack** that supports three operations: pop(), push_trivial(*begin*) and push_non_trivial(*begin,end*). The latter two distinguish whether the SCC being pushed is trivial or not. They can be implemented as a normal push(*begin*), but in Section 4.2 we will see how to use these to compress the stack. Initially, any newly visited state constitutes a trivial SCC (line 14) with respect to the explored part of the automaton; non-trivial SCCs are only created when merging SCCs because of a back-edge (line 24).

DEAD states are stored in a *dead* store as in the previous algorithm, and for the same reason.

4.2 Compressing the *roots* Stack

The *roots* stack represents two kinds of SCCs: trivial and non-trivial. We suggest to compress this stack by representing ranges of consecutive trivial SCCs in a single entry. Each stack entry should have an additional Boolean indicating whether it represents of range of trivial SCCs or a non-trivial SCC, and should store the position of the last state seen before moving to the next entry. Figure 1 shows the effect of this compression.

In the worst case, it appears that we are simply adding one extra bit per entry, but as we shall see in our experiments, merging consecutive trivial SCCs is really effective.

4.3 Emptiness Checks

Dijkstra's algorithm can be turned into a emptiness check by adding the green dotted boxes. Each SCC is associated to a set of acceptance marks that have been seen inside this SCC. When some SCCs are merged, their acceptance marks are merged along with the marks of the transitions between these SCCs (line 25–26). A counterexample can be reported as soon as this union is $\mathcal{F}$.

Several authors have devised emptiness-check algorithms using this principle [1, 5, 12, 14, 10]. In this scheme, the main DFS can also be adjusted to chose the next transition to visit among all the non-visited outgoing transitions of the topmost SCC [1, 5, 14].

The algorithm proposed by Couvreur [4] is sometimes considered as a Dijkstra-based algorithm [12]: it replaces the *live* stack by a simple hash map (save a tiny bit of memory) and consequently has to rediscover the states that need to be marked DEAD during POP (loosing time). Nevertheless it fit perfectly into the generic canvas of Algorithm 1 and can easily be mixed with bitstate hashing and state space caching by using a *dead* store.

5 Gabow-Based Algorithms

The POP operation of previous algorithms is costly because it has to visit all the states in top SCC to mark them as DEAD.

If we regard Dijkstra's algorithm as partitioning of the set of states, each (live) SCC corresponds to a class in this partition, and an additional class stores all DEAD states. Merging SCCs maps to unions of LIVE classes in this partition, while popping an SCCs should incur a union with the class of dead states.

This observation is the base of Gabow's suggestion [8] to use the Union-Find data structure [20] to discover the SCCs of a graph. In this data structure, a union operation can be achieved in near constant-time (or even constant-time for this particular application [9]), without enumerating all its states.

The Union-Find structure partitions the set $Q' = Q \cup \{DeadState\}$ where *DeadState* represent an extra artificial DEAD state, and offers the following methods: make_set$(s \in Q')$ creates a new class containing the state s; unite$(s_1 \in Q', s_2 \in Q')$ makes the union between two classes given by their representatives s_1 and s_2; and same_set$(s_1 \in Q', s_2 \in Q')$ checks whether two states are in the same class.

Algorithm 4 follows the same schema as Algorithm 3, except that we have replaced *live* and *dead*, by the Union-Find structure *uf*, and that *Position*s stored in *dfs* are now pointers to states. When the root of an SCC is popped (line 28), its class is merged with that of the artificial *DeadState* (line 31). GET_STATUS has to be updated to check deadness using this *DeadState* as well. UPDATE is done easily by uniting all classes representing the SCCs on the cycle.

The main difference with Dijkstra's algorithm is therefore that the use of unite in function POP dispenses from enumerating all states in the SCC. This approach remains compatible with the compression of the *roots* stack presented in Sec. 4.2, and can be turned into an emptiness check in the same way as Dijkstra (adding purple boxes).

As-is, this algorithm is neither compatible with bit-state hashing nor state-space caching, because there is no *dead* store. Compatibility with these techniques is possible, but tricky. We discuss it in the next Section.

6 Bit-State Hashing and State-Space Caching Compatibility

Bit-state hashing [15] and state-space caching [13] are two techniques to save memory. In bit-state hashing, collisions in the hash table storing dead states are ignored, turning the algorithm into a semi-decision procedure. In state-space caching, dead state can be removed from the store at any moment, causing the algorithm to possibly revisit a state several times.

On Tarjan-based and Dijkstra-based algorithms, these techniques can be implemented by replacing the `has` and `add` methods of the *dead* store, implemented as a hash table. Note that for bit-state hashing, it is important to check the membership to *live* before the membership to *dead* in GET_STATUS.

When compatibility with these techniques is not required, we can forgot the use of this extra hash table, and actually store LIVE and DEAD states in the same table, using a extra bit to distinguish LIVE from DEAD. This saves a table lookup in GET_STATUS.

For Gabow's algorithm, compatibility with bit-state hashing and state-space caching is more tricky to achieve and we only give the intuition. First, the Union-Find data structure, which stores states in a vector, has to be made aware of what a DEAD state is: let us assume that the `unite` of line 31 is changed to `make_dead`. The first time `make_dead` is called, the states to be marked as DEAD are all at the end of the vector. The trick is to remember the frontier between LIVE and DEAD states in that vector. Then, every time a new singleton class is created with the `make_set` operation, we can reuse the slot of the first DEAD state (right after the frontier), and move that DEAD state to the DEAD store. GET_STATUS has to be updated as well.

Note that in this approach, the set of DEAD states is distributed in two structures: the end of the Union-Find vector, and the DEAD store, but only this store can be subject to bit-state hashing or state-space caching. However this approach still avoids the enumeration of states to mark them DEAD.

7 Implementation Issues and Benchmarks

All these approaches have been implemented in Spot [7]. The Union-Find structure of Gabow's algorithm uses common optimizations: "Immediate Parent Compression", "Link by Rank", "Path Compression", and "Memory Smart" [17].

When *dead* does not use bit-state hashing nor state-space caching techniques, an optimization consists in marking states as DEAD inside the *live* structure

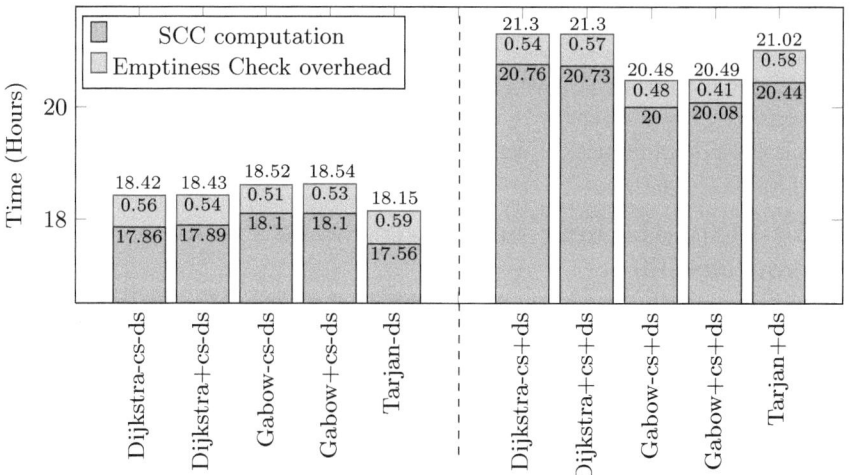

Fig. 2. Overhead of the emptiness checks over the SCC computations on 448 empty products. A total of 2.5×10^9 states, 17.3×10^9 transitions, and 10^9 SCCs were visited.

rather than transferring it into *dead* during a POP. This optimization only requires a special value to tag a state DEAD. Its use is denoted by -ds in tables, while the use of a dedicated *dead* store (as presented previously) is denoted by +ds. Similarly, +cs and -cs indicate whether the *roots* stack optimization (Sec. 4.2) is enabled or disabled.

The models we use come from the BEEM benchmark [18]. We generate the corresponding system automata using a version of DiVinE 2.4 patched by the LTSmin team.[2] Because there are too few LTL formulas supplied by the BEEM benchmark, we opted to generate random formulas for each model. We computed a total number of 860 formulas.[3]

A formula and a model generate a product that may be either empty (the formula is verified) or non-empty (a counterexample exists). To decide that a product is empty, any emptiness check has to explore all the reachable states of the product. Conversely, a non-empty product can be reported as soon as an accepting SCC is detected, avoiding the need to explore the entire product. In our implementation, all algorithms use the same generic DFS traversal and thus visit transitions in the same order.

Among our formulas, 412 result in non-empty product with the model. The remaining 448 formulas, associated to empty products, were selected so that the emptiness check algorithms would take at least 10 seconds on an Intel(R) 64-bit Xeon(R) @2.00GHz with 64GB of RAM.

---

[2] http://fmt.cs.utwente.nl/tools/ltsmin/#divine
[3] For a detailed description of our setup, including selected models and formulas, see http://move.lip6.fr/~Etienne.Renault/benchs/LPAR-2013/results_scc.html.

Figure 2 shows the execution time of all the emptiness check variants presented in this paper (with or without *dead* store, with or without compressed *roots* stack). To measure the overhead of the emptiness check over the SCC computation, we only focus on empty products.

For each bar the lower part represents the SCC computation time while the upper part corresponds to the overhead induced by the emptiness check. The total execution time is indicated atop the bar. The 5 rightmost bars show the emptiness check with a *dead* store enabled (+ds) while the 5 leftmost bars have it disabled (-ds).

For the same +ds/-ds setting, all execution times are very close, and the emptiness check overhead is 3% on the average.

When the *dead* store is disabled, Tarjan is slightly better than Dijkstra, which is itself slightly better than Gabow. Activating the *dead* store generate an overhead of about 15%, and is more favorable to Gabow. This latter point is due to the fact that our handling of the *dead* store for Gabow's algorithm, described in Section 6, will transfer less states from *live* to *dead*; this reduces the overhead to 10% only.

Table 1 reports the memory consumption, based on the size of the data structures used. As for time measurement, these experiments only focuses on verified formulas. The second column gives the formula that computes memory consumption at any time. The third column shows the peak we observed while running our experiments.

From that figure it appears that Dijkstra is the most memory efficient algorithm. Indeed the stack used by Dijkstra is a subset of the *dfs* stack while the *dstack* of Tarjan, storing a *lowlink* and an acceptance set for each element, follows the variations of *dfs*. Gabow's algorithm requires more memory than the two others since it has to maintain the whole structure of the Union-Find. The use of a *dead* store significantly reduces memory consumption (up to 17%).

When bit-state hashing or state-space caching are used, the size of |*dead*| can be fixed arbitrarily, allowing an even greater reduction.

Table 2 reports the the cumulated number of transitions, states and SCC visited by each algorithm for the 412-non empty products. We use this table to compare how quickly each algorithm reports a counterexample.

Gabow's and Dijkstra's algorithms have identical results since they both report a counterexample when a cycle is closed during UPDATE, while Tarjan's algorithm may delay the report of a counterexample to a later POP and visit several states until then. Nonetheless this difference is very small in our experiment: less than 1% additional states, transitions or SCCs have been visited. This negligible difference justifies our decision not to store an additional acceptance set in each element of *live* to report counterexamples earlier in Tarjan's algorithm, as discussed at the end of Sec. 3.2.

Table 3 presents the impact of the lazy transfer into *dead* proposed for Gabow's algorithm. We observe that only half the states are transferred to *dead*; this means that the remaining states have been preserved in the DEAD part of the Union-Find structure. This explains the gain observed from Fig. 2.

Table 1. Comparison of memory consumption for emptiness check algorithms on the 448 empty products. $|roots|$ (resp. $|uf|$, $|dstack|$, $|dead|$) denotes the number of elements in $rstack$ (resp. uf, $dstack$, $dead$). As $rstack$ elements are pairs $(root, \text{acc})$, we count the memory consumption as $2|roots|$ words. The additional bit required for each element of the compressed stack is not accounted for. Since $live$ is constructed using an $hashmap$ and a $stack$, we distinguish these sizes with $|live_{stack}|$ and $|live_{hash}|$: they differ when no $dead$ store is used.

Algorithm	Memory consumption (words)	Observed peak
Dijkstra-cs-ds	$2|roots| + |live_{stack}| + 2|live_{hash}|$	6 225 414 223
Dijkstra+cs-ds		6 225 411 039
Gabow-cs-ds	$2|roots| + 3|uf|$	7 364 856 119
Gabow+cs-ds		7 364 854 033
Tarjan-ds	$2|dstack| + |live_{stack}| + 2|live_{hash}|$	6 325 991 684
Dijkstra-cs+ds	$2|roots| + |live_{stack}| + 2|live_{hash}| + |dead|$	5 160 440 344
Dijkstra+cs+ds		5 160 435 523
Gabow-cs+ds	$2|roots| + 4|uf| + |dead|$	6 608 486 024
Gabow+cs+ds		6 608 482 885
Tarjan+ds	$2|dstack| + |live_{stack}| + 2|live_{hash}| + |dead|$	5 265 484 149

Table 2. Cumulated States, transitions, and SCCs visited by each emptiness check on the 412 non-empty products

	Transitions	States	SCCs
Tarjan	534 471 068	67 230 381	34 622 772
Dijkstra/Gabow	534 338 119	67 187 854	34 582 459

Table 3. Impact of the $dead$ strategy of Gabow's algorithm on the 448 empty products

	Max. $dead$ peak	Cumulated $dead$ peak
Tarjan/Dijkstra (+ds)	29 098 013	2 454 950 318
Gabow (+ds)	21 430 297	1 070 440 670

Table 4. Impact of the compressed $roots$ stack on the 448 empty products

	Max. $roots$ peak	Cumulated $roots$ peak
Dijkstra/Gabow (-cs)	456	98322
Dijkstra/Gabow (+cs)	119	8188

This observation also suggests that a similar optimization could be applied to Tarjan's and Dijkstra's algorithms: each time the $live$ stack is reduced, the residual space (the free list) can be reused to store DEAD states temporarily.

Table 4 shows the impacts of the compression technique proposed in Sec. 4.2. It allows a tenfold memory reduction without run-time overhead according to Fig. 2. Note that such a compression technique is independent of the emptiness check layer, but may apply to Dijkstra's and Gabow's SCC computations.

In Sec. 5, we suggested that using Union-Find was an efficient way to mark all states of an SCC as DEAD in a single operation. Unfortunately, Fig. 2 reveals that these gains are offset by the inherent cost of maintaining the Union-Find structure. Our implementation of the Union-Find uses classical optimizations [17] but we have yet to investiguate wether performances could be improved by the use of a data structure dedicated to the case where each union only concern the last SCCs [9].

8 Conclusion

This paper proposed an overview of existing SCC enumeration algorithms and proposed a generic canvas to transform them into emptiness checks for TGBA.

This lead us to define two new emptiness checks. One is based on Tarjan; it differs from [11] in that it is more memory efficient and generalized. Another one is based on Gabow's suggestion to use the Union-Find data structure: our results with that data structure are mixed, but as far as we know, this is the first time this data structure is used for emptiness check.

We also introduced a couple of optimizations. For Dijkstra's and Gabow's emptiness checks we suggest to compress the *roots* stack to save some memory. Additionally, we discussed a strategy to transfer DEAD state from the Union-Find structure to the *dead* store lazily, resulting in an important gain of time, and this strategy could also be applied to the other algorithms.

We have several leads for future work. One would be to devise a compression technique for the stack of lowlink (*dstack*) used by Tarjan's algorithm to make it more competitive to Dijkstra's algorithm (currently more memory-efficient). Furthermore, the compaction of the *live* stack suggested by Nuutila and Soisalon-Soininen [16] for Tarjan's algorithm could be adapted to Dijkstra's algorithm and (with a more work) to Gabow's. Another idea would be to study the various ways to extract counterexamples from these algorithms; the procedure suggested by Couvreur et al. [5] would work for Dijkstra and Gabow but should not be difficult to adapt to Tarjan. Finally, we would like to investigate the possibility to parallelize these emptiness checks. There are very few parallel emptiness checks based on SCC computations [2], however as Tarjan and Dijkstra use different data structure than Gabow, may be one of them will be more favorable to a parallel setup.

References

[1] Alur, R., Chaudhuri, S., Etessami, K., Madhusudan, P.: On-the-fly reachability and cycle detection for recursive state machines. In: Halbwachs, N., Zuck, L.D. (eds.) TACAS 2005. LNCS, vol. 3440, pp. 61–76. Springer, Heidelberg (2005)

2. Černá, I., Pelánek, R.: Distributed explicit fair cycle detection (set based approach). In: Ball, T., Rajamani, S.K. (eds.) SPIN 2003. LNCS, vol. 2648, pp. 49–73. Springer, Heidelberg (2003)
3. Courcoubetis, C., Vardi, M.Y., Wolper, P., Yannakakis, M.: Memory-efficient algorithm for the verification of temporal properties. In: Clarke, E., Kurshan, R.P. (eds.) CAV 1990. LNCS, vol. 531, pp. 233–242. Springer, Heidelberg (1991)
4. Couvreur, J.-M.: On-the-fly verification of temporal logic. In: Wing, J.M., Woodcock, J. (eds.) FM 1999. LNCS, vol. 1708, pp. 253–271. Springer, Heidelberg (1999)
5. Couvreur, J.-M., Duret-Lutz, A., Poitrenaud, D.: On-the-fly emptiness checks for generalized Büchi automata. In: Godefroid, P. (ed.) SPIN 2005. LNCS, vol. 3639, pp. 169–184. Springer, Heidelberg (2005)
6. Dijkstra, E.W.: EWD 376: Finding the maximum strong components in a directed graph (May 1973), http://www.cs.utexas.edu/users/EWD/ewd03xx/EWD376.PDF
7. Duret-Lutz, A., Poitrenaud, D.: SPOT: an Extensible Model Checking Library using Transition-based Generalized Büchi Automata. In: MASCOTS 2004, pp. 76–83. IEEE Computer Society Press (October 2004)
8. Gabow, H.N.: Path-based depth-first search for strong and biconnected components. Information Processing Letters 74(3-4), 107–114 (2000)
9. Gabow, H.N., Tarjan, R.E.: A linear-time algorithm for a special case of disjoint set union. In: STOC 1983, pp. 246–251. ACM (1983)
10. Gaiser, A., Schwoon, S.: Comparison of algorithms for checking emptiness on Büchi automata. In: MEMICS 2009. OASICS, vol. 13, Schloss Dagstuhl, Leibniz-Zentrum fuer Informatik (2009)
11. Geldenhuys, J., Valmari, A.: Tarjan's algorithm makes on-the-fly LTL verification more efficient. In: Jensen, K., Podelski, A. (eds.) TACAS 2004. LNCS, vol. 2988, pp. 205–219. Springer, Heidelberg (2004)
12. Geldenhuys, J., Valmari, A.: More efficient on-the-fly LTL verification with Tarjan's algorithm. Theoretical Computer Science 345(1), 60–82 (2005)
13. Godefroid, P., Holzmann, G.J., Pirottin, D.: State space caching revisited. In: Probst, D.K., von Bochmann, G. (eds.) CAV 1992. LNCS, vol. 663, pp. 178–191. Springer, Heidelberg (1993)
14. Hansen, H., Geldenhuys, J.: Cheap and small counterexamples. In: SEFM 2008, pp. 53–62. IEEE Computer Society (November 2008)
15. Holzmann, G.J.: On limits and possibilities of automated protocol analysis. In: PSTV 1987, pp. 339–344. North-Holland (May 1987)
16. Nuutila, E., Soisalon-Soininen, E.: On finding the strongly connected components in a directed graph. Information Processing Letters 49(1), 9–14 (1994)
17. Patwary, M. M.A., Blair, J., Manne, F.: Experiments on union-find algorithms for the disjoint-set data structure. In: Festa, P. (ed.) SEA 2010. LNCS, vol. 6049, pp. 411–423. Springer, Heidelberg (2010)
18. Pelánek, R.: BEEM: benchmarks for explicit model checkers. In: Bošnački, D., Edelkamp, S. (eds.) SPIN 2007. LNCS, vol. 4595, pp. 263–267. Springer, Heidelberg (2007)
19. Tarjan, R.: Depth-first search and linear graph algorithms. SIAM Journal on Computing 1(2), 146–160 (1972)
20. Tarjan, R.E.: Efficiency of a good but not linear set union algorithm. Journal of the ACM (JACM) 22(2), 215–225 (1975)

PeRIPLO: A Framework for Producing Effective Interpolants in SAT-Based Software Verification*

Simone Fulvio Rollini, Leonardo Alt, Grigory Fedyukovich,
Antti E.J. Hyvärinen, and Natasha Sharygina

Faculty of Informatics, University of Lugano
Via Giuseppe Buffi 13, CH-6904 Lugano, Switzerland

Abstract. Propositional interpolation is widely used as a means of over-approximation to achieve efficient SAT-based symbolic model checking. Different verification applications exploit interpolants for different purposes; it is unlikely that a single interpolation procedure could provide interpolants fit for all cases. This paper describes the PeRIPLO framework, an interpolating SAT-solver that implements a set of techniques to generate and manipulate interpolants for different model checking tasks. We demonstrate the flexibility of the framework in two software bounded model checking applications: verification of a given source code incrementally with respect to various properties, and verification of software upgrades with respect to a fixed set of properties. Both applications use interpolation for generating function summaries. Our systematic experimental investigation shows that size and logical strength of interpolants significantly affect verification, that these characteristics depend on the role played by interpolants, and that therefore techniques for tuning size and strength can be used to customize interpolants in different applications.

1 Introduction

A common approach for verifying a program is to express its behavior in a symbolic form and to check such representation against a given specification. One of the most appreciated techniques based on symbolic reasoning is SAT-based symbolic model checking [1], where both the program and the specification are encoded as an instance of the propositional satisfiability problem (SAT), and a SAT-solver is used to determine whether the specification is satisfied or violated. The SAT-based approach allows bit-level reasoning, important both in software and hardware applications, e.g., when dealing with pointer arithmetic and overflow. Successful tools exist for SAT-based verification include CBMC, SATABS, and CPAchecker.

In the last years, Craig interpolation [2] has been widely adopted as a means for abstraction in symbolic model checking [3]. Interpolants are usually computed from resolution refutations; several interpolation algorithms exist in the

---

* This work is partially supported by the European Community under the call FP7-ICT-2009-5 project PINCETTE 257647.

literature [3,4,5] and different interpolants can be generated from the same refutation. While interpolation-based verification is critically affected by the quality of the generated interpolants, it is still not clear what makes an interpolant *good* in a particular framework. Two characteristics that have shown promise are logical strength and size: [5,6] suggest that weaker or stronger interpolants might be more appropriate for different applications, while [7] provides evidence that compact interpolants are beneficial in hardware model checking.

This paper addresses the problem of generating effective interpolants in the context of SAT-based Bounded Model Checking (BMC) [8] for software, and studies the impact of size and strength in verification. Specifically, we present the PeRIPLO[1] framework and discuss its ability to drive interpolation by providing routines that act on complementary levels: (i) manipulation (including compression) of the resolution refutations generated by a SAT-solver, from which interpolants are computed, and (ii) systematic variation of the strength of the interpolants, as allowed by the Labeled Interpolation Systems [5].

As case studies we consider two applications of BMC: verification of a C program incrementally with respect to a number of different properties (as in the FunFrog tool [9]), and incremental verification of different versions of a C program with respect to a fixed set of properties (as in the eVolCheck tool [10]). Both applications rely on interpolation to generate abstractions of the behavior of function calls (*function summaries*); the goal of summarization is to store and reuse information about already analyzed portions of a program, to make subsequent verification checks more efficient. If summaries (i.e. interpolants) are fit, a remarkable performance improvement is usually achieved; if spurious errors have been introduced due to over-approximation, (some of) the summaries need to be refined, which might be resource-consuming. The challenge we address is to use PeRIPLO to drive the generation of interpolants so as to obtain effective summaries.

The novelty of our work lies in the following contributions:

- An interpolation framework, PeRIPLO, able to generate individual interpolants and collections of interpolants satisfying particular properties. PeRIPLO offers a set of tunable techniques to manipulate refutations and to obtain interpolants of different strength from them; it can be integrated in any SAT-based verification framework which makes use of interpolants.
- Solid experimental evidence that compact interpolants improve performance in the context of software BMC. To the best of our knowledge, the only previous work to concretely assess the impact of the size of interpolants is [7], which addresses the use of interpolants in hardware model checking.
- A first systematic evaluation of the impact of interpolant strength in a specific verification domain. We target function summarization in software BMC and show that interpolants of different strength are beneficial to different applications; in particular, stronger and weaker interpolants are respectively suitable for the FunFrog and eVolCheck approaches. These results match the intuition behind the use of interpolants as function summaries.

---

[1] PeRIPLO can be found at http://verify.inf.unisi.ch/periplo.html

2 Interpolation

Craig interpolation [2] has found successful application in the context of model checking and it is at the base of techniques like predicate abstraction [6], counterexample guided abstraction refinement [11], interpolation-based function summarization [9], upgrade checking [10], and lazy abstraction with interpolants [12]. Formally, given an unsatisfiable conjunction $A \wedge B$, an interpolant I is a formula implied by A ($A \to I$), unsatisfiable with B (i.e., $B \wedge I \to \bot$) and defined on the common symbols of A and B. In other words an interpolant can be seen as an over-approximation of A that is still unsatisfiable with B.

Several algorithms are available to construct different interpolants for an unsatisfiable conjunction $A \wedge B$; yet, it is still an open problem to identify what characteristics make some interpolants better than others in a particular verification framework. In this paper we target two features which are intuitively relevant to model checking and for which preliminary evidence has been provided in the recent literature: *logical strength* [6,5] and *structural size* [7] (intended as the number of logical connectives in a formula).

Strength. A formula ϕ is said to be *stronger* than ψ if $\phi \to \psi$ (resp. ψ is *weaker* than ϕ). Interpolants are inherently over-approximations, thus a stronger or weaker interpolant is expected to drive verification in terms of a finer or coarser approximation. [5] offers an adequate framework to conduct an investigation of interpolant strength: it in fact presents the *Labeled Interpolation Systems* (LISs) for systematically building propositional interpolants of different strength from a single resolution refutation, generalizing the algorithms previously introduced by Pudlák [4] and McMillan [13]. A LIS is a procedure that, given a refutation of $A \wedge B$ and a labeling function, outputs an interpolant for $A \wedge B$. The authors define a partial order over the labeling functions and relate the corresponding interpolants by strength; [5] proves that the collection of systems represents a *complete lattice*, where McMillan's system M is the greatest element (i.e., it generates the strongest interpolant), the system M' dual to McMillan's is the least (i.e., it generates the weakest interpolant) and Pudlák's P is in between.

Size. Besides semantic features like strength, syntactic features like interpolant size are also likely to affect the verification performance: generating, storing and using smaller and less redundant formulae require fewer computational resources. Supporting evidence is given by [7], where compact interpolants prove beneficial in the context of hardware unbounded model checking. The usefulness of small interpolants is also intuitively clear for the function summarization based approaches considered in this paper, where interpolants correspond to summaries that are used multiple times in subsequent verification attempts.

Reduction of the interpolant size can be achieved both in an indirect and in a direct manner. Interpolants are computed from refutations, and their size is linear in the number of nodes of the DAGs representing the refutations. A simple indirect way to obtain a smaller interpolant is to first compress the refutation and then to apply an interpolation procedure; several compression algorithms exist in the literature, ranging from structural hashing to partial regularization [14,15,16,17,18]. A second way, complementary to proof compression, is to view interpolants as Boolean circuits and address them directly by means of logic synthesis techniques, including BDD sweeping, functional reduction and multi-level structural and functional hashing [19,7].

3 PeRIPLO

PeRIPLO (Proof tRansformer and Interpolator for Propositional LOgic) is an open-source SAT solver, built on MiniSAT 2.2.0 [20], that provides proof logging, proof manipulation routines and propositional interpolation. It can be used as a standalone tool or as a library; its routines are accessible via configuration file or API. Figure 1 illustrates the tool architecture.

PeRIPLO receives as input a propositional formula ϕ from the *verification environment*, and passes it to the *SAT solver*, that checks satisfiability while performing proof logging. If the formula is unsatisfiable, a resolution refutation Π is built in form of a directed acyclic graph.

Π can be further processed by the *proof transformer*, for example it can be compressed or manipulated as a preliminary step to interpolation.

Once Π is available, the environment can ask the *interpolator* for the generation of an individual or a collection of interpolants $\{I_i\}$ by means of an interpolation system *Itp*, providing a subdivision of ϕ into $A \wedge B$; if the collection is related to some interpolation property P, then an additional checking phase can be enabled to ensure that P is satisfied.

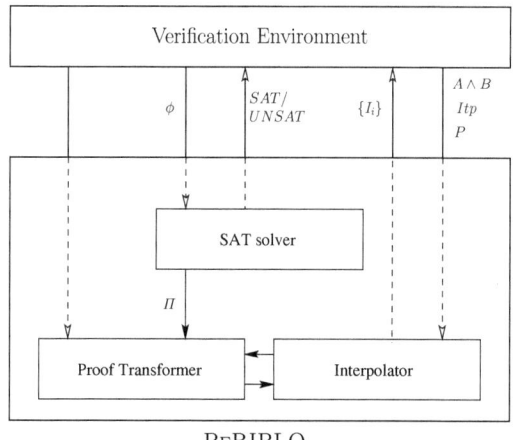

Fig. 1. PeRIPLO architecture

Interpolant Strength. PeRIPLO realizes the Labeled Interpolation Systems of [5] and allows to systematically vary the strength of the interpolants. It is able to produce both individual interpolants and collections of interpolants, w.r.t. various interpolation properties (e.g., tree interpolation, see §5) and in accordance with the constraints posed by the properties on the LISs [21,22].

Proof Compression. PeRIPLO allows to compress refutations by means of the following techniques, which target different kinds of redundancies in proofs: (i) the `RecyclePivotsWithIntersection` (RPI) algorithm of [16,15], (ii) the `LowerUnits` (LU) algorithm of [16], (iii) a structural hashing based approach (SH) similar to that of [14], (iv) the local rewriting rules of [17,18,23]. Some manipulation routines are available depending on the LIS chosen: for example, in case of McMillan's LIS M it is possible to perform a fast transformation of the refutation to achieve a partial CNFization of the interpolant [6,18]. The local rewriting rules can also be applied to further strengthen or weaken the interpolant with respect to a given LIS [6]. PeRIPLO does not implement techniques to directly minimize the interpolants after their generation (as, e.g., in [7]); nevertheless, structural hashing is performed while building formulae, for a more efficient representation in memory.

4 Function Summaries in Bounded Model Checking

SAT-based BMC is one of the most successful approaches to software verification. It checks a program w.r.t. a property by 1) unwinding loops and recursive function calls up to a given bound, 2) encoding program and negated property into a propositional *BMC formula*, and 3) using a SAT-solver to check the BMC formula. If the formula is unsatisfiable, the program is safe w.r.t. the bound; otherwise, a satisfying assignment identifies a behavior that violates the property.

We describe in the following two BMC applications which employ interpolation-based *function summaries* as over-approximations of function calls. These applications, respectively implemented in the FunFrog [24] and eVolCheck [25] tools, prove particularly suitable to PeRIPLO, due to the impact size and strength of interpolants can have on verification.

FunFrog. In [9], Sery et al. present a framework to perform incremental verification of a set of properties. Summaries are used to store information about the already analyzed portions of the program, which helps to check subsequent properties more efficiently.

A summary I_f for a function f is an interpolant constructed from an unsatisfiable BMC formula $\phi \equiv A_f \wedge B_\pi$, where A_f encodes f and its nested calls, B_π the rest of the program and the negated property π (which holds for the program). While checking the program w.r.t. another property π', the BMC formula changes to $A_f \wedge B_{\pi'}$; I_f is used in place of f: if $I_f \wedge B_{\pi'}$ turns out to be unsatisfiable, then the summary is still valid and π' is proved to hold in the program. If instead $I_f \wedge B_{\pi'}$ is satisfiable, satisfiability could be caused by the overapproximation due to I_f: I_f is replaced by the precise encoding of f and the check is repeated. If $A_f \wedge B_{\pi'}$ is satisfiable, the error is real; if $A_f \wedge B_{\pi'}$ is unsatisfiable, then the error is spurious and I_f is *refined* to a new I'_f.

The ability to reuse summaries depends on their quality. According to our intuition, *accurate summaries* (i.e. *strong interpolants*) are effective in FunFrog: a summary in fact over-approximates the behavior of a function call w.r.t. an assertion; the more precise the summary is, the more closely it reflects the behavior of the corresponding function and the more likely it is to be employed in the verification of subsequent assertions.

eVolCheck. The upgrade checking algorithm of [10] uses function summarization for BMC in a different way. Verification is done simultaneously w.r.t. a fixed set of properties, but for a program that undergoes modifications. Summaries $\{I_i\}$ are computed for the function calls $\{A_{f_i}\}$ of the original version of the program, and applied to perform local incremental checks of the new version. If the old summaries are general enough to over-approximate the new behavior of the modified functions $\{A_{f'_j}\}$ (i.e. $A_{f'_j} \to I_j$) then the new version is safe. Otherwise, the summaries of the caller functions of the $\{A_{f'_j}\}$ are checked in the same way. If the check succeeds, new summaries $\{I'_j\}$ are generated that *refine* the old $\{I_j\}$. This process continues up to the call tree root. If in the end the summary of the main function is proven invalid, then the new version is buggy.

In contrast with FunFrog, *coarse summaries* (i.e. *weak interpolants*) are more suitable for eVolCheck; the underlying intuition is that weaker interpolants represent abstractions which are more "tolerant" and are more likely to remain valid when the functions are updated.

Compact summaries are expected to yield a more efficient verification both in the FunFrog and eVolCheck frameworks: on one hand, storing and reusing smaller formulae is less expensive, on the other hand, summary reduction via proof compression allows to remove redundancies while keeping the relevant information; in the FunFrog approach, additionally, new summaries are built when possible from refutations involving previously computed summaries.

5 Experimental Evaluation

We evaluated FunFrog and eVolCheck on a collection of 50 crafted C benchmarks characterized by a non trivial call tree structure reflecting the structure of real C programs used in previous experimentation [24,25]. The benchmarks contain assertions distributed on different levels of the tree, which makes them particularly suitable for summary-based verification. FunFrog and eVolCheck employ PeRIPLO for symbolic reasoning and interpolation; they provide as input BMC formulae and receive as output interpolants, specifying a LIS depending on the desired interpolant strength. Proof compression techniques can also be applied in order to produce smaller summaries. The experiments were carried out on a 64-bit Ubuntu server featuring a Quad-Core 4GHz Xeon CPU, with a memory threshold of 13GB[2].

---

[2] Tools and data are available at http://verify.inf.unisi.ch/files/LPAR.tar.gz

FunFrog. In a first phase, FunFrog was run to check the assertions of each benchmark incrementally w.r.t. the call tree, with the goal of maximizing the reuse of summaries. Consider a program with the following chain of nested calls:

$$main()\{ f()\{ g()\{ h()\{\} \; Assert_g\} \; Assert_f\} \; Assert_{main}\}$$

where $Assert_x$ denotes an assertion in the body of a function x. In a successful scenario, (i) $Assert_g$ is checked and a summary I_h for h is created; (ii) $Assert_f$ is efficiently verified by exploiting I_h (I_g is then built over I_h) and (iii) so is $Assert_{main}$ by means of I_g. Each benchmark was tested in different configurations: with/without performing proof compression before interpolation and choosing one among M, P, M' to compute all the interpolants. Compression consisted of a sequential run of LU,SH,RPI (see §3); this particular combination is effective in reducing proofs, as shown in [18].

eVolCheck. In a second phase, new versions of the benchmarks were created, modifying syntax/semantics of the original programs. First eVolCheck was run to check all assertions at once, yielding a collection of function summaries; then the new program versions were verified w.r.t. the same assertions by using the summaries. As discussed in [10], while performing upgrade checking the interpolants need to satisfy a property known as *tree interpolation*. In [22] it is proved that tree interpolation is satisfied by M, P but not by M'; for this reason we only took into account M and P for experimentation. Compression was performed as in FunFrog.

Experimental Results. Small interpolants indeed have a strong impact on the performance in both frameworks. Figure 2 compares the verification times for the benchmarks in FunFrog (a) and eVolCheck (b), with and without performing proof compression before interpolation. Table 1 provides additional statistics for the individual interpolation systems: *#Refinements* denotes the total amount of summary refinements in FunFrog, while *#Invalid summaries* the total number of summaries that in eVolCheck were made invalid because of program updates; $Avg|I|$ and $Time(s)$ indicate the average size of interpolants and the average verification time over all the benchmarks; $Time_C/Time_V$ ratio is the ratio between the time spent for proof compression and the verification time.

Figure 2 and Table 1 show the remarkable performance improvement achieved by exploiting proof compression; FunFrog, e.g., obtains a reduction in the average interpolants size $Avg|I|$ up to 95% and a speedup up to 54%. Note also in Figure 2 that the effect of compression increases with the complexity of the benchmark; the overhead due to applying compression techniques becomes in fact less and less significant as the benchmark verification time grows.

According to the intuitions discussed in §4, *strong interpolants* prove beneficial in FunFrog, while *weak interpolants* are more suitable for eVolCheck; this is represented in Table 1 by a smaller amount of summary refinements in FunFrog and of invalidated summaries in eVolCheck.

The results show that the size of interpolants seems to have definitely an overall greater impact than interpolant strength. Verification time, in fact, is

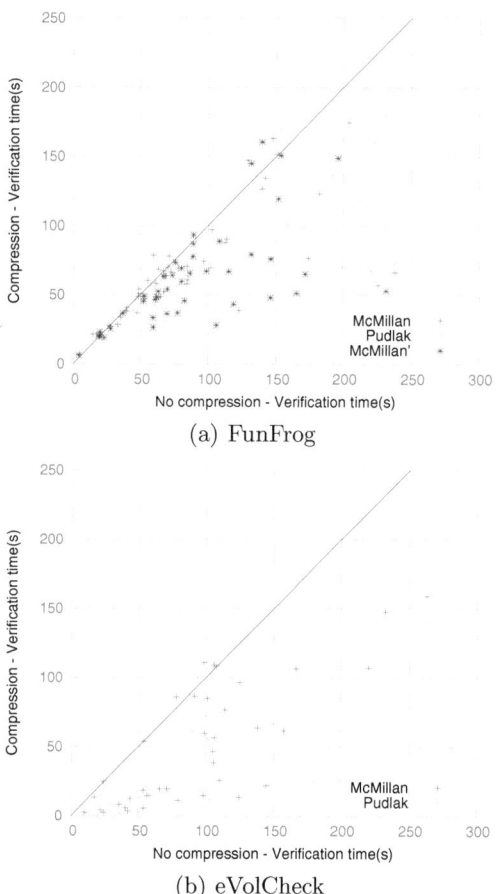

Fig. 2. Proof compression effect on verification time

principally determined by the size of the summaries, so that, even in presence of a larger amount of refinements or invalidated summaries, smaller summaries tend to lead to a better performance.

It is important to remark that both size and strength are dependent on the features of the refutations from which the interpolants are produced, as well as on the specific interpolation algorithms, and that these aspects cannot be considered separately. For example, in our experimentation we found considerable differences in the size of the interpolants generated by the three LISs, and in the effect of proof compression: interpolants generated with M' in FunFrog were on average twice as big as those generated with M, but they benefited the most from compression.

Moreover, among all existing refutations for a certain unsatisfiable formula (including those obtained via compression), there might be some which are of better "quality" w.r.t. interpolation by means of LISs. A good refutation could be characterized by a large logical "distance" between the interpolant I yielded

Table 1. Verification statistics for FunFrog and eVolCheck

(a) FunFrog

No Compression	M	P	M'
#Refinements	290	298	308
Avg $|I|$	38886.62	39372.07	72994.08
Time(s)	4568.08	4929.93	6805.81
Compression	M	P	M'
#Refinements	293	293	294
Avg $|I|$	4336.21	3402.58	3255.69
Time(s)	3327.56	3450.17	3201.72
Time$_C$/Time$_V$ ratio	0.32	0.33	0.32

(b) eVolCheck

No Compression	M	P
#Invalid summaries	65	63
Avg $|I|$	334554.64	377903.11
Time(s)	4322.57	4402.00
Compression	M	P
#Invalid summaries	63	62
Avg $|I|$	12579.89	12929.82
Time(s)	2073.79	2057.34
Time$_C$/Time$_V$ ratio	0.19	0.19

by M and I' yielded by M', where the distance between I and I' — remember that $I \to I'$ — is defined as the number of models of I' that are not models of I. A large distance in this sense would allow for a higher degree of variation in the coarseness of summaries, with direct impact on verification.

6 Conclusions

Craig interpolation is a standard means for abstraction in symbolic model checking, but it is still not clear what makes interpolants good in a particular verification framework. We addressed the problem of generating effective interpolants by evaluating the impact of size and logical strength in the context of software SAT-based BMC. To this end, we introduced PeRIPLO, a novel framework that drives interpolation by providing routines for manipulation of the resolution refutations from which the interpolants are computed and for systematic variation of the interpolants strength. As case studies we considered two BMC applications which use interpolation to generate function summaries: (i) verification of a C program incrementally with respect to a number of different properties, and (ii) incremental verification of different versions of a C program with respect to the fixed set of properties. We provided solid experimental evidence that compact interpolants improve the verification performance in the two applications. We also carried out a first systematic evaluation of the impact of strength in a specific verification domain, showing that different applications benefit from interpolants of different strength: specifically, stronger and weaker interpolants are respectively desirable in (i) and (ii).

References

1. Biere, A., Cimatti, A., Clarke, E., Zhu, Y.: Symbolic Model Checking without BDDs. In: Cleaveland, W.R. (ed.) TACAS 1999. LNCS, vol. 1579, pp. 193–207. Springer, Heidelberg (1999)
2. Craig, W.: Three Uses of the Herbrand-Gentzen Theorem in Relating Model Theory and Proof Theory. Journal of Symbolic Logic 22(3), 269–285 (1957)
3. McMillan, K.L.: Interpolation and SAT-Based Model Checking. In: Hunt Jr., W.A., Somenzi, F. (eds.) CAV 2003. LNCS, vol. 2725, pp. 1–13. Springer, Heidelberg (2003)
4. Pudlák, P.: Lower Bounds for Resolution and Cutting Plane Proofs and Monotone Computations. Journal of Symbolic Logic 62(3), 981–998 (1997)
5. D'Silva, V., Kroening, D., Purandare, M., Weissenbacher, G.: Interpolant Strength. In: Barthe, G., Hermenegildo, M. (eds.) VMCAI 2010. LNCS, vol. 5944, pp. 129–145. Springer, Heidelberg (2010)
6. Jhala, R., McMillan, K.L.: Interpolant-Based Transition Relation Approximation. In: Etessami, K., Rajamani, S.K. (eds.) CAV 2005. LNCS, vol. 3576, pp. 39–51. Springer, Heidelberg (2005)
7. Cabodi, G., Lolacono, C., Vendraminetto, D.: Optimization Techniques for Craig Interpolant Compaction in Unbounded Model Checking. In: DATE 2013 (2013)
8. Biere, A., Cimatti, A., Clarke, E.M., Strichman, O., Zhu, Y.: Bounded Model Checking. Advances in Computers, vol. 58, pp. 117–148. Elsevier (2003)
9. Sery, O., Fedyukovich, G., Sharygina, N.: Interpolation-based Function Summaries in Bounded Model Checking. In: Eder, K., Lourenço, J., Shehory, O. (eds.) HVC 2011. LNCS, vol. 7261, pp. 160–175. Springer, Heidelberg (2012)
10. Sery, O., Fedyukovich, G., Sharygina, N.: Incremental Upgrade Checking by Means of Interpolation-based Function Summaries. In: FMCAD (2012)
11. Henzinger, T., Jhala, R., Majumdar, R., McMillan, K.: Abstractions from Proofs. In: POPL, pp. 232–244 (2004)
12. McMillan, K.L.: Lazy Abstraction with Interpolants. In: Ball, T., Jones, R.B. (eds.) CAV 2006. LNCS, vol. 4144, pp. 123–136. Springer, Heidelberg (2006)
13. McMillan, K.L.: An Interpolating Theorem Prover. In: Jensen, K., Podelski, A. (eds.) TACAS 2004. LNCS, vol. 2988, pp. 16–30. Springer, Heidelberg (2004)
14. Cotton, S.: Two Techniques for Minimizing Resolution Proofs. In: Strichman, O., Szeider, S. (eds.) SAT 2010. LNCS, vol. 6175, pp. 306–312. Springer, Heidelberg (2010)
15. Bar-Ilan, O., Fuhrmann, O., Hoory, S., Shacham, O., Strichman, O.: Linear-Time Reductions of Resolution Proofs. In: Chockler, H., Hu, A.J. (eds.) HVC 2008. LNCS, vol. 5394, pp. 114–128. Springer, Heidelberg (2009)
16. Fontaine, P., Merz, S., Woltzenlogel Paleo, B.: Compression of Propositional Resolution Proofs via Partial Regularization. In: Bjørner, N., Sofronie-Stokkermans, V. (eds.) CADE 2011. LNCS, vol. 6803, pp. 237–251. Springer, Heidelberg (2011)
17. Rollini, S.F., Bruttomesso, R., Sharygina, N.: An Efficient and Flexible Approach to Resolution Proof Reduction. In: Barner, S., Harris, I., Kroening, D., Raz, O. (eds.) HVC 2010. LNCS, vol. 6504, pp. 182–196. Springer, Heidelberg (2010)
18. Rollini, S., Bruttomesso, R., Sharygina, N., Tsitovich, A.: Resolution Proof Transformation for Compression and Interpolation, http://arxiv.org/abs/1307.2028

19. Kuehlmann, A., Paruthi, V., Krohm, F., Ganai, M.: Robust Boolean reasoning for Equivalence Checking and Functional Property Verification. IEEE Transactions on CAD 21(12), 1377–1394 (2002)
20. Eén, N., Sörensson, N.: An Extensible SAT-solver. In: Giunchiglia, E., Tacchella, A. (eds.) SAT 2003. LNCS, vol. 2919, pp. 502–518. Springer, Heidelberg (2004)
21. Rollini, S.F., Sery, O., Sharygina, N.: Leveraging Interpolant Strength in Model Checking. In: Madhusudan, P., Seshia, S.A. (eds.) CAV 2012. LNCS, vol. 7358, pp. 193–209. Springer, Heidelberg (2012)
22. Gurfinkel, A., Rollini, S.F., Sharygina, N.: Interpolation Properties and SAT-Based Model Checking. In: Van Hung, D., Ogawa, M. (eds.) ATVA 2013. LNCS, vol. 8172, pp. 255–271. Springer, Heidelberg (2013)
23. Bruttomesso, R., Rollini, S., Sharygina, N., Tsitovich, A.: Flexible Interpolation with Local Proof Transformations. In: ICCAD, pp. 770–777 (2010)
24. Sery, O., Fedyukovich, G., Sharygina, N.: FunFrog: Bounded Model Checking with Interpolation-based Function Summarization. In: Chakraborty, S., Mukund, M. (eds.) ATVA 2012. LNCS, vol. 7561, pp. 203–207. Springer, Heidelberg (2012)
25. Fedyukovich, G., Sery, O., Sharygina, N.: eVolCheck: Incremental Upgrade Checker for C. In: Piterman, N., Smolka, S.A. (eds.) TACAS 2013 (ETAPS 2013). LNCS, vol. 7795, pp. 292–307. Springer, Heidelberg (2013)

Incremental Tabling for Query-Driven Propagation of Logic Program Updates

Ari Saptawijaya* and Luís Moniz Pereira

Centro de Inteligência Artificial (CENTRIA), Departamento de Informática
Faculdade de Ciências e Tecnologia, Univ. Nova de Lisboa, 2829-516 Caparica, Portugal
ar.saptawijaya@campus.fct.unl.pt, lmp@fct.unl.pt

Abstract. We foster a novel implementation technique for logic program updates, which exploits incremental tabling in logic programming – using XSB Prolog to that effect. Propagation of updates of fluents is controlled by initially keeping any fluent updates pending in the database. And, on the initiative of queries, making active just those updates up to the timestamp of an actual query, by performing incremental assertions of the pending ones. These assertions, in turn, automatically trigger system-implemented incremental bottom-up tabling of other fluents (or their negated complements), with respect to a predefined overall upper time limit, in order to avoid runaway iteration. The frame problem can then be dealt with by inspecting a table for the latest time a fluent is known to be assuredly true, i.e., the latest time it is not supervened by its negated complement, relative to the given query time. To do so, we adopt the dual program transformation for defining and helping propagate, also incrementally and bottom-up, the negated complement of a fluent, in order to establish whether a fluent is still true at some time point, or rather if its complement is. The use of incremental tabling in this approach affords us a form of controlled, but automatic, system level truth-maintenance, up to some actual query time. Consequently, propagation of update side-effects need not employ top-down recursion or bottom-up iteration through a logically defined frame axiom, but can be dealt with by the mechanics of the underlying world. Our approach thus reconciles high-level top-down deliberative reasoning about a query, with autonomous low-level bottom-up world reactivity to ongoing updates, and it might be adopted elsewhere for reasoning in logic.

Keywords: logic program updates, updates propagation, incremental tabling, dual program transformation, XSB Prolog.

1 Introduction

The tabled logic programming paradigm, i.e., logic programming (LP) with tabling mechanisms, is supported by a number of Prolog systems, to different extent. Tabling affords solutions reuse, rather than recomputing them, by keeping in tables subgoals and their answers obtained by query evaluation. Incremental tabling, available in XSB Prolog [23], is an advanced recent tabling feature that ensures the consistency of answers in a table with all dynamic clauses on which the table depends. It does so by incrementally

---
* Affiliated with Fakultas Ilmu Komputer at Universitas Indonesia, Depok, Indonesia.

maintaining the table, rather than by recomputing answers in the table from scratch to keep it updated. The applications of incremental tabling in LP have been demonstrated in pointer analyses of C programs in the context of incremental program analyses [18], data flow analyses [19], static analyses [6], incremental validation of XML documents and push down model checking [17]. This range of applications suggests that incremental tabling lends itself to dynamic environments and evolving systems, including notably logic program updates, as we proceed to show.

In [20], an approach to logic program updates, termed EVOLP/R, theoretically based on Evolving Logic Programs (EVOLP) [1], is proposed. It simplifies EVOLP by restricting updates to fluents only. Rule updates are nevertheless achieved by attaching to each rule, in its body, a name fluent that uniquely identifies that rule (cf. [16]). Updating such a rule name fluent, via its assertion or retraction, permits time-activation or deactivation of the corresponding rule, respectively. Its implementation preliminarily exploits incremental tabling, plus another tabling feature: answer subsumption [22]. Incremental tabling of fluents is employed to automatically maintain the consistency of program states due to assertion and retraction of fluents, whether obtained as updated facts or concluded by rules. On the other hand, answer subsumption of fluents allows to address the frame problem, by automatically keeping track of the latest assertion or retraction of fluents with respect to a given query time. The combined use of incremental tabling and answer subsumption is realized in the tabled predicate $fluent(F, Ht, Qt)$: given query time Qt, it looks for dynamic definitions of fluent F, and returns Ht, the latest time fluent F is true. Predicate $fluent/3$ depends on dynamic fluent definitions of F, and this dependency indicates that $fluent/3$ is tabled incrementally, to avoid abolishing the table each time a Prolog assertion is made and then recomputing from scratch. Moreover, since $fluent/3$ aims at returning only the latest time F is true (with respect to a given Qt), $fluent/3$ can be tabled using answer subsumption on its second argument. While answer subsumption is shown useful in this approach to avoid recursing through the frame axiom by allowing direct access to the latest time when a fluent is true, it requires $fluent/3$ to have query time Qt as its argument. Consequently, it may hinder reuse of tabled answers of $fluent/3$ by similar goals which differ only in their query time. In truth, the state of a fluent in time depends solely on the changes made to the world, and not on whether that world is being queried. For instance, suppose $fluent(a, 2, 4)$ is already tabled, and fluent a is inertially true till it is supervened by its negated complement, say at time $T = 7$. When a new goal $fluent(a, Ht, 5)$ is posed, it cannot reuse the tabled answer $fluent(a, 2, 4)$, as they differ in their query time. Instead, $fluent(a, Ht, 5)$ unnecessarily recomputes the same solution $Ht = 2$ (recall that fluent a is only retracted at $T = 7$), and subsequently tables $fluent(a, 2, 5)$ as a new answer. A similar situation occurs when $fluent(a, Ht, 6)$ is queried, where $fluent(a, 2, 6)$ is eventually added into the table. This is clearly superfluous, as existing tabled answers could actually be reused and such redundancies avoided, if the tabled answers are independent of query time. However, in XSB answer subsumption on argument Ht cannot be made to ignore argument Qt, by its very design.

In this paper we address the aforementioned issue by fostering further incremental tabling, but leaving out the problematic use of the answer subsumption feature by reconceptualizing the issue at hand. The main idea, which was not captured in [20], is the perspective that knowledge updates (either self or world wrought changes) occur whether or not they are queried, i.e., the former take place independently of the latter. That is, when a fluent is true at Ht, its truth lingers on independently of query time: Qt no longer becomes an argument of the tabled $fluent$ predicate, i.e., we now have just $fluent(F, Ht)$. Being independent of query time Qt, $fluent/2$ consequently permits better and more general reuse of its tabled answers than that of [20].

In the present approach, fluent updates are initially kept pending in the database, and on the initiative of top-goal queries, i.e., by need only, incremental assertions make these pending updates active (if not already so), but only those with timestamps up to an actual query time. Such assertions automatically trigger system level incremental upwards propagation and tabling of fluent updates. In order to delimit answers in the table, which in some cases may lead to iterative non-termination, the propagation is bounded by a predefined upper global time limit. Though foregoing answer subsumption, recursion through the frame axiom can thus still be avoided, and a direct access to the latest time a fluent is true is made possible via system table inspection predicates. Benefiting from the automatic upwards propagation of fluent updates, the program transformation in the present approach becomes simpler than our previous one, in [20]. Moreover, it demonstrates how the dual program transformation, initially introduced in the context of abduction [3], is employed for helping propagate the dual negation complement of a fluent incrementally, to establish whether the fluent is still true at some time point or rather if its complement is. Keeping both a fluent and its complement tabled will permit in future to address paraconsistency and counterfactuals.

The paper is organized as follows. Section 2 recaps the EVOLP/R language, and reviews the dual transformation and incremental tabling. We detail the implementation technique in Section 3, discuss related work in Section 4, and conclude in Section 5.

2 Preliminaries

We begin by recapitulating the theoretical basis of our logic program updates.

2.1 The EVOLP/R Language

The syntax of EVOLP/R is simply adapted from that of EVOLP [1], by restricting updates to fluents only. Let $\mathcal{K}$ be an arbitrary set of propositional variables and $\tilde{\mathcal{K}}$ be the *extension* of $\mathcal{K}$, defined as $\tilde{\mathcal{K}} = \{A : A \in \mathcal{K}\} \cup \{\sim A : A \in \mathcal{K}\}$. Atoms $A \in \mathcal{K}$ and $\sim A$ are called *positive fluents* and *negative fluents*, respectively. As in EVOLP, program updates are enacted by having the reserved predicate $assert/1$ in the head of a rule.

Definition 1. *Let $\tilde{\mathcal{K}}$ be the extension of a set $\mathcal{K}$ of propositional variables. The* EVOLP/R *language $\mathcal{L}$ is defined inductively as follows:*

1. *All propositional atoms in $\tilde{\mathcal{K}}$ are propositional atoms in $\mathcal{L}$.*
2. *If A is a propositional atom in $\mathcal{L}$, then $assert(A)$ is a propositional atom in $\mathcal{L}$.*
3. *If A is a propositional atom in $\mathcal{L}$, then $\sim assert(A)$ is a propositional atom in $\mathcal{L}$.*
4. *Nothing else is a propositional atom in $\mathcal{L}$.*

5. If A_0 is a propositional atom in $\mathcal{L}$ and $A_1, \ldots, A_n$, with $n \geq 0$, are literals in $\mathcal{L}$ (i.e. a propositional atom A, or its default negation not A), then $A_0 \leftarrow A_1, \ldots, A_n$ is a rule in $\mathcal{L}$.
6. Nothing else is a rule in $\mathcal{L}$.

An EVOLP/R program *over a language $\mathcal{L}$ is a (possibly infinite) set of rules in $\mathcal{L}$.*

We extend the notion of positive and negative fluents in $\tilde{\mathcal{K}}$ to propositional atoms A and $\sim A$ in $\mathcal{L}$, respectively. They are said to be *complement* each other. When it is clear from the context, we refer both of them as fluents. Retraction of fluent A (or $\sim A$), making it false, is achieved by asserting its complement $\sim A$ (or A, respectively). I.e., no reserved predicate for retraction is needed. Non-monotonicity of a fluent can thus be admitted by asserting its complement, so as to let the latter supervene the former. Observe that the syntax permits embedded assertions of literals, e.g., $assert(assert(a))$, $\sim assert(assert(a))$; the latter being the complement of the former.

In [1], the semantics of EVOLP is given by a set of *evolution stable models*, each of which is a sequence of interpretations or states. Each evolution stable model describes some possible self-evolution of one initial program after a given number of evolution steps, where each self-evolution is represented by a sequence of generalized logic programs (i.e. programs that allow default negation in their heads). By Definition 1, EVOLP/R programs are not generalized logic programs, but they nevertheless permit negative fluents in the rules' heads. Indeed, one may view negative fluents as explicit negations, and due to the coherence principle [2], that states explicit negation entails default negation, negative fluents obey the principle. Therefore, the two forms of rules' heads, i.e. $assert(not\ A)$ in EVOLP and $assert(\sim A)$ in EVOLP/R, can be treated equivalently. This justification allows the semantics of EVOLP/R to be safely based on that of EVOLP, as long as the paraconsistency of simultaneously having A and $\sim A$ is duly detected and user-defined handled, say with integrity constraints or preferences.

In EVOLP, the most recent rule instances are put in force, and the previous rule instances are valid (by inertia) as far as possible, i.e., they are kept for as long as they do not conflict with more recent ones. Though EVOLP/R restricts updates to fluents only, rule updates (like in EVOLP) can nevertheless be achieved, via the mechanism of rule name fluents, placed in rules' bodies, allowing to turn rules on or off, through assertions or retractions of their corresponding unique name fluents. That said, the restriction amounts to saying that all rules are to be known at the start, so that their rule names can be manipulated. Conceivably however, new internally learnt or externally given rules could be associated at such time with corresponding new names, and the association recorded by an update.

We now review the semantics of EVOLP and adapt it for EVOLP/R, restricting updates to fluents only. In the following definitions, $\bigoplus \mathcal{P}$, where $\mathcal{P} = \{P_i \mid 1 \leq i \leq n\}$, denotes a sequence of EVOLP/R programs $P_1 \oplus \cdots \oplus P_n$; each program corresponding to a state $s \in S$.

Definition 2. *Let $\bigoplus \{P_i : i \in S\}$ be an EVOLP/R program over language $\mathcal{L}$, $s \in S$, and M be a set of propositional atoms of $\mathcal{L}$. Then:*

$Default_s(M) = \{not\ A \mid \nexists A \leftarrow Body \in P_i(1 \leq i \leq s) : M \models Body\}$
$Reject_s(M) = \{A \leftarrow Body \in P_i \mid \exists \sim A \leftarrow Body' \in P_j, i < j \leq s \land M \models Body'\}$

where $\sim A$ denotes the *fluent complement* of A, and both $Body$ and $Body'$ are conjunctions of literals.

Definition 3. *Let $P = \bigoplus \{P_i : i \in S\}$ be an EVOLP/R program over language $\mathcal{L}$. A set M of propositional atoms of $\mathcal{L}$ is a* stable model *of P at state $s \in S$ iff:*

$$M' = least\left(\left[\bigcup_{i \leq s} P_i - Reject_s(M)\right] \cup Default_s(M)\right)$$

where $M' = M \cup \{not\_A \mid A \notin M\}$, and $least(.)$ denotes the least model of the definite program obtained from the argument program by replacing every default negated literal not A by a new atom not_A.

Definition 4. *An* evolution interpretation *of length n of an EVOLP/R program P over $\mathcal{L}$ is a finite sequence $\mathcal{I} = \langle I_1, \ldots, I_n \rangle$ of sets of propositional atoms of $\mathcal{L}$. The* evolution trace *associated with an evolution interpretation $\mathcal{I}$ is the sequence of programs $\langle P_1, \ldots, P_n \rangle$ where $P_1 = P$ and $P_i = \{A \mid assert(A) \in I_{i-1}\}$, for $2 \leq i \leq n$.*

Definition 5. *Let $M = \langle I_1, \ldots, I_n \rangle$ be an evolution interpretation of an EVOLP/R program P and $\langle P_1, \ldots, P_n \rangle$ be its evolution trace. M is an* evolution stable model *of P iff for every i ($1 \leq i \leq n$), I_i is a stable model of $\bigoplus \{P_1, \ldots, P_i\}$ at state i.*

Like EVOLP, besides the self-evolution of a program, EVOLP/R also allows influence from the outside, either as an observation of fluents that are perceived at some state, or assertion orders about fluents on the evolving program. Different from EVOLP, the outside influence in EVOLP/R, referred as *external updates*, persist by inertia as long as they do not conflict with the more recent values for them. Nevertheless, we may easily define external updates that do not persist by inertia, called *events* in EVOLP, by defining for every atomic event E the rule: $assert(\sim E) \leftarrow E$, i.e., if event E is imposed at some state i, then it is no longer assumed from the next state, i.e., $(i + 1)$, onwards. In other words, E holds momentarily at state i only.

Definition 6. *Let E_i, for $1 \leq i \leq k$, be a set of propositional atoms in $\mathcal{L}$. An evolution interpretation $\langle I_1, \ldots, I_n \rangle$, with evolution trace $\langle P_1, \ldots, P_n \rangle$, is an* evolution stable model *of P given an external updates sequence $\langle E_1, \ldots, E_k \rangle$ iff for every i ($1 \leq i \leq n$), I_i is a stable model at state i of $(P_1 \cup E_1) \oplus \cdots \oplus (P_i \cup E_i)$.*

The very idea of the paper is to show how an innovative use of tabling in LP, particularly of incremental tabling, may benefit program updates. Our implementation technique, as detailed Section 3, is realized on top of XSB Prolog, which is based on the well-founded semantics (WFS) [25]. Note that in principle, semantics (with a fixpoint definition) other than stable models can be employed in EVOLP/R. For example, it may alternatively be based on WFS, cf. [4]. Currently, EVOLP/R considers only stratified programs, i.e., programs with no loops over negation. The semantics of EVOLP/R for such programs therefore consists of only one evolution stable model, which is also the well-founded model. This is deliberately so, at this point, because we are concentrating rather on the incremental tabling aspects and usage. Indeed, incremental tabling in the current release of XSB Prolog also supports 3-valued WFS. Its use for non-stratified programs in EVOLP/R, i.e., for updating conditional answers and for reasoning with abduction, is a future line of work, as expressed in the Conclusion section.

2.2 The Dual Program Transformation

The dual program transformation is initially introduced in the context of abduction [3] to abduce explanations under negative goals. It is summarized here and adapted to the EVOLP/R language.

The dual program transformation defines for each atom A and its set of rules R in an EVOLP/R program P, a set of dual rules whose head $\sim A$ is true if and only if A is false by R in the employed semantics of P. It relies on the following definition.

Definition 7. *Let L be a literal in EVOLP/R (cf. Definition 1). The conjugate $conj(L)$ of L is defined as follows:*

$$conj(L) = \begin{cases} A & , if\ L = not\ A\ or\ L = \sim A \\ \sim A & , if\ L = A \end{cases}$$

Example 1 illustrates the main idea of the dual transformation in EVOLP/R.

Example 1. Consider the following program: $\quad a \leftarrow \sim b. \quad\quad a \leftarrow c, not\ d.$
The dual transformation creates a set of dual rules for fluent a which falsify a with respect to its two rules, i.e., by falsifying both the first rule *and* the second rule, expressed below by predicate a^{*1} and a^{*2}, respectively:

$$\sim a \leftarrow a^{*1},\ a^{*2}.$$

This single rule is named as the first layer of the dual transformation. The second layer contains the definitions of a^{*1} and a^{*2}, where a^{*1} and a^{*2} are defined by falsifying the body of a's first rule and second rule, respectively; i.e., by taking the conjugate of literals in the body. In case of a^{*1}, the only way the first rule of a can be falsified is by taking the conjugate of $\sim b$. Therefore, we have:

$$a^{*1} \leftarrow b.$$

In case of a^{*2}, the second rule of p is falsified by alternatively failing one subgoal in its body at a time, i.e., by taking the conjugate of c or alternatively, that of $not\ d$.

$$a^{*2} \leftarrow \sim c. \quad\quad a^{*2} \leftarrow d.$$

Note that, if there is only one definition of a, then the first layer dual rule is defined as $\sim a \leftarrow a^{*1}$. In this case, it is preferable to simply unfold a^{*1}'s definitions in the first layer. For instance, if a in Example 1 is defined only by the second rule, the dual rules $\sim a$ can be directly defined as:

$$\sim a \leftarrow \sim c. \quad\quad \sim a \leftarrow d.$$

Dual rules can be added to rules expressing falsity in their heads. This means the use of the dual is what actually enables us to incrementally propagate falsity, as well as truth. The reader is referred to [3] for theoretical details, and to [21] for our tabled implementation. Note that use of the dual program transformation does not preclude undefined fluents, and that incremental tabling is compatible with the WFS of XSB.

2.3 Incremental Tabling

Whenever a tabled predicate depends on dynamic predicates and the latter are updated (with Prolog's assert or retract predicates), these updates are not immediately reflected in the table, i.e., the table becomes out of date. This problem is known as the view maintenance problem in databases and the truth maintenance problem in artificial intelligence. In "classical" tabling, a typical solution to this problem is to rely on the user to explicitly abolish the table whenever a dynamic predicate, on which the table depends, is updated. As several updates may take place on a dynamic predicate, such explicit table abolishment is rather inconvenient and also leads to inefficiency. To overcome this problem, XSB allows maintaining particular tables incrementally, known as *incremental tabling*, i.e., the answers in these tables are ensured to be consistent with all dynamic facts and rules upon which they depend. In XSB, this requires both tabled predicates and the dynamic predicates they depend on to be declared as incremental. For example, if the tabled predicate $r/2$ depends on the dynamic predicate $s/2$, then they are declared as :- table r/2 as incremental and :- dynamic s/2 as incremental, respectively. To update the table of $r/2$ incrementally by a single change to $s/2$, a call such as $incr\_assert(s(a,3))$ or $incr\_retract(s(a,3))$ can be issued, in which case the table of $r/2$ and other tables that depend on $r/2$ and $s/2$ are updated after such a call. Bulk changes are also supported. The reader is referred to [24] for the further options, examples, and details of incremental tabling.

3 Query-Driven Updates Propagation with Incremental Tabling

Since changes by incremental assertions or retractions in incremental tabling update the tables that depend on them, and only those sought – possibly in a chain of dependencies between tabled predicates – this feature can be exploited for automatically propagating the appropriate fluent updates. The use of the frame axiom, with its recursive nature, is thereby avoided. The "world" manages its own consequences, so to speak, and the system provides its history only to the extent needed by queries.

3.1 The Idea

We start with a very simple example to illustrate the basic idea.

Example 2. Consider program P: $b \leftarrow a.$ $c \leftarrow b.$
Given the sequence of external updates $\langle E_1, E_2, E_3 \rangle$, where $E_1 = \{a\}$, $E_2 = \emptyset$, and $E_3 = \{\sim a\}$, the evolution of P in EVOLP/R (cf. definitions in Section 2) is as follows: $P_1 = P$ with $I_1 = \{a, b, c\}$, $P_2 = \emptyset$ with $I_2 = \{a, b, c\}$, and $P_3 = \emptyset$ with $I_3 = \emptyset$.

Observe that a is an external fluent update at state $i = 1$, which propagates to updates of fluents b (by the first rule) and c (by the second rule), making the three fluents true at state $i = 1$. Incremental tabling itself realizes such propagations. A tabled predicate, say $fluent(F, T)$, to record incremental updates of fluent F at state (or time) T is introduced. That is, it depends directly on fluent literals (treated as dynamic incremental predicates), whether extensional or intensional. The external update of fluent a at $i = 1$ is therefore accomplished by an incremental assertion, via $incr\_assert/1$ system predicate, i.e., $incr\_assert(a(1))$ to say that fluent a is incrementally asserted at $i = 1$. Such an incremental assertion results in having entry $fluent(a, 1)$ in the table. Furthermore, due to the dependencies of the three fluents, as defined by the two rules in P, the incremental assertion of a propagates to fluents b and c, leading to tabling $fluent(b, 1)$ and

$fluent(c, 1)$. We thus have $fluent(a, 1)$, $fluent(b, 1)$, and $fluent(c, 1)$, confirming that the three fluents are true at $i = 1$ (cf. I_1).

As there is no update in state $i = 2$, the truths of the three fluents persist by inertia at $i = 2$. From the tabling viewpoint, the previous entries $fluent(a, 1)$, $fluent(b, 1)$, and $fluent(c, 1)$ linger in the table, and a simple check can be performed to verify that the truths of these fluents are not supervened by their complements at $i = 2$. That is, whether there are no $fluent(\sim a, 2)$, $fluent(\sim b, 2)$, and $fluent(\sim c, 2)$ entries in the table, which is indeed the case, and consequently confirms that the three fluents (a, b, and c) are inertially true at $i = 2$ (cf. I_2).

A subsequent update of fluent $\sim a$ at $i = 3$ via $incr\_assert(\sim a(3))$ results in tabling $fluent(\sim a, 3)$. That means, we still have all previous tabled entries, viz., $fluent(a, 1)$, $fluent(b, 1)$, and $fluent(c, 1)$, plus now $fluent(\sim a, 3)$, and a simple state comparison (fluent a at $i = 1$ is supervened by its complement $\sim a$ at a later state $i = 3$) concludes that fluent a is no longer true. Different from before, there is no propagation to fluents $\sim b$ nor $\sim c$ by this incremental assertion, i.e., no $fluent(\sim b, 3)$ and $fluent(\sim c, 3)$ in the table. Indeed, there are no corresponding rules in P for $\sim b$ and $\sim c$; thus failing to conclude that both fluents are also false at $i = 3$ (cf. I_3). We adopt the dual transformation (cf. Section 2.2) to provide rules for $\sim b$ and $\sim c$ from definitions of b and c:
$$\sim b \leftarrow \sim a. \qquad \sim c \leftarrow \sim b.$$

The introduced dual rules now allow the propagations from $\sim a$ to $\sim b$ and then to $\sim c$, resulting in having $fluent(\sim b, 3)$ and $fluent(\sim c, 3)$ in the table. By having the latter two entries in the table, using the same previous reasoning, it can be concluded that fluents b and c are also false at $i = 3$, confirming I_3.

The automatic system level updates propagation, by means of incremental tabling, is driven by a query at a *particular state*, known as a *query time*. Such a query triggers incremental assertions up to the given query time. Indeed, any updates have been kept pending, and only those up to the query time are made actual, if not already so. This mechanism affords us a form of controlled but automatic system level truth-maintenance, up to the given query time. It can be viewed as reconciling a high-level top-down deliberative reasoning (about a query) with low-level bottom-up world reactivity to updates; the latter is relegated to the system enacted incremental tabling feature.

3.2 Implementation

The idea is implemented by a compiled program transformation plus a library of reserved predicates.

Transformation. The transformation adds information and rules to program clauses:

1. *Timestamp* that corresponds to state and serves as the only extra argument of fluents. It denotes the time when a fluent is true (known as *holds time* in [20]). Compared to [20], there is no longer the need to carry the query time as an extra argument of fluents. Conceptually, the state of a fluent in time depends solely on the changes made to the world, and is independent of whether that world is being queried.
2. *Rule name* as a special fluent $\$rule(p/n, id_i)$, which identifies a rule of predicate p with arity n by its unique name identity id_i, and is introduced in its body, for checking that the rule is still active.

3. *Dual rules* that are obtained using the dual transformation for each atom with definitions in the input program.

The transformation technique is illustrated by Example 3, with the extra information and rules figuring in the transform (r and as in the sequel stand for predicates $rule$ and $assert$, respectively). In EVOLP/R, the initial timestamp is set at 1, when a program is inserted. Fluent predicates can be defined as facts (extensional) or by rules (intensional) or both. In Example 3, both fluents b and $as(\sim a)$ are defined intensionally. For such rule regulated intensional fluent instances, unique rule name fluents, i.e., $\$r(b/0, id_1)$ and $\$r(as(\sim a/0), id_1)$ for the first and the second rules, respectively, are introduced. They are extensional fluent instances, and like any other extensional fluent instances, such a rule name fluent is translated (cf. line 1) by adding an extra argument (the third one) that corresponds to its holds time; in this case, each rule name fluent is true at the initial time 1, i.e., the time when its corresponding rule is inserted.

Line 2 shows the translation of rule $b \leftarrow a$ of the input program. The single extra argument in its head is its holds time, H. Call to the goal a in the body is translated into calls to the reserved predicate $fluent/2$ (defined later), that provides their holds time. The subgoal calls $fluent(\$r(b/0, id_1), H_r)$ and $fluent(a, H_a)$ reflect the propagation of the unique rule name fluent $\$r(b/0, id_1)$ and fluent a, respectively, from the body to the head (i.e., fluent b). The holds time H of fluent b in the head is thus determined by which inertial fluent in its body holds latest, via the $latest/2$ reserved predicate (detailed later), assuring that no fluents in the body were subsequently superveneed by their complements at some time before H. Note the inclusion of the unique rule name fluent (i.e., the call $fluent(\$r(b/0, id_1), H_r)$) in the body, whose purpose is to switch the corresponding rule on or off.

The other rule of the input program, viz., $as(\sim a) \leftarrow b$, transforms into two rules: the transform in line 5 is similar to that of rule $b \leftarrow a$, whereas the one in line 8 is derived as the effect of asserting $\sim a$. That is, the truth of $\sim a$ is determined solely by the propagation of fluent $as(\sim a)$, indicated by the call $fluent(as(\sim a), H_{as})$. The holds time H of $\sim a$ is thus determined by $H_{as} + 1$ (rather than H_{as}, because $\sim a$ is actually asserted one time step after the time at which $as(\sim a)$ holds). This transform (line 8) is simpler compared to the one in [20] (cf. line 7 of Example 1 in [20]), because no extra reasoning with respect to query time is needed here (due to independence of the transform from query time). Such a simpler transformation consequently corresponds to less computation time: indeed, the extra reasoning with respect to query time Qt, in [20], requires recursively generating timestamps $T < Qt$, and checking via backtracking whether $assert(\sim a)$ holds at T.

Finally, lines 3 and 4 show the dual rules for b. Line 3 expresses how the conjugate $\sim\$r(b/0, id_1)$ of rule name fluent $\$r(b/0, id_1)$ propagates to fluent $\sim b$, whereas line 4 expresses the other alternative: how the conjugate $\sim a$ of a propagates to fluent $\sim b$. Observe that the dual rules are directly defined by unfolding b^{*1}, because b in the input program has only one definition (cf. the last paragraph of Section 2.2). With similar reasoning, lines 6 and 7 define the dual rules for $as(\sim a)$. Recall that dual rules are defined for each atom with definitions in the input program. Therefore, rules in the transform derived from another rule with $assert/1$ in the head, e.g., rule $\sim a/1$ in line 8 with no definition in the input program, do not have dual rules. From the semantics viewpoint, once $\sim a$ is asserted, its truth remains intact by inertia till superseded, even if $assert(\sim a)$ is retracted at a later time.

Since every fluent occurring in the program is subject to updates, all fluents and their complements should be declared as dynamic and incremental (due to incremental tabling), e.g., :- dynamic a/1,'~a'/1 as incremental (the same for fluents b, $as(\sim a)$, $\$r(b/0, id_1, 1)$, $\$r(as(\sim a/0), id_1, 1)$, as well as their complements).

Example 3. Program: $b \leftarrow a.$ $as(\sim a) \leftarrow b.$ transforms into:

1. $\$r(b/0, id_1, 1).$
2. $b(H) \leftarrow fluent(\$r(b/0, id_1), H_r), fluent(a, H_a),$
   $latest([(\$r(b/0, id_1), H_r), (a, H_a)], H).$
3. $\sim b(H) \leftarrow fluent(\sim\$r(b/0, id_1), H).$
4. $\sim b(H) \leftarrow fluent(\sim a, H).$
5. $as(\sim a, H) \leftarrow fluent(\$r(as(\sim a/0), id_1), H_r), fluent(b, H_b),$
   $latest([(\$r(as(\sim a/0), id_1), H_r), (b, H_b)], H).$
6. $\sim as(\sim a, H) \leftarrow fluent(\sim\$r(as(\sim a/0), id_1), H).$
7. $\sim as(\sim a, H) \leftarrow fluent(\sim b, H).$
8. $\sim a(H) \leftarrow fluent(as(\sim a), H_{as}), H$ is $H_{as} + 1.$

Example 4 focuses on the transformation of a rule with a default negation in its body. Apart from the usual rule name fluent in the body, the goal *not a* with default negation translates into a call to reserved predicate $fluent\_not/2$ (defined later), i.e., $fluent\_not(a, H_a)$; cf. line 2. Lines 3 and 4 are the dual rules for fluent b.

Example 4. Program: $b \leftarrow not\ a.$ transforms into:

1. $\$r(b/0, id_1, 1).$
2. $b(H) \leftarrow fluent(\$r(b/0, id_1), H_r), fluent\_not(a, H_a),$
   $latest([(\$r(b/0, id_1), H_r), (a, H_a)], H).$
3. $\sim b(H) \leftarrow fluent(\sim\$r(b/0, id_1), H).$
4. $\sim b(H) \leftarrow fluent(a, H).$

Reserved Predicates. Predicate $fluent/2$ used in the transformation is a tabled one, as described in Section 3.1. It depends on fluent definitions of F (which are dynamic incremental), and this dependency indicates that $fluent/2$ is tabled incrementally. It is declared as :- table fluent/2 as incremental, and defined as follows:

$$fluent(F, T) \leftarrow upper\_time(Lim), extend(F, [T], F'), call(F'), T \leq Lim.$$

where $extend(F, Args, F')$ extends the arguments of fluent F with those in list $Args$ to obtain F'. The definition requires a predefined upper time limit Lim, which is used to delimit updates propagation, i.e., to delimit answers in the $fluent/2$ table. The motivation for such an upper time limit was explained before, plus illustrated in the sequel.

For updates propagation to take place, initial calls $fluent(F, \_)$, for every fluent F, have to be made in order to initially create the table. Once created, the table is incrementally updated after every $incr\_assert/1$ call by propagating updates on which it depends. Updates propagation are controlled in two innovative ways:

1. *Activating pending updates till some query time.*
   In Section 3.1 we mentioned that updates propagation by incremental tabling is query-driven, within some query time of interest. This means we can use the given query time to control updates propagation by keeping the sequence of updates pending, say in the database, and then making active, through incremental assertions, only those with the states up to the actual query time (if they have not yet been so made already by queries of a later time stamp). For so doing, we may introduce a dynamic predicate $pending(F, T)$ to indicate that update of fluent F at state T is still pending, and use Prolog $assert/1$ predicate, i.e., $assert(pending(F, T))$ to assert such a pending fluent update into the Prolog database. Activating pending updates (up to the given query time Qt), as shown by the code below, can thus be done by calling all $pending(F, T)$ facts with $T \leq Qt$ from the database and actually asserting them incrementally using the system $incr\_assert/1$ predicate:

   $activate\_pending(Qt) \leftarrow pending(F, T), T \leq Qt, extend(F, [T], F'),$
   $\qquad\qquad\qquad\qquad incr\_assert(F'), retract(pending(F, T)), fail.$
   $activate\_pending(\_).$

   Note that a quasi forward-chaining approach [24] of incremental update through the use of $incr\_assert/1$ is employed, as opposed to the use of $incr\_assert\_inval/1$ system predicate of eager and lazy incremental update approaches [24]. Nevertheless, since pending updates are only made active on the initiative of top-goal queries, only those with timestamps up to an actual query time are actually asserted, i.e., by need only. Lazy evaluation by itself would not suffice to delimit actual updates to query time ceilings, and hence the need for pending updates.

2. *Limiting updates propagation to a predefined upper time limit.*
   Activating pending updates up to some query time does not guarantee termination of updates propagation, as Example 5 illustrates.

   Example 5. Consider program P: $\qquad as(\sim a) \leftarrow a. \qquad as(a) \leftarrow \sim a.$
   Given an external update $\langle E_1 \rangle$, where $E_1 = \{a\}$, the evolution of P in EVOLP/R is as follows: $P_1 = P$ with $I_1 = \{a, assert(\sim a)\}$, $P_2 = \{\sim a\}$ with $I_2 = \{\sim a, assert(a)\}$, $P_3 = \{a\}$ with $I_3 = \{a, assert(\sim a)\}$, $P_4 = \{\sim a\}$ with $I_4 = \{\sim a, assert(a)\}$, ... etc. (the evolution continues indefinitely)

   In this example the external update of a at state $i = 1$ leads to non-terminating propagation. From the incremental tabling viewpoint, it indicates that a predefined upper time limit is required to limit updates propagation, thereby avoiding infinite number of answers in the $fluent/2$ table. This requirement is realistic, as our view into the future may be bounded by some time horizon, comparable to bounded rationality. For this purpose, a dynamic predicate $upper\_time(Lim)$ is introduced to indicate the predefined upper time limit Lim, and used in the above $fluent/2$ definition to time-delimit their tabled answers. In the case of Example 5, by setting, e.g., $upper\_time(4)$, the $fluent/2$ table contains a finite number of answers: $fluent(a, 1), fluent(\sim a, 2), fluent(a, 3)$, and $fluent(\sim a, 4)$.

We have seen predicate $latest([(F_1, H_1), \ldots, (F_n, H_n)], H)$ in the transformation, which appears in the body of a rule transform, say of fluent F. This reserved predicate is responsible for obtaining the latest holds time H of F amongst fluents $F_1, \ldots, F_n$ in the body, while also assuring that none of them were subsequently supervened by their complements at some time up to H. It is defined as:

$$latest(Fs, H) \leftarrow greatest(Fs, H), not\_supervened(Fs, H).$$

where $greatest(Fs, H)$ extracts from list Fs, of (F_i, H_i) pairs with $1 \leq i \leq n$, the greatest holds time H among the Hi's, and predicate $not\_supervened(Fs, H)$ subsequently checks, by means of table inspection, that there is no fluent complement F'_i (with holds time H'_i) of F_i in Fs, such that $H_i < H'_i \leq H$.

Recall now Example 4. There, reserved predicate $fluent\_not/2$ is introduced. Its definition is given below:

(1) $fluent\_not(F, T) \leftarrow compl(F, F'), fluent(F', T).$
(2) $fluent\_not(F, T) \leftarrow nonvar(T), !, fail.$
(3) $fluent\_not(\_, 0).$

where $compl(F, F')$ obtains the fluent complement F' from F. Rule (1) captures the coherence principle [2], that states explicit negation entails default negation; in our case, negative fluents are treated as explicit negations, therefore they obey the principle. Rules (2) and (3) are the standard definition of default negation. Note that rule (3) artificially sets the timestamp to $T = 0$ for all fluents; for none are by then (before the "Big Bang" of the starting program update, which initially starts at $T = 1$) known to be true.

Given that an upper time limit has been set, and that the initial calls $fluent(F, \_)$ for every fluent F have been made, and that some pending updates may be available, the EVOLP/R system is ready for a top-goal query. The top-goal query $holds(F, Qt)$ verifies whether fluent F is true at query time Qt within the bounded time horizon (otherwise it is undefined). It does so by first activating pending updates up to Qt and then inspecting $fluent/2$ table to answer the query:

(1) $holds(\_, Qt) \quad \leftarrow upper\_time(Lim), (Qt > Lim ; Qt \leq 0), !, undefined.$
(2) $holds(not\ F, Qt) \leftarrow !, not\ holds(F, Qt).$
(3) $holds(F, Qt) \quad \leftarrow activate\_pending(Qt), compl(F, F'), inspect(F, H, Qt),$
$\quad\quad\quad\quad\quad\quad\quad (H \neq 0 \rightarrow (inspect(F', H', Qt), H \geq H') ; fail).$

where $inspect(F, H, Qt)$ inspects the $fluent/2$ table and looks for entries of fluent F with the highest timestamp $H \leq Qt$. XSB provides various table inspection predicates, e.g., $get\_returns\_for\_call/2$ may be used. If there is no such fluent F in the table, $H = 0$ is returned, making $holds(F, Qt)$ fail, due to the last conditional subgoal in the body. Otherwise, this conditional goal exercises the table inspection of its complement fluent F' to obtain its highest timestamp H', and succeeds only if $H \geq H'$, i.e., checks that fluent F is not supervened at a later time by its complement F'. Note that this allows for paraconsistency (case $H = H'$), to be dealt by the user as desired, e.g., by integrity constraints or preferences, but this matter is beyond the scope of the paper.

Example 6. Recall Example 3, which is loaded initially at time 1. Suppose that the upper time limit is set to $upper\_limit(5)$, and calls $fluent(F, \_)$ and $fluent(F', \_)$, where F' is the complement of F, have been made for every fluent F in the transform, i.e., $F = \{a, b, as(\sim a), \$r(b/0, id_1, 1), \$r(as(\sim a/0), id_1, 1)\}$. Note that, because rule name fluents are already inserted (as fluent facts) in the program (cf. line 1 of Example 3), these $fluent/2$ calls result in having entries $fluent(\$r(b/0, id_1), 1)$ and $fluent(\$r(as(\sim a/0), id_1), 1)$ in the table. Now, assume further that two pending external updates are available, viz., $pending(a, 1)$ and $pending(b, 4)$, that correspond to external updates of fluent a at $i = 1$ and fluent b at $i = 4$, respectively. In other words, $\langle E_1, E_2, E_3, E_4 \rangle$ is the external updates sequence with $E_1 = \{a\}$, $E_2 = E_3 = \emptyset$, and $E_4 = \{b\}$. The following queries show that their answers conform to the evolution model of the program given the above external updates sequence:

1. When $holds(b, 1)$ is queried, it first activates pending updates up to $Qt = 1$, via subgoal $activate\_pending(1)$, thereby incrementally asserting $a(1)$ only, and keeping $pending(b, 4)$ still intact. The incremental assertion of $a(1)$ results in having $fluent(a, 1)$ in the table, and henceforth propagates to update fluents b (by rule 2), $as(\sim a)$ (by rule 5), $\sim a$ (by rule 8), $\sim b$ (by rule 4), and $\sim as(\sim a)$ (by rule 7). These make $fluent(b, 1), fluent(as(\sim a), 1), fluent(\sim a, 2), fluent(\sim b, 2)$, and $fluent(\sim as(\sim a), 2)$ added into the table. When subgoal $inspect(b, H, 1)$ of $holds(b, 1)$ is called, it returns $H = 1$, and since $H \neq 0$, call $inspect(\sim b, H', 1)$ is subsequently made, in which case $H' = 0$ is returned (no $fluent(\sim b, H')$ with $H' \leq 1$ in the table). This eventually makes $holds(b, 1)$ succeed, because condition $H \geq H'$ in the definition of $holds/2$ is satisfied.
2. A similar reasoning applies when $holds(b, 2)$ is queried, but now no more pending updates up to $Qt = 2$ are available. The subgoal calls $inspect(b, H, 2)$ returns $H = 1$ and $inspect(\sim b, H', 2)$ returns $H' = 2$, in which case the condition $H \geq H'$ is unsatisfied, and therefore $holds(a, 2)$ fails, i.e., fluent a does not hold at state $i = 2$.
3. It is easy to confirm, that query $holds(b, 3)$ still fails. Indeed, it persists by inertia.
4. Finally, when $holds(b, 4)$ is queried, the only pending update $pending(b, 4)$ is made active by incrementally asserting $b(4)$ and tabling $fluent(b, 4)$. This propagates to adding several entries into the table: $fluent(as(\sim a), 4), fluent(\sim a, 5)$, $fluent(\sim b, 5)$, and $fluent(\sim as(\sim a), 5)$. Therefore, subgoal call $inspect(b, H, 4)$ now returns $H = 4$, call $inspect(\sim b, H', 2)$ still returns $H' = 2$, and $H \geq H'$ is satisfied, making $holds(b, 4)$ succeed.
5. With the current entries in the $fluent/2$ table, one may verify that $holds(b, 5)$ fails.

4 Related Work

Many Prolog systems are nowadays adopting tabling, though none has gone as far as XSB Prolog, namely in allowing tabling over default negation, and providing together answer subsumption, incremental tabling, and threads with shared tables. Consequently, there are also limited applications of these features, particularly of incremental tabling. Known applications are in pointer analyses of C programs in the context of incremental program analyses [18], data flow analyses [19], static analyses [6], incremental validation of XML documents and push down model checking [17]. But we are not aware of any work on employing incremental tabling for logic program updates as we do here.

Updates propagation has been well studied in the field of deductive databases, e.g., [5, 7, 13]. Similar to what we do here, updates propagation in these works aims at computing implicit changes of derived relations caused by explicit updates of extensional facts. Methods in updates propagation consist of bottom-up and top-down approaches. In [5], both approaches are combined, sharing the same basic idea with ours, i.e., to control bottom-up propagation with a top-down evaluation strategy. But different from ours, it does not use any Prolog tabling features, particularly incremental tabling, but employs instead the Magic Sets approach. Others, like [13], employ a purely top-down approach by querying the relevant portion of the database, whereas [7] focuses on bottom-up methods of updates propagation.

Logic-based Production System (LPS) with abduction [11] is a distinct but somewhat similar and complementary approach to ours. It aims at defining a new logic-based framework for knowledge representation and reasoning, relying on the fundamental role of state transition systems in computing, and involving fluent updates by destructive assignment. It is implemented in LPA Prolog [14] but no details are given about that. Their approach differs from ours in that it defines a new language and an operational semantics, rather than taking an existing one, and implements it on a commercial system (LPA Prolog) with no underlying tabling mechanisms. Moreover, in our work fluent updates are not managed by destructive database assignments, but rather tabled, thereby allowing to inspect their truths at a particular time, e.g., querying the past. Furthermore, full knowledge about each fluent in each state is not presupposed, so that only those fluents are updated for which changes are known about. Subsequent knowledge, say about updates on the world by another agent, or by yet unmeasured world processes, may change the picture of the world to a more complete one. In any case, the emergence and propagation of changes prepare the way for the wider topic of teleo-reactive systems [12, 15].

Regarding other related work, the use of incremental tabling in this paper is very strongly related to the (also incremental, and also tabling-based) algorithms employed in the compile-time analyses of logic programs (e.g., [10] and other connected papers). It could be interesting to compare the algorithms in incremental analysis and our work (which relies on the underlying incremental tabling algorithms of XSB), because some techniques used in incremental analyses might be useful in the context of incremental tabling (and vice-versa). Incremental analyses also table answers (like answers of $fluent/2$ in our work) and include algorithms to incrementally add, delete or modify a clause of a predicate. Furthermore, there exist several specific optimizations and techniques used in these incremental analysis algorithms which may be beneficial in the context of the tabling procedure proposed here, namely: (1) Being cautious about changes in the database that only affect a small subset of it (called local change in Section 5.1 of [10]); (2) Whereas we present in Example 5 a case in which propagation does not terminate, and solve such cases by delimiting propagation to a predefined upper time limit, it may be opportune to consider operators similar to the widening operator of abstract interpretation, which lose precision on the tabling (possibly leading to answers being recomputed), but ensure termination.

Our approach to limit updates propagation, using a predefined time limit as a bound, has the same overall purpose as XSB's recent tabling feature: answer abstraction [8], i.e., to guarantee termination in tabling by ensuring that only a finite number of answers are generated by a query. In answer abstraction, this is achieved via a form of bounded rationality, viz., radial restraint, and is realized by bounding the depth of an answer.

5 Conclusion

We have propounded in detail an implementation technique to logic program updates by further exploiting incremental tabling in logic programming (available in XSB Prolog), which enriches the applicability of the incremental tabling feature to dynamic environments and evolving systems, and that might be adopted elsewhere for reasoning in logic. The implementation technique proposed much refines our previous approach by leaving out the answer subsumption feature that was heretofore employed to address the frame problem. Instead, we rely fully on incremental tabling by separating knowledge updates from queries on them; the former takes place independently from the latter. Incremental tabling allows updates propagation, which is controlled by initially keeping updates pending and making active only those with timestamp up to an actual query time, on the initiative of queries. Possible non-terminating updates propagation is avoided by setting a predefined upper time limit for queries, and the direct access to the latest time a fluent is true is achieved by table inspection predicates. Moreover, we adopt the dual transformation from abduction and adapt it for helping propagate also the complement of fluents incrementally. In summary, our approach affords us a form of controlled (i.e., query-driven) but automatic system level truth-maintenance (i.e., automatic updates propagation via incremental tabling), up to actual query time.

Our future work consists of integrating tabled abduction [21] with EVOLP/R, so as to jointly afford abduction and updating in one integrated XSB system. We intend to apply the system to abductive moral reasoning [9], with updating and argumentation, as a sequel to our ongoing approach to using logic for reasoning.

Acknowledgements. Ari Saptawijaya acknowledges the support of Fundação para a Ciência e a Tecnologia (FCT/MEC) Portugal, grant SFRH/BD/72795/2010. We thank the anonymous reviewers for their helpful suggestions.

References

1. Alferes, J.J., Brogi, A., Leite, J.A., Pereira, L.M.: Evolving logic programs. In: Flesca, S., Greco, S., Leone, N., Ianni, G. (eds.) JELIA 2002. LNCS (LNAI), vol. 2424, pp. 50–61. Springer, Heidelberg (2002)
2. Alferes, J.J., Pereira, L.M. (eds.): Reasoning with Logic Programming. LNCS (LNAI), vol. 1111. Springer, Berlin (1996)
3. Alferes, J.J., Pereira, L.M., Swift, T.: Abduction in well-founded semantics and generalized stable models via tabled dual programs. Theory and Practice of Logic Programming 4(4), 383–428 (2004)
4. Banti, F., Alferes, J.J., Brogi, A.: Well founded semantics for logic program updates. In: Lemaître, C., Reyes, C.A., González, J.A. (eds.) IBERAMIA 2004. LNCS (LNAI), vol. 3315, pp. 397–407. Springer, Heidelberg (2004)

5. Behrend, A., Manthey, R.: Update propagation in deductive databases using soft stratification. In: Benczúr, A.A., Demetrovics, J., Gottlob, G. (eds.) ADBIS 2004. LNCS, vol. 3255, pp. 22–36. Springer, Heidelberg (2004)
6. Eichberg, M., Kahl, M., Saha, D., Mezini, M., Ostermann, K.: Automatic incrementalization of Prolog based static analyses. In: Hanus, M. (ed.) PADL 2007. LNCS, vol. 4354, pp. 109–123. Springer, Heidelberg (2007)
7. Griefahn, U.: Reactive Model Computation - A Uniform Approach to the Implementation of Deductive Databases. PhD thesis, University of Bonn (1997)
8. Grosof, B.N., Swift, T.: Radial restraint: A semantically clean approach to bounded rationality for logic programs. In: AAAI 2013. The AAAI Press (2013)
9. Han, T.A., Saptawijaya, A., Moniz Pereira, L.: Moral reasoning under uncertainty. In: Bjørner, N., Voronkov, A. (eds.) LPAR-18 2012. LNCS, vol. 7180, pp. 212–227. Springer, Heidelberg (2012)
10. Hermenegildo, M., Puebla, G., Marriott, K., Stuckey, P.: Incremental analysis of constraint logic programs. ACM Transactions on Programming Languages and Systems 22(2), 187–223 (2000)
11. Kowalski, R., Sadri, F.: Abductive logic programming agents with destructive databases. Annals of Mathematics and Artificial Intelligence 62(1), 129–158 (2011)
12. Kowalski, R.A., Sadri, F.: Teleo-reactive abductive logic programs. In: Artikis, A., Craven, R., Kesim Çiçekli, N., Sadighi, B., Stathis, K. (eds.) Sergot Festschrift 2012. LNCS, vol. 7360, pp. 12–32. Springer, Heidelberg (2012)
13. Küchenhoff, V.: On the efficient computation of the difference between consecutive database states. In: Delobel, C., Masunaga, Y., Kifer, M. (eds.) DOOD 1991. LNCS, vol. 566, pp. 478–502. Springer, Heidelberg (1991)
14. Logic Programming Associates Ltd. LPA prolog, http://www.lpa.co.uk/
15. Nilsson, N.: Teleo-reactive programs for agent control. Journal of Artificial Intelligence Research 1, 139–158 (1994)
16. Poole, D.L.: A logical framework for default reasoning. Artificial Intelligence 36(1), 27–47 (1988)
17. Saha, D.: Incremental Evaluation of Tabled Logic Programs. PhD thesis, SUNY Stony Brook (2006)
18. Saha, D., Ramakrishnan, C.R.: Incremental and demand-driven points-to analysis using logic programming. In: ACM PPDP 2005, pp. 117–128. ACM (2005)
19. Saha, D., Ramakrishnan, C.R.: A local algorithm for incremental evaluation of tabled logic programs. In: Etalle, S., Truszczyński, M. (eds.) ICLP 2006. LNCS, vol. 4079, pp. 56–71. Springer, Heidelberg (2006)
20. Saptawijaya, A., Pereira, L.M.: Program updating by incremental and answer subsumption tabling. In: Cabalar, P., Son, T.C. (eds.) LPNMR 2013. LNCS, vol. 8148, pp. 479–484. Springer, Heidelberg (2013)
21. Saptawijaya, A., Pereira, L.M.: Tabled abduction in logic programs (technical communication of ICLP 2013). Theory and Practice of Logic Programming, Online Supplement 13(4-5) (2013)
22. Swift, T., Warren, D.S.: Tabling with answer subsumption: Implementation, applications and performance. In: Janhunen, T., Niemelä, I. (eds.) JELIA 2010. LNCS, vol. 6341, pp. 300–312. Springer, Heidelberg (2010)
23. Swift, T., Warren, D.S.: XSB: Extending Prolog with tabled logic programming. Theory and Practice of Logic Programming 12(1-2), 157–187 (2012)
24. Swift, T., Warren, D.S., Sagonas, K., Freire, J., Rao, P., Cui, B., Johnson, E., de Castro, L., Marques, R.F., Saha, D., Dawson, S., Kifer, M.: The XSB System Version 3.3.x, vol. 1. Programmer's Manual (2012)
25. van Gelder, A., Ross, K.A., Schlipf, J.S.: The well-founded semantics for general logic programs. Journal of ACM 38(3), 620–650 (1991)

Tracking Data-Flow with Open Closure Types

Gabriel Scherer[1] and Jan Hoffmann[2]

[1] INRIA Paris-Rocquencourt
[2] Yale University

Abstract. Type systems hide data that is captured by function closures in function types. In most cases this is a beneficial design that enables simplicity and compositionality. However, some applications require explicit information about the data that is captured in closures.

This paper introduces open closure types, that is, function types that are decorated with type contexts. They are used to track data-flow from the environment into the function closure. A simply-typed lambda calculus is used to study the properties of the type theory of open closure types. A distinctive feature of this type theory is that an open closure type of a function can vary in different type contexts. To present an application of the type theory, it is shown that a type derivation establishes a simple non-interference property in the sense of information-flow theory. A publicly available prototype implementation of the system can be used to experiment with type derivations for example programs.

Keywords: Type Systems, Closure Types, Information Flow.

1 Introduction

Function types in traditional type systems only provide information about the arguments and return values of the functions but not about the data that is captured in function closures. Such function types naturally lead to simple and compositional type systems.

Recently, syntax-directed type systems have been increasingly used to statically verify strong program properties such as resource usage [8,7,6], information flow [5,15], and termination [1,3,2]. In such type systems, it is sometimes necessary and natural to include information in the function types about the data that is captured by closures. To see why, assume that we want to design a type system to verify resource usage. Now consider for example the curried append function for integer lists which has the following type in OCaml.

$$\text{append} : \textit{int list} \to \textit{int list} \to \textit{int list}$$

At first glance, we might say that the time complexity of append is $O(n)$ if n is the length of the first argument. But a closer inspection of the definition of append reveals that this is a gross simplification. In fact, the complexity of the partial function call app_par = append ℓ is constant. Moreover, the complexity of the function app_par is linear—not in the length of the argument but in the length of the list ℓ that is captured in the function closure.

In general, we have to describe the resource consumption of a curried function $f : A_1 \to \cdots \to A_n \to A$ with n expressions $c_i(a_1, \ldots, a_i)$ such that c_i describes the complexity of the computation that takes place after f is applied to i arguments $a_1, \ldots, a_i$. We are not aware of any existing type system that can verify a statement of this form.

To express the aforementioned statement in a type system, we have to decorate the function types with additional information about the data that is captured in a function closure. It is however not sufficient to directly describe the complexity of a closure in terms of its arguments and the data captured in the closure. Admittedly, this would work to accurately describe the resource usage in our example function **append** because the first argument is directly captured in the closure. But in general, the data captured in a closure $f a_1 \cdots a_i$ can be any data that is computed from the arguments $a_1, \ldots, a_i$ (and from the data in the environment). To reference this data in the types would not only be meaningless for a user, it would also hamper the compositionality of the type system. It is for instance unclear how to define subtyping for closures that capture different data (which is, e.g., needed in the two branches of a conditional.)

To preserve the compositionality of traditional type systems, we propose to describe the resource usage of a closure as a function of its argument and the data that is visible in the current environment. To this end we introduce *open closure types*, function types that refer to their arguments and to the data in the current environment.

More formally, consider a typing judgment of the form $\Gamma \vdash e : \sigma$, in a type system that tracks fine-grained intensional properties characterizing not only the shape of values, but the behavior of the reduction of e into a value (e.g., resource usage). A typing rule for open closure types, $\Gamma, \Delta \vdash e : [\Gamma'](x{:}\sigma) \to \tau$, captures the idea that, under a weak reduction semantics, the computation of the closure itself, and later the computation of the closure *application*, will have very different behaviors, captured by two different typing environments Γ and Γ' of the same domain, the free variables of e. To describe the complexity of **append**, we might for instance have a statement

$$\ell{:}int\ list \vdash \mathbf{append}\ \ell : [\ell{:}int\ list](y{:}int\ list) \to int\ list\ .$$

This puts us in a position to use type annotations to describe the resource usage of **append** ℓ as a function of ℓ and the future argument y. For example, using type-based amortized analysis [6], we can express a bound on the number of created list notes in **append** with the following open closure type.

$$\mathbf{append} : [](x{:}int\ list^0) \to [x{:}int\ list^1](y{:}int\ list^0) \to int\ list^0\ .$$

The intuitive meaning of this type for **append** is as follows. To pay for the cons operations in the evaluation of **append** ℓ_1 we need $0 \cdot |\ell_1|$ resource units and to pay for the cons operations in the evaluation of **append** $\ell_1\ \ell_2$ we need $0 \cdot |\ell_1| + 1 \cdot |\ell_2|$ resource units.

The development of a type system for open closure types entails some interesting technical challenges: term variables now appear in types, which requires mechanisms for scope management not unlike dependent type theories. If x

appears in σ, the context $\Gamma, x{:}\tau, y{:}\sigma$ is not exchangeable with $\Gamma, y{:}\sigma, x{:}\tau$. Similarly, the judgment $\Gamma, x{:}\tau \vdash e_2 : \sigma$ will not entail $\Gamma \vdash \mathtt{let}\, x = e_1 \,\mathtt{in}\, e_2 : \sigma$, as the return type σ may contain open closures scoping over x, so we need to substitute variables in types.

The main contribution of this paper is a type theory of open closure types and the proof of its main properties. We start from the simply-typed lambda calculus, and consider the simple intensional property of data-flow tracking, annotating each simply-typed lambda-calculus type with a single boolean variable. This allows us to study the metatheory of open closure types in clean and straightforward way. This is the first important step for using such types in more sophisticated type systems for resource usage and termination.

Our type system for data-flow tracking captures higher-order data-flow information. As a byproduct, we get our secondary contribution, a non-interference property in the sense of information flow theory: high-level inputs do not influence the (low-level) results of computations.

To experiment with of our type system, we implemented a software prototype in OCaml (see Section 5). A full version of this article, containing the full proofs and additional details and discussion, is available online.[1]

Related Work. In our type system we maintain the invariant that open closure types only refer to variables that are present in the current typing context. This is a feature that distinguishes open closure types from existing formalisms for closure types.

For example, while our function type $[\Gamma^\Phi](x{:}\sigma_1) \to \sigma_2$ superficially resembles a contextual arrow type $[\Psi](\sigma_1 \to \sigma_2)$ of contextual type theory[12,14,16], we are not aware of any actual connection in application or metatheory with these systems. In particular, the variable in our captured context Γ^Φ are *bound occurrences* of the ambient typing context, while the context Ψ of a contextual type $[\Psi]T$ *binds* metavariables to be used to construct inhabitants. As such a binding can make sense in any context, our substitution judgment has no counterpart in contextual type theory, or other modal type theories for multi-stage programming ([11,17]).

Having closure types carry a set of captured variables has been done in the literature, as for example in Leroy [9], which use closure types to keep track of of *dangerous type variables* that can not be generalized without breaking type safety, or in the higher-order lifetime analysis of Hannan et al. [4], where variable sets denote variables that must be kept in memory. However, these works have no need to vary function types in different typing contexts and subtyping can be defined using set inclusion, which makes the metatheory significantly simpler. On the contrary, our scoping mechanism allows to study more complex properties, such as value dependencies and non-interference.

The classical way to understand value capture in closures in a typed way is through the *typed closure conversion* of Minamide et al. [10]. They use existential types to account for hidden data in function closures without losing

---

[1] http://hal.inria.fr/INRIA-RRRT/hal-00851658

compositionality, by abstracting over the difference between functions capturing from different environments. Our system retains this compositionality, albeit in a less apparent way: we get finer-grained information about the dependency of a closure on the ambient typing environment. Typed closure conversion is still possible, and could be typed in a more precise way, abstracting only over values that are outside the lexical context.

Petricek et al. [13] study *coeffects* systems with judgments of the form $C^r \Gamma \vdash e : \tau$ and function types $C^s \sigma \to \tau$, where r and s are coeffect annotations over an indexed comonad C. Their work is orthogonal to the present one. They study comonadic semantics and algebraic structure of effect indices. These indices are simply booleans in our work but we focus on the syntactic scoping rules that arise from tracking each variable of the context separately.

The non-interference property that we prove is different from the usual treatment in type systems for information flow like the SLam Calculus [5]. In SLam, the information flow into closure is accounted for at abstraction time. In contrast, we account for the information flow into the closure at application time.

2 A Type System for Open Closures

We define a type system for the simplest problem domain that exhibits a need for open closure types. Our goal is to determine statically, for an open term e, on which variables of the environment the value of e depends.

We are interested in weak reduction, and assume a call-by-value reduction strategy. In this context, an abstraction $\lambda x.e$ is already a value, so reducing it does not depend on the environment at all. More generally, for a term e evaluating to a function (closure), we make a distinction between the part of the environment the reduction of e depends on, and the part that will be used when the resulting closure will be applied. For example, the term $(y, \lambda x.z)$ depends on the variable y at evaluation time, but will not need the variable z until the closure in the right pair component is applied.

This is where we need open closure types. Our function types are of the form $[\Gamma^\Phi](x{:}\sigma^\phi) \to \tau$, where the mapping Φ from variables to Booleans indicates on which variables the evaluation depends at application time. The Boolean ϕ indicates whether the argument x is used in the function body. We call Φ the dependency annotation of Γ. Our previous example would for instance be typed as follows.

$$y{:}\sigma^1, z{:}\tau^0 \vdash (y, \lambda x.z) : \sigma * ([y{:}\sigma^0, z{:}\tau^1](x{:}\rho^0) \to \tau)$$

The typing expresses that the result of the computation depends on the variable y but not on the variable z. Moreover, result of the function in the second component of the pair depends on z but not on y.

In general, types are defined by the following grammar.

$$
\begin{aligned}
\textsf{Types} \ni \sigma, \tau, \rho ::= & & \text{types} \\
\mid \ & \alpha & \text{atoms} \\
\mid \ & \tau_1 * \tau_2 & \text{products} \\
\mid \ & [\Gamma^\Phi](x{:}\sigma^\phi) \to \tau & \text{closures}
\end{aligned}
$$

$$\frac{}{\emptyset \vdash} \text{Scope-Context-Nil} \qquad \frac{\Gamma \vdash \sigma}{\Gamma, x{:}\sigma \vdash} \text{Scope-Context} \qquad \frac{\Gamma \vdash}{\Gamma \vdash \alpha} \text{Scope-Atom}$$

$$\frac{\Gamma \vdash \tau_1 \quad \Gamma \vdash \tau_2}{\Gamma \vdash \tau_1 * \tau_2} \text{Scope-Product} \qquad \frac{\Gamma_0, \Gamma_1 \vdash \quad \Gamma_0 \vdash \sigma \quad \Gamma_0, x{:}\sigma \vdash \tau}{\Gamma_0, \Gamma_1 \vdash [\Gamma_0^{\Phi}](x{:}\sigma^{\phi}) \to \tau} \text{Scope-Closure}$$

Fig. 1. Well-scoping of types and contexts

The closure type $[\Gamma^{\Phi}](x{:}\sigma^{\phi}) \to \tau$ binds the new argument variable x, but not the variables occurring in Γ which are reference variables bound in the current typing context. Such a type is *well-scoped* only when all the variables it closes over are actually present in the current context. In particular, it has no meaning in an empty context, unless Γ is itself empty.

We define well-scoping judgments on contexts ($\Gamma \vdash$) and types ($\Gamma \vdash \sigma$). The judgments are defined simultaneously in Figure 1 and refer to each another. They use non-annotated contexts: the dependency annotations characterize data-flow information of *terms*, and are not needed to state the well-formedness of static types and contexts.

Notice that the closure contexts appearing in the return type of a closure, τ in our rule Scope-Closure, may capture the variable x corresponding to the function argument, which is why we chose the dependent-arrow–like notation $(x{:}\sigma) \to \tau$ rather than only $\sigma \to \tau$. There is no dependency of types on terms in this system, this is only used for scope tracking.

Note that $\Gamma \vdash \sigma$ implies $\Gamma \vdash$ (as proved by direct induction until an atom or a function closure is reached). Note also that a context type $[\Gamma_0](x{:}\sigma) \to \tau$ is well-scoped in any larger environment Γ_0, Γ_1: the context information may only mention variables existing in the typing context, but it need not mention all of them. As a result, well-scoping is preserved by context extension: if $\Gamma_0 \vdash \sigma$ and $\Gamma_0, \Gamma_1 \vdash$, then $\Gamma_0, \Gamma_1 \vdash \sigma$.

A Term Language, and a Naive Attempt at a Type System. Our term language, is the lambda calculus with pairs, let bindings and fixpoints. This language is sufficient to discuss the most interesting problems that arise in an application of closure types in a more realistic language.

$$
\begin{array}{rll}
\texttt{Terms} \ni t, u, e ::= & & \text{terms} \\
\mid & x & \text{variables} \\
\mid & (e_1, e_2) & \text{pairs} \\
\mid & \pi_i(e) & \text{projections } (i \in \{1, 2\}) \\
\mid & \lambda x.e & \text{lambda abstractions} \\
\mid & t\ u & \text{applications} \\
\mid & \texttt{let } x = e_1 \texttt{ in } e_2 & \text{let declarations}
\end{array}
$$

For didactic purposes, we start with an intuitive type system presented in Figure 2. The judgment $\Gamma^{\Phi} \vdash e : \sigma$ means that the expression e has type σ, in

$$
\begin{array}{c}
\text{VAR} \\
\dfrac{\Gamma, x{:}\sigma, \Delta \vdash}{\Gamma^0, x{:}\sigma^1, \Delta^0 \vdash x : \sigma}
\end{array}
\qquad
\begin{array}{c}
\text{PRODUCT} \\
\dfrac{\Gamma^{\Phi_1} \vdash e_1 : \tau_1 \quad \Gamma^{\Phi_2} \vdash e_2 : \tau_2}{\Gamma^{\Phi_1+\Phi_2} \vdash (e_1, e_2) : \tau_1 * \tau_2}
\end{array}
\qquad
\begin{array}{c}
\text{PROJ} \\
\dfrac{\Gamma^{\Phi} \vdash e : \tau_1 * \tau_2}{\Gamma^{\Phi} \vdash \pi_i(e) : \tau_i}
\end{array}
$$

$$
\begin{array}{c}
\text{LAM} \\
\dfrac{\Gamma^{\Phi}, x{:}\sigma^{\phi} \vdash t : \tau}{\Gamma^0 \vdash \lambda x.t : [\Gamma^{\Phi}](x{:}\sigma^{\phi}) \to \tau}
\end{array}
\qquad
\begin{array}{c}
\text{LET-TMP} \\
\dfrac{\Gamma^{\Phi_{\text{def}}} \vdash e_1 : \sigma \quad \Gamma^{\Phi_{\text{body}}}, x{:}\sigma^{\phi} \vdash e_2 : \tau}{\Gamma^{\phi.\Phi_{\text{def}}+\Phi_{\text{body}}} \vdash \text{let } x = e_1 \text{ in } e_2 : \tau}
\end{array}
$$

$$
\begin{array}{c}
\text{APP-TMP} \\
\dfrac{(\Gamma_0, \Gamma_1)^{\Phi_{\text{fun}}} \vdash t : [\Gamma_0^{\Phi_{\text{clos}}}](x{:}\sigma^{\phi}) \to \tau \quad (\Gamma_0, \Gamma_1)^{\Phi_{\text{arg}}} \vdash u : \sigma}{(\Gamma_0, \Gamma_1)^{\Phi_{\text{fun}}+\Phi_{\text{clos}}+\phi.\Phi_{\text{arg}}} \vdash t\, u : \tau}
\end{array}
$$

Fig. 2. Naive rules for the type system

the context Γ carrying the intensional information Φ. Context variable mapped to 0 in Φ are not used during the reduction of e to a value. We will show that the rules APP-TMP and LET-TMP are not correct, and introduce a new judgment to develop correct versions of the rules.

In a judgment $\Gamma^0 \vdash \lambda x.t : [\Gamma^{\Phi}](x{:}\sigma^0) \to \tau$, Γ is bound only in one place (the context), and α-renaming any of its variable necessitates a mirroring change in its right-hand-side occurrences (Γ^{Φ} but also in σ and τ), while x is independently bound in the term and in the type, so the aforementioned type is equivalent to $[\Gamma^{\Phi}](y{:}\sigma) \to \tau[y/x]$. In particular, variables occurring in types do *not* reveal implementation details of the underlying term.

The syntax $\phi.\Phi$ used in the APP-TMP and LET-TMP rules is a product, or conjunction, of the single boolean dependency annotation ϕ, and of the vector dependency annotation Φ. The sum $\Phi_1 + \Phi_2$ is the disjunction. In the LET-TMP rule for example, if the typing of e_2 determines that the evaluation of e_2 does not depend on the definition $x = e_1$ (ϕ is 0), then $\phi.\Phi_{\text{def}}$ will mark all the variables used by e_1 as not needed as well (all 0), and only the variables needed by e_2 will be marked in the result annotation $\phi.\Phi_{\text{def}} + \Phi_{\text{body}}$.

In the scoping judgment $\Gamma \vdash [\Gamma^{\Phi}](x{:}\sigma) \to \tau$, the repetition of the judgment Γ is redundant. We could simply write $[\Phi](x{:}\sigma) \to \tau$; – because in our simplified setting the intensional information Φ can be easily separated from the rest of the typing information, corresponding to simply-typed types. However, we found out that such a reformulation made technical developments harder to follow; the Γ^{Φ} form allows one to keep track precisely of the domain of the dependency annotation, and domain changes are precisely the difficult technical aspect of open closure types. For a more detailed discussion of this design point, see the full version of this article.

Maintaining Closure Contexts. As pointed out before, the rules APP-TMP and LET-TMP of the system above are wrong (hence the "temporary" name): the left-hand-side of the rule APP-TMP assumes that the closure captures the same environment Γ that it is computed in. This property is initially true in the closure of the rule LAM, but is not preserved by LET-TMP (for the body type) or

$$\text{Subst-Context-Nil} \quad \Gamma, y{:}\rho, \emptyset \overset{y\backslash\Psi}{\leadsto} \Gamma$$

$$\text{Subst-Context} \quad \frac{\Gamma, y{:}\rho, \Delta \vdash \sigma \overset{y\backslash\Psi}{\leadsto} \Gamma, \Delta' \vdash \tau}{\Gamma, y{:}\rho, \Delta, x{:}\sigma \overset{y\backslash\Psi}{\leadsto} \Gamma, \Delta', x{:}\tau}$$

$$\text{Subst-Atom} \quad \frac{\Gamma, y{:}\rho, \Delta \overset{y\backslash\Psi}{\leadsto} \Gamma, \Delta'}{\Gamma, y{:}\rho, \Delta \vdash \alpha \overset{y\backslash\Psi}{\leadsto} \Gamma, \Delta' \vdash \alpha}$$

$$\text{Subst-Product} \quad \frac{\Gamma, y{:}\rho, \Delta \vdash \sigma_1 \overset{y\backslash\Psi}{\leadsto} \Gamma, \Delta' \vdash \tau_1 \quad \Gamma, y{:}\rho, \Delta \vdash \sigma_2 \overset{y\backslash\Psi}{\leadsto} \Gamma, \Delta' \vdash \tau_2}{\Gamma, y{:}\rho, \Delta \vdash \sigma_1 * \sigma_2 \overset{y\backslash\Psi}{\leadsto} \Gamma, \Delta' \vdash \tau_1 * \tau_2}$$

$$\text{Subst-Closure-NotIn} \quad \frac{\Gamma_0, \Gamma_1, y{:}\rho, \Delta \overset{y\backslash\Psi}{\leadsto} \Gamma_0, \Gamma_1, \Delta'}{\Gamma_0, \Gamma_1, y{:}\rho, \Delta \vdash [\Gamma_0^\Phi](x{:}\sigma_1^\phi) \to \sigma_2 \overset{y\backslash\Psi}{\leadsto} \Gamma_0, \Gamma_1, \Delta' \vdash [\Gamma_0^\Phi](x{:}\sigma_1^\phi) \to \sigma_2}$$

$$\text{Subst-Closure} \quad \frac{\Gamma, y{:}\rho, \Delta, \Gamma_1 \overset{y\backslash\Psi}{\leadsto} \Gamma, \Delta', \Gamma_1' \quad \Gamma, y{:}\rho, \Delta \vdash \sigma_1 \overset{y\backslash\Psi}{\leadsto} \Gamma, \Delta' \vdash \sigma_1 \quad \Gamma, y{:}\rho, \Delta, x{:}\sigma_1 \vdash \sigma_2 \overset{y\backslash\Psi}{\leadsto} \Gamma, \Delta', x{:}\sigma_1 \vdash \tau_2}{\Gamma, y{:}\rho, \Delta, \Gamma_1 \vdash [\Gamma^{\Phi_1}, y{:}\rho^{\chi}, \Delta^{\Phi_2}](x{:}\sigma_1^\phi) \to \sigma_2 \overset{y\backslash\Psi}{\leadsto} \Gamma, \Delta', \Gamma_1' \vdash [\Gamma^{\Phi_1 + \chi.\Psi}, \Delta'^{\Phi_2}](x{:}\sigma_1^\phi) \to \tau_2}$$

Fig. 3. Type substitution

App-Tmp (for the return type). This means that the intensional information in a type may become stale, mentioning variables that have been removed from the context. We will now fix the type system to never mention unbound variables.

We need a *closure substitution mechanism* to explain the closure type $\tau_f = [\Gamma^\Phi, y{:}\rho^\chi](x{:}\sigma^\phi) \to \tau^\psi$ of a closure f in the smaller environment Γ, given dependency information for y in Γ. Assume for example that y was bound in a let binding `let y = e`... and that the type τ_f leaves the scope of y. Then we have to adapt the type rules to express the following. "If f depends on y (at application time) then f depends on the variables of Γ that e depends on."

We define in Figure 3 the judgment $\Gamma, y{:}\rho, \Delta \vdash \sigma \overset{y\backslash\Psi}{\leadsto} \Gamma, \Delta' \vdash \tau$. Assuming that the variable y in the context $\Gamma, y{:}\rho, \Delta$ was let-bound to an definition with usage information Γ^Ψ, this judgment transforms any type σ in this context in a type τ in a context Γ, Δ' that does not mention y anymore. Note that Δ and Δ' have the same domain, only their intensional information changed: any mention of y in a closure type of Δ was removed in Δ'. Also note that $\Gamma, y{:}\rho, \Delta$ and Γ, Δ', or σ and τ, are not annotated with dependency annotations themselves: this is only a scoping transformation that depends on the dependency annotations of y *in the closures* of σ and Δ.

As for the scope-checking judgment, we simultaneously define the substitutions on contexts themselves $\Gamma, y{:}\rho, \Delta \overset{y\backslash\Psi}{\leadsto} \Gamma, \Delta'$. There are two rules for substituting a closure type. If the variable being substituted is not part of the closure type context (rule Subst-Closure-NotIn), this closure type is unchanged. Otherwise (rule Subst-Closure) the substitution is performed in the closure type, and the neededness annotation for y is reported to its definition context Γ_0.

The following lemma verifies that this substitution preserves well-scoping of contexts and types.

Lemma 1 (Substitution and scoping). *If* $\Gamma, y{:}\rho, \Delta \vdash$ *and* $\Gamma, y{:}\rho, \Delta \overset{y\backslash\Psi}{\leadsto} \Gamma, \Delta'$ *then* $\Gamma, \Delta' \vdash$. *If* $\Gamma, y{:}\rho, \Delta \vdash \sigma$ *and* $\Gamma, y{:}\rho, \Delta \vdash \sigma \overset{y\backslash\Psi}{\leadsto} \Gamma, \Delta' \vdash \tau$ *then* $\Gamma, \Delta' \vdash \tau$.

We can now give the correct rules for binders:

LET
$$\frac{\Gamma^{\Phi_{\mathtt{def}}} \vdash e_1 : \sigma \qquad \Gamma^{\Phi_{\mathtt{body}}}, x{:}\sigma^{\phi} \vdash e_2 : \tau \qquad \Gamma, x{:}\sigma \vdash \tau \overset{x\backslash\Phi_{\mathtt{def}}}{\leadsto} \Gamma \vdash \tau'}{\Gamma^{\phi . \Phi_{\mathtt{def}}+\Phi_{\mathtt{body}}} \vdash \mathtt{let}\, x = e_1 \,\mathtt{in}\, e_2 : \tau'}$$

APP
$$\frac{(\Gamma_0, \Gamma_1)^{\Phi_{\mathtt{fun}}} \vdash t : [\Gamma_0^{\Phi_{\mathtt{clos}}}](x{:}\sigma^{\phi}) \to \tau \qquad (\Gamma_0, \Gamma_1)^{\Phi_{\mathtt{arg}}} \vdash u : \sigma \qquad \Gamma_0, \Gamma_1, x{:}\sigma \vdash \tau \overset{x\backslash\Phi_{\mathtt{arg}}}{\leadsto} \Gamma_0, \Gamma_1 \vdash \tau'}{(\Gamma_0, \Gamma_1)^{\Phi_{\mathtt{fun}}+\Phi_{\mathtt{clos}}+\phi.\Phi_{\mathtt{arg}}} \vdash t\, u : \tau'}$$

Lemma 2 (Typing respects scoping). *If* $\Gamma \vdash t : \sigma$ *holds, then* $\Gamma \vdash \sigma$ *holds.*

This lemma guarantees that we fixed the problem of stale intensional information: types appearing in the typing judgment are always well-scoped.

It is handy to introduce a convenient derived notation $\Gamma^{\Phi} \vdash \tau \overset{y\backslash\Psi}{\leadsto} \Gamma'^{\Phi'} \vdash \tau'$ that is defined below. This substitution relation does not only remove y from the open closure types in Γ, it also updates the dependency annotation on Γ to add the dependency Ψ, corresponding to all the variables that y depended on – if it is itself marked as needed.

$$\frac{\Gamma, y{:}\rho, \Delta \vdash \tau \overset{y\backslash\Psi}{\leadsto} \Gamma, \Delta' \vdash \tau'}{\Gamma^{\Phi_1}, y{:}\rho^{\chi}, \Delta^{\Phi_2} \vdash \tau \overset{y\backslash\Psi}{\leadsto} \Gamma^{\Phi_1+\chi.\Psi}, \Delta'^{\Phi_2} \vdash \tau'}$$

3 A Big-Step Operational Semantics

In this section, we will define an operational semantics for our term language, and use it to prove the soundness of the type system (Theorem 1). Our semantics is equivalent to the usual call-by-value big-step reduction semantics for the lambda-calculus in the sense that computation happens at the same time. There is however a notable difference.

Function closures are not built in the same way as they are in classical big-step semantics. Usually, we have a rule of the form $V \vdash \lambda x.t \implies (V, \lambda x.t)$ where the closure for $\lambda x.t$ is a pair of the value environment V (possibly restricted to its subset appearing in t) and the function code. In contrast, we capture no values at closure creation time in our semantics: $V \vdash \lambda x.t \implies (\emptyset, \lambda x.t)$. The captured values will be added to the closure incrementally, during the reduction of binding forms that introduced them in the context.

Consider for example the following two derivations; one in the classic big-step reduction, and the other in our alternative system.

CLASSIC-RED-LET
$$\frac{x{:}v \vdash x \overset{c}{\Longrightarrow} v \qquad x{:}v, y{:}v \vdash \lambda z.y \overset{c}{\Longrightarrow} ((x \mapsto v, y \mapsto v), \lambda z.y)}{x{:}v \vdash \texttt{let } y = x \texttt{ in } \lambda z.y \overset{c}{\Longrightarrow} ((x \mapsto v, y \mapsto v), \lambda z.y)}$$

OUR-RED-LET
$$\frac{x{:}v \vdash x \Longrightarrow v \qquad x{:}v, y{:}v \vdash \lambda z.y \Longrightarrow ([x,y], \emptyset, \lambda z.y) \qquad (\emptyset, \lambda z.y) \overset{y \backslash v}{\leadsto} ([x], y \mapsto v, \lambda z.y)}{x{:}v \vdash \texttt{let } y = x \texttt{ in } \lambda z.y \Longrightarrow ([x], y \mapsto v, \lambda z.y)}$$

Rather than capturing the whole environment in a closure, we store none at all at the beginning (merely record their names), and add values incrementally, just before they get popped from the environment. This is done by the *value substitution* judgment $w \overset{x \backslash v}{\leadsto} w'$ that we will define in this section. The reason for this choice is that this closely corresponds to our typing rules, value substitution being a runtime counterpart to substitution in types $\Gamma \vdash \sigma \overset{x \backslash \Phi}{\leadsto} \Gamma' \vdash \sigma'$; this common structure is essential to prove of the type soundness (Theorem 1).

Note that derivations in this modified system and in the original one are in one-to-one mapping. It should not be considered a new dynamic semantics, rather a reformulation that is convenient for our proofs as it mirrors our static judgment structure.

Values and Value Substitution. Values are defined as follows.

$$\begin{array}{rll}
\texttt{Val} \ni v, w ::= & & \text{values} \\
\mid & v_\alpha & \text{value of atomic type} \\
\mid & (v, w) & \text{value tuples} \\
\mid & ([x_j]_{j \in J}, (x_i \mapsto v_i)_{i \in I}, \lambda x.t) & \text{function closures}
\end{array}$$

The set of variables bound in a closure is split into an ordered mapping $(x_i \mapsto v_i)_{i \in I}$ for variables that have been substituted to their value, and a simple list $[x_j]_{j \in J}$ of variables whose value has not yet been captured. They are both binding occurrences of variables bound in t; α-renaming them is correct as long as t is updated as well.

To formulate our type soundness result, we define a typing judgment on values $\Gamma \vdash v : \sigma$ in Figure 4. An intuition for the rule VALUE-CLOSURE is the following. Internally, the term t has a dependency Γ^Φ on the ambient context, but also dependencies $(\tau_i^{\psi_i})$ on the captured variables. But externally, the type may not mention the captured variables, so it reports a different dependency $\Gamma^{\Phi'}$ that corresponds to the internal dependency Γ^Φ, combined with the dependencies (Ψ_i) of the captured values. Both families $(\psi_i)_{i \in I}$ and $(\Psi_i)_{i \in I}$ are existentially quantified in this rule.

In the judgment rule, the notation $(x_j : \tau_j)_{j < i}$ is meant to define the environment of each $(x_i : \tau_i)$ as Γ^Φ, plus all the $(x_j : \tau_j)$ that come before x_i in the

$$\text{Value-Atom} \quad \frac{\Gamma \vdash}{\Gamma \vdash \mathbf{v}_\alpha : \alpha} \qquad \text{Value-Product} \quad \frac{\Gamma \vdash v_1 : \tau_1 \quad \Gamma \vdash v_2 : \tau_2}{\Gamma \vdash (v_1, v_2) : \tau_1 * \tau_2}$$

Value-Closure
$$\frac{\Gamma, \Gamma_1 \vdash \quad \forall i \in I,\ \Gamma, (x_j{:}\tau_j)_{j<i} \vdash v_i : \tau_i \quad \Gamma^\Phi, (x_i{:}\tau_i^{\psi_i})_{i \in I}, x{:}\sigma^\phi \vdash t : \tau \quad \Gamma^\Phi, (x_i{:}\tau_i^{\psi_i})_{i \in I}, x{:}\sigma^\phi \vdash \tau \overset{(x_i)\backslash(\Psi_i)}{\leadsto} \Gamma^{\Phi'}, x{:}\sigma^\phi \vdash \tau'}{\Gamma, \Gamma_1 \vdash (\text{dom}\,\Gamma, (x_i \mapsto v_i)_{i \in I}, \lambda x.t) : [\Gamma^{\Phi'}](x{:}\sigma^\phi) \to \tau'}$$

Fig. 4. Value typing

Subst-Value-Atom
$$\mathbf{v}_\alpha \overset{y \backslash v}{\leadsto} \mathbf{v}_\alpha$$

Subst-Value-Product
$$\frac{w_1 \overset{y\backslash v}{\leadsto} w_1' \quad w_2 \overset{y\backslash v}{\leadsto} w_2'}{(w_1, w_2) \overset{y\backslash v}{\leadsto} (w_1', w_2')}$$

Subst-Value-Closure
$$([x_{j_1}, \ldots, x_{j_n}, y], (x_i \mapsto w_i)_{i \in I}, t) \overset{y\backslash v}{\leadsto} ([x_{j_1}, \ldots, x_{j_n}], (y \mapsto v)(x_i \mapsto w_i)_i, t)$$

Subst-Value-Closure-NotIn
$$\frac{y \notin (x_j)_{j \in J}}{([x_j]_{j \in J}, (x_i \mapsto w_i)_{i \in I}, t) \overset{y\backslash v}{\leadsto} ([x_j]_{j \in J}, (x_i \mapsto w_i)_{i \in I}, t)}$$

Fig. 5. Value substitution

typing judgment $\Gamma^\Phi, (x_i : \tau_i)_{i \in I}, x : \sigma^\phi \vdash t$. The notation $\ldots \overset{(x_i)\backslash(\Psi_i)}{\leadsto} \ldots$ denotes the sequence of substitutions for all (x_i, Ψ_i), with the rightmost variable (introduced last) substituted first: in our dynamic semantics, values are captured by the closure in the LIFO order in which their binding variables enter and leave the lexical scope.

Substituting Values. The value substitution judgment, define in Figure 5, is an operational counterpart to the substitution of variables in closures types.

Lemma 3 (Value substitution preserves typing). *If* $(\Gamma \vdash v : \rho)$, $(\Gamma, y{:}\rho \vdash w : \sigma)$, $(\Gamma, y{:}\rho \vdash \sigma \overset{y\backslash\Psi}{\leadsto} \Gamma \vdash \tau)$ *and* $(w \overset{y\backslash v}{\leadsto} w')$ *hold, then* $(\Gamma \vdash w' : \tau)$ *holds.*

The Big-Step Reduction Relation. We are now equipped to define in Figure 6 the big-step reduction relation on well-typed terms $V \vdash e \implies v$, where V is a mapping from the variables to values that is assumed to contain at least all the free variables of e. The notation $w \overset{V_2}{\leadsto} w'$ denotes the sequence of substitutions for each (variable, value) pair in V_2, from the last one introduced in the context to the first; the intermediate values are unnamed and existentially quantified.

$$
\begin{array}{ll}
\text{Red-Var} & \text{Red-Lam} \\
V \vdash x \implies V(x) & V \vdash \lambda x.t \implies (\operatorname{dom} V, \emptyset, \lambda x.t)
\end{array}
$$

$$
\text{Red-Pair} \quad \dfrac{V \vdash e_1 \implies v_1 \quad V \vdash e_2 \implies v_2}{V \vdash (e_1, e_2) \implies (v_1, v_2)}
$$

$$
\text{Red-Proj} \quad \dfrac{V \vdash e \implies (v_1, v_2)}{V \vdash \pi_i(e) \implies v_i}
$$

$$
\text{Red-Let} \quad \dfrac{V \vdash e_1 \implies v_1 \quad V, (x \mapsto v_1) \vdash e_2 \implies v_2 \quad v_2 \overset{x \backslash v_1}{\leadsto} v_2'}{V \vdash \texttt{let } x = e_1 \texttt{ in } e_2 \implies v_2'}
$$

$$
\text{Red-App} \quad \dfrac{V, V_1 \vdash u \implies v_{\text{arg}} \quad V, V_1 \vdash t \implies (\operatorname{dom} V, V_2, \lambda y.t') \quad V, V_1, V_2, y \mapsto v_{\text{arg}} \vdash t' \implies w \quad w \overset{y \backslash v_{\text{arg}}}{\leadsto} w' \overset{V_2}{\leadsto} w''}{V, V_1 \vdash t\ u \implies w''}
$$

Fig. 6. Big-step reduction rules

$$
\text{Classic-Red-Lam} \quad W \vdash \lambda x.t \overset{c}{\Longrightarrow} (W, \lambda x.t)
$$

$$
\text{Classic-Red-Let} \quad \dfrac{W \vdash e_1 \overset{c}{\Longrightarrow} w_1 \quad W, x \mapsto w_1 \vdash e_2 \overset{c}{\Longrightarrow} w_2}{W \vdash \texttt{let } x = e_1 \texttt{ in } e_2 \overset{c}{\Longrightarrow} w_2}
$$

$$
\text{Classic-Red-App} \quad \dfrac{W \vdash t \overset{c}{\Longrightarrow} (W', \lambda y.t') \quad W \vdash u \overset{c}{\Longrightarrow} w_{\text{arg}} \quad W', y \mapsto w_{\text{arg}} \vdash t' \overset{c}{\Longrightarrow} w}{W \vdash t\ u \overset{c}{\Longrightarrow} w}
$$

Fig. 7. Classic big-step reduction rules

We write $V : \Gamma \vdash$ if the context valuation V, mapping free variables to values, is well-typed according to the context Γ. The definition of this judgment is given in the full version.

Theorem 1 (Type soundness). *If $\Gamma^\Phi \vdash t : \sigma$, $V : \Gamma \vdash$ and $V \vdash t \implies v$ then $\Gamma \vdash v : \sigma$.*

Finally, we recall the usual big-step semantics for the call-by-value calculus with environments, in Figure 7, and state its equivalence with our utilitarian semantics. Due to space restriction we will only mention the rules that differ, and elide the equivalence proof, but the long version contains all the details.

There is a close correspondence between judgments of both semantics, but as the value differ slightly, in the general cases the value bindings of the environment will also differ. We state the theorem only for closed terms, but the proof will proceed by induction on a stronger induction hypothesis using an equivalence between non-empty contexts.

Theorem 2 (Semantic equivalence). *Our reduction relation is equivalent with the classic one on closed terms: $\emptyset \vdash t \implies v$ holds if and only if $\emptyset \vdash t \overset{c}{\Longrightarrow} v$ also holds.*

To formulate our induction hypothesis, we define the equivalence judgment $V \vdash v = W \overset{c}{\vdash} w$; on each side of the equal sign there is a context and a value, the right-hand side being considered in the classical semantics.

$$\emptyset \vdash\ =\emptyset \overset{c}{\vdash} \qquad \frac{V\vdash\ =W\overset{c}{\vdash} \quad V\vdash v=W\overset{c}{\vdash}w}{V,x\mapsto v\vdash\ =W,x\mapsto w\overset{c}{\vdash}} \qquad \frac{V\vdash\ =W\overset{c}{\vdash}}{V\vdash \mathtt{v}_\alpha=W\overset{c}{\vdash}\mathtt{v}_\alpha}$$

$$\frac{V\vdash v_1=W\overset{c}{\vdash}w_1 \quad V\vdash v_2=W\overset{c}{\vdash}w_2}{V\vdash (v_1,v_2)=W\overset{c}{\vdash}(w_1,w_2)} \qquad \frac{V\vdash\ =W\overset{c}{\vdash} \quad V,x_i\mapsto v_i\vdash\ =W'\overset{c}{\vdash}}{V\vdash ((x_i\mapsto v_i)_{i\in I},\lambda x.t)=W\overset{c}{\vdash}(W',\lambda x.t)}$$

Fig. 8. Equivalence of semantic judgements

The stronger version of the theorem becomes the following: if $V\vdash\ =W\overset{c}{\vdash}$ and $V\vdash t\implies v$ and $W\vdash t\overset{c}{\implies}w$, then $V\vdash v=W\overset{c}{\vdash}w$.

4 Dependency Information as Non-interference

We can formulate our dependency information as a *non-interference* property. Two valuations V and V' are Φ-equivalent, noted $V=_\Phi V'$, if they agree on all variables on which they depend according to Φ. We say that e respects non-interference for Φ when, whenever $V\vdash e\implies v$ holds, then for any V' such that $V=_\Phi V'$ we have that $V'\vdash e\implies v$ also holds. This corresponds to the information-flow security idea that variables marked 1 are low-security, while variables marked 0 are high-security and should not influence the output result.

This non-interference statement requires that the two evaluations of e return the same value v. This raises the question of what is the right notion of equality on values. Values of atomic types have a well-defined equality, but picking the right notion of equality for function types is more difficult. While we can state a non-interference result on atomic values only, the inductive subcases would need to handle higher-order cases as well.

Syntactic equality (even modulo α-equivalence) is not the right notion of equality for closure values. Consider the following example: $x{:}\tau^0\vdash \texttt{let}\,y= x\,\texttt{in}\,\lambda z.z:[x{:}\tau^0](z:\sigma^1)\to\sigma$. This term contains an occurrence of the variable x, but its result does not depend on it. However, evaluating it under two different contexts $x{:}v$ and $x{:}v'$, with $v\neq v'$, returns distinct closures: $(x\mapsto v,\lambda z.z)$ on one hand, and $(x\mapsto v',\lambda z.z)$ on the other. These closures are not structurally equal, but their difference is not essential since they are indistinguishable in any context. Logical relations are the common technique to ignore those internal differences and get a more observational equality on functional values. They involve, however, a fair amount of metatheoretical effort that we would like to avoid.

Consider a different example: $x{:}\tau^0\vdash\lambda y.x:[x{:}\tau^1](y{:}\sigma^0)\to\tau$. Again, we could use two contexts $x{:}v$ and $x{:}v'$ with $v\neq v'$, and we would get as a result two closures: $x{:}v\vdash\lambda y.x\implies(x\mapsto v,\lambda y.x)$ and $x{:}v'\vdash\lambda y.x\implies(x\mapsto v',\lambda y.x)$. Interestingly, these two closures are *not* equivalent under all contexts: any context applying the function will be able to observe the different results. However, our notion of interference requires that they can be considered equal. This is

$$\text{EQUIV-ATOM} \qquad \frac{}{\Gamma \vdash \mathsf{v}_\alpha =_{\Phi_0} \mathsf{v}_\alpha : \alpha}$$

$$\text{EQUIV-PAIR} \qquad \frac{\Gamma \vdash v_1 =_{\Phi_0} v'_1 : \sigma_1 \qquad \Gamma \vdash v_2 =_{\Phi_0} v'_2 : \sigma_2}{\Gamma \vdash (v_1, v_2) =_{\Phi_0} (v'_1, v'_2) : \sigma_1 * \sigma_2}$$

EQUIV-CLOSURE
$$\frac{\forall i \in I,\ \Gamma, (x_j{:}\tau_j)_{j<i} \vdash v_i : \tau_i \qquad \Gamma^\Phi, (x_i{:}\tau_i^{\psi_i})_{i\in I}, x{:}\sigma^\phi \vdash t : \tau \qquad \Gamma^\Phi, (x_i{:}\tau_i^{\psi_i})_{i\in I}, x{:}\sigma^\phi \vdash \tau \overset{(x_i)\setminus(\Psi_i)}{\rightsquigarrow} \Gamma^{\Phi'}, x{:}\sigma^\phi \vdash \tau' \qquad \forall i \in I, \Psi_i \subseteq \Phi_0 \implies v_i =_{\Phi_0} v'_i}{\Gamma \vdash ((x_i \mapsto v_i)_{i\in I}, \lambda y.t) =_{\Phi_0} ((x_i \mapsto v'_i)_{i\in I}, \lambda y.t) : [\Gamma^{\Phi'}](x{:}\sigma) \to \tau'}$$

Fig. 9. Value equivalence

motivated by real-world programming languages that only output a pointer to a closure in a program that returns a function.

While the aforementioned closures are not equal in any context, they are in fact equivalent from the point of view of the particular dependency annotation for which we study non-interference, namely $x{:}\tau^0$. To observe the difference between those closures, we would need to apply the closure of type $[x{:}\tau^1](y:\sigma) \to \tau$, so would be in the different context $x{:}\tau^1$.

This insight leads us to our formulation of value equivalence in Figure 9. Instead of being as modular and general as a logical-relation definition, we fix a *global dependency* Φ_0 that restricts which terms can be used to differentiate values.

Our notion of value equivalence, $\Gamma \vdash v =_{\Phi_0} v' : \sigma$ is typed and includes structural equality. In the rule EQUIV-CLOSURE, we check that the two closures values are well-typed, and only compare captured values whose dependencies are included in those of the global context Φ_0, as we know that the others will not be used. This equality is tailored to the need of the non-interference result, which only compares values resulting from the evaluation of the same subterm – in distinct contexts.

Theorem 3 (Non-interference). *If $\Gamma^{\Phi_0} \vdash e : \sigma$ holds, then for any contexts V, V' such that $V =_{\Phi_0} V'$ and values v, v' such that $V \vdash e \implies v$ and $V' \vdash e \implies v'$, we have $\Gamma \vdash v =_{\Phi_0} v' : \sigma$. In particular, if σ is an atomic type, then $v = v'$ holds.*

5 Prototype Implementation

To experiment with our type system, we implemented a software prototype in OCaml. At around one thousand lines, the implementation mainly contains two parts.

1. For each judgement in this paper, a definition of corresponding set of inference rules along with functions for building and checking derivations.
2. A (rudimentary) command-line interface that is based on a lexer, a parser, and a pretty-printer for the expressions, types, judgments and derivations of our system.

For the scope checking judgments for context and types, the implementation *checks* well-scoping of the given contexts and types. It either builds a derivation using the well-scoping rules or fails to do so because of ill-scoped input.

For the typing judgment, the implementation performs some *inference*. Given a type context Γ and an expression e, it returns Φ, σ, and a derivation $\Gamma^\Phi \vdash e : \sigma$ if such a derivation exists. Otherwise it fails. The substitution and reduction judgments are deterministic and computational in nature. Our implementation takes the left-hand side a judgement (with additional parameters) and *computes* the right-hand-side of the judgment along with a derivation.

Below is an example of interaction with the prototype interface:

```
% make
% ./closures.byte -str "let y = (y1, y2) in (y, \(x:\sigma) z)"
Parsed expression: let y = (y1, y2) in (y, λ(x:σ) z)

The variables (y1, y2, z) were unbound; we add them to the default
environment with dummy types (ty_y1, ty_y2, ty_z) and values
(val_y1, val_y2, val_z).

Inferred typing:
  y1:ty_y1¹,y2:ty_y2¹,z:ty_z⁰ ⊢
    let y = (y1, y2) in (y, λ(x:σ) z)
    : ((ty_y1 * ty_y2) * [y1:ty_y1⁰,y2:ty_y2⁰,z:ty_z¹](x:σ⁰) → ty_z)

Result value:
  ((val_y1, val_y2), ([y1,y2,z], ((y ↦ (val_y1, val_y2))), λ(x) z))
```

In this example, adapted from the starting example of the article, $y{:}\sigma^1, z{:}\tau^0 \vdash (y, \lambda x.z)$, one can observe that the value z is marked as non-needed by the global value judgment, but needed in the type of the closure $\lambda x.z$. Besides, the computed value closure has captured the local variable y, but still references the variables $y1, y2$, and z of the outer context.

The prototype can also produce ASCII rendering of the typing and reduction derivations, when passed `--typing-derivation` or `--reduction-derivation`. This can be useful in particular in the case of typing or reduction errors, as a way to locate the erroneous sub-derivation.

The complete source code of the prototype is available at the following URL: `http://gallium.inria.fr/~scherer/research/open_closure_types`

6 Discussion

Before we conclude, we highlight three technical points that deserve a more in-depth discussion and that are helpful link our work to existing and future work.

Typed Closure Conversion. It is interesting to relate our open closure types and typed closure conversion of Minamide et al. [10]. In the classical semantics, a λ-term $\Gamma \vdash \lambda x.e : \sigma_1 \to \sigma_2$ evaluates under the value binding W to a pair

$(W, \lambda x.e)$, which can be given the type $(\Gamma * (\Gamma \to \sigma_1 \to \sigma_2))$ (writing Γ for the product of all types in the context). To combine closures of the same observable type that capture different environments, one needs to abstract away the environment type by using the existential type $\exists \rho.(\rho * (\rho \to \sigma \to \tau))$.

In our specific semantics, a closure that was originally defined in the environment Γ, Δ but is then seen in the environment Γ, only captures the values of variables in Δ. Typed closure conversion is still possible, but we would need to give it the less abstract type $\forall \Gamma.\exists \rho(\rho * (\Gamma \to \rho \to \sigma_1 \to \sigma_2))$. This reflects how our open closure types allow closure types to contain static information about variables of the current lexical context, while still allowing free composition of closures that were initially defined in distinct environments. Our closure types evolve from a very open type, at the closure construction point, into the usual "closure conversion" type that is completely abstract in captured values, in the empty environment.

Subtyping and Conservativity. As mentioned, our type system is *not* conservative over the simply-typed lambda-calculus because of the restriction on substitution of function types (domain types must be preserved by substitution). This is not a surprise as our types provide more fine-grained information without giving a way to forget some of this more precise information. Regaining conservativity is very simple. One needs a notion of subtyping allowing to hide variables present in closure types (eg., $[\Gamma, \Delta](x : \sigma_1) \to \sigma_2 \leq [\Gamma](x : \sigma_1) \to \sigma_2$ whenever σ_1, σ_2 are well-scoped under Γ alone). Systematically coercing all functions into closures capturing the empty environment then gives us exactly the simply-typed lambda-calculus.

Polymorphism. We feel the two previous points could easily be formally integrated in our work. A more important difference between our prototypical system and a realistic framework for program analysis is the lack of polymorphism. This could require significantly more work and is left for future work. We conjecture that adding abstraction on type variables (and their annotation ϕ) is direct, but a more interesting question is the abstraction over annotated contexts Γ^Φ. For example, we could want to write the following, where κ is a formal context variable:

$$\vdash \lambda f.\lambda x.\lambda y.fyx : \forall \kappa \alpha \beta \gamma.([\kappa](x{:}\alpha) \to [\kappa](y{:}\beta) \to \gamma) \to ([\kappa](y{:}\beta) \to [\kappa](x{:}\alpha) \to \gamma)$$

Polymorphism seems to allow greater flexibility in the analysis of functions taking functions as parameters. This use of polymorphism is related to the "resource polymorphism" of [7], which serves the same purpose of leaving freedom to input functions. Open closure types on the other hand, are motivated by expressions that *return* function closures; the flip side of the higher-order coin.

7 Conclusion

We have introduced open closure types and their type theory. The technical novelty of the type system is the ability to track intensional properties of function application in function closures types. To maintain this information, we have to update function types when they escape to a smaller context. This update is performed by a novel non-trivial substitution operation. We have proved the soundness of this substitution and the type theory for a simply-typed lambda calculus with pairs and let bindings.

To demonstrate how our open closure types can be used in program verification we have applied this technique to track data-flow information and to ensure non-interference in the sense of information-flow theory. We envision open closure types to be applied in the context of type systems for strong intensional properties of higher-order programs, and this simple system to serve as a guideline for more advanced applications.

We already have preliminary results from an application of open closure types in amortized resource analysis [7,6]. Using them, we were for the first time able to express a linear resource bound for the curried append function (see Section 1).

Acknowledgments. This research is based on work supported in part by DARPA CRASH grant FA8750-10-2-0254 and NSF grant CCF-1319671. Any opinions, findings, and conclusions contained in this document are those of the authors and do not reflect the views of these agencies.

References

1. Abel, A.: Semi-continuous Sized Types and Termination. Log. Methods Comput. Sci. 4(2) (2008)
2. Barthe, G., Grégoire, B., Riba, C.: Type-Based Termination with Sized Products. In: Kaminski, M., Martini, S. (eds.) CSL 2008. LNCS, vol. 5213, pp. 493–507. Springer, Heidelberg (2008)
3. Chin, W.N., Khoo, S.C.: Calculating Sized Types. High.-Ord. and Symb. Comp. 14(2-3), 261–300 (2001)
4. Hannan, J., Hicks, P., Liben-Nowell, D.: A Lifetime Analysis for Higher-Order Languages. Tech. rep., The Pennsylvania State University (1997), http://www.cse.psu.edu/~hannan/papers/live.ps.gz
5. Heintze, N., Riecke, J.G.: The SLam Calculus: Programming with Secrecy and Integrity. In: 25th Symp. on Principles of Programming Languages (POPL 1998), pp. 365–377 (1998)
6. Hoffmann, J., Aehlig, K., Hofmann, M.: Multivariate Amortized Resource Analysis. ACM Trans. Program. Lang. Syst. (2012)
7. Jost, S., Hammond, K., Loidl, H.W., Hofmann, M.: Static Determination of Quantitative Resource Usage for Higher-Order Programs. In: 37th Symp. on Principles of Programming Languages (POPL 2010), pp. 223–236 (2010)
8. Lago, U.D., Petit, B.: The Geometry of Types. In: 40th Symp. on Principles of Programming Languages (POPL 2013), pp. 167–178 (2013)
9. Leroy, X.: Polymorphic Typing of an Algorithmic Language. Research report 1778, INRIA (1992)
10. Minamide, Y., Morrisett, J.G., Harper, R.: Typed Closure Conversion. In: 23rd Symp. on Principles of Programming Languages (POPL 1996), pp. 271–283 (1996)

11. Moggi, E., Taha, W., Benaissa, Z.E.-A., Sheard, T.: An idealized metaml: Simpler, and more expressive. In: 8th Europ. Symp. on Programming (ESOP 1999), pp. 193–207 (1999)
12. Nanevski, A., Pfenning, F., Pientka, B.: Contextual Modal Type Theory. ACM Trans. Comput. Log. 9(3) (2008)
13. Petricek, T., Orchard, D., Mycroft, A.: Coeffects: Unified static analysis of context-dependence. In: Fomin, F.V., Freivalds, R., Kwiatkowska, M., Peleg, D. (eds.) ICALP 2013, Part II. LNCS, vol. 7966, pp. 385–397. Springer, Heidelberg (2013)
14. Pientka, B., Dunfield, J.: Programming with Proofs and Explicit Contexts. In: 10th International Conference on Principles and Practice of Declarative Programming (PPDP 2008), pp. 163–173 (2008)
15. Sabelfeld, A., Myers, A.C.: Language-based information-flow security. IEEE Journal on Selected Areas in Communications 21(1), 5–19 (2003)
16. Stampoulis, A., Shao, Z.: Static and User-Extensible Proof Checking. In: 39th Symp. on Principles of Programming Languages (POPL 2012), pp. 273–284 (2012)
17. Tsukada, T., Igarashi, A.: A Logical Foundation for Environment Classifiers. Logical Methods in Computer Science 6(4) (2010)

Putting Newton into Practice: A Solver for Polynomial Equations over Semirings*

Maximilian Schlund[1], Michał Terepeta[2], and Michael Luttenberger[1]

[1] Technische Universität München
{schlund,luttenbe}@model.in.tum.de
[2] Technical University of Denmark
mtte@dtu.dk

Abstract. We present the first implementation of Newton's method for solving systems of equations over ω-continuous semirings (based on [5,11]). For instance, such equation systems arise naturally in the analysis of interprocedural programs or the provenance computation for Datalog. Our implementation provides an attractive alternative for computing their exact least solution in some cases where the ascending chain condition is not met and hence, standard fixed-point iteration needs to be combined with some over-approximation (e.g., widening techniques) to terminate. We present a generic C++ library along with the main algorithms and analyze their complexity. Furthermore, we describe our implementation of the counting semiring based on semilinear sets. Finally, we discuss motivating examples as well as performance benchmarks.

1 Introduction

Given a system composed of several components (e.g. the procedures of a recursive program), the interaction of the components can be naturally described by a system of equations where for every component we have a variable X_i and an equation $X_i = F_i(X)$ which is formulated over some algebraic structure. The behavior of the complete system, or some particular aspect of it, can then be obtained as a solution of this system of equations. Especially the problem of finding the least or the greatest solution arises often in applications like program analysis, formal languages, or database theory [5,7,11]

When the algebraic structure exhibits a complete partial order (with least element 0), and F is continuous, then fixed-point iteration yields a monotonically increasing sequence (ω-chain) $0, F(0), F(F(0)), \ldots$ which converges to the least solution. However, in order to guarantee termination in general, one either needs to require that *every* ω-chain is eventually constant (ascending-chain condition) or resort to over-approximation e.g. by using a widening operator.

---

* This work was partially funded by the DFG project "Polynomial Systems on Semirings: Foundations, Algorithms, Applications" and MT-LAB (http://www.mt-lab.dk/).

Recently, Newton's method – the standard method to approximate the roots of nonlinear functions over the reals – was generalized to systems of equations over so called ω-continuous semirings (see e.g. [5]). In this particular setting it was shown that (1) Newton's method starting from 0 always converges to the least solution (in contrast to the reals where it is usually non-trivial to find a suitable initial approximation), (2) it converges at least as fast as the standard fixed-point iteration, and (3) it converges within a finite number of iterations for several interesting instances of ω-continuous semirings, e.g., commutative and idempotent semirings, for which fixed-point iteration does not reach the fixed-point in a finite number of steps. Thus, Newton's method allows to compute precise solutions of equation systems over many domains where the standard fixed-point iteration does not terminate.

Contributions, Features. We present here the first implementation of Newton's method for ω-continuous semirings; it is freely available from https://github.com/mschlund/newton. Our library is implemented in C++ and leverages templates to offer a very flexible interface to instantiate Newton's method for a concrete semiring. To this end, all algorithms and data structures (e.g. the generic Newton solver, polynomials, matrices) are parametrized, for instance by the semiring (in case of polynomials) or the method to solve linear equations (for the generic Newton solver). Hence, the library can be easily extended (without changing the main algorithms) by user-defined semirings, linear solvers, etc.—of course, it also features a set of predefined ones and some generic constructions like product and matrix semirings to build complex semirings from simpler ones. To handle systems efficiently that are very large but sparse, our implementation offers the option to preprocess systems by decomposing them into strongly connected components (cf. [6,5]). The library can be accessed by its API, but also includes a stand-alone solver together with a parser for equations over a number of predefined semirings (e.g. the counting semiring, non-negative reals, commutative regular expressions).

2 Preliminaries

We briefly recall some facts on *semirings*, for details see e.g. [3]. A *semiring* $\langle S, +, \cdot, 0, 1 \rangle$ consists of a commutative, additively written monoid $\langle S, +, 0 \rangle$ and a (not necessarily commutative) monoid $\langle S, \cdot, 1 \rangle$ written multiplicatively where multiplication distributes over addition from both sides, and for all $a \in S$ we have $0 \cdot a = a \cdot 0 = 0$. The semiring is *commutative* resp. *idempotent* if multiplication is commutative (i.e. $a \cdot b = b \cdot a$) resp. addition is idempotent (i.e. $a + a = a$). In the following we will only consider ω-*continuous* semirings: these come equipped with a complete partial order $\sqsubseteq$ with 0 the least element, and both multiplication and addition are continuous in both arguments. Further, the sum of any countable sequence is well-defined and behaves as absolutely convergent series do over the reals. In particular, the *Kleene star* is defined by $a^* := \sum_{i \in \mathbb{N}} a^i$.

An *algebraic system* $X = F(X)$ over a semiring $\langle S, +, \cdot, 0, 1 \rangle$ is a system of equations where the right-hand sides F_i are *polynomials*, i.e. finite terms constructed from $+$, $\cdot$, the semiring elements and the variables. Let n denote the number of variables occurring in a given algebraic system. Then F induces a continuous map over S^n, and the least solution of $X = F(X)$ is the least fixed-point μF of this map which is the limit of the sequence obtained by standard fixed-point iteration. As shown in [5], μF is also the limit of the sequence $\nu^{(k)}$ defined by

$$\nu^{(k+1)} = \nu^{(k)} + \Delta^{(k)} \text{ with } \Delta^{(k)} := J_F|_{\nu^{(k)}}^* \cdot \delta^{(k)} \text{ and } \nu^{(0)} := 0 \qquad (1)$$

where J_F denotes the Jacobian of F (suitably generalized to the setting of semirings) and $\delta^{(k)}$ denotes *any* element satisfying $\nu^{(k)} + \delta^{(k)} = F(\nu^{(k)})$. This iteration scheme is the generalization [1] of *Newton's method* to algebraic systems over ω-continuous semirings, and it usually converges much faster to μF then the standard fixed-point iteration. In the next section, we present the implementation of this definition, i.e. how to compute $\delta^{(k)}$ and $\Delta^{(k)}$.

3 Algorithms and Data Structures

Once the semiring is fixed the central computational problems for implementing Newton's method (Eq. 1) are (1) the computation of $\delta^{(k)}$, (2) the efficient computation of the Kleene star of the Jacobian $J_F|_{\nu^{(k)}}$ based on the Kleene star provided by the underlying semiring, and (3) the efficient representation of the semiring and its elements. We will discuss (1) and (2) in general in the following. As (3) depends on the actual semiring, we will discuss these topics for the special case of the counting semiring; we deem this semiring particularly interesting as Newton's method reaches μF within a finite number of steps.

3.1 Computing $\delta^{(k)}$

Recently, it was shown that $\delta^{(k)}$ is computable for general (also non-commutative) semirings since it corresponds to one part of an unfolding of the equation system [11]. In the special case of idempotent semirings, one can set $\delta^{(k)} := F(0)$ in every iteration (and even simplify the whole definition to $\nu^{(k+1)} = J_F|_{\nu^{(k)}}^* F(\nu^{(0)})$) as shown in [4]. If the semiring is commutative we can collect common terms and express the j-th component of $\delta^{(k)}$ succinctly using higher-order derivatives:

$$\delta_j^{(k)} = \sum_{\|i\|_1 \geq 2} \frac{1}{i!} \left(\frac{\partial}{\partial X^i} F_j \right) \bigg|_{\nu^{(k-1)}} \cdot X^i \bigg|_{\Delta^{(k-1)}}.$$

Note that $i \in \mathbb{N}^n$ is a multi-index, so we sum over all derivatives of at least second order evaluated at the previous Newton approximation. The crucial point when implementing this equation is to avoid generating unnecessary multi-indices i

---

[1] Over $\mathbb{R}_{\geq 0}$ it coincides with the standard definition of Newton's method.

(those for which the derivative will be zero anyways) like a naive implementation which generates $(\deg(F_j))^n$ many vectors. Note that the derivative is a linear operator, so we only need to focus on the case where $F_j = aX_1^{d_1} \cdots X_n^{d_n}$ is a monomial of degree $D = \sum_k d_k$. Any element from the set $\{(i_1, \ldots, i_n) \in \mathbb{N}^n : \forall_k i_k \leq d_k \land 2 \leq \sum_k i_k \leq D\}$ constitutes a valid multi-index. This set contains less than $\prod_k (d_k + 1) \leq \left(1 + \frac{D}{n}\right)^n \leq e^D$ elements and can be enumerated without repetition leading to an implementation in $\leq |\mathcal{M}_j| \cdot e^D$ many steps where $\mathcal{M}_j$ is the set of monomials of F_j.

3.2 Solving Linear Equation Systems

We have implemented two main variants of the Kleene star computation: one is the well-known Floyd-Warshall algorithm [2] and another one is a recursive divide-and-conquer algorithm [10,1]. This algorithm can be seen as an implementation of a star identity from [3]. We take a subdivision of our input matrix **M**, and compute **M*** recursively:

$$\mathbf{M} = \begin{bmatrix} \mathbf{A} & \mathbf{B} \\ \mathbf{C} & \mathbf{D} \end{bmatrix} \quad \mathbf{M}^* = \begin{bmatrix} \mathbf{F} & \alpha \mathbf{G}^* \\ \mathbf{G}^* \beta & \mathbf{G}^* \end{bmatrix} \quad \text{with} \quad \begin{array}{l} \alpha = \mathbf{A}^* \mathbf{B} \\ \beta = \mathbf{C} \mathbf{A}^* \\ \mathbf{G} = \mathbf{D} + \mathbf{C} \alpha \\ \mathbf{F} = \alpha \mathbf{G}^* \beta + \mathbf{A}^* \end{array}.$$

Both algorithms need $\Theta(n^3)$ semiring operations (which is optimal for general semirings if only $+$ and $\cdot$ are allowed [8]), but create slightly different semiring expressions during computation and thus the optimal choice between them depends on the semiring in question.

We also included the option to solve the system only once symbolically and then in each iteration substitute the values $\nu^{(k-1)}$ into this symbolic solution. Symbolic solving can be understood as interpreting the linear system over the free semiring and computing the Kleene star there. Of course, this does not change the asymptotic complexity of the procedure, but allows us to detect common subexpressions (see Fig. 1 for an illustration) and thus greatly reduces the number of semiring operations required to compute the solution. Sharing can reduce this number by 70–90% which is significant for semirings where each operation is expensive, e.g., for the counting semiring presented in Sec. 3.3.

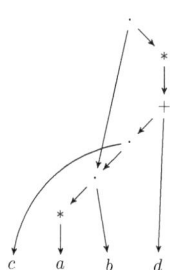

Fig. 1. Succinctly representing $a^*b(ca^*b + d)^*$ by sharing subexpressions

3.3 Implementation of the Counting Semiring

The counting semiring $\mathcal{C} = \langle 2^{|\Sigma|}, \cup, \cdot, \emptyset, \{\mathbf{0}\}\rangle$, consisting of the Parikh images of the formal languages over Σ, is a prime example of an ω-continuous semiring which admits infinite ascending chains. It is known that Newton's method reaches μF on this semiring in at most n steps and that all $\nu^{(i)}$ are rational [4]. Thus, it suffices to give *effective* definitions of the operations on the rational subsets $\mathcal{C}^{\text{rat}}$. Our implementation follows these definitions closely.

Operations. A subset $L \subseteq \mathbb{N}^k$ is called *linear*, if $L = \boldsymbol{v_0} + \mathbb{N}\boldsymbol{v_1} + \cdots + \mathbb{N}\boldsymbol{v_n}$ for $\boldsymbol{v_i} \in \mathbb{N}^k$. A set S is called *semilinear* if it is a finite union of linear sets (i.e. a finite sets of linear sets in our implementation). Let us denote the semilinear sets of $\mathbb{N}^k$ by $\mathcal{S}$. We represent linear sets L as pairs $(\boldsymbol{v_0}, G)$ with $\boldsymbol{v_0}$ the *offset* and $G := \{\boldsymbol{v_1}, \ldots, \boldsymbol{v_n}\}$ the *generators* of L.

$\mathcal{C}^{\text{rat}}$ is the (commutative, idempotent) semiring $\mathcal{C}^{\text{rat}} := \langle \mathcal{S}, \cup, \cdot, \emptyset, \{\boldsymbol{0}\}\rangle$. Multiplication is defined by $S_1 \cdot S_2 := \{L_1 \cdot L_2 \mid L_1 \in S_1, L_2 \in S_2\}$ where $(v, G) \cdot (w, H) := (v + w, G \cup H)$ for two linear sets. The Kleene star over $\mathcal{C}^{\text{rat}}$ can be computed inductively by: $S^* := \textbf{if } S = \emptyset \textbf{ then } \{\boldsymbol{0}\} \textbf{ else } L^* \cdot (S \setminus \{L\})^*$ (**where** $L \in S$) having the star of a linear set $L = (\boldsymbol{v}, G)$ defined by $(\boldsymbol{v}, G)^* = \{\boldsymbol{0}\} \cup (\boldsymbol{v}, \{\boldsymbol{v}\} \cup G)$. It should be clear that the space complexity of the Kleene star for $\mathcal{C}^{\text{rat}}$ is exponential. All these definitions can be regarded as implementations of well-known identities that hold over any commutative, idempotent semiring (cf. [3])

Optimizations. Due to the complexity of $\cdot$ and $(-)^*$ a practical implementation of semilinear sets is challenging and usually requires exponential space (e.g. in the number of Newton steps). Since explicit representations of the Parikh image of a CFG can be exponential in the size of the grammar, some exponential blowup is essentially unavoidable (cf. [9] for a detailed analysis). However, the representation of the Newton approximations exhibits a lot of redundancy, e.g., often linear sets subsume each other and generators can be linearly combined (with coefficients in $\mathbb{N}$) from others. Therefore, we implemented several optimizations: We use extensive sharing and store only one copy of each vector and linear set in memory. Furthermore, we try to determine whether a generator can be combined from other generators, and similarly try to simplify the linear sets. Despite the fact that the latter two "simplification" steps require to solve an NP-complete problem (essentially subset-sum [2]), our implementation based on memoization performs very well since the vectors usually contain small numbers.

These simplifications are necessary to get concise solutions for most equation systems and their impact is illustrated in Table 1 in Sec. 4.

Approximations. Finally, we have developed two approaches to over-approximate semilinear sets. These significantly improve the performance of the semilinear sets and still yield valuable information in many cases. For a simple example, both preserve finiteness and emptiness.

One of the ideas is to to "collapse" a semilinear set into a pair two sets — one of offsets and the other one of generators. We call this structure a *multilinear set*. The intuition behind it is that we can choose any of the offsets and then use the generators as in the case of linear sets. This approximation is precise if the generator sets attached at different offsets are the same. Otherwise this approximation still keeps "asymptotic upper/lower" bounds on the relationship of different components (i.e. when the offsets are negligible). Consider a semilinear set consisting of two linear ones: $(v_1, \{v_2\})$ and $(v'_1, \{v'_2\})$, the corresponding abstraction would be $(\{v_1, v'_1\}, \{v_2, v'_2\})$. Clearly (unless $v_2 = v'_2$) we add some "spurious" points by additionally admitting, e.g., $v_1 + \mathbb{N}v'_2$.

Another idea is to divide every generator v by the greatest common divisor of its elements to obtain a (shorter) vector $\tilde{v}$. For a generator v the set $\mathbb{N}v \subseteq \mathbb{N}^k$ describes a one dimensional discrete "line with gaps". Our approximation corresponds to filling these gaps with more integer points but does not change the direction of the generators, i.e. $\mathbb{N}v \subseteq \mathbb{N}\tilde{v} \subseteq \mathbb{Q}v \cap \mathbb{N}^k$.

4 Experiments

One of the potential applications for counting analyses is to analyze the use of certain resources in a program. For instance, a reentrant lock should be released the same number of times that it has been acquired. Below is a simple example of a recursive program that will obey these rules.

```
proc AcquireRelease                    proc Release
  Lock!();                               if
  if                                     :: true => Unlock!()
  :: true => AcquireRelease()            :: true => Release()
  :: true => skip                        fi
  fi;                                  end
  Release()
end                                    proc main
                                         AcquireRelease()
                                       end
```

However, it is using the stack to ensure that it acquires and releases the lock the same number of times. Even though the stack is unbounded, our solver can verify that — the result of counting the Lock and Unlock actions is: $\{(\langle 1, 1 \rangle, \{\langle 1, 1 \rangle\})\}$. In other words, the behavior is characterized by a linear set with offset $\langle 1, 1 \rangle$ (there is at least one Lock and one Unlock action) and generator $\langle 1, 1 \rangle$ (the number of those actions can be arbitrarily large, but equal in number).

Next we show the behavior of our implementation on two sets of examples over different semirings. We compiled the tool using gcc 4.7 with optimizations (-O2) and ran it on a machine with an Intel 2.7 GHz CPU and 8 GB RAM.

For the first benchmark we computed the Parikh images of all 1,932 grammars provided with the tool cfg-analyzer from http://www2.tcs.ifi.lmu.de/~mlange/cfganalyzer/. We simply interpret the grammars as equation systems over the counting semiring and solve them. The grammars are quite simple—at most three terminal, and less than ten nonterminal symbols. We used a timeout of 15 seconds, but for most examples computation took only a few milliseconds (see Tab. 1). In all but the timeout-cases, memory usage was negligible (less than 1MB). Since the Parikh image can be viewed as an overapproximation, this could be used as an (incomplete) method to check for non-equivalence of context-free grammars in some cases.

Table 1. Parikh image computation for the cfg-analyzer benchmarks; Number of instances solved in the respective times for semi- resp. multilinear sets with and without the optimizations from Sec.3.3.

		> 15s (timeout)	(0.01s, 5s)	≤ 0.01s
Exact	sl-sets, w/o simp	55	35	1842
	sl-sets, simp	0	30	1902
Approx.	ml-sets, w/o simp	2	0	1930
	ml-sets, simp	0	0	1932

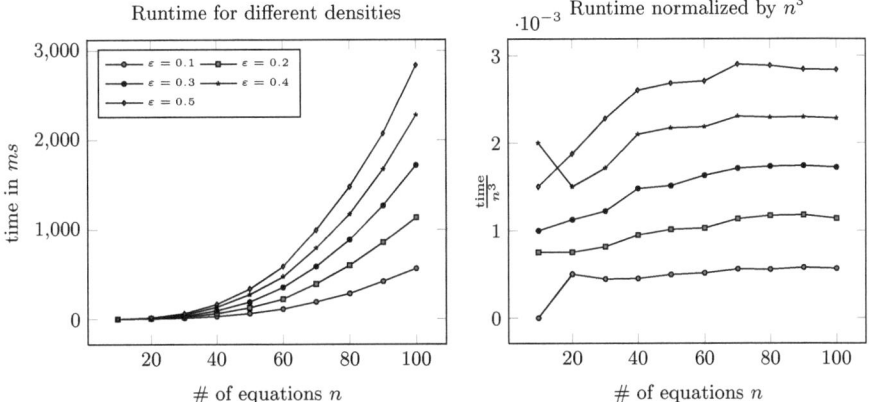

Fig. 2. Approximating the solution (doing 10 Newton steps) of n quadratic equations over $\mathbb{R}_{\geq 0}$ with $\varepsilon \binom{n}{2}$ monomials in each equation. Left: Average solving time (taken over 5 runs) in milliseconds. Right: Numbers from the left divided by n^3.

The second benchmark studies a problem that is important in natural language processing and the study of branching processes. The task is to compute the extinction probabilities for stochastic context-free grammars, i.e. the probability for each non-terminal to derive the empty word [6]. To solve this problem we just have to change the semiring in our implementation. This setting also allows us to demonstrate the scalability of our generic algorithms and to show that our implementation faithfully implements all algorithms with a running time that matches the theoretical analysis. To this end, we randomly generated quadratic equations over $[0, 1]$ and record the running time needed to solve the equations.[2] As we are only interested how the performance varies with the size of the system we fixed the number of Newton iterations to 10. Each equation has $\varepsilon \binom{n}{2}$ monomials and we vary the "density" ε from 0.1 to 0.5—note that these systems are rather dense and large (e.g. the textual description of the system with 100 variables and density 0.5 needs 7.6 MB). For these systems we expect a cubic runtime which is well supported by the data (cf. Fig. 2).

---

[2] These benchmarks are available at https://github.com/mschlund/newton/tree/master/c/test/grammars/float-random .

5 Conclusions and Future Work

In this paper we have presented the first implementation of the Newton's method generalized to ω-continuous semirings [5]. We have briefly described the main algorithms behind our library as well as the implementation of the counting semiring based on semilinear sets. One of our goals was to make the library generic and flexible—new semirings can be defined and used without changing the main algorithms. Furthermore, we have implemented and discussed various optimizations such as common subexpression elimination during Kleene star computation or simplification of semilinear sets. We have provided motivating applications and discussed initial benchmarks of our library.

Concerning future work, computing the Kleene star for matrices is a problem well suited for parallelization [1] and a generic parallel implementation for general semirings would be useful but does not exist yet to the best of our knowledge. Furthermore, there are well-known symbolic representations of semilinear sets described in the literature, e.g., NDDs or Presburger formulae which we plan to integrate into our library. The main challenge there is to compute the Kleene star efficiently which has not yet been addressed for these representations. Finally, we plan on using our library to solve more involved program analysis problems like pointer may-alias analysis.

Acknowledgments. We would like to thank Michael Kerscher for his help with the implementation and Javier Esparza for helpful comments and suggestions.

References

1. Buluç, A., Gilbert, J.R., Budak, C.: Solving Path Problems on the GPU. Parallel Comput. 36(5-6), 241–253 (2010)
2. Cormen, T.H., Leiserson, C.E., Rivest, R.L., Stein, C.: Introduction to Algorithms, 3rd edn. MIT Press (2009)
3. Droste, M., Kuich, W., Vogler, H.: Handbook of Weighted Automata. Springer (2009)
4. Esparza, J., Kiefer, S., Luttenberger, M.: On Fixed Point Equations over Commutative Semirings. In: Thomas, W., Weil, P. (eds.) STACS 2007. LNCS, vol. 4393, pp. 296–307. Springer, Heidelberg (2007)
5. Esparza, J., Kiefer, S., Luttenberger, M.: Newtonian Program Analysis. J. ACM 57(6), 33 (2010)
6. Etessami, K., Yannakakis, M.: Recursive Markov Chains, Stochastic Grammars, and Monotone Systems of Nonlinear Equations. J. ACM 56(1) (2009)
7. Green, T.J., Karvounarakis, G., Tannen, V.: Provenance semirings. In: PODS, pp. 31–40 (2007)
8. Kerr, L.R.: The Effect of Algebraic Structure on the Computational Complexity of Matrix Multiplication. Ph.D. thesis, Cornell University, Ithaca, NY, USA (1970)
9. Kopczynski, E., To, A.: Parikh Images of Grammars: Complexity and Applications. In: LICS 2010, pp. 80–89 (2010)
10. Kot, L., Kozen, D.: Kleene Algebra and Bytecode Verification. Electr. Notes Theor. Comput. Sci. 141(1), 221–236 (2005)
11. Luttenberger, M., Schlund, M.: Convergence of Newton's Method over Commutative Semirings. In: Dediu, A.-H., Martín-Vide, C., Truthe, B. (eds.) LATA 2013. LNCS, vol. 7810, pp. 407–418. Springer, Heidelberg (2013)

System Description: E 1.8

Stephan Schulz

Institut für Informatik, Technische Universität München,
D-80290 München, Germany
schulz@eprover.org

Abstract. E is a theorem prover for full first-order logic with equality. It reduces first-order problems to clause normal form and employs a saturation algorithm based on the equational superposition calculus. E is built on shared terms with cached rewriting, and employs several innovations for efficient clause indexing. Major strengths of the system are automatic problem analysis and highly flexible search heuristics. The prover can provide verifiable proof objects and answer substitutions with very little overhead. E performs well, solving more than 69% of TPTP-5.4.0 FOF and CNF problems in automatic mode.

1 Introduction

E is a theorem prover for full first-order logic with equality, built around a fully equational implementation of the superposition calculus. For the last 12 years the prover has been one of the major participants at the CADE ATP System Competition in the MIX, CNF, FOF, UEQ and LTB categories, usually finishing among the top systems in all these categories. E is available as Free Software under the GNU GPL. It is implemented in C, widely portable, and has been used, in whole or part, as a component in many other systems.

Fig. 1 shows the high-level functional decomposition of the theorem prover, and the data flow between the components. A proof problem is read into main memory, and is passed through several different processing stages:

- The problem is parsed and converted into a set of clauses and formulas by a simple but efficient recursive descent parser. The parser supports E-LOP, and the TPTP CNF/FOF syntax [13].
- In the next stage, *Relevancy Pruning*, the problem is optionally simplified by discarding clauses and formulas deemed unlikely to contribute to a proof. E implements both strict relevancy pruning and a configurable variant of the SInE algorithm [4].
- The third stage, *Clausification*, converts the problem from full first-order logic to clausal form. Clausification uses a slightly simplified version of the algorithm presented by Nonnengart and Weidenbach [8]. The implementation takes advantage of E's shared term/shared formula representation
- The resulting clause set can be pre-processed. Preprocessing removes redundant literals and tautologies, and optionally expands equational definitions. If requested, preprocessing can also perform complete interreduction of the problem specification.

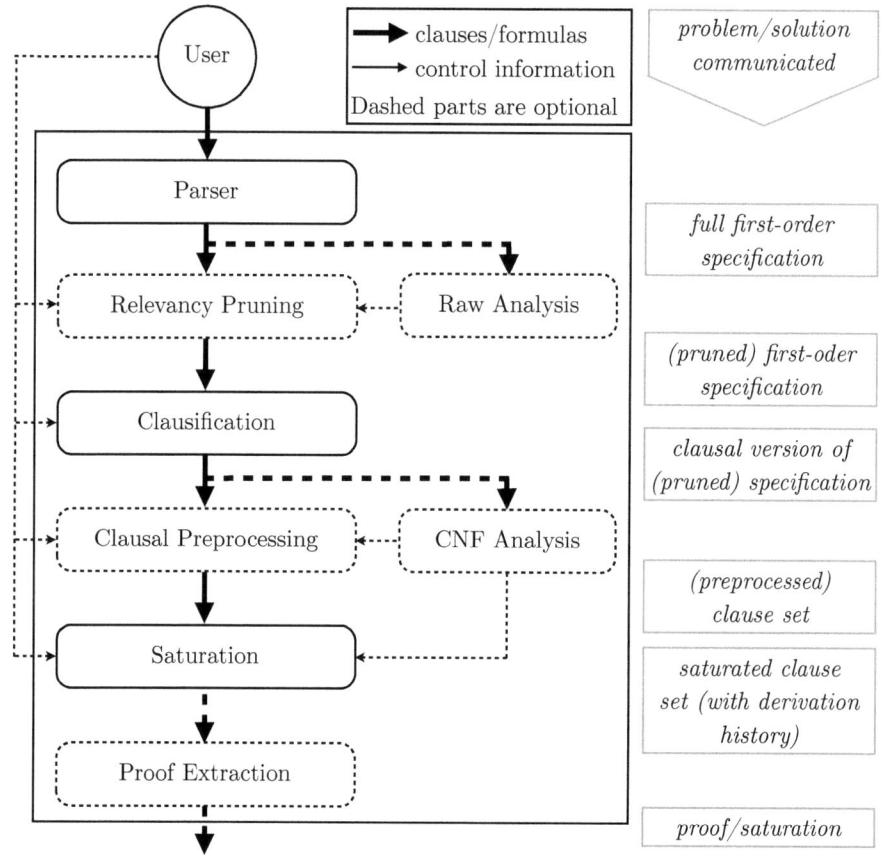

Fig. 1. Decomposition of E and major data flows

- After preprocessing, the clause set is passed to the main saturation algorithm. This is realized as an instance of the DISCOUNT variant of the given-clause algorithm and implements a variant of the superposition calculus with a number of contraction techniques. The saturation ends when the empty clause has been derived, the set is saturated, or a user-defined resource limit is reached.
- The prover can store enough information to generate a checkable proof object. In the final (optional) step, this information is collected into a proof tree (or saturation derivation), which can be printed in E's original PCL-2 or TPTP-3/TSTP syntax.

Various aspects of the process are controlled by parameters that are either provided by the user or heuristically determined by the *automatic mode* of the prover.

2 Saturation

The core of the prover is a saturation procedure that tries to show the inconsistency of a set of clauses (the *search state*). New clauses are deduced using generating inference rules, and existing clauses are simplified or discarded using contraction rules. The algorithm terminates either when it has derived the empty clause as an explicit witness of inconsistency, or if all non-redundant inferences have been computed. In this case, the resulting saturated set describes a model of the clause set.

2.1 Calculus

E implements an instance of the superposition calculus with negative literal selection, as originally described by Bachmair and Ganzinger [2]. It uses the rules *equality resolution* (ER), *equality factoring* (EF), and *superposition into positive and negative literals*, (SP) and (SN). Alternatively, the latter two rules can be replaced by *simultaneous superposition* (SSP and SSN), which often results in slightly better search behaviour and hence is the default. Simultaneous superposition is inspired by simultaneous paramodulation [3], and maintains completeness[1].

Contraction is critical for practical performance. E implements deletion of duplicate and resolved literals (DD, DR), syntactic and semantic tautology deletion (TD1, TD2, SD), *destructive equality resolution* (DR), unconditional rewriting (RP, RN), equational literal cutting (PS, NS), subsumption (CS, ES), *contextual literal cutting* (CLC), condensing (CD), AC-tautology deletion (ACD) and AC-simplification (ACS). The last two rules handle associative and commutative function symbols as suggested in [1].

2.2 Implementation

Fig. 2 sketches the proof procedure. The algorithm maintains the invariant that the set P of unprocessed clauses is interreduced, and that all generating inferences between clauses from P have been performed. Derivations are *fair* if no clause remains unprocessed forever.

The implementation is built around perfectly shared terms. Each distinct term is represented exactly once in a *term bank*. Unconditional rewriting is cached. Whenever a possible simplification is detected, it is recorded in the term bank. Future simplifications simply follow these *rewrite links* before trying new equations.

Indexing enables the prover to quickly find inference partners for a given premise. E indexes the set P of processed clauses. It uses *Perfect Discrimination Trees* [7] with size- and age-constraints for forward rewriting (finding positive

---

[1] On the ground level, a simultaneous superposition inference can be simulated by a single conventional superposition step, followed by a series of (simplifying) conditional rewrite steps.

Search state: $U \cup P$ U contains *unprocessed* clauses, P contains *processed* clauses. Initially, all clauses are in U, P is empty. The *given clause* is denoted by g.

while $U \neq \{\}$
  $g = \text{delete\_best}(U)$
  $g = \text{simplify}(g, P)$
  if $g == \square$
    SUCCESS, Proof found
  if g is not subsumed by any clause in P (or otherwise redundant w.r.t. P)
    $P = P \backslash \{c \in P \mid c \text{ subsumed by (or otherwise redundant w.r.t.) } g\}$
    $T = \{c \in P \mid c \text{ can be simplified with } g\}$
    $P = (P \backslash T) \cup \{g\}$
    $T = T \cup \text{generate}(g, P)$
    foreach $c \in T$
      $c = \text{cheap\_simplify}(c, P)$
      if c is not trivial
        $U = U \cup \{c\}$
SUCCESS, original U is satisfiable

Remarks: delete_best(U) finds and extracts the clause with the best heuristic evaluation (see 3.3) from U. generate(g, P) performs all generating inferences using g as one premise, and clauses from P as additional premises. It uses inference rules (SP) or (SSP), (SN) or (SSN), (ER) and (EF). simplify(c, S) applies all simplification inferences in which the main (simplified) premise is c and all the other premises are clauses from S. This typically includes full rewriting, (CD) and (CLC). cheap_simplify(c, S) works similarly, but only applies inference rules with a particularly low cost implementation, usually including rewriting with orientable units, but not (CLC). The exact set of contraction rules used is configurable in either case.

Fig. 2. Saturation procedure of E

unit clauses that can rewrite new clauses), *Fingerprint Indexing* [10] for backward rewriting (finding clauses in P that can be rewritten with the given clause) and superposition, and *Feature Vector Indexing* [11] for subsumption and contextual literal cutting.

Term orderings (LPO and KBO) are implemented using the elegant and efficient reformulations presented by Löchner [5,6].

3 Search Control

Proof search depends on a number of different parameters. The three major choice points are the selection of a term ordering, the (optional) selection of inference literals, and the order in which clauses from U are picked for processing.

3.1 Term Orderings

E supports KBO and LPO. Both orderings are parameterized. KBO uses a weight function assigning weights to individual function symbols (and a fixed weight to all variables), and both orderings use a precedence on the function symbols. E currently supports about a dozen precedence generation schemes, and more than two dozen weight generation schemes. Orderings showing the best performance use the frequency of symbols in the specification, making terms with rarer symbols larger in the ordering.

3.2 Literal Selection

Literal selection is a major strength of E. Even quite naive approaches (always select the largest negative literal, if any) lead to a significant improvement over the plain superposition calculus. Good literal selection strategies seem to prefer ground literals, literals that are large in the term ordering, and to avoid literals that contain little structure, e.g. literals of the form $p(X, Y, Z)$.

3.3 Clause Evaluation

The given-clause algorithm selects clauses according to a heuristic evaluation. In the simplest case, this is a single value, representing the number of symbols in the clause (smaller is better). E generalizes this concept and allows the user to specify an arbitrary number of priority queues and a weighted round-robin scheme that determines how many clauses are picked from each queue. A major feature is the use of goal-directed evaluation functions. These give a lower weight to symbols that occur in the goal, and a higher weight to other symbols, thus preferring clauses which a likely connection to the conjecture. As an alternative, E can also *learn* good clause evaluations from previous proof experience [9].

3.4 Automatic Prover Configuration

Performance of first-order theorem provers critically depends on the search strategy and heuristics. Finding good heuristics for a given problem is challenging even for an experienced user. E supports a number of *automatic modes* that analyze the problem and apply either a single strategy or a schedule of several strategies. The selection of strategies and generation of schedules for each class of problems is determined automatically by analyzing previous performance of the prover on similar problems.

4 Proofs and Answers

4.1 Proofs

E 1.8 can internally record all necessary information for proof output. It makes use of the DISCOUNT loop property that only processed clauses (usually a

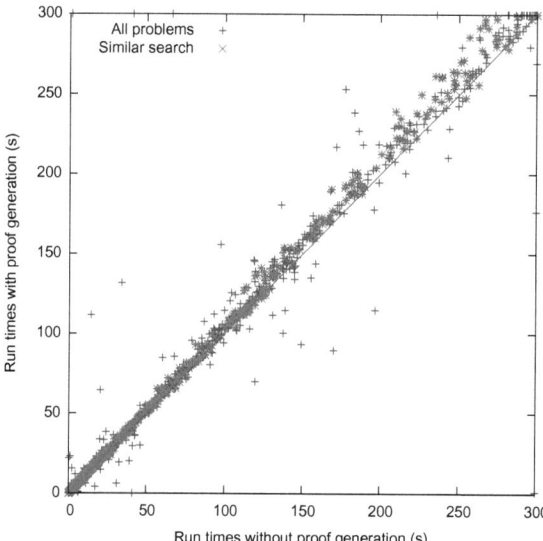

Fig. 3. Comparison of run times

small subset of all clauses in the search state) can ever participate in generating inferences or be used to simplify other clauses. For each clause, the system stores its origin (usually a generating inference and the parents), and a history of simplifications (inference rules and side premises). A processed clause is archived and replaced by a simplified copy (pointing to the original as the parent) only if it itself is back-simplified.

When the empty clause has been derived and hence a proof concluded, the proof tree is extracted by tracing the recorded dependencies. Proof steps are topologically sorted, ensuring that all dependencies of a step are listed before the step itself. The linearized proof can then be printed.

Recording of the derivation history does not systematically change the search behaviour. However, changes in memory usage and layout can cause some operations (e.g. iteration over a set) to be performed differently, potentially disturbing the proof search. Fig. 3 shows the run times of the prover in automatic mode with and without proof generation over TPTP 5.4.0, for both the majority of problems where both versions performed the same search and the small number with differing search behaviour. Performing a simple linear regression over the problems with the same search suggests an overhead of only 0.24% for proof generation.

4.2 Answers

The system supports the proposed TPTP standard for answers [14]. An *answer* is an instantiation for an existential conjecture (or *query*) that makes the conjecture true. In practice, E supplies bindings for the outermost existentially quantified variables in a TPTP formula with type question.

The implementation is straightforward. The query is extended by adding the atomic formula ~$answer(new_fun(<varlist>)), where new_fun is a previously unused function symbol, and <varlist> is the list of outermost existentially quantified variables. This atom is carried through clausification and ends up as a positive literal in the CNF. The literal ordering is automatically chosen so that the answer literal never participates in inferences. Semantically, the $answer predicate always evaluates to false. It is evaluated only in clauses where all remaining literals are answer literals. Answers are extracted and printed in tuple form at the time of the evaluation. Consider the following example:

Specification
fof(greeks, axiom, (philosopher(socrates)|philosopher(plato))).
fof(scot, axiom, (philosopher(hume))).
fof(phils_wise, axiom, (![X]:(philosopher(X) => wise(X)))).
fof(is_there_wisdom, question, (?[X]:wise(X))).
Answers (eprover --tptp3-format -s --answers)
SZS status Theorem
SZS answers Tuple [[hume]|_]
SZS answers Tuple [([socrates]|[plato])|_]
Proof found!

The system correctly handles disjunctive answers (at least one of socrates or plato is a philosopher and hence wise, but the theory does not allow us to decide who is). While the example has been kept intentionally simple, the system also supports complex terms and variables as parts of answers, in that case representing the set of all instances.

5 Performance

Table 1 lists the performance of E for 4 different search regimens and different classes of problems. Tests were run on the University of Miami *Pegasus cluster*. Each node of the cluster is equipped with 8 Intel Xeon cores, running at 2.5 GHz, and 16 GB of RAM. Test runs were done with a CPU time limit of 300 seconds per job, a memory limit of 1024 MB per job, and with 8 jobs scheduled per node. All 15560 untyped first-order problems (including CNF, FOF and UEQ) from TPTP 5.4.0 were used as test examples.

Best is the currently strongest single strategy known. *SatAuto* analyses the input problem and picks an appropriate strategy based on the performance on similar problems. *Auto* additionally performs problem pruning, potentially losing completeness, but improving behaviour on very large problems. Finally, *Auto-Scheduling* runs up to 5 complementary strategies for each problem class.

Search performance over time is visualized in Fig. 4 for all 15560 problems. In all cases, the first 7000 solutions are found within less than 1 second. Of the 10783 solutions found by AutoScheduling, 1000 are saturations, 9783 are proofs.

Table 1. Number of proofs/models found within 300 seconds CPU limit

Strategy	UEQ	CNE	CEQ	FNE	FEQ	All
Class size	(1179)	(2352)	(5867)	(1713)	(5867)	(15560)
Best	764	1642	3211	1251	3211	9305
...with proof object	764	1648	3210	1251	3210	9301
SatAuto	800	1833	3671	1418	3671	10334
...with proof object	799	1833	3664	1421	3664	10326
Auto	801	1834	3758	1424	3758	10432
...with proof object	799	1834	3749	1424	3749	10415
Auto-Scheduling	824	1867	3939	1430	3939	10783
...with proof object	823	1864	3936	1430	3936	10776

UEQ: Unit equational problems, CNE: (non-unit) CNF problems without equality, CEQ: CNF problems with equality, FNE: Full first-order problems without equality, FEQ: Full first-order problems with equality

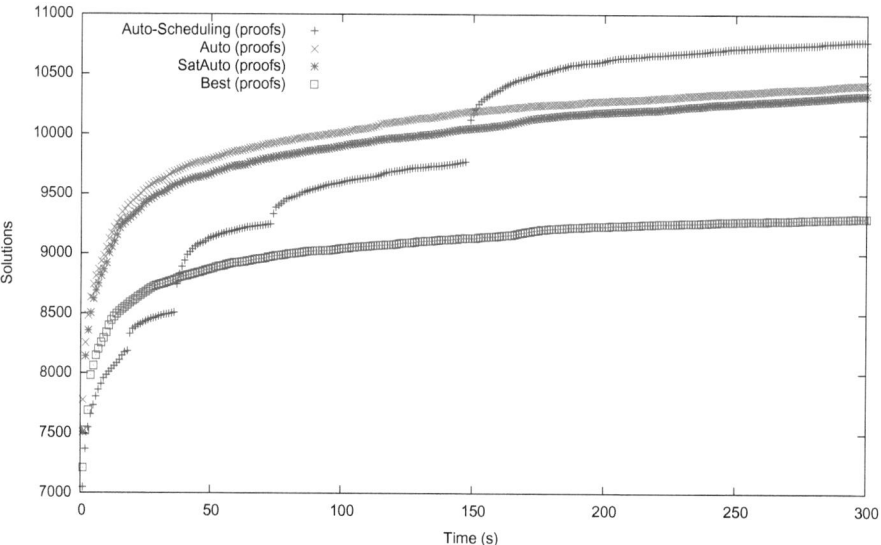

Fig. 4. Performance (number of solutions over time) of E with different strategies and meta-strategies

6 Conclusion

E has reached good maturity for untyped first-order logic. It is stable, reliable, and has improved usability with strong automatic search, proof object generation and answer substitutions.

Future planned changes include support for simply typed first-order logic with arithmetic as defined in [12], improved support for repetitive queries against large axiom sets, and the use of new data-driven methods for search control.

Acknowledgements. I thank the University of Miami's *Center for Computational Science* HPC team for making their cluster available for the evaluation.

References

1. Avenhaus, J., Hillenbrand, T., Löchner, B.: On Using Ground Joinable Equations in Equational Theorem Proving. Journal of Symbolic Computation 36(1-2), 217–233 (2003)
2. Bachmair, L., Ganzinger, H.: Rewrite-Based Equational Theorem Proving with Selection and Simplification. Journal of Logic and Computation 3(4), 217–247 (1994)
3. Benanav, D.: Simultaneous paramodulation. In: Stickel, M.E. (ed.) CADE 1990. LNCS, vol. 449, pp. 442–455. Springer, Heidelberg (1990)
4. Hoder, K., Voronkov, A.: Sine Qua Non for Large Theory Reasoning. In: Bjørner, N., Sofronie-Stokkermans, V. (eds.) CADE 2011. LNCS (LNAI), vol. 6803, pp. 299–314. Springer, Heidelberg (2011)
5. Löchner, B.: Things to Know when Implementing KBO. Journal of Automated Reasoning 36(4), 289–310 (2006)
6. Löchner, B.: Things to Know When Implementing LPO. International Journal on Artificial Intelligence Tools 15(1), 53–80 (2006)
7. McCune, W.: Experiments with Discrimination-Tree Indexing and Path Indexing for Term Retrieval. Journal of Automated Reasoning 9(2), 147–167 (1992)
8. Nonnengart, A., Weidenbach, C.: Computing Small Clause Normal Forms. In: Robinson, A., Voronkov, A. (eds.) Handbook of Automated Reasoning, ch. 5, vol. I, pp. 335–367. Elsevier Science and MIT Press (2001)
9. Schulz, S.: Learning Search Control Knowledge for Equational Theorem Proving. In: Baader, F., Brewka, G., Eiter, T. (eds.) KI 2001. LNCS (LNAI), vol. 2174, pp. 320–334. Springer, Heidelberg (2001)
10. Schulz, S.: Fingerprint Indexing for Paramodulation and Rewriting. In: Gramlich, B., Miller, D., Sattler, U. (eds.) IJCAR 2012. LNCS (LNAI), vol. 7364, pp. 477–483. Springer, Heidelberg (2012)
11. Schulz, S.: Simple and Efficient Clause Subsumption with Feature Vector Indexing. In: Bonacina, M.P., Stickel, M.E. (eds.) McCune Festschrift. LNCS (LNAI), vol. 7788, pp. 45–67. Springer, Heidelberg (2013)
12. Sutcliffe, G., Schulz, S., Claessen, K., Baumgartner, P.: The TPTP Typed First-order Form with Arithmetic. In: Bjørner, N., Voronkov, A. (eds.) LPAR-18 2012. LNCS (LNAI), vol. 7180, pp. 406–419. Springer, Heidelberg (2012)
13. Sutcliffe, G., Schulz, S., Claessen, K., Van Gelder, A.: Using the TPTP Language for Writing Derivations and Finite Interpretations. In: Furbach, U., Shankar, N. (eds.) IJCAR 2006. LNCS (LNAI), vol. 4130, pp. 67–81. Springer, Heidelberg (2006)
14. Sutcliffe, G., Stickel, M., Schulz, S., Urban, J.: Answer Extraction for TPTP, http://www.cs.miami.edu/~tptp/TPTP/Proposals/AnswerExtraction.html (accessed July 08, 2013)

Formalization of Laplace Transform Using the Multivariable Calculus Theory of HOL-Light

Syeda Hira Taqdees and Osman Hasan

School of Electrical Engineering and Computer Science (SEECS),
National University of Sciences and Technology (NUST),
Islamabad, Pakistan
{11mseestaqdees,osman.hasan}@seecs.nust.edu.pk

Abstract. Algebraic techniques based on Laplace transform are widely used for solving differential equations and evaluating transfer of signals while analyzing physical aspects of many safety-critical systems. To facilitate formal analysis of these systems, we present the formalization of Laplace transform using the multivariable calculus theories of HOL-Light. In particular, we use integral, differential, transcendental and topological theories of multivariable calculus to formally define Laplace transform in higher-order logic and reason about the correctness of Laplace transform properties, such as existence, linearity, frequency shifting and differentiation and integration in time domain. In order to demonstrate the practical effectiveness of this formalization, we use it to formally verify the transfer function of Linear Transfer Converter (LTC) circuit, which is a commonly used electrical circuit.

1 Introduction

Laplace transform [12] is an integral transform method that is used to convert the time varying functions to their corresponding s-domain representations, where s represents the angular frequency [1]. This transformation provides a very compact representation of the overall behavior of the given time varying function and is frequently used for analyzing systems that exhibit a deterministic relationship between continuously changing quantities and their rates of change. Laplace transform theory allows us to solve linear Ordinary Differential Equations (ODEs) [19] using simple algebraic techniques since the transformation allows us to convert the integration and differentiation functions from the time-domain to multiplication and division functions in the s-domain. Moreover, the s-domain representations of ODEs are also used for transfer function analysis of the corresponding systems. Due to these unique features, Laplace transform theory has been an integral part of engineering and physical system analysis and is widely used in the design and analysis of electrical networks, control systems, communication systems, optical systems, analogue filters and mechanical networks.

Mathematically, Laplace transform is a complex function defined for a function f, which can be either real or complex-valued, as follows

$$F(s) = \int_0^\infty f(t)e^{-st}dt, \ s \in \mathbb{C} \tag{1}$$

The first step in analyzing differential equations using Laplace transform is to take the Laplace transform of the given equation on both sides. Next, the corresponding s-domain equation is simplified using various properties of Laplace transform, such as existence, linearity, Laplace of a differential and Laplace of an integral. The objective is to either solve the differential equation to obtain values for the variable s or obtain the transfer function of the system corresponding to the given differential equation.

Traditionally, the above mentioned Laplace transform based analysis is performed using computer based numerical techniques or symbolic methods. However, both of these techniques cannot guarantee accurate analysis. Numerical methods cannot ascertain an accurate value of the improper integral of Equation (1) as there is always a limited number of iterations allowed depending on the available memory and computation resources. The round-off errors due to the usage of computer arithmetics also introduce some inaccuracies in the results. Symbolic methods, provided by Symbolic Math Toolbox of Matlab and other computer algebra systems like Maple and Mathematica, are based on algorithms that consider the improper integral of Equation (1) as the continuous analog of the power series, i.e., the integral is discretized to summation and the complex exponentials are sampled. Moreover, the presence of huge symbolic manipulation algorithms, which are usually unverified, in the core of computer algebra systems also makes the accuracy of their analysis results questionable. For-instance, a couple of examples for using Matlab or Maple for control and electrical engineering systems can be found in [3,16]. However, the results of these analyses cannot be termed as 100% accurate. Therefore, these traditional techniques should not be relied upon for the analysis of systems using the Laplace transform method, especially when they are used in safety-critical areas, such as medicine and transportation, where inaccuracies in the analysis could result in system design bugs that in turn may even lead to the loss of human lives in worst cases.

To overcome the above mentioned inaccuracy limitations, we propose to perform the Laplace transform based analysis using a higher-order-logic theorem prover. The main idea is to leverage upon the high expressiveness of higher-order logic to formalize Equation (1) and use it to verify the classical properties of Laplace transform within a theorem prover. These foundations can be built upon to reason about the exact solution of a differential equation or its transfer function within the sound core of a theorem prover. In particular, the paper presents the formal verification of existence, linearity and scaling properties of Laplace transform. It also presents the formal verification of the Laplace transforms of an arbitrary order differential and integral functions. The main advantage of these results is that they greatly minimize the user intervention for formal reasoning about the correctness of many properties of physical systems. In order to illustrate the practical effectiveness and utilization of this formalization, we use it to verify the transfer function of a Linear Transfer Converter (LTC) circuit, which is commonly used analog circuit. Formal verification of analog circuits is of utmost importance [8]. However, to the best of our knowledge, all the existing formal verification approaches work with abstracted discretized models of analog circuits (e.g., [4],[2]). This is mainly because of the inability to model and analyze the properties of differential equations in their true continuous form by the existing formal methods. The formalization of Laplace transform, presented in this paper, overcomes this limitation and we have been able to formally verify the transfer function of the LTC circuit using its differential equation.

The work described in this paper is done using the HOL-Light theorem prover [6], which supports formal reasoning about higher-order logic. The main motivation behind this choice is the availability of reasoning support about multivariable integral, differential, transcendental and topological theories [7], which are the foremost foundations required for the formalization of Laplace transform theory.

The rest of the paper is organized as follows: We provide a brief introduction about the multivariable calculus theories of HOL-Light in Section 2. The formalization of the Laplace transform function is provided in Section 3. We utilize this formalization to formally verify the classical properties of Laplace transform in Section 4. The formal verification of the LTC circuit is given in Section 5. Finally, Section 6 concludes the paper.

2 Multivariable Calculus Theories in HOL-Light

HOL-Light is a higher-order-logic theorem prover that belongs to the HOL family of theorem provers. Its unique features include an efficient set of inference rules and the usage of Objective CAML (OCaml) language [6], which is a variant of the strongly-typed functional programming language ML [11], for its development and interaction. HOL-Light provides formal reasoning support for many mathematical theories, including sets, natural numbers, real analysis, complex analysis and vector calculus, and has been particularly successful in verifying many challenging mathematical theorems. The main motivation behind choosing HOL-Light for the formalization of Laplace transform theory in this paper is the availability of a rich set of formalized multivariable calculus theories on the Euclidean space [7].

In HOL-Light, a n-dimensional vector is represented as a $\mathbb{R}^n$ column matrix with individual elements as real numbers. All of the vector operations are then handled as matrix manipulations. This way, complex numbers can be represented by the data-type $\mathbb{R}^2$, i.e, a column matrix having two elements. Similarly, pure real numbers can be represented by two different data-types, i.e., by a 1-dimensional vector $\mathbb{R}^1$ or a number on the real line $\mathbb{R}$. All the vector algebraic theorems have been formally verified using HOL-Light for arbitrary functions with a flexible data-type $\mathbb{R}^n \to \mathbb{R}^m$. For the formalization of Laplace transform, we have utilized several vector algebraic theorems for complex functions ($\mathbb{R}^2 \to \mathbb{R}^2$) and complex-valued functions ($\mathbb{R}^1 \to \mathbb{R}^2$).

In order to facilitate the understanding of the rest of the paper, some of the frequently used functions of the HOL-Light Multivariable calculus libraries [7] are described below:

Definition 1: *Cx*
⊢ ∀ a. Cx a = complex(a,&0)

The function Cx accepts a real number and return its corresponding complex number with the imaginary part as zero. It uses the function complex, which accepts a pair of real numbers and returns the corresponding complex number such that the real part of the complex number is equal to the first element of the given pair and the imaginary part of the complex number is the second element of the given pair. The operator & maps a natural number to its corresponding real number.

Definition 2: *Re and Im*
⊢ ∀ z. Re z = z$1
⊢ ∀ z. Im z = z$2

The functions Re and Im accept a complex number and return its real and imaginary parts, respectively. The notation z$n represents the nth component of a vector z.

Definition 3: *drop and lift*
⊢ ∀ x. drop x = x$1
⊢ ∀ x. lift x = (lambda i. x)

The function drop accepts a 1-dimensional vector and returns its single component as a real number. The function lift maps a real number to a 1-dimensional vector with its single component equal to the given real number.

Definition 4: *Exponential Functions*
⊢ ∀ x. exp x = Re(cexp (Cx x))

The functions exp and cexp represent the real and complex exponential functions in HOL-Light with data-types $\mathbb{R} \to \mathbb{R}$ and $\mathbb{R}^2 \to \mathbb{R}^2$, respectively.

Definition 5: *Limit of a function*
⊢ ∀ f net. lim net f = (@l. (f→l) net)

The function lim is defined using the Hilbert choice operator @ in the functional form. It accepts a *net* with elements of arbitrary data-type A and a function f, of data-type $A \to \mathbb{R}^m$, and returns $l : \mathbb{R}^m$, i.e., the value to which f converges at the given *net*. To formalize the improper integral of Equation (1), we will use the at_posinfinity, which models positive infinity, as our *net*,

Definition 6: *Integral*
⊢ ∀ f i. integral i f = (@y.(f has_integral y) i)
⊢ ∀ f i. real_integral i f = (@y.(f has_real_integral y) i)

The function integral accepts an integrand function $f : \mathbb{R}^n \to \mathbb{R}^m$ and a vector-space $i : \mathbb{R}^n \to \mathbb{B}$, which defines the region of integration. Here, $\mathbb{B}$ represents boolean data-type. It returns a vector of data-type $\mathbb{R}^m$, which represents the integral of f over i. The function has_integral defines the same relationship in the relational form. In a similar way, the function real_integral represents the integral of a function $f : \mathbb{R} \to \mathbb{R}$, over a set of real numbers $i : \mathbb{R} \to \mathbb{B}$. The regions of integration, for both of the above integrals, can be defined to be bounded by a vector interval $[a, b]$ or real interval $[a, b]$ using the HOL-Light functions interval [a,b] and real_interval [a,b], respectively.

Definition 7: *Derivative*
⊢ ∀ f net. vector_derivative f net =
    (@f'.(f has_vector_derivative f') net)

The function vector_derivative accepts a function $f : \mathbb{R}^1 \to \mathbb{R}^m$, which needs to be differentiated, and a *net* of data-type $\mathbb{R}^1 \to \mathbb{B}$, that defines the point at which f has to be differentiated. It returns a vector of data-type $\mathbb{R}^m$, which represents the differential of f at *net*. The function has_vector_derivative defines the same relationship in the relational form.

We will build upon the above mentioned foundational definitions to formalize the Laplace transform function in the next section.

3 Formalization of Laplace Transform

Based on the theory of improper integrals [18], Equation (1) can be alternatively expressed as follows:

$$F(s) = \lim_{b \to \infty} \int_0^b f(t)e^{-st}dt \qquad (2)$$

This definition holds under the conditions that the integral

$$f(b) = \int_0^b f(t)e^{-st}dt \qquad (3)$$

exists for every $b > 0$ and the limit also exists as b approaches positive infinity.

Now, the Laplace transform function can be formalized in HOL-Light as follows:

Definition 8: *Laplace Transform*
⊢ ∀ s f. laplace f s =
    lim at_posinfinity (λb. integral (interval [lift(&0),lift(b)])
    (λt. cexp (-(s * Cx(drop t))) * f t))

The function laplace accepts a complex number s and a complex-valued function $f : \mathbb{R}^1 \to \mathbb{R}^2$. It returns a complex number that represents the laplace transform of f according to Equation (2). The complex exponential function cexp: $\mathbb{R}^2 \to \mathbb{R}^2$ is used in this definition because the data-type for $f(t)$ is $\mathbb{R}^2$. Similarly, in order to multiply variable $t : \mathbb{R}^1$ with the complex number s, it is first converted to $\mathbb{R}$ by using the function drop and then converted to data-type $\mathbb{R}^2$ by using Cx. Then, we use the vector integration function integral to integrate the expression $f(t)e^{-st}$ over the interval $[0, b]$ since the return type of this expression is $\mathbb{R}^2$. The limit of the upper interval b of this integral is then taken at positive infinity using the lim function with the at_posinfinity net. Based on the definition of at_posinfinity, the variable b must have a data-type $\mathbb{R}$. However, the region of integration of the vector integral function must be a vector space. Therefore, for data-type consistency, we lift the value 0 and variable b in the interval of the integral to the data-type $\mathbb{R}^1$ using the function lift.

The Laplace transform of a function f exists, i.e., the integral of Equation (3) is integrable and the limit of Equation (2) is convergent, if f is piecewise smooth and of exponential order on the positive real axis [1]. A function is said to be piecewise smooth on an interval if it is piecewise differentiable on that interval. Similarly, a causal function $f : \mathbb{R} \to \mathbb{C}$ is of exponential order if there exist constants $\alpha \in \mathbb{R}$ and $M>0$ such that $|f(t)| \leq Me^{\alpha t}$ for all $t \geq 0$. We formalize the Laplace transform existence conditions in HOL-Light as follows:

Definition 9: *Laplace Exists*
⊢ ∀ s f. laplace_exists f s ⇔
(∀ b. f piecewise_differentiable_on interval [lift (&0),lift b])
∧ (∃ M a. Re s > drop a ∧ exp_order f M a)

The first conjunct in the above predicate ensures that f is piecewise differentiable on the positive real axis. The second conjunct expresses the exponential order condition of f for $\alpha < Re\ s$ using the following predicate:

Definition 10: *Exponential Order Function*
⊢ ∀ f M a. exp_order f M a ⇔ &0 < M ∧
(∀ t. &0 ≤ t ⇒ norm (f (lift t)) ≤ M * exp (drop a * t))

The function exp_order accepts a function $f : \mathbb{R}^1 \to \mathbb{R}^2$, a real number M and a complex number s and returns a $True$ if M is positive and f is bounded by Me^{at} for all $0 < t$.

4 Formal Verification of Laplace Transform Properties

In this section, we use Definition 8 to verify some of the classical properties of Laplace transform in HOL-Light. The formal verification of these properties not only ensures the correctness of our definition but also plays a vital role in minimizing the user intervention in reasoning about Laplace transform based analysis of systems, as will be depicted in Section 5 of this paper.

4.1 Limit Existence of the Improper Integral

According to the limit existence of the improper integral of Laplace transform property, if the given function $f : \mathbb{R} \to \mathbb{C}$ fulfills the conditions for the existence of its Laplace transform, i.e., it is of exponential order and piecewise smooth, then there will certainly exists a complex number l, to which the complex-valued integral of Equation (3) converges at positive infinity [1]. This property can be formalized based on Definitions 8 and 9 as follows:

Theorem 1: *Limit Existence of Integral of Laplace Transform*
⊢ ∀ f s. laplace_exists f s ⇒
 (∃l. ((λb. integral (interval [lift (&0),lift b])
  (λt. cexp (-(s * Cx (drop t))) * f t)) → l) at_posinfinity)

We proceed with the verification of the above theorem by first splitting the complex-valued integrand, i.e., $f(t)e^{-st}$, into its corresponding real and imaginary parts. Now using the linearity property of integral, the conclusion of the theorem can be expressed in terms of two integrals as follows:

∃l.((λb. integral (interval [lift (&0),lift b])
   (λt. Cx (Re (cexp (-(s * Cx (drop t))) * f t))) +
 ii * integral (interval [lift (&0),lift b])
   (λt. Cx (Im (cexp (-(s * Cx (drop t))) * f t)))) → l)
   at_posinfinity

where, ii represents the constant value $\sqrt{-1}$ that is multiplied with the imaginary part of a complex number. Next, we verified the following two lemmas that allow us to break the above subgoal into two subgoals involving the limit existence of two real-valued integrals.

Lemma 1: *Relationship between the Real and Complex Integral*
⊢ ∀ f s t l. (f has_real_integral l) (real_interval [&0,t]) ⇒
 ((λt. Cx (f (drop t))) has_integral Cx l)
  (interval [lift (&0),lift t])

Lemma 2: *Limit of a Complex-Valued Function*
⊢ ∀ f L1 L2.
 ((λt. Re (f t)) ⇒ L1) at_posinfinity ∧
 ((λt. Im (f t)) ⇒ L2) at_posinfinity ⇒
 (f → complex (L1,L2)) at_posinfinity

The subgoal for the limit existence of the first real-valued integral is as follows:

laplace_exists f s ⇒
 ∃k. ((λb. real_integral (real_interval [&0,b])
   (λx. abs (Re (cexp (-s * Cx (x)) * f(lift x))))) → k)
   at_posinfinity

The proof of the above subgoal is primarily based on the Comparison Test for Improper Integrals [18], which has been formally verified as part of our development as follows:

Lemma 3: *Comparison Test for Improper Integrals*
⊢ ∀ f g a. (&0 ≤ a) ∧ (∀x. a ≤ x ⇒ &0 ≤ f x ∧ f x ≤ g x) ∧
  (∀ b. g real_integrable_on real_interval [a,b]) ∧
  (∀ b. f real_integrable_on real_interval [a,b]) ∧
  (∃ k.((λb. real_integral (real_interval [a,b]) g)⇒ k)
     at_posinfinity) ⇒
        (∃ k.((λb. real_integral (real_interval [a,b]) f) ⇒ k)
           at_posinfinity)

The laplace_exists f s assumption of Theorem 1 ensures that the integrand fe^{-st}, of our subgoal, is upper bounded by $Me^{-(Re(s)-\alpha)t}$, which in turn can also be verified to be integrable and having a convergent integral for $Re\ s > \alpha$ as the upper limit of integration approaches positive infinity. Moreover, the piecewise differentiability condition in the predicate laplace_exists f s ensures the integrability of f. These results allow us to fulfill the assumptions of Lemma 3 and thus conclude the limit existence subgoal for the real-valued integral of the real part. The proof of the subgoal for the limit existence of the real-valued integral corresponding to the imaginary part is very similar and its verification concludes the proof of Theorem 1.

4.2 Linearity

The linearity of Laplace transform can be expressed mathematically for two functions f and g and two complex numbers α and β as follows [1]:

$$\Big(\mathcal{L}\ \alpha f(x) + \beta g(x)\ \Big)(s) = \alpha(\mathcal{L}f)(s) + \beta(\mathcal{L}g)(s) \tag{4}$$

We verified this property as the following theorem:

Theorem 2: *Linearity of Laplace Transform*
⊢ ∀ f g s a b. laplace_exists f s ∧ laplace_exists g s ⇒
  laplace (λx. a * f x + b * g x) s =
    a * laplace f s + b * laplace g s

The proof is based on Theorem 1 and the linearity properties of integration and limit.

4.3 Frequency Shifting

The Frequency shifting property of Laplace transform deals with the case when the Laplace transform of the composition of a function f with the exponential function is required [1].

$$\Big(\mathcal{L}\ e^{bt}f(t)\Big)(s) = (\mathcal{L}f)(s-b) \tag{5}$$

These type of functions, called the *damping functions*, frequently occur in the analysis of many natural systems like harmonic oscillators. Frequency shifting property is used to analyze and measure the damping effects on the systems in the corresponding s-domain [17]. We verified the property as the following theorem:

Theorem 3: *Frequency Shifting*
⊢ ∀ f s b. laplace_exists f s ⇒
  laplace (λt. cexp (b * Cx (drop t)) * f t) s = laplace f (s - b)

4.4 Integration in Time Domain

The Laplace transform of an integral of a continuous function can be evaluated using the integration in time domain property

$$\left(\mathcal{L}\int_0^t f(\tau)d\tau\right)(s) = \frac{1}{s}(\mathcal{L}f)(s) \tag{6}$$

where Re s > 0 [1]. Such type of functions extensively occur in control and electrical systems and their s-domain analysis is greatly simplified by using the above relation [10]. This property has been verified in HOL-Light as follows:

Theorem 4: *Integration in Time Domain*
⊢ ∀ f s. (&0 < Re s) ∧ laplace_exists f s ∧
  laplace_exists (λx. integral (interval [lift (&0),x]) f) s ∧
  (∀x. f continuous_on interval [lift (&0),x]) ⇒
    laplace (λx. integral (interval [lift (&0),x]) f) s =
    inv(s) * laplace f s

where the function inv represents the reciprocal of a given vector. The proof of the above theorem is primarily based on the Integration-by-parts property, which was verified as part of the reported development as follows:

Lemma 4: *Integration by Parts*
⊢ ∀ f g f' g' a b. (drop a ≤ drop b) ∧
  (∀ x. (f has_vector_derivative f' x)
    (at x within interval [a,b])) ∧
  (∀ x. (g has_vector_derivative g' x)
    (at x within interval [a,b])) ∧
  (λx. f' x * g x) integrable_on interval [a,b] ∧
  (λx. f x * g' x) integrable_on interval [a,b] ⇒
    integral (interval [a,b]) (λx. f x * g' x) =
      f b * g b - f a * g a - integral (interval [a,b])
        (λx. f' x * g x)

where the function integrable_on formally represents the integrability of a vector function on a vector space. The integrand of Theorem 4, which is the product of a complex exponential and the function $\int_0^t f(\tau) d\tau$, can be simplified using Lemma 4 to obtain the following subgoal:

```
(&0 < Re s) ⇒
  lim at_posinfinity (λb. integral (interval [lift &0,lift b]) f *
    -inv s * cexp (-(s * Cx (drop (lift b))))) -
  lim at_posinfinity (λb. integral (interval [lift &0,lift b])
    (λx. f x * -inv s * cexp (-(s * Cx (drop x))))) =
  inv s * lim at_posinfinity (λb. integral
    (interval[lift &0,lift b])(λt. cexp (-(s * Cx(drop t))) * f t))
```

The first term on the left-hand-side of the above subgoal can be verified to approach zero at positive infinity since, based on the existence of Laplace transform condition, $f(t)$ grows more slowly than an exponential. The remaining two terms can then verified to be equivalent based on simple arithmetic reasoning.

4.5 First Order Differentiation in Time Domain

The Laplace of a differential of a continuous function f is given as follows [1]:

$$\left(\mathcal{L}\frac{df}{dx}\right)(s) = s(\mathcal{L}f)(s) - f(0) \tag{7}$$

We verified it as the following theorem:

Theorem 5: *First Order Differentiation in Time Domain*
```
⊢ ∀ f s. laplace_exists f s ∧
  laplace_exists (λx. vector_derivative f (at x)) s ∧
  (∀ x. f differentiable at x) ⇒
    laplace (λx. vector_derivative f (at x)) s =
      s * laplace f s - f (lift (&0))
```
using Theorem 1, Lemma 4 and the fact that $f(t)e^{-st}|_0^\infty = [0 - f(0)]$.

4.6 Higher Order Differentiation in Time Domain

The Laplace of a n-times continuously differentiable function f is given as the following mathematical relation [1]:

$$\left(\mathcal{L}\frac{d^n f}{dx^n}\right)(s) = s^n(\mathcal{L}f)(s) - \sum_{k=1}^{n} s^{k-1}\frac{d^{n-k}f(0)}{dx^{n-k}} \tag{8}$$

This property forms the foremost foundation for analyzing higher-order differential equations based on Laplace transform and is verified as follows:

Theorem 6: *Higher Order Differentiation in Time Domain*
```
⊢ ∀ f s n. laplace_exists_higher_derivative n f s ∧
  (∀x. higher_derivative_differentiable n f x) ⇒
    laplace (λx. higher_order_derivative n f x) s =
      s pow n * laplace f s - vsum (1..n) (λx. s pow (x-1) *
      higher_order_derivative (n-x) f (lift (&0)))
```

The first assumption ensures the Laplace existence of f and its first n higher-order derivatives. Similarly, the second assumption ensures the differentiability of f and its first n higher-order derivatives on $x \in \mathbb{R}$. The expressions `higher_order_derivative n f x` and `vsum (1..n) f` recursively model the nth order derivative of f with respect to x and the vector summation of the n terms from 1 to n of function f, respectively. The proof of Theorem 6 is based on induction on variable n. The proof of the base case is based on simple arithmetic reasoning and the step case is discharged using Theorem 5 and summation properties along with some arithmetic reasoning.

The formalization, presented in this section, had to be done in an interactive way due to the undecidable nature of higher-order logic and took around 5000 lines of HOL-Light code and approximately 800 man-hours. One of the major challenges faced during this formalization is the non-availability of detailed proof steps for Laplace transform properties in the literature. The mathematical texts on Laplace transform properties provide very abstract proof steps and often ignore the subtle reasoning details. For instance, all the mathematical texts that we came across (e.g. [1,14]) provide the exponential order condition as the only condition for the limit existence of the improper integral of Laplace transform. However, as described in Section 4.1, the actual formal proof is based on splitting the complex-valued integrand into the corresponding real and imaginary parts and using the Integral comparison test and we had to find this reasoning on our own. Similarly, in verifying the integration in time property (Theorem 4), the exact reasoning about the convergence of the term $e^{-st} \int_0^t f(\tau)\,d\tau$ to zero, which was the main bottleneck in the proof, could not be found in any mathematical text on Laplace transform.

Other time-consuming factors, associated with our formalization, include the formal verification many multivariable calculus related theorems, which were required in our formalization but were not available in the current HOL-Light distribution. These generic results can be very useful for other similar formalizations and some of the ones of common interest are given below and others can be found in our proof script [15].

Lemma 5: *Upper Bound of Monotonically Increasing and Convergent f*
⊢ ∀ f n k. (&0 ≤ n) ∧ (∀n m. n ≤ m ⇒ f n ≤ f m) ∧
((f → k) at_posinfinity) ⇒ f n ≤ k

Lemma 6: *Limit at Positive Infinity of f implies Limit of abs(f)*
⊢ ∀ f l. (f → l) at_posinfinity ⇔
((λi. f (abs i)) → l) at_posinfinity

Lemma 7: *Relationship between Real and Vector Derivative*
⊢ ∀ f f' x s. ((f has_real_derivative f') (atreal x within s)) ⇒
((Cx o f o drop has_vector_derivative Cx f')
(at (lift x) within IMAGE lift s))

Lemma 8: *Chain Rule of Differentiation for Complex-valued Functions*
⊢ ∀ f g f' g' x s.((f has_vector_derivative f') (at x within s)) ∧
((g has_complex_derivative g') (at (f x) within IMAGE f s)) ⇔
((g o f has_vector_derivative f' * g') (at x within s))

The main advantage of the formal verification of Laplace transform properties is that our proof script, available for download at [15], can be built upon to facilitate formal reasoning about the Laplace transform based analysis of safety-critical systems, as depicted in the next section.

5 Application: Linear Transfer Converter (LTC) circuit

As an illustrative example of our work, we formally verify the transfer function of a Linear Transfer Converter (LTC) circuit, depicted in Figure (1), which is widely used for converting the voltage and current levels in power electronics systems [13]. The functional correctness of power systems mainly depends on the design and stability of LTCs and thus the accuracy of LTC analysis is of dire need. Standard design techniques of LTCs are based on the transfer function analysis, i.e., the differential equation of a LTC circuit is first converted into its corresponding s-domain equivalent, and then depending upon the required stability requirements, the values of circuit components, like resistors and inductors are calculated [9]. We perform this analysis using our formalization of Laplace transform within the sound core of HOL-Light theorem prover in this paper. The behavior of the LTC circuit, with input complex voltage $u(t)$ across

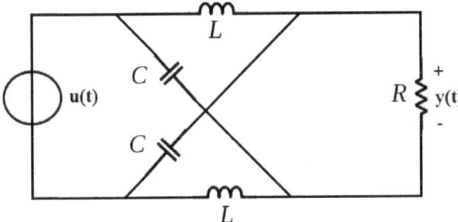

Fig. 1. Linear Transfer Converter Circuit

the voltage generator, and the output complex voltage $y(t)$, across the resistor R, can be expressed using the following differential equation [1]:

$$\frac{d^2y}{dt^2} - \frac{2}{RC}\frac{dy}{dt} + \frac{1}{LC}y = \frac{d^2u}{dt^2} - \frac{1}{LC}u \qquad (9)$$

The corresponding transfer function of this given circuit is as follows [1]:

$$\frac{Y(s)}{U(s)} = \frac{s^2 - \frac{1}{LC}}{s^2 - \frac{2s}{RC} + \frac{1}{LC}} \qquad (10)$$

The objective of this section is to verify this transfer function using Equation (9). In order to be able to formally express Equation (9), we formalized the following function to model an n-order differential equation in HOL-Light:

Definition 11: *Differential Equation*
⊢ ∀ n A f x. diff_eq n A f x ⇔
  vsum (0..n) (λt. EL t L x * higher_order_derivative t f x)

The function diff_eq accepts the order of the differential equation n, a list of coefficients A, differentiable function f and the differentiation variable x. It utilizes the functions vsum n f and EL m L, which return the vector summation ($\sum_{i=0}^{n} f_i$) and the mth element of a list L, respectively, to generate the differential equation corresponding to the given parameters. Now, Equation (9) can be formalized as follows:

Definition 12: *Differential Equation of LTC*
⊢ ∀ y u x L C R. diff_eq_LTC y u x L C R ⇔
diff_eq 2 [Cx (&1 / L * C); --Cx (&2 / R * C); Cx (&1)] y x =
diff_eq 2 [--Cx (&1 / L * C); Cx (&0); Cx (&1)] u x

The function diff_eq_LTC accepts the output voltage function $y : \mathbb{R}^1 \to \mathbb{R}^2$, the input voltage function $u : \mathbb{R}^1 \to \mathbb{R}^2$, the resistance $R : \mathbb{R}$, the inductance $L : \mathbb{R}$ and the capacitance $C : \mathbb{R}$ being the capacitance and $x : \mathbb{R}^1$ being time. It then returns Equation (9) in the summation form.

Now, the transfer function of the given LTC circuit, given in Equation (10), can be verified as the following theorem in HOL-Light.

Theorem 7: *Transfer function of LTC*
⊢ ∀ y u s R L C. (&0 < R) ∧ (&0 < L) ∧ (&0 < C) ∧
  (zero_initial_conditions 1 u) ∧ (zero_initial_conditions 1 y) ∧
  (∀x. higher_derivative_differentiable 2 y x) ∧
  (∀x. higher_derivative_differentiable 2 u x) ∧
  (higher_derivative_laplace_exists 2 y s) ∧
  (higher_derivative_laplace_exists 2 u s) ∧
  (∀t. diff_eq_LTC y u t L C R) ∧ ~(laplace u s = Cx(&0)) ∧
  ~((Cx(&1/(L*C)) - Cx(&2/(R*C))*s) + s pow 2 = Cx(&0)) ⇒
  (laplace y s / laplace u s =
  (s pow 2 - Cx(&1/(L*C))) / ((Cx(&1/(L*C)) -
  Cx(&2/(R*C))*s) + s pow 2))

The first three assumptions ensure the positive values for resistor, inductor and capacitor, respectively. The predicate zero_initial_conditions is used to define the initial conditions, i.e., to assign a value 0 to the given function and its n derivatives at time equal to zero. In our case, we need zero initial conditions for the functions u and y up to the first-order derivative, which are modeled using the fourth and fifth assumptions. The next four assumptions ensure that the functions y and u are differentiable up to the second-order and the Laplace transform exists up to the second order derivatives of these functions. The next assumption represents the formalization of Equation (9), the next two assumptions provide some interesting design related relationships, which must hold for constructing a reliable LTC, and the conclusion of the theorem represents Equation (10). The reasoning about the correctness of Theorem 7 is very straightforward and is primarily based on Definition 8 and Theorem 6 and some simple arithmetic reasoning. The proof script consists of approximately 650 lines of HOL-Light code [15] and the proof process took just a couple of hours, which clearly indicates the usefulness of our work in conducting the formal analysis of real-world applications using the Laplace transform method.

6 Conclusion

This paper advocates the usage of higher-order-logic theorem proving for conducting Laplace transform based analysis, which is an essential design step for almost all physical systems. Due to the high expressiveness of the underlying logic, we can formally model the differential equation depicting the behaviour of the given physical system in its true form, i.e., without compromising on the precision of the model. The Laplace transform method can then be used in a theorem prover to deduce interesting design parameters from this equation. The inherent soundness of theorem proving guarantees correctness of this analysis and ensures the availability of all pre-conditions of the analysis as assumptions of the formally verified theorems. To the best of our knowledge, these features are not shared by any other existing computerized Laplace transform based analysis technique and thus the proposed approach can be very useful for the analysis of physical systems used in safety-critical domains.

The main challenge in the proposed approach is the enormous amount of user intervention required due to the undecidable nature of the higher-order logic. We propose to overcome this limitation by formalizing Laplace transform theory in higher-order logic and thus minimizing the user guidance in the reasoning process by building upon the already available results. As a first step towards this direction, this paper presents the formalization of Laplace transform and the formal verification of some of its classical properties, such as existence, linearity, frequency shifting and differentiation and integration in time domain, using the multivariable calculus theories of HOL-Light. Based on this work, we are able to conduct the formal analysis of a Linear Transfer Converter (LTC) circuit, which is commonly used electronic circuit in a very straightforward way.

This paper opens the doors towards a novel and promising usage of theorem proving. The formalization of Laplace transform foundations, presented in this paper, can be directly used to reason about the transfer functions of many systems used in the domains of control engineering and analog and mixed signal (AMS) circuits, where the usage of formal verification is a dire need given their safety-critical nature. Our formalization can also be built upon to formalize the inverse Laplace transform function and its associated properties, which can be very useful in analyzing the behavior of engineering systems in the time-domain [1]. Our formalization can also be used to formalize other mathematical transforms. For instance, Fourier transform [5], which is a foundational mathematical theory for analyzing digital signal processing applications, can be easily formalized by restricting the variable s of the Laplace transform definition to acquire pure imaginary values only.

Acknowledgements. This work was supported by the National Research Program for Universities grant (number 1543) of Higher Education Commission (HEC), Pakistan.

References

1. Beerends, R.J., Morsche, H.G., Van den Berg, J.C., Van de Vrie, E.M.: Fourier and Laplace Transforms. Cambridge University Press, Cambridge (2003)
2. Denman, W., Akbarpour, B., Tahar, S., Zaki, M., Paulson, L.C.: Formal Verification of Analog Designs using MetiTarski. In: Formal Methods in Computer Aided Design, pp. 93–100. IEEE (2009)
3. Dorcak, L., Petras, I., Gonzalez, E., Valsa, J., Terpak, J., Zecova, M.: Application of PID Retuning Method for Laboratory Feedback Control System Incorporating FO Dynamics. In: International Carpathian Control Conference (ICCC), pp. 38–43. IEEE (2013)
4. Frehse, G., Le Guernic, C., Donzé, A., Cotton, S., Ray, R., Lebeltel, O., Ripado, R., Girard, A., Dang, T., Maler, O.: Spaceex: Scalable Verification of Hybrid Systems. In: Gopalakrishnan, G., Qadeer, S. (eds.) CAV 2011. LNCS, vol. 6806, pp. 379–395. Springer, Heidelberg (2011)
5. Gaydecki, P.: Foundations of Digital Signal Processing: Theory, Algorithms and Hardware Design. IET (2004)
6. Harrison, J.: HOL Light: An overview. In: Berghofer, S., Nipkow, T., Urban, C., Wenzel, M. (eds.) TPHOLs 2009. LNCS, vol. 5674, pp. 60–66. Springer, Heidelberg (2009)
7. Harrison, J.: The HOL Light Theory of Euclidean Space. Automated Reasoning 50(2), 173–190 (2013)
8. Zaki, M.H., Tahar, S., Boisr, G.: Formal Verification of Analog and Mixed Signal Designs: A survey. Microelectronics Journal 39, 1395–1404 (2008)
9. Ioinovici, A.: Power Electronics and Energy Conversion Systems, Fundamentals and Hard-switching Converters. John Wiley & Sons (2013)
10. Paul, B.: Industrial Electronics and Control. PHI Learning Pvt. Ltd. (2004)
11. Paulson, L.C.: ML for the Working Programmer. Cambridge University Press, Cambridge (1996)
12. Podlubny, I.: The Laplace Transform Method for Linear Differential Equations of the Fractional Order. Technical report, Slovak Acad. Sci., Kosice (1994)
13. Rashid, M.: Power Electronics Handbook. Elsevier (2011)
14. Schiff, J.L.: The Laplace Transform: Theory and Applications. Springer (1999)
15. Taqdees, S.H.: Formalization of Laplace Transform using the Multivariable Calculus Theory of HOL-Light (2013),
    http://save.seecs.nust.edu.pk/shtaqdees/laplace.html
16. Ucar, A., Cetin, E., Kale, I.: A Continuous-Time Delta-Sigma Modulator for RF Subsampling Receivers. In: IEEE Transactions on Circuits and Systems, pp. 272–276. IEEE (2012)
17. Westra, J.R., Verhoeven, C.J.M., van Roermund, A.H.M.: Oscillators and Oscillator Systems: Classification, Analysis and Synthesis. Springer (1999)
18. Xiao, J.: Integral and Functional Analysis. Nova Publishers (2008)
19. Yang, X.: Mathematical Modeling with Multidisciplinary Applications. John Wiley & Sons (2013)

On Minimality and Integrity Constraints in Probabilistic Abduction

Calin-Rares Turliuc, Nataly Maimari, Alessandra Russo, and Krysia Broda

Department of Computing, Imperial College London, United Kingdom
{ct1810,nataly.maimari08,a.russo,k.broda}@imperial.ac.uk

Abstract. Abduction is a type of logical inference that can be successfully combined with probabilistic reasoning. However, the role of integrity constraints has not received much attention when performing logical-probabilistic inference. The contribution of our paper is a probabilistic abductive framework based on the distribution semantics for normal logic programs that handles negation as failure and integrity constraints in the form of denials. Integrity constraints are treated as evidence from the perspective of probabilistic inference. An implementation is provided that computes alternative (non-minimal) abductive solutions, using an appropriately modified abductive system, and generates the probability of a query, for given solutions. An example application of the framework is given, where gene network topologies are abduced according to biological expert knowledge, to probabilistically explain observed gene expressions. The example shows the practical utility of the proposed framework.

Keywords: abductive logic programming, probabilistic abduction, distribution semantics.

1 Introduction

Abductive reasoning is a method of logical inference which explains observations (or queries) by making assumptions on possible facts, called abducible atoms. Abduction has been used in various applications [13], e.g. diagnosis, high-level vision, natural language understanding, planning, knowledge assimilation, etc. The choice of the assumptions is often filtered through integrity constraints, i.e. rules which eliminate certain solutions. A solution of an abductive task is therefore a set of abducible atoms that do not violate the integrity constraints and that if true make the query valid. Abductive solutions are hypotheses and as such are inherently uncertain. For a given abductive task there may be multiple solutions which may be ranked according to some notion of plausibility.

In a model governed by uncertainty, it is reasonable to consider a probability distribution over the truth values of each (ground) abducible. This probabilistic perspective provides a method of quantitatively estimating the quality of the abductive solutions, and, consequently, that of the solved query. Introducing probability in abduction essentially redefines the notion of abductive solutions as no longer the minimal but the *most preferred* (possibly non minimal) assumptions, based on their probability, needed to explain a given query. Most existing work in probabilistic abduction (cf. Section 5) does not discuss minimality, nor the role of integrity constraints. In this paper, we treat integrity constraints as evidence from the perspective of probabilistic inference (i.e. the goal is to compute $P(Q|E)$, where Q is the query, and E the evidence). Typically, the query is a set of random variables, and the evidence is a set of random variables whose outcome is observed. We extend this notion of evidence to a set of constraints imposed on the model, expressed as a logical formula. To motivate the main features of our probabilistic abductive approach, including dropping the minimality requirement, consider the following example of an abductive task:

Example 1. In the rules below the abducible atoms are rained_last_night and sprinkler_was_on.

$$grass\_is\_wet \leftarrow rained\_last\_night$$
$$grass\_is\_wet \leftarrow sprinkler\_was\_on$$
$$shoes\_are\_wet \leftarrow grass\_is\_wet$$

The explanations of the observation that the shoes_are_wet are that either it rained_last_night or the sprinkler_was_on.

In the above example, the explanation that it rained_last_night *and* the sprinkler_was_on is non-minimal. We argue that if abduction is augmented with probability using the distribution semantics, non-minimal solutions contribute to the probability of the query, and thus cannot be discarded. Suppose that we know that there is a probability 0.6 that it rained_last_night (with the complementary probability if the abducible is false), and 0.7 that the sprinkler_was_on (with the same remark). One might be tempted to choose the latter explanation, based on its higher probability. However, if rained_last_night and sprinkler_was_on are independent random events, the joint probability of rained_last_night and sprinkler_was_on is computed as shown in Table 1. Under this assumption, the most probable scenario is that it rained last night *and* the sprinkler was on. So the explanation with highest probability is not necessarily the minimal one.

Table 1. Joint probability on the abducibles in Example 1

rained_last_night	sprinkler_was_on	P(rained_last_night, sprinkler_was_on)
false	false	0.12
false	true	0.28
true	false	0.18
true	true	0.42

Furthermore, most semantics for abduction would interpret the explanation rained_last_night as rained_last_night is true and sprinkler_was_on is false, and similarly for the explanation sprinkler_was_on, i.e. all the abducibles in the explanation are true, and all that are not in it are false. The probability of the observation shoes_are_wet is 0.88 (i.e. sum of the join probabilities in the last three rows) as in the last three interpretations in Table 1 shoes_are_wet is true. Computing this probability means, therefore, asking the probability that shoes_are_wet is true under any explanation. This implies that choosing one explanation over another is no longer arbitrary, or according to minimality or other criteria (e.g. Example 2.1 in [13]). Instead, each explanation contributes with a probability mass towards the probability of the observation and all possible explanations should be considered. If a choice of particular explanations is required, then the one with the highest probability should be preferred.

Example 1 shows also that to compute the correct probability of a given observation or query, the closed world assumption (CWA) on abducibles is insufficient. In Table 1, the last interpretation would not be covered by the CWA over minimal explanations. In our approach, we propose an open world interpretation of abducibles (cf. Section 3).

Let us now assume Example 1 to be extended with the integrity constraint ← sprinkler_was_on., expressing the statement that the sprinkler was off. This implies that the only explanation will be rained_last_night. Treating integrity constraints as evidence means computing the probabilistic inference $P(Q|IC)$. In our example $Q = \{$shoes_are_wet$\}$ and the conditional probability $\frac{P(Q,IC)}{P(IC)}$ is, in this case, given by $\frac{0.18}{0.18+0.12} = 0.6$, which is indeed the expected result of the probability of rained_last_night. If we, instead, extend Example 1 with the integrity constraint ← not rained_last_night., meaning that we know that it rained last night, then the probability of shoes_are_wet is $\frac{0.18+0.42}{0.18+0.42} = 1$. In summary, the contributions of this papers are:

1. a probabilistic abductive framework, based on the distribution semantics for normal logic programs [20,22], that handles negation as failure and integrity constraints in the form of denials, and provides an open world interpretation of abducibles;
2. a procedure for logical-probabilistic inference, based on the ASystem [14,17];
3. a practical application in the context of gene networks.

The paper is organized as follows. Section 2 introduces our framework and define our probability model by adapting the distribution semantics for normal logic programs under Fitting semantics [22]. In Section 3 we provide an implementation of our framework that uses an existing state-of-the-art abductive system, appropriately modified in order to support the computation of non-minimal abductive solutions. Section 4 illustrates the applicability of our framework to the real world problem of gene network inference from observed data. Networks are abduced as directed graphs with probabilistic edges to explain observed gene expressions. We learn the probabilities of the edges (gene interactions) that would maximize the probability of a given query and interpret the results. Section 5 discusses related work. In Section 6 we present future work and conclude.

2 Distribution Semantics for an Abductive Framework

An *abductive framework* is a tuple $\langle P, AB, IC \rangle$, where P is a normal logic program, AB is a possibly infinite set of ground atoms called *abducibles*, and IC is a set of integrity constraints expressed as denials, each having the form $\forall \overline{X} \leftarrow \Gamma$., where Γ is a set of literals and $\overline{X}$ is a set of variables. A query Q is a conjunction of existentially quantified literals and denials. An abductive solution for a query Q is a set of abducibles Δ, such that the ground instantiations of Δ, denoted $ground(\Delta)$ are elements in AB and:

- $comp_3(P \cup \Delta) \models Q$.
- $comp_3(P \cup \Delta) \models IC$.
- $comp_3(P \cup \Delta) \models CET$

where CET denotes the Clark Equality Theory axioms [2], and $comp_3(\Pi)$ the Fitting three-valued completion of a program Π [9].

We define our probabilistic abductive framework by integrating distribution semantics [22] into the above notion of an abductive framework. Informally, distribution semantics defines a probability distribution over the set of interpretations over a set of facts F and extends it to a probability distribution over interpretations of a program Π by applying the Fitting fixpoint operator [9]. This extension implies that the probability of an interpretation of the facts $I \subseteq F$ will have the same value as the probability of an interpretation I_Π of Π, given that I_Π is the fixpoint of I according to the rules in Π. In a similar fashion, we consider a two-valued interpretation over abducibles $I \subseteq AB$ and extend it to interpretations I_Π of the Herbrand base of the whole program Π. The interpretation I_Π is in general three-valued, however we impose the restriction that I_Π is two-valued, and in what follows we will treat it as such. We then consider a probability distribution P_{AB} with the sample space the set of all ground interpretations of abducibles (i.e. the powerset of AB) and we extend P_{AB} to a probability distribution P_Π with the sample space the set of all the ground interpretations of the Herbrand base of Π. To compute P_{AB}, we assume that the assignments of truth values to an abducible are independent events, and that all abducibles are *basic*, i.e. they do not appear in the heads of the rules in Π [13]. If each abducible $\delta \in AB$ has a probability $P(\delta)$ of being true (and a probability $1 - P(\delta)$ of being false), then P_{AB} is computed as:

$$P_{AB}(I) = \prod_{\delta \in I} P(\delta) \prod_{\delta \notin I} (1 - P(\delta))$$

P_{AB} is then extended to a probability distribution P_Π by applying Fitting's fixpoint operator Φ_Π to reach the fixpoint Φ_Π^∞ [9].

$$P_\Pi(I_\Pi) = \begin{cases} P_{AB}(I) & \text{if } I_\Pi = \Phi_\Pi^\infty(I) \\ 0 & \text{otherwise} \end{cases} \quad (1)$$

Given the above probability distribution, it is possible to compute the probability of a two-valued interpretation I_B of a set B of ground atoms in Π by marginalization:

$$P_\Pi(I_B) = \sum_{I_\Pi \text{ s.t. } I_B \subseteq I_\Pi} P_\Pi(I_\Pi)$$

For a single atom a, we write $P_\Pi(a)$ with the meaning $P_\Pi(\{a\})$ and $P_\Pi(\neg a)$ with the meaning $P_\Pi(\emptyset)$.

In Example 1, P_{AB} is the last column of Table 1, and the sample space is given by the other columns. P_Π is obtained by extending P_{AB} over grass_is_wet and shoes_are_wet, with the appropriate truth values, i.e. the or function of rained_last_night and sprinkler_was_on. For all other interpretations, P_Π is 0 (Equation 1).

The probability of a query Q given evidence expressed as integrity constraints IC is then:

$$P_\Pi(Q|IC) = \frac{P_\Pi(Q, IC)}{P_\Pi(IC)} \quad (2)$$

$$P_\Pi(Q, IC) = \sum_{\substack{I_\Pi \text{ s.t. } Q \subseteq I_\Pi \\ I_\Pi \models IC}} P_\Pi(I_\Pi) \quad (3)$$

$$P_\Pi(IC) = \sum_{I_\Pi \models IC} P_\Pi(I_\Pi) \quad (4)$$

Informally, $P_\Pi(Q|IC)$ is the ratio of the probability of the interpretations that agree with Q and do not violate the integrity constraints (Equation 3) over the probability of the interpretations that do not violate the integrity constraints (Equation 4).

The novel aspect of our approach is the definition of evidence as a set of integrity constraints, inspired by Markov Logic Networks [7] where the notions of query and evidence are generalized to first-order formulae. This is more expressive than traditional definitions of evidence (i.e. conjunction of random variables taking particular values), because denials can express statements like "random variables X and Y cannot take values x, respectively y at the same time".

In the following section, we describe a logical-probabilistic procedure based on the ASystem [14,17] which can be used for the inference of $P_\Pi(Q|IC)$.

3 A Probabilistic Abductive System

This section describes the implementation of our probabilistic abductive framework. It builds upon an existing abductive system, called ASystem [14,17], briefly described in Section 3.1, and adapts it in Section 3.2 to allow non minimal abductive solutions. Section 3.3 shows how the abductive answers are used for probabilistic inference.

3.1 A Brief Description of the ASystem

The proof procedure of the ASystem [14,17] can be viewed as a *state rewriting* process, where each state rewrite is driven by the application of *inference rules*. The latter handle also *finite domain and real constraints* using a constraint solver. The system can compute *non-ground answers* and uses *constructive negation*, instead of standard negation as failure. Its development was inspired by other abductive systems such as SLDNFA [6], ACLP [12], IFF [10]. The semantics used in the ASystem is the three-valued completion semantics ($comp_3$) [9]: an interpretation of the abducibles is implicitly two-valued, whereas the interpretation of the predicates in P is three-valued. The proof procedure can be viewed as a tree, where the nodes are *ASystem states* and each node generates children nodes according to a set of *inference rules* and a *selection strategy*. The root of the tree is the *initial state*, and the leaves are *failure states* or *success states*.

Definition 1 (ASystem state). *An ASystem state S is a tuple $(\mathcal{G}, \mathcal{ST})$.*

- *$\mathcal{G}$ is a set of goals where each goal can be a literal or a denial. All the variables except the ones universally quantified in the denials are existentially quantified.*
- *$\mathcal{ST}$ is a tuple $(\Delta, \mathcal{N}, \mathcal{E}, \mathcal{C})$ of four stores: Δ is the abducible store, a set of (non-ground) abducible atoms, $\mathcal{N}$ is the denial store, a set of denials (or dynamic integrity constraints), $\mathcal{E}$ is a set of (in)equalities, $\mathcal{C}$ is a set of finite domain or real constraints.*

A *selection strategy* Ξ has a two-fold role: it selects a goal G_i from the set $\mathcal{G}$, and if the goal is a denial $\forall \overline{Y} \leftarrow \Gamma$. it further selects a literal from Γ. A selection strategy is called *safe* if, in a failure goal, it never selects a negative literal or a constraint literal, if the arguments of the predicate include a universally quantified variable. If a failure goal contains only universally quantified negative literals and universally quantified constraint literals, the derivation using a safe selection strategy *flounders* and fails.

Definition 2 (Meaning of an ASystem state). *The meaning of an ASystem state $\mathcal{M}(S)$, $S = (\mathcal{G}, (\Delta, \mathcal{N}, \mathcal{E}, \mathcal{C}))$ is the first-order formula:*

$$\mathcal{M}(S) = \exists \overline{X} (\bigwedge_{g \in \mathcal{G}} g \wedge \bigwedge_{\delta \in \Delta} \delta \wedge \bigwedge_{\forall \overline{Y_\Gamma} \leftarrow \Gamma \in \mathcal{N}} (\forall \overline{Y_\Gamma} \leftarrow \Gamma.) \wedge \bigwedge_{e \in \mathcal{E}} e \wedge \bigwedge_{c \in \mathcal{C}} c)$$

$\overline{Y_\Gamma}$ *is the set of the universally quantified variables in the denial body Γ, and $\overline{X}$ is the set of all the other variables in $\mathcal{M}(S)$.*

Definition 3 (ASystem derivation tree). *Given an abductive framework $\langle P, AB, IC \rangle$, a query Q and a selection strategy Ξ, an ASystem derivation tree is a tree such that:*

- *every node of the tree is an ASystem state.*

- children nodes are generated by selecting a goal (and if the goal is a denial, further selecting a literal in the denial) according to Ξ, and then applying the inference rules on the selected goal.
- the initial state is $S_0 = \langle Q \cup IC, \mathcal{ST}_0 \rangle$, and $\mathcal{ST}_0 = (\emptyset, \emptyset, \emptyset, \emptyset)$.
- a success state is one in which $\mathcal{G} = \emptyset$, and $\mathcal{ST}$ is consistent. If $\mathcal{ST}$ is inconsistent or the derivation flounders, then that state is a failure state. A state is a leaf of the tree iff it is either a success or failure state.

Details of the inference rules and soundness and completeness results are described in [16].

3.2 A Richer Set of Interpretations

According to the definition of our probabilistic semantics (cf. Section 2), every interpretation of abducibles $I \subseteq AB$ has a probability value. This implies that the minimality of abductive solutions, as defined in [13], is no longer a desired property. Since the ASystem incorporates minimality through its rules and interpretations of abducibles, it needs to be modified in order to lift this restriction. To achieve this goal, we will propose an open world interpretation of abducibles via *consistent extended interpretations (CEIs)*. Additionally, since probabilistic inference is currently performed using ground predicates, the ASystem must also be modified such that its success states contain only abducibles, since these are groundable.

The latter modification will be realized using a new safe selection strategy. In order to discuss it, we need to introduce the concept of ASystem types.

Definition 4 (ASystem types). *We distinguish the following types of atoms in the abductive context of the ASystem: (i) abducibles (ii) defined predicates and (iii) constraints. The constraint predicates are of the form $X = Y$ and $X \neq Y$ for in/equality constraints, and $X = Y$, $X > Y$, $X < Y$, ... for real constraints.*

Given a denial $\forall \overline{Y} \leftarrow \Gamma$, the set Γ of body literals is split into three disjoint sets $\Gamma = ABL \cup NGL \cup OL$. The set ABL contains abducible literals. NGL contains negative non-ground defined predicates and non-ground constraint literals. OL consists of the remaining literals: positive defined literals, negative ground defined literals, and ground constraint literals. Let $\overline{Y}_{NGL}$ denote the set of variables appearing in the elements of NGL and $\overline{Y}_{ABL}$ the set of variables in the elements of ABL.

Definition 5 (Unfolding Safe Selection Strategy). *An unfolding safe selection strategy ξ is a safe selection strategy that given the current goal $G = G^- \cup \{\forall \overline{Y} \leftarrow \Gamma\}$ and the selected denial $\forall \overline{Y} \leftarrow \Gamma$, safely selects a literal from Γ in the following manner:*

- *if $OL \neq \emptyset$, select an element from it.*
- *else, if $\overline{Y}_{NGL} \cap \overline{Y}_{ABL} \neq \emptyset$, (i) ground all the abducibles containing at least a variable from $\overline{Y}_{NGL} \cap \overline{Y}_{ABL}$; (ii) set the new goal to be $G^+ =*

$G^- \cup \{ground(\forall \overline{Y} \leftarrow \Gamma)\}$, where $ground(\forall \overline{Y} \leftarrow \Gamma)$ is the grounding of the selected denial goal with respect to $\overline{Y}_{NGL} \cap \overline{Y}_{ABL}$ and the non-ground negative abducible literals in NGL, (iii) apply the unfolding safe selection strategy to the new goal G^+.
- else ($OL = \emptyset$ and $\overline{Y}_{NGL} \cap \overline{Y}_{ABL} = \emptyset$), if $ABL \neq \emptyset$, select an element from ABL. If the selected literal is negative and non-ground, we ground it and apply the unfolding safe selection strategy to the newly generated goal.
- else fail.

The new safe selection strategy allows us to prove assumptions on what the denial store $\mathcal{N}$ of any state would contain (see Proposition 1).

Proposition 1. *Given an unfolding safe selection strategy ξ, the denial store in a derivation tree is either empty or its denials have in their body only literals of the following types: abducibles, universally quantified constraints or universally quantified negative literals. Furthermore, for all denials $\forall \overline{Y} \leftarrow \Gamma$ in the denial store it holds that there are no common variables between the abducible literals and the negative non-ground literals and positive non-ground constraint literals ($\overline{Y}_{NGL} \cap \overline{Y}_{ABL} = \emptyset$).*

Example 2. Consider an abductive task with the empty program P, integrity constraints $IC = \{\forall X, Y \leftarrow a(X), not\ p(X), not\ b(Y).\}$ where p is a defined predicate, a is an abducible with domain $\{1, 2\}$ and $b/1$ an abducible with domain $\{3, 4\}$. Applying our system with an empty goal yields a success state in which the denial is moved to the denial store, and nothing is abduced. Given our abducible types and the unfolding selection strategy, our approach first grounds the shared variable X, generating the new goal:

$$\{\forall Y \leftarrow a(1), not\ p(1), not\ b(Y)., \forall Y \leftarrow a(2), not\ p(2), not\ b(Y).\}$$

Let us assume that the first denial is selected as current denial goal[1]. The literal $not\ p(1)$ is selected, and since the predicate p has not definition $not\ p(1)$ succeeds, reducing the goal to $\forall Y \leftarrow a(1), not\ b(Y)$. In this new goal, we can either select $a(1)$, completing the proof with the denial store $\{\forall Y \leftarrow a(1), not\ b(Y).\}$, or we can ground $not\ b(Y)$ to generate the goal $\{\forall Y \leftarrow a(1), not\ b(3)., \forall Y \leftarrow a(1), not\ b(4).\}$.

The unfolding safe selection strategy imposes an important restriction on the denials: the variables that appear both in abducible and non-abducible atoms have a finite domain, according to the domains of the abducible atoms. If one were to lift this restriction, then the denial $\leftarrow a(X), not\ p(X).$ would always fail, assuming that $a(X)$ is an abducible and $p(X)$ is a defined predicate.

Our goal is to have only states whose meanings are *(groundable) formulae containing only abducible predicates*, since the success states and the probability of the abducibles will be used for inference. The unfolding safe selection strategy allows us to remove from the denial store any non-abducible, i.e. according to

---
[1] The second one is handled similarly.

Proposition 1, universally quantified constraints or negative literals. This is possible due to the second property stated by the proposition claiming that there are no common variables between abducibles and non-abducibles. For example, in a denial such as $\forall Y \leftarrow a, not\ p(Y).$, where a is an abducible and $p(Y)$ is a defined predicate, $p(Y)$ cannot be failed for all Y, so $not\ p(Y)$ is true, and the denial is equivalent to: $\forall Y \leftarrow a$. The same holds for universally quantified constraints in denials. From now on, we assume the denial stores of all states contain only abducibles.

The ASystem interpretations of a success state $S = (\emptyset, (\Delta, \mathcal{N}, \mathcal{E}, \mathcal{C}))$ is simply: $ground(\Delta)$, i.e. all the abducibles in $ground(\Delta)$ are true, and the rest are false. We propose a different understanding of an abductive solution corresponding to a success state, while assuming the use of an unfolding safe selection strategy. The reason we introduce this concept is that the definition of an open world interpretation of abducibles is necessary for correct inference in our probabilistic semantics.

Definition 6 (Consistent Extended Interpretations (CEIs)). *Let S be a success state in the proof of a query Q using an unfolding safe selection strategy and $M(S)$ the meaning of that success state, a ground formula containing only abducibles. The* consistent extended interpretations (CEIs) *of S, denoted by $\mathcal{I}_S$ is the set of models of $M(S)$. Since Δ is part of the conjunction in $M(S)$, all CEIs make the abducibles in Δ true. However, there may be other abducibles which are true in a CEI, hence the title* extended. *These extensions are not arbitrary, instead they must not violate the integrity constraints, encoded in the denial store $\mathcal{N}$, which is part of $M(S)$, hence the title* consistent.

For a query Q, the CEIs $\mathcal{I}_Q$ are simply the union of the all success states, or equivalently, the models of $\bigvee_{i=1}^{n} M(S_i)$, assuming S_i, $i = 1, \ldots, n$ are all the success states for Q.

Changing the perspective on how interpretations of abductive solutions are constructed requires a theoretical justification. Theorem 1 shows that a CEI corresponds to an ASystem interpretation of a success state for an extended query. The extended query is the original query plus the extended part of the CEI, i.e. the abducibles that are true, but not in the abducible store.

Theorem 1. *Consider an abductive framework $\langle P, AB, IC \rangle$ with query Q. Let Δ_i, $i = 1, \ldots, n$ be the abductive solutions. Let $\mathcal{I}_Q$ be the set of consistent extended interpretations of Q. For every $\Delta_i^* \subseteq AB \setminus ground(\Delta_i)$ let $I = ground(\Delta_i) \cup \Delta_i^*$ be a interpretation for the abductive solution to query $Q' = Q \cup \Delta_i^*$ and let $\mathcal{I}_{\Delta^*}$ be the set of all of all such interpretations.*

Then $\mathcal{I}_Q = \mathcal{I}_{\Delta^*}$.

Due to Theorem 1, it is not difficult to extend and prove the notions of soundness and completeness to CEIs.

Theorem 2 (Soundness for CEIs). *Given an abductive framework $\langle P, AB, IC \rangle$ with query Q, and the set $\mathcal{I}_Q$ of consistent extended interpretations, then*

$\forall I \in \mathcal{I}_Q$, $comp_3(P \cup I) \models Q$, and $comp_3(P \cup I)$ is consistent.

Theorem 3 (Completeness for CEIs). *Given an abductive framework $\langle P, AB, IC \rangle$ with query Q, and the set $\mathcal{I}_Q$ of consistent extended interpretations.*
(1) If $\mathcal{I}_Q = \emptyset$, then $comp_3(P) \models \forall \overline{X}(\neg Q)$; and
(2) If $comp_3(P \cup \exists \overline{X}(Q))$ is satisfiable, then $\mathcal{I}_Q \neq \emptyset$.

Example 3. We illustrate the concept of CEIs through the example of "Friends and Smokers" social network analysis, in the variant presented in the ProbLog 2 tutorial[2], using the standard Prolog syntax. Suppose there are 4 people: person(i), $\forall i = 1, \ldots, 4$ in a social network:

$$\{\text{friend}(i,j) | (i,j) \in \{(1,2), (2,1), (2,4), (3,2), (4,2)\}$$

Furthermore, people smoke either because they are stressed, or they are influenced by a friend who smokes, and smoking may cause asthma. We encode this in Prolog as:

```
smokes(X) :- smokes(X, [X]).
smokes(X, _L) :- stress(X).
smokes(X, L) :-
  friend(X,Y),
  \+ member(Y,L),
  influences(Y,X),
  smokes(Y, [Y|L]).
asthma(X) :- smokes(X), smoke_asthma(X).
```

The abducibles in this problem are: stress/1, influences/2, and smoke_asthma/1, where the arguments are of type person.

Assume the query is asthma(1), and the evidence is:
$\{\leftarrow not\ smokes(2)., \leftarrow influences(4,2).\}$. This means we are interested if person 1 has asthma, having observed that person 2 smokes, and person 4 has no influence on person 2. The proof procedure returns four success states, as possible explanations for the query, with the following abducible and denial stores:
$\Delta_1 = \{\text{stress}(1), \text{influences}(1,2), \text{smoke\_asthma}(1), \text{stress}(2), \text{influences}(2,1)\}$
$\mathcal{N}_1 = \{\leftarrow \text{influences}(4,2)\}$
$\Delta_2 = \{\text{smoke\_asthma}(1), \text{stress}(2), \text{influences}(2,1)\}$
$\mathcal{N}_2 = \{\leftarrow \text{influences}(4,2)\}$
$\Delta_3 = \{\text{smoke\_asthma}(1), \text{stress}(1), \text{influences}(1,2)\}$
$\mathcal{N}_3 = \{\leftarrow \text{influences}(4,2)\}$
$\Delta_4 = \{\text{smoke\_asthma}(1), \text{stress}(1), \text{stress}(2)\}$
$\mathcal{N}_4 = \{\leftarrow \text{influences}(4,2)\}$

The CEIs for the second success state are the models of the meaning of the state:

$$\text{smoke\_asthma}(1) \wedge \text{stress}(2) \wedge \text{influences}(2,1) \wedge \neg\text{influences}(4,2)$$

---

[2] http://dtai.cs.kuleuven.be/problog/v2/tutorial.html#tut_part1_smokers

instead of the single interpretation Δ_2. The same holds for the other success states, and the CEIs for the query are the models of the disjunction of all the formulae. This allows the correct inference of the probability of the query, as shown in the next section.

3.3 Probabilistic Inference

The previous subsection has presented the appropriate modification to the ASystem to enable the computation of consistent extended interpretations (CEIs) for a particular success state as the models of the meaning of that success state, and, consequently, for an arbitrary query. The CEIs will be used to compute the probability of a query, given the evidence as integrity constraints. The definition of this quantity is given in Equation 2, Section2. At a first glance, it seems two proofs are necessary, one in order to compute the numerator, using as initial goal the query and the integrity constraints ($Q \cup IC$) and one for the denominator, using as initial goal just the integrity constraints. However, in this manner we prove the integrity constraints twice. To avoid this redundancy, we refine the unfolding safe selection strategy, such that the initial goals and the following subgoals generated by the integrity constraints are solved before the goals and subgoals obtained processing the query[3].

The inference is divided into two parts. The initial goal is $Q \cup IC$ and we stop expanding the proof tree once the integrity constraints are solved. This process ends in *pseudo-success states* of the form: $(Q, (\Delta, \mathcal{N}, \mathcal{E}, \mathcal{C}))$. To compute the CEIs needed for the denominator in Equation 2, we use the models of $\bigvee_j M(S'_j)$, where $S'_j = (\emptyset, (\Delta_j, \mathcal{N}_j, \mathcal{E}_j, \mathcal{C}_j))$ is constructed from the pseudo-success state indexed j by eliminating the query Q from the goal.

The second part of the proof, which is needed to compute Equation 3, resumes the application of the inference rules on the partially developed tree from the pseudo-success states (the other leaves are failure states). Finally, we obtain the needed CEIs from the (true) success states.

We discuss the exact probability computation from the meaning of the success states. In our current implementation, we use the idea of ProbLog I [15,4]: we compile $\bigvee_{i=1}^{n} M(S_i)$ (and similarly for $M(S'_j)$ in the case of pseudo-success states) to a BDD, and compute the probability of the BDD.

Example 4. Extending Example 3, suppose that there is 0.3 probability that a person is stressed, 0.4 probability that smoke causes asthma, and 0.2 probability that one friend influences another. Compiling the disjunction of the meaning of the states in a BDD and computing its probability yields the value: 0.2035 as the probability that person 1 has asthma under any explanation.

---

[3] Note that this refinement concerns the goal selection rather than selecting a literal from a denial, the main feature of an unfolding safe selection strategy.

Furthermore, we can extend the example with more complex forms of evidence. If one observes that in the studied social network, people with asthma don't influence other people to smoke, we can encode this as:
$\leftarrow asthma(X), influences(X,Y)$.

Running the same query after adding this integrity constraint to the program yields a probability of 0.0677, which, as expected, is lower than the probability of person 1 having asthma without this observation. This can be explained also by examining the two success states, with the abducible stores:
$\Delta_1 = \{\text{smoke\_asthma}(1), \text{stress}(2), \text{influences}(2,1)\}$
$\Delta_2 = \{\text{stress}(1), \text{smoke\_asthma}(1), \text{stress}(2)\}$

These solutions correspond to the second and fourth success states in Example 3. The other two are no longer inferred since in both solutions person 1 influences person 2, and person 1 has asthma, thus violating the newly introduced integrity constraint.

In principle, we could use different approaches to compile and evaluate the ground formulae, such as weighted model counting on DNNFs used in ProbLog 2 [8], or, for approximate inference, the MaxWalkSAT procedure used in Markov logic networks [7].

Probabilistic inference assumes that the probabilities of the abducibles are known. Nevertheless, in many situations, these are not known. Instead, queries or explanations are observed, and the probabilities of the abducibles are learned to maximize the likelihood of the observed data. Based on the encoding of the ground formulae, we can use existing algorithms for parameter learning, e.g. in Section 4 we use the EM algorithm for BDDs proposed in [11] to rank abductive solutions.

4 Evaluation

4.1 Friends and Smokers

In order to scale Examples 3 and 4, we simulate synthetic social networks by generating power law random graphs using Python Web Graph Generator[4]. We vary the maximum nodes from 5 to 200 with a step of 5, and the maximum edges are double the maximum nodes. The obtained graphs are then parsed into appropriate input files for our system, and for ProbLog 2. The initial files contain only one random query atom with predicate asthma, which we enrich with 10 random evidence literals, 5 with the smokers predicate name, and 5 with smokers. We then run the abduction (without BDD compilation and evaluation) and compare our performance with the ProbLog 2 counterpart, the grounding step[5].

---

[4] http://pywebgraph.sourceforge.net/
[5] ProbLog 2 has four steps: grounding, CNF conversion, compilation and evaluation, and our modified ASystem can be used as an alternative to the first step. We run ProbLog 2 with default parameters.

Without evidence, our probabilistic abductive system slightly outperforms grounding on large graphs. This result is expected since our top-down proof grounds only what is needed in the proof of the query, rather than the whole program. In the presence of evidence, however, our current prototype implementation suffers from the lack of tabling, and the time for the proof of the denials increases exponentially in the number of denials. The grounding step of ProbLog 2 has the same complexity when incorporating evidence as in the previous case, since the evidence is treated in a different way[6].

In future work, we plan to improve the runtime of handling integrity constraints by either developing a tabling mechanism for abduction, or solving each integrity constraint separately and assembling the final ground formula as a conjunction of the formulae of the query, resp. of each integrity constraint.

4.2 Gene Interaction

We further evaluate our probabilistic abductive system on the problem of finding network structures in the context of gene interaction networks based on observed data and constraints determined by biological expertise. Our application is motivated by the availability of high-throughput data. The task of analysing such complex data requires computational tools to automatically infer networks from data. Key challenges in network inference include incomplete and noisy input, detection of complex network structures that capture fundamental properties (e.g., robustness oscillations, bistability) of biological systems and computational complexity. An abductive framework caters for constraint checks and prior knowledge incorporation, thus partially dealing with the problems [18].

Our probabilistic abductive system has been used to generate a network of 11 genes, shaped by the nature of the interactions between genes. The different types of interactions between any pair of genes represent our abducibles: $compatible\_regulator(G1, G2, E)$ and $overpowered\_regulator(G2, G2, E2)$ (abbreviated to $r(G1, G2, E)$ and $or(G1, G2, E)$). The first two arguments of these abducibles are genes, whereas the third argument E is a binary variable over the set $\{1, -1\}$ denoting the causal effect of the interaction between two genes. For example, $r(g1, g2, 1)$ (resp. $r(g1, g2, -1)$) means that gene $g1$ activates (resp. inhibits) gene $g2$. Compatible regulators represent regulators that satisfy the sign consistency principle which postulates that the state of a target gene $G2$ is directly related to the state of an activator $G1$ and inversely related to the state of an inhibitor. Overpowered regulators are regulators that are overpowered by a compatible regulator acting on the same target and thus are inconsistent with the sign consistency principle. The probability of the abducibles can be interpreted as the the strength of the knowledge that led to this link being present. The higher the probability the higher the chance that the link is true.

Our perspective on probabilistic abduction as requiring non-minimal solutions is reflected in this experiment as biologists are interested in maximal networks

---

[6] If our understanding is correct, the truth values of the atoms are propagated in the ground program.

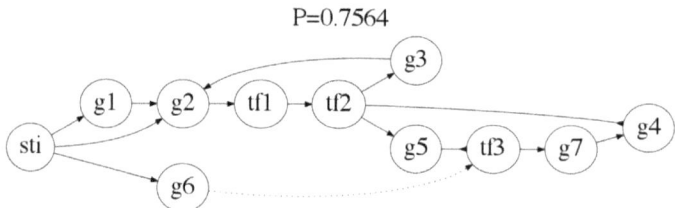

Fig. 1. Normal (resp. dashed) edges are r (resp. or) abducibles. Normal (resp. inverted) arrow heads are activation (resp. inhibition).

to distinguish between interactions that are allowed and interactions which are not biologically justified. During the inference process many different instances of the abducibles can be generated and constraints expressing expert knowledge are required to restrict the computation to possible biologically plausible networks. For instance, abducibles have to satisfy existing knowledge of sets of potential gene interactions:

$\leftarrow r(X,Y,E), not\ interactive\_potential(Y,X).$
$\leftarrow or(X,Y,E), not\ interactive\_potential(Y,X).$

It is also important to guarantee that a gene is not assumed to be at the same time a compatible and an overpowered regulator of another gene, and that for each overpowered regulator, there is at least one compatible regulator that can overpower it. These are captured in our model by the constraints: $\leftarrow r(X,Y,E), or(X,Y,E).$

$\leftarrow or(X,Y,E), not\ exists\_overpowered(X,Y).$
$\leftarrow or(X,Y,E), overpowered(Z,X,Y), not\ r(Z,Y,W).$

The biological problem in hand has also insufficient known biological data to provide reliable probabilities on the gene interactions. So instead of applying direct inference, we have used the BDD-based expectation maximization (EM) learning algorithm [11]. Using our probabilistic abductive system we obtain 36 plausible networks. Learning the probabilities of the interaction is done in order to maximize the probability of each network (i.e. the success probability), and this allows the ranking of the networks in terms of their likelihood. We initialize the probabilities to 0.5 and the learning algorithm takes 135 iterations to converge. In the abduced networks the *compatible_regulator* links appear more frequently than *overpowered_regulator*, which is reflected in the learned parameters and, consequently, the ranking of the networks. For example, the top ranked network contains only *compatible_regulator* links. Figure 1 shows a network validated by biological experiments.

A probabilistic abductive framework such as the one proposed in this paper extends the benefits of abductive inference to capturing noise in the input data and dealing with the problem of model selection. Given the number of variables involved, there are a vast number of possible network topologies, and the problem of model selection is combinatorial. Validating each of them would far exceed practical resources. Our probabilistic approach provides preference measures over links within a network and over networks, thus helping in the design of follow up experiments to discriminate between models.

5 Related Work

Logical-probabilistic reasoning has been defined in the context of deduction, induction and abduction. In this section, we compare our approach to existing work that focuses on probabilistic abduction or uses distribution semantics.

Probabilistic Horn abduction, later developed into the independent choice logic (ICL) [19], is one of the first probabilistic abduction frameworks. ICL accepts as input normal logic programs, but does not support integrity constraints. PRiSM [21] is a system created by the authors of distribution semantics that allows negation as failure, yet probabilistic abduction in PRiSM does not handle integrity constraints, and explanations are required to be mutually exclusive. ProbLog [5,15] is defined in a deductive setting, so it does not feature integrity constraints, and furthermore, the use of negation is limited to probabilistic facts or predicates which are not defined based on probabilistic facts. The latter issue has been addressed in ProbLog 2 [8], a system which, similarly to answer set programming, relies on grounding. Our system postpones grounding as much as possible, and the defined predicates in the program are not required to be groundable. Probabilistic abduction has also been defined in the context of constraint-handling rules (CHR) systems [1] where clauses are definite, and the integrity constraints can contain only abducibles. A probabilistic abduction method for classical negation which allows the encoding of integrity constraints is introduced in [11], but does not propose a probabilistic semantics in an abductive setting.

Markov logic networks (MLNs) [7] provide a different framework for combining probabilistic and logical reasoning. Markov networks are used as a probabilistic model and first-order theories encode the knowledge. Our approach is significantly different in the sense that it is based on abductive logic programming and the distribution semantics. In a MLN all formulas are treated as soft constraints, while in our approach we clearly distinguish between the rules in the logic program and the integrity constraints expressed as denials. Furthermore, we treat the integrity constraints as hard constraints: the consistent extended interpretations never violate the constraints. The possibility of viewing denials as soft constraints is a direction we wish to pursue in future work.

6 Conclusions

In this paper, we have proposed a method for applying distribution semantics in an abductive framework and provided an implementation based on the abductive procedure ASystem, showing how it can be adapted for probabilistic inference by removing the requirement that an abductive solution should be minimal. We have formally shown that our framework is correct with respect to distribution semantics. Advantages of our approach include the ability to handle negation as failure and integrity constraints as denials, as well as numerical constraints and term (in-)equality. We have evaluated our implementation by applying it to the task of finding biologically plausible networks describing gene interactions, which requires discovering non-minimal solutions.

Future work includes making probabilistic inference in our system feasible for larger problems through improved efficiency by tabling mechanisms. Due to the similarity between abduction and induction, the former can be used as an inference mechanism in inductive logic programming (ILP). We plan to integrate our probabilistic abduction framework in a probabilistic ILP context, building on results in [3] where the ASystem is used to explore the hypothesis space in order to find solutions to an ILP task.

References

1. Christiansen, H.: Implementing Probabilistic Abductive Logic Programming with Constraint Handling Rules. In: Schrijvers, T., Frühwirth, T. (eds.) Constraint Handling Rules. LNCS (LNAI), vol. 5388, pp. 85–118. Springer, Heidelberg (2008), http://dx.doi.org/10.1007/978-3-540-92243-8_5
2. Clark, K.L.: Negation as failure. In: Logic and Data Bases, pp. 293–322 (1977)
3. Corapi, D., Russo, A., Lupu, E.: Inductive logic programming as abductive search. In: ICLP (Technical Communications), pp. 54–63 (2010)
4. De Raedt, L., Kimmig, A., Gutmann, B., Kersting, K., Santos Costa, V., Toivonen, H.: Probabilistic inductive querying using ProbLog. Springer (2010), https://lirias.kuleuven.be/handle/123456789/284080
5. De Raedt, L., Kimmig, A., Toivonen, H.: ProbLog: A probabilistic Prolog and its application in link discovery. In: Proceedings of the 20th International Joint Conference on Artificial Intelligence, IJCAI 2007, pp. 2462–2467 (2007)
6. Denecker, M.: Knowledge representation and reasoning in incomplete logic programming. Ph.D. thesis, Department of Computer Science, K.U.Leuven, Leuven, Belgium, de Schreye, Danny and Denef, Jan (supervisors) (September 1993), https://lirias.kuleuven.be/handle/123456789/131431
7. Domingos, P., Kok, S., Poon, H., Richardson, M., Singla, P.: Unifying logical and statistical ai. In: Proceedings of the 21st National Conference on Artificial Intelligence, AAAI 2006, vol. 1, pp. 2–7. AAAI Press (2006), http://dl.acm.org/citation.cfm?id=1597538.1597540
8. Fierens, D., den Broeck, G.V., Thon, I., Gutmann, B., Raedt, L.D.: Inference in probabilistic logic programs using weighted cnf's. In: Proceedings of the Twenty-Seventh Conference Annual Conference on Uncertainty in Artificial Intelligence (UAI 2011), pp. 211–220. AUAI Press, Corvallis (2011)
9. Fitting, M.: A kripke-kleene semantics for logic programs. J. Log. Program. 2(4), 295–312 (1985)
10. Fung, T.H., Kowalski, R.: The iff proof procedure for abductive logic programming. The Journal of Logic Programming 33(2), 151–165 (1997), http://www.sciencedirect.com/science/article/pii/S0743106697000265
11. Inoue, K., Sato, T., Ishihata, M., Kameya, Y., Nabeshima, H.: Evaluating abductive hypotheses using an em algorithm on bdds. In: Proceedings of the 21st International Jont Conference on Artifical Intelligence, IJCAI 2009, pp. 810–815. Morgan Kaufmann Publishers Inc., San Francisco (2009), http://dl.acm.org/citation.cfm?id=1661445.1661574

12. Kakas, A., Michael, A., Mourlas, C.: Aclp: Abductive constraint logic programming. The Journal of Logic Programming 44(1-3), 129–177 (2000), http://www.sciencedirect.com/science/article/pii/S0743106699000758
13. Kakas, A.C., Kowalski, R.A., Toni, F.: Abductive logic programming. J. Log. Comput. 2(6), 719–770 (1992)
14. Kakas, A.C., Van Nuffelen, B., Denecker, M.: A-system: Problem solving through abduction. In: Proceedings of the Seventeenth International Joint Conference on Artificial Intelligence, vol. 1, pp. 591–596. IJCAI, inc. and AAAI, Morgan Kaufmann Publishers, Inc. (2001), http://www.cs.kuleuven.ac.be/cgi-bin-dtai/publ_info.pl?id=34862
15. Kimmig, A.: A Probabilistic Prolog and its Applications. Ph.D. thesis, K.U. Leuven (2010)
16. Ma, J.: Distributed Abductive Reasoning: Theory, Implementation and Application. Ph.D. thesis, Imperial College London (2011)
17. Ma, J.: Abductive reasoning module for sicstus prolog (2012), http://www-dse.doc.ic.ac.uk/cgi-bin/moin.cgi/abduction
18. Maimari, N., Broda, K., Kakas, A., Krams, R., Russo, A.: Arni: Abductive inference of complex regulatory network structures (poster). In: 21st Annual International Conference on Intelligent Systems for Molecular Biology, 12th European Conference on Computational Biology, ISMB/ECCB 2013 (2013)
19. Poole, D.: Abducing through negation as failure: stable models within the independent choice logic. J. Log. Program. 44(1-3), 5–35 (2000)
20. Sato, T.: A statistical learning method for logic programs with distribution semantics. In: Proceedings of the 12th International Conference on Logic Programming, pp. 715–729. MIT Press (1995)
21. Sato, T., Kameya, Y.: Parameter learning of logic programs for symbolic-statistical modeling. J. Artif. Intell. Res. (JAIR) 15, 391–454 (2001)
22. Sato, T., Kameya, Y., Zhou, N.F.: Generative modeling with failure in prism. In: IJCAI, pp. 847–852 (2005)

POLAR: A Framework for Proof Refactoring

Dominik Dietrich[1], Iain Whiteside[2], and David Aspinall[3]

[1] Cyber-Physical Systems, DFKI Bremen, Germany
[2] School of Computing Science, Newcastle University
[3] School of Informatics, The University of Edinburgh

Abstract. We present a prototype refactoring framework based on graph rewriting and bidirectional transformations that is designed to be *generic*, *extensible*, and *declarative*. Our approach uses a language-independent graph meta-model to represent proof developments in a generic way. We use graph rewriting to enrich the meta-model with dependency information and to perform refactorings, which are written as declarative rewrite rules. Our framework, called POLAR, is implemented in the GRGEN rewriting engine.

1 Introduction

Interactive theorem proving (ITP) is the science and art of constructing formal proofs on a computer, using a formal logical language to state properties and a *proof language* to construct the proof, with the assistance of a human guide. ITP is maturing rapidly. Recent work on operating system kernel verification has seen the size of the largest development leap past 500,000 lines of proof [18], [6] and Gonthier and his team recently announced the completion of their formalisation of the famous Feit-Thompson theorem, which weighs in at 170,000 lines and contains 4,300 theorems [14], [13]. The original informal proof was part of the categorisation of finite simple groups in which Aschbacher quipped that 'the probability of an error in the proof is one' [2], which makes a fully verified version of this proof all the more important. Furthermore, Tom Hales' Flyspeck project to formally prove Kepler's famous conjecture about sphere packing is in the final stages and may become the largest formal proof yet [16].

As proofs grow ever larger and more ambitious, the need for tool support to aid development becomes more important. However, while software engineers have a wide variety of tools at their disposal, budding proof engineers have had to 'make do' with basic environments that are akin to those used for programming in the 80's. Over thirty years of research into Software Engineering has resulted in a wide variety of tools and techniques to support the software life-cycle. Large proof developments have a similar life-cycle, but it is not yet well-supported. This paper takes a modest step towards developing the tools of the trade for *Proof Engineering* by adapting the popular technique of *refactoring*.

The term refactoring was coined by Opdyke in his seminal thesis to describe behaviour preserving transformations that improve the readability, maintainability, and efficiency of software [20]. Many refactorings, such as *rename method* and *delete method*, are integrated into modern IDEs, and a refactoring engine is seen as a crucial tool as programs regularly reach many thousands of lines.

Similarly, there is an urgent need to support *proof refactoring* in proof development environments [6], [12]. In previous work, we have shown that proof refactoring is feasible and given it a firm theoretical grounding, [24], [25]. With the work reported here, we take a further step and provide a prototype tool for refactoring called POLAR (PrOof LAnguage Refactoring)[1]. In designing POLAR, we had four key requirements:
 (i) With many ITP systems that each have a reasonably small userbase, we wished it to be as widely applicable as possible.
 (ii) It's infeasible to implement all refactorings that may be required. Therefore, we wished proof engineers to be able to implement custom refactorings.
 (iii) We wanted to provide guarantees that the tool will not cause unexpected *semantic* changes to the proof development.
 (iv) Finally, refactorings should be specified in a natural way, so simple refactorings should require only a few lines to implement.

Based on the observation that many refactorings (e.g., those described in [24]) simply traverse through the abstract syntax to find the appropriate part to refactor (and backed by recent programming language refactoring research [19]), we based our approach on *graph rewriting*, where declarative rules can directly match the location to refactor. We transform a theory to a graph representation where unnecessary details are abstracted away, then *declarative* rewrite rules are used to transform the graph. Finally, a bidirectional transformation mechanism allows us to regain a refactored theory. By providing a graph meta-model, we ensure our approach is *generic*: attaching a new proof language involves writing an appropriate translation to the graph model. Furthermore, we have built POLAR on top of the GRGEN graph rewriting engine, which provides a robust and efficient basis. Furthermore, additional refactorings can be implemented using GRGEN's DSL for writing transformations. The result is a refactoring framework that is *generic, extensible,* and *declarative*. Specifically, we identify the following contributions:
(1) The design and implementation of a prototype framework for refactoring proof. POLAR currently supports two proof languages and ten refactorings.
(2) Furthermore, POLAR is extensible in two directions: new proof languages and new refactorings can be added.
(3) We believe our framework is the only approach in the refactoring community to combine abstraction of irrelevant details with a bidirectional transformation mechanism for obtaining a refactored source theory.

A more detailed presentation of POLAR can be found in the second author's PhD thesis [24, Chapter 11].

Outline of paper In the next section (Section 2), we introduce refactoring by an example. Then, Section 3 gives an overview of our approach. The full details of

---

[1] Our prototype tool is available at
http://homepages.inf.ed.ac.uk/s0569509/refactoring.html

POLAR are given in Section 4. Finally, we sketch related and future work and conclude in Section 5.

2 Introducing Refactoring

POLAR is connected to two proof languages: Hiscript, as described in Whiteside's PhD thesis [24]; and, ΩSCRIPT, as described in Dietrich's PhD thesis [9]. Throughout this paper, we use a simple theory in these languages as a running example. The running example for Hiscript and ΩSCRIPT is shown in Figs. 1 and 2 respectively.

The languages are similar, being both based on Isar [23], but have some minor differences: (1) The syntax differs: backward steps, for example, are handled in Hiscript using the **show** command; however, in ΩSCRIPT the command is **subgoal**. (2) Hiscript is a *generic* proof language, which we instantiate with a sequent style notation to describe the proof context. ΩSCRIPT uses a natural deduction style syntax to describe changes of the proof context. Thus, the number of available proof commands differ; ΩSCRIPT, for example, allows assumptions to be named and used directly but this is not possible in Hiscript. (3) In Hiscript, theory items, such as tactics and lemmas, are annotated with a visibility. Only **public** items are exported. In ΩSCRIPT, all items are exported.

```
theory set
begin
  public tac intro := ⊆−def | ∩−def | id

  public lemma comm: A ∩ B ⊆ B ∩ A
  proof( intro )
  show x ∈ A ∩ B ⊢ x ∈ B ∩ A
    proof( intro )
      show B: x ∈ A ∩ B ⊢ x ∈ B
        by ∩−elim ; ax
      show A: x ∈ A ∩ B ⊢ x ∈ A
        by ∩−elim ; ax
    qed
  qed
end
```

Fig. 1. Hiscript running example

```
theory set
  strategy intro := ⊆−def | ∩−def | Id

  lemma comm: A ∩ B ⊆ B ∩ A
  proof( intro )
    assume hyp: x ∈ A ∩ B
    subgoal x ∈ B ∩ A
    proof ( intro )
      subgoal x ∈ B from hyp
        by auto
      subgoal x ∈ A from hyp
        by auto
    qed
  qed
end
```

Fig. 2. ΩSCRIPT running example

The Hiscript theory, for example, introduces a single tactic definition called *intro*, which attempts to apply either the definition of subset or intersection; if both fail, the identity tactic is applied, leaving the goal unchanged. The lemma is proved in a backwards fashion, using a familiar declarative-style inside a *proof block*, which operates on a single goal, applying the initial rule before solving the resulting subgoals by the statements inside it.

Example Refactorings. A proof refactoring is a behaviour preserving transformation of a theory. Following [25], we say it preserves behaviour if at least the same lemmas are proved before and after the refactoring. We observe that in this (albeit contrived) example theory, the pattern *intro*: 'try an introduction rule and if it fails, do nothing' is quite general. In fact, 'try a tactic and if it fails, do nothing' is exactly the LCF TRY tactical [15]. Rather than (a) leave things as they are (bad design); or, (b) manually generalise and change all occurrences (tedious and error-prone) a refactoring called *generalise tactic* could be used to make a structured, automated change to the theory.

Generalising a tactic requires the proof engineer to supply a sub-expression to generalise over ($\subseteq$-def | ∩-def in this case); and a fresh name for the generalised tactic (*try*). The result is a new, parameterised tactic and the replacement of the body of the original tactic with a call to the more general tactic. Now, however, the name *intro* is (slightly) inconsistent, so we decide to use *rename tactic* to change it to *tryintro*. This refactoring will rename *intro* and any uses of it later in the theory. The result of applying these refactorings on our running examples are shown in Figs. 3 and 4.

```
theory set
begin
  private tac try(X) := X | id
  public tac tryintro := try(⊆−def |
     ∩−def)

  public lemma comm: A ∩ B ⊆ B ∩ A
  proof( tryintro )
  show x ∈ A ∩ B ⊢ x ∈ B ∩ A
    proof( tryintro )
      show B: x ∈ A ∩ B ⊢ x ∈ B
        by ∩−elim ; ax
      show A: x ∈ A ∩ B ⊢ x ∈ A
        by ∩−elim ; ax
    qed
  qed
end
```

```
theory set
  strategy try(X) := X | id
  strategy tryintro := try(⊆−def |
     ∩−def)

  lemma comm: A ∩ B ⊆ B ∩ A
  proof( tryintro )
    assume xinAB: x ∈ A ∩ B
    subgoal x ∈ B ∩ A
    proof ( tryintro )
      subgoal x ∈ B from hyp
        by auto
      subgoal x ∈ A from hyp
        by auto
    qed
  qed
end
```

Fig. 3. Refactored Hiscript theory

Fig. 4. Refactored ΩSCRIPT theory

These examples exhibit the general structure of a refactoring. A set of *parameters* provide information about the object to refactor and any additional information. Preconditions restrict applicability to ensure behaviour is preserved. Finally, a transformation is applied to make the required change. In our framework, parameters for refactorings are simply parameters of the rewrite rules, and preconditions and transformations are written uniformly as rewrite rules.

3 Approach

Our approach is based on graph rewriting and bidirectional transformation. We provide a graph meta-model into which proofs from different languages can be mapped. We then allow the specification of *abstraction* rules to create an abstract *view* that includes only details relevant to a particular refactoring. This abstracted graph can be enriched with semantic information, such as dependencies and it is to this annotated, abstract graph that refactorings, specified as rewrite rules, can be applied. An experimental transformation mechanism provides a means to propagate changes back from the abstract representation to the concrete graph and finally to the syntax. Our meta-model is expressive enough to allow many different proof languages to be mapped to it, thus making our approach generic. Furthermore, the combination of abstraction and the use of graph rewrite rules makes our refactoring specifications compact and declarative.

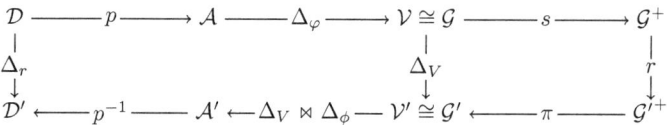

Fig. 5. Overall workflow of our approach

The details of our approach are best described by the workflow in Fig. 5, which consists of the following steps:
(1) A theory $\mathcal{D}$ is parsed to obtain the abstract syntax tree (AST), $\mathcal{A}$.
(2) A user-defined abstraction function φ computes the *view* $\mathcal{V}$ of the theory. We denote the difference between $\mathcal{A}$ and $\mathcal{V}$ by Δ_φ.
(3) The view $\mathcal{V}$ is translated to an isomorphic unordered attributed graph representation $\mathcal{G}$ that is used by the graph rewriting tool by making the ordering relations among children explicit as shown in Fig. 6.
(4) Using a proof language-specific function s, $\mathcal{G}$ is enriched by semantic information, such as dependencies, resulting in a semantic view $\mathcal{G}^+$. This enrichment of the view is an important part of our approach and allows, e.g., edges to be added between references to lemmas and their definition. These edges can then be followed in a *renaming* refactoring.

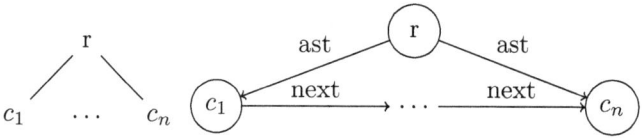

Fig. 6. Representation of ordered trees as directed graphs

(5) $\mathcal{G}^+$ is refactored, resulting in a modified view $\mathcal{G'}^+$. The refactoring performed is selected by the proof engineer and may require additional information, e.g., a renaming refactoring would require the new name to be supplied.
(6) Apply the syntactic projection function π to obtain the modified view $\mathcal{V}'$.
(7) The modifications $\Delta_V \bowtie \Delta_\phi$ between $\mathcal{V}$ and $\mathcal{V}'$ are propagated back to obtain a modified abstract syntax tree $\mathcal{A}'$. The information from Δ_ϕ is used to transform the Δ_V so that modifications to the view are transformed to modifications of the AST $\mathcal{A}$.
(8) $\mathcal{A}'$ is printed to obtain a modified theory $\mathcal{D}'$.

The problem of propagating back the modified view (our step 7) to the source is the well-known *view-update problem* [7].

Thus, our approach to refactoring combines two techniques: (i) *graph rewriting* and (ii) a bidirectional *transformation* mechanism. The main advantages of (i) are the use of a formal language to describe refactorings in a language independent format, and the existence of efficient tools. The advantages of (ii) are independence of the actual syntax of the proof language and the support of information hiding, resulting in a lightweight graph representation.

4 The POLAR Framework

4.1 Graph Meta-model

Our graph model provides a source-language independent format, such that different languages can be connected to the refactoring framework. Formally, we use attributed, typed graphs with inheritance (see [8] for a formal definition). Attributes that can be attached to nodes and edges to store primitive types such as integers or strings. The inheritance on node and edge types allows us to define classes of nodes to simplify analysis and rewriting.

An example graph. Before describing the formalities of our graph, we provide an example instance for the Hiscript theory in Fig. 1. A particular view of the graph obtained from the example theory is given in Fig. 7. It is clear that the constructed graph is similar to an abstract syntax tree for the theory; however, there are some notable differences. We store the names of objects in the theory as attributes in their corresponding node. Additionally, we *abstract* away individual formula representations and visibility annotations. The motivation behind this is to only present required details for a refactoring. In this graph we see the node types for Lemmas's, Tacdef's and Theory's. What is not visible is the inheritance structure of types. We have a type ThyItem, of which Lemma, Tactic, Definition, Axiom, etc are subtypes. We write Lemma < TheoryItem to represent this relationship. Thus, a rewrite rule to match theory items can be written uniformly.

Fig. 8 represents the proof block solving the goal $x \in A \cap B \vdash x \in B \cap A$. The proof block subgraph introduces two additional elements of the graph structure. Firstly, the proof block introduction tactic (in this case *intro*) is represented as a subgraph. The Def node type represents defined tactics in the language.

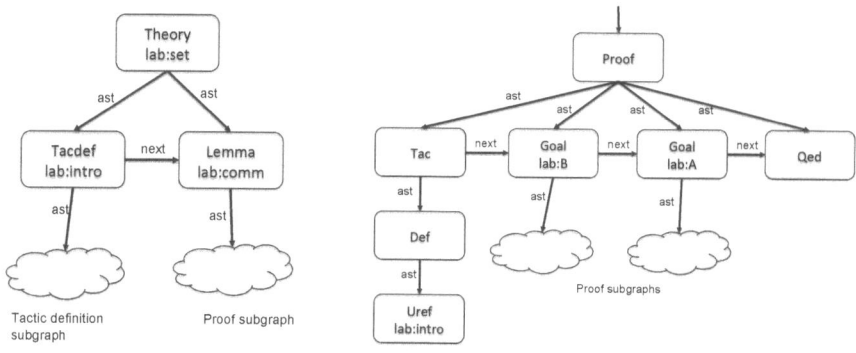

Fig. 7. The proof graph of Fig. 1   **Fig. 8.** The graph representation of a block

Secondly, in order to represent *named references*—to assumptions, tactics, other lemmas etc.—we use the node type Uref, with a lab attribute.

Graph Model. The allowable structure of a graph is captured in the form of an *attributed type graph*. The type graph restricts the node and edge types that can occur and link together in the graph, and describes the attributes for each node together with their types. Thus, it describes the structure of all its instances in an abstract way and allows us to study relations between different languages. Given a proof language $\mathcal{L}$ and a type graph t, we call an abstraction function φ *admissible wrt.* t and $\mathcal{L}$ iff for all ASTs $l \in \mathcal{L}$ the abstraction $\varphi(l)$ satisfies the requirements imposed by the type graph (formally, the existence of a total graph morphism into a type graph [8]).

Fig. 9 shows an excerpt of our type graph. In the figure, $a \to b$ indicates that a is a subtype of b and inherits all the attributes of b, whereas $a \xrightarrow{\text{type}} b$ indicates that edges of type type are allowed between nodes of type a to type b. This

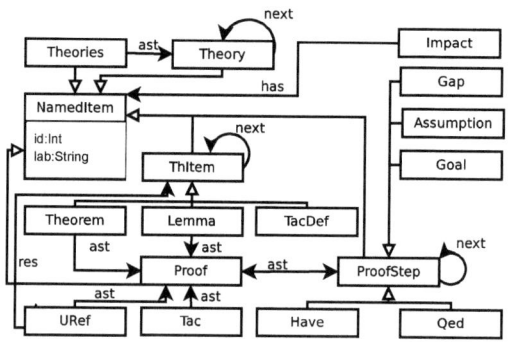

Fig. 9. Type Graph

graph shows the main type graph structure for a theory and its containing items as well as the type graph structure for proofs of lemmas. We elide the type graph corresponding to tactic expressions, but it is similar. The graph model is based on an abstract node type *NamedItem* which has two attributes: a label that represents its name and an identifier that is used internally to uniquely identify a node. It then introduces nodes according to the structure of a typical proof development: a node for theories, tactics, proofs and proof steps. Additionally, a node of type *Impact* is introduced, which is used to attach additional information to the nodes, e.g., failures that are detected by the dependency analysis. We finally point out that we do not consider the current meta-model to be a 'final' representation. We expect that the process of writing more refactorings and connecting additional languages will induce changes.

4.2 Abstraction and Back Translation

Since we allow different mappings to the meta-model for each language, we provide a generic abstraction mechanism to perform simple manipulations on the original AST, such as hiding specific subtrees. This allows us to experiment with different graph representations for different refactorings—in particular, to work with small and human-readable graphs—but it also requires a more sophisticated change model that propagates back the changes made by a refactoring on the abstract graph representation to the original AST. We first describe the process by which we transform an AST into the view, then from the view to the graph, and finally describe the back translation process.

Obtaining the View. ASTs are transformed to their view by the application of abstraction rules, which operate on the AST of a well-formed theory and result in an attributed tree. Abstraction functions are specified by a list of rewrite rules. For example, the rule:

(TAC visib label tac arg?) —> (TACDEF (AT "lab" label) tac arg?)

is used to abstract tactic definitions in a theory. We read this rule as matching a tree rooted with the lexer type TAC and at least three subtrees: one for the visibility, one for the name of the tactic, and one for the tactic definition itself. There is also an optional subtree for any parameter for the tactic, matched with the optional ? attribute. The special symbol AT is used to introduce an attribute "lab" with value *label*. To illustrate the abstraction process, Fig. 10 shows a small portion of the full AST corresponding to the tactic definition and Fig. 11 shows the view resulting from applying the rule above. This abstraction rule performs three changes:
(1) It performs a renaming of the lexer type TAC to TACDEF, which is the type of the equivalent node in the graph model.
(2) It deletes the visibility subtree from the AST.
(3) Finally, it introduces an *attribute* for the name of the tactic being defined.

Fig. 10. AST of a tactic definition   **Fig. 11.** AST after applying rule

The view is obtained by traversing the list of abstraction rules top-down. The full set of abstraction rules for Hiscript can be seen in [24, Chap. 11], alongside the full and the abstracted ASTs for Fig. 1.

View to the Graph. The view is then translated to an isomorphic graph representation. This transformation simply involves translating any subtrees rooted with an AT to attributes and making ordering explicit, cf. Fig. 6.

Back Translation: From the View to Concrete. Assuming we have already refactored our abstracted graph, the changes in the abstract representation must be propagated back to the AST and finally back to the theory. The key problem for propagating the modified view back to its source is that the abstraction is not one-to-one, meaning that some information is lost: the formulae, for example.

In general, given a proof node to be translated, there are two possibilities: (i) the proof node existed already in the original graph. In this case, the abstracted information can be reconstructed from the original graph; and, (ii) the proof node was added by the refactoring operation. In this case, we ensure that, if necessary, a default value is provided to keep the theory well-formed.

Our solution is based on the computation of differences using an *edit script*:

Definition 1 (edit operation, edit script). *An **edit script** is a sequence of the following basic **edit operations** that convert one tree into another*
*(1) **delete**(m) deletes the tree rooted in node m, where m is not the root node.*
*(2) **insert**(n, k, m) inserts the tree rooted by m to be the kth child of the node n.*
*(3) **insert-after**(n, k, m) inserts the tree rooted by m to be the right sibling of k with parent n.*
*(4) **move-before**(n, k, m) moves the tree rooted by m to be the left sibling of k with parent n.*
*(5) **move-after**(n, k, m) moves the tree rooted by m to be the right sibling of k with parent n.*
*(6) **update**(m, n, v), which changes the attribute n of node m to v.*

In our approach, two edit scripts are generated: one between the concrete AST and the view (written Δ_φ)—obtained by the abstraction—and the other between the view and the modified view (written Δ_V)—obtained by the refactoring.

As a simple example, the edit script generated by the abstraction rule for tactic definitions is shown:

delete(25)   Delete node 25: the **public** node
insert(24, 0, 129)   Insert node 129 as the zeroth child of node 24
update(24, con, Tacdef)   Update the attribute of node 24 to 'Tacdef'
moveAfter(129, 130, 26)   Move the tree rooted at 26 to be the right sibling
                                       of node 130, with parent 129. This moves the name
                                       to the value position of the attribute.

This edit script transforms the AST in Fig. 10 to the view in Fig. 11. The refactoring process constructs its own edit script. The complexity of the back propagation process lies in the fact that the refactoring process induces *changes* in the edit script Δ_φ. To compute the differences efficiently, we use persistent identifiers for nodes. These identifiers are used to track the origins of the nodes, i.e. the changes of the theory. Within our implementation, the identifiers correspond to the internal identifiers that are constructed during the parsing of the theory and are never touched by the user (see, e.g. Fig. 10). To translate the modified view back to the source level, we proceed by the following steps: (i) deletes and updates on the view are applied to the source. (ii) Moves of the view are translated to moves of the source; child positions are adapted based on the diff computed by the abstraction function. (iii) Inserts on the view are propagated to inserts on the source, child positions are adapted as well. (iv) Finally, attributes are translated back to name nodes.

Our back-translation approach is experimental and we plan to further develop the theory and practice behind the approach, but has been sufficient for the refactorings that we have implemented for both the Hiscript and ΩSCRIPT languages. In particular, we wish to compare our approach with the approaches used in the field of bidirectional transformations, for example, [21,17,4].

4.3 Dependency Analysis

At this point in the POLAR framework, we have abstracted a theory into its *view* and translated that view to the isomorphic graph representation that was described in Section 4.1. The next step is to enrich the graph with semantic dependencies before applying the refactoring. Both these tasks are performed by graph rewriting. This section describes the dependency analysis and the next describes the refactorings themselves.

Types of Dependencies. Within a theory, there are many dependencies between the statements that need to be respected when applying a behaviour-preserving transformation. For example, changing a name of a variable at some place might require to change it at another place as well. *Dependency analysis* aims to make dependencies due to interconnections between statements explicit. Usually, these dependencies are statically identified using control flow and data flow analysis, which can be performed based on a program dependency graph (see [10]). A systematic review of existing solutions can be found in [1]. We follow this common approach of static analysis, and enrich the syntactic graph by semantic edges, resulting in an abstract semantic graph. These edges are used to check whether a refactoring can be applied, and to propagate changes.

We distinguish two kinds of dependencies: *explicit* and *implicit* dependencies. Explicit dependencies hold between two objects and can thus be represented in the graph by an edge. Implicit dependencies hold between several other items, such as the requirement that each label must be unique inside its context. Such dependencies are not explicitly introduced into the graph but are realised by graph patterns inside our refactoring specifications.

Dependency Analysis in POLAR. We enrich the graph by performing graph rewrites to add edges of type res (for resolve) *from* the reference *to* the definition. To illustrate the result, Fig. 12 shows a part of the enriched graph from our running example. The graph shows the top level of the theory and part of the first proof block of the lemma, including the *intro* tactic. The dependency analysis has added an edge of type res linking the Uref node to the Tacdef node. Furthermore, the analysis adds a second reference from the nested proof block.

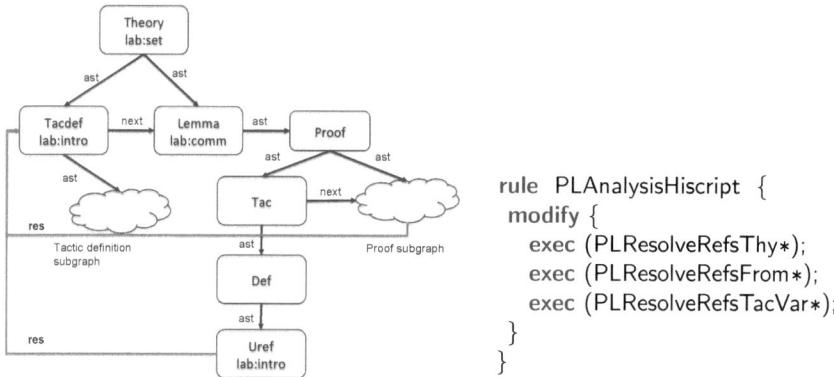

Fig. 12. Partial enriched graph   **Fig. 13.** Top-level analysis rule

We represent the dependency analysis as rewrite rules. Fig. 13 shows the top-level analysis function for Hiscript. The syntax we use is that of GRGEN, the graph rewriting tool that POLAR is built on top of [11]. Rules in GRGEN typically have two sections: a **pattern** to match, which forms the precondition of the rewrite rule and binds variables to graph elements; and a **modify** part that performs the rewriting. The rule PLAnalysisHiscript has no preconditions, so we omit the pattern in this case. The modifications are then performed sequentially and the ∗ operator means apply the rule until it fails. Thus, this rewrite rule will:
(1) Apply the PLResolveRefsThy rule as often as possible. This rewrite rule matches references to theory items, such as lemmas and tactic definitions and then recurses through the graph to find the definition. Its behaviour is general in three ways: (a) It operates on the body of tactic definitions and in

proofs; (b) It resolves references to both tactics and lemmas; (c) It resolves references to locally defined tactics and lemmas.
(2) Then, apply the PLResolveRefsFrom rule as often as possible, which resolves dependencies introduced by **from** statements.
(3) Finally, the PLResolveRefsTacVar rule analyses the local dependencies between tactic variables and their parameters. In the definition below, for example, it adds res edges between the formal parameter X and its uses.
  public tac ALL(X) := X ⊗ ALL(X) | ⟨⟩

Since Hiscript has a single namespace—tactics and lemmas can't have the same names—the rule PLResolveRefsThy is suitable for all theory items. We say that analysis rules are proof language specific because this may not always be the case and a separate namespace will require different analysis rules; furthermore, a language with different scoping rules may need its own analysis rules. The genericity in our approach stems from the fact that once these dependencies are calculated, the same refactoring should be applicable to different languages.

4.4 Refactoring

To this enriched graph, we apply the refactorings. To illustrate the approach, we describe the *rename item* refactoring. The full details of *generalise tactic* can be seen in [24, Chap. 11].

Rename an Item. The refactoring rewrite rule, again in the GRGEN syntax, is shown in Fig. 14. The rule takes two parameters: the *item* to rename, as a reference to a graph node, and the new name that has been supplied. The rule itself contains two **negative** conditions that express the precondition for this refactoring: that no object already exists with the supplied name. There is one rule for searching above the item and the second for searching above the item. Then, the rewriting part of the rule first matches every instance of a res dependency edge to a reference and renames the reference using the **iterated** language construct. Finally, the name of the definition is itself changed.

The refactoring definition itself is a bit of an anti-climax: the power of graph matching and rewriting means the actual transformation is only about four lines and clearly describes the transformation. Furthermore this refactoring is applicable to renaming many different items. The most complicated part of this refactoring is checking the implicit dependency on name-freshness, but this is a common precondition check and is often reused. Other refactorings that we have implemented are similarly compact; for example, the *move item* refactoring is based on repetition of a *swap items* refactoring that is written in one line. Some refactorings that perform complicated changes to the graph, such as *generalise tactic* require a larger rewrite rule, but the complexity is usually low.

5 Conclusion and Future Work

In this paper, we presented a concrete framework for refactoring formal proof developments in a generic, formal, and declarative way. The genericity is achieved

```
rule PLRenameLabel(item:NamedItem, var newname:string)
{
  negative {
    defnode:NamedItem;
    :SearchContextAbove(item, newname, defnode);
  }
  negative {
    defnode:NamedItem;
    :SearchContextBelow(item, newname, defnode);
  }
  iterated {
    item <−:res− uref:Uref;
    modify { eval { uref.name = newname; }}
  }
  modify { eval { item.name = newname; }}
}
```

Fig. 14. Rename item refactoring rewrite rule

by relying on a proof language independent graph meta-model and proof language-dependent dependencies that are available in the preconditions of a refactoring. Thus, to add a proof language, one simply needs to define abstractions into the meta-model and analysis functions for the dependencies.

To study the feasibility of the approach, we have implemented translations for the proof languages ΩSCRIPT and Hiscript and implemented several non-trivial refactorings. To keep the graph representation clean and tidy, our approach allows for information hiding. The tool is also extensible as users can implement their own refactorings in an intuitive way using a declarative language and the graph representation allows for succinct presentations of many refactorings.

5.1 Related Work

In the domain of programming languages, Mens has shown that graph rewriting provides a suitable framework to express refactorings [19]. Our approach is similar, but focuses on genericity, which is achieved by a language-independent graph meta-model. Proof language-specific semantic dependencies are explicitly represented in the graph, similar to [5] which introduces abstract semantic graphs. However, in contrast to existing approaches, we explicitly allow for information hiding by abstraction, based on bidirectional transformation [21]. To our best knowledge, this combination has not yet been explored in the literature. Moreover, due to the restricted complexity of proof languages, refactorings can be proved to be correct. Closely related to our work is a domain-specific programming language called JunGL, designed to enable a programmer to write their own refactorings [22]. This approach is similar to ours as the language is also generic. Where we use graph rewriting to perform the refactorings, JunGL has a number of built in language constructs for adding, removing and modifying edges making the refactorings arguably less understandable. In joint work with Autexier et al, Dietrich employed similar ideas in the SmartTies system for management of change in informal documents [3]. The SmartTies system was also based on GRGEN, and utilised graph rewriting to analyse dependencies between documents.

5.2 Future Work

Besides expanding the number of implemented refactorings and proof languages that are supported by our framework, future work will include a dynamic connection to the theorem prover. This would allow us to attempt to close gaps introduced by refactorings such as *add a constructor*. Furthermore, we would like to establish a connection between the abstract proof language and the resulting proof terms (e.g. to see whether a referenced label is indeed needed). Moreover, we plan to provide a means to automatically refactor a theory according to a specified style. We would also like to further investigate how we could use our graph meta-model. One possibility is to use it as a bridge between different proof languages allowing us to transform proofs in one language into another language. Whilst the meta-model is suitable for declarative and procedural proof languages, we would like to see if it holds tight for a language like SSReflect, which facilitates a very different type of proof style.

Acknowledgements. The authors would like to thank the reviewers for their constructive comments. This research was carried out while the first author a visiting researcher at the University of Edinburgh, supported by EPSRC Platform Grant EP/J001058/1: 'The Integration and Interaction of Multiple Mathematical Reasoning Processes'. The second author was supported by a Microsoft PhD scholarship and is now supported by EPSRC grant EP/H024050/1 'AI4FM: using AI to aid automation of proof search in Formal Methods'.

References

1. Arias, T.B.C., van der Spek, P., Avgeriou, P.: A practice-driven systematic review of dependency analysis solutions. Empirical Software Engineering 16(5), 544–586 (2011)
2. Aschbacher, M.: Highly complex proofs and implications of such proofs. Philosophical Transactions of the Royal Society A: Mathematical, Physical and Engineering Sciences 363, 2401–2406 (2005)
3. Autexier, S., Dietrich, D., Hutter, D., Lüth, C., Maeder, C.: Smartties - management of safety-critical developments. In: Margaria, T., Steffen, B. (eds.) ISoLA 2012, Part I. LNCS, vol. 7609, pp. 238–252. Springer, Heidelberg (2012)
4. Bancilhon, F., Spyratos, N.: Update semantics of relational views. ACM Trans. Database Syst. 6(4), 557–575 (1981)

5. Bell Canada. DATRIX abstract semantic graph reference manual (version 1.4). Technical report (2000)
6. Bourke, T., Daum, M., Klein, G., Kolanski, R.: Challenges and experiences in managing large-scale proofs. In: Jeuring, J., Campbell, J.A., Carette, J., Dos Reis, G., Sojka, P., Wenzel, M., Sorge, V. (eds.) CICM 2012. LNCS (LNAI), vol. 7362, pp. 32–48. Springer, Heidelberg (2012)
7. Chen, H., Liao, H.: A comparative study of view update problem. In: Data Storage and Data Engineering (DSDE), pp. 83–89 (2010)
8. de Lara, J., Bardohl, R., Ehrig, H., Ehrig, K., Prange, U., Taentzer, G.: Attributed graph transformation with node type inheritance. Theor. Comput. Sci. 376(3), 139–163 (2007)
9. Dietrich, D.: Assertion Level Proof Planning with Compiled Strategies. PhD thesis, Saarland University (2011)
10. Ferrante, J., Ottenstein, K.J., Warren, J.D.: The program dependence graph and its use in optimization. ACM Trans. Program. Lang. Syst. 9(3), 319–349 (1987)
11. Geiß, R., Batz, G.V., Grund, D., Hack, S., Szalkowski, A.: GrGen: A fast SPO-based graph rewriting tool. In: Corradini, A., Ehrig, H., Montanari, U., Ribeiro, L., Rozenberg, G. (eds.) ICGT 2006. LNCS, vol. 4178, pp. 383–397. Springer, Heidelberg (2006)
12. Gonthier, G.: The Four Colour Theorem: Engineering of a formal proof. In: Kapur, D. (ed.) ASCM 2007. LNCS (LNAI), vol. 5081, p. 333. Springer, Heidelberg (2008)
13. Gonthier, G., et al.: A machine-checked proof of the odd order theorem. In: Blazy, S., Paulin-Mohring, C., Pichardie, D. (eds.) ITP 2013. LNCS, vol. 7998, pp. 163–179. Springer, Heidelberg (2013)
14. Gonthier, G., Mahboubi, A., Rideau, L., Tassi, E., Théry, L.: A Modular Formalisation of Finite Group Theory. Rapport de recherche RR-6156, INRIA (2007)
15. Gordon, M., Milner, R., Morris, L., Newey, M., Wadsworth, C.: A metalanguage for interactive proof in LCF. In: Proceedings of the 5th ACM SIGACT-SIGPLAN Symposium on Principles of Programming Languages, POPL 1978, pp. 119–130. ACM, New York (1978)
16. Hales, T.C.: Introduction to the Flyspeck project. In: Coquand, T., Lombardi, H., Roy, M.-F. (eds.) Mathematics, Algorithms, Proofs. Dagstuhl Seminar Proceedings, vol. 05021 (2006)
17. Hofmann, M., Pierce, B., Wagner, D.: Edit lenses. In: ACM SIGPLAN Notices, vol. 47, pp. 495–508. ACM (2012)
18. Klein, G., Elphinstone, K., Heiser, G., Andronick, J., Cock, D., Derrin, P., Elkaduwe, D., Engelhardt, K., Kolanski, R., Norrish, M., et al.: seL4: Formal verification of an OS kernel. In: Proceedings of the ACM SIGOPS 22nd Symposium on Operating Systems Principles, pp. 207–220. ACM (2009)
19. Mens, T., Eetvelde, N.V., Demeyer, S., Janssens, D.: Formalizing refactorings with graph transformations. Journal of Software Maintenance 17(4), 247–276 (2005)
20. Opdyke, W.F.: Refactoring object-oriented frameworks. PhD thesis, Champaign, IL, USA (1992)
21. Stevens, P.: A landscape of bidirectional model transformations. In: Lämmel, R., Visser, J., Saraiva, J. (eds.) GTTSE 2007. LNCS, vol. 5235, pp. 408–424. Springer, Heidelberg (2008)
22. Verbaere, M., Ettinger, R., de Moor, O.: JunGL: a scripting language for refactoring. In: Rombach, D., Soffa, M.L. (eds.) ICSE 2006: Proceedings of the 28th International Conference on Software Engineering, pp. 172–181. ACM Press, New York (2006)

23. Wenzel, M.T.: Isar - a generic interpretative approach to readable formal proof documents. In: Bertot, Y., Dowek, G., Hirschowitz, A., Paulin, C., Théry, L. (eds.) TPHOLs 1999. LNCS, vol. 1690, pp. 167–184. Springer, Heidelberg (1999)
24. Whiteside, I.: Refactoring Proofs. PhD thesis, University of Edinburgh (2013)
25. Whiteside, I., Aspinall, D., Dixon, L., Grov, G.: Towards formal proof script refactoring. In: Davenport, J.H., Farmer, W.M., Urban, J., Rabe, F. (eds.) Calculemus/MKM 2011. LNCS (LNAI), vol. 6824, pp. 260–275. Springer, Heidelberg (2011)

Author Index

Aceto, Luca 1
Albert, Elvira 18
Allali, Lisa 407
Alt, Leonardo 683
Artale, Alessandro 35
Aspinall, David 53, 776

Barceló, Pablo 71
Baumgartner, Peter 86
Bax, Joshua 86
Belov, Anton 96
Benhamou, Belaïd 112
Benzmüller, Christoph 127
Berdine, Josh 137
Biere, Armin 423
Bjørner, Nikolaj 137
Blackburn, Patrick 147
Blahoudek, František 164
Blanc, Régis 173
Bolander, Thomas 147
Boudard, Mélanie 182
Braüner, Torben 147
Britz, Katarina 636
Broda, Krysia 759

Casal, Filipe 198
Casini, Giovanni 213
Chatterjee, Krishnendu 228
Cintula, Petr 584
Cruz-Filipe, Luís 243

Dal Lago, Ugo 258
Delahaye, David 274
Della Monica, Dario 1
Denney, Ewen 53
Dietrich, Dominik 776
Doligez, Damien 274
Duret-Lutz, Alexandre 668

Egly, Uwe 291

Fedyukovich, Grigory 683
Fontaine, Gaelle 71
Forejt, Vojtěch 228
French, Tim 309

Genaim, Samir 18
Gilbert, Frédéric 274
Grigore, Radu 473
Groß, Thomas 619
Grov, Gudmund 324
Gulwani, Sumit 457
Gundersen, Tom 340
Gupta, Ashutosh 173

Halmagrand, Pierre 274
Harel, David 355
Hasan, Osman 744
Heijltjes, Willem 340
Heinemann, Bernhard 373
Henriques, Rita 243
Heras, Jónathan 389
Hermant, Olivier 182, 274, 407
Heule, Marijn J.H. 423
Hoffmann, Jan 710
Hyvärinen, Antti E.J. 683

Ignatiev, Alexey 439
Immerman, Neil 457
Ingólfsdóttir, Anna 1
Ishtiaq, Samin 137
Itzhaky, Shachar 457

Janota, Mikoláš 473
Jiang, Chuan 490
Jørgensen, Klaus Frovin 147
Johansson, Moa 389
Junttila, Tommi 568

Kaliszyk, Cezary 503
Kantor, Amir 355
Katz, Guy 355, 518
Kissinger, Aleks 324
Klarman, Szymon 536
Komendantskaya, Ekaterina 389
Kontchakov, Roman 35
Koopmann, Patrick 552
Kordon, Fabrice 668
Kovács, Laura 173
Kragl, Bernhard 173
Křetínský, Mojmír 164
Kriener, Jael E. 137

Author Index

Laitinen, Tero 568
Lin, Anthony Widjaja 71
Lin, Yuhui 324
Lonsing, Florian 291
Lüth, Christoph 53
Luttenberger, Michael 727

Maclean, Ewen 389
Maimari, Nataly 759
Marques-Silva, Joao 96, 439, 473
Martin-Martin, Enrique 18
McCabe-Dansted, John 309
McIver, Annabelle 653
Metcalfe, George 584
Meyer, Thomas 536, 636
Mödersheim, Sebastian A. 619
Mogavero, Fabio 601
Montanari, Angelo 1
Morgado, António 96
Morgado, Antonio 439
Murano, Aniello 601

Niemelä, Ilkka 568
Nortje, Riku 636
Nunes, Isabel 243

Parigot, Michel 340
Pellitta, Giulio 258
Pereira, Luís Moniz 694
Planes, Jordi 439
Poitrenaud, Denis 668

Rabehaja, Tahiry 653
Rasga, João 198
Raths, Thomas 127

Renault, Etienne 668
Reynolds, Mark 309
Rollini, Simone Fulvio 683
Russo, Alessandra 759
Ryzhikov, Vladislav 35

Sagiv, Mooly 457
Saptawijaya, Ari 694
Scherer, Gabriel 710
Schlund, Maximilian 727
Schmidt, Renate A. 552
Schulz, Stephan 735
Sciavicco, Guido 1
Sharygina, Natasha 683
Sorrentino, Loredana 601
Straccia, Umberto 213
Strejček, Jan 164
Struth, Georg 653

Taqdees, Syeda Hira 744
Terepeta, Michał 727
Turliuc, Calin-Rares 759

Urban, Josef 503

Viganò, Luca 619

Whiteside, Iain 776
Widl, Magdalena 291
Wintersteiger, Christoph M. 137
Wojtczak, Dominik 228

Zakharyaschev, Michael 35
Zhang, Ting 490

MIX
Papier aus verantwortungsvollen Quellen
Paper from responsible sources
FSC® C105338

If you have any concerns about our products,
you can contact us on
ProductSafety@springernature.com

In case Publisher is established outside the EU,
the EU authorized representative is:
**Springer Nature Customer Service Center GmbH
Europaplatz 3, 69115 Heidelberg, Germany**

Printed by Libri Plureos GmbH
in Hamburg, Germany